القرآن الحكيم

THE HOLY QUR'ĀN

ARABIC TEXT
AND
ENGLISH TRANSLATION

Translated by:
The late Maulawi Sher Ali

Published under the auspices of

HADHRAT MIRZA TAHIR AHMAD
Fourth Successor of the Promised Messiah and
Supreme Head of the Ahmadiyya Movement in Islam

1997
Islam International Publications Limited

THE HOLY QUR'ĀN

ARABIC TEXT AND ENGLISH TRANSLATION

Translated by: The late Maulawi Sher Ali

First published in Holland in 1955. Since then many editions have been published in different countries.
Present edition 1997

Published by:
Islam International Publications Ltd.
Islamabad, Sheephatch Lane,
Tilford, Surrey GU10 2AQ
U.K.

Printed in U.K. by:
THE BATH PRESS
Lower Bristol Road,
Bath BA2 3BL

British Library Cataloguing in Publication data:
[Koran. English and Arabic. 1989]
The Holy Quran with English translation.
1. Ali, Maulawi Sher
297'. 122

ISBN 1 85372 314 2

Publisher's Note

The late Maulawi Sher Ali's English translation of The Holy Quran which is being produced here is presented exactly in it's original form with no alteration whatsoever. Yet it has been deemed useful that some alternative translations and suggestions and some explanatory notes wherever necessary, should also be provided separately, in the form of an appendix . This we have done with the hope that it will help the reader to understand the meaning more conveniently.

The simple method we have adopted is to mark with a star′let all such verses which are included in the appendix .

CONTENTS

سُوْرَةُ الْفَاتِحَةِ مَكِّيَّةٌ (١) اٰيَاتُهَا ٧ رُكُوْعُهَا ١

AL-FĀTIḤAH

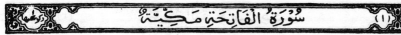

(Revealed before Hijra)

1. In the name of Allah, the Gracious, the Merciful.

المنزل ١ بِسْمِ اللّٰهِ الرَّحْمٰنِ الرَّحِيْمِ ①

2. All praise belongs to Allah, Lord of all the worlds,

اَلْحَمْدُ لِلّٰهِ رَبِّ الْعٰلَمِيْنَ ②

3. The Gracious, the Merciful,

الرَّحْمٰنِ الرَّحِيْمِ ③

4. Master of the Day of Judgment.

مٰلِكِ يَوْمِ الدِّيْنِ ④

5. Thee alone do we worship and Thee alone do we implore for help.

اِيَّاكَ نَعْبُدُ وَاِيَّاكَ نَسْتَعِيْنُ ⑤

6. Guide us in the right path—

اِهْدِنَا الصِّرَاطَ الْمُسْتَقِيْمَ ⑥

* 7. The path of those on whom Thou hast bestowed *Thy* blessings, those who have not incurred *Thy* displeasure, and those who have not gone astray.

صِرَاطَ الَّذِيْنَ اَنْعَمْتَ عَلَيْهِمْ ۙ غَيْرِ الْمَغْضُوْبِ
ع عَلَيْهِمْ وَلَا الضَّآلِّيْنَ ⑦

سُوْرَةُ الْبَقَرَةِ مَدَنِيَّةٌ (٢)

AL-BAQARAH

(Revealed after Hijra)

1. In the name of Allah, the Gracious, the Merciful.

بِسْمِ اللّٰهِ الرَّحْمٰنِ الرَّحِيْمِ ﴿١﴾

2. Alif Lām Mīm *.

الٓمّٓ ﴿٢﴾

3. This is a perfect Book; there is no doubt in it; *it is* a guidance for the righteous,

ذٰلِكَ الْكِتٰبُ لَا رَيْبَ ۛۚ فِيْهِ ۚ هُدًى لِّلْمُتَّقِيْنَ ﴿٣﴾

4. Who believe in the unseen and observe Prayer, and spend out of what We have provided for them;

الَّذِيْنَ يُؤْمِنُوْنَ بِالْغَيْبِ وَيُقِيْمُوْنَ الصَّلٰوةَ وَمِمَّا رَزَقْنٰهُمْ يُنْفِقُوْنَ ﴿٤﴾

5. And who believe in that which has been revealed to thee, and that which was revealed before thee, and they have firm faith in what is *yet* to come.

وَالَّذِيْنَ يُؤْمِنُوْنَ بِمَآ اُنْزِلَ اِلَيْكَ وَمَآ اُنْزِلَ مِنْ قَبْلِكَ ۚ وَبِالْاٰخِرَةِ هُمْ يُوْقِنُوْنَ ﴿٥﴾

6. It is they who follow the guidance of their Lord and it is they who shall prosper.

اُولٰٓئِكَ عَلٰى هُدًى مِّنْ رَّبِّهِمْ ۗ وَاُولٰٓئِكَ هُمُ الْمُفْلِحُوْنَ ﴿٦﴾

7. Those who have disbelieved—it being equal to them whether thou warn them or warn them not—they will not believe.

اِنَّ الَّذِيْنَ كَفَرُوْا سَوَآءٌ عَلَيْهِمْ ءَاَنْذَرْتَهُمْ اَمْ لَمْ تُنْذِرْهُمْ لَا يُؤْمِنُوْنَ ﴿٧﴾

8. Allah has set a seal on their hearts and their ears, and over their eyes is a covering; and for them is a great punishment.

خَتَمَ اللّٰهُ عَلٰى قُلُوْبِهِمْ وَعَلٰى سَمْعِهِمْ ۗ وَعَلٰٓى اَبْصَارِهِمْ غِشَاوَةٌ ۫ وَّلَهُمْ عَذَابٌ عَظِيْمٌ ﴿٨﴾

R. 2.

9. And of the people there are some who say, 'We believe in Allah and the Last Day;' while they are not believers at all.

وَمِنَ النَّاسِ مَنْ يَّقُوْلُ اٰمَنَّا بِاللّٰهِ وَبِالْيَوْمِ الْاٰخِرِ وَمَا هُمْ بِمُؤْمِنِيْنَ ﴿٩﴾

10. They would deceive Allah and those who believe, and they deceive none but themselves; only they perceive *it* not.

يُخٰدِعُوْنَ اللّٰهَ وَالَّذِيْنَ اٰمَنُوْا ۚ وَمَا يَخْدَعُوْنَ اِلَّآ اَنْفُسَهُمْ وَمَا يَشْعُرُوْنَ ﴿١٠﴾

11. In their hearts was a disease, and Allah has increased their disease to them; and for them is a grievous punishment because they lied.

فِيْ قُلُوْبِهِمْ مَّرَضٌ ۙ فَزَادَهُمُ اللّٰهُ مَرَضًا ۚ وَلَهُمْ عَذَابٌ اَلِيْمٌ ۢ بِمَا كَانُوْا يَكْذِبُوْنَ ﴿١١﴾

* I am Allah, the All-Knowing.

12. And when it is said to them: 'Create not disorder on the earth,' they say: 'We are only promoters of peace.'

وَإِذَا قِيلَ لَهُمْ لَا تُفْسِدُوا فِي الْأَرْضِ قَالُوا إِنَّمَا
نَحْنُ مُصْلِحُونَ ﴿١٢﴾

13. Beware! it is surely they who create disorder, but they do not perceive *it*.

أَلَا إِنَّهُمْ هُمُ الْمُفْسِدُونَ وَلَٰكِنْ لَا يَشْعُرُونَ ﴿١٣﴾

14. And when it is said to them, 'Believe as *other* people have believed,' they say: 'Shall we believe as the foolish have believed?' Beware! it is surely they that are foolish, but they do not know.

وَإِذَا قِيلَ لَهُمْ آمِنُوا كَمَا آمَنَ النَّاسُ قَالُوا أَنُؤْمِنُ
كَمَا آمَنَ السُّفَهَاءُ ۗ أَلَا إِنَّهُمْ هُمُ السُّفَهَاءُ وَلَٰكِنْ
لَا يَعْلَمُونَ ﴿١٤﴾

15. And when they meet those who believe, they say: 'We believe;' but when they are alone with their ringleaders, they say: 'We are certainly with you; we are only mocking.'

وَإِذَا لَقُوا الَّذِينَ آمَنُوا قَالُوا آمَنَّا ۖ وَإِذَا خَلَوْا إِلَىٰ
شَيَاطِينِهِمْ قَالُوا إِنَّا مَعَكُمْ إِنَّمَا نَحْنُ مُسْتَهْزِئُونَ ﴿١٥﴾

16. Allah will punish their mockery and will let them continue in their transgression, wandering blindly.

اللَّهُ يَسْتَهْزِئُ بِهِمْ وَيَمُدُّهُمْ فِي طُغْيَانِهِمْ
يَعْمَهُونَ ﴿١٦﴾

17. These are they who have taken error in exchange for guidance; but their traffic has brought them no gain, nor are they rightly guided.

أُولَٰئِكَ الَّذِينَ اشْتَرَوُا الضَّلَالَةَ بِالْهُدَىٰ فَمَا
رَبِحَتْ تِجَارَتُهُمْ وَمَا كَانُوا مُهْتَدِينَ ﴿١٧﴾

18. Their case is like the case of a person who kindled a fire, and when it lighted up all around him, Allah took away their light and left them in thick darkness; they see not.

مَثَلُهُمْ كَمَثَلِ الَّذِي اسْتَوْقَدَ نَارًا فَلَمَّا أَضَاءَتْ
مَا حَوْلَهُ ذَهَبَ اللَّهُ بِنُورِهِمْ وَتَرَكَهُمْ فِي ظُلُمَاتٍ
لَا يُبْصِرُونَ ﴿١٨﴾

* 19. *They are* deaf, dumb *and* blind; so they will not return.

صُمٌّ بُكْمٌ عُمْيٌ فَهُمْ لَا يَرْجِعُونَ ﴿١٩﴾

20. Or *it is* like a heavy rain from the clouds, wherein is thick darkness and thunder and lightning; they put their fingers into their ears because of the thunder-claps for fear of death, and Allah encompasses the disbelievers.

أَوْ كَصَيِّبٍ مِنَ السَّمَاءِ فِيهِ ظُلُمَاتٌ وَرَعْدٌ وَبَرْقٌ
يَجْعَلُونَ أَصَابِعَهُمْ فِي آذَانِهِمْ مِنَ الصَّوَاعِقِ حَذَرَ
الْمَوْتِ ۚ وَاللَّهُ مُحِيطٌ بِالْكَافِرِينَ ﴿٢٠﴾

21. The lightning might well-nigh snatch away their sight; whenever it shines upon them, they walk therein; and when it becomes dark to them, they stand still. And if Allah willed, He could take away their hearing and their sight; surely, Allah has the power to do all that He wills.

يَكَادُ الْبَرْقُ يَخْطَفُ أَبْصَارَهُمْ ۖ كُلَّمَا أَضَاءَ لَهُمْ مَشَوْا
فِيهِ وَإِذَا أَظْلَمَ عَلَيْهِمْ قَامُوا ۚ وَلَوْ شَاءَ اللَّهُ لَذَهَبَ
بِسَمْعِهِمْ وَأَبْصَارِهِمْ ۚ إِنَّ اللَّهَ عَلَىٰ كُلِّ شَيْءٍ قَدِيرٌ ﴿٢١﴾

R. 3.

22. O ye men, worship your Lord Who created you and those who were before you, that you may become righteous;

يٰۤاَيُّهَا النَّاسُ اعۡبُدُوۡا رَبَّكُمُ الَّذِىۡ خَلَقَكُمۡ وَالَّذِيۡنَ
مِنۡ قَبۡلِكُمۡ لَعَلَّكُمۡ تَتَّقُوۡنَ ۙ﴿۲۲﴾

23. Who made the earth a bed for you, and the heaven a roof, and caused water to come down from the clouds and therewith brought forth fruits for your sustenance. Set not up, therefore, equals to Allah, while you know.

الَّذِىۡ جَعَلَ لَـكُمُ الۡاَرۡضَ فِرَاشًا وَّالسَّمَآءَ بِنَآءً وَّ
اَنۡزَلَ مِنَ السَّمَآءِ مَآءً فَاَخۡرَجَ بِهٖ مِنَ الثَّمَرٰتِ
رِزۡقًا لَّكُمۡ‌ۚ فَلَا تَجۡعَلُوۡا لِلّٰهِ اَنۡدَادًا وَّاَنۡتُمۡ تَعۡلَمُوۡنَ﴿۲۳﴾

24. And if you are in doubt as to what We have sent down to Our servant, then produce a Chapter like it, and call upon your helpers beside Allah, if you are truthful.

وَاِنۡ كُنۡتُمۡ فِىۡ رَيۡبٍ مِّمَّا نَزَّلۡنَا عَلٰى عَبۡدِنَا فَاۡتُوۡا
بِسُوۡرَةٍ مِّنۡ مِّثۡلِهٖ وَادۡعُوۡا شُهَدَآءَكُمۡ مِّنۡ دُوۡنِ
اللّٰهِ اِنۡ كُنۡتُمۡ صٰدِقِيۡنَ﴿۲۴﴾

25. But if you do *it* not – and never shall you do *it* – then guard against the Fire, whose fuel is men and stones, *which is* prepared for the disbelievers.

فَاِنۡ لَّمۡ تَفۡعَلُوۡا وَلَنۡ تَفۡعَلُوۡا فَاتَّقُوا النَّارَ الَّتِىۡ وَقُوۡدُهَا
النَّاسُ وَالۡحِجَارَةُ ۖۚ اُعِدَّتۡ لِلۡكٰفِرِيۡنَ﴿۲۵﴾

*26. And give glad tidings to those who believe and do good works, that for them are Gardens beneath which flow streams. Whenever they are given a portion of fruit therefrom, they will say: 'This is what was given us before,' and gifts mutually resembling shall be brought to them. And they will have therein mates perfectly pure, and therein will they abide.

وَبَشِّرِ الَّذِيۡنَ اٰمَنُوۡا وَعَمِلُوا الصّٰلِحٰتِ اَنَّ لَهُمۡ جَنّٰتٍ
تَجۡرِىۡ مِنۡ تَحۡتِهَا الۡاَنۡهٰرُ‌ؕ كُلَّمَا رُزِقُوۡا مِنۡهَا مِنۡ
ثَمَرَةٍ رِّزۡقًا ۙ قَالُوۡا هٰذَا الَّذِىۡ رُزِقۡنَا مِنۡ قَبۡلُ وَ
اُتُوۡا بِهٖ مُتَشَابِهًا ؕ وَلَهُمۡ فِيۡهَآ اَزۡوَاجٌ مُّطَهَّرَةٌ ۙ وَّهُمۡ
فِيۡهَا خٰلِدُوۡنَ﴿۲۶﴾

27. Allah disdains not to give an illustration as small as a gnat or even smaller. Those who believe know that it is the truth from their Lord, while those who disbelieve say: 'What does Allah mean by such an illustration?' Many does He adjudge by it to be erring and many by it does He guide, and none does He adjudge thereby to be erring except the disobedient,

اِنَّ اللّٰهَ لَا يَسۡتَحۡىٖۤ اَنۡ يَّضۡرِبَ مَثَلًا مَّا بَعُوۡضَةً
فَمَا فَوۡقَهَا ؕ فَاَمَّا الَّذِيۡنَ اٰمَنُوۡا فَيَعۡلَمُوۡنَ اَنَّهُ الۡحَـقُّ مِنۡ
رَّبِّهِمۡ‌ۚ وَاَمَّا الَّذِيۡنَ كَفَرُوۡا فَيَقُوۡلُوۡنَ مَاذَآ اَرَادَ اللّٰهُ
بِهٰذَا مَثَلًا ۘ يُضِلُّ بِهٖ كَثِيۡرًا وَّيَهۡدِىۡ بِهٖ كَثِيۡرًا ؕ وَمَا وقف لازم
يُضِلُّ بِهٖۤ اِلَّا الۡفٰسِقِيۡنَ ۙ﴿۲۷﴾

28. Who break the covenant of Allah after having established it, and cut asunder what Allah has bidden to be joined, and

الَّذِيۡنَ يَنۡقُضُوۡنَ عَهۡدَ اللّٰهِ مِنۡۢ بَعۡدِ مِيۡثَاقِهٖ وَ
يَقۡطَعُوۡنَ مَآ اَمَرَ اللّٰهُ بِهٖۤ اَنۡ يُّوۡصَلَ وَيُفۡسِدُوۡنَ

create disorder in the earth; it is these that are the losers.

فِي الْاَرْضِ اُولٰٓئِكَ هُمُ الْخٰسِرُوْنَ ﴿٢٨﴾

29. How can you disbelieve in Allah? When you were without life, He gave you life, and then He will cause you to die, then restore you to life, and then to Him shall you be made to return.

كَيْفَ تَكْفُرُوْنَ بِاللّٰهِ وَكُنْتُمْ اَمْوَاتًا فَاَحْيَاكُمْ ثُمَّ
يُمِيْتُكُمْ ثُمَّ يُحْيِيْكُمْ ثُمَّ اِلَيْهِ تُرْجَعُوْنَ ﴿٢٩﴾

30. He it is Who created for you all that is in the earth; then He turned towards the heavens, and He perfected them as seven heavens; and He knows all things.

هُوَ الَّذِيْ خَلَقَ لَكُمْ مَّا فِي الْاَرْضِ جَمِيْعًا ۗ ثُمَّ
اسْتَوٰٓى اِلَى السَّمَآءِ فَسَوّٰىهُنَّ سَبْعَ سَمٰوٰتٍ ۗ وَهُوَ
بِكُلِّ شَيْءٍ عَلِيْمٌ ﴿٣٠﴾ ع ٤

R. 4.

* 31. And when thy Lord said to the angels: 'I am about to place a vicegerent in the earth,' they said: 'Wilt Thou place therein such as will cause disorder in it, and shed blood?—and we glorify Thee with Thy praise and extol Thy holiness.' He answered: 'I know what you know not.'

وَاِذْ قَالَ رَبُّكَ لِلْمَلٰٓئِكَةِ اِنِّيْ جَاعِلٌ فِي الْاَرْضِ خَلِيْفَةً ۗ
قَالُوْٓا اَتَجْعَلُ فِيْهَا مَنْ يُّفْسِدُ فِيْهَا وَيَسْفِكُ الدِّمَآءَ ۚ
وَنَحْنُ نُسَبِّحُ بِحَمْدِكَ وَنُقَدِّسُ لَكَ ۗ قَالَ اِنِّيْٓ اَعْلَمُ
مَا لَا تَعْلَمُوْنَ ﴿٣١﴾

32. And He taught Adam all the names, then He put *the objects of* these *names* before the angels and said: 'Tell Me the names of these, if you are right.'

وَعَلَّمَ اٰدَمَ الْاَسْمَآءَ كُلَّهَا ثُمَّ عَرَضَهُمْ عَلَى الْمَلٰٓئِكَةِ ۙ
فَقَالَ اَنْۢبِئُوْنِيْ بِاَسْمَآءِ هٰٓؤُلَآءِ اِنْ كُنْتُمْ صٰدِقِيْنَ ﴿٣٢﴾

33. They said: 'Holy art Thou! No knowledge have we except what Thou hast taught us; surely, Thou art the All-Knowing, the Wise.'

قَالُوْا سُبْحٰنَكَ لَا عِلْمَ لَنَآ اِلَّا مَا عَلَّمْتَنَا ۗ اِنَّكَ اَنْتَ
الْعَلِيْمُ الْحَكِيْمُ ﴿٣٣﴾

34. He said: 'O Adam, tell them their names;' and when he had told them their names, He said: 'Did I not say to you, I know the secrets of the heavens and of the earth, and I know what you reveal and what you conceal?'

قَالَ يٰٓاٰدَمُ اَنْۢبِئْهُمْ بِاَسْمَآئِهِمْ ۚ فَلَمَّآ اَنْۢبَاَهُمْ بِاَسْمَآئِهِمْ ۙ
قَالَ اَلَمْ اَقُلْ لَّكُمْ اِنِّيْٓ اَعْلَمُ غَيْبَ السَّمٰوٰتِ وَالْاَرْضِ ۙ
وَاَعْلَمُ مَا تُبْدُوْنَ وَمَا كُنْتُمْ تَكْتُمُوْنَ ﴿٣٤﴾

* 35. And *remember the time* when We said to the angels: 'Submit to Adam,' and they *all* submitted. But Iblīs *did not*. He refused and was too proud; and he was of the disbelievers.

وَاِذْ قُلْنَا لِلْمَلٰٓئِكَةِ اسْجُدُوْا لِاٰدَمَ فَسَجَدُوْٓا اِلَّآ اِبْلِيْسَ ۭ
اَبٰى وَاسْتَكْبَرَ ۤ وَكَانَ مِنَ الْكٰفِرِيْنَ ﴿٣٥﴾

36. And We said: 'O Adam, dwell thou and thy wife in the garden, and eat therefrom plentifully wherever you will, but approach not this tree, lest you be of the wrongdoers.'

وَقُلْنَا يٰٓاٰدَمُ اسْكُنْ اَنْتَ وَزَوْجُكَ الْجَنَّةَ وَكُلَا مِنْهَا
رَغَدًا حَيْثُ شِئْتُمَا ۠ وَلَا تَقْرَبَا هٰذِهِ الشَّجَرَةَ فَتَكُوْنَا
مِنَ الظّٰلِمِيْنَ ﴿٣٦﴾

37. But Satan caused them both to slip by means of it and drove them out of *the state* in which they were. And We said: 'Go forth; some of you are enemies of others, and for you there is an abode in the earth and a provision for a time.'

فازلهما الشيطن عنها فاخرجهما مما كانا فيه وقلنا اهبطوا بعضكم لبعض عدو ولكم في الارض مستقر ومتاع الى حين ﴿٣٧﴾

38. Then Adam learnt from his Lord certain words *of prayer*. So He turned towards him with mercy. Surely, He is Oft-Returning *with compassion, and is* Merciful.

فتلقى ادم من ربه كلمت فتاب عليه انه هو التواب الرحيم ﴿٣٨﴾

39. We said: 'Go forth, all of you, from here. And if there comes to you guidance from Me, then whoso shall follow My guidance, on them *shall come* no fear, nor shall they grieve.'

قلنا اهبطوا منها جميعا فاما يأتينكم مني هدى فمن تبع هداي فلا خوف عليهم ولا هم يحزنون ﴿٣٩﴾

40. But they who will disbelieve and treat Our Signs as lies, these shall be the inmates of the Fire; therein shall they abide.

والذين كفروا وكذبوا بايتنا اولئك اصحب النار هم فيها خلدون ﴿٤٠﴾

R. 5.

41. O children of Israel! remember My favour which I bestowed upon you, and fulfil your covenant with Me, I will fulfil My covenant with you, and Me alone should you fear.

يبني اسراءيل اذكروا نعمتي التي انعمت عليكم واوفوا بعهدي اوف بعهدكم واياي فارهبون ﴿٤١﴾

42. And believe in what I have sent down which fulfils that which is with you, and be not the first to disbelieve therein, and barter not My Signs for a paltry price, and take protection in Me alone.

وامنوا بما انزلت مصدقا لما معكم ولا تكونوا اول كافر به ولا تشتروا بايتي ثمنا قليلا واياي فاتقون ﴿٤٢﴾

43. And confound not truth with falsehood nor hide the truth, knowingly.

ولا تلبسوا الحق بالباطل وتكتموا الحق وانتم تعلمون ﴿٤٣﴾

44. And observe Prayer and pay the Zakāt, and bow down with those who bow.

واقيموا الصلوة واتوا الزكوة واركعوا مع الركعين ﴿٤٤﴾

45. Do you enjoin others to do what is good and forget your own selves, while you read the Book? Will you not then understand?

اتامرون الناس بالبر وتنسون انفسكم وانتم تتلون الكتب افلا تعقلون ﴿٤٥﴾

46. And seek help with patience and Prayer; and this indeed is hard except for the humble in spirit,

واستعينوا بالصبر والصلوة وانها لكبيرة الا على الخشعين ﴿٤٦﴾

47. Who know for certain that they will

الذين يظنون انهم ملقوا ربهم وانهم اليه

meet their Lord, and that to Him will they return.

رٰجِعُوْنَ ﴿۴۷﴾

R. 6.

48. O children of Israel! remember My favour which I bestowed upon you and that I exalted you above the peoples.

يٰبَنِيْٓ اِسْرَآءِيْلَ اذْكُرُوْا نِعْمَتِيَ الَّتِيْٓ اَنْعَمْتُ عَلَيْكُمْ وَاَنِّيْ فَضَّلْتُكُمْ عَلَى الْعٰلَمِيْنَ ﴿۴۸﴾

49. And fear the day when no soul shall serve as a substitute for another soul at all, nor shall intercession be accepted for it; nor shall ransom be taken from it; nor shall they be helped.

وَاتَّقُوْا يَوْمًا لَّا تَجْزِيْ نَفْسٌ عَنْ نَّفْسٍ شَيْـًٔا وَّلَا يُقْبَلُ مِنْهَا شَفَاعَةٌ وَّلَا يُؤْخَذُ مِنْهَا عَدْلٌ وَّلَا هُمْ يُنْصَرُوْنَ ﴿۴۹﴾

50. And *remember the time* when We delivered you from Pharaoh's people who afflicted you with grievous torment, slaying your sons and sparing your women; and in that there was a great trial for you from your Lord.

وَاِذْ نَجَّيْنٰكُمْ مِّنْ اٰلِ فِرْعَوْنَ يَسُوْمُوْنَكُمْ سُوْٓءَ الْعَذَابِ يُذَبِّحُوْنَ اَبْنَآءَكُمْ وَيَسْتَحْيُوْنَ نِسَآءَكُمْ وَفِيْ ذٰلِكُمْ بَلَآءٌ مِّنْ رَّبِّكُمْ عَظِيْمٌ ﴿۵۰﴾

51. And *remember the time* when We divided the sea for you and saved you and drowned Pharaoh's people, while you looked on.

وَاِذْ فَرَقْنَا بِكُمُ الْبَحْرَ فَاَنْجَيْنٰكُمْ وَاَغْرَقْنَآ اٰلَ فِرْعَوْنَ وَاَنْتُمْ تَنْظُرُوْنَ ﴿۵۱﴾

52. And *remember the time* when We made Moses a promise of forty nights; then you took the calf *for worship* in his absence and you were transgressors.

وَاِذْ وٰعَدْنَا مُوْسٰٓى اَرْبَعِيْنَ لَيْلَةً ثُمَّ اتَّخَذْتُمُ الْعِجْلَ مِنْۢ بَعْدِهٖ وَاَنْتُمْ ظٰلِمُوْنَ ﴿۵۲﴾

53. Then We forgave you thereafter, that you might be grateful.

ثُمَّ عَفَوْنَا عَنْكُمْ مِّنْۢ بَعْدِ ذٰلِكَ لَعَلَّكُمْ تَشْكُرُوْنَ ﴿۵۳﴾

54. And *remember the time* when We gave Moses the Book and the Discrimination, that you might be rightly guided.

وَاِذْ اٰتَيْنَا مُوْسَى الْكِتٰبَ وَالْفُرْقَانَ لَعَلَّكُمْ تَهْتَدُوْنَ ﴿۵۴﴾

55. And *remember the time* when Moses said to his people: 'O my people, you have indeed wronged yourselves by taking the calf *for worship;* turn you therefore to your Maker, and slay your own people; that is the best for you with your Maker.' Then He turned towards you with compassion. Surely, He is Oft-Returning *with compassion, and is* Merciful.

وَاِذْ قَالَ مُوْسٰى لِقَوْمِهٖ يٰقَوْمِ اِنَّكُمْ ظَلَمْتُمْ اَنْفُسَكُمْ بِاتِّخَاذِكُمُ الْعِجْلَ فَتُوْبُوْٓا اِلٰى بَارِئِكُمْ فَاقْتُلُوْٓا اَنْفُسَكُمْ ذٰلِكُمْ خَيْرٌ لَّكُمْ عِنْدَ بَارِئِكُمْ فَتَابَ عَلَيْكُمْ اِنَّهٗ هُوَ التَّوَّابُ الرَّحِيْمُ ﴿۵۵﴾

56. And *remember* when you said: 'O Moses, we will by no means believe thee until we see Allah face to face;' then the thunderbolt overtook you, while you gazed.

وَاِذْ قُلْتُمْ يٰمُوْسٰى لَنْ نُّؤْمِنَ لَكَ حَتّٰى نَرَى اللّٰهَ جَهْرَةً فَاَخَذَتْكُمُ الصّٰعِقَةُ وَاَنْتُمْ تَنْظُرُوْنَ ﴿۵۶﴾

57. Then We raised you up after your death, that you might be grateful.

ثُمَّ بَعَثْنٰكُمْ مِّنْۢ بَعْدِ مَوْتِكُمْ لَعَلَّكُمْ تَشْكُرُوْنَ ﴿۵۷﴾

58. And We caused the clouds to be a shade over you and sent down on you Manna and Salwā, *saying:* 'Eat of the good things We have provided for you.' And they wronged Us not, but it was themselves that they wronged.

وَظَلَّلْنَا عَلَيْكُمُ الْغَمَامَ وَاَنْزَلْنَا عَلَيْكُمُ الْمَنَّ وَ
السَّلْوٰى كُلُوْا مِنْ طَيِّبٰتِ مَا رَزَقْنٰكُمْ وَمَا ظَلَمُوْنَا وَ
لٰكِنْ كَانُوْٓا اَنْفُسَهُمْ يَظْلِمُوْنَ ﴿۵۸﴾

59. And *remember the time* when We said: "Enter this village and eat therefrom—wherever you will—plentifully; and enter the gate submissively and say: '*God!* forgive us our sins.' We shall forgive you your sins and We shall give increase to those who do good."

وَاِذْ قُلْنَا ادْخُلُوْا هٰذِهِ الْقَرْيَةَ فَكُلُوْا مِنْهَا حَيْثُ شِئْتُمْ
رَغَدًا وَّادْخُلُوا الْبَابَ سُجَّدًا وَّقُوْلُوْا حِطَّةٌ نَّغْفِرْ لَكُمْ
خَطٰيٰكُمْ وَسَنَزِيْدُ الْمُحْسِنِيْنَ ﴿۵۹﴾

60. The transgressors changed *it* for a word other than that which was said to them. So We sent down upon the transgressors a punishment from heaven, because they were disobedient.

فَبَدَّلَ الَّذِيْنَ ظَلَمُوْا قَوْلًا غَيْرَ الَّذِيْ قِيْلَ لَهُمْ
فَاَنْزَلْنَا عَلَى الَّذِيْنَ ظَلَمُوْا رِجْزًا مِّنَ السَّمَآءِ بِمَا
كَانُوْا يَفْسُقُوْنَ ﴿۶۰﴾ ع

R. 7.

61. And *remember the time* when Moses prayed for water for his people, and We said: 'Strike the rock with thy rod,' and there gushed forth from it twelve springs, *so that* every tribe knew their drinking place. 'Eat and drink of what Allah has provided, and commit not iniquity in the earth, creating disorder.'

وَاِذِ اسْتَسْقٰى مُوْسٰى لِقَوْمِهٖ فَقُلْنَا اضْرِبْ بِّعَصَاكَ
الْحَجَرَ فَانْفَجَرَتْ مِنْهُ اثْنَتَا عَشْرَةَ عَيْنًا قَدْ
عَلِمَ كُلُّ اُنَاسٍ مَّشْرَبَهُمْ كُلُوْا وَاشْرَبُوْا مِنْ رِّزْقِ
اللّٰهِ وَلَا تَعْثَوْا فِي الْاَرْضِ مُفْسِدِيْنَ ﴿۶۱﴾

62. And *remember the time* when you said: 'O Moses, surely, we will not remain content with one *kind of* food; pray, then, to thy Lord for us that He bring forth for us of what the earth grows—of its herbs and its cucumbers and its wheat and its lentils and its onions.' He said: 'Would you take in exchange that which is inferior for that which is superior? Go down to some town, and there is for you what you ask.' And they were smitten with abasement and destitution, and they incurred the wrath of Allah: that was because they rejected the Signs of Allah and would kill the Prophets unjustly; that was because they rebelled and transgressed.

وَاِذْ قُلْتُمْ يٰمُوْسٰى لَنْ نَّصْبِرَ عَلٰى طَعَامٍ وَّاحِدٍ فَادْعُ
لَنَا رَبَّكَ يُخْرِجْ لَنَا مِمَّا تُنْۢبِتُ الْاَرْضُ مِنْۢ بَقْلِهَا وَ
قِثَّآئِهَا وَفُوْمِهَا وَعَدَسِهَا وَبَصَلِهَا قَالَ اَتَسْتَبْدِلُوْنَ
الَّذِيْ هُوَ اَدْنٰى بِالَّذِيْ هُوَ خَيْرٌ اِهْبِطُوْا مِصْرًا فَاِنَّ
لَكُمْ مَّا سَاَلْتُمْ وَضُرِبَتْ عَلَيْهِمُ الذِّلَّةُ وَالْمَسْكَنَةُ
وَبَآءُوْ بِغَضَبٍ مِّنَ اللّٰهِ ذٰلِكَ بِاَنَّهُمْ كَانُوْا يَكْفُرُوْنَ
بِاٰيٰتِ اللّٰهِ وَيَقْتُلُوْنَ النَّبِيّٖنَ بِغَيْرِ الْحَقِّ ذٰلِكَ بِمَا
عَصَوْا وَّكَانُوْا يَعْتَدُوْنَ ﴿۶۲﴾ ع

R. 8.

63. Surely, the Believers, and the Jews, and the Christians and the Sabians —

اِنَّ الَّذِيْنَ اٰمَنُوْا وَالَّذِيْنَ هَادُوْا وَالنَّصٰرٰى وَ

whichever party *from among these truly* believes in Allah and the Last Day and does good deeds — shall have their reward with their Lord, and no fear *shall come* upon them, nor shall they grieve.

الصّٰبِـِٔيْنَ مَنْ اٰمَنَ بِاللّٰهِ وَالْيَوْمِ الْاٰخِرِ وَعَمِلَ
صَالِحًا فَلَهُمْ اَجْرُهُمْ عِنْدَ رَبِّهِمْ ۚ وَلَا خَوْفٌ عَلَيْهِمْ
وَلَا هُمْ يَحْزَنُوْنَ ﴿٦٣﴾

64. And *remember the time* when We took a covenant from you and raised high above you the Mount, *saying*: 'Hold fast that which We have given you and bear in mind what is therein, that you may be saved.'

وَاِذْ اَخَذْنَا مِيْثَاقَكُمْ وَرَفَعْنَا فَوْقَكُمُ الطُّوْرَ ؕ خُذُوْا
مَآ اٰتَيْنٰكُمْ بِقُوَّةٍ وَّاذْكُرُوْا مَا فِيْهِ لَعَلَّكُمْ تَتَّقُوْنَ ﴿٦٤﴾

65. Then you turned back thereafter; and had it not been for Allah's grace towards you and His mercy, you would surely have been of the losers.

ثُمَّ تَوَلَّيْتُمْ مِّنْ بَعْدِ ذٰلِكَ ۚ فَلَوْلَا فَضْلُ اللّٰهِ عَلَيْكُمْ
وَرَحْمَتُهٗ لَكُنْتُمْ مِّنَ الْخٰسِرِيْنَ ﴿٦٥﴾

66. And surely, you have known *the end of* those amongst you, who transgressed in the matter of the Sabbath. So We said to them: 'Be ye apes, despised.'

وَلَقَدْ عَلِمْتُمُ الَّذِيْنَ اعْتَدَوْا مِنْكُمْ فِي السَّبْتِ
فَقُلْنَا لَهُمْ كُوْنُوْا قِرَدَةً خٰسِـِٕيْنَ ﴿٦٦﴾

67. Thus We made it an example to those of its time and to those who came after it, and a lesson to those who fear God.

فَجَعَلْنٰهَا نَكَالًا لِّمَا بَيْنَ يَدَيْهَا وَمَا خَلْفَهَا وَ
مَوْعِظَةً لِّلْمُتَّقِيْنَ ﴿٦٧﴾

68. And *remember* when Moses said to his people: 'Allah commands you to slaughter a cow,' they said: 'Dost thou make a jest of us?' He said: 'I seek refuge with Allah from being one of the ignorant.'

وَاِذْ قَالَ مُوْسٰى لِقَوْمِهٖٓ اِنَّ اللّٰهَ يَاْمُرُكُمْ اَنْ تَذْبَحُوْا
بَقَرَةً ؕ قَالُوْٓا اَتَتَّخِذُنَا هُزُوًا ؕ قَالَ اَعُوْذُ بِاللّٰهِ اَنْ اَكُوْنَ
مِنَ الْجٰهِلِيْنَ ﴿٦٨﴾

69. They said: 'Pray for us to thy Lord that He make plain to us what she is.' He answered: '*God* says, it is a cow, neither old nor young, full-grown, between the two; now do what you are commanded.'

قَالُوا ادْعُ لَنَا رَبَّكَ يُبَيِّنْ لَّنَا مَا هِيَ ؕ قَالَ اِنَّهٗ يَقُوْلُ
اِنَّهَا بَقَرَةٌ لَّا فَارِضٌ وَّلَا بِكْرٌ ؕ عَوَانٌۢ بَيْنَ ذٰلِكَ ؕ
فَافْعَلُوْا مَا تُؤْمَرُوْنَ ﴿٦٩﴾

70. They said: 'Pray for us to thy Lord that He make plain to us what colour she is.' He answered: '*God* says, it is a cow of a dun colour, pure and rich *in tone;* delighting the beholders.'

قَالُوا ادْعُ لَنَا رَبَّكَ يُبَيِّنْ لَّنَا مَا لَوْنُهَا ؕ قَالَ اِنَّهٗ يَقُوْلُ
اِنَّهَا بَقَرَةٌ صَفْرَآءُ ۙ فَاقِعٌ لَّوْنُهَا تَسُرُّ النّٰظِرِيْنَ ﴿٧٠﴾

71. They said: 'Pray for us to thy Lord that He make plain to us what she is, for *all such* cows appear to us alike; and if Allah please, we shall indeed be guided.'

قَالُوا ادْعُ لَنَا رَبَّكَ يُبَيِّنْ لَّنَا مَا هِيَ ۙ اِنَّ الْبَقَرَ تَشٰبَهَ
عَلَيْنَا ؕ وَاِنَّآ اِنْ شَآءَ اللّٰهُ لَمُهْتَدُوْنَ ﴿٧١﴾

72. He answered: '*God* says, it is a cow not broken in to plough the earth or water

قَالَ اِنَّهٗ يَقُوْلُ اِنَّهَا بَقَرَةٌ لَّا ذَلُوْلٌ تُثِيْرُ الْاَرْضَ

the tilth; one without blemish; of one colour.' They said: 'Now hast thou brought the truth.' Then they slaughtered her, though they would rather not do so.

وَلَا تَسْقِي الْحَرْثَ مُسَلَّمَةٌ لَّا شِيَةَ فِيهَا قَالُوا الْـٰٔنَ
جِئْتَ بِالْحَقِّ فَذَبَحُوهَا وَمَا كَادُوا يَفْعَلُونَ ﴿٧٢﴾

R. 9.

73. And *remember the time* when you slew a person and differed among yourselves about it; and Allah would bring to light what you concealed.

وَإِذْ قَتَلْتُمْ نَفْسًا فَادَّارَءْتُمْ فِيهَا وَاللّٰهُ مُخْرِجٌ مَّا
كُنتُمْ تَكْتُمُونَ ﴿٧٣﴾

74. Then We said: 'Smite him (the murderer) for a part of *the offence against* him (the murdered person).' Thus Allah gives life to the dead and shows you His Signs that you may understand.

فَقُلْنَا اضْرِبُوهُ بِبَعْضِهَا كَذٰلِكَ يُحْيِ اللّٰهُ الْمَوْتٰى
وَيُرِيكُمْ اٰيٰتِهِ لَعَلَّكُمْ تَعْقِلُونَ ﴿٧٤﴾

75. Then your hearts became hardened after that, till they were like stones or harder still; for of stones indeed there are some out of which gush forth streams, and of them there are some out of which flows water when they cleave asunder. And indeed, of them there are some that humble themselves for fear of Allah. And Allah is not unmindful of what you do.

ثُمَّ قَسَتْ قُلُوبُكُم مِّنْ بَعْدِ ذٰلِكَ فَهِيَ كَالْحِجَارَةِ
أَوْ أَشَدُّ قَسْوَةً وَإِنَّ مِنَ الْحِجَارَةِ لَمَا يَتَفَجَّرُ مِنْهُ
الْأَنْهٰرُ وَإِنَّ مِنْهَا لَمَا يَشَّقَّقُ فَيَخْرُجُ مِنْهُ الْمَاءُ
وَإِنَّ مِنْهَا لَمَا يَهْبِطُ مِنْ خَشْيَةِ اللّٰهِ وَمَا اللّٰهُ
بِغٰفِلٍ عَمَّا تَعْمَلُونَ ﴿٧٥﴾

* 76. Do you expect that they will believe you when a party of them hear the word of Allah, then pervert it after they have understood it, and they know *the consequences thereof?*

أَفَتَطْمَعُونَ أَن يُؤْمِنُوا لَكُمْ وَقَدْ كَانَ فَرِيقٌ مِّنْهُمْ
يَسْمَعُونَ كَلٰمَ اللّٰهِ ثُمَّ يُحَرِّفُونَهُ مِنْ بَعْدِ مَا عَقَلُوهُ
وَهُمْ يَعْلَمُونَ ﴿٧٦﴾

77. And when they meet those who believe, they say: 'We believe,' and when they meet one another in private, they say: 'Do you inform them of what Allah has unfolded to you, that they may thereby argue with you before your Lord? Will you not then understand?'

وَإِذَا لَقُوا الَّذِينَ اٰمَنُوا قَالُوا اٰمَنَّا وَإِذَا خَلَا بَعْضُهُمْ
إِلٰى بَعْضٍ قَالُوا أَتُحَدِّثُونَهُم بِمَا فَتَحَ اللّٰهُ عَلَيْكُمْ
لِيُحَاجُّوكُم بِهِ عِندَ رَبِّكُمْ أَفَلَا تَعْقِلُونَ ﴿٧٧﴾

78. Do they not know that Allah knows what they conceal and what they disclose?

أَوَلَا يَعْلَمُونَ أَنَّ اللّٰهَ يَعْلَمُ مَا يُسِرُّونَ وَمَا يُعْلِنُونَ ﴿٧٨﴾

79. And some of them are illiterate; they know not the Book but *their own* false notions, and they *do nothing* but conjecture.

وَمِنْهُمْ أُمِّيُّونَ لَا يَعْلَمُونَ الْكِتٰبَ إِلَّا أَمَانِيَّ وَإِنْ هُمْ
إِلَّا يَظُنُّونَ ﴿٧٩﴾ النصف

80. Woe, therefore, to those who write the Book with their own hands, and then say: 'This is from Allah,' that they may take for it a paltry price. Woe, then, to them for

فَوَيْلٌ لِّلَّذِينَ يَكْتُبُونَ الْكِتٰبَ بِأَيْدِيهِمْ ثُمَّ يَقُولُونَ
هٰذَا مِنْ عِندِ اللّٰهِ لِيَشْتَرُوا بِهِ ثَمَنًا قَلِيلًا فَوَيْلٌ

what their hands have written, and woe to them for what they earn.

لَهُمْ مِّمَّا كَتَبَتْ اَيْدِيْهِمْ وَوَيْلٌ لَّهُمْ مِّمَّا يَكْسِبُوْنَ ﴿٨٠﴾

81. And they say: 'The Fire shall not touch us except for a *small* number of days.' Say: 'Have you taken a promise from Allah? Then, Allah will never break His promise. Or, do you say of Allah what you know not?'

وَقَالُوْا لَنْ تَمَسَّنَا النَّارُ اِلَّاۤ اَيَّامًا مَّعْدُوْدَةً ؕ قُلْ
اَتَّخَذْتُمْ عِنْدَ اللّٰهِ عَهْدًا فَلَنْ يُّخْلِفَ اللّٰهُ عَهْدَهٗۤ
اَمْ تَقُوْلُوْنَ عَلَى اللّٰهِ مَا لَا تَعْلَمُوْنَ ﴿٨١﴾

82. Aye, whoso does evil and is encompassed by his sins—those are the inmates of the Fire; therein shall they abide.

بَلٰى مَنْ كَسَبَ سَيِّئَةً وَّاَحَاطَتْ بِهٖ خَطِيْٓئَتُهٗ فَاُولٰٓئِكَ
اَصْحٰبُ النَّارِ ۚ هُمْ فِيْهَا خٰلِدُوْنَ ﴿٨٢﴾

83. But they who believe and do good works—those are the dwellers of Heaven; therein shall they abide.

وَالَّذِيْنَ اٰمَنُوْا وَعَمِلُوا الصّٰلِحٰتِ اُولٰٓئِكَ اَصْحٰبُ الْجَنَّةِ ۚ
هُمْ فِيْهَا خٰلِدُوْنَ ﴿٨٣﴾ ع ٩

R. 10.

84. And *remember the time* when We took a covenant from the children of Israel: 'You shall worship *nothing* but Allah and *show* kindness to parents and to kindred and orphans and the poor, and speak to men kindly and observe Prayer, and pay the Zakāt;' then you turned away in aversion, except a few of you.

وَاِذْ اَخَذْنَا مِيْثَاقَ بَنِيْٓ اِسْرَآءِيْلَ لَا تَعْبُدُوْنَ اِلَّا
اللّٰهَ ۟ وَبِالْوَالِدَيْنِ اِحْسَانًا وَّذِي الْقُرْبٰى وَالْيَتٰمٰى
وَالْمَسٰكِيْنِ وَقُوْلُوْا لِلنَّاسِ حُسْنًا وَّاَقِيْمُوا الصَّلٰوةَ
وَاٰتُوا الزَّكٰوةَ ؕ ثُمَّ تَوَلَّيْتُمْ اِلَّا قَلِيْلًا مِّنْكُمْ وَاَنْتُمْ
مُّعْرِضُوْنَ ﴿٨٤﴾

85. And *remember the time* when We took a covenant from you: 'You shall not shed your blood or turn your people out of your homes;' then you confirmed *it;* and you have been witness *to it*.

وَاِذْ اَخَذْنَا مِيْثَاقَكُمْ لَا تَسْفِكُوْنَ دِمَآءَكُمْ وَلَا
تُخْرِجُوْنَ اَنْفُسَكُمْ مِّنْ دِيَارِكُمْ ثُمَّ اَقْرَرْتُمْ وَاَنْتُمْ
تَشْهَدُوْنَ ﴿٨٥﴾

86. Yet you are the people who slay your own brethren and turn out a section of your people from their homes, backing up one another against them with sin and transgression. And if they come to you as captives, you ransom them, while their *very* expulsion was unlawful for you. Do you, then, believe in part of the Book and disbelieve in part? There is, therefore, no reward for such among you as do this, except disgrace in the present life; and on

ثُمَّ اَنْتُمْ هٰٓؤُلَآءِ تَقْتُلُوْنَ اَنْفُسَكُمْ وَتُخْرِجُوْنَ فَرِيْقًا
مِّنْكُمْ مِّنْ دِيَارِهِمْ ۫ تَظٰهَرُوْنَ عَلَيْهِمْ بِالْاِثْمِ
وَالْعُدْوَانِ ؕ وَاِنْ يَّاْتُوْكُمْ اُسٰرٰى تُفٰدُوْهُمْ وَهُوَ
مُحَرَّمٌ عَلَيْكُمْ اِخْرَاجُهُمْ ؕ اَفَتُؤْمِنُوْنَ بِبَعْضِ
الْكِتٰبِ وَتَكْفُرُوْنَ بِبَعْضٍ ۚ فَمَا جَزَآءُ مَنْ يَّفْعَلُ
ذٰلِكَ مِنْكُمْ اِلَّا خِزْيٌ فِي الْحَيٰوةِ الدُّنْيَا ۚ وَيَوْمَ الْقِيٰمَةِ

the Day of Judgment they shall be driven to a most severe chastisement; and surely, Allah is not unmindful of what you do.

يُرَدُّوْنَ اِلٰۤى اَشَدِّ الْعَذَابِ ؕ وَ مَا اللّٰهُ بِغَافِلٍ عَمَّا
تَعْمَلُوْنَ ﴿۸۶﴾

87. These are they who have preferred the present life to the Hereafter. Their punishment shall not therefore be lightened, nor shall they be helped *in any other way*.

اُولٰٓئِكَ الَّذِيْنَ اشْتَرَوُا الْحَيٰوةَ الدُّنْيَا بِالْاٰخِرَةِ ؗ فَلَا
يُخَفَّفُ عَنْهُمُ الْعَذَابُ وَ لَا هُمْ يُنْصَرُوْنَ ﴿۸۷﴾ ع

R. 11.

88. And verily, We gave Moses the Book and caused after him Messengers to follow in his footsteps; and to Jesus, son of Mary, We gave manifest Signs, and strengthened him with the Spirit of holiness. Will you then, every time a Messenger comes to you with what you yourselves desire not, behave arrogantly and treat some as liars and slay others?

وَ لَقَدْ اٰتَيْنَا مُوْسَى الْكِتٰبَ وَ قَفَّيْنَا مِنْۢ بَعْدِهٖ بِالرُّسُلِ ؗ
وَ اٰتَيْنَا عِيْسَى ابْنَ مَرْيَمَ الْبَيِّنٰتِ وَ اَيَّدْنٰهُ بِرُوْحِ الْقُدُسِ ؕ
اَفَكُلَّمَا جَآءَكُمْ رَسُوْلٌۢ بِمَا لَا تَهْوٰۤى اَنْفُسُكُمُ اسْتَكْبَرْتُمْ ۚ
فَفَرِيْقًا كَذَّبْتُمْ ؗ وَ فَرِيْقًا تَقْتُلُوْنَ ﴿۸۸﴾

89. They said: 'Our hearts are wrapped in covers.' Nay, Allah has cursed them for their disbelief. Little is that which they believe.

وَ قَالُوْا قُلُوْبُنَا غُلْفٌ ؕ بَلْ لَّعَنَهُمُ اللّٰهُ بِكُفْرِهِمْ فَقَلِيْلًا
مَّا يُؤْمِنُوْنَ ﴿۸۹﴾

90. And when there came to them a Book from Allah, fulfilling that which is with them—and before that they had prayed for victory over the disbelievers—yet when there came to them that which they knew, they rejected it. The curse of Allah be on the disbelievers.

وَ لَمَّا جَآءَهُمْ كِتٰبٌ مِّنْ عِنْدِ اللّٰهِ مُصَدِّقٌ لِّمَا مَعَهُمْ ۙ
وَ كَانُوْا مِنْ قَبْلُ يَسْتَفْتِحُوْنَ عَلَى الَّذِيْنَ كَفَرُوْا ۚۖ
فَلَمَّا جَآءَهُمْ مَّا عَرَفُوْا كَفَرُوْا بِهٖ ؗ فَلَعْنَةُ اللّٰهِ عَلَى
الْكٰفِرِيْنَ ﴿۹۰﴾

91. Evil is that for which they have sold their souls: that they should disbelieve in what Allah has revealed, grudging that Allah should send down His grace on whomsoever of His servants He pleases. So they incurred wrath upon wrath; and there is an humiliating chastisement for the disbelievers.

بِئْسَمَا اشْتَرَوْا بِهٖۤ اَنْفُسَهُمْ اَنْ يَّكْفُرُوْا بِمَاۤ اَنْزَلَ اللّٰهُ
بَغْيًا اَنْ يُّنَزِّلَ اللّٰهُ مِنْ فَضْلِهٖ عَلٰى مَنْ يَّشَآءُ مِنْ
عِبَادِهٖ ۚ فَبَآءُوْ بِغَضَبٍ عَلٰى غَضَبٍ ؕ وَ لِلْكٰفِرِيْنَ عَذَابٌ
مُّهِيْنٌ ﴿۹۱﴾

92. And when it is said to them: 'Believe in what Allah has sent down,' they say: 'We believe in what has been sent down to us;' and they disbelieve in what *has been sent down* after that, yet it is the Truth, fulfilling that which is with them. Say: 'Why, then, did you attempt to slay the Prophets of Allah before this, if you were believers?'

وَ اِذَا قِيْلَ لَهُمْ اٰمِنُوْا بِمَاۤ اَنْزَلَ اللّٰهُ قَالُوْا نُؤْمِنُ بِمَاۤ
اُنْزِلَ عَلَيْنَا وَ يَكْفُرُوْنَ بِمَا وَرَآءَهٗ ۗ وَ هُوَ الْحَقُّ
مُصَدِّقًا لِّمَا مَعَهُمْ ؕ قُلْ فَلِمَ تَقْتُلُوْنَ اَنْۢبِيَآءَ اللّٰهِ
مِنْ قَبْلُ اِنْ كُنْتُمْ مُّؤْمِنِيْنَ ﴿۹۲﴾

93. And Moses came to you with manifest Signs, then you took the calf *for worship* in his absence and you were transgressors.

وَلَقَدْ جَآءَكُمْ مُّوْسٰى بِالْبَيِّنٰتِ ثُمَّ اتَّخَذْتُمُ الْعِجْلَ مِنْ بَعْدِهٖ وَاَنْتُمْ ظٰلِمُوْنَ ﴿۹۳﴾

94. And *remember the time*, when We took a covenant from you and raised high above you the Mount, *saying:* 'Hold firmly to what We have given you and hearken;' they said: 'We hear and we disobey;' and their hearts were permeated with *the love of* the calf because of their disbelief. Say: 'Evil is that which your faith enjoins on you, if you have any faith!'

وَاِذْ اَخَذْنَا مِيْثَاقَكُمْ وَرَفَعْنَا فَوْقَكُمُ الطُّوْرَ خُذُوْا مَآ اٰتَيْنٰكُمْ بِقُوَّةٍ وَّاسْمَعُوْا قَالُوْا سَمِعْنَا وَعَصَيْنَا وَاُشْرِبُوْا فِيْ قُلُوْبِهِمُ الْعِجْلَ بِكُفْرِهِمْ قُلْ بِئْسَمَا يَاْمُرُكُمْ بِهٖٓ اِيْمَانُكُمْ اِنْ كُنْتُمْ مُّؤْمِنِيْنَ ﴿۹۴﴾

95. Say: 'If the abode of the Hereafter, with Allah, is solely for you to the exclusion of *all* other people, then wish for death, if you are truthful.'

قُلْ اِنْ كَانَتْ لَكُمُ الدَّارُ الْاٰخِرَةُ عِنْدَ اللّٰهِ خَالِصَةً مِّنْ دُوْنِ النَّاسِ فَتَمَنَّوُا الْمَوْتَ اِنْ كُنْتُمْ صٰدِقِيْنَ ﴿۹۵﴾

96. But never shall they wish for it, because of what their own hands have sent on before *them;* and Allah knows the wrongdoers well.

وَلَنْ يَّتَمَنَّوْهُ اَبَدًا بِمَا قَدَّمَتْ اَيْدِيْهِمْ وَاللّٰهُ عَلِيْمٌ بِالظّٰلِمِيْنَ ﴿۹۶﴾

97. And thou shalt surely find them of all people, the most covetous of life, even *more* than those who set up equals *with God.* Every one of them wishes that he may be granted a life of a thousand years, but his being granted *such* life shall not keep him away from the punishment; and Allah sees all that they do.

وَلَتَجِدَنَّهُمْ اَحْرَصَ النَّاسِ عَلٰى حَيٰوةٍ وَمِنَ الَّذِيْنَ اَشْرَكُوْا يَوَدُّ اَحَدُهُمْ لَوْ يُعَمَّرُ اَلْفَ سَنَةٍ وَمَا هُوَ بِمُزَحْزِحِهٖ مِنَ الْعَذَابِ اَنْ يُّعَمَّرَ وَاللّٰهُ بَصِيْرٌ بِمَا يَعْمَلُوْنَ ﴿۹۷﴾ ع

R. 12.

98. Say: 'Whoever is an enemy to Gabriel—for he it is who has caused it to descend on thy heart by the command of Allah, which fulfils that which precedes it, and is a guidance and glad tidings to the believers—

قُلْ مَنْ كَانَ عَدُوًّا لِّجِبْرِيْلَ فَاِنَّهٗ نَزَّلَهٗ عَلٰى قَلْبِكَ بِاِذْنِ اللّٰهِ مُصَدِّقًا لِّمَا بَيْنَ يَدَيْهِ وَهُدًى وَّبُشْرٰى لِلْمُؤْمِنِيْنَ ﴿۹۸﴾

99. 'Whoever is an enemy to Allah, and His angels, and His Messengers, and Gabriel, and Michael, then surely, Allah is an enemy to *such* disbelievers.'

مَنْ كَانَ عَدُوًّا لِّلّٰهِ وَمَلٰٓئِكَتِهٖ وَرُسُلِهٖ وَجِبْرِيْلَ وَمِيْكٰلَ فَاِنَّ اللّٰهَ عَدُوٌّ لِّلْكٰفِرِيْنَ ﴿۹۹﴾

100. And surely, We have sent down to thee manifest Signs, and no one disbelieves in them but the disobedient.

وَلَقَدْ اَنْزَلْنَآ اِلَيْكَ اٰيٰتٍۭ بَيِّنٰتٍ وَمَا يَكْفُرُ بِهَآ اِلَّا الْفٰسِقُوْنَ ﴿۱۰۰﴾

101. What! every time they make a covenant, will a party among them throw it

اَوَكُلَّمَا عٰهَدُوْا عَهْدًا نَّبَذَهٗ فَرِيْقٌ مِّنْهُمْ بَلْ

aside? Nay, most of them have no faith.

أَكْثَرُهُمْ لَا يُؤْمِنُونَ ﴿١٠١﴾

102. And *now* when there has come to them a Messenger from Allah, fulfilling that which is with them, a party of the people to whom the Book was given have thrown the Book of Allah behind their backs, as if they knew *it* not.

وَلَمَّا جَاءَهُمْ رَسُولٌ مِّنْ عِندِ اللَّهِ مُصَدِّقٌ لِّمَا
مَعَهُمْ نَبَذَ فَرِيقٌ مِّنَ الَّذِينَ أُوتُوا الْكِتَابَ كِتَابَ
اللَّهِ وَرَاءَ ظُهُورِهِمْ كَأَنَّهُمْ لَا يَعْلَمُونَ ﴿١٠٢﴾

103. And they pursue *the course* which the rebellious *men* followed during the reign of Solomon. And Solomon did not disbelieve; but *it was* the rebellious ones *who* disbelieved, teaching people falsehood and deception. And *they pursue* what was revealed to the two angels in Babylon, Hārūt and Mārūt. But these two taught no one until they had said: 'We are but a trial, do not therefore disbelieve.' So men learnt from them that by which they made a difference between a man and his wife, but they harmed no one thereby, except by the command of Allah; *on the contrary*, these people are learning that which would harm them and do them no good. And they have certainly known that he who trafficks therein has no share of good in the Hereafter; and surely, evil is that for which they have sold their souls; had they but known!

وَاتَّبَعُوا مَا تَتْلُو الشَّيَاطِينُ عَلَىٰ مُلْكِ سُلَيْمَانَ وَ
مَا كَفَرَ سُلَيْمَانُ وَلَٰكِنَّ الشَّيَاطِينَ كَفَرُوا يُعَلِّمُونَ
النَّاسَ السِّحْرَ وَمَا أُنزِلَ عَلَى الْمَلَكَيْنِ بِبَابِلَ
هَارُوتَ وَمَارُوتَ وَمَا يُعَلِّمَانِ مِنْ أَحَدٍ حَتَّىٰ
يَقُولَا إِنَّمَا نَحْنُ فِتْنَةٌ فَلَا تَكْفُرْ فَيَتَعَلَّمُونَ مِنْهُمَا
مَا يُفَرِّقُونَ بِهِ بَيْنَ الْمَرْءِ وَزَوْجِهِ وَمَا هُم بِضَارِّينَ
بِهِ مِنْ أَحَدٍ إِلَّا بِإِذْنِ اللَّهِ وَيَتَعَلَّمُونَ مَا يَضُرُّهُمْ
وَلَا يَنفَعُهُمْ وَلَقَدْ عَلِمُوا لَمَنِ اشْتَرَاهُ مَا لَهُ فِي
الْآخِرَةِ مِنْ خَلَاقٍ وَلَبِئْسَ مَا شَرَوْا بِهِ أَنفُسَهُمْ
لَوْ كَانُوا يَعْلَمُونَ ﴿١٠٣﴾

104. And if they had believed and acted righteously, better surely would have been the reward from Allah, had they but known!

وَلَوْ أَنَّهُمْ آمَنُوا وَاتَّقَوْا لَمَثُوبَةٌ مِّنْ عِندِ اللَّهِ خَيْرٌ
لَّوْ كَانُوا يَعْلَمُونَ ﴿١٠٤﴾ ع ١٢ ١٢

R. 13.

105. O ye who believe! say not 'Rā'inā', but say, 'Unẓurnā' and hearken. And for the disbelievers is a painful punishment.

يَا أَيُّهَا الَّذِينَ آمَنُوا لَا تَقُولُوا رَاعِنَا وَقُولُوا انظُرْنَا
وَاسْمَعُوا وَلِلْكَافِرِينَ عَذَابٌ أَلِيمٌ ﴿١٠٥﴾

106. They who disbelieve from among the People of the Book, or from among those who associate gods *with Allah*, desire not that any good should be sent down to you from your Lord; but Allah chooses for His mercy whomsoever He pleases; and Allah is of exceeding bounty.

مَا يَوَدُّ الَّذِينَ كَفَرُوا مِنْ أَهْلِ الْكِتَابِ وَلَا الْمُشْرِكِينَ
أَن يُنَزَّلَ عَلَيْكُم مِّنْ خَيْرٍ مِّن رَّبِّكُمْ وَاللَّهُ يَخْتَصُّ
بِرَحْمَتِهِ مَن يَشَاءُ وَاللَّهُ ذُو الْفَضْلِ الْعَظِيمِ ﴿١٠٦﴾

107. Whatever Sign We abrogate or cause to be forgotten, We bring one better

مَا نَنسَخْ مِنْ آيَةٍ أَوْ نُنسِهَا نَأْتِ بِخَيْرٍ مِّنْهَا أَوْ

than that or the like thereof. Dost thou not know that Allah has the power to do all that He wills?

108. Dost thou not know that the kingdom of the heavens and the earth belongs to Allah alone? And there is no protector or helper for you beside Allah.

109. Would you question the Messenger sent to you as Moses was questioned before this? And whoever takes disbelief in exchange for belief has undoubtedly gone astray from the right path.

110. Many of the People of the Book wish out of *sheer* envy from their own selves that, after you have believed, they could turn you again into disbelievers after the truth has become manifest to them. But forgive and turn away *from them*, till Allah brings about His decree. Surely, Allah has the power to do all that He wills.

111. And observe Prayer and pay the Zakāt; and whatever good you send on before you for yourselves, you shall find it with Allah; surely, Allah sees all that you do.

112. And they say, 'None shall ever enter Heaven unless he be a Jew or a Christian.' These are their vain desires. Say, 'Produce your proof, if you are truthful.'

* 113. Nay, whoever submits himself completely to Allah, and is the doer of good, shall have his reward with his Lord. No fear *shall come* upon such, neither shall they grieve.

R. 14.

114. And the Jews say, 'The Christians stand on nothing;' and the Christians say, 'The Jews stand on nothing;' while they *both* read the *same* Book. Even thus said those who had no knowledge, like what they say. But Allah shall judge between them on the Day of Resurrection concerning that wherein they disagree.

مِثْلِهَا ۗ أَلَمْ تَعْلَمْ أَنَّ اللَّهَ عَلَىٰ كُلِّ شَيْءٍ قَدِيرٌ ﴿١٠٧﴾
أَلَمْ تَعْلَمْ أَنَّ اللَّهَ لَهُ مُلْكُ السَّمَاوَاتِ وَالْأَرْضِ ۗ وَ
مَا لَكُمْ مِنْ دُونِ اللَّهِ مِنْ وَلِيٍّ وَلَا نَصِيرٍ ﴿١٠٨﴾
أَمْ تُرِيدُونَ أَنْ تَسْأَلُوا رَسُولَكُمْ كَمَا سُئِلَ مُوسَىٰ مِنْ
قَبْلُ ۗ وَمَنْ يَتَبَدَّلِ الْكُفْرَ بِالْإِيمَانِ فَقَدْ ضَلَّ سَوَاءَ
السَّبِيلِ ﴿١٠٩﴾
وَدَّ كَثِيرٌ مِنْ أَهْلِ الْكِتَابِ لَوْ يَرُدُّونَكُمْ مِنْ بَعْدِ
إِيمَانِكُمْ كُفَّارًا حَسَدًا مِنْ عِنْدِ أَنْفُسِهِمْ
مِنْ بَعْدِ مَا تَبَيَّنَ لَهُمُ الْحَقُّ ۖ فَاعْفُوا وَاصْفَحُوا
حَتَّىٰ يَأْتِيَ اللَّهُ بِأَمْرِهِ ۗ إِنَّ اللَّهَ عَلَىٰ كُلِّ شَيْءٍ قَدِيرٌ ﴿١١٠﴾
وَأَقِيمُوا الصَّلَاةَ وَآتُوا الزَّكَاةَ ۚ وَمَا تُقَدِّمُوا لِأَنْفُسِكُمْ
مِنْ خَيْرٍ تَجِدُوهُ عِنْدَ اللَّهِ ۗ إِنَّ اللَّهَ بِمَا تَعْمَلُونَ
بَصِيرٌ ﴿١١١﴾
وَقَالُوا لَنْ يَدْخُلَ الْجَنَّةَ إِلَّا مَنْ كَانَ هُودًا أَوْ
نَصَارَىٰ ۗ تِلْكَ أَمَانِيُّهُمْ ۗ قُلْ هَاتُوا بُرْهَانَكُمْ إِنْ
كُنْتُمْ صَادِقِينَ ﴿١١٢﴾
بَلَىٰ مَنْ أَسْلَمَ وَجْهَهُ لِلَّهِ وَهُوَ مُحْسِنٌ فَلَهُ أَجْرُهُ
عِنْدَ رَبِّهِ وَلَا خَوْفٌ عَلَيْهِمْ وَلَا هُمْ يَحْزَنُونَ ﴿١١٣﴾
وَقَالَتِ الْيَهُودُ لَيْسَتِ النَّصَارَىٰ عَلَىٰ شَيْءٍ وَقَالَتِ
النَّصَارَىٰ لَيْسَتِ الْيَهُودُ عَلَىٰ شَيْءٍ وَهُمْ يَتْلُونَ الْكِتَابَ ۗ
كَذَٰلِكَ قَالَ الَّذِينَ لَا يَعْلَمُونَ مِثْلَ قَوْلِهِمْ ۚ فَاللَّهُ
يَحْكُمُ بَيْنَهُمْ يَوْمَ الْقِيَامَةِ فِيمَا كَانُوا فِيهِ يَخْتَلِفُونَ ﴿١١٤﴾

115. And who is more unjust than he who prohibits the name of Allah being glorified in Allah's temples and seeks to ruin them? It was not proper for such men to enter therein except in fear. For them is disgrace in this world; and theirs shall be a great punishment in the next.

وَمَنْ اَظْلَمُ مِمَّنْ مَّنَعَ مَسٰجِدَ اللّٰهِ اَنْ يُّذْكَرَ فِيْهَا
اسْمُهٗ وَسَعٰى فِيْ خَرَابِهَا ؕ اُولٰٓئِكَ مَا كَانَ لَهُمْ اَنْ
يَّدْخُلُوْهَآ اِلَّا خَآئِفِيْنَ ؕ لَهُمْ فِي الدُّنْيَا خِزْيٌ وَّلَهُمْ
فِي الْاٰخِرَةِ عَذَابٌ عَظِيْمٌ ﴿۱۱۵﴾

116. To Allah belong the East and the West; so whithersoever you turn, there will be the face of Allah. Surely, Allah is Bountiful, All-Knowing.

وَلِلّٰهِ الْمَشْرِقُ وَالْمَغْرِبُ ۚ فَاَيْنَمَا تُوَلُّوْا فَثَمَّ وَجْهُ
اللّٰهِ ؕ اِنَّ اللّٰهَ وَاسِعٌ عَلِيْمٌ ﴿۱۱۶﴾

117. And they say, 'Allah has taken *to Himself* a son.' Holy is He! Nay, everything in the heavens and the earth belongs to Him. To Him are all obedient.

وَقَالُوا اتَّخَذَ اللّٰهُ وَلَدًا ۙ سُبْحٰنَهٗ ؕ بَلْ لَّهٗ مَا فِي السَّمٰوٰتِ
وَالْاَرْضِ ؕ كُلٌّ لَّهٗ قٰنِتُوْنَ ﴿۱۱۷﴾

118. *He is* the Originator of the heavens and the earth. When He decrees a thing, He does only say to it, 'Be!' and it is.

بَدِيْعُ السَّمٰوٰتِ وَالْاَرْضِ ؕ وَاِذَا قَضٰٓى اَمْرًا فَاِنَّمَا
يَقُوْلُ لَهٗ كُنْ فَيَكُوْنُ ﴿۱۱۸﴾

119. And those who have no knowledge say, 'Why does not Allah speak to us, or a Sign come to us?' Likewise said those before them similar to their saying. Their hearts are alike. We have certainly made the Signs plain for a people who firmly believe.

وَقَالَ الَّذِيْنَ لَا يَعْلَمُوْنَ لَوْلَا يُكَلِّمُنَا اللّٰهُ اَوْ تَاْتِيْنَآ
اٰيَةٌ ؕ كَذٰلِكَ قَالَ الَّذِيْنَ مِنْ قَبْلِهِمْ مِّثْلَ قَوْلِهِمْ ؕ
تَشَابَهَتْ قُلُوْبُهُمْ ؕ قَدْ بَيَّنَّا الْاٰيٰتِ لِقَوْمٍ يُّوْقِنُوْنَ ﴿۱۱۹﴾

120. We have sent thee with the Truth, as a bearer of glad tidings and a warner. And thou wilt not be questioned about the inmates of Hell.

اِنَّآ اَرْسَلْنٰكَ بِالْحَقِّ بَشِيْرًا وَّنَذِيْرًا ۙ وَّلَا تُسْئَلُ عَنْ
اَصْحٰبِ الْجَحِيْمِ ﴿۱۲۰﴾

121. And the Jews will by no means be pleased with thee, nor the Christians, unless thou follow their creed. Say, 'Surely, Allah's guidance alone is the guidance.' And if thou follow their evil desires after the knowledge that has come to thee, thou shalt have, from Allah, no friend nor helper.

وَلَنْ تَرْضٰى عَنْكَ الْيَهُوْدُ وَلَا النَّصٰرٰى حَتّٰى تَتَّبِعَ
مِلَّتَهُمْ ؕ قُلْ اِنَّ هُدَى اللّٰهِ هُوَ الْهُدٰى ؕ وَلَئِنِ
اتَّبَعْتَ اَهْوَآءَهُمْ بَعْدَ الَّذِيْ جَآءَكَ مِنَ الْعِلْمِ ۙ
مَا لَكَ مِنَ اللّٰهِ مِنْ وَّلِيٍّ وَّلَا نَصِيْرٍ ﴿۱۲۱﴾

122. They to whom We have given the Book follow it as it ought to be followed; it is these that believe therein. And whoso believes not therein, these are they who are the losers.

اَلَّذِيْنَ اٰتَيْنٰهُمُ الْكِتٰبَ يَتْلُوْنَهٗ حَقَّ تِلَاوَتِهٖ ؕ اُولٰٓئِكَ
يُؤْمِنُوْنَ بِهٖ ؕ وَمَنْ يَّكْفُرْ بِهٖ فَاُولٰٓئِكَ هُمُ الْخٰسِرُوْنَ ﴿۱۲۲﴾ ع ۱۴ ۱۴

R. 15.

123. O ye children of Israel! remember My favour which I bestowed upon you,

يٰبَنِيْٓ اِسْرَآءِيْلَ اذْكُرُوْا نِعْمَتِيَ الَّتِيْٓ اَنْعَمْتُ عَلَيْكُمْ

and that I exalted you above all peoples.

وانّي فضّلتكم على العٰلمين ﴿١٢٣﴾

124. And fear the day when no soul shall serve as a substitute for another soul at all, nor shall any ransom be accepted from it, nor any intercession avail it, nor shall they be helped.

واتّقوا يومًا لّا تجزي نفس عن نّفسٍ شيـًٔا وّ
لا يقبل منها عدل وّلا تنفعها شفاعة وّلا هم
ينصرون ﴿١٢٤﴾

125. And *remember* when his Lord tried Abraham with certain commands which he fulfilled. He said, 'I will make thee a Leader of men.' *Abraham* asked, 'And from among my offspring?' He said, 'My covenant does not embrace the transgressors.'

واذ ابتلٰى ابرٰهم ربّه بكلمٰتٍ فاتمّهنّ قال انّي
جاعلك للنّاس امامًا قال ومن ذرّيّتي قال
لا ينال عهدي الظّٰلمين ﴿١٢٥﴾

126. And *remember the time* when We made the House a resort for mankind and *a place of* security; and take ye the station of Abraham as a place of Prayer. And We commanded Abraham and Ishmael, *saying*, 'Purify My House for those who perform the circuit and those who remain *therein* for devotion and those who bow down and fall prostrate *in Prayer*.'

واذ جعلنا البيت مثابةً لّلنّاس وامنًا واتّخذوا
من مّقام ابرٰهم مصلًّى وعهدنا الٰى ابرٰهم
واسمٰعيل ان طهّرا بيتي للطّآئفين والعٰكفين
والرّكّع السّجود ﴿١٢٦﴾

127. And *remember* when Abraham said, 'My Lord, make this a town of peace and provide with fruits such of its dwellers as believe in Allah and the Last Day,' He said, 'And on him too who believes not will I bestow benefits for a little while; then will I drive him to the punishment of the Fire, and an evil destination it is.'

واذ قال ابرٰهم ربّ اجعل هٰذا بلدًا امنًا وّارزق
اهله من الثّمرٰت من امن منهم باللّٰه واليوم
الاخر قال ومن كفر فامتّعه قليلًا ثمّ اضطرّه
الٰى عذاب النّار وبئس المصير ﴿١٢٧﴾

128. And *remember the time* when Abraham and Ishmael raised the foundations of the House, *praying*, 'Our Lord, accept *this* from us; for Thou art All-Hearing, All-Knowing.

واذ يرفع ابرٰهم القواعد من البيت واسمٰعيل
ربّنا تقبّل منّا انّك انت السّميع العليم ﴿١٢٨﴾

129. 'Our Lord, make us submissive to Thee and *make* of our offspring a people submissive to Thee. And show us our ways of worship, and turn to us with mercy; for Thou art Oft-Returning *with compassion and* Merciful.

ربّنا واجعلنا مسلمين لك ومن ذرّيّتنآ امّةً
مّسلمةً لّك وارنا مناسكنا وتب علينا انّك انت
التّوّاب الرّحيم ﴿١٢٩﴾

130. 'And, our Lord, raise up among them a Messenger from among themselves, who may recite to them Thy Signs and teach them the Book and Wisdom and

ربّنا وابعث فيهم رسولًا مّنهم يتلوا عليهم
اٰيٰتك ويعلّمهم الكتٰب والحكمة ويزكّيهم

may purify them; surely, Thou art the Mighty, the Wise.'

R. 16.

131. And who will turn away from the religion of Abraham but he who is foolish of mind? Him did We choose in this world, and in the next he will surely be among the righteous.

132. When his Lord said to him, 'Submit,' he said, 'I have submitted to the Lord of the worlds.'

133. The same did Abraham enjoin upon his sons—and *so did* Jacob—*saying*: 'O my sons, truly Allah has chosen this religion for you; so let not death overtake you except when you are in a state of submission.'

134. Were you present when death came to Jacob, when he said to his sons, 'What will you worship after me?' They answered, 'We will worship thy God, the God of thy fathers, Abraham and Ishmael and Isaac, the One God; and to Him we submit ourselves.'

135. Those are a people that have passed away; for them is what they earned, and for you shall be what you earn; and you shall not be questioned as to what they did.

136. And they say, 'Be ye Jews or Christians that you may be rightly guided.' Say: 'Nay, *follow ye* the religion of Abraham who was ever inclined *to God*; he was not of those who set up gods *with God*.'

137. Say ye: 'We believe in Allah and what has been revealed to us, and what was revealed to Abraham and Ishmael, and Isaac, and Jacob and *his* children, and what was given to Moses and Jesus, and what was given to *all other* Prophets from their Lord. We make no difference between any of them; and to Him we submit ourselves.'

138. And if they believe as you have believed, then are they surely guided; but if they turn back, then they are only creating a schism, and Allah will surely suffice thee against them, for He is All-Hearing, All-Knowing.

إِنَّكَ أَنْتَ الْعَزِيزُ الْحَكِيمُ ﴿١٣٠﴾
وَمَنْ يَرْغَبُ عَنْ مِلَّةِ إِبْرٰهِيمَ إِلَّا مَنْ سَفِهَ نَفْسَهُ
وَلَقَدِ اصْطَفَيْنٰهُ فِي الدُّنْيَا وَإِنَّهُ فِي الْآخِرَةِ
لَمِنَ الصّٰلِحِينَ ﴿١٣١﴾
إِذْ قَالَ لَهُ رَبُّهُ أَسْلِمْ قَالَ أَسْلَمْتُ لِرَبِّ الْعٰلَمِينَ ﴿١٣٢﴾
وَوَصّٰى بِهَا إِبْرٰهِيمُ بَنِيهِ وَيَعْقُوبُ يٰبَنِيَّ إِنَّ اللّٰهَ
اصْطَفٰى لَكُمُ الدِّينَ فَلَا تَمُوتُنَّ إِلَّا وَأَنْتُمْ مُسْلِمُونَ ﴿١٣٣﴾
أَمْ كُنْتُمْ شُهَدَاءَ إِذْ حَضَرَ يَعْقُوبَ الْمَوْتُ إِذْ قَالَ
لِبَنِيهِ مَا تَعْبُدُونَ مِنْ بَعْدِي قَالُوا نَعْبُدُ إِلٰهَكَ
وَإِلٰهَ آبَائِكَ إِبْرٰهِيمَ وَإِسْمٰعِيلَ وَإِسْحٰقَ إِلٰهًا وَاحِدًا
وَنَحْنُ لَهُ مُسْلِمُونَ ﴿١٣٤﴾
تِلْكَ أُمَّةٌ قَدْ خَلَتْ لَهَا مَا كَسَبَتْ وَلَكُمْ مَا
كَسَبْتُمْ وَلَا تُسْئَلُونَ عَمَّا كَانُوا يَعْمَلُونَ ﴿١٣٥﴾
وَقَالُوا كُونُوا هُودًا أَوْ نَصٰرٰى تَهْتَدُوا قُلْ بَلْ
مِلَّةَ إِبْرٰهِيمَ حَنِيفًا وَمَا كَانَ مِنَ الْمُشْرِكِينَ ﴿١٣٦﴾
قُولُوا آمَنَّا بِاللّٰهِ وَمَا أُنْزِلَ إِلَيْنَا وَمَا أُنْزِلَ إِلٰى
إِبْرٰهِيمَ وَإِسْمٰعِيلَ وَإِسْحٰقَ وَيَعْقُوبَ وَالْأَسْبَاطِ
وَمَا أُوتِيَ مُوسٰى وَعِيسٰى وَمَا أُوتِيَ النَّبِيُّونَ مِنْ رَبِّهِمْ
لَا نُفَرِّقُ بَيْنَ أَحَدٍ مِنْهُمْ وَنَحْنُ لَهُ مُسْلِمُونَ ﴿١٣٧﴾
فَإِنْ آمَنُوا بِمِثْلِ مَا آمَنْتُمْ بِهِ فَقَدِ اهْتَدَوْا وَإِنْ
تَوَلَّوْا فَإِنَّمَا هُمْ فِي شِقَاقٍ فَسَيَكْفِيكَهُمُ اللّٰهُ وَهُوَ
السَّمِيعُ الْعَلِيمُ ﴿١٣٨﴾

139. *Say*, '*We will adopt* the religion of Allah; and who is better than Allah in *teaching* religion, and Him alone do we worship.'

140. Say: 'Do you dispute with us concerning Allah, while He is our Lord and your Lord? And for us are our works, and for you your works; and to Him alone we are sincerely devoted.'

141. Do you say that Abraham, and Ishmael, and Isaac, and Jacob, and *his* children were Jews or Christians? Say, 'Do you know better or Allah?' And who is more unjust than he who conceals the testimony that he has from Allah? And Allah is not unaware of what you do.

142. Those are a people that have passed away; for them is what they earned, and for you shall be what you earn; and you shall not be questioned as to what they did.

R. 17.

143. The foolish among the people will say: 'What has turned them away from their Qibla which they followed?' Say: 'To Allah belong the East and the West. He guides whom He pleases to the right path.'

144. And thus have We made you an exalted nation, that you may be guardians over men, and the Messenger *of God* may be a guardian over you. And We did not appoint the Qibla which thou didst follow, except that We might know him who follows the Messenger *of God* from him who turns upon his heels. And this is indeed hard, except for those whom Allah has guided. And it does not behove Allah to let your faith go in vain; surely, Allah is Compassionate *and* Merciful to the people.

145. Verily, We see thee turning thy face often to heaven; surely, then, will We make thee turn to the Qibla which thou likest. So, turn thy face towards the

صِبْغَةَ اللّٰهِ ۚ وَمَنْ اَحْسَنُ مِنَ اللّٰهِ صِبْغَةً ۫ وَّنَحْنُ
لَهٗ عٰبِدُوْنَ ﴿۱۳۹﴾
قُلْ اَتُحَآجُّوْنَنَا فِي اللّٰهِ وَهُوَ رَبُّنَا وَرَبُّكُمْ ۚ وَلَنَآ
اَعْمَالُنَا وَلَكُمْ اَعْمَالُكُمْ ۚ وَنَحْنُ لَهٗ مُخْلِصُوْنَ ﴿۱۴۰﴾
اَمْ تَقُوْلُوْنَ اِنَّ اِبْرٰهٖمَ وَاِسْمٰعِيْلَ وَاِسْحٰقَ وَ
يَعْقُوْبَ وَالْاَسْبَاطَ كَانُوْا هُوْدًا اَوْ نَصٰرٰى ۗ قُلْ
ءَاَنْتُمْ اَعْلَمُ اَمِ اللّٰهُ ۗ وَمَنْ اَظْلَمُ مِمَّنْ كَتَمَ
شَهَادَةً عِنْدَهٗ مِنَ اللّٰهِ ۗ وَمَا اللّٰهُ بِغَافِلٍ عَمَّا
تَعْمَلُوْنَ ﴿۱۴۱﴾
تِلْكَ اُمَّةٌ قَدْ خَلَتْ ۚ لَهَا مَا كَسَبَتْ وَلَكُمْ مَّا
كَسَبْتُمْ ۚ وَلَا تُسْـَٔلُوْنَ عَمَّا كَانُوْا يَعْمَلُوْنَ ﴿۱۴۲﴾ ع
سَيَقُوْلُ السُّفَهَآءُ مِنَ النَّاسِ مَا وَلّٰىهُمْ عَنْ
قِبْلَتِهِمُ الَّتِيْ كَانُوْا عَلَيْهَا ۗ قُلْ لِّلّٰهِ الْمَشْرِقُ وَ
الْمَغْرِبُ ۗ يَهْدِيْ مَنْ يَّشَآءُ اِلٰى صِرَاطٍ مُّسْتَقِيْمٍ ﴿۱۴۳﴾
وَكَذٰلِكَ جَعَلْنٰكُمْ اُمَّةً وَّسَطًا لِّتَكُوْنُوْا شُهَدَآءَ عَلَى
النَّاسِ وَيَكُوْنَ الرَّسُوْلُ عَلَيْكُمْ شَهِيْدًا ۗ وَمَا جَعَلْنَا
الْقِبْلَةَ الَّتِيْ كُنْتَ عَلَيْهَآ اِلَّا لِنَعْلَمَ مَنْ يَّتَّبِعُ الرَّسُوْلَ
مِمَّنْ يَّنْقَلِبُ عَلٰى عَقِبَيْهِ ۗ وَاِنْ كَانَتْ لَكَبِيْرَةً اِلَّا
عَلَى الَّذِيْنَ هَدَى اللّٰهُ ۗ وَمَا كَانَ اللّٰهُ لِيُضِيْعَ اِيْمَانَكُمْ ۗ
اِنَّ اللّٰهَ بِالنَّاسِ لَرَءُوْفٌ رَّحِيْمٌ ﴿۱۴۴﴾
قَدْ نَرٰى تَقَلُّبَ وَجْهِكَ فِي السَّمَآءِ ۚ فَلَنُوَلِّيَنَّكَ
قِبْلَةً تَرْضٰىهَا ۠ فَوَلِّ وَجْهَكَ شَطْرَ الْمَسْجِدِ الْحَرَامِ ۗ

الجزء ٢

Sacred Mosque; and wherever you be, turn your faces towards it. And they to whom the Book has been given know that this is the truth from their Lord; and Allah is not unmindful of what they do.

وَحَيْثُ مَا كُنْتُمْ فَوَلُّوا وُجُوهَكُمْ شَطْرَهُ ۗ وَإِنَّ
الَّذِينَ أُوتُوا الْكِتٰبَ لَيَعْلَمُونَ أَنَّهُ الْحَقُّ مِنْ رَبِّهِمْ ۗ
وَمَا اللّٰهُ بِغَافِلٍ عَمَّا يَعْمَلُونَ ﴿١٤٥﴾

146. And even if thou shouldst bring every Sign to those who have been given the Book, they would never follow thy Qibla; nor wouldst thou follow their Qibla; nor would some of them follow the Qibla of others. And if thou shouldst follow their desires after the knowledge that has come to thee, then thou shalt surely be of the transgressors.

وَلَئِنْ أَتَيْتَ الَّذِينَ أُوتُوا الْكِتٰبَ بِكُلِّ اٰيَةٍ مَّا تَبِعُوا
قِبْلَتَكَ ۚ وَمَا أَنْتَ بِتَابِعٍ قِبْلَتَهُمْ ۚ وَمَا بَعْضُهُمْ بِتَابِعٍ
قِبْلَةَ بَعْضٍ ۚ وَلَئِنِ اتَّبَعْتَ أَهْوَاءَهُمْ مِّنْ بَعْدِ مَا
جَاءَكَ مِنَ الْعِلْمِ ۙ إِنَّكَ إِذًا لَّمِنَ الظّٰلِمِينَ ﴿١٤٦﴾

وقف لازم

* 147. Those to whom We have given the Book recognize it even as they recognize their sons, but surely some of them conceal the truth knowingly.

الَّذِينَ اٰتَيْنٰهُمُ الْكِتٰبَ يَعْرِفُونَهُ كَمَا يَعْرِفُونَ أَبْنَاءَهُمْ ۖ
وَإِنَّ فَرِيقًا مِّنْهُمْ لَيَكْتُمُونَ الْحَقَّ وَهُمْ يَعْلَمُونَ ﴿١٤٧﴾

148. *It is* the truth from thy Lord; be not therefore of those who doubt.

الْحَقُّ مِنْ رَّبِّكَ فَلَا تَكُونَنَّ مِنَ الْمُمْتَرِينَ ﴿١٤٨﴾

R. 18.

149. And every one has a goal which dominates him; vie, then, with one another in good works. Wherever you be, Allah will bring you all together. Surely, Allah has the power to do all that He wills.

وَلِكُلٍّ وِّجْهَةٌ هُوَ مُوَلِّيهَا فَاسْتَبِقُوا الْخَيْرٰتِ ۗ أَيْنَ
مَا تَكُونُوا يَأْتِ بِكُمُ اللّٰهُ جَمِيعًا ۗ إِنَّ اللّٰهَ عَلٰى كُلِّ
شَيْءٍ قَدِيرٌ ﴿١٤٩﴾

وقف النبي صلى الله عليه وسلم

150. And from wheresoever thou comest forth, turn thy face towards the Sacred Mosque; for that is indeed the truth from thy Lord. And Allah is not unmindful of what you do.

وَمِنْ حَيْثُ خَرَجْتَ فَوَلِّ وَجْهَكَ شَطْرَ الْمَسْجِدِ
الْحَرَامِ ۖ وَإِنَّهُ لَلْحَقُّ مِنْ رَّبِّكَ ۗ وَمَا اللّٰهُ بِغَافِلٍ
عَمَّا تَعْمَلُونَ ﴿١٥٠﴾

151. And from wheresoever thou comest forth, turn thy face towards the Sacred Mosque; and wherever you be, turn your faces towards it that people may have no argument against you, except those who are unjust — so fear them not, but fear Me — and that I may perfect My favour upon you; and that you may be rightly guided.

وَمِنْ حَيْثُ خَرَجْتَ فَوَلِّ وَجْهَكَ شَطْرَ الْمَسْجِدِ
الْحَرَامِ ۖ وَحَيْثُ مَا كُنْتُمْ فَوَلُّوا وُجُوهَكُمْ شَطْرَهُ ۙ
لِئَلَّا يَكُونَ لِلنَّاسِ عَلَيْكُمْ حُجَّةٌ ۙ إِلَّا الَّذِينَ ظَلَمُوا
مِنْهُمْ فَلَا تَخْشَوْهُمْ وَاخْشَوْنِي ۗ وَلِأُتِمَّ نِعْمَتِي
عَلَيْكُمْ وَلَعَلَّكُمْ تَهْتَدُونَ ﴿١٥١﴾

152. Even as We have sent to you a Messenger from among yourselves who recites Our Signs to you, and purifies you,

كَمَا أَرْسَلْنَا فِيكُمْ رَسُولًا مِّنْكُمْ يَتْلُوا عَلَيْكُمْ اٰيٰتِنَا

and teaches you the Book and Wisdom, and teaches you that which you did not know.

وَيُزَكِّيكُمْ وَيُعَلِّمُكُمُ الْكِتٰبَ وَالْحِكْمَةَ وَيُعَلِّمُكُمْ مَّا لَمْ تَكُوْنُوْا تَعْلَمُوْنَ ﴿١٥٢﴾

153. Therefore remember Me, and I will remember you; and be thankful to Me and do not be ungrateful to Me.

فَاذْكُرُوْنِيْٓ اَذْكُرْكُمْ وَاشْكُرُوْا لِيْ وَلَا تَكْفُرُوْنِ ﴿١٥٣﴾

R. 19.

154. O ye who believe! seek help with patience and Prayer; surely, Allah is with the steadfast.

يٰٓاَيُّهَا الَّذِيْنَ اٰمَنُوا اسْتَعِيْنُوْا بِالصَّبْرِ وَالصَّلٰوةِ ۭ اِنَّ اللّٰهَ مَعَ الصّٰبِرِيْنَ ﴿١٥٤﴾

155. And say not of those who are killed in the cause of Allah that they are dead; nay, they are living; only you perceive not.

وَلَا تَقُوْلُوْا لِمَنْ يُّقْتَلُ فِيْ سَبِيْلِ اللّٰهِ اَمْوَاتٌ ۭ بَلْ اَحْيَاۗءٌ وَّلٰكِنْ لَّا تَشْعُرُوْنَ ﴿١٥٥﴾

156. And We will try you with something of fear and hunger, and loss of wealth and lives, and fruits; but give glad tidings to the patient,

وَلَنَبْلُوَنَّكُمْ بِشَيْءٍ مِّنَ الْخَوْفِ وَالْجُوْعِ وَنَقْصٍ مِّنَ الْاَمْوَالِ وَالْاَنْفُسِ وَالثَّمَرٰتِ ۭ وَبَشِّرِ الصّٰبِرِيْنَ ﴿١٥٦﴾

157. Who, when a misfortune overtakes them, say, 'Surely, to Allah we belong and to Him shall we return.'

الَّذِيْنَ اِذَآ اَصَابَتْهُمْ مُّصِيْبَةٌ ۙ قَالُوْٓا اِنَّا لِلّٰهِ وَاِنَّآ اِلَيْهِ رٰجِعُوْنَ ﴿١٥٧﴾

158. It is these on whom are blessings from their Lord and mercy, and it is these who are rightly guided.

اُولٰۗىِٕكَ عَلَيْهِمْ صَلَوٰتٌ مِّنْ رَّبِّهِمْ وَرَحْمَةٌ ۣ وَاُولٰۗىِٕكَ هُمُ الْمُهْتَدُوْنَ ﴿١٥٨﴾

159. Surely, Al-Ṣafā and Al-Marwa are among the Signs of Allah. It is, therefore, no sin for him who is on pilgrimage to the House, or performs 'Umra, to go round the two. And whoso does good beyond what is obligatory, surely then, Allah is Appreciating, All-Knowing.

اِنَّ الصَّفَا وَالْمَرْوَةَ مِنْ شَعَاۗىِٕرِ اللّٰهِ ۚ فَمَنْ حَجَّ الْبَيْتَ اَوِ اعْتَمَرَ فَلَا جُنَاحَ عَلَيْهِ اَنْ يَّطَّوَّفَ بِهِمَا ۭ وَمَنْ تَطَوَّعَ خَيْرًا ۙ فَاِنَّ اللّٰهَ شَاكِرٌ عَلِيْمٌ ﴿١٥٩﴾

160. Those who conceal what We have sent down of Signs and guidance after We have made it clear for the people in the Book, it is these whom Allah curses; and *so* curse them those who curse.

اِنَّ الَّذِيْنَ يَكْتُمُوْنَ مَآ اَنْزَلْنَا مِنَ الْبَيِّنٰتِ وَالْهُدٰى مِنْۢ بَعْدِ مَا بَيَّنّٰهُ لِلنَّاسِ فِي الْكِتٰبِ ۙ اُولٰۗىِٕكَ يَلْعَنُهُمُ اللّٰهُ وَيَلْعَنُهُمُ اللّٰعِنُوْنَ ﴿١٦٠﴾

161. But they who repent and amend and openly declare *the truth*, it is these to whom I turn with forgiveness, and I am Oft-Returning *with compassion and* Merciful.

اِلَّا الَّذِيْنَ تَابُوْا وَاَصْلَحُوْا وَبَيَّنُوْا فَاُولٰۗىِٕكَ اَتُوْبُ عَلَيْهِمْ ۚ وَاَنَا التَّوَّابُ الرَّحِيْمُ ﴿١٦١﴾

162. Those who disbelieve and die while they are disbelievers, on them shall be the curse of Allah and of angels and of men all together.

إِنَّ الَّذِينَ كَفَرُوا وَمَاتُوا وَهُمْ كُفَّارٌ أُولَٰئِكَ
عَلَيْهِمْ لَعْنَةُ اللَّهِ وَالْمَلَائِكَةِ وَالنَّاسِ أَجْمَعِينَ ﴿١٦٢﴾

163. They shall remain under it. The punishment shall not be lightened for them, nor shall they be granted respite.

خَالِدِينَ فِيهَا ۖ لَا يُخَفَّفُ عَنْهُمُ الْعَذَابُ وَلَا
هُمْ يُنْظَرُونَ ﴿١٦٣﴾

164. And your God is One God; there is no God but He, the Gracious, the Merciful.

وَإِلَٰهُكُمْ إِلَٰهٌ وَاحِدٌ ۖ لَا إِلَٰهَ إِلَّا هُوَ الرَّحْمَٰنُ الرَّحِيمُ ﴿١٦٤﴾

R. 20.

165. Verily, in the creation of the heavens and the earth and in the alternation of night and day, and in the ships which sail in the sea with that which profits men, and in the water which Allah sends down from the sky and quickens therewith the earth after its death and scatters therein all kinds of beasts, and in the change of the winds, and the clouds pressed into service between the heaven and the earth — are indeed Signs for the people who understand.

إِنَّ فِي خَلْقِ السَّمَاوَاتِ وَالْأَرْضِ وَاخْتِلَافِ اللَّيْلِ وَ
النَّهَارِ وَالْفُلْكِ الَّتِي تَجْرِي فِي الْبَحْرِ بِمَا يَنْفَعُ
النَّاسَ وَمَا أَنْزَلَ اللَّهُ مِنَ السَّمَاءِ مِنْ مَاءٍ فَأَحْيَا
بِهِ الْأَرْضَ بَعْدَ مَوْتِهَا وَبَثَّ فِيهَا مِنْ كُلِّ دَابَّةٍ
وَتَصْرِيفِ الرِّيَاحِ وَالسَّحَابِ الْمُسَخَّرِ بَيْنَ السَّمَاءِ
وَالْأَرْضِ لَآيَاتٍ لِقَوْمٍ يَعْقِلُونَ ﴿١٦٥﴾

166. And there are some among men who take for themselves objects of worship other than Allah, loving them as they should love Allah. But those who believe are stronger in *their* love for Allah. And if those who transgress could *now* see *the time* when they shall see the punishment, *they would realize* that all power belongs to Allah and that Allah is severe in punishing.

وَمِنَ النَّاسِ مَنْ يَتَّخِذُ مِنْ دُونِ اللَّهِ أَنْدَادًا
يُحِبُّونَهُمْ كَحُبِّ اللَّهِ ۖ وَالَّذِينَ آمَنُوا أَشَدُّ حُبًّا
لِلَّهِ ۗ وَلَوْ يَرَى الَّذِينَ ظَلَمُوا إِذْ يَرَوْنَ الْعَذَابَ
أَنَّ الْقُوَّةَ لِلَّهِ جَمِيعًا وَأَنَّ اللَّهَ شَدِيدُ الْعَذَابِ ﴿١٦٦﴾

* 167. *Aye, they would certainly realize if they could see the time* when those who were followed shall disown their followers and shall see the punishment, and all their ties shall be cut asunder.

إِذْ تَبَرَّأَ الَّذِينَ اتُّبِعُوا مِنَ الَّذِينَ اتَّبَعُوا وَرَأَوُا الْعَذَابَ
وَتَقَطَّعَتْ بِهِمُ الْأَسْبَابُ ﴿١٦٧﴾

168. And those who followed shall say: 'If we could only return, we would disown them as they have disowned us.' Thus will Allah show them their works as anguish for them, and they shall not get out of the Fire.

وَقَالَ الَّذِينَ اتَّبَعُوا لَوْ أَنَّ لَنَا كَرَّةً فَنَتَبَرَّأَ مِنْهُمْ
كَمَا تَبَرَّءُوا مِنَّا ۗ كَذَٰلِكَ يُرِيهِمُ اللَّهُ أَعْمَالَهُمْ حَسَرَاتٍ
عَلَيْهِمْ ۖ وَمَا هُمْ بِخَارِجِينَ مِنَ النَّارِ ﴿١٦٨﴾

R. 21.

* 169. O ye men! eat of what is lawful *and* good in the earth; and follow not the footsteps of Satan; surely, he is to you an open enemy.

يَا أَيُّهَا النَّاسُ كُلُوا مِمَّا فِي الْأَرْضِ حَلَالًا طَيِّبًا وَلَا
تَتَّبِعُوا خُطُوَاتِ الشَّيْطَانِ ۚ إِنَّهُ لَكُمْ عَدُوٌّ مُبِينٌ ﴿١٦٩﴾

170. He only enjoins upon you what is evil and what is foul, and that you say of Allah what you do not know.

إِنَّمَا يَأْمُرُكُمْ بِالسُّوْءِ وَالْفَحْشَاءِ وَأَنْ تَقُوْلُوْا عَلَى
اللّٰهِ مَا لَا تَعْلَمُوْنَ ۝١٧٠

171. And when it is said to them, 'Follow that which Allah has sent down,' they say: 'Nay, we will follow that wherein we found our fathers.' What! even if their fathers had no sense at all and no guidance?

وَإِذَا قِيْلَ لَهُمُ اتَّبِعُوْا مَآ أَنْزَلَ اللّٰهُ قَالُوْا بَلْ
نَتَّبِعُ مَآ أَلْفَيْنَا عَلَيْهِ آبَآءَنَا ۚ أَوَلَوْ كَانَ آبَآؤُهُمْ
لَا يَعْقِلُوْنَ شَيْئًا وَّلَا يَهْتَدُوْنَ ۝١٧١

172. And the case of those who disbelieve is like the case of one who shouts to that which hears nothing but a call and a cry. *They are* deaf, dumb, *and* blind—so they do not understand.

وَمَثَلُ الَّذِيْنَ كَفَرُوْا كَمَثَلِ الَّذِيْ يَنْعِقُ بِمَا لَا يَسْمَعُ
إِلَّا دُعَآءً وَّنِدَآءً ۚ صُمٌّۢ بُكْمٌ عُمْيٌ فَهُمْ لَا
يَعْقِلُوْنَ ۝١٧٢

173. O ye who believe! eat of the good things We have provided for you, and render thanks to Allah, if it is He Whom you worship.

يٰٓأَيُّهَا الَّذِيْنَ آمَنُوْا كُلُوْا مِنْ طَيِّبٰتِ مَا رَزَقْنٰكُمْ
وَاشْكُرُوْا لِلّٰهِ إِنْ كُنْتُمْ إِيَّاهُ تَعْبُدُوْنَ ۝١٧٣

174. He has made unlawful to you only that which dies of itself, and blood and the flesh of swine, and that on which the name of any other than Allah has been invoked. But he who is driven by necessity, being neither disobedient nor exceeding the limit, it shall be no sin for him. Surely, Allah is Most Forgiving, Merciful.

إِنَّمَا حَرَّمَ عَلَيْكُمُ الْمَيْتَةَ وَالدَّمَ وَلَحْمَ الْخِنْزِيْرِ
وَمَآ أُهِلَّ بِهٖ لِغَيْرِ اللّٰهِ ۚ فَمَنِ اضْطُرَّ غَيْرَ بَاغٍ وَّ
لَا عَادٍ فَلَآ إِثْمَ عَلَيْهِ ۚ إِنَّ اللّٰهَ غَفُوْرٌ رَّحِيْمٌ ۝١٧٤

175. Those who conceal that which Allah has sent down of the Book and take in exchange for that a paltry price, they fill their bellies with nothing but fire. Allah will not speak to them on the Day of Resurrection, nor will He purify them. And for them is a grievous punishment.

إِنَّ الَّذِيْنَ يَكْتُمُوْنَ مَآ أَنْزَلَ اللّٰهُ مِنَ الْكِتٰبِ وَ
يَشْتَرُوْنَ بِهٖ ثَمَنًا قَلِيْلًا ۙ أُولٰٓئِكَ مَا يَأْكُلُوْنَ فِيْ بُطُوْنِهِمْ
إِلَّا النَّارَ وَلَا يُكَلِّمُهُمُ اللّٰهُ يَوْمَ الْقِيٰمَةِ وَلَا يُزَكِّيْهِمْ ۚ
وَلَهُمْ عَذَابٌ أَلِيْمٌ ۝١٧٥

176. It is they who have taken error in exchange for guidance and punishment for forgiveness. How great is their endurance of the Fire!

أُولٰٓئِكَ الَّذِيْنَ اشْتَرَوُا الضَّلٰلَةَ بِالْهُدٰى وَالْعَذَابَ
بِالْمَغْفِرَةِ ۚ فَمَآ أَصْبَرَهُمْ عَلَى النَّارِ ۝١٧٦

177. That is because Allah has sent down the Book with the truth; and surely, they who disagree concerning the Book are gone far in enmity.

ذٰلِكَ بِأَنَّ اللّٰهَ نَزَّلَ الْكِتٰبَ بِالْحَقِّ ۗ وَإِنَّ الَّذِيْنَ اخْتَلَفُوْا
فِي الْكِتٰبِ لَفِيْ شِقَاقٍۢ بَعِيْدٍ ۝١٧٧ ع ٢١ ٩ ٥

R. 22.

178. It is not righteousness that you turn your faces to the East or the West,

لَيْسَ الْبِرَّ أَنْ تُوَلُّوْا وُجُوْهَكُمْ قِبَلَ الْمَشْرِقِ وَ

but *truly* righteous is he who believes in Allah and the Last Day and the angels and the Book and the Prophets, and spends his money for love of Him, on the kindred and the orphans and the needy and the wayfarer and those who ask *for charity,* and for *ransoming* the captives; and who observes Prayer and pays the Zakāt; and those who fulfil their promise when they have made one, and the patient in poverty and afflictions and *the steadfast* in time of war; it is these who have proved truthful and it is these who are the God-fearing.

* 179. O ye who believe! *equitable* retaliation in *the matter of* the slain is prescribed for you: the free man for the free man, and the slave for the slave, and the female for the female. But if one is granted any remission by one's brother, then pursuing *the matter for the realization of the blood-money* shall be done with fairness and *the murderer* shall pay him the blood-money in a handsome manner. This is an alleviation from your Lord and a mercy. And whoso transgresses thereafter, for him there shall be a grievous punishment.

180. And there is life for you in *the law of* retaliation, O men of understanding, that you may enjoy security.

181. It is prescribed for you, when death comes to any one of you, if he leave much wealth, *that he make* a will to parents and near relatives to act with fairness; *it is* an obligation on those who fear God.

182. And he who alters it after he has heard it, the sin thereof shall surely lie on those who alter it. Surely, Allah is All-Hearing, All-Knowing.

183. But whoso apprehends from a testator a partiality or a wrong, and makes peace between them (the parties affected), it shall be no sin for him. Surely, Allah is Most Forgiving, Merciful.

R. 23.

184. O ye who believe! fasting is prescribed for you, as it was prescribed for

الْمَغْرِبِ وَلٰكِنَّ الْبِرَّ مَنْ اٰمَنَ بِاللّٰهِ وَالْيَوْمِ الْاٰخِرِ
وَالْمَلٰٓئِكَةِ وَالْكِتٰبِ وَالنَّبِيّٖنَ ۚ وَاٰتَى الْمَالَ عَلٰى
حُبِّهٖ ذَوِي الْقُرْبٰى وَالْيَتٰمٰى وَالْمَسٰكِيْنَ وَابْنَ السَّبِيْلِ ۙ
وَالسَّآئِلِيْنَ وَفِي الرِّقَابِ ۚ وَاَقَامَ الصَّلٰوةَ وَاٰتَى
الزَّكٰوةَ ۚ وَالْمُوْفُوْنَ بِعَهْدِهِمْ اِذَا عٰهَدُوْا ۚ وَالصّٰبِرِيْنَ
فِي الْبَاْسَآءِ وَالضَّرَّآءِ وَحِيْنَ الْبَاْسِ ؕ اُولٰٓئِكَ الَّذِيْنَ
صَدَقُوْا ؕ وَاُولٰٓئِكَ هُمُ الْمُتَّقُوْنَ ﴿۱۷۸﴾
يٰٓاَيُّهَا الَّذِيْنَ اٰمَنُوْا كُتِبَ عَلَيْكُمُ الْقِصَاصُ فِي الْقَتْلٰى ؕ
اَلْحُرُّ بِالْحُرِّ وَالْعَبْدُ بِالْعَبْدِ وَالْاُنْثٰى بِالْاُنْثٰى ؕ فَمَنْ
عُفِيَ لَهٗ مِنْ اَخِيْهِ شَيْءٌ فَاتِّبَاعٌ ۢ بِالْمَعْرُوْفِ وَاَدَآءٌ
اِلَيْهِ بِاِحْسَانٍ ؕ ذٰلِكَ تَخْفِيْفٌ مِّنْ رَّبِّكُمْ وَرَحْمَةٌ ؕ
فَمَنِ اعْتَدٰى بَعْدَ ذٰلِكَ فَلَهٗ عَذَابٌ اَلِيْمٌ ﴿۱۷۹﴾
وَلَكُمْ فِي الْقِصَاصِ حَيٰوةٌ يّٰٓاُولِي الْاَلْبَابِ لَعَلَّكُمْ
تَتَّقُوْنَ ﴿۱۸۰﴾
كُتِبَ عَلَيْكُمْ اِذَا حَضَرَ اَحَدَكُمُ الْمَوْتُ اِنْ تَرَكَ
خَيْرَا ۖۚ ۨالْوَصِيَّةُ لِلْوَالِدَيْنِ وَالْاَقْرَبِيْنَ بِالْمَعْرُوْفِ ۚ
حَقًّا عَلَى الْمُتَّقِيْنَ ﴿۱۸۱﴾ ؕ
فَمَنْ بَدَّلَهٗ بَعْدَ مَا سَمِعَهٗ فَاِنَّمَآ اِثْمُهٗ عَلَى الَّذِيْنَ
يُبَدِّلُوْنَهٗ ؕ اِنَّ اللّٰهَ سَمِيْعٌ عَلِيْمٌ ﴿۱۸۲﴾ ؕ
فَمَنْ خَافَ مِنْ مُّوْصٍ جَنَفًا اَوْ اِثْمًا فَاَصْلَحَ بَيْنَهُمْ
ع ۲۲ فَلَآ اِثْمَ عَلَيْهِ ؕ اِنَّ اللّٰهَ غَفُوْرٌ رَّحِيْمٌ ﴿۱۸۳﴾ ع
يٰٓاَيُّهَا الَّذِيْنَ اٰمَنُوْا كُتِبَ عَلَيْكُمُ الصِّيَامُ كَمَا كُتِبَ

those before you, so that you may become righteous.

185. *The prescribed fasting is* for a fixed number of days, but whoso among you is sick or is on a journey *shall fast* the same number of other days; and for those who are able to fast *only* with great difficulty is an expiation—the feeding of a poor man. And whoso performs a good work with willing obedience, it is better for him. And fasting is good for you, if you only knew.

186. The month of Ramaḍān is that in which the Qur'ān was sent down as a guidance for mankind with clear proofs of guidance and discrimination. Therefore, whosoever of you is present *at home* in this month, let him fast therein. But whoso is sick or is on a journey, *shall fast* the same number of other days. Allah desires *to give* you facility and He desires not hardship for you, and that you may complete the number, and that you may exalt Allah for His having guided you and that you may be grateful.

187. And when My servants ask thee about Me, *say:* I am near. I answer the prayer of the supplicant when he prays to Me. So they should hearken to Me and believe in Me, that they may follow the right way.

* 188. It is made lawful for you to go in unto your wives on the night of the fast. They are a garment for you, and you are a garment for them. Allah knows that you have been acting unjustly to yourselves, wherefore He has turned to you with mercy and afforded you relief. So you may now go in unto them and seek what Allah has ordained for you; and eat and drink until the white thread becomes distinct to you from the black thread of the dawn. Then complete the fast till nightfall and do not go in unto them while you remain in the mosques for devotion. These are the limits *fixed* by Allah, so approach them not. Thus does Allah make His commandments

عَلَى الَّذِيْنَ مِنْ قَبْلِكُمْ لَعَلَّكُمْ تَتَّقُوْنَ ﴿١٨٤﴾
اَيَّامًا مَّعْدُوْدٰتٍ ۭ فَمَنْ كَانَ مِنْكُمْ مَّرِيْضًا اَوْ عَلٰى
سَفَرٍ فَعِدَّةٌ مِّنْ اَيَّامٍ اُخَرَ ۭ وَعَلَى الَّذِيْنَ يُطِيْقُوْنَهٗ
فِدْيَةٌ طَعَامُ مِسْكِيْنٍ ۭ فَمَنْ تَطَوَّعَ خَيْرًا فَهُوَ خَيْرٌ
لَّهٗ ۭ وَاَنْ تَصُوْمُوْا خَيْرٌ لَّكُمْ اِنْ كُنْتُمْ تَعْلَمُوْنَ ﴿١٨٥﴾
شَهْرُ رَمَضَانَ الَّذِيْٓ اُنْزِلَ فِيْهِ الْقُرْاٰنُ هُدًى
لِّلنَّاسِ وَبَيِّنٰتٍ مِّنَ الْهُدٰى وَالْفُرْقَانِ ۚ فَمَنْ شَهِدَ
مِنْكُمُ الشَّهْرَ فَلْيَصُمْهُ ۭ وَمَنْ كَانَ مَرِيْضًا اَوْ عَلٰى
سَفَرٍ فَعِدَّةٌ مِّنْ اَيَّامٍ اُخَرَ ۭ يُرِيْدُ اللّٰهُ بِكُمُ
الْيُسْرَ وَلَا يُرِيْدُ بِكُمُ الْعُسْرَ ۡ وَلِتُكْمِلُوا الْعِدَّةَ
وَلِتُكَبِّرُوا اللّٰهَ عَلٰى مَا هَدٰىكُمْ وَلَعَلَّكُمْ تَشْكُرُوْنَ ﴿١٨٦﴾
وَاِذَا سَاَلَكَ عِبَادِيْ عَنِّيْ فَاِنِّيْ قَرِيْبٌ ۭ اُجِيْبُ دَعْوَةَ
الدَّاعِ اِذَا دَعَانِ ۙ فَلْيَسْتَجِيْبُوْا لِيْ وَلْيُؤْمِنُوْا بِيْ لَعَلَّهُمْ
يَرْشُدُوْنَ ﴿١٨٧﴾
اُحِلَّ لَكُمْ لَيْلَةَ الصِّيَامِ الرَّفَثُ اِلٰى نِسَاۗىِٕكُمْ ۭ هُنَّ
لِبَاسٌ لَّكُمْ وَاَنْتُمْ لِبَاسٌ لَّهُنَّ ۭ عَلِمَ اللّٰهُ اَنَّكُمْ
كُنْتُمْ تَخْتَانُوْنَ اَنْفُسَكُمْ فَتَابَ عَلَيْكُمْ وَعَفَا
عَنْكُمْ ۚ فَالْـٰٔنَ بَاشِرُوْهُنَّ وَابْتَغُوْا مَا كَتَبَ اللّٰهُ لَكُمْ
وَكُلُوْا وَاشْرَبُوْا حَتّٰى يَتَبَيَّنَ لَكُمُ الْخَيْطُ الْاَبْيَضُ
مِنَ الْخَيْطِ الْاَسْوَدِ مِنَ الْفَجْرِ ۠ ثُمَّ اَتِمُّوا الصِّيَامَ
اِلَى الَّيْلِ ۚ وَلَا تُبَاشِرُوْهُنَّ وَاَنْتُمْ عٰكِفُوْنَ ۙ فِي الْمَسٰجِدِ ۭ
تِلْكَ حُدُوْدُ اللّٰهِ فَلَا تَقْرَبُوْهَا ۭ كَذٰلِكَ يُبَيِّنُ اللّٰهُ

clear to men that they may become secure against evil.

* 189. And do not devour your wealth among yourselves through falsehood, and offer it not *as bribe* to the authorities that you may knowingly devour a part of the wealth of *other* people with injustice.

R. 24.

190. They ask thee about the new moons. Say, 'They are means for measuring time for *the general good of* mankind and for the Pilgrimage.' And it is not righteousness that you come into houses by the backs thereof; but *truly* righteous is he who fears God. And you should come into houses by the doors thereof; and fear Allah that you may prosper.

191. And fight in the cause of Allah against those who fight against you, but do not transgress. Surely, Allah loves not the transgressors.

192. And kill them wherever you meet them and drive them out from where they have driven you out; for persecution is worse than killing. And fight them not *in, and* near, the Sacred Mosque until they fight you therein. But if they fight you, then fight them: such is the requital for the disbelievers.

193. But if they desist, then surely Allah is Most Forgiving, Merciful.

194. And fight them until there is no persecution, and religion is *freely professed* for Allah. But if they desist, then *remember* that no hostility is allowed except against the aggressors.

195. The *violation of a* Sacred Month *should be retaliated* in the Sacred Month; and for *all* sacred things there is *the law of* retaliation. So, whoso transgresses against you, punish him for his transgression to the extent to which he has transgressed against you. And fear Allah and know that Allah is with those who fear Him.

196. And spend for the cause of Allah, and cast not yourselves into ruin with your own hands, and do good; surely, Allah loves those who do good.

اٰيٰتِهٖ لِلنَّاسِ لَعَلَّهُمْ يَتَّقُوْنَ ﴿۱۸۸﴾
وَلَا تَاْكُلُوْٓا اَمْوَالَكُمْ بَيْنَكُمْ بِالْبَاطِلِ وَتُدْلُوْا بِهَآ
اِلَى الْحُكَّامِ لِتَاْكُلُوْا فَرِيْقًا مِّنْ اَمْوَالِ النَّاسِ بِالْاِثْمِ
وَاَنْتُمْ تَعْلَمُوْنَ ﴿۱۸۹﴾ ع ٢٣
يَسْـَٔلُوْنَكَ عَنِ الْاَهِلَّةِ ۭ قُلْ هِيَ مَوَاقِيْتُ لِلنَّاسِ
وَالْحَجِّ ۭ وَلَيْسَ الْبِرُّ بِاَنْ تَاْتُوا الْبُيُوْتَ مِنْ ظُهُوْرِهَا
وَلٰكِنَّ الْبِرَّ مَنِ اتَّقٰى ۚ وَاْتُوا الْبُيُوْتَ مِنْ اَبْوَابِهَا ۠
وَاتَّقُوا اللّٰهَ لَعَلَّكُمْ تُفْلِحُوْنَ ﴿۱۹۰﴾
وَقَاتِلُوْا فِيْ سَبِيْلِ اللّٰهِ الَّذِيْنَ يُقَاتِلُوْنَكُمْ وَلَا
تَعْتَدُوْا ۭ اِنَّ اللّٰهَ لَا يُحِبُّ الْمُعْتَدِيْنَ ﴿۱۹۱﴾
وَاقْتُلُوْهُمْ حَيْثُ ثَقِفْتُمُوْهُمْ وَاَخْرِجُوْهُمْ مِّنْ
حَيْثُ اَخْرَجُوْكُمْ وَالْفِتْنَةُ اَشَدُّ مِنَ الْقَتْلِ ۚ وَ
لَا تُقٰتِلُوْهُمْ عِنْدَ الْمَسْجِدِ الْحَرَامِ حَتّٰى يُقٰتِلُوْكُمْ
فِيْهِ ۚ فَاِنْ قٰتَلُوْكُمْ فَاقْتُلُوْهُمْ ۭ كَذٰلِكَ جَزَاۗءُ الْكٰفِرِيْنَ ﴿۱۹۲﴾
فَاِنِ انْتَهَوْا فَاِنَّ اللّٰهَ غَفُوْرٌ رَّحِيْمٌ ﴿۱۹۳﴾
وَقٰتِلُوْهُمْ حَتّٰى لَا تَكُوْنَ فِتْنَةٌ وَّيَكُوْنَ الدِّيْنُ لِلّٰهِ ۭ
فَاِنِ انْتَهَوْا فَلَا عُدْوَانَ اِلَّا عَلَى الظّٰلِمِيْنَ ﴿۱۹۴﴾
اَلشَّهْرُ الْحَرَامُ بِالشَّهْرِ الْحَرَامِ وَالْحُرُمٰتُ قِصَاصٌ ۭ
فَمَنِ اعْتَدٰى عَلَيْكُمْ فَاعْتَدُوْا عَلَيْهِ بِمِثْلِ مَا اعْتَدٰى
عَلَيْكُمْ ۠ وَاتَّقُوا اللّٰهَ وَاعْلَمُوْٓا اَنَّ اللّٰهَ مَعَ الْمُتَّقِيْنَ ﴿۱۹۵﴾
وَاَنْفِقُوْا فِيْ سَبِيْلِ اللّٰهِ وَلَا تُلْقُوْا بِاَيْدِيْكُمْ اِلَى التَّهْلُكَةِ ۚۖ
وَاَحْسِنُوْا ۚ اِنَّ اللّٰهَ يُحِبُّ الْمُحْسِنِيْنَ ﴿۱۹۶﴾

197. And complete the Ḥajj and the 'Umra for the sake of Allah: but if you are kept back, then *make* whatever offering is easily available; and do not shave your heads until the offering reaches its destination. And whoever among you is sick or has an ailment of the head, *should make* an expiation either by fasting or almsgiving or a sacrifice. But when you are safe, then he, who would avail himself of the 'Umra together with the Ḥajj, *should make* whatever offering is easily obtainable. But such *of you* as cannot find *an offering* should fast three days during the Pilgrimage, and seven when you return home; these are ten complete. This is for him whose family does not reside near the Sacred Mosque. And fear Allah and know that Allah is severe in punishing.

وَاَتِمُّوا الْحَجَّ وَالْعُمْرَةَ لِلّٰهِ ۚ فَاِنْ اُحْصِرْتُمْ فَمَا اسْتَيْسَرَ
مِنَ الْهَدْيِ ۚ وَلَا تَحْلِقُوْا رُءُوْسَكُمْ حَتّٰى يَبْلُغَ الْهَدْيُ
مَحِلَّهٗ ۚ فَمَنْ كَانَ مِنْكُمْ مَّرِيْضًا اَوْ بِهٖٓ اَذًى مِّنْ رَّاْسِهٖ
فَفِدْيَةٌ مِّنْ صِيَامٍ اَوْ صَدَقَةٍ اَوْ نُسُكٍ ۚ فَاِذَآ اَمِنْتُمْ
فَمَنْ تَمَتَّعَ بِالْعُمْرَةِ اِلَى الْحَجِّ فَمَا اسْتَيْسَرَ مِنَ
الْهَدْيِ ۚ فَمَنْ لَّمْ يَجِدْ فَصِيَامُ ثَلٰثَةِ اَيَّامٍ فِي الْحَجِّ
وَسَبْعَةٍ اِذَا رَجَعْتُمْ ۭ تِلْكَ عَشَرَةٌ كَامِلَةٌ ۭ ذٰلِكَ لِمَنْ
لَّمْ يَكُنْ اَهْلُهٗ حَاضِرِي الْمَسْجِدِ الْحَرَامِ ۭ وَاتَّقُوا اللّٰهَ
وَاعْلَمُوْٓا اَنَّ اللّٰهَ شَدِيْدُ الْعِقَابِ ﴿۱۹۷﴾ ع ۲۴

R. 25.

198. The months of the Ḥajj are well known; so whoever determines to perform the Pilgrimage in these months, *should remember that* there is *to be* no foul talk, nor any transgression, nor any quarrelling during the Pilgrimage. And whatever good you do, Allah knows it. And furnish yourselves with *necessary* provisions, and surely, the best provision is righteousness. And fear Me *alone*, O men of understanding.

اَلْحَجُّ اَشْهُرٌ مَّعْلُوْمٰتٌ ۚ فَمَنْ فَرَضَ فِيْهِنَّ الْحَجَّ
فَلَا رَفَثَ وَلَا فُسُوْقَ ۙ وَلَا جِدَالَ فِي الْحَجِّ ۭ وَمَا
تَفْعَلُوْا مِنْ خَيْرٍ يَّعْلَمْهُ اللّٰهُ ۭ وَتَزَوَّدُوْا فَاِنَّ خَيْرَ
الزَّادِ التَّقْوٰى ۡ وَاتَّقُوْنِ يٰٓاُولِي الْاَلْبَابِ ﴿۱۹۸﴾

وقف النبي صلى الله عليه وسلم

199. It is no sin for you that you seek the bounty of your Lord. But when you pour forth from 'Arafāt, remember Allah at Mash'ar al-Ḥarām; and remember Him as He has guided you, although, before this, you were of those gone astray.

لَيْسَ عَلَيْكُمْ جُنَاحٌ اَنْ تَبْتَغُوْا فَضْلًا مِّنْ رَّبِّكُمْ ۭ
فَاِذَآ اَفَضْتُمْ مِّنْ عَرَفٰتٍ فَاذْكُرُوا اللّٰهَ عِنْدَ الْمَشْعَرِ
الْحَرَامِ ۠ وَاذْكُرُوْهُ كَمَا هَدٰىكُمْ ۚ وَاِنْ كُنْتُمْ مِّنْ
قَبْلِهٖ لَمِنَ الضَّاۗلِّيْنَ ﴿۱۹۹﴾

200. Then pour forth from where the people pour forth, and seek forgiveness from Allah; surely, Allah is Most Forgiving, Merciful.

ثُمَّ اَفِيْضُوْا مِنْ حَيْثُ اَفَاضَ النَّاسُ وَاسْتَغْفِرُوا
اللّٰهَ ۭ اِنَّ اللّٰهَ غَفُوْرٌ رَّحِيْمٌ ﴿۲۰۰﴾

201. And when you have performed the acts of worship prescribed for you, celebrate the praises of Allah as you celebrated the praises of your fathers, or even more than that. And of men there are some who say, 'Our Lord, grant us *good things* in this world;' and such a one shall have no share in the Hereafter.

فَاِذَا قَضَيْتُمْ مَّنَاسِكَكُمْ فَاذْكُرُوا اللّٰهَ كَذِكْرِكُمْ
اٰبَاۗءَكُمْ اَوْ اَشَدَّ ذِكْرًا ۭ فَمِنَ النَّاسِ مَنْ يَّقُوْلُ
رَبَّنَآ اٰتِنَا فِي الدُّنْيَا وَمَا لَهٗ فِي الْاٰخِرَةِ مِنْ خَلَاقٍ ﴿۲۰۱﴾

202. And of them there are some who say: 'Our Lord, grant us good in this world as well as good in the world to come, and protect us from the torment of the Fire.'

203. For these there shall be a *goodly* share because of what they have earned. And Allah is swift at reckoning.

204. And remember Allah during the appointed number of days; but whoso hastens *to leave* in two days, it shall be no sin for him; and whoso stays behind, it shall be no sin for him. *This is* for him who fears God. And fear Allah and know that you shall be brought together before Him.

205. And of men there is he whose talk on this life would please thee, and he would call Allah to witness as to that which is in his heart, and yet he is the most contentious of quarrellers.

206. And when he is in authority, he runs about in the land to create disorder in it and destroy the crops and the progeny *of man*; and Allah loves not disorder.

207. And when it is said to him, 'Fear Allah,' pride incites him to *further* sin. So Hell shall be his sufficient reward; and surely, it is an evil place of rest.

208. And of men there is he who would sell himself to seek the pleasure of Allah; and Allah is Compassionate to *His* servants.

209. O ye who believe! come into submission wholly and follow not the footsteps of Satan; surely, he is your open enemy.

210. But if you slip after the clear Signs that have come to you, then know that Allah is Mighty, Wise.

211. Are they waiting for anything but that Allah should come to them in the coverings of the clouds with angels, and the matter be decided? And to Allah do all things return.

R. 26.

212. Ask of the children of Israel how many clear Signs We gave them. But

وَمِنْهُمْ مَّنْ يَّقُوْلُ رَبَّنَآ اٰتِنَا فِي الدُّنْيَا حَسَنَةً وَّ
فِي الْاٰخِرَةِ حَسَنَةً وَّقِنَا عَذَابَ النَّارِ (٢٠٢) النصف
اُولٰٓئِكَ لَهُمْ نَصِيْبٌ مِّمَّا كَسَبُوْا ؕ وَاللّٰهُ سَرِيْعُ الْحِسَابِ (٢٠٣)
وَاذْكُرُوا اللّٰهَ فِيْٓ اَيَّامٍ مَّعْدُوْدٰتٍ ؕ فَمَنْ تَعَجَّلَ فِيْ
يَوْمَيْنِ فَلَآ اِثْمَ عَلَيْهِ ۚ وَمَنْ تَاَخَّرَ فَلَآ اِثْمَ عَلَيْهِ ۙ
لِمَنِ اتَّقٰى ؕ وَاتَّقُوا اللّٰهَ وَاعْلَمُوْٓا اَنَّكُمْ اِلَيْهِ تُحْشَرُوْنَ (٢٠٤)
وَمِنَ النَّاسِ مَنْ يُّعْجِبُكَ قَوْلُهٗ فِي الْحَيٰوةِ الدُّنْيَا
وَيُشْهِدُ اللّٰهَ عَلٰى مَا فِيْ قَلْبِهٖ ۙ وَهُوَ اَلَدُّ الْخِصَامِ (٢٠٥)
وَاِذَا تَوَلّٰى سَعٰى فِي الْاَرْضِ لِيُفْسِدَ فِيْهَا وَيُهْلِكَ
الْحَرْثَ وَالنَّسْلَ ؕ وَاللّٰهُ لَا يُحِبُّ الْفَسَادَ (٢٠٦)
وَاِذَا قِيْلَ لَهُ اتَّقِ اللّٰهَ اَخَذَتْهُ الْعِزَّةُ بِالْاِثْمِ فَحَسْبُهٗ
جَهَنَّمُ ؕ وَلَبِئْسَ الْمِهَادُ (٢٠٧)
وَمِنَ النَّاسِ مَنْ يَّشْرِيْ نَفْسَهُ ابْتِغَآءَ مَرْضَاتِ اللّٰهِ ؕ
وَاللّٰهُ رَءُوْفٌ ۢ بِالْعِبَادِ (٢٠٨)
يٰٓاَيُّهَا الَّذِيْنَ اٰمَنُوا ادْخُلُوْا فِي السِّلْمِ كَآفَّةً ۠ وَّلَا
تَتَّبِعُوْا خُطُوٰتِ الشَّيْطٰنِ ؕ اِنَّهٗ لَكُمْ عَدُوٌّ مُّبِيْنٌ (٢٠٩)
فَاِنْ زَلَلْتُمْ مِّنْۢ بَعْدِ مَا جَآءَتْكُمُ الْبَيِّنٰتُ فَاعْلَمُوْٓا
اَنَّ اللّٰهَ عَزِيْزٌ حَكِيْمٌ (٢١٠)
هَلْ يَنْظُرُوْنَ اِلَّآ اَنْ يَّاْتِيَهُمُ اللّٰهُ فِيْ ظُلَلٍ مِّنَ
الْغَمَامِ وَالْمَلٰٓئِكَةُ وَقُضِيَ الْاَمْرُ ؕ وَاِلَى اللّٰهِ تُرْجَعُ
الْاُمُوْرُ (٢١١) ع ٢٥ ع ١٣ ٩
سَلْ بَنِيْٓ اِسْرَآءِيْلَ كَمْ اٰتَيْنٰهُمْ مِّنْ اٰيَةٍ ۢ بَيِّنَةٍ ؕ

whoso changes the gift of Allah after it has come to him, surely, then, Allah is severe in punishing.

وَمَنْ يُّبَدِّلْ نِعْمَةَ اللّٰهِ مِنْ بَعْدِ مَا جَآءَتْهُ فَاِنَّ
اللّٰهَ شَدِيْدُ الْعِقَابِ ﴿٢١٢﴾

213. The life of this world is made *to appear* attractive to those who disbelieve; and they scoff at those who believe. But those who fear *God* shall be above them on the Day of Resurrection; and Allah bestows *His gifts* on whomsoever He pleases without reckoning.

زُيِّنَ لِلَّذِيْنَ كَفَرُوا الْحَيٰوةُ الدُّنْيَا وَيَسْخَرُوْنَ مِنَ
الَّذِيْنَ اٰمَنُوْا ۘ وَالَّذِيْنَ اتَّقَوْا فَوْقَهُمْ يَوْمَ الْقِيٰمَةِ ۗ
وَاللّٰهُ يَرْزُقُ مَنْ يَّشَآءُ بِغَيْرِ حِسَابٍ ﴿٢١٣﴾

وقف لازم

214. Mankind were one community, *then they differed among themselves*, so Allah raised Prophets as bearers of good tidings and as warners, and sent down with them the Book containing the truth that He might judge between the people wherein they differed. *But now they began to differ about the Book*, and none differed about it except those to whom it was given, after clear Signs had come to them, out of envy towards one another. Now has Allah, by His command, guided the believers to the truth in regard to which they (the unbelievers) differed; and Allah guides whomsoever He pleases to the right path.

كَانَ النَّاسُ اُمَّةً وَّاحِدَةً ۟ فَبَعَثَ اللّٰهُ النَّبِيّٖنَ
مُبَشِّرِيْنَ وَمُنْذِرِيْنَ ۖ وَاَنْزَلَ مَعَهُمُ الْكِتٰبَ بِالْحَقِّ
لِيَحْكُمَ بَيْنَ النَّاسِ فِيْمَا اخْتَلَفُوْا فِيْهِ ۭ وَمَا اخْتَلَفَ
فِيْهِ اِلَّا الَّذِيْنَ اُوْتُوْهُ مِنْۢ بَعْدِ مَا جَآءَتْهُمُ الْبَيِّنٰتُ
بَغْيًۢا بَيْنَهُمْ ۚ فَهَدَى اللّٰهُ الَّذِيْنَ اٰمَنُوْا لِمَا اخْتَلَفُوْا
فِيْهِ مِنَ الْحَقِّ بِاِذْنِهٖ ۭ وَاللّٰهُ يَهْدِيْ مَنْ يَّشَآءُ
اِلٰى صِرَاطٍ مُّسْتَقِيْمٍ ﴿٢١٤﴾

215. Do you think that you will enter Heaven while there has not come over you the condition of those who passed away before you? Poverty and afflictions befell them, and they were violently shaken until the Messenger and those who believed along with him said: 'When *will come* the help of Allah?' Yea, surely the help of Allah is nigh.

اَمْ حَسِبْتُمْ اَنْ تَدْخُلُوا الْجَنَّةَ وَلَمَّا يَاْتِكُمْ مَّثَلُ
الَّذِيْنَ خَلَوْا مِنْ قَبْلِكُمْ ۭ مَسَّتْهُمُ الْبَاْسَآءُ وَالضَّرَّآءُ
وَزُلْزِلُوْا حَتّٰى يَقُوْلَ الرَّسُوْلُ وَالَّذِيْنَ اٰمَنُوْا مَعَهٗ
مَتٰى نَصْرُ اللّٰهِ ۭ اَلَآ اِنَّ نَصْرَ اللّٰهِ قَرِيْبٌ ﴿٢١٥﴾

216. They ask thee what they shall spend. Say: 'Whatever of good and abundant wealth you spend should be for parents and near relatives and orphans and the needy and the wayfarer. And whatever good you do, surely Allah knows it well.'

يَسْـَٔلُوْنَكَ مَاذَا يُنْفِقُوْنَ ۭ قُلْ مَآ اَنْفَقْتُمْ مِّنْ
خَيْرٍ فَلِلْوَالِدَيْنِ وَالْاَقْرَبِيْنَ وَالْيَتٰمٰى وَالْمَسٰكِيْنِ
وَابْنِ السَّبِيْلِ ۭ وَمَا تَفْعَلُوْا مِنْ خَيْرٍ فَاِنَّ اللّٰهَ بِهٖ
عَلِيْمٌ ﴿٢١٦﴾

217. Fighting is ordained for you, though it is repugnant to you; but it may be that you dislike a thing while it is good for you, and it may be that you like a

كُتِبَ عَلَيْكُمُ الْقِتَالُ وَهُوَ كُرْهٌ لَّكُمْ ۚ وَعَسٰٓى اَنْ
تَكْرَهُوْا شَيْـًٔا وَّهُوَ خَيْرٌ لَّكُمْ ۚ وَعَسٰٓى اَنْ تُحِبُّوْا

thing while it is bad for you. Allah knows *all things*, and you know not.

R. 27.

218. They ask thee about fighting in the Sacred Month. Say: 'Fighting therein is *a* great *transgression*, but to hinder *men* from the way of Allah, and to be ungrateful to Him and *to hinder men from* the Sacred Mosque, and to turn out its people therefrom, is *a* greater *sin* with Allah; and persecution is worse than killing.' And they will not cease fighting you until they turn you back from your faith, if they can. And whoso from among you turns back from his faith and dies while he is a disbeliever, it is they whose works shall be vain in this world and the next. These are the inmates of the Fire and therein shall they abide.

219. Those who believe and those who emigrate and strive hard in the cause of Allah, it is these who hope for Allah's mercy; and Allah is Most Forgiving, Merciful.

220. They ask thee concerning wine and the game of hazard. Say: 'In both there is great sin and also *some* advantages for men; but their sin is greater than their advantage.' And they ask thee what they should spend. Say: 'What you can spare.' Thus does Allah make His commandments clear to you that you may reflect

221. Upon this world and the next. And they ask thee concerning the orphans. Say: 'Promotion of their welfare is *an act of* great goodness. And if you intermix with them, they are your brethren. And Allah knows the mischief-maker from the reformer. And if Allah had so willed, He would have put you to hardship. Surely, Allah is Mighty, Wise.'

222. And marry not idolatrous women until they believe; even a believing bondwoman is better than an idolatress, although she may *highly* please you. And give not *believing women* in marriage to idolaters until they believe; *even* a believ-

شَيْـًٔا وَهُوَ شَرٌّ لَّكُمْ ۗ وَاللّٰهُ يَعْلَمُ وَاَنْتُمْ لَا تَعْلَمُوْنَ ﴿۲۱۷﴾
يَسْـَٔلُوْنَكَ عَنِ الشَّهْرِ الْحَرَامِ قِتَالٍ فِيْهِ ۗ قُلْ قِتَالٌ
فِيْهِ كَبِيْرٌ ۗ وَصَدٌّ عَنْ سَبِيْلِ اللّٰهِ وَكُفْرٌۢ بِهٖ وَ
الْمَسْجِدِ الْحَرَامِ ۗ وَاِخْرَاجُ اَهْلِهٖ مِنْهُ اَكْبَرُ عِنْدَ
اللّٰهِ ۚ وَالْفِتْنَةُ اَكْبَرُ مِنَ الْقَتْلِ ۗ وَلَا يَزَالُوْنَ
يُقَاتِلُوْنَكُمْ حَتّٰى يَرُدُّوْكُمْ عَنْ دِيْنِكُمْ اِنِ اسْتَطَاعُوْا ۗ
وَمَنْ يَّرْتَدِدْ مِنْكُمْ عَنْ دِيْنِهٖ فَيَمُتْ وَهُوَ كَافِرٌ
فَاُولٰٓئِكَ حَبِطَتْ اَعْمَالُهُمْ فِي الدُّنْيَا وَالْاٰخِرَةِ ۚ وَاُولٰٓئِكَ
اَصْحٰبُ النَّارِ ۚ هُمْ فِيْهَا خٰلِدُوْنَ ﴿۲۱۸﴾
اِنَّ الَّذِيْنَ اٰمَنُوْا وَالَّذِيْنَ هَاجَرُوْا وَجٰهَدُوْا فِيْ
سَبِيْلِ اللّٰهِ ۙ اُولٰٓئِكَ يَرْجُوْنَ رَحْمَتَ اللّٰهِ ۗ وَاللّٰهُ
غَفُوْرٌ رَّحِيْمٌ ﴿۲۱۹﴾
يَسْـَٔلُوْنَكَ عَنِ الْخَمْرِ وَالْمَيْسِرِ ۗ قُلْ فِيْهِمَآ اِثْمٌ
كَبِيْرٌ وَّمَنَافِعُ لِلنَّاسِ ۡ وَاِثْمُهُمَآ اَكْبَرُ مِنْ نَّفْعِهِمَا ۗ وَ
يَسْـَٔلُوْنَكَ مَاذَا يُنْفِقُوْنَ ۬ قُلِ الْعَفْوَ ۗ كَذٰلِكَ يُبَيِّنُ اللّٰهُ
لَكُمُ الْاٰيٰتِ لَعَلَّكُمْ تَتَفَكَّرُوْنَ ﴿۲۲۰﴾
فِي الدُّنْيَا وَالْاٰخِرَةِ ۗ وَيَسْـَٔلُوْنَكَ عَنِ الْيَتٰمٰى ۗ قُلْ اِصْلَاحٌ
لَّهُمْ خَيْرٌ ۗ وَاِنْ تُخَالِطُوْهُمْ فَاِخْوَانُكُمْ ۗ وَاللّٰهُ يَعْلَمُ
الْمُفْسِدَ مِنَ الْمُصْلِحِ ۗ وَلَوْ شَآءَ اللّٰهُ لَاَعْنَتَكُمْ ۗ اِنَّ اللّٰهَ
عَزِيْزٌ حَكِيْمٌ ﴿۲۲۱﴾
وَلَا تَنْكِحُوا الْمُشْرِكٰتِ حَتّٰى يُؤْمِنَّ ۗ وَلَاَمَةٌ مُّؤْمِنَةٌ
خَيْرٌ مِّنْ مُّشْرِكَةٍ وَّلَوْ اَعْجَبَتْكُمْ ۚ وَلَا تُنْكِحُوا الْمُشْرِكِيْنَ

ing slave is better than an idolater, although he may *highly* please you. These call to the Fire, but Allah calls to Heaven and to forgiveness by His command. And He makes His Signs clear to the people that they may remember.

R. 28.

* 223. And they ask thee concerning menstruation. Say: 'It is a harmful thing, so keep away from women during menstruation, and go not in unto them until they are clean. But when they have cleansed themselves, go in unto them as Allah has commanded you. Allah loves those who turn to Him and loves those who keep themselves clean.'

224. Your wives are a tilth for you; so approach your tilth when and how you like and send ahead *some good* for yourselves; and fear Allah and know that you shall meet Him; and give good tidings to those who obey.

225. And make not Allah a target for your oaths that you may *thereby* abstain from doing good and acting righteously and making peace between men. And Allah is All-Hearing, All-Knowing.

226. Allah will not call you to account for such of your oaths as are vain, but He will call you to account for what your hearts have earned. And Allah is Most Forgiving, Forbearing.

227. For those who vow *abstinence* from their wives, the *maximum* period of waiting is four months; then if they go back from the vow, surely, Allah is Most Forgiving, Merciful.

228. And if they decide upon divorce, then surely, Allah is All-Hearing, All-Knowing.

229. And the divorced women shall wait concerning themselves for three courses; and it is not lawful for them that they conceal what Allah has created in their wombs, if they believe in Allah and the Last Day; and their husbands have the greater right to take them back during that period, provided they desire reconciliation. And they (the women) have rights similar

حَتّٰى يُؤْمِنُوْا ۭ وَلَعَبْدٌ مُّؤْمِنٌ خَيْرٌ مِّنْ مُّشْرِكٍ وَّلَوْ
اَعْجَبَكُمْ ۭ اُولٰۗىِٕكَ يَدْعُوْنَ اِلَى النَّارِ ښ وَاللّٰهُ يَدْعُوْٓا
اِلَى الْجَنَّةِ وَالْمَغْفِرَةِ بِاِذْنِهٖ ۚ وَيُبَيِّنُ اٰيٰتِهٖ لِلنَّاسِ
لَعَلَّهُمْ يَتَذَكَّرُوْنَ ﴿۲۲۲﴾ ۲۸ ع
وَيَسْـَٔلُوْنَكَ عَنِ الْمَحِيْضِ ۭ قُلْ هُوَ اَذًى ۙ فَاعْتَزِلُوا
النِّسَاۗءَ فِي الْمَحِيْضِ ۙ وَلَا تَقْرَبُوْهُنَّ حَتّٰى يَطْهُرْنَ ۚ
فَاِذَا تَطَهَّرْنَ فَاْتُوْهُنَّ مِنْ حَيْثُ اَمَرَكُمُ اللّٰهُ ۭ اِنَّ
اللّٰهَ يُحِبُّ التَّوَّابِيْنَ وَيُحِبُّ الْمُتَطَهِّرِيْنَ ﴿۲۲۳﴾
نِسَاۗؤُكُمْ حَرْثٌ لَّكُمْ ۠ فَاْتُوْا حَرْثَكُمْ اَنّٰى شِئْتُمْ ۡ وَ
قَدِّمُوْا لِاَنْفُسِكُمْ ۭ وَاتَّقُوا اللّٰهَ وَاعْلَمُوْٓا اَنَّكُمْ مُّلٰقُوْهُ ۭ
وَبَشِّرِ الْمُؤْمِنِيْنَ ﴿۲۲۴﴾
وَلَا تَجْعَلُوا اللّٰهَ عُرْضَةً لِّاَيْمَانِكُمْ اَنْ تَبَرُّوْا وَتَتَّقُوْا
وَتُصْلِحُوْا بَيْنَ النَّاسِ ۭ وَاللّٰهُ سَمِيْعٌ عَلِيْمٌ ﴿۲۲۵﴾
لَا يُؤَاخِذُكُمُ اللّٰهُ بِاللَّغْوِ فِيْٓ اَيْمَانِكُمْ وَلٰكِنْ يُّؤَاخِذُكُمْ
بِمَا كَسَبَتْ قُلُوْبُكُمْ ۭ وَاللّٰهُ غَفُوْرٌ حَلِيْمٌ ﴿۲۲۶﴾
لِلَّذِيْنَ يُؤْلُوْنَ مِنْ نِّسَاۗىِٕهِمْ تَرَبُّصُ اَرْبَعَةِ اَشْهُرٍ ۚ
فَاِنْ فَاۗءُوْ فَاِنَّ اللّٰهَ غَفُوْرٌ رَّحِيْمٌ ﴿۲۲۷﴾
وَاِنْ عَزَمُوا الطَّلَاقَ فَاِنَّ اللّٰهَ سَمِيْعٌ عَلِيْمٌ ﴿۲۲۸﴾
وَالْمُطَلَّقٰتُ يَتَرَبَّصْنَ بِاَنْفُسِهِنَّ ثَلٰثَةَ قُرُوْۗءٍ ۭ وَ
لَا يَحِلُّ لَهُنَّ اَنْ يَّكْتُمْنَ مَا خَلَقَ اللّٰهُ فِيْٓ اَرْحَامِهِنَّ
اِنْ كُنَّ يُؤْمِنَّ بِاللّٰهِ وَالْيَوْمِ الْاٰخِرِ ۭ وَبُعُوْلَتُهُنَّ اَحَقُّ
بِرَدِّهِنَّ فِيْ ذٰلِكَ اِنْ اَرَادُوْٓا اِصْلَاحًا ۭ وَلَهُنَّ مِثْلُ

to those (of men) over them in equity; but men have a rank above them. And Allah is Mighty, Wise.

R. 29.

230. Such divorce may be *pronounced* twice; then, either retain *them* in a becoming manner or send *them* away with kindness. And it is not lawful for you that you take anything of what you have given them (your wives) unless both fear that they cannot observe the limits *prescribed* by Allah. But, if you fear that they cannot observe the limits *prescribed* by Allah, then it shall be no sin for either of them in what she gives to get her freedom. These are the limits *prescribed* by Allah, so transgress them not; and whoso transgresses the limits *prescribed* by Allah, it is they that are the wrongdoers.

231. And if he divorce her *the third time*, then she is not lawful for him thereafter, until she marries another husband; and, if he *also* divorce her, then it shall be no sin for them to return to each other, provided they are sure that they would be able to observe the limits *prescribed* by Allah. And these are the limits *prescribed* by Allah which He makes clear to the people who have knowledge.

232. And when you divorce* your wives and they approach the end of their *appointed* period, then either retain them in a becoming manner; or send them away in a becoming manner; but retain them not wrongfully so that you may transgress. And whoso does that, surely wrongs his own soul. And do not make a jest of the commandments of Allah, and remember the favour of Allah upon you and the Book and the Wisdom which He has sent down to you, whereby He exhorts you. And fear Allah and know that Allah knows all things well.

R. 30.

233. And when you divorce women and they reach the end of their period, prevent them not from marrying their husbands, if they agree between themselves in a decent manner. This is an admonition for him among you who believes in Allah and the Last Day. It is more blessed for you

الَّذِيْ عَلَيْهِنَّ بِالْمَعْرُوْفِ ۪ وَلِلرِّجَالِ عَلَيْهِنَّ دَرَجَةٌ ؕ
وَاللّٰهُ عَزِيْزٌ حَكِيْمٌ ﴿٢٢٩﴾ ع ٢٨ ١٢
اَلطَّلَاقُ مَرَّتٰنِ ۪ فَاِمْسَاكٌۢ بِمَعْرُوْفٍ اَوْ تَسْرِيْحٌۢ بِاِحْسَانٍ ؕ
وَلَا يَحِلُّ لَكُمْ اَنْ تَاْخُذُوْا مِمَّآ اٰتَيْتُمُوْهُنَّ شَيْـًٔا اِلَّآ
اَنْ يَّخَافَآ اَلَّا يُقِيْمَا حُدُوْدَ اللّٰهِ ؕ فَاِنْ خِفْتُمْ اَلَّا يُقِيْمَا
حُدُوْدَ اللّٰهِ ۙ فَلَا جُنَاحَ عَلَيْهِمَا فِيْمَا افْتَدَتْ بِهٖ ؕ تِلْكَ
حُدُوْدُ اللّٰهِ فَلَا تَعْتَدُوْهَا ۚ وَمَنْ يَّتَعَدَّ حُدُوْدَ اللّٰهِ
فَاُولٰٓئِكَ هُمُ الظّٰلِمُوْنَ ﴿٢٣٠﴾
فَاِنْ طَلَّقَهَا فَلَا تَحِلُّ لَهٗ مِنْۢ بَعْدُ حَتّٰى تَنْكِحَ زَوْجًا
غَيْرَهٗ ؕ فَاِنْ طَلَّقَهَا فَلَا جُنَاحَ عَلَيْهِمَآ اَنْ يَّتَرَاجَعَآ
اِنْ ظَنَّآ اَنْ يُّقِيْمَا حُدُوْدَ اللّٰهِ ؕ وَتِلْكَ حُدُوْدُ اللّٰهِ
يُبَيِّنُهَا لِقَوْمٍ يَّعْلَمُوْنَ ﴿٢٣١﴾
وَاِذَا طَلَّقْتُمُ النِّسَآءَ فَبَلَغْنَ اَجَلَهُنَّ فَاَمْسِكُوْهُنَّ
بِمَعْرُوْفٍ اَوْ سَرِّحُوْهُنَّ بِمَعْرُوْفٍ ۪ وَلَا تُمْسِكُوْهُنَّ
ضِرَارًا لِّتَعْتَدُوْا ۚ وَمَنْ يَّفْعَلْ ذٰلِكَ فَقَدْ ظَلَمَ نَفْسَهٗ ؕ
وَلَا تَتَّخِذُوْٓا اٰيٰتِ اللّٰهِ هُزُوًا ؗ وَّاذْكُرُوْا نِعْمَتَ اللّٰهِ عَلَيْكُمْ
وَمَآ اَنْزَلَ عَلَيْكُمْ مِّنَ الْكِتٰبِ وَالْحِكْمَةِ يَعِظُكُمْ
بِهٖ ؕ وَاتَّقُوا اللّٰهَ وَاعْلَمُوْٓا اَنَّ اللّٰهَ بِكُلِّ شَيْءٍ عَلِيْمٌ ﴿٢٣٢﴾ الربع ع ٢٩ ١٣
وَاِذَا طَلَّقْتُمُ النِّسَآءَ فَبَلَغْنَ اَجَلَهُنَّ فَلَا تَعْضُلُوْهُنَّ
اَنْ يَّنْكِحْنَ اَزْوَاجَهُنَّ اِذَا تَرَاضَوْا بَيْنَهُمْ بِالْمَعْرُوْفِ ؕ
ذٰلِكَ يُوْعَظُ بِهٖ مَنْ كَانَ مِنْكُمْ يُؤْمِنُ بِاللّٰهِ وَالْيَوْمِ
الْاٰخِرِ ؕ ذٰلِكُمْ اَزْكٰى لَكُمْ وَاَطْهَرُ ؕ وَاللّٰهُ يَعْلَمُ وَاَنْتُمْ

* The revocable divorce.

and purer; and Allah knows but you do not know.

234. And mothers shall give suck to their children for two whole years; *this is* for those who desire to complete the suckling. And the man to whom the child belongs shall be responsible for their (the mothers') food and clothing according to usage. No soul is burdened beyond its capacity. The mother shall not make *the father* suffer on account of her child, nor shall he to whom the child belongs make *the mother* suffer on account of his child, and the same is incumbent on the heir. If they both decide upon weaning *the child* by mutual consent and consultation, there is no blame on them. And if you desire to engage a wet-nurse for your children, there shall be no blame on you, provided you pay what you have agreed to pay, in a fair manner. And fear Allah and know that Allah sees what you do.

235. And those of you who die and leave wives behind, these (wives) shall wait concerning themselves four months and ten *days*. And when they have reached the end of their period, no sin shall lie on you in anything that they do with regard to themselves according to what is fair. And Allah is aware of what you do.

236. And there shall be no blame on you in throwing out a hint regarding a proposal of marriage to *these* women or in keeping *the desire* hidden in your minds. Allah knows that you will think of them *in this connection*. But make not a contract with them in secret, except that you say a fair word. And resolve not on the marriage tie until the prescribed period reaches its end. And know that Allah knows what is in your minds; so beware of it. And know that Allah is Most Forgiving, Forbearing.

R. 31.

237. It shall be no sin for you if you divorce women while you have not touched them, nor settled for them a dowry. But provdie for them—the rich man according

لَا تَعْلَمُوْنَ ﴿٢٣٣﴾
وَالْوَالِدٰتُ يُرْضِعْنَ اَوْلَادَهُنَّ حَوْلَيْنِ كَامِلَيْنِ
لِمَنْ اَرَادَ اَنْ يُّتِمَّ الرَّضَاعَةَ ؕ وَعَلَى الْمَوْلُوْدِ لَهٗ
رِزْقُهُنَّ وَكِسْوَتُهُنَّ بِالْمَعْرُوْفِ ؕ لَا تُكَلَّفُ نَفْسٌ
اِلَّا وُسْعَهَا ۚ لَا تُضَآرَّ وَالِدَةٌ ۢ بِوَلَدِهَا وَلَا مَوْلُوْدٌ
لَّهٗ بِوَلَدِهٖ ۗ وَعَلَى الْوَارِثِ مِثْلُ ذٰلِكَ ۚ فَاِنْ اَرَادَا
فِصَالًا عَنْ تَرَاضٍ مِّنْهُمَا وَتَشَاوُرٍ فَلَا جُنَاحَ عَلَيْهِمَا ؕ
وَاِنْ اَرَدْتُّمْ اَنْ تَسْتَرْضِعُوْٓا اَوْلَادَكُمْ فَلَا جُنَاحَ
عَلَيْكُمْ اِذَا سَلَّمْتُمْ مَّآ اٰتَيْتُمْ بِالْمَعْرُوْفِ ؕ وَاتَّقُوا
اللّٰهَ وَاعْلَمُوْٓا اَنَّ اللّٰهَ بِمَا تَعْمَلُوْنَ بَصِيْرٌ ﴿٢٣٤﴾
وَالَّذِيْنَ يُتَوَفَّوْنَ مِنْكُمْ وَيَذَرُوْنَ اَزْوَاجًا يَّتَرَبَّصْنَ
بِاَنْفُسِهِنَّ اَرْبَعَةَ اَشْهُرٍ وَّعَشْرًا ۚ فَاِذَا بَلَغْنَ اَجَلَهُنَّ
فَلَا جُنَاحَ عَلَيْكُمْ فِيْمَا فَعَلْنَ فِيْٓ اَنْفُسِهِنَّ بِالْمَعْرُوْفِ ؕ
وَاللّٰهُ بِمَا تَعْمَلُوْنَ خَبِيْرٌ ﴿٢٣٥﴾
وَلَا جُنَاحَ عَلَيْكُمْ فِيْمَا عَرَّضْتُمْ بِهٖ مِنْ خِطْبَةِ النِّسَآءِ
اَوْ اَكْنَنْتُمْ فِيْٓ اَنْفُسِكُمْ ؕ عَلِمَ اللّٰهُ اَنَّكُمْ سَتَذْكُرُوْنَهُنَّ
وَلٰكِنْ لَّا تُوَاعِدُوْهُنَّ سِرًّا اِلَّآ اَنْ تَقُوْلُوْا قَوْلًا
مَّعْرُوْفًا ؕ وَلَا تَعْزِمُوْا عُقْدَةَ النِّكَاحِ حَتّٰى يَبْلُغَ
الْكِتٰبُ اَجَلَهٗ ؕ وَاعْلَمُوْٓا اَنَّ اللّٰهَ يَعْلَمُ مَا فِيْٓ اَنْفُسِكُمْ
فَاحْذَرُوْهُ ۚ وَاعْلَمُوْٓا اَنَّ اللّٰهَ غَفُوْرٌ حَلِيْمٌ ﴿٢٣٦﴾ ع
لَا جُنَاحَ عَلَيْكُمْ اِنْ طَلَّقْتُمُ النِّسَآءَ مَا لَمْ تَمَسُّوْهُنَّ
اَوْ تَفْرِضُوْا لَهُنَّ فَرِيْضَةً ۖۚ وَّمَتِّعُوْهُنَّ عَلَى الْمُوْسِعِ

to his means and the poor man according to his means—a provision in a becoming manner, an obligation upon the virtuous.

قَدَرُهٗ وَعَلَى الْمُقْتِرِ قَدَرُهٗ ۚ مَتَاعًا بِالْمَعْرُوْفِ ۚ حَقًّا
عَلَى الْمُحْسِنِيْنَ ﴿۲۳۷﴾

238. And if you divorce them before you have touched them, but have settled for them a dowry, then half of what you have settled *shall be due from you*, unless they remit, or he, in whose hand is the tie of marriage, should remit. And that you should remit is nearer to righteousness. And do not forget to do good to one another. Surely, Allah sees what you do.

وَاِنْ طَلَّقْتُمُوْهُنَّ مِنْ قَبْلِ اَنْ تَمَسُّوْهُنَّ وَقَدْ
فَرَضْتُمْ لَهُنَّ فَرِيْضَةً فَنِصْفُ مَا فَرَضْتُمْ اِلَّآ اَنْ
يَّعْفُوْنَ اَوْ يَعْفُوَا الَّذِيْ بِيَدِهٖ عُقْدَةُ النِّكَاحِ ۭ وَ
اَنْ تَعْفُوْٓا اَقْرَبُ لِلتَّقْوٰى ۭ وَلَا تَنْسَوُا الْفَضْلَ بَيْنَكُمْ ۭ
اِنَّ اللّٰهَ بِمَا تَعْمَلُوْنَ بَصِيْرٌ ﴿۲۳۸﴾

239. Watch over Prayers, and the middle Prayer, and stand before Allah submissively.

حٰفِظُوْا عَلَى الصَّلَوٰتِ وَالصَّلٰوةِ الْوُسْطٰى ۚ وَقُوْمُوْا
لِلّٰهِ قٰنِتِيْنَ ﴿۲۳۹﴾

240. If you are in *a state of* fear, then *say your Prayer* on foot or riding; but when you are safe, remember Allah as He has taught you that which you did not know.

فَاِنْ خِفْتُمْ فَرِجَالًا اَوْ رُكْبَانًا ۚ فَاِذَآ اَمِنْتُمْ فَاذْكُرُوا
اللّٰهَ كَمَا عَلَّمَكُمْ مَّا لَمْ تَكُوْنُوْا تَعْلَمُوْنَ ﴿۲۴۰﴾

241. And those of you who die and leave behind wives shall bequeath to their wives provision for a year without *their* being turned out. But if they *themselves* go out, there shall be no blame upon you in regard to any proper thing which they do concerning themselves. And Allah is Mighty, Wise.

وَالَّذِيْنَ يُتَوَفَّوْنَ مِنْكُمْ وَيَذَرُوْنَ اَزْوَاجًا ښ وَّصِيَّةً
لِّاَزْوَاجِهِمْ مَّتَاعًا اِلَى الْحَوْلِ غَيْرَ اِخْرَاجٍ ۚ فَاِنْ
خَرَجْنَ فَلَا جُنَاحَ عَلَيْكُمْ فِيْ مَا فَعَلْنَ فِيْٓ اَنْفُسِهِنَّ
مِنْ مَّعْرُوْفٍ ۭ وَاللّٰهُ عَزِيْزٌ حَكِيْمٌ ﴿۲۴۱﴾

242. And for the divorced women *also* there should be a provision according to what is fair—an obligation on the God-fearing.

وَلِلْمُطَلَّقٰتِ مَتَاعٌ بِالْمَعْرُوْفِ ۭ حَقًّا عَلَى الْمُتَّقِيْنَ ﴿۲۴۲﴾

243. Thus does Allah make His commandments clear to you that you may understand.

كَذٰلِكَ يُبَيِّنُ اللّٰهُ لَكُمْ اٰيٰتِهٖ لَعَلَّكُمْ تَعْقِلُوْنَ ﴿۲۴۳﴾ ع ۳۱ ۱۵

R. 32.

244. Dost thou not know of those who went forth from their homes, and they were thousands, fearing death? And Allah said to them: 'Die'; then He brought them to life. Surely, Allah is Munificent to men, but most men are not grateful.

اَلَمْ تَرَ اِلَى الَّذِيْنَ خَرَجُوْا مِنْ دِيَارِهِمْ وَهُمْ اُلُوْفٌ
حَذَرَ الْمَوْتِ ۠ فَقَالَ لَهُمُ اللّٰهُ مُوْتُوْا ۣ ثُمَّ اَحْيَاهُمْ ۭ
اِنَّ اللّٰهَ لَذُوْ فَضْلٍ عَلَى النَّاسِ وَلٰكِنَّ اَكْثَرَ
النَّاسِ لَا يَشْكُرُوْنَ ﴿۲۴۴﴾

245. And fight in the cause of Allah and

وَقَاتِلُوْا فِيْ سَبِيْلِ اللّٰهِ وَاعْلَمُوْٓا اَنَّ اللّٰهَ سَمِيْعٌ

know that Allah is All-Hearing, All-Knowing.

عَلِيْمٌ ﴿٢٤٥﴾

246. Who is it that will lend Allah a goodly loan that He may multiply it for him manifold? And Allah receives and enlarges, and to Him shall you be made to return.

مَنْ ذَا الَّذِيْ يُقْرِضُ اللّٰهَ قَرْضًا حَسَنًا فَيُضٰعِفَهٗ
لَهٗٓ اَضْعَافًا كَثِيْرَةً ؕ وَاللّٰهُ يَقْبِضُ وَيَبْصُۜطُ وَ
اِلَيْهِ تُرْجَعُوْنَ ﴿٢٤٦﴾

247. Hast thou not heard of the chiefs of the children of Israel after Moses, when they said to a Prophet of theirs: 'Appoint for us a king that we may fight in the cause of Allah?' He said: 'Is it not likely that you will not fight, if fighting is prescribed for you?' They said: 'What reason have we to abstain from fighting in the cause of Allah when we have been driven forth from our homes and our sons?' But when fighting was ordained for them, they turned back except a small number of them. And Allah knows the transgressors well.

اَلَمْ تَرَ اِلَى الْمَلَاِ مِنْۢ بَنِيْٓ اِسْرَآءِيْلَ مِنْۢ بَعْدِ
مُوْسٰى ۘ اِذْ قَالُوْا لِنَبِيٍّ لَّهُمُ ابْعَثْ لَنَا مَلِكًا نُّقَاتِلْ وقف لازم
فِيْ سَبِيْلِ اللّٰهِ ؕ قَالَ هَلْ عَسَيْتُمْ اِنْ كُتِبَ عَلَيْكُمُ
الْقِتَالُ اَلَّا تُقَاتِلُوْا ؕ قَالُوْا وَمَا لَنَآ اَلَّا نُقَاتِلَ فِيْ
سَبِيْلِ اللّٰهِ وَقَدْ اُخْرِجْنَا مِنْ دِيَارِنَا وَاَبْنَآئِنَا ؕ
فَلَمَّا كُتِبَ عَلَيْهِمُ الْقِتَالُ تَوَلَّوْا اِلَّا قَلِيْلًا مِّنْهُمْ ؕ
وَاللّٰهُ عَلِيْمٌۢ بِالظّٰلِمِيْنَ ﴿٢٤٧﴾

248. And their Prophet said to them: 'Allah has appointed for you Ṭālūt as a king.' They said: 'How can he have sovereignty over us while we are better entitled to sovereignty than he, and he is not given abundance of wealth?' He said: 'Surely, Allah has chosen him above you and has increased him abundantly in knowledge and body.' And Allah gives sovereignty to whom He pleases and Allah is Bountiful, All-Knowing.

وَقَالَ لَهُمْ نَبِيُّهُمْ اِنَّ اللّٰهَ قَدْ بَعَثَ لَكُمْ طَالُوْتَ
مَلِكًا ؕ قَالُوْٓا اَنّٰى يَكُوْنُ لَهُ الْمُلْكُ عَلَيْنَا وَنَحْنُ
اَحَقُّ بِالْمُلْكِ مِنْهُ وَلَمْ يُؤْتَ سَعَةً مِّنَ الْمَالِ ؕ
قَالَ اِنَّ اللّٰهَ اصْطَفٰهُ عَلَيْكُمْ وَزَادَهٗ بَسْطَةً فِي
الْعِلْمِ وَالْجِسْمِ ؕ وَاللّٰهُ يُؤْتِيْ مُلْكَهٗ مَنْ يَّشَآءُ ؕ
وَاللّٰهُ وَاسِعٌ عَلِيْمٌ ﴿٢٤٨﴾

249. And their Prophet said to them: 'The sign of his sovereignty is that there shall be given you a heart wherein there will be tranquillity from your Lord and a legacy *of good* left by the family of Moses and the family of Aaron – the angels bearing it. Surely, in this there is a Sign for you if you are believers.'

وَقَالَ لَهُمْ نَبِيُّهُمْ اِنَّ اٰيَةَ مُلْكِهٖٓ اَنْ يَّاْتِيَكُمُ
التَّابُوْتُ فِيْهِ سَكِيْنَةٌ مِّنْ رَّبِّكُمْ وَبَقِيَّةٌ مِّمَّا
تَرَكَ اٰلُ مُوْسٰى وَاٰلُ هٰرُوْنَ تَحْمِلُهُ الْمَلٰٓئِكَةُ ؕ اِنَّ
فِيْ ذٰلِكَ لَاٰيَةً لَّكُمْ اِنْ كُنْتُمْ مُّؤْمِنِيْنَ ﴿٢٤٩﴾ ٣٢ ع ١٧

R. 33.

250. And when Ṭālūt set out with the forces, he said: 'Surely, Allah will try you

فَلَمَّا فَصَلَ طَالُوْتُ بِالْجُنُوْدِ ۙ قَالَ اِنَّ اللّٰهَ مُبْتَلِيْكُمْ

with a river. So he who drinks therefrom is not of me; and he who tastes it not is assuredly of me, except him who takes a handful of water with his hand.' But they drank of it, except a few of them. And when they crossed it—he and those who believed along with him—they said: 'We have no power today against Jālūt and his forces.' But those who knew for certain that they would *one day* meet Allah said: 'How many a small party has triumphed over a large party by Allah's command! And Allah is with the steadfast.'

بنهر فمن شرب منه فليس مني ومن لم
يطعمه فإنه مني إلا من اغترف غرفة بيده
فشربوا منه إلا قليلا منهم فلما جاوزه هو
والذين آمنوا معه قالوا لا طاقة لنا اليوم
بجالوت وجنوده قال الذين يظنون أنهم ملاقوا
الله كم من فئة قليلة غلبت فئة كثيرة بإذن
الله والله مع الصابرين ﴿٢٥٠﴾

251. And when they issued forth to *encounter* Jālūt and his forces, they said: 'O our Lord, pour forth steadfastness upon us, and make our steps firm, and help us against the disbelieving people.'

ولما برزوا لجالوت وجنوده قالوا ربنا أفرغ
علينا صبرا وثبت أقدامنا وانصرنا على القوم
الكافرين ﴿٢٥١﴾

252. So they routed them by the command of Allah; and David slew Jālūt, and Allah gave him sovereignty and wisdom, and taught him of what He pleased. And had it not been for Allah's repelling men, some of them by the others, the earth would have become filled with disorder. But Allah is Munificent to *all* peoples.

فهزموهم بإذن الله وقتل داود جالوت و
آتاه الله الملك والحكمة وعلمه مما يشاء و
لولا دفع الله الناس بعضهم ببعض لفسدت
الأرض ولكن الله ذو فضل على العالمين ﴿٢٥٢﴾

253. These are the Signs of Allah; We recite them unto thee with truth. Surely, thou art *one* of the Messengers.

تلك آيات الله نتلوها عليك بالحق وإنك لمن
المرسلين ﴿٢٥٣﴾

* 254. These Messengers have We exalted, some of them above others: among them there are those to whom Allah spoke*; and some of them He exalted by degrees of rank. And We gave Jesus, son of Mary, clear proofs and strengthened him with the Spirit of holiness. And if Allah had *so* willed, those *that came* after them would not have fought with one another after clear Signs had come to them; but they did disagree. Of them were some who believed, and of them were some who disbelieved. And if Allah had *so* willed, they would not

تلك الرسل فضلنا بعضهم على بعض منهم
من كلم الله ورفع بعضهم درجات وآتينا
عيسى ابن مريم البينات وأيدناه بروح القدس
ولو شاء الله ما اقتتل الذين من بعدهم من
بعد ما جاءتهم البينات ولكن اختلفوا فمنهم من
آمن ومنهم من كفر ولو شاء الله ما اقتتلوا

* i. e. gave them a new Law.

have fought with one another; but Allah does what He desires.

R. 34.

255. O ye who believe! spend out of what We have bestowed on you before the day comes wherein there shall be no buying and selling, nor friendship, nor intercession; and it is those who disbelieve that do wrong *to themselves*.

* 256. Allah—there is no God but He, the Living, the Self-Subsisting and All-Sustaining. Slumber seizes Him not, nor sleep. To Him belongs whatsoever is in the heavens and whatsoever is in the earth. Who is he that will intercede with Him except by His permission? He knows what is before them and what is behind them; and they encompass nothing of His knowledge except what He pleases. His knowledge extends over the heavens and the earth; and the care of them burdens Him not; and He is the High, the Great.

257. There should be no compulsion in religion. Surely, right has become distinct from wrong; so whosoever refuses to be led by those who transgress, and believes in Allah, has surely grasped a strong handle which knows no breaking. And Allah is All-Hearing, All-Knowing.

258. Allah is the friend of those who believe: He brings them out of every *kind of* darkness into light. And those who disbelieve, their friends are the transgressors who bring them out of light into every *kind of* darkness. These are the inmates of the Fire; therein shall they abide.

R. 35.

259. Hast thou not heard of him who disputed with Abraham about his Lord, because Allah had given him kingdom? When Abraham said, 'My Lord is He Who gives life and causes death,' he said, 'I *also* give life and cause death.' Abraham said, 'Well, Allah brings the sun from the East; bring it thou from the West.'

وَلٰكِنَّ اللّٰهَ يَفْعَلُ مَا يُرِيْدُ ﴿٢٥٤﴾ ع ٣٣
يٰٓاَيُّهَا الَّذِيْنَ اٰمَنُوْٓا اَنْفِقُوْا مِمَّا رَزَقْنٰكُمْ مِّنْ قَبْلِ
اَنْ يَّاْتِيَ يَوْمٌ لَّا بَيْعٌ فِيْهِ وَلَا خُلَّةٌ وَّلَا شَفَاعَةٌ ؕ
وَالْكٰفِرُوْنَ هُمُ الظّٰلِمُوْنَ ﴿٢٥٥﴾
اَللّٰهُ لَآ اِلٰهَ اِلَّا هُوَ ۚ اَلْحَيُّ الْقَيُّوْمُ ۚ لَا تَاْخُذُهٗ سِنَةٌ
وَّلَا نَوْمٌ ؕ لَهٗ مَا فِي السَّمٰوٰتِ وَمَا فِي الْاَرْضِ ؕ مَنْ
ذَا الَّذِيْ يَشْفَعُ عِنْدَهٗٓ اِلَّا بِاِذْنِهٖ ؕ يَعْلَمُ مَا بَيْنَ
اَيْدِيْهِمْ وَمَا خَلْفَهُمْ ۚ وَلَا يُحِيْطُوْنَ بِشَيْءٍ مِّنْ
عِلْمِهٖٓ اِلَّا بِمَا شَآءَ ۚ وَسِعَ كُرْسِيُّهُ السَّمٰوٰتِ وَالْاَرْضَ ۚ
وَلَا يَئُوْدُهٗ حِفْظُهُمَا ۚ وَهُوَ الْعَلِيُّ الْعَظِيْمُ ﴿٢٥٦﴾
لَآ اِكْرَاهَ فِي الدِّيْنِ ۟ۙ قَدْ تَّبَيَّنَ الرُّشْدُ مِنَ الْغَيِّ ۚ
فَمَنْ يَّكْفُرْ بِالطَّاغُوْتِ وَيُؤْمِنْۢ بِاللّٰهِ فَقَدِ
اسْتَمْسَكَ بِالْعُرْوَةِ الْوُثْقٰى ۗ لَا انْفِصَامَ لَهَا ؕ
وَاللّٰهُ سَمِيْعٌ عَلِيْمٌ ﴿٢٥٧﴾
اَللّٰهُ وَلِيُّ الَّذِيْنَ اٰمَنُوْا ۙ يُخْرِجُهُمْ مِّنَ الظُّلُمٰتِ اِلَى
النُّوْرِ ؕ وَالَّذِيْنَ كَفَرُوْٓا اَوْلِيٰٓـُٔهُمُ الطَّاغُوْتُ ۙ
يُخْرِجُوْنَهُمْ مِّنَ النُّوْرِ اِلَى الظُّلُمٰتِ ؕ اُولٰٓئِكَ اَصْحٰبُ
النَّارِ ۚ هُمْ فِيْهَا خٰلِدُوْنَ ﴿٢٥٨﴾ ع ٣٤
اَلَمْ تَرَ اِلَى الَّذِيْ حَآجَّ اِبْرٰهٖمَ فِيْ رَبِّهٖٓ اَنْ اٰتٰىهُ
اللّٰهُ الْمُلْكَ ۘ اِذْ قَالَ اِبْرٰهٖمُ رَبِّيَ الَّذِيْ يُحْيٖ وَيُمِيْتُ ۙ وقف لازم
قَالَ اَنَا اُحْيٖ وَاُمِيْتُ ؕ قَالَ اِبْرٰهٖمُ فَاِنَّ اللّٰهَ يَاْتِيْ
بِالشَّمْسِ مِنَ الْمَشْرِقِ فَاْتِ بِهَا مِنَ الْمَغْرِبِ

Thereupon the infidel was dumbfounded. And Allah guides not the unjust people.

260. Or like him who passed by a town which had fallen down upon its roofs, *and* exclaimed, 'When will Allah restore it to life after its destruction?' Then Allah caused him to die for a hundred years; then He raised him, and said: 'How long hast thou remained *in this state*?' He answered, 'I have remained a day or part of a day.' He said: 'Nay, thou hast remained *in this state* for a hundred years. Now look at thy food and thy drink; they have not rotted. And look at thy ass. And *We have done this* that We may make thee a Sign unto men. And look at the bones, how We set them and then clothe them with flesh.' And when this became clear to him, he said, 'I know that Allah has the power to do all that He wills.'

261. And *remember* when Abraham said, 'My Lord, show me how Thou givest life to the dead.' He said, 'Hast thou not believed?' He said, 'Yes, but *I ask this* that my heart may be at rest.' He answered, 'Take four birds and make them attached to thyself. Then put each of them on a hill; then call them; they will come to thee in haste. And know that Allah is Mighty, Wise.'

R. 36.

262. The similitude of those who spend their wealth for the cause of Allah is like the similitude of a grain of corn which grows seven ears, in each ear a hundred grains. And Allah multiplies *it* further for whomsoever He pleases; and Allah is Bountiful, All-Knowing.

263. They who spend their wealth for the cause of Allah, then follow not up what they have spent with taunt or injury, for them is their reward with their Lord, and they shall have no fear, nor shall they grieve.

264. A kind word and forgiveness are better than charity followed by injury. And Allah is Self-Sufficient, Forbearing.

فَبُهِتَ الَّذِيْ كَفَرَ ۗ وَاللّٰهُ لَا يَهْدِي الْقَوْمَ الظّٰلِمِيْنَ ﴿٢٥٩﴾
اَوْ كَالَّذِيْ مَرَّ عَلٰى قَرْيَةٍ وَّهِيَ خَاوِيَةٌ عَلٰى
عُرُوْشِهَا ۚ قَالَ اَنّٰى يُحْيٖ هٰذِهِ اللّٰهُ بَعْدَ مَوْتِهَا ۚ
فَاَمَاتَهُ اللّٰهُ مِائَةَ عَامٍ ثُمَّ بَعَثَهٗ ۗ قَالَ كَمْ لَبِثْتَ ۗ
قَالَ لَبِثْتُ يَوْمًا اَوْ بَعْضَ يَوْمٍ ۗ قَالَ بَلْ لَّبِثْتَ
مِائَةَ عَامٍ فَانْظُرْ اِلٰى طَعَامِكَ وَشَرَابِكَ لَمْ يَتَسَنَّهْ ۚ
وَانْظُرْ اِلٰى حِمَارِكَ وَلِنَجْعَلَكَ اٰيَةً لِّلنَّاسِ وَانْظُرْ اِلَى
الْعِظَامِ كَيْفَ نُنْشِزُهَا ثُمَّ نَكْسُوْهَا لَحْمًا ۗ فَلَمَّا تَبَيَّنَ
لَهٗ ۙ قَالَ اَعْلَمُ اَنَّ اللّٰهَ عَلٰى كُلِّ شَيْءٍ قَدِيْرٌ ﴿٢٦٠﴾
وَاِذْ قَالَ اِبْرٰهٖمُ رَبِّ اَرِنِيْ كَيْفَ تُحْيِ الْمَوْتٰى ۗ قَالَ
اَوَلَمْ تُؤْمِنْ ۗ قَالَ بَلٰى وَلٰكِنْ لِّيَطْمَئِنَّ قَلْبِيْ ۗ قَالَ
فَخُذْ اَرْبَعَةً مِّنَ الطَّيْرِ فَصُرْهُنَّ اِلَيْكَ ثُمَّ اجْعَلْ
عَلٰى كُلِّ جَبَلٍ مِّنْهُنَّ جُزْءًا ثُمَّ ادْعُهُنَّ يَاْتِيْنَكَ
سَعْيًا ۗ وَاعْلَمْ اَنَّ اللّٰهَ عَزِيْزٌ حَكِيْمٌ ﴿٢٦١﴾
مَثَلُ الَّذِيْنَ يُنْفِقُوْنَ اَمْوَالَهُمْ فِيْ سَبِيْلِ اللّٰهِ كَمَثَلِ
حَبَّةٍ اَنْۢبَتَتْ سَبْعَ سَنَابِلَ فِيْ كُلِّ سُنْۢبُلَةٍ مِّائَةُ
حَبَّةٍ ۗ وَاللّٰهُ يُضٰعِفُ لِمَنْ يَّشَآءُ ۗ وَاللّٰهُ وَاسِعٌ عَلِيْمٌ ﴿٢٦٢﴾
اَلَّذِيْنَ يُنْفِقُوْنَ اَمْوَالَهُمْ فِيْ سَبِيْلِ اللّٰهِ ثُمَّ لَا
يُتْبِعُوْنَ مَآ اَنْفَقُوْا مَنًّا وَّلَآ اَذًى ۙ لَّهُمْ اَجْرُهُمْ
عِنْدَ رَبِّهِمْ ۚ وَلَا خَوْفٌ عَلَيْهِمْ وَلَا هُمْ يَحْزَنُوْنَ ﴿٢٦٣﴾
قَوْلٌ مَّعْرُوْفٌ وَّمَغْفِرَةٌ خَيْرٌ مِّنْ صَدَقَةٍ يَّتْبَعُهَآ
اَذًى ۗ وَاللّٰهُ غَنِيٌّ حَلِيْمٌ ﴿٢٦٤﴾

265. O ye who believe! render not vain your alms by taunt and injury, like him who spends his wealth to be seen of men, and he believes not in Allah and the Last Day. His case is like the case of a smooth rock *covered* with earth, on which heavy rain falls, leaving it bare, smooth and hard. They shall not secure aught of what they earn. And Allah guides not the disbelieving people.

يٰۤاَيُّهَا الَّذِيۡنَ اٰمَنُوۡا لَا تُبۡطِلُوۡا صَدَقٰتِكُمۡ بِالۡمَنِّ
وَالۡاَذٰى كَالَّذِىۡ يُنۡفِقُ مَالَهٗ رِئَآءَ النَّاسِ وَلَا
يُؤۡمِنُ بِاللّٰهِ وَالۡيَوۡمِ الۡاٰخِرِ ؕ فَمَثَلُهٗ كَمَثَلِ صَفۡوَانٍ
عَلَيۡهِ تُرَابٌ فَاَصَابَهٗ وَابِلٌ فَتَرَكَهٗ صَلۡدًا ؕ لَا
يَقۡدِرُوۡنَ عَلٰى شَىۡءٍ مِّمَّا كَسَبُوۡا ؕ وَاللّٰهُ لَا يَهۡدِى
الۡقَوۡمَ الۡكٰفِرِيۡنَ ﴿۲۶۵﴾

266. And the case of those who spend their wealth to seek the pleasure of Allah and to strengthen their souls is like the case of a garden on elevated ground. Heavy rain falls on it so that it brings forth its fruit twofold. And if heavy rain does not fall on it, then light rain *suffices*. And Allah sees what you do.

وَمَثَلُ الَّذِيۡنَ يُنۡفِقُوۡنَ اَمۡوَالَهُمُ ابۡتِغَآءَ مَرۡضَاتِ
اللّٰهِ وَتَثۡبِيۡتًا مِّنۡ اَنۡفُسِهِمۡ كَمَثَلِ جَنَّةٍ بِرَبۡوَةٍ
اَصَابَهَا وَابِلٌ فَاٰتَتۡ اُكُلَهَا ضِعۡفَيۡنِ ۚ فَاِنۡ لَّمۡ يُصِبۡهَا
وَابِلٌ فَطَلٌّ ؕ وَاللّٰهُ بِمَا تَعۡمَلُوۡنَ بَصِيۡرٌ ﴿۲۶۶﴾

267. Does any of you desire that there should be for him a garden of palm trees and vines with streams flowing beneath it, and with all kinds of fruit for him therein —while old age has stricken him and he has weak offspring—and that a fiery whirlwind should smite it and it be *all* burnt? Thus does Allah make His Signs clear to you that you may ponder.

اَيَوَدُّ اَحَدُكُمۡ اَنۡ تَكُوۡنَ لَهٗ جَنَّةٌ مِّنۡ نَّخِيۡلٍ وَّاَعۡنَابٍ
تَجۡرِىۡ مِنۡ تَحۡتِهَا الۡاَنۡهٰرُ لَهٗ فِيۡهَا مِنۡ كُلِّ الثَّمَرٰتِ
وَاَصَابَهُ الۡكِبَرُ وَلَهٗ ذُرِّيَّةٌ ضُعَفَآءُ ۖ فَاَصَابَهَاۤ
اِعۡصَارٌ فِيۡهِ نَارٌ فَاحۡتَرَقَتۡ ؕ كَذٰلِكَ يُبَيِّنُ اللّٰهُ لَكُمُ
الۡاٰيٰتِ لَعَلَّكُمۡ تَتَفَكَّرُوۡنَ ﴿۲۶۷﴾ ع

R. 37.

* 268. O ye who believe! spend of the good things that you have earned, and of what We produce for you from the earth; and seek not what is bad to spend out of it when you would not take it yourselves except that you connive at it. And know that Allah is Self-Sufficient, Praiseworthy.

يٰۤاَيُّهَا الَّذِيۡنَ اٰمَنُوۡۤا اَنۡفِقُوۡا مِنۡ طَيِّبٰتِ مَا كَسَبۡتُمۡ
وَمِمَّاۤ اَخۡرَجۡنَا لَكُمۡ مِّنَ الۡاَرۡضِ ۖ وَلَا تَيَمَّمُوا الۡخَبِيۡثَ
مِنۡهُ تُنۡفِقُوۡنَ وَلَسۡتُمۡ بِاٰخِذِيۡهِ اِلَّاۤ اَنۡ تُغۡمِضُوۡا فِيۡهِ ؕ
وَاعۡلَمُوۡۤا اَنَّ اللّٰهَ غَنِىٌّ حَمِيۡدٌ ﴿۲۶۸﴾

269. Satan threatens you with poverty and enjoins upon you what is foul, whereas Allah promises you forgiveness from Himself and bounty. And Allah is Bountiful, All-Knowing.

اَلشَّيۡطٰنُ يَعِدُكُمُ الۡفَقۡرَ وَيَاۡمُرُكُمۡ بِالۡفَحۡشَآءِ ۚ وَاللّٰهُ
يَعِدُكُمۡ مَّغۡفِرَةً مِّنۡهُ وَفَضۡلًا ؕ وَاللّٰهُ وَاسِعٌ عَلِيۡمٌ ۖ ﴿۲۶۹﴾

270. He grants wisdom to whom He pleases, and whoever is granted wisdom

يُّؤۡتِى الۡحِكۡمَةَ مَنۡ يَّشَآءُ ۚ وَمَنۡ يُّؤۡتَ الۡحِكۡمَةَ فَقَدۡ

has indeed been granted abundant good; and none would be reminded except those endowed with understanding.

أُوتِيَ خَيْرًا كَثِيرًا ۗ وَمَا يَذَّكَّرُ إِلَّآ أُولُوا الْأَلْبَابِ ﴿٢٧٠﴾

271. And whatsoever you spend or whatsoever vow you vow, Allah surely knows it; and for the wrongdoers there shall be no helpers.

وَمَآ أَنْفَقْتُمْ مِّنْ نَّفَقَةٍ أَوْ نَذَرْتُمْ مِّنْ نَّذْرٍ فَإِنَّ
اللّٰهَ يَعْلَمُهُ ۗ وَمَا لِلظّٰلِمِينَ مِنْ أَنْصَارٍ ﴿٢٧١﴾

272. If you give alms openly, it is well *and good*; but if you conceal them and give them to the poor, it is better for you; and He will remove from you *many* of your sins. And Allah is aware of what you do.

إِنْ تُبْدُوا الصَّدَقٰتِ فَنِعِمَّا هِيَ ۚ وَإِنْ تُخْفُوهَا وَ
تُؤْتُوهَا الْفُقَرَآءَ فَهُوَ خَيْرٌ لَّكُمْ ۗ وَيُكَفِّرُ عَنْكُمْ مِّنْ
سَيِّاٰتِكُمْ ۗ وَاللّٰهُ بِمَا تَعْمَلُونَ خَبِيرٌ ﴿٢٧٢﴾

273. It is not thy responsibility to make them follow the right path; but Allah guides whomsoever He pleases. And whatever of wealth you spend, it is for yourselves, while you spend not but to seek the favour of Allah. And whatever of wealth you spend, it shall be paid back to you in full and you shall not be wronged.

لَيْسَ عَلَيْكَ هُدٰىهُمْ وَلٰكِنَّ اللّٰهَ يَهْدِي مَنْ يَّشَآءُ ۗ
وَمَا تُنْفِقُوا مِنْ خَيْرٍ فَلِأَنْفُسِكُمْ ۗ وَمَا تُنْفِقُونَ إِلَّا
ابْتِغَآءَ وَجْهِ اللّٰهِ ۗ وَمَا تُنْفِقُوا مِنْ خَيْرٍ يُّوَفَّ إِلَيْكُمْ
وَأَنْتُمْ لَا تُظْلَمُونَ ﴿٢٧٣﴾

274. *These alms are* for the poor who are detained in the cause of Allah and are unable to move about in the land. The ignorant man thinks them to be free from want because of *their* abstaining *from begging*. Thou shalt know them by their appearance; they do not beg of men with importunity. And whatever of wealth you spend, surely, Allah has perfect knowledge thereof.

لِلْفُقَرَآءِ الَّذِينَ أُحْصِرُوا فِي سَبِيلِ اللّٰهِ لَا يَسْتَطِيعُونَ
ضَرْبًا فِي الْأَرْضِ ۫ يَحْسَبُهُمُ الْجَاهِلُ أَغْنِيَآءَ مِنَ
التَّعَفُّفِ ۚ تَعْرِفُهُمْ بِسِيمٰهُمْ ۚ لَا يَسْـَٔلُونَ النَّاسَ
إِلْحَافًا ۗ وَمَا تُنْفِقُوا مِنْ خَيْرٍ فَإِنَّ اللّٰهَ بِهِ عَلِيمٌ ﴿٢٧٤﴾

R. 38.

275. Those who spend their wealth by night and day, secretly and openly, have their reward with their Lord; on them *shall come* no fear, nor shall they grieve.

الَّذِينَ يُنْفِقُونَ أَمْوَالَهُمْ بِالَّيْلِ وَالنَّهَارِ سِرًّا وَّ
عَلَانِيَةً فَلَهُمْ أَجْرُهُمْ عِنْدَ رَبِّهِمْ ۚ وَلَا خَوْفٌ عَلَيْهِمْ
وَلَا هُمْ يَحْزَنُونَ ﴿٢٧٥﴾

276. Those who devour interest do not rise except as rises one whom Satan has smitten with insanity. That is because they say: 'Trade *also* is like interest;' whereas Allah has made trade lawful and made interest unlawful. So he to whom an admonition comes from his Lord and he desists, then will that *which he received* in the past be his; and his affair is with Allah. And those who revert *to it*, they are

الَّذِينَ يَأْكُلُونَ الرِّبٰوا لَا يَقُومُونَ إِلَّا كَمَا يَقُومُ الَّذِي
يَتَخَبَّطُهُ الشَّيْطٰنُ مِنَ الْمَسِّ ۗ ذٰلِكَ بِأَنَّهُمْ قَالُوٓا إِنَّمَا
الْبَيْعُ مِثْلُ الرِّبٰوا ۘ وَأَحَلَّ اللّٰهُ الْبَيْعَ وَحَرَّمَ الرِّبٰوا ۗ
فَمَنْ جَآءَهُ مَوْعِظَةٌ مِّنْ رَّبِّهِ فَانْتَهٰى فَلَهُ مَا سَلَفَ ۗ
وَأَمْرُهُ إِلَى اللّٰهِ ۗ وَمَنْ عَادَ فَأُولٰٓئِكَ أَصْحٰبُ النَّارِ ۚ

the inmates of the Fire; therein shall they abide.

هُمْ فِيهَا خٰلِدُونَ ﴿٢٧٦﴾

* 277. Allah will abolish interest and will cause charity to increase. And Allah loves not anyone who is a confirmed disbeliever and an arch-sinner.

يَمْحَقُ اللّٰهُ الرِّبٰوا وَيُرْبِي الصَّدَقٰتِ ۗ وَاللّٰهُ لَا يُحِبُّ
كُلَّ كَفَّارٍ اَثِيْمٍ ﴿٢٧٧﴾

278. Surely, those who believe and do good deeds, and observe Prayer and pay the Zakāt, shall have their reward from their Lord, and no fear *shall come* on them, nor shall they grieve.

اِنَّ الَّذِيْنَ اٰمَنُوْا وَعَمِلُوا الصّٰلِحٰتِ وَاَقَامُوا الصَّلٰوةَ
وَاٰتَوُا الزَّكٰوةَ لَهُمْ اَجْرُهُمْ عِنْدَ رَبِّهِمْ ۚ وَلَا خَوْفٌ
عَلَيْهِمْ وَلَا هُمْ يَحْزَنُوْنَ ﴿٢٧٨﴾

279. O ye who believe! fear Allah and relinquish what remains of interest, if you are believers.

يٰۤاَيُّهَا الَّذِيْنَ اٰمَنُوا اتَّقُوا اللّٰهَ وَذَرُوْا مَا بَقِيَ مِنَ
الرِّبٰوۤا اِنْ كُنْتُمْ مُّؤْمِنِيْنَ ﴿٢٧٩﴾

280. But if you do *it* not, then beware of war from Allah and His Messenger; and if you repent, then you shall have your original sums; *thus* you shall not wrong, nor shall you be wronged.

فَاِنْ لَّمْ تَفْعَلُوْا فَاْذَنُوْا بِحَرْبٍ مِّنَ اللّٰهِ وَرَسُوْلِهٖ ۚ
وَاِنْ تُبْتُمْ فَلَكُمْ رُءُوْسُ اَمْوَالِكُمْ ۚ لَا تَظْلِمُوْنَ
وَلَا تُظْلَمُوْنَ ﴿٢٨٠﴾

281. And if any *debtor* be in straitened circumstances, then *grant him* respite till a time of ease. And that you remit it as charity shall be better for you, if only you knew.

وَاِنْ كَانَ ذُوْ عُسْرَةٍ فَنَظِرَةٌ اِلٰى مَيْسَرَةٍ ۗ وَاَنْ
تَصَدَّقُوْا خَيْرٌ لَّكُمْ اِنْ كُنْتُمْ تَعْلَمُوْنَ ﴿٢٨١﴾

282. And fear the day when you shall be made to return to Allah; then shall every soul be paid in full what it has earned; and they shall not be wronged.

وَاتَّقُوْا يَوْمًا تُرْجَعُوْنَ فِيْهِ اِلَى اللّٰهِ ۗ ثُمَّ تُوَفّٰى كُلُّ
نَفْسٍ مَّا كَسَبَتْ وَهُمْ لَا يُظْلَمُوْنَ ﴿٢٨٢﴾ ٣٨ ع ٨ ٦

R. 39.

283. O ye who believe! when you borrow one from another for a fixed period, then write it down. And let a scribe write *it* in your presence faithfully; and no scribe should refuse to write, because Allah has taught him, so let him write and let him who incurs the liability dictate; and he should fear Allah, his Lord, and not diminish anything therefrom. But if the person incurring the liability be of low understanding or be weak or be unable himself to dictate, then let someone who can watch his interest dictate with justice. And call two witnesses from among your men; and if two men be not *available*, then a man and two women, of such as you like as

يٰۤاَيُّهَا الَّذِيْنَ اٰمَنُوْۤا اِذَا تَدَايَنْتُمْ بِدَيْنٍ اِلٰۤى اَجَلٍ
مُّسَمًّى فَاكْتُبُوْهُ ؕ وَلْيَكْتُبْ بَّيْنَكُمْ كَاتِبٌ ۢ بِالْعَدْلِ ۪ وَ
لَا يَاْبَ كَاتِبٌ اَنْ يَّكْتُبَ كَمَا عَلَّمَهُ اللّٰهُ فَلْيَكْتُبْ ۚ
وَلْيُمْلِلِ الَّذِيْ عَلَيْهِ الْحَقُّ وَلْيَتَّقِ اللّٰهَ رَبَّهٗ وَلَا
يَبْخَسْ مِنْهُ شَيْـًٔا ؕ فَاِنْ كَانَ الَّذِيْ عَلَيْهِ الْحَقُّ سَفِيْهًا
اَوْ ضَعِيْفًا اَوْ لَا يَسْتَطِيْعُ اَنْ يُّمِلَّ هُوَ فَلْيُمْلِلْ
وَلِيُّهٗ بِالْعَدْلِ ؕ وَاسْتَشْهِدُوْا شَهِيْدَيْنِ مِنْ رِّجَالِكُمْ ۚ

witnesses, so that if either of the two *women* should err *in memory*, then one may remind the other. And the witnesses should not refuse when they are called. And do not feel weary of writing it down, whether it be small or large, along with its appointed time *of payment*. This is more equitable in the sight of Allah and makes testimony surer and is more likely to keep you away from doubts; *therefore omit not to write* except that it be ready merchandise which you give or take from hand to hand, in which case it shall be no sin for you that you write it not. And have witnesses when you sell one to another; and let no harm be done to the scribe or the witness. And if you do *that*, then certainly it shall be disobedience on your part. And fear Allah. And Allah grants you knowledge and Allah knows all things well.

فَاِنْ لَّمْ يَكُوْنَا رَجُلَيْنِ فَرَجُلٌ وَّامْرَاَتٰنِ مِمَّنْ تَرْضَوْنَ
مِنَ الشُّهَدَآءِ اَنْ تَضِلَّ اِحْدٰىهُمَا فَتُذَكِّرَ اِحْدٰىهُمَا
الْاُخْرٰى ؕ وَلَا يَاْبَ الشُّهَدَآءُ اِذَا مَا دُعُوْا ؕ وَلَا تَسْـَٔمُوْٓا
اَنْ تَكْتُبُوْهُ صَغِيْرًا اَوْ كَبِيْرًا اِلٰٓى اَجَلِهٖ ؕ ذٰلِكُمْ اَقْسَطُ
عِنْدَ اللّٰهِ وَاَقْوَمُ لِلشَّهَادَةِ وَاَدْنٰٓى اَلَّا تَرْتَابُوْٓا اِلَّآ اَنْ
تَكُوْنَ تِجَارَةً حَاضِرَةً تُدِيْرُوْنَهَا بَيْنَكُمْ فَلَيْسَ عَلَيْكُمْ
جُنَاحٌ اَلَّا تَكْتُبُوْهَا ؕ وَاَشْهِدُوْٓا اِذَا تَبَايَعْتُمْ ۖ وَلَا
يُضَآرَّ كَاتِبٌ وَّلَا شَهِيْدٌ ؕ وَاِنْ تَفْعَلُوْا فَاِنَّهٗ فُسُوْقٌ
بِكُمْ ؕ وَاتَّقُوا اللّٰهَ ؕ وَيُعَلِّمُكُمُ اللّٰهُ ؕ وَاللّٰهُ بِكُلِّ شَيْءٍ
عَلِيْمٌ ﴿۲۸۳﴾

284. And if you be on a journey, and you find not a scribe, then let there be a pledge with possession. And if one of you entrusts another with something, then let him who is entrusted surrender his trust and let him fear Allah, his Lord. And conceal not testimony; and whoever conceals it, his heart is certainly sinful. And Allah is well aware of what you do.

وَاِنْ كُنْتُمْ عَلٰى سَفَرٍ وَّلَمْ تَجِدُوْا كَاتِبًا فَرِهٰنٌ
مَّقْبُوْضَةٌ ؕ فَاِنْ اَمِنَ بَعْضُكُمْ بَعْضًا فَلْيُؤَدِّ الَّذِى
اؤْتُمِنَ اَمَانَتَهٗ وَلْيَتَّقِ اللّٰهَ رَبَّهٗ ؕ وَلَا تَكْتُمُوا الشَّهَادَةَ ؕ
وَمَنْ يَّكْتُمْهَا فَاِنَّهٗٓ اٰثِمٌ قَلْبُهٗ ؕ وَاللّٰهُ بِمَا تَعْمَلُوْنَ
عَلِيْمٌ ﴿۲۸۴﴾ ع ۳۹ ۷

R. 40.

285. To Allah belongs whatever is in the heavens and whatever is in the earth; and whether you disclose what is in your minds or keep it hidden, Allah will call you to account for it; then will He forgive whomsoever He pleases and punish whomsoever He pleases; and Allah has the power to do all that He wills.

لِلّٰهِ مَا فِى السَّمٰوٰتِ وَمَا فِى الْاَرْضِ ؕ وَاِنْ تُبْدُوْا
مَا فِىْٓ اَنْفُسِكُمْ اَوْ تُخْفُوْهُ يُحَاسِبْكُمْ بِهِ اللّٰهُ ؕ فَيَغْفِرُ
لِمَنْ يَّشَآءُ وَيُعَذِّبُ مَنْ يَّشَآءُ ؕ وَاللّٰهُ عَلٰى كُلِّ شَيْءٍ
قَدِيْرٌ ﴿۲۸۵﴾

286. This Messenger *of Ours* believes in that which has been revealed to him from his Lord, and *so do* the believers: all *of them* believe in Allah, and in His angels, and in His Books, and in His Messengers, *saying*, 'We make no distinction between any of His Messengers;' and they say, 'We hear, and we obey. *We implore* Thy

اٰمَنَ الرَّسُوْلُ بِمَآ اُنْزِلَ اِلَيْهِ مِنْ رَّبِّهٖ وَالْمُؤْمِنُوْنَ ؕ
كُلٌّ اٰمَنَ بِاللّٰهِ وَمَلٰٓئِكَتِهٖ وَكُتُبِهٖ وَرُسُلِهٖ ۟ لَا نُفَرِّقُ
بَيْنَ اَحَدٍ مِّنْ رُّسُلِهٖ ۟ وَقَالُوْا سَمِعْنَا وَاَطَعْنَا ۗ غُفْرَانَكَ

forgiveness, O our Lord, and to Thee is the returning.'

* 287. Allah burdens not any soul beyond its capacity. It shall have *the reward* it earns, and it shall get *the punishment* it incurs. Our Lord, do not punish us, if we forget or fall into error; and our Lord, lay not on us a responsibility as Thou didst lay upon those before us. Our Lord, burden us not with what we have not the strength to bear; and efface our *sins*, and grant us forgiveness and have mercy on us; Thou art our Master; so help us Thou against the disbelieving people.

رَبَّنَا وَاِلَيْكَ الْمَصِيْرُ ﴿٢٨٦﴾

لَا يُكَلِّفُ اللّٰهُ نَفْسًا اِلَّا وُسْعَهَا ۭ لَهَا مَا كَسَبَتْ وَعَلَيْهَا

مَا اكْتَسَبَتْ ۭ رَبَّنَا لَا تُؤَاخِذْنَآ اِنْ نَّسِيْنَآ اَوْ اَخْطَاْنَا ۚ

رَبَّنَا وَلَا تَحْمِلْ عَلَيْنَآ اِصْرًا كَمَا حَمَلْتَهٗ عَلَى الَّذِيْنَ

مِنْ قَبْلِنَا ۚ رَبَّنَا وَلَا تُحَمِّلْنَا مَا لَا طَاقَةَ لَنَا بِهٖ ۚ

وَاعْفُ عَنَّا ۪ وَاغْفِرْ لَنَا ۪ وَارْحَمْنَا ۪ اَنْتَ مَوْلٰىنَا

فَانْصُرْنَا عَلَى الْقَوْمِ الْكٰفِرِيْنَ ﴿٢٨٧﴾ ع

(٣) سُوْرَةُ اٰلِ عِمْرٰنَ مَدَنِيَّةٌ

ĀL-'IMRĀN

(Revealed after Hijra)

1. In the name of Allah, the Gracious, the Merciful.

بِسْمِ اللّٰهِ الرَّحْمٰنِ الرَّحِيْمِ ﴿١﴾

2. Alif Lām Mīm*.

الٓمّٓ ﴿٢﴾

3. Allah is He beside Whom there is no God, the Living, the Self-Subsisting and All-Sustaining.

اللّٰهُ لَآ اِلٰهَ اِلَّا هُوَ الْحَيُّ الْقَيُّوْمُ ﴿٣﴾

4. He has sent down to thee the Book containing the truth *and* fulfilling that which precedes it; and He sent down the Torah and the Gospel before *this*, as a guidance to the people; and He has sent down the Discrimination.

نَزَّلَ عَلَيْكَ الْكِتٰبَ بِالْحَقِّ مُصَدِّقًا لِّمَا بَيْنَ يَدَيْهِ
وَاَنْزَلَ التَّوْرٰىةَ وَالْاِنْجِيْلَ ﴿٤﴾
مِنْ قَبْلُ هُدًى لِّلنَّاسِ وَاَنْزَلَ الْفُرْقَانَ

5. Surely, those who deny the Signs of Allah shall have a severe punishment. And Allah is Mighty, Possessor of the power to requite.

اِنَّ الَّذِيْنَ كَفَرُوْا بِاٰيٰتِ اللّٰهِ لَهُمْ عَذَابٌ شَدِيْدٌ
وَاللّٰهُ عَزِيْزٌ ذُو انْتِقَامٍ ﴿٥﴾

6. Surely, nothing in the earth or in the heaven is hidden from Allah.

اِنَّ اللّٰهَ لَا يَخْفٰى عَلَيْهِ شَيْءٌ فِي الْاَرْضِ وَلَا فِي
السَّمَآءِ ﴿٦﴾

7. He it is Who fashions you in the wombs as He wills; there is no God but He, the Mighty, the Wise.

هُوَ الَّذِيْ يُصَوِّرُكُمْ فِي الْاَرْحَامِ كَيْفَ يَشَآءُ لَآ اِلٰهَ
اِلَّا هُوَ الْعَزِيْزُ الْحَكِيْمُ ﴿٧﴾

8. He it is Who has sent down to thee the Book; in it there are verses that are decisive in meaning – they are the basis of the Book – and there are others that are susceptible of different interpretations. But those in whose hearts is perversity pursue such thereof as are susceptible of different interpretations, seeking discord and seeking *wrong* interpretation of it. And none knows its *right* interpretation except Allah and those who are firmly grounded in knowledge; they say, 'We believe in it; the whole is from our Lord.' – And none heed except those gifted with understanding. –

هُوَ الَّذِيْٓ اَنْزَلَ عَلَيْكَ الْكِتٰبَ مِنْهُ اٰيٰتٌ مُّحْكَمٰتٌ
هُنَّ اُمُّ الْكِتٰبِ وَاُخَرُ مُتَشٰبِهٰتٌ فَاَمَّا الَّذِيْنَ فِيْ
قُلُوْبِهِمْ زَيْغٌ فَيَتَّبِعُوْنَ مَا تَشَابَهَ مِنْهُ ابْتِغَآءَ
الْفِتْنَةِ وَابْتِغَآءَ تَاْوِيْلِهٖ وَمَا يَعْلَمُ تَاْوِيْلَهٗٓ
اِلَّا اللّٰهُ وَالرّٰسِخُوْنَ فِي الْعِلْمِ يَقُوْلُوْنَ اٰمَنَّا بِهٖ كُلٌّ
مِّنْ عِنْدِ رَبِّنَا وَمَا يَذَّكَّرُ اِلَّآ اُولُوا الْاَلْبَابِ ﴿٨﴾

9. 'Our Lord, let not our hearts become perverse after Thou hast guided us; and

رَبَّنَا لَا تُزِغْ قُلُوْبَنَا بَعْدَ اِذْ هَدَيْتَنَا وَهَبْ لَنَا مِنْ

* I am Allah, the All-Knowing.

bestow on us mercy from Thyself; surely, Thou alone art the Bestower.

لَدُنْكَ رَحْمَةً ۚ إِنَّكَ أَنْتَ الْوَهَّابُ ﴿٩﴾

10. 'Our Lord, Thou wilt certainly assemble mankind together on the Day about which there is no doubt; surely, Allah breaks not *His* promise.'

رَبَّنَآ إِنَّكَ جَامِعُ النَّاسِ لِيَوْمٍ لَّا رَيْبَ فِيهِ ۚ إِنَّ اللّٰهَ
لَا يُخْلِفُ الْمِيعَادَ ﴿١٠﴾

R. 2.

11. Those who disbelieve—their possessions and their children shall not avail them at all against Allah; and it is they that are the fuel of the Fire.

إِنَّ الَّذِينَ كَفَرُوا لَنْ تُغْنِيَ عَنْهُمْ أَمْوَالُهُمْ وَلَآ أَوْلَادُهُمْ
مِّنَ اللّٰهِ شَيْئًا ۖ وَأُولٰٓئِكَ هُمْ وَقُودُ النَّارِ ﴿١١﴾

12. *Their case is* like the case of the people of Pharaoh and those before them; they rejected Our Signs; so Allah punished them for their sins, and Allah is severe in punishing.

كَدَأْبِ آلِ فِرْعَوْنَ ۙ وَالَّذِينَ مِنْ قَبْلِهِمْ ۚ كَذَّبُوا
بِآيَاتِنَا ۚ فَأَخَذَهُمُ اللّٰهُ بِذُنُوبِهِمْ ۗ وَاللّٰهُ شَدِيدُ
الْعِقَابِ ﴿١٢﴾

13. Say to those who disbelieve, 'You shall be overcome and gathered unto Hell; and an evil place of rest it is.'

قُلْ لِّلَّذِينَ كَفَرُوا سَتُغْلَبُونَ وَتُحْشَرُونَ إِلٰى جَهَنَّمَ ۚ
وَبِئْسَ الْمِهَادُ ﴿١٣﴾

14. Certainly there was for you a Sign in the two armies that encountered each other, one army fighting in the cause of Allah and the other disbelieving, whom they saw to be twice as many as themselves, actually with *their* eyes. *Thus* Allah strengthens with His aid whomsoever He pleases. In that surely is a lesson for those who have eyes.

قَدْ كَانَ لَكُمْ آيَةٌ فِي فِئَتَيْنِ الْتَقَتَا ۖ فِئَةٌ تُقَاتِلُ فِي
سَبِيلِ اللّٰهِ وَأُخْرٰى كَافِرَةٌ يَرَوْنَهُمْ مِّثْلَيْهِمْ رَأْيَ
الْعَيْنِ ۚ وَاللّٰهُ يُؤَيِّدُ بِنَصْرِهٖ مَنْ يَّشَآءُ ۗ إِنَّ فِي ذٰلِكَ
لَعِبْرَةً لِّأُولِي الْأَبْصَارِ ﴿١٤﴾

15. Beautified for men is the love of desired things—women and children, and stored-up heaps of gold and silver, and pastured horses and cattle and crops. That is the provision of the present life; but it is Allah with Whom is an excellent home.

زُيِّنَ لِلنَّاسِ حُبُّ الشَّهَوَاتِ مِنَ النِّسَآءِ وَالْبَنِينَ
وَالْقَنَاطِيرِ الْمُقَنْطَرَةِ مِنَ الذَّهَبِ وَالْفِضَّةِ وَالْخَيْلِ
الْمُسَوَّمَةِ وَالْأَنْعَامِ وَالْحَرْثِ ۗ ذٰلِكَ مَتَاعُ الْحَيٰوةِ
الدُّنْيَا ۚ وَاللّٰهُ عِنْدَهٗ حُسْنُ الْمَاٰبِ ﴿١٥﴾

* 16. Say, 'Shall I inform you of something better than that?' For those who fear God, there are Gardens with their Lord, beneath which rivers flow; therein shall they abide; and pure spouses and Allah's pleasure. And Allah is Mindful of *His* servants,

قُلْ أَؤُنَبِّئُكُمْ بِخَيْرٍ مِّنْ ذٰلِكُمْ ۚ لِلَّذِينَ اتَّقَوْا عِنْدَ
رَبِّهِمْ جَنّٰتٌ تَجْرِي مِنْ تَحْتِهَا الْأَنْهٰرُ خٰلِدِينَ فِيهَا
وَأَزْوَاجٌ مُّطَهَّرَةٌ وَّرِضْوَانٌ مِّنَ اللّٰهِ ۗ وَاللّٰهُ بَصِيرٌ ۢ
بِالْعِبَادِ ﴿١٦﴾

17. Those who say, 'Our Lord, we do believe; forgive us, therefore, our sins and save us from the punishment of the Fire;'

الَّذِينَ يَقُولُونَ رَبَّنَآ إِنَّنَآ اٰمَنَّا فَاغْفِرْ لَنَا ذُنُوبَنَا وَقِنَا عَذَابَ النَّارِ ﴿١٧﴾

18. The steadfast, and the truthful, and the humble, and those who spend in the way of God, and those who seek forgiveness in the latter part of the night.

الصّٰبِرِينَ وَالصّٰدِقِينَ وَالْقٰنِتِينَ وَالْمُنْفِقِينَ وَالْمُسْتَغْفِرِينَ بِالْاَسْحَارِ ﴿١٨﴾

* 19. Allah bears witness that there is no God but He—and *also do* the angels and those possessed of knowledge—Maintainer of justice; there is no God but He, the Mighty, the Wise.

شَهِدَ اللّٰهُ اَنَّهٗ لَآ اِلٰهَ اِلَّا هُوَ وَالْمَلٰٓئِكَةُ وَاُولُوا الْعِلْمِ قَآئِمًا بِالْقِسْطِ لَآ اِلٰهَ اِلَّا هُوَ الْعَزِيزُ الْحَكِيمُ ﴿١٩﴾ النصف

20. Surely, the *true* religion with Allah is Islam (complete submission). And those who were given the Book did not disagree but after knowledge had come to them, out of mutual envy. And whoso denies the Signs of Allah, then surely, Allah is quick at reckoning.

اِنَّ الدِّينَ عِنْدَ اللّٰهِ الْاِسْلَامُ وَمَا اخْتَلَفَ الَّذِينَ اُوتُوا الْكِتٰبَ اِلَّا مِنْ بَعْدِ مَا جَآءَهُمُ الْعِلْمُ بَغْيًا بَيْنَهُمْ وَمَنْ يَّكْفُرْ بِاٰيٰتِ اللّٰهِ فَاِنَّ اللّٰهَ سَرِيعُ الْحِسَابِ ﴿٢٠﴾

21. But if they dispute with thee, say, 'I have submitted myself to Allah, and *also* those who follow me.' And say to those who have been given the Book and to the unlearned, 'Have you submitted?' If they submit, then they will surely be guided; but if they turn back, then thy duty is only to convey the message. And Allah is Watchful of *His* servants.

فَاِنْ حَآجُّوكَ فَقُلْ اَسْلَمْتُ وَجْهِيَ لِلّٰهِ وَمَنِ اتَّبَعَنِ وَقُلْ لِّلَّذِينَ اُوتُوا الْكِتٰبَ وَالْاُمِّيّٖنَ ءَاَسْلَمْتُمْ فَاِنْ اَسْلَمُوا فَقَدِ اهْتَدَوْا وَاِنْ تَوَلَّوْا فَاِنَّمَا عَلَيْكَ الْبَلٰغُ وَاللّٰهُ بَصِيرٌ بِالْعِبَادِ ﴿٢١﴾ ع

R. 3

22. Surely, those who deny the Signs of Allah and seek to kill the Prophets unjustly, and seek to kill such men as enjoin equity—announce to them a painful punishment.

اِنَّ الَّذِينَ يَكْفُرُونَ بِاٰيٰتِ اللّٰهِ وَيَقْتُلُونَ النَّبِيّٖنَ بِغَيْرِ حَقٍّ وَّيَقْتُلُونَ الَّذِينَ يَاْمُرُونَ بِالْقِسْطِ مِنَ النَّاسِ فَبَشِّرْهُمْ بِعَذَابٍ اَلِيمٍ ﴿٢٢﴾

23. Those are they whose deeds shall come to naught in this world and in the next, and they shall have no helpers.

اُولٰٓئِكَ الَّذِينَ حَبِطَتْ اَعْمَالُهُمْ فِي الدُّنْيَا وَالْاٰخِرَةِ وَمَا لَهُمْ مِّنْ نّٰصِرِينَ ﴿٢٣﴾

24. Dost thou not know of those who have been given *their* portion of the Book? They are called to the Book of Allah that it may judge between them, but a party of them turn away in aversion.

اَلَمْ تَرَ اِلَى الَّذِينَ اُوتُوا نَصِيبًا مِّنَ الْكِتٰبِ يُدْعَوْنَ اِلٰى كِتٰبِ اللّٰهِ لِيَحْكُمَ بَيْنَهُمْ ثُمَّ يَتَوَلّٰى فَرِيقٌ مِّنْهُمْ وَهُمْ مُّعْرِضُونَ ﴿٢٤﴾

25. That is because they say, 'The Fire shall not touch us, except for a limited number of days.' And what they used to forge has deceived them regarding their religion.

ذٰلِكَ بِاَنَّهُمْ قَالُوْا لَنْ تَمَسَّنَا النَّارُ اِلَّآ اَيَّامًا مَّعْدُوْدٰتٍ ۪
وَّغَرَّهُمْ فِيْ دِيْنِهِمْ مَّا كَانُوْا يَفْتَرُوْنَ ﴿٢٥﴾

26. How *will they fare* when We will gather them together on the Day about which there is no doubt; and when every soul shall be paid in full what it has earned, and they shall not be wronged?

فَكَيْفَ اِذَا جَمَعْنٰهُمْ لِيَوْمٍ لَّا رَيْبَ فِيْهِ ۣ وَوُفِّيَتْ
كُلُّ نَفْسٍ مَّا كَسَبَتْ وَهُمْ لَا يُظْلَمُوْنَ ﴿٢٦﴾

27. Say, 'O Allah, Lord of sovereignty, Thou givest sovereignty to whomsoever Thou pleasest; and Thou takest away sovereignty from whomsoever Thou pleasest. Thou exaltest whomsoever Thou pleasest and Thou abasest whomsoever Thou pleasest. In Thy hand is all good. Thou surely hast power to do all things.

قُلِ اللّٰهُمَّ مٰلِكَ الْمُلْكِ تُؤْتِي الْمُلْكَ مَنْ تَشَآءُ وَتَنْزِعُ
الْمُلْكَ مِمَّنْ تَشَآءُ ۫ وَتُعِزُّ مَنْ تَشَآءُ وَتُذِلُّ مَنْ
تَشَآءُ ؕ بِيَدِكَ الْخَيْرُ ؕ اِنَّكَ عَلٰى كُلِّ شَيْءٍ قَدِيْرٌ ﴿٢٧﴾

28. 'Thou makest the night pass into the day and makest the day pass into the night. And Thou bringest forth the living from the dead and bringest forth the dead from the living. And Thou givest to whomsoever Thou pleasest without measure.'

تُوْلِجُ الَّيْلَ فِي النَّهَارِ وَتُوْلِجُ النَّهَارَ فِي الَّيْلِ ۫
وَتُخْرِجُ الْحَيَّ مِنَ الْمَيِّتِ وَتُخْرِجُ الْمَيِّتَ مِنَ الْحَيِّ
وَتَرْزُقُ مَنْ تَشَآءُ بِغَيْرِ حِسَابٍ ﴿٢٨﴾

* 29. Let not the believers take disbelievers for friends in preference to believers—and whoever does that has no connection with Allah—except that you cautiously guard against them. And Allah cautions you against His punishment; and to Allah is the returning.

لَا يَتَّخِذِ الْمُؤْمِنُوْنَ الْكٰفِرِيْنَ اَوْلِيَآءَ مِنْ دُوْنِ
الْمُؤْمِنِيْنَ ۚ وَمَنْ يَّفْعَلْ ذٰلِكَ فَلَيْسَ مِنَ اللّٰهِ
فِيْ شَيْءٍ اِلَّآ اَنْ تَتَّقُوْا مِنْهُمْ تُقٰىةً ؕ وَيُحَذِّرُكُمُ
اللّٰهُ نَفْسَهٗ ؕ وَاِلَى اللّٰهِ الْمَصِيْرُ ﴿٢٩﴾

30. Say, 'Whether you conceal what is in your breasts or reveal it, Allah knows it; and He knows whatever is in the heavens and whatever is in the earth. And Allah has power to do all things.'

قُلْ اِنْ تُخْفُوْا مَا فِيْ صُدُوْرِكُمْ اَوْ تُبْدُوْهُ يَعْلَمْهُ
اللّٰهُ ؕ وَيَعْلَمُ مَا فِي السَّمٰوٰتِ وَمَا فِي الْاَرْضِ ؕ وَ
اللّٰهُ عَلٰى كُلِّ شَيْءٍ قَدِيْرٌ ﴿٣٠﴾

31. *Beware of* the Day when every soul shall find itself confronted with *all* the good it has done and *all* the evil it has done. It will wish there were a great distance between it and that *evil*. And Allah cautions you against His punishment. And Allah is Most Compassionate to *His* servants.

يَوْمَ تَجِدُ كُلُّ نَفْسٍ مَّا عَمِلَتْ مِنْ خَيْرٍ مُّحْضَرًا ۖۚ
وَّمَا عَمِلَتْ مِنْ سُوْٓءٍ ۚ تَوَدُّ لَوْ اَنَّ بَيْنَهَا وَبَيْنَهٗۤ
اَمَدًا بَعِيْدًا ؕ وَيُحَذِّرُكُمُ اللّٰهُ نَفْسَهٗ ؕ وَاللّٰهُ رَءُوْفٌۢ
بِالْعِبَادِ ﴿٣١﴾ ع

R. 4.

32. Say, 'If you love Allah, follow me: *then* will Allah love you and forgive you

قُلْ اِنْ كُنْتُمْ تُحِبُّوْنَ اللّٰهَ فَاتَّبِعُوْنِيْ يُحْبِبْكُمُ

your faults. And Allah is Most Forgiving, Merciful.'

اللّٰهُ وَ يَغْفِرْ لَكُمْ ذُنُوْبَكُمْ ۚ وَاللّٰهُ غَفُوْرٌ رَّحِيْمٌ ﴿۳۲﴾

33. Say, 'Obey Allah and the Messenger;' but if they turn away, then *remember that* Allah loves not the disbelievers.

قُلْ اَطِيْعُوا اللّٰهَ وَ الرَّسُوْلَ ۚ فَاِنْ تَوَلَّوْا فَاِنَّ اللّٰهَ لَا يُحِبُّ
الْكٰفِرِيْنَ ﴿۳۳﴾

34. Allah did choose Adam and Noah and the family of Abraham and the family of 'Imrān above all peoples —

اِنَّ اللّٰهَ اصْطَفٰۤى اٰدَمَ وَ نُوْحًا وَّ اٰلَ اِبْرٰهِيْمَ وَ اٰلَ
عِمْرٰنَ عَلَى الْعٰلَمِيْنَ ﴿۳۴﴾

35. A race, co-related with one another. And Allah is All-Hearing, All-Knowing.

ذُرِّيَّةً ۢ بَعْضُهَا مِنْۢ بَعْضٍ ۚ وَاللّٰهُ سَمِيْعٌ عَلِيْمٌ ﴿۳۵﴾

36. *Remember* when *the* woman of 'Imrān said, 'My Lord, I have vowed to Thee what is in my womb to be dedicated to Thy service. So do accept *it* of me; verily, Thou alone art All-Hearing, All-Knowing.'

اِذْ قَالَتِ امْرَاَتُ عِمْرٰنَ رَبِّ اِنِّيْ نَذَرْتُ لَكَ مَا
فِيْ بَطْنِيْ مُحَرَّرًا فَتَقَبَّلْ مِنِّيْ ۚ اِنَّكَ اَنْتَ السَّمِيْعُ
الْعَلِيْمُ ﴿۳۶﴾

* 37. But when she was delivered of it, she said, 'My Lord, I am delivered of a female'—and Allah knew best what she had brought forth and the male *she was thinking of* was not like the female *she had brought forth*—'and I have named her Mary, and I commit her and her offspring to Thy protection from Satan, the rejected.'

فَلَمَّا وَضَعَتْهَا قَالَتْ رَبِّ اِنِّيْ وَضَعْتُهَاۤ اُنْثٰى ؕ وَاللّٰهُ
اَعْلَمُ بِمَا وَضَعَتْ ؕ وَ لَيْسَ الذَّكَرُ كَالْاُنْثٰى ۚ وَاِنِّيْ
سَمَّيْتُهَا مَرْيَمَ وَاِنِّيْۤ اُعِيْذُهَا بِكَ وَ ذُرِّيَّتَهَا
مِنَ الشَّيْطٰنِ الرَّجِيْمِ ﴿۳۷﴾

38. So her Lord accepted her with a gracious acceptance and caused her to grow an excellent growth and made Zachariah her guardian. Whenever Zachariah visited her in the chamber, he found with her provisions. He said, 'O Mary, whence hast thou this?' She replied, 'It is from Allah.' Surely, Allah gives to whomsoever He pleases without measure.

فَتَقَبَّلَهَا رَبُّهَا بِقَبُوْلٍ حَسَنٍ وَّ اَنْۢبَتَهَا نَبَاتًا حَسَنًا ۙ
وَّ كَفَّلَهَا زَكَرِيَّا ۚ كُلَّمَا دَخَلَ عَلَيْهَا زَكَرِيَّا الْمِحْرَابَ ۙ
وَجَدَ عِنْدَهَا رِزْقًا ۚ قَالَ يٰمَرْيَمُ اَنّٰى لَكِ هٰذَا ؕ
قَالَتْ هُوَ مِنْ عِنْدِ اللّٰهِ ؕ اِنَّ اللّٰهَ يَرْزُقُ مَنْ يَّشَآءُ
بِغَيْرِ حِسَابٍ ﴿۳۸﴾

39. There *and then* did Zachariah pray to his Lord, saying, 'My Lord, grant me from Thyself pure offspring; surely, Thou art the Hearer of prayer.'

هُنَالِكَ دَعَا زَكَرِيَّا رَبَّهٗ ۚ قَالَ رَبِّ هَبْ لِيْ مِنْ
لَّدُنْكَ ذُرِّيَّةً طَيِّبَةً ۚ اِنَّكَ سَمِيْعُ الدُّعَآءِ ﴿۳۹﴾

40. And the angels called to him as he stood praying in the chamber: 'Allah gives thee glad tidings of Yaḥyā, who shall testify to the truth of a word from Allah —

فَنَادَتْهُ الْمَلٰٓئِكَةُ وَهُوَ قَآئِمٌ يُّصَلِّيْ فِي الْمِحْرَابِ ۙ
اَنَّ اللّٰهَ يُبَشِّرُكَ بِيَحْيٰى مُصَدِّقًۢا بِكَلِمَةٍ مِّنَ اللّٰهِ

noble and chaste and a Prophet, from among the righteous.'

وَسَيِّدًا وَّحَصُوْرًا وَّنَبِيًّا مِّنَ الصّٰلِحِيْنَ ﴿٤٠﴾

41. He said, 'My Lord, how shall I have a son, when age has overtaken me, and my wife is barren?' He answered, 'Such is *the way of* Allah: He does what He pleases.'

قَالَ رَبِّ اَنّٰى يَكُوْنُ لِيْ غُلٰمٌ وَّقَدْ بَلَغَنِيَ الْكِبَرُ
وَامْرَاَتِيْ عَاقِرٌ ؕ قَالَ كَذٰلِكَ اللّٰهُ يَفْعَلُ مَا يَشَآءُ ﴿٤١﴾

42. He said, 'My Lord, appoint a token for me.' He replied, 'Thy token shall be that thou shalt not speak to men for three days except by signs. And remember thy Lord much and glorify Him in the evening and in the early morning.'

قَالَ رَبِّ اجْعَلْ لِّيْۤ اٰيَةً ؕ قَالَ اٰيَتُكَ اَلَّا تُكَلِّمَ النَّاسَ
ثَلٰثَةَ اَيَّامٍ اِلَّا رَمْزًا ؕ وَاذْكُرْ رَّبَّكَ كَثِيْرًا وَّسَبِّحْ بِالْعَشِيِّ
وَالْاِبْكَارِ ﴿٤٢﴾ ٤ ع

R. 5.

43. And *remember* when the angels said, 'O Mary, Allah has chosen thee and purified thee and chosen thee above the women of all peoples.

وَاِذْ قَالَتِ الْمَلٰٓئِكَةُ يٰمَرْيَمُ اِنَّ اللّٰهَ اصْطَفٰكِ وَ
طَهَّرَكِ وَاصْطَفٰكِ عَلٰى نِسَآءِ الْعٰلَمِيْنَ ﴿٤٣﴾

44. 'O Mary, be obedient to thy Lord and prostrate thyself and worship *God alone* with those who worship.'

يٰمَرْيَمُ اقْنُتِيْ لِرَبِّكِ وَاسْجُدِيْ وَارْكَعِيْ مَعَ
الرّٰكِعِيْنَ ﴿٤٤﴾

45. This is of the tidings of things unseen which We reveal to thee. And thou wast not with them when they cast their arrows, as to which of them should be the guardian of Mary, nor wast thou with them when they disputed with one another.

ذٰلِكَ مِنْ اَنْۢبَآءِ الْغَيْبِ نُوْحِيْهِ اِلَيْكَ ؕ وَمَا كُنْتَ
لَدَيْهِمْ اِذْ يُلْقُوْنَ اَقْلَامَهُمْ اَيُّهُمْ يَكْفُلُ مَرْيَمَ ۪
وَمَا كُنْتَ لَدَيْهِمْ اِذْ يَخْتَصِمُوْنَ ﴿٤٥﴾

46. When the angels said, 'O Mary, Allah gives thee glad tidings of a word from Him; his name *shall be* the Messiah, Jesus, son of Mary, honoured in this world and in the next, and of those who are granted nearness *to God;*

اِذْ قَالَتِ الْمَلٰٓئِكَةُ يٰمَرْيَمُ اِنَّ اللّٰهَ يُبَشِّرُكِ بِكَلِمَةٍ
مِّنْهُ ۖۗ اسْمُهُ الْمَسِيْحُ عِيْسَى ابْنُ مَرْيَمَ وَجِيْهًا
فِي الدُّنْيَا وَالْاٰخِرَةِ وَمِنَ الْمُقَرَّبِيْنَ ۙ ﴿٤٦﴾

47. 'And he shall speak to the people in the cradle and when of middle age, and he shall be of the righteous.'

وَيُكَلِّمُ النَّاسَ فِي الْمَهْدِ وَكَهْلًا وَّمِنَ الصّٰلِحِيْنَ ﴿٤٧﴾

* 48. She said, 'My Lord, how shall I have a son, when no man has touched me?' He said, "Such is *the way of* Allah, He creates what He pleases. When He decrees a thing, He says to it, 'Be!' and it is.

قَالَتْ رَبِّ اَنّٰى يَكُوْنُ لِيْ وَلَدٌ وَّلَمْ يَمْسَسْنِيْ بَشَرٌ ؕ
قَالَ كَذٰلِكِ اللّٰهُ يَخْلُقُ مَا يَشَآءُ ؕ اِذَا قَضٰٓى اَمْرًا فَاِنَّمَا
يَقُوْلُ لَهٗ كُنْ فَيَكُوْنُ ﴿٤٨﴾

49. "And He will teach him the Book and the Wisdom and the Torah and the Gospel;

وَيُعَلِّمُهُ الْكِتٰبَ وَالْحِكْمَةَ وَالتَّوْرٰىةَ وَالْاِنْجِيْلَ ﴿٤٩﴾

50. "And *will make him* a Messenger to the children of Israel (to say): 'I come to you with a Sign from your Lord, *which is,*

وَرَسُوْلًا اِلٰى بَنِيْٓ اِسْرَآءِيْلَ ۙ اَنِّيْ قَدْ جِئْتُكُمْ بِاٰيَةٍ

that I will fashion out for you *a creation* out of clay after the manner of a bird, then I will breathe into it *a new spirit* and it will become a soaring being by the command of Allah; and I will heal the night-blind and the leprous, and I will quicken the dead, by the command of Allah; and I will announce to you what you will eat and what you will store up in your houses. Surely, therein is a Sign for you, if you be believers.

مِّنْ رَّبِّكُمْ ۙ اَنِّیْۤ اَخْلُقُ لَكُمْ مِّنَ الطِّیْنِ كَهَیْـَٔةِ الطَّیْرِ
فَاَنْفُخُ فِیْهِ فَیَكُوْنُ طَیْرًۢا بِاِذْنِ اللّٰهِ ۚ وَاُبْرِئُ
الْاَكْمَهَ وَالْاَبْرَصَ وَاُحْیِ الْمَوْتٰى بِاِذْنِ اللّٰهِ ۚ وَ
اُنَبِّئُكُمْ بِمَا تَاْكُلُوْنَ وَمَا تَدَّخِرُوْنَ ۙ فِیْ بُیُوْتِكُمْ ؕ
اِنَّ فِیْ ذٰلِكَ لَاٰیَةً لَّكُمْ اِنْ كُنْتُمْ مُّؤْمِنِیْنَ ۚ﴿۵۰﴾

51. 'And *I come* fulfilling that which is before me, namely, the Torah; and to allow you some of that which was forbidden you; and I come to you with a Sign from your Lord; so fear Allah and obey me.

وَمُصَدِّقًا لِّمَا بَیْنَ یَدَیَّ مِنَ التَّوْرٰىةِ وَلِاُحِلَّ
لَكُمْ بَعْضَ الَّذِیْ حُرِّمَ عَلَیْكُمْ وَجِئْتُكُمْ بِاٰیَةٍ
مِّنْ رَّبِّكُمْ ۟ فَاتَّقُوا اللّٰهَ وَاَطِیْعُوْنِ ﴿۵۱﴾

52. 'Surely, Allah is my Lord and your Lord; so worship Him: this is the right path.' "

اِنَّ اللّٰهَ رَبِّیْ وَرَبُّكُمْ فَاعْبُدُوْهُ ؕ هٰذَا صِرَاطٌ
مُّسْتَقِیْمٌ ﴿۵۲﴾

53. And when Jesus perceived their disbelief, he said, 'Who will be my helpers in the cause of Allah?' The disciples answered, 'We are the helpers of Allah. We have believed in Allah. And bear thou witness that we are obedient.

فَلَمَّاۤ اَحَسَّ عِیْسٰى مِنْهُمُ الْكُفْرَ قَالَ مَنْ اَنْصَارِیْۤ
اِلَى اللّٰهِ ؕ قَالَ الْحَوَارِیُّوْنَ نَحْنُ اَنْصَارُ اللّٰهِ ۚ اٰمَنَّا
بِاللّٰهِ ۚ وَاشْهَدْ بِاَنَّا مُسْلِمُوْنَ ﴿۵۳﴾

54. 'Our Lord, we believe in that which Thou hast sent down and we follow this Messenger. So write us down among those who bear witness.'

رَبَّنَاۤ اٰمَنَّا بِمَاۤ اَنْزَلْتَ وَاتَّبَعْنَا الرَّسُوْلَ فَاكْتُبْنَا
مَعَ الشّٰهِدِیْنَ ﴿۵۴﴾

55. And they planned, and Allah *also* planned; and Allah is the Best of planners.

وَمَكَرُوْا وَمَكَرَ اللّٰهُ ؕ وَاللّٰهُ خَیْرُ الْمٰكِرِیْنَ ﴿۵۵﴾

R. 6.

56. When Allah said, 'O Jesus, I will cause thee to die *a natural death* and will exalt thee to Myself, and will clear thee from *the charges of* those who disbelieve, and will place those who follow thee above those who disbelieve, until the Day of Resurrection; then to Me shall be your return, and I will judge between you concerning that wherein you differ.

اِذْ قَالَ اللّٰهُ یٰعِیْسٰۤى اِنِّیْ مُتَوَفِّیْكَ وَرَافِعُكَ اِلَیَّ
وَمُطَهِّرُكَ مِنَ الَّذِیْنَ كَفَرُوْا وَجَاعِلُ الَّذِیْنَ
اتَّبَعُوْكَ فَوْقَ الَّذِیْنَ كَفَرُوْۤا اِلٰى یَوْمِ الْقِیٰمَةِ ۚ ثُمَّ
اِلَیَّ مَرْجِعُكُمْ فَاَحْكُمُ بَیْنَكُمْ فِیْمَا كُنْتُمْ فِیْهِ
تَخْتَلِفُوْنَ ﴿۵۶﴾

57. 'Then as for those who disbelieve, I will punish them with a severe punish-

فَاَمَّا الَّذِیْنَ كَفَرُوْا فَاُعَذِّبُهُمْ عَذَابًا شَدِیْدًا فِی

ment in this world and in the next, and they shall have no helpers.

58. 'And as for those who believe and do good works, He will pay them their full rewards. And Allah loves not the wrong-doers.'

59. That is what We recite unto thee of the Signs and the wise Reminder.

60. Surely, the case of Jesus with Allah is like the case of Adam. He created him out of dust, then He said to him, 'Be!', and he was.

61. *This is* the truth from thy Lord, so be thou not of those who doubt.

62. Now whoso disputes with thee concerning him, after what has come to thee of knowledge, say *to him*, 'Come, let us call our sons and your sons, and our women and your women, and our people and your people; then let us pray fervently and invoke the curse of Allah on those who lie.'

63. This certainly is the true account. There is none worthy of worship save Allah; and surely, it is Allah Who is the Mighty, the Wise.

64. But if they turn away, then *remember that* Allah knows the mischief-makers well.

R. 7.

65. Say, 'O People of the Book! come to a word equal between us and you—that we worship none but Allah, and that we associate no partner with Him, and that some of us take not others for Lords beside Allah.' But if they turn away, then say, 'Bear witness that we have submitted *to God*.'

66. O People of the Book! why do you dispute concerning Abraham, when the Torah and the Gospel were not revealed till after him? Will you not then understand?

67. Behold! you are those who disputed about that whereof you had knowledge. Why then do you *now* dispute about that

الدُّنْيَا وَالْاٰخِرَةِ ۫ وَمَا لَهُمْ مِّنْ نّٰصِرِيْنَ ﴿۵۷﴾
وَاَمَّا الَّذِيْنَ اٰمَنُوْا وَعَمِلُوا الصّٰلِحٰتِ فَيُوَفِّيْهِمْ اُجُوْرَهُمْ ؕ
وَاللّٰهُ لَا يُحِبُّ الظّٰلِمِيْنَ ﴿۵۸﴾
ذٰلِكَ نَتْلُوْهُ عَلَيْكَ مِنَ الْاٰيٰتِ وَالذِّكْرِ الْحَكِيْمِ ﴿۵۹﴾
اِنَّ مَثَلَ عِيْسٰى عِنْدَ اللّٰهِ كَمَثَلِ اٰدَمَ ؕ خَلَقَهٗ مِنْ
تُرَابٍ ثُمَّ قَالَ لَهٗ كُنْ فَيَكُوْنُ ﴿۶۰﴾
اَلْحَقُّ مِنْ رَّبِّكَ فَلَا تَكُنْ مِّنَ الْمُمْتَرِيْنَ ﴿۶۱﴾
فَمَنْ حَآجَّكَ فِيْهِ مِنْۢ بَعْدِ مَا جَآءَكَ مِنَ الْعِلْمِ
فَقُلْ تَعَالَوْا نَدْعُ اَبْنَآءَنَا وَاَبْنَآءَكُمْ وَنِسَآءَنَا وَ
نِسَآءَكُمْ وَاَنْفُسَنَا وَاَنْفُسَكُمْ ۟ ثُمَّ نَبْتَهِلْ فَنَجْعَلْ
لَّعْنَتَ اللّٰهِ عَلَى الْكٰذِبِيْنَ ﴿۶۲﴾
اِنَّ هٰذَا لَهُوَ الْقَصَصُ الْحَقُّ ۚ وَمَا مِنْ اِلٰهٍ اِلَّا اللّٰهُ ؕ
وَاِنَّ اللّٰهَ لَهُوَ الْعَزِيْزُ الْحَكِيْمُ ﴿۶۳﴾
ع فَاِنْ تَوَلَّوْا فَاِنَّ اللّٰهَ عَلِيْمٌۢ بِالْمُفْسِدِيْنَ ﴿۶۴﴾
قُلْ يٰۤاَهْلَ الْكِتٰبِ تَعَالَوْا اِلٰى كَلِمَةٍ سَوَآءٍۢ بَيْنَنَا وَبَيْنَكُمْ
اَلَّا نَعْبُدَ اِلَّا اللّٰهَ وَلَا نُشْرِكَ بِهٖ شَيْـًٔا وَّلَا يَتَّخِذَ بَعْضُنَا
بَعْضًا اَرْبَابًا مِّنْ دُوْنِ اللّٰهِ ؕ فَاِنْ تَوَلَّوْا فَقُوْلُوا اشْهَدُوْا
بِاَنَّا مُسْلِمُوْنَ ﴿۶۵﴾
يٰۤاَهْلَ الْكِتٰبِ لِمَ تُحَآجُّوْنَ فِيْۤ اِبْرٰهِيْمَ وَمَاۤ اُنْزِلَتِ
التَّوْرٰىةُ وَالْاِنْجِيْلُ اِلَّا مِنْۢ بَعْدِهٖ ؕ اَفَلَا تَعْقِلُوْنَ ﴿۶۶﴾
هٰۤاَنْتُمْ هٰۤؤُلَآءِ حَاجَجْتُمْ فِيْمَا لَكُمْ بِهٖ عِلْمٌ فَلِمَ
تُحَآجُّوْنَ فِيْمَا لَيْسَ لَكُمْ بِهٖ عِلْمٌ ؕ وَاللّٰهُ يَعْلَمُ وَ

whereof you have no knowledge *at all?* Allah knows, and you know not.

أَنْتُمْ لَا تَعْلَمُونَ ٦٧

68. Abraham was neither a Jew nor a Christian, but he was ever inclined *to God and* obedient *to Him*, and he was not of those who associate gods *with God*.

مَا كَانَ إِبْرٰهِيمُ يَهُودِيًّا وَّلَا نَصْرَانِيًّا وَّلٰكِنْ كَانَ
حَنِيفًا مُّسْلِمًا ۗ وَمَا كَانَ مِنَ الْمُشْرِكِينَ ٦٨

69. Surely, the nearest of men to Abraham are those who followed him, and this Prophet and those who believe; and Allah is the friend of believers.

إِنَّ أَوْلَى النَّاسِ بِإِبْرٰهِيمَ لَلَّذِينَ اتَّبَعُوهُ وَهٰذَا
النَّبِيُّ وَالَّذِينَ آمَنُوا ۗ وَاللّٰهُ وَلِيُّ الْمُؤْمِنِينَ ٦٩

70. A section of the People of the Book would fain lead you astray; but they lead astray none except themselves, only they perceive not.

وَدَّتْ طَّائِفَةٌ مِّنْ أَهْلِ الْكِتٰبِ لَوْ يُضِلُّونَكُمْ ۖ وَمَا
يُضِلُّونَ إِلَّا أَنْفُسَهُمْ وَمَا يَشْعُرُونَ ٧٠

71. O People of the Book! why do you deny the Signs of Allah, while you are witnesses thereof?

يٰأَهْلَ الْكِتٰبِ لِمَ تَكْفُرُونَ بِآيٰتِ اللّٰهِ وَأَنْتُمْ
تَشْهَدُونَ ٧١

72. O People of the Book! why do you confound truth with falsehood and hide the truth knowingly?

يٰأَهْلَ الْكِتٰبِ لِمَ تَلْبِسُونَ الْحَقَّ بِالْبٰطِلِ وَتَكْتُمُونَ
الْحَقَّ وَأَنْتُمْ تَعْلَمُونَ ٧٢ ع ٨ ١٥

R. 8.

73. And a section of the People of the Book say, 'Believe in that which has been revealed unto the believers, in the early part of day, and disbelieve in the latter part thereof; perchance they may return;

وَقَالَتْ طَّائِفَةٌ مِّنْ أَهْلِ الْكِتٰبِ آمِنُوا بِالَّذِي أُنْزِلَ
عَلَى الَّذِينَ آمَنُوا وَجْهَ النَّهَارِ وَاكْفُرُوا آخِرَهُ لَعَلَّهُمْ
يَرْجِعُونَ ٧٣

* 74. 'And obey none but him who follows your religion;' – Say, 'Surely, the *true* guidance, the guidance of Allah, is that one may be given the like of that which has been given to you'—'or they would dispute with you before your Lord.' Say, 'All bounty is in the hand of Allah. He gives it to whomsoever He pleases. And Allah is Bountiful, All-Knowing.

وَلَا تُؤْمِنُوا إِلَّا لِمَنْ تَبِعَ دِينَكُمْ ۗ قُلْ إِنَّ الْهُدٰى
هُدَى اللّٰهِ ۙ أَنْ يُؤْتٰى أَحَدٌ مِّثْلَ مَا أُوتِيتُمْ أَوْ
يُحَاجُّوكُمْ عِنْدَ رَبِّكُمْ ۗ قُلْ إِنَّ الْفَضْلَ بِيَدِ اللّٰهِ ۚ
يُؤْتِيهِ مَنْ يَشَاءُ ۗ وَاللّٰهُ وَاسِعٌ عَلِيمٌ ٧٤

75. 'He chooses for His mercy whomsoever He pleases. And Allah is Lord of exceeding bounty.'

يَخْتَصُّ بِرَحْمَتِهِ مَنْ يَشَاءُ ۗ وَاللّٰهُ ذُو الْفَضْلِ
الْعَظِيمِ ٧٥

76. Among the People of the Book there is he who, if thou trust him with a treasure, will return it to thee; and among them there is he who, if thou trust him with a

وَمِنْ أَهْلِ الْكِتٰبِ مَنْ إِنْ تَأْمَنْهُ بِقِنْطَارٍ يُؤَدِّهِ
إِلَيْكَ ۚ وَمِنْهُمْ مَّنْ إِنْ تَأْمَنْهُ بِدِينَارٍ لَّا يُؤَدِّهِ

dīnār, will not return it to thee, unless thou keep standing over him. That is because they say, 'We are not liable to blame in the matter of the unlearned;' and they utter a lie against Allah knowingly.

77. Nay, but whoso fulfils his pledge and fears God – verily, Allah loves the God-fearing.

78. *As for* those who take a paltry price in exchange for *their* covenant with Allah and their oaths, they shall have no portion in the life to come, and Allah will neither speak to them nor look upon them on the Day of Resurrection, nor will He purify them; and for them shall be a grievous punishment.

79. And, surely, among them is a section who twist their tongues while reciting the Book; that you may think it *to be part* of the Book, while it is not *part* of the Book. And they say, 'It is from Allah;' while it is not from Allah; and they utter a lie against Allah knowingly.

* 80. It is not *possible* for a man that Allah should give him the Book and dominion and prophethood, *and* then he should say to men: 'Be servants to me and not to Allah;' but *he would say*: 'Be solely devoted to the Lord because you teach the Book and because you study *it*.'

81. Nor *is it possible for him* that he should bid you take the angels and the Prophets for Lords. Would he enjoin you to disbelieve after you have submitted *to God?*

R. 9.

82. And *remember the time* when Allah took a covenant from *the people through* the Prophets, *saying*: 'Whatever I give you of the Book and Wisdom *and* then there comes to you a Messenger, fulfilling that which is with you, you shall believe in him and help him.' *And* He said: 'Do you agree, and do you accept the responsibility

اِلَيْكَ اِلَّا مَا دُمْتَ عَلَيْهِ قَآئِمًا ۗ ذٰلِكَ بِاَنَّهُمْ قَالُوْا
لَيْسَ عَلَيْنَا فِي الْاُمِّيّٖنَ سَبِيْلٌ ۚ وَيَقُوْلُوْنَ عَلَى اللّٰهِ
الْكَذِبَ وَهُمْ يَعْلَمُوْنَ ﴿٧٦﴾
بَلٰى مَنْ اَوْفٰى بِعَهْدِهٖ وَاتَّقٰى فَاِنَّ اللّٰهَ يُحِبُّ
الْمُتَّقِيْنَ ﴿٧٧﴾
اِنَّ الَّذِيْنَ يَشْتَرُوْنَ بِعَهْدِ اللّٰهِ وَاَيْمَانِهِمْ ثَمَنًا
قَلِيْلًا اُولٰٓئِكَ لَا خَلَاقَ لَهُمْ فِي الْاٰخِرَةِ وَلَا يُكَلِّمُهُمُ
اللّٰهُ وَلَا يَنْظُرُ اِلَيْهِمْ يَوْمَ الْقِيٰمَةِ وَلَا يُزَكِّيْهِمْ ۖ
وَلَهُمْ عَذَابٌ اَلِيْمٌ ﴿٧٨﴾
وَاِنَّ مِنْهُمْ لَفَرِيْقًا يَّلْوٗنَ اَلْسِنَتَهُمْ بِالْكِتٰبِ
لِتَحْسَبُوْهُ مِنَ الْكِتٰبِ وَمَا هُوَ مِنَ الْكِتٰبِ ۚ وَيَقُوْلُوْنَ
هُوَ مِنْ عِنْدِ اللّٰهِ وَمَا هُوَ مِنْ عِنْدِ اللّٰهِ ۚ وَيَقُوْلُوْنَ
عَلَى اللّٰهِ الْكَذِبَ وَهُمْ يَعْلَمُوْنَ ﴿٧٩﴾
مَا كَانَ لِبَشَرٍ اَنْ يُّؤْتِيَهُ اللّٰهُ الْكِتٰبَ وَالْحُكْمَ وَ
النُّبُوَّةَ ثُمَّ يَقُوْلَ لِلنَّاسِ كُوْنُوْا عِبَادًا لِّيْ مِنْ دُوْنِ
اللّٰهِ وَلٰكِنْ كُوْنُوْا رَبَّانِيّٖنَ بِمَا كُنْتُمْ تُعَلِّمُوْنَ الْكِتٰبَ
وَبِمَا كُنْتُمْ تَدْرُسُوْنَ ﴿٨٠﴾
وَلَا يَاْمُرَكُمْ اَنْ تَتَّخِذُوا الْمَلٰٓئِكَةَ وَالنَّبِيّٖنَ اَرْبَابًا ۗ
اَيَاْمُرُكُمْ بِالْكُفْرِ بَعْدَ اِذْ اَنْتُمْ مُّسْلِمُوْنَ ﴿٨١﴾
وَاِذْ اَخَذَ اللّٰهُ مِيْثَاقَ النَّبِيّٖنَ لَمَآ اٰتَيْتُكُمْ مِّنْ
كِتٰبٍ وَّحِكْمَةٍ ثُمَّ جَآءَكُمْ رَسُوْلٌ مُّصَدِّقٌ لِّمَا
مَعَكُمْ لَتُؤْمِنُنَّ بِهٖ وَلَتَنْصُرُنَّهٗ ۗ قَالَ ءَاَقْرَرْتُمْ

which I lay upon you in this *matter?*' They said, 'We agree;' He said, 'Then bear witness, and I am with you among the witnesses.'

وَأَخَذْتُمْ عَلٰى ذٰلِكُمْ إِصْرِيْ قَالُوْٓا أَقْرَرْنَا قَالَ
فَاشْهَدُوْا وَأَنَا مَعَكُمْ مِّنَ الشّٰهِدِيْنَ ﴿٨٢﴾

83. Now whoso turns away after this, then, surely, those are the transgressors.

فَمَنْ تَوَلّٰى بَعْدَ ذٰلِكَ فَأُولٰٓئِكَ هُمُ الْفٰسِقُوْنَ ﴿٨٣﴾

84. Do they seek a religion other than Allah's, while to Him submits whosoever is in the heavens and the earth, willingly or unwillingly, and to Him shall they be returned?

أَفَغَيْرَ دِيْنِ اللّٰهِ يَبْغُوْنَ وَلَهٗٓ أَسْلَمَ مَنْ فِي السَّمٰوٰتِ
وَالْأَرْضِ طَوْعًا وَّكَرْهًا وَّإِلَيْهِ يُرْجَعُوْنَ ﴿٨٤﴾

85. Say, 'We believe in Allah and in that which has been revealed to us, and that which was revealed to Abraham and Ishmael and Isaac and Jacob and the Tribes, and that which was given to Moses and Jesus and *other* Prophets from their Lord. We make no distinction between any of them, and to Him we submit.'

قُلْ اٰمَنَّا بِاللّٰهِ وَمَآ أُنْزِلَ عَلَيْنَا وَمَآ أُنْزِلَ عَلٰٓى إِبْرٰهِيْمَ
وَإِسْمٰعِيْلَ وَإِسْحٰقَ وَيَعْقُوْبَ وَالْأَسْبَاطِ وَمَآ
أُوْتِيَ مُوْسٰى وَعِيْسٰى وَالنَّبِيُّوْنَ مِنْ رَّبِّهِمْ لَا نُفَرِّقُ
بَيْنَ أَحَدٍ مِّنْهُمْ وَنَحْنُ لَهٗ مُسْلِمُوْنَ ﴿٨٥﴾

86. And whoso seeks a religion other than Islam, it shall not be accepted from him, and in the life to come he shall be among the losers.

وَمَنْ يَّبْتَغِ غَيْرَ الْإِسْلَامِ دِيْنًا فَلَنْ يُّقْبَلَ مِنْهُ
وَهُوَ فِي الْاٰخِرَةِ مِنَ الْخٰسِرِيْنَ ﴿٨٦﴾

87. How shall Allah guide a people who have disbelieved after believing and who had borne witness that the Messenger was true and to whom clear proofs had come? And Allah guides not the wrongdoing people.

كَيْفَ يَهْدِي اللّٰهُ قَوْمًا كَفَرُوْا بَعْدَ إِيْمَانِهِمْ وَ
شَهِدُوْٓا أَنَّ الرَّسُوْلَ حَقٌّ وَّجَآءَهُمُ الْبَيِّنٰتُ وَاللّٰهُ
لَا يَهْدِي الْقَوْمَ الظّٰلِمِيْنَ ﴿٨٧﴾

88. Of such the reward is that on them shall be the curse of Allah and of angels and of men, all together.

أُولٰٓئِكَ جَزَآؤُهُمْ أَنَّ عَلَيْهِمْ لَعْنَةَ اللّٰهِ وَالْمَلٰٓئِكَةِ
وَالنَّاسِ أَجْمَعِيْنَ ﴿٨٨﴾

89. They shall abide thereunder. Their punishment shall not be lightened nor shall they be reprieved;

خٰلِدِيْنَ فِيْهَا لَا يُخَفَّفُ عَنْهُمُ الْعَذَابُ وَ
لَا هُمْ يُنْظَرُوْنَ ﴿٨٩﴾

90. Except those who repent thereafter and amend. And surely, Allah is Most Forgiving, Merciful.

إِلَّا الَّذِيْنَ تَابُوْا مِنْ بَعْدِ ذٰلِكَ وَأَصْلَحُوْا فَإِنَّ
اللّٰهَ غَفُوْرٌ رَّحِيْمٌ ﴿٩٠﴾

91. Surely, those who disbelieve after they have believed and then increase in disbelief, their repentance shall not be accepted, and these are they who have gone astray.

إِنَّ الَّذِيْنَ كَفَرُوْا بَعْدَ إِيْمَانِهِمْ ثُمَّ ازْدَادُوْا كُفْرًا
لَّنْ تُقْبَلَ تَوْبَتُهُمْ وَأُولٰٓئِكَ هُمُ الضَّآلُّوْنَ ﴿٩١﴾

92. *As for* those who have disbelieved, and die while they are disbelievers, there shall not be accepted from any one of them *even* an earthful of gold, though he offer it in ransom. It is these for whom shall be a grievous punishment, and they shall have no helpers.

إِنَّ الَّذِينَ كَفَرُوا وَمَاتُوا وَهُمْ كُفَّارٌ فَلَن يُقْبَلَ
مِنْ أَحَدِهِم مِّلْءُ الْأَرْضِ ذَهَبًا وَلَوِ افْتَدَىٰ بِهِ ۗ
أُولَٰئِكَ لَهُمْ عَذَابٌ أَلِيمٌ وَمَا لَهُم مِّن نَّاصِرِينَ ﴿٩٢﴾

R. 10.

93. Never shall you attain to righteousness unless you spend out of that which you love; and whatever you spend, Allah surely knows it well.

لَن تَنَالُوا الْبِرَّ حَتَّىٰ تُنفِقُوا مِمَّا تُحِبُّونَ ۚ وَمَا
تُنفِقُوا مِن شَيْءٍ فَإِنَّ اللَّهَ بِهِ عَلِيمٌ ﴿٩٣﴾

94. All food was lawful to the children of Israel, except what Israel forbade himself before the Torah was sent down. Say, 'Bring, then, the Torah and read it, if you are truthful.'

كُلُّ الطَّعَامِ كَانَ حِلًّا لِّبَنِي إِسْرَائِيلَ إِلَّا مَا حَرَّمَ
إِسْرَائِيلُ عَلَىٰ نَفْسِهِ مِن قَبْلِ أَن تُنَزَّلَ التَّوْرَاةُ ۗ
قُلْ فَأْتُوا بِالتَّوْرَاةِ فَاتْلُوهَا إِن كُنتُمْ صَادِقِينَ ﴿٩٤﴾

95. Now whoso forges a lie against Allah after this, then it is these that are the wrongdoers.

فَمَنِ افْتَرَىٰ عَلَى اللَّهِ الْكَذِبَ مِن بَعْدِ ذَٰلِكَ فَأُولَٰئِكَ
هُمُ الظَّالِمُونَ ﴿٩٥﴾

96. Say, 'Allah has spoken the truth: follow, therefore, the religion of Abraham, *who was* ever inclined *to God;* and he was not of those who associate gods *with God*.'

قُلْ صَدَقَ اللَّهُ ۗ فَاتَّبِعُوا مِلَّةَ إِبْرَاهِيمَ حَنِيفًا ۖ وَمَا
كَانَ مِنَ الْمُشْرِكِينَ ﴿٩٦﴾

97. Surely, the first House founded for mankind is that at Becca*, abounding in blessings and a guidance for all peoples.

إِنَّ أَوَّلَ بَيْتٍ وُضِعَ لِلنَّاسِ لَلَّذِي بِبَكَّةَ مُبَارَكًا
وَهُدًى لِّلْعَالَمِينَ ﴿٩٧﴾

98. In it are manifest Signs; it is the place of Abraham; and whoso enters it, enters peace. And pilgrimage to the House is a duty which men—those who can find a way thither—owe to Allah. And whoever disbelieves, *let him remember* that Allah is surely independent of all creatures.

فِيهِ آيَاتٌ بَيِّنَاتٌ مَّقَامُ إِبْرَاهِيمَ ۖ وَمَن دَخَلَهُ كَانَ
آمِنًا ۗ وَلِلَّهِ عَلَى النَّاسِ حِجُّ الْبَيْتِ مَنِ اسْتَطَاعَ
إِلَيْهِ سَبِيلًا ۚ وَمَن كَفَرَ فَإِنَّ اللَّهَ غَنِيٌّ عَنِ الْعَالَمِينَ ﴿٩٨﴾

99. Say, 'O People of the Book! why deny ye the Signs of Allah, while Allah is Watchful of what you do?'

قُلْ يَا أَهْلَ الْكِتَابِ لِمَ تَكْفُرُونَ بِآيَاتِ اللَّهِ وَاللَّهُ
شَهِيدٌ عَلَىٰ مَا تَعْمَلُونَ ﴿٩٩﴾

100. Say, 'O People of the Book! why hinder ye the believers from the path of Allah, seeking to make it crooked, while you are witnesses *thereof?* And Allah is not unmindful of what you do.'

قُلْ يَا أَهْلَ الْكِتَابِ لِمَ تَصُدُّونَ عَن سَبِيلِ اللَّهِ
مَنْ آمَنَ تَبْغُونَهَا عِوَجًا وَأَنتُمْ شُهَدَاءُ ۗ وَمَا اللَّهُ
بِغَافِلٍ عَمَّا تَعْمَلُونَ ﴿١٠٠﴾

* The valley of Mecca.

101. O ye who believe! if you obey any party of those who have been given the Book, they will turn you again into disbelievers after you have believed.

يٰۤاَيُّهَا الَّذِيْنَ اٰمَنُوْۤا اِنْ تُطِيْعُوْا فَرِيْقًا مِّنَ الَّذِيْنَ
اُوْتُوا الْكِتٰبَ يَرُدُّوْكُمْ بَعْدَ اِيْمَانِكُمْ كٰفِرِيْنَ ﴿١٠١﴾

102. How would you disbelieve, while to you are rehearsed the Signs of Allah, and His Messenger is present among you? And he who holds fast to Allah is indeed guided to the right path.

وَكَيْفَ تَكْفُرُوْنَ وَاَنْتُمْ تُتْلٰى عَلَيْكُمْ اٰيٰتُ اللّٰهِ وَ
فِيْكُمْ رَسُوْلُهٗ ؕ وَمَنْ يَّعْتَصِمْ بِاللّٰهِ فَقَدْ هُدِيَ
اِلٰى صِرَاطٍ مُّسْتَقِيْمٍ ﴿١٠٢﴾ ع

R. 11.

103. O ye who believe! fear Allah as He should be feared; and let not death overtake you except when you are in a state of submission.

يٰۤاَيُّهَا الَّذِيْنَ اٰمَنُوا اتَّقُوا اللّٰهَ حَقَّ تُقٰتِهٖ وَلَا
تَمُوْتُنَّ اِلَّا وَاَنْتُمْ مُّسْلِمُوْنَ ﴿١٠٣﴾

104. And hold fast, all together, by the rope of Allah and be not divided; and remember the favour of Allah which He bestowed upon you when you were enemies and He united your hearts in love, so that by His grace you became *as* brothers; and you were on the brink of a pit of fire and He saved you from it. Thus does Allah explain to you His commandments that you may be guided.

وَاعْتَصِمُوْا بِحَبْلِ اللّٰهِ جَمِيْعًا وَّلَا تَفَرَّقُوْا ۠
وَاذْكُرُوْا نِعْمَتَ اللّٰهِ عَلَيْكُمْ اِذْ كُنْتُمْ اَعْدَآءً
فَاَلَّفَ بَيْنَ قُلُوْبِكُمْ فَاَصْبَحْتُمْ بِنِعْمَتِهٖۤ اِخْوَانًا ۚ
وَكُنْتُمْ عَلٰى شَفَا حُفْرَةٍ مِّنَ النَّارِ فَاَنْقَذَكُمْ
مِّنْهَا ؕ كَذٰلِكَ يُبَيِّنُ اللّٰهُ لَكُمْ اٰيٰتِهٖ لَعَلَّكُمْ
تَهْتَدُوْنَ ﴿١٠٤﴾

105. And let there be among you a body of men who should invite to goodness, and enjoin equity and forbid evil. And it is they who shall prosper.

وَلْتَكُنْ مِّنْكُمْ اُمَّةٌ يَّدْعُوْنَ اِلَى الْخَيْرِ وَيَاْمُرُوْنَ
بِالْمَعْرُوْفِ وَيَنْهَوْنَ عَنِ الْمُنْكَرِ ؕ وَاُولٰٓئِكَ هُمُ
الْمُفْلِحُوْنَ ﴿١٠٥﴾

106. And be not like those who became divided and who disagreed *among themselves* after clear proofs had come to them. And it is they for whom there shall be a great punishment,

وَلَا تَكُوْنُوْا كَالَّذِيْنَ تَفَرَّقُوْا وَاخْتَلَفُوْا مِنْۢ بَعْدِ
مَا جَآءَهُمُ الْبَيِّنٰتُ ؕ وَاُولٰٓئِكَ لَهُمْ عَذَابٌ
عَظِيْمٌ ﴿١٠٦﴾

107. On the day when some faces shall be white, and some faces shall be black. As for those whose faces will be black, *it will be said to them*: 'Did you disbelieve after believing? Taste, then, the punishment because you disbelieved.'

يَّوْمَ تَبْيَضُّ وُجُوْهٌ وَّتَسْوَدُّ وُجُوْهٌ ۚ فَاَمَّا الَّذِيْنَ
اسْوَدَّتْ وُجُوْهُهُمْ ۟ اَكَفَرْتُمْ بَعْدَ اِيْمَانِكُمْ فَذُوْقُوا
الْعَذَابَ بِمَا كُنْتُمْ تَكْفُرُوْنَ ﴿١٠٧﴾

108. And as for those whose faces will be white, they will be in the mercy of Allah; therein will they abide.

وَأَمَّا الَّذِينَ ابْيَضَّتْ وُجُوهُهُمْ فَفِي رَحْمَةِ اللَّهِ
هُمْ فِيهَا خَالِدُونَ (١٠٨)

109. These are the Signs of Allah, We rehearse them to thee while they comprise the truth; and Allah wills not any wrong to *His* creatures.

تِلْكَ آيَاتُ اللَّهِ نَتْلُوهَا عَلَيْكَ بِالْحَقِّ ۗ وَمَا اللَّهُ يُرِيدُ
ظُلْمًا لِلْعَالَمِينَ (١٠٩)

110. And to Allah belongs whatever is in the heavens and whatever is in the earth, and to Allah shall all affairs be returned *for decision*.

وَلِلَّهِ مَا فِي السَّمَاوَاتِ وَمَا فِي الْأَرْضِ ۚ وَإِلَى اللَّهِ تُرْجَعُ
الْأُمُورُ (١١٠)

R. 12.

111. You are the best people raised for the good of mankind; you enjoin what is good and forbid evil and believe in Allah. And if the People of the Book had believed, it would have surely been better for them. Some of them are believers, but most of them are disobedient.

كُنْتُمْ خَيْرَ أُمَّةٍ أُخْرِجَتْ لِلنَّاسِ تَأْمُرُونَ بِالْمَعْرُوفِ
وَتَنْهَوْنَ عَنِ الْمُنْكَرِ وَتُؤْمِنُونَ بِاللَّهِ ۗ وَلَوْ آمَنَ
أَهْلُ الْكِتَابِ لَكَانَ خَيْرًا لَهُمْ ۚ مِنْهُمُ الْمُؤْمِنُونَ وَ
أَكْثَرُهُمُ الْفَاسِقُونَ (١١١)

112. They cannot harm you save a slight hurt; and if they fight you, they shall show you their backs. Then they shall not be helped.

لَنْ يَضُرُّوكُمْ إِلَّا أَذًى ۖ وَإِنْ يُقَاتِلُوكُمْ يُوَلُّوكُمُ
الْأَدْبَارَ ثُمَّ لَا يُنْصَرُونَ (١١٢)

113. Smitten shall they be with abasement wherever they are found, unless they have protection from Allah, or protection from men. They have incurred the wrath of Allah, and smitten are they with wretchedness. That is because they would reject the Signs of Allah and kill the Prophets unjustly. That is because they rebelled and used to transgress.

ضُرِبَتْ عَلَيْهِمُ الذِّلَّةُ أَيْنَ مَا ثُقِفُوا إِلَّا بِحَبْلٍ مِنَ اللَّهِ
وَحَبْلٍ مِنَ النَّاسِ وَبَاءُوا بِغَضَبٍ مِنَ اللَّهِ وَضُرِبَتْ
عَلَيْهِمُ الْمَسْكَنَةُ ۚ ذَٰلِكَ بِأَنَّهُمْ كَانُوا يَكْفُرُونَ بِآيَاتِ اللَّهِ وَيَقْتُلُونَ
الْأَنْبِيَاءَ بِغَيْرِ حَقٍّ ۚ ذَٰلِكَ بِمَا عَصَوْا وَكَانُوا يَعْتَدُونَ (١١٣)

* 114. They are not *all* alike. Among the People of the Book there is a party who stand *by their covenant*; they recite the word of Allah in the hours of night and prostrate themselves *before Him*.

لَيْسُوا سَوَاءً ۗ مِنْ أَهْلِ الْكِتَابِ أُمَّةٌ قَائِمَةٌ يَتْلُونَ
آيَاتِ اللَّهِ آنَاءَ اللَّيْلِ وَهُمْ يَسْجُدُونَ (١١٤)

115. They believe in Allah and the Last Day, and enjoin what is good and forbid evil, and hasten, vying with one another, in good works. And these are among the righteous.

يُؤْمِنُونَ بِاللَّهِ وَالْيَوْمِ الْآخِرِ وَيَأْمُرُونَ بِالْمَعْرُوفِ
وَيَنْهَوْنَ عَنِ الْمُنْكَرِ وَيُسَارِعُونَ فِي الْخَيْرَاتِ ۖ
وَأُولَٰئِكَ مِنَ الصَّالِحِينَ (١١٥)

116. And whatever good they do, they shall not be denied its due reward; and

وَمَا يَفْعَلُوا مِنْ خَيْرٍ فَلَنْ يُكْفَرُوهُ ۗ وَاللَّهُ عَلِيمٌ

Allah well knows the God-fearing.

بِالْمُتَّقِيْنَ ﴿١١٦﴾

117. As for those who disbelieve, their possessions and their children shall not avail them aught against Allah; and these are the inmates of the Fire; therein shall they abide.

إِنَّ الَّذِيْنَ كَفَرُوْا لَنْ تُغْنِيَ عَنْهُمْ أَمْوَالُهُمْ وَلَا
أَوْلَادُهُمْ مِّنَ اللّٰهِ شَيْئًا ۖ وَأُولٰٓئِكَ أَصْحٰبُ النَّارِ ۚ
هُمْ فِيْهَا خٰلِدُوْنَ ﴿١١٧﴾

118. The likeness of what they spend for the present life is as the likeness of a wind wherein there is intense cold which smites the harvest of a people who have wronged themselves, and destroys it. And Allah has not wronged them, but they wrong themselves.

مَثَلُ مَا يُنْفِقُوْنَ فِيْ هٰذِهِ الْحَيٰوةِ الدُّنْيَا كَمَثَلِ
رِيْحٍ فِيْهَا صِرٌّ أَصَابَتْ حَرْثَ قَوْمٍ ظَلَمُوْٓا أَنْفُسَهُمْ
فَأَهْلَكَتْهُ ۚ وَمَا ظَلَمَهُمُ اللّٰهُ وَلٰكِنْ أَنْفُسَهُمْ
يَظْلِمُوْنَ ﴿١١٨﴾

119. O ye who believe! take not *others* than your own people as intimate friends; they will not fail to corrupt you. They love to see you in trouble. Hatred has already shown itself through *the utterances of* their mouths, and what their breasts conceal is greater still. We have made clear to you Our commandments, if you will understand.

يٰٓأَيُّهَا الَّذِيْنَ اٰمَنُوْا لَا تَتَّخِذُوْا بِطَانَةً مِّنْ دُوْنِكُمْ
لَا يَأْلُوْنَكُمْ خَبَالًا ۖ وَدُّوْا مَا عَنِتُّمْ ۚ قَدْ بَدَتِ
الْبَغْضَآءُ مِنْ أَفْوَاهِهِمْ ۖ وَمَا تُخْفِيْ صُدُوْرُهُمْ
أَكْبَرُ ۚ قَدْ بَيَّنَّا لَكُمُ الْاٰيٰتِ إِنْ كُنْتُمْ
تَعْقِلُوْنَ ﴿١١٩﴾

120. Behold, you are those who love them, but they love you not. And you believe in all the Book. When they meet you, they say, 'We believe;' but when they are alone, they bite their finger-tips at you for rage. Say, 'Perish in your rage. Surely, Allah knows well what is hidden in *your* breasts.'

هٰٓأَنْتُمْ أُولَآءِ تُحِبُّوْنَهُمْ وَلَا يُحِبُّوْنَكُمْ وَتُؤْمِنُوْنَ
بِالْكِتٰبِ كُلِّهٖ ۚ وَإِذَا لَقُوْكُمْ قَالُوْٓا اٰمَنَّا ۖ وَإِذَا خَلَوْا
عَضُّوْا عَلَيْكُمُ الْأَنَامِلَ مِنَ الْغَيْظِ ۚ قُلْ مُوْتُوْا
بِغَيْظِكُمْ ۚ إِنَّ اللّٰهَ عَلِيْمٌ بِذَاتِ الصُّدُوْرِ ﴿١٢٠﴾

121. If anything good befall you, it grieves them; and if an evil befall you, they rejoice thereat. But if you be steadfast and righteous, their designs will not harm you at all; surely, Allah encompasses *all* that they do.

إِنْ تَمْسَسْكُمْ حَسَنَةٌ تَسُؤْهُمْ ۖ وَإِنْ تُصِبْكُمْ
سَيِّئَةٌ يَفْرَحُوْا بِهَا ۖ وَإِنْ تَصْبِرُوْا وَتَتَّقُوْا لَا
يَضُرُّكُمْ كَيْدُهُمْ شَيْئًا ۚ إِنَّ اللّٰهَ بِمَا يَعْمَلُوْنَ
مُحِيْطٌ ﴿١٢١﴾ ع ١٢ ١٣

R. 13.

122. And *remember the time* when thou didst go forth early in the morning from

وَإِذْ غَدَوْتَ مِنْ أَهْلِكَ تُبَوِّئُ الْمُؤْمِنِيْنَ مَقَاعِدَ

thy household, assigning to the believers their positions for battle. And Allah is All-Hearing, All-Knowing;

لِلْقِتَالِ ۗ وَاللّٰهُ سَمِيْعٌ عَلِيْمٌ ﴿١٢٢﴾

123. When two of your groups meditated cowardice, although Allah was their friend. And upon Allah should the believers rely.

اِذْ هَمَّتْ طَّآئِفَتٰنِ مِنْكُمْ اَنْ تَفْشَلَا ۙ وَاللّٰهُ وَلِيُّهُمَا ۭ
وَعَلَى اللّٰهِ فَلْيَتَوَكَّلِ الْمُؤْمِنُوْنَ ﴿١٢٣﴾

124. And Allah had *already* helped you at Badr when you were weak. So take Allah for your Protector that you may be grateful.

وَلَقَدْ نَصَرَكُمُ اللّٰهُ بِبَدْرٍ وَّاَنْتُمْ اَذِلَّةٌ ۚ فَاتَّقُوا
اللّٰهَ لَعَلَّكُمْ تَشْكُرُوْنَ ﴿١٢٤﴾

125. When thou didst say to the believers, 'Will it not suffice you that your Lord should help you with three thousand angels sent down *from on high?'*

اِذْ تَقُوْلُ لِلْمُؤْمِنِيْنَ اَلَنْ يَّكْفِيَكُمْ اَنْ يُّمِدَّكُمْ
رَبُّكُمْ بِثَلٰثَةِ اٰلٰفٍ مِّنَ الْمَلٰٓئِكَةِ مُنْزَلِيْنَ ﴿١٢٥﴾

126. Yea, if you be steadfast and righteous and they come upon you immediately in hot haste, your Lord will help you with five thousand angels, attacking vehemently.

بَلٰٓى ۙ اِنْ تَصْبِرُوْا وَتَتَّقُوْا وَيَاْتُوْكُمْ مِّنْ فَوْرِهِمْ
هٰذَا يُمْدِدْكُمْ رَبُّكُمْ بِخَمْسَةِ اٰلٰفٍ مِّنَ الْمَلٰٓئِكَةِ
مُسَوِّمِيْنَ ﴿١٢٦﴾

127. And Allah has made it only as glad tidings for you and that your hearts might be at rest thereby; and help comes from Allah alone, the Mighty, the Wise.

وَمَا جَعَلَهُ اللّٰهُ اِلَّا بُشْرٰى لَكُمْ وَلِتَطْمَئِنَّ قُلُوْبُكُمْ بِهٖ ۭ
وَمَا النَّصْرُ اِلَّا مِنْ عِنْدِ اللّٰهِ الْعَزِيْزِ الْحَكِيْمِ ﴿١٢٧﴾

128. *God will do so* that He might cut off a part of the disbelievers or abase them so that they might go back frustrated.

لِيَقْطَعَ طَرَفًا مِّنَ الَّذِيْنَ كَفَرُوْٓا اَوْ يَكْبِتَهُمْ فَيَنْقَلِبُوْا
خَآئِبِيْنَ ﴿١٢٨﴾

129. Thou hast no concern in the matter: He may turn to them in mercy or punish them, for they are wrongdoers.

لَيْسَ لَكَ مِنَ الْاَمْرِ شَيْءٌ اَوْ يَتُوْبَ عَلَيْهِمْ اَوْ يُعَذِّبَهُمْ
فَاِنَّهُمْ ظٰلِمُوْنَ ﴿١٢٩﴾

130. And to Allah belongs whatever is in the heavens and whatever is in the earth. He forgives whomsoever He pleases and punishes whomsoever He pleases, and Allah is Most Forgiving, Merciful.

وَلِلّٰهِ مَا فِي السَّمٰوٰتِ وَمَا فِي الْاَرْضِ ۭ يَغْفِرُ لِمَنْ
يَّشَآءُ وَيُعَذِّبُ مَنْ يَّشَآءُ ۭ وَاللّٰهُ غَفُوْرٌ رَّحِيْمٌ ﴿١٣٠﴾ ع

R. 14.

* 131. O ye who believe! devour not interest involving diverse additions; and fear Allah that you may prosper.

يٰٓاَيُّهَا الَّذِيْنَ اٰمَنُوْا لَا تَاْكُلُوا الرِّبٰٓوا اَضْعَافًا مُّضٰعَفَةً ۠
وَّاتَّقُوا اللّٰهَ لَعَلَّكُمْ تُفْلِحُوْنَ ﴿١٣١﴾

132. And fear the Fire prepared for the disbelievers.

وَاتَّقُوا النَّارَ الَّتِيْٓ اُعِدَّتْ لِلْكٰفِرِيْنَ ﴿١٣٢﴾

133. And obey Allah and the Messenger that you be shown mercy.

وَاَطِيْعُوا اللّٰهَ وَالرَّسُوْلَ لَعَلَّكُمْ تُرْحَمُوْنَ ﴿١٣٣﴾

134. And vie with one another in asking for forgiveness from your Lord, and for a Paradise whose price is the heavens and the earth, prepared for the God-fearing—

وَسَارِعُوْٓا اِلٰى مَغْفِرَةٍ مِّنْ رَّبِّكُمْ وَجَنَّةٍ عَرْضُهَا
السَّمٰوٰتُ وَالْاَرْضُ ۙ اُعِدَّتْ لِلْمُتَّقِيْنَ ﴿۱۳۴﴾

135. Those who spend in prosperity and adversity, and those who suppress anger and pardon men; and Allah loves those who do good;

الَّذِيْنَ يُنْفِقُوْنَ فِي السَّرَّآءِ وَالضَّرَّآءِ وَالْكٰظِمِيْنَ
الْغَيْظَ وَالْعَافِيْنَ عَنِ النَّاسِ ۗ وَاللّٰهُ يُحِبُّ الْمُحْسِنِيْنَ ﴿۱۳۵﴾

136. And those who, when they commit a foul deed or wrong themselves, remember Allah and implore forgiveness for their sins—and who can forgive sins except Allah?—and do not persist knowingly in what they have done.

وَالَّذِيْنَ اِذَا فَعَلُوْا فَاحِشَةً اَوْ ظَلَمُوْٓا اَنْفُسَهُمْ ذَكَرُوا اللّٰهَ فَاسْتَغْفَرُوْا
لِذُنُوْبِهِمْ ۠ وَمَنْ يَّغْفِرُ الذُّنُوْبَ اِلَّا اللّٰهُ ۫ وَلَمْ
يُصِرُّوْا عَلٰى مَا فَعَلُوْا وَهُمْ يَعْلَمُوْنَ ﴿۱۳۶﴾

137. It is these whose reward is forgiveness from their Lord, and Gardens beneath which rivers flow, wherein they shall abide; and how good is the reward of those who work!

اُولٰٓئِكَ جَزَآؤُهُمْ مَّغْفِرَةٌ مِّنْ رَّبِّهِمْ وَجَنّٰتٌ تَجْرِيْ
مِنْ تَحْتِهَا الْاَنْهٰرُ خٰلِدِيْنَ فِيْهَا ۗ وَنِعْمَ اَجْرُ
الْعٰمِلِيْنَ ﴿۱۳۷﴾

138. Surely, there have been *many* dispensations before you; so travel through the earth and see how *evil* was the end of those who treated *the Prophets* as liars.

قَدْ خَلَتْ مِنْ قَبْلِكُمْ سُنَنٌ ۙ فَسِيْرُوْا فِي الْاَرْضِ
فَانْظُرُوْا كَيْفَ كَانَ عَاقِبَةُ الْمُكَذِّبِيْنَ ﴿۱۳۸﴾

* 139. This (the Qur'ān) is a clear demonstration to men, and a guidance and an admonition to the God-fearing.

هٰذَا بَيَانٌ لِّلنَّاسِ وَهُدًى وَّمَوْعِظَةٌ لِّلْمُتَّقِيْنَ ﴿۱۳۹﴾

140. Slacken not, nor grieve; and you shall certainly have the upper hand, if you are believers.

وَلَا تَهِنُوْا وَلَا تَحْزَنُوْا وَاَنْتُمُ الْاَعْلَوْنَ اِنْ كُنْتُمْ
مُّؤْمِنِيْنَ ﴿۱۴۰﴾

141. If you have received an injury, surely the *disbelieving* people have *already* received a similar injury. And such days We cause to alternate among men *that they may be admonished*, and that Allah may distinguish those who believe and may take witnesses from among you; and Allah loves not the unjust;

اِنْ يَّمْسَسْكُمْ قَرْحٌ فَقَدْ مَسَّ الْقَوْمَ قَرْحٌ مِّثْلُهٗ ۗ
وَتِلْكَ الْاَيَّامُ نُدَاوِلُهَا بَيْنَ النَّاسِ ۚ وَلِيَعْلَمَ اللّٰهُ
الَّذِيْنَ اٰمَنُوْا وَيَتَّخِذَ مِنْكُمْ شُهَدَآءَ ۗ وَاللّٰهُ لَا يُحِبُّ
الظّٰلِمِيْنَ ۙ ﴿۱۴۱﴾

142. And that Allah may purify those who believe, and destroy the disbelievers.

وَلِيُمَحِّصَ اللّٰهُ الَّذِيْنَ اٰمَنُوْا وَيَمْحَقَ الْكٰفِرِيْنَ ﴿۱۴۲﴾

143. Do you suppose that you will enter Heaven while Allah has not yet distinguished those of you that strive *in the way of Allah* and has not yet distinguished the steadfast?

اَمْ حَسِبْتُمْ اَنْ تَدْخُلُوا الْجَنَّةَ وَلَمَّا يَعْلَمِ اللّٰهُ الَّذِيْنَ
جٰهَدُوْا مِنْكُمْ وَيَعْلَمَ الصّٰبِرِيْنَ ﴿۱۴۳﴾

* **144.** And you used to wish for this death before you met it; now you have seen it while you were *actually* looking for *it*.

وَلَقَدْ كُنْتُمْ تَمَنَّوْنَ الْمَوْتَ مِنْ قَبْلِ أَنْ تَلْقَوْهُ فَقَدْ رَأَيْتُمُوهُ وَأَنْتُمْ تَنْظُرُونَ ﴿١٤٤﴾

R. 15.

145. And Muḥammad is only a Messenger. Verily, *all* Messengers have passed away before him. If then he die or be slain, will you turn back on your heels? And he who turns back on his heels shall not harm Allah at all. And Allah will certainly reward the grateful.

وَمَا مُحَمَّدٌ إِلَّا رَسُولٌ قَدْ خَلَتْ مِنْ قَبْلِهِ الرُّسُلُ أَفَإِنْ مَاتَ أَوْ قُتِلَ انْقَلَبْتُمْ عَلَىٰ أَعْقَابِكُمْ وَمَنْ يَنْقَلِبْ عَلَىٰ عَقِبَيْهِ فَلَنْ يَضُرَّ اللَّهَ شَيْئًا وَسَيَجْزِي اللَّهُ الشَّاكِرِينَ ﴿١٤٥﴾

146. And no soul can die except by Allah's leave—a decree with a fixed term. And whoever desires the reward of the present world, We will give him thereof; and whoever desires the reward of the life to come, We will give him thereof; and We will surely reward the grateful.

وَمَا كَانَ لِنَفْسٍ أَنْ تَمُوتَ إِلَّا بِإِذْنِ اللَّهِ كِتَابًا مُؤَجَّلًا وَمَنْ يُرِدْ ثَوَابَ الدُّنْيَا نُؤْتِهِ مِنْهَا وَمَنْ يُرِدْ ثَوَابَ الْآخِرَةِ نُؤْتِهِ مِنْهَا وَسَنَجْزِي الشَّاكِرِينَ ﴿١٤٦﴾

* **147.** And many a Prophet there has been beside whom fought numerous companies *of their followers*. They slackened not for aught that befell them in the way of Allah, nor did they weaken, nor did they humiliate themselves *before the enemy*. And Allah loves the steadfast.

وَكَأَيِّنْ مِنْ نَبِيٍّ قُتِلَ مَعَهُ رِبِّيُّونَ كَثِيرٌ فَمَا وَهَنُوا لِمَا أَصَابَهُمْ فِي سَبِيلِ اللَّهِ وَمَا ضَعُفُوا وَمَا اسْتَكَانُوا وَاللَّهُ يُحِبُّ الصَّابِرِينَ ﴿١٤٧﴾

148. And they uttered not a word except that they said: 'Our Lord, forgive us our errors and our excesses in our conduct, and make firm our steps and help us against the disbelieving people.'

وَمَا كَانَ قَوْلَهُمْ إِلَّا أَنْ قَالُوا رَبَّنَا اغْفِرْ لَنَا ذُنُوبَنَا وَإِسْرَافَنَا فِي أَمْرِنَا وَثَبِّتْ أَقْدَامَنَا وَانْصُرْنَا عَلَى الْقَوْمِ الْكَافِرِينَ ﴿١٤٨﴾

149. So Allah gave them the reward of this world, as also an excellent reward of the next; and Allah loves those who do good.

فَآتَاهُمُ اللَّهُ ثَوَابَ الدُّنْيَا وَحُسْنَ ثَوَابِ الْآخِرَةِ وَاللَّهُ يُحِبُّ الْمُحْسِنِينَ ﴿١٤٩﴾

R. 16.

150. O ye who believe! if you obey those who have disbelieved, they will cause you to turn back on your heels, and you will become losers.

يَا أَيُّهَا الَّذِينَ آمَنُوا إِنْ تُطِيعُوا الَّذِينَ كَفَرُوا يَرُدُّوكُمْ عَلَىٰ أَعْقَابِكُمْ فَتَنْقَلِبُوا خَاسِرِينَ ﴿١٥٠﴾

151. Nay, Allah is your Protector, and He is the Best of helpers.

بَلِ اللَّهُ مَوْلَاكُمْ وَهُوَ خَيْرُ النَّاصِرِينَ ﴿١٥١﴾

152. We shall strike terror into the

سَنُلْقِي فِي قُلُوبِ الَّذِينَ كَفَرُوا الرُّعْبَ بِمَا أَشْرَكُوا

hearts of those that have disbelieved because they associate partners with Allah for which He has sent down no authority. Their abode is the Fire; and evil is the habitation of the wrongdoers.

* 153. And Allah had surely made good to you His promise when you were slaying and destroying them by His leave, until, when you became lax and disagreed among yourselves concerning the order and you disobeyed after He had shown you that which you loved, *He withdrew His help*. Among you were those who desired the present world, and among you were those who desired the next. Then He turned you away from them, that He might try you —and He has surely pardoned you, and Allah is Gracious to the believers.—

* 154. When you were running away and looked not back at anyone while the Messenger was calling out to you from your rear, then He gave you a sorrow in recompense for a sorrow, that you might not grieve for what escaped you, nor for what befell you. And Allah is well aware of what you do.

155. Then, after the sorrow, He sent down peace on you—a slumber that overcame a party of you—while the other party was anxious concerning their own selves, thinking wrongly of Allah *like unto* the thought of ignorance. They said, 'Is there for us any part in the government *of affairs?*' Say, 'All government belongs to Allah.' They hide in their minds what they disclose not to thee. They say, 'If we had any part in the government *of affairs*, we should not have been killed here.' Say, 'If you had remained in your homes, surely those on whom fighting had been enjoined would have gone forth to their deathbeds,' *that Allah might bring about His decree* and that Allah might test what was in your breasts and that He might purge what was in your hearts. And Allah knows well what is in the minds;

بِاللّٰهِ مَا لَمْ يُنَزِّلْ بِهٖ سُلْطٰنًا ۚ وَمَاْوٰىهُمُ النَّارُ ؕ
وَبِئْسَ مَثْوَى الظّٰلِمِيْنَ ﴿۱۵۲﴾
وَلَقَدْ صَدَقَكُمُ اللّٰهُ وَعْدَهٗۤ اِذْ تَحُسُّوْنَهُمْ بِاِذْنِهٖ ۚ
حَتّٰۤى اِذَا فَشِلْتُمْ وَتَنَازَعْتُمْ فِى الْاَمْرِ وَعَصَيْتُمْ مِّنْۢ
بَعْدِ مَاۤ اَرٰىكُمْ مَّا تُحِبُّوْنَ ؕ مِنْكُمْ مَّنْ يُّرِيْدُ الدُّنْيَا
وَمِنْكُمْ مَّنْ يُّرِيْدُ الْاٰخِرَةَ ۚ ثُمَّ صَرَفَكُمْ عَنْهُمْ
لِيَبْتَلِيَكُمْ ۚ وَلَقَدْ عَفَا عَنْكُمْ ؕ وَاللّٰهُ ذُوْ فَضْلٍ
عَلَى الْمُؤْمِنِيْنَ ﴿۱۵۳﴾
اِذْ تُصْعِدُوْنَ وَلَا تَلْوٗنَ عَلٰۤى اَحَدٍ وَّالرَّسُوْلُ
يَدْعُوْكُمْ فِىْۤ اُخْرٰىكُمْ فَاَثَابَكُمْ غَمًّاۢ بِغَمٍّ لِّكَيْلَا
تَحْزَنُوْا عَلٰى مَا فَاتَكُمْ وَلَا مَاۤ اَصَابَكُمْ ؕ وَاللّٰهُ خَبِيْرٌۢ
بِمَا تَعْمَلُوْنَ ﴿۱۵۴﴾
ثُمَّ اَنْزَلَ عَلَيْكُمْ مِّنْۢ بَعْدِ الْغَمِّ اَمَنَةً نُّعَاسًا يَّغْشٰى
طَآئِفَةً مِّنْكُمْ ۙ وَطَآئِفَةٌ قَدْ اَهَمَّتْهُمْ اَنْفُسُهُمْ
يَظُنُّوْنَ بِاللّٰهِ غَيْرَ الْحَقِّ ظَنَّ الْجَاهِلِيَّةِ ؕ يَقُوْلُوْنَ
هَلْ لَّنَا مِنَ الْاَمْرِ مِنْ شَىْءٍ ؕ قُلْ اِنَّ الْاَمْرَ كُلَّهٗ لِلّٰهِ ؕ
يُخْفُوْنَ فِىْۤ اَنْفُسِهِمْ مَّا لَا يُبْدُوْنَ لَكَ ؕ يَقُوْلُوْنَ لَوْ
كَانَ لَنَا مِنَ الْاَمْرِ شَىْءٌ مَّا قُتِلْنَا هٰهُنَا ؕ قُلْ لَّوْ
كُنْتُمْ فِىْ بُيُوْتِكُمْ لَبَرَزَ الَّذِيْنَ كُتِبَ عَلَيْهِمُ الْقَتْلُ
اِلٰى مَضَاجِعِهِمْ ۚ وَلِيَبْتَلِىَ اللّٰهُ مَا فِىْ صُدُوْرِكُمْ
وَلِيُمَحِّصَ مَا فِىْ قُلُوْبِكُمْ ؕ وَاللّٰهُ عَلِيْمٌۢ بِذَاتِ
الصُّدُوْرِ ﴿۱۵۵﴾

156. Those of you who turned their backs on the day when the two hosts met,* surely it was Satan who sought to make them slip because of certain doings of theirs. But certainly Allah has already pardoned them. Verily, Allah is Most Forgiving, Forbearing.

R. 17.

157. O ye who believe! be not like those who have disbelieved, and who say of their brethren when they travel in the land or go forth to war: 'Had they been with us, they would not have died or been slain.' *This is so,* that Allah may make it a cause of regret in their hearts. And Allah gives life and causes death and Allah is Mindful of what you do.

158. And if you are slain in the cause of Allah or you die, surely forgiveness from Allah and mercy shall be better than what they hoard.

159. And if you die or be slain, surely unto Allah shall you be gathered together.

* 160. And it is by the *great* mercy of Allah that thou art kind towards them, and if thou hadst been rough *and* hard-hearted, they would surely have dispersed from around thee. So pardon them and ask forgiveness for them, and consult them in matters *of administration*; and when thou art determined, then put thy trust in Allah. Surely, Allah loves those who put their trust *in Him.*

161. If Allah help you, none shall overcome you; but if He forsake you, then who is there that can help you beside Him? In Allah, then, let the believers put their trust.

162. And it is not possible for a Prophet to act dishonestly, and whoever acts dishonestly shall bring *with him* that about which he has been dishonest, on the Day of Resurrection. Then shall every soul be fully paid what it has earned; and they shall not be wronged.

163. Is he who follows the pleasure of Allah like him who draws on himself the

إِنَّ الَّذِينَ تَوَلَّوْا مِنْكُمْ يَوْمَ الْتَقَى الْجَمْعٰنِ إِنَّمَا
اسْتَزَلَّهُمُ الشَّيْطٰنُ بِبَعْضِ مَا كَسَبُوا ۚ وَلَقَدْ عَفَا
اللّٰهُ عَنْهُمْ ۗ إِنَّ اللّٰهَ غَفُورٌ حَلِيمٌ ﴿١٥٦﴾ ع
يٰٓأَيُّهَا الَّذِينَ اٰمَنُوا لَا تَكُونُوا كَالَّذِينَ كَفَرُوا وَقَالُوا
لِإِخْوَانِهِمْ إِذَا ضَرَبُوا فِي الْأَرْضِ أَوْ كَانُوا غُزًّى لَّوْ
كَانُوا عِنْدَنَا مَا مَاتُوا وَمَا قُتِلُوا لِيَجْعَلَ اللّٰهُ ذٰلِكَ
حَسْرَةً فِي قُلُوبِهِمْ ۗ وَاللّٰهُ يُحْيِي وَيُمِيتُ ۗ وَاللّٰهُ بِمَا
تَعْمَلُونَ بَصِيرٌ ﴿١٥٧﴾
وَلَئِنْ قُتِلْتُمْ فِي سَبِيلِ اللّٰهِ أَوْ مُتُّمْ لَمَغْفِرَةٌ مِّنَ
اللّٰهِ وَرَحْمَةٌ خَيْرٌ مِّمَّا يَجْمَعُونَ ﴿١٥٨﴾
وَلَئِنْ مُّتُّمْ أَوْ قُتِلْتُمْ لَإِلَى اللّٰهِ تُحْشَرُونَ ﴿١٥٩﴾
فَبِمَا رَحْمَةٍ مِّنَ اللّٰهِ لِنْتَ لَهُمْ ۚ وَلَوْ كُنْتَ فَظًّا
غَلِيظَ الْقَلْبِ لَانْفَضُّوا مِنْ حَوْلِكَ ۖ فَاعْفُ عَنْهُمْ
وَاسْتَغْفِرْ لَهُمْ وَشَاوِرْهُمْ فِي الْأَمْرِ ۚ فَإِذَا عَزَمْتَ
فَتَوَكَّلْ عَلَى اللّٰهِ ۗ إِنَّ اللّٰهَ يُحِبُّ الْمُتَوَكِّلِينَ ﴿١٦٠﴾
إِنْ يَنْصُرْكُمُ اللّٰهُ فَلَا غَالِبَ لَكُمْ ۚ وَإِنْ يَخْذُلْكُمْ
فَمَنْ ذَا الَّذِي يَنْصُرُكُمْ مِّنْ بَعْدِهِ ۗ وَعَلَى اللّٰهِ فَلْيَتَوَكَّلِ
الْمُؤْمِنُونَ ﴿١٦١﴾
وَمَا كَانَ لِنَبِيٍّ أَنْ يَغُلَّ ۗ وَمَنْ يَغْلُلْ يَأْتِ بِمَا
غَلَّ يَوْمَ الْقِيٰمَةِ ۚ ثُمَّ تُوَفّٰى كُلُّ نَفْسٍ مَّا كَسَبَتْ
وَهُمْ لَا يُظْلَمُونَ ﴿١٦٢﴾
أَفَمَنِ اتَّبَعَ رِضْوَانَ اللّٰهِ كَمَنْ بَآءَ بِسَخَطٍ مِّنَ اللّٰهِ

* The battle of Uḥad.

wrath of Allah and whose abode is Hell? And an evil retreat it is!	وماوىه جهنم وبئس المصير ﴿١٦٣﴾
164. They have *different* grades *of grace* with Allah; and Allah sees what they do.	هم درجت عند الله والله بصير بما يعملون ﴿١٦٤﴾
165. Verily, Allah has conferred a favour on the believers by raising among them a Messenger from among themselves, who recites to them His Signs, and purifies them and teaches them the Book and Wisdom; and, before that, they were surely in manifest error.	لقد من الله على المؤمنين اذ بعث فيهم رسولا من انفسهم يتلوا عليهم ايته ويزكيهم و يعلمهم الكتب والحكمة وان كانوا من قبل لفي ضلل مبين ﴿١٦٥﴾
166. What! when a misfortune befalls you—and you had inflicted the double of that—you say, whence is this? Say, 'It is from your own selves.' Surely, Allah has power over all things.	اولما اصابتكم مصيبة قد اصبتم مثليها قلتم انى هذا قل هو من عند انفسكم ان الله على كل شيء قدير ﴿١٦٦﴾
167. And that which befell you, on the day when the two parties met*, was by Allah's command; and *this was so* that He might distinguish the believers;	وما اصابكم يوم التقى الجمعن فباذن الله وليعلم المؤمنين ﴿١٦٧﴾
168. And that He might distinguish the hypocrites. And it was said to them, 'Come ye, fight in the cause of Allah and repel *the attack of the enemy;*' they said, 'If we knew how to fight, we would surely follow you.' They were, that day, nearer to disbelief than to belief. They say with their mouths what is not in their hearts. And Allah knows well what they conceal.	وليعلم الذين نافقوا وقيل لهم تعالوا قاتلوا في سبيل الله او ادفعوا قالوا لو نعلم قتالا لاتبعنكم هم للكفر يومئذ اقرب منهم للايمان يقولون بافواههم ما ليس في قلوبهم والله اعلم بما يكتمون ﴿١٦٨﴾
169. *It is these* who said of their brethren, while they *themselves* remained behind, 'If they had obeyed us, they would not have been slain.' Say, 'Then avert death from yourselves, if you are truthful.'	الذين قالوا لاخوانهم وقعدوا لو اطاعونا ما قتلوا قل فادرءوا عن انفسكم الموت ان كنتم صدقين ﴿١٦٩﴾
* 170. Think not of those, who have been slain in the cause of Allah, as dead. Nay, they are living, in the presence of their Lord, *and* are granted gifts *from Him*,	ولا تحسبن الذين قتلوا في سبيل الله امواتا بل احياء عند ربهم يرزقون ﴿١٧٠﴾
171. Jubilant because of that which Allah has given them of His bounty; and	فرحين بما اتىهم الله من فضله ويستبشرون بالذين

* The battle of Uḥad.

rejoicing for those who have not yet joined them from behind them, because on them *shall come* no fear, nor shall they grieve.

لَمْ يَلْحَقُوا بِهِمْ مِّنْ خَلْفِهِمْ أَلَّا خَوْفٌ عَلَيْهِمْ وَلَا هُمْ
يَحْزَنُونَ ﴿١٧١﴾

172. They rejoice at the favour of Allah and *His* bounty, and *at the fact* that Allah suffers not the reward of the believers to be lost.

يَسْتَبْشِرُونَ بِنِعْمَةٍ مِّنَ اللَّهِ وَفَضْلٍ وَأَنَّ اللَّهَ لَا يُضِيعُ
أَجْرَ الْمُؤْمِنِينَ ﴿١٧٢﴾

R. 18.

173. *As to* those who answered the call of Allah and the Messenger after they had received an injury—such of them as do good and act righteously shall have a great reward;

الَّذِينَ اسْتَجَابُوا لِلَّهِ وَالرَّسُولِ مِن بَعْدِ مَا أَصَابَهُمُ
الْقَرْحُ ۚ لِلَّذِينَ أَحْسَنُوا مِنْهُمْ وَاتَّقَوْا أَجْرٌ عَظِيمٌ ﴿١٧٣﴾

174. Those to whom men said, 'People have mustered against you, therefore fear them,' but this *only* increased their faith, and they said, 'Sufficient for us is Allah, and an excellent Guardian is He.'

الَّذِينَ قَالَ لَهُمُ النَّاسُ إِنَّ النَّاسَ قَدْ جَمَعُوا لَكُمْ
فَاخْشَوْهُمْ فَزَادَهُمْ إِيمَانًا ۖ وَقَالُوا حَسْبُنَا اللَّهُ
وَنِعْمَ الْوَكِيلُ ﴿١٧٤﴾

175. So they returned with a *mighty* favour from Allah and a *great* bounty, while no evil had touched them; and they followed the pleasure of Allah; and Allah is the Lord of great bounty.

فَانقَلَبُوا بِنِعْمَةٍ مِّنَ اللَّهِ وَفَضْلٍ لَّمْ يَمْسَسْهُمْ سُوءٌ
وَاتَّبَعُوا رِضْوَانَ اللَّهِ ۗ وَاللَّهُ ذُو فَضْلٍ عَظِيمٍ ﴿١٧٥﴾

176. It is Satan who only frightens his friends; so fear them not but fear Me, if you are believers.

إِنَّمَا ذَٰلِكُمُ الشَّيْطَانُ يُخَوِّفُ أَوْلِيَاءَهُ فَلَا تَخَافُوهُمْ
وَخَافُونِ إِن كُنتُم مُّؤْمِنِينَ ﴿١٧٦﴾

177. And let not those who hastily fall into disbelief grieve thee; surely, they cannot harm Allah in any way. Allah desires not to assign any portion for them in the life to come; and they shall have a severe punishment.

وَلَا يَحْزُنكَ الَّذِينَ يُسَارِعُونَ فِي الْكُفْرِ ۚ إِنَّهُمْ لَن
يَضُرُّوا اللَّهَ شَيْئًا ۗ يُرِيدُ اللَّهُ أَلَّا يَجْعَلَ لَهُمْ حَظًّا فِي
الْآخِرَةِ ۖ وَلَهُمْ عَذَابٌ عَظِيمٌ ﴿١٧٧﴾

178. Surely, those who have purchased disbelief at the price of faith cannot harm Allah at all; and they shall have a grievous punishment.

إِنَّ الَّذِينَ اشْتَرَوُا الْكُفْرَ بِالْإِيمَانِ لَن يَضُرُّوا اللَّهَ
شَيْئًا ۚ وَلَهُمْ عَذَابٌ أَلِيمٌ ﴿١٧٨﴾

179. And let not the disbelievers think that Our granting them respite is good for them; *the result of* Our granting them respite will only be that they will increase in sin; and they shall have an humiliating punishment.

وَلَا يَحْسَبَنَّ الَّذِينَ كَفَرُوا أَنَّمَا نُمْلِي لَهُمْ خَيْرٌ لِّأَنفُسِهِمْ ۚ
إِنَّمَا نُمْلِي لَهُمْ لِيَزْدَادُوا إِثْمًا ۚ وَلَهُمْ عَذَابٌ
مُّهِينٌ ﴿١٧٩﴾

180. Allah would not leave the believers as you are, until He separated the wicked

مَّا كَانَ اللَّهُ لِيَذَرَ الْمُؤْمِنِينَ عَلَىٰ مَا أَنتُمْ عَلَيْهِ

from the good. Nor would Allah reveal to you the unseen. But Allah chooses of His Messengers whom He pleases. Believe, therefore, in Allah and His Messengers. If you believe and be righteous, you shall have a great reward.

حَتّٰى يَمِيْزَ الْخَبِيْثَ مِنَ الطَّيِّبِ ۭ وَمَا كَانَ اللّٰهُ لِيُطْلِعَكُمْ عَلَى الْغَيْبِ وَلٰكِنَّ اللّٰهَ يَجْتَبِيْ مِنْ رُّسُلِهٖ مَنْ يَّشَاۗءُ ۠ فَاٰمِنُوْا بِاللّٰهِ وَرُسُلِهٖ ۚ وَاِنْ تُؤْمِنُوْا وَتَتَّقُوْا فَلَكُمْ اَجْرٌ عَظِيْمٌ ﴿۱۸۰﴾

181. And let not those, who are niggardly with respect to what Allah has given them of His bounty, think that it is good for them; nay, it is evil for them. That with respect to which they were niggardly shall be put as a collar round their necks on the Day of Resurrection. And to Allah belongs the heritage of the heavens and the earth, and Allah is well aware of what you do.

وَلَا يَحْسَبَنَّ الَّذِيْنَ يَبْخَلُوْنَ بِمَاۗ اٰتٰىھُمُ اللّٰهُ مِنْ فَضْلِهٖ ھُوَ خَيْرًا لَّھُمْ ۭ بَلْ ھُوَ شَرٌّ لَّھُمْ ۭ سَيُطَوَّقُوْنَ مَا بَخِلُوْا بِهٖ يَوْمَ الْقِيٰمَةِ ۭ وَلِلّٰهِ مِيْرَاثُ السَّمٰوٰتِ وَالْاَرْضِ ۭ وَاللّٰهُ بِمَا تَعْمَلُوْنَ خَبِيْرٌ ﴿۱۸۱﴾

R. 19.

182. And surely Allah has heard the utterance of those who said, 'Allah is poor and we are rich.' We shall record what they have said, and their attempts to kill the Prophets unjustly; and We shall say, 'Taste ye the punishment of burning.'

لَقَدْ سَمِعَ اللّٰهُ قَوْلَ الَّذِيْنَ قَالُوْۗا اِنَّ اللّٰهَ فَقِيْرٌ وَّنَحْنُ اَغْنِيَاۗءُ ۘ سَنَكْتُبُ مَا قَالُوْا وَقَتْلَھُمُ الْاَنْۢبِيَاۗءَ بِغَيْرِ حَقٍّ ۙ وَّنَقُوْلُ ذُوْقُوْا عَذَابَ الْحَرِيْقِ ﴿۱۸۲﴾

183. That is because of that which your hands have sent on before *yourselves*, and *the truth is* that Allah is not at all unjust to *His* servants.

ذٰلِكَ بِمَا قَدَّمَتْ اَيْدِيْكُمْ وَاَنَّ اللّٰهَ لَيْسَ بِظَلَّامٍ لِّلْعَبِيْدِ ﴿۱۸۳﴾

184. Those who say, 'Allah has charged us not to believe in any Messenger until he bring us an offering which fire devours.' Say, 'There have already come to you Messengers before me with clear Signs and with that which you speak of. Why, then, did you seek to kill them, if you are truthful?'

اَلَّذِيْنَ قَالُوْۗا اِنَّ اللّٰهَ عَهِدَ اِلَيْنَاۗ اَلَّا نُؤْمِنَ لِرَسُوْلٍ حَتّٰى يَاْتِيَنَا بِقُرْبَانٍ تَاْكُلُهُ النَّارُ ۭ قُلْ قَدْ جَاۗءَكُمْ رُسُلٌ مِّنْ قَبْلِيْ بِالْبَيِّنٰتِ وَبِالَّذِيْ قُلْتُمْ فَلِمَ قَتَلْتُمُوْھُمْ اِنْ كُنْتُمْ صٰدِقِيْنَ ﴿۱۸۴﴾

* 185. And if they accuse thee of lying, even so were accused of lying Messengers before thee who came with clear Signs and books of wisdom and the shining Book.

فَاِنْ كَذَّبُوْكَ فَقَدْ كُذِّبَ رُسُلٌ مِّنْ قَبْلِكَ جَاۗءُوْ بِالْبَيِّنٰتِ وَالزُّبُرِ وَالْكِتٰبِ الْمُنِيْرِ ﴿۱۸۵﴾

186. Every soul shall taste of death. And you shall be paid in full your rewards only on the Day of Resurrection. So whosoever is removed away from the Fire and is made to enter Heaven has indeed attained his goal. And the life of this world is nothing but an illusory enjoyment.

كُلُّ نَفْسٍ ذَاۗىِٕقَةُ الْمَوْتِ ۭ وَاِنَّمَا تُوَفَّوْنَ اُجُوْرَكُمْ يَوْمَ الْقِيٰمَةِ ۭ فَمَنْ زُحْزِحَ عَنِ النَّارِ وَاُدْخِلَ الْجَنَّةَ فَقَدْ فَازَ ۭ وَمَا الْحَيٰوةُ الدُّنْيَاۗ اِلَّا مَتَاعُ الْغُرُوْرِ ﴿۱۸۶﴾

187. You shall surely be tried in your possessions and in your persons and you shall surely hear many hurtful things from those who were given the Book before you and from those who set up equals *to God*. But if you show fortitude and act righteously, that indeed is *a matter* of strong determination.

لَتُبْلَوُنَّ فِيْٓ اَمْوَالِكُمْ وَاَنْفُسِكُمْ وَلَتَسْمَعُنَّ مِنَ الَّذِيْنَ
اُوْتُوا الْكِتٰبَ مِنْ قَبْلِكُمْ وَمِنَ الَّذِيْنَ اَشْرَكُوْٓا اَذًى
كَثِيْرًا ۭ وَاِنْ تَصْبِرُوْا وَتَتَّقُوْا فَاِنَّ ذٰلِكَ مِنْ عَزْمِ
الْاُمُوْرِ ﴿١٨٧﴾

188. And *remember* when Allah took a covenant from those who were given the Book, *saying*, 'You shall make this *Book* known to the people and not conceal it.' But they threw it away behind their backs, and bartered it for a paltry price. Evil is that which they have purchased.

وَاِذْ اَخَذَ اللّٰهُ مِيْثَاقَ الَّذِيْنَ اُوْتُوا الْكِتٰبَ لَتُبَيِّنُنَّهٗ
لِلنَّاسِ وَلَا تَكْتُمُوْنَهٗ ۡ فَنَبَذُوْهُ وَرَآءَ ظُهُوْرِهِمْ
وَاشْتَرَوْا بِهٖ ثَمَنًا قَلِيْلًا ۭ فَبِئْسَ مَا يَشْتَرُوْنَ ﴿١٨٨﴾

189. Think not that those who exult in what they have done, and love to be praised for what they have not done—think not that they are secure from punishment. They shall suffer a grievous chastisement.

لَا تَحْسَبَنَّ الَّذِيْنَ يَفْرَحُوْنَ بِمَآ اَتَوْا وَّيُحِبُّوْنَ اَنْ
يُّحْمَدُوْا بِمَا لَمْ يَفْعَلُوْا فَلَا تَحْسَبَنَّهُمْ بِمَفَازَةٍ مِّنَ
الْعَذَابِ ۚ وَلَهُمْ عَذَابٌ اَلِيْمٌ ﴿١٨٩﴾

190. And to Allah belongs the kingdom of the heavens and the earth; and Allah has power over all things.

وَلِلّٰهِ مُلْكُ السَّمٰوٰتِ وَالْاَرْضِ ۭ وَاللّٰهُ عَلٰى كُلِّ شَيْءٍ
قَدِيْرٌ ﴿١٩٠﴾

R. 20.

191. In the creation of the heavens and the earth and in the alternation of the night and the day there are indeed Signs for men of understanding;

اِنَّ فِيْ خَلْقِ السَّمٰوٰتِ وَالْاَرْضِ وَاخْتِلَافِ الَّيْلِ
وَالنَّهَارِ لَاٰيٰتٍ لِّاُولِي الْاَلْبَابِ ﴿١٩١﴾

192. Those who remember Allah while standing, sitting, and *lying* on their sides, and ponder over the creation of the heavens and the earth: "Our Lord, Thou hast not created this in vain; *nay*, Holy art Thou; save us, then, from the punishment of the Fire.

الَّذِيْنَ يَذْكُرُوْنَ اللّٰهَ قِيٰمًا وَّقُعُوْدًا وَّعَلٰى جُنُوْبِهِمْ
وَيَتَفَكَّرُوْنَ فِيْ خَلْقِ السَّمٰوٰتِ وَالْاَرْضِ ۚ رَبَّنَا مَا
خَلَقْتَ هٰذَا بَاطِلًا ۚ سُبْحٰنَكَ فَقِنَا عَذَابَ النَّارِ ﴿١٩٢﴾

193. "Our Lord, whomsoever Thou causest to enter the Fire, him hast Thou surely disgraced. And the wrongdoers shall have no helpers.

رَبَّنَآ اِنَّكَ مَنْ تُدْخِلِ النَّارَ فَقَدْ اَخْزَيْتَهٗ ۭ وَمَا
لِلظّٰلِمِيْنَ مِنْ اَنْصَارٍ ﴿١٩٣﴾

* 194. "Our Lord, we have heard a Crier calling *us* unto faith, 'Believe ye in your Lord,' and we have believed. Our Lord, forgive us, therefore, our errors and remove from us our evils, and in death number us with the righteous.

رَبَّنَآ اِنَّنَا سَمِعْنَا مُنَادِيًا يُّنَادِيْ لِلْاِيْمَانِ اَنْ اٰمِنُوْا
بِرَبِّكُمْ فَاٰمَنَّا ۖ رَبَّنَا فَاغْفِرْ لَنَا ذُنُوْبَنَا وَكَفِّرْ عَنَّا
سَيِّاٰتِنَا وَتَوَفَّنَا مَعَ الْاَبْرَارِ ﴿١٩٤﴾

195. "Our Lord, give us what Thou hast promised to us through Thy Messengers; and disgrace us not on the Day of Resurrection. Surely, Thou breakest not Thy promise."

رَبَّنَا وَاٰتِنَا مَا وَعَدْتَّنَا عَلٰى رُسُلِكَ وَلَا تُخْزِنَا يَوْمَ
الْقِيٰمَةِ ؕ اِنَّكَ لَا تُخْلِفُ الْمِيْعَادَ ﴿۱۹۵﴾

196. So their Lord answered their *prayers, saying*, 'I will allow not the work of any worker from among you, whether male or female, to be lost. You are from one another. Those, therefore, who have emigrated, and have been driven out from their homes, and have been persecuted in My cause, and have fought and been killed, I will surely remove from them their evils and will cause them to enter Gardens through which streams flow—a reward from Allah, and with Allah is the best of rewards.'

فَاسْتَجَابَ لَهُمْ رَبُّهُمْ اَنِّيْ لَاۤ اُضِيْعُ عَمَلَ عَامِلٍ
مِّنْكُمْ مِّنْ ذَكَرٍ اَوْ اُنْثٰى ۚ بَعْضُكُمْ مِّنْۢ بَعْضٍ ۚ فَالَّذِيْنَ
هَاجَرُوْا وَاُخْرِجُوْا مِنْ دِيَارِهِمْ وَاُوْذُوْا فِيْ سَبِيْلِيْ
وَقٰتَلُوْا وَقُتِلُوْا لَاُكَفِّرَنَّ عَنْهُمْ سَيِّاٰتِهِمْ وَلَاُدْخِلَنَّهُمْ
جَنّٰتٍ تَجْرِيْ مِنْ تَحْتِهَا الْاَنْهٰرُ ۚ ثَوَابًا مِّنْ عِنْدِ
اللّٰهِ ؕ وَاللّٰهُ عِنْدَهٗ حُسْنُ الثَّوَابِ ﴿۱۹۶﴾

197. Let not the moving about of the disbelievers in the land deceive thee.

لَا يَغُرَّنَّكَ تَقَلُّبُ الَّذِيْنَ كَفَرُوْا فِي الْبِلَادِ ؕ ﴿۱۹۷﴾

198. *It is* a small *and brief* advantage, then Hell shall be their abode. What an evil place of rest!

مَتَاعٌ قَلِيْلٌ ۟ ثُمَّ مَاْوٰىهُمْ جَهَنَّمُ ؕ وَبِئْسَ الْمِهَادُ ﴿۱۹۸﴾

199. But those who fear their Lord shall have Gardens through which streams flow; therein shall they abide—an entertainment from Allah. And that which is with Allah is still better for the righteous.

لٰكِنِ الَّذِيْنَ اتَّقَوْا رَبَّهُمْ لَهُمْ جَنّٰتٌ تَجْرِيْ مِنْ تَحْتِهَا
الْاَنْهٰرُ خٰلِدِيْنَ فِيْهَا نُزُلًا مِّنْ عِنْدِ اللّٰهِ ؕ وَمَا عِنْدَ
اللّٰهِ خَيْرٌ لِّلْاَبْرَارِ ﴿۱۹۹﴾ الثلث

200. And surely among the People of the Book there are some who believe in Allah and in what has been sent down to you and in what was sent down to them, humbling themselves before Allah. They barter not the Signs of Allah for a paltry price. It is these who shall have their reward with their Lord. Surely, Allah is swift to take account.

وَاِنَّ مِنْ اَهْلِ الْكِتٰبِ لَمَنْ يُّؤْمِنُ بِاللّٰهِ وَمَاۤ اُنْزِلَ
اِلَيْكُمْ وَمَاۤ اُنْزِلَ اِلَيْهِمْ خٰشِعِيْنَ لِلّٰهِ ۙ لَا يَشْتَرُوْنَ
بِاٰيٰتِ اللّٰهِ ثَمَنًا قَلِيْلًا ؕ اُولٰٓئِكَ لَهُمْ اَجْرُهُمْ عِنْدَ
رَبِّهِمْ ؕ اِنَّ اللّٰهَ سَرِيْعُ الْحِسَابِ ﴿۲۰۰﴾

201. O ye who believe! be steadfast and strive to excel in steadfastness and be on *your* guard and fear Allah that you may prosper.

يٰۤاَيُّهَا الَّذِيْنَ اٰمَنُوا اصْبِرُوْا وَصَابِرُوْا وَرَابِطُوْا ۟ وَ
اتَّقُوا اللّٰهَ لَعَلَّكُمْ تُفْلِحُوْنَ ﴿۲۰۱﴾ ع ٢٠ ١١

سُوْرَةُ النِّسَآءِ مَدَنِيَّةٌ

AL-NISĀ

(Revealed after Hijra)

1. In the name of Allah, the Gracious, the Merciful.

بِسْمِ اللّٰهِ الرَّحْمٰنِ الرَّحِيْمِ ۝١

* 2. O ye people! fear your Lord, Who created you from a single soul and created therefrom its mate, and from them twain spread many men and women; and fear Allah, in Whose name you appeal to one another, and *fear Him particularly respecting* ties of relationship. Verily, Allah watches over you.

يٰٓاَيُّهَا النَّاسُ اتَّقُوْا رَبَّكُمُ الَّذِيْ خَلَقَكُمْ مِّنْ نَّفْسٍ
وَّاحِدَةٍ وَّخَلَقَ مِنْهَا زَوْجَهَا وَبَثَّ مِنْهُمَا رِجَالًا كَثِيْرًا
وَّنِسَآءً ۚ وَاتَّقُوا اللّٰهَ الَّذِيْ تَسَآءَلُوْنَ بِهٖ وَالْاَرْحَامَ ؕ
اِنَّ اللّٰهَ كَانَ عَلَيْكُمْ رَقِيْبًا ۝٢

3. And give to the orphans their property and exchange not the bad for the good, and devour not their property with your own. Surely, it is a great sin.

وَاٰتُوا الْيَتٰمٰٓى اَمْوَالَهُمْ وَلَا تَتَبَدَّلُوا الْخَبِيْثَ بِالطَّيِّبِ ۪
وَلَا تَاْكُلُوْٓا اَمْوَالَهُمْ اِلٰٓى اَمْوَالِكُمْ ؕ اِنَّهٗ كَانَ حُوْبًا
كَبِيْرًا ۝٣

* 4. And if you fear that you will not be fair in dealing with the orphans, then marry of women as may be agreeable to you, two, or three, or four; and if you fear you will not deal justly, then *marry only* one or what your right hands possess. That is the nearest *way* for you to avoid injustice.

وَاِنْ خِفْتُمْ اَلَّا تُقْسِطُوْا فِي الْيَتٰمٰى فَانْكِحُوْا مَا طَابَ
لَكُمْ مِّنَ النِّسَآءِ مَثْنٰى وَثُلٰثَ وَرُبٰعَ ۚ فَاِنْ خِفْتُمْ
اَلَّا تَعْدِلُوْا فَوَاحِدَةً اَوْ مَا مَلَكَتْ اَيْمَانُكُمْ ؕ ذٰلِكَ
اَدْنٰٓى اَلَّا تَعُوْلُوْا ؕ ۝٤

5. And give the women their dowries willingly. But if they, of their own pleasure, remit to you a part thereof, then enjoy it as something pleasant and wholesome.

وَاٰتُوا النِّسَآءَ صَدُقٰتِهِنَّ نِحْلَةً ؕ فَاِنْ طِبْنَ لَكُمْ
عَنْ شَيْءٍ مِّنْهُ نَفْسًا فَكُلُوْهُ هَنِيْٓـًٔا مَّرِيْٓـًٔا ۝٥

* 6. And give not to the foolish your property which Allah has made for you a means of support; but feed them therewith and clothe them and speak to them words of kind advice.

وَلَا تُؤْتُوا السُّفَهَآءَ اَمْوَالَكُمُ الَّتِيْ جَعَلَ اللّٰهُ لَكُمْ
قِيٰمًا وَّارْزُقُوْهُمْ فِيْهَا وَاكْسُوْهُمْ وَقُوْلُوْا لَهُمْ
قَوْلًا مَّعْرُوْفًا ۝٦

* 7. And prove the orphans until they attain *the age of* marriage; then, if you find in them sound judgment, deliver to them their property; and devour it not in

وَابْتَلُوا الْيَتٰمٰى حَتّٰٓى اِذَا بَلَغُوا النِّكَاحَ ۚ فَاِنْ اٰنَسْتُمْ
مِّنْهُمْ رُشْدًا فَادْفَعُوْٓا اِلَيْهِمْ اَمْوَالَهُمْ ۚ وَلَا تَاْكُلُوْهَآ

extravagance and haste against their growing up. And whoso is rich, let him abstain; and whoso is poor, let him eat *thereof* with equity. And when you deliver to them their property, then call witnesses in their presence. And Allah is sufficient as a Reckoner.

8. For men is a share of that which parents and near relations leave; and for women is a share of that which parents and near relations leave, whether it be little or much—a determined share.

9. And when *other* relations and orphans and the poor are present at the division *of heritage*, give them *something* therefrom and speak to them words of kindness.

10. And let those fear *God* who, if they should leave behind them their own weak offspring, would be anxious for them. Let them, therefore, fear Allah and let them say the right word.

11. Surely, they who devour the property of orphans unjustly, only swallow fire into their bellies, and they shall burn in a blazing fire.

R. 2.

12. Allah commands you concerning your children: a male shall have as much as the share of two females; but if there be females *only, numbering* more than two, then they shall have two-thirds of what the *deceased* leaves; and if there be one, she shall have the half. And his parents shall have each of them a sixth of the inheritance, if he have a child; but if he have no child and his parents be his heirs, then his mother shall have a third; and if he have brothers and sisters, then his mother shall have a sixth, after *the payment of* any bequests he may have bequeathed or of debt. Your fathers and your children, you know not which of them is nearest to you in benefit. *This* fixing *of portions* is from Allah. Surely, Allah is All-Knowing, Wise.

* 13. And you shall have half of that which your wives leave, if they have no child; but if they have a child, then you

إِسْرَافًا وَبِدَارًا أَنْ يَكْبَرُوا ۚ وَمَنْ كَانَ غَنِيًّا فَلْيَسْتَعْفِفْ ۖ
وَمَنْ كَانَ فَقِيرًا فَلْيَأْكُلْ بِالْمَعْرُوفِ ۚ فَإِذَا دَفَعْتُمْ
إِلَيْهِمْ أَمْوَالَهُمْ فَأَشْهِدُوا عَلَيْهِمْ ۚ وَكَفَىٰ بِاللَّهِ حَسِيبًا ﴿٧﴾
لِلرِّجَالِ نَصِيبٌ مِمَّا تَرَكَ الْوَالِدَانِ وَالْأَقْرَبُونَ وَلِلنِّسَاءِ نَصِيبٌ مِمَّا
تَرَكَ الْوَالِدَانِ وَالْأَقْرَبُونَ مِمَّا قَلَّ مِنْهُ أَوْ كَثُرَ ۚ نَصِيبًا مَفْرُوضًا ﴿٨﴾
وَإِذَا حَضَرَ الْقِسْمَةَ أُولُو الْقُرْبَىٰ وَالْيَتَامَىٰ وَالْمَسَاكِينُ
فَارْزُقُوهُمْ مِنْهُ وَقُولُوا لَهُمْ قَوْلًا مَعْرُوفًا ﴿٩﴾
وَلْيَخْشَ الَّذِينَ لَوْ تَرَكُوا مِنْ خَلْفِهِمْ ذُرِّيَّةً ضِعَافًا
خَافُوا عَلَيْهِمْ فَلْيَتَّقُوا اللَّهَ وَلْيَقُولُوا قَوْلًا سَدِيدًا ﴿١٠﴾
إِنَّ الَّذِينَ يَأْكُلُونَ أَمْوَالَ الْيَتَامَىٰ ظُلْمًا إِنَّمَا يَأْكُلُونَ
فِي بُطُونِهِمْ نَارًا ۖ وَسَيَصْلَوْنَ سَعِيرًا ﴿١١﴾ ع
يُوصِيكُمُ اللَّهُ فِي أَوْلَادِكُمْ ۖ لِلذَّكَرِ مِثْلُ حَظِّ الْأُنْثَيَيْنِ ۚ
فَإِنْ كُنَّ نِسَاءً فَوْقَ اثْنَتَيْنِ فَلَهُنَّ ثُلُثَا مَا تَرَكَ ۖ
وَإِنْ كَانَتْ وَاحِدَةً فَلَهَا النِّصْفُ ۚ وَلِأَبَوَيْهِ لِكُلِّ
وَاحِدٍ مِنْهُمَا السُّدُسُ مِمَّا تَرَكَ إِنْ كَانَ لَهُ وَلَدٌ ۚ
فَإِنْ لَمْ يَكُنْ لَهُ وَلَدٌ وَوَرِثَهُ أَبَوَاهُ فَلِأُمِّهِ الثُّلُثُ ۚ
فَإِنْ كَانَ لَهُ إِخْوَةٌ فَلِأُمِّهِ السُّدُسُ ۚ مِنْ بَعْدِ وَصِيَّةٍ
يُوصِي بِهَا أَوْ دَيْنٍ ۗ آبَاؤُكُمْ وَأَبْنَاؤُكُمْ لَا تَدْرُونَ
أَيُّهُمْ أَقْرَبُ لَكُمْ نَفْعًا ۚ فَرِيضَةً مِنَ اللَّهِ ۗ إِنَّ اللَّهَ كَانَ
عَلِيمًا حَكِيمًا ﴿١٢﴾
وَلَكُمْ نِصْفُ مَا تَرَكَ أَزْوَاجُكُمْ إِنْ لَمْ يَكُنْ لَهُنَّ
وَلَدٌ ۚ فَإِنْ كَانَ لَهُنَّ وَلَدٌ فَلَكُمُ الرُّبُعُ مِمَّا تَرَكْنَ

shall have a fourth of that which they leave, after *the payment of* any bequests they may have bequeathed or of debt. And they shall have a fourth of that which you leave, if you have no child; but if you have a child, then they shall have an eighth of that which you leave, after *the payment of* any bequests you may have bequeathed or of debt. And if there be a man or a woman whose heritage is to be divided and he *or she* has neither parent nor child, and he *or she* has a brother or a sister, then each one of them shall have a sixth. But if they be more than that, then they shall be *equal* sharers in one-third, after *the payment of* any bequests which may have been bequeathed or of debt, without prejudice *to the debt. This is* an injunction from Allah, and Allah is All-Knowing, Forbearing.

14. These are the limits *set* by Allah; and whoso obeys Allah and His Messenger, He will make him enter Gardens through which streams flow; therein shall they abide; and that is a great triumph.

15. And whoso disobeys Allah and His Messenger and transgresses His limits, He will make him enter into Fire; therein shall he abide; and he shall have an humiliating punishment.

R. 3.

16. And those of your women who are guilty of lewdness—call to witness four of you against them; and if they bear witness, then confine them to the houses until death overtake them or Allah open for them a way.

17. And if two men from among you are guilty of it, punish them both. And if they repent and amend, then leave them alone; surely, Allah is Oft-Returning *with compassion and is* Merciful.

18. Verily, Allah undertakes to accept the repentance of only those who do evil ignorantly and then repent soon after. These are they to whom Allah turns with mercy; and Allah is All-Knowing, Wise.

مِنۢ بَعۡدِ وَصِيَّةٍ يُّوۡصِيۡنَ بِهَاۤ اَوۡ دَيۡنٍ ؕ وَلَهُنَّ الرُّبُعُ
مِمَّا تَرَكۡتُمۡ اِنۡ لَّمۡ يَكُنۡ لَّكُمۡ وَلَدٌ ۚ فَاِنۡ كَانَ لَكُمۡ وَلَدٌ
فَلَهُنَّ الثُّمُنُ مِمَّا تَرَكۡتُمۡ مِّنۢ بَعۡدِ وَصِيَّةٍ تُوۡصُوۡنَ
بِهَاۤ اَوۡ دَيۡنٍ ؕ وَاِنۡ كَانَ رَجُلٌ يُّوۡرَثُ كَلٰلَةً اَوِ امۡرَاَةٌ
وَّلَهٗۤ اَخٌ اَوۡ اُخۡتٌ فَلِكُلِّ وَاحِدٍ مِّنۡهُمَا السُّدُسُ ۚ فَاِنۡ
كَانُوۡۤا اَكۡثَرَ مِنۡ ذٰلِكَ فَهُمۡ شُرَكَآءُ فِى الثُّلُثِ مِنۢ
بَعۡدِ وَصِيَّةٍ يُّوۡصٰى بِهَاۤ اَوۡ دَيۡنٍ ۙ غَيۡرَ مُضَآرٍّ ۚ وَصِيَّةً
مِّنَ اللّٰهِ ؕ وَاللّٰهُ عَلِيۡمٌ حَلِيۡمٌ ﴿۱۳﴾ ؕ
تِلۡكَ حُدُوۡدُ اللّٰهِ ؕ وَمَنۡ يُّطِعِ اللّٰهَ وَرَسُوۡلَهٗ يُدۡخِلۡهُ
جَنّٰتٍ تَجۡرِىۡ مِنۡ تَحۡتِهَا الۡاَنۡهٰرُ خٰلِدِيۡنَ فِيۡهَا ؕ وَ
ذٰلِكَ الۡفَوۡزُ الۡعَظِيۡمُ ﴿۱۴﴾
وَمَنۡ يَّعۡصِ اللّٰهَ وَرَسُوۡلَهٗ وَيَتَعَدَّ حُدُوۡدَهٗ يُدۡخِلۡهُ
نَارًا خَالِدًا فِيۡهَا ۖ وَلَهٗ عَذَابٌ مُّهِيۡنٌ ﴿۱۵﴾ ع ۲ ۳ ۱۳
وَالّٰتِىۡ يَاۡتِيۡنَ الۡفَاحِشَةَ مِنۡ نِّسَآٮِٕكُمۡ فَاسۡتَشۡهِدُوۡا
عَلَيۡهِنَّ اَرۡبَعَةً مِّنۡكُمۡ ۚ فَاِنۡ شَهِدُوۡا فَاَمۡسِكُوۡهُنَّ
فِى الۡبُيُوۡتِ حَتّٰى يَتَوَفّٰٮهُنَّ الۡمَوۡتُ اَوۡ يَجۡعَلَ اللّٰهُ
لَهُنَّ سَبِيۡلًا ﴿۱۶﴾
وَالَّذٰنِ يَاۡتِيٰنِهَا مِنۡكُمۡ فَاٰذُوۡهُمَا ۚ فَاِنۡ تَابَا وَاَصۡلَحَا
فَاَعۡرِضُوۡا عَنۡهُمَا ؕ اِنَّ اللّٰهَ كَانَ تَوَّابًا رَّحِيۡمًا ﴿۱۷﴾
اِنَّمَا التَّوۡبَةُ عَلَى اللّٰهِ لِلَّذِيۡنَ يَعۡمَلُوۡنَ السُّوۡٓءَ بِجَهَالَةٍ
ثُمَّ يَتُوۡبُوۡنَ مِنۡ قَرِيۡبٍ فَاُولٰٓٮِٕكَ يَتُوۡبُ اللّٰهُ عَلَيۡهِمۡ ؕ
وَكَانَ اللّٰهُ عَلِيۡمًا حَكِيۡمًا ﴿۱۸﴾

19. There is no *acceptance of* repentance for those who *continue to* do evil until, when death faces one of them, he says, 'I do repent now;' nor for those who die disbelievers. It is these for whom We have prepared a painful punishment.

وَلَيْسَتِ التَّوْبَةُ لِلَّذِيْنَ يَعْمَلُوْنَ السَّيِّاٰتِ ۚ حَتّٰۤى اِذَا
حَضَرَ اَحَدَهُمُ الْمَوْتُ قَالَ اِنِّيْ تُبْتُ الْـٰٔنَ وَ لَا
الَّذِيْنَ يَمُوْتُوْنَ وَ هُمْ كُفَّارٌ ؕ اُولٰٓئِكَ اَعْتَدْنَا
لَهُمْ عَذَابًا اَلِيْمًا ﴿۱۹﴾

20. O ye who believe! it is not lawful for you to inherit women against their will; nor should you detain them wrongfully that you may take away part of that which you have given them, except that they be guilty of a flagrant evil; and consort with them in kindness; and if you dislike them, it may be that you dislike a thing wherein Allah has placed much good.

يٰۤاَيُّهَا الَّذِيْنَ اٰمَنُوْا لَا يَحِلُّ لَكُمْ اَنْ تَرِثُوا النِّسَآءَ كَرْهًا ؕ
وَ لَا تَعْضُلُوْهُنَّ لِتَذْهَبُوْا بِبَعْضِ مَاۤ اٰتَيْتُمُوْهُنَّ
اِلَّاۤ اَنْ يَّاْتِيْنَ بِفَاحِشَةٍ مُّبَيِّنَةٍ ۚ وَعَاشِرُوْهُنَّ بِالْمَعْرُوْفِ ۚ
فَاِنْ كَرِهْتُمُوْهُنَّ فَعَسٰۤى اَنْ تَكْرَهُوْا شَيْـًٔا وَّ يَجْعَلَ اللّٰهُ
فِيْهِ خَيْرًا كَثِيْرًا ﴿۲۰﴾

21. And if you desire to take one wife in place of another and you have given one of them a treasure, take not aught therefrom. Will you take it by lying and with manifest sinfulness?

وَاِنْ اَرَدْتُّمُ اسْتِبْدَالَ زَوْجٍ مَّكَانَ زَوْجٍ ۙ وَّ
اٰتَيْتُمْ اِحْدٰىهُنَّ قِنْطَارًا فَلَا تَاْخُذُوْا مِنْهُ شَيْـًٔا ؕ
اَتَاْخُذُوْنَهٗ بُهْتَانًا وَّ اِثْمًا مُّبِيْنًا ﴿۲۱﴾

22. And how can you take it when one of you has been alone with the other, and they (the women) have taken from you a strong covenant?

وَ كَيْفَ تَاْخُذُوْنَهٗ وَقَدْ اَفْضٰى بَعْضُكُمْ اِلٰى بَعْضٍ
وَّاَخَذْنَ مِنْكُمْ مِّيْثَاقًا غَلِيْظًا ﴿۲۲﴾

23. And marry not those women whom your fathers married, except what has already passed. It is a thing foul and hateful and an evil way.

وَ لَا تَنْكِحُوْا مَا نَكَحَ اٰبَآؤُكُمْ مِّنَ النِّسَآءِ اِلَّا مَا قَدْ
سَلَفَ ؕ اِنَّهٗ كَانَ فَاحِشَةً وَّ مَقْتًا ؕ وَسَآءَ سَبِيْلًا ﴿۲۳﴾ ع ۴

R. 4.

24. Forbidden to you are your mothers, and your daughters, and your sisters, and your fathers' sisters, and your mothers' sisters, and brother's daughters, and sister's daughters, and your *foster*-mothers that have given you suck, and your foster-sisters, and the mothers of your wives, and your step-daughters, who are your wards by your wives unto whom you have gone in —but if you have not gone in unto them, there shall be no sin upon you—and the wives of your sons that are from your loins;

حُرِّمَتْ عَلَيْكُمْ اُمَّهٰتُكُمْ وَ بَنٰتُكُمْ وَاَخَوٰتُكُمْ وَعَمّٰتُكُمْ
وَخٰلٰتُكُمْ وَ بَنٰتُ الْاَخِ وَ بَنٰتُ الْاُخْتِ وَاُمَّهٰتُكُمُ
الّٰتِيْۤ اَرْضَعْنَكُمْ وَ اَخَوٰتُكُمْ مِّنَ الرَّضَاعَةِ وَ اُمَّهٰتُ
نِسَآئِكُمْ وَ رَبَآئِبُكُمُ الّٰتِيْ فِيْ حُجُوْرِكُمْ مِّنْ نِّسَآئِكُمُ
الّٰتِيْ دَخَلْتُمْ بِهِنَّ ۫ فَاِنْ لَّمْ تَكُوْنُوْا دَخَلْتُمْ بِهِنَّ فَلَا
جُنَاحَ عَلَيْكُمْ ۫ وَحَلَآئِلُ اَبْنَآئِكُمُ الَّذِيْنَ مِنْ

and *it is forbidden to you* to have two sisters together *in marriage*, except what has already passed; surely, Allah is Most Forgiving, Merciful.

اَصْلَابِكُمْ وَاَنْ تَجْمَعُوْا بَيْنَ الْاُخْتَيْنِ اِلَّا مَا قَدْ
سَلَفَ اِنَّ اللّٰهَ كَانَ غَفُوْرًا رَّحِيْمًا ﴿٢٤﴾

25. And *forbidden to you are* married women, except such as your right hands possess. This has Allah enjoined on you. And allowed to you are those beyond that, that you seek *them* by means of your property, marrying them properly and not committing fornication. And for the benefit you receive from them, give them their dowries, as fixed, and there shall be no sin for you in anything you mutually agree upon, after the fixing *of the dowry*. Surely, Allah is All-Knowing, Wise.

الجزء ٥
وَالْمُحْصَنٰتُ مِنَ النِّسَآءِ اِلَّا مَا مَلَكَتْ اَيْمَانُكُمْ
كِتٰبَ اللّٰهِ عَلَيْكُمْ وَاُحِلَّ لَكُمْ مَّا وَرَآءَ ذٰلِكُمْ اَنْ
تَبْتَغُوْا بِاَمْوَالِكُمْ مُّحْصِنِيْنَ غَيْرَ مُسٰفِحِيْنَ فَمَا
اسْتَمْتَعْتُمْ بِهٖ مِنْهُنَّ فَاٰتُوْهُنَّ اُجُوْرَهُنَّ فَرِيْضَةً
وَلَا جُنَاحَ عَلَيْكُمْ فِيْمَا تَرٰضَيْتُمْ بِهٖ مِنْۢ بَعْدِ الْفَرِيْضَةِ
اِنَّ اللّٰهَ كَانَ عَلِيْمًا حَكِيْمًا ﴿٢٥﴾

26. And whoso of you cannot afford to marry free, believing women, *let him* marry what your right hands possess, namely, your believing handmaids. And Allah knows your faith best; you are *all* one from another; so marry them with the leave of their masters and give them their dowries according to what is fair, they being chaste, not committing fornication, nor taking secret paramours. And if, after they are married, they are guilty of lewdness, they shall have half the punishment prescribed for free women. This is for him among you who fears lest he should commit sin. And that you restrain yourselves is better for you; and Allah is Most Forgiving, Merciful.

وَمَنْ لَّمْ يَسْتَطِعْ مِنْكُمْ طَوْلًا اَنْ يَّنْكِحَ الْمُحْصَنٰتِ
الْمُؤْمِنٰتِ فَمِنْ مَّا مَلَكَتْ اَيْمَانُكُمْ مِّنْ فَتَيٰتِكُمُ
الْمُؤْمِنٰتِ وَاللّٰهُ اَعْلَمُ بِاِيْمَانِكُمْ بَعْضُكُمْ مِّنْۢ
بَعْضٍ فَانْكِحُوْهُنَّ بِاِذْنِ اَهْلِهِنَّ وَاٰتُوْهُنَّ
اُجُوْرَهُنَّ بِالْمَعْرُوْفِ مُحْصَنٰتٍ غَيْرَ مُسٰفِحٰتٍ
وَّلَا مُتَّخِذٰتِ اَخْدَانٍ فَاِذَآ اُحْصِنَّ فَاِنْ اَتَيْنَ
بِفَاحِشَةٍ فَعَلَيْهِنَّ نِصْفُ مَا عَلَى الْمُحْصَنٰتِ مِنَ
الْعَذَابِ ذٰلِكَ لِمَنْ خَشِيَ الْعَنَتَ مِنْكُمْ وَاَنْ
تَصْبِرُوْا خَيْرٌ لَّكُمْ وَاللّٰهُ غَفُوْرٌ رَّحِيْمٌ ﴿٢٦﴾ ع ٤

R. 5.

27. Allah desires to make clear to you, and guide you to, the paths of those before you, and to turn to you in mercy. And Allah is All-Knowing, Wise.

يُرِيْدُ اللّٰهُ لِيُبَيِّنَ لَكُمْ وَيَهْدِيَكُمْ سُنَنَ الَّذِيْنَ
مِنْ قَبْلِكُمْ وَيَتُوْبَ عَلَيْكُمْ وَاللّٰهُ عَلِيْمٌ حَكِيْمٌ ﴿٢٧﴾

28. And Allah wishes to turn to you in mercy, but those who follow *their* low desires wish that you should stray far away.

وَاللّٰهُ يُرِيْدُ اَنْ يَّتُوْبَ عَلَيْكُمْ وَيُرِيْدُ الَّذِيْنَ يَتَّبِعُوْنَ
الشَّهَوٰتِ اَنْ تَمِيْلُوْا مَيْلًا عَظِيْمًا ﴿٢٨﴾

29. Allah desires to lighten your burden, for man has been created weak.

يُرِيْدُ اللّٰهُ اَنْ يُّخَفِّفَ عَنْكُمْ وَخُلِقَ الْاِنْسَانُ ضَعِيْفًا ﴿٢٩﴾

30. O ye who believe! devour not your property among yourselves by unlawful means, except that *you earn* by trade with mutual consent. And kill not yourselves. Surely, Allah is Merciful to you.

يٰٓاَيُّهَا الَّذِيْنَ اٰمَنُوْا لَا تَاْكُلُوْٓا اَمْوَالَكُمْ بَيْنَكُمْ
بِالْبَاطِلِ اِلَّآ اَنْ تَكُوْنَ تِجَارَةً عَنْ تَرَاضٍ مِّنْكُمْ
وَلَا تَقْتُلُوْٓا اَنْفُسَكُمْ ؕ اِنَّ اللّٰهَ كَانَ بِكُمْ رَحِيْمًا ﴿۳۰﴾

31. And whosoever does that by way of transgression and injustice, We shall cast him into Fire; and that is easy with Allah.

وَمَنْ يَّفْعَلْ ذٰلِكَ عُدْوَانًا وَّظُلْمًا فَسَوْفَ نُصْلِيْهِ
نَارًا ؕ وَكَانَ ذٰلِكَ عَلَى اللّٰهِ يَسِيْرًا ﴿۳۱﴾

32. If you keep away from the more grievous of the things which are forbidden you, We will remove from you your *minor* evils and admit you to a place of great honour.

اِنْ تَجْتَنِبُوْا كَبَآئِرَ مَا تُنْهَوْنَ عَنْهُ نُكَفِّرْ عَنْكُمْ سَيِّاٰتِكُمْ
وَنُدْخِلْكُمْ مُّدْخَلًا كَرِيْمًا ﴿۳۲﴾

33. And covet not that whereby Allah has made some of you excel others. Men shall have a share of that which they have earned, and women a share of that which they have earned. And ask Allah of His bounty. Surely, Allah has perfect knowledge of all things.

وَلَا تَتَمَنَّوْا مَا فَضَّلَ اللّٰهُ بِهٖ بَعْضَكُمْ عَلٰى بَعْضٍ ؕ
لِلرِّجَالِ نَصِيْبٌ مِّمَّا اكْتَسَبُوْا ؕ وَلِلنِّسَآءِ نَصِيْبٌ مِّمَّا
اكْتَسَبْنَ ؕ وَسْـَٔلُوا اللّٰهَ مِنْ فَضْلِهٖ ؕ اِنَّ اللّٰهَ كَانَ
بِكُلِّ شَيْءٍ عَلِيْمًا ﴿۳۳﴾

34. And to every one We have appointed heirs to what the parents and the relations leave, and *also* those with whom your oaths have ratified a contract. So give them their portion. Surely, Allah watches over all things.

وَلِكُلٍّ جَعَلْنَا مَوَالِيَ مِمَّا تَرَكَ الْوَالِدٰنِ وَالْاَقْرَبُوْنَ ؕ
وَالَّذِيْنَ عَقَدَتْ اَيْمَانُكُمْ فَاٰتُوْهُمْ نَصِيْبَهُمْ ؕ اِنَّ
اللّٰهَ كَانَ عَلٰى كُلِّ شَيْءٍ شَهِيْدًا ﴿۳۴﴾ ع

R. 6.

35. Men are guardians over women because Allah has made some of them excel others, and because they (men) spend of their wealth. So virtuous women *are those who* are obedient, and guard the secrets *of their husbands* with Allah's protection. And *as for* those on whose part you fear disobedience, admonish them and leave them alone in their beds, and chastise them. Then if they obey you, seek not a way against them. Surely, Allah is High, Great.

اَلرِّجَالُ قَوّٰمُوْنَ عَلَى النِّسَآءِ بِمَا فَضَّلَ اللّٰهُ بَعْضَهُمْ
عَلٰى بَعْضٍ وَّبِمَآ اَنْفَقُوْا مِنْ اَمْوَالِهِمْ ؕ فَالصّٰلِحٰتُ
قٰنِتٰتٌ حٰفِظٰتٌ لِّلْغَيْبِ بِمَا حَفِظَ اللّٰهُ ؕ وَالّٰتِيْ تَخَافُوْنَ
نُشُوْزَهُنَّ فَعِظُوْهُنَّ وَاهْجُرُوْهُنَّ فِي الْمَضَاجِعِ
وَاضْرِبُوْهُنَّ ۚ فَاِنْ اَطَعْنَكُمْ فَلَا تَبْغُوْا عَلَيْهِنَّ
سَبِيْلًا ؕ اِنَّ اللّٰهَ كَانَ عَلِيًّا كَبِيْرًا ﴿۳۵﴾

* 36. And if you fear a breach between them, then appoint an arbiter from his folk and an arbiter from her folk. If they (the arbiters) desire reconciliation, Allah

وَاِنْ خِفْتُمْ شِقَاقَ بَيْنِهِمَا فَابْعَثُوْا حَكَمًا مِّنْ
اَهْلِهٖ وَحَكَمًا مِّنْ اَهْلِهَا ۚ اِنْ يُّرِيْدَآ اِصْلَاحًا يُّوَفِّقِ

will effect it between them. Surely, Allah is All-Knowing, All-Aware.

اللّٰهُ بَيْنَهُمَا ۭ اِنَّ اللّٰهَ كَانَ عَلِيْمًا خَبِيْرًا ﴿٣٦﴾

37. And worship Allah and associate naught with Him, and *show* kindness to parents, and to kindred, and orphans, and the needy, and to the neighbour that is a kinsman and the neighbour that is a stranger, and the companion by *your* side, and the wayfarer, and those whom your right hands possess. Surely, Allah loves not the proud *and* the boastful,

وَاعْبُدُوا اللّٰهَ وَلَا تُشْرِكُوْا بِهٖ شَيْـًٔا وَّبِالْوَالِدَيْنِ
اِحْسَانًا وَّبِذِي الْقُرْبٰى وَالْيَتٰمٰى وَالْمَسٰكِيْنِ وَالْجَارِ
ذِي الْقُرْبٰى وَالْجَارِ الْجُنُبِ وَالصَّاحِبِ بِالْجَنْۢبِ
وَابْنِ السَّبِيْلِ ۙ وَمَا مَلَكَتْ اَيْمَانُكُمْ ۭ اِنَّ اللّٰهَ لَا يُحِبُّ
مَنْ كَانَ مُخْتَالًا فَخُوْرَا ۙ ﴿٣٧﴾

38. Who are niggardly and enjoin people to be niggardly, and conceal that which Allah has given them of His bounty. And We have prepared for the disbelievers an humiliating punishment,

اۨلَّذِيْنَ يَبْخَلُوْنَ وَيَاْمُرُوْنَ النَّاسَ بِالْبُخْلِ وَيَكْتُمُوْنَ
مَآ اٰتٰىهُمُ اللّٰهُ مِنْ فَضْلِهٖ ۭ وَاَعْتَدْنَا لِلْكٰفِرِيْنَ عَذَابًا
مُّهِيْنًا ﴿٣٨﴾

39. And for those who spend their wealth to be seen of men, and believe not in Allah nor the Last Day. And whoso has Satan for his companion, *let him remember that* an evil companion is he.

وَالَّذِيْنَ يُنْفِقُوْنَ اَمْوَالَهُمْ رِئَاۗءَ النَّاسِ وَلَا يُؤْمِنُوْنَ
بِاللّٰهِ وَلَا بِالْيَوْمِ الْاٰخِرِ ۭ وَمَنْ يَّكُنِ الشَّيْطٰنُ لَهٗ قَرِيْنًا
فَسَاۗءَ قَرِيْنًا ﴿٣٩﴾

40. And what *harm* would have befallen them, if they had believed in Allah and the Last Day and spent out of what Allah has given them? And Allah knows them full well.

وَمَاذَا عَلَيْهِمْ لَوْ اٰمَنُوْا بِاللّٰهِ وَالْيَوْمِ الْاٰخِرِ وَاَنْفَقُوْا
مِمَّا رَزَقَهُمُ اللّٰهُ ۭ وَكَانَ اللّٰهُ بِهِمْ عَلِيْمًا ﴿٤٠﴾

41. Surely, Allah wrongs not *any one even* by the weight of an atom. And if there be a good deed, He multiplies it and gives from Himself a great reward.

اِنَّ اللّٰهَ لَا يَظْلِمُ مِثْقَالَ ذَرَّةٍ ۚ وَاِنْ تَكُ حَسَنَةً
يُّضٰعِفْهَا وَيُؤْتِ مِنْ لَّدُنْهُ اَجْرًا عَظِيْمًا ﴿٤١﴾

42. And how *will it fare with them* when We shall bring a witness from every people, and shall bring thee as a witness against these!

فَكَيْفَ اِذَا جِئْنَا مِنْ كُلِّ اُمَّةٍۢ بِشَهِيْدٍ وَّجِئْنَا بِكَ
عَلٰى هٰٓؤُلَاۗءِ شَهِيْدًا ﴿٤٢﴾ وقف النبي صلى الله عليه وسلم

43. On that day those who disbelieved and disobeyed the Messenger will wish that the earth were made level with them, and they shall not *be able to* conceal anything from Allah.

يَوْمَىِٕذٍ يَّوَدُّ الَّذِيْنَ كَفَرُوْا وَعَصَوُا الرَّسُوْلَ لَوْ تُسَوّٰى
بِهِمُ الْاَرْضُ ۭ وَلَا يَكْتُمُوْنَ اللّٰهَ حَدِيْثًا ﴿٤٣﴾ ع

R. 7.

* 44. O ye who believe! approach not Prayer when you are not in *full* possession of your senses, until you know what you say, nor when you are unclean, except

يٰٓاَيُّهَا الَّذِيْنَ اٰمَنُوْا لَا تَقْرَبُوا الصَّلٰوةَ وَاَنْتُمْ سُكٰرٰى
حَتّٰى تَعْلَمُوْا مَا تَقُوْلُوْنَ وَلَا جُنُبًا اِلَّا عَابِرِيْ سَبِيْلٍ

when you are travelling along a way, until you have bathed. And if you are ill or *you are* on a journey *while unclean*, or *if* one of you comes from the privy or you have touched women and you find no water, then betake yourselves to pure dust and wipe therewith your faces and your hands. Surely, Allah is Most Indulgent, Most Forgiving.

حَتّٰى تَغْتَسِلُوْا ؕ وَاِنْ كُنْتُمْ مَّرْضٰۤى اَوْ عَلٰى سَفَرٍ اَوْ جَآءَ
اَحَدٌ مِّنْكُمْ مِّنَ الْغَآئِطِ اَوْ لٰمَسْتُمُ النِّسَآءَ فَلَمْ تَجِدُوْا
مَآءً فَتَيَمَّمُوْا صَعِيْدًا طَيِّبًا فَامْسَحُوْا بِوُجُوْهِكُمْ وَ
اَيْدِيْكُمْ ؕ اِنَّ اللّٰهَ كَانَ عَفُوًّا غَفُوْرًا ﴿۴۴﴾

45. Dost thou not know of those who were given a portion of the Book? They buy error and desire that you *too* may lose the way.

اَلَمْ تَرَ اِلَى الَّذِيْنَ اُوْتُوْا نَصِيْبًا مِّنَ الْكِتٰبِ يَشْتَرُوْنَ
الضَّلٰلَةَ وَيُرِيْدُوْنَ اَنْ تَضِلُّوا السَّبِيْلَ ﴿۴۵﴾

46. And Allah knows your enemies full well. And sufficient is Allah as a Friend, and sufficient is Allah as a Helper.

وَاللّٰهُ اَعْلَمُ بِاَعْدَآئِكُمْ ؕ وَكَفٰى بِاللّٰهِ وَلِيًّا ۙ وَّكَفٰى
بِاللّٰهِ نَصِيْرًا ﴿۴۶﴾

* 47. There are some among the Jews who pervert words from their *proper* places. And they say, 'We hear and we disobey,' and 'hear *thou* without being heard,' and 'Rā'inā,' screening with their tongues *what is in their minds* and *seeking* to injure the Faith. And if they had said, 'We hear and we obey,' and 'hear *thou*,' and 'Unẓurnā,' it would have been better for them and more upright. But Allah has cursed them for their disbelief; so they believe but little.

مِنَ الَّذِيْنَ هَادُوْا يُحَرِّفُوْنَ الْكَلِمَ عَنْ مَّوَاضِعِهٖ
وَيَقُوْلُوْنَ سَمِعْنَا وَعَصَيْنَا وَاسْمَعْ غَيْرَ مُسْمَعٍ وَّ
رَاعِنَا لَيًّۢا بِاَلْسِنَتِهِمْ وَطَعْنًا فِى الدِّيْنِ ؕ وَلَوْ اَنَّهُمْ
قَالُوْا سَمِعْنَا وَاَطَعْنَا وَاسْمَعْ وَانْظُرْنَا لَكَانَ خَيْرًا
لَّهُمْ وَاَقْوَمَ ۙ وَلٰكِنْ لَّعَنَهُمُ اللّٰهُ بِكُفْرِهِمْ فَلَا
يُؤْمِنُوْنَ اِلَّا قَلِيْلًا ﴿۴۷﴾

* 48. O ye People of the Book! believe in what We have sent down, fulfilling that which is with you, before We destroy *some of* the leaders and turn them on their backs or curse them as We cursed the People of the Sabbath. And the decree of Allah is *bound* to be carried out.

يٰۤاَيُّهَا الَّذِيْنَ اُوْتُوا الْكِتٰبَ اٰمِنُوْا بِمَا نَزَّلْنَا مُصَدِّقًا
لِّمَا مَعَكُمْ مِّنْ قَبْلِ اَنْ نَّطْمِسَ وُجُوْهًا فَنَرُدَّهَا عَلٰۤى
اَدْبَارِهَاۤ اَوْ نَلْعَنَهُمْ كَمَا لَعَنَّاۤ اَصْحٰبَ السَّبْتِ ؕ وَكَانَ
اَمْرُ اللّٰهِ مَفْعُوْلًا ﴿۴۸﴾

49. Surely, Allah will not forgive that any partner be associated with Him; but He will forgive whatever is short of that to whomsoever He pleases. And whoso associates partners with Allah has indeed devised a very great sin.

اِنَّ اللّٰهَ لَا يَغْفِرُ اَنْ يُّشْرَكَ بِهٖ وَيَغْفِرُ مَا دُوْنَ
ذٰلِكَ لِمَنْ يَّشَآءُ ۚ وَمَنْ يُّشْرِكْ بِاللّٰهِ فَقَدِ افْتَرٰۤى
اِثْمًا عَظِيْمًا ﴿۴۹﴾

50. Dost thou not know of those who hold themselves to be pure? Nay, it is

اَلَمْ تَرَ اِلَى الَّذِيْنَ يُزَكُّوْنَ اَنْفُسَهُمْ ؕ بَلِ اللّٰهُ يُزَكِّيْ

Allah Who purifies whomsoever He pleases, and they will not be wronged a whit.

مَنْ يَّشَآءُ وَلَا يُظْلَمُوْنَ فَتِيْلًا ﴿٥٠﴾

51. Behold, how they forge a lie against Allah! And sufficient is that as a manifest sin.

اُنْظُرْ كَيْفَ يَفْتَرُوْنَ عَلَى اللّٰهِ الْكَذِبَ ؕ وَكَفٰى بِهٖۤ
اِثْمًا مُّبِيْنًا ﴿٥١﴾

R. 8.

52. Dost thou not know of those who were given a portion of the Book? They believe in evil things and *follow* those who transgress, and they say of the disbelievers, 'These are better guided in religion than those who believe.'

اَلَمْ تَرَ اِلَى الَّذِيْنَ اُوْتُوْا نَصِيْبًا مِّنَ الْكِتٰبِ يُؤْمِنُوْنَ
بِالْجِبْتِ وَالطَّاغُوْتِ وَيَقُوْلُوْنَ لِلَّذِيْنَ كَفَرُوْا هٰۤؤُلَآءِ
اَهْدٰى مِنَ الَّذِيْنَ اٰمَنُوْا سَبِيْلًا ﴿٥٢﴾

53. They it is whom Allah has cursed; and he whom Allah curses, thou shalt not find for him a helper.

اُولٰٓئِكَ الَّذِيْنَ لَعَنَهُمُ اللّٰهُ ؕ وَمَنْ يَّلْعَنِ اللّٰهُ فَلَنْ
تَجِدَ لَهٗ نَصِيْرًا ﴿٥٣﴾

54. Have they a share in the kingdom? Then would they not give men *even so much as* the little hollow in the back of a date-stone.

اَمْ لَهُمْ نَصِيْبٌ مِّنَ الْمُلْكِ فَاِذًا لَّا يُؤْتُوْنَ النَّاسَ
نَقِيْرًا ﴿٥٤﴾

55. Or do they envy men for what Allah has given them out of His bounty? *If that is so*, surely, We gave the Book and Wisdom to the children of Abraham *also* and We *also* gave them a great kingdom.

اَمْ يَحْسُدُوْنَ النَّاسَ عَلٰى مَآ اٰتٰىهُمُ اللّٰهُ مِنْ فَضْلِهٖ ۚ
فَقَدْ اٰتَيْنَآ اٰلَ اِبْرٰهِيْمَ الْكِتٰبَ وَالْحِكْمَةَ وَاٰتَيْنٰهُمْ
مُّلْكًا عَظِيْمًا ﴿٥٥﴾

56. And of them were some who believed in him; and of them were others who turned away from him. And sufficient is Hell as a blazing fire.

فَمِنْهُمْ مَّنْ اٰمَنَ بِهٖ وَمِنْهُمْ مَّنْ صَدَّ عَنْهُ ؕ وَ
كَفٰى بِجَهَنَّمَ سَعِيْرًا ﴿٥٦﴾

57. Those who disbelieve in Our Signs, We shall soon cause them to enter Fire. As often as their skins are burnt up, We shall give them in exchange other skins that they may taste the punishment. Surely, Allah is Mighty, Wise.

اِنَّ الَّذِيْنَ كَفَرُوْا بِاٰيٰتِنَا سَوْفَ نُصْلِيْهِمْ نَارًا ؕ كُلَّمَا
نَضِجَتْ جُلُوْدُهُمْ بَدَّلْنٰهُمْ جُلُوْدًا غَيْرَهَا لِيَذُوْقُوا
الْعَذَابَ ؕ اِنَّ اللّٰهَ كَانَ عَزِيْزًا حَكِيْمًا ﴿٥٧﴾

* 58. And those who believe and do good works, We shall make them enter Gardens through which streams flow, to abide therein for ever; therein shall they have pure spouses; and We shall admit them to a *place of* pleasant and plenteous shade.

وَالَّذِيْنَ اٰمَنُوْا وَعَمِلُوا الصّٰلِحٰتِ سَنُدْخِلُهُمْ جَنّٰتٍ
تَجْرِيْ مِنْ تَحْتِهَا الْاَنْهٰرُ خٰلِدِيْنَ فِيْهَآ اَبَدًا ؕ لَهُمْ
فِيْهَآ اَزْوَاجٌ مُّطَهَّرَةٌ ۫ وَّنُدْخِلُهُمْ ظِلًّا ظَلِيْلًا ﴿٥٨﴾

59. Verily, Allah commands you to make over the trusts to those entitled to them,

اِنَّ اللّٰهَ يَاْمُرُكُمْ اَنْ تُؤَدُّوا الْاَمٰنٰتِ اِلٰۤى اَهْلِهَا ۙ وَ

and that, when you judge between men, you judge with justice. And surely excellent is that with which Allah admonishes you! Allah is All-Hearing, All-Seeing.

إِذَا حَكَمْتُمْ بَيْنَ النَّاسِ أَنْ تَحْكُمُوا بِالْعَدْلِ ۚ إِنَّ اللّٰهَ
نِعِمَّا يَعِظُكُمْ بِهٖ ۗ إِنَّ اللّٰهَ كَانَ سَمِيعًا بَصِيرًا ﴿٥٩﴾

* 60. O ye who believe! obey Allah, and obey *His* Messenger and those who are in authority among you. And if you differ in anything among yourselves, refer it to Allah and *His* Messenger if you are believers in Allah and the Last Day. That is best and most commendable in the end.

يٰٓأَيُّهَا الَّذِينَ اٰمَنُوٓا أَطِيعُوا اللّٰهَ وَأَطِيعُوا الرَّسُولَ وَ
أُولِي الْأَمْرِ مِنْكُمْ ۚ فَإِنْ تَنَازَعْتُمْ فِي شَيْءٍ فَرُدُّوهُ
إِلَى اللّٰهِ وَالرَّسُولِ إِنْ كُنْتُمْ تُؤْمِنُونَ بِاللّٰهِ وَالْيَوْمِ
الْاٰخِرِ ۚ ذٰلِكَ خَيْرٌ وَّأَحْسَنُ تَأْوِيلًا ﴿٦٠﴾ ع ٨ ٥

R. 9.

61. Dost thou not know of those who pretend that they believe in what has been revealed to thee and what has been revealed before thee? They desire to seek judgment from the rebellious, although they were commanded not to obey them. And Satan desires to lead them far astray.

أَلَمْ تَرَ إِلَى الَّذِينَ يَزْعُمُونَ أَنَّهُمْ اٰمَنُوا بِمَآ أُنْزِلَ
إِلَيْكَ وَمَآ أُنْزِلَ مِنْ قَبْلِكَ يُرِيدُونَ أَنْ يَتَحَاكَمُوٓا
إِلَى الطَّاغُوتِ وَقَدْ أُمِرُوٓا أَنْ يَكْفُرُوا بِهٖ ۗ وَيُرِيدُ
الشَّيْطٰنُ أَنْ يُضِلَّهُمْ ضَلٰلًا بَعِيدًا ﴿٦١﴾

62. And when it is said to them, 'Come ye to what Allah has sent down and to *His* Messenger,' thou seest the hypocrites turn away from thee with aversion.

وَإِذَا قِيلَ لَهُمْ تَعَالَوْا إِلٰى مَآ أَنْزَلَ اللّٰهُ وَإِلَى الرَّسُولِ
رَأَيْتَ الْمُنٰفِقِينَ يَصُدُّونَ عَنْكَ صُدُودًا ﴿٦٢﴾

* 63. Then how is it that when an affliction befalls them because of what their hands have sent on before them, they come to thee swearing by Allah, *saying*, 'We meant nothing but the doing of good and reconciliation?'

فَكَيْفَ إِذَآ أَصَابَتْهُمْ مُّصِيبَةٌ ۢ بِمَا قَدَّمَتْ أَيْدِيهِمْ
ثُمَّ جَآءُوكَ يَحْلِفُونَ ۖ بِاللّٰهِ إِنْ أَرَدْنَآ إِلَّآ إِحْسَانًا
وَّتَوْفِيقًا ﴿٦٣﴾

64. These are they, the secrets of whose hearts Allah knows well. So turn away from them and admonish them and speak to them an effective word concerning their own selves.

أُولٰٓئِكَ الَّذِينَ يَعْلَمُ اللّٰهُ مَا فِي قُلُوبِهِمْ ۗ فَأَعْرِضْ
عَنْهُمْ وَعِظْهُمْ وَقُلْ لَّهُمْ فِيٓ أَنْفُسِهِمْ قَوْلًا بَلِيغًا ﴿٦٤﴾

65. And We have sent no Messenger but that he should be obeyed by the command of Allah. And if they had come to thee when they had wronged their souls, and asked forgiveness of Allah, and *if* the Messenger *also* had asked forgiveness for them, they would have surely found Allah Oft-Returning *with compassion and* Merciful.

وَمَآ أَرْسَلْنَا مِنْ رَّسُولٍ إِلَّا لِيُطَاعَ بِإِذْنِ اللّٰهِ ۗ وَلَوْ
أَنَّهُمْ إِذْ ظَّلَمُوٓا أَنْفُسَهُمْ جَآءُوكَ فَاسْتَغْفَرُوا اللّٰهَ
وَاسْتَغْفَرَ لَهُمُ الرَّسُولُ لَوَجَدُوا اللّٰهَ تَوَّابًا رَّحِيمًا ﴿٦٥﴾

66. But no, by thy Lord, they are not believers until they make thee judge in all that is in dispute between them and then find not in their hearts any demur

فَلَا وَرَبِّكَ لَا يُؤْمِنُونَ حَتّٰى يُحَكِّمُوكَ فِيمَا شَجَرَ
بَيْنَهُمْ ثُمَّ لَا يَجِدُوا فِيٓ أَنْفُسِهِمْ حَرَجًا مِّمَّا قَضَيْتَ

concerning that which thou decidest and submit with full submission.

وَيُسَلِّمُوْا تَسْلِيْمًا ﴿٦٦﴾

* 67. And if We had commanded them, 'Kill your people or leave your homes,' they would not have done it except a few of them; and if they had done what they are exhorted to do, it would surely have been better for them and conducive to greater strength.

وَلَوْ اَنَّا كَتَبْنَا عَلَيْهِمْ اَنِ اقْتُلُوْٓا اَنْفُسَكُمْ اَوِ اخْرُجُوْا
مِنْ دِيَارِكُمْ مَّا فَعَلُوْهُ اِلَّا قَلِيْلٌ مِّنْهُمْ ۭ وَلَوْ اَنَّهُمْ
فَعَلُوْا مَا يُوْعَظُوْنَ بِهٖ لَكَانَ خَيْرًا لَّهُمْ وَاَشَدَّ
تَثْبِيْتًا ﴿٦٧﴾

68. And then We would have surely given them a great reward from Ourself;

وَّاِذًا لَّاٰتَيْنٰهُمْ مِّنْ لَّدُنَّآ اَجْرًا عَظِيْمًا ﴿٦٨﴾

69. And We would surely have guided them in the right path.

وَّلَهَدَيْنٰهُمْ صِرَاطًا مُّسْتَقِيْمًا ﴿٦٩﴾

70. And whoso obeys Allah and this Messenger *of His* shall be among those on whom Allah has bestowed His blessings, namely, the Prophets, the Truthful, the Martyrs, and the Righteous. And excellent companions are these.

وَمَنْ يُّطِعِ اللّٰهَ وَالرَّسُوْلَ فَاُولٰٓئِكَ مَعَ الَّذِيْنَ اَنْعَمَ
اللّٰهُ عَلَيْهِمْ مِّنَ النَّبِيّٖنَ وَالصِّدِّيْقِيْنَ وَالشُّهَدَاۤءِ
وَالصّٰلِحِيْنَ ۚ وَحَسُنَ اُولٰٓئِكَ رَفِيْقًا ﴿٧٠﴾

71. This grace is from Allah, and sufficient is Allah, the All-Knowing.

ع ذٰلِكَ الْفَضْلُ مِنَ اللّٰهِ ۭ وَكَفٰى بِاللّٰهِ عَلِيْمًا ﴿٧١﴾

R. 10.

72. O ye who believe! take your precautions; then either go forth in separate parties or go forth all together.

يٰٓاَيُّهَا الَّذِيْنَ اٰمَنُوْا خُذُوْا حِذْرَكُمْ فَانْفِرُوْا ثُبَاتٍ
اَوِ انْفِرُوْا جَمِيْعًا ﴿٧٢﴾

73. And among you there is he who will tarry behind, and if a misfortune befall you, he says, 'Surely, Allah has been gracious to me, since I was not present with them.'

وَاِنَّ مِنْكُمْ لَمَنْ لَّيُبَطِّئَنَّ ۚ فَاِنْ اَصَابَتْكُمْ مُّصِيْبَةٌ
قَالَ قَدْ اَنْعَمَ اللّٰهُ عَلَيَّ اِذْ لَمْ اَكُنْ مَّعَهُمْ شَهِيْدًا ﴿٧٣﴾

74. But if there comes to you some good fortune from Allah, he says, as if there were no love between you and him, 'Would that I had been with them, then should I have indeed achieved a great success!'

وَلَئِنْ اَصَابَكُمْ فَضْلٌ مِّنَ اللّٰهِ لَيَقُوْلَنَّ كَاَنْ لَّمْ
تَكُنْ بَيْنَكُمْ وَبَيْنَهٗ مَوَدَّةٌ يّٰلَيْتَنِيْ كُنْتُ مَعَهُمْ
فَاَفُوْزَ فَوْزًا عَظِيْمًا ﴿٧٤﴾

75. Let those then fight in the cause of Allah who would sell the present life for the Hereafter. And whoso fights in the cause of Allah, be he slain or be he victorious, We shall soon give him a great reward.

فَلْيُقَاتِلْ فِيْ سَبِيْلِ اللّٰهِ الَّذِيْنَ يَشْرُوْنَ الْحَيٰوةَ الدُّنْيَا
بِالْاٰخِرَةِ ۭ وَمَنْ يُّقَاتِلْ فِيْ سَبِيْلِ اللّٰهِ فَيُقْتَلْ اَوْ
يَغْلِبْ فَسَوْفَ نُؤْتِيْهِ اَجْرًا عَظِيْمًا ﴿٧٥﴾

76. And what is the matter with you *that* you fight not in the cause of Allah and

وَمَا لَكُمْ لَا تُقَاتِلُوْنَ فِيْ سَبِيْلِ اللّٰهِ وَالْمُسْتَضْعَفِيْنَ

of the weak—men, women and children—who say, 'Our Lord, take us out of this town, whose people are oppressors, and make for us some friend from Thyself, and make for us from Thyself some helper?'

مِنَ الرِّجَالِ وَالنِّسَآءِ وَالْوِلْدَانِ الَّذِيْنَ يَقُوْلُوْنَ
رَبَّنَآ اَخْرِجْنَا مِنْ هٰذِهِ الْقَرْيَةِ الظَّالِمِ اَهْلُهَا
وَاجْعَلْ لَّنَا مِنْ لَّدُنْكَ وَلِيًّا ۚ وَّاجْعَلْ لَّنَا مِنْ
لَّدُنْكَ نَصِيْرًا ﴿٧٦﴾

77. Those who believe fight in the cause of Allah, and those who disbelieve fight in the cause of the Evil One. Fight ye therefore against the friends of Satan; surely, Satan's strategy is weak!

اَلَّذِيْنَ اٰمَنُوْا يُقَاتِلُوْنَ فِيْ سَبِيْلِ اللّٰهِ ۚ وَالَّذِيْنَ كَفَرُوْا
يُقَاتِلُوْنَ فِيْ سَبِيْلِ الطَّاغُوْتِ فَقَاتِلُوْٓا اَوْلِيَآءَ الشَّيْطٰنِ ۚ
اِنَّ كَيْدَ الشَّيْطٰنِ كَانَ ضَعِيْفًا ﴿٧٧﴾

R. 11.

78. Dost thou not know of those to whom it was said: 'Restrain your hands, observe Prayer and pay the Zakāt?' And when fighting has been prescribed for them, behold! a section of them fear men as they should fear Allah, or with still greater fear; and they say, 'Our Lord, why hast Thou prescribed fighting for us? Wouldst Thou not grant us respite yet a while?' Say, 'The benefit of this world is little and the Hereafter will be better for him who fears *God;* and you shall not be wronged a whit.'

اَلَمْ تَرَ اِلَى الَّذِيْنَ قِيْلَ لَهُمْ كُفُّوْٓا اَيْدِيَكُمْ وَاَقِيْمُوا
الصَّلٰوةَ وَاٰتُوا الزَّكٰوةَ ۚ فَلَمَّا كُتِبَ عَلَيْهِمُ الْقِتَالُ
اِذَا فَرِيْقٌ مِّنْهُمْ يَخْشَوْنَ النَّاسَ كَخَشْيَةِ اللّٰهِ
اَوْ اَشَدَّ خَشْيَةً ۚ وَقَالُوْا رَبَّنَا لِمَ كَتَبْتَ عَلَيْنَا
الْقِتَالَ ۚ لَوْلَآ اَخَّرْتَنَآ اِلٰٓى اَجَلٍ قَرِيْبٍ ۗ قُلْ مَتَاعُ
الدُّنْيَا قَلِيْلٌ ۚ وَالْاٰخِرَةُ خَيْرٌ لِّمَنِ اتَّقٰى ۟ وَلَا
تُظْلَمُوْنَ فَتِيْلًا ﴿٧٨﴾

79. Wheresoever you may be, death will overtake you, even if you be in strongly built towers. And if some good befalls them, they say, 'This is from Allah;' and if evil befalls them, they say, 'This is from thee.' Say, 'All is from Allah.' What has happened to these people that they come not near understanding anything?

اَيْنَ مَا تَكُوْنُوْا يُدْرِكْكُّمُ الْمَوْتُ وَلَوْ كُنْتُمْ فِيْ بُرُوْجٍ
مُّشَيَّدَةٍ ۗ وَاِنْ تُصِبْهُمْ حَسَنَةٌ يَّقُوْلُوْا هٰذِهٖ مِنْ
عِنْدِ اللّٰهِ ۚ وَاِنْ تُصِبْهُمْ سَيِّئَةٌ يَّقُوْلُوْا هٰذِهٖ مِنْ
عِنْدِكَ ۗ قُلْ كُلٌّ مِّنْ عِنْدِ اللّٰهِ ۗ فَمَالِ هٰٓؤُلَآءِ الْقَوْمِ
لَا يَكَادُوْنَ يَفْقَهُوْنَ حَدِيْثًا ﴿٧٩﴾

80. Whatever of good comes to thee is from Allah; and whatever of evil befalls thee is from thyself. And We have sent thee as a Messenger to mankind. And sufficient is Allah as a Witness.

مَآ اَصَابَكَ مِنْ حَسَنَةٍ فَمِنَ اللّٰهِ ۫ وَمَآ اَصَابَكَ مِنْ
سَيِّئَةٍ فَمِنْ نَّفْسِكَ ۗ وَاَرْسَلْنٰكَ لِلنَّاسِ رَسُوْلًا ۗ
وَكَفٰى بِاللّٰهِ شَهِيْدًا ﴿٨٠﴾

81. Whoso obeys the Messenger obeys Allah indeed; and whoso turns away, then We have not sent thee as a keeper over them.

82. And they say: 'Obedience *is our guiding principle;*' but when they go forth from thy presence, a section of them spends the night scheming against what thou sayest. Allah records whatever they scheme by night. So turn away from them, and put *thy* trust in Allah. And sufficient is Allah as a Disposer of affairs.

* 83. Will they not, then, meditate upon the Qur'ān? Had it been from anyone other than Allah, they would surely have found therein much disagreement.

* 84. And when there comes to them any tidings *whether* of peace or of fear, they spread it about; whereas if they had referred it to the Messenger and to those in authority among them, surely those of them, who can elicit *the truth from* it, would have understood it. And had it not been for the grace of Allah upon you and His mercy, you would have followed Satan, save a few.

85. Fight, therefore, in the cause of Allah—thou art not made responsible except for thyself—and urge on the believers. It may be that Allah will restrain the might of those that disbelieve; and Allah is stronger in might and stronger in inflicting punishment.

* 86. Whoso makes a righteous intercession shall have a share thereof, and whoso makes an evil intercession, shall have a like portion thereof; and Allah is Powerful over everything.

* 87. And when you are greeted with a prayer, greet ye with a better prayer or *at least* return it. Surely, Allah takes account of all things.

88. Allah is He beside Whom there is none worthy of worship. He will certainly *continue to* assemble you till the Day of Resurrection, about which there is no doubt. And who is more truthful in his word than Allah?

مَنْ يُّطِعِ الرَّسُوْلَ فَقَدْ اَطَاعَ اللّٰهَ ۚ وَمَنْ تَوَلّٰى فَمَآ
اَرْسَلْنٰكَ عَلَيْهِمْ حَفِيْظًا ﴿٨١﴾
وَيَقُوْلُوْنَ طَاعَةٌ ۖ فَاِذَا بَرَزُوْا مِنْ عِنْدِكَ بَيَّتَ طَآئِفَةٌ
مِّنْهُمْ غَيْرَ الَّذِيْ تَقُوْلُ ۚ وَاللّٰهُ يَكْتُبُ مَا يُبَيِّتُوْنَ ۚ
فَاَعْرِضْ عَنْهُمْ وَتَوَكَّلْ عَلَى اللّٰهِ ۗ وَكَفٰى بِاللّٰهِ
وَكِيْلًا ﴿٨٢﴾
اَفَلَا يَتَدَبَّرُوْنَ الْقُرْاٰنَ ۗ وَلَوْ كَانَ مِنْ عِنْدِ غَيْرِ اللّٰهِ
لَوَجَدُوْا فِيْهِ اخْتِلَافًا كَثِيْرًا ﴿٨٣﴾
وَاِذَا جَآءَهُمْ اَمْرٌ مِّنَ الْاَمْنِ اَوِ الْخَوْفِ اَذَاعُوْا
بِهٖ ۗ وَلَوْ رَدُّوْهُ اِلَى الرَّسُوْلِ وَاِلٰٓى اُولِى الْاَمْرِ مِنْهُمْ
لَعَلِمَهُ الَّذِيْنَ يَسْتَنْۢبِطُوْنَهٗ مِنْهُمْ ۗ وَلَوْلَا فَضْلُ اللّٰهِ
عَلَيْكُمْ وَرَحْمَتُهٗ لَاتَّبَعْتُمُ الشَّيْطٰنَ اِلَّا قَلِيْلًا ﴿٨٤﴾
فَقَاتِلْ فِيْ سَبِيْلِ اللّٰهِ ۚ لَا تُكَلَّفُ اِلَّا نَفْسَكَ وَ
حَرِّضِ الْمُؤْمِنِيْنَ ۚ عَسَى اللّٰهُ اَنْ يَّكُفَّ بَاْسَ الَّذِيْنَ
كَفَرُوْا ۗ وَاللّٰهُ اَشَدُّ بَاْسًا وَّاَشَدُّ تَنْكِيْلًا ﴿٨٥﴾
مَنْ يَّشْفَعْ شَفَاعَةً حَسَنَةً يَّكُنْ لَّهٗ نَصِيْبٌ مِّنْهَا ۚ
وَمَنْ يَّشْفَعْ شَفَاعَةً سَيِّئَةً يَّكُنْ لَّهٗ كِفْلٌ مِّنْهَا ۗ
وَكَانَ اللّٰهُ عَلٰى كُلِّ شَيْءٍ مُّقِيْتًا ﴿٨٦﴾
وَاِذَا حُيِّيْتُمْ بِتَحِيَّةٍ فَحَيُّوْا بِاَحْسَنَ مِنْهَآ اَوْ رُدُّوْهَا ۗ
اِنَّ اللّٰهَ كَانَ عَلٰى كُلِّ شَيْءٍ حَسِيْبًا ﴿٨٧﴾ النصف
اَللّٰهُ لَآ اِلٰهَ اِلَّا هُوَ ۗ لَيَجْمَعَنَّكُمْ اِلٰى يَوْمِ الْقِيٰمَةِ لَا
رَيْبَ فِيْهِ ۗ وَمَنْ اَصْدَقُ مِنَ اللّٰهِ حَدِيْثًا ﴿٨٨﴾ ع ٨

R. 12.

89. What has happened to you that you are divided into two parties regarding the hypocrites? And Allah has overthrown them because of what they earned. Desire ye to guide him whom Allah has caused to perish? And for him whom Allah causes to perish thou shalt not find a way.

90. They wish that you should disbelieve as they have disbelieved, so that you may become all alike. Take not, therefore, friends from among them, until they emigrate in the way of Allah. And if they turn away, then seize them and kill them wherever you find them; and take no friend nor helper from among them;

91. Except those who are connected with a people between whom and you there is a pact, or those who come to you, while their hearts shrink from fighting you or fighting their own people. And if Allah had so pleased, He would have given them power over you, then they would have surely fought you. So, if they keep aloof from you and fight you not, and make you an offer of peace, then *remember that* Allah has allowed you no way *of aggression* against them.

92. You will find others who desire to be secure from you and to be secure from their own people. Whenever they are made to revert to hostility, they fall headlong into it. Therefore, if they do not keep aloof from you nor offer you peace nor restrain their hands, then seize them and kill them, wherever you find them. Against these We have given you clear authority.

R. 13.

* 93. It does not become a believer to kill a believer unless it be by mistake. And he who kills a believer by mistake shall free a believing slave, and *pay* blood-money to be handed over to his heirs, unless they remit it as charity. But if *the person slain* be of a people hostile to you, and be a believer, then *the offender* shall free a believing slave; and if he be of a people between whom and you is a pact, then *the offender shall pay* blood-money to be

فَمَا لَكُمْ فِي الْمُنٰفِقِيْنَ فِئَتَيْنِ وَاللّٰهُ اَرْكَسَهُمْ
بِمَا كَسَبُوْا ۭ اَتُرِيْدُوْنَ اَنْ تَهْدُوْا مَنْ اَضَلَّ اللّٰهُ ۭ
وَمَنْ يُّضْلِلِ اللّٰهُ فَلَنْ تَجِدَ لَهٗ سَبِيْلًا ﴿۸۹﴾
وَدُّوْا لَوْ تَكْفُرُوْنَ كَمَا كَفَرُوْا فَتَكُوْنُوْنَ سَوَاۗءً فَلَا
تَتَّخِذُوْا مِنْهُمْ اَوْلِيَاۗءَ حَتّٰى يُهَاجِرُوْا فِيْ سَبِيْلِ اللّٰهِ ۭ
فَاِنْ تَوَلَّوْا فَخُذُوْهُمْ وَاقْتُلُوْهُمْ حَيْثُ وَجَدْتُّمُوْهُمْ
وَلَا تَتَّخِذُوْا مِنْهُمْ وَلِيًّا وَّلَا نَصِيْرًا ﴿۹۰﴾
اِلَّا الَّذِيْنَ يَصِلُوْنَ اِلٰى قَوْمٍۢ بَيْنَكُمْ وَبَيْنَهُمْ مِّيْثَاقٌ
اَوْ جَاۗءُوْكُمْ حَصِرَتْ صُدُوْرُهُمْ اَنْ يُّقَاتِلُوْكُمْ اَوْ
يُقَاتِلُوْا قَوْمَهُمْ ۭ وَلَوْ شَاۗءَ اللّٰهُ لَسَلَّطَهُمْ عَلَيْكُمْ
فَلَقٰتَلُوْكُمْ ۚ فَاِنِ اعْتَزَلُوْكُمْ فَلَمْ يُقَاتِلُوْكُمْ وَاَلْقَوْا
اِلَيْكُمُ السَّلَمَ ۙ فَمَا جَعَلَ اللّٰهُ لَكُمْ عَلَيْهِمْ سَبِيْلًا ﴿۹۱﴾
سَتَجِدُوْنَ اٰخَرِيْنَ يُرِيْدُوْنَ اَنْ يَّاْمَنُوْكُمْ وَيَاْمَنُوْا
قَوْمَهُمْ ۭ كُلَّمَا رُدُّوْٓا اِلَى الْفِتْنَةِ اُرْكِسُوْا فِيْهَا ۚ فَاِنْ لَّمْ
يَعْتَزِلُوْكُمْ وَيُلْقُوْٓا اِلَيْكُمُ السَّلَمَ وَيَكُفُّوْٓا اَيْدِيَهُمْ
فَخُذُوْهُمْ وَاقْتُلُوْهُمْ حَيْثُ ثَقِفْتُمُوْهُمْ ۭ وَاُولٰۗىِٕكُمْ
جَعَلْنَا لَكُمْ عَلَيْهِمْ سُلْطٰنًا مُّبِيْنًا ﴿۹۲﴾ ع ۱۲
وَمَا كَانَ لِمُؤْمِنٍ اَنْ يَّقْتُلَ مُؤْمِنًا اِلَّا خَطَــــًٔا ۚ وَمَنْ
قَتَلَ مُؤْمِنًا خَطَــــًٔا فَتَحْرِيْرُ رَقَبَةٍ مُّؤْمِنَةٍ وَّدِيَةٌ
مُّسَلَّمَةٌ اِلٰٓى اَهْلِهٖٓ اِلَّآ اَنْ يَّصَّدَّقُوْا ۭ فَاِنْ كَانَ مِنْ
قَوْمٍ عَدُوٍّ لَّكُمْ وَهُوَ مُؤْمِنٌ فَتَحْرِيْرُ رَقَبَةٍ مُّؤْمِنَةٍ ۭ
وَاِنْ كَانَ مِنْ قَوْمٍۢ بَيْنَكُمْ وَبَيْنَهُمْ مِّيْثَاقٌ فَدِيَةٌ

handed over to his heirs, and free a believing slave. But whoso finds not *one*, then he shall fast for two consecutive months—a mercy from Allah. And Allah is All-Knowing, Wise.

مُسَلَّمَةٌ اِلٰۤى اَهۡلِهٖ وَ تَحۡرِيۡرُ رَقَبَةٍ مُّؤۡمِنَةٍ ۚ فَمَنۡ
لَّمۡ يَجِدۡ فَصِيَامُ شَهۡرَيۡنِ مُتَتَابِعَيۡنِ ۫ تَوۡبَةً مِّنَ
اللّٰهِ ؕ وَ كَانَ اللّٰهُ عَلِيۡمًا حَكِيۡمًا ﴿۹۳﴾

94. And whoso kills a believer intentionally, his reward shall be Hell wherein he shall abide. And Allah will be wroth with him and will curse him and will prepare for him a great punishment.

وَ مَنۡ يَّقۡتُلۡ مُؤۡمِنًا مُّتَعَمِّدًا فَجَزَآؤُهٗ جَهَنَّمُ خٰلِدًا
فِيۡهَا وَ غَضِبَ اللّٰهُ عَلَيۡهِ وَ لَعَنَهٗ وَ اَعَدَّ لَهٗ عَذَابًا
عَظِيۡمًا ﴿۹۴﴾

95. O ye who believe! when you go forth in the cause of Allah, make proper investigation and say not to anyone who greets you with the greeting of peace, 'Thou art not a believer.' You seek the goods of this life, but with Allah are good things in plenty. Such were you before this, but Allah conferred His *special* favour on you; so do make proper investigation. Surely, Allah is well aware of what you do.

يٰۤاَيُّهَا الَّذِيۡنَ اٰمَنُوۡۤا اِذَا ضَرَبۡتُمۡ فِىۡ سَبِيۡلِ اللّٰهِ فَتَبَيَّنُوۡا
وَ لَا تَقُوۡلُوۡا لِمَنۡ اَلۡقٰٓى اِلَيۡكُمُ السَّلٰمَ لَسۡتَ مُؤۡمِنًا ۚ
تَبۡتَغُوۡنَ عَرَضَ الۡحَيٰوةِ الدُّنۡيَا ۫ فَعِنۡدَ اللّٰهِ مَغَانِمُ
كَثِيۡرَةٌ ؕ كَذٰلِكَ كُنۡتُمۡ مِّنۡ قَبۡلُ فَمَنَّ اللّٰهُ عَلَيۡكُمۡ
فَتَبَيَّنُوۡا ؕ اِنَّ اللّٰهَ كَانَ بِمَا تَعۡمَلُوۡنَ خَبِيۡرًا ﴿۹۵﴾

96. Those of the believers who sit *still*, excepting the disabled ones, and those who strive in the cause of Allah with their wealth and their persons, are not equal. Allah has exalted in rank those who strive with their wealth and their persons above those who sit *still*. And to each Allah has promised good. And Allah has exalted those who strive above those who sit *still*, by a great reward,

لَا يَسۡتَوِى الۡقٰعِدُوۡنَ مِنَ الۡمُؤۡمِنِيۡنَ غَيۡرُ اُولِى الضَّرَرِ
وَ الۡمُجٰهِدُوۡنَ فِىۡ سَبِيۡلِ اللّٰهِ بِاَمۡوَالِهِمۡ وَ اَنۡفُسِهِمۡ ؕ
فَضَّلَ اللّٰهُ الۡمُجٰهِدِيۡنَ بِاَمۡوَالِهِمۡ وَ اَنۡفُسِهِمۡ عَلَى
الۡقٰعِدِيۡنَ دَرَجَةً ؕ وَ كُلًّا وَّعَدَ اللّٰهُ الۡحُسۡنٰى ؕ وَ فَضَّلَ
اللّٰهُ الۡمُجٰهِدِيۡنَ عَلَى الۡقٰعِدِيۡنَ اَجۡرًا عَظِيۡمًا ۙ﴿۹۶﴾

97. *Namely, by* degrees of excellence *bestowed* by Him, and *by special* forgiveness and mercy. And Allah is Most Forgiving, Merciful.

دَرَجٰتٍ مِّنۡهُ وَ مَغۡفِرَةً وَّ رَحۡمَةً ؕ وَ كَانَ اللّٰهُ غَفُوۡرًا
رَّحِيۡمًا ﴿۹۷﴾ ع ١٣ ٥

R. 14.

98. Verily, those whom the angels cause to die while they are wronging their own souls, they (the angels) will say *to them*: 'What were you after?' They will reply: 'We were treated as weak in the land.' They will say, 'Was not Allah's earth vast enough for you to emigrate therein?' It is these whose abode shall be Hell, and an evil destination it is;

اِنَّ الَّذِيۡنَ تَوَفّٰٮهُمُ الۡمَلٰٓئِكَةُ ظَالِمِىۡۤ اَنۡفُسِهِمۡ قَالُوۡا
فِيۡمَ كُنۡتُمۡ ؕ قَالُوۡا كُنَّا مُسۡتَضۡعَفِيۡنَ فِى الۡاَرۡضِ ؕ قَالُوۡۤا
اَلَمۡ تَكُنۡ اَرۡضُ اللّٰهِ وَاسِعَةً فَتُهَاجِرُوۡا فِيۡهَا ؕ فَاُولٰٓئِكَ
مَاۡوٰٮهُمۡ جَهَنَّمُ ؕ وَ سَآءَتۡ مَصِيۡرًا ۙ﴿۹۸﴾

99. Except such weak ones among men, women and children, as are incapable of adopting any plan or of finding any way.

إِلَّا الْمُسْتَضْعَفِينَ مِنَ الرِّجَالِ وَالنِّسَاءِ وَالْوِلْدَانِ لَا يَسْتَطِيعُونَ حِيلَةً وَلَا يَهْتَدُونَ سَبِيلًا (٩٩)

100. As to these, maybe Allah will efface their sins; for Allah is the Effacer of sins, *and is* Most Forgiving.

فَأُولَٰئِكَ عَسَى اللَّهُ أَنْ يَعْفُوَ عَنْهُمْ وَكَانَ اللَّهُ عَفُوًّا غَفُورًا (١٠٠)

* 101. And whoso emigrates from his country in the cause of Allah will find in the earth an abundant place of refuge and plentifulness. And whoso goes forth from his home, emigrating in the cause of Allah and His Messenger, and death overtakes him, his reward lies on Allah, and Allah is Most Forgiving, Merciful.

وَمَنْ يُهَاجِرْ فِي سَبِيلِ اللَّهِ يَجِدْ فِي الْأَرْضِ مُرَاغَمًا كَثِيرًا وَسَعَةً وَمَنْ يَخْرُجْ مِنْ بَيْتِهِ مُهَاجِرًا إِلَى اللَّهِ وَرَسُولِهِ ثُمَّ يُدْرِكْهُ الْمَوْتُ فَقَدْ وَقَعَ أَجْرُهُ عَلَى اللَّهِ وَكَانَ اللَّهُ غَفُورًا رَحِيمًا (١٠١)

R. 15.

102. And when you journey in the land, it shall be no sin on you to shorten the Prayer, if you fear that those who disbelieve may give you trouble. Verily, the disbelievers are an open enemy to you.

وَإِذَا ضَرَبْتُمْ فِي الْأَرْضِ فَلَيْسَ عَلَيْكُمْ جُنَاحٌ أَنْ تَقْصُرُوا مِنَ الصَّلَاةِ إِنْ خِفْتُمْ أَنْ يَفْتِنَكُمُ الَّذِينَ كَفَرُوا إِنَّ الْكَافِرِينَ كَانُوا لَكُمْ عَدُوًّا مُبِينًا (١٠٢)

103. And when thou art among them, and leadest the Prayer for them, let a party of them stand with thee and let them take their arms. And when they have performed their prostrations, let them go to your rear, and let another party, who have not yet prayed, come forward and pray with thee; and let them take their means of defence and their arms. The disbelievers wish that you be neglectful of your arms and your baggage that they may fall upon you at once. And it shall be no sin on you, if you are in trouble on account of rain or if you are sick, that you lay aside your arms. But you should *always* take your means of defence. Surely, Allah has prepared an humiliating punishment for the disbelievers.

وَإِذَا كُنْتَ فِيهِمْ فَأَقَمْتَ لَهُمُ الصَّلَاةَ فَلْتَقُمْ طَائِفَةٌ مِنْهُمْ مَعَكَ وَلْيَأْخُذُوا أَسْلِحَتَهُمْ فَإِذَا سَجَدُوا فَلْيَكُونُوا مِنْ وَرَائِكُمْ وَلْتَأْتِ طَائِفَةٌ أُخْرَىٰ لَمْ يُصَلُّوا فَلْيُصَلُّوا مَعَكَ وَلْيَأْخُذُوا حِذْرَهُمْ وَأَسْلِحَتَهُمْ وَدَّ الَّذِينَ كَفَرُوا لَوْ تَغْفُلُونَ عَنْ أَسْلِحَتِكُمْ وَأَمْتِعَتِكُمْ فَيَمِيلُونَ عَلَيْكُمْ مَيْلَةً وَاحِدَةً وَلَا جُنَاحَ عَلَيْكُمْ إِنْ كَانَ بِكُمْ أَذًى مِنْ مَطَرٍ أَوْ كُنْتُمْ مَرْضَىٰ أَنْ تَضَعُوا أَسْلِحَتَكُمْ وَخُذُوا حِذْرَكُمْ إِنَّ اللَّهَ أَعَدَّ لِلْكَافِرِينَ عَذَابًا مُهِينًا (١٠٣)

* 104. And when you have finished the Prayer, remember Allah while standing, and sitting, and *lying* on your sides. And when you are secure *from danger*, then observe

فَإِذَا قَضَيْتُمُ الصَّلَاةَ فَاذْكُرُوا اللَّهَ قِيَامًا وَقُعُودًا وَعَلَىٰ جُنُوبِكُمْ فَإِذَا اطْمَأْنَنْتُمْ فَأَقِيمُوا الصَّلَاةَ إِنَّ

Prayer *in the prescribed form*; verily Prayer is enjoined on the believers *to be performed* at fixed hours.

105. And slacken not in seeking these people. If you suffer, they too suffer even as you suffer. But you hope from Allah what they hope not. And Allah is All-Knowing, Wise.

R. 16.

* 106. We have surely sent down to thee the Book comprising the truth, that thou mayest judge between men by that which Allah has taught thee. And be not thou a disputer for the faithless;

107. And ask forgiveness of Allah. Surely, Allah is Most Forgiving, Merciful.

108. And plead not on behalf of those who are dishonest to themselves. Surely, Allah loves not one who is perfidious *and* a great sinner.

109. They seek to hide from men, but they cannot hide from Allah; and He is with them when they spend the night plotting about matters of which He does not approve. And Allah encompasses what they do.

110. Behold! you are they who pleaded for them in the present life. But who will plead with Allah for them on the Day of Resurrection, or who will be a guardian over them?

111. And whoso does evil or wrongs his soul, and then asks forgiveness of Allah, will *surely* find Allah Most Forgiving, Merciful.

112. And whoso commits a sin commits it only against his own soul. And Allah is All-Knowing, Wise.

113. And whoso commits a fault or a sin, then imputes it to an innocent person, certainly bears *the burden of* a calumny and a manifest sin.

R. 17.

* 114. And but for the grace of Allah upon

الصَّلٰوةَ كَانَتْ عَلَى الْمُؤْمِنِيْنَ كِتٰبًا مَّوْقُوْتًا ﴿١٠٤﴾
وَلَا تَهِنُوْا فِي ابْتِغَآءِ الْقَوْمِ ؕ اِنْ تَكُوْنُوْا تَاْلَمُوْنَ
فَاِنَّهُمْ يَاْلَمُوْنَ كَمَا تَاْلَمُوْنَ ۚ وَتَرْجُوْنَ مِنَ اللّٰهِ مَا
لَا يَرْجُوْنَ ؕ وَكَانَ اللّٰهُ عَلِيْمًا حَكِيْمًا ﴿١٠٥﴾ ع ١٥ ١٢
اِنَّآ اَنْزَلْنَآ اِلَيْكَ الْكِتٰبَ بِالْحَقِّ لِتَحْكُمَ بَيْنَ النَّاسِ
بِمَآ اَرٰىكَ اللّٰهُ ؕ وَلَا تَكُنْ لِّلْخَآئِنِيْنَ خَصِيْمًا ﴿١٠٦﴾
وَّاسْتَغْفِرِ اللّٰهَ ؕ اِنَّ اللّٰهَ كَانَ غَفُوْرًا رَّحِيْمًا ﴿١٠٧﴾
وَلَا تُجَادِلْ عَنِ الَّذِيْنَ يَخْتَانُوْنَ اَنْفُسَهُمْ ؕ اِنَّ اللّٰهَ
لَا يُحِبُّ مَنْ كَانَ خَوَّانًا اَثِيْمًا ﴿١٠٨﴾
يَّسْتَخْفُوْنَ مِنَ النَّاسِ وَلَا يَسْتَخْفُوْنَ مِنَ اللّٰهِ
وَهُوَ مَعَهُمْ اِذْ يُبَيِّتُوْنَ مَا لَا يَرْضٰى مِنَ الْقَوْلِ ؕ
وَكَانَ اللّٰهُ بِمَا يَعْمَلُوْنَ مُحِيْطًا ﴿١٠٩﴾
هٰٓاَنْتُمْ هٰٓؤُلَآءِ جٰدَلْتُمْ عَنْهُمْ فِي الْحَيٰوةِ الدُّنْيَا ۫
فَمَنْ يُّجَادِلُ اللّٰهَ عَنْهُمْ يَوْمَ الْقِيٰمَةِ اَمْ مَّنْ يَّكُوْنُ
عَلَيْهِمْ وَكِيْلًا ﴿١١٠﴾
وَمَنْ يَّعْمَلْ سُوْٓءًا اَوْ يَظْلِمْ نَفْسَهٗ ثُمَّ يَسْتَغْفِرِ اللّٰهَ
يَجِدِ اللّٰهَ غَفُوْرًا رَّحِيْمًا ﴿١١١﴾
وَمَنْ يَّكْسِبْ اِثْمًا فَاِنَّمَا يَكْسِبُهٗ عَلٰى نَفْسِهٖ ؕ وَكَانَ
اللّٰهُ عَلِيْمًا حَكِيْمًا ﴿١١٢﴾
وَمَنْ يَّكْسِبْ خَطِيْٓئَةً اَوْ اِثْمًا ثُمَّ يَرْمِ بِهٖ بَرِيْٓـًٔا
فَقَدِ احْتَمَلَ بُهْتَانًا وَّاِثْمًا مُّبِيْنًا ﴿١١٣﴾ ع ١٦ ١٣
وَلَوْلَا فَضْلُ اللّٰهِ عَلَيْكَ وَرَحْمَتُهٗ لَهَمَّتْ طَّآئِفَةٌ

thee and His mercy, a party of them had resolved to bring about thy ruin. And they ruin none but themselves and they cannot harm thee at all. Allah has sent down to thee the Book and Wisdom and has taught thee what thou knewest not, and great is Allah's grace on thee.

مِّنۡهُمۡ اَنۡ يُّضِلُّوۡكَ ؕ وَمَا يُضِلُّوۡنَ اِلَّاۤ اَنۡفُسَهُمۡ وَمَا
يَضُرُّوۡنَكَ مِنۡ شَیۡءٍ ؕ وَاَنۡزَلَ اللّٰهُ عَلَيۡكَ الۡكِتٰبَ وَ
الۡحِكۡمَةَ وَعَلَّمَكَ مَا لَمۡ تَكُنۡ تَعۡلَمُ ؕ وَكَانَ فَضۡلُ اللّٰهِ
عَلَيۡكَ عَظِيۡمًا ﴿۱۱۴﴾

* 115. There is no good in many of their conferences except *the conferences of* such as enjoin charity, or goodness, or the making of peace among men. And whoso does that, seeking the pleasure of Allah, We shall soon bestow on him a great reward.

لَا خَيۡرَ فِىۡ كَثِيۡرٍ مِّنۡ نَّجۡوٰٮهُمۡ اِلَّا مَنۡ اَمَرَ بِصَدَقَةٍ
اَوۡ مَعۡرُوۡفٍ اَوۡ اِصۡلَاحٍۢ بَيۡنَ النَّاسِ ؕ وَمَنۡ يَّفۡعَلۡ
ذٰلِكَ ابۡتِغَآءَ مَرۡضَاتِ اللّٰهِ فَسَوۡفَ نُؤۡتِيۡهِ اَجۡرًا
عَظِيۡمًا ﴿۱۱۵﴾

116. And *as to* him who opposes the Messenger after guidance has become clear to him, and follows a way other than that of the believers, We shall let him pursue the way he is pursuing and shall cast him into Hell; and an evil destination it is.

وَمَنۡ يُّشَاقِقِ الرَّسُوۡلَ مِنۡۢ بَعۡدِ مَا تَبَيَّنَ لَهُ الۡهُدٰى
وَيَتَّبِعۡ غَيۡرَ سَبِيۡلِ الۡمُؤۡمِنِيۡنَ نُوَلِّهٖ مَا تَوَلّٰى وَنُصۡلِهٖ
جَهَنَّمَ ؕ وَسَآءَتۡ مَصِيۡرًا ﴿۱۱۶﴾ ع

R. 18.

117. Allah will not forgive that anything be associated with Him as partner, but He will forgive what is short of that to whomsoever He pleases. And whos associates anything as partner with Allah has indeed strayed far away.

اِنَّ اللّٰهَ لَا يَغۡفِرُ اَنۡ يُّشۡرَكَ بِهٖ وَيَغۡفِرُ مَا دُوۡنَ
ذٰلِكَ لِمَنۡ يَّشَآءُ ؕ وَمَنۡ يُّشۡرِكۡ بِاللّٰهِ فَقَدۡ ضَلَّ
ضَلٰلًاۢ بَعِيۡدًا ﴿۱۱۷﴾

* 118. They invoke beside Him none but lifeless objects; and they invoke none but Satan, the rebellious,

اِنۡ يَّدۡعُوۡنَ مِنۡ دُوۡنِهٖۤ اِلَّاۤ اِنٰـثًا ۚ وَاِنۡ يَّدۡعُوۡنَ اِلَّا شَيۡطٰنًا مَّرِيۡدًا ۙ﴿۱۱۸﴾

119. Whom Allah has cursed. And he said, 'I will assuredly take a fixed portion from Thy servants;

لَّعَنَهُ اللّٰهُ ۘ وَقَالَ لَاَ تَّخِذَنَّ مِنۡ عِبَادِكَ نَصِيۡبًا وقف لازم
مَّفۡرُوۡضًا ۙ﴿۱۱۹﴾

* 120. 'And assuredly I will lead them astray and assuredly I will excite in them vain desires, and assuredly I will incite them and they will cut the ears of cattle; and assuredly I will incite them and they will alter Allah's creation.' And he who takes Satan for a friend beside Allah has certainly suffered a manifest loss.

وَّلَاُضِلَّنَّهُمۡ وَلَاُمَنِّيَنَّهُمۡ وَلَاٰمُرَنَّهُمۡ فَلَيُبَتِّكُنَّ
اٰذَانَ الۡاَنۡعَامِ وَلَاٰمُرَنَّهُمۡ فَلَيُغَيِّرُنَّ خَلۡقَ اللّٰهِ ؕ
وَمَنۡ يَّتَّخِذِ الشَّيۡطٰنَ وَلِيًّا مِّنۡ دُوۡنِ اللّٰهِ فَقَدۡ
خَسِرَ خُسۡرَانًا مُّبِيۡنًا ؕ﴿۱۲۰﴾

121. He holds out promises to them and raises vain desires in them, and Satan

يَعِدُهُمۡ وَيُمَنِّيۡهِمۡ ؕ وَمَا يَعِدُهُمُ الشَّيۡطٰنُ اِلَّا

promises them nothing but vain things.

غُرُوْرًا ﴿١٢١﴾

122. These are they whose abode shall be Hell and they shall find no way of escape from it.

أُولٰٓئِكَ مَأْوٰىهُمْ جَهَنَّمُ ۫ وَلَا يَجِدُوْنَ عَنْهَا
مَحِيْصًا ﴿١٢٢﴾

123. But *as to* those who believe and do good works, We will admit them into Gardens, beneath which streams flow, abiding therein for ever. *It is* Allah's unfailing promise; and who can be more truthful than Allah in word?

وَالَّذِيْنَ اٰمَنُوْا وَعَمِلُوا الصّٰلِحٰتِ سَنُدْخِلُهُمْ جَنّٰتٍ
تَجْرِيْ مِنْ تَحْتِهَا الْاَنْهٰرُ خٰلِدِيْنَ فِيْهَآ اَبَدًا ؕ
وَعْدَ اللّٰهِ حَقًّا ؕ وَمَنْ اَصْدَقُ مِنَ اللّٰهِ قِيْلًا ﴿١٢٣﴾

124. It shall not be according to your desires, nor according to the desires of the People of the Book. Whoso does evil shall be rewarded for it; and he shall find for himself no friend or helper beside Allah.

لَيْسَ بِاَمَانِيِّكُمْ وَلَآ اَمَانِيِّ اَهْلِ الْكِتٰبِ ؕ مَنْ يَّعْمَلْ
سُوْٓءًا يُّجْزَ بِهٖ ۙ وَلَا يَجِدْ لَهٗ مِنْ دُوْنِ اللّٰهِ وَلِيًّا
وَّلَا نَصِيْرًا ﴿١٢٤﴾

125. But whoso does good works, whether male or female, and is a believer, such shall enter Heaven, and shall not be wronged even *as much as* the little hollow in the back of a date-stone.

وَمَنْ يَّعْمَلْ مِنَ الصّٰلِحٰتِ مِنْ ذَكَرٍ اَوْ اُنْثٰى وَهُوَ
مُؤْمِنٌ فَاُولٰٓئِكَ يَدْخُلُوْنَ الْجَنَّةَ وَلَا يُظْلَمُوْنَ
نَقِيْرًا ﴿١٢٥﴾

126. And who is better in faith than he who submits himself to Allah, and he is a doer of good, and follows the religion of Abraham, the upright? And Allah took Abraham for a special friend.

وَمَنْ اَحْسَنُ دِيْنًا مِّمَّنْ اَسْلَمَ وَجْهَهٗ لِلّٰهِ وَهُوَ
مُحْسِنٌ وَّاتَّبَعَ مِلَّةَ اِبْرٰهِيْمَ حَنِيْفًا ؕ وَاتَّخَذَ
اللّٰهُ اِبْرٰهِيْمَ خَلِيْلًا ﴿١٢٦﴾

127. And to Allah belongs all that is in the heavens and all that is in the earth; and Allah encompasses all things.

وَلِلّٰهِ مَا فِي السَّمٰوٰتِ وَمَا فِي الْاَرْضِ ؕ وَكَانَ اللّٰهُ
بِكُلِّ شَيْءٍ مُّحِيْطًا ﴿١٢٧﴾ ع ١٥

R. 19.

128. And they seek of thee the decision *of the Law* with regard to women. Say, Allah gives you His decision regarding them. And so does that which is recited to you in the Book concerning the orphan girls whom you give not what is prescribed for them and whom you desire to marry, and *concerning* the weak among children. And *He enjoins you to* observe equity towards the orphans. And whatever good

وَيَسْتَفْتُوْنَكَ فِي النِّسَآءِ ؕ قُلِ اللّٰهُ يُفْتِيْكُمْ فِيْهِنَّ ۙ وَ
مَا يُتْلٰى عَلَيْكُمْ فِي الْكِتٰبِ فِيْ يَتٰمَى النِّسَآءِ الّٰتِيْ لَا
تُؤْتُوْنَهُنَّ مَا كُتِبَ لَهُنَّ وَتَرْغَبُوْنَ اَنْ تَنْكِحُوْهُنَّ
وَالْمُسْتَضْعَفِيْنَ مِنَ الْوِلْدَانِ ۙ وَاَنْ تَقُوْمُوْا لِلْيَتٰمٰى
بِالْقِسْطِ ؕ وَمَا تَفْعَلُوْا مِنْ خَيْرٍ فَاِنَّ اللّٰهَ كَانَ بِهٖ

you do, surely Allah knows it well.

عليما ﴿١٢٨﴾

129. And if a woman fear ill-treatment or indifference on the part of her husband, it shall be no sin on them that they be suitably reconciled to each other; and reconciliation is best. And people are prone to covetousness. If you do good and are righteous, surely Allah is aware of what you do.

وان امرأة خافت من بعلها نشوزا او اعراضا
فلا جناح عليهما ان يصلحا بينهما صلحا والصلح
خير واحضرت الانفس الشح وان تحسنوا
وتتقوا فان الله كان بما تعملون خبيرا ﴿١٢٩﴾

* 130. And you cannot keep *perfect* balance between wives, however much you may desire it. But incline not wholly *to one* so that you leave the other like a thing suspended. And if you amend and act righteously, surely Allah is Most Forgiving, Merciful.

ولن تستطيعوا ان تعدلوا بين النساء ولو حرصتم
فلا تميلوا كل الميل فتذروها كالمعلقة وان
تصلحوا وتتقوا فان الله كان غفورا رحيما ﴿١٣٠﴾

131. And if they separate, Allah will make both independent out of His abundance; and Allah is Bountiful, Wise.

وان يتفرقا يغن الله كلا من سعته وكان الله
واسعا حكيما ﴿١٣١﴾

132. And to Allah belongs whatever is in the heavens and whatever is in the earth. And We have assuredly commanded those who were given the Book before you, and *commanded* you also, to fear Allah. But if you disbelieve, then *remember that* to Allah belongs whatever is in the heavens and whatever is in the earth, and Allah is Self-Sufficient, Praiseworthy.

ولله ما في السموت وما في الارض ولقد وصينا
الذين اوتوا الكتب من قبلكم واياكم ان اتقوا الله
وان تكفروا فان لله ما في السموت وما في الارض
وكان الله غنيا حميدا ﴿١٣٢﴾

133. And to Allah belongs whatever is in the heavens and whatever is in the earth, and sufficient is Allah as a Guardian.

ولله ما في السموت وما في الارض وكفى بالله
وكيلا ﴿١٣٣﴾

134. If He please, He can take you away, O people, and bring others *in your stead;* and Allah has full power to do that.

ان يشا يذهبكم ايها الناس ويات باخرين
وكان الله على ذلك قديرا ﴿١٣٤﴾

135. Whoso desires the reward of this world, then *let him remember that* with Allah is the reward of this world and of the next; and Allah is All-Hearing, All-Seeing.

من كان يريد ثواب الدنيا فعند الله ثواب الدنيا
والاخرة وكان الله سميعا بصيرا ﴿١٣٥﴾ ع ١٩ ١٤

R. 20.

* 136. O ye who believe! be strict in observing justice, *and be* witnesses for Allah, even though it be against yourselves or *against* parents and kindred. Whether he

يايها الذين امنوا كونوا قومين بالقسط شهداء
لله ولو على انفسكم او الوالدين والاقربين ان

be rich or poor, Allah is more regardful of them both *than you are*. Therefore follow not low desires so that you may *be able to* act equitably. And if you conceal *the truth* or evade *it*, then *remember that* Allah is well aware of what you do.

يَكُنْ غَنِيًّا أَوْ فَقِيرًا فَاللَّهُ أَوْلَىٰ بِهِمَا ۖ فَلَا تَتَّبِعُوا
الْهَوَىٰ أَنْ تَعْدِلُوا ۚ وَإِنْ تَلْوُوا أَوْ تُعْرِضُوا فَإِنَّ اللَّهَ
كَانَ بِمَا تَعْمَلُونَ خَبِيرًا ﴿١٣٦﴾

137. O ye who believe! believe in Allah and His Messenger, and in the Book which He has revealed to His Messenger, and the Book which He revealed before *it*. And whoso disbelieves in Allah and His angels, and His Books, and His Messengers, and the Last Day, has surely strayed far away.

يَا أَيُّهَا الَّذِينَ آمَنُوا آمِنُوا بِاللَّهِ وَرَسُولِهِ وَالْكِتَابِ الَّذِي
نَزَّلَ عَلَىٰ رَسُولِهِ وَالْكِتَابِ الَّذِي أَنْزَلَ مِنْ قَبْلُ ۚ وَمَنْ
يَكْفُرْ بِاللَّهِ وَمَلَائِكَتِهِ وَكُتُبِهِ وَرُسُلِهِ وَالْيَوْمِ الْآخِرِ فَقَدْ
ضَلَّ ضَلَالًا بَعِيدًا ﴿١٣٧﴾

138. Those who believe, then disbelieve, then *again* believe, then disbelieve, *and* then increase in disbelief, Allah will never forgive them nor will He guide them to the way.

إِنَّ الَّذِينَ آمَنُوا ثُمَّ كَفَرُوا ثُمَّ آمَنُوا ثُمَّ كَفَرُوا ثُمَّ ازْدَادُوا كُفْرًا
لَمْ يَكُنِ اللَّهُ لِيَغْفِرَ لَهُمْ وَلَا لِيَهْدِيَهُمْ سَبِيلًا ﴿١٣٨﴾

139. Give to the hypocrites the tidings that for them is a grievous punishment,

بَشِّرِ الْمُنَافِقِينَ بِأَنَّ لَهُمْ عَذَابًا أَلِيمًا ﴿١٣٩﴾

140. Those who take disbelievers for friends rather than believers. Do they seek honour at their hands? Then *let them remember that* all honour belongs to Allah.

الَّذِينَ يَتَّخِذُونَ الْكَافِرِينَ أَوْلِيَاءَ مِنْ دُونِ
الْمُؤْمِنِينَ ۚ أَيَبْتَغُونَ عِنْدَهُمُ الْعِزَّةَ فَإِنَّ الْعِزَّةَ
لِلَّهِ جَمِيعًا ﴿١٤٠﴾

141. And He has already revealed to you in the Book that, when you hear the Signs of Allah being denied and mocked at, sit not with them until they engage in a talk other than that; for in that case you would be like them. Surely, Allah will assemble the hypocrites and the disbelievers in Hell, all together;

وَقَدْ نَزَّلَ عَلَيْكُمْ فِي الْكِتَابِ أَنْ إِذَا سَمِعْتُمْ آيَاتِ
اللَّهِ يُكْفَرُ بِهَا وَيُسْتَهْزَأُ بِهَا فَلَا تَقْعُدُوا مَعَهُمْ
حَتَّىٰ يَخُوضُوا فِي حَدِيثٍ غَيْرِهِ ۚ إِنَّكُمْ إِذًا مِثْلُهُمْ ۗ
إِنَّ اللَّهَ جَامِعُ الْمُنَافِقِينَ وَالْكَافِرِينَ فِي جَهَنَّمَ
جَمِيعًا ﴿١٤١﴾

142. Those who wait *for news* concerning you. If you have a victory from Allah, they say, 'Were we not with you?' And if the disbelievers have a share *of it*, they say *to them*, 'Did we not get the better of you, and protect you against the believers?' Allah will judge between you on the Day of Resurrection; and Allah will not grant the

الَّذِينَ يَتَرَبَّصُونَ بِكُمْ فَإِنْ كَانَ لَكُمْ فَتْحٌ مِنَ اللَّهِ
قَالُوا أَلَمْ نَكُنْ مَعَكُمْ وَإِنْ كَانَ لِلْكَافِرِينَ نَصِيبٌ
قَالُوا أَلَمْ نَسْتَحْوِذْ عَلَيْكُمْ وَنَمْنَعْكُمْ مِنَ الْمُؤْمِنِينَ ۚ
فَاللَّهُ يَحْكُمُ بَيْنَكُمْ يَوْمَ الْقِيَامَةِ ۗ وَلَنْ يَجْعَلَ اللَّهُ

disbelievers a way *to prevail* against the believers.

لِلْكٰفِرِيْنَ عَلَى الْمُؤْمِنِيْنَ سَبِيْلًا ﴿١٤٢﴾ ع

R. 21.

* 143. The hypocrites seek to deceive Allah, but He will punish them for their deception. And when they stand up for Prayer, they stand lazily *and* to be seen of men, and they remember Allah but little,

اِنَّ الْمُنٰفِقِيْنَ يُخٰدِعُوْنَ اللّٰهَ وَهُوَ خَادِعُهُمْ ۚ وَاِذَا
قَامُوْٓا اِلَى الصَّلٰوةِ قَامُوْا كُسَالٰى ۙ يُرَآءُوْنَ النَّاسَ
وَلَا يَذْكُرُوْنَ اللّٰهَ اِلَّا قَلِيْلًا ﴿١٤٣﴾

144. Wavering between *this and* that, *belonging* neither to these nor to those. And he whom Allah causes to perish, for him thou shalt not find a way.

مُّذَبْذَبِيْنَ بَيْنَ ذٰلِكَ ۖ لَآ اِلٰى هٰٓؤُلَآءِ وَلَآ اِلٰى هٰٓؤُلَآءِ ۗ
وَمَنْ يُّضْلِلِ اللّٰهُ فَلَنْ تَجِدَ لَهٗ سَبِيْلًا ﴿١٤٤﴾

145. O ye who believe! take not disbelievers for friends, in preference to believers. Do you mean to give Allah a manifest proof against yourselves?

يٰٓاَيُّهَا الَّذِيْنَ اٰمَنُوْا لَا تَتَّخِذُوا الْكٰفِرِيْنَ اَوْلِيَآءَ مِنْ
دُوْنِ الْمُؤْمِنِيْنَ ۗ اَتُرِيْدُوْنَ اَنْ تَجْعَلُوْا لِلّٰهِ عَلَيْكُمْ
سُلْطٰنًا مُّبِيْنًا ﴿١٤٥﴾

146. The hypocrites shall surely be in the lowest depth of the Fire; and thou shalt find no helper for them,

اِنَّ الْمُنٰفِقِيْنَ فِى الدَّرْكِ الْاَسْفَلِ مِنَ النَّارِ ۚ وَلَنْ
تَجِدَ لَهُمْ نَصِيْرًا ﴿١٤٦﴾

147. Except those who repent and amend and hold fast to Allah and are sincere in their obedience to Allah. These are among the believers. And Allah will soon bestow a great reward upon the believers.

اِلَّا الَّذِيْنَ تَابُوْا وَاَصْلَحُوْا وَاعْتَصَمُوْا بِاللّٰهِ وَاَخْلَصُوْا
دِيْنَهُمْ لِلّٰهِ فَاُولٰٓئِكَ مَعَ الْمُؤْمِنِيْنَ ۗ وَسَوْفَ يُؤْتِ
اللّٰهُ الْمُؤْمِنِيْنَ اَجْرًا عَظِيْمًا ﴿١٤٧﴾

148. Why should Allah punish you, if you are thankful and *if* you believe? And Allah is Appreciating, All-Knowing.

مَا يَفْعَلُ اللّٰهُ بِعَذَابِكُمْ اِنْ شَكَرْتُمْ وَاٰمَنْتُمْ ۗ وَ
كَانَ اللّٰهُ شَاكِرًا عَلِيْمًا ﴿١٤٨﴾

149. Allah likes not the uttering of unseemly speech in public, except *on the part of* one who is *being* wronged. Verily, Allah is All-Hearing, All-Knowing.

لَا يُحِبُّ اللّٰهُ الْجَهْرَ بِالسُّوْٓءِ مِنَ الْقَوْلِ اِلَّا الجزء ٦
مَنْ ظُلِمَ ۗ وَكَانَ اللّٰهُ سَمِيْعًا عَلِيْمًا ﴿١٤٩﴾

150. Whether you make public a good deed or conceal it, or pardon an evil, Allah is certainly the Effacer of sins, *and is* All-Powerful.

اِنْ تُبْدُوْا خَيْرًا اَوْ تُخْفُوْهُ اَوْ تَعْفُوْا عَنْ سُوْٓءٍ
فَاِنَّ اللّٰهَ كَانَ عَفُوًّا قَدِيْرًا ﴿١٥٠﴾

151. Surely, those who disbelieve in Allah and His Messengers and desire to make a distinction between Allah and His Messengers, and say, 'We believe in some

اِنَّ الَّذِيْنَ يَكْفُرُوْنَ بِاللّٰهِ وَرُسُلِهٖ وَيُرِيْدُوْنَ اَنْ
يُّفَرِّقُوْا بَيْنَ اللّٰهِ وَرُسُلِهٖ وَيَقُوْلُوْنَ نُؤْمِنُ بِبَعْضٍ

and disbelieve in others,' and desire to take a way in between,

وَ نَكْفُرُ بِبَعْضٍ ۙ وَّ يُرِيْدُوْنَ اَنْ يَّتَّخِذُوْا بَيْنَ
ذٰلِكَ سَبِيْلًا ۙ ﴿۱۵۱﴾

152. These indeed are veritable disbelievers, and We have prepared for the disbelievers an humiliating punishment.

اُولٰٓئِكَ هُمُ الْكٰفِرُوْنَ حَقًّا ۚ وَ اَعْتَدْنَا لِلْكٰفِرِيْنَ
عَذَابًا مُّهِيْنًا ﴿۱۵۲﴾

* 153. And *as for* those who believe in Allah and *in all of* His Messengers and make no distinction between any of them, these are they whom He will soon give their rewards. And Allah is Most Forgiving, Merciful.

وَ الَّذِيْنَ اٰمَنُوْا بِاللّٰهِ وَ رُسُلِهٖ وَ لَمْ يُفَرِّقُوْا بَيْنَ
اَحَدٍ مِّنْهُمْ اُولٰٓئِكَ سَوْفَ يُؤْتِيْهِمْ اُجُوْرَهُمْ ؕ وَ
كَانَ اللّٰهُ غَفُوْرًا رَّحِيْمًا ﴿۱۵۳﴾ ع ٢١

R. 22.

* 154. The People of the Book ask thee to cause a Book to descend on them from heaven. They asked Moses a greater thing than this: they said, 'Show us Allah openly.' Then a destructive punishment overtook them because of their transgression. Then they took the calf *for worship* after clear Signs had come to them, but We pardoned *even* that. And We gave Moses manifest authority.

يَسْـَٔلُكَ اَهْلُ الْكِتٰبِ اَنْ تُنَزِّلَ عَلَيْهِمْ كِتٰبًا مِّنَ
السَّمَآءِ فَقَدْ سَاَلُوْا مُوْسٰٓى اَكْبَرَ مِنْ ذٰلِكَ فَقَالُوْٓا
اَرِنَا اللّٰهَ جَهْرَةً فَاَخَذَتْهُمُ الصّٰعِقَةُ بِظُلْمِهِمْ ۚ
ثُمَّ اتَّخَذُوا الْعِجْلَ مِنْۢ بَعْدِ مَا جَآءَتْهُمُ الْبَيِّنٰتُ
فَعَفَوْنَا عَنْ ذٰلِكَ ۚ وَ اٰتَيْنَا مُوْسٰى سُلْطٰنًا
مُّبِيْنًا ﴿۱۵۴﴾

155. And We raised high above them the Mount while making a covenant with them, and We said to them, 'Enter the gate submissively,' and We said to them, 'Transgress not in *the matter of* the Sabbath.' And We took from them a firm covenant.

وَ رَفَعْنَا فَوْقَهُمُ الطُّوْرَ بِمِيْثَاقِهِمْ وَ قُلْنَا لَهُمُ
ادْخُلُوا الْبَابَ سُجَّدًا وَّ قُلْنَا لَهُمْ لَا تَعْدُوْا فِي
السَّبْتِ وَ اَخَذْنَا مِنْهُمْ مِّيْثَاقًا غَلِيْظًا ﴿۱۵۵﴾

156. Then, because of their breaking of their covenant, and their denial of the Signs of Allah, and their seeking to kill the Prophets unjustly, and their saying: 'Our hearts are wrapped in covers,'—nay, but Allah has sealed them because of their disbelief, so they believe not but little—

فَبِمَا نَقْضِهِمْ مِّيْثَاقَهُمْ وَ كُفْرِهِمْ بِاٰيٰتِ اللّٰهِ
وَ قَتْلِهِمُ الْاَنْۢبِيَآءَ بِغَيْرِ حَقٍّ وَّ قَوْلِهِمْ قُلُوْبُنَا
غُلْفٌ ؕ بَلْ طَبَعَ اللّٰهُ عَلَيْهَا بِكُفْرِهِمْ فَلَا يُؤْمِنُوْنَ
اِلَّا قَلِيْلًا ﴿۱۵۶﴾

157. And because of their disbelief and their uttering against Mary a grievous calumny,

وَّ بِكُفْرِهِمْ وَ قَوْلِهِمْ عَلٰى مَرْيَمَ بُهْتَانًا
عَظِيْمًا ۙ ﴿۱۵۷﴾

* 158. And their saying, 'We did kill the Messiah, Jesus, son of Mary, the Messenger of Allah;' whereas they slew him not, nor crucified * him, but he was made to appear to them like *one crucified*; and those who differ therein are certainly in *a state of* doubt about it; they have no *definite* knowledge thereof, but only follow a conjecture; and they did not convert this *conjecture* into a certainty;

وَّ قَوْلِهِمْ اِنَّا قَتَلْنَا الْمَسِيْحَ عِيْسَى ابْنَ مَرْيَمَ
رَسُوْلَ اللّٰهِ ۚ وَمَا قَتَلُوْهُ وَمَا صَلَبُوْهُ وَلٰكِنْ شُبِّهَ
لَهُمْ ۗ وَاِنَّ الَّذِيْنَ اخْتَلَفُوْا فِيْهِ لَفِيْ شَكٍّ مِّنْهُ ۗ
مَا لَهُمْ بِهٖ مِنْ عِلْمٍ اِلَّا اتِّبَاعَ الظَّنِّ ۚ وَمَا قَتَلُوْهُ
يَقِيْنًا ۙ ﴿١٥٨﴾

159. On the contrary, Allah exalted him to Himself. And Allah is Mighty, Wise.

بَلْ رَّفَعَهُ اللّٰهُ اِلَيْهِ ۗ وَكَانَ اللّٰهُ عَزِيْزًا حَكِيْمًا ﴿١٥٩﴾

* 160. And there is none among the People of the Book but will believe in it before his death; and on the Day of Resurrection, he (Jesus) shall be a witness against them—

وَاِنْ مِّنْ اَهْلِ الْكِتٰبِ اِلَّا لَيُؤْمِنَنَّ بِهٖ قَبْلَ مَوْتِهٖ ۚ
وَيَوْمَ الْقِيٰمَةِ يَكُوْنُ عَلَيْهِمْ شَهِيْدًا ۚ ﴿١٦٠﴾

161. So, because of the transgression of the Jews, We forbade them pure things which had been allowed to them, and *also* because of their hindering many *men* from Allah's way,

فَبِظُلْمٍ مِّنَ الَّذِيْنَ هَادُوْا حَرَّمْنَا عَلَيْهِمْ طَيِّبٰتٍ
اُحِلَّتْ لَهُمْ وَبِصَدِّهِمْ عَنْ سَبِيْلِ اللّٰهِ كَثِيْرًا ۙ ﴿١٦١﴾

162. And *because of* their taking interest, although they had been forbidden it, and *because of* their devouring people's wealth wrongfully. And We have prepared for those of them who disbelieve a painful punishment.

وَّاَخْذِهِمُ الرِّبٰوا وَقَدْ نُهُوْا عَنْهُ وَاَكْلِهِمْ اَمْوَالَ
النَّاسِ بِالْبَاطِلِ ۗ وَاَعْتَدْنَا لِلْكٰفِرِيْنَ مِنْهُمْ
عَذَابًا اَلِيْمًا ﴿١٦٢﴾

163. But those among them who are firmly grounded in knowledge, and the believers, believe in what has been sent down to thee and what was sent down before thee, and *especially* those who observe Prayer and those who pay the Zakāt and those who believe in Allah and the Last Day. To these will We surely give a great reward.

لٰكِنِ الرّٰسِخُوْنَ فِي الْعِلْمِ مِنْهُمْ وَالْمُؤْمِنُوْنَ يُؤْمِنُوْنَ
بِمَآ اُنْزِلَ اِلَيْكَ وَمَآ اُنْزِلَ مِنْ قَبْلِكَ وَالْمُقِيْمِيْنَ
الصَّلٰوةَ وَالْمُؤْتُوْنَ الزَّكٰوةَ وَالْمُؤْمِنُوْنَ بِاللّٰهِ وَ
الْيَوْمِ الْاٰخِرِ ۭ اُولٰۗىِٕكَ سَنُؤْتِيْهِمْ اَجْرًا عَظِيْمًا ﴿١٦٣﴾ ع ٢٣

R. 23.

* 164. Surely, We have sent revelation to thee, as We sent revelation to Noah and the Prophets after him; and We sent revelation to Abraham and Ishmael and Isaac and Jacob and *his* children and *to* Jesus and Job and Jonah and Aaron and Solomon, and We gave David a Book.

اِنَّآ اَوْحَيْنَآ اِلَيْكَ كَمَآ اَوْحَيْنَآ اِلٰى نُوْحٍ وَّالنَّبِيّٖنَ
مِنْۢ بَعْدِهٖ ۚ وَاَوْحَيْنَآ اِلٰٓى اِبْرٰهِيْمَ وَاِسْمٰعِيْلَ وَ
اِسْحٰقَ وَيَعْقُوْبَ وَالْاَسْبَاطِ وَعِيْسٰى وَاَيُّوْبَ
وَيُوْنُسَ وَهٰرُوْنَ وَسُلَيْمٰنَ ۚ وَاٰتَيْنَا دَاوٗدَ
زَبُوْرًا ۚ ﴿١٦٤﴾

---

* i. e. killed him by crucifixion.

* 165. And *We sent some* Messengers whom We have already mentioned to thee and *some* Messengers whom We have not mentioned to thee— and Allah spoke to Moses particularly—

166. Messengers, bearers of glad tidings and warners, so that people may have no plea against Allah after *the coming of* the Messengers. And Allah is Mighty, Wise.

167. But Allah bears witness by means of *the revelation* which He has sent down to thee that He has sent it down *pregnant* with His knowledge; and the angels *also* bear witness; and sufficient is Allah as a Witness.

168. Those who disbelieve and hinder *others* from the way of Allah, have certainly strayed far away.

169. Surely, those who have disbelieved and have acted unjustly, Allah is not going to forgive them, nor will He show them any way,

170. Except the way of Hell, wherein they shall abide for a long, long period. And that is easy for Allah.

171. O mankind, the Messenger has indeed come to you with Truth from your Lord; believe therefore, *it will be* better for you. But if you disbelieve, verily, to Allah belongs whatever is in the heavens and in the earth. And Allah is All-Knowing, Wise.

172. O People of the Book, exceed not the limits in your religion, and say not of Allah anything but the truth. Verily, the Messiah, Jesus, son of Mary, was only a Messenger of Allah and *a fulfilment of* His word which He sent down to Mary, and a mercy from Him. So believe in Allah and His Messengers, and say not *'They are three.'* Desist, *it will be* better for you. Verily, Allah is the only One God. Far is it from His Holiness that He should have a son. To Him belongs whatever is in the heavens and whatever is in the earth. And

وَ رُسُلًا قَدْ قَصَصْنٰهُمْ عَلَيْكَ مِنْ قَبْلُ وَ رُسُلًا
لَّمْ نَقْصُصْهُمْ عَلَيْكَ ؕ وَ كَلَّمَ اللّٰهُ مُوْسٰى تَكْلِيْمًا ﴿۱۶۵﴾
رُسُلًا مُّبَشِّرِيْنَ وَ مُنْذِرِيْنَ لِئَلَّا يَكُوْنَ لِلنَّاسِ
عَلَى اللّٰهِ حُجَّةٌۢ بَعْدَ الرُّسُلِ ؕ وَ كَانَ اللّٰهُ عَزِيْزًا
حَكِيْمًا ﴿۱۶۶﴾
لٰكِنِ اللّٰهُ يَشْهَدُ بِمَآ اَنْزَلَ اِلَيْكَ اَنْزَلَهٗ بِعِلْمِهٖ ۚ
وَ الْمَلٰٓئِكَةُ يَشْهَدُوْنَ ؕ وَ كَفٰى بِاللّٰهِ شَهِيْدًا ﴿۱۶۷﴾
اِنَّ الَّذِيْنَ كَفَرُوْا وَ صَدُّوْا عَنْ سَبِيْلِ اللّٰهِ قَدْ ضَلُّوْا
ضَلٰلًۢا بَعِيْدًا ﴿۱۶۸﴾
اِنَّ الَّذِيْنَ كَفَرُوْا وَ ظَلَمُوْا لَمْ يَكُنِ اللّٰهُ لِيَغْفِرَ لَهُمْ
وَ لَا لِيَهْدِيَهُمْ طَرِيْقًا ﴿۱۶۹﴾
اِلَّا طَرِيْقَ جَهَنَّمَ خٰلِدِيْنَ فِيْهَآ اَبَدًا ؕ وَ كَانَ ذٰلِكَ
عَلَى اللّٰهِ يَسِيْرًا ﴿۱۷۰﴾
يٰٓاَيُّهَا النَّاسُ قَدْ جَآءَكُمُ الرَّسُوْلُ بِالْحَقِّ مِنْ
رَّبِّكُمْ فَاٰمِنُوْا خَيْرًا لَّكُمْ ؕ وَ اِنْ تَكْفُرُوْا فَاِنَّ لِلّٰهِ مَا
فِي السَّمٰوٰتِ وَ الْاَرْضِ ؕ وَ كَانَ اللّٰهُ عَلِيْمًا حَكِيْمًا ﴿۱۷۱﴾
يٰٓاَهْلَ الْكِتٰبِ لَا تَغْلُوْا فِيْ دِيْنِكُمْ وَ لَا تَقُوْلُوْا عَلَى
اللّٰهِ اِلَّا الْحَقَّ ؕ اِنَّمَا الْمَسِيْحُ عِيْسَى ابْنُ مَرْيَمَ
رَسُوْلُ اللّٰهِ وَ كَلِمَتُهٗ ۚ اَلْقٰهَآ اِلٰى مَرْيَمَ وَ رُوْحٌ مِّنْهُ ۫
فَاٰمِنُوْا بِاللّٰهِ وَ رُسُلِهٖ ۚ وَ لَا تَقُوْلُوْا ثَلٰثَةٌ ؕ اِنْتَهُوْا
خَيْرًا لَّكُمْ ؕ اِنَّمَا اللّٰهُ اِلٰهٌ وَّاحِدٌ ؕ سُبْحٰنَهٗٓ اَنْ يَّكُوْنَ
لَهٗ وَلَدٌ ۘ لَهٗ مَا فِي السَّمٰوٰتِ وَ مَا فِي الْاَرْضِ ؕ وَ كَفٰى وقف لازم

sufficient is Allah as a Guardian.

٢٣ ع بِاللّٰهِ وَكِيْلًا ۝١٧٢ ع

R. 24.

173. Surely, the Messiah will never disdain to be a servant of Allah, nor will the angels near *unto God;* and whoso disdains to worship Him and feels proud, He will gather them all to Himself.

٣ لَنْ يَّسْتَنْكِفَ الْمَسِيْحُ اَنْ يَّكُوْنَ عَبْدًا لِّلّٰهِ وَلَا
الْمَلٰٓئِكَةُ الْمُقَرَّبُوْنَ ۭ وَمَنْ يَّسْتَنْكِفْ عَنْ عِبَادَتِهٖ وَ
يَسْتَكْبِرْ فَسَيَحْشُرُهُمْ اِلَيْهِ جَمِيْعًا ۝١٧٣

174. Then as for those who believed and did good works, He will give them their rewards in full and will give them more out of His bounty; but as for those who disdained and were proud, He will punish them with a painful punishment. And they shall find for themselves beside Allah no friend nor helper.

فَاَمَّا الَّذِيْنَ اٰمَنُوْا وَعَمِلُوا الصّٰلِحٰتِ فَيُوَفِّيْهِمْ اُجُوْرَهُمْ
وَيَزِيْدُهُمْ مِّنْ فَضْلِهٖ ۚ وَاَمَّا الَّذِيْنَ اسْتَنْكَفُوْا وَ
اسْتَكْبَرُوْا فَيُعَذِّبُهُمْ عَذَابًا اَلِيْمًا ۙ وَّلَا يَجِدُوْنَ
لَهُمْ مِّنْ دُوْنِ اللّٰهِ وَلِيًّا وَّلَا نَصِيْرًا ۝١٧٤

175. O ye people, a manifest proof has indeed come to you from your Lord, and We have sent down to you a clear light.

يٰٓاَيُّهَا النَّاسُ قَدْ جَآءَكُمْ بُرْهَانٌ مِّنْ رَّبِّكُمْ وَ
اَنْزَلْنَآ اِلَيْكُمْ نُوْرًا مُّبِيْنًا ۝١٧٥

176. So, as for those who believe in Allah and hold fast to Him, He will surely admit them to His mercy and grace and will guide them on a straight path *leading* to Himself.

فَاَمَّا الَّذِيْنَ اٰمَنُوْا بِاللّٰهِ وَاعْتَصَمُوْا بِهٖ فَسَيُدْخِلُهُمْ
فِيْ رَحْمَةٍ مِّنْهُ وَفَضْلٍ ۙ وَّيَهْدِيْهِمْ اِلَيْهِ صِرَاطًا
مُّسْتَقِيْمًا ۝١٧٦

177. They ask thee for instructions. Say, Allah gives you *His* instructions concerning 'Kalāla': If a man dies leaving no child and he has a sister, then she shall have half of what he leaves; and he shall inherit her if she has no child. But if there be two sisters, then they shall have two-thirds of what he leaves. And if *the heirs* be brethren—*both* men and women—then the male shall have as much as the portion of two females. Allah explains *this* to you lest you go astray, and Allah knows all things well.

يَسْتَفْتُوْنَكَ ۭ قُلِ اللّٰهُ يُفْتِيْكُمْ فِي الْكَلٰلَةِ ۭ اِنِ امْرُؤٌا
هَلَكَ لَيْسَ لَهٗ وَلَدٌ وَّلَهٗٓ اُخْتٌ فَلَهَا نِصْفُ مَا تَرَكَ ۚ
وَهُوَ يَرِثُهَآ اِنْ لَّمْ يَكُنْ لَّهَا وَلَدٌ ۭ فَاِنْ كَانَتَا اثْنَتَيْنِ
فَلَهُمَا الثُّلُثٰنِ مِمَّا تَرَكَ ۭ وَاِنْ كَانُوْٓا اِخْوَةً رِّجَالًا
وَّنِسَآءً فَلِلذَّكَرِ مِثْلُ حَظِّ الْاُنْثَيَيْنِ ۭ يُبَيِّنُ اللّٰهُ
٢٤ ع ٤ لَكُمْ اَنْ تَضِلُّوْا ۭ وَاللّٰهُ بِكُلِّ شَيْءٍ عَلِيْمٌ ۝١٧٧ ع

سُوْرَةُ الْمَآئِدَةِ مَدَنِيَّةٌ (٥) آياتها ١٢١ ركوعاتها ١٦

AL-MĀ'IDAH

(Revealed after Hijra)

1. In the name of Allah, the Gracious, the Merciful.

2. O ye who believe! fulfil *your* compacts. Lawful are made to you quadrupeds *of the class* of cattle other than those which are being announced to you, except that you should not hold game to be lawful while you are in a state of pilgrimage; verily, Allah decrees what He wills.

* 3. O ye who believe! profane not the Signs of Allah, nor the Sacred Month, nor the animals brought as an offering, nor the *animals of sacrifice wearing* collars, nor those repairing to the Sacred House, seeking grace from their Lord, and *His* pleasure. And when you put off the pilgrims' garb *and are clear of the Sacred Territory,* you may hunt. And let not the enmity of a people, that they hindered you from the Sacred Mosque, incite you to transgress. And help one another in righteousness and piety; but help not one another in sin and transgression. And fear Allah; surely, Allah is severe in punishment.

4. Forbidden to you is *the flesh of an animal* which dies of itself, and blood and the flesh of swine; and that on which is invoked the name of one other than Allah; and that which has been strangled; and that beaten to death; and that killed by a fall; and that which has been gored to death; and that of which a wild animal has eaten, except that which you have properly slaughtered; and that which has been slaughtered at an altar. *And forbidden is also* that you seek to know your lot by the divining arrows. That is *an act of* disobedience. This day have those who disbelieve despaired of *harming* your religion. So fear them not, but fear Me. This day have I perfected your religion for you and completed My favour upon you and have chosen for you Islam as religion. But whoso is forced by hunger, without being wilfully inclined to sin, then, surely, Allah is Most Forgiving, Merciful.

بِسْمِ اللّٰهِ الرَّحْمٰنِ الرَّحِيْمِ ①
يٰٓاَيُّهَا الَّذِيْنَ اٰمَنُوْٓا اَوْفُوْا بِالْعُقُوْدِ ۛ اُحِلَّتْ لَكُمْ
بَهِيْمَةُ الْاَنْعَامِ اِلَّا مَا يُتْلٰى عَلَيْكُمْ غَيْرَ مُحِلِّي الصَّيْدِ
وَاَنْتُمْ حُرُمٌ اِنَّ اللّٰهَ يَحْكُمُ مَا يُرِيْدُ ②
يٰٓاَيُّهَا الَّذِيْنَ اٰمَنُوْا لَا تُحِلُّوْا شَعَآئِرَ اللّٰهِ وَلَا الشَّهْرَ
الْحَرَامَ وَلَا الْهَدْيَ وَلَا الْقَلَآئِدَ وَلَآ اٰمِّيْنَ الْبَيْتَ
الْحَرَامَ يَبْتَغُوْنَ فَضْلًا مِّنْ رَّبِّهِمْ وَرِضْوَانًا وَاِذَا
حَلَلْتُمْ فَاصْطَادُوْا وَلَا يَجْرِمَنَّكُمْ شَنَاٰنُ قَوْمٍ اَنْ
صَدُّوْكُمْ عَنِ الْمَسْجِدِ الْحَرَامِ اَنْ تَعْتَدُوْا وَتَعَاوَنُوْا
عَلَى الْبِرِّ وَالتَّقْوٰى وَلَا تَعَاوَنُوْا عَلَى الْاِثْمِ وَالْعُدْوَانِ
وَاتَّقُوا اللّٰهَ اِنَّ اللّٰهَ شَدِيْدُ الْعِقَابِ ③
حُرِّمَتْ عَلَيْكُمُ الْمَيْتَةُ وَالدَّمُ وَلَحْمُ الْخِنْزِيْرِ وَ
مَآ اُهِلَّ لِغَيْرِ اللّٰهِ بِهٖ وَالْمُنْخَنِقَةُ وَالْمَوْقُوْذَةُ وَالْمُتَرَدِّيَةُ
وَالنَّطِيْحَةُ وَمَآ اَكَلَ السَّبُعُ اِلَّا مَا ذَكَّيْتُمْ وَمَا ذُبِحَ
عَلَى النُّصُبِ وَاَنْ تَسْتَقْسِمُوْا بِالْاَزْلَامِ ذٰلِكُمْ فِسْقٌ
اَلْيَوْمَ يَئِسَ الَّذِيْنَ كَفَرُوْا مِنْ دِيْنِكُمْ فَلَا تَخْشَوْهُمْ
وَاخْشَوْنِ اَلْيَوْمَ اَكْمَلْتُ لَكُمْ دِيْنَكُمْ وَاَتْمَمْتُ عَلَيْكُمْ
نِعْمَتِيْ وَرَضِيْتُ لَكُمُ الْاِسْلَامَ دِيْنًا فَمَنِ اضْطُرَّ فِيْ
مَخْمَصَةٍ غَيْرَ مُتَجَانِفٍ لِّاِثْمٍ فَاِنَّ اللّٰهَ غَفُوْرٌ رَّحِيْمٌ ④

المنزل ٢ وقف لازم الربع

5. They ask thee what is made lawful for them. Say, 'All good things have been made lawful for you; and what you have taught the beasts and birds of prey *to catch for you*, training *them* for hunting *and* teaching them of what Allah has taught you. So eat of that which they catch for you, and pronounce thereon the name of Allah. And fear Allah. Surely, Allah is quick in reckoning.'

يَسْـَٔلُونَكَ مَاذَآ أُحِلَّ لَهُمْ ۖ قُلْ أُحِلَّ لَكُمُ ٱلطَّيِّبَٰتُ ۙ
وَمَا عَلَّمْتُم مِّنَ ٱلْجَوَارِحِ مُكَلِّبِينَ تُعَلِّمُونَهُنَّ مِمَّا
عَلَّمَكُمُ ٱللَّهُ ۖ فَكُلُوا۟ مِمَّآ أَمْسَكْنَ عَلَيْكُمْ وَٱذْكُرُوا۟ ٱسْمَ
ٱللَّهِ عَلَيْهِ ۖ وَٱتَّقُوا۟ ٱللَّهَ ۚ إِنَّ ٱللَّهَ سَرِيعُ ٱلْحِسَابِ ٥

6. This day all good things have been made lawful for you. And the food of the People of the Book is lawful for you, and your food is lawful for them. And *lawful for you are* chaste believing women and chaste women from among those who were given the Book before you, when you give them their dowries, contracting valid marriage and not committing fornication nor taking secret paramours. And whoever rejects the faith, his work has doubtless come to naught, and in the Hereafter he will be among the losers.

ٱلْيَوْمَ أُحِلَّ لَكُمُ ٱلطَّيِّبَٰتُ ۖ وَطَعَامُ ٱلَّذِينَ أُوتُوا۟ ٱلْكِتَٰبَ
حِلٌّ لَّكُمْ وَطَعَامُكُمْ حِلٌّ لَّهُمْ ۖ وَٱلْمُحْصَنَٰتُ مِنَ
ٱلْمُؤْمِنَٰتِ وَٱلْمُحْصَنَٰتُ مِنَ ٱلَّذِينَ أُوتُوا۟ ٱلْكِتَٰبَ
مِن قَبْلِكُمْ إِذَآ ءَاتَيْتُمُوهُنَّ أُجُورَهُنَّ مُحْصِنِينَ
غَيْرَ مُسَٰفِحِينَ وَلَا مُتَّخِذِىٓ أَخْدَانٍ ۗ وَمَن يَكْفُرْ
بِٱلْإِيمَٰنِ فَقَدْ حَبِطَ عَمَلُهُۥ وَهُوَ فِى ٱلْـَٔاخِرَةِ مِنَ
ٱلْخَٰسِرِينَ ٦ ع ٦ ٥

R. 2.

7. O ye who believe! when you stand up for Prayer, wash your faces, and your hands up to the elbows, and pass your *wet* hands over your heads, and *wash* your feet to the ankles. And if you be unclean, purify yourselves *by bathing*. And if you are ill or *you are* on a journey *while unclean*, or one of you comes from the privy or you have touched women, and you find not water, betake yourselves to pure dust and wipe therewith your faces and your hands. Allah desires not that He should place you in a difficulty, but He desires to purify you and to complete His favour upon you, so that you may be grateful.

يَٰٓأَيُّهَا ٱلَّذِينَ ءَامَنُوٓا۟ إِذَا قُمْتُمْ إِلَى ٱلصَّلَوٰةِ فَٱغْسِلُوا۟
وُجُوهَكُمْ وَأَيْدِيَكُمْ إِلَى ٱلْمَرَافِقِ وَٱمْسَحُوا۟ بِرُءُوسِكُمْ
وَأَرْجُلَكُمْ إِلَى ٱلْكَعْبَيْنِ ۚ وَإِن كُنتُمْ جُنُبًا فَٱطَّهَّرُوا۟ ۚ
وَإِن كُنتُم مَّرْضَىٰٓ أَوْ عَلَىٰ سَفَرٍ أَوْ جَآءَ أَحَدٌ مِّنكُم مِّنَ
ٱلْغَآئِطِ أَوْ لَٰمَسْتُمُ ٱلنِّسَآءَ فَلَمْ تَجِدُوا۟ مَآءً فَتَيَمَّمُوا۟
صَعِيدًا طَيِّبًا فَٱمْسَحُوا۟ بِوُجُوهِكُمْ وَأَيْدِيكُم مِّنْهُ ۚ
مَا يُرِيدُ ٱللَّهُ لِيَجْعَلَ عَلَيْكُم مِّنْ حَرَجٍ وَلَٰكِن يُرِيدُ
لِيُطَهِّرَكُمْ وَلِيُتِمَّ نِعْمَتَهُۥ عَلَيْكُمْ لَعَلَّكُمْ تَشْكُرُونَ ٧

8. And remember Allah's favour upon you and the covenant which He made with you, when you said, 'We hear and we obey.' And fear Allah. Surely, Allah knows well what is in the minds.

وَٱذْكُرُوا۟ نِعْمَةَ ٱللَّهِ عَلَيْكُمْ وَمِيثَٰقَهُ ٱلَّذِى وَاثَقَكُم
بِهِۦٓ إِذْ قُلْتُمْ سَمِعْنَا وَأَطَعْنَا ۖ وَٱتَّقُوا۟ ٱللَّهَ ۚ إِنَّ ٱللَّهَ
عَلِيمٌۢ بِذَاتِ ٱلصُّدُورِ ٨

9. O ye who believe! be steadfast in the cause of Allah, bearing witness in equity; and let not a people's enmity incite you to act otherwise than with justice. Be *always* just, that is nearer to righteousness. And fear Allah. Surely, Allah is aware of what you do.

يٰٓاَيُّهَا الَّذِيْنَ اٰمَنُوْا كُوْنُوْا قَوّٰمِيْنَ لِلّٰهِ شُهَدَآءَ بِالْقِسْطِ
وَلَا يَجْرِمَنَّكُمْ شَنَاٰنُ قَوْمٍ عَلٰٓى اَلَّا تَعْدِلُوْا ؕ اِعْدِلُوْا ۟
هُوَ اَقْرَبُ لِلتَّقْوٰى ۫ وَاتَّقُوا اللّٰهَ ؕ اِنَّ اللّٰهَ خَبِيْرٌۢ بِمَا
تَعْمَلُوْنَ ﴿٩﴾

10. Allah has promised those who believe and do good deeds that they shall have forgiveness and a great reward.

وَعَدَ اللّٰهُ الَّذِيْنَ اٰمَنُوْا وَعَمِلُوا الصّٰلِحٰتِ ۙ لَهُمْ
مَّغْفِرَةٌ وَّاَجْرٌ عَظِيْمٌ ﴿١٠﴾

11. And *as for* those who disbelieve and reject Our Signs, they are the people of Hell.

وَالَّذِيْنَ كَفَرُوْا وَكَذَّبُوْا بِاٰيٰتِنَآ اُولٰٓئِكَ اَصْحٰبُ الْجَحِيْمِ ﴿١١﴾

12. O ye who believe! remember Allah's favour upon you when a people intended to stretch out their hands against you, but He withheld their hands from you; and fear Allah. And on Allah should the believers rely.

يٰٓاَيُّهَا الَّذِيْنَ اٰمَنُوا اذْكُرُوْا نِعْمَتَ اللّٰهِ عَلَيْكُمْ اِذْ هَمَّ
قَوْمٌ اَنْ يَّبْسُطُوْٓا اِلَيْكُمْ اَيْدِيَهُمْ فَكَفَّ اَيْدِيَهُمْ
عَنْكُمْ ۚ وَاتَّقُوا اللّٰهَ ؕ وَعَلَى اللّٰهِ فَلْيَتَوَكَّلِ الْمُؤْمِنُوْنَ ﴿١٢﴾ ع

R. 3.

* 13. And indeed Allah did take a covenant from the children of Israel; and We raised among them twelve leaders. And Allah said, 'Surely, I am with you. If you observe Prayer, and pay the Zakāt, and believe in My Messengers and support them, and lend to Allah a goodly loan, I will remove your evils from you and admit you into Gardens beneath which streams flow. But whoso from among you disbelieves thereafter does indeed stray away from the right path.'

وَلَقَدْ اَخَذَ اللّٰهُ مِيْثَاقَ بَنِيْٓ اِسْرَآءِيْلَ ۚ وَبَعَثْنَا مِنْهُمُ
اثْنَيْ عَشَرَ نَقِيْبًا ؕ وَقَالَ اللّٰهُ اِنِّيْ مَعَكُمْ ؕ لَئِنْ اَقَمْتُمُ
الصَّلٰوةَ وَاٰتَيْتُمُ الزَّكٰوةَ وَاٰمَنْتُمْ بِرُسُلِيْ وَعَزَّرْتُمُوْهُمْ
وَاَقْرَضْتُمُ اللّٰهَ قَرْضًا حَسَنًا لَّاُكَفِّرَنَّ عَنْكُمْ سَيِّاٰتِكُمْ
وَلَاُدْخِلَنَّكُمْ جَنّٰتٍ تَجْرِيْ مِنْ تَحْتِهَا الْاَنْهٰرُ ۚ فَمَنْ
كَفَرَ بَعْدَ ذٰلِكَ مِنْكُمْ فَقَدْ ضَلَّ سَوَآءَ السَّبِيْلِ ﴿١٣﴾

* 14. So, because of their breaking their covenant, We have cursed them, and have hardened their hearts. They pervert the words from their *proper* places and have forgotten a *good* part of that with which they were exhorted. And thou wilt not cease to discover treachery on their part, except *in* a few of them. So pardon them and turn away *from them*. Surely, Allah loves those who do good.

فَبِمَا نَقْضِهِمْ مِّيْثَاقَهُمْ لَعَنّٰهُمْ وَجَعَلْنَا قُلُوْبَهُمْ
قٰسِيَةً ۚ يُحَرِّفُوْنَ الْكَلِمَ عَنْ مَّوَاضِعِهٖ ۙ وَنَسُوْا حَظًّا
مِّمَّا ذُكِّرُوْا بِهٖ ۚ وَلَا تَزَالُ تَطَّلِعُ عَلٰى خَآئِنَةٍ مِّنْهُمْ
اِلَّا قَلِيْلًا مِّنْهُمْ فَاعْفُ عَنْهُمْ وَاصْفَحْ ؕ اِنَّ اللّٰهَ يُحِبُّ
الْمُحْسِنِيْنَ ﴿١٤﴾

* 15. And from those *also* who say, 'We are Christians,' We took a covenant, but

وَمِنَ الَّذِيْنَ قَالُوْٓا اِنَّا نَصٰرٰٓى اَخَذْنَا مِيْثَاقَهُمْ فَنَسُوْا

they too have forgotten a *good* part of that with which they were exhorted. So We have caused enmity and hatred among them till the Day of Resurrection. And Allah will soon let them know what they have been doing.

حَظًّا مِّمَّا ذُكِّرُوْا بِهٖ فَاَغْرَيْنَا بَيْنَهُمُ الْعَدَاوَةَ وَالْبَغْضَآءَ
اِلٰى يَوْمِ الْقِيٰمَةِ ۭ وَسَوْفَ يُنَبِّئُهُمُ اللّٰهُ بِمَا كَانُوْا
يَصْنَعُوْنَ ﴿١٥﴾

16. O People of the Book! there has come to you Our Messenger who unfolds to you much of what you had kept hidden of the Book and passes over much. There has come to you indeed from Allah a Light and a clear Book.

يٰٓاَهْلَ الْكِتٰبِ قَدْ جَآءَكُمْ رَسُوْلُنَا يُبَيِّنُ لَكُمْ كَثِيْرًا
مِّمَّا كُنْتُمْ تُخْفُوْنَ مِنَ الْكِتٰبِ وَيَعْفُوْا عَنْ كَثِيْرٍ ۭ
قَدْ جَآءَكُمْ مِّنَ اللّٰهِ نُوْرٌ وَّكِتٰبٌ مُّبِيْنٌ ﴿١٦﴾

17. Thereby does Allah guide those who seek His pleasure on the paths of peace, and leads them out of every *kind of* darkness into light by His will, and guides them to the right path.

يَّهْدِيْ بِهِ اللّٰهُ مَنِ اتَّبَعَ رِضْوَانَهٗ سُبُلَ السَّلٰمِ
وَيُخْرِجُهُمْ مِّنَ الظُّلُمٰتِ اِلَى النُّوْرِ بِاِذْنِهٖ وَيَهْدِيْهِمْ
اِلٰى صِرَاطٍ مُّسْتَقِيْمٍ ﴿١٧﴾

18. They have indeed disbelieved who say, 'Surely, Allah is none but the Messiah, son of Mary.' Say, 'Who then has any power against Allah, if He desire to bring to naught the Messiah, son of Mary, and his mother and all those that are in the earth?' And to Allah belongs the kingdom of the heavens and the earth and what is between them. He creates what He pleases; and Allah has power to do all things.

لَقَدْ كَفَرَ الَّذِيْنَ قَالُوْٓا اِنَّ اللّٰهَ هُوَ الْمَسِيْحُ ابْنُ مَرْيَمَ ۭ
قُلْ فَمَنْ يَّمْلِكُ مِنَ اللّٰهِ شَيْـًٔا اِنْ اَرَادَ اَنْ يُّهْلِكَ
الْمَسِيْحَ ابْنَ مَرْيَمَ وَاُمَّهٗ وَمَنْ فِي الْاَرْضِ جَمِيْعًا ۭ
وَلِلّٰهِ مُلْكُ السَّمٰوٰتِ وَالْاَرْضِ وَمَا بَيْنَهُمَا ۭ يَخْلُقُ
مَا يَشَآءُ ۭ وَاللّٰهُ عَلٰى كُلِّ شَيْءٍ قَدِيْرٌ ﴿١٨﴾

19. The Jews and the Christians say, 'We are sons of Allah and His loved ones.' Say, 'Why then does He punish you for your sins? Nay, you are *only* human beings among those He has created.' He forgives whom He pleases and punishes whom He pleases. And to Allah belongs the kingdom of the heavens and the earth and what is between them, and to Him shall be the return.

وَقَالَتِ الْيَهُوْدُ وَالنَّصٰرٰى نَحْنُ اَبْنٰٓؤُا اللّٰهِ وَاَحِبَّآؤُهٗ ۭ
قُلْ فَلِمَ يُعَذِّبُكُمْ بِذُنُوْبِكُمْ ۭ بَلْ اَنْتُمْ بَشَرٌ مِّمَّنْ
خَلَقَ ۭ يَغْفِرُ لِمَنْ يَّشَآءُ وَيُعَذِّبُ مَنْ يَّشَآءُ ۭ وَلِلّٰهِ مُلْكُ
السَّمٰوٰتِ وَالْاَرْضِ وَمَا بَيْنَهُمَا ۡ وَاِلَيْهِ الْمَصِيْرُ ﴿١٩﴾

20. O People of the Book! there has come to you Our Messenger, after a break in *the series of* Messengers, who makes *things* clear to you lest you say, 'There has come to us no bearer of glad tidings and no warner.' So a bearer of glad tidings and a warner has indeed come to you. And Allah has power to do all things.

يٰٓاَهْلَ الْكِتٰبِ قَدْ جَآءَكُمْ رَسُوْلُنَا يُبَيِّنُ لَكُمْ عَلٰى
فَتْرَةٍ مِّنَ الرُّسُلِ اَنْ تَقُوْلُوْا مَا جَآءَنَا مِنْ بَشِيْرٍ وَّ
لَا نَذِيْرٍ ۡ فَقَدْ جَآءَكُمْ بَشِيْرٌ وَّنَذِيْرٌ ۭ وَاللّٰهُ عَلٰى
كُلِّ شَيْءٍ قَدِيْرٌ ﴿٢٠﴾

R. 4.

* 21. And *remember* when Moses said to his people, 'O my people, call to mind Allah's favour upon you when He appointed Prophets among you and made you kings, and gave you what He gave not to any other among the peoples.

22. 'O my people, enter the Holy Land which Allah has ordained for you and do not turn back, for then you will turn losers.'

23. They said, 'O Moses, there is in that *land* a haughty and powerful people, and we shall not enter it until they go forth from it. But if they go forth from it, then we will enter *it*.'

24. Thereupon two men from among those who feared *their Lord*, on whom Allah had conferred His favour, said, 'Enter the gate, *advancing* against them; when *once* you have entered it, then surely you will be victorious. And put your trust in Allah, if you are believers.'

25. They said, 'O Moses, we will never enter it so long as they remain in it. Therefore, go thou and thy Lord and fight, *and* here we sit.'

26. He said, 'My Lord, I have power over none but myself and my brother; therefore make Thou a distinction between us and the rebellious people.'

27. *God* said: 'Verily, it shall be forbidden them for forty years; in distraction shall they wander through the land. So grieve not over the rebellious people.'

R. 5.

28. And relate to them truly the story of the two sons of Adam, when they *each* offered an offering, and it was accepted from one of them and was not accepted from the other. The latter said, 'I will surely kill thee.' The former replied, 'Allah accepts only from the righteous.

29. 'If thou stretch out thy hand against me to kill me, I am not going to stretch out my hand against thee to kill thee. I do fear Allah, the Lord of the universe.

وَاِذْ قَالَ مُوْسٰی لِقَوْمِهٖ يٰقَوْمِ اذْكُرُوْا نِعْمَةَ اللّٰهِ
عَلَيْكُمْ اِذْ جَعَلَ فِيْكُمْ اَنْۢبِيَآءَ وَجَعَلَكُمْ مُّلُوْكًا ۖۗ
وَّاٰتٰىكُمْ مَّا لَمْ يُؤْتِ اَحَدًا مِّنَ الْعٰلَمِيْنَ ﴿٢١﴾
يٰقَوْمِ ادْخُلُوا الْاَرْضَ الْمُقَدَّسَةَ الَّتِيْ كَتَبَ اللّٰهُ لَكُمْ
وَلَا تَرْتَدُّوْا عَلٰۤى اَدْبَارِكُمْ فَتَنْقَلِبُوْا خٰسِرِيْنَ ﴿٢٢﴾
قَالُوْا يٰمُوْسٰۤى اِنَّ فِيْهَا قَوْمًا جَبَّارِيْنَ ۖۗ وَاِنَّا لَنْ
نَّدْخُلَهَا حَتّٰى يَخْرُجُوْا مِنْهَا ۚ فَاِنْ يَّخْرُجُوْا مِنْهَا
فَاِنَّا دٰخِلُوْنَ ﴿٢٣﴾
قَالَ رَجُلٰنِ مِنَ الَّذِيْنَ يَخَافُوْنَ اَنْعَمَ اللّٰهُ عَلَيْهِمَا
ادْخُلُوْا عَلَيْهِمُ الْبَابَ ۚ فَاِذَا دَخَلْتُمُوْهُ فَاِنَّكُمْ غٰلِبُوْنَ ۚ
وَعَلَى اللّٰهِ فَتَوَكَّلُوْۤا اِنْ كُنْتُمْ مُّؤْمِنِيْنَ ﴿٢٤﴾
قَالُوْا يٰمُوْسٰۤى اِنَّا لَنْ نَّدْخُلَهَاۤ اَبَدًا مَّا دَامُوْا فِيْهَا
فَاذْهَبْ اَنْتَ وَرَبُّكَ فَقَاتِلَاۤ اِنَّا هٰهُنَا قٰعِدُوْنَ ﴿٢٥﴾
قَالَ رَبِّ اِنِّيْ لَاۤ اَمْلِكُ اِلَّا نَفْسِيْ وَاَخِيْ فَافْرُقْ بَيْنَنَا
وَبَيْنَ الْقَوْمِ الْفٰسِقِيْنَ ﴿٢٦﴾
قَالَ فَاِنَّهَا مُحَرَّمَةٌ عَلَيْهِمْ اَرْبَعِيْنَ سَنَةً ۚ يَتِيْهُوْنَ
فِي الْاَرْضِ ؕ فَلَا تَاْسَ عَلَى الْقَوْمِ الْفٰسِقِيْنَ ﴿٢٧﴾
وَاتْلُ عَلَيْهِمْ نَبَاَ ابْنَيْ اٰدَمَ بِالْحَقِّ ۘ اِذْ قَرَّبَا قُرْبَانًا
فَتُقُبِّلَ مِنْ اَحَدِهِمَا وَلَمْ يُتَقَبَّلْ مِنَ الْاٰخَرِ ؕ قَالَ
لَاَقْتُلَنَّكَ ؕ قَالَ اِنَّمَا يَتَقَبَّلُ اللّٰهُ مِنَ الْمُتَّقِيْنَ ﴿٢٨﴾
لَئِنْۢ بَسَطْتَّ اِلَيَّ يَدَكَ لِتَقْتُلَنِيْ مَاۤ اَنَا بِبَاسِطٍ يَّدِيَ
اِلَيْكَ لِاَقْتُلَكَ ۚ اِنِّيْۤ اَخَافُ اللّٰهَ رَبَّ الْعٰلَمِيْنَ ﴿٢٩﴾

30. 'I wish that thou shouldst bear my sin as well as thy sin, and thus be among the inmates of the Fire, and that is the reward of those who do wrong.'

إِنِّيٓ أُرِيدُ أَن تَبُوٓأَ بِإِثۡمِي وَإِثۡمِكَ فَتَكُونَ مِنۡ
أَصۡحَٰبِ ٱلنَّارِۚ وَذَٰلِكَ جَزَٰٓؤُاْ ٱلظَّٰلِمِينَ ﴿٣٠﴾

31. But his mind induced him to kill his brother, so he killed him and became one of the losers.

فَطَوَّعَتۡ لَهُۥ نَفۡسُهُۥ قَتۡلَ أَخِيهِ فَقَتَلَهُۥ فَأَصۡبَحَ
مِنَ ٱلۡخَٰسِرِينَ ﴿٣١﴾

32. Then Allah sent a raven which scratched in the ground, that He might show him how to hide the corpse of his brother. He said, 'Woe is me! Am I not able to be even like this raven so that I may hide the corpse of my brother?' And then he became regretful.

فَبَعَثَ ٱللَّهُ غُرَابٗا يَبۡحَثُ فِي ٱلۡأَرۡضِ لِيُرِيَهُۥ كَيۡفَ
يُوَٰرِي سَوۡءَةَ أَخِيهِۚ قَالَ يَٰوَيۡلَتَىٰٓ أَعَجَزۡتُ أَنۡ أَكُونَ
مِثۡلَ هَٰذَا ٱلۡغُرَابِ فَأُوَٰرِيَ سَوۡءَةَ أَخِيۖ فَأَصۡبَحَ
مِنَ ٱلنَّٰدِمِينَ ﴿٣٢﴾

33. On account of this, We prescribed for the children of Israel that whosoever killed a person—unless it be for *killing* a person or for creating disorder in the land—it shall be as if he had killed all mankind; and whoso gave life to one, it shall be as if he had given life to all mankind. And Our Messengers came to them with clear Signs, yet even after that, many of them commit excesses in the land.

مِنۡ أَجۡلِ ذَٰلِكَ كَتَبۡنَا عَلَىٰ بَنِيٓ إِسۡرَٰٓءِيلَ أَنَّهُۥ مَن
قَتَلَ نَفۡسَۢا بِغَيۡرِ نَفۡسٍ أَوۡ فَسَادٖ فِي ٱلۡأَرۡضِ فَكَأَنَّمَا
قَتَلَ ٱلنَّاسَ جَمِيعٗا وَمَنۡ أَحۡيَاهَا فَكَأَنَّمَآ أَحۡيَا ٱلنَّاسَ
جَمِيعٗاۚ وَلَقَدۡ جَآءَتۡهُمۡ رُسُلُنَا بِٱلۡبَيِّنَٰتِ ثُمَّ إِنَّ
كَثِيرٗا مِّنۡهُم بَعۡدَ ذَٰلِكَ فِي ٱلۡأَرۡضِ لَمُسۡرِفُونَ ﴿٣٣﴾

34. The reward of those who wage war against Allah and His Messenger and strive to create disorder in the land is *only this* that they be slain or crucified or their hands and their feet be cut off on alternate sides, or they be expelled from the land. That shall be a disgrace for them in this world, and in the Hereafter they shall have a great punishment;

إِنَّمَا جَزَٰٓؤُاْ ٱلَّذِينَ يُحَارِبُونَ ٱللَّهَ وَرَسُولَهُۥ وَيَسۡعَوۡنَ
فِي ٱلۡأَرۡضِ فَسَادًا أَن يُقَتَّلُوٓاْ أَوۡ يُصَلَّبُوٓاْ أَوۡ تُقَطَّعَ
أَيۡدِيهِمۡ وَأَرۡجُلُهُم مِّنۡ خِلَٰفٍ أَوۡ يُنفَوۡاْ مِنَ ٱلۡأَرۡضِۚ
ذَٰلِكَ لَهُمۡ خِزۡيٞ فِي ٱلدُّنۡيَاۖ وَلَهُمۡ فِي ٱلۡأٓخِرَةِ عَذَابٌ
عَظِيمٌ ﴿٣٤﴾

35. Except those who repent before you have them in your power. So know that Allah is Most Forgiving, Merciful.

إِلَّا ٱلَّذِينَ تَابُواْ مِن قَبۡلِ أَن تَقۡدِرُواْ عَلَيۡهِمۡۖ فَٱعۡلَمُوٓاْ
أَنَّ ٱللَّهَ غَفُورٞ رَّحِيمٞ ﴿٣٥﴾

R. 6.

36. O ye who believe! fear Allah and seek the way of approach unto Him and strive in His way that you may prosper.

يَٰٓأَيُّهَا ٱلَّذِينَ ءَامَنُواْ ٱتَّقُواْ ٱللَّهَ وَٱبۡتَغُوٓاْ إِلَيۡهِ ٱلۡوَسِيلَةَ
وَجَٰهِدُواْ فِي سَبِيلِهِۦ لَعَلَّكُمۡ تُفۡلِحُونَ ﴿٣٦﴾

37. Surely, if those who disbelieve had all that is in the earth and as much over again, to ransom themselves therewith from the punishment of the Day of Resurrection, it would not be accepted from them; and they shall have a painful punishment.

إِنَّ الَّذِينَ كَفَرُوا لَوْ أَنَّ لَهُم مَّا فِي الْأَرْضِ جَمِيعًا
وَمِثْلَهُ مَعَهُ لِيَفْتَدُوا بِهِ مِنْ عَذَابِ يَوْمِ الْقِيَامَةِ
مَا تُقُبِّلَ مِنْهُمْ ۖ وَلَهُمْ عَذَابٌ أَلِيمٌ ﴿٣٧﴾

38. They will wish to come out of the Fire, but they will not be able to come out of it, and they shall have a lasting punishment.

يُرِيدُونَ أَن يَخْرُجُوا مِنَ النَّارِ وَمَا هُم بِخَارِجِينَ
مِنْهَا ۖ وَلَهُمْ عَذَابٌ مُّقِيمٌ ﴿٣٨﴾

39. And *as for* the man who steals and the woman who steals, cut off their hands in retribution of their offence as an exemplary punishment from Allah. And Allah is Mighty, Wise.

وَالسَّارِقُ وَالسَّارِقَةُ فَاقْطَعُوا أَيْدِيَهُمَا جَزَاءً بِمَا
كَسَبَا نَكَالًا مِّنَ اللَّهِ ۗ وَاللَّهُ عَزِيزٌ حَكِيمٌ ﴿٣٩﴾

40. But whoso repents after his transgression and amends, then will Allah surely turn to him in mercy; verily, Allah is Most Forgiving, Merciful.

فَمَن تَابَ مِن بَعْدِ ظُلْمِهِ وَأَصْلَحَ فَإِنَّ اللَّهَ يَتُوبُ
عَلَيْهِ ۗ إِنَّ اللَّهَ غَفُورٌ رَّحِيمٌ ﴿٤٠﴾

41. Dost thou not know that Allah is He to Whom belongs the kingdom of the heavens and the earth? He punishes whom He pleases and forgives whom He pleases; and Allah has power to do all things.

أَلَمْ تَعْلَمْ أَنَّ اللَّهَ لَهُ مُلْكُ السَّمَاوَاتِ وَالْأَرْضِ يُعَذِّبُ
مَن يَشَاءُ وَيَغْفِرُ لِمَن يَشَاءُ ۗ وَاللَّهُ عَلَىٰ كُلِّ شَيْءٍ
قَدِيرٌ ﴿٤١﴾

* 42. O Messenger! let not those grieve thee who hastily fall into disbelief—those who say with their mouths, 'We believe,' but their hearts believe not. And among the Jews *too* are those who would fondly listen to *any* lie—who listen for *conveying it to* another people who have not come to thee. They pervert words after their being put in their *right* places, and say, 'If you are given this, then accept it, but if you are not given this, then beware!' And as for him whom Allah desires to try, thou shalt not avail him aught against Allah. These are they whose hearts Allah has not been pleased to purify; they shall have disgrace in this world, and in the Hereafter they shall have a severe punishment.

يَا أَيُّهَا الرَّسُولُ لَا يَحْزُنكَ الَّذِينَ يُسَارِعُونَ فِي
الْكُفْرِ مِنَ الَّذِينَ قَالُوا آمَنَّا بِأَفْوَاهِهِمْ وَلَمْ تُؤْمِن
قُلُوبُهُمْ ۛ وَمِنَ الَّذِينَ هَادُوا ۛ سَمَّاعُونَ لِلْكَذِبِ
سَمَّاعُونَ لِقَوْمٍ آخَرِينَ لَمْ يَأْتُوكَ ۖ يُحَرِّفُونَ الْكَلِمَ
مِن بَعْدِ مَوَاضِعِهِ ۖ يَقُولُونَ إِنْ أُوتِيتُمْ هَٰذَا فَخُذُوهُ
وَإِن لَّمْ تُؤْتَوْهُ فَاحْذَرُوا ۚ وَمَن يُرِدِ اللَّهُ فِتْنَتَهُ
فَلَن تَمْلِكَ لَهُ مِنَ اللَّهِ شَيْئًا ۚ أُولَٰئِكَ الَّذِينَ لَمْ يُرِدِ
اللَّهُ أَن يُطَهِّرَ قُلُوبَهُمْ ۚ لَهُمْ فِي الدُّنْيَا خِزْيٌ ۖ وَ
لَهُمْ فِي الْآخِرَةِ عَذَابٌ عَظِيمٌ ﴿٤٢﴾

43. They are habitual listeners to falsehood, devourers of things forbidden. If, then, they come to thee *for judgment*,

سَمَّاعُونَ لِلْكَذِبِ أَكَّالُونَ لِلسُّحْتِ ۚ فَإِن جَاءُوكَ

judge between them or turn aside from them. And if thou turn aside from them, they cannot harm thee at all. And if thou judge, judge between them with justice. Surely, Allah loves those who are just.

فَاحْكُمْ بَيْنَهُمْ أَوْ أَعْرِضْ عَنْهُمْ ۚ وَإِنْ تُعْرِضْ عَنْهُمْ فَلَنْ يَضُرُّوكَ شَيْئًا ۖ وَإِنْ حَكَمْتَ فَاحْكُمْ بَيْنَهُمْ بِالْقِسْطِ ۖ إِنَّ اللّٰهَ يُحِبُّ الْمُقْسِطِينَ ﴿٤٣﴾

44. And how will they make thee *their* judge when they have with them the Torah, wherein is Allah's judgment? Yet, in spite of that they turn their backs; and certainly they will not believe.

وَكَيْفَ يُحَكِّمُونَكَ وَعِنْدَهُمُ التَّوْرٰىةُ فِيهَا حُكْمُ اللّٰهِ ثُمَّ يَتَوَلَّوْنَ مِنْ بَعْدِ ذٰلِكَ ۖ وَمَا أُولٰٓئِكَ بِالْمُؤْمِنِينَ ﴿٤٤﴾ ع

R. 7.

45. Surely, We sent down the Torah wherein was guidance and light. By it did the Prophets, who were obedient *to Us*, judge for the Jews, as did the godly people and those learned *in the Law;* for they were required to preserve the Book of Allah, and *because* they were guardians over it. Therefore fear not men but fear Me; and barter not My Signs for a paltry price. And whoso judges not by that which Allah has sent down, these it is who are the disbelievers.

إِنَّآ أَنْزَلْنَا التَّوْرٰىةَ فِيهَا هُدًى وَّنُورٌ ۚ يَحْكُمُ بِهَا النَّبِيُّونَ الَّذِينَ أَسْلَمُوا لِلَّذِينَ هَادُوا وَالرَّبّٰنِيُّونَ وَالْأَحْبَارُ بِمَا اسْتُحْفِظُوا مِنْ كِتٰبِ اللّٰهِ وَكَانُوا عَلَيْهِ شُهَدَآءَ ۚ فَلَا تَخْشَوُا النَّاسَ وَاخْشَوْنِ وَلَا تَشْتَرُوا بِاٰيٰتِي ثَمَنًا قَلِيلًا ۗ وَمَنْ لَّمْ يَحْكُمْ بِمَآ أَنْزَلَ اللّٰهُ فَأُولٰٓئِكَ هُمُ الْكٰفِرُونَ ﴿٤٥﴾

46. And therein We prescribed for them: A life for a life, and an eye for an eye, and a nose for a nose, and an ear for an ear, and a tooth for a tooth, and for *other* injuries equitable retaliation. And whoso waives the right thereto, it shall be an expiation for his *sins*; and whoso judges not by what Allah has sent down, these it is who are wrongdoers.

وَكَتَبْنَا عَلَيْهِمْ فِيهَآ أَنَّ النَّفْسَ بِالنَّفْسِ وَالْعَيْنَ بِالْعَيْنِ وَالْأَنْفَ بِالْأَنْفِ وَالْأُذُنَ بِالْأُذُنِ وَالسِّنَّ بِالسِّنِّ ۙ وَالْجُرُوحَ قِصَاصٌ ۗ فَمَنْ تَصَدَّقَ بِهِ فَهُوَ كَفَّارَةٌ لَّهُ ۗ وَمَنْ لَّمْ يَحْكُمْ بِمَآ أَنْزَلَ اللّٰهُ فَأُولٰٓئِكَ هُمُ الظّٰلِمُونَ ﴿٤٦﴾

47. And We caused Jesus, son of Mary, to follow in their footsteps, fulfilling that which was *revealed* before him in the Torah; and We gave him the Gospel which contained guidance and light, fulfilling that which was *revealed* before it in the Torah, and a guidance and an admonition for the God-fearing.

وَقَفَّيْنَا عَلٰٓى اٰثَارِهِمْ بِعِيسَى ابْنِ مَرْيَمَ مُصَدِّقًا لِّمَا بَيْنَ يَدَيْهِ مِنَ التَّوْرٰىةِ ۖ وَاٰتَيْنٰهُ الْإِنْجِيلَ فِيهِ هُدًى وَّنُورٌ ۙ وَّمُصَدِّقًا لِّمَا بَيْنَ يَدَيْهِ مِنَ التَّوْرٰىةِ وَهُدًى وَّمَوْعِظَةً لِّلْمُتَّقِينَ ﴿٤٧﴾

48. And let the People of the Gospel judge according to what Allah has revealed therein, and whoso judges not by what

وَلْيَحْكُمْ أَهْلُ الْإِنْجِيلِ بِمَآ أَنْزَلَ اللّٰهُ فِيهِ ۗ وَمَنْ لَّمْ

Allah has revealed, these it is who are the rebellious.

49. And We have revealed unto thee the Book comprising the truth *and* fulfilling that which was *revealed* before it in the Book, and as a guardian over it. Judge, therefore, between them by what Allah has revealed, and follow not their evil inclinations, *turning away* from the truth which has come to thee. For each of you We prescribed a clear spiritual Law and a manifest way *in secular matters*. And if Allah had *enforced* His will, He would have made you *all* one people, but *He wishes* to try you by that which He has given you. Vie, then, with one another in good works. To Allah shall you all return; then will He inform you of that wherein you differed.

50. And *We have revealed the Book to thee bidding thee* to judge between them by that which Allah has revealed and not to follow their evil inclinations, and to be on thy guard against them, lest they cause thee *to fall into* affliction on account of part of what Allah has revealed to thee. But if they turn away, then know that Allah intends to smite them for some of their sins. And indeed a large number of men are disobedient.

51. Do they then seek the judgment of *the days of* Ignorance? And who is better than Allah as a Judge for a people who have firm faith?

R. 8.

52. O ye who believe! take not the Jews and the Christians for friends. They are friends one to another. And whoso among you takes them for friends is indeed one of them. Verily, Allah guides not the unjust people.

53. And thou wilt see those in whose hearts is a disease, hastening towards them, saying, 'We fear lest a misfortune befall us.' Maybe, Allah will bring about victory or some *other* event from Himself. Then will they become regretful of what they concealed in their minds.

54. And those who believe will say, 'Are these they who swore by Allah with their

يَحْكُمْ بِمَآ اَنْزَلَ اللّٰهُ فَاُولٰٓئِكَ هُمُ الْفٰسِقُوْنَ ﴿۴۸﴾
وَ اَنْزَلْنَآ اِلَيْكَ الْكِتٰبَ بِالْحَقِّ مُصَدِّقًا لِّمَا بَيْنَ يَدَيْهِ
مِنَ الْكِتٰبِ وَ مُهَيْمِنًا عَلَيْهِ فَاحْكُمْ بَيْنَهُمْ بِمَآ اَنْزَلَ
اللّٰهُ وَلَا تَتَّبِعْ اَهْوَآءَهُمْ عَمَّا جَآءَكَ مِنَ الْحَقِّ لِكُلٍّ
جَعَلْنَا مِنْكُمْ شِرْعَةً وَّمِنْهَاجًا وَلَوْ شَآءَ اللّٰهُ لَجَعَلَكُمْ
اُمَّةً وَّاحِدَةً وَّلٰكِنْ لِّيَبْلُوَكُمْ فِيْ مَآ اٰتٰىكُمْ فَاسْتَبِقُوا
الْخَيْرٰتِ اِلَى اللّٰهِ مَرْجِعُكُمْ جَمِيْعًا فَيُنَبِّئُكُمْ بِمَا
كُنْتُمْ فِيْهِ تَخْتَلِفُوْنَ ﴿۴۹﴾
وَ اَنِ احْكُمْ بَيْنَهُمْ بِمَآ اَنْزَلَ اللّٰهُ وَلَا تَتَّبِعْ اَهْوَآءَهُمْ
وَاحْذَرْهُمْ اَنْ يَّفْتِنُوْكَ عَنْ بَعْضِ مَآ اَنْزَلَ اللّٰهُ اِلَيْكَ
فَاِنْ تَوَلَّوْا فَاعْلَمْ اَنَّمَا يُرِيْدُ اللّٰهُ اَنْ يُّصِيْبَهُمْ بِبَعْضِ
ذُنُوْبِهِمْ وَاِنَّ كَثِيْرًا مِّنَ النَّاسِ لَفٰسِقُوْنَ ﴿۵۰﴾
اَفَحُكْمَ الْجَاهِلِيَّةِ يَبْغُوْنَ وَمَنْ اَحْسَنُ مِنَ اللّٰهِ
حُكْمًا لِّقَوْمٍ يُّوْقِنُوْنَ ﴿۵۱﴾ ع
يٰٓاَيُّهَا الَّذِيْنَ اٰمَنُوْا لَا تَتَّخِذُوا الْيَهُوْدَ وَالنَّصٰرٰٓى اَوْلِيَآءَ
بَعْضُهُمْ اَوْلِيَآءُ بَعْضٍ وَمَنْ يَّتَوَلَّهُمْ مِّنْكُمْ فَاِنَّهٗ
مِنْهُمْ اِنَّ اللّٰهَ لَا يَهْدِي الْقَوْمَ الظّٰلِمِيْنَ ﴿۵۲﴾
فَتَرَى الَّذِيْنَ فِيْ قُلُوْبِهِمْ مَّرَضٌ يُّسَارِعُوْنَ فِيْهِمْ
يَقُوْلُوْنَ نَخْشٰٓى اَنْ تُصِيْبَنَا دَآئِرَةٌ فَعَسَى اللّٰهُ اَنْ يَّاْتِيَ
بِالْفَتْحِ اَوْ اَمْرٍ مِّنْ عِنْدِهٖ فَيُصْبِحُوْا عَلٰى مَآ اَسَرُّوْا فِيْٓ
اَنْفُسِهِمْ نٰدِمِيْنَ ﴿۵۳﴾
وَ يَقُوْلُ الَّذِيْنَ اٰمَنُوْٓا اَهٰٓؤُلَآءِ الَّذِيْنَ اَقْسَمُوْا بِاللّٰهِ جَهْدَ

most solemn oaths that they were surely with you?' Their works are vain and they have become the losers.

55. O ye who believe! whoso among you turns back from his religion, then *let it be known that in his stead* Allah will soon bring a people whom He will love and who will love Him, *and who will be* kind and humble towards believers, hard and firm against disbelievers. They will strive in the cause of Allah and will not fear the reproach of a fault-finder. That is Allah's grace; He bestows it upon whomsoever He pleases; and Allah is Bountiful, All-Knowing.

* 56. Your friend is only Allah and His Messenger and the believers who observe Prayer and pay the Zakāt and worship God alone.

57. And those who take Allah and His Messenger and the believers for friends *should rest assured* that it is the party of Allah that must triumph.

R. 9.

58. O ye who believe! take not those for friends who make a jest and sport of your religion from among those who were given the Book before you, and the disbelievers. And fear Allah if you are believers;

59. And *who*, when you call *people* to Prayer, take it as jest and sport. That is because they are a people who do not understand.

60. Say, 'O People of the Book! do you find fault with us because we believe in Allah and what has been sent down to us and what was sent down previously? Or *is it* because most of you are disobedient *to God?*'

61. Say, 'Shall I inform you of those whose reward with Allah is worse than that? *They are* those whom Allah has cursed and on whom His wrath has fallen and of whom He has made apes and swine and *who* worship the Evil One. These indeed are in a worse plight, and farther astray from the right path.

62. And when they come to you, they say, 'We believe,' while they enter with

أَيْمَانِهِمْ إِنَّهُمْ لَمَعَكُمْ حَبِطَتْ أَعْمَالُهُمْ فَأَصْبَحُوا
خٰسِرِينَ ﴿٥٤﴾
يٰٓأَيُّهَا الَّذِينَ اٰمَنُوا مَنْ يَّرْتَدَّ مِنْكُمْ عَنْ دِينِهٖ فَسَوْفَ
يَأْتِي اللّٰهُ بِقَوْمٍ يُّحِبُّهُمْ وَيُحِبُّونَهٗٓ أَذِلَّةٍ عَلَى الْمُؤْمِنِينَ
أَعِزَّةٍ عَلَى الْكٰفِرِينَ يُجَاهِدُونَ فِي سَبِيلِ اللّٰهِ وَلَا
يَخَافُونَ لَوْمَةَ لَآئِمٍ ذٰلِكَ فَضْلُ اللّٰهِ يُؤْتِيهِ مَنْ يَّشَآءُ
وَاللّٰهُ وَاسِعٌ عَلِيمٌ ﴿٥٥﴾
إِنَّمَا وَلِيُّكُمُ اللّٰهُ وَرَسُولُهٗ وَالَّذِينَ اٰمَنُوا الَّذِينَ يُقِيمُونَ
الصَّلٰوةَ وَيُؤْتُونَ الزَّكٰوةَ وَهُمْ رٰكِعُونَ ﴿٥٦﴾
وَمَنْ يَّتَوَلَّ اللّٰهَ وَرَسُولَهٗ وَالَّذِينَ اٰمَنُوا فَإِنَّ حِزْبَ
اللّٰهِ هُمُ الْغٰلِبُونَ ﴿٥٧﴾
يٰٓأَيُّهَا الَّذِينَ اٰمَنُوا لَا تَتَّخِذُوا الَّذِينَ اتَّخَذُوا دِينَكُمْ
هُزُوًا وَّلَعِبًا مِّنَ الَّذِينَ أُوتُوا الْكِتٰبَ مِنْ قَبْلِكُمْ وَالْكُفَّارَ
أَوْلِيَآءَ وَاتَّقُوا اللّٰهَ إِنْ كُنْتُمْ مُّؤْمِنِينَ ﴿٥٨﴾
وَإِذَا نَادَيْتُمْ إِلَى الصَّلٰوةِ اتَّخَذُوهَا هُزُوًا وَّلَعِبًا
ذٰلِكَ بِأَنَّهُمْ قَوْمٌ لَّا يَعْقِلُونَ ﴿٥٩﴾
قُلْ يٰٓأَهْلَ الْكِتٰبِ هَلْ تَنْقِمُونَ مِنَّآ إِلَّآ أَنْ اٰمَنَّا بِاللّٰهِ وَمَآ أُنْزِلَ
إِلَيْنَا وَمَآ أُنْزِلَ مِنْ قَبْلُ وَأَنَّ أَكْثَرَكُمْ فٰسِقُونَ ﴿٦٠﴾
قُلْ هَلْ أُنَبِّئُكُمْ بِشَرٍّ مِّنْ ذٰلِكَ مَثُوبَةً عِنْدَ اللّٰهِ مَنْ
لَّعَنَهُ اللّٰهُ وَغَضِبَ عَلَيْهِ وَجَعَلَ مِنْهُمُ الْقِرَدَةَ وَالْخَنَازِيرَ وَعَبَدَ
الطَّاغُوتَ أُولٰٓئِكَ شَرٌّ مَّكَانًا وَّأَضَلُّ عَنْ سَوَآءِ السَّبِيلِ ﴿٦١﴾
وَإِذَا جَآءُوكُمْ قَالُوٓا اٰمَنَّا وَقَدْ دَّخَلُوا بِالْكُفْرِ وَهُمْ قَدْ خَرَجُوا

unbelief and go out therewith; and Allah knows best what they conceal.

63. And thou seest many of them hastening towards sin and transgression and the eating of things forbidden. Evil indeed is that which they practise.

64. Why do not the divines and those learned in the Law prohibit them from uttering falsehood and eating things forbidden? Evil indeed is that which they do.

* 65. And the Jews say, 'The hand of Allah is tied up.' Their *own* hands shall be tied up and they shall be cursed for what they say. Nay, both His hands are wide open; He spends how He pleases. And what has been sent down to thee from thy Lord will most surely increase many of them in rebellion and disbelief. And We have cast among them enmity and hatred till the Day of Resurrection. Whenever they kindle a fire for war, Allah extinguishes it. And they strive to create disorder in the earth, and Allah loves not those who create disorder.

66. And if the People of the Book had believed and been righteous, We would surely have removed from them their evils and We would surely have admitted them into Gardens of Bliss.

* 67. And if they had observed the Torah and the Gospel and what has been *now* sent down to them from their Lord, they would, surely, have eaten *of good things* from above them and from under their feet. Among them are a people who are moderate; but many of them—evil indeed is that which they do.

R. 10.

68. O Messenger! convey *to the people* what has been revealed to thee from thy Lord; and if thou do it not, thou hast not conveyed His Message *at all*. And Allah will protect thee from men. Surely, Allah guides not the disbelieving people.

69. Say, 'O People of the Book! you *stand* on nothing until you observe the

بِهٖ ۭ وَاللّٰهُ اَعْلَمُ بِمَا كَانُوْا يَكْتُمُوْنَ ﴿٦٢﴾
وَتَرٰى كَثِيْرًا مِّنْهُمْ يُسَارِعُوْنَ فِي الْاِثْمِ وَالْعُدْوَانِ وَ
اَكْلِهِمُ السُّحْتَ ۭ لَبِئْسَ مَا كَانُوْا يَعْمَلُوْنَ ﴿٦٣﴾
لَوْلَا يَنْهٰىهُمُ الرَّبّٰنِيُّوْنَ وَالْاَحْبَارُ عَنْ قَوْلِهِمُ الْاِثْمَ
وَاَكْلِهِمُ السُّحْتَ ۭ لَبِئْسَ مَا كَانُوْا يَصْنَعُوْنَ ﴿٦٤﴾
وَقَالَتِ الْيَهُوْدُ يَدُ اللّٰهِ مَغْلُوْلَةٌ ۭ غُلَّتْ اَيْدِيْهِمْ
وَلُعِنُوْا بِمَا قَالُوْا ۘ بَلْ يَدٰهُ مَبْسُوْطَتٰنِ ۙ يُنْفِقُ كَيْفَ ربع
يَشَاۗءُ ۭ وَلَيَزِيْدَنَّ كَثِيْرًا مِّنْهُمْ مَّاۤ اُنْزِلَ اِلَيْكَ مِنْ
رَّبِّكَ طُغْيَانًا وَّكُفْرًا ۭ وَاَلْقَيْنَا بَيْنَهُمُ الْعَدَاوَةَ
وَالْبَغْضَاۗءَ اِلٰى يَوْمِ الْقِيٰمَةِ ۭ كُلَّمَاۤ اَوْقَدُوْا نَارًا
لِّلْحَرْبِ اَطْفَاَهَا اللّٰهُ ۙ وَيَسْعَوْنَ فِي الْاَرْضِ فَسَادًا ۭ
وَاللّٰهُ لَا يُحِبُّ الْمُفْسِدِيْنَ ﴿٦٥﴾
وَلَوْ اَنَّ اَهْلَ الْكِتٰبِ اٰمَنُوْا وَاتَّقَوْا لَكَفَّرْنَا عَنْهُمْ
سَيِّاٰتِهِمْ وَلَاَدْخَلْنٰهُمْ جَنّٰتِ النَّعِيْمِ ﴿٦٦﴾
وَلَوْ اَنَّهُمْ اَقَامُوا التَّوْرٰىةَ وَالْاِنْجِيْلَ وَمَاۤ اُنْزِلَ
اِلَيْهِمْ مِّنْ رَّبِّهِمْ لَاَكَلُوْا مِنْ فَوْقِهِمْ وَمِنْ تَحْتِ
اَرْجُلِهِمْ ۭ مِنْهُمْ اُمَّةٌ مُّقْتَصِدَةٌ ۭ وَكَثِيْرٌ مِّنْهُمْ سَاۗءَ
مَا يَعْمَلُوْنَ ﴿٦٧﴾ ع ٩ ١٤
يٰۤاَيُّهَا الرَّسُوْلُ بَلِّغْ مَاۤ اُنْزِلَ اِلَيْكَ مِنْ رَّبِّكَ ۭ وَاِنْ لَّمْ
تَفْعَلْ فَمَا بَلَّغْتَ رِسَالَتَهٗ ۭ وَاللّٰهُ يَعْصِمُكَ مِنَ النَّاسِ ۭ
اِنَّ اللّٰهَ لَا يَهْدِي الْقَوْمَ الْكٰفِرِيْنَ ﴿٦٨﴾
قُلْ يٰۤاَهْلَ الْكِتٰبِ لَسْتُمْ عَلٰى شَيْءٍ حَتّٰى تُقِيْمُوا التَّوْرٰىةَ

Torah and the Gospel and what has *now* been sent down to you from your Lord.' And surely, what has been sent down to thee from thy Lord will increase many of them in rebellion and disbelief; so grieve not for the disbelieving people.

والانجيل وما انزل اليكم من ربكم وليزيدن
كثيرا منهم ما انزل اليك من ربك طغيانا وكفرا
فلا تاس على القوم الكفرين ﴿٦٩﴾

70. Surely, those who have believed, and the Jews, and the Sabians, and the Christians—whoso believes in Allah and the Last Day and does good deeds, on them *shall come* no fear, nor shall they grieve.

ان الذين امنوا والذين هادوا والصبئون والنصرى
من امن بالله واليوم الاخر وعمل صالحا فلا خوف
عليهم ولا هم يحزنون ﴿٧٠﴾

71. Surely, We took a covenant from the children of Israel, and We sent Messengers to them. But every time there came to them a Messenger with what their hearts desired not, they treated some as liars, and some they sought to kill.

لقد اخذنا ميثاق بني اسراءيل وارسلنا اليهم
رسلا كلما جاءهم رسول بما لا تهوى انفسهم
فريقا كذبوا وفريقا يقتلون ﴿٧١﴾

72. And they thought there would be no punishment, so they became blind and deaf. But Allah turned to them in mercy; yet again many of them became blind and deaf; and Allah is Watchful of what they do.

وحسبوا الا تكون فتنة فعموا وصموا ثم تاب الله
عليهم ثم عموا وصموا كثير منهم والله بصير بما
يعملون ﴿٧٢﴾

73. Indeed they are disbelievers who say, 'Surely, Allah is none but the Messiah, son of Mary,' whereas the Messiah *himself* said, 'O children of Israel, worship Allah Who is my Lord and your Lord.' Surely, whoso associates partners with Allah, him has Allah forbidden Heaven, and the Fire will be his resort. And the wrongdoers shall have no helpers.

لقد كفر الذين قالوا ان الله هو المسيح ابن مريم
وقال المسيح يبني اسراءيل اعبدوا الله ربي
وربكم انه من يشرك بالله فقد حرم الله عليه
الجنة وماوىه النار وما للظلمين من انصار ﴿٧٣﴾

* 74. They are surely disbelievers who say, 'Allah is the third of three;' there is no God but the One God. And if they do not desist from what they say, a grievous punishment shall surely befall those of them that disbelieve.

لقد كفر الذين قالوا ان الله ثالث ثلثة وما من
اله الا اله واحد وان لم ينتهوا عما يقولون
ليمسن الذين كفروا منهم عذاب اليم ﴿٧٤﴾

75. Will they not then turn to Allah and beg His forgiveness, while Allah is Most Forgiving, Merciful?

افلا يتوبون الى الله ويستغفرونه والله غفور
رحيم ﴿٧٥﴾

* 76. The Messiah, son of Mary, was only a Messenger; surely, Messengers *like unto*

ما المسيح ابن مريم الا رسول قد خلت من

him had indeed passed away before him. And his mother was a truthful woman. They both used to eat food. See how We explain the Signs for their good, and see how they are turned away.

77. Say, 'Will you worship beside Allah that which has no power to do you harm or good?' And it is Allah Who is All-Hearing, All-Knowing.

78. Say, 'O People of the Book! exceed not the limits in *the matter of* your religion unjustly, nor follow the evil inclinations of a people who went astray before and caused many to go astray, and *who* have strayed away from the right path.'

R. 11.

79. Those amongst the children of Israel who disbelieved were cursed by the tongue of David, and of Jesus, son of Mary. That was because they disobeyed and used to transgress.

* 80. They did not prohibit one another from the iniquity which they committed. Evil indeed was that which they used to do.

81. Thou shalt see many of them taking the disbelievers as *their* friends. Surely, evil is that which they themselves have sent on before for themselves; *with the result* that Allah is displeased with them; and in *this* punishment they shall abide.

82. And if they had believed in Allah and this Prophet, and *in* that which has been revealed to him, they would not have taken them as *their* friends, but many of them are disobedient.

83. Thou shalt certainly find the Jews and those who associate partners *with God* to be the most vehement of men in enmity against the believers. And thou shalt assuredly find those who say, 'We are Christians,' to be the nearest of them in love to the believers. That is because amongst them are savants and monks and because they are not proud.

84. And when they hear what has been revealed to this Messenger, thou seest their

قَبْلِهِ الرُّسُلُ ۚ وَأُمُّهُ صِدِّيقَةٌ ۖ كَانَا يَأْكُلَانِ الطَّعَامَ ۗ
انْظُرْ كَيْفَ نُبَيِّنُ لَهُمُ الْآيٰتِ ثُمَّ انْظُرْ أَنّٰى يُؤْفَكُونَ ٧٦
قُلْ أَتَعْبُدُونَ مِنْ دُونِ اللّٰهِ مَا لَا يَمْلِكُ لَكُمْ ضَرًّا
وَلَا نَفْعًا ۚ وَاللّٰهُ هُوَ السَّمِيعُ الْعَلِيمُ ٧٧
قُلْ يٰأَهْلَ الْكِتٰبِ لَا تَغْلُوا فِي دِينِكُمْ غَيْرَ الْحَقِّ وَلَا تَتَّبِعُوا
أَهْوَاءَ قَوْمٍ قَدْ ضَلُّوا مِنْ قَبْلُ وَأَضَلُّوا كَثِيرًا وَضَلُّوا
عَنْ سَوَاءِ السَّبِيلِ ٧٨
لُعِنَ الَّذِينَ كَفَرُوا مِنْ بَنِي إِسْرَائِيلَ عَلٰى لِسَانِ
دَاوُدَ وَعِيسَى ابْنِ مَرْيَمَ ۚ ذٰلِكَ بِمَا عَصَوْا وَكَانُوا
يَعْتَدُونَ ٧٩
كَانُوا لَا يَتَنَاهَوْنَ عَنْ مُنْكَرٍ فَعَلُوهُ ۚ لَبِئْسَ مَا كَانُوا
يَفْعَلُونَ ٨٠
تَرٰى كَثِيرًا مِنْهُمْ يَتَوَلَّوْنَ الَّذِينَ كَفَرُوا ۚ لَبِئْسَ مَا
قَدَّمَتْ لَهُمْ أَنْفُسُهُمْ أَنْ سَخِطَ اللّٰهُ عَلَيْهِمْ وَفِي
الْعَذَابِ هُمْ خٰلِدُونَ ٨١
وَلَوْ كَانُوا يُؤْمِنُونَ بِاللّٰهِ وَالنَّبِيِّ وَمَا أُنْزِلَ إِلَيْهِ
مَا اتَّخَذُوهُمْ أَوْلِيَاءَ وَلٰكِنَّ كَثِيرًا مِنْهُمْ فٰسِقُونَ ٨٢
لَتَجِدَنَّ أَشَدَّ النَّاسِ عَدَاوَةً لِلَّذِينَ آمَنُوا الْيَهُودَ
وَالَّذِينَ أَشْرَكُوا ۚ وَلَتَجِدَنَّ أَقْرَبَهُمْ مَوَدَّةً لِلَّذِينَ
آمَنُوا الَّذِينَ قَالُوا إِنَّا نَصٰرٰى ۚ ذٰلِكَ بِأَنَّ مِنْهُمْ قِسِّيسِينَ
وَرُهْبَانًا وَأَنَّهُمْ لَا يَسْتَكْبِرُونَ ٨٣
وَإِذَا سَمِعُوا مَا أُنْزِلَ إِلَى الرَّسُولِ تَرٰى أَعْيُنَهُمْ

eyes overflow with tears, because of the truth which they have recognized. They say, 'Our Lord, we believe, so write us down among those who bear witness.

85. 'And why should we not believe in Allah and in the truth which has come to us, while we earnestly wish that our Lord should include us among the righteous people?'

86. So Allah rewarded them, for what they said, with Gardens beneath which streams flow. Therein shall they abide; and that is the reward of those who do good.

87. And those who have disbelieved and rejected Our Signs, these are they who are the inmates of Hell.

R. 12.

88. O ye who believe! make not unlawful the good things which Allah has made lawful for you, and do not transgress. Surely, Allah loves not the transgressors.

89. And eat of that which Allah has provided for you of what is lawful and good. And fear Allah in Whom you believe.

90. Allah will not call you to account for *such of* your oaths as are vain, but He will call you to account for the oaths which you take in earnest. The expiation for this is the feeding of ten poor persons with *such* average *food* as you feed your families with, or the clothing of them or the freeing of a neck. But whoso finds not *the means* shall fast for three days. That is the expiation of your oaths when you have sworn *them*. And do keep your oaths. Thus does Allah explain to you His Signs that you may be grateful.

* 91. O ye who believe! wine and the game of hazard and idols and divining arrows are only an abomination of Satan's handiwork. So shun *each one of* them that you may prosper.

* 92. Satan desires only to create enmity and hatred among you by means of wine and the game of hazard, and to keep you

تَفِيْضُ مِنَ الدَّمْعِ مِمَّا عَرَفُوْا مِنَ الْحَقِّ ۚ يَقُوْلُوْنَ
رَبَّنَآ اٰمَنَّا فَاكْتُبْنَا مَعَ الشّٰهِدِيْنَ ﴿۸۴﴾
وَمَا لَنَا لَا نُؤْمِنُ بِاللّٰهِ وَمَا جَآءَنَا مِنَ الْحَقِّ ۙ وَ
نَطْمَعُ اَنْ يُّدْخِلَنَا رَبُّنَا مَعَ الْقَوْمِ الصّٰلِحِيْنَ ﴿۸۵﴾
فَاَثَابَهُمُ اللّٰهُ بِمَا قَالُوْا جَنّٰتٍ تَجْرِيْ مِنْ تَحْتِهَا الْاَنْهٰرُ
خٰلِدِيْنَ فِيْهَا ۭ وَذٰلِكَ جَزَآءُ الْمُحْسِنِيْنَ ﴿۸۶﴾
وَالَّذِيْنَ كَفَرُوْا وَكَذَّبُوْا بِاٰيٰتِنَآ اُولٰٓئِكَ اَصْحٰبُ الْجَحِيْمِ ﴿۸۷﴾ ع
يٰٓاَيُّهَا الَّذِيْنَ اٰمَنُوْا لَا تُحَرِّمُوْا طَيِّبٰتِ مَآ اَحَلَّ اللّٰهُ لَكُمْ
وَلَا تَعْتَدُوْا ۭ اِنَّ اللّٰهَ لَا يُحِبُّ الْمُعْتَدِيْنَ ﴿۸۸﴾
وَكُلُوْا مِمَّا رَزَقَكُمُ اللّٰهُ حَلٰلًا طَيِّبًا ۠ وَّاتَّقُوا اللّٰهَ الَّذِيْٓ
اَنْتُمْ بِهٖ مُؤْمِنُوْنَ ﴿۸۹﴾
لَا يُؤَاخِذُكُمُ اللّٰهُ بِاللَّغْوِ فِيْٓ اَيْمَانِكُمْ وَلٰكِنْ يُّؤَاخِذُكُمْ
بِمَا عَقَّدْتُّمُ الْاَيْمَانَ ۚ فَكَفَّارَتُهٗٓ اِطْعَامُ عَشَرَةِ مَسٰكِيْنَ
مِنْ اَوْسَطِ مَا تُطْعِمُوْنَ اَهْلِيْكُمْ اَوْ كِسْوَتُهُمْ اَوْ تَحْرِيْرُ
رَقَبَةٍ ۭ فَمَنْ لَّمْ يَجِدْ فَصِيَامُ ثَلٰثَةِ اَيَّامٍ ۭ ذٰلِكَ كَفَّارَةُ
اَيْمَانِكُمْ اِذَا حَلَفْتُمْ ۭ وَاحْفَظُوْٓا اَيْمَانَكُمْ ۭ كَذٰلِكَ
يُبَيِّنُ اللّٰهُ لَكُمْ اٰيٰتِهٖ لَعَلَّكُمْ تَشْكُرُوْنَ ﴿۹۰﴾
يٰٓاَيُّهَا الَّذِيْنَ اٰمَنُوْٓا اِنَّمَا الْخَمْرُ وَالْمَيْسِرُ وَالْاَنْصَابُ
وَالْاَزْلَامُ رِجْسٌ مِّنْ عَمَلِ الشَّيْطٰنِ فَاجْتَنِبُوْهُ لَعَلَّكُمْ
تُفْلِحُوْنَ ﴿۹۱﴾
اِنَّمَا يُرِيْدُ الشَّيْطٰنُ اَنْ يُّوْقِعَ بَيْنَكُمُ الْعَدَاوَةَ
وَالْبَغْضَآءَ فِي الْخَمْرِ وَالْمَيْسِرِ وَيَصُدَّكُمْ عَنْ

back from the remembrance of Allah and from Prayer. But will you keep back?

93. And obey Allah and obey the Messenger, and be on *your* guard. But if you turn away, then know that on Our Messenger lies only the clear conveyance of the Message.

94. On those who believe and do good works there shall be no sin for what they eat, provided they fear *God* and believe and do good works, *and* again fear *God* and believe, yet again fear *God* and do good. And Allah loves those who do good.

R. 13.

95. O ye who believe! Allah will surely try you in a *little* matter: the game which your hands and your lances can reach, so that Allah may distinguish those who fear Him in secret. Whoso, therefore, will transgress after this shall have a grievous punishment.

96. O ye who believe! kill not game while you are in a state of pilgrimage. And whoso amongst you kills it intentionally, its compensation is a quadruped like unto that which he has killed, as determined by two just men from among you, *the same* to be brought as an offering to the Ka'ba; or as an expiation *he shall have* to feed *a number of* poor persons, or fast an equivalent number *of days*, so that he may taste the penalty of his deed. *As for* the past, Allah forgives *it;* but whoso reverts to it, Allah will punish him *for his offence*. And Allah is Mighty, Lord of retribution.

97. The game of the sea and the eating thereof have been made lawful for you as a provision for you and the travellers; but forbidden to you is the game of the land as long as you are in a state of pilgrimage. And fear Allah to Whom you shall be gathered.

98. Allah has made the Ka'ba, the inviolable House, as a means of support and uplift for mankind, as also the Sacred Month and the offerings and the *animals with* collars. That is so that you may know that Allah knows what is in the heavens

ذِكْرِ اللّٰهِ وَعَنِ الصَّلٰوةِ ۚ فَهَلْ اَنْتُمْ مُّنْتَهُوْنَ ﴿۹۲﴾

وَاَطِيْعُوا اللّٰهَ وَاَطِيْعُوا الرَّسُوْلَ وَاحْذَرُوْا ۚ فَاِنْ تَوَلَّيْتُمْ
فَاعْلَمُوْٓا اَنَّمَا عَلٰى رَسُوْلِنَا الْبَلٰغُ الْمُبِيْنُ ﴿۹۳﴾

لَيْسَ عَلَى الَّذِيْنَ اٰمَنُوْا وَعَمِلُوا الصّٰلِحٰتِ جُنَاحٌ
فِيْمَا طَعِمُوْٓا اِذَا مَا اتَّقَوْا وَّاٰمَنُوْا وَعَمِلُوا الصّٰلِحٰتِ
ثُمَّ اتَّقَوْا وَّاٰمَنُوْا ثُمَّ اتَّقَوْا وَّاَحْسَنُوْا ۗ وَاللّٰهُ يُحِبُّ
الْمُحْسِنِيْنَ ﴿۹۴﴾ ع ۲

يٰٓاَيُّهَا الَّذِيْنَ اٰمَنُوْا لَيَبْلُوَنَّكُمُ اللّٰهُ بِشَيْءٍ مِّنَ الصَّيْدِ
تَنَالُهٗٓ اَيْدِيْكُمْ وَرِمَاحُكُمْ لِيَعْلَمَ اللّٰهُ مَنْ يَّخَافُهٗ
بِالْغَيْبِ ۚ فَمَنِ اعْتَدٰى بَعْدَ ذٰلِكَ فَلَهٗ عَذَابٌ اَلِيْمٌ ﴿۹۵﴾

يٰٓاَيُّهَا الَّذِيْنَ اٰمَنُوْا لَا تَقْتُلُوا الصَّيْدَ وَاَنْتُمْ حُرُمٌ ۗ
وَمَنْ قَتَلَهٗ مِنْكُمْ مُّتَعَمِّدًا فَجَزَآءٌ مِّثْلُ مَا قَتَلَ مِنَ
النَّعَمِ يَحْكُمُ بِهٖ ذَوَا عَدْلٍ مِّنْكُمْ هَدْيًا ۢ بٰلِغَ الْكَعْبَةِ
اَوْ كَفَّارَةٌ طَعَامُ مَسٰكِيْنَ اَوْ عَدْلُ ذٰلِكَ صِيَامًا
لِّيَذُوْقَ وَبَالَ اَمْرِهٖ ۗ عَفَا اللّٰهُ عَمَّا سَلَفَ ۗ وَمَنْ عَادَ
فَيَنْتَقِمُ اللّٰهُ مِنْهُ ۗ وَاللّٰهُ عَزِيْزٌ ذُو انْتِقَامٍ ﴿۹۶﴾

اُحِلَّ لَكُمْ صَيْدُ الْبَحْرِ وَطَعَامُهٗ مَتَاعًا لَّكُمْ وَ
لِلسَّيَّارَةِ ۚ وَحُرِّمَ عَلَيْكُمْ صَيْدُ الْبَرِّ مَا دُمْتُمْ حُرُمًا ۗ
وَاتَّقُوا اللّٰهَ الَّذِيْٓ اِلَيْهِ تُحْشَرُوْنَ ﴿۹۷﴾

جَعَلَ اللّٰهُ الْكَعْبَةَ الْبَيْتَ الْحَرَامَ قِيٰمًا لِّلنَّاسِ وَ
الشَّهْرَ الْحَرَامَ وَالْهَدْيَ وَالْقَلَآئِدَ ۗ ذٰلِكَ لِتَعْلَمُوْٓا
اَنَّ اللّٰهَ يَعْلَمُ مَا فِي السَّمٰوٰتِ وَمَا فِي الْاَرْضِ وَاَنَّ

and what is in the earth, and that Allah knows all things well.

اللّٰهَ بِكُلِّ شَيْءٍ عَلِيْمٌ ﴿٩٨﴾

99. Know that Allah is severe in punishment and that Allah is *also* Most Forgiving, Merciful.

اِعْلَمُوْٓا اَنَّ اللّٰهَ شَدِيْدُ الْعِقَابِ وَ اَنَّ اللّٰهَ غَفُوْرٌ
رَّحِيْمٌ ﴿٩٩﴾

100. On the Messenger lies only the conveying of the Message. And Allah knows what you reveal and what you hide.

مَا عَلَى الرَّسُوْلِ اِلَّا الْبَلٰغُ ۗ وَ اللّٰهُ يَعْلَمُ مَا تُبْدُوْنَ
وَ مَا تَكْتُمُوْنَ ﴿١٠٠﴾

101. Say, 'The bad and the good are not alike,' even though the abundance of the bad may cause thee to wonder. So fear Allah, O men of understanding, that you may prosper.

قُلْ لَّا يَسْتَوِي الْخَبِيْثُ وَ الطَّيِّبُ وَلَوْ اَعْجَبَكَ كَثْرَةُ
الْخَبِيْثِ ۚ فَاتَّقُوا اللّٰهَ يٰٓاُولِي الْاَلْبَابِ لَعَلَّكُمْ
تُفْلِحُوْنَ ﴿١٠١﴾ ع٤

R. 14.

* 102. O ye who believe! ask not about things which, if revealed to you, would cause you trouble; though if you ask about them while the Qur'ān is being sent down, they will be revealed to you. Allah has left them out. And Allah is Most Forgiving, Forbearing.

يٰٓاَيُّهَا الَّذِيْنَ اٰمَنُوْا لَا تَسْـَٔلُوْا عَنْ اَشْيَآءَ اِنْ تُبْدَ لَكُمْ
تَسُؤْكُمْ ۚ وَ اِنْ تَسْـَٔلُوْا عَنْهَا حِيْنَ يُنَزَّلُ الْقُرْاٰنُ
تُبْدَ لَكُمْ ۗ عَفَا اللّٰهُ عَنْهَا ۗ وَ اللّٰهُ غَفُوْرٌ حَلِيْمٌ ﴿١٠٢﴾

103. A people before you asked about such *things*, *but* then they became disbelievers therein.

قَدْ سَاَلَهَا قَوْمٌ مِّنْ قَبْلِكُمْ ثُمَّ اَصْبَحُوْا بِهَا
كٰفِرِيْنَ ﴿١٠٣﴾

* 104. Allah has not ordained any 'Baḥīra' or 'Sā'iba' or 'Waṣīla' or 'Ḥāmī'; but those who disbelieve forge a lie against Allah, and most of them do not make use of their understanding.

مَا جَعَلَ اللّٰهُ مِنْۢ بَحِيْرَةٍ وَّ لَا سَآئِبَةٍ وَّ لَا وَصِيْلَةٍ
وَّ لَا حَامٍ ۙ وَّ لٰكِنَّ الَّذِيْنَ كَفَرُوْا يَفْتَرُوْنَ عَلَى اللّٰهِ
الْكَذِبَ ۗ وَ اَكْثَرُهُمْ لَا يَعْقِلُوْنَ ﴿١٠٤﴾

105. And when it is said to them, 'Come to what Allah has revealed, and to the Messenger,' they say, 'Sufficient for us is that wherein we found our fathers.' What! even though their fathers had no knowledge and no guidance?

وَ اِذَا قِيْلَ لَهُمْ تَعَالَوْا اِلٰى مَآ اَنْزَلَ اللّٰهُ وَ اِلَى
الرَّسُوْلِ قَالُوْا حَسْبُنَا مَا وَجَدْنَا عَلَيْهِ اٰبَآءَنَا ۗ اَوَلَوْ
كَانَ اٰبَآؤُهُمْ لَا يَعْلَمُوْنَ شَيْـًٔا وَّ لَا يَهْتَدُوْنَ ﴿١٠٥﴾

* 106. O ye who believe! be heedful of your own selves. He who goes astray cannot harm you when you *yourselves* are rightly guided. To Allah will you all return; then will He disclose to you what you used to do.

يٰٓاَيُّهَا الَّذِيْنَ اٰمَنُوْا عَلَيْكُمْ اَنْفُسَكُمْ ۚ لَا يَضُرُّكُمْ مَّنْ
ضَلَّ اِذَا اهْتَدَيْتُمْ ۗ اِلَى اللّٰهِ مَرْجِعُكُمْ جَمِيْعًا
فَيُنَبِّئُكُمْ بِمَا كُنْتُمْ تَعْمَلُوْنَ ﴿١٠٦﴾

107. O ye who believe! the *right* evidence among you, when death presents itself to one of you, at the time of making a bequest, is of two just men from among you; or of two others not from among you, if you be journeying in the land and the calamity of death befall you. You shall detain them both after Prayer *for giving evidence;* if you doubt, they shall both swear by Allah, *saying*, 'We take not in exchange for this any price, even though he be a near relation, and we conceal not the testimony *enjoined* by Allah; surely, in that case, we should be among the sinners.'

يٰٓاَيُّهَا الَّذِيْنَ اٰمَنُوْا شَهَادَةُ بَيْنِكُمْ اِذَا حَضَرَ اَحَدَكُمُ
الْمَوْتُ حِيْنَ الْوَصِيَّةِ اثْنٰنِ ذَوَا عَدْلٍ مِّنْكُمْ اَوْ
اٰخَرٰنِ مِنْ غَيْرِكُمْ اِنْ اَنْتُمْ ضَرَبْتُمْ فِي الْاَرْضِ
فَاَصَابَتْكُمْ مُّصِيْبَةُ الْمَوْتِ تَحْبِسُوْنَهُمَا مِنْۢ بَعْدِ
الصَّلٰوةِ فَيُقْسِمٰنِ بِاللّٰهِ اِنِ ارْتَبْتُمْ لَا نَشْتَرِيْ بِهٖ
ثَمَنًا وَّلَوْ كَانَ ذَا قُرْبٰى وَلَا نَكْتُمُ شَهَادَةَ اللّٰهِ
اِنَّآ اِذًا لَّمِنَ الْاٰثِمِيْنَ ﴿١٠٧﴾

* 108. But if it be discovered that the two *witnesses* are guilty of sin, then two others shall take their place from among those against whom the *former* two *witnesses*—who were in a better position *to give true evidence—sinfully* deposed, and the two *latter witnesses* shall swear by Allah, *saying*, 'Surely, our testimony is truer than the testimony of the *former* two, and we have not been unfair *in any way;* for then, indeed, we should be of the unjust.'

فَاِنْ عُثِرَ عَلٰٓى اَنَّهُمَا اسْتَحَقَّآ اِثْمًا فَاٰخَرٰنِ يَقُوْمٰنِ
مَقَامَهُمَا مِنَ الَّذِيْنَ اسْتَحَقَّ عَلَيْهِمُ الْاَوْلَيٰنِ فَيُقْسِمٰنِ
بِاللّٰهِ لَشَهَادَتُنَآ اَحَقُّ مِنْ شَهَادَتِهِمَا وَمَا اعْتَدَيْنَآ
اِنَّآ اِذًا لَّمِنَ الظّٰلِمِيْنَ ﴿١٠٨﴾

* 109. Thus it is more likely that they will give evidence according to facts or that they will fear that other oaths will be taken after their oaths. And fear Allah and hearken. And Allah guides not the disobedient people.

ذٰلِكَ اَدْنٰٓى اَنْ يَّاْتُوْا بِالشَّهَادَةِ عَلٰى وَجْهِهَآ اَوْ يَخَافُوْٓا
اَنْ تُرَدَّ اَيْمَانٌۢ بَعْدَ اَيْمَانِهِمْ وَاتَّقُوا اللّٰهَ وَاسْمَعُوْا
وَاللّٰهُ لَا يَهْدِي الْقَوْمَ الْفٰسِقِيْنَ ﴿١٠٩﴾

R. 15.

* 110. *Think of* the day when Allah will assemble the Messengers and say, 'What reply was made to you?' They will say, 'We have no knowledge, it is only Thou Who art the Knower of hidden things.'

يَوْمَ يَجْمَعُ اللّٰهُ الرُّسُلَ فَيَقُوْلُ مَاذَآ اُجِبْتُمْ قَالُوْا
لَا عِلْمَ لَنَا اِنَّكَ اَنْتَ عَلَّامُ الْغُيُوْبِ ﴿١١٠﴾

* 111. When Allah will say, "O Jesus, son of Mary, remember My favour upon thee and upon thy mother; when I strengthened thee with the Spirit of holiness *so that* thou didst speak to the people in the cradle and in middle age; and when I taught thee the Book and Wisdom and the Torah and the Gospel; and when thou didst fashion *a creation* out of clay, in the likeness of a bird, by My command; then thou didst breathe into it *a new spirit* and it became a soaring being by My

اِذْ قَالَ اللّٰهُ يٰعِيْسَى ابْنَ مَرْيَمَ اذْكُرْ نِعْمَتِيْ عَلَيْكَ
وَعَلٰى وَالِدَتِكَ اِذْ اَيَّدْتُّكَ بِرُوْحِ الْقُدُسِ تُكَلِّمُ
النَّاسَ فِي الْمَهْدِ وَكَهْلًا وَاِذْ عَلَّمْتُكَ الْكِتٰبَ وَ
الْحِكْمَةَ وَالتَّوْرٰىةَ وَالْاِنْجِيْلَ وَاِذْ تَخْلُقُ مِنَ الطِّيْنِ
كَهَيْـَٔةِ الطَّيْرِ بِاِذْنِيْ فَتَنْفُخُ فِيْهَا فَتَكُوْنُ طَيْرًۢا بِاِذْنِيْ
وَتُبْرِئُ الْاَكْمَهَ وَالْاَبْرَصَ بِاِذْنِيْ وَاِذْ تُخْرِجُ الْمَوْتٰى

command; and thou didst heal the night-blind and the leprous by My command; and when thou didst raise the dead by My command; and when I restrained the children of Israel from *putting* thee *to death* when thou didst come to them with clear Signs; and those who disbelieved from among them said, 'This is nothing but clear deception.' "

112. And when I inspired the disciples *of Jesus* to believe in Me and in My Messenger, they said, 'We believe and bear Thou witness that we have submitted.'

113. When the disciples said, 'O Jesus, son of Mary, is thy Lord able to send down to us a table spread with food from heaven?' he said, 'Fear Allah, if you are believers.'

114. They said, 'We desire that we may eat of it, and that our hearts be at rest and that we may know that thou hast spoken truth to us, and that we may be witnesses thereto.'

115. Said Jesus, son of Mary, 'O Allah, our Lord, send down to us a table from heaven spread with food that it may be to us a festival, to the first of us and to the last of us, and a Sign from Thee; and provide sustenance for us, for Thou art the Best of sustainers.'

116. Allah said, 'Surely, I will send it down to you, but whosoever of you disbelieves afterwards—I will surely punish them with a punishment wherewith I will not punish any other of the peoples.'

R. 16.

117. And when Allah will say, "O Jesus, son of Mary, didst thou say to men, 'Take me and my mother for two gods beside Allah?' " he will answer, "Holy art Thou. I could never say that to which I had no right. If I had said it, Thou wouldst have surely known it. Thou knowest what is in my mind, and I know not what is in Thy mind. It is only Thou Who art the Knower of hidden things.

118. "I said nothing to them except that which Thou didst command me—'Worship Allah, my Lord and your Lord.' And I was a witness over them as long as I remained among them, but since Thou

بِإِذْنِيْ وَإِذْ كَفَفْتُ بَنِيْٓ إِسْرَآءِيْلَ عَنْكَ إِذْ جِئْتَهُمْ
بِالْبَيِّنٰتِ فَقَالَ الَّذِيْنَ كَفَرُوْا مِنْهُمْ إِنْ هٰذَآ إِلَّا
سِحْرٌ مُّبِيْنٌ ﴿١١١﴾
وَإِذْ أَوْحَيْتُ إِلَى الْحَوَارِيّٖنَ أَنْ اٰمِنُوْا بِيْ وَبِرَسُوْلِيْ
قَالُوْٓا اٰمَنَّا وَاشْهَدْ بِأَنَّنَا مُسْلِمُوْنَ ﴿١١٢﴾
إِذْ قَالَ الْحَوَارِيُّوْنَ يٰعِيْسَى ابْنَ مَرْيَمَ هَلْ يَسْتَطِيْعُ
رَبُّكَ أَنْ يُّنَزِّلَ عَلَيْنَا مَآئِدَةً مِّنَ السَّمَآءِ قَالَ اتَّقُوا
اللّٰهَ إِنْ كُنْتُمْ مُّؤْمِنِيْنَ ﴿١١٣﴾
قَالُوْا نُرِيْدُ أَنْ نَّأْكُلَ مِنْهَا وَتَطْمَئِنَّ قُلُوْبُنَا وَنَعْلَمَ
أَنْ قَدْ صَدَقْتَنَا وَنَكُوْنَ عَلَيْهَا مِنَ الشّٰهِدِيْنَ ﴿١١٤﴾
قَالَ عِيْسَى ابْنُ مَرْيَمَ اللّٰهُمَّ رَبَّنَآ أَنْزِلْ عَلَيْنَا مَآئِدَةً
مِّنَ السَّمَآءِ تَكُوْنُ لَنَا عِيْدًا لِّأَوَّلِنَا وَاٰخِرِنَا وَاٰيَةً
مِّنْكَ وَارْزُقْنَا وَأَنْتَ خَيْرُ الرّٰزِقِيْنَ ﴿١١٥﴾
قَالَ اللّٰهُ إِنِّيْ مُنَزِّلُهَا عَلَيْكُمْ فَمَنْ يَّكْفُرْ بَعْدُ مِنْكُمْ
فَإِنِّيْٓ أُعَذِّبُهٗ عَذَابًا لَّآ أُعَذِّبُهٗٓ أَحَدًا مِّنَ الْعٰلَمِيْنَ ﴿١١٦﴾
وَإِذْ قَالَ اللّٰهُ يٰعِيْسَى ابْنَ مَرْيَمَ ءَأَنْتَ قُلْتَ لِلنَّاسِ
اتَّخِذُوْنِيْ وَأُمِّيَ إِلٰهَيْنِ مِنْ دُوْنِ اللّٰهِ قَالَ سُبْحٰنَكَ
مَا يَكُوْنُ لِيْٓ أَنْ أَقُوْلَ مَا لَيْسَ لِيْ بِحَقٍّ إِنْ كُنْتُ
قُلْتُهٗ فَقَدْ عَلِمْتَهٗ تَعْلَمُ مَا فِيْ نَفْسِيْ وَلَآ أَعْلَمُ
مَا فِيْ نَفْسِكَ إِنَّكَ أَنْتَ عَلَّامُ الْغُيُوْبِ ﴿١١٧﴾
مَا قُلْتُ لَهُمْ إِلَّا مَآ أَمَرْتَنِيْ بِهٖٓ أَنِ اعْبُدُوا اللّٰهَ رَبِّيْ
وَرَبَّكُمْ وَكُنْتُ عَلَيْهِمْ شَهِيْدًا مَّا دُمْتُ فِيْهِمْ فَلَمَّا

didst cause me to die, Thou hast been the Watcher over them; and Thou art Witness over all things.

توفيتني كنت انت الرقيب عليهم ۚ وانت على كل
شيء شهيد ﴿١١٨﴾

119. "If Thou punish them, they are Thy servants; and if Thou forgive them, Thou surely art the Mighty, the Wise."

ان تعذبهم فانهم عبادك ۚ وان تغفر لهم فانك
انت العزيز الحكيم ﴿١١٩﴾

120. Allah will say, 'This is a day when *only* the truthful shall profit by their truthfulness. For them are Gardens beneath which streams flow; therein shall they abide for ever. Allah is well pleased with them, and they are well pleased with Him; that indeed is the great triumph.'

قال الله هذا يوم ينفع الصدقين صدقهم ۚ
لهم جنت تجري من تحتها الانهر خلدين
فيها ابدا ۚ رضي الله عنهم ورضوا عنه ۚ ذلك
الفوز العظيم ﴿١٢٠﴾

121. To Allah belongs the kingdom of the heavens and the earth and whatever is in them; and He has power over all things.

لله ملك السموت والارض وما فيهن ۚ وهو على
كل شيء قدير ﴿١٢١﴾

سُوۡرَۃُ الۡاَنۡعَامِ مَکِّیَّۃٌ (٦)

AL-AN'ĀM

(Revealed before Hijra)

1. In the name of Allah, the Gracious, the Merciful.

بِسۡمِ اللّٰہِ الرَّحۡمٰنِ الرَّحِیۡمِ ﴿۱﴾

2. All praise belongs to Allah Who created the heavens and the earth and brought into being every *kind of* darkness and light; yet those who disbelieve set up equals to their Lord.

اَلۡحَمۡدُ لِلّٰہِ الَّذِیۡ خَلَقَ السَّمٰوٰتِ وَ الۡاَرۡضَ وَ جَعَلَ
الظُّلُمٰتِ وَ النُّوۡرَ ۬ؕ ثُمَّ الَّذِیۡنَ کَفَرُوۡا بِرَبِّہِمۡ یَعۡدِلُوۡنَ ﴿۲﴾

3. He it is Who created you from clay, and then He decreed a term. And there is *another* term fixed with Him. Yet you doubt!

ہُوَ الَّذِیۡ خَلَقَکُمۡ مِّنۡ طِیۡنٍ ثُمَّ قَضٰۤی اَجَلًا ؕ وَ اَجَلٌ
مُّسَمًّی عِنۡدَہٗ ثُمَّ اَنۡتُمۡ تَمۡتَرُوۡنَ ﴿۳﴾

* 4. And He is Allah, *the God, both* in the heavens and in the earth. He knows your inside and your outside. And He knows what you earn.

وَ ہُوَ اللّٰہُ فِی السَّمٰوٰتِ وَ فِی الۡاَرۡضِ ؕ یَعۡلَمُ سِرَّکُمۡ
وَ جَہۡرَکُمۡ وَ یَعۡلَمُ مَا تَکۡسِبُوۡنَ ﴿۴﴾

5. And there comes not to them any Sign of the Signs of their Lord, but they turn away from it.

وَ مَا تَاۡتِیۡہِمۡ مِّنۡ اٰیَۃٍ مِّنۡ اٰیٰتِ رَبِّہِمۡ اِلَّا کَانُوۡا عَنۡہَا
مُعۡرِضِیۡنَ ﴿۵﴾

6. So they rejected the truth when it came to them; but soon shall come to them the tidings of that at which they mocked.

فَقَدۡ کَذَّبُوۡا بِالۡحَقِّ لَمَّا جَآءَہُمۡ ؕ فَسَوۡفَ یَاۡتِیۡہِمۡ
اَنۡۢبٰٓؤُا مَا کَانُوۡا بِہٖ یَسۡتَہۡزِءُوۡنَ ﴿۶﴾

* 7. See they not how many a generation We have destroyed before them? We had established them in the earth as We have established you not, and We sent the clouds over them, pouring down abundant rain; and We caused streams to flow beneath them; then did We destroy them because of their sins and raised up after them another generation.

اَلَمۡ یَرَوۡا کَمۡ اَہۡلَکۡنَا مِنۡ قَبۡلِہِمۡ مِّنۡ قَرۡنٍ مَّکَّنّٰہُمۡ
فِی الۡاَرۡضِ مَا لَمۡ نُمَکِّنۡ لَّکُمۡ وَ اَرۡسَلۡنَا السَّمَآءَ عَلَیۡہِمۡ
مِّدۡرَارًا ۪ وَّ جَعَلۡنَا الۡاَنۡہٰرَ تَجۡرِیۡ مِنۡ تَحۡتِہِمۡ فَاَہۡلَکۡنٰہُمۡ
بِذُنُوۡبِہِمۡ وَ اَنۡشَاۡنَا مِنۡۢ بَعۡدِہِمۡ قَرۡنًا اٰخَرِیۡنَ ﴿۷﴾

8. And if We had sent down to thee a writing upon parchment and they had felt it with their hands, *even then* the disbelievers would have surely said, 'This is nothing but manifest sorcery.'

وَ لَوۡ نَزَّلۡنَا عَلَیۡکَ کِتٰبًا فِیۡ قِرۡطَاسٍ فَلَمَسُوۡہُ بِاَیۡدِیۡہِمۡ
لَقَالَ الَّذِیۡنَ کَفَرُوۡۤا اِنۡ ہٰذَاۤ اِلَّا سِحۡرٌ مُّبِیۡنٌ ﴿۸﴾

9. And they say, 'Why has not an angel been sent down to him?' But if We had sent down an angel, the matter would have been settled, *and* then they would not have been granted a respite.

وَ قَالُوۡا لَوۡ لَاۤ اُنۡزِلَ عَلَیۡہِ مَلَکٌ ؕ وَ لَوۡ اَنۡزَلۡنَا مَلَکًا لَّقُضِیَ
الۡاَمۡرُ ثُمَّ لَا یُنۡظَرُوۡنَ ﴿۹﴾

10. And if We had appointed *as Messenger* an angel, We would have made him *appear as* a man; and *thus* We would have made confused to them what they are *themselves* confusing.

وَلَوْ جَعَلْنٰهُ مَلَكًا لَّجَعَلْنٰهُ رَجُلًا وَّلَلَبَسْنَا عَلَيْهِمْ
مَّا يَلْبِسُوْنَ ﴿١٠﴾

11. And surely have the Messengers been mocked at before thee, but that which they mocked at encompassed those of them who scoffed.

وَلَقَدِ اسْتُهْزِئَ بِرُسُلٍ مِّنْ قَبْلِكَ فَحَاقَ بِالَّذِيْنَ
سَخِرُوْا مِنْهُمْ مَّا كَانُوْا بِهٖ يَسْتَهْزِءُوْنَ ﴿١١﴾ ع

R. 2.

12. Say, 'Go about in the earth, and see what was the end of those who treated *the Prophets* as liars.'

قُلْ سِيْرُوْا فِي الْاَرْضِ ثُمَّ انْظُرُوْا كَيْفَ كَانَ عَاقِبَةُ
الْمُكَذِّبِيْنَ ﴿١٢﴾

* 13. Say, 'To whom belongs what is in the heavens and the earth?' Say, 'To Allah.' He has taken upon Himself *to show* mercy. He will certainly *continue to* assemble you till the Day of Resurrection. There is no doubt in it. Those who ruin their souls will not believe.

قُلْ لِّمَنْ مَّا فِي السَّمٰوٰتِ وَالْاَرْضِ قُلْ لِّلّٰهِ كَتَبَ عَلٰى
نَفْسِهِ الرَّحْمَةَ لَيَجْمَعَنَّكُمْ اِلٰى يَوْمِ الْقِيٰمَةِ لَا رَيْبَ
فِيْهِ اَلَّذِيْنَ خَسِرُوْٓا اَنْفُسَهُمْ فَهُمْ لَا يُؤْمِنُوْنَ ﴿١٣﴾

14. To Him belongs whatever dwells in the night and the day. And He is the All-Hearing, the All-Knowing.

وَلَهٗ مَا سَكَنَ فِي الَّيْلِ وَالنَّهَارِ وَهُوَ السَّمِيْعُ الْعَلِيْمُ ﴿١٤﴾

15. Say, 'Shall I take any protector other than Allah, the Maker of the heavens and the earth, Who feeds and is not fed?' Say, 'I have been commanded to be the first of those who submit.' And be thou not of those who associate partners *with God*.

قُلْ اَغَيْرَ اللّٰهِ اَتَّخِذُ وَلِيًّا فَاطِرِ السَّمٰوٰتِ وَالْاَرْضِ
وَهُوَ يُطْعِمُ وَلَا يُطْعَمُ قُلْ اِنِّيْٓ اُمِرْتُ اَنْ اَكُوْنَ
اَوَّلَ مَنْ اَسْلَمَ وَلَا تَكُوْنَنَّ مِنَ الْمُشْرِكِيْنَ ﴿١٥﴾

* 16. Say, 'Of a truth, I fear, if I disobey my Lord, the punishment of an awful day.'

قُلْ اِنِّيْٓ اَخَافُ اِنْ عَصَيْتُ رَبِّيْ عَذَابَ يَوْمٍ عَظِيْمٍ ﴿١٦﴾

17. He from whom it is averted on that day, *God* indeed has had mercy on him. And that indeed is a manifest triumph.

مَنْ يُّصْرَفْ عَنْهُ يَوْمَئِذٍ فَقَدْ رَحِمَهٗ وَذٰلِكَ الْفَوْزُ
الْمُبِيْنُ ﴿١٧﴾

* 18. And if Allah touch thee with affliction, there is none that can remove it but He; and if He touch thee with happiness, then He has power to do all that He wills.

وَاِنْ يَّمْسَسْكَ اللّٰهُ بِضُرٍّ فَلَا كَاشِفَ لَهٗٓ اِلَّا هُوَ
وَاِنْ يَّمْسَسْكَ بِخَيْرٍ فَهُوَ عَلٰى كُلِّ شَيْءٍ قَدِيْرٌ ﴿١٨﴾

* 19. And He is Supreme over His servants; and He is the Wise, the All-Aware.

وَهُوَ الْقَاهِرُ فَوْقَ عِبَادِهٖ وَهُوَ الْحَكِيْمُ الْخَبِيْرُ ﴿١٩﴾

* 20. Say, 'What thing is most weighty as a witness?' Say, 'Allah is a Witness between me and you. And this Qur'ān has been revealed to me so that with it I may warn you and whomsoever it reaches. What! do you really bear witness that

قُلْ اَيُّ شَيْءٍ اَكْبَرُ شَهَادَةً قُلِ اللّٰهُ شَهِيْدٌ بَيْنِيْ
وَبَيْنَكُمْ وَاُوْحِيَ اِلَيَّ هٰذَا الْقُرْاٰنُ لِاُنْذِرَكُمْ بِهٖ
وَمَنْ بَلَغَ اَئِنَّكُمْ لَتَشْهَدُوْنَ اَنَّ مَعَ اللّٰهِ اٰلِهَةً

there are other gods beside Allah?' Say, 'I bear not witness *thereto*.' Say, 'He is the One God, and certainly I am far removed from that which you associate *with Him*.'

21. Those to whom We gave the Book recognize him as they recognize their sons. But those who ruin their souls will not believe.

R. 3.

22. And who is more unjust than he who forges a lie against Allah or gives the lie to His Signs? Surely, the unjust shall not prosper.

23. And *think of* the day when We shall gather them all together; then shall We say to those who associated partners *with God*, 'Where are the partners you spoke of, those whom you used to assert?'

24. Then *the end of* their mischief will be naught save that they shall say, 'By Allah, our Lord, we were not idolaters.'

* 25. See how they lie against themselves. And that which they fabricated has failed them.

26. And among them are some who give ear to thee; but We have put veils on their hearts, that they should not understand, and deafness in their ears. And *even* if they see every Sign, they would not believe therein, so much so, that when they come to thee, disputing with thee, those who disbelieve say, 'This is nothing but fables of the ancients.'

27. And they forbid *others* to *believe* it and *themselves too* they keep away from it. And they ruin none but their own selves; only they perceive not.

28. And if thou couldst only see when they are made to stand before the Fire! They will say, 'Oh, would that we might be sent back! And *then* we would not treat the Signs of our Lord as lies, and we would be of the believers.'

29. Nay, that which they used to conceal before has *now* become clear to them. And if they were sent back, they would surely return to that which they were forbidden. And they are certainly liars.

أُخْرٰى قُلْ لَّآ أَشْهَدُ قُلْ إِنَّمَا هُوَ إِلٰهٌ وَّاحِدٌ وَّ
إِنَّنِي بَرِيٓءٌ مِّمَّا تُشْرِكُونَ ﴿٢٠﴾
اَلَّذِينَ اٰتَيْنٰهُمُ الْكِتٰبَ يَعْرِفُوْنَهٗ كَمَا يَعْرِفُوْنَ
اَبْنَآءَهُمْ اَلَّذِينَ خَسِرُوْٓا اَنْفُسَهُمْ فَهُمْ لَا يُؤْمِنُوْنَ ﴿٢١﴾
وَمَنْ اَظْلَمُ مِمَّنِ افْتَرٰى عَلَى اللّٰهِ كَذِبًا اَوْ كَذَّبَ
بِاٰيٰتِهٖ اِنَّهٗ لَا يُفْلِحُ الظّٰلِمُوْنَ ﴿٢٢﴾
وَيَوْمَ نَحْشُرُهُمْ جَمِيْعًا ثُمَّ نَقُوْلُ لِلَّذِيْنَ اَشْرَكُوْٓا
اَيْنَ شُرَكَآؤُكُمُ الَّذِيْنَ كُنْتُمْ تَزْعُمُوْنَ ﴿٢٣﴾
ثُمَّ لَمْ تَكُنْ فِتْنَتُهُمْ اِلَّآ اَنْ قَالُوْا وَاللّٰهِ رَبِّنَا مَا
كُنَّا مُشْرِكِيْنَ ﴿٢٤﴾
اُنْظُرْ كَيْفَ كَذَبُوْا عَلٰٓى اَنْفُسِهِمْ وَضَلَّ عَنْهُمْ مَّا كَانُوْا
يَفْتَرُوْنَ ﴿٢٥﴾
وَمِنْهُمْ مَّنْ يَّسْتَمِعُ اِلَيْكَ وَجَعَلْنَا عَلٰى قُلُوْبِهِمْ
اَكِنَّةً اَنْ يَّفْقَهُوْهُ وَفِيْٓ اٰذَانِهِمْ وَقْرًا وَاِنْ يَّرَوْا
كُلَّ اٰيَةٍ لَّا يُؤْمِنُوْا بِهَا حَتّٰٓى اِذَا جَآءُوْكَ يُجَادِلُوْنَكَ
يَقُوْلُ الَّذِيْنَ كَفَرُوْٓا اِنْ هٰذَآ اِلَّآ اَسَاطِيْرُ الْاَوَّلِيْنَ ﴿٢٦﴾
وَهُمْ يَنْهَوْنَ عَنْهُ وَيَنْـَٔوْنَ عَنْهُ وَاِنْ يُّهْلِكُوْنَ
اِلَّآ اَنْفُسَهُمْ وَمَا يَشْعُرُوْنَ ﴿٢٧﴾
وَلَوْ تَرٰٓى اِذْ وُقِفُوْا عَلَى النَّارِ فَقَالُوْا يٰلَيْتَنَا نُرَدُّ وَ
لَا نُكَذِّبَ بِاٰيٰتِ رَبِّنَا وَنَكُوْنَ مِنَ الْمُؤْمِنِيْنَ ﴿٢٨﴾
بَلْ بَدَا لَهُمْ مَّا كَانُوْا يُخْفُوْنَ مِنْ قَبْلُ وَلَوْ رُدُّوْا
لَعَادُوْا لِمَا نُهُوْا عَنْهُ وَاِنَّهُمْ لَكٰذِبُوْنَ ﴿٢٩﴾

30. And they say, 'There is nothing except *this* our present life, and we shall not be raised again.'

31. And if thou couldst only see when they are made to stand before their Lord! He will say, 'Is not this *second life* the truth?' They will say, 'Yea, by our Lord.' He will say, 'Then taste the punishment because you disbelieved.'

R. 4.

32. Those indeed are the losers who deny the meeting with Allah, so much so, that when the Hour shall come on them unawares, they will say, 'O our grief for our neglecting this *Hour!*' And they shall bear their burdens on their backs. Surely, evil is that which they bear.

33. And worldly life is nothing but a sport and a pastime. And surely the abode of the Hereafter is better for those who are righteous. Will you not then understand?

34. We know *full well* that what they say verily grieves thee; for surely it is not thee that they charge with falsehood but it is the Signs of Allah that the evil-doers reject.

35. And Messengers indeed have been rejected before thee; but notwithstanding their rejection and persecution they remained patient until Our help came to them. There is none that can change the words of Allah. And there have already come to thee tidings of *past* Messengers.

36. And if their aversion is grievous to thee, then, if thou art able to seek a passage into the earth or a ladder unto heaven, and bring them a Sign, *thou canst do so*. And had Allah *enforced* His will, He could surely have brought them together into the guidance. So be thou not of those who lack knowledge.

* 37. Only those can accept who listen. And *as for* the dead, Allah will raise them *to life*, then to Him shall they be brought back.

38. And they say, 'Why has not a Sign been sent down to him from his Lord?'

وَقَالُوْٓا اِنْ هِيَ اِلَّا حَيَاتُنَا الدُّنْيَا وَمَا نَحْنُ بِمَبْعُوْثِيْنَ ﴿۳۰﴾
وَلَوْ تَرٰٓى اِذْ وُقِفُوْا عَلٰى رَبِّهِمْ ۭ قَالَ اَلَيْسَ هٰذَا بِالْحَقِّ ۭ
قَالُوْا بَلٰى وَرَبِّنَا ۭ قَالَ فَذُوْقُوا الْعَذَابَ بِمَا كُنْتُمْ
تَكْفُرُوْنَ ﴿۳۱﴾ ع
قَدْ خَسِرَ الَّذِيْنَ كَذَّبُوْا بِلِقَاۗءِ اللّٰهِ ۭ حَتّٰٓى اِذَا جَاۗءَتْهُمُ
السَّاعَةُ بَغْتَةً قَالُوْا يٰحَسْرَتَنَا عَلٰي مَا فَرَّطْنَا فِيْهَا ۙ
وَهُمْ يَحْمِلُوْنَ اَوْزَارَهُمْ عَلٰي ظُهُوْرِهِمْ ۭ اَلَا سَاۗءَ مَا
يَزِرُوْنَ ﴿۳۲﴾
وَمَا الْحَيٰوةُ الدُّنْيَآ اِلَّا لَعِبٌ وَّلَهْوٌ ۭ وَلَلدَّارُ الْاٰخِرَةُ
خَيْرٌ لِّلَّذِيْنَ يَتَّقُوْنَ ۭ اَفَلَا تَعْقِلُوْنَ ﴿۳۳﴾
قَدْ نَعْلَمُ اِنَّهٗ لَيَحْزُنُكَ الَّذِيْ يَقُوْلُوْنَ فَاِنَّهُمْ لَا
يُكَذِّبُوْنَكَ وَلٰكِنَّ الظّٰلِمِيْنَ بِاٰيٰتِ اللّٰهِ يَجْحَدُوْنَ ﴿۳۴﴾
وَلَقَدْ كُذِّبَتْ رُسُلٌ مِّنْ قَبْلِكَ فَصَبَرُوْا عَلٰي مَا كُذِّبُوْا
وَاُوْذُوْا حَتّٰٓى اَتٰىهُمْ نَصْرُنَا ۚ وَلَا مُبَدِّلَ لِكَلِمٰتِ اللّٰهِ ۚ
وَلَقَدْ جَاۗءَكَ مِنْ نَّبَاِي الْمُرْسَلِيْنَ ﴿۳۵﴾
وَاِنْ كَانَ كَبُرَ عَلَيْكَ اِعْرَاضُهُمْ فَاِنِ اسْتَطَعْتَ اَنْ
تَبْتَغِيَ نَفَقًا فِي الْاَرْضِ اَوْ سُلَّمًا فِي السَّمَاۗءِ فَتَاْتِيَهُمْ
بِاٰيَةٍ ۭ وَلَوْ شَاۗءَ اللّٰهُ لَجَمَعَهُمْ عَلَي الْهُدٰي فَلَا
تَكُوْنَنَّ مِنَ الْجٰهِلِيْنَ ﴿۳۶﴾ النصف
اِنَّمَا يَسْتَجِيْبُ الَّذِيْنَ يَسْمَعُوْنَ ۭ وَالْمَوْتٰى يَبْعَثُهُمُ
اللّٰهُ ثُمَّ اِلَيْهِ يُرْجَعُوْنَ ﴿۳۷﴾
وَقَالُوْا لَوْلَا نُزِّلَ عَلَيْهِ اٰيَةٌ مِّنْ رَّبِّهٖ ۭ قُلْ اِنَّ اللّٰهَ

Say, 'Surely, Allah has power to send down a Sign, but most of them do not know.'

قَادِرٌ عَلٰٓى اَنْ يُّنَزِّلَ اٰيَةً وَّلٰكِنَّ اَكْثَرَهُمْ لَا
يَعْلَمُوْنَ ﴿۳۸﴾

39. There is not an animal *that crawls* in the earth, nor a bird that flies on its two wings, but they are communities like you. We have left out nothing in the Book. Then to their Lord shall they be gathered together.

وَمَا مِنْ دَآبَّةٍ فِى الْاَرْضِ وَلَا طٰٓئِرٍ يَّطِيْرُ بِجَنَاحَيْهِ
اِلَّآ اُمَمٌ اَمْثَالُكُمْ مَا فَرَّطْنَا فِى الْكِتٰبِ مِنْ شَیْءٍ ثُمَّ
اِلٰى رَبِّهِمْ يُحْشَرُوْنَ ﴿۳۹﴾

* 40. Those who have rejected Our Signs are deaf and dumb, in utter darkness. Whom Allah wills He allows to perish and whom He wills He places on the right path.

وَالَّذِيْنَ كَذَّبُوْا بِاٰيٰتِنَا صُمٌّ وَّبُكْمٌ فِى الظُّلُمٰتِ
مَنْ يَّشَاِ اللّٰهُ يُضْلِلْهُ وَمَنْ يَّشَاْ يَجْعَلْهُ عَلٰى صِرَاطٍ
مُّسْتَقِيْمٍ ﴿۴۰﴾

* 41. Say, 'What think ye? If the punishment of Allah come upon you or there come upon you the Hour, will you call upon any other than Allah, if you are truthful?'

قُلْ اَرَءَيْتَكُمْ اِنْ اَتٰىكُمْ عَذَابُ اللّٰهِ اَوْ اَتَتْكُمُ السَّاعَةُ
اَغَيْرَ اللّٰهِ تَدْعُوْنَ اِنْ كُنْتُمْ صٰدِقِيْنَ ﴿۴۱﴾

42. Nay, but on Him alone will you call; then will He remove that which you call on Him *to remove*, if He please, and you will forget what you associate *with Him*.

بَلْ اِيَّاهُ تَدْعُوْنَ فَيَكْشِفُ مَا تَدْعُوْنَ اِلَيْهِ اِنْ شَآءَ
وَتَنْسَوْنَ مَا تُشْرِكُوْنَ ﴿۴۲﴾ ع

R. 5.

43. And indeed We sent *Messengers* to peoples before thee; then We afflicted them with poverty and adversity that they might humble themselves.

وَلَقَدْ اَرْسَلْنَآ اِلٰٓى اُمَمٍ مِّنْ قَبْلِكَ فَاَخَذْنٰهُمْ بِالْبَاْسَآءِ
وَالضَّرَّآءِ لَعَلَّهُمْ يَتَضَرَّعُوْنَ ﴿۴۳﴾

44. Why, then, when Our punishment came upon them, did they not grow humble? But their hearts were hardened and Satan made all that they did *seem* fair to them.

فَلَوْلَآ اِذْ جَآءَهُمْ بَاْسُنَا تَضَرَّعُوْا وَلٰكِنْ قَسَتْ قُلُوْبُهُمْ
وَزَيَّنَ لَهُمُ الشَّيْطٰنُ مَا كَانُوْا يَعْمَلُوْنَ ﴿۴۴﴾

45. Then, when they forgot that with which they had been admonished, We opened unto them the gates of all things, until, when they became exultant at what they were given, We seized them suddenly, and lo! they were plunged into despair.

فَلَمَّا نَسُوْا مَا ذُكِّرُوْا بِهٖ فَتَحْنَا عَلَيْهِمْ اَبْوَابَ كُلِّ
شَیْءٍ حَتّٰٓى اِذَا فَرِحُوْا بِمَآ اُوْتُوْٓا اَخَذْنٰهُمْ بَغْتَةً
فَاِذَا هُمْ مُّبْلِسُوْنَ ﴿۴۵﴾

* 46. So the last remnant of the people who did wrong was cut off; and all praise belongs to Allah, the Lord of all the worlds.

فَقُطِعَ دَابِرُ الْقَوْمِ الَّذِيْنَ ظَلَمُوْا وَالْحَمْدُ لِلّٰهِ رَبِّ
الْعٰلَمِيْنَ ﴿۴۶﴾

47. Say, 'What think ye? If Allah should take away your hearing and your

قُلْ اَرَءَيْتُمْ اِنْ اَخَذَ اللّٰهُ سَمْعَكُمْ وَاَبْصَارَكُمْ وَخَتَمَ

sight, and seal up your hearts, who is the God other than Allah who could bring it *back* to you?' See how We vary the Signs, yet they turn away.

عَلٰى قُلُوْبِكُمْ مَّنْ اِلٰهٌ غَيْرُ اللّٰهِ يَاْتِيْكُمْ بِهٖ ۭ اُنْظُرْ
كَيْفَ نُصَرِّفُ الْاٰيٰتِ ثُمَّ هُمْ يَصْدِفُوْنَ ﴿٤٧﴾

48. Say, 'What think ye? If the punishment of Allah come upon you suddenly or openly, will any be destroyed save the wrongdoing people?'

قُلْ اَرَءَيْتَكُمْ اِنْ اَتٰىكُمْ عَذَابُ اللّٰهِ بَغْتَةً اَوْ
جَهْرَةً هَلْ يُهْلَكُ اِلَّا الْقَوْمُ الظّٰلِمُوْنَ ﴿٤٨﴾

49. And We send not the Messengers but as bearers of glad tidings and as warners. So those who believe and reform *themselves*, on them *shall come* no fear nor shall they grieve.

وَمَا نُرْسِلُ الْمُرْسَلِيْنَ اِلَّا مُبَشِّرِيْنَ وَمُنْذِرِيْنَ ۚ
فَمَنْ اٰمَنَ وَاَصْلَحَ فَلَا خَوْفٌ عَلَيْهِمْ وَلَا هُمْ
يَحْزَنُوْنَ ﴿٤٩﴾

* 50. And those who reject Our Signs, punishment will touch them, because they disobeyed.

وَالَّذِيْنَ كَذَّبُوْا بِاٰيٰتِنَا يَمَسُّهُمُ الْعَذَابُ بِمَا كَانُوْا
يَفْسُقُوْنَ ﴿٥٠﴾

51. Say: "I do not say to you: 'I possess the treasures of Allah,' nor do I know the unseen; nor do I say to you: 'I am an angel.' I follow only that which is revealed to me." Say: 'Can a blind man and one who sees be alike?' Will you not then reflect?

قُلْ لَّاۤ اَقُوْلُ لَكُمْ عِنْدِيْ خَزَآئِنُ اللّٰهِ وَلَاۤ اَعْلَمُ
الْغَيْبَ وَلَاۤ اَقُوْلُ لَكُمْ اِنِّيْ مَلَكٌ ۚ اِنْ اَتَّبِعُ اِلَّا مَا
يُوْحٰۤى اِلَيَّ ۭ قُلْ هَلْ يَسْتَوِي الْاَعْمٰى وَالْبَصِيْرُ ۭ اَفَلَا
تَتَفَكَّرُوْنَ ﴿٥١﴾ ع ٦

R. 6.

52. And warn thereby those who fear that they shall be gathered to their Lord, that they shall have no friend nor intercessor beside Him, so that they may become righteous.

وَاَنْذِرْ بِهِ الَّذِيْنَ يَخَافُوْنَ اَنْ يُّحْشَرُوْۤا اِلٰى رَبِّهِمْ
لَيْسَ لَهُمْ مِّنْ دُوْنِهٖ وَلِيٌّ وَّلَا شَفِيْعٌ لَّعَلَّهُمْ
يَتَّقُوْنَ ﴿٥٢﴾

53. And drive not away those who call upon their Lord morning and evening, seeking His countenance. Thou art not at all accountable for them nor are they at all accountable for thee, that thou shouldst drive them away and be of the unjust.

وَلَا تَطْرُدِ الَّذِيْنَ يَدْعُوْنَ رَبَّهُمْ بِالْغَدٰوةِ وَالْعَشِيِّ
يُرِيْدُوْنَ وَجْهَهٗ ۭ مَا عَلَيْكَ مِنْ حِسَابِهِمْ مِّنْ شَيْءٍ
وَّمَا مِنْ حِسَابِكَ عَلَيْهِمْ مِّنْ شَيْءٍ فَتَطْرُدَهُمْ فَتَكُوْنَ
مِنَ الظّٰلِمِيْنَ ﴿٥٣﴾

54. And in like manner have We tried some of them by others, that they may say, 'Is it these whom Allah has favoured from among us?' Does not Allah know

وَكَذٰلِكَ فَتَنَّا بَعْضَهُمْ بِبَعْضٍ لِّيَقُوْلُوْۤا اَهٰۤؤُلَاۤءِ
مَنَّ اللّٰهُ عَلَيْهِمْ مِّنْ بَيْنِنَا ۭ اَلَيْسَ اللّٰهُ بِاَعْلَمَ

best those who are grateful?

بِالشّٰكِرِيْنَ ﴿۵۴﴾

55. And when those who believe in Our Signs come to thee, say: 'Peace be unto you! Your Lord has taken it upon Himself *to show* mercy, so that whoso among you does evil ignorantly, and repents thereafter and amends, then He is Most Forgiving, Merciful.'

وَاِذَا جَآءَكَ الَّذِيْنَ يُؤْمِنُوْنَ بِاٰيٰتِنَا فَقُلْ سَلٰمٌ
عَلَيْكُمْ كَتَبَ رَبُّكُمْ عَلٰى نَفْسِهِ الرَّحْمَةَ ۙ اَنَّهٗ مَنْ
عَمِلَ مِنْكُمْ سُوْٓءًا ۢ بِجَهَالَةٍ ثُمَّ تَابَ مِنْ ۢ بَعْدِهٖ
وَاَصْلَحَ فَاَنَّهٗ غَفُوْرٌ رَّحِيْمٌ ﴿۵۵﴾

56. And thus do We expound the Signs *that you may seek forgiveness* and that the way of the sinners may become manifest.

وَكَذٰلِكَ نُفَصِّلُ الْاٰيٰتِ وَلِتَسْتَبِيْنَ سَبِيْلُ الْمُجْرِمِيْنَ ﴿۵۶﴾

R. 7.

* 57. Say: 'I am forbidden to worship those on whom you call beside Allah.' Say: 'I will not follow your evil inclinations. In that case, I shall become lost and I shall not be of the guided.'

قُلْ اِنِّيْ نُهِيْتُ اَنْ اَعْبُدَ الَّذِيْنَ تَدْعُوْنَ مِنْ دُوْنِ
اللّٰهِ ۭ قُلْ لَّآ اَتَّبِعُ اَهْوَآءَكُمْ ۙ قَدْ ضَلَلْتُ اِذًا وَّمَآ
اَنَا مِنَ الْمُهْتَدِيْنَ ﴿۵۷﴾

58. Say: 'I *take my stand* on a clear evidence from my Lord and you reject it. That which you desire to be hastened is not in my *power*. The decision rests with none but Allah. He explains the truth, and He is Best of judges.'

قُلْ اِنِّيْ عَلٰى بَيِّنَةٍ مِّنْ رَّبِّيْ وَكَذَّبْتُمْ بِهٖ ۭ مَا عِنْدِيْ
مَا تَسْتَعْجِلُوْنَ بِهٖ ۭ اِنِ الْحُكْمُ اِلَّا لِلّٰهِ ۭ يَقُصُّ الْحَقَّ
وَهُوَ خَيْرُ الْفٰصِلِيْنَ ﴿۵۸﴾

59. Say: 'If that which you desire to be hastened were in my *power*, surely the matter would be decided between me and you. And Allah knows best the unjust.'

قُلْ لَّوْ اَنَّ عِنْدِيْ مَا تَسْتَعْجِلُوْنَ بِهٖ لَقُضِيَ الْاَمْرُ
بَيْنِيْ وَبَيْنَكُمْ ۭ وَاللّٰهُ اَعْلَمُ بِالظّٰلِمِيْنَ ﴿۵۹﴾

60. And with Him are the keys of the unseen; none knows them but He. And He knows whatsoever is in the land and *in* the sea. And there falls not a leaf but He knows it; nor is there a grain in the deep darkness of the earth, nor anything green or dry, but is *recorded* in a clear Book.

وَعِنْدَهٗ مَفَاتِحُ الْغَيْبِ لَا يَعْلَمُهَآ اِلَّا هُوَ ۭ وَيَعْلَمُ
مَا فِي الْبَرِّ وَالْبَحْرِ ۭ وَمَا تَسْقُطُ مِنْ وَّرَقَةٍ اِلَّا يَعْلَمُهَا
وَلَا حَبَّةٍ فِيْ ظُلُمٰتِ الْاَرْضِ وَلَا رَطْبٍ وَّلَا يَابِسٍ
اِلَّا فِيْ كِتٰبٍ مُّبِيْنٍ ﴿۶۰﴾

61. And He it is Who takes your souls by night and knows that which you do by day; then He raises you up again therein, that the appointed term may be completed. Then to Him is your return. Then will He inform you of what you used to do.

وَهُوَ الَّذِيْ يَتَوَفّٰىكُمْ بِالَّيْلِ وَيَعْلَمُ مَا جَرَحْتُمْ
بِالنَّهَارِ ثُمَّ يَبْعَثُكُمْ فِيْهِ لِيُقْضٰٓى اَجَلٌ مُّسَمًّى ۚ ثُمَّ
اِلَيْهِ مَرْجِعُكُمْ ثُمَّ يُنَبِّئُكُمْ بِمَا كُنْتُمْ تَعْمَلُوْنَ ﴿۶۱﴾

R. 8.

62. And He is Supreme over His servants, and He sends guardians *to watch*

وَهُوَ الْقَاهِرُ فَوْقَ عِبَادِهٖ وَيُرْسِلُ عَلَيْكُمْ حَفَظَةً ۭ

over you, until, when death comes to anyone of you, Our messengers take his soul, and they fail not.

حَتّٰۤى اِذَا جَآءَ اَحَدَكُمُ الْمَوْتُ تَوَفَّتْهُ رُسُلُنَا وَهُمْ
لَا يُفَرِّطُوْنَ ﴿۶۲﴾

63. Then are they returned to Allah, their true Lord. Surely, His is the judgment. And He is the Quickest of reckoners.

ثُمَّ رُدُّوْۤا اِلَى اللّٰهِ مَوْلٰىهُمُ الْحَقِّ ؕ اَلَا لَهُ الْحُكْمُ وَهُوَ
اَسْرَعُ الْحٰسِبِيْنَ ﴿۶۳﴾

64. Say, "Who delivers you from the calamities of the land and the sea, *when* you call upon Him in humility and in secret, *saying*, 'If He deliver us from this, we will surely be of those who are grateful?' "

قُلْ مَنْ يُّنَجِّيْكُمْ مِّنْ ظُلُمٰتِ الْبَرِّ وَالْبَحْرِ تَدْعُوْنَهٗ
تَضَرُّعًا وَّخُفْيَةً ۚ لَئِنْ اَنْجٰىنَا مِنْ هٰذِهٖ لَنَكُوْنَنَّ
مِنَ الشّٰكِرِيْنَ ﴿۶۴﴾

65. Say, 'Allah delivers you from them and from every distress, yet you associate partners *with Him*.'

قُلِ اللّٰهُ يُنَجِّيْكُمْ مِّنْهَا وَمِنْ كُلِّ كَرْبٍ ثُمَّ اَنْتُمْ
تُشْرِكُوْنَ ﴿۶۵﴾

* 66. Say, 'He has power to send punishment upon you from above you or from beneath your feet, or to confound you by *splitting you into* sects and make you taste the violence of one another.' See how We expound the Signs in various ways that they may understand!

قُلْ هُوَ الْقَادِرُ عَلٰۤى اَنْ يَّبْعَثَ عَلَيْكُمْ عَذَابًا مِّنْ
فَوْقِكُمْ اَوْ مِنْ تَحْتِ اَرْجُلِكُمْ اَوْ يَلْبِسَكُمْ شِيَعًا
وَّيُذِيْقَ بَعْضَكُمْ بَاْسَ بَعْضٍ ؕ اُنْظُرْ كَيْفَ نُصَرِّفُ
الْاٰيٰتِ لَعَلَّهُمْ يَفْقَهُوْنَ ﴿۶۶﴾

67. And thy people have rejected it, though it is the truth. Say, 'I am not a guardian over you.'

وَكَذَّبَ بِهٖ قَوْمُكَ وَهُوَ الْحَقُّ ؕ قُلْ لَّسْتُ عَلَيْكُمْ
بِوَكِيْلٍ ﴿۶۷﴾

68. For every prophecy there is a fixed time; and soon will you come to know.

لِكُلِّ نَبَاٍ مُّسْتَقَرٌّ وَّسَوْفَ تَعْلَمُوْنَ ﴿۶۸﴾

* 69. And when thou seest those who engage in *vain discourse concerning* Our Signs, then turn thou away from them until they engage in a discourse other than that. And if Satan cause thee to forget, then sit not, after recollection, with the unjust people.

وَاِذَا رَاَيْتَ الَّذِيْنَ يَخُوْضُوْنَ فِيْۤ اٰيٰتِنَا فَاَعْرِضْ
عَنْهُمْ حَتّٰى يَخُوْضُوْا فِيْ حَدِيْثٍ غَيْرِهٖ ؕ وَاِمَّا
يُنْسِيَنَّكَ الشَّيْطٰنُ فَلَا تَقْعُدْ بَعْدَ الذِّكْرٰى مَعَ
الْقَوْمِ الظّٰلِمِيْنَ ﴿۶۹﴾

70. And those who are righteous are not at all accountable for them, but *their duty is* to admonish them, that they may fear *God*.

وَمَا عَلَى الَّذِيْنَ يَتَّقُوْنَ مِنْ حِسَابِهِمْ مِّنْ شَيْءٍ
وَّلٰكِنْ ذِكْرٰى لَعَلَّهُمْ يَتَّقُوْنَ ﴿۷۰﴾

وَذَرِ الَّذِينَ اتَّخَذُوا دِينَهُمْ لَعِبًا وَّلَهْوًا وَّغَرَّتْهُمُ
الْحَيٰوةُ الدُّنْيَا وَذَكِّرْ بِهٖٓ اَنْ تُبْسَلَ نَفْسٌۢ بِمَا كَسَبَتْ
لَيْسَ لَهَا مِنْ دُوْنِ اللّٰهِ وَلِيٌّ وَّلَا شَفِيْعٌ ۚ وَاِنْ
تَعْدِلْ كُلَّ عَدْلٍ لَّا يُؤْخَذْ مِنْهَا ۗ اُولٰٓئِكَ الَّذِيْنَ
اُبْسِلُوْا بِمَا كَسَبُوْا ۚ لَهُمْ شَرَابٌ مِّنْ حَمِيْمٍ وَّعَذَابٌ
ع اَلِيْمٌۢ بِمَا كَانُوْا يَكْفُرُوْنَ ﴿٧١﴾

71. And let alone those who take their religion for a sport and a pastime, and whom worldly life has beguiled. And admonish *people* thereby lest a soul be consigned to perdition for what it has wrought. It shall have no helper nor intercessor beside Allah; and even if it offer every ransom, it shall not be accepted from it. These are they who have been delivered over to destruction for their own acts. They will have a drink of boiling water and a grievous punishment, because they disbelieved.

R. 9.

قُلْ اَنَدْعُوْا مِنْ دُوْنِ اللّٰهِ مَا لَا يَنْفَعُنَا وَلَا يَضُرُّنَا
وَنُرَدُّ عَلٰٓى اَعْقَابِنَا بَعْدَ اِذْ هَدٰىنَا اللّٰهُ كَالَّذِي
اسْتَهْوَتْهُ الشَّيٰطِيْنُ فِي الْاَرْضِ حَيْرَانَ لَهٗٓ اَصْحٰبٌ
يَّدْعُوْنَهٗٓ اِلَى الْهُدَى ائْتِنَا ۗ قُلْ اِنَّ هُدَى اللّٰهِ
هُوَ الْهُدٰى ۗ وَاُمِرْنَا لِنُسْلِمَ لِرَبِّ الْعٰلَمِيْنَ ﴿٧٢﴾

72. Say: "Shall we call, beside Allah, upon that which can neither profit us nor harm us, and shall we be turned back on our heels after Allah has guided us, like one whom the evil ones entice away *leaving him* bewildered in the land, *and* who has companions who call him to guidance, *saying*, 'Come to us?'" Say: "Surely, the guidance of Allah is the only guidance and we have been commanded to submit to the Lord of all the worlds.

وَاَنْ اَقِيْمُوا الصَّلٰوةَ وَاتَّقُوْهُ ۗ وَهُوَ الَّذِيْٓ اِلَيْهِ
تُحْشَرُوْنَ ﴿٧٣﴾

73. "And *we have been given the command*: 'Observe Prayer and fear Him;' and He it is to Whom you shall be gathered."

وَهُوَ الَّذِيْ خَلَقَ السَّمٰوٰتِ وَالْاَرْضَ بِالْحَقِّ ۗ وَيَوْمَ
يَقُوْلُ كُنْ فَيَكُوْنُ ۚ قَوْلُهُ الْحَقُّ ۗ وَلَهُ الْمُلْكُ يَوْمَ
يُنْفَخُ فِي الصُّوْرِ ۗ عٰلِمُ الْغَيْبِ وَالشَّهَادَةِ ۗ وَهُوَ
الْحَكِيْمُ الْخَبِيْرُ ﴿٧٤﴾

* 74. And He it is Who created the heavens and the earth in accordance with the requirements of wisdom; and the day He says, 'Be!,' it will be. His word is the truth, and His will be the kingdom on the day when the trumpet will be blown. *He is* the Knower of the unseen and the seen. And He is the Wise, the All-Aware.

وَاِذْ قَالَ اِبْرٰهِيْمُ لِاَبِيْهِ اٰزَرَ اَتَتَّخِذُ اَصْنَامًا اٰلِهَةً
اِنِّيْٓ اَرٰىكَ وَقَوْمَكَ فِيْ ضَلٰلٍ مُّبِيْنٍ ﴿٧٥﴾

75. And *remember the time* when Abraham said to his father, Āzar: 'Dost thou take idols for gods? Surely, I see thee and thy people in manifest error.'

وَكَذٰلِكَ نُرِيْٓ اِبْرٰهِيْمَ مَلَكُوْتَ السَّمٰوٰتِ
وَالْاَرْضِ وَلِيَكُوْنَ مِنَ الْمُوْقِنِيْنَ ﴿٧٦﴾

76. And thus did We show Abraham the kingdom of the heavens and the earth *that he might be rightly guided* and that he might be of those who have certainty of faith.

فَلَمَّا جَنَّ عَلَيْهِ الَّيْلُ رَاٰ كَوْكَبًا ۚ قَالَ هٰذَا رَبِّيْ

77. And when the night darkened upon

him, he saw a star. He said: 'This is my Lord!' But when it set, he said: 'I like not those that set.'

78. And when he saw the moon rise with spreading light, he said: 'This is my Lord.' But when it set, he said, 'If my Lord guide me not, I shall surely be of the people who go astray.'

79. And when he saw the sun rise with spreading light, he said: 'This is my Lord, this is the greatest.' But when it set, he said, 'O my people, surely I am clear of that which you associate *with God*.

80. 'I have turned my face toward Him Who created the heavens and the earth, being ever inclined *to God*, and I am not of those who associate gods *with God*.'

81. And his people argued with him. He said: 'Do you argue with me concerning Allah when He has guided me aright? And I fear not that which you associate with Him, unless my Lord will something. My Lord comprehends all things in His knowledge. Will you not then be admonished?

82. 'And why should I fear that which you associate *with God*, when you fear not to associate with Allah that for which He has sent down to you no authority?' Which, then, of the two parties has greater right to security, if indeed you know?

83. Those who believe and mix not up their belief with injustice—it is they who shall have peace, and who are rightly guided.

R. 10.

84. And that is Our argument which We gave to Abraham against his people. We exalt in degrees of rank whomso We please. Thy Lord is indeed Wise, All-Knowing.

85. And We gave him Isaac and Jacob; each did We guide aright, and Noah did We guide aright aforetime, and of his progeny, David and Solomon and Job and Joseph and Moses and Aaron. Thus do We reward those who do good.

فَلَمَّآ اَفَلَ قَالَ لَآ اُحِبُّ الْاٰفِلِيْنَ ﴿٧٧﴾
فَلَمَّا رَاَ الْقَمَرَ بَازِغًا قَالَ هٰذَا رَبِّيْ ۚ فَلَمَّآ اَفَلَ
قَالَ لَئِنْ لَّمْ يَهْدِنِيْ رَبِّيْ لَاَكُوْنَنَّ مِنَ الْقَوْمِ
الضَّآلِّيْنَ ﴿٧٨﴾
فَلَمَّا رَاَ الشَّمْسَ بَازِغَةً قَالَ هٰذَا رَبِّيْ هٰذَآ اَكْبَرُ ۚ
فَلَمَّآ اَفَلَتْ قَالَ يٰقَوْمِ اِنِّيْ بَرِيْٓءٌ مِّمَّا تُشْرِكُوْنَ ﴿٧٩﴾
اِنِّيْ وَجَّهْتُ وَجْهِيَ لِلَّذِيْ فَطَرَ السَّمٰوٰتِ وَالْاَرْضَ
حَنِيْفًا وَّمَآ اَنَا مِنَ الْمُشْرِكِيْنَ ﴿٨٠﴾
وَحَآجَّهٗ قَوْمُهٗ ؕ قَالَ اَتُحَآجُّوْٓنِّيْ فِي اللّٰهِ وَقَدْ
هَدٰىنِ ؕ وَلَآ اَخَافُ مَا تُشْرِكُوْنَ بِهٖٓ اِلَّآ اَنْ يَّشَآءَ
رَبِّيْ شَيْـًٔا ؕ وَسِعَ رَبِّيْ كُلَّ شَيْءٍ عِلْمًا ؕ اَفَلَا تَتَذَكَّرُوْنَ ﴿٨١﴾
وَكَيْفَ اَخَافُ مَآ اَشْرَكْتُمْ وَلَا تَخَافُوْنَ اَنَّكُمْ
اَشْرَكْتُمْ بِاللّٰهِ مَا لَمْ يُنَزِّلْ بِهٖ عَلَيْكُمْ سُلْطٰنًا ؕ
فَاَيُّ الْفَرِيْقَيْنِ اَحَقُّ بِالْاَمْنِ ۚ اِنْ كُنْتُمْ تَعْلَمُوْنَ ﴿٨٢﴾
اَلَّذِيْنَ اٰمَنُوْا وَلَمْ يَلْبِسُوْٓا اِيْمَانَهُمْ بِظُلْمٍ اُولٰٓئِكَ
لَهُمُ الْاَمْنُ وَهُمْ مُّهْتَدُوْنَ ﴿٨٣﴾
وَتِلْكَ حُجَّتُنَآ اٰتَيْنٰهَآ اِبْرٰهِيْمَ عَلٰى قَوْمِهٖ ؕ نَرْفَعُ
دَرَجٰتٍ مَّنْ نَّشَآءُ ؕ اِنَّ رَبَّكَ حَكِيْمٌ عَلِيْمٌ ﴿٨٤﴾
وَوَهَبْنَا لَهٗٓ اِسْحٰقَ وَيَعْقُوْبَ ؕ كُلًّا هَدَيْنَا ۚ وَنُوْحًا
هَدَيْنَا مِنْ قَبْلُ وَمِنْ ذُرِّيَّتِهٖ دَاوٗدَ وَسُلَيْمٰنَ
وَاَيُّوْبَ وَيُوْسُفَ وَمُوْسٰى وَهٰرُوْنَ ۚ وَكَذٰلِكَ
نَجْزِي الْمُحْسِنِيْنَ ﴿٨٥﴾

86. And *We guided* Zachariah and John and Jesus and Elias; each *one of them* was of the virtuous.

وَزَكَرِيَّا وَيَحْيٰى وَعِيسٰى وَإِلْيَاسَ ۖ كُلٌّ مِّنَ الصّٰلِحِينَ ﴿٨٦﴾

87. And *We also guided* Ishmael and Elisha and Jonah and Lot; and each one did We exalt above the people.

وَإِسْمٰعِيلَ وَالْيَسَعَ وَيُونُسَ وَلُوطًا ۚ وَكُلًّا فَضَّلْنَا عَلَى الْعٰلَمِينَ ﴿٨٧﴾

88. And *We exalted* some of their fathers and their children and their brethren, and We chose them and We guided them in the straight path.

وَمِنْ اٰبَآئِهِمْ وَذُرِّيّٰتِهِمْ وَإِخْوَانِهِمْ ۚ وَاجْتَبَيْنٰهُمْ وَهَدَيْنٰهُمْ إِلٰى صِرَاطٍ مُّسْتَقِيمٍ ﴿٨٨﴾

89. That is the guidance of Allah. He guides thereby those of His servants whom He pleases. And if they had worshipped aught beside Him, surely all they did would have been of no avail to them.

ذٰلِكَ هُدَى اللّٰهِ يَهْدِي بِهٖ مَنْ يَّشَآءُ مِنْ عِبَادِهٖ ۚ وَلَوْ أَشْرَكُوا لَحَبِطَ عَنْهُمْ مَّا كَانُوا يَعْمَلُونَ ﴿٨٩﴾

* 90. It is these to whom We gave the Book and dominion and prophethood. But if these *people* are ungrateful for them, *it matters not*, for We have now entrusted them to a people who are not ungrateful for them.

أُولٰٓئِكَ الَّذِينَ اٰتَيْنٰهُمُ الْكِتٰبَ وَالْحُكْمَ وَالنُّبُوَّةَ ۚ فَإِنْ يَّكْفُرْ بِهَا هٰٓؤُلَآءِ فَقَدْ وَكَّلْنَا بِهَا قَوْمًا لَّيْسُوا بِهَا بِكٰفِرِينَ ﴿٩٠﴾

91. These it is whom Allah guided aright, so follow thou their guidance. Say: 'I ask not of you any reward for it. This is naught but an admonition for all mankind.'

أُولٰٓئِكَ الَّذِينَ هَدَى اللّٰهُ فَبِهُدٰىهُمُ اقْتَدِهْ ۗ قُلْ لَّآ
ع ٤ ١٢ أَسْـَٔلُكُمْ عَلَيْهِ أَجْرًا ۗ إِنْ هُوَ إِلَّا ذِكْرٰى لِلْعٰلَمِينَ ﴿٩١﴾

R. 11.

* 92. And they do not make a just estimate of Allah, when they say: 'Allah has not revealed anything to any man.' Say: 'Who revealed the Book which Moses brought, a light and guidance for the people — though you treat it as scraps of paper which you show while you conceal much; and you have been taught that which neither you nor your fathers knew?'— Say: 'Allah'. Then leave them to amuse themselves with their *vain* discourse.

وَمَا قَدَرُوا اللّٰهَ حَقَّ قَدْرِهٖٓ إِذْ قَالُوا مَآ أَنْزَلَ اللّٰهُ عَلٰى بَشَرٍ مِّنْ شَيْءٍ ۗ قُلْ مَنْ أَنْزَلَ الْكِتٰبَ الَّذِي جَآءَ بِهٖ مُوسٰى نُورًا وَّهُدًى لِّلنَّاسِ تَجْعَلُونَهٗ قَرَاطِيسَ تُبْدُونَهَا وَتُخْفُونَ كَثِيرًا ۚ وَعُلِّمْتُمْ مَّا لَمْ تَعْلَمُوٓا أَنْتُمْ وَلَآ اٰبَآؤُكُمْ ۗ قُلِ اللّٰهُ ۙ ثُمَّ ذَرْهُمْ فِي خَوْضِهِمْ يَلْعَبُونَ ﴿٩٢﴾

93. And this is a Book which We have revealed, full of blessings, to fulfil that which preceded it, and to enable thee to warn the Mother of towns and those around her. And those who believe in the Hereafter believe therein and they keep

وَهٰذَا كِتٰبٌ أَنْزَلْنٰهُ مُبٰرَكٌ مُّصَدِّقُ الَّذِي بَيْنَ يَدَيْهِ وَلِتُنْذِرَ أُمَّ الْقُرٰى وَمَنْ حَوْلَهَا ۚ وَالَّذِينَ يُؤْمِنُونَ بِالْاٰخِرَةِ يُؤْمِنُونَ بِهٖ وَهُمْ عَلٰى صَلَاتِهِمْ

a watch over their Prayer.

94. And who is more unjust than he who forges a lie against Allah, or says, 'It has been revealed to me,' while nothing has been revealed to him; and who says, 'I will send down the like of that which Allah has sent down?' And if thou couldst only see, when the wrongdoers are in the agonies of death, and the angels stretch forth their hands, *saying*, 'Yield up your souls. This day shall you be awarded the punishment of disgrace, because of that which you spoke against Allah falsely and *because* you turned away from His Signs with disdain.'

95. And now you come to Us one by one even as We created you at first, and you have left behind you that which We bestowed upon you, and We see not with you your intercessors of whom you asserted that they were partners *with God* in your *affairs*. Now you have been cut off from one another and that which you presumed has failed you.

R. 12.

96. Verily, it is Allah Who causes the grain and the date-stones to sprout. He brings forth the living from the dead, and *He* is the Bringer forth of the dead from the living. That is Allah; wherefore, then, are you turned back?

97. He causes the break of day; and He made the night for rest and the sun and the moon for reckoning *time*. That is the decree of the Mighty, the Wise.

98. And He it is Who has made the stars for you that you may follow the right direction with their help amid the deep darkness of the land and the sea. We have explained the Signs in detail for a people who possess knowledge.

99. And He it is Who has produced you from a single person and there is *for you* a home and a lodging. We have explained the Signs in detail for a people who understand.

100. And it is He Who sends down water from the cloud; and We bring forth there-

يُحَافِظُونَ ﴿٩٣﴾
وَمَنْ أَظْلَمُ مِمَّنِ افْتَرَىٰ عَلَى اللَّهِ كَذِبًا أَوْ قَالَ أُوحِيَ
إِلَيَّ وَلَمْ يُوحَ إِلَيْهِ شَيْءٌ وَمَنْ قَالَ سَأُنْزِلُ مِثْلَ
مَا أَنْزَلَ اللَّهُ ۗ وَلَوْ تَرَىٰ إِذِ الظَّالِمُونَ فِي غَمَرَاتِ الْمَوْتِ
وَالْمَلَائِكَةُ بَاسِطُو أَيْدِيهِمْ أَخْرِجُوا أَنْفُسَكُمُ ۖ الْيَوْمَ
تُجْزَوْنَ عَذَابَ الْهُونِ بِمَا كُنْتُمْ تَقُولُونَ عَلَى
اللَّهِ غَيْرَ الْحَقِّ وَكُنْتُمْ عَنْ آيَاتِهِ تَسْتَكْبِرُونَ ﴿٩٤﴾
وَلَقَدْ جِئْتُمُونَا فُرَادَىٰ كَمَا خَلَقْنَاكُمْ أَوَّلَ مَرَّةٍ
وَتَرَكْتُمْ مَا خَوَّلْنَاكُمْ وَرَاءَ ظُهُورِكُمْ ۖ وَمَا نَرَىٰ مَعَكُمْ
شُفَعَاءَكُمُ الَّذِينَ زَعَمْتُمْ أَنَّهُمْ فِيكُمْ شُرَكَاءُ ۚ
ع لَقَدْ تَقَطَّعَ بَيْنَكُمْ وَضَلَّ عَنْكُمْ مَا كُنْتُمْ تَزْعُمُونَ ﴿٩٥﴾
إِنَّ اللَّهَ فَالِقُ الْحَبِّ وَالنَّوَىٰ ۖ يُخْرِجُ الْحَيَّ مِنَ
الْمَيِّتِ وَمُخْرِجُ الْمَيِّتِ مِنَ الْحَيِّ ۚ ذَٰلِكُمُ اللَّهُ ۖ فَأَنَّىٰ
تُؤْفَكُونَ ﴿٩٦﴾
فَالِقُ الْإِصْبَاحِ وَجَعَلَ اللَّيْلَ سَكَنًا وَالشَّمْسَ وَالْقَمَرَ
حُسْبَانًا ۚ ذَٰلِكَ تَقْدِيرُ الْعَزِيزِ الْعَلِيمِ ﴿٩٧﴾
وَهُوَ الَّذِي جَعَلَ لَكُمُ النُّجُومَ لِتَهْتَدُوا بِهَا فِي
ظُلُمَاتِ الْبَرِّ وَالْبَحْرِ ۗ قَدْ فَصَّلْنَا الْآيَاتِ لِقَوْمٍ
يَعْلَمُونَ ﴿٩٨﴾
وَهُوَ الَّذِي أَنْشَأَكُمْ مِنْ نَفْسٍ وَاحِدَةٍ فَمُسْتَقَرٌّ
وَمُسْتَوْدَعٌ ۗ قَدْ فَصَّلْنَا الْآيَاتِ لِقَوْمٍ يَفْقَهُونَ ﴿٩٩﴾
وَهُوَ الَّذِي أَنْزَلَ مِنَ السَّمَاءِ مَاءً فَأَخْرَجْنَا بِهِ

with every kind of growth; then We bring forth with that green foliage wherefrom We produce clustered grain. And from the date-palm, out of its sheaths, *come forth* bunches hanging low. And *We produce therewith* gardens of grapes, and the olive and the pomegranate—similar and dissimilar. Look at the fruit thereof when it bears fruit, and the ripening thereof. Surely, in this are Signs for a people who believe.

نَبَاتَ كُلِّ شَيْءٍ فَأَخْرَجْنَا مِنْهُ خَضِرًا نُّخْرِجُ مِنْهُ
حَبًّا مُّتَرَاكِبًا ۚ وَمِنَ النَّخْلِ مِن طَلْعِهَا قِنْوَانٌ دَانِيَةٌ
وَّجَنّٰتٍ مِّنْ اَعْنَابٍ وَّالزَّيْتُوْنَ وَالرُّمَّانَ مُشْتَبِهًا
وَّغَيْرَ مُتَشَابِهٍ ۗ اُنْظُرُوْٓا اِلٰى ثَمَرِهٖٓ اِذَآ اَثْمَرَ وَيَنْعِهٖ ۗ
اِنَّ فِيْ ذٰلِكُمْ لَاٰيٰتٍ لِّقَوْمٍ يُّؤْمِنُوْنَ ﴿١٠٠﴾

101. And they hold the Jinn to be partners with Allah, although He created them; and they falsely ascribe to Him sons and daughters without any knowledge. Holy is He and exalted *far* above what they attribute *to Him!*

وَجَعَلُوْا لِلّٰهِ شُرَكَآءَ الْجِنَّ وَخَلَقَهُمْ وَخَرَقُوْا لَهٗ
بَنِيْنَ وَبَنٰتٍۢ بِغَيْرِ عِلْمٍ ۗ سُبْحٰنَهٗ وَتَعٰلٰى عَمَّا
يَصِفُوْنَ ﴿١٠١﴾ ع ١٣/١٨

R. 13.

102. The Originator of the heavens and the earth! How can He have a son when He has no consort, and *when* He has created everything and has knowledge of all things?

بَدِيْعُ السَّمٰوٰتِ وَالْاَرْضِ ۗ اَنّٰى يَكُوْنُ لَهٗ وَلَدٌ وَّ
لَمْ تَكُنْ لَّهٗ صَاحِبَةٌ ۗ وَخَلَقَ كُلَّ شَيْءٍ ۚ وَهُوَ بِكُلِّ
شَيْءٍ عَلِيْمٌ ﴿١٠٢﴾

103. Such is Allah, your Lord. There is no God but He, the Creator of all things, so worship Him. And He is Guardian over everything.

ذٰلِكُمُ اللّٰهُ رَبُّكُمْ ۚ لَآ اِلٰهَ اِلَّا هُوَ ۚ خَالِقُ كُلِّ شَيْءٍ
فَاعْبُدُوْهُ ۚ وَهُوَ عَلٰى كُلِّ شَيْءٍ وَّكِيْلٌ ﴿١٠٣﴾

104. Eyes cannot reach Him but He reaches the eyes. And He is the Incomprehensible, the All-Aware.

لَا تُدْرِكُهُ الْاَبْصَارُ ۫ وَهُوَ يُدْرِكُ الْاَبْصَارَ ۚ وَهُوَ
اللَّطِيْفُ الْخَبِيْرُ ﴿١٠٤﴾

105. Proofs have indeed come to you from your Lord; so whoever sees, it is for his own good; and whoever becomes blind, it is to his own harm. And I am not a guardian over you.

قَدْ جَآءَكُمْ بَصَآئِرُ مِنْ رَّبِّكُمْ ۚ فَمَنْ اَبْصَرَ فَلِنَفْسِهٖ ۚ
وَمَنْ عَمِيَ فَعَلَيْهَا ۗ وَمَآ اَنَا عَلَيْكُمْ بِحَفِيْظٍ ﴿١٠٥﴾

106. And thus do We vary the Signs *that the truth may become established*, but *the result is* that they say, 'Thou hast learnt *well;*' and *We vary the Signs* that We may explain it to a people who have knowledge.

وَكَذٰلِكَ نُصَرِّفُ الْاٰيٰتِ وَلِيَقُوْلُوْا دَرَسْتَ وَلِنُبَيِّنَهٗ
لِقَوْمٍ يَّعْلَمُوْنَ ﴿١٠٦﴾

107. Follow that which has been revealed to thee from thy Lord; there is no God but He; and turn aside from the idolaters.

اِتَّبِعْ مَآ اُوْحِيَ اِلَيْكَ مِنْ رَّبِّكَ ۚ لَآ اِلٰهَ اِلَّا هُوَ ۚ وَ
اَعْرِضْ عَنِ الْمُشْرِكِيْنَ ﴿١٠٧﴾

108. And if Allah had *enforced* His will, they would not have set up gods *with Him*.

وَلَوْ شَآءَ اللّٰهُ مَآ اَشْرَكُوْا ۗ وَمَا جَعَلْنٰكَ عَلَيْهِمْ

And We have not made thee a keeper over them nor art thou over them a guardian.

109. And revile not those whom they call upon beside Allah, lest they, out of spite, revile Allah in *their* ignorance. Thus unto every people have We caused their doing *to seem* fair. Then unto their Lord is their return; and He will inform them of what they used to do.

110. And they swear their strongest oaths by Allah that if there came to them a Sign, they would surely believe therein. Say, 'Surely, Signs are with Allah. But what should make you understand that when the Signs come, they will not believe?'

* 111. And We shall confound their hearts and their eyes, as they believed not therein at the first time, and We shall leave them in their transgression to wander in distraction.

R. 14.

112. And even if We send down unto them angels, and the dead speak to them, and We gather to them all things face to face, they would not believe, unless Allah *enforced* His will. But most of them behave ignorantly.

113. And in like manner have We made for every Prophet an enemy, evil ones from among men and Jinn. They suggest one to another gilded speech in order to deceive—and if thy Lord had *enforced* His will, they would not have done it; so leave them alone with that which they fabricate—

114. And in order that the hearts of those who believe not in the Hereafter may incline thereto and that they may be pleased therewith and that they may *continue to* earn what they are earning.

115. Shall I seek for judge other than Allah, when He it is Who has sent down to you the Book, clearly explained? And those to whom We gave the Book know that it has been sent down from thy Lord with truth; so be thou not of those who doubt.

116. And the word of thy Lord has been fulfilled in truth and justice. None can

حفيظا ۚ وما انت عليهم بوكيل ﴿١٠٨﴾
ولا تسبوا الذين يدعون من دون الله فيسبوا
الله عدوا بغير علم ۗ كذلك زينا لكل امة
عملهم ثم الى ربهم مرجعهم فينبئهم بما
كانوا يعملون ﴿١٠٩﴾
واقسموا بالله جهد ايمانهم لئن جاءتهم اية
ليؤمنن بها ۚ قل انما الايت عند الله وما يشعركم
انها اذا جاءت لا يؤمنون ﴿١١٠﴾
ونقلب افـدتهم وابصارهم كما لم يؤمنوا به اول
مرة ونذرهم في طغيانهم يعمهون ﴿١١١﴾ ع ١٣ الجزء ٨
ولو اننا نزلنا اليهم الملئكة وكلمهم الموتى
وحشرنا عليهم كل شيء قبلا ما كانوا ليؤمنوا الا
ان يشاء الله ولكن اكثرهم يجهلون ﴿١١٢﴾
وكذلك جعلنا لكل نبي عدوا شيطين الانس و
الجن يوحي بعضهم الى بعض زخرف القول غرورا ۚ
ولو شاء ربك ما فعلوه فذرهم وما يفترون ﴿١١٣﴾
ولتصغى اليه افـدة الذين لا يؤمنون بالاخرة و
ليرضوه وليقترفوا ما هم مقترفون ﴿١١٤﴾
افغير الله ابتغي حكما وهو الذي انزل اليكم
الكتب مفصلا ۚ والذين اتينهم الكتب يعلمون
انه منزل من ربك بالحق فلا تكونن من الممترين ﴿١١٥﴾
وتمت كلمت ربك صدقا وعدلا ۚ لا مبدل ل

change His words; and He is the All-Hearing, the All-Knowing.

لِكَلِمٰتِهٖ ۚ وَهُوَ السَّمِيْعُ الْعَلِيْمُ ﴿١١٦﴾

* 117. And if thou obey the majority of those on earth, they will lead thee astray from Allah's way. They follow nothing but *mere* conjecture, and they do nothing but lie.

وَاِنْ تُطِعْ اَكْثَرَ مَنْ فِي الْاَرْضِ يُضِلُّوْكَ عَنْ
سَبِيْلِ اللّٰهِ ۚ اِنْ يَّتَّبِعُوْنَ اِلَّا الظَّنَّ وَاِنْ هُمْ
اِلَّا يَخْرُصُوْنَ ﴿١١٧﴾

118. Surely, thy Lord knows best those who go astray from His way; and He knows best those who are rightly guided.

اِنَّ رَبَّكَ هُوَ اَعْلَمُ مَنْ يَّضِلُّ عَنْ سَبِيْلِهٖ ۚ وَهُوَ
اَعْلَمُ بِالْمُهْتَدِيْنَ ﴿١١٨﴾

119. Eat, then, of that over which the name of Allah has been pronounced, if you are believers in His Signs.

فَكُلُوْا مِمَّا ذُكِرَ اسْمُ اللّٰهِ عَلَيْهِ اِنْ كُنْتُمْ بِاٰيٰتِهٖ
مُؤْمِنِيْنَ ﴿١١٩﴾

120. And what reason have you that you should not eat of that over which the name of Allah has been pronounced, when He has already explained to you that which He has forbidden unto you—save that which you are forced to? And surely many mislead *others* by their evil desires through lack of knowledge. Assuredly, thy Lord knows best the transgressors.

وَمَا لَكُمْ اَلَّا تَاْكُلُوْا مِمَّا ذُكِرَ اسْمُ اللّٰهِ عَلَيْهِ وَ
قَدْ فَصَّلَ لَكُمْ مَّا حَرَّمَ عَلَيْكُمْ اِلَّا مَا اضْطُرِرْتُمْ
اِلَيْهِ ۗ وَاِنَّ كَثِيْرًا لَّيُضِلُّوْنَ بِاَهْوَآئِهِمْ بِغَيْرِ عِلْمٍ ۗ
اِنَّ رَبَّكَ هُوَ اَعْلَمُ بِالْمُعْتَدِيْنَ ﴿١٢٠﴾

* 121. And eschew open sins as well as secret ones. Surely, those who earn sin will be rewarded for that which they have earned.

وَذَرُوْا ظَاهِرَ الْاِثْمِ وَبَاطِنَهٗ ۗ اِنَّ الَّذِيْنَ يَكْسِبُوْنَ
الْاِثْمَ سَيُجْزَوْنَ بِمَا كَانُوْا يَقْتَرِفُوْنَ ﴿١٢١﴾

122. And eat not of that on which the name of Allah has not been pronounced, for surely that is disobedience. And certainly the evil ones inspire their friends that they may dispute with you. And if you obey them, you will indeed be setting up gods *with God*.

وَلَا تَاْكُلُوْا مِمَّا لَمْ يُذْكَرِ اسْمُ اللّٰهِ عَلَيْهِ وَاِنَّهٗ
لَفِسْقٌ ۗ وَاِنَّ الشَّيٰطِيْنَ لَيُوْحُوْنَ اِلٰٓى اَوْلِيٰٓئِهِمْ
لِيُجَادِلُوْكُمْ ۚ وَاِنْ اَطَعْتُمُوْهُمْ اِنَّكُمْ لَمُشْرِكُوْنَ ﴿١٢٢﴾

R. 15.

123. Can he, who was dead and We gave him life and made for him a light whereby he walks among men, be like him whose condition is *that he is* in utter darkness whence he cannot come forth? Thus have the doings of the disbelievers been made *to seem* fair to them.

اَوَمَنْ كَانَ مَيْتًا فَاَحْيَيْنٰهُ وَجَعَلْنَا لَهٗ نُوْرًا
يَّمْشِيْ بِهٖ فِي النَّاسِ كَمَنْ مَّثَلُهٗ فِي الظُّلُمٰتِ لَيْسَ
بِخَارِجٍ مِّنْهَا ۗ كَذٰلِكَ زُيِّنَ لِلْكٰفِرِيْنَ مَا كَانُوْا
يَعْمَلُوْنَ ﴿١٢٣﴾

* 124. And thus have We made in every town the great ones from among its sinners

وَكَذٰلِكَ جَعَلْنَا فِيْ كُلِّ قَرْيَةٍ اَكٰبِرَ مُجْرِمِيْهَا لِيَمْكُرُوْا

such as are in utter darkness with the result that they plot therein; and they plot not except against their own souls; but they perceive not.

125. And when there comes to them a Sign, they say, 'We will not believe until we are given the like of that which Allah's Messengers have been given.' Allah knows best where to place His Message. Surely, humiliation before Allah and a severe punishment shall smite the offenders because of their plotting.

* 126. So, whomsoever Allah wishes to guide, He expands his bosom for *the acceptance of* Islam; and as to him whom He wishes to *let* go astray, He makes his bosom narrow *and* close, as though he were mounting up into the skies. Thus does Allah inflict punishment on those who do not believe.

127. And this is the path of thy Lord *leading* straight *to Him*. We have indeed explained the Signs in detail for a people who would be admonished.

128. For them is the abode of peace with their Lord, and He is their Friend because of what they did.

129. And on the day when He will gather them all together, *He will say*, 'O company of Jinn! you sought *to make subservient to yourselves* a great many from among men!' And their friends from among men will say, 'Our Lord! we profited from one another but *now* we have reached our term which Thou didst appoint for us.' He will say, 'The Fire is your abode, wherein you shall abide, save what Allah may will.' Surely, thy Lord is Wise, All-Knowing.

130. And in like manner do We set some of the wrongdoers over the others because of what they earned.

R. 16.

131. 'O company of Jinn and men! did not Messengers come to you from among

فيها وما يمكرون الا بانفسهم وما يشعرون ﴿١٢٤﴾
وإذا جاءتهم آية قالوا لن نؤمن حتى نؤتى
مثل ما أوتي رسل الله الله أعلم حيث يجعل
رسالته سيصيب الذين أجرموا صغار عند
الله وعذاب شديد بما كانوا يمكرون ﴿١٢٥﴾
فمن يرد الله أن يهديه يشرح صدره للإسلام
ومن يرد أن يضله يجعل صدره ضيقا حرجا
كأنما يصعد في السماء كذلك يجعل الله الرجس
على الذين لا يؤمنون ﴿١٢٦﴾
وهذا صراط ربك مستقيما قد فصلنا الآيات
لقوم يذكرون ﴿١٢٧﴾
لهم دار السلام عند ربهم وهو وليهم بما
كانوا يعملون ﴿١٢٨﴾
ويوم يحشرهم جميعا يمعشر الجن قد
استكثرتم من الإنس وقال أولياؤهم من
الإنس ربنا استمتع بعضنا ببعض وبلغنا
أجلنا الذي أجلت لنا قال النار مثواكم
خالدين فيها إلا ما شاء الله إن ربك حكيم
عليم ﴿١٢٩﴾
وكذلك نولي بعض الظالمين بعضا بما كانوا
يكسبون ﴿١٣٠﴾
يمعشر الجن والإنس ألم يأتكم رسل منكم

yourselves who related to you My Signs and who warned you of the meeting of this your day?' They will say, 'We bear witness against ourselves.' And the worldly life deceived them. And they will bear witness against themselves that they were disbelievers.

132. That is because thy Lord would not destroy the towns unjustly while their people were unwarned.

133. And for all are degrees *of rank* according to what they do, and thy Lord is not unmindful of what they do.

134. And thy Lord is Self-Sufficient, full of mercy. If He please, He can do away with you and cause to succeed you what He pleases, even as He raised you from the offspring of other people.

135. Surely, that which you are promised shall come to pass and you cannot frustrate *it*.

136. Say, 'O my people, act as best you can. I, too, am acting. Soon will you know whose will be the ultimate reward of the abode.' Surely, the wrongdoers shall not prosper.

* 137. And they have assigned Allah a portion of the crops and cattle which He has produced, and they say, 'This is for Allah,' as they imagine, 'and this is for our idols.' But that which is for their idols reaches not Allah, while that which is for Allah reaches their idols. Evil is what they judge.

* 138. And in like manner have their associate-gods made the killing of their children *appear* beautiful to many of the idolaters that they may ruin them and cause them confusion in their religion. And if Allah had *enforced* His will, they would not have done this; so leave them alone with that which they invent.

139. And they say, 'Such and such cattle and crops are forbidden. None shall

يَقُصُّوْنَ عَلَيْكُمْ اٰيٰتِيْ وَيُنْذِرُوْنَكُمْ لِقَآءَ يَوْمِكُمْ
هٰذَا ۚ قَالُوْا شَهِدْنَا عَلٰٓى اَنْفُسِنَا وَغَرَّتْهُمُ الْحَيٰوةُ
الدُّنْيَا وَشَهِدُوْا عَلٰٓى اَنْفُسِهِمْ اَنَّهُمْ كَانُوْا كٰفِرِيْنَ ﴿١٣١﴾
ذٰلِكَ اَنْ لَّمْ يَكُنْ رَّبُّكَ مُهْلِكَ الْقُرٰى بِظُلْمٍ وَّ
اَهْلُهَا غٰفِلُوْنَ ﴿١٣٢﴾
وَلِكُلٍّ دَرَجٰتٌ مِّمَّا عَمِلُوْا ۗ وَمَا رَبُّكَ بِغَافِلٍ عَمَّا
يَعْمَلُوْنَ ﴿١٣٣﴾
وَرَبُّكَ الْغَنِيُّ ذُو الرَّحْمَةِ ۗ اِنْ يَّشَاْ يُذْهِبْكُمْ
وَيَسْتَخْلِفْ مِنْۢ بَعْدِكُمْ مَّا يَشَآءُ كَمَآ اَنْشَاَكُمْ
مِّنْ ذُرِّيَّةِ قَوْمٍ اٰخَرِيْنَ ﴿١٣٤﴾
اِنَّ مَا تُوْعَدُوْنَ لَاٰتٍ ۙ وَّمَآ اَنْتُمْ بِمُعْجِزِيْنَ ﴿١٣٥﴾
قُلْ يٰقَوْمِ اعْمَلُوْا عَلٰى مَكَانَتِكُمْ اِنِّيْ عَامِلٌ ۚ فَسَوْفَ
تَعْلَمُوْنَ ۙ مَنْ تَكُوْنُ لَهٗ عَاقِبَةُ الدَّارِ ۗ اِنَّهٗ لَا يُفْلِحُ
الظّٰلِمُوْنَ ﴿١٣٦﴾
وَجَعَلُوْا لِلّٰهِ مِمَّا ذَرَاَ مِنَ الْحَرْثِ وَالْاَنْعَامِ نَصِيْبًا
فَقَالُوْا هٰذَا لِلّٰهِ بِزَعْمِهِمْ وَهٰذَا لِشُرَكَآئِنَا ۚ فَمَا
كَانَ لِشُرَكَآئِهِمْ فَلَا يَصِلُ اِلَى اللّٰهِ ۚ وَمَا كَانَ
لِلّٰهِ فَهُوَ يَصِلُ اِلٰى شُرَكَآئِهِمْ ۗ سَآءَ مَا يَحْكُمُوْنَ ﴿١٣٧﴾
وَكَذٰلِكَ زَيَّنَ لِكَثِيْرٍ مِّنَ الْمُشْرِكِيْنَ قَتْلَ اَوْلَادِهِمْ
شُرَكَآؤُهُمْ لِيُرْدُوْهُمْ وَلِيَلْبِسُوْا عَلَيْهِمْ دِيْنَهُمْ ۗ
وَلَوْ شَآءَ اللّٰهُ مَا فَعَلُوْهُ فَذَرْهُمْ وَمَا يَفْتَرُوْنَ ﴿١٣٨﴾
وَقَالُوْا هٰذِهٖٓ اَنْعَامٌ وَّحَرْثٌ حِجْرٌ ۖ لَّا يَطْعَمُهَآ اِلَّا

eat thereof save whom we please'—so they allege—and there are cattle whose backs are forbidden, and there are cattle over which they pronounce not the name of Allah, forging a lie against Him. Soon will He requite them for that which they have fabricated.

مَنْ نَّشَآءُ بِزَعْمِهِمْ وَاَنْعَامٌ حُرِّمَتْ ظُهُوْرُهَا وَاَنْعَامٌ
لَّا يَذْكُرُوْنَ اسْمَ اللّٰهِ عَلَيْهَا افْتِرَآءً عَلَيْهِ سَيَجْزِيْهِمْ
بِمَا كَانُوْا يَفْتَرُوْنَ ﴿١٣٩﴾

* 140. And they say, 'That which is in the wombs of such and such cattle is exclusively *reserved* for our males and is forbidden to our wives; but if it be *born* dead, then they are *all* partakers thereof. He will reward them for their assertion. Surely, He is Wise, All-Knowing.

وَقَالُوْا مَا فِيْ بُطُوْنِ هٰذِهِ الْاَنْعَامِ خَالِصَةٌ لِّذُكُوْرِنَا
وَمُحَرَّمٌ عَلٰٓى اَزْوَاجِنَا ۚ وَاِنْ يَّكُنْ مَّيْتَةً فَهُمْ فِيْهِ
شُرَكَآءُ ۗ سَيَجْزِيْهِمْ وَصْفَهُمْ ۗ اِنَّهٗ حَكِيْمٌ عَلِيْمٌ ﴿١٤٠﴾

141. Losers indeed are they who kill their children foolishly for lack of knowledge, and make unlawful what Allah has provided for them, forging a lie against Allah. They have indeed gone astray and are not rightly guided.

قَدْ خَسِرَ الَّذِيْنَ قَتَلُوْٓا اَوْلَادَهُمْ سَفَهًا ۢ بِغَيْرِ عِلْمٍ
وَّحَرَّمُوْا مَا رَزَقَهُمُ اللّٰهُ افْتِرَآءً عَلَى اللّٰهِ ۗ قَدْ ضَلُّوْا
وَمَا كَانُوْا مُهْتَدِيْنَ ﴿١٤١﴾

R. 17.

142. And He it is Who brings into being gardens, trellised and untrellised, and the date-palm and cornfields whose fruits are of diverse kinds, and the olive and the pomegranate, alike and unlike. Eat of the fruit of each when it bears fruit, but pay His due on the day of harvest and exceed not the bounds. Surely, Allah loves not those who exceed the bounds.

وَهُوَ الَّذِيْٓ اَنْشَاَ جَنّٰتٍ مَّعْرُوْشٰتٍ وَّغَيْرَ مَعْرُوْشٰتٍ
وَّالنَّخْلَ وَالزَّرْعَ مُخْتَلِفًا اُكُلُهٗ وَالزَّيْتُوْنَ وَالرُّمَّانَ
مُتَشَابِهًا وَّغَيْرَ مُتَشَابِهٍ ۗ كُلُوْا مِنْ ثَمَرِهٖٓ اِذَآ اَثْمَرَ
وَاٰتُوْا حَقَّهٗ يَوْمَ حَصَادِهٖ ۖ وَلَا تُسْرِفُوْا ۗ اِنَّهٗ لَا يُحِبُّ
الْمُسْرِفِيْنَ ﴿١٤٢﴾

143. And of the cattle *He has created some* for burden and *some* for slaughter. Eat of that which Allah has provided for you, and follow not the footsteps of Satan. Surely, he is to you an open foe.

وَمِنَ الْاَنْعَامِ حَمُوْلَةً وَّفَرْشًا ۗ كُلُوْا مِمَّا رَزَقَكُمُ اللّٰهُ
وَلَا تَتَّبِعُوْا خُطُوٰتِ الشَّيْطٰنِ ۗ اِنَّهٗ لَكُمْ عَدُوٌّ
مُّبِيْنٌ ﴿١٤٣﴾

* 144. *And of the cattle He has created* eight mates: of the sheep two, and of the goats two;—say, 'Is it the two males that He has forbidden or the two females or that which the wombs of the two females contain? Inform me with knowledge, if you are truthful.'

ثَمٰنِيَةَ اَزْوَاجٍ ۚ مِنَ الضَّاْنِ اثْنَيْنِ وَمِنَ الْمَعْزِ
اثْنَيْنِ ۗ قُلْ ءٰٓالذَّكَرَيْنِ حَرَّمَ اَمِ الْاُنْثَيَيْنِ اَمَّا
اشْتَمَلَتْ عَلَيْهِ اَرْحَامُ الْاُنْثَيَيْنِ ۗ نَبِّـُٔوْنِيْ بِعِلْمٍ
اِنْ كُنْتُمْ صٰدِقِيْنَ ﴿١٤٤﴾

145. And of the camels two, and of the oxen two. Say, 'Is it the two males that

وَمِنَ الْاِبِلِ اثْنَيْنِ وَمِنَ الْبَقَرِ اثْنَيْنِ ۗ قُلْ ءٰٓالذَّكَرَيْنِ

He has forbidden or the two females or that which the wombs of the two females contain? Were you present when Allah enjoined this on you?' Who is then more unjust than he who forges a lie against Allah that he may lead men astray without knowledge? Surely, Allah guides not the unjust people.

حَرَّمَ أَمِ الْأُنْثَيَيْنِ أَمَّا اشْتَمَلَتْ عَلَيْهِ أَرْحَامُ
الْأُنْثَيَيْنِ أَمْ كُنْتُمْ شُهَدَاءَ إِذْ وَصَّاكُمُ اللَّهُ بِهَٰذَا
فَمَنْ أَظْلَمُ مِمَّنِ افْتَرَىٰ عَلَى اللَّهِ كَذِبًا لِيُضِلَّ النَّاسَ
بِغَيْرِ عِلْمٍ إِنَّ اللَّهَ لَا يَهْدِي الْقَوْمَ الظَّالِمِينَ ﴿١٤٥﴾

R. 18.

* 146. Say, 'I find not in what has been revealed to me aught forbidden to an eater *who wishes* to eat it, except it be that which dies of itself, or blood poured forth, or the flesh of swine—for *all* that is unclean—or what is profane, on which is invoked the name of other than Allah. But whoso is driven by necessity, being neither disobedient nor exceeding *the limit*, then surely thy Lord is Most Forgiving, Merciful.'

قُلْ لَا أَجِدُ فِي مَا أُوحِيَ إِلَيَّ مُحَرَّمًا عَلَىٰ طَاعِمٍ يَطْعَمُهُ
إِلَّا أَنْ يَكُونَ مَيْتَةً أَوْ دَمًا مَسْفُوحًا أَوْ لَحْمَ خِنْزِيرٍ
فَإِنَّهُ رِجْسٌ أَوْ فِسْقًا أُهِلَّ لِغَيْرِ اللَّهِ بِهِ ۚ فَمَنِ اضْطُرَّ
غَيْرَ بَاغٍ وَلَا عَادٍ فَإِنَّ رَبَّكَ غَفُورٌ رَحِيمٌ ﴿١٤٦﴾

147. And to those who are Jews We forbade all animals having claws; and of the oxen and the sheep and goats did We forbid them their fats, save that which their backs bear or the intestines, or that which is mixed with a bone. That is the reward We gave them for their rebellion. And most surely We are truthful.

وَعَلَى الَّذِينَ هَادُوا حَرَّمْنَا كُلَّ ذِي ظُفُرٍ ۖ وَمِنَ
الْبَقَرِ وَالْغَنَمِ حَرَّمْنَا عَلَيْهِمْ شُحُومَهُمَا إِلَّا مَا
حَمَلَتْ ظُهُورُهُمَا أَوِ الْحَوَايَا أَوْ مَا اخْتَلَطَ بِعَظْمٍ ۚ ذَٰلِكَ
جَزَيْنَاهُمْ بِبَغْيِهِمْ ۖ وَإِنَّا لَصَادِقُونَ ﴿١٤٧﴾

148. But if they accuse thee of falsehood, say, 'Your Lord is possessed of all-embracing mercy, and His wrath shall not be turned back from the guilty people.'

فَإِنْ كَذَّبُوكَ فَقُلْ رَبُّكُمْ ذُو رَحْمَةٍ وَاسِعَةٍ ۚ وَلَا
يُرَدُّ بَأْسُهُ عَنِ الْقَوْمِ الْمُجْرِمِينَ ﴿١٤٨﴾

* 149. Those who join gods *with God* will say, 'If Allah had pleased, we could not have joined gods *with Him*, nor could our fathers; nor could we have made anything unlawful.' In like manner did those who were before them accuse *God's Messengers* of falsehood, until they tasted of Our wrath. Say, 'Have you any knowledge? Then produce it for us. You follow nothing but *mere* conjecture. And you do nothing but lie.'

سَيَقُولُ الَّذِينَ أَشْرَكُوا لَوْ شَاءَ اللَّهُ مَا أَشْرَكْنَا وَ
لَا آبَاؤُنَا وَلَا حَرَّمْنَا مِنْ شَيْءٍ ۚ كَذَٰلِكَ كَذَّبَ الَّذِينَ
مِنْ قَبْلِهِمْ حَتَّىٰ ذَاقُوا بَأْسَنَا ۗ قُلْ هَلْ عِنْدَكُمْ
مِنْ عِلْمٍ فَتُخْرِجُوهُ لَنَا ۖ إِنْ تَتَّبِعُونَ إِلَّا الظَّنَّ وَ
إِنْ أَنْتُمْ إِلَّا تَخْرُصُونَ ﴿١٤٩﴾

* 150. Say, 'Allah's is the argument that reaches *home*. If He had *enforced* His will, He could have surely guided you all.'

قُلْ فَلِلَّهِ الْحُجَّةُ الْبَالِغَةُ ۖ فَلَوْ شَاءَ لَهَدَاكُمْ
أَجْمَعِينَ ﴿١٥٠﴾

151. Say, 'Bring forward your witnesses who testify that Allah has forbidden this.'

قُلْ هَلُمَّ شُهَدَاءَكُمُ الَّذِينَ يَشْهَدُونَ أَنَّ اللَّهَ

If they bear witness, bear thou not witness with them, nor follow thou the evil inclinations of those who treat Our Signs as lies and those who believe not in the Hereafter and who set up equals to their Lord.

حَرَّمَ هٰذَا ۚ فَاِنْ شَهِدُوْا فَلَا تَشْهَدْ مَعَهُمْ ۚ وَلَا تَتَّبِعْ اَهْوَآءَ الَّذِيْنَ كَذَّبُوْا بِاٰيٰتِنَا وَالَّذِيْنَ لَا يُؤْمِنُوْنَ بِالْاٰخِرَةِ وَهُمْ بِرَبِّهِمْ يَعْدِلُوْنَ (١٥١) ع ١٨ ٥

R. 19.

* 152. Say, 'Come, I will rehearse to you what your Lord has forbidden: that you associate not anything as partner with Him and *that you do* good to parents, and that you kill not your children for *fear of* poverty – it is We Who provide for you and for them – and that you approach not foul deeds, whether open or secret; and that you kill not the life which Allah has made sacred, save by right. That is what He has enjoined upon you, that you may understand.

قُلْ تَعَالَوْا اَتْلُ مَا حَرَّمَ رَبُّكُمْ عَلَيْكُمْ اَلَّا تُشْرِكُوْا بِهٖ شَيْـًٔا وَّبِالْوَالِدَيْنِ اِحْسَانًا ۚ وَلَا تَقْتُلُوْٓا اَوْلَادَكُمْ مِّنْ اِمْلَاقٍ ۚ نَحْنُ نَرْزُقُكُمْ وَاِيَّاهُمْ ۚ وَلَا تَقْرَبُوا الْفَوَاحِشَ مَا ظَهَرَ مِنْهَا وَمَا بَطَنَ ۚ وَلَا تَقْتُلُوا النَّفْسَ الَّتِيْ حَرَّمَ اللّٰهُ اِلَّا بِالْحَقِّ ؕ ذٰلِكُمْ وَصّٰكُمْ بِهٖ لَعَلَّكُمْ تَعْقِلُوْنَ (١٥٢)

153. 'And approach not the property of the orphan, except in *a way* which is best, till he attains his maturity. And give full measure and weight with equity. We task not any soul except according to its capacity. And when you speak, observe justice, even if *the concerned person* be a relative, and fulfil the covenant of Allah. That is what He enjoins upon you, that you may remember.'

وَلَا تَقْرَبُوْا مَالَ الْيَتِيْمِ اِلَّا بِالَّتِيْ هِيَ اَحْسَنُ حَتّٰى يَبْلُغَ اَشُدَّهٗ ۚ وَاَوْفُوا الْكَيْلَ وَالْمِيْزَانَ بِالْقِسْطِ ۚ لَا نُكَلِّفُ نَفْسًا اِلَّا وُسْعَهَا ۚ وَاِذَا قُلْتُمْ فَاعْدِلُوْا وَلَوْ كَانَ ذَا قُرْبٰى ۚ وَبِعَهْدِ اللّٰهِ اَوْفُوْا ؕ ذٰلِكُمْ وَصّٰكُمْ بِهٖ لَعَلَّكُمْ تَذَكَّرُوْنَ (١٥٣)

154. And *say*, 'This is My path *leading* straight. So follow it; and follow not *other* ways, lest they lead you away from His way. That is what He enjoins upon you, that you may *become able to* guard *against evils*.'

وَاَنَّ هٰذَا صِرَاطِيْ مُسْتَقِيْمًا فَاتَّبِعُوْهُ ۚ وَلَا تَتَّبِعُوا السُّبُلَ فَتَفَرَّقَ بِكُمْ عَنْ سَبِيْلِهٖ ؕ ذٰلِكُمْ وَصّٰكُمْ بِهٖ لَعَلَّكُمْ تَتَّقُوْنَ (١٥٤)

* 155. Again, We gave Moses the Book —completing the favour upon him who did good, and an explanation of all *necessary* things, and a guidance and a mercy — that they might believe in the meeting with their Lord.

ثُمَّ اٰتَيْنَا مُوْسَى الْكِتٰبَ تَمَامًا عَلَى الَّذِيْٓ اَحْسَنَ وَتَفْصِيْلًا لِّكُلِّ شَيْءٍ وَّهُدًى وَّرَحْمَةً لَّعَلَّهُمْ بِلِقَآءِ رَبِّهِمْ يُؤْمِنُوْنَ (١٥٥) ع ١٩ ٦

R. 20.

156. And this is a Book which We have sent down; *it is* full of blessings. So follow it, and guard against *sin* that you may be shown mercy;

وَهٰذَا كِتٰبٌ اَنْزَلْنٰهُ مُبٰرَكٌ فَاتَّبِعُوْهُ وَاتَّقُوْا لَعَلَّكُمْ تُرْحَمُوْنَ (١٥٦)

157. Lest you should say, 'The Book was sent down only to two peoples before us, and we were indeed unaware of their reading;'

أَنْ تَقُوْلُوْٓا إِنَّمَآ أُنْزِلَ الْكِتٰبُ عَلٰى طَآئِفَتَيْنِ مِنْ
قَبْلِنَا ۠ وَإِنْ كُنَّا عَنْ دِرَاسَتِهِمْ لَغٰفِلِيْنَ ﴿۱۵۷﴾

158. Or lest you should say, 'Had the Book been sent down to us, we should surely have been better guided than they.' There has *now* come to you a clear evidence from your Lord, and a guidance and a mercy. Who, then, is more unjust than he who rejects the Signs of Allah and turns away from them? We will requite those who turn away from Our Signs with an evil punishment because of their turning away.

أَوْ تَقُوْلُوْا لَوْ أَنَّآ أُنْزِلَ عَلَيْنَا الْكِتٰبُ لَكُنَّآ أَهْدٰى
مِنْهُمْ ۚ فَقَدْ جَآءَكُمْ بَيِّنَةٌ مِّنْ رَّبِّكُمْ وَهُدًى وَّ
رَحْمَةٌ ۚ فَمَنْ أَظْلَمُ مِمَّنْ كَذَّبَ بِاٰيٰتِ اللّٰهِ وَصَدَفَ
عَنْهَا ۗ سَنَجْزِي الَّذِيْنَ يَصْدِفُوْنَ عَنْ اٰيٰتِنَا سُوْٓءَ
الْعَذَابِ بِمَا كَانُوْا يَصْدِفُوْنَ ﴿۱۵۸﴾

159. Do they expect aught but that angels should come to them or that thy Lord should come or that some of the Signs of thy Lord should come? The day when some of the Signs of thy Lord shall come, to believe in them shall not profit a soul which believed not before, nor earned any good by its faith. Say, 'Wait ye, we *too* are waiting.'

هَلْ يَنْظُرُوْنَ إِلَّآ أَنْ تَأْتِيَهُمُ الْمَلٰٓئِكَةُ أَوْ يَأْتِيَ
رَبُّكَ أَوْ يَأْتِيَ بَعْضُ اٰيٰتِ رَبِّكَ ۗ يَوْمَ يَأْتِيْ بَعْضُ
اٰيٰتِ رَبِّكَ لَا يَنْفَعُ نَفْسًا إِيْمَانُهَا لَمْ تَكُنْ اٰمَنَتْ
مِنْ قَبْلُ أَوْ كَسَبَتْ فِيْٓ إِيْمَانِهَا خَيْرًا ۗ قُلِ انْتَظِرُوْٓا
إِنَّا مُنْتَظِرُوْنَ ﴿۱۵۹﴾

160. *As for* those who split up their religion and became *divided into* sects, thou hast no concern at all with them. Surely their case will come before Allah, then will He inform them of what they used to do.

إِنَّ الَّذِيْنَ فَرَّقُوْا دِيْنَهُمْ وَكَانُوْا شِيَعًا لَّسْتَ مِنْهُمْ
فِيْ شَيْءٍ ۗ إِنَّمَآ أَمْرُهُمْ إِلَى اللّٰهِ ثُمَّ يُنَبِّئُهُمْ بِمَا كَانُوْا
يَفْعَلُوْنَ ﴿۱۶۰﴾

161. Whoso does a good deed shall have ten times as much; but he who does an evil deed, shall have only a like reward; and they shall not be wronged.

مَنْ جَآءَ بِالْحَسَنَةِ فَلَهٗ عَشْرُ أَمْثَالِهَا ۚ وَمَنْ جَآءَ
بِالسَّيِّئَةِ فَلَا يُجْزٰٓى إِلَّا مِثْلَهَا وَهُمْ لَا يُظْلَمُوْنَ ﴿۱۶۱﴾

* 162. Say, 'As for me, my Lord has guided me unto a straight path—a right religion, the religion of Abraham, the upright. And he was not of those who join gods *with God*.'

قُلْ إِنَّنِيْ هَدٰىنِيْ رَبِّيْٓ إِلٰى صِرَاطٍ مُّسْتَقِيْمٍ ۚ دِيْنًا
قِيَمًا مِّلَّةَ إِبْرٰهِيْمَ حَنِيْفًا ۚ وَمَا كَانَ مِنَ الْمُشْرِكِيْنَ ﴿۱۶۲﴾

163. Say, 'My Prayer and my sacrifice and my life and my death are *all* for Allah, the Lord of the worlds.

قُلْ إِنَّ صَلَاتِيْ وَنُسُكِيْ وَمَحْيَايَ وَمَمَاتِيْ لِلّٰهِ رَبِّ
الْعٰلَمِيْنَ ﴿۱۶۳﴾

164. 'He has no partner. And so am I commanded, and I am the first of those who submit.'

لَا شَرِيْكَ لَهٗ ۚ وَبِذٰلِكَ أُمِرْتُ وَأَنَا أَوَّلُ الْمُسْلِمِيْنَ ﴿۱۶۴﴾

* 165. Say, 'Shall I seek a lord other than Allah, while He is the Lord of all things?' And no soul acts but only against itself; nor does any bearer of burden bear the burden of another. Then to your Lord will be your return, and He will inform you of that wherein you used to differ.

* 166. And He it is Who has made you successors *of others* on the earth and has exalted some of you over the others in degrees *of rank*, that He may try you by that which He has given you. Surely, thy Lord is quick in punishment; and surely He is Most Forgiving, Merciful.

قُلْ أَغَيْرَ اللّٰهِ أَبْغِي رَبًّا وَّهُوَ رَبُّ كُلِّ شَيْءٍ ۚ وَلَا تَكْسِبُ
كُلُّ نَفْسٍ إِلَّا عَلَيْهَا ۚ وَلَا تَزِرُ وَازِرَةٌ وِّزْرَ أُخْرٰى ۚ
ثُمَّ إِلٰى رَبِّكُمْ مَّرْجِعُكُمْ فَيُنَبِّئُكُمْ بِمَا كُنْتُمْ فِيهِ
تَخْتَلِفُوْنَ ﴿١٦٥﴾

وَهُوَ الَّذِي جَعَلَكُمْ خَلٰٓئِفَ الْأَرْضِ وَرَفَعَ بَعْضَكُمْ
فَوْقَ بَعْضٍ دَرَجٰتٍ لِّيَبْلُوَكُمْ فِي مَآ اٰتٰكُمْ ۗ إِنَّ رَبَّكَ
ع النصف سَرِيْعُ الْعِقَابِ ۖ وَإِنَّهُ لَغَفُوْرٌ رَّحِيْمٌ ﴿١٦٦﴾ ع

سُورَةُ الْأَعْرَافِ مَكِّيَّةٌ (٧)

ركوعاتها ٢٤ — آياتها ٢٠٦

AL-A'RĀF

(Revealed before Hijra)

1. In the name of Allah, the Gracious, the Merciful.

2. Alif Lām Mīm Ṣād*.

3. *This is* a Book revealed unto thee —so let there be no straitness in thy bosom concerning it—that thou mayest warn thereby, and *that it be* an exhortation to the believers.

4. Follow that which has been sent down to you from your Lord, and follow no protectors other than Him. How little do you remember!

* 5. How many a town have We destroyed! And Our punishment came upon it by night or while they slept at noon.

6. So when Our punishment came upon them, their cry was nothing but that they said: 'We were indeed wrongdoers!'

7. And We will certainly question those to whom *the Messengers* were sent, and We will certainly question the Messengers.

8. Then will We certainly relate to them *their deeds* with knowledge, for We were never absent.

9. And the weighing on that day will be true. Then as for those whose scales are heavy, it is they who shall prosper.

10. And as for those whose scales are light, it is they who shall have ruined their souls because of their being unjust to Our Signs.

11. And We have established you in the earth and provided for you therein the means of subsistence. How little thanks you give!

R. 2.

12. And We did create you *and* then We gave you shape; then said We to the angels, 'Submit to Adam;' and they *all* submitted but Iblīs *did not;* he would not be of those who submit.

بِسْمِ اللّٰهِ الرَّحْمٰنِ الرَّحِيْمِ ﴿١﴾

الٓمّٓصٓ ﴿٢﴾

كِتٰبٌ اُنْزِلَ اِلَيْكَ فَلَا يَكُنْ فِيْ صَدْرِكَ حَرَجٌ مِّنْهُ

لِتُنْذِرَ بِهٖ وَذِكْرٰى لِلْمُؤْمِنِيْنَ ﴿٣﴾

اِتَّبِعُوْا مَآ اُنْزِلَ اِلَيْكُمْ مِّنْ رَّبِّكُمْ وَلَا تَتَّبِعُوْا مِنْ دُوْنِهٖٓ

اَوْلِيَآءَ ؕ قَلِيْلًا مَّا تَذَكَّرُوْنَ ﴿٤﴾

وَكَمْ مِّنْ قَرْيَةٍ اَهْلَكْنٰهَا فَجَآءَهَا بَاْسُنَا بَيَاتًا اَوْ هُمْ قَآئِلُوْنَ ﴿٥﴾

فَمَا كَانَ دَعْوٰىهُمْ اِذْ جَآءَهُمْ بَاْسُنَآ اِلَّآ اَنْ قَالُوْٓا اِنَّا

كُنَّا ظٰلِمِيْنَ ﴿٦﴾

فَلَنَسْـَٔلَنَّ الَّذِيْنَ اُرْسِلَ اِلَيْهِمْ وَلَنَسْـَٔلَنَّ الْمُرْسَلِيْنَ ﴿٧﴾

فَلَنَقُصَّنَّ عَلَيْهِمْ بِعِلْمٍ وَّمَا كُنَّا غَآئِبِيْنَ ﴿٨﴾

وَالْوَزْنُ يَوْمَئِذِ ۣالْحَقُّ ۚ فَمَنْ ثَقُلَتْ مَوَازِيْنُهٗ فَاُولٰٓئِكَ

هُمُ الْمُفْلِحُوْنَ ﴿٩﴾

وَمَنْ خَفَّتْ مَوَازِيْنُهٗ فَاُولٰٓئِكَ الَّذِيْنَ خَسِرُوْٓا اَنْفُسَهُمْ

بِمَا كَانُوْا بِاٰيٰتِنَا يَظْلِمُوْنَ ﴿١٠﴾

وَلَقَدْ مَكَّنّٰكُمْ فِي الْاَرْضِ وَجَعَلْنَا لَكُمْ فِيْهَا مَعَايِشَ ؕ

قَلِيْلًا مَّا تَشْكُرُوْنَ ﴿١١﴾

وَلَقَدْ خَلَقْنٰكُمْ ثُمَّ صَوَّرْنٰكُمْ ثُمَّ قُلْنَا لِلْمَلٰٓئِكَةِ اسْجُدُوْا

لِاٰدَمَ ۖ فَسَجَدُوْٓا اِلَّآ اِبْلِيْسَ ؕ لَمْ يَكُنْ مِّنَ السّٰجِدِيْنَ ﴿١٢﴾

---

* I am Allah, I know and I explain.

13. *God* said, 'What prevented thee from submitting when I commanded thee?' He said, 'I am better than he. Thou hast created me of fire while him hast Thou created of clay.'

قَالَ مَا مَنَعَكَ اَلَّا تَسْجُدَ اِذْ اَمَرْتُكَ ؕ قَالَ اَنَا خَيْرٌ مِّنْهُ ۚ
خَلَقْتَنِيْ مِنْ نَّارٍ وَّ خَلَقْتَهٗ مِنْ طِيْنٍ ﴿۱۳﴾

14. *God* said, 'Then go down hence; it is not for thee to be arrogant here. Get out; thou art certainly of those who are abased.'

قَالَ فَاهْبِطْ مِنْهَا فَمَا يَكُوْنُ لَكَ اَنْ تَتَكَبَّرَ فِيْهَا فَاخْرُجْ
اِنَّكَ مِنَ الصّٰغِرِيْنَ ﴿۱۴﴾

15. He said, 'Grant me respite till the day when they will be raised up.'

قَالَ اَنْظِرْنِيْۤ اِلٰى يَوْمِ يُبْعَثُوْنَ ﴿۱۵﴾

16. *God* said, 'Thou shalt be of those who are given respite.'

قَالَ اِنَّكَ مِنَ الْمُنْظَرِيْنَ ﴿۱۶﴾

17. He said: 'Now, since Thou hast adjudged me as lost, I will assuredly lie in wait for them on Thy straight path.

قَالَ فَبِمَاۤ اَغْوَيْتَنِيْ لَاَقْعُدَنَّ لَهُمْ صِرَاطَكَ
الْمُسْتَقِيْمَ ﴿۱۷﴾ ۙ

18. 'Then will I surely come upon them from before them and from behind them and from their right and from their left, and Thou wilt not find most of them to be grateful."

ثُمَّ لَاٰتِيَنَّهُمْ مِّنْ بَيْنِ اَيْدِيْهِمْ وَ مِنْ خَلْفِهِمْ
وَ عَنْ اَيْمَانِهِمْ وَ عَنْ شَمَآئِلِهِمْ ؕ وَ لَا تَجِدُ اَكْثَرَهُمْ
شٰكِرِيْنَ ﴿۱۸﴾

19. *God* said: 'Get out hence, despised and banished. Whosoever of them shall follow thee, I will surely fill Hell with you all.'

قَالَ اخْرُجْ مِنْهَا مَذْءُوْمًا مَّدْحُوْرًا ؕ لَمَنْ تَبِعَكَ
مِنْهُمْ لَاَمْلَـَٔنَّ جَهَنَّمَ مِنْكُمْ اَجْمَعِيْنَ ﴿۱۹﴾

20. 'And O Adam, dwell thou and thy wife in the garden and eat therefrom wherever you will, but approach not this tree lest you be among the wrongdoers.'

وَ يٰۤاٰدَمُ اسْكُنْ اَنْتَ وَ زَوْجُكَ الْجَنَّةَ فَكُلَا مِنْ حَيْثُ
شِئْتُمَا وَ لَا تَقْرَبَا هٰذِهِ الشَّجَرَةَ فَتَكُوْنَا مِنَ
الظّٰلِمِيْنَ ﴿۲۰﴾

* 21. But Satan whispered *evil suggestions* to them so that he might make known to them what was hidden from them of their shame, and said, 'Your Lord has only forbidden you this tree, lest you should become angels or such *beings* as live for ever.'

فَوَسْوَسَ لَهُمَا الشَّيْطٰنُ لِيُبْدِيَ لَهُمَا مَا وٗرِيَ
عَنْهُمَا مِنْ سَوْاٰتِهِمَا وَ قَالَ مَا نَهٰىكُمَا رَبُّكُمَا عَنْ
هٰذِهِ الشَّجَرَةِ اِلَّاۤ اَنْ تَكُوْنَا مَلَكَيْنِ اَوْ تَكُوْنَا مِنَ
الْخٰلِدِيْنَ ﴿۲۱﴾

22. And he swore to them, *saying*, 'Surely, I am a sincere counsellor unto you.'

وَ قَاسَمَهُمَاۤ اِنِّيْ لَكُمَا لَمِنَ النّٰصِحِيْنَ ﴿۲۲﴾ ۙ

23. So he caused them to fall *into disobedience* by deceit. And when they tasted

فَدَلّٰىهُمَا بِغُرُوْرٍ ۚ فَلَمَّا ذَاقَا الشَّجَرَةَ بَدَتْ لَهُمَا

of the tree, their shame became manifest to them and they began to stick the leaves of the garden *together* over themselves. And their Lord called them, *saying*, 'Did I not forbid you that tree and tell you: verily, Satan is to you an open foe?'

سَوْاٰتُهُمَا وَطَفِقَا يَخْصِفٰنِ عَلَيْهِمَا مِنْ وَّرَقِ
الْجَنَّةِ ۖ وَنَادٰىهُمَا رَبُّهُمَآ اَلَمْ اَنْهَكُمَا عَنْ تِلْكُمَا
الشَّجَرَةِ وَاَقُلْ لَّكُمَآ اِنَّ الشَّيْطٰنَ لَكُمَا عَدُوٌّ
مُّبِيْنٌ ﴿۲۳﴾

24. They said, 'Our Lord, we have wronged ourselves; and if Thou forgive us not and have not mercy on us, we shall surely be of the lost.'

قَالَا رَبَّنَا ظَلَمْنَآ اَنْفُسَنَا ٚ وَاِنْ لَّمْ تَغْفِرْ لَنَا وَ
تَرْحَمْنَا لَنَكُوْنَنَّ مِنَ الْخٰسِرِيْنَ ﴿۲۴﴾

25. He said, 'Go forth, some of you *being* enemies of others. And for you there is an abode on the earth and a provision for a time.'

قَالَ اهْبِطُوْا بَعْضُكُمْ لِبَعْضٍ عَدُوٌّ ۚ وَلَكُمْ فِي الْاَرْضِ
مُسْتَقَرٌّ وَّمَتَاعٌ اِلٰى حِيْنٍ ﴿۲۵﴾

26. He said, 'Therein shall you live, and therein shall you die, and therefrom shall you be brought forth.'

قَالَ فِيْهَا تَحْيَوْنَ وَفِيْهَا تَمُوْتُوْنَ وَمِنْهَا
تُخْرَجُوْنَ ﴿۲۶﴾ ع ۲ ۹

R. 3.

27. O children of Adam! We have indeed sent down to you raiment to cover your shame, and to be an elegant dress; but the raiment of righteousness—that is the best. That is *one* of the Signs of Allah, that they may remember.

يٰبَنِيْٓ اٰدَمَ قَدْ اَنْزَلْنَا عَلَيْكُمْ لِبَاسًا يُّوَارِيْ سَوْاٰتِكُمْ
وَرِيْشًا ۖ وَلِبَاسُ التَّقْوٰى ۙ ذٰلِكَ خَيْرٌ ۖ ذٰلِكَ مِنْ
اٰيٰتِ اللّٰهِ لَعَلَّهُمْ يَذَّكَّرُوْنَ ﴿۲۷﴾

28. O children of Adam! let not Satan seduce you, even as he turned your parents out of the garden, stripping them of their raiment that he might show them their shame. Truly he sees you, he and his tribe, from where you see them not. Surely, We have made satans friends for those who believe not.

يٰبَنِيْٓ اٰدَمَ لَا يَفْتِنَنَّكُمُ الشَّيْطٰنُ كَمَآ اَخْرَجَ اَبَوَيْكُمْ
مِّنَ الْجَنَّةِ يَنْزِعُ عَنْهُمَا لِبَاسَهُمَا لِيُرِيَهُمَا
سَوْاٰتِهِمَا ۖ اِنَّهٗ يَرٰىكُمْ هُوَ وَقَبِيْلُهٗ مِنْ حَيْثُ لَا
تَرَوْنَهُمْ ۖ اِنَّا جَعَلْنَا الشَّيٰطِيْنَ اَوْلِيَآءَ لِلَّذِيْنَ لَا
يُؤْمِنُوْنَ ﴿۲۸﴾

29. And when they commit a foul deed, they say: 'We found our fathers doing it, and Allah has enjoined it upon us.' Say, 'Allah never enjoins foul deeds. Do you say of Allah what you know not?'

وَاِذَا فَعَلُوْا فَاحِشَةً قَالُوْا وَجَدْنَا عَلَيْهَآ اٰبَآءَنَا
وَاللّٰهُ اَمَرَنَا بِهَا ۖ قُلْ اِنَّ اللّٰهَ لَا يَاْمُرُ بِالْفَحْشَآءِ ۖ
اَتَقُوْلُوْنَ عَلَى اللّٰهِ مَا لَا تَعْلَمُوْنَ ﴿۲۹﴾

30. Say, 'My Lord has enjoined justice. And fix your attention aright at every

قُلْ اَمَرَ رَبِّيْ بِالْقِسْطِ ۗ وَاَقِيْمُوْا وُجُوْهَكُمْ عِنْدَ كُلِّ

مَسْجِدٍ وَّادْعُوْهُ مُخْلِصِيْنَ لَهُ الدِّيْنَ ۬ؕ كَمَا بَدَاَكُمْ
تَعُوْدُوْنَ ﴿۳۰﴾

time and place of worship, and call upon Him, making yourselves sincere towards Him in religion. As He brought you into being, so shall you return.'

فَرِيْقًا هَدٰى وَفَرِيْقًا حَقَّ عَلَيْهِمُ الضَّلٰلَةُ ؕ اِنَّهُمُ
اتَّخَذُوا الشَّيٰطِيْنَ اَوْلِيَآءَ مِنْ دُوْنِ اللّٰهِ وَيَحْسَبُوْنَ
اَنَّهُمْ مُّهْتَدُوْنَ ﴿۳۱﴾

31. Some has He guided, and *as for* others error has become their desert. They have taken evil ones for friends to the exclusion of Allah, and they think that they are rightly guided.

يٰبَنِيْۤ اٰدَمَ خُذُوْا زِيْنَتَكُمْ عِنْدَ كُلِّ مَسْجِدٍ وَّكُلُوْا
وَاشْرَبُوْا وَلَا تُسْرِفُوْا ۚ اِنَّهٗ لَا يُحِبُّ الْمُسْرِفِيْنَ ﴿۳۲﴾ ع

32. O children of Adam! look to your adornment at every *time and* place of worship, and eat and drink but exceed not the bounds; surely, He does not love those who exceed the bounds.

R. 4.

قُلْ مَنْ حَرَّمَ زِيْنَةَ اللّٰهِ الَّتِيْۤ اَخْرَجَ لِعِبَادِهٖ وَالطَّيِّبٰتِ
مِنَ الرِّزْقِ ؕ قُلْ هِيَ لِلَّذِيْنَ اٰمَنُوْا فِي الْحَيٰوةِ الدُّنْيَا
خَالِصَةً يَّوْمَ الْقِيٰمَةِ ؕ كَذٰلِكَ نُفَصِّلُ الْاٰيٰتِ لِقَوْمٍ
يَّعْلَمُوْنَ ﴿۳۳﴾

33. Say, 'Who has forbidden the adornment of Allah which He has produced for His servants, and the good things of *His* providing?' Say, 'They are for the believers in the present life *and* exclusively *for them* on the Day of Resurrection. Thus do We explain the Signs for a people who have knowledge.'

قُلْ اِنَّمَا حَرَّمَ رَبِّيَ الْفَوَاحِشَ مَا ظَهَرَ مِنْهَا وَمَا بَطَنَ
وَالْاِثْمَ وَالْبَغْيَ بِغَيْرِ الْحَقِّ وَاَنْ تُشْرِكُوْا بِاللّٰهِ مَا لَمْ
يُنَزِّلْ بِهٖ سُلْطٰنًا وَّاَنْ تَقُوْلُوْا عَلَى اللّٰهِ مَا لَا تَعْلَمُوْنَ ﴿۳۴﴾

34. Say, 'My Lord has only forbidden foul deeds, whether open or secret, and sin and wrongful transgression, and that you associate with Allah that for which He has sent down no authority, and that you say of Allah that of which you have no knowledge.'

وَلِكُلِّ اُمَّةٍ اَجَلٌ ۚ فَاِذَا جَآءَ اَجَلُهُمْ لَا يَسْتَاْخِرُوْنَ
سَاعَةً وَّلَا يَسْتَقْدِمُوْنَ ﴿۳۵﴾

35. And for every people there is a term, and when their term is come, they cannot remain behind a single moment, nor can they get ahead *of it*.

يٰبَنِيْۤ اٰدَمَ اِمَّا يَاْتِيَنَّكُمْ رُسُلٌ مِّنْكُمْ يَقُصُّوْنَ عَلَيْكُمْ
اٰيٰتِيْ ۙ فَمَنِ اتَّقٰى وَاَصْلَحَ فَلَا خَوْفٌ عَلَيْهِمْ وَلَا
هُمْ يَحْزَنُوْنَ ﴿۳۶﴾

36. O children of Adam! if Messengers come to you from among yourselves, rehearsing My Signs unto you, then whoso shall fear God and do good deeds, on them *shall come* no fear nor shall they grieve.

وَالَّذِيْنَ كَذَّبُوْا بِاٰيٰتِنَا وَاسْتَكْبَرُوْا عَنْهَاۤ اُولٰٓئِكَ
اَصْحٰبُ النَّارِ ۚ هُمْ فِيْهَا خٰلِدُوْنَ ﴿۳۷﴾

37. But those who reject Our Signs and turn away from them with disdain, these shall be the inmates of the Fire; they shall abide therein.

فَمَنْ اَظْلَمُ مِمَّنِ افْتَرٰى عَلَى اللّٰهِ كَذِبًا اَوْ كَذَّبَ

* 38. Who is, then, more unjust than he who forges a lie against Allah or gives the

lie to His Signs? It is these who shall have their lot as ordained till when Our messengers shall visit them to take away their souls, they shall say, 'Where is that which you used to call upon beside Allah?' They will answer, 'We cannot find them;' and they will bear witness against themselves that they were disbelievers.

بِاٰيٰتِهٖ ۭ اُولٰۗىِٕكَ يَنَالُهُمْ نَصِيْبُهُمْ مِّنَ الْكِتٰبِ ۭ حَتّٰٓى
اِذَا جَاۗءَتْهُمْ رُسُلُنَا يَتَوَفَّوْنَهُمْ ۙ قَالُوْٓا اَيْنَ مَا كُنْتُمْ
تَدْعُوْنَ مِنْ دُوْنِ اللّٰهِ ۭ قَالُوْا ضَلُّوْا عَنَّا وَشَهِدُوْا
عَلٰٓي اَنْفُسِهِمْ اَنَّهُمْ كَانُوْا كٰفِرِيْنَ ﴿٣٨﴾

39. He will say, 'Enter ye into the Fire among the nations of Jinn and men who passed away before you.' Every time a people enters, it shall curse its sister (people) until, when they have all successively arrived therein, the last of them will say of the first of them: 'Our Lord, these led us astray, so give them a double punishment of the Fire.' He will say, 'For each *preceding party* there shall be double *punishment*, but you do not know.'

قَالَ ادْخُلُوْا فِيْٓ اُمَمٍ قَدْ خَلَتْ مِنْ قَبْلِكُمْ مِّنَ الْجِنِّ
وَالْاِنْسِ فِي النَّارِ ۭ كُلَّمَا دَخَلَتْ اُمَّةٌ لَّعَنَتْ اُخْتَهَا ۭ
حَتّٰٓي اِذَا ادَّارَكُوْا فِيْهَا جَمِيْعًا ۙ قَالَتْ اُخْرٰىهُمْ لِاُوْلٰىهُمْ
رَبَّنَا هٰٓؤُلَاۗءِ اَضَلُّوْنَا فَاٰتِهِمْ عَذَابًا ضِعْفًا مِّنَ النَّارِ ۥ
قَالَ لِكُلٍّ ضِعْفٌ وَّلٰكِنْ لَّا تَعْلَمُوْنَ ﴿٣٩﴾

40. And the first of them will say to the last of them: 'You have then no superiority over us; taste therefore the punishment for all that you did.'

وَقَالَتْ اُوْلٰىهُمْ لِاُخْرٰىهُمْ فَمَا كَانَ لَكُمْ عَلَيْنَا مِنْ
فَضْلٍ فَذُوْقُوا الْعَذَابَ بِمَا كُنْتُمْ تَكْسِبُوْنَ ﴿٤٠﴾ ع

R. 5.

* 41. Those who reject Our Signs and turn away from them with disdain, the gates of the *spiritual* firmament will not be opened for them, nor will they enter Heaven until a camel goes through the eye of a needle. And thus do We requite the offenders.

اِنَّ الَّذِيْنَ كَذَّبُوْا بِاٰيٰتِنَا وَاسْتَكْبَرُوْا عَنْهَا لَا تُفَتَّحُ
لَهُمْ اَبْوَابُ السَّمَاۗءِ وَلَا يَدْخُلُوْنَ الْجَنَّةَ حَتّٰي يَلِجَ
الْجَمَلُ فِيْ سَمِّ الْخِيَاطِ ۭ وَكَذٰلِكَ نَجْزِي الْمُجْرِمِيْنَ ﴿٤١﴾

42. They shall have a bed of Hell, and over them coverings *of the same*. And thus do We requite the unjust.

لَهُمْ مِّنْ جَهَنَّمَ مِهَادٌ وَّمِنْ فَوْقِهِمْ غَوَاشٍ ۭ وَ
كَذٰلِكَ نَجْزِي الظّٰلِمِيْنَ ﴿٤٢﴾

43. But *as to* those who believe and do good works—*and* We task not any soul beyond its capacity—these are the inmates of Heaven; they shall abide therein.

وَالَّذِيْنَ اٰمَنُوْا وَعَمِلُوا الصّٰلِحٰتِ لَا نُكَلِّفُ نَفْسًا اِلَّا
وُسْعَهَآ ۡ اُولٰۗىِٕكَ اَصْحٰبُ الْجَنَّةِ ۚ هُمْ فِيْهَا خٰلِدُوْنَ ﴿٤٣﴾

44. And We shall remove whatever rancour may be in their hearts. Beneath them shall flow rivers. And they shall say, 'All praise belongs to Allah Who has guided us to this. And we could not have found guidance, if Allah had not guided us. The Messengers of our Lord did indeed bring the truth.' And it shall be proclaimed unto them: 'This is the Heaven which you

وَنَزَعْنَا مَا فِيْ صُدُوْرِهِمْ مِّنْ غِلٍّ تَجْرِيْ مِنْ تَحْتِهِمُ
الْاَنْهٰرُ ۚ وَقَالُوا الْحَمْدُ لِلّٰهِ الَّذِيْ هَدٰىنَا لِهٰذَا ۣ وَمَا
كُنَّا لِنَهْتَدِيَ لَوْلَآ اَنْ هَدٰىنَا اللّٰهُ ۚ لَقَدْ جَاۗءَتْ
رُسُلُ رَبِّنَا بِالْحَقِّ ۭ وَنُوْدُوْٓا اَنْ تِلْكُمُ الْجَنَّةُ اُوْرِثْتُمُوْهَا

have been given for an inheritance *as a reward* for what you used to do.'

بِمَا كُنْتُمْ تَعْمَلُوْنَ ﴿٤٤﴾

45. And the inmates of Heaven will call out to the inmates of Hell: 'We have indeed found what our Lord promised us to be true. Have you too found what your Lord promised you to be true?' They shall say: 'Yes'. Then a proclaimer shall proclaim between them *saying*, 'The curse of Allah is on the wrongdoers—

وَنَادٰٓى اَصْحٰبُ الْجَنَّةِ اَصْحٰبَ النَّارِ اَنْ قَدْ وَجَدْنَا
مَا وَعَدَنَا رَبُّنَا حَقًّا فَهَلْ وَجَدْتُّمْ مَّا وَعَدَ رَبُّكُمْ
حَقًّا ۚ قَالُوْا نَعَمْ ۚ فَاَذَّنَ مُؤَذِّنٌۢ بَيْنَهُمْ اَنْ لَّعْنَةُ اللّٰهِ
عَلَى الظّٰلِمِيْنَ ﴿٤٥﴾

46. 'Who turn *men* away from the path of Allah and seek to make it crooked, and who are disbelievers in the Hereafter.'

الَّذِيْنَ يَصُدُّوْنَ عَنْ سَبِيْلِ اللّٰهِ وَيَبْغُوْنَهَا عِوَجًا ۚ
وَهُمْ بِالْاٰخِرَةِ كٰفِرُوْنَ ﴿٤٦﴾

47. And between the two there shall be a partition, and on the elevated places there shall be men who will know all by their marks. And they will call out to the people of Heaven: 'Peace be on you.' These will not have *yet* entered it although they will be hoping *to do so*.

وَبَيْنَهُمَا حِجَابٌ ۚ وَعَلَى الْاَعْرَافِ رِجَالٌ يَّعْرِفُوْنَ كُلًّا
بِسِيْمٰهُمْ ۚ وَنَادَوْا اَصْحٰبَ الْجَنَّةِ اَنْ سَلٰمٌ عَلَيْكُمْ
لَمْ يَدْخُلُوْهَا وَهُمْ يَطْمَعُوْنَ ﴿٤٧﴾

48. And when their eyes are turned towards the people of the Fire, they will say, 'Our Lord, put us not with the unjust people.'

وَاِذَا صُرِفَتْ اَبْصَارُهُمْ تِلْقَآءَ اَصْحٰبِ النَّارِ ۙ قَالُوْا رَبَّنَا
لَا تَجْعَلْنَا مَعَ الْقَوْمِ الظّٰلِمِيْنَ ﴿٤٨﴾

R. 6.

49. And the occupants of the elevated places will call out to men whom they will know by their marks, *and* say, "Your multitude availed you not, nor your arrogance.

وَنَادٰٓى اَصْحٰبُ الْاَعْرَافِ رِجَالًا يَّعْرِفُوْنَهُمْ بِسِيْمٰهُمْ
قَالُوْا مَآ اَغْنٰى عَنْكُمْ جَمْعُكُمْ وَمَا كُنْتُمْ تَسْتَكْبِرُوْنَ ﴿٤٩﴾

50. "Are these the men about whom you swore that Allah would not extend mercy to them? *To them it has been said*, 'Enter Paradise; no fear *shall come* upon you, nor shall you grieve.' "

اَهٰٓؤُلَآءِ الَّذِيْنَ اَقْسَمْتُمْ لَا يَنَالُهُمُ اللّٰهُ بِرَحْمَةٍ ۭ
اُدْخُلُوا الْجَنَّةَ لَا خَوْفٌ عَلَيْكُمْ وَلَآ اَنْتُمْ تَحْزَنُوْنَ ﴿٥٠﴾

51. And the inmates of the Fire will call out to the inmates of Heaven, 'Pour out on us some water or some of that which Allah has provided for you.' They will say, 'Verily, Allah has forbidden them both to disbelievers—

وَنَادٰٓى اَصْحٰبُ النَّارِ اَصْحٰبَ الْجَنَّةِ اَنْ اَفِيْضُوْا عَلَيْنَا
مِنَ الْمَآءِ اَوْ مِمَّا رَزَقَكُمُ اللّٰهُ ۭ قَالُوْٓا اِنَّ اللّٰهَ حَرَّمَهُمَا
عَلَى الْكٰفِرِيْنَ ﴿٥١﴾

52. 'Those who took their religion for a pastime and a sport, and whom th life of the world beguiled.' This day, then, shall We forget them as they forgot the meeting of this day of theirs, and as they used to deny Our Signs.

الَّذِيْنَ اتَّخَذُوْا دِيْنَهُمْ لَهْوًا وَّلَعِبًا وَّغَرَّتْهُمُ الْحَيٰوةُ
الدُّنْيَا ۚ فَالْيَوْمَ نَنْسٰىهُمْ كَمَا نَسُوْا لِقَآءَ يَوْمِهِمْ هٰذَا ۙ
وَمَا كَانُوْا بِاٰيٰتِنَا يَجْحَدُوْنَ ﴿٥٢﴾

53. And surely We have brought them a Book which We have expounded with knowledge, a guidance and a mercy for a people who believe.

وَ لَقَدْ جِئْنٰهُمْ بِكِتٰبٍ فَصَّلْنٰهُ عَلٰى عِلْمٍ هُدًى وَّ
رَحْمَةً لِّقَوْمٍ يُّؤْمِنُوْنَ ﴿۵۳﴾

54. Do they wait only for the fulfilment *of warnings* thereof? On the day when the fulfilment thereof shall come, those who had forgotten it before shall say, 'The Messengers of our Lord did indeed bring the truth. Have we then any intercessors to intercede for us? Or could we be sent back so that we might do *deeds* other than that which we used to do?' They have indeed ruined their souls and that which they used to fabricate has failed them.

هَلْ يَنْظُرُوْنَ اِلَّا تَاْوِيْلَهٗ ؕ يَوْمَ يَاْتِيْ تَاْوِيْلُهٗ يَقُوْلُ
الَّذِيْنَ نَسُوْهُ مِنْ قَبْلُ قَدْ جَآءَتْ رُسُلُ رَبِّنَا بِالْحَقِّ ۚ
فَهَلْ لَّنَا مِنْ شُفَعَآءَ فَيَشْفَعُوْا لَنَآ اَوْ نُرَدُّ فَنَعْمَلَ
غَيْرَ الَّذِيْ كُنَّا نَعْمَلُ ؕ قَدْ خَسِرُوْٓا اَنْفُسَهُمْ وَ ضَلَّ
عَنْهُمْ مَّا كَانُوْا يَفْتَرُوْنَ ﴿۵۴﴾ ع ١٣

R. 7.

55. Surely, your Lord is Allah Who created the heavens and the earth in six periods; then He settled Himself on the Throne. He makes the night cover the day, which pursues it swiftly. And *He created* the sun and the moon and the stars, *all* made subservient by His command. Verily, His is the creation and the command. Blessed is Allah, the Lord of the worlds.

اِنَّ رَبَّكُمُ اللّٰهُ الَّذِيْ خَلَقَ السَّمٰوٰتِ وَ الْاَرْضَ فِيْ
سِتَّةِ اَيَّامٍ ثُمَّ اسْتَوٰى عَلَى الْعَرْشِ ۟ يُغْشِي الَّيْلَ النَّهَارَ
يَطْلُبُهٗ حَثِيْثًا ۙ وَّ الشَّمْسَ وَ الْقَمَرَ وَ النُّجُوْمَ مُسَخَّرٰتٍۭ
بِاَمْرِهٖ ؕ اَلَا لَهُ الْخَلْقُ وَ الْاَمْرُ ؕ تَبٰرَكَ اللّٰهُ رَبُّ
الْعٰلَمِيْنَ ﴿۵۵﴾

56. Call upon your Lord in humility and in secret. Surely, He does not love the transgressors.

اُدْعُوْا رَبَّكُمْ تَضَرُّعًا وَّ خُفْيَةً ؕ اِنَّهٗ لَا يُحِبُّ
الْمُعْتَدِيْنَ ﴿۵۶﴾

57. And create not disorder in the earth after it has been set in order, and call upon Him in fear and hope. Surely, the mercy of Allah is nigh unto those who do good.

وَ لَا تُفْسِدُوْا فِي الْاَرْضِ بَعْدَ اِصْلَاحِهَا وَ ادْعُوْهُ
خَوْفًا وَّ طَمَعًا ؕ اِنَّ رَحْمَتَ اللّٰهِ قَرِيْبٌ مِّنَ الْمُحْسِنِيْنَ ﴿۵۷﴾

58. And He it is Who sends the winds as glad tidings before His mercy, till, when they bear a heavy cloud, We drive it to a dead land, then We send down water therefrom, and We bring forth therewith fruits of every kind. In like manner do We bring forth the dead that you may remember.

وَ هُوَ الَّذِيْ يُرْسِلُ الرِّيٰحَ بُشْرًۢا بَيْنَ يَدَيْ رَحْمَتِهٖ ؕ
حَتّٰٓى اِذَآ اَقَلَّتْ سَحَابًا ثِقَالًا سُقْنٰهُ لِبَلَدٍ مَّيِّتٍ فَاَنْزَلْنَا
بِهِ الْمَآءَ فَاَخْرَجْنَا بِهٖ مِنْ كُلِّ الثَّمَرٰتِ ؕ كَذٰلِكَ نُخْرِجُ
الْمَوْتٰى لَعَلَّكُمْ تَذَكَّرُوْنَ ﴿۵۸﴾

59. And *as for* the good land, its vegetation comes forth *plentifully* by the command of its Lord; and that which is bad, *its vegetation* does not come forth but

وَ الْبَلَدُ الطَّيِّبُ يَخْرُجُ نَبَاتُهٗ بِاِذْنِ رَبِّهٖ ۚ وَ الَّذِيْ
خَبُثَ لَا يَخْرُجُ اِلَّا نَكِدًا ؕ كَذٰلِكَ نُصَرِّفُ الْاٰيٰتِ

scantily. In like manner do We vary the Signs for a people who are grateful.

لِقَوْمٍ يَّشْكُرُوْنَ ﴿۵۹﴾ ع ٧ ٥ ١٤

R. 8.

60. We sent Noah to his people and he said, 'O my people, worship Allah, you have no other God but Him. Indeed, I fear for you the punishment of the great day.'

لَقَدْ اَرْسَلْنَا نُوْحًا اِلٰى قَوْمِهٖ فَقَالَ يٰقَوْمِ اعْبُدُوا
اللّٰهَ مَا لَكُمْ مِّنْ اِلٰهٍ غَيْرُهٗ اِنِّيْٓ اَخَافُ عَلَيْكُمْ
عَذَابَ يَوْمٍ عَظِيْمٍ ﴿۶۰﴾

61. The chiefs of his people said, 'Surely, we see thee to be in manifest error.'

قَالَ الْمَلَاُ مِنْ قَوْمِهٖٓ اِنَّا لَنَرٰىكَ فِيْ ضَلٰلٍ مُّبِيْنٍ ﴿۶۱﴾

62. He said, 'O my people, there is no error in me, but I am a Messenger from the Lord of the worlds.

قَالَ يٰقَوْمِ لَيْسَ بِيْ ضَلٰلَةٌ وَّ لٰكِنِّيْ رَسُوْلٌ مِّنْ رَّبِّ
الْعٰلَمِيْنَ ﴿۶۲﴾

63. 'I deliver to you the messages of my Lord and give you sincere advice, and I know from Allah what you do not know.

اُبَلِّغُكُمْ رِسٰلٰتِ رَبِّيْ وَاَنْصَحُ لَكُمْ وَاَعْلَمُ مِنَ اللّٰهِ
مَا لَا تَعْلَمُوْنَ ﴿۶۳﴾

64. 'Do you wonder that an exhortation has come to you from your Lord through a man from among yourselves, that he may warn you and that you may become righteous and that you may be shown mercy?'

اَوَعَجِبْتُمْ اَنْ جَآءَكُمْ ذِكْرٌ مِّنْ رَّبِّكُمْ عَلٰى رَجُلٍ مِّنْكُمْ
لِيُنْذِرَكُمْ وَلِتَتَّقُوْا وَلَعَلَّكُمْ تُرْحَمُوْنَ ﴿۶۴﴾

65. But they accused him of falsehood, so We saved him and those with him in the Ark, and We drowned those who rejected Our Signs. They were indeed a blind people.

فَكَذَّبُوْهُ فَاَنْجَيْنٰهُ وَالَّذِيْنَ مَعَهٗ فِي الْفُلْكِ وَاَغْرَقْنَا
الَّذِيْنَ كَذَّبُوْا بِاٰيٰتِنَا اِنَّهُمْ كَانُوْا قَوْمًا عَمِيْنَ ﴿۶۵﴾ ع ٨ ٦ ١٥

R. 9.

66. And unto 'Ād *We sent* their brother Hūd. He said, 'O my people, worship Allah; you have no other deity but Him. Will you not then be God-fearing?'

وَاِلٰى عَادٍ اَخَاهُمْ هُوْدًا قَالَ يٰقَوْمِ اعْبُدُوا اللّٰهَ
مَا لَكُمْ مِّنْ اِلٰهٍ غَيْرُهٗ اَفَلَا تَتَّقُوْنَ ﴿۶۶﴾

67. The disbelieving chiefs of his people said, 'We surely see thee *lost* in foolishness, and we surely think thee to be *one* of the liars.'

قَالَ الْمَلَاُ الَّذِيْنَ كَفَرُوْا مِنْ قَوْمِهٖٓ اِنَّا لَنَرٰىكَ فِيْ
سَفَاهَةٍ وَّاِنَّا لَنَظُنُّكَ مِنَ الْكٰذِبِيْنَ ﴿۶۷﴾

68. He replied, 'O my people, there is no foolishness in me, but I am a Messenger from the Lord of the worlds.

قَالَ يٰقَوْمِ لَيْسَ بِيْ سَفَاهَةٌ وَّ لٰكِنِّيْ رَسُوْلٌ مِّنْ رَّبِّ
الْعٰلَمِيْنَ ﴿۶۸﴾

69. 'I deliver to you the messages of my Lord and I am to you a sincere and faithful counsellor.

اُبَلِّغُكُمْ رِسٰلٰتِ رَبِّيْ وَاَنَا لَكُمْ نَاصِحٌ اَمِيْنٌ ﴿۶۹﴾

70. 'Do you wonder that an exhortation has come to you from your Lord through a man from among yourselves that he may warn you? And remember *the*

اَوَعَجِبْتُمْ اَنْ جَآءَكُمْ ذِكْرٌ مِّنْ رَّبِّكُمْ عَلٰى رَجُلٍ
مِّنْكُمْ لِيُنْذِرَكُمْ وَاذْكُرُوْٓا اِذْ جَعَلَكُمْ خُلَفَآءَ مِنْ

time when He made you inheritors *of His favours* after the people of Noah, and increased you abundantly in constitution. Remember, then, the favours of Allah, that you may prosper.'

بَعْدِ قَوْمِ نُوْحٍ وَّ زَادَكُمْ فِي الْخَلْقِ بَصْطَةً ۚ فَاذْكُرُوْٓا
اٰلَآءَ اللّٰهِ لَعَلَّكُمْ تُفْلِحُوْنَ ﴿٧٠﴾

71. They said, 'Hast thou come to us that we may worship Allah alone and forsake what our fathers used to worship? Bring us, then, that which thou threatenest us with, if thou art of the truthful.'

قَالُوْٓا اَجِئْتَنَا لِنَعْبُدَ اللّٰهَ وَحْدَهٗ وَنَذَرَ مَا كَانَ
يَعْبُدُ اٰبَآؤُنَا ۚ فَاْتِنَا بِمَا تَعِدُنَآ اِنْ كُنْتَ مِنَ
الصّٰدِقِيْنَ ﴿٧١﴾

72. He replied, 'Indeed there have *already* fallen on you punishment and wrath from your Lord. Do you dispute with me about names which you have named—you and your fathers—for which Allah has sent down no authority? Wait then, I am with you among those who wait.'

قَالَ قَدْ وَقَعَ عَلَيْكُمْ مِّنْ رَّبِّكُمْ رِجْسٌ وَّغَضَبٌ ۚ
اَتُجَادِلُوْنَنِيْ فِيْٓ اَسْمَآءٍ سَمَّيْتُمُوْهَآ اَنْتُمْ وَاٰبَآؤُكُمْ
مَّا نَزَّلَ اللّٰهُ بِهَا مِنْ سُلْطٰنٍ ۚ فَانْتَظِرُوْٓا اِنِّيْ مَعَكُمْ
مِّنَ الْمُنْتَظِرِيْنَ ﴿٧٢﴾

73. And We saved him and those who were with him, by Our mercy, and We cut off the last remnant of those who rejected Our Signs. And they were not believers.

فَاَنْجَيْنٰهُ وَالَّذِيْنَ مَعَهٗ بِرَحْمَةٍ مِّنَّا وَقَطَعْنَا دَابِرَ
الَّذِيْنَ كَذَّبُوْا بِاٰيٰتِنَا وَمَا كَانُوْا مُؤْمِنِيْنَ ﴿٧٣﴾

R. 10.

74. And to Thamūd *We sent* their brother Ṣāliḥ. He said, 'O my people, worship Allah; you have no other deity but Him. Verily there has come to you a clear evidence from your Lord—this she-camel of Allah, a Sign for you. So leave her that she may feed in Allah's earth, and do her no harm, lest a painful punishment seize you.

وَاِلٰى ثَمُوْدَ اَخَاهُمْ صٰلِحًا ۘ قَالَ يٰقَوْمِ اعْبُدُوا اللّٰهَ مَا
لَكُمْ مِّنْ اِلٰهٍ غَيْرُهٗ ؕ قَدْ جَآءَتْكُمْ بَيِّنَةٌ مِّنْ رَّبِّكُمْ ؕ
هٰذِهٖ نَاقَةُ اللّٰهِ لَكُمْ اٰيَةً فَذَرُوْهَا تَاْكُلْ فِيْٓ اَرْضِ
اللّٰهِ وَلَا تَمَسُّوْهَا بِسُوْٓءٍ فَيَاْخُذَكُمْ عَذَابٌ اَلِيْمٌ ﴿٧٤﴾

75. And remember *the time* when He made you inheritors *of His favours* after 'Ād, and assigned you an abode in the land; you build palaces in its plains, and you hew the mountains into houses. Remember, therefore, the favours of Allah and commit not iniquity in the earth, causing disorder.'

وَاذْكُرُوْٓا اِذْ جَعَلَكُمْ خُلَفَآءَ مِنْ بَعْدِ عَادٍ وَّبَوَّاَكُمْ
فِي الْاَرْضِ تَتَّخِذُوْنَ مِنْ سُهُوْلِهَا قُصُوْرًا وَّتَنْحِتُوْنَ
الْجِبَالَ بُيُوْتًا ۚ فَاذْكُرُوْٓا اٰلَآءَ اللّٰهِ وَلَا تَعْثَوْا فِي
الْاَرْضِ مُفْسِدِيْنَ ﴿٧٥﴾

76. The chief men of his people who were arrogant said to those who were reckoned weak—those among them who believed—'Do you know *for certain* that Ṣāliḥ is one sent by his Lord?' They answered, 'Surely, we believe in that with which he has been sent.'

قَالَ الْمَلَاُ الَّذِيْنَ اسْتَكْبَرُوْا مِنْ قَوْمِهٖ لِلَّذِيْنَ
اسْتُضْعِفُوْا لِمَنْ اٰمَنَ مِنْهُمْ اَتَعْلَمُوْنَ اَنَّ صٰلِحًا
مُّرْسَلٌ مِّنْ رَّبِّهٖ ؕ قَالُوْٓا اِنَّا بِمَآ اُرْسِلَ بِهٖ مُؤْمِنُوْنَ ﴿٧٦﴾

77. Those who were arrogant said, ‘Verily, we do disbelieve in that in which you believe.’

قَالَ الَّذِيْنَ اسْتَكْبَرُوْٓا اِنَّا بِالَّذِيْٓ اٰمَنْتُمْ بِهٖ كٰفِرُوْنَ ﴿۷۷﴾

78. Then they hamstrung the she-camel and rebelled against the command of their Lord, and said, ‘O Ṣāliḥ, bring us that which thou threatenest us with, if thou art *indeed one* of the Messengers.’

فَعَقَرُوا النَّاقَةَ وَعَتَوْا عَنْ اَمْرِ رَبِّهِمْ وَقَالُوْا يٰصٰلِحُ
ائْتِنَا بِمَا تَعِدُنَآ اِنْ كُنْتَ مِنَ الْمُرْسَلِيْنَ ﴿۷۸﴾

* 79. So the earthquake seized them and in their homes they lay prostrate upon the ground.

فَاَخَذَتْهُمُ الرَّجْفَةُ فَاَصْبَحُوْا فِيْ دَارِهِمْ جٰثِمِيْنَ ﴿۷۹﴾

80. Then *Ṣāliḥ* turned away from them and said, ‘O my people, I did deliver the message of my Lord unto you and offered you sincere counsel, but you love not sincere counsellors.’

فَتَوَلّٰى عَنْهُمْ وَقَالَ يٰقَوْمِ لَقَدْ اَبْلَغْتُكُمْ رِسَالَةَ
رَبِّيْ وَنَصَحْتُ لَكُمْ وَلٰكِنْ لَّا تُحِبُّوْنَ النّٰصِحِيْنَ ﴿۸۰﴾

81. And *We sent* Lot—when he said to his people, ‘Do you commit an abomination such as no one in the world ever did before you?

وَلُوْطًا اِذْ قَالَ لِقَوْمِهٖٓ اَتَاْتُوْنَ الْفَاحِشَةَ مَا سَبَقَكُمْ
بِهَا مِنْ اَحَدٍ مِّنَ الْعٰلَمِيْنَ ﴿۸۱﴾

82. ‘You approach men with lust instead of women. Nay, you are a people who exceed *all* bounds.’

اِنَّكُمْ لَتَاْتُوْنَ الرِّجَالَ شَهْوَةً مِّنْ دُوْنِ النِّسَآءِ ۭ
بَلْ اَنْتُمْ قَوْمٌ مُّسْرِفُوْنَ ﴿۸۲﴾

83. And the answer of his people was no other than that they said, ‘Turn them out of your town, for they are men who would keep pure.’

وَمَا كَانَ جَوَابَ قَوْمِهٖٓ اِلَّآ اَنْ قَالُوْٓا اَخْرِجُوْهُمْ
مِّنْ قَرْيَتِكُمْ ۚ اِنَّهُمْ اُنَاسٌ يَّتَطَهَّرُوْنَ ﴿۸۳﴾

84. And We saved him and his family, except his wife: she was of those who stayed behind.

فَاَنْجَيْنٰهُ وَاَهْلَهٗٓ اِلَّا امْرَاَتَهٗ ۖ كَانَتْ مِنَ الْغٰبِرِيْنَ ﴿۸۴﴾

85. And We rained upon them a rain. Now see, what was the end of the sinners!

وَاَمْطَرْنَا عَلَيْهِمْ مَّطَرًا ۭ فَانْظُرْ كَيْفَ كَانَ عَاقِبَةُ
الْمُجْرِمِيْنَ ﴿۸۵﴾ ع

R. 11.

* 86. And to Midian *We sent* their brother Shu‘aib. He said, ‘O my people, worship Allah; you have no other deity but Him. A clear Sign has indeed come to you from your Lord. So give full measure and full weight, and diminish not unto people their things, and create not disorder in the earth after it has been set in order. This is better for you, if you are believers.

وَاِلٰى مَدْيَنَ اَخَاهُمْ شُعَيْبًا ۭ قَالَ يٰقَوْمِ اعْبُدُوا اللّٰهَ
مَا لَكُمْ مِّنْ اِلٰهٍ غَيْرُهٗ ۭ قَدْ جَآءَتْكُمْ بَيِّنَةٌ مِّنْ رَّبِّكُمْ
فَاَوْفُوا الْكَيْلَ وَالْمِيْزَانَ وَلَا تَبْخَسُوا النَّاسَ اَشْيَآءَهُمْ
وَلَا تُفْسِدُوْا فِي الْاَرْضِ بَعْدَ اِصْلَاحِهَا ۭ ذٰلِكُمْ خَيْرٌ
لَّكُمْ اِنْ كُنْتُمْ مُّؤْمِنِيْنَ ﴿۸۶﴾

87. ‘And sit not on every path, threatening and turning away from the path of Allah those who believe in Him, and seeking to make it crooked. And remember

وَلَا تَقْعُدُوْا بِكُلِّ صِرَاطٍ تُوْعِدُوْنَ وَتَصُدُّوْنَ
عَنْ سَبِيْلِ اللّٰهِ مَنْ اٰمَنَ بِهٖ وَتَبْغُوْنَهَا عِوَجًا ۚ

when you were few and He multiplied you. And behold, what was the end of those who created disorder!

وَاذْكُرُوا إِذْ كُنْتُمْ قَلِيلًا فَكَثَّرَكُمْ وَانْظُرُوا كَيْفَ كَانَ عَاقِبَةُ الْمُفْسِدِينَ ﴿٨٧﴾

88. 'And if there is a party among you who believes in that with which I have been sent, and a party who does not believe, then have patience until Allah judges between us. And He is the Best of judges.'

وَإِنْ كَانَ طَائِفَةٌ مِنْكُمْ آمَنُوا بِالَّذِي أُرْسِلْتُ بِهِ وَطَائِفَةٌ لَمْ يُؤْمِنُوا فَاصْبِرُوا حَتَّىٰ يَحْكُمَ اللَّهُ بَيْنَنَا ۚ وَهُوَ خَيْرُ الْحَاكِمِينَ ﴿٨٨﴾

89. The chief men of his people who were arrogant said, 'Assuredly, we will drive thee out, O Shu'aib, and the believers *that are* with thee, from our town, or you shall have to return to our religion.' He said: 'Even though we be unwilling?

قَالَ الْمَلَأُ الَّذِينَ اسْتَكْبَرُوا مِنْ قَوْمِهِ لَنُخْرِجَنَّكَ يَا شُعَيْبُ وَالَّذِينَ آمَنُوا مَعَكَ مِنْ قَرْيَتِنَا أَوْ لَتَعُودُنَّ فِي مِلَّتِنَا ۚ قَالَ أَوَلَوْ كُنَّا كَارِهِينَ ﴿٨٩﴾

* 90. 'We have indeed been forging a lie against Allah, if we *now* return to your religion after Allah has saved us therefrom. And it behoves us not to return thereto except that Allah, our Lord, should *so* will. Our Lord comprehends all things in *His* knowledge. In Allah have we put our trust. *So* O our Lord, decide Thou between us and between our people with truth, and Thou art the Best of those who decide.'

قَدِ افْتَرَيْنَا عَلَى اللَّهِ كَذِبًا إِنْ عُدْنَا فِي مِلَّتِكُمْ بَعْدَ إِذْ نَجَّانَا اللَّهُ مِنْهَا ۚ وَمَا يَكُونُ لَنَا أَنْ نَعُودَ فِيهَا إِلَّا أَنْ يَشَاءَ اللَّهُ رَبُّنَا ۚ وَسِعَ رَبُّنَا كُلَّ شَيْءٍ عِلْمًا ۚ عَلَى اللَّهِ تَوَكَّلْنَا ۚ رَبَّنَا افْتَحْ بَيْنَنَا وَبَيْنَ قَوْمِنَا بِالْحَقِّ وَأَنْتَ خَيْرُ الْفَاتِحِينَ ﴿٩٠﴾

91. And the chief men of his people who disbelieved said, 'If you follow Shu'aib, you shall then certainly be the losers.'

وَقَالَ الْمَلَأُ الَّذِينَ كَفَرُوا مِنْ قَوْمِهِ لَئِنِ اتَّبَعْتُمْ شُعَيْبًا إِنَّكُمْ إِذًا لَخَاسِرُونَ ﴿٩١﴾

92. So the earthquake seized them and in their homes they lay prostrate upon the ground.

فَأَخَذَتْهُمُ الرَّجْفَةُ فَأَصْبَحُوا فِي دَارِهِمْ جَاثِمِينَ ﴿٩٢﴾

93. Those who accused Shu'aib of lying became as if they had never dwelt therein. Those who accused Shu'aib of lying—it was they who were the losers.

الَّذِينَ كَذَّبُوا شُعَيْبًا كَأَنْ لَمْ يَغْنَوْا فِيهَا ۚ الَّذِينَ كَذَّبُوا شُعَيْبًا كَانُوا هُمُ الْخَاسِرِينَ ﴿٩٣﴾

94. Then he turned away from them and said, 'O my people, indeed, I delivered to you the messages of my Lord and gave you sincere counsel. How then should I sorrow for a disbelieving people?'

فَتَوَلَّىٰ عَنْهُمْ وَقَالَ يَا قَوْمِ لَقَدْ أَبْلَغْتُكُمْ رِسَالَاتِ رَبِّي وَنَصَحْتُ لَكُمْ ۖ فَكَيْفَ آسَىٰ عَلَىٰ قَوْمٍ كَافِرِينَ ﴿٩٤﴾

R. 12.

95. And never did We send a Prophet to any town but We seized the people thereof with adversity and suffering, that they might become humble.

وَمَا أَرْسَلْنَا فِي قَرْيَةٍ مِنْ نَبِيٍّ إِلَّا أَخَذْنَا أَهْلَهَا بِالْبَأْسَاءِ وَالضَّرَّاءِ لَعَلَّهُمْ يَضَّرَّعُونَ ﴿٩٥﴾

96. Then We changed *their* evil *condition* into good until they grew *in affluence and number* and said, 'Suffering and happiness betided our fathers *also*.' Then We seized them suddenly, while they perceived not.

ثُمَّ بَدَّلْنَا مَكَانَ السَّيِّئَةِ الْحَسَنَةَ حَتّٰى عَفَوْا وَّ قَالُوْا
قَدْ مَسَّ اٰبَآءَنَا الضَّرَّآءُ وَ السَّرَّآءُ فَاَخَذْنٰهُمْ بَغْتَةً
وَّهُمْ لَا يَشْعُرُوْنَ ﴿٩٦﴾

97. And if the people of *those* towns had believed and been righteous, We would have surely opened for them blessings from heaven and earth; but they disbelieved, so We seized them because of that which they used to earn.

وَلَوْ اَنَّ اَهْلَ الْقُرٰۤى اٰمَنُوْا وَ اتَّقَوْا لَفَتَحْنَا عَلَيْهِمْ
بَرَكٰتٍ مِّنَ السَّمَآءِ وَ الْاَرْضِ وَلٰكِنْ كَذَّبُوْا فَاَخَذْنٰهُمْ
بِمَا كَانُوْا يَكْسِبُوْنَ ﴿٩٧﴾

98. Are the people of *these* towns, then, secure from the coming of Our punishment upon them by night while they are asleep?

اَفَاَمِنَ اَهْلُ الْقُرٰۤى اَنْ يَّاْتِيَهُمْ بَاْسُنَا بَيَاتًا وَّهُمْ نَآئِمُوْنَ ﴿٩٨﴾

99. And are the people of *these* towns secure from the coming of Our punishment upon them in the early part of the forenoon while they are engaged in play?

اَوَ اَمِنَ اَهْلُ الْقُرٰۤى اَنْ يَّاْتِيَهُمْ بَاْسُنَا ضُحًى وَّهُمْ يَلْعَبُوْنَ ﴿٩٩﴾

100. Are they then secure from the design of Allah? And none feels secure from the design of Allah save the people that perish.

اَفَاَمِنُوْا مَكْرَ اللّٰهِ ۚ فَلَا يَاْمَنُ مَكْرَ اللّٰهِ اِلَّا الْقَوْمُ
الْخٰسِرُوْنَ ﴿١٠٠﴾ ع

R. 13.

101. Does it not afford guidance to those who have inherited the earth in succession to its *former* inhabitants, that if We please, We can smite them for their sins and seal up their hearts, so that they should not hear?

اَوَلَمْ يَهْدِ لِلَّذِيْنَ يَرِثُوْنَ الْاَرْضَ مِنْۢ بَعْدِ اَهْلِهَاۤ
اَنْ لَّوْ نَشَآءُ اَصَبْنٰهُمْ بِذُنُوْبِهِمْ ۚ وَنَطْبَعُ عَلٰى قُلُوْبِهِمْ
فَهُمْ لَا يَسْمَعُوْنَ ﴿١٠١﴾

102. Such were the towns some of whose news We have related to thee. And their Messengers did indeed come to them with clear Signs. But they would not believe what they had disbelieved before. In this manner does Allah seal up the hearts of the disbelievers.

تِلْكَ الْقُرٰى نَقُصُّ عَلَيْكَ مِنْ اَنْۢبَآئِهَا ۚ وَلَقَدْ
جَآءَتْهُمْ رُسُلُهُمْ بِالْبَيِّنٰتِ ۚ فَمَا كَانُوْا لِيُؤْمِنُوْا بِمَا
كَذَّبُوْا مِنْ قَبْلُ ؕ كَذٰلِكَ يَطْبَعُ اللّٰهُ عَلٰى قُلُوْبِ
الْكٰفِرِيْنَ ﴿١٠٢﴾

* 103. And We found not in most of them any *observance of* covenant and surely We found most of them to be evil-doers.

وَمَا وَجَدْنَا لِاَكْثَرِهِمْ مِّنْ عَهْدٍ ۚ وَاِنْ وَّجَدْنَاۤ
اَكْثَرَهُمْ لَفٰسِقِيْنَ ﴿١٠٣﴾

104. Then, after them, We sent Moses with Our Signs to Pharaoh and his chiefs, but they unjustly *rejected* them. Behold, then, what was the end of those who created disorder!

ثُمَّ بَعَثْنَا مِنْۢ بَعْدِهِمْ مُّوْسٰى بِاٰيٰتِنَاۤ اِلٰى فِرْعَوْنَ
وَمَلَا۠ئِهٖ فَظَلَمُوْا بِهَا ۚ فَانْظُرْ كَيْفَ كَانَ عَاقِبَةُ
الْمُفْسِدِيْنَ ﴿١٠٤﴾

105. And Moses said, 'O Pharaoh, *truly*, I am a Messenger from the Lord of the worlds.

وَقَالَ مُوسٰى يٰفِرْعَوْنُ اِنِّيْ رَسُوْلٌ مِّنْ رَّبِّ الْعٰلَمِيْنَ ﴿١٠٥﴾

106. 'It is not meet that I should say anything of Allah except the truth. I have come to you with a clear Sign from your Lord; therefore, let the children of Israel go with me.'

حَقِيْقٌ عَلٰٓى اَنْ لَّآ اَقُوْلَ عَلَى اللّٰهِ اِلَّا الْحَقَّ قَدْ جِئْتُكُمْ بِبَيِّنَةٍ مِّنْ رَّبِّكُمْ فَاَرْسِلْ مَعِيَ بَنِيْٓ اِسْرَآءِيْلَ ﴿١٠٦﴾

107. *Pharaoh* replied, 'If thou hast indeed come with a Sign, then produce it, if thou art of the truthful.'

قَالَ اِنْ كُنْتَ جِئْتَ بِاٰيَةٍ فَاْتِ بِهَآ اِنْ كُنْتَ مِنَ الصّٰدِقِيْنَ ﴿١٠٧﴾

108. So he flung down his rod, and behold! it was a serpent plainly visible.

فَاَلْقٰى عَصَاهُ فَاِذَا هِيَ ثُعْبَانٌ مُّبِيْنٌ ﴿١٠٨﴾

109. And He drew forth his hand, and lo! it was white for the beholders.

وَّنَزَعَ يَدَهٗ فَاِذَا هِيَ بَيْضَآءُ لِلنّٰظِرِيْنَ ﴿١٠٩﴾

R. 14.

110. The chiefs of Pharaoh's people said, 'This is most surely a skilful magician.

قَالَ الْمَلَاُ مِنْ قَوْمِ فِرْعَوْنَ اِنَّ هٰذَا لَسٰحِرٌ عَلِيْمٌ ﴿١١٠﴾

111. 'He desires to turn you out from your land. Now what do you advise?'

يُّرِيْدُ اَنْ يُّخْرِجَكُمْ مِّنْ اَرْضِكُمْ فَمَاذَا تَاْمُرُوْنَ ﴿١١١﴾

112. They said, 'Put him off and his brother *awhile*, and send into the cities summoners,

قَالُوْٓا اَرْجِهْ وَاَخَاهُ وَاَرْسِلْ فِي الْمَدَآئِنِ حٰشِرِيْنَ ﴿١١٢﴾

113. 'Who should bring to thee every skilful magician.'

يَاْتُوْكَ بِكُلِّ سٰحِرٍ عَلِيْمٍ ﴿١١٣﴾

114. And the magicians came to Pharaoh *and* said: 'We shall, of course, have a reward, if we prevail.'

وَجَآءَ السَّحَرَةُ فِرْعَوْنَ قَالُوْٓا اِنَّ لَنَا لَاَجْرًا اِنْ كُنَّا نَحْنُ الْغٰلِبِيْنَ ﴿١١٤﴾

115. He said, 'Yes, and you shall *also* be of those who are placed near *me*.'

قَالَ نَعَمْ وَاِنَّكُمْ لَمِنَ الْمُقَرَّبِيْنَ ﴿١١٥﴾

116. They said, 'O Moses, either throw thou *first*, or we shall be the *first* throwers.'

قَالُوْا يٰمُوْسٰٓى اِمَّآ اَنْ تُلْقِيَ وَاِمَّآ اَنْ نَّكُوْنَ نَحْنُ الْمُلْقِيْنَ ﴿١١٦﴾

117. He replied, 'Throw ye.' And when they threw, they enchanted the eyes of the people, and struck them with awe and brought forth a great magic.

قَالَ اَلْقُوْا فَلَمَّآ اَلْقَوْا سَحَرُوْٓا اَعْيُنَ النَّاسِ وَاسْتَرْهَبُوْهُمْ وَجَآءُوْ بِسِحْرٍ عَظِيْمٍ ﴿١١٧﴾

118. And We inspired Moses, *saying*, 'Throw thy rod,' and lo! it swallowed up whatever they feigned.

وَاَوْحَيْنَآ اِلٰى مُوْسٰٓى اَنْ اَلْقِ عَصَاكَ فَاِذَا هِيَ تَلْقَفُ مَا يَاْفِكُوْنَ ﴿١١٨﴾

119. So was the Truth established, and their works proved vain.

فَوَقَعَ الْحَقُّ وَبَطَلَ مَا كَانُوْا يَعْمَلُوْنَ ﴿١١٩﴾

120. Thus were they vanquished there, and they returned humiliated.

فَغُلِبُوْا هُنَالِكَ وَانْقَلَبُوْا صٰغِرِيْنَ ﴿١٢٠﴾

121. And the magicians were impelled to fall down prostrate.

وَأُلْقِيَ السَّحَرَةُ سٰجِدِيْنَ ﴿١٢١﴾

122. *And* they said, 'We believe in the Lord of the worlds,

قَالُوْٓا اٰمَنَّا بِرَبِّ الْعٰلَمِيْنَ ﴿١٢٢﴾

123. 'The Lord of Moses and Aaron.'

رَبِّ مُوْسٰى وَهٰرُوْنَ ﴿١٢٣﴾

124. Pharaoh said, 'You have believed in him before I gave you leave. Surely, this is a plot that you have plotted in the city, that you may turn out therefrom its inhabitants, but you shall soon know *the consequences*.

قَالَ فِرْعَوْنُ اٰمَنْتُمْ بِهٖ قَبْلَ اَنْ اٰذَنَ لَكُمْ ۚ اِنَّ
هٰذَا لَمَكْرٌ مَّكَرْتُمُوْهُ فِى الْمَدِيْنَةِ لِتُخْرِجُوْا مِنْهَآ
اَهْلَهَا ۚ فَسَوْفَ تَعْلَمُوْنَ ﴿١٢٤﴾

125. 'Most surely will I cut off your hands and your feet on alternate sides. Then will I surely crucify you all together.

لَاُقَطِّعَنَّ اَيْدِيَكُمْ وَاَرْجُلَكُمْ مِّنْ خِلَافٍ ثُمَّ لَاُصَلِّبَنَّكُمْ
اَجْمَعِيْنَ ﴿١٢٥﴾

126. They answered, 'To our Lord *then* shall we return.

قَالُوْٓا اِنَّآ اِلٰى رَبِّنَا مُنْقَلِبُوْنَ ﴿١٢٦﴾

127. 'And thou dost not wreak vengeance on us but because we have believed in the Signs of our Lord, when they came to us. Our Lord, pour forth upon us steadfastness and cause us to die resigned *unto Thee*.'

وَمَا تَنْقِمُ مِنَّآ اِلَّآ اَنْ اٰمَنَّا بِاٰيٰتِ رَبِّنَا لَمَّا جَآءَتْنَا ۗ
رَبَّنَآ اَفْرِغْ عَلَيْنَا صَبْرًا وَّتَوَفَّنَا مُسْلِمِيْنَ ﴿١٢٧﴾ ع ١٤ ٤

R. 15.

128. And the chiefs of Pharaoh's people said, 'Wilt thou leave Moses and his people to create disorder in the land, and forsake thee and thy gods?' He answered, 'We will ruthlessly slay their sons and let their women live. And surely we are dominant over them.'

وَقَالَ الْمَلَاُ مِنْ قَوْمِ فِرْعَوْنَ اَتَذَرُ مُوْسٰى وَقَوْمَهٗ
لِيُفْسِدُوْا فِى الْاَرْضِ وَيَذَرَكَ وَاٰلِهَتَكَ ۗ قَالَ
سَنُقَتِّلُ اَبْنَآءَهُمْ وَنَسْتَحْيٖ نِسَآءَهُمْ ۚ وَاِنَّا فَوْقَهُمْ
قٰهِرُوْنَ ﴿١٢٨﴾

129. Moses said to his people, 'Seek help from Allah and be steadfast. Verily, the earth is Allah's; He gives it as a heritage to whomsoever He pleases of His servants, and the end is for the God-fearing.'

قَالَ مُوْسٰى لِقَوْمِهِ اسْتَعِيْنُوْا بِاللّٰهِ وَاصْبِرُوْا ۚ اِنَّ
الْاَرْضَ لِلّٰهِ ۙ يُوْرِثُهَا مَنْ يَّشَآءُ مِنْ عِبَادِهٖ ۗ وَ
الْعَاقِبَةُ لِلْمُتَّقِيْنَ ﴿١٢٩﴾

130. They replied, 'We were persecuted before thou camest to us und *even* after thou camest to us.' He said, 'Your Lord is about to destroy your enemy and make you rulers in the land, *that* He may then see how you act.'

قَالُوْٓا اُوْذِيْنَا مِنْ قَبْلِ اَنْ تَاْتِيَنَا وَمِنْ بَعْدِ مَا
جِئْتَنَا ۗ قَالَ عَسٰى رَبُّكُمْ اَنْ يُّهْلِكَ عَدُوَّكُمْ وَ
يَسْتَخْلِفَكُمْ فِى الْاَرْضِ فَيَنْظُرَ كَيْفَ تَعْمَلُوْنَ ﴿١٣٠﴾ ع ١٥ ٥

R. 16.

131. And We punished Pharaoh's people with drought and scarcity of fruits, that

وَلَقَدْ اَخَذْنَآ اٰلَ فِرْعَوْنَ بِالسِّنِيْنَ وَنَقْصٍ مِّنْ

they might be admonished.

الثَّمَرٰتِ لَعَلَّهُمْ يَذَّكَّرُوْنَ ﴿١٣١﴾

132. But when there came to them good, they said, 'This is for us.' And if evil befell them, they ascribed the evil fortune to Moses and those with him. Now, surely, *the cause of* their evil fortune is with Allah. But most of them do not know.

فَاِذَا جَآءَتْهُمُ الْحَسَنَةُ قَالُوْا لَنَا هٰذِهٖ ۚ وَاِنْ تُصِبْهُمْ
سَيِّئَةٌ يَّطَّيَّرُوْا بِمُوْسٰى وَمَنْ مَّعَهٗ ؕ اَلَآ اِنَّمَا
طٰٓئِرُهُمْ عِنْدَ اللّٰهِ وَلٰكِنَّ اَكْثَرَهُمْ لَا يَعْلَمُوْنَ ﴿١٣٢﴾

133. And they said, 'Whatever Sign thou mayest bring us to bewitch us with, we will not believe in thee.'

وَقَالُوْا مَهْمَا تَاْتِنَا بِهٖ مِنْ اٰيَةٍ لِّتَسْحَرَنَا بِهَا ۙ
فَمَا نَحْنُ لَكَ بِمُؤْمِنِيْنَ ﴿١٣٣﴾

134. Then We sent upon them the storm and the locusts, and the lice, and the frogs, and the blood—clear Signs; but they behaved proudly and were a sinful people.

فَاَرْسَلْنَا عَلَيْهِمُ الطُّوْفَانَ وَالْجَرَادَ وَالْقُمَّلَ
وَالضَّفَادِعَ وَالدَّمَ اٰيٰتٍ مُّفَصَّلٰتٍ ۟ فَاسْتَكْبَرُوْا
وَكَانُوْا قَوْمًا مُّجْرِمِيْنَ ﴿١٣٤﴾

135. And when there fell upon them the punishment, they said, 'O Moses, pray for us to thy Lord according to that which He has promised to thee. If thou remove from us the punishment, we will surely believe in thee and we will surely send with thee the children of Israel.'

وَلَمَّا وَقَعَ عَلَيْهِمُ الرِّجْزُ قَالُوْا يٰمُوْسَى ادْعُ لَنَا رَبَّكَ
بِمَا عَهِدَ عِنْدَكَ ۚ لَئِنْ كَشَفْتَ عَنَّا الرِّجْزَ لَنُؤْمِنَنَّ
لَكَ وَلَنُرْسِلَنَّ مَعَكَ بَنِيْٓ اِسْرَآءِيْلَ ۚ ﴿١٣٥﴾

136. But when We removed from them the punishment for a term which they were to reach, lo! they broke their promise.

فَلَمَّا كَشَفْنَا عَنْهُمُ الرِّجْزَ اِلٰٓى اَجَلٍ هُمْ بٰلِغُوْهُ
اِذَا هُمْ يَنْكُثُوْنَ ﴿١٣٦﴾

137. So We took vengeance upon them and drowned them in the sea, because they treated Our Signs as lies and were heedless of them.

فَانْتَقَمْنَا مِنْهُمْ فَاَغْرَقْنٰهُمْ فِى الْيَمِّ بِاَنَّهُمْ كَذَّبُوْا
بِاٰيٰتِنَا وَكَانُوْا عَنْهَا غٰفِلِيْنَ ﴿١٣٧﴾

138. And We caused the people who were considered weak to inherit the eastern parts of the land and the western parts thereof, which We blessed. And the gracious word of thy Lord was fulfilled for the children of Israel because they were steadfast; and We destroyed all that Pharaoh and his people had built and all that they had erected.

وَاَوْرَثْنَا الْقَوْمَ الَّذِيْنَ كَانُوْا يُسْتَضْعَفُوْنَ مَشَارِقَ
الْاَرْضِ وَمَغَارِبَهَا الَّتِيْ بٰرَكْنَا فِيْهَا ؕ وَتَمَّتْ
كَلِمَتُ رَبِّكَ الْحُسْنٰى عَلٰى بَنِيْٓ اِسْرَآءِيْلَ ۙ۬ بِمَا صَبَرُوْا ؕ
وَدَمَّرْنَا مَا كَانَ يَصْنَعُ فِرْعَوْنُ وَقَوْمُهٗ وَمَا كَانُوْا
يَعْرِشُوْنَ ﴿١٣٨﴾

139. And We brought the children of Israel across the sea, and they came to a

وَجٰوَزْنَا بِبَنِيْٓ اِسْرَآءِيْلَ الْبَحْرَ فَاَتَوْا عَلٰى قَوْمٍ

people who were devoted to their idols. They said, 'O Moses, make for us a god just as they have gods.' He said, 'Surely, you are an ignorant people.

يَعْكُفُوْنَ عَلٰٓى اَصْنَامٍ لَّهُمْ ۚ قَالُوْا يٰمُوْسَى اجْعَلْ
لَّنَآ اِلٰهًا كَمَا لَهُمْ اٰلِهَةٌ ۭ قَالَ اِنَّكُمْ قَوْمٌ تَجْهَلُوْنَ ﴿١٣٩﴾

140. '*As to* these, surely destroyed shall be all that they are engaged in, and vain shall be all that they do.'

اِنَّ هٰٓؤُلَآءِ مُتَبَّرٌ مَّا هُمْ فِيْهِ وَبٰطِلٌ مَّا كَانُوْا
يَعْمَلُوْنَ ﴿١٤٠﴾

141. He said, 'Shall I seek for you a god other than Allah, while He has exalted you above all peoples?'

قَالَ اَغَيْرَ اللّٰهِ اَبْغِيْكُمْ اِلٰهًا وَّهُوَ فَضَّلَكُمْ عَلَى
الْعٰلَمِيْنَ ﴿١٤١﴾

142. And *remember the time* when We delivered you from Pharaoh's people who afflicted you with grievous torment, slaughtering your sons and sparing your women. And therein was a great trial for you from your Lord.

وَاِذْ اَنْجَيْنٰكُمْ مِّنْ اٰلِ فِرْعَوْنَ يَسُوْمُوْنَكُمْ سُوْٓءَ
الْعَذَابِ ۚ يُقَتِّلُوْنَ اَبْنَآءَكُمْ وَيَسْتَحْيُوْنَ نِسَآءَكُمْ ۭ
وَفِيْ ذٰلِكُمْ بَلَآءٌ مِّنْ رَّبِّكُمْ عَظِيْمٌ ﴿١٤٢﴾

R. 17.

143. And We made Moses a promise of thirty nights and supplemented them with ten. Thus the period appointed by his Lord was completed—forty nights. And Moses said to his brother, Aaron, 'Act for me among my people in my absence, and manage *them* well, and follow not the way of those who cause disorder.'

وَوٰعَدْنَا مُوْسٰى ثَلٰثِيْنَ لَيْلَةً وَّاَتْمَمْنٰهَا بِعَشْرٍ
فَتَمَّ مِيْقَاتُ رَبِّهٖٓ اَرْبَعِيْنَ لَيْلَةً ۚ وَقَالَ مُوْسٰى
لِاَخِيْهِ هٰرُوْنَ اخْلُفْنِيْ فِيْ قَوْمِيْ وَاَصْلِحْ وَلَا تَتَّبِعْ
سَبِيْلَ الْمُفْسِدِيْنَ ﴿١٤٣﴾

144. And when Moses came at Our appointed time and his Lord spoke to him, he said, 'My Lord, show *Thyself* to me that I may look at Thee.' He replied, 'Thou shalt not see Me, but look at the mountain; if it remains in its place, then shalt thou see Me.' And when his Lord manifested Himself on the mountain, He broke it into pieces and Moses fell down unconscious. And when he recovered, he said, 'Holy art Thou, I turn towards Thee, and I am the first to believe.'

وَلَمَّا جَآءَ مُوْسٰى لِمِيْقَاتِنَا وَكَلَّمَهٗ رَبُّهٗ ۙ قَالَ رَبِّ
اَرِنِيْٓ اَنْظُرْ اِلَيْكَ ۭ قَالَ لَنْ تَرٰىنِيْ وَلٰكِنِ انْظُرْ
اِلَى الْجَبَلِ فَاِنِ اسْتَقَرَّ مَكَانَهٗ فَسَوْفَ تَرٰىنِيْ ۚ فَلَمَّا
تَجَلّٰى رَبُّهٗ لِلْجَبَلِ جَعَلَهٗ دَكًّا وَّخَرَّ مُوْسٰى صَعِقًا ۚ
فَلَمَّآ اَفَاقَ قَالَ سُبْحٰنَكَ تُبْتُ اِلَيْكَ وَاَنَا اَوَّلُ
الْمُؤْمِنِيْنَ ﴿١٤٤﴾

145. *God* said, 'O Moses, I have chosen thee above the people *of thy time* by My messages and by My word. So take hold of that which I have given thee and be of the grateful.'

قَالَ يٰمُوْسٰٓى اِنِّي اصْطَفَيْتُكَ عَلَى النَّاسِ بِرِسٰلٰتِيْ
وَبِكَلَامِيْ ۖ فَخُذْ مَآ اٰتَيْتُكَ وَكُنْ مِّنَ الشّٰكِرِيْنَ ﴿١٤٥﴾

146. And We wrote for him upon the tablets about everything—an admonition

وَكَتَبْنَا لَهٗ فِي الْاَلْوَاحِ مِنْ كُلِّ شَيْءٍ مَّوْعِظَةً وَّتَفْصِيْلًا

and an explanation of all things. 'So hold them fast and bid thy people follow the best thereof. Soon shall I show you the abode of the transgressors.'

147. I shall soon turn away from My Signs those who behave proudly in the land in an unjust manner; and even if they see all the Signs, they will not believe therein; and if they see the way of righteousness, they will not adopt it as *their* way; but if they see the way of error, they will adopt it as *their* way. That is because they treated Our Signs as lies and were heedless of them.

148. And those who disbelieve in Our Signs and the meeting of the Hereafter—their works are vain. Can they *expect to* be rewarded *for anything* except for what they do?

R. 18.

149. And the people of Moses made, in his absence, out of their ornaments a calf—a *lifeless* body producing a lowing sound. Did they not see that it spoke not to them, nor guided them to any way? They took it *for worship* and they were transgressors.

150. And when they were smitten with remorse and saw that they had indeed gone astray, they said, 'If our Lord do not have mercy on us and forgive us, we shall surely be among the losers.'

151. And when Moses returned to his people, indignant and grieved, he said, 'Evil is that which you did in my place in my absence. Did you hasten *to devise a way for yourselves without waiting for* the command of your Lord?' And he put down the tablets, and caught hold of his brother's head, dragging him towards himself. He (Aaron) said, 'Son of my mother, the people indeed deemed me weak, and were about to kill me. Therefore make not the enemies rejoice over me, and place me not with the unjust people.'

152. He (Moses) said, 'My Lord, forgive me and my brother, and admit us to Thy

لِكُلِّ شَيْءٍ ۚ فَخُذْهَا بِقُوَّةٍ وَّأْمُرْ قَوْمَكَ يَأْخُذُوا بِأَحْسَنِهَا ۚ
سَأُورِيكُمْ دَارَ الْفٰسِقِينَ ﴿١٤٦﴾
سَأَصْرِفُ عَنْ اٰيٰتِيَ الَّذِينَ يَتَكَبَّرُونَ فِي الْأَرْضِ
بِغَيْرِ الْحَقِّ ۖ وَإِنْ يَّرَوْا كُلَّ اٰيَةٍ لَّا يُؤْمِنُوا بِهَا ۚ وَإِنْ
يَّرَوْا سَبِيلَ الرُّشْدِ لَا يَتَّخِذُوهُ سَبِيلًا ۚ وَإِنْ يَّرَوْا
سَبِيلَ الْغَيِّ يَتَّخِذُوهُ سَبِيلًا ۚ ذٰلِكَ بِأَنَّهُمْ كَذَّبُوا
بِاٰيٰتِنَا وَكَانُوا عَنْهَا غٰفِلِينَ ﴿١٤٧﴾
وَالَّذِينَ كَذَّبُوا بِاٰيٰتِنَا وَلِقَاءِ الْاٰخِرَةِ حَبِطَتْ أَعْمَالُهُمْ ۚ
هَلْ يُجْزَوْنَ إِلَّا مَا كَانُوا يَعْمَلُونَ ﴿١٤٨﴾ ع
وَاتَّخَذَ قَوْمُ مُوسٰى مِنْ بَعْدِهٖ مِنْ حُلِيِّهِمْ عِجْلًا
جَسَدًا لَّهٗ خُوَارٌ ۚ أَلَمْ يَرَوْا أَنَّهٗ لَا يُكَلِّمُهُمْ وَلَا
يَهْدِيهِمْ سَبِيلًا ۘ اِتَّخَذُوهُ وَكَانُوا ظٰلِمِينَ ﴿١٤٩﴾
وَلَمَّا سُقِطَ فِي أَيْدِيهِمْ وَرَأَوْا أَنَّهُمْ قَدْ ضَلُّوا ۙ
قَالُوا لَئِنْ لَّمْ يَرْحَمْنَا رَبُّنَا وَيَغْفِرْ لَنَا لَنَكُونَنَّ مِنَ
الْخٰسِرِينَ ﴿١٥٠﴾
وَلَمَّا رَجَعَ مُوسٰى إِلٰى قَوْمِهٖ غَضْبَانَ أَسِفًا ۙ قَالَ
بِئْسَمَا خَلَفْتُمُونِي مِنْ بَعْدِي ۚ أَعَجِلْتُمْ أَمْرَ رَبِّكُمْ ۚ
وَأَلْقَى الْأَلْوَاحَ وَأَخَذَ بِرَأْسِ أَخِيهِ يَجُرُّهٗ إِلَيْهِ ۚ
قَالَ ابْنَ أُمَّ إِنَّ الْقَوْمَ اسْتَضْعَفُونِي وَكَادُوا
يَقْتُلُونَنِي ۖ فَلَا تُشْمِتْ بِيَ الْأَعْدَاءَ وَلَا تَجْعَلْنِي
مَعَ الْقَوْمِ الظّٰلِمِينَ ﴿١٥١﴾
قَالَ رَبِّ اغْفِرْ لِي وَلِأَخِي وَأَدْخِلْنَا فِي رَحْمَتِكَ ۖ

mercy, and Thou art the Most Merciful of those who show mercy.'

R. 19.

153. *As to* those who took the calf *for worship*, wrath from their Lord shall overtake them and abasement in the present life. And thus do We reward those who invent lies.

154. But those who did evil deeds and repented after that and believed, surely thy Lord is thereafter Most Forgiving, Merciful.

155. And when the anger of Moses was appeased, he took the tablets, and in their writing there was guidance and mercy for those who fear their Lord.

156. And Moses chose of his people seventy men for Our appointment. But when the earthquake overtook them, he said, 'My Lord, if Thou hadst pleased, Thou couldst have destroyed them before *this*, and me *also*. Wilt Thou destroy us for that which the foolish among us have done? This is nothing but a trial from Thee. Thou causest to perish thereby whom Thou pleasest and Thou guidest whom Thou pleasest. Thou art our Protector; forgive us then and have mercy on us, for Thou art the Best of those who forgive.

157. 'And ordain for us good in this world, as well as in the next; we have turned to Thee *with repentance*.' *God* replied, 'I will inflict My punishment on whom I will; but My mercy encompasses all things; so I will ordain it for those who act righteously, and pay the Zakāt and those who believe in Our Signs—

* 158. 'Those who follow the Messenger, the Prophet, the Immaculate one, whom they find mentioned in the Torah and the Gospel *which are* with them. He enjoins on them good and forbids them evil, and makes lawful for them the good things and forbids them the bad, and removes from them their burden and the shackles that were upon them. So those who shall believe in him, and honour and support

ع ١٨ ٨ وَ اَنْتَ اَرْحَمُ الرّٰحِمِيْنَ ﴿١٥٢﴾
اِنَّ الَّذِيْنَ اتَّخَذُوا الْعِجْلَ سَيَنَالُهُمْ غَضَبٌ مِّنْ رَّبِّهِمْ
وَ ذِلَّةٌ فِي الْحَيٰوةِ الدُّنْيَا ؕ وَ كَذٰلِكَ نَجْزِي الْمُفْتَرِيْنَ ﴿١٥٣﴾
وَ الَّذِيْنَ عَمِلُوا السَّيِّاٰتِ ثُمَّ تَابُوْا مِنْۢ بَعْدِهَا وَ
اٰمَنُوْۤا ۫ اِنَّ رَبَّكَ مِنْۢ بَعْدِهَا لَغَفُوْرٌ رَّحِيْمٌ ﴿١٥٤﴾
وَ لَمَّا سَكَتَ عَنْ مُّوْسَى الْغَضَبُ اَخَذَ الْاَلْوَاحَ ۚۖ وَ فِيْ
نُسْخَتِهَا هُدًى وَّ رَحْمَةٌ لِّلَّذِيْنَ هُمْ لِرَبِّهِمْ يَرْهَبُوْنَ ﴿١٥٥﴾
وَ اخْتَارَ مُوْسٰى قَوْمَهٗ سَبْعِيْنَ رَجُلًا لِّمِيْقَاتِنَا ۚ فَلَمَّاۤ
اَخَذَتْهُمُ الرَّجْفَةُ قَالَ رَبِّ لَوْ شِئْتَ اَهْلَكْتَهُمْ مِّنْ
قَبْلُ وَ اِيَّايَ ؕ اَتُهْلِكُنَا بِمَا فَعَلَ السُّفَهَآءُ مِنَّا ۚ
اِنْ هِيَ اِلَّا فِتْنَتُكَ ؕ تُضِلُّ بِهَا مَنْ تَشَآءُ وَ تَهْدِيْ
مَنْ تَشَآءُ ؕ اَنْتَ وَلِيُّنَا فَاغْفِرْ لَنَا وَ ارْحَمْنَا وَ اَنْتَ
خَيْرُ الْغٰفِرِيْنَ ﴿١٥٦﴾
وَ اكْتُبْ لَنَا فِيْ هٰذِهِ الدُّنْيَا حَسَنَةً وَّ فِي الْاٰخِرَةِ
اِنَّا هُدْنَاۤ اِلَيْكَ ؕ قَالَ عَذَابِيْۤ اُصِيْبُ بِهٖ مَنْ اَشَآءُ ۚ
وَ رَحْمَتِيْ وَسِعَتْ كُلَّ شَيْءٍ ؕ فَسَاَكْتُبُهَا لِلَّذِيْنَ يَتَّقُوْنَ
وَ يُؤْتُوْنَ الزَّكٰوةَ وَ الَّذِيْنَ هُمْ بِاٰيٰتِنَا يُؤْمِنُوْنَ ﴿١٥٧﴾ ۚ
اَلَّذِيْنَ يَتَّبِعُوْنَ الرَّسُوْلَ النَّبِيَّ الْاُمِّيَّ الَّذِيْ يَجِدُوْنَهٗ
مَكْتُوْبًا عِنْدَهُمْ فِي التَّوْرٰىةِ وَ الْاِنْجِيْلِ ۫ يَاْمُرُهُمْ
بِالْمَعْرُوْفِ وَ يَنْهٰهُمْ عَنِ الْمُنْكَرِ وَ يُحِلُّ لَهُمُ الطَّيِّبٰتِ
وَ يُحَرِّمُ عَلَيْهِمُ الْخَبٰٓئِثَ وَ يَضَعُ عَنْهُمْ اِصْرَهُمْ
وَ الْاَغْلٰلَ الَّتِيْ كَانَتْ عَلَيْهِمْ ؕ فَالَّذِيْنَ اٰمَنُوْا بِهٖ وَ

him, and help him, and follow the light that has been sent down with him—these shall prosper.'

عَزَّرُوْهُ وَنَصَرُوْهُ وَاتَّبَعُوا النُّوْرَ الَّذِيْٓ اُنْزِلَ مَعَهٗٓ
اُولٰٓئِكَ هُمُ الْمُفْلِحُوْنَ ﴿۱۵۸﴾

R. 20.

159. Say, 'O mankind! truly I am a Messenger to you all from Allah to Whom belongs the kingdom of the heavens and the earth. There is no God but He. He gives life, and He causes death. So believe in Allah and His Messenger, the Prophet, the Immaculate one, who believes in Allah and His words; and follow him that you may be rightly guided.'

قُلْ يٰٓاَيُّهَا النَّاسُ اِنِّيْ رَسُوْلُ اللّٰهِ اِلَيْكُمْ جَمِيْعَا ِالَّذِيْ
لَهٗ مُلْكُ السَّمٰوٰتِ وَالْاَرْضِ ۚ لَآ اِلٰهَ اِلَّا هُوَ يُحْيٖ وَ
يُمِيْتُ ۖ فَاٰمِنُوْا بِاللّٰهِ وَرَسُوْلِهِ النَّبِيِّ الْاُمِّيِّ الَّذِيْ
يُؤْمِنُ بِاللّٰهِ وَكَلِمٰتِهٖ وَاتَّبِعُوْهُ لَعَلَّكُمْ تَهْتَدُوْنَ ﴿۱۵۹﴾

* 160. And of the people of Moses there is a party that exhorts *people* to truth and does justice therewith.

وَمِنْ قَوْمِ مُوْسٰٓى اُمَّةٌ يَّهْدُوْنَ بِالْحَقِّ وَبِهٖ يَعْدِلُوْنَ ﴿۱۶۰﴾

161. And We divided them into twelve tribes, *distinct* peoples. And We revealed to Moses, when his people asked drink of him, *saying*, 'Strike the rock with thy rod;' and from it there gushed forth twelve springs; every tribe knew their drinking place. And We caused the clouds to overshadow them, and We sent down for them Manna and Salwā: 'Eat of the good things We have provided for you.' And they wronged Us not, but it was themselves that they wronged.

وَقَطَّعْنٰهُمُ اثْنَتَيْ عَشْرَةَ اَسْبَاطًا اُمَمًا ۚ وَاَوْحَيْنَآ
اِلٰى مُوْسٰٓى اِذِ اسْتَسْقٰىهُ قَوْمُهٗٓ اَنِ اضْرِبْ بِّعَصَاكَ
الْحَجَرَ ۚ فَانْۢبَجَسَتْ مِنْهُ اثْنَتَا عَشْرَةَ عَيْنًا ۭ قَدْ
عَلِمَ كُلُّ اُنَاسٍ مَّشْرَبَهُمْ ۭ وَظَلَّلْنَا عَلَيْهِمُ الْغَمَامَ
وَاَنْزَلْنَا عَلَيْهِمُ الْمَنَّ وَالسَّلْوٰى ۭ كُلُوْا مِنْ طَيِّبٰتِ مَا
رَزَقْنٰكُمْ ۭ وَمَا ظَلَمُوْنَا وَلٰكِنْ كَانُوْٓا اَنْفُسَهُمْ
يَظْلِمُوْنَ ﴿۱۶۱﴾

162. And when it was said to them, "Dwell in this town and eat therefrom wherever you will, and say, *'God!* lighten *our* burden,' and enter the gate in humility, We shall forgive you your sins, *and* surely We shall give increase to those who do good."

وَاِذْ قِيْلَ لَهُمُ اسْكُنُوْا هٰذِهِ الْقَرْيَةَ وَكُلُوْا مِنْهَا
حَيْثُ شِئْتُمْ وَقُوْلُوْا حِطَّةٌ وَّادْخُلُوا الْبَابَ سُجَّدًا
نَّغْفِرْ لَكُمْ خَطِيْٓـٰٔتِكُمْ ۭ سَنَزِيْدُ الْمُحْسِنِيْنَ ﴿۱۶۲﴾

163. But the transgressors among them changed *it* for a word other than that which was said to them. So We sent upon them a punishment from heaven, because of their wrongdoing.

فَبَدَّلَ الَّذِيْنَ ظَلَمُوْا مِنْهُمْ قَوْلًا غَيْرَ الَّذِيْ قِيْلَ
لَهُمْ فَاَرْسَلْنَا عَلَيْهِمْ رِجْزًا مِّنَ السَّمَاۗءِ بِمَا كَانُوْا
يَظْلِمُوْنَ ﴿۱۶۳﴾

R. 21.

164. And ask them concerning the town which stood by the sea. When they profaned the Sabbath; when their fish came to them on their Sabbath day

وَسْـَٔـلْهُمْ عَنِ الْقَرْيَةِ الَّتِيْ كَانَتْ حَاضِرَةَ الْبَحْرِ ۘ
اِذْ يَعْدُوْنَ فِي السَّبْتِ اِذْ تَاْتِيْهِمْ حِيْتَانُهُمْ يَوْمَ

appearing on the surface *of the water*, but on the day when they did not keep the Sabbath, they came not to them. Thus did We try them because they were rebellious.

سَبْتِهِمْ شُرَّعًا وَّيَوْمَ لَا يَسْبِتُوْنَ لَا تَاْتِيْهِمْ كَذٰلِكَ
نَبْلُوْهُمْ بِمَا كَانُوْا يَفْسُقُوْنَ ﴿١٦٤﴾ النصف

* 165. And when a party among them said, ‘Wherefore do you preach to a people whom Allah is going to destroy or punish with a severe punishment?’ They said, ‘As an excuse before your Lord, and that they may become righteous.’

وَاِذْ قَالَتْ اُمَّةٌ مِّنْهُمْ لِمَ تَعِظُوْنَ قَوْمًا ۙ اللّٰهُ
مُهْلِكُهُمْ اَوْ مُعَذِّبُهُمْ عَذَابًا شَدِيْدًا ؕ قَالُوْا
مَعْذِرَةً اِلٰى رَبِّكُمْ وَلَعَلَّهُمْ يَتَّقُوْنَ ﴿١٦٥﴾

* 166. And when they forgot all that with which they had been admonished, We saved those who forbade evil, and We seized the transgressors with a severe punishment because they were rebellious.

فَلَمَّا نَسُوْا مَا ذُكِّرُوْا بِهٖۤ اَنْجَيْنَا الَّذِيْنَ يَنْهَوْنَ عَنِ
السُّوْٓءِ وَاَخَذْنَا الَّذِيْنَ ظَلَمُوْا بِعَذَابٍۭ بَىِٕيْسٍۭ بِمَا
كَانُوْا يَفْسُقُوْنَ ﴿١٦٦﴾

167. And when they insolently rebelled against that which they had been forbidden, We said to them, ‘Be ye apes, despised!’

فَلَمَّا عَتَوْا عَنْ مَّا نُهُوْا عَنْهُ قُلْنَا لَهُمْ كُوْنُوْا قِرَدَةً
خٰسِـِٕيْنَ ﴿١٦٧﴾

168. And *remember the time* when thy Lord proclaimed that He would truly raise against them, till the Day of Resurrection, those who would afflict them with grievous torment. Surely, thy Lord is quick in retribution, and surely He is *also* Most Forgiving, Merciful.

وَاِذْ تَاَذَّنَ رَبُّكَ لَيَبْعَثَنَّ عَلَيْهِمْ اِلٰى يَوْمِ الْقِيٰمَةِ
مَنْ يَّسُوْمُهُمْ سُوْٓءَ الْعَذَابِ ؕ اِنَّ رَبَّكَ لَسَرِيْعُ
الْعِقَابِ ۖۚ وَاِنَّهٗ لَغَفُوْرٌ رَّحِيْمٌ ﴿١٦٨﴾

169. And We broke them up into *separate* peoples in the earth. Among them are those that are righteous and among them are those that are otherwise. And We tried them with good things and bad things that they might return.

وَقَطَّعْنٰهُمْ فِى الْاَرْضِ اُمَمًا ۚ مِنْهُمُ الصّٰلِحُوْنَ وَمِنْهُمْ
دُوْنَ ذٰلِكَ ۫ وَبَلَوْنٰهُمْ بِالْحَسَنٰتِ وَالسَّيِّاٰتِ لَعَلَّهُمْ
يَرْجِعُوْنَ ﴿١٦٩﴾

170. Then there has come an *evil* generation after them who inherited the Book. They take the paltry goods of this low *world* and say, ‘It will be forgiven us.’ But if there came to them similar goods *again*, they would take them. Was not the covenant of the Book taken from them, that they would not say of Allah *anything* but the truth? And they have studied what is therein. And the abode of the Hereafter is better for those who are righteous. Will you not then understand?

فَخَلَفَ مِنْۢ بَعْدِهِمْ خَلْفٌ وَّرِثُوا الْكِتٰبَ يَاْخُذُوْنَ
عَرَضَ هٰذَا الْاَدْنٰى وَيَقُوْلُوْنَ سَيُغْفَرُ لَنَا ۚ وَاِنْ
يَّاْتِهِمْ عَرَضٌ مِّثْلُهٗ يَاْخُذُوْهُ ؕ اَلَمْ يُؤْخَذْ عَلَيْهِمْ مِّيْثَاقُ
الْكِتٰبِ اَنْ لَّا يَقُوْلُوْا عَلَى اللّٰهِ اِلَّا الْحَقَّ وَدَرَسُوْا مَا
فِيْهِ ؕ وَالدَّارُ الْاٰخِرَةُ خَيْرٌ لِّلَّذِيْنَ يَتَّقُوْنَ ؕ اَفَلَا
تَعْقِلُوْنَ ﴿١٧٠﴾

171. And *as to* those who hold fast by the Book, and observe Prayer, surely We suffer not the reward of *such* righteous *people* to perish.

وَالَّذِيْنَ يُمَسِّكُوْنَ بِالْكِتٰبِ وَاَقَامُوا الصَّلٰوةَ ؕ اِنَّا لَا نُضِيْعُ اَجْرَ الْمُصْلِحِيْنَ ﴿۱۷۱﴾

* 172. And when We shook the mountain over them as though it were a covering, and they thought it was going to fall on them, *We said*, 'Hold fast that which We have given you, and remember what is therein that you may be saved.'

وَاِذْ نَتَقْنَا الْجَبَلَ فَوْقَهُمْ كَاَنَّهٗ ظُلَّةٌ وَّظَنُّوْٓا اَنَّهٗ وَاقِعٌۢ بِهِمْ ۚ خُذُوْا مَآ اٰتَيْنٰكُمْ بِقُوَّةٍ وَّاذْكُرُوْا مَا فِيْهِ لَعَلَّكُمْ تَتَّقُوْنَ ﴿۱۷۲﴾ ع

ع ۲۱ ۱۱

R. 22.

173. And when thy Lord brings forth from Adam's children—out of their loins—their offspring and makes them witnesses against their own selves *by saying:* 'Am I not your Lord?' they say, 'Yea, we do bear witness.' *This He does* lest you should say on the Day of Resurrection, 'We were surely unaware of this.'

وَاِذْ اَخَذَ رَبُّكَ مِنْۢ بَنِيْٓ اٰدَمَ مِنْ ظُهُوْرِهِمْ ذُرِّيَّتَهُمْ وَاَشْهَدَهُمْ عَلٰٓى اَنْفُسِهِمْ ۚ اَلَسْتُ بِرَبِّكُمْ ؕ قَالُوْا بَلٰى ۛۚ شَهِدْنَا ۛۚ اَنْ تَقُوْلُوْا يَوْمَ الْقِيٰمَةِ اِنَّا كُنَّا عَنْ هٰذَا غٰفِلِيْنَ ﴿۱۷۳﴾

174. Or *lest* you should say, 'It was only our fathers who attributed co-partners *to God* in the past and we were *merely* a generation after them. Wilt Thou then destroy us for what was done by those who lied?'

اَوْ تَقُوْلُوْٓا اِنَّمَآ اَشْرَكَ اٰبَآؤُنَا مِنْ قَبْلُ وَكُنَّا ذُرِّيَّةً مِّنْۢ بَعْدِهِمْ ۚ اَفَتُهْلِكُنَا بِمَا فَعَلَ الْمُبْطِلُوْنَ ﴿۱۷۴﴾

175. And thus do We make clear the Signs, *that they may be admonished* and that they may return *to Us*.

وَكَذٰلِكَ نُفَصِّلُ الْاٰيٰتِ وَلَعَلَّهُمْ يَرْجِعُوْنَ ﴿۱۷۵﴾

176. And relate to them the story of him to whom We gave Our Signs, but he stepped away from them; so Satan followed him up, and he became *one* of those who go astray.

وَاتْلُ عَلَيْهِمْ نَبَاَ الَّذِيْٓ اٰتَيْنٰهُ اٰيٰتِنَا فَانْسَلَخَ مِنْهَا فَاَتْبَعَهُ الشَّيْطٰنُ فَكَانَ مِنَ الْغٰوِيْنَ ﴿۱۷۶﴾

* 177. And if We had pleased, We could have exalted him thereby; but he inclined to the earth and followed his evil inclination. His case therefore is like the case of a *thirsty* dog; if thou drive him away, he hangs out his tongue; and if thou leave him, he hangs out his tongue. Such is the case of the people who disbelieve in Our Signs. So give *them* the description that they may ponder.

وَلَوْ شِئْنَا لَرَفَعْنٰهُ بِهَا وَلٰكِنَّهٗٓ اَخْلَدَ اِلَى الْاَرْضِ وَاتَّبَعَ هَوٰىهُ ۚ فَمَثَلُهٗ كَمَثَلِ الْكَلْبِ ۚ اِنْ تَحْمِلْ عَلَيْهِ يَلْهَثْ اَوْ تَتْرُكْهُ يَلْهَثْ ؕ ذٰلِكَ مَثَلُ الْقَوْمِ الَّذِيْنَ كَذَّبُوْا بِاٰيٰتِنَا ۚ فَاقْصُصِ الْقَصَصَ لَعَلَّهُمْ يَتَفَكَّرُوْنَ ﴿۱۷۷﴾

178. Evil is the case of the people who treat Our Signs as lies. And it was their own selves that they wronged.

سَآءَ مَثَلَا ۨالْقَوْمُ الَّذِيْنَ كَذَّبُوْا بِاٰيٰتِنَا وَاَنْفُسَهُمْ كَانُوْا يَظْلِمُوْنَ ﴿۱۷۸﴾

179. He whom Allah guides is on the right path. And they whom He adjudges astray, these it is who shall be the losers.

مَنْ يَّهْدِ اللّٰهُ فَهُوَ الْمُهْتَدِيْ ۚ وَمَنْ يُّضْلِلْ فَاُولٰٓئِكَ هُمُ الْخٰسِرُوْنَ ﴿۱۷۹﴾

180. Verily, We have created many of the Jinn and men whose end shall be Hell! They have hearts *but* they understand not therewith, and they have eyes *but* they see not therewith, and they have ears *but* they hear not therewith. They are like cattle; nay, they are *even* more astray. They are indeed *quite* heedless.

181. And to Allah *alone* belong *all* perfect attributes. So call on Him by these. And leave alone those who deviate from the right way with respect to His attributes. They shall be repaid for what they do.

182. And of those We have created there are a people that guide *men* with truth and do justice therewith.

R. 23.

183. And those who reject Our Signs, We will draw them *to destruction* step by step in a manner which they do not know.

184. And I give them the rein; surely, My plan is mighty.

185. Have they not considered *that* there is no insanity about their companion? He is only a plain Warner.

186. And have they not looked into the kingdom of the heavens and the earth, and all things that Allah has created? And *do they not see* that, maybe their *own* term has already drawn nigh? Then in what thing will they believe thereafter?

187. Whomsoever Allah adjudges astray, there can be no guide for him. And He leaves such in their transgression, wandering in distraction.

188. They ask thee respecting the Hour: 'When will it come to pass?' Say, 'The knowledge thereof is only with my Lord. None can manifest it at its time but He. It lies heavy on the heavens and the earth. It shall not come upon you but of a sudden.' They ask thee as if thou wert well acquainted therewith. Say, 'The knowledge thereof is only with Allah; but most men do not know.'

وَلَقَدْ ذَرَأْنَا لِجَهَنَّمَ كَثِيرًا مِّنَ الْجِنِّ وَالْإِنْسِ ۖ
لَهُمْ قُلُوبٌ لَّا يَفْقَهُونَ بِهَا وَلَهُمْ أَعْيُنٌ لَّا يُبْصِرُونَ
بِهَا وَلَهُمْ آذَانٌ لَّا يَسْمَعُونَ بِهَا ۚ أُولَٰئِكَ كَالْأَنْعَامِ
بَلْ هُمْ أَضَلُّ ۚ أُولَٰئِكَ هُمُ الْغَافِلُونَ ﴿١٨٠﴾
وَلِلَّهِ الْأَسْمَاءُ الْحُسْنَىٰ فَادْعُوهُ بِهَا ۖ وَذَرُوا الَّذِينَ
يُلْحِدُونَ فِي أَسْمَائِهِ ۚ سَيُجْزَوْنَ مَا كَانُوا يَعْمَلُونَ ﴿١٨١﴾
وَمِمَّنْ خَلَقْنَا أُمَّةٌ يَهْدُونَ بِالْحَقِّ وَبِهِ يَعْدِلُونَ ﴿١٨٢﴾ ع ٢٣
وَالَّذِينَ كَذَّبُوا بِآيَاتِنَا سَنَسْتَدْرِجُهُمْ مِّنْ حَيْثُ لَا
يَعْلَمُونَ ﴿١٨٣﴾
وَأُمْلِي لَهُمْ ۚ إِنَّ كَيْدِي مَتِينٌ ﴿١٨٤﴾
أَوَلَمْ يَتَفَكَّرُوا ۗ مَا بِصَاحِبِهِمْ مِّنْ جِنَّةٍ ۚ إِنْ هُوَ إِلَّا
نَذِيرٌ مُّبِينٌ ﴿١٨٥﴾
أَوَلَمْ يَنْظُرُوا فِي مَلَكُوتِ السَّمَاوَاتِ وَالْأَرْضِ وَمَا
خَلَقَ اللَّهُ مِنْ شَيْءٍ وَأَنْ عَسَىٰ أَنْ يَكُونَ قَدِ اقْتَرَبَ
أَجَلُهُمْ ۖ فَبِأَيِّ حَدِيثٍ بَعْدَهُ يُؤْمِنُونَ ﴿١٨٦﴾
مَنْ يُضْلِلِ اللَّهُ فَلَا هَادِيَ لَهُ ۚ وَيَذَرُهُمْ فِي طُغْيَانِهِمْ
يَعْمَهُونَ ﴿١٨٧﴾
يَسْأَلُونَكَ عَنِ السَّاعَةِ أَيَّانَ مُرْسَاهَا ۖ قُلْ إِنَّمَا عِلْمُهَا
عِنْدَ رَبِّي ۖ لَا يُجَلِّيهَا لِوَقْتِهَا إِلَّا هُوَ ۚ ثَقُلَتْ فِي
السَّمَاوَاتِ وَالْأَرْضِ ۚ لَا تَأْتِيكُمْ إِلَّا بَغْتَةً ۗ يَسْأَلُونَكَ
كَأَنَّكَ حَفِيٌّ عَنْهَا ۖ قُلْ إِنَّمَا عِلْمُهَا عِنْدَ اللَّهِ وَلَٰكِنَّ
أَكْثَرَ النَّاسِ لَا يَعْلَمُونَ ﴿١٨٨﴾

189. Say, 'I have no power to do good or harm to myself, save as Allah please. And if I had knowledge of the unseen, I should have secured abundance of good; and evil would not have touched me. I am only a warner and a bearer of good tidings to a people who believe.'

قُلْ لَّآ اَمْلِكُ لِنَفْسِيْ نَفْعًا وَّلَا ضَرًّا اِلَّا مَا شَآءَ اللّٰهُ ۭ
وَلَوْ كُنْتُ اَعْلَمُ الْغَيْبَ لَاسْتَكْثَرْتُ مِنَ الْخَيْرِ ۚۖ
وَمَا مَسَّنِيَ السُّوْٓءُ ۚ اِنْ اَنَا اِلَّا نَذِيْرٌ وَّبَشِيْرٌ لِّقَوْمٍ
يُّؤْمِنُوْنَ ﴿١٨٩﴾ ع ٢٣ ١٣

R. 24.

* 190. He it is Who has created you from a single soul, and made therefrom its mate, that he might find comfort in her. And when he knows her, she bears a light burden, and goes about with it. And when she grows heavy, they both pray to Allah, their Lord, *saying:* 'If Thou give us a good *child,* we will surely be of the thankful.'

هُوَ الَّذِيْ خَلَقَكُمْ مِّنْ نَّفْسٍ وَّاحِدَةٍ وَّجَعَلَ مِنْهَا
زَوْجَهَا لِيَسْكُنَ اِلَيْهَا ۚ فَلَمَّا تَغَشّٰىهَا حَمَلَتْ حَمْلًا
خَفِيْفًا فَمَرَّتْ بِهٖ ۚ فَلَمَّآ اَثْقَلَتْ دَّعَوَا اللّٰهَ رَبَّهُمَا
لَئِنْ اٰتَيْتَنَا صَالِحًا لَّنَكُوْنَنَّ مِنَ الشّٰكِرِيْنَ ﴿١٩٠﴾

191. But when He gives them a good *child,* they attribute to Him partners in respect of that which He has given them. But exalted is Allah above what they associate *with Him.*

فَلَمَّآ اٰتٰىهُمَا صَالِحًا جَعَلَا لَهٗ شُرَكَآءَ فِيْمَآ اٰتٰىهُمَا ۚ
فَتَعٰلَى اللّٰهُ عَمَّا يُشْرِكُوْنَ ﴿١٩١﴾

192. Do they associate *with Him* as partners those who create nothing, and are themselves created?

اَيُشْرِكُوْنَ مَا لَا يَخْلُقُ شَيْئًا وَّهُمْ يُخْلَقُوْنَ ﴿١٩٢﴾ۡۖ

193. And they can give them no help, nor can they help themselves.

وَلَا يَسْتَطِيْعُوْنَ لَهُمْ نَصْرًا وَّلَآ اَنْفُسَهُمْ يَنْصُرُوْنَ ﴿١٩٣﴾

194. And if you call them to guidance, they will not follow you. It is the same to you whether you call them or you remain silent.

وَاِنْ تَدْعُوْهُمْ اِلَى الْهُدٰى لَا يَتَّبِعُوْكُمْ ۭ سَوَآءٌ عَلَيْكُمْ
اَدَعَوْتُمُوْهُمْ اَمْ اَنْتُمْ صَامِتُوْنَ ﴿١٩٤﴾

195. Surely, those whom you call on beside Allah are *mere* servants like you. Then call on them and let them answer you, if you are truthful.

اِنَّ الَّذِيْنَ تَدْعُوْنَ مِنْ دُوْنِ اللّٰهِ عِبَادٌ اَمْثَالُكُمْ
فَادْعُوْهُمْ فَلْيَسْتَجِيْبُوْا لَكُمْ اِنْ كُنْتُمْ صٰدِقِيْنَ ﴿١٩٥﴾

196. Have they feet wherewith they walk, or have they hands wherewith they hold, or have they eyes wherewith they see, or have they ears wherewith they hear? Say, 'Call upon the partners you associate *with God,* then contrive *ye all* against me, and give me no time.

اَلَهُمْ اَرْجُلٌ يَّمْشُوْنَ بِهَآ ۡ اَمْ لَهُمْ اَيْدٍ يَّبْطِشُوْنَ بِهَآ ۡ
اَمْ لَهُمْ اَعْيُنٌ يُّبْصِرُوْنَ بِهَآ ۡ اَمْ لَهُمْ اٰذَانٌ يَّسْمَعُوْنَ
بِهَا ۭ قُلِ ادْعُوْا شُرَكَآءَكُمْ ثُمَّ كِيْدُوْنِ فَلَا تُنْظِرُوْنِ ﴿١٩٦﴾

197. 'Truly, my protector is Allah Who revealed the Book. And He protects the righteous.

اِنَّ وَلِيِّ َۦ اللّٰهُ الَّذِيْ نَزَّلَ الْكِتٰبَ ڮ وَهُوَ يَتَوَلَّى
الصّٰلِحِيْنَ ﴿١٩٧﴾

198. 'And they whom you call on beside Him have no power to help you, nor can

وَالَّذِيْنَ تَدْعُوْنَ مِنْ دُوْنِهٖ لَا يَسْتَطِيْعُوْنَ نَصْرَكُمْ

they help themselves.'

وَلَآ أَنْفُسَهُمْ يَنْصُرُونَ ﴿١٩٨﴾

199. And if you invite them to guidance, they hear not. And thou seest them looking towards thee, but they see not.

وَإِنْ تَدْعُوهُمْ إِلَى الْهُدٰى لَا يَسْمَعُوا ۖ وَتَرٰىهُمْ
يَنْظُرُونَ إِلَيْكَ وَهُمْ لَا يُبْصِرُونَ ﴿١٩٩﴾

200. Take to forgiveness, and enjoin kindness, and turn away from the ignorant.

خُذِ الْعَفْوَ وَأْمُرْ بِالْعُرْفِ وَأَعْرِضْ عَنِ الْجٰهِلِيْنَ ﴿٢٠٠﴾

201. And if an evil suggestion from Satan incite thee, then seek refuge in Allah; surely, He is All-Hearing, All-Knowing.

وَإِمَّا يَنْزَغَنَّكَ مِنَ الشَّيْطٰنِ نَزْغٌ فَاسْتَعِذْ بِاللّٰهِ ۚ
إِنَّهٗ سَمِيْعٌ عَلِيْمٌ ﴿٢٠١﴾

202. *As to* those who are righteous, when a suggestion from Satan assails them, they remember *God:* and behold! they begin to see *things rightly*.

إِنَّ الَّذِيْنَ اتَّقَوْا إِذَا مَسَّهُمْ طَيْفٌ مِّنَ الشَّيْطٰنِ
تَذَكَّرُوْا فَإِذَا هُمْ مُّبْصِرُوْنَ ﴿٢٠٢﴾

203. And their brethren make them continue in error, and then they relax not.

وَإِخْوَانُهُمْ يَمُدُّوْنَهُمْ فِي الْغَيِّ ثُمَّ لَا يُقْصِرُوْنَ ﴿٢٠٣﴾

* 204. And when thou bringest not to them a Sign, they say, 'Wherefore dost thou not forge it?' Say, 'I follow only that which is revealed to me from my Lord. These are evidences from your Lord, and guidance and mercy for a people that believe.'

وَإِذَا لَمْ تَأْتِهِمْ بِاٰيَةٍ قَالُوْا لَوْلَا اجْتَبَيْتَهَا ۚ قُلْ إِنَّمَآ
أَتَّبِعُ مَا يُوْحٰٓى إِلَيَّ مِنْ رَّبِّيْ ۚ هٰذَا بَصَآئِرُ مِنْ رَّبِّكُمْ
وَهُدًى وَّرَحْمَةٌ لِّقَوْمٍ يُّؤْمِنُوْنَ ﴿٢٠٤﴾

205. And when the Qur'ān is recited, give ear to it and keep silence, that you may be shown mercy.

وَإِذَا قُرِئَ الْقُرْاٰنُ فَاسْتَمِعُوْا لَهٗ وَأَنْصِتُوْا لَعَلَّكُمْ
تُرْحَمُوْنَ ﴿٢٠٥﴾

206. And remember thy Lord in thy mind with humility and fear, and without loudness of speech, in the mornings and evenings; and be not of the neglectful.

وَاذْكُرْ رَّبَّكَ فِيْ نَفْسِكَ تَضَرُّعًا وَّخِيْفَةً وَّدُوْنَ الْجَهْرِ
مِنَ الْقَوْلِ بِالْغُدُوِّ وَالْاٰصَالِ وَلَا تَكُنْ مِّنَ الْغٰفِلِيْنَ ﴿٢٠٦﴾

207. Truly, those who are near to thy Lord, turn not away with pride from His worship, but they glorify Him and prostrate themselves before Him.

إِنَّ الَّذِيْنَ عِنْدَ رَبِّكَ لَا يَسْتَكْبِرُوْنَ عَنْ عِبَادَتِهٖ
وَيُسَبِّحُوْنَهٗ وَلَهٗ يَسْجُدُوْنَ ۩ ﴿٢٠٧﴾

سُوْرَةُ الْاَنْفَالِ مَدَنِيَّةٌ

اٰيَاتُهَا (٨) رُكُوْعَاتُهَا

AL-ANFĀL

(Revealed after Hijra)

1. In the name of Allah, the Gracious, the Merciful.

2. They ask thee concerning the spoils *of war*. Say, 'The spoils belong to Allah and the Messenger. So fear Allah, and set things right among yourselves, and obey Allah and His Messenger, if you are believers.'

3. *True* believers are only those whose hearts tremble when *the name of* Allah is mentioned, and when His Signs are recited to them they increase their faith, and who put their trust in their Lord,

4. Who observe Prayer and spend out of that which We have provided for them.

5. These it is who are true believers. They have grades *of rank* with their Lord, as well as forgiveness and an honourable provision.

6. As *it was* thy Lord *Who* rightfully brought thee forth from thy house, while a party of the believers were averse, *therefore He helped thee against thy enemy*.

7. They dispute with thee concerning the truth after it has become manifest, as though they are being driven to death while they actually see *it*.

8. And *remember the time* when Allah promised you one of the two parties * that it should be yours, and you wished that the one without sting should be yours, but Allah desired to establish the truth by His words and to cut off the root of the disbelievers,

9. That He might establish the truth and bring to naught that which is false, although the guilty might dislike it.

10. When you implored the assistance of your Lord, and He answered you,

بِسْمِ اللّٰهِ الرَّحْمٰنِ الرَّحِيْمِ (1)

يَسْـَٔلُوْنَكَ عَنِ الْاَنْفَالِ ؕ قُلِ الْاَنْفَالُ لِلّٰهِ وَالرَّسُوْلِ ۚ

فَاتَّقُوا اللّٰهَ وَاَصْلِحُوْا ذَاتَ بَيْنِكُمْ ۪ وَاَطِيْعُوا اللّٰهَ وَ

رَسُوْلَهٗۤ اِنْ كُنْتُمْ مُّؤْمِنِيْنَ (2)

اِنَّمَا الْمُؤْمِنُوْنَ الَّذِيْنَ اِذَا ذُكِرَ اللّٰهُ وَجِلَتْ قُلُوْبُهُمْ

وَاِذَا تُلِيَتْ عَلَيْهِمْ اٰيٰتُهٗ زَادَتْهُمْ اِيْمَانًا وَّعَلٰى

رَبِّهِمْ يَتَوَكَّلُوْنَ (3)

الَّذِيْنَ يُقِيْمُوْنَ الصَّلٰوةَ وَمِمَّا رَزَقْنٰهُمْ يُنْفِقُوْنَ (4) ؕ

اُولٰٓئِكَ هُمُ الْمُؤْمِنُوْنَ حَقًّا ؕ لَهُمْ دَرَجٰتٌ عِنْدَ رَبِّهِمْ

وَمَغْفِرَةٌ وَّرِزْقٌ كَرِيْمٌ (5)

كَمَآ اَخْرَجَكَ رَبُّكَ مِنْۢ بَيْتِكَ بِالْحَقِّ ۪ وَاِنَّ فَرِيْقًا

مِّنَ الْمُؤْمِنِيْنَ لَكٰرِهُوْنَ (6)

يُجَادِلُوْنَكَ فِي الْحَقِّ بَعْدَ مَا تَبَيَّنَ كَاَنَّمَا يُسَاقُوْنَ

اِلَى الْمَوْتِ وَهُمْ يَنْظُرُوْنَ (7)

وَاِذْ يَعِدُكُمُ اللّٰهُ اِحْدَى الطَّآئِفَتَيْنِ اَنَّهَا لَكُمْ وَ

تَوَدُّوْنَ اَنَّ غَيْرَ ذَاتِ الشَّوْكَةِ تَكُوْنُ لَكُمْ وَيُرِيْدُ

اللّٰهُ اَنْ يُّحِقَّ الْحَقَّ بِكَلِمٰتِهٖ وَيَقْطَعَ دَابِرَ الْكٰفِرِيْنَ (8)

لِيُحِقَّ الْحَقَّ وَيُبْطِلَ الْبَاطِلَ وَلَوْ كَرِهَ الْمُجْرِمُوْنَ (9)

اِذْ تَسْتَغِيْثُوْنَ رَبَّكُمْ فَاسْتَجَابَ لَكُمْ اَنِّيْ مُمِدُّكُمْ

---

* i.e. The well-equipped Meccan army and the caravan which, only lightly armed, was proceeding to Mecca from the north.

saying, 'I will assist you with a thousand of the angels, following one another.'

11. And Allah made it only as glad tidings, and that your hearts might thereby be set at rest. But help comes from Allah alone; surely, Allah is Mighty, Wise.

R. 2.

12. When He caused sleep to come upon you as a *sign of* security from Him, and He sent down water upon you from the clouds, that thereby He might purify you, and remove from you the filth of Satan, and that He might strengthen your hearts and make *your* steps firm therewith.

13. When thy Lord revealed to the angels, *saying*, 'I am with you; so give firmness to those who believe. I will cast terror into the hearts of those who disbelieve. Smite, then, the upper parts of *their* necks, and smite off all finger-tips.'

14. That is because they have opposed Allah and His Messenger. And whoso opposes Allah and His Messenger, then Allah is surely severe in retribution.

15. That *is your punishment*, taste it then; and *know* that for disbelievers there is the punishment of the Fire.

16. O ye who believe! when you meet those who disbelieve, advancing in force, turn not *your* backs to them.

17. And whoso turns his back to them on such a day, unless manoeuvring for battle or turning to *join another* company, he indeed draws upon himself the wrath of Allah, and Hell shall be his abode. And an evil resort it is.

* 18. So you killed them not, but it was Allah Who killed them. And thou threwest not when thou didst throw, but it was Allah Who threw, *that He might overthrow the disbelievers* and that He might confer on the believers a great favour from Himself. Surely, Allah is All-Hearing, All-Knowing.

19. That *is what happened*; and *know* that Allah is He Who weakens the design of the disbelievers.

20. If you sought a judgment, then judgment has indeed come to you. And if you desist, it will be better for you; but

بِأَلْفٍ مِّنَ الْمَلٰٓئِكَةِ مُرْدِفِيْنَ ﴿١٠﴾
وَمَا جَعَلَهُ اللّٰهُ اِلَّا بُشْرٰى وَلِتَطْمَئِنَّ بِهٖ قُلُوْبُكُمْ ۚ
وَمَا النَّصْرُ اِلَّا مِنْ عِنْدِ اللّٰهِ ۭ اِنَّ اللّٰهَ عَزِيْزٌ حَكِيْمٌ ﴿١١﴾ ع ١٥
اِذْ يُغَشِّيْكُمُ النُّعَاسَ اَمَنَةً مِّنْهُ وَيُنَزِّلُ عَلَيْكُمْ مِّنَ
السَّمَآءِ مَآءً لِّيُطَهِّرَكُمْ بِهٖ وَيُذْهِبَ عَنْكُمْ رِجْزَ الشَّيْطٰنِ
وَلِيَرْبِطَ عَلٰى قُلُوْبِكُمْ وَيُثَبِّتَ بِهِ الْاَقْدَامَ ﴿١٢﴾ ۭ
اِذْ يُوْحِيْ رَبُّكَ اِلَى الْمَلٰٓئِكَةِ اَنِّيْ مَعَكُمْ فَثَبِّتُوا الَّذِيْنَ
اٰمَنُوْا ۭ سَاُلْقِيْ فِيْ قُلُوْبِ الَّذِيْنَ كَفَرُوا الرُّعْبَ فَاضْرِبُوْا
فَوْقَ الْاَعْنَاقِ وَاضْرِبُوْا مِنْهُمْ كُلَّ بَنَانٍ ﴿١٣﴾
ذٰلِكَ بِاَنَّهُمْ شَآقُّوا اللّٰهَ وَرَسُوْلَهٗ ۚ وَمَنْ يُّشَاقِقِ
اللّٰهَ وَرَسُوْلَهٗ فَاِنَّ اللّٰهَ شَدِيْدُ الْعِقَابِ ﴿١٤﴾
ذٰلِكُمْ فَذُوْقُوْهُ وَاَنَّ لِلْكٰفِرِيْنَ عَذَابَ النَّارِ ﴿١٥﴾
يٰٓاَيُّهَا الَّذِيْنَ اٰمَنُوْٓا اِذَا لَقِيْتُمُ الَّذِيْنَ كَفَرُوْا زَحْفًا
فَلَا تُوَلُّوْهُمُ الْاَدْبَارَ ﴿١٦﴾ ۚ
وَمَنْ يُّوَلِّهِمْ يَوْمَئِذٍ دُبُرَهٗٓ اِلَّا مُتَحَرِّفًا لِّقِتَالٍ اَوْ
مُتَحَيِّزًا اِلٰى فِئَةٍ فَقَدْ بَآءَ بِغَضَبٍ مِّنَ اللّٰهِ وَمَاْوٰىهُ
جَهَنَّمُ ۭ وَبِئْسَ الْمَصِيْرُ ﴿١٧﴾
فَلَمْ تَقْتُلُوْهُمْ وَلٰكِنَّ اللّٰهَ قَتَلَهُمْ ۠ وَمَا رَمَيْتَ اِذْ
رَمَيْتَ وَلٰكِنَّ اللّٰهَ رَمٰى ۚ وَلِيُبْلِيَ الْمُؤْمِنِيْنَ مِنْهُ
بَلَآءً حَسَنًا ۭ اِنَّ اللّٰهَ سَمِيْعٌ عَلِيْمٌ ﴿١٨﴾
ذٰلِكُمْ وَاَنَّ اللّٰهَ مُوْهِنُ كَيْدِ الْكٰفِرِيْنَ ﴿١٩﴾
اِنْ تَسْتَفْتِحُوْا فَقَدْ جَآءَكُمُ الْفَتْحُ ۚ وَاِنْ تَنْتَهُوْا فَهُوَ

if you return *to hostility*, We *too* will return. And your party shall be of no avail at all to you, however numerous it be, and *know* that Allah is with the believers.

خَيْرٌ لَّكُمْ ۚ وَإِن تَعُودُوا نَعُدْ ۚ وَلَن تُغْنِيَ عَنكُمْ فِئَتُكُمْ
شَيْئًا وَلَوْ كَثُرَتْ ۙ وَأَنَّ اللَّهَ مَعَ الْمُؤْمِنِينَ ﴿٢٠﴾

R. 3.

21. O ye who believe! obey Allah and His Messenger, and do not turn away from him while you hear *him speak*.

يَا أَيُّهَا الَّذِينَ آمَنُوا أَطِيعُوا اللَّهَ وَرَسُولَهُ وَلَا تَوَلَّوْا
عَنْهُ وَأَنتُمْ تَسْمَعُونَ ﴿٢١﴾

22. And be not like those who say, 'We hear,' but they hear not.

وَلَا تَكُونُوا كَالَّذِينَ قَالُوا سَمِعْنَا وَهُمْ لَا يَسْمَعُونَ ﴿٢٢﴾

23. Surely, the worst of beasts in the sight of Allah are the deaf *and* the dumb, who have no sense.

إِنَّ شَرَّ الدَّوَابِّ عِندَ اللَّهِ الصُّمُّ الْبُكْمُ الَّذِينَ
لَا يَعْقِلُونَ ﴿٢٣﴾

24. And if Allah had known any good in them, He would certainly have made them hear. And if He *now* makes them hear, they will turn away, in aversion.

وَلَوْ عَلِمَ اللَّهُ فِيهِمْ خَيْرًا لَّأَسْمَعَهُمْ ۖ وَلَوْ أَسْمَعَهُمْ
لَتَوَلَّوا وَّهُم مُّعْرِضُونَ ﴿٢٤﴾

25. O ye who believe! respond to Allah, and the Messenger when he calls you that he may give you life, and know that Allah comes in between a man and his heart, and that He it is unto Whom you shall be gathered.

يَا أَيُّهَا الَّذِينَ آمَنُوا اسْتَجِيبُوا لِلَّهِ وَلِلرَّسُولِ إِذَا
دَعَاكُمْ لِمَا يُحْيِيكُمْ ۖ وَاعْلَمُوا أَنَّ اللَّهَ يَحُولُ بَيْنَ
الْمَرْءِ وَقَلْبِهِ وَأَنَّهُ إِلَيْهِ تُحْشَرُونَ ﴿٢٥﴾

26. And beware of an affliction which will not smite exclusively those among you who have done wrong. And know that Allah is severe in requiting.

وَاتَّقُوا فِتْنَةً لَّا تُصِيبَنَّ الَّذِينَ ظَلَمُوا مِنكُمْ
خَاصَّةً ۖ وَاعْلَمُوا أَنَّ اللَّهَ شَدِيدُ الْعِقَابِ ﴿٢٦﴾

27. And remember *the time* when you were few *and* deemed weak in the land, *and* were in fear lest people should snatch you away, but He sheltered you and strengthened you with His help, and provided you with good things that you might be thankful.

وَاذْكُرُوا إِذْ أَنتُمْ قَلِيلٌ مُّسْتَضْعَفُونَ فِي الْأَرْضِ
تَخَافُونَ أَن يَتَخَطَّفَكُمُ النَّاسُ فَآوَاكُمْ وَأَيَّدَكُم
بِنَصْرِهِ وَرَزَقَكُم مِّنَ الطَّيِّبَاتِ لَعَلَّكُمْ تَشْكُرُونَ ﴿٢٧﴾

∴ 28. O ye who believe! prove not false to Allah and the Messenger, nor prove false to your trusts knowingly.

يَا أَيُّهَا الَّذِينَ آمَنُوا لَا تَخُونُوا اللَّهَ وَالرَّسُولَ وَتَخُونُوا
أَمَانَاتِكُمْ وَأَنتُمْ تَعْلَمُونَ ﴿٢٨﴾

29. And know that your possessions and your children are but a trial and that it is Allah with Whom is a great reward.

وَاعْلَمُوا أَنَّمَا أَمْوَالُكُمْ وَأَوْلَادُكُمْ فِتْنَةٌ ۙ وَأَنَّ
اللَّهَ عِندَهُ أَجْرٌ عَظِيمٌ ﴿٢٩﴾

R. 4.

30. O ye who believe! if you fear Allah, He will grant you a distinction and will

يَا أَيُّهَا الَّذِينَ آمَنُوا إِن تَتَّقُوا اللَّهَ يَجْعَل لَّكُمْ

remove your evils from you and will forgive you; and Allah is *Lord* of great bounty.

فُرْقَانًا وَّيُكَفِّرْ عَنْكُمْ سَيِّاٰتِكُمْ وَيَغْفِرْ لَكُمْ ۗ وَاللّٰهُ
ذُو الْفَضْلِ الْعَظِيْمِ ﴿٣٠﴾

31. And *remember the time* when the disbelievers plotted against thee that they might imprison thee or kill thee or expel thee. And they planned and Allah *also* planned, and Allah is the Best of planners.

وَاِذْ يَمْكُرُ بِكَ الَّذِيْنَ كَفَرُوْا لِيُثْبِتُوْكَ اَوْ يَقْتُلُوْكَ اَوْ
يُخْرِجُوْكَ ۗ وَيَمْكُرُوْنَ وَيَمْكُرُ اللّٰهُ ۗ وَاللّٰهُ خَيْرُ
الْمٰكِرِيْنَ ﴿٣١﴾

32. And when Our verses are recited to them, they say, 'We have heard. If we wished we could certainly utter the like of this. This is nothing but *mere* tales of the ancients.'

وَاِذَا تُتْلٰى عَلَيْهِمْ اٰيٰتُنَا قَالُوْا قَدْ سَمِعْنَا لَوْ نَشَآءُ
لَقُلْنَا مِثْلَ هٰذَآ ۙ اِنْ هٰذَآ اِلَّآ اَسَاطِيْرُ الْاَوَّلِيْنَ ﴿٣٢﴾

33. And *remember the time* when they said, 'O Allah, if this be indeed the truth from Thee, then rain down upon us stones from heaven or bring down upon us a grievous punishment.'

وَاِذْ قَالُوا اللّٰهُمَّ اِنْ كَانَ هٰذَا هُوَ الْحَقَّ مِنْ عِنْدِكَ
فَاَمْطِرْ عَلَيْنَا حِجَارَةً مِّنَ السَّمَآءِ اَوِ ائْتِنَا بِعَذَابٍ
اَلِيْمٍ ﴿٣٣﴾

34. But Allah would not punish them while thou wast among them, and Allah would not punish them while they sought forgiveness.

وَمَا كَانَ اللّٰهُ لِيُعَذِّبَهُمْ وَاَنْتَ فِيْهِمْ ۗ وَمَا كَانَ
اللّٰهُ مُعَذِّبَهُمْ وَهُمْ يَسْتَغْفِرُوْنَ ﴿٣٤﴾

35. And what excuse have they *now* that Allah should not punish them, when they hinder *men* from the Sacred Mosque, and they are not its *true* guardians? Its *true* guardians are only those who are righteous, but most of them know not.

وَمَا لَهُمْ اَلَّا يُعَذِّبَهُمُ اللّٰهُ وَهُمْ يَصُدُّوْنَ عَنِ
الْمَسْجِدِ الْحَرَامِ وَمَا كَانُوْٓا اَوْلِيَآءَهٗ ۗ اِنْ اَوْلِيَآؤُهٗ
اِلَّا الْمُتَّقُوْنَ وَلٰكِنَّ اَكْثَرَهُمْ لَا يَعْلَمُوْنَ ﴿٣٥﴾

36. And their prayer at the House is nothing but whistling and clapping of hands. 'Taste then the punishment because you disbelieved.'

وَمَا كَانَ صَلَاتُهُمْ عِنْدَ الْبَيْتِ اِلَّا مُكَآءً وَّتَصْدِيَةً ۗ
فَذُوْقُوا الْعَذَابَ بِمَا كُنْتُمْ تَكْفُرُوْنَ ﴿٣٦﴾

* 37. Surely, those who disbelieve spend their wealth to turn *men* away from the way of Allah. They will surely continue to spend it; *but* then shall it become a *source of* regret for them, *and* then shall they be overcome. And the disbelievers shall be gathered unto Hell;

اِنَّ الَّذِيْنَ كَفَرُوْا يُنْفِقُوْنَ اَمْوَالَهُمْ لِيَصُدُّوْا عَنْ
سَبِيْلِ اللّٰهِ ۗ فَسَيُنْفِقُوْنَهَا ثُمَّ تَكُوْنُ عَلَيْهِمْ حَسْرَةً
ثُمَّ يُغْلَبُوْنَ ۗ وَالَّذِيْنَ كَفَرُوْٓا اِلٰى جَهَنَّمَ يُحْشَرُوْنَ ﴿٣٧﴾

38. That Allah may separate the bad from the good, and put the bad, one upon another, and heap them up all together,

لِيَمِيْزَ اللّٰهُ الْخَبِيْثَ مِنَ الطَّيِّبِ وَيَجْعَلَ الْخَبِيْثَ
بَعْضَهٗ عَلٰى بَعْضٍ فَيَرْكُمَهٗ جَمِيْعًا فَيَجْعَلَهٗ فِيْ جَهَنَّمَ

and then cast them into Hell. These indeed are the losers.

R. 5.

39. Say to those who disbelieve, if they desist, that which is past will be forgiven them; and if they return *thereto*, then verily, the example of the former peoples has already gone *before them.*

40. And fight them until there is no persecution and religion is wholly for Allah. But if they desist, then surely Allah is Watchful of what they do.

41. And if they turn their backs, then know that Allah is your Protector. What an excellent Protector and what an excellent Helper!

42. And know that whatever you take as spoils *in war*, a fifth thereof shall go to Allah and to the Messenger and to the kindred and orphans and the needy and the wayfarer, if you believe in Allah and in what We sent down to Our servant on the Day of Distinction*—the day when the two armies met—and Allah has the power to do all things.

43. When you were on the nearer bank *of the valley*, and they were on the farther bank, and the caravan was below you. And if you had to make a mutual appointment, you would have certainly differed with regard to the appointment. But *the encounter was brought about* that Allah might accomplish the thing that was decreed; so that he who had *already* perished through a clear Sign might perish, and he who had *already* come to life through a clear Sign might live. And certainly Allah is All-Hearing, All-Knowing.

44. When Allah showed them to thee in thy dream as few; and if He had shown them to thee as many, you would have surely faltered and would have disagreed with one another about the matter; but Allah saved *you*. Surely, He has full knowledge of what is in *your* breasts.

45. And when at the time of your encounter He made them appear to you as few in your eyes, and made you appear as few in their eyes, that Allah

أُولٰٓئِكَ هُمُ الْخٰسِرُوْنَ ﴿٣٨﴾
قُلْ لِّلَّذِيْنَ كَفَرُوْٓا اِنْ يَّنْتَهُوْا يُغْفَرْ لَهُمْ مَّا قَدْ
سَلَفَ ۚ وَاِنْ يَّعُوْدُوْا فَقَدْ مَضَتْ سُنَّتُ الْاَوَّلِيْنَ ﴿٣٩﴾
وَقٰتِلُوْهُمْ حَتّٰى لَا تَكُوْنَ فِتْنَةٌ وَّيَكُوْنَ الدِّيْنُ
كُلُّهٗ لِلّٰهِ ۚ فَاِنِ انْتَهَوْا فَاِنَّ اللّٰهَ بِمَا يَعْمَلُوْنَ بَصِيْرٌ ﴿٤٠﴾
وَاِنْ تَوَلَّوْا فَاعْلَمُوْٓا اَنَّ اللّٰهَ مَوْلٰىكُمْ ۭ نِعْمَ الْمَوْلٰى
وَنِعْمَ النَّصِيْرُ ﴿٤١﴾
وَاعْلَمُوْٓا اَنَّمَا غَنِمْتُمْ مِّنْ شَيْءٍ فَاَنَّ لِلّٰهِ خُمُسَهٗ
وَلِلرَّسُوْلِ وَلِذِي الْقُرْبٰى وَالْيَتٰمٰى وَالْمَسٰكِيْنِ
وَابْنِ السَّبِيْلِ ۙ اِنْ كُنْتُمْ اٰمَنْتُمْ بِاللّٰهِ وَمَآ اَنْزَلْنَا
عَلٰى عَبْدِنَا يَوْمَ الْفُرْقَانِ يَوْمَ الْتَقَى الْجَمْعٰنِ ۭ وَاللّٰهُ
عَلٰى كُلِّ شَيْءٍ قَدِيْرٌ ﴿٤٢﴾
اِذْ اَنْتُمْ بِالْعُدْوَةِ الدُّنْيَا وَهُمْ بِالْعُدْوَةِ الْقُصْوٰى
وَالرَّكْبُ اَسْفَلَ مِنْكُمْ ۭ وَلَوْ تَوَاعَدْتُّمْ لَاخْتَلَفْتُمْ فِي
الْمِيْعٰدِ ۙ وَلٰكِنْ لِّيَقْضِيَ اللّٰهُ اَمْرًا كَانَ مَفْعُوْلًا ۙ لِّيَهْلِكَ
مَنْ هَلَكَ عَنْۢ بَيِّنَةٍ وَّيَحْيٰى مَنْ حَيَّ عَنْۢ بَيِّنَةٍ ۭ وَاِنَّ
اللّٰهَ لَسَمِيْعٌ عَلِيْمٌ ﴿٤٣﴾
اِذْ يُرِيْكَهُمُ اللّٰهُ فِيْ مَنَامِكَ قَلِيْلًا ۭ وَلَوْ اَرٰىكَهُمْ
كَثِيْرًا لَّفَشِلْتُمْ وَلَتَنَازَعْتُمْ فِي الْاَمْرِ وَلٰكِنَّ اللّٰهَ سَلَّمَ ۭ
اِنَّهٗ عَلِيْمٌۢ بِذَاتِ الصُّدُوْرِ ﴿٤٤﴾
وَاِذْ يُرِيْكُمُوْهُمْ اِذِ الْتَقَيْتُمْ فِيْٓ اَعْيُنِكُمْ قَلِيْلًا وَّ
يُقَلِّلُكُمْ فِيْٓ اَعْيُنِهِمْ لِيَقْضِيَ اللّٰهُ اَمْرًا كَانَ مَفْعُوْلًا

* The battle of Badr.

might bring about the thing that was decreed. And to Allah are all affairs referred *for final decision*.

R. 6.

46. O ye who believe! when you encounter an army, remain firm, and remember Allah much that you may prosper.

47. And obey Allah and His Messenger and dispute not with one another, lest you falter and your power depart *from you*. And be steadfast; surely, Allah is with the steadfast.

* 48. And be not like those who came forth from their homes boastfully, and to be seen of men, and who turn *men* away from the path of Allah, and Allah encompasses all that they do.

49. And when Satan made their deeds *seem* fair to them and said, 'None among men shall prevail against you this day, and I am your protector.' But when the two armies came in sight of each other, he turned on his heels, and said, 'Surely, I have nothing to do with you; surely, I see what you see not. Surely, I fear Allah; and Allah is severe in punishing.'

R. 7.

50. When the hypocrites and those in whose hearts is a disease said, 'Their religion has deluded these *men*.' And whoso puts his trust in Allah, then surely, Allah is Mighty, Wise.

51. And if thou couldst see, when the angels take away the souls of those who disbelieve, smiting their faces and their backs, *saying*: 'Taste ye the punishment of burning!

52. 'That is because of that which your hands have sent on before *yourselves*, and *know* that Allah is not at all unjust to *His* servants.'

53. *Their case is* like the case of the people of Pharaoh and those before them: they disbelieved in the Signs of Allah; so Allah punished them for their sins. Surely,

ع وَإِلَى اللّٰهِ تُرْجَعُ الْأُمُورُ ﴿٤٥﴾
يَا أَيُّهَا الَّذِينَ آمَنُوا إِذَا لَقِيتُمْ فِئَةً فَاثْبُتُوا وَاذْكُرُوا
اللّٰهَ كَثِيرًا لَعَلَّكُمْ تُفْلِحُونَ ﴿٤٦﴾
وَأَطِيعُوا اللّٰهَ وَرَسُولَهُ وَلَا تَنَازَعُوا فَتَفْشَلُوا وَتَذْهَبَ
رِيحُكُمْ وَاصْبِرُوا إِنَّ اللّٰهَ مَعَ الصَّابِرِينَ ﴿٤٧﴾
وَلَا تَكُونُوا كَالَّذِينَ خَرَجُوا مِنْ دِيَارِهِمْ بَطَرًا وَ
رِئَاءَ النَّاسِ وَيَصُدُّونَ عَنْ سَبِيلِ اللّٰهِ وَاللّٰهُ
بِمَا يَعْمَلُونَ مُحِيطٌ ﴿٤٨﴾
وَإِذْ زَيَّنَ لَهُمُ الشَّيْطَانُ أَعْمَالَهُمْ وَقَالَ لَا غَالِبَ
لَكُمُ الْيَوْمَ مِنَ النَّاسِ وَإِنِّي جَارٌ لَكُمْ فَلَمَّا تَرَاءَتِ
الْفِئَتَانِ نَكَصَ عَلَى عَقِبَيْهِ وَقَالَ إِنِّي بَرِيءٌ مِنْكُمْ
إِنِّي أَرَى مَا لَا تَرَوْنَ إِنِّي أَخَافُ اللّٰهَ وَاللّٰهُ شَدِيدُ
ع الْعِقَابِ ﴿٤٩﴾
إِذْ يَقُولُ الْمُنَافِقُونَ وَالَّذِينَ فِي قُلُوبِهِمْ مَرَضٌ غَرَّ
هَؤُلَاءِ دِينُهُمْ وَمَنْ يَتَوَكَّلْ عَلَى اللّٰهِ فَإِنَّ اللّٰهَ عَزِيزٌ
حَكِيمٌ ﴿٥٠﴾
وَلَوْ تَرَى إِذْ يَتَوَفَّى الَّذِينَ كَفَرُوا الْمَلَائِكَةُ يَضْرِبُونَ
وُجُوهَهُمْ وَأَدْبَارَهُمْ وَذُوقُوا عَذَابَ الْحَرِيقِ ﴿٥١﴾
ذَلِكَ بِمَا قَدَّمَتْ أَيْدِيكُمْ وَأَنَّ اللّٰهَ لَيْسَ بِظَلَّامٍ
لِلْعَبِيدِ ﴿٥٢﴾
كَدَأْبِ آلِ فِرْعَوْنَ وَالَّذِينَ مِنْ قَبْلِهِمْ كَفَرُوا
بِآيَاتِ اللّٰهِ فَأَخَذَهُمُ اللّٰهُ بِذُنُوبِهِمْ إِنَّ اللّٰهَ

Allah is Powerful *and* severe in punishing.

قَوِيٌّ شَدِيْدُ الْعِقَابِ ﴿٥٣﴾

54. This is because Allah would never change a favour that He has conferred upon a people until they change their own condition, and *know* that Allah is All-Hearing, All-Knowing.

ذٰلِكَ بِاَنَّ اللّٰهَ لَمْ يَكُ مُغَيِّرًا نِّعْمَةً اَنْعَمَهَا عَلٰى قَوْمٍ
حَتّٰى يُغَيِّرُوْا مَا بِاَنْفُسِهِمْ ۙ وَاَنَّ اللّٰهَ سَمِيْعٌ عَلِيْمٌ ﴿٥٤﴾

55. *Their case is* like the case of the people of Pharaoh and those before them: they rejected the Signs of their Lord, so We destroyed them for their sins. And We drowned the people of Pharaoh, for they were all wrongdoers.

كَدَاْبِ اٰلِ فِرْعَوْنَ ۙ وَالَّذِيْنَ مِنْ قَبْلِهِمْ ؕ كَذَّبُوْا
بِاٰيٰتِ رَبِّهِمْ فَاَهْلَكْنٰهُمْ بِذُنُوْبِهِمْ وَاَغْرَقْنَاۤ اٰلَ
فِرْعَوْنَ ۚ وَكُلٌّ كَانُوْا ظٰلِمِيْنَ ﴿٥٥﴾

* 56. Surely, the worst of beasts in the sight of Allah are those who are ungrateful. So they will not believe,

اِنَّ شَرَّ الدَّوَآبِّ عِنْدَ اللّٰهِ الَّذِيْنَ كَفَرُوْا فَهُمْ لَا
يُؤْمِنُوْنَ ﴿٥٦﴾

57. Those with whom thou didst make a covenant; then they break their covenant every time, and they do not fear God.

اَلَّذِيْنَ عٰهَدْتَّ مِنْهُمْ ثُمَّ يَنْقُضُوْنَ عَهْدَهُمْ
فِيْ كُلِّ مَرَّةٍ وَّهُمْ لَا يَتَّقُوْنَ ﴿٥٧﴾

58. So, if thou catchest them in war, then by *routing* them strike fear in those that are behind them, that they may be admonished.

فَاِمَّا تَثْقَفَنَّهُمْ فِي الْحَرْبِ فَشَرِّدْ بِهِمْ مَّنْ خَلْفَهُمْ
لَعَلَّهُمْ يَذَّكَّرُوْنَ ﴿٥٨﴾

59. And if thou fearest treachery from a people, throw back to them *their covenant* with equity. Surely, Allah loves not the treacherous.

وَاِمَّا تَخَافَنَّ مِنْ قَوْمٍ خِيَانَةً فَانْۢبِذْ اِلَيْهِمْ عَلٰى
سَوَآءٍ ؕ اِنَّ اللّٰهَ لَا يُحِبُّ الْخَآئِنِيْنَ ﴿٥٩﴾

R. 8.

60. And let not those who disbelieve think that they have outstripped *Us*. Surely, they cannot frustrate *God's purpose*.

وَلَا يَحْسَبَنَّ الَّذِيْنَ كَفَرُوْا سَبَقُوْا ؕ اِنَّهُمْ لَا
يُعْجِزُوْنَ ﴿٦٠﴾

61. And make ready for them whatever you can of *armed* force and of mounted pickets at the frontier, whereby you may frighten the enemy of Allah and your enemy and others besides them whom you know not, *but* Allah knows them. And whatever you spend in the way of Allah, it shall be repaid to you in full and you shall not be wronged.

وَاَعِدُّوْا لَهُمْ مَّا اسْتَطَعْتُمْ مِّنْ قُوَّةٍ وَّمِنْ رِّبَاطِ
الْخَيْلِ تُرْهِبُوْنَ بِهٖ عَدُوَّ اللّٰهِ وَعَدُوَّكُمْ وَاٰخَرِيْنَ
مِنْ دُوْنِهِمْ ۚ لَا تَعْلَمُوْنَهُمْ ۚ اَللّٰهُ يَعْلَمُهُمْ ؕ وَمَا
تُنْفِقُوْا مِنْ شَيْءٍ فِيْ سَبِيْلِ اللّٰهِ يُوَفَّ اِلَيْكُمْ وَاَنْتُمْ
لَا تُظْلَمُوْنَ ﴿٦١﴾

62. And if they incline towards peace, incline thou also towards it, and put thy

وَاِنْ جَنَحُوْا لِلسَّلْمِ فَاجْنَحْ لَهَا وَتَوَكَّلْ عَلَى اللّٰهِ ؕ

trust in Allah. Surely, it is He Who is All-Hearing, All-Knowing.

63. And if they intend to deceive thee, then surely Allah is sufficient for thee. He it is Who has strengthened thee with His help and with the believers;

64. And He has put affection between their hearts. If thou hadst expended all that is in the earth, thou couldst not have put affection between their hearts, but Allah has put affection between them. Surely, He is Mighty, Wise.

R. 9.

65. O Prophet, Allah is sufficient for thee and for those who follow thee of the believers.

66. O Prophet, urge the believers to fight. If there be of you twenty who are steadfast, they shall overcome two hundred; and if there be a hundred of you, they shall overcome a thousand of those who disbelieve, because they are a people who do not understand.

67. For the present Allah has lightened your burden, for He knows that there is weakness in you. So, if there be a hundred of you who are steadfast, they shall overcome two hundred; and if there be a thousand of you, they shall overcome two thousand by the command of Allah. And Allah is with those who are steadfast.

68. It does not behove a Prophet that he should have captives until he engages in regular fighting in the land. You desire the goods of the world, while Allah desires *for you* the Hereafter. And Allah is Mighty, Wise.

69. Had there not been a decree from Allah which had gone before, great distress would have surely overtaken you in *connection with that* which you took.

70. So eat of that which you have won *in war* as lawful and good, and fear Allah. Surely, Allah is Most Forgiving, Merciful.

R. 10.

71. O Prophet, say to the captives who are in your hands, 'If Allah knows any

إِنَّهُ هُوَ السَّمِيعُ الْعَلِيمُ ﴿٦٢﴾

وَإِنْ يُرِيدُوا أَنْ يَخْدَعُوكَ فَإِنَّ حَسْبَكَ اللَّهُ هُوَ
الَّذِي أَيَّدَكَ بِنَصْرِهِ وَبِالْمُؤْمِنِينَ ﴿٦٣﴾

وَأَلَّفَ بَيْنَ قُلُوبِهِمْ لَوْ أَنْفَقْتَ مَا فِي الْأَرْضِ جَمِيعًا
مَا أَلَّفْتَ بَيْنَ قُلُوبِهِمْ وَلَٰكِنَّ اللَّهَ أَلَّفَ بَيْنَهُمْ إِنَّهُ
عَزِيزٌ حَكِيمٌ ﴿٦٤﴾

يَا أَيُّهَا النَّبِيُّ حَسْبُكَ اللَّهُ وَمَنِ اتَّبَعَكَ مِنَ الْمُؤْمِنِينَ ﴿٦٥﴾

يَا أَيُّهَا النَّبِيُّ حَرِّضِ الْمُؤْمِنِينَ عَلَى الْقِتَالِ إِنْ يَكُنْ
مِنْكُمْ عِشْرُونَ صَابِرُونَ يَغْلِبُوا مِائَتَيْنِ وَإِنْ
يَكُنْ مِنْكُمْ مِائَةٌ يَغْلِبُوا أَلْفًا مِنَ الَّذِينَ كَفَرُوا
بِأَنَّهُمْ قَوْمٌ لَا يَفْقَهُونَ ﴿٦٦﴾

الْآنَ خَفَّفَ اللَّهُ عَنْكُمْ وَعَلِمَ أَنَّ فِيكُمْ ضَعْفًا فَإِنْ
يَكُنْ مِنْكُمْ مِائَةٌ صَابِرَةٌ يَغْلِبُوا مِائَتَيْنِ وَإِنْ يَكُنْ مِنْكُمْ
أَلْفٌ يَغْلِبُوا أَلْفَيْنِ بِإِذْنِ اللَّهِ وَاللَّهُ مَعَ الصَّابِرِينَ ﴿٦٧﴾

مَا كَانَ لِنَبِيٍّ أَنْ يَكُونَ لَهُ أَسْرَىٰ حَتَّىٰ يُثْخِنَ فِي
الْأَرْضِ تُرِيدُونَ عَرَضَ الدُّنْيَا وَاللَّهُ يُرِيدُ الْآخِرَةَ
وَاللَّهُ عَزِيزٌ حَكِيمٌ ﴿٦٨﴾

لَوْلَا كِتَابٌ مِنَ اللَّهِ سَبَقَ لَمَسَّكُمْ فِيمَا أَخَذْتُمْ
عَذَابٌ عَظِيمٌ ﴿٦٩﴾

فَكُلُوا مِمَّا غَنِمْتُمْ حَلَالًا طَيِّبًا وَاتَّقُوا اللَّهَ إِنَّ اللَّهَ
غَفُورٌ رَحِيمٌ ﴿٧٠﴾

يَا أَيُّهَا النَّبِيُّ قُلْ لِمَنْ فِي أَيْدِيكُمْ مِنَ الْأَسْرَىٰ

good in your hearts, He will give you better than that which has been taken from you, and will forgive you. And Allah is Most Forgiving, Merciful.'

إِنْ يَعْلَمِ اللّٰهُ فِي قُلُوبِكُمْ خَيْرًا يُؤْتِكُمْ خَيْرًا مِمَّا أُخِذَ
مِنْكُمْ وَيَغْفِرْ لَكُمْ وَاللّٰهُ غَفُورٌ رَحِيمٌ ﴿٧١﴾

* 72. And if they intend to deal treacherously with thee, they have already dealt treacherously with Allah before, but He gave *thee* power over them. And Allah is All-Knowing, Wise.

وَإِنْ يُرِيدُوا خِيَانَتَكَ فَقَدْ خَانُوا اللّٰهَ مِنْ قَبْلُ
فَأَمْكَنَ مِنْهُمْ وَاللّٰهُ عَلِيمٌ حَكِيمٌ ﴿٧٢﴾

* 73. Surely, those who have believed and fled from their homes and striven with their property and their persons for the cause of Allah, and those who have given *them* shelter and help—these are friends one of another. But as for those who have believed but have not left their homes, you are not at all responsible for their protection until they leave their homes. But if they seek your help in *the matter of* religion, then it is your duty to help them, except against a people between whom and yourselves there is a treaty. And Allah sees what you do.

إِنَّ الَّذِينَ آمَنُوا وَهَاجَرُوا وَجَاهَدُوا بِأَمْوَالِهِمْ وَ
أَنْفُسِهِمْ فِي سَبِيلِ اللّٰهِ وَالَّذِينَ آوَوْا وَنَصَرُوا
أُولٰئِكَ بَعْضُهُمْ أَوْلِيَاءُ بَعْضٍ وَالَّذِينَ آمَنُوا وَ
لَمْ يُهَاجِرُوا مَا لَكُمْ مِنْ وَلَايَتِهِمْ مِنْ شَيْءٍ حَتّٰى
يُهَاجِرُوا وَإِنِ اسْتَنْصَرُوكُمْ فِي الدِّينِ فَعَلَيْكُمُ
النَّصْرُ إِلَّا عَلٰى قَوْمٍ بَيْنَكُمْ وَبَيْنَهُمْ مِيثَاقٌ وَاللّٰهُ
بِمَا تَعْمَلُونَ بَصِيرٌ ﴿٧٣﴾

74. And those who disbelieve—they are friends one of another. If you do it not, there will be mischief in the land and great disorder.

وَالَّذِينَ كَفَرُوا بَعْضُهُمْ أَوْلِيَاءُ بَعْضٍ إِلَّا تَفْعَلُوهُ
تَكُنْ فِتْنَةٌ فِي الْأَرْضِ وَفَسَادٌ كَبِيرٌ ﴿٧٤﴾

75. And those who have believed and left their homes and striven for the cause of Allah, and those who have given *them* shelter and help—these indeed are true believers. For them is forgiveness and an honourable provision.

وَالَّذِينَ آمَنُوا وَهَاجَرُوا وَجَاهَدُوا فِي سَبِيلِ اللّٰهِ
وَالَّذِينَ آوَوْا وَنَصَرُوا أُولٰئِكَ هُمُ الْمُؤْمِنُونَ حَقًّا
لَهُمْ مَغْفِرَةٌ وَرِزْقٌ كَرِيمٌ ﴿٧٥﴾

76. And those who have believed since then and left their homes and striven *for the cause of Allah* along with you—these are of you; and *as to* blood relations, they are nearer one to another in the Book of Allah. Surely, Allah knows all things well.

وَالَّذِينَ آمَنُوا مِنْ بَعْدُ وَهَاجَرُوا وَجَاهَدُوا مَعَكُمْ
فَأُولٰئِكَ مِنْكُمْ وَأُولُو الْأَرْحَامِ بَعْضُهُمْ أَوْلٰى بِبَعْضٍ
فِي كِتَابِ اللّٰهِ إِنَّ اللّٰهَ بِكُلِّ شَيْءٍ عَلِيمٌ ﴿٧٦﴾ ع

اٰیاتہا ۱۲۹ (۹) سُوْرَةُ التَّوْبَةِ مَدَنِيَّةٌ رکوعاتہا ۱۶

AL-TAUBA

(Revealed after Hijra)

1. *This is* a declaration of *complete* absolution on the part of Allah and His Messenger *from all obligation* to the idolaters with whom you had made promises.

بَرَاۗءَةٌ مِّنَ اللّٰهِ وَرَسُوْلِهٖۤ اِلَى الَّذِيْنَ عٰهَدْتُّمْ مِّنَ
الْمُشْرِكِيْنَ ۝١

2. So go about in the land for four months, and know that you cannot frustrate *the plan of* Allah and that Allah will humiliate the disbelievers.

فَسِيْحُوْا فِى الْاَرْضِ اَرْبَعَةَ اَشْهُرٍ وَّاعْلَمُوْۤا اَنَّكُمْ
غَيْرُ مُعْجِزِى اللّٰهِ ۙ وَاَنَّ اللّٰهَ مُخْزِى الْكٰفِرِيْنَ ۝٢

* 3. And *this is* a proclamation from Allah and His Messenger to the people on the day of the Greater Pilgrimage, that Allah is clear of the idolaters, and so is His Messenger. So if you repent, it will be better for you; but if you turn away, then know that you cannot frustrate *the plan of* Allah. And give tidings of a painful punishment to those who disbelieve,

وَاَذَانٌ مِّنَ اللّٰهِ وَرَسُوْلِهٖۤ اِلَى النَّاسِ يَوْمَ الْحَجِّ
الْاَكْبَرِ اَنَّ اللّٰهَ بَرِىۤءٌ مِّنَ الْمُشْرِكِيْنَ ۙ وَرَسُوْلُهٗ ۗ
فَاِنْ تُبْتُمْ فَهُوَ خَيْرٌ لَّكُمْ ۚ وَاِنْ تَوَلَّيْتُمْ فَاعْلَمُوْۤا
اَنَّكُمْ غَيْرُ مُعْجِزِى اللّٰهِ ۗ وَبَشِّرِ الَّذِيْنَ كَفَرُوْا
بِعَذَابٍ اَلِيْمٍ ۝٣

* 4. Excepting those of the idolaters with whom you have entered into a treaty and who have not *subsequently* failed you in anything nor aided anyone against you. So fulfil to these the treaty *you have* made with them till their term. Surely, Allah loves those who are righteous.

اِلَّا الَّذِيْنَ عٰهَدْتُّمْ مِّنَ الْمُشْرِكِيْنَ ثُمَّ لَمْ يَنْقُصُوْكُمْ
شَيْـًٔا وَّلَمْ يُظَاهِرُوْا عَلَيْكُمْ اَحَدًا فَاَتِمُّوْۤا اِلَيْهِمْ
عَهْدَهُمْ اِلٰى مُدَّتِهِمْ ۗ اِنَّ اللّٰهَ يُحِبُّ الْمُتَّقِيْنَ ۝٤

* 5. And when the forbidden months have passed, kill the idolaters wherever you find them and take them *prisoners*, and beleaguer them, and lie in wait for them at every place of ambush. But if they repent and observe Prayer and pay the Zakāt, then leave their way *free*. Surely, Allah is Most Forgiving, Merciful.

فَاِذَا انْسَلَخَ الْاَشْهُرُ الْحُرُمُ فَاقْتُلُوا الْمُشْرِكِيْنَ
حَيْثُ وَجَدْتُّمُوْهُمْ وَخُذُوْهُمْ وَاحْصُرُوْهُمْ وَاقْعُدُوْا
لَهُمْ كُلَّ مَرْصَدٍ ۚ فَاِنْ تَابُوْا وَاَقَامُوا الصَّلٰوةَ وَاٰتَوُا
الزَّكٰوةَ فَخَلُّوْا سَبِيْلَهُمْ ۗ اِنَّ اللّٰهَ غَفُوْرٌ رَّحِيْمٌ ۝٥

6. And if anyone of the idolaters ask protection of thee, grant him protection so that he may hear the word of Allah; then convey him to his place of security. That is because they are a people who have no knowledge.

وَاِنْ اَحَدٌ مِّنَ الْمُشْرِكِيْنَ اسْتَجَارَكَ فَاَجِرْهُ حَتّٰى يَسْمَعَ
كَلٰمَ اللّٰهِ ثُمَّ اَبْلِغْهُ مَاْمَنَهٗ ۗ ذٰلِكَ بِاَنَّهُمْ قَوْمٌ لَّا
يَعْلَمُوْنَ ۝٦ ع

R. 2.

7. How can there be a treaty of *these* idolaters with Allah and His Messenger, except those with whom you entered into a treaty at the Sacred Mosque? So, as long as they stand true to you, stand true to them. Surely, Allah loves those who are righteous.

كَيْفَ يَكُوْنُ لِلْمُشْرِكِيْنَ عَهْدٌ عِنْدَ اللّٰهِ وَعِنْدَ رَسُوْلِهٖٓ
اِلَّا الَّذِيْنَ عٰهَدْتُّمْ عِنْدَ الْمَسْجِدِ الْحَرَامِ ۚ فَمَا
اسْتَقَامُوْا لَكُمْ فَاسْتَقِيْمُوْا لَهُمْ ۭ اِنَّ اللّٰهَ يُحِبُّ
الْمُتَّقِيْنَ ٧

8. How *can it be* when, if they prevail against you, they would not observe any tie of relationship or covenant in respect of you? They would please you with their mouths, while their hearts refuse, and most of them are perfidious.

كَيْفَ وَاِنْ يَّظْهَرُوْا عَلَيْكُمْ لَا يَرْقُبُوْا فِيْكُمْ اِلًّا
وَّلَا ذِمَّةً ۭ يُرْضُوْنَكُمْ بِاَفْوَاهِهِمْ وَتَاْبٰى قُلُوْبُهُمْ
وَاَكْثَرُهُمْ فٰسِقُوْنَ ٨

9. They barter the Signs of Allah for a paltry price and turn *men* away from His way. Evil indeed is that which they do.

اِشْتَرَوْا بِاٰيٰتِ اللّٰهِ ثَمَنًا قَلِيْلًا فَصَدُّوْا عَنْ سَبِيْلِهٖ ۭ
اِنَّهُمْ سَاۗءَ مَا كَانُوْا يَعْمَلُوْنَ ٩

10. They observe not any tie of relationship or covenant in respect of anyone who trusts *them*. And it is they who are transgressors.

لَا يَرْقُبُوْنَ فِيْ مُؤْمِنٍ اِلًّا وَّلَا ذِمَّةً ۭ وَاُولٰۗىِٕكَ هُمُ
الْمُعْتَدُوْنَ ١٠

11. But if they repent and observe Prayer and pay the Zakāt, then they are your brethren in faith. And We explain the Signs for a people who have knowledge.

فَاِنْ تَابُوْا وَاَقَامُوا الصَّلٰوةَ وَاٰتَوُا الزَّكٰوةَ فَاِخْوَانُكُمْ
فِي الدِّيْنِ ۭ وَنُفَصِّلُ الْاٰيٰتِ لِقَوْمٍ يَّعْلَمُوْنَ ١١

* 12. And if they break their oaths after their covenant, and attack your religion, then fight *these* leaders of disbelief—surely, they have no regard for their oaths—that they may desist.

وَاِنْ نَّكَثُوْٓا اَيْمَانَهُمْ مِّنْۢ بَعْدِ عَهْدِهِمْ وَطَعَنُوْا
فِيْ دِيْنِكُمْ فَقَاتِلُوْٓا اَىِٕمَّةَ الْكُفْرِ ۙ اِنَّهُمْ لَآ اَيْمَانَ
لَهُمْ لَعَلَّهُمْ يَنْتَهُوْنَ ١٢

13. Will you not fight a people who have broken their oaths, and who plotted to turn out the Messenger, and they were the first to commence *hostilities* against you? Do you fear them? Nay, Allah is most worthy that you should fear Him, if you are believers.

اَلَا تُقَاتِلُوْنَ قَوْمًا نَّكَثُوْٓا اَيْمَانَهُمْ وَهَمُّوْا بِاِخْرَاجِ
الرَّسُوْلِ وَهُمْ بَدَءُوْكُمْ اَوَّلَ مَرَّةٍ ۭ اَتَخْشَوْنَهُمْ ۚ فَاللّٰهُ
اَحَقُّ اَنْ تَخْشَوْهُ اِنْ كُنْتُمْ مُّؤْمِنِيْنَ ١٣

14. Fight them, that Allah may punish them at your hands, and humiliate them, and help you *to victory* over them, and relieve the minds of a people who believe;

قَاتِلُوْهُمْ يُعَذِّبْهُمُ اللّٰهُ بِاَيْدِيْكُمْ وَيُخْزِهِمْ وَيَنْصُرْكُمْ
عَلَيْهِمْ وَيَشْفِ صُدُوْرَ قَوْمٍ مُّؤْمِنِيْنَ ١٤

15. And that He may take away the wrath of their hearts. And Allah turns with

وَيُذْهِبْ غَيْظَ قُلُوْبِهِمْ ۭ وَيَتُوْبُ اللّٰهُ عَلٰي مَنْ يَّشَاۗءُ

mercy to whomsoever He pleases. And Allah is All-Knowing, Wise.

16. Do you think that you would be left alone, while Allah has not yet known those of you who strive *in the cause of Allah* and do not take *anyone* for an intimate friend beside Allah and His Messenger and the believers? Allah is well aware of what you do.

R. 3.

* 17. The idolaters cannot keep the Mosques of Allah in a good and flourishing condition while they bear witness against themselves to disbelief. It is they whose works shall be vain, and in the Fire shall they abide.

* 18. He alone can keep the Mosques of Allah in a good and flourishing condition who believes in Allah, and the Last Day, and observes Prayer, and pays the Zakāt, and fears none but Allah; so these it is who may be among those who reach the goal.

19. Do you hold the giving of drink to the pilgrims, and the maintenance of the Sacred Mosque as *equal to the works of* him who believes in Allah and the Last Day and strives in the path of Allah? They are not *at all* equal in the sight of Allah. And Allah guides not the unjust people.

20. Those who believe and emigrate *from their homes for the sake of God* and strive in the cause of Allah with their property and their persons have the highest rank in the sight of Allah. And it is they who shall triumph.

21. Their Lord gives them glad tidings of mercy from Him, and of *His* pleasure, and of Gardens wherein there shall be lasting bliss for them;

22. They will abide therein for ever. Verily, with Allah there is a great reward.

23. O ye who believe! take not your fathers and your brothers for friends, if they prefer disbelief to faith. And whoso

وَاللّٰهُ عَلِيْمٌ حَكِيْمٌ ﴿١٥﴾

اَمْ حَسِبْتُمْ اَنْ تُتْرَكُوْا وَلَمَّا يَعْلَمِ اللّٰهُ الَّذِيْنَ جٰهَدُوْا
مِنْكُمْ وَلَمْ يَتَّخِذُوْا مِنْ دُوْنِ اللّٰهِ وَلَا رَسُوْلِهٖ وَ
لَا الْمُؤْمِنِيْنَ وَلِيْجَةً ۭ وَاللّٰهُ خَبِيْرٌۢ بِمَا تَعْمَلُوْنَ ﴿١٦﴾ ع

مَا كَانَ لِلْمُشْرِكِيْنَ اَنْ يَّعْمُرُوْا مَسٰجِدَ اللّٰهِ شٰهِدِيْنَ
عَلٰٓى اَنْفُسِهِمْ بِالْكُفْرِ ۭ اُولٰۗىِٕكَ حَبِطَتْ اَعْمَالُهُمْ ښ وَ
فِي النَّارِ هُمْ خٰلِدُوْنَ ﴿١٧﴾

اِنَّمَا يَعْمُرُ مَسٰجِدَ اللّٰهِ مَنْ اٰمَنَ بِاللّٰهِ وَالْيَوْمِ الْاٰخِرِ
وَاَقَامَ الصَّلٰوةَ وَاٰتَى الزَّكٰوةَ وَلَمْ يَخْشَ اِلَّا اللّٰهَ فَعَسٰٓى
اُولٰۗىِٕكَ اَنْ يَّكُوْنُوْا مِنَ الْمُهْتَدِيْنَ ﴿١٨﴾

اَجَعَلْتُمْ سِقَايَةَ الْحَاۗجِّ وَعِمَارَةَ الْمَسْجِدِ الْحَرَامِ
كَمَنْ اٰمَنَ بِاللّٰهِ وَالْيَوْمِ الْاٰخِرِ وَجٰهَدَ فِيْ سَبِيْلِ
اللّٰهِ ۭ لَا يَسْتَوٗنَ عِنْدَ اللّٰهِ ۭ وَاللّٰهُ لَا يَهْدِي الْقَوْمَ
الظّٰلِمِيْنَ ﴿١٩﴾ وقف لازم

اَلَّذِيْنَ اٰمَنُوْا وَهَاجَرُوْا وَجٰهَدُوْا فِيْ سَبِيْلِ اللّٰهِ
بِاَمْوَالِهِمْ وَاَنْفُسِهِمْ ۙ اَعْظَمُ دَرَجَةً عِنْدَ اللّٰهِ ۭ وَ
اُولٰۗىِٕكَ هُمُ الْفَاۗىِٕزُوْنَ ﴿٢٠﴾

يُبَشِّرُهُمْ رَبُّهُمْ بِرَحْمَةٍ مِّنْهُ وَرِضْوَانٍ وَّجَنّٰتٍ لَّهُمْ
فِيْهَا نَعِيْمٌ مُّقِيْمٌ ﴿٢١﴾

خٰلِدِيْنَ فِيْهَآ اَبَدًا ۭ اِنَّ اللّٰهَ عِنْدَهٗٓ اَجْرٌ عَظِيْمٌ ﴿٢٢﴾

يٰٓاَيُّهَا الَّذِيْنَ اٰمَنُوْا لَا تَتَّخِذُوْٓا اٰبَاۗءَكُمْ وَاِخْوَانَكُمْ
اَوْلِيَاۗءَ اِنِ اسْتَحَبُّوا الْكُفْرَ عَلَي الْاِيْمَانِ ۭ وَمَنْ يَّتَوَلَّهُمْ

befriends them from among you, it is they that are wrongdoers.

مِنْكُمْ فَاُولٰٓئِكَ هُمُ الظّٰلِمُوْنَ ۝٢٣

24. Say, if your fathers, and your sons, and your brethren, and your wives, and your kinsfolk, and the wealth you have acquired, and the trade whose dullness you fear, and the dwellings which you love are dearer to you than Allah and His Messenger and striving in His cause, then wait until Allah comes with His judgment; and Allah guides not the disobedient people.

قُلْ اِنْ كَانَ اٰبَآؤُكُمْ وَاَبْنَآؤُكُمْ وَاِخْوَانُكُمْ وَاَزْوَاجُكُمْ
وَعَشِيْرَتُكُمْ وَاَمْوَالُ اقْتَرَفْتُمُوْهَا وَتِجَارَةٌ تَخْشَوْنَ
كَسَادَهَا وَمَسٰكِنُ تَرْضَوْنَهَآ اَحَبَّ اِلَيْكُمْ مِّنَ اللّٰهِ
وَرَسُوْلِهٖ وَجِهَادٍ فِيْ سَبِيْلِهٖ فَتَرَبَّصُوْا حَتّٰى يَاْتِيَ
اللّٰهُ بِاَمْرِهٖ ؕ وَاللّٰهُ لَا يَهْدِي الْقَوْمَ الْفٰسِقِيْنَ ۝٢٤ ع ٣

R. 4.

25. Surely, Allah had helped you on many a battlefield, and on the Day of Ḥunain, when your great numbers made you proud, but they availed you nought; and the earth, with *all* its vastness, became straitened for you, *and* then you turned your backs retreating.

لَقَدْ نَصَرَكُمُ اللّٰهُ فِيْ مَوَاطِنَ كَثِيْرَةٍ ۙ وَّيَوْمَ حُنَيْنٍ ۙ
اِذْ اَعْجَبَتْكُمْ كَثْرَتُكُمْ فَلَمْ تُغْنِ عَنْكُمْ شَيْـًٔا وَّ
ضَاقَتْ عَلَيْكُمُ الْاَرْضُ بِمَا رَحُبَتْ ثُمَّ وَلَّيْتُمْ
مُّدْبِرِيْنَ ۝٢٥

* 26. Then Allah sent down His peace upon His Messenger and upon the believers, and He sent down hosts which you did not see, and He punished those who disbelieved. And this is the reward of the disbelievers.

ثُمَّ اَنْزَلَ اللّٰهُ سَكِيْنَتَهٗ عَلٰى رَسُوْلِهٖ وَعَلَى الْمُؤْمِنِيْنَ
وَاَنْزَلَ جُنُوْدًا لَّمْ تَرَوْهَا وَعَذَّبَ الَّذِيْنَ كَفَرُوْا
وَذٰلِكَ جَزَآءُ الْكٰفِرِيْنَ ۝٢٦

27. Then will Allah, after that, turn with compassion to whomsoever He pleases; and Allah is Most Forgiving, Merciful.

ثُمَّ يَتُوْبُ اللّٰهُ مِنْ بَعْدِ ذٰلِكَ عَلٰى مَنْ يَّشَآءُ ؕ وَاللّٰهُ
غَفُوْرٌ رَّحِيْمٌ ۝٢٧

28. O ye who believe! surely, the idolaters are unclean. So they shall not approach the Sacred Mosque after this year of theirs. And if you fear poverty, Allah will enrich you out of His bounty, if He pleases. Surely, Allah is All-Knowing, Wise.

يٰٓاَيُّهَا الَّذِيْنَ اٰمَنُوْٓا اِنَّمَا الْمُشْرِكُوْنَ نَجَسٌ فَلَا يَقْرَبُوا
الْمَسْجِدَ الْحَرَامَ بَعْدَ عَامِهِمْ هٰذَا ۚ وَاِنْ خِفْتُمْ
عَيْلَةً فَسَوْفَ يُغْنِيْكُمُ اللّٰهُ مِنْ فَضْلِهٖٓ اِنْ شَآءَ ؕ
اِنَّ اللّٰهَ عَلِيْمٌ حَكِيْمٌ ۝٢٨

* 29. Fight those from among the People of the Book who believe not in Allah, nor in the Last Day, nor hold as unlawful what Allah and His Messenger have declared to be unlawful, nor follow the true religion, until they pay the tax with

قَاتِلُوا الَّذِيْنَ لَا يُؤْمِنُوْنَ بِاللّٰهِ وَلَا بِالْيَوْمِ الْاٰخِرِ
وَلَا يُحَرِّمُوْنَ مَا حَرَّمَ اللّٰهُ وَرَسُوْلُهٗ وَلَا يَدِيْنُوْنَ
دِيْنَ الْحَقِّ مِنَ الَّذِيْنَ اُوْتُوا الْكِتٰبَ حَتّٰى يُعْطُوا الْجِزْيَةَ

their own hand and acknowledge their subjection.

R. 5.

* 30. And the Jews say, Ezra is the son of Allah, and the Christians say, the Messiah is the son of Allah; that is what they say with their mouths. They imitate the saying of those who disbelieved before them. Allah's curse be on them! How are they turned away!

31. They have taken their learned men and their monks for lords beside Allah. And *so have they taken* the Messiah, son of Mary. And they were not commanded but to worship the One God. There is no God but He. Too Holy is He for what they associate *with Him!*

32. They desire to extinguish the light of Allah with their mouths; but Allah will permit nothing except that He will perfect His light, though the disbelievers may dislike *it*.

33. He it is Who sent His Messenger with guidance and the religion of truth, that He may make it prevail over every *other* religion, even though the idolaters may dislike *it*.

34. O ye who believe! surely, many of the priests and monks devour the wealth of men by false means and turn *men* away from the way of Allah. And those who hoard up gold and silver and spend it not in the way of Allah—give to them the tidings of a painful punishment,

35. On the day when it shall be made hot in the fire of Hell, and their foreheads and their sides and their backs shall be branded therewith *and it shall be said to them:* 'This is what you treasured up for yourselves; so now taste what you used to treasure up.'

* 36. The reckoning of months with Allah has been twelve months by Allah's ordinance since the day when He created the heavens and the earth. Of these, four are sacred. That is the right creed. So wrong not yourselves therein. And fight

عَنْ يَدٍ وَّهُمْ صٰغِرُوْنَ ﴿۲۹﴾ ع

وَقَالَتِ الْيَهُوْدُ عُزَيْرُ ابْنُ اللّٰهِ وَقَالَتِ النَّصٰرَى الْمَسِيْحُ
ابْنُ اللّٰهِ ؕ ذٰلِكَ قَوْلُهُمْ بِاَفْوَاهِهِمْ ۚ يُضَاهِـُٔوْنَ قَوْلَ
الَّذِيْنَ كَفَرُوْا مِنْ قَبْلُ ؕ قٰتَلَهُمُ اللّٰهُ ۚ اَنّٰى يُؤْفَكُوْنَ ﴿۳۰﴾
اِتَّخَذُوْۤا اَحْبَارَهُمْ وَرُهْبَانَهُمْ اَرْبَابًا مِّنْ دُوْنِ
اللّٰهِ وَالْمَسِيْحَ ابْنَ مَرْيَمَ ۚ وَمَاۤ اُمِرُوْۤا اِلَّا لِيَعْبُدُوْۤا
اِلٰهًا وَّاحِدًا ۚ لَاۤ اِلٰهَ اِلَّا هُوَ ؕ سُبْحٰنَهٗ عَمَّا يُشْرِكُوْنَ ﴿۳۱﴾
يُرِيْدُوْنَ اَنْ يُّطْفِـُٔوْا نُوْرَ اللّٰهِ بِاَفْوَاهِهِمْ وَيَاْبَى اللّٰهُ
اِلَّاۤ اَنْ يُّتِمَّ نُوْرَهٗ وَلَوْ كَرِهَ الْكٰفِرُوْنَ ﴿۳۲﴾
هُوَ الَّذِيْۤ اَرْسَلَ رَسُوْلَهٗ بِالْهُدٰى وَدِيْنِ الْحَقِّ لِيُظْهِرَهٗ
عَلَى الدِّيْنِ كُلِّهٖ ۙ وَلَوْ كَرِهَ الْمُشْرِكُوْنَ ﴿۳۳﴾ النصف
يٰۤاَيُّهَا الَّذِيْنَ اٰمَنُوْۤا اِنَّ كَثِيْرًا مِّنَ الْاَحْبَارِ وَالرُّهْبَانِ
لَيَاْكُلُوْنَ اَمْوَالَ النَّاسِ بِالْبَاطِلِ وَيَصُدُّوْنَ عَنْ
سَبِيْلِ اللّٰهِ ؕ وَالَّذِيْنَ يَكْنِزُوْنَ الذَّهَبَ وَالْفِضَّةَ
وَلَا يُنْفِقُوْنَهَا فِيْ سَبِيْلِ اللّٰهِ ۙ فَبَشِّرْهُمْ بِعَذَابٍ
اَلِيْمٍ ﴿۳۴﴾

يَّوْمَ يُحْمٰى عَلَيْهَا فِيْ نَارِ جَهَنَّمَ فَتُكْوٰى بِهَا جِبَاهُهُمْ
وَجُنُوْبُهُمْ وَظُهُوْرُهُمْ ؕ هٰذَا مَا كَنَزْتُمْ لِاَنْفُسِكُمْ
فَذُوْقُوْا مَا كُنْتُمْ تَكْنِزُوْنَ ﴿۳۵﴾

اِنَّ عِدَّةَ الشُّهُوْرِ عِنْدَ اللّٰهِ اثْنَا عَشَرَ شَهْرًا فِيْ كِتٰبِ
اللّٰهِ يَوْمَ خَلَقَ السَّمٰوٰتِ وَالْاَرْضَ مِنْهَاۤ اَرْبَعَةٌ حُرُمٌ ؕ
ذٰلِكَ الدِّيْنُ الْقَيِّمُ ۙ فَلَا تَظْلِمُوْا فِيْهِنَّ اَنْفُسَكُمْ

the idolaters all together as they fight you all together; and know that Allah is with the righteous.

37. Surely, the postponement *of a Sacred Month* is an addition to disbelief. Those who disbelieve are led astray thereby. They allow it one year and forbid it another year, that they may agree in the number of *the months* which Allah has made sacred, and thus may make lawful what Allah has forbidden. The evil of their deeds is made *to seem* fair to them. And Allah guides not the disbelieving people.

R. 6.

* 38. O ye who believe! what is the matter with you that, when it is said to you, go forth in the way of Allah, you sink heavily towards the earth? Would you be contented with the present life in preference to the Hereafter? But the enjoyment of the present life is but little, as compared with the Hereafter.

39. If you do not go forth *to fight*, He will punish you with a painful punishment, and will choose in your stead a people other than you, and you shall do Him no harm at all. And Allah has full power over all things.

40. If you help him not, then *know that* Allah helped him *even* when the disbelievers drove him forth while he was one of the two when they were both in the cave, when he said to his companion, 'Grieve not, for Allah is with us.' Then Allah sent down His peace on him, and strengthened him with hosts which you did not see, and humbled the word of those who disbelieved, and it is the word of Allah alone which is supreme. And Allah is Mighty, Wise.

41. Go forth, light and heavy, and strive with your property and your persons in the cause of Allah. That is better for you, if only you knew.

42. If it had been an immediate gain and a short journey, they would certainly have followed thee, but the hard journey seemed too long to them. Yet they will

وقاتلوا المشركين كافة كما يقاتلونكم كافة
واعلموا أن الله مع المتقين ﴿٣٦﴾
إنما النسيء زيادة في الكفر يضل به الذين كفروا
يحلونه عاما ويحرمونه عاما ليواطئوا عدة ما
حرم الله فيحلوا ما حرم الله زين لهم سوء
ع أعمالهم والله لا يهدي القوم الكافرين ﴿٣٧﴾
يا أيها الذين آمنوا ما لكم إذا قيل لكم انفروا
في سبيل الله اثاقلتم إلى الأرض أرضيتم بالحياة
الدنيا من الآخرة فما متاع الحياة الدنيا في
الآخرة إلا قليل ﴿٣٨﴾
إلا تنفروا يعذبكم عذابا أليما ويستبدل قوما
غيركم ولا تضروه شيئا والله على كل شيء قدير ﴿٣٩﴾
إلا تنصروه فقد نصره الله إذ أخرجه الذين كفروا
ثاني اثنين إذ هما في الغار إذ يقول لصاحبه
لا تحزن إن الله معنا فأنزل الله سكينته عليه
وأيده بجنود لم تروها وجعل كلمة الذين
كفروا السفلى وكلمة الله هي العليا والله عزيز
حكيم ﴿٤٠﴾
انفروا خفافا وثقالا وجاهدوا بأموالكم وأنفسكم
في سبيل الله ذلكم خير لكم إن كنتم تعلمون ﴿٤١﴾
لو كان عرضا قريبا وسفرا قاصدا لاتبعوك و
لكن بعدت عليهم الشقة وسيحلفون بالله

swear by Allah, *saying*, 'If we had been able, we would surely have gone forth with you.' They ruin their souls; and Allah knows that they are liars.

لَوِ اسْتَطَعْنَا لَخَرَجْنَا مَعَكُمْ يُهْلِكُوْنَ أَنْفُسَهُمْ
وَاللّٰهُ يَعْلَمُ إِنَّهُمْ لَكٰذِبُوْنَ ﴿٤٢﴾ ع ١٢

R. 7.

43. Allah remove thy *cares*. Why didst thou permit them *to stay behind* until those who spoke the truth had become known to thee and *until* thou hadst known the liars?

عَفَا اللّٰهُ عَنْكَ لِمَ أَذِنْتَ لَهُمْ حَتّٰى يَتَبَيَّنَ لَكَ
الَّذِيْنَ صَدَقُوْا وَتَعْلَمَ الْكٰذِبِيْنَ ﴿٤٣﴾

44. Those who believe in Allah and the Last Day will not ask leave of thee *to be exempted* from striving with their property and their persons. And Allah well knows the righteous.

لَا يَسْتَأْذِنُكَ الَّذِيْنَ يُؤْمِنُوْنَ بِاللّٰهِ وَالْيَوْمِ الْاٰخِرِ
أَنْ يُّجَاهِدُوْا بِأَمْوَالِهِمْ وَأَنْفُسِهِمْ وَاللّٰهُ عَلِيْمٌۢ
بِالْمُتَّقِيْنَ ﴿٤٤﴾

45. Only those will ask leave of thee *to be exempted* who do not believe in Allah and the Last Day, and whose hearts are full of doubt, and in their doubt they waver.

إِنَّمَا يَسْتَأْذِنُكَ الَّذِيْنَ لَا يُؤْمِنُوْنَ بِاللّٰهِ وَالْيَوْمِ
الْاٰخِرِ وَارْتَابَتْ قُلُوْبُهُمْ فَهُمْ فِيْ رَيْبِهِمْ يَتَرَدَّدُوْنَ ﴿٤٥﴾

46. And if they had intended to go forth they would certainly have made some preparation for it; but Allah was averse to their marching forth. So He kept them back, and it was said: 'Sit ye *at home* with those who sit.'

وَلَوْ أَرَادُوا الْخُرُوْجَ لَأَعَدُّوْا لَهٗ عُدَّةً وَّلٰكِنْ كَرِهَ
اللّٰهُ انْبِعَاثَهُمْ فَثَبَّطَهُمْ وَقِيْلَ اقْعُدُوْا مَعَ
الْقٰعِدِيْنَ ﴿٤٦﴾

* 47. If they had gone forth with you, they would have added to you nothing but trouble, and would have hurried to and fro in your midst, seeking *to create* discord among you. And there are among you those who would listen to them. And Allah well knows the wrongdoers.

لَوْ خَرَجُوْا فِيْكُمْ مَّا زَادُوْكُمْ إِلَّا خَبَالًا وَّلَأَوْضَعُوْا
خِلٰلَكُمْ يَبْغُوْنَكُمُ الْفِتْنَةَ وَفِيْكُمْ سَمّٰعُوْنَ لَهُمْ
وَاللّٰهُ عَلِيْمٌۢ بِالظّٰلِمِيْنَ ﴿٤٧﴾

48. They sought *to create* disorder even before *this*, and they devised plots against thee till the truth came and the purpose of Allah prevailed, though they did not like *it*.

لَقَدِ ابْتَغَوُا الْفِتْنَةَ مِنْ قَبْلُ وَقَلَّبُوْا لَكَ الْأُمُوْرَ
حَتّٰى جَآءَ الْحَقُّ وَظَهَرَ أَمْرُ اللّٰهِ وَهُمْ كٰرِهُوْنَ ﴿٤٨﴾

49. And among them is he who says, 'Permit me *to stay behind* and put me not to trial.' Surely, they have already fallen into trial. And surely, Hell shall encompass the disbelievers.

وَمِنْهُمْ مَّنْ يَّقُوْلُ ائْذَنْ لِّيْ وَلَا تَفْتِنِّيْ أَلَا فِي
الْفِتْنَةِ سَقَطُوْا وَإِنَّ جَهَنَّمَ لَمُحِيْطَةٌۢ بِالْكٰفِرِيْنَ ﴿٤٩﴾

50. If good befall thee, it grieves them, but if a misfortune befall thee, they say, 'We had indeed taken our precaution beforehand.' And they turn away rejoicing.

إِنْ تُصِبْكَ حَسَنَةٌ تَسُؤْهُمْ وَإِنْ تُصِبْكَ مُصِيْبَةٌ
يَّقُوْلُوْا قَدْ أَخَذْنَا أَمْرَنَا مِنْ قَبْلُ وَيَتَوَلَّوْا وَّهُمْ
فَرِحُوْنَ ﴿٥٠﴾

51. Say, 'Nothing shall befall us save that which Allah has ordained for us. He is our Protector. And in Allah then should the believers put their trust.'

قُل لَّن يُصِيبَنَآ إِلَّا مَا كَتَبَ ٱللَّهُ لَنَا هُوَ مَوْلَىٰنَا ۚ
وَعَلَى ٱللَّهِ فَلْيَتَوَكَّلِ ٱلْمُؤْمِنُونَ ﴿٥١﴾

52. Say, 'You do not await for us anything except one of the two good things; while as regards you, we await that Allah will afflict you with a punishment either from Himself or at our hands. Wait then; we *also* are waiting with you.'

قُلْ هَلْ تَرَبَّصُونَ بِنَآ إِلَّآ إِحْدَى ٱلْحُسْنَيَيْنِ ۖ
وَنَحْنُ نَتَرَبَّصُ بِكُمْ أَن يُصِيبَكُمُ ٱللَّهُ بِعَذَابٍ
مِّنْ عِندِهِۦٓ أَوْ بِأَيْدِينَا ۖ فَتَرَبَّصُوٓا۟ إِنَّا مَعَكُم
مُّتَرَبِّصُونَ ﴿٥٢﴾

53. Say, 'Spend willingly or unwillingly, it shall not be accepted from you. You are indeed a disobedient people.'

قُلْ أَنفِقُوا۟ طَوْعًا أَوْ كَرْهًا لَّن يُتَقَبَّلَ مِنكُمْ ۖ إِنَّكُمْ
كُنتُمْ قَوْمًا فَٰسِقِينَ ﴿٥٣﴾

54. And nothing has deprived them of the acceptance of their contributions save that they disbelieve in Allah and His Messenger. And they come not to Prayer except lazily and they make no contribution save reluctantly.

وَمَا مَنَعَهُمْ أَن تُقْبَلَ مِنْهُمْ نَفَقَٰتُهُمْ إِلَّآ أَنَّهُمْ
كَفَرُوا۟ بِٱللَّهِ وَبِرَسُولِهِۦ وَلَا يَأْتُونَ ٱلصَّلَوٰةَ إِلَّا وَهُمْ
كُسَالَىٰ وَلَا يُنفِقُونَ إِلَّا وَهُمْ كَٰرِهُونَ ﴿٥٤﴾

55. So let not their wealth nor their children excite thy wonder. Allah only intends to punish them therewith in the present life and that their souls may depart while they are disbelievers.

فَلَا تُعْجِبْكَ أَمْوَٰلُهُمْ وَلَآ أَوْلَٰدُهُمْ ۚ إِنَّمَا يُرِيدُ
ٱللَّهُ لِيُعَذِّبَهُم بِهَا فِى ٱلْحَيَوٰةِ ٱلدُّنْيَا وَتَزْهَقَ
أَنفُسُهُمْ وَهُمْ كَٰفِرُونَ ﴿٥٥﴾

56. And they swear by Allah that they are indeed of you, while they are not of you, but they are a people who are timorous.

وَيَحْلِفُونَ بِٱللَّهِ إِنَّهُمْ لَمِنكُمْ وَمَا هُم مِّنكُمْ وَ
لَٰكِنَّهُمْ قَوْمٌ يَفْرَقُونَ ﴿٥٦﴾

57. If they could find a place of refuge, or caves, or *even* a hole to enter, they would surely turn thereto, rushing uncontrollably.

لَوْ يَجِدُونَ مَلْجَـًٔا أَوْ مَغَٰرَٰتٍ أَوْ مُدَّخَلًا لَّوَلَّوْا۟
إِلَيْهِ وَهُمْ يَجْمَحُونَ ﴿٥٧﴾

58. And among them are those who find fault with thee in *the matter of* alms. If they are given thereof, they are content; but if they are not given thereof, behold! they are discontented.

وَمِنْهُم مَّن يَلْمِزُكَ فِى ٱلصَّدَقَٰتِ فَإِنْ أُعْطُوا۟
مِنْهَا رَضُوا۟ وَإِن لَّمْ يُعْطَوْا۟ مِنْهَآ إِذَا هُمْ يَسْخَطُونَ ﴿٥٨﴾

* 59. Had they but been content with what Allah and His Messenger had given them and said, 'Sufficient for us is Allah; Allah will give us of His bounty, and so will

وَلَوْ أَنَّهُمْ رَضُوا۟ مَآ ءَاتَىٰهُمُ ٱللَّهُ وَرَسُولُهُۥ وَقَالُوا۟
حَسْبُنَا ٱللَّهُ سَيُؤْتِينَا ٱللَّهُ مِن فَضْلِهِۦ وَرَسُولُهُۥٓ

His Messenger; to Allah do we turn in supplication,' *it would have been better for them.*

R. 8.

60. The alms are only for the poor and the needy, and for those employed in connection therewith, and for those whose hearts are to be reconciled, and for the *freeing of* slaves, and for those in debt, and for the cause of Allah, and for the wayfarer—an ordinance from Allah. And Allah is All-Knowing, Wise.

* 61. And among them are those who annoy the Prophet and say, 'He *gives* ear *to all.*' Say, '*His giving* ear *to all* is good for you; he believes in Allah and believes the Faithful, and is a mercy for those of you who believe.' And those who annoy the Messenger of Allah shall have a grievous punishment.

62. They swear by Allah to you to please you; but Allah and His Messenger are more worthy that they should please him *and God,* if they are believers.

63. Have they not known that whoso opposes Allah and His Messenger, for him is the fire of Hell, wherein he shall abide? That is the great humiliation.

64. The hypocrites fear lest a Sūra should be revealed against them, informing them of what is in their hearts. Say, 'Mock ye! surely, Allah will bring to light what you fear.'

65. And if thou question them, they will most surely say, 'We were only talking idly and jesting.' Say, 'Was it Allah and His Signs and His Messenger that you mocked at?

66. 'Offer no excuse. You have certainly disbelieved after your believing. If We forgive a party from among you, a party shall We punish, for they have been guilty.'

R. 9.

67. The hypocrites, men and women, are *all connected* one with another. They enjoin evil and forbid good, and keep their hands closed. They neglected Allah, so He

إنا إلى الله رٰغبون ﴿٥٩﴾
إنما الصدقٰت للفقراء والمسٰكين والعٰملين
عليها والمؤلفة قلوبهم وفي الرقاب والغٰرمين
وفي سبيل الله وابن السبيل فريضة من الله
والله عليم حكيم ﴿٦٠﴾
ومنهم الذين يؤذون النبي ويقولون هو أذن
قل أذن خير لكم يؤمن بالله ويؤمن للمؤمنين
ورحمة للذين آمنوا منكم والذين يؤذون رسول
الله لهم عذاب أليم ﴿٦١﴾
يحلفون بالله لكم ليرضوكم والله ورسوله أحق
أن يرضوه إن كانوا مؤمنين ﴿٦٢﴾
ألم يعلموا أنه من يحادد الله ورسوله فأن
له نار جهنم خٰلدا فيها ذٰلك الخزي العظيم ﴿٦٣﴾
يحذر المنٰفقون أن تنزل عليهم سورة تنبئهم
بما في قلوبهم قل استهزءوا إن الله مخرج
ما تحذرون ﴿٦٤﴾
ولئن سألتهم ليقولن إنما كنا نخوض ونلعب
قل أبالله وآيٰته ورسوله كنتم تستهزءون ﴿٦٥﴾
لا تعتذروا قد كفرتم بعد إيمٰنكم إن نعف عن
طائفة منكم نعذب طائفة بأنهم كانوا مجرمين ﴿٦٦﴾
المنٰفقون والمنٰفقٰت بعضهم من بعض يأمرون
بالمنكر وينهون عن المعروف ويقبضون أيديهم

has neglected them. Surely, it is the hypocrites who are the disobedient.

نَسُوا اللّٰهَ فَنَسِيَهُمْ ۗ اِنَّ الْمُنٰفِقِيْنَ هُمُ الْفٰسِقُوْنَ ﴿٦٧﴾

68. Allah promises the hypocrites, men and women, and the disbelievers the fire of Hell, wherein they shall abide. It will suffice them. And Allah has cursed them. And they shall have a lasting punishment,

وَعَدَ اللّٰهُ الْمُنٰفِقِيْنَ وَالْمُنٰفِقٰتِ وَالْكُفَّارَ نَارَ جَهَنَّمَ
خٰلِدِيْنَ فِيْهَا ۗ هِيَ حَسْبُهُمْ ۚ وَلَعَنَهُمُ اللّٰهُ ۚ وَلَهُمْ
عَذَابٌ مُّقِيْمٌ ﴿٦٨﴾

69. Even as those before you. They were mightier than you in power and richer in possessions and children. They enjoyed their lot for a short time, so have you enjoyed your lot as those before you enjoyed their lot. And you indulged in idle talk as they indulged in idle talk. It is they whose works shall be of no avail in this world and the Hereafter. And it is they who are the losers.

كَالَّذِيْنَ مِنْ قَبْلِكُمْ كَانُوْٓا اَشَدَّ مِنْكُمْ قُوَّةً وَّاَكْثَرَ
اَمْوَالًا وَّاَوْلَادًا ۗ فَاسْتَمْتَعُوْا بِخَلَاقِهِمْ فَاسْتَمْتَعْتُمْ
بِخَلَاقِكُمْ كَمَا اسْتَمْتَعَ الَّذِيْنَ مِنْ قَبْلِكُمْ بِخَلَاقِهِمْ
وَخُضْتُمْ كَالَّذِيْ خَاضُوْا ۗ اُولٰٓئِكَ حَبِطَتْ اَعْمَالُهُمْ
فِي الدُّنْيَا وَالْاٰخِرَةِ ۚ وَاُولٰٓئِكَ هُمُ الْخٰسِرُوْنَ ﴿٦٩﴾

70. Has not the story reached them of those before them—the people of Noah, 'Ād, and Thamūd, and the people of Abraham, and the dwellers of Midian, and the cities which were overthrown? Their Messengers came to them with clear Signs. So Allah would not wrong them, but they wronged themselves.

اَلَمْ يَاْتِهِمْ نَبَاُ الَّذِيْنَ مِنْ قَبْلِهِمْ قَوْمِ نُوْحٍ وَّعَادٍ
وَّثَمُوْدَ ۙ وَقَوْمِ اِبْرٰهِيْمَ وَاَصْحٰبِ مَدْيَنَ وَالْمُؤْتَفِكٰتِ ۗ
اَتَتْهُمْ رُسُلُهُمْ بِالْبَيِّنٰتِ ۚ فَمَا كَانَ اللّٰهُ لِيَظْلِمَهُمْ
وَلٰكِنْ كَانُوْٓا اَنْفُسَهُمْ يَظْلِمُوْنَ ﴿٧٠﴾

71. And the believers, men and women, are friends one of another. They enjoin good and forbid evil and observe Prayer and pay the Zakāt and obey Allah and His Messenger. It is these on whom Allah will have mercy. Surely, Allah is Mighty, Wise.

وَالْمُؤْمِنُوْنَ وَالْمُؤْمِنٰتُ بَعْضُهُمْ اَوْلِيَآءُ بَعْضٍ ۘ وقف لازم
يَاْمُرُوْنَ بِالْمَعْرُوْفِ وَيَنْهَوْنَ عَنِ الْمُنْكَرِ وَ
يُقِيْمُوْنَ الصَّلٰوةَ وَيُؤْتُوْنَ الزَّكٰوةَ وَيُطِيْعُوْنَ اللّٰهَ
وَرَسُوْلَهٗ ۗ اُولٰٓئِكَ سَيَرْحَمُهُمُ اللّٰهُ ۗ اِنَّ اللّٰهَ عَزِيْزٌ
حَكِيْمٌ ﴿٧١﴾

72. Allah has promised to believers, men and women, Gardens beneath which rivers flow, wherein they will abide, and delightful dwelling-places in Gardens of Eternity. And the pleasure of Allah is the greatest of all. That is the supreme triumph.

وَعَدَ اللّٰهُ الْمُؤْمِنِيْنَ وَالْمُؤْمِنٰتِ جَنّٰتٍ تَجْرِيْ مِنْ
تَحْتِهَا الْاَنْهٰرُ خٰلِدِيْنَ فِيْهَا وَمَسٰكِنَ طَيِّبَةً فِيْ
جَنّٰتِ عَدْنٍ ۗ وَرِضْوَانٌ مِّنَ اللّٰهِ اَكْبَرُ ۗ ذٰلِكَ هُوَ
الْفَوْزُ الْعَظِيْمُ ﴿٧٢﴾ ع ٩ ١٥

R. 10.

يايها النبي جاهد الكفار والمنفقين واغلظ
عليهم وماوىهم جهنم وبئس المصير ٧٣

73. O Prophet, strive against the disbelievers and the hypocrites. And be severe to them. Their abode is Hell, and an evil destination it is.

يحلفون بالله ما قالوا ولقد قالوا كلمة الكفر و
كفروا بعد اسلامهم وهموا بما لم ينالوا وما
نقموا الا ان اغنىهم الله ورسوله من فضله
فان يتوبوا يك خيرا لهم وان يتولوا يعذبهم الله
عذابا اليما في الدنيا والاخرة وما لهم في الارض
من ولي ولا نصير ٧٤

* 74. They swear by Allah that they said nothing, but they did certainly use blasphemous language, and disbelieved after they had embraced Islam. And they meditated that which they could not attain. And they cherished hatred only because Allah and His Messenger had enriched them out of His bounty. So if they repent, it will be better for them; but if they turn away, Allah will punish them with a grievous punishment in this world and the Hereafter, and they shall have neither friend nor helper in the earth.

ومنهم من عهد الله لئن اتىنا من فضله لنصدقن
ولنكونن من الصلحين ٧٥

75. And among them there are those who made a covenant with Allah, *saying*, 'If He give us of His bounty, we would most surely give alms and be of the virtuous.'

فلما اتىهم من فضله بخلوا به وتولوا وهم معرضون ٧٦

76. But when He gave them of His bounty, they became niggardly of it, and they turned away in aversion.

فاعقبهم نفاقا في قلوبهم الى يوم يلقونه بما اخلفوا
الله ما وعدوه وبما كانوا يكذبون ٧٧

77. So He requited them with hypocrisy *which shall last* in their hearts until the day when they shall meet Him, because they broke their promise to Allah, and because they lied.

الم يعلموا ان الله يعلم سرهم ونجوىهم وان
الله علام الغيوب ٧٨

* 78. Know they not that Allah knows their secrets as well as their private counsels and that Allah is the Best Knower of all unseen things?

الذين يلمزون المطوعين من المؤمنين في
الصدقت والذين لا يجدون الا جهدهم فيسخرون
منهم سخر الله منهم ولهم عذاب اليم ٧٩

79. Those who find fault with such of the believers as give alms of their own free will and with such as find nothing *to give* save *the earnings of* their toil. They thus deride them. Allah shall requite them for their derision, and for them is a grievous punishment.

استغفر لهم او لا تستغفر لهم ان تستغفر لهم
سبعين مرة فلن يغفر الله لهم ذلك بانهم كفروا
بالله ورسوله والله لا يهدي القوم الفسقين ٨٠

80. Ask thou forgiveness for them, or ask thou not forgiveness for them; even if thou ask forgiveness for them seventy times, Allah will never forgive them. That is because they disbelieved in Allah and His Messenger. And Allah guides not the perfidious people.

R. 11.

فرح المخلفون بمقعدهم خلف رسول الله و

* 81. Those who were left behind rejoiced

in their sitting *at home* behind *the back of* the Messenger of Allah, and were averse to striving with their property and their persons in the cause of Allah. And they said, 'Go not forth in the heat.' Say, 'The fire of Hell is more intense in heat.' Could they but understand!

كَرِهُوٓا اَنْ يُّجَاهِدُوْا بِاَمْوَالِهِمْ وَاَنْفُسِهِمْ فِيْ سَبِيْلِ
اللّٰهِ وَقَالُوْا لَا تَنْفِرُوْا فِي الْحَرِّ ۗ قُلْ نَارُ جَهَنَّمَ اَشَدُّ
حَرًّا ۗ لَوْ كَانُوْا يَفْقَهُوْنَ ﴿٨١﴾

82. They must laugh little and weep much as a reward for that which they used to earn.

فَلْيَضْحَكُوْا قَلِيْلًا وَّلْيَبْكُوْا كَثِيْرًا ۚ جَزَآءً ۢ بِمَا
كَانُوْا يَكْسِبُوْنَ ﴿٨٢﴾

83. And if Allah return thee to a party of them, and they ask of thee leave to go forth *to fight*, say then, 'You shall never go forth with me and shall never fight an enemy with me. You chose to sit *at home* the first time, so sit now with those who remain behind.'

فَاِنْ رَّجَعَكَ اللّٰهُ اِلٰى طَآئِفَةٍ مِّنْهُمْ فَاسْتَاْذَنُوْكَ
لِلْخُرُوْجِ فَقُلْ لَّنْ تَخْرُجُوْا مَعِيَ اَبَدًا وَّلَنْ تُقَاتِلُوْا
مَعِيَ عَدُوًّا ۗ اِنَّكُمْ رَضِيْتُمْ بِالْقُعُوْدِ اَوَّلَ مَرَّةٍ
فَاقْعُدُوْا مَعَ الْخٰلِفِيْنَ ﴿٨٣﴾

* 84. And never pray thou for any of them that dies, nor stand by his grave; for they disbelieved in Allah and His Messenger and died while they were disobedient.

وَلَا تُصَلِّ عَلٰٓى اَحَدٍ مِّنْهُمْ مَّاتَ اَبَدًا وَّلَا تَقُمْ
عَلٰى قَبْرِهٖ ۗ اِنَّهُمْ كَفَرُوْا بِاللّٰهِ وَرَسُوْلِهٖ وَمَاتُوْا وَ
هُمْ فٰسِقُوْنَ ﴿٨٤﴾

85. And their possessions and their children should not excite thy wonder; Allah only intends to punish them therewith in this world and that their souls may depart while they are disbelievers.

وَلَا تُعْجِبْكَ اَمْوَالُهُمْ وَاَوْلَادُهُمْ ۗ اِنَّمَا يُرِيْدُ
اللّٰهُ اَنْ يُّعَذِّبَهُمْ بِهَا فِي الدُّنْيَا وَتَزْهَقَ اَنْفُسُهُمْ
وَهُمْ كٰفِرُوْنَ ﴿٨٥﴾

86. And when a Sūra is revealed, *enjoining*, 'Believe in Allah and strive *in the cause of Allah* in company with His Messenger,' those of them who possess affluence ask leave of thee and say, 'Leave us that we be with those who sit *at home*.'

وَاِذَآ اُنْزِلَتْ سُوْرَةٌ اَنْ اٰمِنُوْا بِاللّٰهِ وَجَاهِدُوْا مَعَ
رَسُوْلِهِ اسْتَاْذَنَكَ اُولُوا الطَّوْلِ مِنْهُمْ وَقَالُوْا ذَرْنَا
نَكُنْ مَّعَ الْقٰعِدِيْنَ ﴿٨٦﴾

87. They are content to be with the womenfolk, and their hearts are sealed so that they understand not.

رَضُوْا بِاَنْ يَّكُوْنُوْا مَعَ الْخَوَالِفِ وَطُبِعَ عَلٰى قُلُوْبِهِمْ
فَهُمْ لَا يَفْقَهُوْنَ ﴿٨٧﴾

88. But the Messenger and those who believe with him strive *in the cause of Allah* with their property and their persons, and it is they who shall have good things,

لٰكِنِ الرَّسُوْلُ وَالَّذِيْنَ اٰمَنُوْا مَعَهٗ جٰهَدُوْا بِاَمْوَالِهِمْ
وَاَنْفُسِهِمْ ۗ وَاُولٰٓئِكَ لَهُمُ الْخَيْرٰتُ ۡ وَاُولٰٓئِكَ هُمُ

and it is they who shall prosper.

الْمُفْلِحُونَ ﴿٨٨﴾

89. Allah has prepared for them Gardens underneath which flow rivers; therein they shall abide. That is the supreme triumph.

أَعَدَّ اللَّهُ لَهُمْ جَنَّاتٍ تَجْرِي مِنْ تَحْتِهَا الْأَنْهَارُ
خَالِدِينَ فِيهَا ۚ ذَٰلِكَ الْفَوْزُ الْعَظِيمُ ﴿٨٩﴾

R. 12.

90. And those who make excuses from among the desert Arabs, came that exemption might be granted them. And those who were false to Allah and His Messenger stayed *at home*. A grievous punishment shall befall those of them who disbelieve.

وَجَاءَ الْمُعَذِّرُونَ مِنَ الْأَعْرَابِ لِيُؤْذَنَ لَهُمْ
وَقَعَدَ الَّذِينَ كَذَبُوا اللَّهَ وَرَسُولَهُ ۚ سَيُصِيبُ الَّذِينَ
كَفَرُوا مِنْهُمْ عَذَابٌ أَلِيمٌ ﴿٩٠﴾

91. No blame lies on the weak, nor on the sick, nor on those who find naught to spend, if they are sincere to Allah and His Messenger. There is no cause of reproach against those who do good deeds; and Allah is Most Forgiving, Merciful.

لَيْسَ عَلَى الضُّعَفَاءِ وَلَا عَلَى الْمَرْضَىٰ وَلَا عَلَى
الَّذِينَ لَا يَجِدُونَ مَا يُنْفِقُونَ حَرَجٌ إِذَا نَصَحُوا
لِلَّهِ وَرَسُولِهِ ۚ مَا عَلَى الْمُحْسِنِينَ مِنْ سَبِيلٍ ۚ وَ
اللَّهُ غَفُورٌ رَحِيمٌ ﴿٩١﴾

92. Nor against those to whom, when they came to thee that thou shouldst mount them, thou didst say, 'I cannot find whereon I can mount you;' they turned back, their eyes overflowing with tears, out of grief that they could not find what they might spend.

وَلَا عَلَى الَّذِينَ إِذَا مَا أَتَوْكَ لِتَحْمِلَهُمْ قُلْتَ لَا
أَجِدُ مَا أَحْمِلُكُمْ عَلَيْهِ تَوَلَّوْا وَأَعْيُنُهُمْ تَفِيضُ مِنَ
الدَّمْعِ حَزَنًا أَلَّا يَجِدُوا مَا يُنْفِقُونَ ﴿٩٢﴾

93. The cause of reproach is only against those who ask leave of thee, while they are rich. They are content to be with the womenfolk. And Allah has set a seal upon their hearts so that they know not.

إِنَّمَا السَّبِيلُ عَلَى الَّذِينَ يَسْتَأْذِنُونَكَ وَهُمْ
أَغْنِيَاءُ ۚ رَضُوا بِأَنْ يَكُونُوا مَعَ الْخَوَالِفِ وَطَبَعَ
اللَّهُ عَلَىٰ قُلُوبِهِمْ فَهُمْ لَا يَعْلَمُونَ ﴿٩٣﴾

94. They will make excuses to you when you return to them. Say, 'Make no excuses; we will not believe you. Allah has already informed us of the facts about you. And Allah will observe your conduct, and *also* His Messenger; then you will be brought back to Him Who knows the unseen and the seen, and He will tell you all that you used to do.'

يَعْتَذِرُونَ إِلَيْكُمْ إِذَا رَجَعْتُمْ إِلَيْهِمْ ۚ قُلْ
لَا تَعْتَذِرُوا لَنْ نُؤْمِنَ لَكُمْ قَدْ نَبَّأَنَا اللَّهُ مِنْ
أَخْبَارِكُمْ ۚ وَسَيَرَى اللَّهُ عَمَلَكُمْ وَرَسُولُهُ ثُمَّ تُرَدُّونَ
إِلَىٰ عَالِمِ الْغَيْبِ وَالشَّهَادَةِ فَيُنَبِّئُكُمْ بِمَا كُنْتُمْ
تَعْمَلُونَ ﴿٩٤﴾

* 95. They will swear to you by Allah, when you return to them, that you may

سَيَحْلِفُونَ بِاللَّهِ لَكُمْ إِذَا انْقَلَبْتُمْ إِلَيْهِمْ لِتُعْرِضُوا

leave them alone. So leave them alone. Surely, they are an abomination, and their abode is Hell—a *fit* recompense for that which they used to earn.

عَنْهُمْ فَاَعْرِضُوْا عَنْهُمْ اِنَّهُمْ رِجْسٌ وَّ مَاْوٰىهُمْ
جَهَنَّمُ جَزَآءً بِمَا كَانُوْا يَكْسِبُوْنَ ﴿٩٥﴾

96. They will swear to you that you may be pleased with them. But *even* if you be pleased with them, Allah will not be pleased with the rebellious people.

يَحْلِفُوْنَ لَكُمْ لِتَرْضَوْا عَنْهُمْ فَاِنْ تَرْضَوْا عَنْهُمْ
فَاِنَّ اللّٰهَ لَا يَرْضٰى عَنِ الْقَوْمِ الْفٰسِقِيْنَ ﴿٩٦﴾

97. The Arabs of the desert are the worst in disbelief and hypocrisy, and most apt not to know the ordinances *of the Revelation* which Allah has sent down to His Messenger. And Allah is All-Knowing, Wise.

اَلْاَعْرَابُ اَشَدُّ كُفْرًا وَّ نِفَاقًا وَّ اَجْدَرُ اَلَّا يَعْلَمُوْا
حُدُوْدَ مَآ اَنْزَلَ اللّٰهُ عَلٰى رَسُوْلِهٖ وَاللّٰهُ عَلِيْمٌ حَكِيْمٌ ﴿٩٧﴾

* 98. And among the Arabs of the desert are those who regard that which they spend *for God* as a fine and they wait for calamities to *befall* you. On themselves shall fall an evil calamity. And Allah is All-Hearing, All-Knowing.

وَمِنَ الْاَعْرَابِ مَنْ يَّتَّخِذُ مَا يُنْفِقُ مَغْرَمًا وَّ يَتَرَبَّصُ
بِكُمُ الدَّوَآئِرَ عَلَيْهِمْ دَآئِرَةُ السَّوْءِ وَاللّٰهُ سَمِيْعٌ
عَلِيْمٌ ﴿٩٨﴾

99. And among the Arabs of the desert are those who believe in Allah and the Last Day and regard that which they spend as means of drawing near to Allah and *of receiving* the blessings of the Prophet. Aye! it is for them certainly a means of drawing near *to God*. Allah will soon admit them to His mercy. Surely, Allah is Most Forgiving, Merciful.

وَمِنَ الْاَعْرَابِ مَنْ يُّؤْمِنُ بِاللّٰهِ وَالْيَوْمِ الْاٰخِرِ
وَيَتَّخِذُ مَا يُنْفِقُ قُرُبٰتٍ عِنْدَ اللّٰهِ وَصَلَوٰتِ الرَّسُوْلِ
اَلَآ اِنَّهَا قُرْبَةٌ لَّهُمْ سَيُدْخِلُهُمُ اللّٰهُ فِيْ رَحْمَتِهٖ
اِنَّ اللّٰهَ غَفُوْرٌ رَّحِيْمٌ ﴿٩٩﴾

R. 13.

* 100. And *as for* the foremost *among the believers*, the first of the Emigrants* and the Helpers**, and those who followed them in the best possible manner, Allah is well pleased with them and they are well pleased with Him; and He has prepared for them Gardens beneath which flow rivers. They will abide therein for ever. That is the supreme triumph.

وَالسّٰبِقُوْنَ الْاَوَّلُوْنَ مِنَ الْمُهٰجِرِيْنَ وَالْاَنْصَارِ
وَالَّذِيْنَ اتَّبَعُوْهُمْ بِاِحْسَانٍ رَّضِيَ اللّٰهُ عَنْهُمْ
وَرَضُوْا عَنْهُ وَاَعَدَّ لَهُمْ جَنّٰتٍ تَجْرِيْ تَحْتَهَا
الْاَنْهٰرُ خٰلِدِيْنَ فِيْهَآ اَبَدًا ذٰلِكَ الْفَوْزُ الْعَظِيْمُ ﴿١٠٠﴾

101. And of the desert Arabs around you *some* are hypocrites; and of the people of Medina *also*. They persist in hypocrisy. Thou knowest them not; We know them. We will punish them twice; then shall they be given over to a great punishment.

وَمِمَّنْ حَوْلَكُمْ مِّنَ الْاَعْرَابِ مُنٰفِقُوْنَ وَمِنْ
اَهْلِ الْمَدِيْنَةِ مَرَدُوْا عَلَى النِّفَاقِ لَا تَعْلَمُهُمْ
نَحْنُ نَعْلَمُهُمْ سَنُعَذِّبُهُمْ مَّرَّتَيْنِ ثُمَّ يُرَدُّوْنَ اِلٰى
عَذَابٍ عَظِيْمٍ ﴿١٠١﴾

102. And *there are* others who have acknowledged their faults. They mixed a

وَاٰخَرُوْنَ اعْتَرَفُوْا بِذُنُوْبِهِمْ خَلَطُوْا عَمَلًا صَالِحًا

* from Mecca. ** in Medina.

good work with another *that was* evil. It may be that Allah will turn to them with compassion. Surely, Allah is Most Forgiving, Merciful.

وَاٰخَرَ سَيِّئًا عَسَى اللّٰهُ اَنْ يَّتُوْبَ عَلَيْهِمْ اِنَّ اللّٰهَ
غَفُوْرٌ رَّحِيْمٌ ﴿١٠٢﴾

103. Take alms out of their wealth, so that thou mayest cleanse them and purify them thereby. And pray for them; thy prayer is indeed a *source of* tranquillity for them. And Allah is All-Hearing, All-Knowing.

خُذْ مِنْ اَمْوَالِهِمْ صَدَقَةً تُطَهِّرُهُمْ وَتُزَكِّيْهِمْ
بِهَا وَصَلِّ عَلَيْهِمْ اِنَّ صَلٰوتَكَ سَكَنٌ لَّهُمْ وَاللّٰهُ
سَمِيْعٌ عَلِيْمٌ ﴿١٠٣﴾

* 104. Know they not that Allah is He Who accepts repentance from His servants and takes alms, and that Allah is He Who is Oft-Returning *with compassion, and is* Merciful?

اَلَمْ يَعْلَمُوْٓا اَنَّ اللّٰهَ هُوَ يَقْبَلُ التَّوْبَةَ عَنْ عِبَادِهٖ وَ
يَاْخُذُ الصَّدَقٰتِ وَاَنَّ اللّٰهَ هُوَ التَّوَّابُ الرَّحِيْمُ ﴿١٠٤﴾

* 105. And say, 'Work, and Allah will surely see your work and *also* His Messenger and the believers. And you shall be brought back to Him Who knows the unseen and the seen; then He will tell you what you used to do.'

وَقُلِ اعْمَلُوْا فَسَيَرَى اللّٰهُ عَمَلَكُمْ وَرَسُوْلُهٗ وَالْمُؤْمِنُوْنَ
وَسَتُرَدُّوْنَ اِلٰى عٰلِمِ الْغَيْبِ وَالشَّهَادَةِ فَيُنَبِّئُكُمْ بِمَا
كُنْتُمْ تَعْمَلُوْنَ ﴿١٠٥﴾

* 106. And *there are* others *whose* case has been postponed for the decree of Allah. He may punish them or He may turn to them with compassion. And Allah is All-Knowing, Wise.

وَاٰخَرُوْنَ مُرْجَوْنَ لِاَمْرِ اللّٰهِ اِمَّا يُعَذِّبُهُمْ وَاِمَّا يَتُوْبُ
عَلَيْهِمْ وَاللّٰهُ عَلِيْمٌ حَكِيْمٌ ﴿١٠٦﴾

* 107. And *among the hypocrites are* those who have built a mosque in order to injure *Islam* and *help* disbelief and cause a division among the believers, and prepare an ambush for him who warred against Allah and His Messenger before *this*. And they will surely swear: 'We meant nothing but good;' but Allah bears witness that they are certainly liars.

وَالَّذِيْنَ اتَّخَذُوْا مَسْجِدًا ضِرَارًا وَّكُفْرًا وَّتَفْرِيْقًا
بَيْنَ الْمُؤْمِنِيْنَ وَاِرْصَادًا لِّمَنْ حَارَبَ اللّٰهَ وَرَسُوْلَهٗ
مِنْ قَبْلُ وَلَيَحْلِفُنَّ اِنْ اَرَدْنَآ اِلَّا الْحُسْنٰى وَاللّٰهُ يَشْهَدُ
اِنَّهُمْ لَكٰذِبُوْنَ ﴿١٠٧﴾

108. Never stand *to pray* therein. A mosque which was founded upon piety from the *very* first day is surely more worthy that thou shouldst stand *to pray* therein. In it are men who love to become purified, and Allah loves those who purify themselves.

لَا تَقُمْ فِيْهِ اَبَدًا لَمَسْجِدٌ اُسِّسَ عَلَى التَّقْوٰى مِنْ اَوَّلِ
يَوْمٍ اَحَقُّ اَنْ تَقُوْمَ فِيْهِ فِيْهِ رِجَالٌ يُّحِبُّوْنَ اَنْ يَّتَطَهَّرُوْا
وَاللّٰهُ يُحِبُّ الْمُطَّهِّرِيْنَ ﴿١٠٨﴾

* 109. Is he, then, who founded his building on fear of Allah and His pleasure better or he who founded his building on the brink of a tottering water-worn bank which tumbled down with him into

اَفَمَنْ اَسَّسَ بُنْيَانَهٗ عَلٰى تَقْوٰى مِنَ اللّٰهِ وَرِضْوَانٍ
خَيْرٌ اَمْ مَّنْ اَسَّسَ بُنْيَانَهٗ عَلٰى شَفَا جُرُفٍ هَارٍ
فَانْهَارَ بِهٖ فِيْ نَارِ جَهَنَّمَ وَاللّٰهُ لَا يَهْدِي الْقَوْمَ

the fire of Hell? And Allah guides not the wrongdoing people.

* 110. *This* building of theirs, which they have built, will ever continue to be a *source of* disquiet in their hearts, unless their hearts be torn to pieces. And Allah is All-Knowing, Wise.

R. 14.

111. Surely, Allah has purchased of the believers their persons and their property in return for the Garden they shall have; they fight in the cause of Allah, and they slay and are slain—a promise *that He has made* incumbent on Himself in the Torah, and the Gospel, and the Qur'ān. And who is more faithful to his promise than Allah? Rejoice, then, in your bargain which you have made with Him; and that it is which is the supreme triumph.

112. *They are* the ones who turn *to God in repentance*, who worship *Him*, who praise *Him*, who go about in the land *serving Him*, who bow down *to God*, who prostrate themselves *in prayer*, who enjoin good and forbid evil, and who watch the limits *set* by Allah. And give glad tidings to those who believe.

113. It is not for the Prophet and those who believe that they should ask *of God* forgiveness for the idolaters, even though they may be kinsmen, after it has become plain to them that they are the people of Hell.

114. And Abraham's asking forgiveness for his father was only because of a promise he had made to him, but when it became clear to him that he was an enemy to Allah, he dissociated himself from him. Surely, Abraham was most tender-hearted, forbearing.

115. And it is not for Allah to cause a people to go astray after He has guided them until He makes clear to them that which they ought to guard against. Surely, Allah knows all things full well.

116. Surely, it is Allah to Whom belongs the kingdom of the heavens and the earth. He gives life and causes death. And you have no friend nor helper beside Allah.

الظّٰلِمِيْنَ ﴿١٠٩﴾
لَا يَزَالُ بُنْيَانُهُمُ الَّذِيْ بَنَوْا رِيْبَةً فِيْ قُلُوْبِهِمْ
إِلَّآ أَنْ تَقَطَّعَ قُلُوْبُهُمْ ۚ وَاللّٰهُ عَلِيْمٌ حَكِيْمٌ ﴿١١٠﴾ ع
إِنَّ اللّٰهَ اشْتَرٰى مِنَ الْمُؤْمِنِيْنَ أَنْفُسَهُمْ وَأَمْوَالَهُمْ
بِأَنَّ لَهُمُ الْجَنَّةَ ۚ يُقَاتِلُوْنَ فِيْ سَبِيْلِ اللّٰهِ فَيَقْتُلُوْنَ
وَيُقْتَلُوْنَ وَعْدًا عَلَيْهِ حَقًّا فِي التَّوْرٰىةِ وَالْإِنْجِيْلِ
وَالْقُرْاٰنِ ۚ وَمَنْ أَوْفٰى بِعَهْدِهٖ مِنَ اللّٰهِ فَاسْتَبْشِرُوْا
بِبَيْعِكُمُ الَّذِيْ بَايَعْتُمْ بِهٖ ۚ وَذٰلِكَ هُوَ الْفَوْزُ الْعَظِيْمُ ﴿١١١﴾
اَلتَّآئِبُوْنَ الْعٰبِدُوْنَ الْحٰمِدُوْنَ السَّآئِحُوْنَ الرّٰكِعُوْنَ
السّٰجِدُوْنَ الْاٰمِرُوْنَ بِالْمَعْرُوْفِ وَالنَّاهُوْنَ عَنِ
الْمُنْكَرِ وَالْحٰفِظُوْنَ لِحُدُوْدِ اللّٰهِ ۗ وَبَشِّرِ الْمُؤْمِنِيْنَ ﴿١١٢﴾
مَا كَانَ لِلنَّبِيِّ وَالَّذِيْنَ اٰمَنُوْٓا أَنْ يَّسْتَغْفِرُوْا لِلْمُشْرِكِيْنَ
وَلَوْ كَانُوْٓا أُولِيْ قُرْبٰى مِنْۢ بَعْدِ مَا تَبَيَّنَ لَهُمْ أَنَّهُمْ
أَصْحٰبُ الْجَحِيْمِ ﴿١١٣﴾
وَمَا كَانَ اسْتِغْفَارُ إِبْرٰهِيْمَ لِأَبِيْهِ إِلَّا عَنْ مَّوْعِدَةٍ
وَّعَدَهَآ إِيَّاهُ ۚ فَلَمَّا تَبَيَّنَ لَهٗٓ أَنَّهٗ عَدُوٌّ لِّلّٰهِ تَبَرَّأَ مِنْهُ ۚ
إِنَّ إِبْرٰهِيْمَ لَأَوَّاهٌ حَلِيْمٌ ﴿١١٤﴾
وَمَا كَانَ اللّٰهُ لِيُضِلَّ قَوْمًۢا بَعْدَ إِذْ هَدٰىهُمْ
حَتّٰى يُبَيِّنَ لَهُمْ مَّا يَتَّقُوْنَ ۚ إِنَّ اللّٰهَ بِكُلِّ شَيْءٍ عَلِيْمٌ ﴿١١٥﴾
إِنَّ اللّٰهَ لَهٗ مُلْكُ السَّمٰوٰتِ وَالْأَرْضِ ۚ يُحْيٖ
وَيُمِيْتُ ۚ وَمَا لَكُمْ مِّنْ دُوْنِ اللّٰهِ مِنْ
وَّلِيٍّ وَّلَا نَصِيْرٍ ﴿١١٦﴾

117. Allah has certainly turned with mercy to the Prophet and *to* the Emigrants and the Helpers who followed him in the hour of distress after the hearts of a party of them had well-nigh swerved. He again turned to them with mercy. Surely, He is to them Compassionate, Merciful.

* 118. And *He has turned with mercy* to the three whose *case* was deferred, until the earth became too strait for them with *all* its vastness, and their souls were *also* straitened for them, and they became convinced that there was no refuge from Allah save unto Himself. Then He turned to them with mercy that they might turn *to Him*. Surely, it is Allah Who is Oft-Returning *with compassion and is* Merciful.

R. 15.

119. O ye who believe! fear Allah and be with the truthful.

* 120. It was not proper for the people of Medina and those around them from among the Arabs of the desert that they should have remained behind the Messenger of Allah or that they should have preferred their own lives to his. That is because there distresses them neither thirst nor fatigue nor hunger in the way of Allah, nor do they tread a track which enrages the disbelievers, nor do they cause an enemy any injury whatsoever, but there is written down for them a good work on account of it. Surely, Allah suffers not the reward of those who do good to be lost.

121. And they spend not any sum, small or great, nor do they traverse a valley, but it is written down for them, that Allah may give them the best reward for what they did.

* 122. It is not possible for the believers to go forth all together. Why, then, does not a party from every section of them go forth that they may become well versed in religion, and that they may warn their people when they return to them, so that they may guard *against evil?*

لَقَدْ تَّابَ اللّٰهُ عَلَى النَّبِيِّ وَالْمُهٰجِرِيْنَ وَالْاَنْصَارِ
الَّذِيْنَ اتَّبَعُوْهُ فِيْ سَاعَةِ الْعُسْرَةِ مِنْۢ بَعْدِ مَا
كَادَ يَزِيْغُ قُلُوْبُ فَرِيْقٍ مِّنْهُمْ ثُمَّ تَابَ عَلَيْهِمْ
اِنَّهٗ بِهِمْ رَءُوْفٌ رَّحِيْمٌ ﴿۱۱۷﴾
وَّعَلَى الثَّلٰثَةِ الَّذِيْنَ خُلِّفُوْا حَتّٰۤى اِذَا ضَاقَتْ عَلَيْهِمُ الْاَرْضُ بِمَا
رَحُبَتْ وَضَاقَتْ عَلَيْهِمْ اَنْفُسُهُمْ وَظَنُّوْۤا اَنْ لَّا مَلْجَاَ
مِنَ اللّٰهِ اِلَّاۤ اِلَيْهِ ثُمَّ تَابَ عَلَيْهِمْ لِيَتُوْبُوْا اِنَّ اللّٰهَ
هُوَ التَّوَّابُ الرَّحِيْمُ ﴿۱۱۸﴾ ع ۱۴
يٰۤاَيُّهَا الَّذِيْنَ اٰمَنُوا اتَّقُوا اللّٰهَ وَكُوْنُوْا مَعَ الصّٰدِقِيْنَ ﴿۱۱۹﴾
مَا كَانَ لِاَهْلِ الْمَدِيْنَةِ وَمَنْ حَوْلَهُمْ مِّنَ الْاَعْرَابِ
اَنْ يَّتَخَلَّفُوْا عَنْ رَّسُوْلِ اللّٰهِ وَلَا يَرْغَبُوْا بِاَنْفُسِهِمْ عَنْ
نَّفْسِهٖ ذٰلِكَ بِاَنَّهُمْ لَا يُصِيْبُهُمْ ظَمَاٌ وَّلَا نَصَبٌ وَّلَا
مَخْمَصَةٌ فِيْ سَبِيْلِ اللّٰهِ وَلَا يَطَـُٔوْنَ مَوْطِئًا يَّغِيْظُ
الْكُفَّارَ وَلَا يَنَالُوْنَ مِنْ عَدُوٍّ نَّيْلًا اِلَّا كُتِبَ لَهُمْ بِهٖ
عَمَلٌ صَالِحٌ اِنَّ اللّٰهَ لَا يُضِيْعُ اَجْرَ الْمُحْسِنِيْنَ ﴿۱۲۰﴾
وَلَا يُنْفِقُوْنَ نَفَقَةً صَغِيْرَةً وَّلَا كَبِيْرَةً وَّلَا يَقْطَعُوْنَ
وَادِيًا اِلَّا كُتِبَ لَهُمْ لِيَجْزِيَهُمُ اللّٰهُ اَحْسَنَ مَا كَانُوْا
يَعْمَلُوْنَ ﴿۱۲۱﴾
وَمَا كَانَ الْمُؤْمِنُوْنَ لِيَنْفِرُوْا كَآفَّةً فَلَوْلَا نَفَرَ مِنْ
كُلِّ فِرْقَةٍ مِّنْهُمْ طَآئِفَةٌ لِّيَتَفَقَّهُوْا فِي الدِّيْنِ
وَلِيُنْذِرُوْا قَوْمَهُمْ اِذَا رَجَعُوْۤا اِلَيْهِمْ لَعَلَّهُمْ
يَحْذَرُوْنَ ﴿۱۲۲﴾ ع ۱۵

R. 16.

* 123. O ye who believe! fight such of the disbelievers as are near to you and let them find hardness in you; and know that Allah is with the righteous.

124. And whenever a Sūra is sent down, there are some of them who say: 'Which of you has this *Sūra* increased in faith?' But, as to those who believe, it increases their faith and they rejoice.

125. But as for those in whose hearts is a disease, it adds *further* filth to their *present* filth, and they die while they are disbelievers.

* 126. Do they not see that they are tried every year once or twice? Yet they do not repent, nor would they be admonished.

127. And whenever a Sūra is sent down, they look at one another, *saying*, 'Does any one see you?' Then they turn away. Allah has turned away their hearts because they are a people who would not understand.

128. Surely, a Messenger has come unto you from among yourselves; grievous to him is that you should fall into trouble; *he is* ardently desirous of your *welfare; and* to the believers *he is* compassionate, merciful.

129. But if they turn away, say, 'Allah is sufficient for me. There is no God but He. In Him do I put my trust, and He is the Lord of the mighty Throne.'

يٰٓاَيُّهَا الَّذِيْنَ اٰمَنُوْا قَاتِلُوا الَّذِيْنَ يَلُوْنَكُمْ مِّنَ الْكُفَّارِ
وَلْيَجِدُوْا فِيْكُمْ غِلْظَةً ۭ وَاعْلَمُوْٓا اَنَّ اللّٰهَ مَعَ الْمُتَّقِيْنَ ﴿١٢٣﴾
وَاِذَا مَآ اُنْزِلَتْ سُوْرَةٌ فَمِنْهُمْ مَّنْ يَّقُوْلُ اَيُّكُمْ زَادَتْهُ
هٰذِهٖٓ اِيْمَانًا ۚ فَاَمَّا الَّذِيْنَ اٰمَنُوْا فَزَادَتْهُمْ اِيْمَانًا
وَّهُمْ يَسْتَبْشِرُوْنَ ﴿١٢٤﴾
وَاَمَّا الَّذِيْنَ فِيْ قُلُوْبِهِمْ مَّرَضٌ فَزَادَتْهُمْ رِجْسًا
اِلٰى رِجْسِهِمْ وَمَاتُوْا وَهُمْ كٰفِرُوْنَ ﴿١٢٥﴾
اَوَلَا يَرَوْنَ اَنَّهُمْ يُفْتَنُوْنَ فِيْ كُلِّ عَامٍ مَّرَّةً اَوْ
مَرَّتَيْنِ ثُمَّ لَا يَتُوْبُوْنَ وَلَا هُمْ يَذَّكَّرُوْنَ ﴿١٢٦﴾
وَاِذَا مَآ اُنْزِلَتْ سُوْرَةٌ نَّظَرَ بَعْضُهُمْ اِلٰى بَعْضٍ ۭ هَلْ
يَرٰىكُمْ مِّنْ اَحَدٍ ثُمَّ انْصَرَفُوْا ۭ صَرَفَ اللّٰهُ قُلُوْبَهُمْ
بِاَنَّهُمْ قَوْمٌ لَّا يَفْقَهُوْنَ ﴿١٢٧﴾
لَقَدْ جَاۗءَكُمْ رَسُوْلٌ مِّنْ اَنْفُسِكُمْ عَزِيْزٌ عَلَيْهِ مَا
عَنِتُّمْ حَرِيْصٌ عَلَيْكُمْ بِالْمُؤْمِنِيْنَ رَءُوْفٌ
رَّحِيْمٌ ﴿١٢٨﴾
فَاِنْ تَوَلَّوْا فَقُلْ حَسْبِيَ اللّٰهُ ڮ لَآ اِلٰهَ اِلَّا هُوَ ۭ
عَلَيْهِ تَوَكَّلْتُ وَهُوَ رَبُّ الْعَرْشِ الْعَظِيْمِ ﴿١٢٩﴾

رُكُوْعَاتُهَا ١١ سُوْرَةُ يُوْنُسَ مَكِّيَّةٌ (١٠) اٰيَاتُهَا ١١١

YŪNUS

(Revealed before Hijra)

1. In the name of Allah, the Gracious, the Merciful.

بِسْمِ اللّٰهِ الرَّحْمٰنِ الرَّحِيْمِ ①

2. Alif Lām Rā*. These are the verses of the Book that is full of wisdom.

الٓرٰ تِلْكَ اٰيٰتُ الْكِتٰبِ الْحَكِيْمِ ②

* 3. Is it a *matter of* wonder for men that We have inspired a man from among them, *saying*, 'Warn mankind and give glad tidings to those who believe that they have a true rank *of honour* with their Lord?' The disbelievers say, 'Surely, this is a manifest enchanter.'

اَكَانَ لِلنَّاسِ عَجَبًا اَنْ اَوْحَيْنَاۤ اِلٰى رَجُلٍ مِّنْهُمْ اَنْ اَنْذِرِ النَّاسَ وَ بَشِّرِ الَّذِيْنَ اٰمَنُوْۤا اَنَّ لَهُمْ قَدَمَ صِدْقٍ عِنْدَ رَبِّهِمْ ؕ قَالَ الْكٰفِرُوْنَ اِنَّ هٰذَا لَسٰحِرٌ مُّبِيْنٌ ③

* 4. Verily, your Lord is Allah Who created the heavens and the earth in six periods, then He settled Himself on the Throne; He governs everything. There is no intercessor *with Him* save after His permission. That is Allah, your Lord, so worship Him. Will you not, then, be admonished?

اِنَّ رَبَّكُمُ اللّٰهُ الَّذِيْ خَلَقَ السَّمٰوٰتِ وَ الْاَرْضَ فِيْ سِتَّةِ اَيَّامٍ ثُمَّ اسْتَوٰى عَلَى الْعَرْشِ يُدَبِّرُ الْاَمْرَ ؕ مَا مِنْ شَفِيْعٍ اِلَّا مِنْۢ بَعْدِ اِذْنِهٖ ؕ ذٰلِكُمُ اللّٰهُ رَبُّكُمْ فَاعْبُدُوْهُ ؕ اَفَلَا تَذَكَّرُوْنَ ④

5. To Him shall you all return. The promise of Allah is true. Surely, He originates the creation; then He reproduces it, that He may reward those who believe and do good works, with equity; and *as for* those who disbelieve, they shall have a drink of boiling water, and a painful punishment, because they disbelieved.

اِلَيْهِ مَرْجِعُكُمْ جَمِيْعًا ؕ وَعْدَ اللّٰهِ حَقًّا ؕ اِنَّهٗ يَبْدَؤُا الْخَلْقَ ثُمَّ يُعِيْدُهٗ لِيَجْزِيَ الَّذِيْنَ اٰمَنُوْا وَ عَمِلُوا الصّٰلِحٰتِ بِالْقِسْطِ ؕ وَ الَّذِيْنَ كَفَرُوْا لَهُمْ شَرَابٌ مِّنْ حَمِيْمٍ وَّ عَذَابٌ اَلِيْمٌۢ بِمَا كَانُوْا يَكْفُرُوْنَ ⑤

* 6. He it is Who made the sun *radiate* a brilliant light and the moon *reflect* a lustre, and ordained for it stages, that you might know the number of years and the reckoning *of time*. Allah has not created this but in truth. He details the Signs for a people who have knowledge.

هُوَ الَّذِيْ جَعَلَ الشَّمْسَ ضِيَآءً وَّ الْقَمَرَ نُوْرًا وَّ قَدَّرَهٗ مَنَازِلَ لِتَعْلَمُوْا عَدَدَ السِّنِيْنَ وَ الْحِسَابَ ؕ مَا خَلَقَ اللّٰهُ ذٰلِكَ اِلَّا بِالْحَقِّ ۚ يُفَصِّلُ الْاٰيٰتِ لِقَوْمٍ يَّعْلَمُوْنَ ⑥

7. Verily, in the alternation of night and day, and in all that Allah has created

اِنَّ فِي اخْتِلَافِ الَّيْلِ وَ النَّهَارِ وَ مَا خَلَقَ اللّٰهُ فِي

---

* I am Allah Who is All-Seeing.

in the heavens and the earth there are Signs for a God-fearing people.

8. Those who look not for the meeting with Us and are content with the life of this world and feel at rest therewith, and those who are heedless of Our Signs –

9. It is these whose abode is Fire, because of what they earned.

10. But *as for* those who believe, and do good works—their Lord will guide them because of their faith. Rivers shall flow beneath them in the Gardens of Bliss.

11. Their prayer therein shall be, 'Glory be to Thee, O Allah!' and their greeting therein shall be, 'Peace.' And the conclusion of their prayer shall be, 'All praise be to Allah, the Lord of the worlds.'

R. 2.

12. And if Allah were to hasten for men the ill *they have earned* as they would hasten on the *acquisition of* wealth, *the end of* their term *of life* would have been already brought upon them. But We leave those who look not for the meeting with Us to wander distractedly in their transgression.

* 13. And when trouble befalls a man, he calls on Us, lying on his side, or sitting, or standing; but when We have removed his trouble from him, he goes his way as though he had never called on Us for the *removal of the* trouble that befell him. Thus it is that the doings of the extravagant are given a fair appearance in their eyes.

* 14. And We destroyed the generations before you when they did wrong; and there came to them their Messengers with clear Signs, but they would not believe. Thus do We requite the guilty people.

15. Then, We made you *their* successors in the earth after them, that We might see how you would act.

* 16. And when Our clear Signs are recited unto them, those who look not for the

السَّمٰوٰتِ وَالْاَرْضِ لَاٰيٰتٍ لِّقَوْمٍ يَّتَّقُوْنَ ۝٧

اِنَّ الَّذِيْنَ لَا يَرْجُوْنَ لِقَآءَنَا وَرَضُوْا بِالْحَيٰوةِ الدُّنْيَا
وَاطْمَاَنُّوْا بِهَا وَالَّذِيْنَ هُمْ عَنْ اٰيٰتِنَا غٰفِلُوْنَ ۝٨

اُولٰٓئِكَ مَاْوٰىهُمُ النَّارُ بِمَا كَانُوْا يَكْسِبُوْنَ ۝٩

اِنَّ الَّذِيْنَ اٰمَنُوْا وَعَمِلُوا الصّٰلِحٰتِ يَهْدِيْهِمْ رَبُّهُمْ
بِاِيْمَانِهِمْ تَجْرِيْ مِنْ تَحْتِهِمُ الْاَنْهٰرُ فِيْ جَنّٰتِ
النَّعِيْمِ ۝١٠

دَعْوٰىهُمْ فِيْهَا سُبْحٰنَكَ اللّٰهُمَّ وَتَحِيَّتُهُمْ فِيْهَا سَلٰمٌ
وَاٰخِرُ دَعْوٰىهُمْ اَنِ الْحَمْدُ لِلّٰهِ رَبِّ الْعٰلَمِيْنَ ۝١١

وَلَوْ يُعَجِّلُ اللّٰهُ لِلنَّاسِ الشَّرَّ اسْتِعْجَالَهُمْ بِالْخَيْرِ
لَقُضِيَ اِلَيْهِمْ اَجَلُهُمْ فَنَذَرُ الَّذِيْنَ لَا يَرْجُوْنَ لِقَآءَنَا
فِيْ طُغْيَانِهِمْ يَعْمَهُوْنَ ۝١٢

وَاِذَا مَسَّ الْاِنْسَانَ الضُّرُّ دَعَانَا لِجَنْۢبِهٖٓ اَوْ قَاعِدًا
اَوْ قَآئِمًا فَلَمَّا كَشَفْنَا عَنْهُ ضُرَّهٗ مَرَّ كَاَنْ لَّمْ يَدْعُنَآ
اِلٰى ضُرٍّ مَّسَّهٗ كَذٰلِكَ زُيِّنَ لِلْمُسْرِفِيْنَ مَا كَانُوْا
يَعْمَلُوْنَ ۝١٣

وَلَقَدْ اَهْلَكْنَا الْقُرُوْنَ مِنْ قَبْلِكُمْ لَمَّا ظَلَمُوْا
وَجَآءَتْهُمْ رُسُلُهُمْ بِالْبَيِّنٰتِ وَمَا كَانُوْا لِيُؤْمِنُوْا
كَذٰلِكَ نَجْزِي الْقَوْمَ الْمُجْرِمِيْنَ ۝١٤

ثُمَّ جَعَلْنٰكُمْ خَلٰٓئِفَ فِي الْاَرْضِ مِنْۢ بَعْدِهِمْ لِنَنْظُرَ
كَيْفَ تَعْمَلُوْنَ ۝١٥

وَاِذَا تُتْلٰى عَلَيْهِمْ اٰيَاتُنَا بَيِّنٰتٍ قَالَ الَّذِيْنَ لَا يَرْجُوْنَ

meeting with Us say, 'Bring a Qur'ān other than this or change it.' Say, 'It is not for me to change it of my own accord. I only follow what is revealed to me. Indeed, I fear, if I disobey my Lord, the punishment of an awful day.'

لِقَآءَنَا ائْتِ بِقُرْاٰنٍ غَيْرِ هٰذَآ اَوْ بَدِّلْهُ ؕ قُلْ مَا يَكُوْنُ
لِيْٓ اَنْ اُبَدِّلَهٗ مِنْ تِلْقَآئِ نَفْسِيْ ۚ اِنْ اَتَّبِعُ اِلَّا مَا يُوْحٰٓى
اِلَيَّ ۚ اِنِّيْٓ اَخَافُ اِنْ عَصَيْتُ رَبِّيْ عَذَابَ يَوْمٍ عَظِيْمٍ ﴿١٦﴾

17. Say, 'If Allah had *so* willed, I should not have recited it to you nor would He have made it known to you. I have indeed lived among you a *whole* lifetime before this. Will you not then understand?'

قُلْ لَّوْ شَآءَ اللّٰهُ مَا تَلَوْتُهٗ عَلَيْكُمْ وَلَآ اَدْرٰىكُمْ بِهٖ ۖ
فَقَدْ لَبِثْتُ فِيْكُمْ عُمُرًا مِّنْ قَبْلِهٖ ؕ اَفَلَا تَعْقِلُوْنَ ﴿١٧﴾

* 18. Who is then more unjust than he who forges a lie against Allah or *he* who treats His Signs as lies? Surely, the guilty shall never prosper.

فَمَنْ اَظْلَمُ مِمَّنِ افْتَرٰى عَلَى اللّٰهِ كَذِبًا اَوْ كَذَّبَ بِاٰيٰتِهٖ ؕ
اِنَّهٗ لَا يُفْلِحُ الْمُجْرِمُوْنَ ﴿١٨﴾

* 19. And they worship, instead of Allah, that which neither harms them nor profits them; and they say, 'These are our intercessors with Allah.' Say, 'Would you inform Allah of something He knows not in the heavens or in the earth?' Holy is He, and high exalted above *all* that which they associate *with Him*.

وَيَعْبُدُوْنَ مِنْ دُوْنِ اللّٰهِ مَا لَا يَضُرُّهُمْ وَلَا يَنْفَعُهُمْ
وَيَقُوْلُوْنَ هٰٓؤُلَآءِ شُفَعَآؤُنَا عِنْدَ اللّٰهِ ؕ قُلْ اَتُنَبِّـُٔوْنَ
اللّٰهَ بِمَا لَا يَعْلَمُ فِي السَّمٰوٰتِ وَلَا فِي الْاَرْضِ ؕ سُبْحٰنَهٗ
وَتَعٰلٰى عَمَّا يُشْرِكُوْنَ ﴿١٩﴾

* 20. And mankind were but one community, then they differed *among themselves;* and had it not been for a word that had gone before from thy Lord, it would have *already* been judged between them concerning that in which they differed.

وَمَا كَانَ النَّاسُ اِلَّآ اُمَّةً وَّاحِدَةً فَاخْتَلَفُوْا ؕ وَلَوْلَا
كَلِمَةٌ سَبَقَتْ مِنْ رَّبِّكَ لَقُضِيَ بَيْنَهُمْ فِيْمَا فِيْهِ
يَخْتَلِفُوْنَ ﴿٢٠﴾

* 21. And they say, 'Why has not a Sign been sent down to him from his Lord?' Say, 'The unseen belongs only to Allah. So wait; I am with you among those who wait.'

وَيَقُوْلُوْنَ لَوْلَآ اُنْزِلَ عَلَيْهِ اٰيَةٌ مِّنْ رَّبِّهٖ ۚ فَقُلْ اِنَّمَا
الْغَيْبُ لِلّٰهِ فَانْتَظِرُوْا ۚ اِنِّيْ مَعَكُمْ مِّنَ الْمُنْتَظِرِيْنَ ﴿٢١﴾ ع

R. 3.

* 22. And when We make people taste of mercy after adversity has touched them, behold, they begin to plan against Our Signs. Say, 'Allah is swifter in planning.' Surely, Our messengers write down all that you plan.

وَاِذَآ اَذَقْنَا النَّاسَ رَحْمَةً مِّنْۢ بَعْدِ ضَرَّآءَ مَسَّتْهُمْ
اِذَا لَهُمْ مَّكْرٌ فِيْٓ اٰيَاتِنَا ؕ قُلِ اللّٰهُ اَسْرَعُ مَكْرًا ؕ اِنَّ
رُسُلَنَا يَكْتُبُوْنَ مَا تَمْكُرُوْنَ ﴿٢٢﴾

* 23. He it is Who enables you to journey through land and sea until, when you are on *board* the ships and they sail with them with a fair breeze and they rejoice in it, there overtakes them (the ships) a violent wind and the waves come on them from

هُوَ الَّذِيْ يُسَيِّرُكُمْ فِي الْبَرِّ وَالْبَحْرِ ؕ حَتّٰٓى اِذَا كُنْتُمْ
فِي الْفُلْكِ ۚ وَجَرَيْنَ بِهِمْ بِرِيْحٍ طَيِّبَةٍ وَّفَرِحُوْا بِهَا
جَآءَتْهَا رِيْحٌ عَاصِفٌ وَّجَآءَهُمُ الْمَوْجُ مِنْ كُلِّ

every side and they think they are encompassed, *then* they call upon Allah, purifying *their* religion for Him, *saying*, 'If Thou deliver us from this, we will surely be of the thankful.'

مَكَانٍ وَّظَنُّوْٓا اَنَّهُمْ اُحِيْطَ بِهِمْ ۙ دَعَوُا اللّٰهَ مُخْلِصِيْنَ
لَهُ الدِّيْنَ ۚ لَئِنْ اَنْجَيْتَنَا مِنْ هٰذِهٖ لَنَكُوْنَنَّ مِنَ
الشّٰكِرِيْنَ ﴿٢٣﴾

* 24. But when He has delivered them, lo! they begin to commit excesses in the earth wrongfully. O ye men, your excesses are only against your own selves. *Have* the enjoyment of the present life. Then to Us shall be your return; and We will inform you of what you used to do.

فَلَمَّآ اَنْجٰهُمْ اِذَا هُمْ يَبْغُوْنَ فِي الْاَرْضِ بِغَيْرِ الْحَقِّ ؕ
يٰٓاَيُّهَا النَّاسُ اِنَّمَا بَغْيُكُمْ عَلٰٓى اَنْفُسِكُمْ ۙ مَّتَاعَ الْحَيٰوةِ
الدُّنْيَا ۫ ثُمَّ اِلَيْنَا مَرْجِعُكُمْ فَنُنَبِّئُكُمْ بِمَا كُنْتُمْ
تَعْمَلُوْنَ ﴿٢٤﴾

* 25. The likeness of the present life is only as water which We send down from the clouds, then there mingles with it the produce of the earth, of which men and cattle eat till, when the earth receives its ornature and looks beautiful and its owners think that they have power over it, there comes to it Our command by night or by day and We render it a field that is mown down, as if nothing had existed there the day before. Thus do We expound the Signs for a people who reflect.

اِنَّمَا مَثَلُ الْحَيٰوةِ الدُّنْيَا كَمَآءٍ اَنْزَلْنٰهُ مِنَ السَّمَآءِ
فَاخْتَلَطَ بِهٖ نَبَاتُ الْاَرْضِ مِمَّا يَاْكُلُ النَّاسُ وَ
الْاَنْعَامُ ؕ حَتّٰٓى اِذَآ اَخَذَتِ الْاَرْضُ زُخْرُفَهَا وَ
ازَّيَّنَتْ وَظَنَّ اَهْلُهَآ اَنَّهُمْ قٰدِرُوْنَ عَلَيْهَآ ۙ اَتٰىهَآ
اَمْرُنَا لَيْلًا اَوْ نَهَارًا فَجَعَلْنٰهَا حَصِيْدًا كَاَنْ لَّمْ تَغْنَ
بِالْاَمْسِ ؕ كَذٰلِكَ نُفَصِّلُ الْاٰيٰتِ لِقَوْمٍ يَّتَفَكَّرُوْنَ ﴿٢٥﴾

26. And Allah calls to the abode of peace, and guides whom He pleases to the straight path.

وَاللّٰهُ يَدْعُوْٓا اِلٰى دَارِ السَّلٰمِ ؕ وَيَهْدِيْ مَنْ يَّشَآءُ
اِلٰى صِرَاطٍ مُّسْتَقِيْمٍ ﴿٢٦﴾

27. For those who do good deeds, there shall be the best *reward* and *yet* more *blessings*. And neither darkness nor ignominy shall cover their faces. It is these who are the inmates of Heaven; therein shall they abide.

لِلَّذِيْنَ اَحْسَنُوا الْحُسْنٰى وَزِيَادَةٌ ؕ وَلَا يَرْهَقُ وُجُوْهَهُمْ
قَتَرٌ وَّلَا ذِلَّةٌ ؕ اُولٰٓئِكَ اَصْحٰبُ الْجَنَّةِ ۚ هُمْ فِيْهَا
خٰلِدُوْنَ ﴿٢٧﴾

28. And *as for* those who do evil deeds, the punishment of an evil shall be the like thereof, and ignominy shall cover them. They shall have none to protect them against Allah. *And they shall look* as if their faces had been covered with dark patches of night. It is these who are the inmates of the Fire; therein shall they abide.

وَالَّذِيْنَ كَسَبُوا السَّيِّاٰتِ جَزَآءُ سَيِّئَةٍۭ بِمِثْلِهَا ۙ وَ
تَرْهَقُهُمْ ذِلَّةٌ ؕ مَا لَهُمْ مِّنَ اللّٰهِ مِنْ عَاصِمٍ ۚ كَاَنَّمَآ
اُغْشِيَتْ وُجُوْهُهُمْ قِطَعًا مِّنَ الَّيْلِ مُظْلِمًا ؕ اُولٰٓئِكَ
اَصْحٰبُ النَّارِ ۚ هُمْ فِيْهَا خٰلِدُوْنَ ﴿٢٨﴾

* 29. And *remember* the day when We shall gather them all together, then shall We say to those who ascribed partners *to God*, "*Stand back in* your places, you and your 'partners". Then We shall separate them widely, one from another, and their 'partners' will say: 'It was not us that you worshipped.

وَيَوْمَ نَحْشُرُهُمْ جَمِيعًا ثُمَّ نَقُولُ لِلَّذِينَ أَشْرَكُوا
مَكَانَكُمْ أَنتُمْ وَشُرَكَاؤُكُمْ فَزَيَّلْنَا بَيْنَهُمْ وَقَالَ
شُرَكَاؤُهُم مَّا كُنتُمْ إِيَّانَا تَعْبُدُونَ ﴿٢٩﴾

* 30. 'So Allah is *now* sufficient as a Witness between us and you. We were certainly unaware of your worship.'

فَكَفَىٰ بِاللَّهِ شَهِيدًا بَيْنَنَا وَبَيْنَكُمْ إِن كُنَّا عَنْ
عِبَادَتِكُمْ لَغَافِلِينَ ﴿٣٠﴾

31. There shall every soul realize what it shall have sent on before. And they shall be brought back to Allah, their true Master, and all that they used to forge shall be lost to them.

هُنَالِكَ تَبْلُوا كُلُّ نَفْسٍ مَّا أَسْلَفَتْ وَرُدُّوا إِلَى اللَّهِ
مَوْلَاهُمُ الْحَقِّ وَضَلَّ عَنْهُم مَّا كَانُوا يَفْتَرُونَ ﴿٣١﴾ ع النصف

R. 4.

* 32. Say, 'Who provides sustenance for you from the heaven and the earth? Or who is it that has power over the ears and the eyes? And who brings forth the living from the dead and brings the dead out of the living? And who governs all affairs?' They will say, 'Allah'. Then say, 'Will you not then seek *His* protection?'

قُلْ مَن يَرْزُقُكُم مِّنَ السَّمَاءِ وَالْأَرْضِ أَمَّن يَمْلِكُ
السَّمْعَ وَالْأَبْصَارَ وَمَن يُخْرِجُ الْحَيَّ مِنَ الْمَيِّتِ
وَيُخْرِجُ الْمَيِّتَ مِنَ الْحَيِّ وَمَن يُدَبِّرُ الْأَمْرَ
فَسَيَقُولُونَ اللَّهُ فَقُلْ أَفَلَا تَتَّقُونَ ﴿٣٢﴾

* 33. Such is Allah, your true Lord. So what *would you have* after *discarding* the truth except error? How then are you being turned away *from the truth?*

فَذَٰلِكُمُ اللَّهُ رَبُّكُمُ الْحَقُّ فَمَاذَا بَعْدَ الْحَقِّ إِلَّا
الضَّلَالُ فَأَنَّىٰ تُصْرَفُونَ ﴿٣٣﴾

34. Thus is the word of thy Lord proved true against those who rebel, that they believe not.

كَذَٰلِكَ حَقَّتْ كَلِمَتُ رَبِّكَ عَلَى الَّذِينَ فَسَقُوا
أَنَّهُمْ لَا يُؤْمِنُونَ ﴿٣٤﴾

* 35. Say, 'Is there any of your associate-gods who originates creation and then reproduces it?' Say, 'It is Allah *alone* Who originates creation and then reproduces it. Whither then are you turned away?'

قُلْ هَلْ مِن شُرَكَائِكُم مَّن يَبْدَأُ الْخَلْقَ ثُمَّ
يُعِيدُهُ قُلِ اللَّهُ يَبْدَأُ الْخَلْقَ ثُمَّ يُعِيدُهُ فَأَنَّىٰ
تُؤْفَكُونَ ﴿٣٥﴾

36. Say, 'Is there any of your associate-gods who leads to the truth?' Say, 'It is Allah Who leads to the truth. Is then He Who leads to the truth more worthy to be followed or he who finds not the way *himself* unless he be guided? What, then, is the matter with you? How judge ye?'

قُلْ هَلْ مِن شُرَكَائِكُم مَّن يَهْدِي إِلَى الْحَقِّ قُلِ
اللَّهُ يَهْدِي لِلْحَقِّ أَفَمَن يَهْدِي إِلَى الْحَقِّ أَحَقُّ
أَن يُتَّبَعَ أَمَّن لَّا يَهِدِّي إِلَّا أَن يُهْدَىٰ فَمَا لَكُمْ
كَيْفَ تَحْكُمُونَ ﴿٣٦﴾

* 37. And most of them follow nothing but conjecture. Surely, conjecture avails nothing against truth. Verily, Allah is well aware of what they do.

وَمَا يَتَّبِعُ أَكْثَرُهُمْ إِلَّا ظَنًّا ۚ إِنَّ الظَّنَّ لَا يُغْنِي مِنَ الْحَقِّ شَيْئًا ۚ إِنَّ اللَّهَ عَلِيمٌ بِمَا يَفْعَلُونَ ﴿٣٧﴾

38. And this Qur'ān is not such as might be devised by any one except Allah. On the contrary, it fulfils that which is before it and is an exposition of the Law *of God*. There is no doubt about it. *It is* from the Lord of the worlds.

وَمَا كَانَ هَٰذَا الْقُرْآنُ أَنْ يُفْتَرَىٰ مِنْ دُونِ اللَّهِ وَلَٰكِنْ تَصْدِيقَ الَّذِي بَيْنَ يَدَيْهِ وَتَفْصِيلَ الْكِتَابِ لَا رَيْبَ فِيهِ مِنْ رَبِّ الْعَالَمِينَ ﴿٣٨﴾

39. Do they say, 'He has forged it?' Say, 'Bring then a Sūra like unto it, and call for help on all you can besides Allah, if you are truthful.'

أَمْ يَقُولُونَ افْتَرَاهُ ۖ قُلْ فَأْتُوا بِسُورَةٍ مِثْلِهِ وَادْعُوا مَنِ اسْتَطَعْتُمْ مِنْ دُونِ اللَّهِ إِنْ كُنْتُمْ صَادِقِينَ ﴿٣٩﴾

40. Nay, but they have rejected that the knowledge of which they did not encompass nor has the *true* significance thereof yet come to them. In like manner did those before them reject *the truth*. But see what was the end of those who did wrong!

بَلْ كَذَّبُوا بِمَا لَمْ يُحِيطُوا بِعِلْمِهِ وَلَمَّا يَأْتِهِمْ تَأْوِيلُهُ ۚ كَذَٰلِكَ كَذَّبَ الَّذِينَ مِنْ قَبْلِهِمْ ۖ فَانْظُرْ كَيْفَ كَانَ عَاقِبَةُ الظَّالِمِينَ ﴿٤٠﴾

* 41. And of them there are *some* who believe therein, and of them there are *others* who do not believe therein, and thy Lord well knows those who act corruptly.

وَمِنْهُمْ مَنْ يُؤْمِنُ بِهِ وَمِنْهُمْ مَنْ لَا يُؤْمِنُ بِهِ ۚ وَرَبُّكَ أَعْلَمُ بِالْمُفْسِدِينَ ﴿٤١﴾ ع

R. 5.

* 42. And if they accuse thee of lying, say, 'For me is my work and for you is your work. You are not responsible for what I do and I am not responsible for what you do.'

وَإِنْ كَذَّبُوكَ فَقُلْ لِي عَمَلِي وَلَكُمْ عَمَلُكُمْ ۖ أَنْتُمْ بَرِيئُونَ مِمَّا أَعْمَلُ وَأَنَا بَرِيءٌ مِمَّا تَعْمَلُونَ ﴿٤٢﴾

43. And among them are *some* who give ear to thee. But canst thou make the deaf hear, even though they understand not?

وَمِنْهُمْ مَنْ يَسْتَمِعُونَ إِلَيْكَ ۚ أَفَأَنْتَ تُسْمِعُ الصُّمَّ وَلَوْ كَانُوا لَا يَعْقِلُونَ ﴿٤٣﴾

44. And among them are *some* who look towards thee. But canst thou guide the blind, even though they see not?

وَمِنْهُمْ مَنْ يَنْظُرُ إِلَيْكَ ۚ أَفَأَنْتَ تَهْدِي الْعُمْيَ وَلَوْ كَانُوا لَا يُبْصِرُونَ ﴿٤٤﴾

45. Certainly, Allah wrongs not men at all, but men wrong their own souls.

إِنَّ اللَّهَ لَا يَظْلِمُ النَّاسَ شَيْئًا وَلَٰكِنَّ النَّاسَ أَنْفُسَهُمْ يَظْلِمُونَ ﴿٤٥﴾

* 46. And on the day when He will gather them together, *it will appear to them* as though they had not tarried in the world save for an hour of a day. They will recognize one another. Losers indeed are

وَيَوْمَ يَحْشُرُهُمْ كَأَنْ لَمْ يَلْبَثُوا إِلَّا سَاعَةً مِنَ النَّهَارِ يَتَعَارَفُونَ بَيْنَهُمْ ۚ قَدْ خَسِرَ الَّذِينَ كَذَّبُوا

those who deny the meeting with Allah and would not follow guidance.

* 47. And if We show thee *in thy lifetime the fulfilment of* some of the things with which We have threatened them, *thou wilt know it;* or if We cause thee to die *before that*, then to Us is their return, *and thou wilt see the fulfilment in the next world;* and Allah is Witness to all that they do.

48. And for every people there is a Messenger. So when their Messenger comes, it is judged between them with equity, and they are not wronged.

49. And they say, 'When will this promise be *fulfilled*, if you are truthful?'

50. Say, 'I have no power for myself over any harm or benefit, save that which Allah wills. For every *disbelieving* people there is an appointed term. When their term is come, they cannot remain behind a single moment, nor can they get ahead *of it*.'

* 51. Say, 'Tell me, if His punishment comes upon you by night or by day, how will the guilty run away from it?

52. 'Is it then when it has befallen you that you will believe in it? What! Now! And *before this* you used to demand its speedy coming?'

53. Then will it be said to those who did wrong, 'Taste ye the abiding punishment. You are not requited save for that which you used to earn.'

54. And they enquire of thee, 'Is it true?' Say, 'Yea, by my Lord! It is most surely true; and you cannot frustrate *it*.'

R. 6.

55. And if every soul that does wrong possessed all that is in the earth, it would surely offer to ransom *itself* therewith. And they will conceal *their* remorse when they see the punishment. And judgment shall be passed between them with equity, and they shall not be wronged.

* 56. Know ye! to Allah, surely, belongs whatever is in the heavens and the earth. Know ye, that Allah's promise is surely true! But most of them understand not.

بِلِقَآءِ اللّٰهِ وَمَا كَانُوْا مُهْتَدِيْنَ ﴿٤٦﴾

وَاِمَّا نُرِيَنَّكَ بَعْضَ الَّذِيْ نَعِدُهُمْ اَوْ نَتَوَفَّيَنَّكَ فَاِلَيْنَا

مَرْجِعُهُمْ ثُمَّ اللّٰهُ شَهِيْدٌ عَلٰى مَا يَفْعَلُوْنَ ﴿٤٧﴾

وَلِكُلِّ اُمَّةٍ رَّسُوْلٌ ۚ فَاِذَا جَآءَ رَسُوْلُهُمْ قُضِيَ بَيْنَهُمْ

بِالْقِسْطِ وَهُمْ لَا يُظْلَمُوْنَ ﴿٤٨﴾

وَيَقُوْلُوْنَ مَتٰى هٰذَا الْوَعْدُ اِنْ كُنْتُمْ صٰدِقِيْنَ ﴿٤٩﴾

قُلْ لَّآ اَمْلِكُ لِنَفْسِيْ ضَرًّا وَّلَا نَفْعًا اِلَّا مَا شَآءَ اللّٰهُ

لِكُلِّ اُمَّةٍ اَجَلٌ ۚ اِذَا جَآءَ اَجَلُهُمْ فَلَا يَسْتَاْخِرُوْنَ

سَاعَةً وَّلَا يَسْتَقْدِمُوْنَ ﴿٥٠﴾

قُلْ اَرَءَيْتُمْ اِنْ اَتٰىكُمْ عَذَابُهٗ بَيَاتًا اَوْ نَهَارًا مَّاذَا

يَسْتَعْجِلُ مِنْهُ الْمُجْرِمُوْنَ ﴿٥١﴾

اَثُمَّ اِذَا مَا وَقَعَ اٰمَنْتُمْ بِهٖ ؕ آٰلْـٰٔنَ وَقَدْ كُنْتُمْ بِهٖ

تَسْتَعْجِلُوْنَ ﴿٥٢﴾

ثُمَّ قِيْلَ لِلَّذِيْنَ ظَلَمُوْا ذُوْقُوْا عَذَابَ الْخُلْدِ ۚ هَلْ

تُجْزَوْنَ اِلَّا بِمَا كُنْتُمْ تَكْسِبُوْنَ ﴿٥٣﴾ وقف النبي صلى الله عليه وسلم

وَيَسْتَنْۢبِـُٔوْنَكَ اَحَقٌّ هُوَ ؕ قُلْ اِيْ وَرَبِّيْٓ اِنَّهٗ لَحَقٌّ ؕۚ

وَمَآ اَنْتُمْ بِمُعْجِزِيْنَ ﴿٥٤﴾ ع ٥

وَلَوْ اَنَّ لِكُلِّ نَفْسٍ ظَلَمَتْ مَا فِي الْاَرْضِ لَافْتَدَتْ

بِهٖ ؕ وَاَسَرُّوا النَّدَامَةَ لَمَّا رَاَوُا الْعَذَابَ ۚ وَقُضِيَ

بَيْنَهُمْ بِالْقِسْطِ وَهُمْ لَا يُظْلَمُوْنَ ﴿٥٥﴾

اَلَآ اِنَّ لِلّٰهِ مَا فِي السَّمٰوٰتِ وَالْاَرْضِ ؕ اَلَآ اِنَّ وَعْدَ

اللّٰهِ حَقٌّ وَّلٰكِنَّ اَكْثَرَهُمْ لَا يَعْلَمُوْنَ ﴿٥٦﴾

57. He it is Who gives life and causes death, and to Him shall you be brought back.

هُوَ يُحْيٖ وَيُمِيْتُ وَاِلَيْهِ تُرْجَعُوْنَ (٥٧)

58. O mankind! there has indeed come to you an exhortation from your Lord and a cure for whatever *disease* there is in the hearts, and a guidance and a mercy to the believers.

يٰۤاَيُّهَا النَّاسُ قَدْ جَآءَتْكُمْ مَّوْعِظَةٌ مِّنْ رَّبِّكُمْ وَشِفَآءٌ لِّمَا فِي الصُّدُوْرِ ۙ وَهُدًى وَّرَحْمَةٌ لِّلْمُؤْمِنِيْنَ (٥٨)

59. Say, '*All this is* through the grace of Allah and through His mercy; therein, therefore, let them rejoice. That is better than what they hoard.'

قُلْ بِفَضْلِ اللّٰهِ وَبِرَحْمَتِهٖ فَبِذٰلِكَ فَلْيَفْرَحُوْا ؕ هُوَ خَيْرٌ مِّمَّا يَجْمَعُوْنَ (٥٩)

60. Say, 'Have you considered that Allah sent down provision to you, then you made *some* of it unlawful and *some* lawful?' Say, 'Has Allah permitted you *that* or do you invent lies against Allah?'

قُلْ اَرَءَيْتُمْ مَّاۤ اَنْزَلَ اللّٰهُ لَكُمْ مِّنْ رِّزْقٍ فَجَعَلْتُمْ مِّنْهُ حَرَامًا وَّحَلٰلًا ؕ قُلْ آٰللّٰهُ اَذِنَ لَكُمْ اَمْ عَلَى اللّٰهِ تَفْتَرُوْنَ (٦٠)

61. What think those who invent lies against Allah of the Day of Resurrection? Surely, Allah is gracious towards mankind, but most of them are not thankful.

وَمَا ظَنُّ الَّذِيْنَ يَفْتَرُوْنَ عَلَى اللّٰهِ الْكَذِبَ يَوْمَ الْقِيٰمَةِ ؕ اِنَّ اللّٰهَ لَذُوْ فَضْلٍ عَلَى النَّاسِ وَلٰكِنَّ اَكْثَرَهُمْ لَا يَشْكُرُوْنَ (٦١)

R. 7.

* 62. And thou art not engaged in anything, and thou recitest not from Him any portion of the Qur'ān, and you do no work, but We are witnesses of you when you are engrossed therein. And there is not hidden from thy Lord even an atom's weight in the earth or in heaven. And there is nothing smaller than that or greater, but it is *recorded* in a clear Book.

وَمَا تَكُوْنُ فِيْ شَاْنٍ وَّمَا تَتْلُوْا مِنْهُ مِنْ قُرْاٰنٍ وَّلَا تَعْمَلُوْنَ مِنْ عَمَلٍ اِلَّا كُنَّا عَلَيْكُمْ شُهُوْدًا اِذْ تُفِيْضُوْنَ فِيْهِ ؕ وَمَا يَعْزُبُ عَنْ رَّبِّكَ مِنْ مِّثْقَالِ ذَرَّةٍ فِي الْاَرْضِ وَلَا فِي السَّمَآءِ وَلَاۤ اَصْغَرَ مِنْ ذٰلِكَ وَلَاۤ اَكْبَرَ اِلَّا فِيْ كِتٰبٍ مُّبِيْنٍ (٦٢)

63. Behold! the friends of Allah shall certainly have no fear, nor shall they grieve—

اَلَاۤ اِنَّ اَوْلِيَآءَ اللّٰهِ لَا خَوْفٌ عَلَيْهِمْ وَلَا هُمْ يَحْزَنُوْنَ (٦٣)

* 64. Those who believed and kept to righteousness—

الَّذِيْنَ اٰمَنُوْا وَكَانُوْا يَتَّقُوْنَ (٦٤)

65. For them are glad tidings in the present life and *also* in the Hereafter—there is no changing the words of Allah; that indeed is the supreme triumph.

لَهُمُ الْبُشْرٰى فِي الْحَيٰوةِ الدُّنْيَا وَفِي الْاٰخِرَةِ ؕ لَا تَبْدِيْلَ لِكَلِمٰتِ اللّٰهِ ؕ ذٰلِكَ هُوَ الْفَوْزُ الْعَظِيْمُ (٦٥)

* 66. And let not their words grieve thee. Surely, all power belongs to Allah. He is

وَلَا يَحْزُنْكَ قَوْلُهُمْ ۘ اِنَّ الْعِزَّةَ لِلّٰهِ جَمِيْعًا ؕ هُوَ السَّمِيْعُ

the All-Hearing, the All-Knowing.

الْعَلِيْمُ ٦٦

* 67. Behold! whoever is in the heavens and whoever is in the earth is Allah's. Those who call on others than Allah do not *really* follow *these* 'partners'; they follow only a conjecture, and they do nothing but guess.

أَلَآ إِنَّ لِلّٰهِ مَنْ فِي السَّمٰوٰتِ وَمَنْ فِي الْأَرْضِ ۗ وَمَا يَتَّبِعُ الَّذِيْنَ يَدْعُوْنَ مِنْ دُوْنِ اللّٰهِ شُرَكَآءَ ۗ إِنْ يَّتَّبِعُوْنَ إِلَّا الظَّنَّ وَإِنْ هُمْ إِلَّا يَخْرُصُوْنَ ٦٧

* 68. He it is Who has made for you the night *dark* that you may rest therein, and the day full of light. Surely, therein are Signs for a people who listen.

هُوَ الَّذِيْ جَعَلَ لَكُمُ الَّيْلَ لِتَسْكُنُوْا فِيْهِ وَالنَّهَارَ مُبْصِرًا ۗ إِنَّ فِيْ ذٰلِكَ لَاٰيٰتٍ لِّقَوْمٍ يَّسْمَعُوْنَ ٦٨

69. They say, 'Allah has taken unto Himself a son.' Holy is He! He is Self-Sufficient. To Him belongs whatsoever is in the heavens and whatsoever is in the earth. You have no authority for this. Do you say against Allah what you know not?

قَالُوا اتَّخَذَ اللّٰهُ وَلَدًا سُبْحٰنَهٗ ۗ هُوَ الْغَنِيُّ ۗ لَهٗ مَا فِي السَّمٰوٰتِ وَمَا فِي الْأَرْضِ ۗ إِنْ عِنْدَكُمْ مِّنْ سُلْطٰنٍ بِهٰذَا ۗ أَتَقُوْلُوْنَ عَلَى اللّٰهِ مَا لَا تَعْلَمُوْنَ ٦٩

70. Say, 'Those who invent a lie against Allah shall not prosper.'

قُلْ إِنَّ الَّذِيْنَ يَفْتَرُوْنَ عَلَى اللّٰهِ الْكَذِبَ لَا يُفْلِحُوْنَ ٧٠

* 71. *They will have some* enjoyment in this world. Then to Us is their return. Then shall We make them taste a severe punishment, because they used to disbelieve.

مَتَاعٌ فِي الدُّنْيَا ثُمَّ إِلَيْنَا مَرْجِعُهُمْ ثُمَّ نُذِيْقُهُمُ الْعَذَابَ الشَّدِيْدَ بِمَا كَانُوْا يَكْفُرُوْنَ ٧١

R. 8.

72. And recite unto them the story of Noah, when he said to his people, 'O my people, if my station *with God* and my reminding you *of your duty* through the Signs of Allah offend you—and in Allah do I put my trust—muster then *all* your designs, *you* and your 'partners'; then let not your course of action be obscure to you; then carry out *your designs* against me and give me no respite.

وَاتْلُ عَلَيْهِمْ نَبَأَ نُوْحٍ ۘ إِذْ قَالَ لِقَوْمِهٖ يٰقَوْمِ إِنْ كَانَ كَبُرَ عَلَيْكُمْ مَّقَامِيْ وَتَذْكِيْرِيْ بِاٰيٰتِ اللّٰهِ فَعَلَى اللّٰهِ تَوَكَّلْتُ فَأَجْمِعُوْٓا أَمْرَكُمْ وَشُرَكَآءَكُمْ ثُمَّ لَا يَكُنْ أَمْرُكُمْ عَلَيْكُمْ غُمَّةً ثُمَّ اقْضُوْٓا إِلَيَّ وَلَا تُنْظِرُوْنِ ٧٢

* 73. 'But if you turn back, *remember*, I have not asked of you any reward. My reward is with Allah alone, and I have been commanded to be of those who are resigned *to Him*.'

فَإِنْ تَوَلَّيْتُمْ فَمَا سَأَلْتُكُمْ مِّنْ أَجْرٍ ۗ إِنْ أَجْرِيَ إِلَّا عَلَى اللّٰهِ ۙ وَأُمِرْتُ أَنْ أَكُوْنَ مِنَ الْمُسْلِمِيْنَ ٧٣

* 74. But they rejected him, so We saved him and those who were with him in the Ark. And We made them inheritors *of Our favours*, while We drowned those who rejected Our Signs. See then, how was the end of those who had been warned!

فَكَذَّبُوْهُ فَنَجَّيْنٰهُ وَمَنْ مَّعَهٗ فِي الْفُلْكِ وَجَعَلْنٰهُمْ خَلٰٓئِفَ وَأَغْرَقْنَا الَّذِيْنَ كَذَّبُوْا بِاٰيٰتِنَا ۚ فَانْظُرْ كَيْفَ كَانَ عَاقِبَةُ الْمُنْذَرِيْنَ ٧٤

75. Then We sent, after him, *other* Messengers to their *respective* peoples, and they brought them clear proofs. But they would not believe *in them*, because they had rejected them before. Thus do We seal the hearts of transgressors.

ثم بعثنا من بعده رسلا الى قومهم فجاءوهم
بالبينت فما كانوا ليؤمنوا بما كذبوا به من قبل
كذلك نطبع على قلوب المعتدين ٧٥

76. Then did We send, after them, Moses and Aaron to Pharaoh and his chiefs with Our Signs, but they behaved arrogantly. And they were a sinful people.

ثم بعثنا من بعدهم موسى وهرون الى فرعون
وملايه بايتنا فاستكبروا وكانوا قوما مجرمين ٧٦

77. And when there came to them the truth from Us, they said, 'This is surely a manifest enchantment.'

فلما جاءهم الحق من عندنا قالوا ان هذا لسحر
مبين ٧٧

78. Moses said, 'Do you say *this* of the truth when it has come to you? Is this enchantment? And the enchanters never prosper.'

قال موسى اتقولون للحق لما جاءكم اسحر هذا
ولا يفلح السحرون ٧٨

79. They said, 'Hast thou come to us that thou mayest turn us away from what we found our fathers following, and that you two may have greatness in the land? But we will not believe in either of you.'

قالوا اجئتنا لتلفتنا عما وجدنا عليه اباءنا و
تكون لكما الكبرياء في الارض وما نحن لكما
بمؤمنين ٧٩

80. And Pharaoh said, 'Bring to me every expert magician.'

وقال فرعون ائتوني بكل سحر عليم ٨٠

81. And when the magicians came, Moses said to them, 'Cast ye what you would cast.'

فلما جاء السحرة قال لهم موسى القوا ما انتم
ملقون ٨١

82. And when they had cast, Moses said, 'What you have brought is *mere* sorcery. Surely, Allah will make it vain. Verily, Allah does not allow the work of mischief-makers to prosper.

فلما القوا قال موسى ما جئتم به السحر ان الله
سيبطله ان الله لا يصلح عمل المفسدين ٨٢

83. 'And Allah establishes the truth by His words, even though the sinners be averse *to it*.'

ويحق الله الحق بكلمته ولو كره المجرمون ٨٣ ع ٨ ١٢ ١٣

R. 9.

* 84. And none obeyed Moses save some youths from among his people, because of the fear of Pharaoh and their chiefs, lest he should persecute them. And of a truth, Pharaoh was a tyrant in the land and surely he was of the transgressors.

فما امن لموسى الا ذرية من قومه على خوف
من فرعون وملايهم ان يفتنهم وان فرعون
لعال في الارض وانه لمن المسرفين ٨٤

85. And Moses said, 'O my people, if you have believed in Allah, then in Him

وقال موسى يقوم ان كنتم امنتم بالله فعليه

put your trust, if you indeed submit *to His will*.'

86. And they said, 'In Allah do we put our trust. Our Lord, make us not a trial for the wrongdoing people.

87. 'And deliver us by Thy mercy from the disbelieving people.'

* 88. And We spoke to Moses and his brother, *saying*, 'Take, ye twain, *some* houses for your people in *the* town, and make your houses so as to face one another, and observe Prayer. And give glad tidings to the believers.'

* 89. And Moses said, 'Our Lord, Thou hast bestowed upon Pharaoh and his chiefs embellishment and wealth in the present life, with the result, our Lord, that they are leading *men* astray from Thy path. Our Lord! destroy their riches and attack their hearts—and they are not going to believe until they see the grievous punishment.'

90. He said, 'Your prayer is accepted. So be ye twain steadfast, and follow not the path of those who know not.'

* 91. And We brought the children of Israel across the sea; and Pharaoh and his hosts pursued them wrongfully and aggressively, till, when *the calamity of* drowning overtook him, he said, 'I believe that there is no God but He in Whom the children of Israel believe, and I am of those who submit *to Him*.'

* 92. What! Now! while thou wast disobedient before *this* and wast of those who create disorder.

93. So this day We will save thee in thy body *alone* that thou mayest be a Sign to those *who come* after thee. And surely, many of mankind are heedless of Our Signs.

R. 10.

94. And We assigned to the children of Israel an excellent abode, and We provided them with good things, and they differed not until there came to

تَوَكَّلُوْٓا اِنْ كُنْتُمْ مُّسْلِمِيْنَ ﴿۸۵﴾
فَقَالُوْا عَلَى اللّٰهِ تَوَكَّلْنَا ۚ رَبَّنَا لَا تَجْعَلْنَا فِتْنَةً لِّلْقَوْمِ
الظّٰلِمِيْنَ ﴿۸۶﴾
وَنَجِّنَا بِرَحْمَتِكَ مِنَ الْقَوْمِ الْكٰفِرِيْنَ ﴿۸۷﴾
وَاَوْحَيْنَآ اِلٰى مُوْسٰى وَاَخِيْهِ اَنْ تَبَوَّاٰ لِقَوْمِكُمَا
بِمِصْرَ بُيُوْتًا وَّاجْعَلُوْا بُيُوْتَكُمْ قِبْلَةً وَّاَقِيْمُوا الصَّلٰوةَ ۗ
وَبَشِّرِ الْمُؤْمِنِيْنَ ﴿۸۸﴾
وَقَالَ مُوْسٰى رَبَّنَآ اِنَّكَ اٰتَيْتَ فِرْعَوْنَ وَمَلَاَهٗ
زِيْنَةً وَّاَمْوَالًا فِي الْحَيٰوةِ الدُّنْيَا ۙ رَبَّنَا لِيُضِلُّوْا
عَنْ سَبِيْلِكَ ۚ رَبَّنَا اطْمِسْ عَلٰٓى اَمْوَالِهِمْ وَاشْدُدْ
عَلٰى قُلُوْبِهِمْ فَلَا يُؤْمِنُوْا حَتّٰى يَرَوُا الْعَذَابَ الْاَلِيْمَ ﴿۸۹﴾
قَالَ قَدْ اُجِيْبَتْ دَّعْوَتُكُمَا فَاسْتَقِيْمَا وَلَا تَتَّبِعٰٓنِّ
سَبِيْلَ الَّذِيْنَ لَا يَعْلَمُوْنَ ﴿۹۰﴾
وَجٰوَزْنَا بِبَنِيْٓ اِسْرَآءِيْلَ الْبَحْرَ فَاَتْبَعَهُمْ فِرْعَوْنُ
وَجُنُوْدُهٗ بَغْيًا وَّعَدْوًا ۭ حَتّٰٓى اِذَآ اَدْرَكَهُ الْغَرَقُ ۙ قَالَ
اٰمَنْتُ اَنَّهٗ لَآ اِلٰهَ اِلَّا الَّذِيْٓ اٰمَنَتْ بِهٖ بَنُوْٓا اِسْرَآءِيْلَ
وَاَنَا مِنَ الْمُسْلِمِيْنَ ﴿۹۱﴾
آٰلْـٰٔنَ وَقَدْ عَصَيْتَ قَبْلُ وَكُنْتَ مِنَ الْمُفْسِدِيْنَ ﴿۹۲﴾
فَالْيَوْمَ نُنَجِّيْكَ بِبَدَنِكَ لِتَكُوْنَ لِمَنْ خَلْفَكَ اٰيَةً ۭ
وَاِنَّ كَثِيْرًا مِّنَ النَّاسِ عَنْ اٰيٰتِنَا لَغٰفِلُوْنَ ﴿۹۳﴾ ع
وَلَقَدْ بَوَّاْنَا بَنِيْٓ اِسْرَآءِيْلَ مُبَوَّاَ صِدْقٍ وَّرَزَقْنٰهُمْ
مِّنَ الطَّيِّبٰتِ ۚ فَمَا اخْتَلَفُوْا حَتّٰى جَآءَهُمُ الْعِلْمُ ۭ اِنَّ

them the knowledge. Surely, thy Lord will judge between them on the Day of Resurrection concerning that in which they differed.

رَبَّكَ يَقْضِيْ بَيْنَهُمْ يَوْمَ الْقِيٰمَةِ فِيْمَا كَانُوْا فِيْهِ
يَخْتَلِفُوْنَ ﴿٩٤﴾

95. And if thou art in doubt concerning that which We have sent down to thee, ask those who have been reading the Book before thee. Indeed the truth has come to thee from thy Lord; be not, therefore, of those who doubt.

فَاِنْ كُنْتَ فِيْ شَكٍّ مِّمَّاۤ اَنْزَلْنَاۤ اِلَيْكَ فَسْـَٔلِ الَّذِيْنَ
يَقْرَءُوْنَ الْكِتٰبَ مِنْ قَبْلِكَ لَقَدْ جَآءَكَ الْحَقُّ مِنْ
رَّبِّكَ فَلَا تَكُوْنَنَّ مِنَ الْمُمْتَرِيْنَ ﴿٩٥﴾

96. And be not thou of those who reject the Signs of Allah, or thou shalt be of the losers.

وَلَا تَكُوْنَنَّ مِنَ الَّذِيْنَ كَذَّبُوْا بِاٰيٰتِ اللّٰهِ فَتَكُوْنَ
مِنَ الْخٰسِرِيْنَ ﴿٩٦﴾

97. Surely, those against whom the word of thy Lord has taken effect will not believe,

اِنَّ الَّذِيْنَ حَقَّتْ عَلَيْهِمْ كَلِمَتُ رَبِّكَ لَا يُؤْمِنُوْنَ ﴿٩٧﴾

98. Even if there come to them every Sign, till they see the grievous punishment.

وَلَوْ جَآءَتْهُمْ كُلُّ اٰيَةٍ حَتّٰى يَرَوُا الْعَذَابَ الْاَلِيْمَ ﴿٩٨﴾

99. Why was there no *other* people, save the people of Jonah, who should have believed so that their belief would have profited them? When they believed, We removed from them the punishment of disgrace in the present life, and We gave them provision for a while.

فَلَوْلَا كَانَتْ قَرْيَةٌ اٰمَنَتْ فَنَفَعَهَاۤ اِيْمَانُهَاۤ اِلَّا قَوْمَ
يُوْنُسَ لَمَّاۤ اٰمَنُوْا كَشَفْنَا عَنْهُمْ عَذَابَ الْخِزْيِ فِي
الْحَيٰوةِ الدُّنْيَا وَمَتَّعْنٰهُمْ اِلٰى حِيْنٍ ﴿٩٩﴾

100. And if thy Lord had *enforced* His will, surely, all who are on the earth would have believed together. Wilt thou, then, force men to become believers?

وَلَوْ شَآءَ رَبُّكَ لَاٰمَنَ مَنْ فِي الْاَرْضِ كُلُّهُمْ جَمِيْعًا
اَفَاَنْتَ تُكْرِهُ النَّاسَ حَتّٰى يَكُوْنُوْا مُؤْمِنِيْنَ ﴿١٠٠﴾

101. And no soul can believe except by the permission of Allah. And He makes *His* wrath *descend* on those who will not use their reason.

وَمَا كَانَ لِنَفْسٍ اَنْ تُؤْمِنَ اِلَّا بِاِذْنِ اللّٰهِ وَيَجْعَلُ
الرِّجْسَ عَلَى الَّذِيْنَ لَا يَعْقِلُوْنَ ﴿١٠١﴾

102. Say, 'Consider what is *happening* in the heavens and the earth.' But Signs and Warners avail not a people who will not believe.

قُلِ انْظُرُوْا مَاذَا فِي السَّمٰوٰتِ وَالْاَرْضِ وَمَا تُغْنِي
الْاٰيٰتُ وَالنُّذُرُ عَنْ قَوْمٍ لَّا يُؤْمِنُوْنَ ﴿١٠٢﴾

103. What then do they expect save the like of the days of *punishment suffered by* those who passed away before them? Say, 'Wait then, *and* I am with you among those who wait.'

فَهَلْ يَنْتَظِرُوْنَ اِلَّا مِثْلَ اَيَّامِ الَّذِيْنَ خَلَوْا مِنْ
قَبْلِهِمْ قُلْ فَانْتَظِرُوْۤا اِنِّيْ مَعَكُمْ مِّنَ الْمُنْتَظِرِيْنَ ﴿١٠٣﴾

104. Then shall We save Our Messengers and those who believe. Thus *does it always happen;* it is incumbent on Us to save believers.

ثُمَّ نُنَجِّيْ رُسُلَنَا وَالَّذِيْنَ اٰمَنُوْا كَذٰلِكَ حَقًّا عَلَيْنَا
نُنْجِ الْمُؤْمِنِيْنَ ﴿١٠٤﴾ ع ١٠/١١ ١٥

R. 11.

105. Say, "O ye men, if you are in doubt as to my religion, then *know that* I worship not those whom you worship beside Allah, but I worship Allah *alone* Who causes you to die, and I have been commanded to be of the believers,

قُلْ يٰٓاَيُّهَا النَّاسُ اِنْ كُنْتُمْ فِيْ شَكٍّ مِّنْ دِيْنِيْ
فَلَآ اَعْبُدُ الَّذِيْنَ تَعْبُدُوْنَ مِنْ دُوْنِ اللّٰهِ وَلٰكِنْ
اَعْبُدُ اللّٰهَ الَّذِيْ يَتَوَفّٰىكُمْ ۖۚ وَاُمِرْتُ اَنْ اَكُوْنَ
مِنَ الْمُؤْمِنِيْنَ ﴿١٠٥﴾

106. "And *I have also been commanded to say*: 'Set thy face toward religion as one ever inclined *to God*, and be not thou of those who ascribe partners *to Him*.

وَاَنْ اَقِمْ وَجْهَكَ لِلدِّيْنِ حَنِيْفًا ۚ وَلَا تَكُوْنَنَّ مِنَ
الْمُشْرِكِيْنَ ﴿١٠٦﴾

107. 'And call not, beside Allah, on any other that can neither profit thee nor harm thee. And if thou didst so, thou wouldst then certainly be of the wrongdoers.'"

وَلَا تَدْعُ مِنْ دُوْنِ اللّٰهِ مَا لَا يَنْفَعُكَ وَلَا يَضُرُّكَ ۚ
فَاِنْ فَعَلْتَ فَاِنَّكَ اِذًا مِّنَ الظّٰلِمِيْنَ ﴿١٠٧﴾

108. And if Allah touch thee with harm, there is none who can remove it but He: and if He desire good for thee, there is none who can repel His grace. He causes it to reach whomsoever of His servants He wills. And He is the Most Forgiving, Merciful.

وَاِنْ يَّمْسَسْكَ اللّٰهُ بِضُرٍّ فَلَا كَاشِفَ لَهٗٓ اِلَّا هُوَ ۚ وَ
اِنْ يُّرِدْكَ بِخَيْرٍ فَلَا رَآدَّ لِفَضْلِهٖ ۗ يُصِيْبُ بِهٖ مَنْ
يَّشَآءُ مِنْ عِبَادِهٖ ۗ وَهُوَ الْغَفُوْرُ الرَّحِيْمُ ﴿١٠٨﴾

109. Say, 'O ye men, now has the truth come to you from your Lord. So whosoever follows the guidance, follows it only for the good of his own soul, and whosoever errs, errs only against it. And I am not a keeper over you.'

قُلْ يٰٓاَيُّهَا النَّاسُ قَدْ جَآءَكُمُ الْحَقُّ مِنْ رَّبِّكُمْ ۚ فَمَنِ
اهْتَدٰى فَاِنَّمَا يَهْتَدِيْ لِنَفْسِهٖ ۚ وَمَنْ ضَلَّ فَاِنَّمَا
يَضِلُّ عَلَيْهَا ۚ وَمَآ اَنَا عَلَيْكُمْ بِوَكِيْلٍ ﴿١٠٩﴾

110. And follow that which is revealed to thee and be steadfast until Allah give His judgment. And He is the Best of judges.

وَاتَّبِعْ مَا يُوْحٰٓى اِلَيْكَ وَاصْبِرْ حَتّٰى يَحْكُمَ اللّٰهُ ۖۚ وَهُوَ
خَيْرُ الْحٰكِمِيْنَ ﴿١١٠﴾ ع ١١

رکوعاتها ١٠ — سُوْرَةُ هُوْدٍ مَّكِّيَّةٌ — (١١) — اٰياتها ١٢٤

HŪD

(Revealed before Hijra)

1. In the name of Allah, the Gracious, the Merciful.

* 2. Alif Lām Rā*. *This is* a Book whose verses have been made unchangeable *and* then they have been expounded in detail. *It is* from One Wise, *and* All-Aware.

3. *It teaches* that you should worship none but Allah. I am to you a Warner, and a bearer of glad tidings from Him;

* 4. And that you seek forgiveness of your Lord, *and* then turn to Him. He will provide for you a goodly provision until an appointed term. And He will grant His grace to every one possessed of merit. And if you turn away, then surely, I fear for you the punishment of a dreadful day.

5. To Allah is your return; and He has power over all things.

6. Now surely, they fold up their breasts that they may hide themselves from Him. Aye, *even* when they cover themselves with their garments, He knows what they conceal and what they reveal. Surely, He is well aware of what is in *their* breasts.

* 7. And there is no creature that moves in the earth but it is for Allah to provide it with sustenance. And He knows its lodging and its home. All *this* is *recorded* in a clear Book.

8. And He it is Who created the heavens and the earth in six periods, and His throne rests on water, that He might prove you *to show* which of you is best in conduct. And if thou say, 'You shall surely be raised after death,' those who disbelieve will certainly say, 'This is nothing but clear deception.'

بِسْمِ اللّٰهِ الرَّحْمٰنِ الرَّحِيْمِ ①

الٓرٰ كِتٰبٌ اُحْكِمَتْ اٰيٰتُهٗ ثُمَّ فُصِّلَتْ مِنْ لَّدُنْ
حَكِيْمٍ خَبِيْرٍ ②
اَلَّا تَعْبُدُوْٓا اِلَّا اللّٰهَ ؕ اِنَّنِيْ لَكُمْ مِّنْهُ نَذِيْرٌ وَّ بَشِيْرٌ ③
وَّ اَنِ اسْتَغْفِرُوْا رَبَّكُمْ ثُمَّ تُوْبُوْٓا اِلَيْهِ يُمَتِّعْكُمْ
مَّتَاعًا حَسَنًا اِلٰٓى اَجَلٍ مُّسَمًّى وَّ يُؤْتِ كُلَّ ذِيْ فَضْلٍ
فَضْلَهٗ ؕ وَ اِنْ تَوَلَّوْا فَاِنِّيْٓ اَخَافُ عَلَيْكُمْ عَذَابَ
يَوْمٍ كَبِيْرٍ ④
اِلَى اللّٰهِ مَرْجِعُكُمْ ۚ وَهُوَ عَلٰى كُلِّ شَيْءٍ قَدِيْرٌ ⑤
اَلَآ اِنَّهُمْ يَثْنُوْنَ صُدُوْرَهُمْ لِيَسْتَخْفُوْا مِنْهُ ؕ اَلَا
حِيْنَ يَسْتَغْشُوْنَ ثِيَابَهُمْ ۙ يَعْلَمُ مَا يُسِرُّوْنَ وَ مَا
يُعْلِنُوْنَ ۚ اِنَّهٗ عَلِيْمٌۢ بِذَاتِ الصُّدُوْرِ ⑥
الجزء ١٢ وَمَا مِنْ دَآبَّةٍ فِي الْاَرْضِ اِلَّا عَلَى اللّٰهِ رِزْقُهَا
وَ يَعْلَمُ مُسْتَقَرَّهَا وَ مُسْتَوْدَعَهَا ؕ كُلٌّ فِيْ كِتٰبٍ
مُّبِيْنٍ ⑦
وَ هُوَ الَّذِيْ خَلَقَ السَّمٰوٰتِ وَ الْاَرْضَ فِيْ سِتَّةِ
اَيَّامٍ وَّ كَانَ عَرْشُهٗ عَلَى الْمَآءِ لِيَبْلُوَكُمْ اَيُّكُمْ
اَحْسَنُ عَمَلًا ؕ وَ لَئِنْ قُلْتَ اِنَّكُمْ مَّبْعُوْثُوْنَ مِنْۢ بَعْدِ
الْمَوْتِ لَيَقُوْلَنَّ الَّذِيْنَ كَفَرُوْٓا اِنْ هٰذَآ اِلَّا سِحْرٌ

* I am Allah Who is All-Seeing.

مُّبِيْنٌ ۝٨

9. And if We put off their punishment until a reckoned time, they would certainly say, 'What withholds it?' Now surely, on the day that it shall come unto them, it shall not be averted from them, and that which they used to mock at shall encompass them.

وَلَئِنْ أَخَّرْنَا عَنْهُمُ الْعَذَابَ إِلَىٰ أُمَّةٍ مَّعْدُودَةٍ لَّيَقُولُنَّ مَا يَحْبِسُهُ ۗ أَلَا يَوْمَ يَأْتِيهِمْ لَيْسَ مَصْرُوفًا عَنْهُمْ وَحَاقَ بِهِم مَّا كَانُوا بِهِ يَسْتَهْزِئُونَ ۝٩

R. 2.

10. And if We make man taste of mercy from Us, and then take it away from him, verily, he is despairing, ungrateful.

وَلَئِنْ أَذَقْنَا الْإِنسَانَ مِنَّا رَحْمَةً ثُمَّ نَزَعْنَاهَا مِنْهُ إِنَّهُ لَيَئُوسٌ كَفُورٌ ۝١٠

11. And if after an adversity has touched him We cause him to taste of prosperity, he will assuredly say, 'Gone are the ills from me.' Lo! he is exultant, boastful;

وَلَئِنْ أَذَقْنَاهُ نَعْمَاءَ بَعْدَ ضَرَّاءَ مَسَّتْهُ لَيَقُولَنَّ ذَهَبَ السَّيِّئَاتُ عَنِّي ۚ إِنَّهُ لَفَرِحٌ فَخُورٌ ۝١١

12. Save those who are steadfast and do good works. It is they who will have forgiveness and a great reward.

إِلَّا الَّذِينَ صَبَرُوا وَعَمِلُوا الصَّالِحَاتِ أُولَٰئِكَ لَهُم مَّغْفِرَةٌ وَأَجْرٌ كَبِيرٌ ۝١٢

13. *They imagine that* thou art now perhaps going to abandon part of that which has been revealed to thee; and thy bosom is becoming straitened thereby because they say, 'Wherefore has not a treasure been sent down to him or an angel come with him?' Verily, thou art only a Warner, and Allah is Guardian over all things.

فَلَعَلَّكَ تَارِكٌ بَعْضَ مَا يُوحَىٰ إِلَيْكَ وَضَائِقٌ بِهِ صَدْرُكَ أَن يَقُولُوا لَوْلَا أُنزِلَ عَلَيْهِ كَنزٌ أَوْ جَاءَ مَعَهُ مَلَكٌ ۚ إِنَّمَا أَنتَ نَذِيرٌ ۚ وَاللَّهُ عَلَىٰ كُلِّ شَيْءٍ وَكِيلٌ ۝١٣

14. Do they say, 'He has forged it?' Say, 'Then bring ten Chapters like it, forged, and call on whom you can beside Allah, if you are truthful.'

أَمْ يَقُولُونَ افْتَرَاهُ ۖ قُلْ فَأْتُوا بِعَشْرِ سُوَرٍ مِّثْلِهِ مُفْتَرَيَاتٍ وَادْعُوا مَنِ اسْتَطَعْتُم مِّن دُونِ اللَّهِ إِن كُنتُمْ صَادِقِينَ ۝١٤

15. And if they do not respond to you, then know that it has been revealed *replete* with Allah's knowledge and that there is no God but He. Will you then submit?

فَإِلَّمْ يَسْتَجِيبُوا لَكُمْ فَاعْلَمُوا أَنَّمَا أُنزِلَ بِعِلْمِ اللَّهِ وَأَن لَّا إِلَٰهَ إِلَّا هُوَ ۖ فَهَلْ أَنتُم مُّسْلِمُونَ ۝١٥

16. Whoso desires the present life and its embellishment, We will fully repay them for their works in this *life* and they shall not be wronged therein.

مَن كَانَ يُرِيدُ الْحَيَاةَ الدُّنْيَا وَزِينَتَهَا نُوَفِّ إِلَيْهِمْ أَعْمَالَهُمْ فِيهَا وَهُمْ فِيهَا لَا يُبْخَسُونَ ۝١٦

17. Those are they who shall have nothing in the Hereafter save the Fire,

أُولَٰئِكَ الَّذِينَ لَيْسَ لَهُمْ فِي الْآخِرَةِ إِلَّا النَّارُ

and that which they wrought in this *life* shall come to naught, and vain shall be that which they used to do.

وحبط ما صنعوا فيها وبطل ما كانوا يعملون ﴿١٧﴾

* 18. Can he, then, who possesses a clear proof from his Lord, and *to testify to whose truth* a witness from Him shall follow him, and who was preceded by the Book of Moses, a guide and a mercy, *be an impostor?* Those *who consider these matters* believe therein, and whoever of the *opposing* parties disbelieves in it, Fire shall be his promised place. So be not thou in doubt about it. Surely, it is the truth from thy Lord; but most men do not believe.

افمن كان على بينة من ربه ويتلوه شاهد منه ومن قبله كتب موسى اماما ورحمة اولٓئك يؤمنون به ومن يكفر به من الاحزاب فالنار موعده فلا تك في مرية منه انه الحق من ربك ولكن اكثر الناس لا يؤمنون ﴿١٨﴾

19. And who is more unjust than he who forges a lie against Allah? Such shall be presented before their Lord, and the witnesses will say, 'These are they who lied against their Lord.' Now surely, the curse of Allah is on the unjust:

ومن اظلم ممن افترى على الله كذبا اولٓئك يعرضون على ربهم ويقول الاشهاد هٓؤلاء الذين كذبوا على ربهم الا لعنة الله على الظلمين ﴿١٩﴾

20. Who turn *men* away from the path of Allah and seek to make it crooked. And these it is who disbelieve in the Hereafter.

الذين يصدون عن سبيل الله ويبغونها عوجا وهم بالاخرة هم كفرون ﴿٢٠﴾

21. Such can never frustrate *God's plans* in the land, nor have they any friends beside Allah. Punishment will be doubled for them. They can neither hear, nor can they see.

اولٓئك لم يكونوا معجزين في الارض وما كان لهم من دون الله من اولياء يضعف لهم العذاب ما كانوا يستطيعون السمع وما كانوا يبصرون ﴿٢١﴾

22. It is these who have ruined their souls, and that which they fabricated shall fail them.

اولٓئك الذين خسروا انفسهم وضل عنهم ما كانوا يفترون ﴿٢٢﴾

23. Undoubtedly, it is they who shall be the greatest losers in the Hereafter.

لا جرم انهم في الاخرة هم الاخسرون ﴿٢٣﴾

24. Verily, those who believe and do good works, and humble themselves before their Lord—these are the inmates of Heaven; therein shall they abide.

ان الذين امنوا وعملوا الصلحت واخبتوا الى ربهم اولٓئك اصحب الجنة هم فيها خلدون ﴿٢٤﴾

25. The case of the two parties is like *that of* the blind and the deaf, and the

مثل الفريقين كالاعمى والاصم والبصير و

seeing and the hearing. Is the case of the two alike? Will you not then understand?

السَّمِيعِ هَلْ يَسْتَوِيَانِ مَثَلًا أَفَلَا تَذَكَّرُونَ ﴿٢٥﴾ ع

R. 3.

26. And We sent Noah to his people, *and he said,* 'Truly, I am a plain Warner to you,

وَلَقَدْ أَرْسَلْنَا نُوحًا إِلَىٰ قَوْمِهِ إِنِّي لَكُمْ نَذِيرٌ
مُبِينٌ ﴿٢٦﴾

27. 'That you worship none but Allah. Indeed, I fear for you the punishment of a grievous day.'

أَنْ لَا تَعْبُدُوا إِلَّا اللَّهَ إِنِّي أَخَافُ عَلَيْكُمْ عَذَابَ
يَوْمٍ أَلِيمٍ ﴿٢٧﴾

28. The chiefs of his people, who disbelieved, replied, 'We see in thee nothing but a man like ourselves, and we see that none have followed thee but those who, to all outward appearance, are the meanest of us. And we do not see in you any superiority over us; nay, we believe you to be liars.'

فَقَالَ الْمَلَأُ الَّذِينَ كَفَرُوا مِنْ قَوْمِهِ مَا نَرَاكَ إِلَّا
بَشَرًا مِثْلَنَا وَمَا نَرَاكَ اتَّبَعَكَ إِلَّا الَّذِينَ هُمْ
أَرَاذِلُنَا بَادِيَ الرَّأْيِ وَمَا نَرَىٰ لَكُمْ عَلَيْنَا مِنْ فَضْلٍ
بَلْ نَظُنُّكُمْ كَاذِبِينَ ﴿٢٨﴾

29. He said, "O my people, tell me: if I stand on a clear proof from my Lord and He has bestowed upon me from Himself a great mercy which has been rendered obscure to you, shall we force it upon you, while you are averse thereto?

قَالَ يَا قَوْمِ أَرَأَيْتُمْ إِنْ كُنْتُ عَلَىٰ بَيِّنَةٍ مِنْ رَبِّي
وَآتَانِي رَحْمَةً مِنْ عِنْدِهِ فَعُمِّيَتْ عَلَيْكُمْ
أَنُلْزِمُكُمُوهَا وَأَنْتُمْ لَهَا كَارِهُونَ ﴿٢٩﴾

30. "And O my people, I ask not of you any wealth in return for it. My reward is due from Allah alone. And I am not going to drive away those who believe. They shall certainly meet their Lord. But I consider you to be a people who act ignorantly.

وَيَا قَوْمِ لَا أَسْأَلُكُمْ عَلَيْهِ مَالًا إِنْ أَجْرِيَ إِلَّا
عَلَى اللَّهِ وَمَا أَنَا بِطَارِدِ الَّذِينَ آمَنُوا إِنَّهُمْ مُلَاقُو
رَبِّهِمْ وَلَٰكِنِّي أَرَاكُمْ قَوْمًا تَجْهَلُونَ ﴿٣٠﴾

31. "And O my people, who would help me against Allah, if I were to drive them away? Will you not then consider?

وَيَا قَوْمِ مَنْ يَنْصُرُنِي مِنَ اللَّهِ إِنْ طَرَدْتُهُمْ أَفَلَا
تَذَكَّرُونَ ﴿٣١﴾

32. "And I say not to you, 'I possess the treasures of Allah,' nor do I know the unseen, nor say I, 'I am an angel.' Nor say I concerning those whom your eyes despise, 'Allah will not bestow any good upon them'—Allah knows best whatever is in their minds—Surely, I should then be of the unjust."

وَلَا أَقُولُ لَكُمْ عِنْدِي خَزَائِنُ اللَّهِ وَلَا أَعْلَمُ
الْغَيْبَ وَلَا أَقُولُ إِنِّي مَلَكٌ وَلَا أَقُولُ لِلَّذِينَ
تَزْدَرِي أَعْيُنُكُمْ لَنْ يُؤْتِيَهُمُ اللَّهُ خَيْرًا اللَّهُ
أَعْلَمُ بِمَا فِي أَنْفُسِهِمْ إِنِّي إِذًا لَمِنَ الظَّالِمِينَ ﴿٣٢﴾

33. They said, 'O Noah, thou hast indeed disputed with us *long* and hast

قَالُوا يَا نُوحُ قَدْ جَادَلْتَنَا فَأَكْثَرْتَ جِدَالَنَا فَأْتِنَا

disputed with us many a time; bring us now that with which thou threatenest us, if thou art of those who speak the truth.'

بِمَا تَعِدُنَآ اِنْ كُنْتَ مِنَ الصّٰدِقِيْنَ ﴿٣٣﴾

34. He said, 'Allah alone will bring it to you, if He please, and you cannot frustrate *God's purpose*.

قَالَ اِنَّمَا يَاْتِيْكُمْ بِهِ اللّٰهُ اِنْ شَآءَ وَمَآ اَنْتُمْ
بِمُعْجِزِيْنَ ﴿٣٤﴾

* 35. 'And my advice will profit you not if I desire to advise you, if Allah intends to destroy you. He is your Lord and to Him shall you be made to return.'

وَلَا يَنْفَعُكُمْ نُصْحِيْٓ اِنْ اَرَدْتُّ اَنْ اَنْصَحَ لَكُمْ
اِنْ كَانَ اللّٰهُ يُرِيْدُ اَنْ يُّغْوِيَكُمْ هُوَ رَبُّكُمْ
وَاِلَيْهِ تُرْجَعُوْنَ ﴿٣٥﴾

36. Do they say, 'He has forged it?' Say, 'If I have forged it, on me be my sin and I am clear of the sins you commit.'

اَمْ يَقُوْلُوْنَ افْتَرٰىهُ قُلْ اِنِ افْتَرَيْتُهٗ فَعَلَيَّ اِجْرَامِيْ
وَاَنَا بَرِيْٓءٌ مِّمَّا تُجْرِمُوْنَ ﴿٣٦﴾

R. 4.

37. And it was revealed to Noah, 'None of thy people will believe except those who have already believed; grieve not therefore at what they have been doing.

وَاُوْحِيَ اِلٰى نُوْحٍ اَنَّهٗ لَنْ يُّؤْمِنَ مِنْ قَوْمِكَ اِلَّا
مَنْ قَدْ اٰمَنَ فَلَا تَبْتَئِسْ بِمَا كَانُوْا يَفْعَلُوْنَ ﴿٣٧﴾

38. 'And build thou the Ark under Our eyes and *as commanded by* Our revelation. And address not Me concerning the wrongdoers. They are surely going to be drowned.'

وَاصْنَعِ الْفُلْكَ بِاَعْيُنِنَا وَوَحْيِنَا وَلَا تُخَاطِبْنِيْ فِي
الَّذِيْنَ ظَلَمُوْا اِنَّهُمْ مُّغْرَقُوْنَ ﴿٣٨﴾

39. And he was making the Ark; and every time the chiefs of his people passed by him, they mocked at him. He said, 'If *now* you mock at us, *the time is coming when* we shall mock at you even just as you mock *now*.

وَيَصْنَعُ الْفُلْكَ وَكُلَّمَا مَرَّ عَلَيْهِ مَلَاٌ مِّنْ قَوْمِهٖ
سَخِرُوْا مِنْهُ قَالَ اِنْ تَسْخَرُوْا مِنَّا فَاِنَّا نَسْخَرُ مِنْكُمْ
كَمَا تَسْخَرُوْنَ ﴿٣٩﴾

40. 'Then you shall know who it is on whom will come a punishment that will disgrace him, and on whom will fall a lasting punishment.'

فَسَوْفَ تَعْلَمُوْنَ مَنْ يَّاْتِيْهِ عَذَابٌ يُّخْزِيْهِ وَ
يَحِلُّ عَلَيْهِ عَذَابٌ مُّقِيْمٌ ﴿٤٠﴾

41. Till, when Our command came and the fountains *of the earth* gushed forth, We said, 'Embark therein two of every kind, male and female, and thy family, except those against whom the word has already gone forth, and those who believe.' And there did not believe *and live* with him except a few.

حَتّٰٓى اِذَا جَآءَ اَمْرُنَا وَفَارَ التَّنُّوْرُ قُلْنَا احْمِلْ فِيْهَا
مِنْ كُلٍّ زَوْجَيْنِ اثْنَيْنِ وَاَهْلَكَ اِلَّا مَنْ سَبَقَ
عَلَيْهِ الْقَوْلُ وَمَنْ اٰمَنَ وَمَآ اٰمَنَ مَعَهٗٓ اِلَّا قَلِيْلٌ ﴿٤١﴾

42. And he said, 'Embark therein. In the name of Allah be its course and its mooring. My Lord is assuredly Most Forgiving, Merciful.'

وَقَالَ ارْكَبُوْا فِيْهَا بِسْمِ اللّٰهِ مَجْرٖىهَا وَمُرْسٰىهَا
اِنَّ رَبِّيْ لَغَفُوْرٌ رَّحِيْمٌ ﴿٤٢﴾

43. And it moved along with them on waves like mountains. And Noah cried unto his son, while he was *keeping* apart, 'O my son, embark with us and be not with the disbelievers.'

وَهِيَ تَجْرِي بِهِمْ فِي مَوْجٍ كَالْجِبَالِ وَنَادَىٰ
نُوحٌ ابْنَهُ وَكَانَ فِي مَعْزِلٍ يَٰبُنَيَّ ارْكَبْ مَعَنَا وَ
لَا تَكُنْ مَعَ الْكٰفِرِينَ ﴿٤٣﴾

44. He replied, 'I shall soon betake myself to a mountain which will shelter me from the water.' He said, 'There is no shelter *for anyone* this day, from the decree of Allah, excepting those to whom He shows mercy.' And the wave came in between the two; so he was among the drowned.

قَالَ سَاٰوِيْ إِلَىٰ جَبَلٍ يَعْصِمُنِي مِنَ الْمَآءِ قَالَ
لَا عَاصِمَ الْيَوْمَ مِنْ أَمْرِ اللّٰهِ إِلَّا مَنْ رَّحِمَ وَحَالَ
بَيْنَهُمَا الْمَوْجُ فَكَانَ مِنَ الْمُغْرَقِينَ ﴿٤٤﴾

45. And it was said, 'O earth, swallow thy water, and O sky, cease *raining*.' And the water was made to subside and the matter was ended. And *the Ark* came to rest on al-Jūdī. And it was said, 'Cursed be the wrongdoing people.'

وَقِيلَ يٰأَرْضُ ابْلَعِي مَآءَكِ وَيٰسَمَآءُ أَقْلِعِي
وَغِيضَ الْمَآءُ وَقُضِيَ الْأَمْرُ وَاسْتَوَتْ عَلَى الْجُودِيِّ
وَقِيلَ بُعْدًا لِّلْقَوْمِ الظّٰلِمِينَ ﴿٤٥﴾

46. And Noah cried unto his Lord and said: 'My Lord, verily, my son is of my family, and surely, Thy promise is true, and Thou art the Most Just of judges.'

وَنَادَىٰ نُوحٌ رَّبَّهُ فَقَالَ رَبِّ إِنَّ ابْنِي مِنْ أَهْلِي
وَإِنَّ وَعْدَكَ الْحَقُّ وَأَنْتَ أَحْكَمُ الْحٰكِمِينَ ﴿٤٦﴾

47. He said: 'O Noah, he is surely not of thy family; he is indeed *a man of* unrighteous conduct. So ask not of Me that of which thou hast no knowledge. I advise thee lest thou become *one* of the ignorant.'

قَالَ يٰنُوحُ إِنَّهُ لَيْسَ مِنْ أَهْلِكَ إِنَّهُ عَمَلٌ غَيْرُ
صَالِحٍ فَلَا تَسْـَٔلْنِ مَا لَيْسَ لَكَ بِهِ عِلْمٌ إِنِّيْ
أَعِظُكَ أَنْ تَكُونَ مِنَ الْجٰهِلِينَ ﴿٤٧﴾

48. He said: 'My Lord, I beg Thee to protect me from asking Thee that whereof I have no knowledge. And unless Thou forgive me and have mercy on me, I shall be among the losers.'

قَالَ رَبِّ إِنِّيْ أَعُوذُ بِكَ أَنْ أَسْـَٔلَكَ مَا لَيْسَ لِي بِهِ
عِلْمٌ وَإِلَّا تَغْفِرْ لِي وَتَرْحَمْنِيْ أَكُنْ مِّنَ
الْخٰسِرِينَ ﴿٤٨﴾

49. It was said, 'O Noah, descend *then* with peace from Us and blessings upon thee and upon peoples *to be born* of those with thee. And there will be *other* peoples whom We shall grant provision *for a time*, then shall a grievous punishment touch them from Us.'

قِيلَ يٰنُوحُ اهْبِطْ بِسَلٰمٍ مِّنَّا وَبَرَكٰتٍ عَلَيْكَ وَ
عَلٰىٓ أُمَمٍ مِّمَّنْ مَّعَكَ وَأُمَمٌ سَنُمَتِّعُهُمْ ثُمَّ يَمَسُّهُمْ
مِّنَّا عَذَابٌ أَلِيمٌ ﴿٤٩﴾

50. This is of the tidings of the unseen which We reveal to thee. Thou didst not know them, neither thou nor thy people,

تِلْكَ مِنْ أَنْبَآءِ الْغَيْبِ نُوحِيهَآ إِلَيْكَ مَا كُنْتَ
تَعْلَمُهَآ أَنْتَ وَلَا قَوْمُكَ مِنْ قَبْلِ هٰذَا فَاصْبِرْ

before this. So be thou patient; for the end is for the God-fearing.

R. 5.

51. And to 'Ād *We sent* their brother Hūd. He said, 'O my people, worship Allah *alone*. You have no God beside Him. You are but forgers of lies.

52. 'O my people, I do not ask of you any reward therefor. My reward is not due except from Him Who created me. Will you not then understand?

53. 'And O my people, ask forgiveness of your Lord, then turn to Him, He will send over you clouds pouring down abundant rain, and will add strength to your strength. And turn not away sinners.'

54. They said, 'O Hūd, thou hast not brought us any clear proof, and we are not going to forsake our gods *merely* because of thy saying, nor are we going to believe in thee.

55. 'We can only say that some of our gods have visited thee with evil.' He replied, 'Surely, I call Allah to witness, and do ye also bear witness that I am clear of that which you associate as partners *with God*

56. 'Beside Him. So devise plans against me, all *of you*, and give me no respite.

57. 'I have indeed put my trust in Allah, my Lord and your Lord. There is no creature that moves *on the earth* but He holds it by the forelock. Surely, my Lord *stands* on the straight path.

58. 'If then, you turn away, I have already conveyed to you that with which I have been sent to you, and my Lord will make another people take your place. And you cannot harm Him at all. Surely, my Lord is Guardian over all things.'

59. And when Our command came, We saved Hūd and those who believed with him, by Our *special* mercy. And We saved them from a severe torment.

60. And these were 'Ād. They denied the Signs of their Lord and disobeyed

ع إِنَّ الْعَاقِبَةَ لِلْمُتَّقِينَ ﴿٥٠﴾
وَإِلَىٰ عَادٍ أَخَاهُمْ هُودًا ۚ قَالَ يَا قَوْمِ اعْبُدُوا اللَّهَ
مَا لَكُم مِّنْ إِلَٰهٍ غَيْرُهُ ۖ إِنْ أَنتُمْ إِلَّا مُفْتَرُونَ ﴿٥١﴾
يَا قَوْمِ لَا أَسْأَلُكُمْ عَلَيْهِ أَجْرًا ۖ إِنْ أَجْرِيَ إِلَّا عَلَى
الَّذِي فَطَرَنِي ۚ أَفَلَا تَعْقِلُونَ ﴿٥٢﴾
وَيَا قَوْمِ اسْتَغْفِرُوا رَبَّكُمْ ثُمَّ تُوبُوا إِلَيْهِ يُرْسِلِ
السَّمَاءَ عَلَيْكُم مِّدْرَارًا وَيَزِدْكُمْ قُوَّةً إِلَىٰ قُوَّتِكُمْ
وَلَا تَتَوَلَّوْا مُجْرِمِينَ ﴿٥٣﴾
قَالُوا يَا هُودُ مَا جِئْتَنَا بِبَيِّنَةٍ وَمَا نَحْنُ بِتَارِكِي
آلِهَتِنَا عَن قَوْلِكَ وَمَا نَحْنُ لَكَ بِمُؤْمِنِينَ ﴿٥٤﴾
إِن نَّقُولُ إِلَّا اعْتَرَاكَ بَعْضُ آلِهَتِنَا بِسُوءٍ ۗ قَالَ إِنِّي
أُشْهِدُ اللَّهَ وَاشْهَدُوا أَنِّي بَرِيءٌ مِّمَّا تُشْرِكُونَ ﴿٥٥﴾
مِن دُونِهِ ۖ فَكِيدُونِي جَمِيعًا ثُمَّ لَا تُنظِرُونِ ﴿٥٦﴾
إِنِّي تَوَكَّلْتُ عَلَى اللَّهِ رَبِّي وَرَبِّكُم ۚ مَّا مِن دَابَّةٍ
إِلَّا هُوَ آخِذٌ بِنَاصِيَتِهَا ۚ إِنَّ رَبِّي عَلَىٰ صِرَاطٍ
مُّسْتَقِيمٍ ﴿٥٧﴾
فَإِن تَوَلَّوْا فَقَدْ أَبْلَغْتُكُم مَّا أُرْسِلْتُ بِهِ إِلَيْكُمْ ۚ
وَيَسْتَخْلِفُ رَبِّي قَوْمًا غَيْرَكُمْ وَلَا تَضُرُّونَهُ شَيْئًا ۚ إِنَّ
رَبِّي عَلَىٰ كُلِّ شَيْءٍ حَفِيظٌ ﴿٥٨﴾
وَلَمَّا جَاءَ أَمْرُنَا نَجَّيْنَا هُودًا وَالَّذِينَ آمَنُوا مَعَهُ
بِرَحْمَةٍ مِّنَّا وَنَجَّيْنَاهُم مِّنْ عَذَابٍ غَلِيظٍ ﴿٥٩﴾
وَتِلْكَ عَادٌ ۖ جَحَدُوا بِآيَاتِ رَبِّهِمْ وَعَصَوْا رُسُلَهُ

His Messengers and followed the bidding of every haughty enemy *of truth*.

وَاتَّبَعُوٓا أَمْرَ كُلِّ جَبَّارٍ عَنِيدٍ ﴿٦٠﴾

61. And a curse was made to follow them in this world, and on the Day of Resurrection. Behold! *the tribe of* 'Ād behaved ungratefully to their Lord. Behold! cursed are 'Ād, the people of Hūd!

وَأُتْبِعُوا فِي هَٰذِهِ الدُّنْيَا لَعْنَةً وَيَوْمَ الْقِيَامَةِ أَلَا
إِنَّ عَادًا كَفَرُوا رَبَّهُمْ أَلَا بُعْدًا لِّعَادٍ قَوْمِ هُودٍ ﴿٦١﴾

R. 6.

62. And to *the tribe of* Thamūd *We sent* their brother Ṣāliḥ. He said, 'O my people, worship Allah; you have no God but Him. He raised you up from the earth, and settled you therein. So ask forgiveness of Him, then turn to Him *whole-heartedly*. Verily, my Lord is nigh, *and* answers *prayers*.'

وَإِلَىٰ ثَمُودَ أَخَاهُمْ صَالِحًا قَالَ يَا قَوْمِ اعْبُدُوا اللَّهَ
مَا لَكُم مِّنْ إِلَٰهٍ غَيْرُهُ هُوَ أَنشَأَكُم مِّنَ الْأَرْضِ
وَاسْتَعْمَرَكُمْ فِيهَا فَاسْتَغْفِرُوهُ ثُمَّ تُوبُوا إِلَيْهِ
إِنَّ رَبِّي قَرِيبٌ مُّجِيبٌ ﴿٦٢﴾

63. They said, 'O Ṣāliḥ, thou wast among us one in whom we placed our hopes. Dost thou forbid us to worship what our fathers worshipped? And we are surely in disquieting doubt concerning that to which thou callest us.'

قَالُوا يَا صَالِحُ قَدْ كُنتَ فِينَا مَرْجُوًّا قَبْلَ هَٰذَا أَتَنْهَانَا
أَن نَّعْبُدَ مَا يَعْبُدُ آبَاؤُنَا وَإِنَّنَا لَفِي شَكٍّ مِّمَّا
تَدْعُونَا إِلَيْهِ مُرِيبٍ ﴿٦٣﴾

64. He said, 'O my people, tell me: if I stand on a clear proof from my Lord, and He has granted me mercy from Himself, who then will help me against Allah, if I disobey Him? So you will not but add to my destruction.

قَالَ يَا قَوْمِ أَرَأَيْتُمْ إِن كُنتُ عَلَىٰ بَيِّنَةٍ مِّن رَّبِّي
وَآتَانِي مِنْهُ رَحْمَةً فَمَن يَنصُرُنِي مِنَ اللَّهِ إِنْ
عَصَيْتُهُ فَمَا تَزِيدُونَنِي غَيْرَ تَخْسِيرٍ ﴿٦٤﴾

65. 'And O my people, this is the she-camel of Allah as a Sign for you, so let her alone that she may feed in Allah's earth, and touch her not with harm lest a near punishment seize you.'

وَيَا قَوْمِ هَٰذِهِ نَاقَةُ اللَّهِ لَكُمْ آيَةً فَذَرُوهَا تَأْكُلْ
فِي أَرْضِ اللَّهِ وَلَا تَمَسُّوهَا بِسُوءٍ فَيَأْخُذَكُمْ عَذَابٌ
قَرِيبٌ ﴿٦٥﴾

66. But they hamstrung her; then he said, 'Enjoy yourselves in your houses for three days. This is a promise which is not a lie.'

فَعَقَرُوهَا فَقَالَ تَمَتَّعُوا فِي دَارِكُمْ ثَلَاثَةَ أَيَّامٍ
ذَٰلِكَ وَعْدٌ غَيْرُ مَكْذُوبٍ ﴿٦٦﴾

67. So when Our command came, we saved Ṣāliḥ and those who believed with him by Our *special* mercy, and *We saved them* from the ignominy of that day. Surely, thy Lord is Powerful, Mighty.

فَلَمَّا جَاءَ أَمْرُنَا نَجَّيْنَا صَالِحًا وَالَّذِينَ آمَنُوا مَعَهُ
بِرَحْمَةٍ مِّنَّا وَمِنْ خِزْيِ يَوْمِئِذٍ إِنَّ رَبَّكَ هُوَ
الْقَوِيُّ الْعَزِيزُ ﴿٦٧﴾

* 68. And punishment overtook those who had done wrong, and they lay pros-

وَأَخَذَ الَّذِينَ ظَلَمُوا الصَّيْحَةُ فَأَصْبَحُوا فِي دِيَارِهِمْ

trate in their houses,

جٰثِمِيْنَ ﴿٦٨﴾

69. As though they had never dwelt therein. Behold! Thamūd behaved ungratefully to their Lord; Behold! cursed are *the tribe of* Thamūd.

كَاَنْ لَّمْ يَغْنَوْا فِيْهَا ۗ اَلَآ اِنَّ ثَمُوْدَاۡ كَفَرُوْا رَبَّهُمْ

ع اَلَا بُعْدًا لِّثَمُوْدَ ﴿٦٩﴾

R. 7.

70. And surely, Our messengers came to Abraham with glad tidings. They said, '*We bid you* peace.' He answered, 'Peace *be on you*,' and was not long in bringing a roasted calf.

وَلَقَدْ جَآءَتْ رُسُلُنَآ اِبْرٰهِيْمَ بِالْبُشْرٰى قَالُوْا سَلٰمًا ۗ

قَالَ سَلٰمٌ فَمَا لَبِثَ اَنْ جَآءَ بِعِجْلٍ حَنِيْذٍ ﴿٧٠﴾

* 71. But when he saw their hands not reaching thereto, he knew not what they were, and conceived a fear of them. They said, 'Fear not, for we have been sent to the people of Lot.'

فَلَمَّا رَاٰۤ اَيْدِيَهُمْ لَا تَصِلُ اِلَيْهِ نَكِرَهُمْ وَاَوْجَسَ

مِنْهُمْ خِيْفَةً ۗ قَالُوْا لَا تَخَفْ اِنَّآ اُرْسِلْنَآ اِلٰى

قَوْمِ لُوْطٍ ﴿٧١﴾

* 72. And his wife was standing *by*, and she *too* was frightened, whereupon We gave her glad tidings of the birth of Isaac and, after Isaac, of Jacob.

وَامْرَاَتُهٗ قَآئِمَةٌ فَضَحِكَتْ فَبَشَّرْنٰهَا بِاِسْحٰقَ ۙ وَ

مِنْ وَّرَآءِ اِسْحٰقَ يَعْقُوْبَ ﴿٧٢﴾

73. She said, 'Oh, woe is me! Shall I bear a child when I am an old woman, and this my husband is an old man? This is indeed a strange thing!'

قَالَتْ يٰوَيْلَتٰۤى ءَاَلِدُ وَاَنَا عَجُوْزٌ وَّهٰذَا بَعْلِىْ شَيْخًا ۗ

اِنَّ هٰذَا لَشَىْءٌ عَجِيْبٌ ﴿٧٣﴾

74. They said, 'Dost thou wonder at Allah's decree? The mercy of Allah and His blessings are upon you, O people of the House. Surely, He is Praiseworthy, Glorious.'

قَالُوْۤا اَتَعْجَبِيْنَ مِنْ اَمْرِ اللّٰهِ رَحْمَتُ اللّٰهِ وَبَرَكٰتُهٗ

عَلَيْكُمْ اَهْلَ الْبَيْتِ ۗ اِنَّهٗ حَمِيْدٌ مَّجِيْدٌ ﴿٧٤﴾

75. And when fear left Abraham, and the glad tidings came to him, he began disputing with Us about the people of Lot.

فَلَمَّا ذَهَبَ عَنْ اِبْرٰهِيْمَ الرَّوْعُ وَجَآءَتْهُ الْبُشْرٰى

يُجَادِلُنَا فِىْ قَوْمِ لُوْطٍ ﴿٧٥﴾

76. Indeed, Abraham was clement, tender-hearted, and oft-turning *to God*.

اِنَّ اِبْرٰهِيْمَ لَحَلِيْمٌ اَوَّاهٌ مُّنِيْبٌ ﴿٧٦﴾

77. 'O Abraham, turn away from this. Surely, the command of thy Lord has gone forth, and surely, there is coming to them a punishment that cannot be averted.'

يٰۤاِبْرٰهِيْمُ اَعْرِضْ عَنْ هٰذَا ۚ اِنَّهٗ قَدْ جَآءَ اَمْرُ

رَبِّكَ ۚ وَاِنَّهُمْ اٰتِيْهِمْ عَذَابٌ غَيْرُ مَرْدُوْدٍ ﴿٧٧﴾

78. And when Our messengers came to Lot, he was grieved on account of them and felt helpless on their behalf and said, 'This is a distressful day.'

وَلَمَّا جَآءَتْ رُسُلُنَا لُوْطًا سِىْٓءَ بِهِمْ وَضَاقَ بِهِمْ

ذَرْعًا وَّقَالَ هٰذَا يَوْمٌ عَصِيْبٌ ﴿٧٨﴾

* 79. And his people came running towards him, trembling *with rage;* and

وَجَآءَهٗ قَوْمُهٗ يُهْرَعُوْنَ اِلَيْهِ ۗ وَمِنْ قَبْلُ كَانُوْا

before this *too* they used to do evil. He said, 'O my people, these are my daughters; they are purer for you. So fear Allah and disgrace me not in the presence of my guests. Is there not among you any right-minded man?'

يَعْمَلُوْنَ السَّيِّاٰتِ ۭ قَالَ يٰقَوْمِ هٰٓؤُلَاۗءِ بَنَاتِيْ هُنَّ
اَطْهَرُ لَكُمْ فَاتَّقُوا اللّٰهَ وَلَا تُخْزُوْنِ فِيْ ضَيْفِيْ ۭ اَلَيْسَ
مِنْكُمْ رَجُلٌ رَّشِيْدٌ ﴿۷۹﴾

80. They answered, 'Thou surely knowest that we have no claim on thy daughters, and thou surely knowest what we desire.'

قَالُوْا لَقَدْ عَلِمْتَ مَا لَنَا فِيْ بَنٰتِكَ مِنْ حَقٍّ ۚ وَاِنَّكَ
لَتَعْلَمُ مَا نُرِيْدُ ﴿۸۰﴾

81. He said, 'Would that I had power *to deal* with you, or I should betake myself to a mighty support *for shelter*.'

قَالَ لَوْ اَنَّ لِيْ بِكُمْ قُوَّةً اَوْ اٰوِيْٓ اِلٰى رُكْنٍ شَدِيْدٍ ﴿۸۱﴾

* 82. *The messengers* said, 'O Lot, we are the messengers of thy Lord. They shall by no means reach thee. So depart with thy family in a part of the night, and let none of you look back, but thy wife. Surely, what is going to befall them shall *also* befall her. Verily, their appointed time is the morning. Is not the morning nigh?'

قَالُوْا يٰلُوْطُ اِنَّا رُسُلُ رَبِّكَ لَنْ يَّصِلُوْٓا اِلَيْكَ فَاَسْرِ
بِاَهْلِكَ بِقِطْعٍ مِّنَ الَّيْلِ وَلَا يَلْتَفِتْ مِنْكُمْ اَحَدٌ
اِلَّا امْرَاَتَكَ ۭ اِنَّهٗ مُصِيْبُهَا مَآ اَصَابَهُمْ ۭ اِنَّ مَوْعِدَهُمُ
الصُّبْحُ ۭ اَلَيْسَ الصُّبْحُ بِقَرِيْبٍ ﴿۸۲﴾

83. So when Our command came, We turned that *town* upside down and We rained upon it stones of clay, layer upon layer,

فَلَمَّا جَاۗءَ اَمْرُنَا جَعَلْنَا عَالِيَهَا سَافِلَهَا وَاَمْطَرْنَا
عَلَيْهَا حِجَارَةً مِّنْ سِجِّيْلٍ ۥ مَّنْضُوْدٍ ﴿۸۳﴾

84. Marked *for them* in the decree of thy Lord. And such *punishment* is not far from the wrongdoers *of the present age*.

مُّسَوَّمَةً عِنْدَ رَبِّكَ ۭ وَمَا هِيَ مِنَ الظّٰلِمِيْنَ
بِبَعِيْدٍ ﴿۸۴﴾ ع النصف

R. 8.

85. And to Midian *We sent* their brother Shu'aib. He said, 'O my people, worship Allah. You have no God other than Him. And give not short measure and short weight. I see you in *a state of* prosperity and I fear for you the punishment of a destructive day.

وَاِلٰى مَدْيَنَ اَخَاهُمْ شُعَيْبًا ۭ قَالَ يٰقَوْمِ اعْبُدُوا
اللّٰهَ مَا لَكُمْ مِّنْ اِلٰهٍ غَيْرُهٗ ۭ وَلَا تَنْقُصُوا الْمِكْيَالَ
وَالْمِيْزَانَ اِنِّيْٓ اَرٰىكُمْ بِخَيْرٍ وَّاِنِّيْٓ اَخَافُ عَلَيْكُمْ
عَذَابَ يَوْمٍ مُّحِيْطٍ ﴿۸۵﴾

* 86. 'And O my people, give full measure and full weight with equity, and defraud not people of their things and commit not iniquity in the earth, causing disorder.

وَيٰقَوْمِ اَوْفُوا الْمِكْيَالَ وَالْمِيْزَانَ بِالْقِسْطِ وَلَا
تَبْخَسُوا النَّاسَ اَشْيَاۗءَهُمْ وَلَا تَعْثَوْا فِي الْاَرْضِ
مُفْسِدِيْنَ ﴿۸۶﴾

87. 'That which is left *with you* by Allah is better for you, if you are believers.

بَقِيَّتُ اللّٰهِ خَيْرٌ لَّكُمْ اِنْ كُنْتُمْ مُّؤْمِنِيْنَ ڬ وَمَآ اَنَا

And I am not a keeper over you.'

عليكم بحفيظ ﴿٨٧﴾

88. They replied, 'O Shu'aib, does thy Prayer bid thee that we should leave what our fathers worshipped, or that we cease to do with our property what we please? Thou art *indeed* very intelligent *and* right-minded.'

قالوا يشعيب اصلوتك تامرك ان نترك ما يعبد اباؤنا او ان نفعل في اموالنا ما نشؤا انك لانت الحليم الرشيد ﴿٨٨﴾

89. He said, 'O my people, tell me: if I stand on a clear evidence from my Lord, and He has provided me from Himself with a handsome provision, *what answer will you give to Him?* And I do not desire to do against you the *very* thing which I ask you not to do. I only desire reform as far as I can. There is no power in me save through Allah. In Him do I trust and to Him do I return.

قال يقوم ارءيتم ان كنت على بينة من ربي ورزقني منه رزقا حسنا وما اريد ان اخالفكم الى ما انهكم عنه ان اريد الا الاصلاح ما استطعت وما توفيقي الا بالله عليه توكلت واليه انيب ﴿٨٩﴾

90. 'And O my people, let not *your* hostility towards me lead you *to this* that there should befall you the like of that which befell the people of Noah or the people of Hūd or the people of Ṣāliḥ; and the people of Lot are not far from you.

ويقوم لا يجرمنكم شقاقي ان يصيبكم مثل ما اصاب قوم نوح او قوم هود او قوم صلح وما قوم لوط منكم ببعيد ﴿٩٠﴾

91. 'And seek forgiveness of your Lord; then turn to Him *whole-heartedly*. Verily, my Lord is Merciful, Most Loving.'

واستغفروا ربكم ثم توبوا اليه ان ربي رحيم ودود ﴿٩١﴾

* 92. They replied, 'O Shu'aib, we do not understand much of that which thou sayest, and surely, we see that thou art weak among us. And were it not for thy tribe, we would surely stone thee. And thou holdest no strong position among us.'

قالوا يشعيب ما نفقه كثيرا مما تقول وانا لنرىك فينا ضعيفا ولولا رهطك لرجمنك وما انت علينا بعزيز ﴿٩٢﴾

93. He said, 'O my people, is my tribe mightier with you than Allah? And you have cast Him behind your backs as neglected. Surely, my Lord encompasses all that you do.

قال يقوم ارهطي اعز عليكم من الله واتخذتموه وراءكم ظهريا ان ربي بما تعملون محيط ﴿٩٣﴾

94. 'And O my people, act as best you can, I *too* am acting. You will soon know on whom lights a punishment that will disgrace him, and who it is that is a liar. And wait; surely, I wait with you.'

ويقوم اعملوا على مكانتكم اني عامل سوف تعلمون من ياتيه عذاب يخزيه ومن هو كاذب وارتقبوا اني معكم رقيب ﴿٩٤﴾

95. And when Our command came, We saved Shu‘aib and those who had believed with him by Our *special* mercy; and chastisement seized those who had done wrong, so that they lay prostrate in their houses,

وَلَمَّا جَآءَ اَمْرُنَا نَجَّيْنَا شُعَيْبًا وَّالَّذِيْنَ اٰمَنُوْا مَعَهٗ
بِرَحْمَةٍ مِّنَّا وَاَخَذَتِ الَّذِيْنَ ظَلَمُوا الصَّيْحَةُ فَاَصْبَحُوْا
فِيْ دِيَارِهِمْ جٰثِمِيْنَ ﴿٩٥﴾

96. As though they had never dwelt therein. Behold! how Midian was cut off, even as Thamūd had been cut off.

كَاَنْ لَّمْ يَغْنَوْا فِيْهَا ۭ اَلَا بُعْدًا لِّمَدْيَنَ كَمَا بَعِدَتْ
ثَمُوْدُ ﴿٩٦﴾

R. 9.

97. And, surely, We sent Moses with Our Signs and manifest authority

وَلَقَدْ اَرْسَلْنَا مُوْسٰى بِاٰيٰتِنَا وَسُلْطٰنٍ مُّبِيْنٍ ﴿٩٧﴾

98. To Pharaoh and his chiefs; but they followed the command of Pharaoh, and the command of Pharaoh was not at all rightful.

اِلٰى فِرْعَوْنَ وَمَلَا۟ئِهٖ فَاتَّبَعُوْٓا اَمْرَ فِرْعَوْنَ ۚ وَمَآ
اَمْرُ فِرْعَوْنَ بِرَشِيْدٍ ﴿٩٨﴾

* 99. He will go before his people on the Day of Resurrection and will bring them down into the Fire, *even as cattle are brought to a watering-place*. And evil is the watering-place arrived at.

يَقْدُمُ قَوْمَهٗ يَوْمَ الْقِيٰمَةِ فَاَوْرَدَهُمُ النَّارَ ۭ وَبِئْسَ
الْوِرْدُ الْمَوْرُوْدُ ﴿٩٩﴾

* 100. And a curse was made to follow them in this *life* and on the Day of Resurrection. Evil is the gift which shall be given *them*.

وَاُتْبِعُوْا فِيْ هٰذِهٖ لَعْنَةً وَّيَوْمَ الْقِيٰمَةِ ۭ بِئْسَ الرِّفْدُ
الْمَرْفُوْدُ ﴿١٠٠﴾

101. That is of the tidings of the *ruined* cities, We relate it to thee. Of them *some* are standing and *some* have been mown down *like the harvest*.

ذٰلِكَ مِنْ اَنْۢبَآءِ الْقُرٰى نَقُصُّهٗ عَلَيْكَ مِنْهَا قَآئِمٌ
وَّحَصِيْدٌ ﴿١٠١﴾

102. And We did not wrong them, but they wronged themselves; and their gods on whom they called beside Allah were of no avail to them at all when the command of thy Lord came; and they added to them naught but perdition.

وَمَا ظَلَمْنٰهُمْ وَلٰكِنْ ظَلَمُوْٓا اَنْفُسَهُمْ فَمَآ اَغْنَتْ
عَنْهُمْ اٰلِهَتُهُمُ الَّتِيْ يَدْعُوْنَ مِنْ دُوْنِ اللّٰهِ مِنْ
شَيْءٍ لَّمَّا جَآءَ اَمْرُ رَبِّكَ ۭ وَمَا زَادُوْهُمْ غَيْرَ تَتْبِيْبٍ ﴿١٠٢﴾

103. Such is the grasp of thy Lord when He seizes the cities while they are doing wrong. Surely, His grasp is grievous *and* severe.

وَكَذٰلِكَ اَخْذُ رَبِّكَ اِذَآ اَخَذَ الْقُرٰى وَهِيَ ظٰلِمَةٌ ۭ
اِنَّ اَخْذَهٗٓ اَلِيْمٌ شَدِيْدٌ ﴿١٠٣﴾

104. In that surely is a Sign for him who fears the punishment of the Hereafter. That is a day for which *all* mankind shall be gathered together and that is a day *the proceedings of* which shall be witnessed *by all*.

اِنَّ فِيْ ذٰلِكَ لَاٰيَةً لِّمَنْ خَافَ عَذَابَ الْاٰخِرَةِ ۭ ذٰلِكَ
يَوْمٌ مَّجْمُوْعٌ ۙ لَّهُ النَّاسُ وَذٰلِكَ يَوْمٌ مَّشْهُوْدٌ ﴿١٠٤﴾

105. And We delay it not save for a computed term.

وَمَا نُؤَخِّرُهٗٓ اِلَّا لِاَجَلٍ مَّعْدُوْدٍ ﴿١٠٥﴾

106. The day it comes, no soul shall speak except by His permission; then *some* of them will prove unfortunate and *others* fortunate.

107. As for those who will prove unfortunate, they shall be in the Fire, wherein there shall be for them sighing and sobbing,

108. Abiding therein so long as the heavens and the earth endure, excepting what thy Lord may will. Surely, thy Lord does bring about what He pleases.

109. But as for those who will prove fortunate, they shall be in Heaven; abiding therein so long as the heavens and the earth endure, excepting what thy Lord may will—a gift that shall not be cut off.

110. So be not in doubt concerning that which these *people* worship. They only worship as their fathers worshipped before, and We shall surely pay them in full their portion undiminished.

R. 10.

111. And We certainly gave Moses the Book, but differences were created therein; and had it not been for a word already gone forth from thy Lord, surely, the matter would have been decided between them *long before;* and *now* these *people* are in a disquieting doubt concerning it.

112. And surely, *the works of* all *these have* not yet *been requited but* thy Lord will certainly repay them in full, according to their works. He is surely well aware of all that they do.

113. So stand thou upright, as thou hast been commanded, and *also* those who have turned *to God* with thee; and exceed ye not the bounds, *O believers; for* surely, He sees what you do.

114. And incline not toward those who do wrong, lest the Fire touch you. And you shall have no friends beside Allah, nor shall you be helped.

* 115. And observe Prayer at the two ends of the day, and in the hours of the

يَوْمَ يَأْتِ لَا تَكَلَّمُ نَفْسٌ إِلَّا بِإِذْنِهٖ فَمِنْهُمْ شَقِيٌّ
وَّسَعِيْدٌ ﴿١٠٦﴾
فَأَمَّا الَّذِيْنَ شَقُوْا فَفِي النَّارِ لَهُمْ فِيْهَا زَفِيْرٌ وَّ
شَهِيْقٌ ﴿١٠٧﴾
خٰلِدِيْنَ فِيْهَا مَا دَامَتِ السَّمٰوٰتُ وَالْأَرْضُ إِلَّا مَا
شَآءَ رَبُّكَ إِنَّ رَبَّكَ فَعَّالٌ لِّمَا يُرِيْدُ ﴿١٠٨﴾
وَأَمَّا الَّذِيْنَ سُعِدُوْا فَفِي الْجَنَّةِ خٰلِدِيْنَ فِيْهَا مَا
دَامَتِ السَّمٰوٰتُ وَالْأَرْضُ إِلَّا مَا شَآءَ رَبُّكَ
عَطَآءً غَيْرَ مَجْذُوْذٍ ﴿١٠٩﴾
فَلَا تَكُ فِيْ مِرْيَةٍ مِّمَّا يَعْبُدُ هٰٓؤُلَآءِ مَا يَعْبُدُوْنَ
إِلَّا كَمَا يَعْبُدُ اٰبَآؤُهُمْ مِّنْ قَبْلُ وَإِنَّا لَمُوَفُّوْهُمْ
ع ٩ نَصِيْبَهُمْ غَيْرَ مَنْقُوْصٍ ﴿١١٠﴾
وَلَقَدْ اٰتَيْنَا مُوْسَى الْكِتٰبَ فَاخْتُلِفَ فِيْهِ وَلَوْلَا
كَلِمَةٌ سَبَقَتْ مِنْ رَّبِّكَ لَقُضِيَ بَيْنَهُمْ وَإِنَّهُمْ لَفِيْ
شَكٍّ مِّنْهُ مُرِيْبٍ ﴿١١١﴾
وَإِنَّ كُلًّا لَّمَّا لَيُوَفِّيَنَّهُمْ رَبُّكَ أَعْمَالَهُمْ إِنَّهٗ بِمَا
يَعْمَلُوْنَ خَبِيْرٌ ﴿١١٢﴾
فَاسْتَقِمْ كَمَآ أُمِرْتَ وَمَنْ تَابَ مَعَكَ وَلَا تَطْغَوْا
إِنَّهٗ بِمَا تَعْمَلُوْنَ بَصِيْرٌ ﴿١١٣﴾
وَلَا تَرْكَنُوْٓا إِلَى الَّذِيْنَ ظَلَمُوْا فَتَمَسَّكُمُ النَّارُ وَمَا
لَكُمْ مِّنْ دُوْنِ اللّٰهِ مِنْ أَوْلِيَآءَ ثُمَّ لَا تُنْصَرُوْنَ ﴿١١٤﴾
وَأَقِمِ الصَّلٰوةَ طَرَفَيِ النَّهَارِ وَزُلَفًا مِّنَ الَّيْلِ إِنَّ

الْحَسَنٰتِ يُذْهِبْنَ السَّيِّاٰتِ ۭ ذٰلِكَ ذِكْرٰى
لِلذّٰكِرِيْنَ (١١٥)

night *that are nearer the day*. Surely, good works drive away evil works. This is a reminder for those who would remember.

وَاصْبِرْ فَاِنَّ اللّٰهَ لَا يُضِيْعُ اَجْرَ الْمُحْسِنِيْنَ (١١٦)

116. And be thou steadfast; for surely, Allah suffers not the reward of the righteous to perish.

فَلَوْلَا كَانَ مِنَ الْقُرُوْنِ مِنْ قَبْلِكُمْ اُولُوْا بَقِيَّةٍ
يَّنْهَوْنَ عَنِ الْفَسَادِ فِي الْاَرْضِ اِلَّا قَلِيْلًا مِّمَّنْ
اَنْجَيْنَا مِنْهُمْ ۚ وَاتَّبَعَ الَّذِيْنَ ظَلَمُوْا مَآ اُتْرِفُوْا فِيْهِ
وَكَانُوْا مُجْرِمِيْنَ (١١٧)

117. Why, then, were there not among the generations before you persons possessed of understanding who would have forbidden corruption in the earth—except a few of those whom We saved from among them? But the wrongdoers followed that by which they were afforded ease and comfort, and they became guilty.

وَمَا كَانَ رَبُّكَ لِيُهْلِكَ الْقُرٰى بِظُلْمٍ وَّاَهْلُهَا
مُصْلِحُوْنَ (١١٨)

118. And thy Lord would not destroy the cities unjustly while the people thereof were righteous.

وَلَوْ شَآءَ رَبُّكَ لَجَعَلَ النَّاسَ اُمَّةً وَّاحِدَةً وَّلَا
يَزَالُوْنَ مُخْتَلِفِيْنَ (١١٩)

119. And if thy Lord had *enforced* His will, He would have surely made mankind one people; but they would not cease to differ,

اِلَّا مَنْ رَّحِمَ رَبُّكَ ۭ وَلِذٰلِكَ خَلَقَهُمْ ۭ وَتَمَّتْ كَلِمَةُ
رَبِّكَ لَاَمْلَئَنَّ جَهَنَّمَ مِنَ الْجِنَّةِ وَالنَّاسِ اَجْمَعِيْنَ (١٢٠)

120. Save those on whom thy Lord has had mercy, and for this has He created them. But the word of thy Lord shall be fulfilled: 'Verily, I will fill Hell with *the disobedient* Jinn and men all together.'

وَكُلًّا نَّقُصُّ عَلَيْكَ مِنْ اَنْۢبَاۗءِ الرُّسُلِ مَا نُثَبِّتُ بِهٖ
فُؤَادَكَ ۚ وَجَاۗءَكَ فِيْ هٰذِهِ الْحَقُّ وَمَوْعِظَةٌ وَّذِكْرٰى
لِلْمُؤْمِنِيْنَ (١٢١)

121. And all of the tidings of the Messengers, whereby We make thy heart firm, We relate unto thee. And herein has come to thee the truth and an exhortation and a reminder for believers.

وَقُلْ لِّلَّذِيْنَ لَا يُؤْمِنُوْنَ اعْمَلُوْا عَلٰى مَكَانَتِكُمْ ۭ اِنَّا عٰمِلُوْنَ (١٢٢)

122. And say to those who believe not: 'Act as best you can, we *too* are acting.

وَانْتَظِرُوْا ۚ اِنَّا مُنْتَظِرُوْنَ (١٢٣)

123. 'And wait ye, we *too* are waiting.'

وَلِلّٰهِ غَيْبُ السَّمٰوٰتِ وَالْاَرْضِ وَاِلَيْهِ يُرْجَعُ الْاَمْرُ كُلُّهٗ
فَاعْبُدْهُ وَتَوَكَّلْ عَلَيْهِ ۭ وَمَا رَبُّكَ بِغَافِلٍ عَمَّا تَعْمَلُوْنَ (١٢٤)

124. And to Allah belong the hidden things of the heavens and the earth, and to Him shall the whole affair be referred. So worship Him and put thy trust in Him *alone*. And thy Lord is not unmindful of what you do.

سُوْرَةُ يُوْسُفَ مَكِّيَّةٌ

(١٢) اٰيَاتُهَا ١١٢ — رُكُوْعَاتُهَا ١٢

YŪSUF

(Revealed before Hijra)

1\. In the name of Allah, the Gracious, the Merciful.

بِسْمِ اللّٰهِ الرَّحْمٰنِ الرَّحِيْمِ (١)

2\. Alif Lām Rā*. These are verses of the clear Book.

الٓرٰ ۫ تِلْكَ اٰيٰتُ الْكِتٰبِ الْمُبِيْنِ (٢)

* 3. We have revealed it—the Qur'ān in Arabic—that you may understand.

اِنَّآ اَنْزَلْنٰهُ قُرْءٰنًا عَرَبِيًّا لَّعَلَّكُمْ تَعْقِلُوْنَ (٣)

* 4. We narrate unto thee the most beautiful narration by revealing to thee this Qur'ān, though thou wast, before this, of those not possessed of *requisite* knowledge.

نَحْنُ نَقُصُّ عَلَيْكَ اَحْسَنَ الْقَصَصِ بِمَآ اَوْحَيْنَآ
اِلَيْكَ هٰذَا الْقُرْاٰنَ ۖ وَاِنْ كُنْتَ مِنْ قَبْلِهٖ لَمِنَ
الْغٰفِلِيْنَ (٤)

5\. *Remember the time* when Joseph said to his father, 'O my father, I saw *in a dream* eleven stars and the sun and the moon, I saw them making obeisance to me.'

اِذْ قَالَ يُوْسُفُ لِاَبِيْهِ يٰۤاَبَتِ اِنِّيْ رَاَيْتُ اَحَدَ عَشَرَ
كَوْكَبًا وَّالشَّمْسَ وَالْقَمَرَ رَاَيْتُهُمْ لِيْ سٰجِدِيْنَ (٥)

6\. He said, 'O my darling son, relate not thy dream to thy brothers, lest they contrive a plot against thee; for Satan is to man an open enemy.

قَالَ يٰبُنَيَّ لَا تَقْصُصْ رُءْيَاكَ عَلٰۤى اِخْوَتِكَ فَيَكِيْدُوْا
لَكَ كَيْدًا ۗ اِنَّ الشَّيْطٰنَ لِلْاِنْسَانِ عَدُوٌّ مُّبِيْنٌ (٦)

* 7. 'And thus *shall it be as thou hast seen*, thy Lord will choose thee and teach thee the interpretation of things and perfect His favour upon thee and upon the family of Jacob as He perfected it upon two of thy forefathers—Abraham and Isaac. Verily, thy Lord is All-Knowing, Wise.'

وَكَذٰلِكَ يَجْتَبِيْكَ رَبُّكَ وَيُعَلِّمُكَ مِنْ تَاْوِيْلِ
الْاَحَادِيْثِ وَيُتِمُّ نِعْمَتَهٗ عَلَيْكَ وَعَلٰۤى اٰلِ يَعْقُوْبَ
كَمَآ اَتَمَّهَا عَلٰۤى اَبَوَيْكَ مِنْ قَبْلُ اِبْرٰهِيْمَ وَاِسْحٰقَ ۗ
ع اِنَّ رَبَّكَ عَلِيْمٌ حَكِيْمٌ (٧)

R. 2.

8\. Surely, in Joseph and his brethren there are Signs for the inquirers.

لَقَدْ كَانَ فِيْ يُوْسُفَ وَاِخْوَتِهٖۤ اٰيٰتٌ لِّلسَّآئِلِيْنَ (٨)

9\. When they said, 'Verily, Joseph and his brother are dearer to our father than we are, although we are a strong party. Surely, our father is in manifest error.

اِذْ قَالُوْا لَيُوْسُفُ وَاَخُوْهُ اَحَبُّ اِلٰۤى اَبِيْنَا مِنَّا وَ
نَحْنُ عُصْبَةٌ ۗ اِنَّ اَبَانَا لَفِيْ ضَلٰلٍ مُّبِيْنِ ۚ (٩)

10\. 'Kill Joseph or cast him out to some *distant* land, so that your father's favour may become exclusively yours and you can thereafter become a righteous people.'

اقْتُلُوْا يُوْسُفَ اَوِ اطْرَحُوْهُ اَرْضًا يَّخْلُ لَكُمْ وَجْهُ
اَبِيْكُمْ وَتَكُوْنُوْا مِنْ بَعْدِهٖ قَوْمًا صٰلِحِيْنَ (١٠)

---

* I am Allah Who is All-Seeing.

11. One of them said, 'Kill not Joseph, but if you must do something, cast him into the bottom of a deep well; some of the travellers will pick him up.'

قَالَ قَآئِلٌ مِّنْهُمْ لَا تَقْتُلُوْا يُوْسُفَ وَاَلْقُوْهُ فِيْ غَيٰبَتِ الْجُبِّ يَلْتَقِطْهُ بَعْضُ السَّيَّارَةِ اِنْ كُنْتُمْ فٰعِلِيْنَ ۝١١

12. They said, 'O our father, why dost thou not trust us with respect to Joseph, when we are certainly his sincere well-wishers?

قَالُوْا يٰۤاَبَانَا مَا لَكَ لَا تَاْمَنَّا عَلٰى يُوْسُفَ وَاِنَّا لَهٗ لَنٰصِحُوْنَ ۝١٢

13. 'Send him with us tomorrow that he may enjoy himself and play, and we shall surely keep guard over him.'

اَرْسِلْهُ مَعَنَا غَدًا يَّرْتَعْ وَيَلْعَبْ وَاِنَّا لَهٗ لَحٰفِظُوْنَ ۝١٣

14. He said, 'It grieves me that you should take him away, and I fear lest the wolf should devour him while you are heedless of him.'

قَالَ اِنِّيْ لَيَحْزُنُنِيْۤ اَنْ تَذْهَبُوْا بِهٖ وَاَخَافُ اَنْ يَّاْكُلَهُ الذِّئْبُ وَاَنْتُمْ عَنْهُ غٰفِلُوْنَ ۝١٤

15. They said, 'Surely, if the wolf devour him while we are a strong party, then we shall indeed be *great* losers.'

قَالُوْا لَئِنْ اَكَلَهُ الذِّئْبُ وَنَحْنُ عُصْبَةٌ اِنَّاۤ اِذًا لَّخٰسِرُوْنَ ۝١٥

* 16. So, when they took him away, and agreed to put him into the bottom of a deep well, *they had their malicious design carried out;* and We sent a revelation to him, *saying*, 'Thou shalt surely *one day* tell them of this affair of theirs and they shall not know.'

فَلَمَّا ذَهَبُوْا بِهٖ وَاَجْمَعُوْۤا اَنْ يَّجْعَلُوْهُ فِيْ غَيٰبَتِ الْجُبِّ وَاَوْحَيْنَاۤ اِلَيْهِ لَتُنَبِّئَنَّهُمْ بِاَمْرِهِمْ هٰذَا وَهُمْ لَا يَشْعُرُوْنَ ۝١٦

17. And they came to their father in the evening, weeping.

وَجَآءُوْۤ اَبَاهُمْ عِشَآءً يَّبْكُوْنَ ۝١٧

18. They said, 'O our father, we went forth racing with one another, and left Joseph with our things, and the wolf devoured him, but thou wilt not believe us even if we speak the truth.'

قَالُوْا يٰۤاَبَانَاۤ اِنَّا ذَهَبْنَا نَسْتَبِقُ وَتَرَكْنَا يُوْسُفَ عِنْدَ مَتَاعِنَا فَاَكَلَهُ الذِّئْبُ وَمَاۤ اَنْتَ بِمُؤْمِنٍ لَّنَا وَلَوْ كُنَّا صٰدِقِيْنَ ۝١٨

* 19. And they came with false blood on his shirt. He said, 'Nay, but your souls have made a *great* thing appear light in your eyes. So *now* comely patience *is good for me*. And it is Allah *alone* Whose help is to be sought against what you assert.'

وَجَآءُوْ عَلٰى قَمِيْصِهٖ بِدَمٍ كَذِبٍ قَالَ بَلْ سَوَّلَتْ لَكُمْ اَنْفُسُكُمْ اَمْرًا فَصَبْرٌ جَمِيْلٌ وَاللّٰهُ الْمُسْتَعَانُ عَلٰى مَا تَصِفُوْنَ ۝١٩

20. And there came a caravan of travellers and they sent their water-drawer. And he let down his bucket *into the well*. 'Oh, good news!' said he, 'Here is a youth!' And they concealed

وَجَآءَتْ سَيَّارَةٌ فَاَرْسَلُوْا وَارِدَهُمْ فَاَدْلٰى دَلْوَهٗ قَالَ يٰبُشْرٰى هٰذَا غُلٰمٌ وَاَسَرُّوْهُ بِضَاعَةً وَاللّٰهُ

him as a piece of merchandise, and Allah knew full well what they did.

عَلِيْمٌۢ بِمَا يَعْمَلُوْنَ ﴿٢٠﴾

* 21. And they sold him for a paltry price, a few dirhems, and they were not desirous of it.

وَشَرَوْهُ بِثَمَنٍۭ بَخْسٍ دَرَاهِمَ مَعْدُوْدَةٍ ۚ وَكَانُوْا
فِيْهِ مِنَ الزَّاهِدِيْنَ ﴿٢١﴾ ع ۲ ۱۲

R. 3.

* 22. And the man from Egypt who bought him said to his wife, 'Make his stay honourable. Maybe he will be of benefit to us; or we shall adopt him as a son.' And thus did We establish Joseph in the land, and *We did so* that We might *also* teach him the interpretation of things. And Allah has full power over His decree, but most men know *it* not.

وَقَالَ الَّذِي اشْتَرٰىهُ مِنْ مِّصْرَ لِامْرَاَتِهٖٓ اَكْرِمِيْ
مَثْوٰىهُ عَسٰٓى اَنْ يَّنْفَعَنَآ اَوْ نَتَّخِذَهٗ وَلَدًا ۚ وَكَذٰلِكَ
مَكَّنَّا لِيُوْسُفَ فِي الْاَرْضِ ۡ وَلِنُعَلِّمَهٗ مِنْ تَاْوِيْلِ
الْاَحَادِيْثِ ۚ وَاللّٰهُ غَالِبٌ عَلٰٓى اَمْرِهٖ وَلٰكِنَّ اَكْثَرَ
النَّاسِ لَا يَعْلَمُوْنَ ﴿٢٢﴾

* 23. And when he attained his *age of* full strength, We granted him judgment and knowledge. And thus do We reward the doers of good.

وَلَمَّا بَلَغَ اَشُدَّهٗٓ اٰتَيْنٰهُ حُكْمًا وَّعِلْمًا ۚ وَكَذٰلِكَ
نَجْزِي الْمُحْسِنِيْنَ ﴿٢٣﴾

24. And she, in whose house he was, sought to seduce him against his will. And she bolted the doors, and said, 'Now come.' He said, 'I seek refuge with Allah. He is my Lord. He has made my stay *with you* honourable. Verily, the wrongdoers never prosper.'

وَرَاوَدَتْهُ الَّتِيْ هُوَ فِيْ بَيْتِهَا عَنْ نَّفْسِهٖ وَغَلَّقَتِ
الْاَبْوَابَ وَقَالَتْ هَيْتَ لَكَ ۚ قَالَ مَعَاذَ اللّٰهِ اِنَّهٗ
رَبِّيْٓ اَحْسَنَ مَثْوَايَ ۚ اِنَّهٗ لَا يُفْلِحُ الظّٰلِمُوْنَ ﴿٢٤﴾

25. And she made up her mind with regard to him, and he made up his mind with regard to her. If he had not seen a manifest Sign of his Lord, *he could not have shown such determination*. Thus was it, that We might turn away from him evil and indecency. Surely, he was *one* of Our chosen servants.

وَلَقَدْ هَمَّتْ بِهٖ ۚ وَهَمَّ بِهَا لَوْلَآ اَنْ رَّاٰ بُرْهَانَ رَبِّهٖ ۚ
كَذٰلِكَ لِنَصْرِفَ عَنْهُ السُّوْٓءَ وَالْفَحْشَآءَ ۚ اِنَّهٗ مِنْ
عِبَادِنَا الْمُخْلَصِيْنَ ﴿٢٥﴾

26. And they both raced to the door, and she tore his shirt from behind, and they found her lord at the door. She said, 'What shall be the punishment of one who intended evil to thy wife, save imprisonment or a grievous chastisement?'

وَاسْتَبَقَا الْبَابَ وَقَدَّتْ قَمِيْصَهٗ مِنْ دُبُرٍ وَّ
اَلْفَيَا سَيِّدَهَا لَدَا الْبَابِ ۚ قَالَتْ مَا جَزَآءُ مَنْ اَرَادَ
بِاَهْلِكَ سُوْٓءًا اِلَّآ اَنْ يُّسْجَنَ اَوْ عَذَابٌ اَلِيْمٌ ﴿٢٦﴾

27. He said, 'She it was who sought to seduce me against my will.' And a witness of her household bore witness *saying*, 'If his shirt is torn from the front, then she has spoken the truth and he is of the liars.

قَالَ هِيَ رَاوَدَتْنِيْ عَنْ نَّفْسِيْ وَشَهِدَ شَاهِدٌ مِّنْ
اَهْلِهَا ۚ اِنْ كَانَ قَمِيْصُهٗ قُدَّ مِنْ قُبُلٍ فَصَدَقَتْ
وَهُوَ مِنَ الْكٰذِبِيْنَ ﴿٢٧﴾

28. 'But if his shirt is torn from behind, then she has lied and he is of the truthful.'

وَاِنْ كَانَ قَمِيْصُهٗ قُدَّ مِنْ دُبُرٍ فَكَذَبَتْ وَهُوَ مِنَ الصّٰدِقِيْنَ ﴿٢٨﴾

29. So when he saw his shirt torn from behind, he said, 'Surely, this is a device of you women. Your device is indeed mighty.

فَلَمَّا رَاٰ قَمِيْصَهٗ قُدَّ مِنْ دُبُرٍ قَالَ اِنَّهٗ مِنْ كَيْدِكُنَّ اِنَّ كَيْدَكُنَّ عَظِيْمٌ ﴿٢٩﴾

30. 'O Joseph, turn away from this and thou, *O woman*, ask forgiveness for thy sin. Certainly, thou art of the guilty.'

يُوْسُفُ اَعْرِضْ عَنْ هٰذَا وَاسْتَغْفِرِيْ لِذَنْۢبِكِ اِنَّكِ كُنْتِ مِنَ الْخٰطِـِٕيْنَ ﴿٣٠﴾ ع ٣ ١٣

R. 4.

31. And women in the city said, 'The wife of the 'Azīz seeks to seduce her slave-boy against his will. He has infatuated her with love. Indeed, we see her in manifest error.'

وَقَالَ نِسْوَةٌ فِي الْمَدِيْنَةِ امْرَاَتُ الْعَزِيْزِ تُرَاوِدُ فَتٰىهَا عَنْ نَّفْسِهٖ قَدْ شَغَفَهَا حُبًّا اِنَّا لَنَرٰىهَا فِيْ ضَلٰلٍ مُّبِيْنٍ ﴿٣١﴾

32. And when she heard of their *crafty* design, she sent for them and prepared for them a repast, and gave every one of them a knife and *then* said *to Joseph*, 'Come forth to them.' And when they saw him they thought much of him and cut their hands, and said, 'Allah be glorified! This is not a human being; this is but a noble angel.'

فَلَمَّا سَمِعَتْ بِمَكْرِهِنَّ اَرْسَلَتْ اِلَيْهِنَّ وَاَعْتَدَتْ لَهُنَّ مُتَّكَاً وَّاٰتَتْ كُلَّ وَاحِدَةٍ مِّنْهُنَّ سِكِّيْنًا وَّقَالَتِ اخْرُجْ عَلَيْهِنَّ فَلَمَّا رَاَيْنَهٗ اَكْبَرْنَهٗ وَقَطَّعْنَ اَيْدِيَهُنَّ وَقُلْنَ حَاشَ لِلّٰهِ مَا هٰذَا بَشَرًا اِنْ هٰذَا اِلَّا مَلَكٌ كَرِيْمٌ ﴿٣٢﴾

33. She said, 'And this is he about whom you blamed me. I did seek to seduce him against his will, but he preserved himself *from sin*. And now if he do not what I bid him, he shall certainly be imprisoned and become *one* of the humbled.'

قَالَتْ فَذٰلِكُنَّ الَّذِيْ لُمْتُنَّنِيْ فِيْهِ وَلَقَدْ رَاوَدْتُّهٗ عَنْ نَّفْسِهٖ فَاسْتَعْصَمَ وَلَئِنْ لَّمْ يَفْعَلْ مَا اٰمُرُهٗ لَيُسْجَنَنَّ وَلَيَكُوْنًا مِّنَ الصّٰغِرِيْنَ ﴿٣٣﴾

34. He said, 'O my Lord, I would prefer prison to that to which they invite me; and unless Thou turn away their guile from me I shall incline towards them and be of the ignorant.'

قَالَ رَبِّ السِّجْنُ اَحَبُّ اِلَيَّ مِمَّا يَدْعُوْنَنِيْ اِلَيْهِ وَاِلَّا تَصْرِفْ عَنِّيْ كَيْدَهُنَّ اَصْبُ اِلَيْهِنَّ وَاَكُنْ مِّنَ الْجٰهِلِيْنَ ﴿٣٤﴾

35. So his Lord heard his prayer, and turned away their guile from him. Verily, He is the All-Hearing, the All-Knowing.

فَاسْتَجَابَ لَهٗ رَبُّهٗ فَصَرَفَ عَنْهُ كَيْدَهُنَّ اِنَّهٗ هُوَ السَّمِيْعُ الْعَلِيْمُ ﴿٣٥﴾

36. Then it occurred to them (the men) after they had seen the signs *of his innocence* that, *to preserve their good name*, they should imprison him for a time.

ثُمَّ بَدَا لَهُمْ مِّنْ بَعْدِ مَا رَاَوُا الْاٰيٰتِ لَيَسْجُنُنَّهٗ
حَتّٰى حِيْنٍ ﴿۳۶﴾ ع

R. 5.

37. And with him there entered the prison two young men. One of them said, 'I saw myself *in a dream* pressing wine.' And the other said, 'I saw myself *in a dream* carrying upon my head bread of which the birds are eating. Inform us of the interpretation thereof; for we see thee to be of the righteous.'

وَدَخَلَ مَعَهُ السِّجْنَ فَتَيٰنِ ؕ قَالَ اَحَدُهُمَآ اِنِّيْٓ
اَرٰىنِيْٓ اَعْصِرُ خَمْرًا ۚ وَقَالَ الْاٰخَرُ اِنِّيْٓ اَرٰىنِيْٓ اَحْمِلُ
فَوْقَ رَاْسِيْ خُبْزًا تَاْكُلُ الطَّيْرُ مِنْهُ ؕ نَبِّئْنَا بِتَاْوِيْلِهٖ ۚ
اِنَّا نَرٰىكَ مِنَ الْمُحْسِنِيْنَ ﴿۳۷﴾

38. He replied, 'The food which you are given shall not come to you but I shall inform you of the interpretation thereof before it comes to you. This is on account of what my Lord has taught me. I have renounced the religion of the people who do not believe in Allah and who are disbelievers in the Hereafter.

قَالَ لَا يَاْتِيْكُمَا طَعَامٌ تُرْزَقٰنِهٖٓ اِلَّا نَبَّاْتُكُمَا بِتَاْوِيْلِهٖ
قَبْلَ اَنْ يَّاْتِيَكُمَا ؕ ذٰلِكُمَا مِمَّا عَلَّمَنِيْ رَبِّيْ ؕ اِنِّيْ تَرَكْتُ
مِلَّةَ قَوْمٍ لَّا يُؤْمِنُوْنَ بِاللّٰهِ وَهُمْ بِالْاٰخِرَةِ هُمْ
كٰفِرُوْنَ ﴿۳۸﴾

39. 'And I have followed the religion of my fathers, Abraham and Isaac and Jacob. We cannot indeed associate anything as partner with Allah. This is of Allah's grace upon us and upon mankind, but most men are ungrateful.

وَاتَّبَعْتُ مِلَّةَ اٰبَآءِيْٓ اِبْرٰهِيْمَ وَاِسْحٰقَ وَيَعْقُوْبَ ؕ
مَا كَانَ لَنَآ اَنْ نُّشْرِكَ بِاللّٰهِ مِنْ شَيْءٍ ؕ ذٰلِكَ مِنْ
فَضْلِ اللّٰهِ عَلَيْنَا وَعَلَى النَّاسِ وَلٰكِنَّ اَكْثَرَ النَّاسِ
لَا يَشْكُرُوْنَ ﴿۳۹﴾

40. 'O my two companions of the prison, are diverse lords better or Allah, the One, the Most Supreme?

يٰصَاحِبَيِ السِّجْنِ ءَاَرْبَابٌ مُّتَفَرِّقُوْنَ خَيْرٌ اَمِ
اللّٰهُ الْوَاحِدُ الْقَهَّارُ ﴿۴۰﴾

* 41. 'You worship nothing beside Allah, but *mere* names that you have named, you and your fathers; Allah has sent down no authority for that. The decision rests with Allah alone. He has commanded that you shall not worship anything save Him. That is the right religion, but most men know *it* not.

مَا تَعْبُدُوْنَ مِنْ دُوْنِهٖٓ اِلَّآ اَسْمَآءً سَمَّيْتُمُوْهَآ
اَنْتُمْ وَاٰبَآؤُكُمْ مَّآ اَنْزَلَ اللّٰهُ بِهَا مِنْ سُلْطٰنٍ ؕ اِنِ
الْحُكْمُ اِلَّا لِلّٰهِ ؕ اَمَرَ اَلَّا تَعْبُدُوْٓا اِلَّآ اِيَّاهُ ؕ ذٰلِكَ
الدِّيْنُ الْقَيِّمُ وَلٰكِنَّ اَكْثَرَ النَّاسِ لَا يَعْلَمُوْنَ ﴿۴۱﴾

42. 'O my two companions of the prison, as for one of you, he will pour out wine for his lord to drink; and as for the other, he will be crucified so that the birds will

يٰصَاحِبَيِ السِّجْنِ اَمَّآ اَحَدُكُمَا فَيَسْقِيْ رَبَّهٗ خَمْرًا ۚ
وَاَمَّا الْاٰخَرُ فَيُصْلَبُ فَتَاْكُلُ الطَّيْرُ مِنْ رَّاْسِهٖ ؕ

eat from off his head. The matter about which you inquired has been decreed.'

قُضِيَ الْاَمْرُ الَّذِيْ فِيْهِ تَسْتَفْتِيٰنِ ﴿٤٢﴾

43. And of the two, he said to him whom he thought to be the one who would escape: 'Mention me to thy lord.' But Satan caused him to forget mentioning *it* to his lord, so he remained in prison for some years.

وَقَالَ لِلَّذِيْ ظَنَّ اَنَّهٗ نَاجٍ مِّنْهُمَا اذْكُرْنِيْ عِنْدَ
رَبِّكَ ۫ فَاَنْسٰىهُ الشَّيْطٰنُ ذِكْرَ رَبِّهٖ فَلَبِثَ فِي السِّجْنِ
بِضْعَ سِنِيْنَ ﴿٤٣﴾ ع

R. 6.

* 44. And the King said, 'I see *in a dream* seven fat kine which seven lean ones eat up, and seven green ears of corn and *seven* others withered. O ye chiefs, explain to me the meaning of my dream if you can interpret a dream.'

وَقَالَ الْمَلِكُ اِنِّيْۤ اَرٰى سَبْعَ بَقَرٰتٍ سِمَانٍ يَّاْكُلُهُنَّ
سَبْعٌ عِجَافٌ وَّسَبْعَ سُنْۢبُلٰتٍ خُضْرٍ وَّاُخَرَ يٰبِسٰتٍ ؕ يٰۤاَيُّهَا
الْمَلَاُ اَفْتُوْنِيْ فِيْ رُءْيَايَ اِنْ كُنْتُمْ لِلرُّءْيَا تَعْبُرُوْنَ ﴿٤٤﴾

45. They replied, 'They are confused dreams, and we do not know the interpretation of such confused dreams.'

قَالُوْۤا اَضْغَاثُ اَحْلَامٍ ۚ وَمَا نَحْنُ بِتَاْوِيْلِ الْاَحْلَامِ
بِعٰلِمِيْنَ ﴿٤٥﴾

46. And he of the two who had escaped, and who *now* remembered after a time, said, 'I will let you know its interpretation, therefore send ye me.'

وَقَالَ الَّذِيْ نَجَا مِنْهُمَا وَادَّكَرَ بَعْدَ اُمَّةٍ اَنَا اُنَبِّئُكُمْ
بِتَاْوِيْلِهٖ فَاَرْسِلُوْنِ ﴿٤٦﴾

47. 'Joseph! O thou man of truth, explain to us the meaning of seven fat kine which seven lean ones devour, and of seven green ears of corn and *seven* others withered; that I may return to the people so that they may know.'

يُوْسُفُ اَيُّهَا الصِّدِّيْقُ اَفْتِنَا فِيْ سَبْعِ بَقَرٰتٍ سِمَانٍ
يَّاْكُلُهُنَّ سَبْعٌ عِجَافٌ وَّسَبْعِ سُنْۢبُلٰتٍ خُضْرٍ وَّاُخَرَ
يٰبِسٰتٍ ۙ لَّعَلِّيْۤ اَرْجِعُ اِلَى النَّاسِ لَعَلَّهُمْ يَعْلَمُوْنَ ﴿٤٧﴾

48. He replied, 'You shall sow for seven years, working hard and continuously, and leave what you reap in its ear, except a little which you shall eat.

قَالَ تَزْرَعُوْنَ سَبْعَ سِنِيْنَ دَاَبًا ۚ فَمَا حَصَدْتُّمْ فَذَرُوْهُ
فِيْ سُنْۢبُلِهٖۤ اِلَّا قَلِيْلًا مِّمَّا تَاْكُلُوْنَ ﴿٤٨﴾

49. 'Then there shall come after that seven hard years which shall consume all that you shall have laid by in advance for them except a little which you may preserve.

ثُمَّ يَاْتِيْ مِنْۢ بَعْدِ ذٰلِكَ سَبْعٌ شِدَادٌ يَّاْكُلْنَ مَا
قَدَّمْتُمْ لَهُنَّ اِلَّا قَلِيْلًا مِّمَّا تُحْصِنُوْنَ ﴿٤٩﴾

* 50. 'Then there shall come after that a year in which people shall be relieved and in which they shall give presents *to each other*.'

ثُمَّ يَاْتِيْ مِنْۢ بَعْدِ ذٰلِكَ عَامٌ فِيْهِ يُغَاثُ النَّاسُ
وَفِيْهِ يَعْصِرُوْنَ ﴿٥٠﴾ ع

R. 7.

* 51. And the King said, 'Bring him to me.' But when the messenger came to him, he said, 'Go back to thy lord and ask him how fare the women who cut

وَقَالَ الْمَلِكُ ائْتُوْنِيْ بِهٖ ۚ فَلَمَّا جَآءَهُ الرَّسُوْلُ قَالَ
ارْجِعْ اِلٰى رَبِّكَ فَسْـَٔلْهُ مَا بَالُ النِّسْوَةِ الّٰتِيْ قَطَّعْنَ

their hands: for, my Lord well knows their crafty design.'

* 52. He (the King) said *to the women*, 'What was the matter with you when you sought to seduce Joseph against his will?' They said, 'He kept away *from sin* for fear of Allah—we have known no evil against him.' The wife of the 'Azīz said, 'Now has the truth come to light. It was I who sought to seduce him against his will, and surely, he is the truthful.'

* 53. *Joseph said, 'I asked for that enquiry to be made* so that he (the 'Azīz) might know that I was not unfaithful to him in *his* absence and that Allah suffers not the device of the unfaithful to succeed.

* 54. 'And I do not hold my own self to be free from weakness; for, the soul is surely prone to enjoin evil, save that whereon my Lord has mercy. Surely, my Lord is Most Forgiving, Merciful.'

55. And the King said, 'Bring him to me that I may take him specially for myself.' And when he had spoken to him, he said, 'Thou art this day *a man* of established position *and* trust with us.'

56. He said, 'Appoint me over the treasures of the land, for I am a good keeper, *and* possessed of knowledge.'

57. And thus did We establish Joseph in the land. He dwelt therein wherever he pleased. We bestow Our mercy on whomsoever We please, and We suffer not the reward of the righteous to perish.

58. And surely, the reward of the Hereafter is better for those who believe and fear God.

R. 8.

* 59. And Joseph's brethren came and entered in unto him; and he knew them, but they knew him not.

* 60. And when he had provided them with their provision, he said, 'Bring me your brother on your father's side. Do you not see that I give you full measure *of corn* and that I am the best of hosts?

61. 'But if you bring him not to me, then there shall be no measure *of corn* for you from me, nor shall you come near me.'

أَيۡدِيَهُنَّ ؕ اِنَّ رَبِّيۡ بِكَيۡدِهِنَّ عَلِيۡمٌ ﴿۵۱﴾
قَالَ مَا خَطۡبُكُنَّ اِذۡ رَاوَدۡتُّنَّ يُوۡسُفَ عَنۡ نَّفۡسِهٖ ؕ
قُلۡنَ حَاشَ لِلّٰهِ مَا عَلِمۡنَا عَلَيۡهِ مِنۡ سُوۡٓءٍ ؕ قَالَتِ امۡرَاَتُ
الۡعَزِيۡزِ الۡـٰٔنَ حَصۡحَصَ الۡحَقُّ اَنَا رَاوَدۡتُّهٗ عَنۡ نَّفۡسِهٖ
وَاِنَّهٗ لَمِنَ الصّٰدِقِيۡنَ ﴿۵۲﴾
ذٰلِكَ لِيَعۡلَمَ اَنِّيۡ لَمۡ اَخُنۡهُ بِالۡغَيۡبِ وَاَنَّ اللّٰهَ لَا يَهۡدِيۡ
كَيۡدَ الۡخَآئِنِيۡنَ ﴿۵۳﴾
وَمَاۤ اُبَرِّئُ نَفۡسِيۡ ۚ اِنَّ النَّفۡسَ لَاَمَّارَةٌۢ بِالسُّوۡٓءِ
اِلَّا مَا رَحِمَ رَبِّيۡ ؕ اِنَّ رَبِّيۡ غَفُوۡرٌ رَّحِيۡمٌ ﴿۵۴﴾
وَقَالَ الۡمَلِكُ ائۡتُوۡنِيۡ بِهٖۤ اَسۡتَخۡلِصۡهُ لِنَفۡسِيۡ ۚ فَلَمَّا
كَلَّمَهٗ قَالَ اِنَّكَ الۡيَوۡمَ لَدَيۡنَا مَكِيۡنٌ اَمِيۡنٌ ﴿۵۵﴾
قَالَ اجۡعَلۡنِيۡ عَلٰى خَزَآئِنِ الۡاَرۡضِ ۚ اِنِّيۡ حَفِيۡظٌ عَلِيۡمٌ ﴿۵۶﴾
وَكَذٰلِكَ مَكَّنَّا لِيُوۡسُفَ فِي الۡاَرۡضِ ۚ يَتَبَوَّاُ مِنۡهَا حَيۡثُ
يَشَآءُ ؕ نُصِيۡبُ بِرَحۡمَتِنَا مَنۡ نَّشَآءُ وَلَا نُضِيۡعُ اَجۡرَ الۡمُحۡسِنِيۡنَ ﴿۵۷﴾
وَلَاَجۡرُ الۡاٰخِرَةِ خَيۡرٌ لِّلَّذِيۡنَ اٰمَنُوۡا وَكَانُوۡا يَتَّقُوۡنَ ﴿۵۸﴾
وَجَآءَ اِخۡوَةُ يُوۡسُفَ فَدَخَلُوۡا عَلَيۡهِ فَعَرَفَهُمۡ وَهُمۡ
لَهٗ مُنۡكِرُوۡنَ ﴿۵۹﴾
وَلَمَّا جَهَّزَهُمۡ بِجَهَازِهِمۡ قَالَ ائۡتُوۡنِيۡ بِاَخٍ لَّكُمۡ
مِّنۡ اَبِيۡكُمۡ ۚ اَلَا تَرَوۡنَ اَنِّيۡۤ اُوۡفِي الۡكَيۡلَ وَاَنَا خَيۡرُ
الۡمُنۡزِلِيۡنَ ﴿۶۰﴾
فَاِنۡ لَّمۡ تَاۡتُوۡنِيۡ بِهٖ فَلَا كَيۡلَ لَكُمۡ عِنۡدِيۡ وَلَا
تَقۡرَبُوۡنِ ﴿۶۱﴾

62. They replied, 'We will try to induce his father to part with him and we will certainly do *it*.'

قالوا سنراود عنه اباه وانا لفعلون ﴿٦٢﴾

63. And he said to his servants, 'Put their money *also* into their saddlebags that they may recognize it when they return to their family; haply they may come back.'

وقال لفتينه اجعلوا بضاعتهم في رحالهم لعلهم يعرفونها اذا انقلبوا الى اهلهم لعلهم يرجعون ﴿٦٣﴾

64. And when they returned to their father, they said, 'O our father, *a further* measure *of corn* has been denied us, so send with us our brother that we may obtain our measure, and we will surely take care of him.'

فلما رجعوا الى ابيهم قالوا يابانا منع منا الكيل فارسل معنا اخانا نكتل وانا له لحفظون ﴿٦٤﴾

65. He said, 'I cannot trust you with him, save as I trusted you with his brother before. But Allah is the best Protector, and He is the Most Merciful of those who show mercy.'

قال هل امنكم عليه الا كما امنتكم على اخيه من قبل فالله خير حفظا وهو ارحم الرحمين ﴿٦٥﴾

66. And when they opened their goods, they found their money returned to them. They said, 'O our father, what more can we desire? Here is our money returned to us. We shall bring provision for our family, and guard our brother and we shall have in addition the measure of a camel-*load*. That is a measure which is easy *to obtain*.'

ولما فتحوا متاعهم وجدوا بضاعتهم ردت اليهم قالوا يابانا ما نبغي هذه بضاعتنا ردت الينا ونمير اهلنا ونحفظ اخانا ونزداد كيل بعير ذلك كيل يسير ﴿٦٦﴾

67. He said, 'I will not send him with you until you give me a solemn promise in the name of Allah that you will surely bring him to me, unless you are encompassed.' And when they gave him their solemn promise, he said, 'Allah watches over what we say.'

قال لن ارسله معكم حتى تؤتون موثقا من الله لتاتنني به الا ان يحاط بكم فلما اتوه موثقهم قال الله على ما نقول وكيل ﴿٦٧﴾

68. And he said, 'O my sons, enter not by one gate, but enter by different gates; and I can avail you nothing against Allah. The decision rests only with Allah. In Him do I put my trust and in Him let all who would trust put their trust.'

وقال يبني لا تدخلوا من باب واحد وادخلوا من ابواب متفرقة وما اغني عنكم من الله من شيء ان الحكم الا لله عليه توكلت وعليه فليتوكل المتوكلون ﴿٦٨﴾

* 69. And when they entered in the manner their father had commanded them, it could not avail them anything against Allah, except that there was a desire in Jacob's mind which he *thus* satisfied; and he was surely possessed of

ولما دخلوا من حيث امرهم ابوهم ما كان يغني عنهم من الله من شيء الا حاجة في نفس يعقوب قضها وانه لذو علم لما علمنه ولكن اكثر

great knowledge because We had taught him, but most men know not.

R. 9.

70. And when they visited Joseph, he lodged his brother with himself. *And* he said, 'I am thy brother; so *now* grieve not at what they have been doing.'

71. And when he had provided them with their provision, he put the drinking-cup in his brother's saddlebag. Then a crier cried, 'O ye *men of the* caravan, you have been guilty of theft.'

72. They said, turning towards them, 'What is it that you miss?'

73. They replied, 'We miss the King's measuring-cup, and whoso brings it shall have a camel-load, and I am surety for it.'

74. They answered, 'By Allah, you know well that we came not to act corruptly in the land, and we are not thieves.'

75. They said, 'What then shall be the punishment for it, if you *are found to* have told a lie?'

76. They replied, 'The punishment for it—he in whose saddlebag it is found shall himself be the penalty for it. Thus do we punish the wrongdoers.'

77. Then he began *the search* with their sacks before the sack of his brother; then he took it out from his brother's sack. Thus did We plan for Joseph. He could not have taken his brother under the King's law unless Allah had *so* willed. We raise in degrees *of rank* whomsoever We please; and over every possessor of knowledge is One, Most-Knowing.

78. They said, 'If he has stolen, a brother of his had *also* committed theft before.' But Joseph kept it secret in his heart and did not disclose it to them. He *simply* said, 'You seem to be in the worst condition; and Allah knows best what you allege.'

79. They said, 'O exalted one, he has a very aged father, so take one of us in his

ع النَّاسِ لَا يَعْلَمُونَ ﴿٦٩﴾
وَلَمَّا دَخَلُوا عَلَىٰ يُوسُفَ آوَىٰ إِلَيْهِ أَخَاهُ قَالَ إِنِّي
أَنَا أَخُوكَ فَلَا تَبْتَئِسْ بِمَا كَانُوا يَعْمَلُونَ ﴿٧٠﴾
فَلَمَّا جَهَّزَهُمْ بِجَهَازِهِمْ جَعَلَ السِّقَايَةَ فِي رَحْلِ
أَخِيهِ ثُمَّ أَذَّنَ مُؤَذِّنٌ أَيَّتُهَا الْعِيرُ إِنَّكُمْ لَسَارِقُونَ ﴿٧١﴾
قَالُوا وَأَقْبَلُوا عَلَيْهِمْ مَاذَا تَفْقِدُونَ ﴿٧٢﴾
قَالُوا نَفْقِدُ صُوَاعَ الْمَلِكِ وَلِمَنْ جَاءَ بِهِ حِمْلُ
بَعِيرٍ وَأَنَا بِهِ زَعِيمٌ ﴿٧٣﴾
قَالُوا تَاللَّهِ لَقَدْ عَلِمْتُمْ مَا جِئْنَا لِنُفْسِدَ فِي الْأَرْضِ
وَمَا كُنَّا سَارِقِينَ ﴿٧٤﴾
قَالُوا فَمَا جَزَاؤُهُ إِنْ كُنْتُمْ كَاذِبِينَ ﴿٧٥﴾
قَالُوا جَزَاؤُهُ مَنْ وُجِدَ فِي رَحْلِهِ فَهُوَ جَزَاؤُهُ كَذَٰلِكَ
نَجْزِي الظَّالِمِينَ ﴿٧٦﴾
فَبَدَأَ بِأَوْعِيَتِهِمْ قَبْلَ وِعَاءِ أَخِيهِ ثُمَّ اسْتَخْرَجَهَا
مِنْ وِعَاءِ أَخِيهِ كَذَٰلِكَ كِدْنَا لِيُوسُفَ مَا كَانَ
لِيَأْخُذَ أَخَاهُ فِي دِينِ الْمَلِكِ إِلَّا أَنْ يَشَاءَ اللَّهُ
نَرْفَعُ دَرَجَاتٍ مَنْ نَشَاءُ وَفَوْقَ كُلِّ ذِي عِلْمٍ
عَلِيمٌ ﴿٧٧﴾
قَالُوا إِنْ يَسْرِقْ فَقَدْ سَرَقَ أَخٌ لَهُ مِنْ قَبْلُ
فَأَسَرَّهَا يُوسُفُ فِي نَفْسِهِ وَلَمْ يُبْدِهَا لَهُمْ قَالَ
أَنْتُمْ شَرٌّ مَكَانًا وَاللَّهُ أَعْلَمُ بِمَا تَصِفُونَ ﴿٧٨﴾
قَالُوا يَا أَيُّهَا الْعَزِيزُ إِنَّ لَهُ أَبًا شَيْخًا كَبِيرًا فَخُذْ

stead; for we see thee to be of those who do good.'

أَحَدَنَا مَكَانَهٗ ۚ إِنَّا نَرٰىكَ مِنَ الْمُحْسِنِيْنَ ﴿٧٩﴾

80. He replied, 'Allah forbid that we should take *any* save him with whom we found our property; for then we should certainly be unjust.'

قَالَ مَعَاذَ اللّٰهِ أَنْ نَّأْخُذَ إِلَّا مَنْ وَّجَدْنَا مَتَاعَنَا
عِنْدَهٗٓ ۙ إِنَّآ إِذًا لَّظٰلِمُوْنَ ﴿٨٠﴾ ع

R. 10.

* 81. And when they despaired of him, they retired, conferring together in private. Their leader said, "Know ye not that your father has taken from you a solemn promise in the name of Allah and how, before this, you failed in your duty with respect to Joseph? I will, therefore, not leave the land until my father permits me or Allah decides for me. And He is the Best of judges.

فَلَمَّا اسْتَيْـَٔسُوْا مِنْهُ خَلَصُوْا نَجِيًّا ۗ قَالَ كَبِيْرُهُمْ أَلَمْ
تَعْلَمُوْٓا أَنَّ أَبَاكُمْ قَدْ أَخَذَ عَلَيْكُمْ مَّوْثِقًا مِّنَ اللّٰهِ
وَمِنْ قَبْلُ مَا فَرَّطْتُّمْ فِيْ يُوْسُفَ ۚ فَلَنْ أَبْرَحَ الْأَرْضَ
حَتّٰى يَأْذَنَ لِيْٓ أَبِيْٓ أَوْ يَحْكُمَ اللّٰهُ لِيْ ۚ وَهُوَ خَيْرُ الْحٰكِمِيْنَ ﴿٨١﴾

82. "Return ye to your father and say, 'O our father, thy son has stolen and we have stated only what we know and we could not be guardians over the unseen.

إِرْجِعُوْٓا إِلٰٓى أَبِيْكُمْ فَقُوْلُوْا يٰٓأَبَانَآ إِنَّ ابْنَكَ سَرَقَ ۚ
وَمَا شَهِدْنَآ إِلَّا بِمَا عَلِمْنَا وَمَا كُنَّا لِلْغَيْبِ
حٰفِظِيْنَ ﴿٨٢﴾

83. 'And inquire of *the people of* the city wherein we were, and of the caravan with which we came, and certainly we are speaking the truth.' "

وَسْـَٔلِ الْقَرْيَةَ الَّتِيْ كُنَّا فِيْهَا وَالْعِيْرَ الَّتِيْٓ أَقْبَلْنَا
فِيْهَا ۗ وَإِنَّا لَصٰدِقُوْنَ ﴿٨٣﴾

* 84. He replied, 'Nay, but your souls have embellished to you this thing. So *now* comely patience *is good for me*. Maybe Allah will bring them all to me; for He is the All-Knowing, the Wise.'

قَالَ بَلْ سَوَّلَتْ لَكُمْ أَنْفُسُكُمْ أَمْرًا ۗ
فَصَبْرٌ جَمِيْلٌ ۗ عَسَى اللّٰهُ أَنْ يَّأْتِيَنِيْ بِهِمْ جَمِيْعًا ۗ
إِنَّهٗ هُوَ الْعَلِيْمُ الْحَكِيْمُ ﴿٨٤﴾

* 85. And he turned away from them and said, 'O my grief for Joseph!' And his eyes became white because of grief, and he was suppressing *his sorrow*.

وَتَوَلّٰى عَنْهُمْ وَقَالَ يٰٓأَسَفٰى عَلٰى يُوْسُفَ وَابْيَضَّتْ
عَيْنٰهُ مِنَ الْحُزْنِ فَهُوَ كَظِيْمٌ ﴿٨٥﴾

* 86. They said, 'By Allah, thou wilt not cease talking of Joseph until thou art wasted away or thou art of those who perish.'

قَالُوْا تَاللّٰهِ تَفْتَؤُا تَذْكُرُ يُوْسُفَ حَتّٰى تَكُوْنَ حَرَضًا
أَوْ تَكُوْنَ مِنَ الْهٰلِكِيْنَ ﴿٨٦﴾

87. He replied, 'I only complain of my sorrow and my grief to Allah, and I know from Allah that which you know not.

قَالَ إِنَّمَآ أَشْكُوْا بَثِّيْ وَحُزْنِيْٓ إِلَى اللّٰهِ وَأَعْلَمُ مِنَ
اللّٰهِ مَا لَا تَعْلَمُوْنَ ﴿٨٧﴾

88. 'O my sons, go ye and search for Joseph and his brother and despair not

يٰبَنِيَّ اذْهَبُوْا فَتَحَسَّسُوْا مِنْ يُّوْسُفَ وَأَخِيْهِ وَلَا

of the mercy of Allah; for none despairs of Allah's mercy save the unbelieving people.'

تَايْـَٔسُوْا مِنْ رَّوْحِ اللّٰهِ ۭ اِنَّهٗ لَا يَايْـَٔسُ مِنْ رَّوْحِ
اللّٰهِ اِلَّا الْقَوْمُ الْكٰفِرُوْنَ ﴿۸۸﴾

89. And, when they came before him (Joseph), they said, 'O exalted one, poverty has smitten us and our family, and we have brought a paltry sum of money, so give us the full measure, and be charitable to us. Surely, Allah rewards the charitable.'

فَلَمَّا دَخَلُوْا عَلَيْهِ قَالُوْا يٰۤاَيُّهَا الْعَزِيْزُ مَسَّنَا وَاَهْلَنَا
الضُّرُّ وَجِئْنَا بِبِضَاعَةٍ مُّزْجٰىةٍ فَاَوْفِ لَنَا الْكَيْلَ
وَتَصَدَّقْ عَلَيْنَا ۭ اِنَّ اللّٰهَ يَجْزِي الْمُتَصَدِّقِيْنَ ﴿۸۹﴾

90. He said, 'Do you know what you did to Joseph and his brother, when you were ignorant?'

قَالَ هَلْ عَلِمْتُمْ مَّا فَعَلْتُمْ بِيُوْسُفَ وَاَخِيْهِ اِذْ
اَنْتُمْ جٰهِلُوْنَ ﴿۹۰﴾

* 91. They replied, 'Art thou Joseph?' He said, '*Yes*, I am Joseph and this is my brother. Allah has indeed been gracious to us. Verily, whoso is righteous and is steadfast—Allah will never suffer the reward of the good to be lost.'

قَالُوْۤا ءَاِنَّكَ لَاَنْتَ يُوْسُفُ ۭ قَالَ اَنَا يُوْسُفُ وَهٰذَاۤ
اَخِيْ ۡ قَدْ مَنَّ اللّٰهُ عَلَيْنَا ۭ اِنَّهٗ مَنْ يَّتَّقِ وَيَصْبِرْ
فَاِنَّ اللّٰهَ لَا يُضِيْعُ اَجْرَ الْمُحْسِنِيْنَ ﴿۹۱﴾

92. They replied, 'By Allah! Surely has Allah preferred thee above us and we have indeed been sinners.'

قَالُوْا تَاللّٰهِ لَقَدْ اٰثَرَكَ اللّٰهُ عَلَيْنَا وَاِنْ كُنَّا
لَخٰطِـِٕيْنَ ﴿۹۲﴾

93. He said, 'No blame *shall lie* on you this day; may Allah forgive you! And He is the Most Merciful of those who show mercy.

قَالَ لَا تَثْرِيْبَ عَلَيْكُمُ الْيَوْمَ ۭ يَغْفِرُ اللّٰهُ لَكُمْ ۡ وَهُوَ
اَرْحَمُ الرّٰحِمِيْنَ ﴿۹۳﴾

94. 'Go with this shirt of mine and lay it before my father: he will come to know. And bring to me the whole of your family.'

اِذْهَبُوْا بِقَمِيْصِيْ هٰذَا فَاَلْقُوْهُ عَلٰى وَجْهِ اَبِيْ يَاْتِ
بَصِيْرًا ۚ وَاْتُوْنِيْ بِاَهْلِكُمْ اَجْمَعِيْنَ ﴿۹۴﴾

R. 11.

95. And when the caravan departed, their father said, 'Surely, I feel the scent of Joseph, even though you take me to be a dotard.'

وَلَمَّا فَصَلَتِ الْعِيْرُ قَالَ اَبُوْهُمْ اِنِّيْ لَاَجِدُ رِيْحَ
يُوْسُفَ لَوْلَاۤ اَنْ تُفَنِّدُوْنِ ﴿۹۵﴾

96. They replied, 'By Allah, thou art assuredly in thy old error.'

قَالُوْا تَاللّٰهِ اِنَّكَ لَفِيْ ضَلٰلِكَ الْقَدِيْمِ ﴿۹۶﴾

97. And when the bearer of glad tidings came, he laid it before him and he became enlightened. *Then* he said, 'Did I not say to you: I know from Allah what you know not?'

فَلَمَّاۤ اَنْ جَآءَ الْبَشِيْرُ اَلْقٰىهُ عَلٰى وَجْهِهٖ فَارْتَدَّ
بَصِيْرًا ۚ قَالَ اَلَمْ اَقُلْ لَّكُمْ ۚ اِنِّيْۤ اَعْلَمُ مِنَ اللّٰهِ مَا
لَا تَعْلَمُوْنَ ﴿۹۷﴾

98. They said, 'O our father, ask forgiveness of our sins for us; we have indeed been sinners.'

قَالُوْا يٰٓاَبَانَا اسْتَغْفِرْ لَنَا ذُنُوْبَنَآ اِنَّا كُنَّا
خٰطِـِٕيْنَ ﴿٩٨﴾

99. He said, 'I will certainly ask forgiveness for you of my Lord. Surely, He is the Most Forgiving, the Merciful.'

قَالَ سَوْفَ اَسْتَغْفِرُ لَكُمْ رَبِّيْ ؕ اِنَّهٗ هُوَ الْغَفُوْرُ
الرَّحِيْمُ ﴿٩٩﴾

100. And when they came to Joseph, he put up his parents with himself, and said, 'Enter Egypt in peace, if it please Allah.'

فَلَمَّا دَخَلُوْا عَلٰى يُوْسُفَ اٰوٰٓى اِلَيْهِ اَبَوَيْهِ وَقَالَ
ادْخُلُوْا مِصْرَ اِنْ شَآءَ اللّٰهُ اٰمِنِيْنَ ﴿١٠٠﴾ؕ

101. And he raised his parents upon the throne, and they *all* fell down prostrate *before God* for him. And he said, 'O my father, this is the fulfilment of my dream of old. My Lord has made it true. And He bestowed a favour upon me when He took me out of the prison and brought you from the desert after Satan had stirred up discord between me and my brethren. Surely, my Lord is Benignant to whomsoever He pleases; for He is the All-Knowing, the Wise.

وَرَفَعَ اَبَوَيْهِ عَلَى الْعَرْشِ وَخَرُّوْا لَهٗ سُجَّدًا ۚ وَ
قَالَ يٰٓاَبَتِ هٰذَا تَاْوِيْلُ رُءْيَايَ مِنْ قَبْلُ ۫ قَدْ
جَعَلَهَا رَبِّيْ حَقًّا ؕ وَقَدْ اَحْسَنَ بِيْٓ اِذْ اَخْرَجَنِيْ مِنَ
السِّجْنِ وَجَآءَ بِكُمْ مِّنَ الْبَدْوِ مِنْۢ بَعْدِ اَنْ نَّزَغَ
الشَّيْطٰنُ بَيْنِيْ وَبَيْنَ اِخْوَتِيْ ؕ اِنَّ رَبِّيْ لَطِيْفٌ لِّمَا
يَشَآءُ ؕ اِنَّهٗ هُوَ الْعَلِيْمُ الْحَكِيْمُ ﴿١٠١﴾

* 102. 'O my Lord, Thou hast bestowed power upon me and taught me the interpretation of dreams. O Maker of the heavens and the earth, Thou art my Protector in this world and the Hereafter. Let death come to me in a state of submission *to Thy will* and join me to the righteous.'

رَبِّ قَدْ اٰتَيْتَنِيْ مِنَ الْمُلْكِ وَعَلَّمْتَنِيْ مِنْ تَاْوِيْلِ
الْاَحَادِيْثِ ۚ فَاطِرَ السَّمٰوٰتِ وَالْاَرْضِ ۟ اَنْتَ وَلِيّٖ فِي
الدُّنْيَا وَالْاٰخِرَةِ ۚ تَوَفَّنِيْ مُسْلِمًا وَّاَلْحِقْنِيْ بِالصّٰلِحِيْنَ ﴿١٠٢﴾

103. That is of the tidings of the unseen, *which* We reveal to thee. And thou wast not with them when they agreed upon their plan while they were plotting.

ذٰلِكَ مِنْ اَنْۢبَآءِ الْغَيْبِ نُوْحِيْهِ اِلَيْكَ ۚ وَمَا كُنْتَ
لَدَيْهِمْ اِذْ اَجْمَعُوْٓا اَمْرَهُمْ وَهُمْ يَمْكُرُوْنَ ﴿١٠٣﴾

104. And most men will not believe even though thou eagerly desire *it*.

وَمَآ اَكْثَرُ النَّاسِ وَلَوْ حَرَصْتَ بِمُؤْمِنِيْنَ ﴿١٠٤﴾

* 105. And thou dost not ask of them any reward for it. *On the contrary*, it is but *a source of* honour for all mankind.

وَمَا تَسْـَٔلُهُمْ عَلَيْهِ مِنْ اَجْرٍ ؕ اِنْ هُوَ اِلَّا ذِكْرٌ لِّلْعٰلَمِيْنَ ﴿١٠٥﴾ ع

R. 12.

106. And how many a Sign is there in the heavens and the earth, which they pass by, turning away from it.

وَكَاَيِّنْ مِّنْ اٰيَةٍ فِي السَّمٰوٰتِ وَالْاَرْضِ يَمُرُّوْنَ عَلَيْهَا
وَهُمْ عَنْهَا مُعْرِضُوْنَ ﴿١٠٦﴾

107. And most of them believe not in Allah without *also* attributing partners *to Him*.

وَمَا يُؤْمِنُ اَكْثَرُهُمْ بِاللّٰهِ اِلَّا وَهُمْ مُّشْرِكُوْنَ ﴿١٠٧﴾

108. Do they, then, feel secure from the coming on them of an overwhelming punishment from Allah or the sudden coming of the Hour upon them while they are unaware?

اَفَاَمِنُوْٓا اَنْ تَاْتِيَهُمْ غَاشِيَةٌ مِّنْ عَذَابِ اللّٰهِ اَوْ
تَاْتِيَهُمُ السَّاعَةُ بَغْتَةً وَّهُمْ لَا يَشْعُرُوْنَ ﴿١٠٨﴾

* 109. Say, 'This is my way: I call unto Allah on sure knowledge, I and those who follow me. And Holy is Allah; and I am not of those who associate gods *with God.*'

قُلْ هٰذِهٖ سَبِيْلِيْٓ اَدْعُوْٓا اِلَى اللّٰهِ ۛ عَلٰى بَصِيْرَةٍ اَنَا وَمَنِ النبی صلی اللہ علیہ وسلم
اتَّبَعَنِيْ ۭ وَسُبْحٰنَ اللّٰهِ وَمَآ اَنَا مِنَ الْمُشْرِكِيْنَ ﴿١٠٩﴾

110. And We sent not before thee *as Messengers* any but men, whom We inspired, from among the people of the towns. Have they not then travelled in the earth and seen what was the end of those before them? And surely, the abode of the Hereafter is better for those who fear God. Will you not then understand?

وَمَآ اَرْسَلْنَا مِنْ قَبْلِكَ اِلَّا رِجَالًا نُّوْحِيْٓ اِلَيْهِمْ مِّنْ
اَهْلِ الْقُرٰى ۭ اَفَلَمْ يَسِيْرُوْا فِي الْاَرْضِ فَيَنْظُرُوْا كَيْفَ
كَانَ عَاقِبَةُ الَّذِيْنَ مِنْ قَبْلِهِمْ ۭ وَلَدَارُ الْاٰخِرَةِ خَيْرٌ
لِّلَّذِيْنَ اتَّقَوْا ۭ اَفَلَا تَعْقِلُوْنَ ﴿١١٠﴾

* 111. Till, when the Messengers despaired *of the disbelievers* and they (the disbelievers) thought that they had been told a lie, Our help came to them, then was saved he whom We pleased. And Our chastisement cannot be averted from the sinful people.

حَتّٰٓى اِذَا اسْتَيْــَٔسَ الرُّسُلُ وَظَنُّوْٓا اَنَّهُمْ قَدْ كُذِبُوْا
جَاۗءَهُمْ نَصْرُنَا ۙ فَنُجِّيَ مَنْ نَّشَاۗءُ ۭ وَلَا يُرَدُّ بَاْسُنَا
عَنِ الْقَوْمِ الْمُجْرِمِيْنَ ﴿١١١﴾

112. Assuredly, in their narrative is a lesson for men of understanding. It is not a thing that has been forged, but a fulfilment of that which is before it and a detailed exposition of all things, and a guidance and a mercy to a people who believe.

لَقَدْ كَانَ فِيْ قَصَصِهِمْ عِبْرَةٌ لِّاُولِي الْاَلْبَابِ ۭ مَا
كَانَ حَدِيْثًا يُّفْتَرٰى وَلٰكِنْ تَصْدِيْقَ الَّذِيْ بَيْنَ
يَدَيْهِ وَتَفْصِيْلَ كُلِّ شَيْءٍ وَّهُدًى وَّرَحْمَةً
لِّقَوْمٍ يُّؤْمِنُوْنَ ﴿١١٢﴾ ع ١٢

سُوْرَةُ الرَّعْدِ مَكِّيَّةٌ

(١٣) ايَاتُهَا رُكُوعَاتُهَا

AL-RA'D

(Revealed before Hijra)

1. In the name of Allah, the Gracious, the Merciful.

2. Alif Lām Mīm Rā*. These are verses of the Book. And that which has been revealed to thee from thy Lord is the truth, but most men believe not.

3. Allah is He Who raised up the heavens without any pillars that you can see. Then He settled Himself on the Throne. And He pressed the sun and the moon into service: each pursues its course until an appointed term. He regulates it all. He clearly explains the Signs, that you may have a firm belief in the meeting with your Lord.

* 4. And He it is Who spread out the earth and made therein mountains and rivers. And fruits of every kind He made therein in two sexes. He causes the night to cover the day. Therein, verily, are Signs for a people who reflect.

* 5. And in the earth are *diverse* tracts, adjoining one another, and gardens of vines, and corn-fields, and date-palms, growing together from one root and *others* not so growing; they are watered with the same water, yet We make some of them excel others in fruit. Therein are Signs for a people who understand.

6. And if thou dost wonder, then wondrous indeed is their saying: 'What! when we have become dust, shall we then be in *a state of* new creation?' These it is who disbelieve in their Lord; and these it is who shall have shackles round their necks, and they shall be the inmates of the Fire, wherein they shall abide.

* 7. And they want thee to hasten on the punishment in preference to good, whereas

---

* I am Allah, the All-Knowing, the All-Seeing.

بِسْمِ اللّٰهِ الرَّحْمٰنِ الرَّحِيْمِ ①

الٓمّٓرٰ تِلْكَ اٰيٰتُ الْكِتٰبِ ؕ وَالَّذِيْٓ اُنْزِلَ اِلَيْكَ مِنْ
رَّبِّكَ الْحَقُّ وَلٰكِنَّ اَكْثَرَ النَّاسِ لَا يُؤْمِنُوْنَ ②

اَللّٰهُ الَّذِيْ رَفَعَ السَّمٰوٰتِ بِغَيْرِ عَمَدٍ تَرَوْنَهَا ثُمَّ اسْتَوٰى
عَلَى الْعَرْشِ وَسَخَّرَ الشَّمْسَ وَالْقَمَرَ ؕ كُلٌّ يَّجْرِيْ لِاَجَلٍ
مُّسَمًّى ؕ يُدَبِّرُ الْاَمْرَ يُفَصِّلُ الْاٰيٰتِ لَعَلَّكُمْ بِلِقَآءِ
رَبِّكُمْ تُوْقِنُوْنَ ③

وَهُوَ الَّذِيْ مَدَّ الْاَرْضَ وَجَعَلَ فِيْهَا رَوَاسِيَ وَ
اَنْهٰرًا ؕ وَمِنْ كُلِّ الثَّمَرٰتِ جَعَلَ فِيْهَا زَوْجَيْنِ اثْنَيْنِ
يُغْشِي الَّيْلَ النَّهَارَ ؕ اِنَّ فِيْ ذٰلِكَ لَاٰيٰتٍ لِّقَوْمٍ يَّتَفَكَّرُوْنَ ④

وَفِي الْاَرْضِ قِطَعٌ مُّتَجٰوِرٰتٌ وَّجَنّٰتٌ مِّنْ اَعْنَابٍ وَّ
زَرْعٌ وَّنَخِيْلٌ صِنْوَانٌ وَّغَيْرُ صِنْوَانٍ يُّسْقٰى بِمَآءٍ
وَّاحِدٍ ۟ وَنُفَضِّلُ بَعْضَهَا عَلٰى بَعْضٍ فِي الْاُكُلِ ؕ اِنَّ
فِيْ ذٰلِكَ لَاٰيٰتٍ لِّقَوْمٍ يَّعْقِلُوْنَ ⑤

وَاِنْ تَعْجَبْ فَعَجَبٌ قَوْلُهُمْ ءَاِذَا كُنَّا تُرٰبًا ءَاِنَّا لَفِيْ
خَلْقٍ جَدِيْدٍ ؕ اُولٰٓئِكَ الَّذِيْنَ كَفَرُوْا بِرَبِّهِمْ ۚ وَاُولٰٓئِكَ
الْاَغْلٰلُ فِيْٓ اَعْنَاقِهِمْ ۚ وَاُولٰٓئِكَ اَصْحٰبُ النَّارِ ۚ هُمْ فِيْهَا
خٰلِدُوْنَ ⑥

وَيَسْتَعْجِلُوْنَكَ بِالسَّيِّئَةِ قَبْلَ الْحَسَنَةِ وَقَدْ خَلَتْ

exemplary punishments have *already* occurred before them. And verily, thy Lord is full of forgiveness for mankind despite their wrongdoing, and verily, thy Lord is *also* strict in condign punishment.

8. And those who disbelieve say, 'Wherefore has not a Sign been sent down to him from his Lord?' Thou art, surely, a Warner. And there is a Guide for every people.

R. 2.

9. Allah knows what every female bears, and what wombs diminish and what they cause to grow. And with Him everything has a *proper* measure.

10. *He is the* Knower of the unseen and the seen, the Incomparably Great, the Most High.

11. He among you who conceals *his* word, and he who utters it openly are equal *in His sight;* and *also* he who hides by night, and he who goes forth *openly* by day.

12. For him (the Messenger) is a succession *of angels* before him and behind him; they guard him by the command of Allah. Surely, Allah changes not the condition of a people until they change that which is in their hearts. And when Allah wishes to punish a people, there is no repelling it, nor have they any helper beside Him.

13. He it is Who shows you the lightning *to inspire* fear and hope, and He raises the heavy clouds.

14. And the thunder glorifies Him with His praise and *likewise do* the angels for awe of Him; and He sends the thunderbolts, and smites therewith whom He wills, yet they dispute concerning Allah, le He is severe in punishing.

* 15. Unto Him is the true prayer. And those on whom they call beside Him answer them not at all, except as he *is answered* who stretches forth his two hands toward water that it may reach his mouth, but it reaches it not. And the prayer of the disbelievers is but a thing wasted.

مِنْ قَبْلِهِمُ الْمَثُلٰتُ ۭ وَاِنَّ رَبَّكَ لَذُوْ مَغْفِرَةٍ لِّلنَّاسِ
عَلٰى ظُلْمِهِمْ ۚ وَاِنَّ رَبَّكَ لَشَدِيْدُ الْعِقَابِ ﴿۷﴾
وَيَقُوْلُ الَّذِيْنَ كَفَرُوْا لَوْلَآ اُنْزِلَ عَلَيْهِ اٰيَةٌ مِّنْ
رَّبِّهٖ ۭ اِنَّمَآ اَنْتَ مُنْذِرٌ وَّلِكُلِّ قَوْمٍ هَادٍ ﴿۸﴾ ع
اَللّٰهُ يَعْلَمُ مَا تَحْمِلُ كُلُّ اُنْثٰى وَمَا تَغِيْضُ الْاَرْحَامُ
وَمَا تَزْدَادُ ۭ وَكُلُّ شَيْءٍ عِنْدَهٗ بِمِقْدَارٍ ﴿۹﴾
عٰلِمُ الْغَيْبِ وَالشَّهَادَةِ الْكَبِيْرُ الْمُتَعَالِ ﴿۱۰﴾
سَوَآءٌ مِّنْكُمْ مَّنْ اَسَرَّ الْقَوْلَ وَمَنْ جَهَرَ بِهٖ وَمَنْ هُوَ
مُسْتَخْفٍ بِالَّيْلِ وَسَارِبٌ بِالنَّهَارِ ﴿۱۱﴾
لَهٗ مُعَقِّبٰتٌ مِّنْ بَيْنِ يَدَيْهِ وَمِنْ خَلْفِهٖ يَحْفَظُوْنَهٗ
مِنْ اَمْرِ اللّٰهِ ۭ اِنَّ اللّٰهَ لَا يُغَيِّرُ مَا بِقَوْمٍ حَتّٰى يُغَيِّرُوْا
مَا بِاَنْفُسِهِمْ ۭ وَاِذَآ اَرَادَ اللّٰهُ بِقَوْمٍ سُوْٓءًا فَلَا مَرَدَّ لَهٗ ۚ
وَمَا لَهُمْ مِّنْ دُوْنِهٖ مِنْ وَّالٍ ﴿۱۲﴾
هُوَ الَّذِيْ يُرِيْكُمُ الْبَرْقَ خَوْفًا وَّطَمَعًا وَّيُنْشِئُ السَّحَابَ
الثِّقَالَ ﴿۱۳﴾ ۚ
وَيُسَبِّحُ الرَّعْدُ بِحَمْدِهٖ وَالْمَلٰٓئِكَةُ مِنْ خِيْفَتِهٖ ۚ وَ
يُرْسِلُ الصَّوَاعِقَ فَيُصِيْبُ بِهَا مَنْ يَّشَآءُ وَهُمْ
يُجَادِلُوْنَ فِي اللّٰهِ ۚ وَهُوَ شَدِيْدُ الْمِحَالِ ﴿۱۴﴾
لَهٗ دَعْوَةُ الْحَقِّ ۭ وَالَّذِيْنَ يَدْعُوْنَ مِنْ دُوْنِهٖ لَا
يَسْتَجِيْبُوْنَ لَهُمْ بِشَيْءٍ اِلَّا كَبَاسِطِ كَفَّيْهِ اِلَى الْمَآءِ
لِيَبْلُغَ فَاهُ وَمَا هُوَ بِبَالِغِهٖ ۭ وَمَا دُعَآءُ الْكٰفِرِيْنَ
اِلَّا فِيْ ضَلٰلٍ ﴿۱۵﴾

16. And to Allah submits whosoever is in the heavens and the earth willingly or unwillingly and *likewise do* their shadows, in the mornings and the evenings.

وَ لِلّٰهِ يَسْجُدُ مَنْ فِي السَّمٰوٰتِ وَالْاَرْضِ طَوْعًا وَّ
السجدة
كَرْهًا وَّظِلٰلُهُمْ بِالْغُدُوِّ وَالْاٰصَالِ ﴿١٦﴾

17. Say, 'Who is the Lord of the heavens and the earth?' Say, 'Allah.' Say, 'Have you then taken beside Him helpers who have no power for good or harm *even* for themselves?' Say, 'Can the blind and the seeing be equal? Or, can darkness be equal to light? Or, do they assign to Allah partners who have created the like of His creation so that the *two* creations appear similar to them?' Say, 'Allah *alone* is the Creator of all things, and He is the One, the Most Supreme.'

قُلْ مَنْ رَّبُّ السَّمٰوٰتِ وَالْاَرْضِ قُلِ اللّٰهُ قُلْ
اَفَاتَّخَذْتُمْ مِّنْ دُوْنِهٖۤ اَوْلِيَآءَ لَا يَمْلِكُوْنَ لِاَنْفُسِهِمْ
نَفْعًا وَّلَا ضَرًّا قُلْ هَلْ يَسْتَوِي الْاَعْمٰى وَالْبَصِيْرُ
اَمْ هَلْ تَسْتَوِي الظُّلُمٰتُ وَالنُّوْرُ اَمْ جَعَلُوْا لِلّٰهِ
شُرَكَآءَ خَلَقُوْا كَخَلْقِهٖ فَتَشَابَهَ الْخَلْقُ عَلَيْهِمْ
قُلِ اللّٰهُ خَالِقُ كُلِّ شَيْءٍ وَّهُوَ الْوَاحِدُ الْقَهَّارُ ﴿١٧﴾

18. He sends down water from the sky, so that valleys flow according to their measure, and the flood bears *on its surface* swelling foam. And from that which they heat in the fire, seeking *to make* ornaments or utensils, *comes out* a foam similar to it. Thus does Allah illustrate truth and falsehood. Now, as to the foam, it goes away as rubbish, but as to that which benefits men, it stays on the earth. Thus does Allah set forth parables.

اَنْزَلَ مِنَ السَّمَآءِ مَآءً فَسَالَتْ اَوْدِيَةٌۢ بِقَدَرِهَا
فَاحْتَمَلَ السَّيْلُ زَبَدًا رَّابِيًا وَمِمَّا يُوْقِدُوْنَ
عَلَيْهِ فِي النَّارِ ابْتِغَآءَ حِلْيَةٍ اَوْ مَتَاعٍ زَبَدٌ مِّثْلُهٗ
كَذٰلِكَ يَضْرِبُ اللّٰهُ الْحَقَّ وَالْبَاطِلَ فَاَمَّا الزَّبَدُ
فَيَذْهَبُ جُفَآءً وَاَمَّا مَا يَنْفَعُ النَّاسَ فَيَمْكُثُ
فِي الْاَرْضِ كَذٰلِكَ يَضْرِبُ اللّٰهُ الْاَمْثَالَ ﴿١٨﴾

19. For those who respond to their Lord is *eternal* good; and *as for* those who respond not to Him, if they had all that is in the earth and the like of it added thereto, they would *readily* ransom themselves therewith. It is these that shall have an evil reckoning, and their abode is Hell. What a wretched place of rest!

وقف النبي صلى الله عليه وسلم
لِلَّذِيْنَ اسْتَجَابُوْا لِرَبِّهِمُ الْحُسْنٰى وَالَّذِيْنَ لَمْ يَسْتَجِيْبُوْا
لَهٗ لَوْ اَنَّ لَهُمْ مَّا فِي الْاَرْضِ جَمِيْعًا وَّمِثْلَهٗ مَعَهٗ
لَافْتَدَوْا بِهٖ اُولٰٓئِكَ لَهُمْ سُوْٓءُ الْحِسَابِ وَمَاْوٰىهُمْ
النصف
ع
جَهَنَّمُ وَبِئْسَ الْمِهَادُ ﴿١٩﴾

R. 3.

20. Is he, then, who knows that what has been revealed to thee from thy Lord is the truth, like one who is blind? *But* only those gifted with understanding will reflect:

اَفَمَنْ يَّعْلَمُ اَنَّمَآ اُنْزِلَ اِلَيْكَ مِنْ رَّبِّكَ الْحَقُّ كَمَنْ
هُوَ اَعْمٰى اِنَّمَا يَتَذَكَّرُ اُولُوا الْاَلْبَابِ ﴿٢٠﴾

21. Those who fulfil Allah's pact, and break not the covenant;

الَّذِيْنَ يُوْفُوْنَ بِعَهْدِ اللّٰهِ وَلَا يَنْقُضُوْنَ الْمِيْثَاقَ ﴿٢١﴾

22. And those who join what Allah has

وَالَّذِيْنَ يَصِلُوْنَ مَآ اَمَرَ اللّٰهُ بِهٖۤ اَنْ يُّوْصَلَ وَ

commanded to be joined, and fear their Lord, and dread the evil reckoning;

يَخْشَوْنَ رَبَّهُمْ وَيَخَافُوْنَ سُوْٓءَ الْحِسَابِ ﴿٢٢﴾

23. And those who persevere in seeking the favour of their Lord, and observe Prayer, and spend out of that with which We have provided them, secretly and openly, and repel evil with good. It is these who shall have the *best* reward of the *final* Abode—

وَالَّذِيْنَ صَبَرُوا ابْتِغَآءَ وَجْهِ رَبِّهِمْ وَأَقَامُوا
الصَّلٰوةَ وَأَنْفَقُوْا مِمَّا رَزَقْنٰهُمْ سِرًّا وَّعَلَانِيَةً وَّ
يَدْرَءُوْنَ بِالْحَسَنَةِ السَّيِّئَةَ أُولٰٓئِكَ لَهُمْ عُقْبَى
الدَّارِ ﴿٢٣﴾

24. Gardens of Eternity. They shall enter them and *also* those who are righteous from among their fathers, and their wives and their children. And angels shall enter unto them from every gate, *saying:*

جَنّٰتُ عَدْنٍ يَّدْخُلُوْنَهَا وَمَنْ صَلَحَ مِنْ اٰبَآئِهِمْ
وَأَزْوَاجِهِمْ وَذُرِّيّٰتِهِمْ وَالْمَلٰٓئِكَةُ يَدْخُلُوْنَ عَلَيْهِمْ
مِّنْ كُلِّ بَابٍ ﴿٢٤﴾

25. 'Peace be unto you, because you were steadfast; behold how excellent is the reward of the *final* Abode!'

سَلٰمٌ عَلَيْكُمْ بِمَا صَبَرْتُمْ فَنِعْمَ عُقْبَى الدَّارِ ﴿٢٥﴾

26. And those who break the covenant of Allah, after having established it and cut asunder what Allah has commanded to be joined, and act corruptly in the earth – on them is the curse and they shall have a grievous abode.

وَالَّذِيْنَ يَنْقُضُوْنَ عَهْدَ اللّٰهِ مِنْ بَعْدِ مِيْثَاقِهٖ
وَيَقْطَعُوْنَ مَآ أَمَرَ اللّٰهُ بِهٖٓ أَنْ يُّوْصَلَ وَيُفْسِدُوْنَ
فِي الْأَرْضِ أُولٰٓئِكَ لَهُمُ اللَّعْنَةُ وَلَهُمْ سُوْٓءُ الدَّارِ ﴿٢٦﴾

27. Allah enlarges *His* provision for whomsoever He pleases and straitens *it for whomsoever He pleases*. And they rejoice in the present life, while the present life is but a *temporary* enjoyment as compared with that which is to come.

اَللّٰهُ يَبْسُطُ الرِّزْقَ لِمَنْ يَّشَآءُ وَيَقْدِرُ وَفَرِحُوْا
بِالْحَيٰوةِ الدُّنْيَا وَمَا الْحَيٰوةُ الدُّنْيَا فِي الْاٰخِرَةِ إِلَّا
مَتَاعٌ ﴿٢٧﴾

R. 4.

28. And those who disbelieve say, 'Why is not a Sign sent down to him from his Lord?' Say, 'Allah lets go astray those whom He wills and guides to Himself those who turn *to Him:*

وَيَقُوْلُ الَّذِيْنَ كَفَرُوْا لَوْلَآ أُنْزِلَ عَلَيْهِ اٰيَةٌ مِّنْ
رَّبِّهٖ قُلْ إِنَّ اللّٰهَ يُضِلُّ مَنْ يَّشَآءُ وَيَهْدِيْٓ إِلَيْهِ
مَنْ أَنَابَ ﴿٢٨﴾

29. 'Those who believe, and whose hearts find comfort in the remembrance of Allah. Aye! it is in the remembrance of Allah that hearts can find comfort;

اَلَّذِيْنَ اٰمَنُوْا وَتَطْمَئِنُّ قُلُوْبُهُمْ بِذِكْرِ اللّٰهِ أَلَا
بِذِكْرِ اللّٰهِ تَطْمَئِنُّ الْقُلُوْبُ ﴿٢٩﴾

30. 'Those who believe and do good works—happiness shall be theirs, and an excellent place of return.'

اَلَّذِيْنَ اٰمَنُوْا وَعَمِلُوا الصّٰلِحٰتِ طُوْبٰى لَهُمْ
وَحُسْنُ مَاٰبٍ ﴿٣٠﴾

31. Thus have We sent thee to a people, before whom other peoples have passed away, that thou mayest recite to them what We have revealed to thee, yet they disbelieve in the Gracious *God*. Say, 'He is my Lord; there is no God but He. In Him do I put my trust and towards Him is my return.'

كَذٰلِكَ اَرْسَلْنٰكَ فِيْۤ اُمَّةٍ قَدْ خَلَتْ مِنْ قَبْلِهَاۤ اُمَمٌ
لِّتَتْلُوَاۡ عَلَيْهِمُ الَّذِيْۤ اَوْحَيْنَاۤ اِلَيْكَ وَهُمْ يَكْفُرُوْنَ
بِالرَّحْمٰنِؕ قُلْ هُوَ رَبِّيْ لَاۤ اِلٰهَ اِلَّا هُوَۚ عَلَيْهِ تَوَكَّلْتُ
وَاِلَيْهِ مَتَابِ ﴿٣١﴾

32. And if there were a Qur'ān by which mountains could be moved or by which the earth could be cut asunder or by which the dead could be spoken to, *they would not believe in it*. Nay, the matter rests entirely with Allah. Have not the believers *yet* come to know that, if Allah had *enforced* His will, He could have surely guided all mankind? And as for those who disbelieve, disaster shall not cease to befall them for what they have wrought or to alight near their home, until the promise of Allah comes to pass. Surely, Allah fails not in *His* promise.

وَلَوْ اَنَّ قُرْاٰنًا سُيِّرَتْ بِهِ الْجِبَالُ اَوْ قُطِّعَتْ بِهِ
الْاَرْضُ اَوْ كُلِّمَ بِهِ الْمَوْتٰىؕ بَلْ لِّلّٰهِ الْاَمْرُ جَمِيْعًاؕ
اَفَلَمْ يَايْـَٔسِ الَّذِيْنَ اٰمَنُوْۤا اَنْ لَّوْ يَشَآءُ اللّٰهُ لَهَدَى
النَّاسَ جَمِيْعًاؕ وَلَا يَزَالُ الَّذِيْنَ كَفَرُوْا تُصِيْبُهُمْ بِمَا
صَنَعُوْا قَارِعَةٌ اَوْ تَحُلُّ قَرِيْبًا مِّنْ دَارِهِمْ حَتّٰى
يَاْتِيَ وَعْدُ اللّٰهِؕ اِنَّ اللّٰهَ لَا يُخْلِفُ الْمِيْعَادَ ﴿٣٢﴾ ع ۴ ۱۰

R. 5.

33. And surely, Messengers have been mocked at before thee; but I granted respite to those who disbelieved. Then I seized them, and how was then My punishment!

وَلَقَدِ اسْتُهْزِئَ بِرُسُلٍ مِّنْ قَبْلِكَ فَاَمْلَيْتُ لِلَّذِيْنَ
كَفَرُوْا ثُمَّ اَخَذْتُهُمْ فَكَيْفَ كَانَ عِقَابِ ﴿٣٣﴾

34. Will then He, Who stands over every soul *to note* what it earns, *let them go unpunished?* Yet, they ascribe partners to Allah. Say, 'Name them.' Would you inform Him of what He does not know in the earth? Or, is it *a mere* empty saying? Nay, but the design of the disbelievers has been made *to appear* beautiful in their eyes, and they have been kept back from the *right* way. And he whom Allah lets go astray shall have no guide.

اَفَمَنْ هُوَ قَآئِمٌ عَلٰى كُلِّ نَفْسٍۢ بِمَا كَسَبَتْۚ وَجَعَلُوْا لِلّٰهِ
شُرَكَآءَؕ قُلْ سَمُّوْهُمْؕ اَمْ تُنَبِّـُٔوْنَهٗ بِمَا لَا يَعْلَمُ فِي
الْاَرْضِ اَمْ بِظَاهِرٍ مِّنَ الْقَوْلِؕ بَلْ زُيِّنَ لِلَّذِيْنَ كَفَرُوْا
مَكْرُهُمْ وَصُدُّوْا عَنِ السَّبِيْلِؕ وَمَنْ يُّضْلِلِ اللّٰهُ فَمَا
لَهٗ مِنْ هَادٍ ﴿٣٤﴾

35. For them is a punishment in the present life; and, surely, the punishment of the Hereafter is harder, and they will have no defender against Allah.

لَهُمْ عَذَابٌ فِي الْحَيٰوةِ الدُّنْيَا وَلَعَذَابُ الْاٰخِرَةِ
اَشَقُّۚ وَمَا لَهُمْ مِّنَ اللّٰهِ مِنْ وَّاقٍ ﴿٣٥﴾

36. The similitude of the Heaven promised to the God-fearing is, that through it flow streams: its fruit is everlasting, and *so is* its shade. That is the reward of those who are righteous; and the reward of the disbelievers is Fire.

مَثَلُ الْجَنَّةِ الَّتِيْ وُعِدَ الْمُتَّقُوْنَؕ تَجْرِيْ مِنْ تَحْتِهَا
الْاَنْهٰرُؕ اُكُلُهَا دَآئِمٌ وَّظِلُّهَاؕ تِلْكَ عُقْبَى الَّذِيْنَ اتَّقَوْا
وَّعُقْبَى الْكٰفِرِيْنَ النَّارُ ﴿٣٦﴾

37. And those to whom We have given the Book rejoice in what has been revealed to thee. And of the *different* parties there are *some* who deny a part thereof. Say, 'I am only commanded to worship Allah and not to set up equals to Him. Unto Him do I call, and unto Him is my return.'

وَالَّذِينَ آتَيْنٰهُمُ الْكِتٰبَ يَفْرَحُونَ بِمَا أُنْزِلَ إِلَيْكَ
وَمِنَ الْأَحْزَابِ مَنْ يُنْكِرُ بَعْضَهُ ۚ قُلْ إِنَّمَا أُمِرْتُ
أَنْ أَعْبُدَ اللّٰهَ وَلَا أُشْرِكَ بِهِ ۚ إِلَيْهِ أَدْعُوا وَإِلَيْهِ
مَآبِ ﴿٣٧﴾

38. And thus have We revealed it as a clear judgment. And if thou follow their evil desires after the knowledge that has come to thee, thou shalt have no friend nor defender against Allah.

وَكَذٰلِكَ أَنْزَلْنٰهُ حُكْمًا عَرَبِيًّا ۚ وَلَئِنِ اتَّبَعْتَ أَهْوَاءَهُمْ
بَعْدَ مَا جَاءَكَ مِنَ الْعِلْمِ ۙ مَا لَكَ مِنَ اللّٰهِ مِنْ وَلِيٍّ
وَلَا وَاقٍ ﴿٣٨﴾ ع ٥ ١١

R. 6.

39. And, indeed, We sent Messengers before thee, and We gave them wives and children. And it is not possible for a Messenger to bring a Sign save by the command of Allah. For every term there is a *divine* decree.

وَلَقَدْ أَرْسَلْنَا رُسُلًا مِنْ قَبْلِكَ وَجَعَلْنَا لَهُمْ أَزْوَاجًا
وَذُرِّيَّةً ۚ وَمَا كَانَ لِرَسُولٍ أَنْ يَأْتِيَ بِآيَةٍ إِلَّا
بِإِذْنِ اللّٰهِ ۗ لِكُلِّ أَجَلٍ كِتَابٌ ﴿٣٩﴾

* 40. Allah effaces what He wills and establishes *what He wills*, and with Him is the source of *all* commandments.

يَمْحُوا اللّٰهُ مَا يَشَاءُ وَيُثْبِتُ ۖ وَعِنْدَهُ أُمُّ الْكِتٰبِ ﴿٤٠﴾

41. And whether We make thee see *the fulfilment of* some of the things with which We threaten them or *whether* We make thee die, *it makes little difference*, for on thee lies only the delivery of the Message, and on Us the reckoning.

وَإِنْ مَا نُرِيَنَّكَ بَعْضَ الَّذِي نَعِدُهُمْ أَوْ نَتَوَفَّيَنَّكَ
فَإِنَّمَا عَلَيْكَ الْبَلٰغُ وَعَلَيْنَا الْحِسَابُ ﴿٤١﴾

42. Do they not see that We are visiting the land, reducing it from its outlying borders? And Allah judges; there is none to reverse His judgment. And He is swift at reckoning.

أَوَلَمْ يَرَوْا أَنَّا نَأْتِي الْأَرْضَ نَنْقُصُهَا مِنْ أَطْرَافِهَا ۚ
وَاللّٰهُ يَحْكُمُ لَا مُعَقِّبَ لِحُكْمِهِ ۚ وَهُوَ سَرِيعُ الْحِسَابِ ﴿٤٢﴾

43. And those who were before them did *also* devise plans, but all *effective* devising of plans belongs to Allah. He knows what every soul earns; and the disbelievers shall soon know whose will be the final reward of *this* abode.

وَقَدْ مَكَرَ الَّذِينَ مِنْ قَبْلِهِمْ فَلِلّٰهِ الْمَكْرُ جَمِيعًا ۖ
يَعْلَمُ مَا تَكْسِبُ كُلُّ نَفْسٍ ۗ وَسَيَعْلَمُ الْكُفّٰرُ لِمَنْ
عُقْبَى الدَّارِ ﴿٤٣﴾

44. And those who disbelieve say, 'Thou art not a Messenger.' Say, 'Sufficient is Allah as a Witness between me and you, and *so is* he who possesses knowledge of the Book.'

وَيَقُولُ الَّذِينَ كَفَرُوا لَسْتَ مُرْسَلًا ۚ قُلْ كَفٰى بِاللّٰهِ
شَهِيدًا بَيْنِي وَبَيْنَكُمْ ۙ وَمَنْ عِنْدَهُ عِلْمُ الْكِتٰبِ ﴿٤٤﴾ ع ٦ ١٢

سُوْرَةُ اِبْرٰهِيْمَ مَكِّيَّةٌ

(١٤) اٰيَاتُهَا — رُكُوْعَاتُهَا

IBRĀHĪM

(Revealed before Hijra)

1. In the name of Allah, the Gracious, the Merciful.

بِسْمِ اللّٰهِ الرَّحْمٰنِ الرَّحِيْمِ ﴿١﴾

2. Alif Lām Rā*. *This is* a Book which We have revealed to thee that thou mayest bring mankind out of every *kind of* darkness into light, by the command of their Lord, to the path of the Mighty, the Praiseworthy—

الٓرٰ كِتٰبٌ اَنْزَلْنٰهُ اِلَيْكَ لِتُخْرِجَ النَّاسَ مِنَ الظُّلُمٰتِ اِلَى النُّوْرِ ۙ بِاِذْنِ رَبِّهِمْ اِلٰى صِرَاطِ الْعَزِيْزِ الْحَمِيْدِ ۙ ﴿٢﴾

3. Allah, to Whom belongs whatsoever is in the heavens and whatsoever is in the earth. And woe to the disbelievers for a terrible punishment:

اللّٰهِ الَّذِيْ لَهٗ مَا فِي السَّمٰوٰتِ وَمَا فِي الْاَرْضِ ؕ وَوَيْلٌ لِّلْكٰفِرِيْنَ مِنْ عَذَابٍ شَدِيْدِ ۙ ﴿٣﴾

4. Those who prefer the present life to the Hereafter, and hinder *men* from the way of Allah and seek to make it crooked. It is these who have gone far off in error.

الَّذِيْنَ يَسْتَحِبُّوْنَ الْحَيٰوةَ الدُّنْيَا عَلَى الْاٰخِرَةِ وَيَصُدُّوْنَ عَنْ سَبِيْلِ اللّٰهِ وَيَبْغُوْنَهَا عِوَجًا ؕ اُولٰٓئِكَ فِيْ ضَلٰلٍۭ بَعِيْدٍ ﴿٤﴾

5. And We have not sent any Messenger except with the language of his people in order that he might make *things* clear to them. Then Allah lets go astray whom He wills, and guides whom He wills. And He is the Mighty, the Wise.

وَمَآ اَرْسَلْنَا مِنْ رَّسُوْلٍ اِلَّا بِلِسَانِ قَوْمِهٖ لِيُبَيِّنَ لَهُمْ ؕ فَيُضِلُّ اللّٰهُ مَنْ يَّشَآءُ وَيَهْدِيْ مَنْ يَّشَآءُ ؕ وَهُوَ الْعَزِيْزُ الْحَكِيْمُ ﴿٥﴾

6. And We did send Moses with Our Signs, *saying*, 'Bring forth thy people from every *kind of* darkness into light, and remind them of the days of Allah.' Surely, therein are Signs for every patient *and* thankful person.

وَلَقَدْ اَرْسَلْنَا مُوْسٰى بِاٰيٰتِنَآ اَنْ اَخْرِجْ قَوْمَكَ مِنَ الظُّلُمٰتِ اِلَى النُّوْرِ ۙ وَذَكِّرْهُمْ بِاَيّٰىمِ اللّٰهِ ؕ اِنَّ فِيْ ذٰلِكَ لَاٰيٰتٍ لِّكُلِّ صَبَّارٍ شَكُوْرٍ ﴿٦﴾

7. And *call to mind* when Moses said to his people, 'Remember Allah's favour upon you when He delivered you from Pharaoh's people who afflicted you with grievous torment, slaying your sons and sparing your women; and in that there was a great trial for you from your Lord.'

وَاِذْ قَالَ مُوْسٰى لِقَوْمِهِ اذْكُرُوْا نِعْمَةَ اللّٰهِ عَلَيْكُمْ اِذْ اَنْجٰىكُمْ مِّنْ اٰلِ فِرْعَوْنَ يَسُوْمُوْنَكُمْ سُوْٓءَ الْعَذَابِ وَيُذَبِّحُوْنَ اَبْنَآءَكُمْ وَيَسْتَحْيُوْنَ نِسَآءَكُمْ ؕ وَفِيْ ذٰلِكُمْ بَلَآءٌ مِّنْ رَّبِّكُمْ عَظِيْمٌ ﴿٧﴾ ع

R. 2.

8. And *remember also the time* when your Lord declared, 'If you are grateful, I will, surely, bestow more *favours* on you;

وَاِذْ تَاَذَّنَ رَبُّكُمْ لَئِنْ شَكَرْتُمْ لَاَزِيْدَنَّكُمْ وَلَئِنْ

* I am Allah, the All-Seeing.

but if you are ungrateful, *then know that* My punishment is severe indeed.'

كفرتم إن عذابي لشديد ⑧

9. And Moses said, 'If you disbelieve, you and those who are in the earth all together, *you can do no harm to God;* verily, Allah is Self-Sufficient, Praiseworthy.'

وقال موسى إن تكفروا أنتم ومن في الأرض جميعا فإن الله لغني حميد ⑨

* 10. Have not the tidings come to you of those before you, the people of Noah, and *the tribes of* 'Ād and Thamūd, and those after them? None knows them *now* save Allah. Their Messengers came to them with clear Signs, but they turned their hands to their mouths, and said, 'We disbelieve in that with which you have been sent and surely, we are in disquieting doubt concerning that to which you call us.'

ألم يأتكم نبؤا الذين من قبلكم قوم نوح وعاد وثمود والذين من بعدهم لا يعلمهم إلا الله جاءتهم رسلهم بالبينت فردوا أيديهم في أفواههم وقالوا إنا كفرنا بما أرسلتم به وإنا لفي شك مما تدعوننا إليه مريب ⑩

11. Their Messengers said, 'Are you in doubt concerning Allah, Maker of the heavens and the earth? He calls you that He may forgive you your sins, and grant you respite till an appointed term.' They said, 'You are but men like ourselves; you desire to turn us away from that which our fathers used to worship. Bring us, then, a clear proof.'

قالت رسلهم أفي الله شك فاطر السموت والأرض يدعوكم ليغفر لكم من ذنوبكم ويؤخركم إلى أجل مسمى قالوا إن أنتم إلا بشر مثلنا تريدون أن تصدونا عما كان يعبد آباؤنا فأتونا بسلطن مبين ⑪

12. Their Messengers said to them, 'We are indeed only men like yourselves, but Allah bestows *His* favour on whomsoever He wills from among His servants. And it is not for us to bring you a proof except by the command of Allah. And in Allah *alone* should the believers put their trust.

قالت لهم رسلهم إن نحن إلا بشر مثلكم ولكن الله يمن على من يشاء من عباده وما كان لنا أن نأتيكم بسلطن إلا بإذن الله وعلى الله فليتوكل المؤمنون ⑫

13. 'And why should we not put our trust in Allah when He has showed us our ways? And we will, surely, bear with patience *all* the harm you do us. So in Allah let those who trust put their trust.'

وما لنا ألا نتوكل على الله وقد هدنا سبلنا ولنصبرن على ما آذيتمونا وعلى الله فليتوكل المتوكلون ⑬

R. 3.

14. And those who disbelieved said to their Messengers, 'We will, surely, expel you from our land unless you return to our religion.' Then their Lord sent unto

وقال الذين كفروا لرسلهم لنخرجنكم من أرضنا أو لتعودن في ملتنا فأوحى إليهم ربهم

them the revelation: 'We will, surely, destroy the wrongdoers.

* 15. 'And We will, surely, make you dwell in the land after them. This is for him who fears to stand before My Tribunal and fears My warning.'

16. And they prayed for victory, and *as a result thereof* every haughty enemy *of truth* came to naught.

17. Before him is Hell; and he shall be made to drink boiling water.

* 18. He shall sip it and shall not be able to swallow it easily. And death shall come to him from every quarter, *yet* he shall not die. And besides that there shall be *for him* a severe chastisement.

* 19. The case of those who disbelieve in their Lord is that their works are like ashes on which the wind blows violently on a stormy day. They shall have no power over what they earned. That, indeed, is extreme ruin.

* 20. Dost thou not see that Allah created the heavens and the earth in accordance with the requirements of wisdom? If He please, He can do away with you, and bring a new creation.

21. And that is not *at all* hard for Allah.

22. They shall all appear before Allah; then shall the weak say to those who behaved proudly: 'Surely, we were your followers; can you not then avail us aught against Allah's punishment?' They will say, 'If Allah had guided us, we would, surely, have guided you. *But* it is *now* equal for us whether we show impatience or remain patient: there is no way of escape for us.'

R. 4.

23. And when the matter is decided, Satan will say, 'Allah promised you a promise of truth, but I promised you and failed you. And I had no power over you except that I called you and you obeyed me. So blame me not, but blame your own selves. I cannot succour you nor can you

لَنُهْلِكَنَّ الظّٰلِمِيْنَ ﴿۱۴﴾
وَلَنُسْكِنَنَّكُمُ الْاَرْضَ مِنْۢ بَعْدِهِمْ ؕ ذٰلِكَ لِمَنْ
خَافَ مَقَامِیْ وَخَافَ وَعِيْدِ ﴿۱۵﴾
وَاسْتَفْتَحُوْا وَخَابَ كُلُّ جَبَّارٍ عَنِيْدٍ ﴿۱۶﴾
مِّنْ وَّرَآئِهٖ جَهَنَّمُ وَيُسْقٰى مِنْ مَّآءٍ صَدِيْدٍ ﴿۱۷﴾
يَّتَجَرَّعُهٗ وَلَا يَكَادُ يُسِيْغُهٗ وَيَاْتِيْهِ الْمَوْتُ مِنْ
كُلِّ مَكَانٍ وَّمَا هُوَ بِمَيِّتٍ ؕ وَمِنْ وَّرَآئِهٖ عَذَابٌ
غَلِيْظٌ ﴿۱۸﴾
مَثَلُ الَّذِيْنَ كَفَرُوْا بِرَبِّهِمْ اَعْمَالُهُمْ كَرَمَادِ
ِاشْتَدَّتْ بِهِ الرِّيْحُ فِيْ يَوْمٍ عَاصِفٍ ؕ لَا يَقْدِرُوْنَ
مِمَّا كَسَبُوْا عَلٰى شَيْءٍ ؕ ذٰلِكَ هُوَ الضَّلٰلُ الْبَعِيْدُ ﴿۱۹﴾
اَلَمْ تَرَ اَنَّ اللّٰهَ خَلَقَ السَّمٰوٰتِ وَالْاَرْضَ بِالْحَقِّ ؕ
اِنْ يَّشَاْ يُذْهِبْكُمْ وَيَاْتِ بِخَلْقٍ جَدِيْدٍ ﴿۲۰﴾
وَّمَا ذٰلِكَ عَلَى اللّٰهِ بِعَزِيْزٍ ﴿۲۱﴾
وَبَرَزُوْا لِلّٰهِ جَمِيْعًا فَقَالَ الضُّعَفٰٓؤُا لِلَّذِيْنَ اسْتَكْبَرُوْٓا
اِنَّا كُنَّا لَكُمْ تَبَعًا فَهَلْ اَنْتُمْ مُّغْنُوْنَ عَنَّا مِنْ
عَذَابِ اللّٰهِ مِنْ شَيْءٍ ؕ قَالُوْا لَوْ هَدٰىنَا اللّٰهُ لَهَدَيْنٰكُمْ ؕ
سَوَآءٌ عَلَيْنَآ اَجَزِعْنَآ اَمْ صَبَرْنَا مَا لَنَا مِنْ مَّحِيْصٍ ﴿۲۲﴾
وَقَالَ الشَّيْطٰنُ لَمَّا قُضِيَ الْاَمْرُ اِنَّ اللّٰهَ وَعَدَكُمْ
وَعْدَ الْحَقِّ وَوَعَدْتُّكُمْ فَاَخْلَفْتُكُمْ ؕ وَمَا كَانَ لِيَ
عَلَيْكُمْ مِّنْ سُلْطٰنٍ اِلَّآ اَنْ دَعَوْتُكُمْ فَاسْتَجَبْتُمْ لِيْ ۚ
فَلَا تَلُوْمُوْنِيْ وَلُوْمُوْٓا اَنْفُسَكُمْ ؕ مَآ اَنَا بِمُصْرِخِكُمْ

succour me. I have already disclaimed your associating me *with God*. For the wrongdoers there shall, surely, be a grievous punishment.'

وَمَآ أَنتُمْ بِمُصْرِخِيَّ ۖ إِنِّي كَفَرْتُ بِمَآ أَشْرَكْتُمُونِ
مِن قَبْلُ ۗ إِنَّ الظّٰلِمِينَ لَهُمْ عَذَابٌ أَلِيمٌ ﴿٢٣﴾

24. And those who believe and do good works will be admitted into Gardens through which rivers flow, wherein they will abide by the command of their Lord. Their greeting therein will be 'Peace.'

وَأُدْخِلَ الَّذِينَ آمَنُوا وَعَمِلُوا الصّٰلِحٰتِ جَنّٰتٍ تَجْرِي
مِن تَحْتِهَا الْأَنْهٰرُ خٰلِدِينَ فِيهَا بِإِذْنِ رَبِّهِمْ ۖ تَحِيَّتُهُمْ
فِيهَا سَلٰمٌ ﴿٢٤﴾

25. Dost thou not see how Allah sets forth the similitude of a good word? *It is* like a good tree, whose root is firm and whose branches *reach* into heaven.

أَلَمْ تَرَ كَيْفَ ضَرَبَ اللّٰهُ مَثَلًا كَلِمَةً طَيِّبَةً كَشَجَرَةٍ
طَيِّبَةٍ أَصْلُهَا ثَابِتٌ وَفَرْعُهَا فِي السَّمَآءِ ﴿٢٥﴾

26. It brings forth its fruit at all times by the command of its Lord. And Allah sets forth similitudes for men that they may reflect.

تُؤْتِيٓ أُكُلَهَا كُلَّ حِينٍ بِإِذْنِ رَبِّهَا ۗ وَيَضْرِبُ اللّٰهُ
الْأَمْثَالَ لِلنَّاسِ لَعَلَّهُمْ يَتَذَكَّرُونَ ﴿٢٦﴾

27. And the case of an evil word is like *that of* an evil tree, which is uprooted from above the earth and has no stability.

وَمَثَلُ كَلِمَةٍ خَبِيثَةٍ كَشَجَرَةٍ خَبِيثَةٍ اجْتُثَّتْ
مِن فَوْقِ الْأَرْضِ مَا لَهَا مِن قَرَارٍ ﴿٢٧﴾

28. Allah strengthens the believers with the word that is firmly established, *both* in the present life and in the Hereafter; and Allah lets the wrongdoers go astray. And Allah does what He wills.

يُثَبِّتُ اللّٰهُ الَّذِينَ آمَنُوا بِالْقَوْلِ الثَّابِتِ فِي الْحَيٰوةِ
الدُّنْيَا وَفِي الْآخِرَةِ ۖ وَيُضِلُّ اللّٰهُ الظّٰلِمِينَ ۚ وَ
ع يَفْعَلُ اللّٰهُ مَا يَشَآءُ ﴿٢٨﴾

R. 5.

29. Dost thou not see those who changed Allah's favour into ingratitude and landed their people into the abode of ruin—

أَلَمْ تَرَ إِلَى الَّذِينَ بَدَّلُوا نِعْمَتَ اللّٰهِ كُفْرًا وَأَحَلُّوا
قَوْمَهُمْ دَارَ الْبَوَارِ ﴿٢٩﴾

30. *Which is* Hell? They shall burn therein; and an evil place of rest is that.

جَهَنَّمَ يَصْلَوْنَهَا ۖ وَبِئْسَ الْقَرَارُ ﴿٣٠﴾

31. And they have set up rivals to Allah to mislead *people* from His way. Say, 'Enjoy yourselves a while, then, surely, your journey is toward the Fire.'

وَجَعَلُوا لِلّٰهِ أَندَادًا لِّيُضِلُّوا عَن سَبِيلِهِ ۗ قُلْ تَمَتَّعُوا
فَإِنَّ مَصِيرَكُمْ إِلَى النَّارِ ﴿٣١﴾

32. Say to My servants who have believed, that they should observe Prayer and spend out of what We have given them, secretly and openly, before there comes a day wherein there will be neither bargaining nor friendship.

قُل لِّعِبَادِيَ الَّذِينَ آمَنُوا يُقِيمُوا الصَّلٰوةَ وَيُنفِقُوا
مِمَّا رَزَقْنٰهُمْ سِرًّا وَعَلَانِيَةً مِّن قَبْلِ أَن يَأْتِيَ
يَوْمٌ لَّا بَيْعٌ فِيهِ وَلَا خِلٰلٌ ﴿٣٢﴾

33. Allah is He Who created the heavens and the earth and caused water to come down from the clouds, and brought forth therewith fruits for your sustenance; and He has subjected to you the ships that they may sail through the sea by His command, and the rivers *too* has He subjected to you.

اللّٰهُ الَّذِي خَلَقَ السَّمٰوٰتِ وَالْأَرْضَ وَأَنْزَلَ مِنَ
السَّمَآءِ مَآءً فَأَخْرَجَ بِهٖ مِنَ الثَّمَرٰتِ رِزْقًا لَّكُمْ
وَسَخَّرَ لَكُمُ الْفُلْكَ لِتَجْرِيَ فِي الْبَحْرِ بِأَمْرِهٖ
وَسَخَّرَ لَكُمُ الْأَنْهٰرَ ﴿٣٣﴾

* 34. And He has *also* subjected to you the sun and the moon, both performing their work constantly. And He has subjected to you the night as well as the day.

وَسَخَّرَ لَكُمُ الشَّمْسَ وَالْقَمَرَ دَآئِبَيْنِ وَسَخَّرَ
لَكُمُ الَّيْلَ وَالنَّهَارَ ﴿٣٤﴾

35. And He gave you all that you wanted of Him; and if you *try to* count the favours of Allah, you will not be able to number them. Verily, man is very unjust, very ungrateful.

وَاٰتٰىكُمْ مِّنْ كُلِّ مَا سَأَلْتُمُوْهُ وَإِنْ تَعُدُّوْا نِعْمَتَ
اللّٰهِ لَا تُحْصُوْهَا إِنَّ الْإِنْسَانَ لَظَلُوْمٌ كَفَّارٌ ﴿٣٥﴾ ع

R. 6.

36. And *remember* when Abraham said, 'My Lord, make this city *a city* of peace, and keep me and my children away from worshipping idols.

وَإِذْ قَالَ إِبْرٰهِيْمُ رَبِّ اجْعَلْ هٰذَا الْبَلَدَ اٰمِنًا
وَّاجْنُبْنِيْ وَبَنِيَّ أَنْ نَّعْبُدَ الْأَصْنَامَ ﴿٣٦﴾

37. 'My Lord, they have indeed led astray many among mankind. So whoever follows me, he is certainly of me; and whoever disobeys me—Thou art, surely, Most Forgiving, Merciful.

رَبِّ إِنَّهُنَّ أَضْلَلْنَ كَثِيْرًا مِّنَ النَّاسِ فَمَنْ تَبِعَنِيْ
فَإِنَّهٗ مِنِّيْ وَمَنْ عَصَانِيْ فَإِنَّكَ غَفُوْرٌ رَّحِيْمٌ ﴿٣٧﴾

38. 'Our Lord, I have settled some of my children in an uncultivable valley near Thy Sacred House—our Lord—that they may observe Prayer. So make men's hearts incline towards them and provide them with fruits, that they may be thankful.

رَبَّنَآ إِنِّيْٓ أَسْكَنْتُ مِنْ ذُرِّيَّتِيْ بِوَادٍ غَيْرِ ذِيْ زَرْعٍ
عِنْدَ بَيْتِكَ الْمُحَرَّمِ رَبَّنَا لِيُقِيْمُوا الصَّلٰوةَ فَاجْعَلْ
أَفْئِدَةً مِّنَ النَّاسِ تَهْوِيْٓ إِلَيْهِمْ وَارْزُقْهُمْ مِّنَ
الثَّمَرٰتِ لَعَلَّهُمْ يَشْكُرُوْنَ ﴿٣٨﴾

39. 'Our Lord, certainly, Thou knowest what we conceal and what we make known. And nothing whatsoever is hidden from Allah, whether in the earth or in the heaven.

رَبَّنَآ إِنَّكَ تَعْلَمُ مَا نُخْفِيْ وَمَا نُعْلِنُ وَمَا يَخْفٰى
عَلَى اللّٰهِ مِنْ شَيْءٍ فِي الْأَرْضِ وَلَا فِي السَّمَآءِ ﴿٣٩﴾

40. 'All praise belongs to Allah Who has given me, despite *my* old age, Ishmael and Isaac. Surely, my Lord is the Hearer of prayer.

اَلْحَمْدُ لِلّٰهِ الَّذِيْ وَهَبَ لِيْ عَلَى الْكِبَرِ إِسْمٰعِيْلَ
وَإِسْحٰقَ إِنَّ رَبِّيْ لَسَمِيْعُ الدُّعَآءِ ﴿٤٠﴾

* 41. 'My Lord, make me observe Prayer, and my children *too*. Our Lord! *bestow Thy grace on me* and accept my prayer.

رَبِّ اجْعَلْنِيْ مُقِيْمَ الصَّلٰوةِ وَمِنْ ذُرِّيَّتِيْ رَبَّنَا
وَتَقَبَّلْ دُعَآءِ ﴿٤١﴾

42. 'Our Lord, grant forgiveness to me and to my parents and to the believers on the day when the reckoning will take place.'

ربنا اغفر لي ولوالدي وللمؤمنين يوم يقوم
الحساب (٤٢)

R. 7.

43. And think not that Allah is unaware of what the wrongdoers do. He only gives them respite till the day on which the eyes will fixedly stare,

ولا تحسبن الله غافلا عما يعمل الظلمون ۚ إنما
يؤخرهم ليوم تشخص فيه الأبصار (٤٣)

44. Hurrying on in fright, raising up their heads, their gaze not returning to them, and their minds *utterly* void.

مهطعين مقنعي رءوسهم لا يرتد إليهم طرفهم ۚ
وأفئدتهم هواء (٤٤)

45. And warn men of the day when *the promised* chastisement will come upon them, and the wrongdoers will say, 'Our Lord, grant us respite for a short term. We will respond to Thy call and will follow the Messengers.' 'Did you not swear before this *that* you would have no fall?

وأنذر الناس يوم يأتيهم العذاب فيقول
الذين ظلموا ربنا أخرنا إلى أجل قريب نجب
دعوتك ونتبع الرسل ۗ أولم تكونوا أقسمتم
من قبل ما لكم من زوال (٤٥)

46. 'And you dwell in the dwellings of those who wronged themselves, and it has become plain to you how We dealt with them; and We have set forth *clear* parables for you.'

وسكنتم في مسكن الذين ظلموا أنفسهم وتبين
لكم كيف فعلنا بهم وضربنا لكم الأمثال (٤٦)

* 47. And they have already made their designs; but their designs are with Allah. And even though their designs be such as to make the mountains move, *they cannot succeed.*

وقد مكروا مكرهم وعند الله مكرهم وإن
كان مكرهم لتزول منه الجبال (٤٧)

48. Think not then that Allah will fail to keep His promise to His Messengers. Surely, Allah is Mighty, Lord of retribution,

فلا تحسبن الله مخلف وعده رسله ۗ إن الله
عزيز ذو انتقام (٤٨)

49. On the day when this earth will be changed into another earth, and the heavens *too;* and they will *all* appear before Allah, the One, the Most Supreme;

يوم تبدل الأرض غير الأرض والسموت وبرزوا
لله الواحد القهار (٤٩)

50. And thou shalt see the guilty on that day bound in chains.

وترى المجرمين يومئذ مقرنين في الأصفاد (٥٠)

51. Their garments shall be of pitch, and the fire shall envelop their faces.

سرابيلهم من قطران وتغشى وجوههم النار (٥١)

52. *It will be so* that Allah may requite each soul for what it has wrought. Surely, Allah is swift at reckoning.

ليجزي الله كل نفس ما كسبت ۚ إن الله سريع الحساب (٥٢)

* 53. This is a sufficient admonition for mankind *that they may benefit by it,* and

هذا بلغ للناس ولينذروا به وليعلموا أنما هو

that they may be warned thereby, and that they may know that He is the only One God, and that those possessed of understanding may ponder.

ع إِلٰهٌ وَّاحِدٌ وَّلِيَذَّكَّرَ أُولُوا الْأَلْبَابِ ﴿٥٣﴾

سُورَةُ الْحِجْرِ مَكِّيَّةٌ (١٥)

AL-ḤIJR

(Revealed before Hijra)

1. In the name of Allah, the Gracious, the Merciful.

2. Alif Lām Rā*. These are verses of the Book and of the illuminating Qur'ān.

3. Often will the disbelievers wish that they were Muslims.

4. Leave them alone that they may eat and enjoy themselves and that vain hope may beguile them; but they will soon know.

5. And We have never destroyed any town but there was for it a known decree.

6. No people can outstrip their appointed time, nor can they remain behind.

7. And they said, 'O thou to whom this Exhortation has been sent down, thou art surely a madman.

8. 'Why dost thou not bring angels to us, if thou art of the truthful?'

9. We do not send down angels but by due right, and then they are granted no respite.

10. Verily, We Ourself have sent down this Exhortation, and most surely We will be its Guardian.

* 11. And We sent *Messengers* before thee among parties of ancient peoples.

12. And there never came to them any Messenger but they mocked at him.

13. Thus do We cause this *habit of mocking* to enter into the hearts of the sinful people;

14. They believe not therein, though the example of the former peoples has gone *before them*.

15. And even if We opened to them a door from heaven, and they began ascending through it,

16. They would surely say, 'Only our eyes are dazed; rather we are a bewitched people.'

R. 2.

* 17. And We have, indeed, made mansions *of stars* in the heaven and have adorned it for beholders.

18. And We have protected it against every rejected satan.

* I am Allah Who is All-Seeing.

بِسْمِ اللّٰهِ الرَّحْمٰنِ الرَّحِيْمِ ﴿١﴾

الٓرٰ تِلْكَ اٰيٰتُ الْكِتٰبِ وَقُرْاٰنٍ مُّبِيْنٍ ﴿٢﴾

رُبَمَا يَوَدُّ الَّذِيْنَ كَفَرُوْا لَوْ كَانُوْا مُسْلِمِيْنَ ﴿٣﴾

ذَرْهُمْ يَاْكُلُوْا وَيَتَمَتَّعُوْا وَيُلْهِهِمُ الْاَمَلُ فَسَوْفَ
يَعْلَمُوْنَ ﴿٤﴾

وَمَآ اَهْلَكْنَا مِنْ قَرْيَةٍ اِلَّا وَلَهَا كِتَابٌ مَّعْلُوْمٌ ﴿٥﴾

مَا تَسْبِقُ مِنْ اُمَّةٍ اَجَلَهَا وَمَا يَسْتَاْخِرُوْنَ ﴿٦﴾

وَقَالُوْا يٰۤاَيُّهَا الَّذِيْ نُزِّلَ عَلَيْهِ الذِّكْرُ اِنَّكَ لَمَجْنُوْنٌ ﴿٧﴾

لَوْ مَا تَاْتِيْنَا بِالْمَلٰٓئِكَةِ اِنْ كُنْتَ مِنَ الصّٰدِقِيْنَ ﴿٨﴾

مَا نُنَزِّلُ الْمَلٰٓئِكَةَ اِلَّا بِالْحَقِّ وَمَا كَانُوْۤا اِذًا مُّنْظَرِيْنَ ﴿٩﴾

اِنَّا نَحْنُ نَزَّلْنَا الذِّكْرَ وَاِنَّا لَهٗ لَحٰفِظُوْنَ ﴿١٠﴾

وَلَقَدْ اَرْسَلْنَا مِنْ قَبْلِكَ فِيْ شِيَعِ الْاَوَّلِيْنَ ﴿١١﴾

وَمَا يَاْتِيْهِمْ مِّنْ رَّسُوْلٍ اِلَّا كَانُوْا بِهٖ يَسْتَهْزِءُوْنَ ﴿١٢﴾

كَذٰلِكَ نَسْلُكُهٗ فِيْ قُلُوْبِ الْمُجْرِمِيْنَ ﴿١٣﴾

لَا يُؤْمِنُوْنَ بِهٖ وَقَدْ خَلَتْ سُنَّةُ الْاَوَّلِيْنَ ﴿١٤﴾

وَلَوْ فَتَحْنَا عَلَيْهِمْ بَابًا مِّنَ السَّمَآءِ فَظَلُّوْا فِيْهِ يَعْرُجُوْنَ ﴿١٥﴾

لَقَالُوْۤا اِنَّمَا سُكِّرَتْ اَبْصَارُنَا بَلْ نَحْنُ قَوْمٌ مَّسْحُوْرُوْنَ ﴿١٦﴾

وَلَقَدْ جَعَلْنَا فِي السَّمَآءِ بُرُوْجًا وَّزَيَّنّٰهَا لِلنّٰظِرِيْنَ ﴿١٧﴾

وَحَفِظْنٰهَا مِنْ كُلِّ شَيْطٰنٍ رَّجِيْمٍ ﴿١٨﴾

19. But if any one hears stealthily, there pursues him a bright flame.

إِلَّا مَنِ اسْتَرَقَ السَّمْعَ فَأَتْبَعَهُ شِهَابٌ مُّبِينٌ ﴿١٩﴾

20. And the earth have We spread out, and set therein firm mountains and caused everything to grow therein in proper proportion.

وَالْأَرْضَ مَدَدْنٰهَا وَأَلْقَيْنَا فِيهَا رَوَاسِيَ وَأَنْبَتْنَا فِيهَا مِنْ كُلِّ شَيْءٍ مَّوْزُونٍ ﴿٢٠﴾

21. And We have made for you therein means of livelihood, and *also* for *all* those for whom you do not provide.

وَجَعَلْنَا لَكُمْ فِيهَا مَعَايِشَ وَمَنْ لَّسْتُمْ لَهُ بِرٰزِقِينَ ﴿٢١﴾

22. And there is not a thing but with Us are the treasures thereof and We send it not down except in a known measure.

وَإِنْ مِّنْ شَيْءٍ إِلَّا عِنْدَنَا خَزَآئِنُهُ وَمَا نُنَزِّلُهُ إِلَّا بِقَدَرٍ مَّعْلُومٍ ﴿٢٢﴾

23. And We send impregnating winds, then We send down water from the clouds, then We give it to you to drink; and you are not the ones to store it up.

وَأَرْسَلْنَا الرِّيٰحَ لَوَاقِحَ فَأَنْزَلْنَا مِنَ السَّمَآءِ مَآءً فَأَسْقَيْنٰكُمُوهُ وَمَآ أَنْتُمْ لَهُ بِخٰزِنِينَ ﴿٢٣﴾

24. And verily, it is We Who give life, and We Who cause death; and it is We Who are the *sole* Inheritor.

وَإِنَّا لَنَحْنُ نُحْيِي وَنُمِيتُ وَنَحْنُ الْوٰرِثُونَ ﴿٢٤﴾

25. And We do know those who go ahead among you and We do know those who lag behind.

وَلَقَدْ عَلِمْنَا الْمُسْتَقْدِمِينَ مِنْكُمْ وَلَقَدْ عَلِمْنَا الْمُسْتَأْخِرِينَ ﴿٢٥﴾

26. And, surely, it is thy Lord Who will gather them together. Surely, He is Wise, All-Knowing.

ع ٢ وَإِنَّ رَبَّكَ هُوَ يَحْشُرُهُمْ إِنَّهُ حَكِيمٌ عَلِيمٌ ﴿٢٦﴾

R. 3.

* 27. And, surely, We created man from dry ringing clay, from black mud wrought into shape.

وَلَقَدْ خَلَقْنَا الْإِنْسَانَ مِنْ صَلْصَالٍ مِّنْ حَمَإٍ مَّسْنُونٍ ﴿٢٧﴾

* 28. And the Jinn We had created before from the fire of hot wind.

وَالْجَآنَّ خَلَقْنٰهُ مِنْ قَبْلُ مِنْ نَّارِ السَّمُومِ ﴿٢٨﴾

29. And *remember* when thy Lord said to the angels, 'I am about to create man from dry ringing clay, from black mud wrought into shape;

وَإِذْ قَالَ رَبُّكَ لِلْمَلٰٓئِكَةِ إِنِّي خَالِقٌ بَشَرًا مِّنْ صَلْصَالٍ مِّنْ حَمَإٍ مَّسْنُونٍ ﴿٢٩﴾

30. 'So when I have fashioned him *in perfection* and have breathed into him of My Spirit, fall ye down in submission to him.'

فَإِذَا سَوَّيْتُهُ وَنَفَخْتُ فِيهِ مِنْ رُّوحِي فَقَعُوا لَهُ سٰجِدِينَ ﴿٣٠﴾

31. So the angels submitted, all of them together,

فَسَجَدَ الْمَلٰٓئِكَةُ كُلُّهُمْ أَجْمَعُونَ ﴿٣١﴾

32. Except Iblīs; he refused to be among those who submit.

إِلَّا إِبْلِيسَ أَبٰى أَنْ يَكُونَ مَعَ السّٰجِدِينَ ﴿٣٢﴾

33. *God* said, 'O Iblīs, what is the matter with thee that thou wouldst not be among those who submit?'

قَالَ يٰٓاِبْلِيْسُ مَا لَكَ اَلَّا تَكُوْنَ مَعَ السّٰجِدِيْنَ ﴿٣٣﴾

34. He answered, 'I am not going to submit to man whom Thou hast created from dry ringing clay, from black mud wrought into shape.'

قَالَ لَمْ اَكُنْ لِّاَسْجُدَ لِبَشَرٍ خَلَقْتَهٗ مِنْ صَلْصَالٍ
مِّنْ حَمَاٍ مَّسْنُوْنٍ ﴿٣٤﴾

35. *God* said, 'Then get out hence, for, surely, thou art rejected.

قَالَ فَاخْرُجْ مِنْهَا فَاِنَّكَ رَجِيْمٌ ﴿٣٥﴾

36. 'And, surely, on thee shall be *My* curse till the Day of Judgment.'

وَّاِنَّ عَلَيْكَ اللَّعْنَةَ اِلٰى يَوْمِ الدِّيْنِ ﴿٣٦﴾

37. He said, 'My Lord, then grant me respite till the day when they shall be raised.'

قَالَ رَبِّ فَاَنْظِرْنِيْٓ اِلٰى يَوْمِ يُبْعَثُوْنَ ﴿٣٧﴾

38. *God* said, 'Thou art of those that are granted respite,

قَالَ فَاِنَّكَ مِنَ الْمُنْظَرِيْنَ ﴿٣٨﴾

39. 'Till the day of the appointed time.'

اِلٰى يَوْمِ الْوَقْتِ الْمَعْلُوْمِ ﴿٣٩﴾

40. He answered, 'My Lord, since Thou hast adjudged me as lost, I will surely make *evil appear* beautiful to them on the earth, and I will surely lead them all astray,

قَالَ رَبِّ بِمَآ اَغْوَيْتَنِيْ لَاُزَيِّنَنَّ لَهُمْ فِي الْاَرْضِ
وَلَاُغْوِيَنَّهُمْ اَجْمَعِيْنَ ﴿٤٠﴾

41. 'Except Thy chosen servants from among them.'

اِلَّا عِبَادَكَ مِنْهُمُ الْمُخْلَصِيْنَ ﴿٤١﴾

42. *God* said, 'This is a path *leading* straight to Me.

قَالَ هٰذَا صِرَاطٌ عَلَيَّ مُسْتَقِيْمٌ ﴿٤٢﴾

43. 'Surely, thou shalt have no power over My servants, except such of the erring ones as *choose to* follow thee.'

اِنَّ عِبَادِيْ لَيْسَ لَكَ عَلَيْهِمْ سُلْطٰنٌ اِلَّا مَنِ
اتَّبَعَكَ مِنَ الْغٰوِيْنَ ﴿٤٣﴾

44. And, surely, Hell is the promised place for them all.

وَاِنَّ جَهَنَّمَ لَمَوْعِدُهُمْ اَجْمَعِيْنَ ﴿٤٤﴾

45. It has seven gates: *and* each gate has a portion of them allotted *to it*.

لَهَا سَبْعَةُ اَبْوَابٍ لِكُلِّ بَابٍ مِّنْهُمْ جُزْءٌ مَّقْسُوْمٌ ﴿٤٥﴾ ع ٣ ١٩

R. 4.

46. Verily, the righteous will be *placed* amid gardens and fountains.

اِنَّ الْمُتَّقِيْنَ فِيْ جَنّٰتٍ وَّعُيُوْنٍ ﴿٤٦﴾

47. 'Enter therein with peace, in safety.'

اُدْخُلُوْهَا بِسَلٰمٍ اٰمِنِيْنَ ﴿٤٧﴾

* 48. And We shall remove whatever of rancour may be in their breasts *so that they will become* as brothers *seated* on thrones, facing one another.

وَنَزَعْنَا مَا فِيْ صُدُوْرِهِمْ مِّنْ غِلٍّ اِخْوَانًا عَلٰى
سُرُرٍ مُّتَقٰبِلِيْنَ ﴿٤٨﴾

49. Fatigue shall not touch them there, nor shall they *ever* be ejected therefrom.

لَا يَمَسُّهُمْ فِيْهَا نَصَبٌ وَّمَا هُمْ مِّنْهَا بِمُخْرَجِيْنَ ﴿٤٩﴾

50. Tell My servants that I am surely the One Most Forgiving, the Merciful;

نَبِّئْ عِبَادِيْٓ اَنِّيْٓ اَنَا الْغَفُوْرُ الرَّحِيْمُ ﴿٥٠﴾

51. And *also* that My punishment is the grievous punishment.

وَاَنَّ عَذَابِیۡ هُوَ الۡعَذَابُ الۡاَلِیۡمُ ﴿۵۱﴾

52. And tell them about Abraham's guests.

وَنَبِّئۡهُمۡ عَنۡ ضَیۡفِ اِبۡرٰهِیۡمَ ﴿۵۲﴾

53. When they entered in unto him and said, 'Peace,' he answered, 'Verily, we feel afraid of you.'

اِذۡ دَخَلُوۡا عَلَیۡهِ فَقَالُوۡا سَلٰمًا ؕ قَالَ اِنَّا مِنۡکُمۡ
وَجِلُوۡنَ ﴿۵۳﴾

54. They said, 'Fear not, we give thee glad tidings of a son *who shall be* endowed with knowledge.'

قَالُوۡا لَا تَوۡجَلۡ اِنَّا نُبَشِّرُکَ بِغُلٰمٍ عَلِیۡمٍ ﴿۵۴﴾

55. He said, 'Do you give me the glad tidings in spite of the fact that old age has overtaken me? Of what then do you give me the glad tidings?'

قَالَ اَبَشَّرۡتُمُوۡنِیۡ عَلٰۤی اَنۡ مَّسَّنِیَ الۡکِبَرُ فَبِمَ تُبَشِّرُوۡنَ ﴿۵۵﴾

* 56. They said, 'We have, indeed, given thee glad tidings in truth; be not therefore of those who despair.'

قَالُوۡا بَشَّرۡنٰکَ بِالۡحَقِّ فَلَا تَکُنۡ مِّنَ الۡقٰنِطِیۡنَ ﴿۵۶﴾

57. He said, 'And who can despair of the mercy of his Lord save those who go astray?'

قَالَ وَمَنۡ یَّقۡنَطُ مِنۡ رَّحۡمَۃِ رَبِّهٖۤ اِلَّا الضَّآلُّوۡنَ ﴿۵۷﴾

58. He said, 'What *now* is your business, O ye messengers?'

قَالَ فَمَا خَطۡبُکُمۡ اَیُّهَا الۡمُرۡسَلُوۡنَ ﴿۵۸﴾

59. They said, 'We have been sent unto a guilty people

قَالُوۡۤا اِنَّاۤ اُرۡسِلۡنَاۤ اِلٰی قَوۡمٍ مُّجۡرِمِیۡنَ ﴿۵۹﴾

60. 'Excepting the family of Lot. Them we shall save all,

اِلَّاۤ اٰلَ لُوۡطٍ ؕ اِنَّا لَمُنَجُّوۡهُمۡ اَجۡمَعِیۡنَ ﴿۶۰﴾

61. 'Except his wife. We surmise that she shall be of those who remain behind.'

اِلَّا امۡرَاَتَهٗ قَدَّرۡنَاۤ ۙ اِنَّهَا لَمِنَ الۡغٰبِرِیۡنَ ﴿۶۱﴾

R. 5.

62. And when the messengers came unto the family of Lot,

فَلَمَّا جَآءَ اٰلَ لُوۡطِ ۣالۡمُرۡسَلُوۡنَ ﴿۶۲﴾

63. He said, 'Verily, you are a party of strangers.'

قَالَ اِنَّکُمۡ قَوۡمٌ مُّنۡکَرُوۡنَ ﴿۶۳﴾

64. They said, 'Nay, but we have come to thee with that about which they doubted.

قَالُوۡا بَلۡ جِئۡنٰکَ بِمَا کَانُوۡا فِیۡهِ یَمۡتَرُوۡنَ ﴿۶۴﴾

65. 'And we have come to thee with the truth, and surely we are truthful.

وَاَتَیۡنٰکَ بِالۡحَقِّ وَاِنَّا لَصٰدِقُوۡنَ ﴿۶۵﴾

66. 'So go forth with thy family in the *latter* part of the night, and follow thou in their rear. And let none of you look back, and *now* proceed to where you are commanded.'

فَاَسۡرِ بِاَهۡلِکَ بِقِطۡعٍ مِّنَ الَّیۡلِ وَاتَّبِعۡ اَدۡبَارَهُمۡ وَلَا یَلۡتَفِتۡ
مِنۡکُمۡ اَحَدٌ وَّامۡضُوۡا حَیۡثُ تُؤۡمَرُوۡنَ ﴿۶۶﴾

67. And We communicated to him this decree that the root of them was to be cut off by the morning.

وَقَضَیۡنَاۤ اِلَیۡهِ ذٰلِکَ الۡاَمۡرَ اَنَّ دَابِرَ هٰۤؤُلَآءِ مَقۡطُوۡعٌ
مُّصۡبِحِیۡنَ ﴿۶۷﴾

68. And the people of the city came rejoicing.

وَجَآءَ اَهۡلُ الۡمَدِیۡنَۃِ یَسۡتَبۡشِرُوۡنَ ﴿۶۸﴾

69. He said, 'These are my guests, so put me not to shame;

قَالَ اِنَّ هٰۤؤُلَآءِ ضَیۡفِیۡ فَلَا تَفۡضَحُوۡنِ ﴿۶۹﴾

70. 'And fear Allah and disgrace me not.'

وَاتَّقُوا اللّٰهَ وَلَا تُخْزُوْنِ ﴿٧٠﴾

71. They said, 'Did we not forbid thee *to entertain* all *sorts of* people?'

قَالُوْٓا اَوَلَمْ نَنْهَكَ عَنِ الْعٰلَمِيْنَ ﴿٧١﴾

* 72. He said, 'These are my daughters if you must do something.'

قَالَ هٰٓؤُلَآءِ بَنٰتِيْٓ اِنْ كُنْتُمْ فٰعِلِيْنَ ﴿٧٢﴾

73. By thy life, these *too* in their *mad* intoxication are wandering in distraction—

لَعَمْرُكَ اِنَّهُمْ لَفِيْ سَكْرَتِهِمْ يَعْمَهُوْنَ ﴿٧٣﴾

74. Then the punishment seized them at sunrise.

فَاَخَذَتْهُمُ الصَّيْحَةُ مُشْرِقِيْنَ ﴿٧٤﴾

75. We turned it upside down, and We rained upon them stones of clay.

فَجَعَلْنَا عَالِيَهَا سَافِلَهَا وَاَمْطَرْنَا عَلَيْهِمْ حِجَارَةً
مِّنْ سِجِّيْلٍ ﴿٧٥﴾

76. Surely, in this are Signs for those who can read *signs.*

اِنَّ فِيْ ذٰلِكَ لَاٰيٰتٍ لِّلْمُتَوَسِّمِيْنَ ﴿٧٦﴾

77. And it lies on a road that *still* exists.

وَاِنَّهَا لَبِسَبِيْلٍ مُّقِيْمٍ ﴿٧٧﴾

78. Surely, in this is a Sign for believers.

اِنَّ فِيْ ذٰلِكَ لَاٰيَةً لِّلْمُؤْمِنِيْنَ ﴿٧٨﴾

79. And the People of the Wood *too* were surely wrongdoers.

وَاِنْ كَانَ اَصْحٰبُ الْاَيْكَةِ لَظٰلِمِيْنَ ﴿٧٩﴾

* 80. So We chastised them *also.* And they both lie on a manifest way.

فَانْتَقَمْنَا مِنْهُمْ وَاِنَّهُمَا لَبِاِمَامٍ مُّبِيْنٍ ﴿٨٠﴾

R. 6.

81. And the People of the Ḥijr *also* did treat the Messengers as liars.

وَلَقَدْ كَذَّبَ اَصْحٰبُ الْحِجْرِ الْمُرْسَلِيْنَ ﴿٨١﴾

82. And We gave them Our Signs, but they turned away from them.

وَاٰتَيْنٰهُمْ اٰيٰتِنَا فَكَانُوْا عَنْهَا مُعْرِضِيْنَ ﴿٨٢﴾

83. And they used to hew out houses in the mountains, in security.

وَكَانُوْا يَنْحِتُوْنَ مِنَ الْجِبَالِ بُيُوْتًا اٰمِنِيْنَ ﴿٨٣﴾

84. But the punishment seized them in the morning,

فَاَخَذَتْهُمُ الصَّيْحَةُ مُصْبِحِيْنَ ﴿٨٤﴾

85. And all that they had earned availed them not.

فَمَآ اَغْنٰى عَنْهُمْ مَّا كَانُوْا يَكْسِبُوْنَ ﴿٨٥﴾

* 86. And We have not created the heavens and the earth and all that is between the two but in accordance with the requirements of wisdom; and the Hour is sure to come. So turn away *from them* in a comely manner.

وَمَا خَلَقْنَا السَّمٰوٰتِ وَالْاَرْضَ وَمَا بَيْنَهُمَآ اِلَّا بِالْحَقِّ
وَاِنَّ السَّاعَةَ لَاٰتِيَةٌ فَاصْفَحِ الصَّفْحَ الْجَمِيْلَ ﴿٨٦﴾

87. Verily, it is thy Lord Who is the Great Creator, the All-Knowing.

اِنَّ رَبَّكَ هُوَ الْخَلّٰقُ الْعَلِيْمُ ﴿٨٧﴾

88. And We have, indeed, given thee the seven oft-repeated *verses,* and the Great Qur'ān.

وَلَقَدْ اٰتَيْنٰكَ سَبْعًا مِّنَ الْمَثَانِيْ وَالْقُرْاٰنَ الْعَظِيْمَ ﴿٨٨﴾

* 89. Stretch not thy eyes towards what We have bestowed on some classes

لَا تَمُدَّنَّ عَيْنَيْكَ اِلٰى مَا مَتَّعْنَا بِهٖٓ اَزْوَاجًا مِّنْهُمْ وَ

of them to enjoy for a short time, and grieve not over them; and lower thy wing *of mercy* for the believers.

* 90. And say, 'I am, indeed, a plain Warner.'

* 91. Because We *have decided to* send down *punishment* on those who have formed themselves into groups *against thee;*

* 92. Who have pronounced the Qur'ān to be *so many* lies;

93. So by thy Lord, We will, surely, question them all

94. Concerning that which they used to do.

95. So declare openly that with which thou art commanded and turn aside from those who ascribe partners *to God*.

96. We will, surely, suffice thee against those who mock:

97. Who set up another God with Allah, but soon shall they come to know.

98. And, indeed, We know that thy bosom becomes straitened because of what they say.

99. But glorify thy Lord praising Him, and be of those who prostrate themselves *before Him*.

100. And continue worshipping thy Lord, till death comes to thee.

لَا تَحْزَنْ عَلَيْهِمْ وَاخْفِضْ جَنَاحَكَ لِلْمُؤْمِنِينَ ﴿٨٩﴾

وَقُلْ إِنِّي أَنَا النَّذِيرُ الْمُبِينُ ﴿٩٠﴾

كَمَا أَنْزَلْنَا عَلَى الْمُقْتَسِمِينَ ﴿٩١﴾

الَّذِينَ جَعَلُوا الْقُرْآنَ عِضِينَ ﴿٩٢﴾

فَوَرَبِّكَ لَنَسْأَلَنَّهُمْ أَجْمَعِينَ ﴿٩٣﴾

عَمَّا كَانُوا يَعْمَلُونَ ﴿٩٤﴾

فَاصْدَعْ بِمَا تُؤْمَرُ وَأَعْرِضْ عَنِ الْمُشْرِكِينَ ﴿٩٥﴾

إِنَّا كَفَيْنَاكَ الْمُسْتَهْزِئِينَ ﴿٩٦﴾

الَّذِينَ يَجْعَلُونَ مَعَ اللَّهِ إِلَٰهًا آخَرَ فَسَوْفَ
يَعْلَمُونَ ﴿٩٧﴾

وَلَقَدْ نَعْلَمُ أَنَّكَ يَضِيقُ صَدْرُكَ بِمَا يَقُولُونَ ﴿٩٨﴾

فَسَبِّحْ بِحَمْدِ رَبِّكَ وَكُنْ مِنَ السَّاجِدِينَ ﴿٩٩﴾

وَاعْبُدْ رَبَّكَ حَتَّىٰ يَأْتِيَكَ الْيَقِينُ ﴿١٠٠﴾

(آیاتہا ١٢٩) سُوْرَةُ النَّحْلِ مَكِّيَّةٌ (١٦) (رکوعاتہا ١٦)

AL-NAḤL

(Revealed before Hijra)

1. In the name of Allah, the Gracious, the Merciful.

بِسْمِ اللّٰهِ الرَّحْمٰنِ الرَّحِيْمِ ۝١

2. The decree of Allah is coming, so seek ye not to hasten it. Holy is He, and exalted above all that which they associate *with Him*.

اَتٰۤى اَمْرُ اللّٰهِ فَلَا تَسْتَعْجِلُوْهُ ؕ سُبْحٰنَهٗ وَتَعٰلٰى عَمَّا
يُشْرِكُوْنَ ۝٢

* 3. He sends down the angels with revelation by His command on whomsoever of His servants He pleases *saying*, 'Warn *people* that there is no God but I, so take Me *alone* for your Protector.'

يُنَزِّلُ الْمَلٰٓئِكَةَ بِالرُّوْحِ مِنْ اَمْرِهٖ عَلٰى مَنْ يَّشَآءُ
مِنْ عِبَادِهٖۤ اَنْ اَنْذِرُوْۤا اَنَّهٗ لَاۤ اِلٰهَ اِلَّاۤ اَنَا فَاتَّقُوْنِ ۝٣

4. He has created the heavens and the earth in accordance with the requirements of wisdom. Exalted is He above all that they associate *with Him*.

خَلَقَ السَّمٰوٰتِ وَالْاَرْضَ بِالْحَقِّ ؕ تَعٰلٰى عَمَّا
يُشْرِكُوْنَ ۝٤

5. He has created man from a drop of fluid, but lo! he is an open disputer.

خَلَقَ الْاِنْسَانَ مِنْ نُّطْفَةٍ فَاِذَا هُوَ خَصِيْمٌ مُّبِيْنٌ ۝٥

* 6. And the cattle too He has created; you find in them warmth and *other* uses; and some of them you eat.

وَالْاَنْعَامَ خَلَقَهَا ۚ لَكُمْ فِيْهَا دِفْءٌ وَّمَنَافِعُ وَمِنْهَا
تَاْكُلُوْنَ ۝٦

7. And in them there is beauty for you when you bring *them* home in the evening, and when you drive *them* forth to pasture in the morning.

وَلَكُمْ فِيْهَا جَمَالٌ حِيْنَ تُرِيْحُوْنَ وَحِيْنَ تَسْرَحُوْنَ ۝٧

8. And they carry your loads to a land which you could not reach except with great hardship to yourselves. Surely, your Lord is Compassionate, Merciful.

وَتَحْمِلُ اَثْقَالَكُمْ اِلٰى بَلَدٍ لَّمْ تَكُوْنُوْا بٰلِغِيْهِ اِلَّا بِشِقِّ
الْاَنْفُسِ ؕ اِنَّ رَبَّكُمْ لَرَءُوْفٌ رَّحِيْمٌ ۝٨

9. And *He has created* horses and mules and asses that you may ride them, and as *a source of* beauty. And He will create what you do not *yet* know.

وَّالْخَيْلَ وَالْبِغَالَ وَالْحَمِيْرَ لِتَرْكَبُوْهَا وَزِيْنَةً ؕ وَيَخْلُقُ
مَا لَا تَعْلَمُوْنَ ۝٩

10. And upon Allah rests the *showing of the* right way, and there are ways which deviate *from the right course*. And if He had *enforced* His will, He would have guided you all.

وَعَلَى اللّٰهِ قَصْدُ السَّبِيْلِ وَمِنْهَا جَآئِرٌ ؕ وَلَوْ شَآءَ
لَهَدٰىكُمْ اَجْمَعِيْنَ ۝١٠ ع

R. 2.

11. He it is Who sends down water for you from the clouds; out of it you have your drink, and there *grow* from it trees on which you pasture *your cattle*.

هُوَ الَّذِيْۤ اَنْزَلَ مِنَ السَّمَآءِ مَآءً لَّكُمْ مِّنْهُ شَرَابٌ
وَّمِنْهُ شَجَرٌ فِيْهِ تُسِيْمُوْنَ ۝١١

* 12. Therewith He grows corn for you, and the olive and the date-palm, and the grapes, and all kinds of fruits. Surely, in that is a Sign for a people who reflect.

ينبت لكم به الزرع والزيتون والنخيل والاعناب ومن كل الثمرت ان في ذلك لاية لقوم يتفكرون ﴿١٢﴾

13. And He has pressed into service for you the night and the day, and the sun and the moon; and the stars *too* have been pressed into service by His command. Surely, in that are Signs for a people who make use of their reason.

وسخر لكم اليل والنهار والشمس والقمر والنجوم مسخرت بامره ان في ذلك لايت لقوم يعقلون ﴿١٣﴾

14. And *He has pressed into service* the things He has created for you in the earth, varying in colours. Surely, in that is a Sign for a people who take heed.

وما ذرا لكم في الارض مختلفا الوانه ان في ذلك لاية لقوم يذكرون ﴿١٤﴾

15. And He it is Who has subjected *to you* the sea that you may eat therefrom fresh flesh, and may take forth therefrom ornaments which you wear. And thou seest the ships ploughing through it, *that you may thereby journey* and that you may seek of His bounty and that you may be grateful.

وهو الذي سخر البحر لتاكلوا منه لحما طريا وتستخرجوا منه حلية تلبسونها وترى الفلك مواخر فيه ولتبتغوا من فضله ولعلكم تشكرون ﴿١٥﴾

* 16. And He has placed in the earth firm mountains lest it quake with you, and rivers and routes that you may take the right way.

والقى في الارض رواسي ان تميد بكم وانهرا وسبلا لعلكم تهتدون ﴿١٦﴾

17. And, *other* marks *too; by them* and by the stars they follow the right direction.

وعلمت وبالنجم هم يهتدون ﴿١٧﴾

18. Is He, then, Who creates like one who creates not? Will you not then take heed?

افمن يخلق كمن لا يخلق افلا تذكرون ﴿١٨﴾

19. And if you *try* to count the favours of Allah, you will not be able to number them. Surely, Allah is Most Forgiving, Merciful.

وان تعدوا نعمة الله لا تحصوها ان الله لغفور رحيم ﴿١٩﴾

20. And Allah knows what you conceal and what you disclose.

والله يعلم ما تسرون وما تعلنون ﴿٢٠﴾

21. And those on whom they call beside Allah create not anything, but they are themselves created.

والذين يدعون من دون الله لا يخلقون شيئا وهم يخلقون ﴿٢١﴾

22. *They are* dead, not living; and they know not when they will be raised.

اموات غير احياء وما يشعرون ايان يبعثون ﴿٢٢﴾

R. 3.

23. Your God is One God. And as to those who believe not in the Hereafter, their hearts are strangers *to truth*, and they are full of pride.

إِلَٰهُكُمْ إِلَٰهٌ وَاحِدٌ ۚ فَالَّذِينَ لَا يُؤْمِنُونَ بِالْآخِرَةِ
قُلُوبُهُم مُّنكِرَةٌ وَهُم مُّسْتَكْبِرُونَ ﴿٢٣﴾

24. Undoubtedly, Allah knows what they conceal and what they disclose. Surely, He loves not the proud.

لَا جَرَمَ أَنَّ اللَّهَ يَعْلَمُ مَا يُسِرُّونَ وَمَا يُعْلِنُونَ ۚ
إِنَّهُ لَا يُحِبُّ الْمُسْتَكْبِرِينَ ﴿٢٤﴾

25. And when it is said to them, 'What *think ye of* that which your Lord has sent down?' they say, 'Stories of the ancients,'

وَإِذَا قِيلَ لَهُم مَّاذَا أَنزَلَ رَبُّكُمْ ۙ قَالُوا أَسَاطِيرُ
الْأَوَّلِينَ ﴿٢٥﴾

26. That they may bear their burdens in full on the Day of Resurrection, and *also* a portion of the burdens of those whom they lead astray without knowledge. Behold! evil is that which they bear.

لِيَحْمِلُوا أَوْزَارَهُمْ كَامِلَةً يَوْمَ الْقِيَامَةِ ۙ وَمِنْ أَوْزَارِ
الَّذِينَ يُضِلُّونَهُم بِغَيْرِ عِلْمٍ ۗ أَلَا سَاءَ مَا يَزِرُونَ ﴿٢٦﴾

R. 4.

27. Those who were before them did *also* plan, but Allah came upon their structure at the *very* foundations, so that the roof fell down upon them from above them; and the punishment came upon them from where they knew not.

قَدْ مَكَرَ الَّذِينَ مِن قَبْلِهِمْ فَأَتَى اللَّهُ بُنْيَانَهُم مِّنَ
الْقَوَاعِدِ فَخَرَّ عَلَيْهِمُ السَّقْفُ مِن فَوْقِهِمْ وَأَتَاهُمُ
الْعَذَابُ مِنْ حَيْثُ لَا يَشْعُرُونَ ﴿٢٧﴾

28. Then on the Day of Resurrection He will disgrace them and will say, "Where are My 'partners' for whose sake you used to oppose *the Prophets?*" Those endowed with knowledge will say, 'This day disgrace and affliction will surely *fall* on the disbelievers,'

ثُمَّ يَوْمَ الْقِيَامَةِ يُخْزِيهِمْ وَيَقُولُ أَيْنَ شُرَكَائِيَ
الَّذِينَ كُنتُمْ تُشَاقُّونَ فِيهِمْ ۚ قَالَ الَّذِينَ أُوتُوا
الْعِلْمَ إِنَّ الْخِزْيَ الْيَوْمَ وَالسُّوءَ عَلَى الْكَافِرِينَ ﴿٢٨﴾

29. Those whom the angels cause to die while they are wronging their souls. Then will they offer submission, *saying*, 'We used not to do any evil.' Nay, surely, Allah knows well what you used to do.

الَّذِينَ تَتَوَفَّاهُمُ الْمَلَائِكَةُ ظَالِمِي أَنفُسِهِمْ ۖ فَأَلْقَوُا
السَّلَمَ مَا كُنَّا نَعْمَلُ مِن سُوءٍ ۚ بَلَىٰ إِنَّ اللَّهَ عَلِيمٌ
بِمَا كُنتُمْ تَعْمَلُونَ ﴿٢٩﴾

30. So enter the gates of Hell, to abide therein. Evil indeed is the abode of the proud.

فَادْخُلُوا أَبْوَابَ جَهَنَّمَ خَالِدِينَ فِيهَا ۖ فَلَبِئْسَ مَثْوَى
الْمُتَكَبِّرِينَ ﴿٣٠﴾

31. And *when* it is said to the righteous, 'What *think ye of* that which your Lord has revealed?' they say, 'The best.' For those who do good there is good in this world, and the home of the Hereafter is even better. Excellent indeed is the abode of the righteous –

وَقِيلَ لِلَّذِينَ اتَّقَوْا مَاذَا أَنزَلَ رَبُّكُمْ ۚ قَالُوا خَيْرًا ۗ
لِّلَّذِينَ أَحْسَنُوا فِي هَٰذِهِ الدُّنْيَا حَسَنَةٌ ۚ وَلَدَارُ
الْآخِرَةِ خَيْرٌ ۚ وَلَنِعْمَ دَارُ الْمُتَّقِينَ ﴿٣١﴾

32. Gardens of Eternity, which they will enter; through them flow streams. They will have therein what they wish for. Thus does Allah reward the righteous,

جَنّٰتُ عَدْنٍ يَّدْخُلُوْنَهَا تَجْرِيْ مِنْ تَحْتِهَا الْاَنْهٰرُ
لَهُمْ فِيْهَا مَا يَشَآءُوْنَ ؕ كَذٰلِكَ يَجْزِي اللّٰهُ
الْمُتَّقِيْنَ ﴿۳۲﴾

33. Those whom the angels cause to die while they are pure. They say: 'Peace be unto you! Enter Heaven because of what you used to do.'

الَّذِيْنَ تَتَوَفّٰىهُمُ الْمَلٰٓئِكَةُ طَيِّبِيْنَ ۙ يَقُوْلُوْنَ سَلٰمٌ
عَلَيْكُمُ ۙ ادْخُلُوا الْجَنَّةَ بِمَا كُنْتُمْ تَعْمَلُوْنَ ﴿۳۳﴾

34. What do they wait for except that the angels should come upon them or that the decree of thy Lord should come to pass? So did those who were before them. Allah did not wrong them, but they used to wrong themselves.

هَلْ يَنْظُرُوْنَ اِلَّآ اَنْ تَاْتِيَهُمُ الْمَلٰٓئِكَةُ اَوْ يَاْتِيَ
اَمْرُ رَبِّكَ ؕ كَذٰلِكَ فَعَلَ الَّذِيْنَ مِنْ قَبْلِهِمْ ؕ وَمَا ظَلَمَهُمُ
اللّٰهُ وَلٰكِنْ كَانُوْٓا اَنْفُسَهُمْ يَظْلِمُوْنَ ﴿۳۴﴾

35. So the evil *result* of what they did befell them, and that which they used to mock at encompassed them.

فَاَصَابَهُمْ سَيِّاٰتُ مَا عَمِلُوْا وَحَاقَ بِهِمْ مَّا كَانُوْا
بِهٖ يَسْتَهْزِءُوْنَ ﴿۳۵﴾ ع

R. 5.

36. Those who set up equals *to God* say: 'If Allah had *so* willed, we should not have worshipped anything beside Him, neither we nor our fathers, nor should we have forbidden anything without *command from* Him.' So did those who were before them. But are the Messengers responsible for anything except the plain delivery of the Message?

وَقَالَ الَّذِيْنَ اَشْرَكُوْا لَوْ شَآءَ اللّٰهُ مَا عَبَدْنَا مِنْ
دُوْنِهٖ مِنْ شَيْءٍ نَّحْنُ وَلَآ اٰبَآؤُنَا وَلَا حَرَّمْنَا مِنْ
دُوْنِهٖ مِنْ شَيْءٍ ؕ كَذٰلِكَ فَعَلَ الَّذِيْنَ مِنْ قَبْلِهِمْ ۚ
فَهَلْ عَلَى الرُّسُلِ اِلَّا الْبَلٰغُ الْمُبِيْنُ ﴿۳۶﴾

37. And We did raise among every people a Messenger, *preaching:* 'Worship Allah and shun the Evil One.' Then among them were *some* whom Allah guided and among them were *some* who became deserving of ruin. So travel through the earth, and see what was the end of those who treated *the Prophets* as liars!

وَلَقَدْ بَعَثْنَا فِيْ كُلِّ اُمَّةٍ رَّسُوْلًا اَنِ اعْبُدُوا اللّٰهَ
وَاجْتَنِبُوا الطَّاغُوْتَ ۚ فَمِنْهُمْ مَّنْ هَدَى اللّٰهُ
وَمِنْهُمْ مَّنْ حَقَّتْ عَلَيْهِ الضَّلٰلَةُ ؕ فَسِيْرُوْا فِي الْاَرْضِ
فَانْظُرُوْا كَيْفَ كَانَ عَاقِبَةُ الْمُكَذِّبِيْنَ ﴿۳۷﴾

38. If thou art solicitous of their guidance, then *know that* Allah surely guides not those who lead *others* astray. And for such there are no helpers.

اِنْ تَحْرِصْ عَلٰى هُدٰىهُمْ فَاِنَّ اللّٰهَ لَا يَهْدِيْ مَنْ
يُّضِلُّ وَمَا لَهُمْ مِّنْ نّٰصِرِيْنَ ﴿۳۸﴾

39. And they swear by Allah their strongest oaths, that Allah will not raise up those who die. Nay, *He will certainly raise them up*— a promise *He has made*

وَاَقْسَمُوْا بِاللّٰهِ جَهْدَ اَيْمَانِهِمْ ۙ لَا يَبْعَثُ اللّٰهُ مَنْ
يَّمُوْتُ ؕ بَلٰى وَعْدًا عَلَيْهِ حَقًّا وَّلٰكِنَّ اَكْثَرَ النَّاسِ

binding on Himself, but most people know not.

لَا يَعْلَمُوْنَ ﴿۳۹﴾

40. *He will raise them up* that He may make clear to them that wherein they differed, and that those who disbelieved may know that they were liars.

لِيُبَيِّنَ لَهُمُ الَّذِيْ يَخْتَلِفُوْنَ فِيْهِ وَلِيَعْلَمَ الَّذِيْنَ
كَفَرُوْٓا اَنَّهُمْ كَانُوْا كٰذِبِيْنَ ﴿۴۰﴾

41. Our word to a thing, when We will it, is only that We say to it, 'Be!', and it is.

اِنَّمَا قَوْلُنَا لِشَيْءٍ اِذَآ اَرَدْنٰهُ اَنْ نَّقُوْلَ لَهٗ كُنْ
فَيَكُوْنُ ﴿۴۱﴾

R. 6.

42. And *as to* those who have left their homes for the sake of Allah after they had been wronged, We will surely give them a goodly abode in this world; and truly the reward of the Hereafter is greater, if they but knew –

وَالَّذِيْنَ هَاجَرُوْا فِي اللّٰهِ مِنْۢ بَعْدِ مَا ظُلِمُوْا لَنُبَوِّئَنَّهُمْ
فِي الدُّنْيَا حَسَنَةً ؕ وَلَاَجْرُ الْاٰخِرَةِ اَكْبَرُ ۘ لَوْ كَانُوْا
يَعْلَمُوْنَ ﴿۴۲﴾

43. Those who are steadfast and put their trust in their Lord.

الَّذِيْنَ صَبَرُوْا وَعَلٰى رَبِّهِمْ يَتَوَكَّلُوْنَ ﴿۴۳﴾

* 44. And We sent not *as Messengers* before thee but men to whom We sent revelation, so ask those who possess the Reminder, if you know not.

وَمَآ اَرْسَلْنَا مِنْ قَبْلِكَ اِلَّا رِجَالًا نُّوْحِيْٓ اِلَيْهِمْ فَسْـَٔلُوْٓا
اَهْلَ الذِّكْرِ اِنْ كُنْتُمْ لَا تَعْلَمُوْنَ ﴿۴۴﴾

* 45. *We sent Our Messengers* with clear Signs and Scriptures. And We have sent down to thee the Reminder that thou mayest explain to mankind that which has been sent down to them, and that they may reflect.

بِالْبَيِّنٰتِ وَالزُّبُرِ ؕ وَاَنْزَلْنَآ اِلَيْكَ الذِّكْرَ لِتُبَيِّنَ
لِلنَّاسِ مَا نُزِّلَ اِلَيْهِمْ وَلَعَلَّهُمْ يَتَفَكَّرُوْنَ ﴿۴۵﴾

46. Do, then, those who devise evil plans feel secure that Allah will not make them sink into the land, or that the punishment will not come upon them from whence they do not know?

اَفَاَمِنَ الَّذِيْنَ مَكَرُوا السَّيِّاٰتِ اَنْ يَّخْسِفَ اللّٰهُ بِهِمُ
الْاَرْضَ اَوْ يَاْتِيَهُمُ الْعَذَابُ مِنْ حَيْثُ لَا يَشْعُرُوْنَ ﴿۴۶﴾

47. Or that He will not seize them in their going to and fro so that they shall not be able to frustrate *God's plans?*

اَوْ يَاْخُذَهُمْ فِيْ تَقَلُّبِهِمْ فَمَا هُمْ بِمُعْجِزِيْنَ ﴿۴۷﴾

48. Or that He will not seize them by *a process of* gradual destruction? Your Lord is indeed Compassionate, Merciful.

اَوْ يَاْخُذَهُمْ عَلٰى تَخَوُّفٍ ؕ فَاِنَّ رَبَّكُمْ لَرَءُوْفٌ رَّحِيْمٌ ﴿۴۸﴾

49. Have they not seen that the shadows of everything which Allah has created shift from the right and *from* the left, prostrating themselves to Allah, while they are being humbled?

اَوَلَمْ يَرَوْا اِلٰى مَا خَلَقَ اللّٰهُ مِنْ شَيْءٍ يَّتَفَيَّؤُا ظِلٰلُهٗ
عَنِ الْيَمِيْنِ وَالشَّمَآئِلِ سُجَّدًا لِّلّٰهِ وَهُمْ دٰخِرُوْنَ ﴿۴۹﴾

50. And whatever is in the heavens and whatever creature is in the earth submits *humbly* to Allah, and the angels *too*, and they do not behave proudly.

وَلِلّٰهِ يَسْجُدُ مَا فِي السَّمٰوٰتِ وَمَا فِي الْاَرْضِ مِنْ
دَآبَّةٍ وَّالْمَلٰٓئِكَةُ وَهُمْ لَا يَسْتَكْبِرُوْنَ ﴿۵۰﴾

51. They fear their Lord above them,

يَخَافُوْنَ رَبَّهُمْ مِّنْ فَوْقِهِمْ وَيَفْعَلُوْنَ مَا

and do what they are commanded.

R. 7.

52. Allah has said, 'Take not *for worship* two gods. There is only One God. So fear Me alone.'

* 53. And to Him belongs whatsoever is in the heavens and the earth and to Him is due obedience for ever. Will you then fear any other than Allah?

54. And whatever blessing you have, it is from Allah. And when affliction befalls you, it is unto Him that you cry *for help*.

55. Then, when He removes the affliction from you, behold! a party among you *begins to* attribute equals to their Lord,

56. So that they deny that which We have bestowed upon them. Well, enjoy yourselves a little; but soon will you know.

57. And they set apart *for the false deities* of which they know nothing a portion of that which We have bestowed on them. By Allah, you shall certainly be called to account for all that you have forged.

58. And they ascribe daughters to Allah —Holy is He!—while they *themselves* have what they desire.

59. And when to one of them is conveyed the tidings of *the birth of* a female, his face darkens, while he suppresses *his inward* grief.

60. He hides himself from the people because of the bad news he has had: 'Shall he keep it in spite of disgrace or bury it in the dust?' Verily, evil is that which they judge.

* 61. The state of those who do not believe in the Hereafter is evil, while Allah's attribute is sublime and He is the Mighty, the Wise.

R. 8.

62. And if Allah were to punish men for their wrongdoing, He would not leave thereon a living creature, but He gives

السجدة
ع يُؤْمَرُوْنَ ﴿٥١﴾
وَقَالَ اللّٰهُ لَا تَتَّخِذُوْٓا اِلٰهَيْنِ اثْنَيْنِ ۚ اِنَّمَا هُوَ اِلٰهٌ
وَّاحِدٌ ۚ فَاِيَّايَ فَارْهَبُوْنِ ﴿٥٢﴾
وَلَهٗ مَا فِي السَّمٰوٰتِ وَالْاَرْضِ وَلَهُ الدِّيْنُ وَاصِبًا ۭ
اَفَغَيْرَ اللّٰهِ تَتَّقُوْنَ ﴿٥٣﴾
وَمَا بِكُمْ مِّنْ نِّعْمَةٍ فَمِنَ اللّٰهِ ثُمَّ اِذَا مَسَّكُمُ الضُّرُّ
فَاِلَيْهِ تَجْـَٔرُوْنَ ﴿٥٤﴾
ثُمَّ اِذَا كَشَفَ الضُّرَّ عَنْكُمْ اِذَا فَرِيْقٌ مِّنْكُمْ بِرَبِّهِمْ
يُشْرِكُوْنَ ﴿٥٥﴾
لِيَكْفُرُوْا بِمَآ اٰتَيْنٰهُمْ ۭ فَتَمَتَّعُوْا ۣ فَسَوْفَ تَعْلَمُوْنَ ﴿٥٦﴾
وَيَجْعَلُوْنَ لِمَا لَا يَعْلَمُوْنَ نَصِيْبًا مِّمَّا رَزَقْنٰهُمْ ۭ
تَاللّٰهِ لَتُسْـَٔلُنَّ عَمَّا كُنْتُمْ تَفْتَرُوْنَ ﴿٥٧﴾
وَيَجْعَلُوْنَ لِلّٰهِ الْبَنٰتِ سُبْحٰنَهٗ ۙ وَلَهُمْ مَّا يَشْتَهُوْنَ ﴿٥٨﴾
وَاِذَا بُشِّرَ اَحَدُهُمْ بِالْاُنْثٰى ظَلَّ وَجْهُهٗ مُسْوَدًّا
وَّهُوَ كَظِيْمٌ ﴿٥٩﴾
يَتَوَارٰى مِنَ الْقَوْمِ مِنْ سُوْۗءِ مَا بُشِّرَ بِهٖ ۭ اَيُمْسِكُهٗ
عَلٰي هُوْنٍ اَمْ يَدُسُّهٗ فِي التُّرَابِ ۭ اَلَا سَاۗءَ مَا
يَحْكُمُوْنَ ﴿٦٠﴾
لِلَّذِيْنَ لَا يُؤْمِنُوْنَ بِالْاٰخِرَةِ مَثَلُ السَّوْءِ ۚ وَلِلّٰهِ
ع الْمَثَلُ الْاَعْلٰى ۭ وَهُوَ الْعَزِيْزُ الْحَكِيْمُ ﴿٦١﴾
وَلَوْ يُؤَاخِذُ اللّٰهُ النَّاسَ بِظُلْمِهِمْ مَّا تَرَكَ عَلَيْهَا
مِنْ دَاۗبَّةٍ وَّلٰكِنْ يُّؤَخِّرُهُمْ اِلٰٓى اَجَلٍ مُّسَمًّى ۚ فَاِذَا

them respite till an appointed term; and when their term is come, they cannot remain behind a single hour, nor can they go ahead *of it*.

جَآءَ اَجَلُهُمْ لَا يَسْتَاْخِرُوْنَ سَاعَةً وَّلَا يَسْتَقْدِمُوْنَ ﴿٦٢﴾

63. And they attribute to Allah what they dislike *for themselves* and their tongues utter the lie that they will have the best *of everything*. Undoubtedly, theirs shall be the Fire, and *therein* shall they be abandoned.

وَيَجْعَلُوْنَ لِلّٰهِ مَا يَكْرَهُوْنَ وَتَصِفُ اَلْسِنَتُهُمُ الْكَذِبَ
اَنَّ لَهُمُ الْحُسْنٰى ؕ لَا جَرَمَ اَنَّ لَهُمُ النَّارَ وَاَنَّهُمْ
مُّفْرَطُوْنَ ﴿٦٣﴾

64. By Allah, We did send *Messengers* to the peoples before thee; but Satan made their works *appear* beautiful to them. So he is their patron this day, and they shall have a grievous punishment.

تَاللّٰهِ لَقَدْ اَرْسَلْنَآ اِلٰٓى اُمَمٍ مِّنْ قَبْلِكَ فَزَيَّنَ لَهُمُ
الشَّيْطٰنُ اَعْمَالَهُمْ فَهُوَ وَلِيُّهُمُ الْيَوْمَ وَلَهُمْ عَذَابٌ
اَلِيْمٌ ﴿٦٤﴾

65. And We have not sent down to thee the Book except that thou mayest explain to them that concerning which they differ, and as a guidance, and a mercy for a people who believe.

وَمَآ اَنْزَلْنَا عَلَيْكَ الْكِتٰبَ اِلَّا لِتُبَيِّنَ لَهُمُ الَّذِى اخْتَلَفُوْا
فِيْهِ ۙ وَهُدًى وَّرَحْمَةً لِّقَوْمٍ يُّؤْمِنُوْنَ ﴿٦٥﴾

66. And Allah has sent down water from the sky, and has quickened therewith the earth after its death. Surely, in that is a Sign for a people who would hear.

وَاللّٰهُ اَنْزَلَ مِنَ السَّمَآءِ مَآءً فَاَحْيَا بِهِ الْاَرْضَ بَعْدَ
مَوْتِهَا ؕ اِنَّ فِىْ ذٰلِكَ لَاٰيَةً لِّقَوْمٍ يَّسْمَعُوْنَ ﴿٦٦﴾ ع ٩

R. 9.

67. And surely in the cattle *too* there is a lesson for you. We give you to drink of what is in their bellies, from betwixt the faeces and the blood, milk pure *and* pleasant for those who drink *it*.

وَاِنَّ لَكُمْ فِى الْاَنْعَامِ لَعِبْرَةً ؕ نُسْقِيْكُمْ مِّمَّا فِىْ بُطُوْنِهٖ
مِنْۢ بَيْنِ فَرْثٍ وَّدَمٍ لَّبَنًا خَالِصًا سَآئِغًا لِّلشّٰرِبِيْنَ ﴿٦٧﴾

68. And of the fruits of the date-palms and the grapes, whence you obtain intoxicating drink and wholesome food. Verily, in that is a Sign for a people who make use of their reason.

وَمِنْ ثَمَرٰتِ النَّخِيْلِ وَالْاَعْنَابِ تَتَّخِذُوْنَ مِنْهُ
سَكَرًا وَّرِزْقًا حَسَنًا ؕ اِنَّ فِىْ ذٰلِكَ لَاٰيَةً لِّقَوْمٍ يَّعْقِلُوْنَ ﴿٦٨﴾

69. And thy Lord has inspired the bee, *saying*, 'Make thou houses in the hills and in the trees and in the trellises which they build.

وَاَوْحٰى رَبُّكَ اِلَى النَّحْلِ اَنِ اتَّخِذِىْ مِنَ الْجِبَالِ بُيُوْتًا
وَّمِنَ الشَّجَرِ وَمِمَّا يَعْرِشُوْنَ ﴿٦٩﴾

* 70. 'Then eat of every *kind of* fruit, and follow the ways of thy Lord *that have been* made easy *for thee*.' There comes forth from their bellies a drink of varying hues. Therein is cure for men. Surely, in that is a Sign for a people who reflect.

ثُمَّ كُلِىْ مِنْ كُلِّ الثَّمَرٰتِ فَاسْلُكِىْ سُبُلَ رَبِّكِ ذُلُلًا ؕ
يَخْرُجُ مِنْۢ بُطُوْنِهَا شَرَابٌ مُّخْتَلِفٌ اَلْوَانُهٗ فِيْهِ شِفَآءٌ
لِّلنَّاسِ ؕ اِنَّ فِىْ ذٰلِكَ لَاٰيَةً لِّقَوْمٍ يَّتَفَكَّرُوْنَ ﴿٧٠﴾

* 71. And Allah creates you, then He causes you to die; and there are *some* among you who are driven to the worst part of life, with the result that they know

وَاللّٰهُ خَلَقَكُمْ ثُمَّ يَتَوَفّٰىكُمْ ۙ وَمِنْكُمْ مَّنْ يُّرَدُّ اِلٰٓى
اَرْذَلِ الْعُمُرِ لِكَىْ لَا يَعْلَمَ بَعْدَ عِلْمٍ شَيْـًٔا ؕ اِنَّ اللّٰهَ عَلِيْمٌ

nothing after *having had* knowledge. Surely, Allah is All-Knowing, Powerful.

قَدِيْرٌ ﴿٧١﴾ ٩ ع ٥ ١٥

R. 10.

72. And Allah has favoured some of you above others in *worldly* gifts. But those more favoured will not restore *any part of* their *worldly* gifts to those whom their right hands possess, so that they may be equal *sharers* in them. Will they then deny the favour of Allah?

وَاللّٰهُ فَضَّلَ بَعْضَكُمْ عَلٰى بَعْضٍ فِي الرِّزْقِ ۚ فَمَا
الَّذِيْنَ فُضِّلُوْا بِرَآدِّيْ رِزْقِهِمْ عَلٰى مَا مَلَكَتْ اَيْمَانُهُمْ
فَهُمْ فِيْهِ سَوَآءٌ ۭ اَفَبِنِعْمَةِ اللّٰهِ يَجْحَدُوْنَ ﴿٧٢﴾

73. And Allah has made for you mates from among yourselves, and has made for you, from your mates, sons and grandsons, and has provided you with good things. Will they then believe in vain things and deny the favour of Allah?

وَاللّٰهُ جَعَلَ لَكُمْ مِّنْ اَنْفُسِكُمْ اَزْوَاجًا وَّجَعَلَ لَكُمْ
مِّنْ اَزْوَاجِكُمْ بَنِيْنَ وَحَفَدَةً وَّرَزَقَكُمْ مِّنَ الطَّيِّبٰتِ ۭ
اَفَبِالْبَاطِلِ يُؤْمِنُوْنَ وَبِنِعْمَتِ اللّٰهِ هُمْ يَكْفُرُوْنَ ﴿٧٣﴾

74. And they worship beside Allah such as have no power to bestow on them any gift from the heavens or the earth, nor can they *ever* have such power.

وَيَعْبُدُوْنَ مِنْ دُوْنِ اللّٰهِ مَا لَا يَمْلِكُ لَهُمْ رِزْقًا
مِّنَ السَّمٰوٰتِ وَالْاَرْضِ شَيْـًٔا وَّلَا يَسْتَطِيْعُوْنَ ﴿٧٤﴾

75. So coin not similitudes for Allah. Surely, Allah knows and you know not.

فَلَا تَضْرِبُوْا لِلّٰهِ الْاَمْثَالَ ۭ اِنَّ اللّٰهَ يَعْلَمُ وَاَنْتُمْ لَا
تَعْلَمُوْنَ ﴿٧٥﴾

76. Allah sets forth the parable of a slave who is owned, having no power over anything; and *a free man* whom We have provided with a fair provision from Ourself, and he spends thereof secretly and openly. Are they equal? Praise be to Allah! But most of them know not.

ضَرَبَ اللّٰهُ مَثَلًا عَبْدًا مَّمْلُوْكًا لَّا يَقْدِرُ عَلٰى شَيْءٍ
وَّمَنْ رَّزَقْنٰهُ مِنَّا رِزْقًا حَسَنًا فَهُوَ يُنْفِقُ مِنْهُ سِرًّا
وَّجَهْرًا ۭ هَلْ يَسْتَوٗنَ ۭ اَلْحَمْدُ لِلّٰهِ ۭ بَلْ اَكْثَرُهُمْ لَا
يَعْلَمُوْنَ ﴿٧٦﴾

77. And Allah sets forth *another* parable of two men: one of them is dumb, having no power over anything, and he is a burden to his master; whithersoever he sends him, he brings no good. Can he be equal to him who enjoins justice and who is himself on the straight path?

وَضَرَبَ اللّٰهُ مَثَلًا رَّجُلَيْنِ اَحَدُهُمَآ اَبْكَمُ لَا يَقْدِرُ
عَلٰى شَيْءٍ وَّهُوَ كَلٌّ عَلٰى مَوْلٰىهُ ۙ اَيْنَمَا يُوَجِّهْهُّ لَا يَاْتِ
بِخَيْرٍ ۭ هَلْ يَسْتَوِيْ هُوَ ۙ وَمَنْ يَّاْمُرُ بِالْعَدْلِ ۙ وَهُوَ
عَلٰى صِرَاطٍ مُّسْتَقِيْمٍ ﴿٧٧﴾ ١٠ ع ٦ ١٦

R. 11.

78. And to Allah belongs the unseen of the heavens and the earth; and the matter of the Hour is but as the twinkling of an eye, nay, it is nearer still. Surely, Allah has power over all things.

وَلِلّٰهِ غَيْبُ السَّمٰوٰتِ وَالْاَرْضِ ۭ وَمَآ اَمْرُ السَّاعَةِ
اِلَّا كَلَمْحِ الْبَصَرِ اَوْ هُوَ اَقْرَبُ ۭ اِنَّ اللّٰهَ عَلٰى كُلِّ شَيْءٍ
قَدِيْرٌ ﴿٧٨﴾

79. And Allah brought you forth from the wombs of your mothers while you knew nothing, and gave you ears and eyes and hearts, that you might be grateful.

وَاللّٰهُ اَخْرَجَكُمْ مِّنْۢ بُطُوْنِ اُمَّهٰتِكُمْ لَا تَعْلَمُوْنَ شَيْـًٔا
وَّجَعَلَ لَكُمُ السَّمْعَ وَالْاَبْصَارَ وَالْاَفْـِٕدَةَ لَعَلَّكُمْ
تَشْكُرُوْنَ ﴿۷۹﴾

* 80. Do they not see the birds held under subjection in the vault of heaven? None keeps them back save Allah. Verily, in that are Signs for a people who believe.

اَلَمْ يَرَوْا اِلَى الطَّيْرِ مُسَخَّرٰتٍ فِيْ جَوِّ السَّمَآءِ ؕ مَا
يُمْسِكُهُنَّ اِلَّا اللّٰهُ ؕ اِنَّ فِيْ ذٰلِكَ لَاٰيٰتٍ لِّقَوْمٍ يُّؤْمِنُوْنَ ﴿۸۰﴾

81. And Allah has made your homes, a place of rest for you and has made for you, of the skins of cattle, abodes which you find light at the time when you travel and at the time when you halt; and of their wool, and their furs, and their hair, *He has supplied you with* household goods and articles of use for a time.

وَاللّٰهُ جَعَلَ لَكُمْ مِّنْۢ بُيُوْتِكُمْ سَكَنًا وَّجَعَلَ لَكُمْ مِّنْ
جُلُوْدِ الْاَنْعَامِ بُيُوْتًا تَسْتَخِفُّوْنَهَا يَوْمَ ظَعْنِكُمْ وَيَوْمَ
اِقَامَتِكُمْ ۙ وَمِنْ اَصْوَافِهَا وَاَوْبَارِهَا وَاَشْعَارِهَاۤ
اَثَاثًا وَّمَتَاعًا اِلٰى حِيْنٍ ﴿۸۱﴾

82. And Allah has made for you, of that which He has created, *things affording* shade; and He has made for you, in the mountains, places of shelter; and He has made for you garments which protect you from heat, and coats of mail which protect you in your wars. Thus does He complete His favour on you, that you may submit *to Him*.

وَاللّٰهُ جَعَلَ لَكُمْ مِّمَّا خَلَقَ ظِلٰلًا وَّجَعَلَ لَكُمْ مِّنَ
الْجِبَالِ اَكْنَانًا وَّجَعَلَ لَكُمْ سَرَابِيْلَ تَقِيْكُمُ الْحَرَّ
وَسَرَابِيْلَ تَقِيْكُمْ بَاْسَكُمْ ؕ كَذٰلِكَ يُتِمُّ نِعْمَتَهٗ عَلَيْكُمْ
لَعَلَّكُمْ تُسْلِمُوْنَ ﴿۸۲﴾

83. But if they turn away, then thou art responsible only for the plain delivery of the Message.

فَاِنْ تَوَلَّوْا فَاِنَّمَا عَلَيْكَ الْبَلٰغُ الْمُبِيْنُ ﴿۸۳﴾

* 84. They recognize the favour of Allah, yet they deny it; and most of them are *confirmed* disbelievers.

يَعْرِفُوْنَ نِعْمَتَ اللّٰهِ ثُمَّ يُنْكِرُوْنَهَا وَاَكْثَرُهُمُ
ع الْكٰفِرُوْنَ ﴿۸۴﴾

R. 12.

* 85. And *remember* the day when We shall raise up a witness from every people, then those who disbelieve shall not be permitted *to make amends*, nor shall they be allowed to solicit *God's* favour.

وَيَوْمَ نَبْعَثُ مِنْ كُلِّ اُمَّةٍ شَهِيْدًا ثُمَّ لَا يُؤْذَنُ
لِلَّذِيْنَ كَفَرُوْا وَلَا هُمْ يُسْتَعْتَبُوْنَ ﴿۸۵﴾

86. And when those who did wrong *actually* see the punishment, it will not be made light for them, nor will they be granted respite.

وَاِذَا رَاَ الَّذِيْنَ ظَلَمُوا الْعَذَابَ فَلَا يُخَفَّفُ عَنْهُمْ
وَلَا هُمْ يُنْظَرُوْنَ ﴿۸۶﴾

87. And when those who associate partners *with God* will see their associate-gods, they will say, 'Our Lord, these are our associate-gods whom we used to call

وَاِذَا رَاَ الَّذِيْنَ اَشْرَكُوْا شُرَكَآءَهُمْ قَالُوْا رَبَّنَا
هٰٓؤُلَآءِ شُرَكَآؤُنَا الَّذِيْنَ كُنَّا نَدْعُوْا مِنْ دُوْنِكَ ۚ

upon instead of Thee.' Thereupon, they will retort on them with the words, 'Surely, you are liars.'

88. And they will offer submission to Allah on that day, and all that they used to forge shall fail them.

89. *As for* those who disbelieve and turn *men* away from the way of Allah, We will add punishment to *their* punishment because they acted corruptly.

90. And *remember* the day when We will raise up in every people a witness against them from amongst themselves, and We will bring thee as a witness against these. And We have sent down to thee the Book to explain everything, and a guidance, and a mercy, and glad tidings to those who submit *to God*.

R. 13.

* 91. Verily, Allah enjoins justice, and the doing of good to others; and giving like kindred; and forbids indecency, and manifest evil, and wrongful transgression. He admonishes you that you may take heed.

92. And fulfil the covenant of Allah when you have made; and break not the oaths after making them firm, while you have made Allah your surety. Certainly, Allah knows what you do.

93. And be not like unto her who, after having made it strong, breaks her yarn into pieces. You make your oaths a means of deceit between you, *for fear* lest one people become more powerful than another. Surely, Allah tries you therewith, and on the Day of Resurrection He will make clear to you that wherein you differed.

94. And if Allah had *enforced* His will, He would surely have made you *all* one people; but He lets go astray him who wishes *it*, and guides him who wishes *it;* and you shall surely be questioned concerning that which you have been doing.

95. And make not your oaths a means of deceit between you; or *your* foot will

فَأَلْقَوْا إِلَيْهِمُ الْقَوْلَ إِنَّكُمْ لَكٰذِبُوْنَ ﴿٨٧﴾
وَأَلْقَوْا إِلَى اللّٰهِ يَوْمَئِذِ السَّلَمَ وَضَلَّ عَنْهُمْ مَّا كَانُوْا
يَفْتَرُوْنَ ﴿٨٨﴾
اَلَّذِيْنَ كَفَرُوْا وَصَدُّوْا عَنْ سَبِيْلِ اللّٰهِ زِدْنٰهُمْ
عَذَابًا فَوْقَ الْعَذَابِ بِمَا كَانُوْا يُفْسِدُوْنَ ﴿٨٩﴾
وَيَوْمَ نَبْعَثُ فِيْ كُلِّ اُمَّةٍ شَهِيْدًا عَلَيْهِمْ مِّنْ اَنْفُسِهِمْ
وَجِئْنَا بِكَ شَهِيْدًا عَلٰى هٰٓؤُلَآءِ ۗ وَنَزَّلْنَا عَلَيْكَ الْكِتٰبَ
تِبْيَانًا لِّكُلِّ شَيْءٍ وَّهُدًى وَّرَحْمَةً وَّبُشْرٰى لِلْمُسْلِمِيْنَ ﴿٩٠﴾
اِنَّ اللّٰهَ يَاْمُرُ بِالْعَدْلِ وَالْاِحْسَانِ وَاِيْتَآئِ ذِي
الْقُرْبٰى وَيَنْهٰى عَنِ الْفَحْشَآءِ وَالْمُنْكَرِ وَالْبَغْيِ ۚ
يَعِظُكُمْ لَعَلَّكُمْ تَذَكَّرُوْنَ ﴿٩١﴾
وَاَوْفُوْا بِعَهْدِ اللّٰهِ اِذَا عٰهَدْتُّمْ وَلَا تَنْقُضُوا الْاَيْمَانَ
بَعْدَ تَوْكِيْدِهَا وَقَدْ جَعَلْتُمُ اللّٰهَ عَلَيْكُمْ كَفِيْلًا ۗ
اِنَّ اللّٰهَ يَعْلَمُ مَا تَفْعَلُوْنَ ﴿٩٢﴾
وَلَا تَكُوْنُوْا كَالَّتِيْ نَقَضَتْ غَزْلَهَا مِنْ بَعْدِ قُوَّةٍ
اَنْكَاثًا ۗ تَتَّخِذُوْنَ اَيْمَانَكُمْ دَخَلًا بَيْنَكُمْ اَنْ تَكُوْنَ
اُمَّةٌ هِيَ اَرْبٰى مِنْ اُمَّةٍ ۗ اِنَّمَا يَبْلُوْكُمُ اللّٰهُ بِهٖ ۗ وَلَيُبَيِّنَنَّ
لَكُمْ يَوْمَ الْقِيٰمَةِ مَا كُنْتُمْ فِيْهِ تَخْتَلِفُوْنَ ﴿٩٣﴾
وَلَوْ شَآءَ اللّٰهُ لَجَعَلَكُمْ اُمَّةً وَّاحِدَةً وَّلٰكِنْ يُّضِلُّ
مَنْ يَّشَآءُ وَيَهْدِيْ مَنْ يَّشَآءُ ۗ وَلَتُسْئَلُنَّ عَمَّا
كُنْتُمْ تَعْمَلُوْنَ ﴿٩٤﴾
وَلَا تَتَّخِذُوْٓا اَيْمَانَكُمْ دَخَلًا بَيْنَكُمْ فَتَزِلَّ قَدَمٌ

slip after it has been firmly established, and you will taste evil because you turned *people* away from the path of Allah, and you will have a severe punishment.

بَعْدَ ثُبُوْتِهَا وَتَذُوْقُوا السُّوْٓءَ بِمَا صَدَدْتُّمْ عَنْ
سَبِيْلِ اللّٰهِ ۚ وَلَكُمْ عَذَابٌ عَظِيْمٌ ﴿۹۵﴾

96. And barter not the covenant of Allah for a paltry price. Surely, that which is with Allah is better for you if you only knew.

وَلَا تَشْتَرُوْا بِعَهْدِ اللّٰهِ ثَمَنًا قَلِيْلًا ۭ اِنَّمَا عِنْدَ اللّٰهِ
هُوَ خَيْرٌ لَّكُمْ اِنْ كُنْتُمْ تَعْلَمُوْنَ ﴿۹۶﴾

* 97. That which you have shall pass away, but that which is with Allah is lasting. And We will certainly give those who are steadfast their reward according to the best of their works.

مَا عِنْدَكُمْ يَنْفَدُ وَمَا عِنْدَ اللّٰهِ بَاقٍ ۭ وَلَنَجْزِيَنَّ
الَّذِيْنَ صَبَرُوْٓا اَجْرَهُمْ بِاَحْسَنِ مَا كَانُوْا
يَعْمَلُوْنَ ﴿۹۷﴾

98. Whoso acts righteously, whether male or female, and is a believer, We will surely grant him a pure life; and We will surely bestow on such their reward according to the best of their works.

مَنْ عَمِلَ صَالِحًا مِّنْ ذَكَرٍ اَوْ اُنْثٰى وَهُوَ مُؤْمِنٌ
فَلَنُحْيِيَنَّهٗ حَيٰوةً طَيِّبَةً ۚ وَلَنَجْزِيَنَّهُمْ اَجْرَهُمْ
بِاَحْسَنِ مَا كَانُوْا يَعْمَلُوْنَ ﴿۹۸﴾

99. And when thou recitest the Qur'ān, seek refuge with Allah from Satan the rejected.

فَاِذَا قَرَاْتَ الْقُرْاٰنَ فَاسْتَعِذْ بِاللّٰهِ مِنَ الشَّيْطٰنِ
الرَّجِيْمِ ﴿۹۹﴾

100. Surely, he has no power over those who believe and who put their trust in their Lord.

اِنَّهٗ لَيْسَ لَهٗ سُلْطٰنٌ عَلَى الَّذِيْنَ اٰمَنُوْا وَعَلٰى رَبِّهِمْ
يَتَوَكَّلُوْنَ ﴿۱۰۰﴾

101. His power is only over those who make friends with him and who set up equals to Him.

اِنَّمَا سُلْطٰنُهٗ عَلَى الَّذِيْنَ يَتَوَلَّوْنَهٗ وَالَّذِيْنَ هُمْ بِهٖ
مُشْرِكُوْنَ ﴿۱۰۱﴾ ع

R. 14.

102. And when We bring one Sign in place of another—and Allah knows best what He reveals—they say, 'Thou art but a fabricator.' Nay, but most of them know not.

وَاِذَا بَدَّلْنَآ اٰيَةً مَّكَانَ اٰيَةٍ ۙ وَّاللّٰهُ اَعْلَمُ بِمَا
يُنَزِّلُ قَالُوْٓا اِنَّمَآ اَنْتَ مُفْتَرٍ ۭ بَلْ اَكْثَرُهُمْ
لَا يَعْلَمُوْنَ ﴿۱۰۲﴾

103. Say, 'The Spirit of holiness has brought it down from thy Lord with truth, that He may strengthen those who believe, and as a guidance and glad tidings for Muslims.'

قُلْ نَزَّلَهٗ رُوْحُ الْقُدُسِ مِنْ رَّبِّكَ بِالْحَقِّ لِيُثَبِّتَ
الَّذِيْنَ اٰمَنُوْا وَهُدًى وَّبُشْرٰى لِلْمُسْلِمِيْنَ ﴿۱۰۳﴾

104. And indeed We know that they say that it is only a man who teaches him.

وَلَقَدْ نَعْلَمُ اَنَّهُمْ يَقُوْلُوْنَ اِنَّمَا يُعَلِّمُهٗ بَشَرٌ

But the tongue of him to whom they *unjustly* incline *in making this insinuation* is foreign, while this is Arabic tongue, plain and clear.	لِسَانُ الَّذِي يُلْحِدُونَ إِلَيْهِ أَعْجَمِيٌّ وَهَٰذَا لِسَانٌ عَرَبِيٌّ مُّبِينٌ ﴿١٠٤﴾
105. *As for* those who do not believe in the Signs of Allah, surely, Allah will not guide them, and they shall have a grievous punishment.	إِنَّ الَّذِينَ لَا يُؤْمِنُونَ بِآيَاتِ اللَّهِ لَا يَهْدِيهِمُ اللَّهُ وَلَهُمْ عَذَابٌ أَلِيمٌ ﴿١٠٥﴾
106. It is only those who believe not in the Signs of Allah, that forge falsehood, and they it is who are the liars.	إِنَّمَا يَفْتَرِي الْكَذِبَ الَّذِينَ لَا يُؤْمِنُونَ بِآيَاتِ اللَّهِ وَأُولَٰئِكَ هُمُ الْكَاذِبُونَ ﴿١٠٦﴾
* 107. Whoso disbelieves in Allah after he has believed—save him who is forced *thereto* while his heart finds peace in the faith—but such as open their breasts to disbelief, on them is Allah's wrath; and they shall have a severe punishment.	مَن كَفَرَ بِاللَّهِ مِن بَعْدِ إِيمَانِهِ إِلَّا مَنْ أُكْرِهَ وَقَلْبُهُ مُطْمَئِنٌّ بِالْإِيمَانِ وَلَٰكِن مَّن شَرَحَ بِالْكُفْرِ صَدْرًا فَعَلَيْهِمْ غَضَبٌ مِّنَ اللَّهِ وَلَهُمْ عَذَابٌ عَظِيمٌ ﴿١٠٧﴾
108. That is because they have preferred the present life to the Hereafter, and because Allah guides not the disbelieving people.	ذَٰلِكَ بِأَنَّهُمُ اسْتَحَبُّوا الْحَيَاةَ الدُّنْيَا عَلَى الْآخِرَةِ وَأَنَّ اللَّهَ لَا يَهْدِي الْقَوْمَ الْكَافِرِينَ ﴿١٠٨﴾
109. It is they on whose hearts and ears and eyes Allah has set a seal. And it is they who are the heedless.	أُولَٰئِكَ الَّذِينَ طَبَعَ اللَّهُ عَلَىٰ قُلُوبِهِمْ وَسَمْعِهِمْ وَأَبْصَارِهِمْ وَأُولَٰئِكَ هُمُ الْغَافِلُونَ ﴿١٠٩﴾
110. Undoubtedly, it is they who will be the losers in the Hereafter.	لَا جَرَمَ أَنَّهُمْ فِي الْآخِرَةِ هُمُ الْخَاسِرُونَ ﴿١١٠﴾
111. Then, surely, thy Lord—to those who fled *their homes* after they had been persecuted and then struggled hard *in the cause of Allah* and remained steadfast—*aye*, surely, after that thy Lord is Most Forgiving, Merciful.	ثُمَّ إِنَّ رَبَّكَ لِلَّذِينَ هَاجَرُوا مِن بَعْدِ مَا فُتِنُوا ثُمَّ جَاهَدُوا وَصَبَرُوا إِنَّ رَبَّكَ مِن بَعْدِهَا لَغَفُورٌ رَّحِيمٌ ﴿١١١﴾ ع
R. 15.	
112. On the day when every soul will come pleading for itself, and every soul will be fully recompensed for what it did, and they will not be wronged.	يَوْمَ تَأْتِي كُلُّ نَفْسٍ تُجَادِلُ عَن نَّفْسِهَا وَتُوَفَّىٰ كُلُّ نَفْسٍ مَّا عَمِلَتْ وَهُمْ لَا يُظْلَمُونَ ﴿١١٢﴾
* 113. And Allah sets forth *for you* the parable of a city which enjoyed security and peace; its provisions came to it in plenty from every quarter; but it denied the favours of Allah, so Allah made it taste hunger and fear *which clothed it like*	وَضَرَبَ اللَّهُ مَثَلًا قَرْيَةً كَانَتْ آمِنَةً مُّطْمَئِنَّةً يَأْتِيهَا رِزْقُهَا رَغَدًا مِّن كُلِّ مَكَانٍ فَكَفَرَتْ بِأَنْعُمِ اللَّهِ فَأَذَاقَهَا اللَّهُ لِبَاسَ الْجُوعِ وَالْخَوْفِ

a garment because of what they used to do.

بِمَا كَانُوا يَصْنَعُونَ ﴿١١٣﴾

114. And indeed there has come to them a Messenger from among themselves, but they treated him as a liar, so punishment overtook them while they were wrongdoers.

وَلَقَدْ جَآءَهُمْ رَسُولٌ مِّنْهُمْ فَكَذَّبُوهُ فَأَخَذَهُمُ
الْعَذَابُ وَهُمْ ظٰلِمُونَ ﴿١١٤﴾

115. So eat of the lawful *and* good things which Allah has provided for you; and be grateful for the bounty of Allah, if it is Him you worship.

فَكُلُوا مِمَّا رَزَقَكُمُ اللّٰهُ حَلٰلًا طَيِّبًا وَّاشْكُرُوا
نِعْمَتَ اللّٰهِ إِنْ كُنْتُمْ إِيَّاهُ تَعْبُدُونَ ﴿١١٥﴾

* 116. He has made unlawful for you only that which dies of itself and blood and the flesh of swine and that on which the name of any other than Allah has been invoked. But he who is driven by necessity, being neither disobedient nor exceeding the limit, then surely, Allah is Most Forgiving, Merciful.

إِنَّمَا حَرَّمَ عَلَيْكُمُ الْمَيْتَةَ وَالدَّمَ وَلَحْمَ الْخِنْزِيرِ
وَمَآ أُهِلَّ لِغَيْرِ اللّٰهِ بِهٖ فَمَنِ اضْطُرَّ غَيْرَ بَاغٍ وَّ
لَا عَادٍ فَإِنَّ اللّٰهَ غَفُورٌ رَّحِيمٌ ﴿١١٦﴾

117. And say not—because of the falsehood which your tongues utter—'This is lawful, and this is unlawful,' so as to forge a lie against Allah. Surely, those who forge a lie against Allah do not prosper.

وَلَا تَقُولُوا لِمَا تَصِفُ أَلْسِنَتُكُمُ الْكَذِبَ هٰذَا
حَلٰلٌ وَّهٰذَا حَرَامٌ لِّتَفْتَرُوا عَلَى اللّٰهِ الْكَذِبَ
إِنَّ الَّذِينَ يَفْتَرُونَ عَلَى اللّٰهِ الْكَذِبَ لَا يُفْلِحُونَ ﴿١١٧﴾

* 118. *It is* a brief enjoyment, and *then* they shall have a grievous punishment.

مَتَاعٌ قَلِيلٌ وَّلَهُمْ عَذَابٌ أَلِيمٌ ﴿١١٨﴾

119. And to those *also* who are Jews, We forbade before *this* all that We have related to thee. And We wronged them not, but they used to wrong themselves.

وَعَلَى الَّذِينَ هَادُوا حَرَّمْنَا مَا قَصَصْنَا عَلَيْكَ
مِنْ قَبْلُ وَمَا ظَلَمْنٰهُمْ وَلٰكِنْ كَانُوٓا أَنْفُسَهُمْ
يَظْلِمُونَ ﴿١١٩﴾

120. Then surely, thy Lord—to those who do evil in ignorance and repent thereafter and make amends—*aye*, surely, after that thy Lord is Most Forgiving, Merciful.

ثُمَّ إِنَّ رَبَّكَ لِلَّذِينَ عَمِلُوا السُّوٓءَ بِجَهَالَةٍ ثُمَّ
تَابُوا مِنْ بَعْدِ ذٰلِكَ وَأَصْلَحُوٓا إِنَّ رَبَّكَ مِنْ بَعْدِهَا
لَغَفُورٌ رَّحِيمٌ ﴿١٢٠﴾

R. 16.

* 121. Abraham was indeed a paragon of virtue, obedient to Allah, ever inclined *to Him*, and he was not of those who set up equals *to God;*

إِنَّ إِبْرٰهِيمَ كَانَ أُمَّةً قَانِتًا لِّلّٰهِ حَنِيفًا وَلَمْ يَكُ
مِنَ الْمُشْرِكِينَ ﴿١٢١﴾

* 122. Grateful for His favours; He chose him and guided him to a straight path.

شَاكِرًا لِّأَنْعُمِهٖ اجْتَبٰهُ وَهَدٰهُ إِلٰى صِرَاطٍ
مُّسْتَقِيمٍ ﴿١٢٢﴾

123. And We bestowed on him good in this world, and in the Hereafter he will surely be among the righteous.

وَ اٰتَيْنٰهُ فِي الدُّنْيَا حَسَنَةً ۭ وَاِنَّهٗ فِي الْاٰخِرَةِ لَمِنَ
الصّٰلِحِيْنَ ﴿۱۲۳﴾

124. And *now* We have revealed to thee, *saying*, 'Follow the way of Abraham *who was* ever inclined *to God* and was not of those who set up equals *to Him*.'

ثُمَّ اَوْحَيْنَآ اِلَيْكَ اَنِ اتَّبِعْ مِلَّةَ اِبْرٰهِيْمَ حَنِيْفًا ۭ
وَمَا كَانَ مِنَ الْمُشْرِكِيْنَ ﴿۱۲۴﴾

* 125. The *punishment for profaning the* Sabbath was imposed only on those who had differed about it, and thy Lord will surely judge between them on the Day of Resurrection about that in which they differed.

اِنَّمَا جُعِلَ السَّبْتُ عَلَى الَّذِيْنَ اخْتَلَفُوْا فِيْهِ ۭ وَاِنَّ
رَبَّكَ لَيَحْكُمُ بَيْنَهُمْ يَوْمَ الْقِيٰمَةِ فِيْمَا كَانُوْا فِيْهِ
يَخْتَلِفُوْنَ ﴿۱۲۵﴾

126. Call unto the way of thy Lord with wisdom and goodly exhortation, and argue with them in a way that is best. Surely, thy Lord knows best who has strayed from His way; and He knows those who are rightly guided.

اُدْعُ اِلٰى سَبِيْلِ رَبِّكَ بِالْحِكْمَةِ وَالْمَوْعِظَةِ الْحَسَنَةِ
وَجَادِلْهُمْ بِالَّتِيْ هِيَ اَحْسَنُ ۭ اِنَّ رَبَّكَ هُوَ اَعْلَمُ
بِمَنْ ضَلَّ عَنْ سَبِيْلِهٖ وَهُوَ اَعْلَمُ بِالْمُهْتَدِيْنَ ﴿۱۲۶﴾

127. And if you *desire to* punish *the oppressors*, then punish *them* to the extent to which you have been wronged; but if you show patience, then, surely, that is best for those who are patient.

وَاِنْ عَاقَبْتُمْ فَعَاقِبُوْا بِمِثْلِ مَا عُوْقِبْتُمْ بِهٖ ۭ
وَلَىِٕنْ صَبَرْتُمْ لَهُوَ خَيْرٌ لِّلصّٰبِرِيْنَ ﴿۱۲۷﴾

128. And endure thou with patience; and verily, thy patience is *possible* only with *the help of* Allah. And grieve not for them, nor feel distressed because of their plots.

وَاصْبِرْ وَمَا صَبْرُكَ اِلَّا بِاللّٰهِ وَلَا تَحْزَنْ عَلَيْهِمْ
وَلَا تَكُ فِيْ ضَيْقٍ مِّمَّا يَمْكُرُوْنَ ﴿۱۲۸﴾

129. Verily, Allah is with those who are righteous and those who do good.

اِنَّ اللّٰهَ مَعَ الَّذِيْنَ اتَّقَوْا وَّالَّذِيْنَ هُمْ
مُّحْسِنُوْنَ ﴿۱۲۹﴾ ع ١٦ ٢٢

آیاتها ۱۱۲ (۱۷) سُوْرَةُ بَنِيْۤ اِسْرَآءِيْلَ مَكِّيَّةٌ رکوعاتها ۱۲

BANĪ ISRĀ'ĪL

(Revealed before Hijra)

1. In the name of Allah, the Gracious, the Merciful.

* 2. Glory be to Him Who carried His servant by night from the Sacred Mosque to the Distant Mosque, the environs of which We have blessed, that We might show him *some* of Our Signs. Surely, He alone is the Hearing, the Seeing.

3. And We gave Moses the Book, and We made it a guidance for the children of Israel, *saying,* 'Take no guardian beside Me,

4. 'O ye the progeny of those whom We carried *in the Ark* with Noah.' He was indeed a grateful servant.

5. And We revealed to the children of Israel in the Book, *saying,* 'You will surely do mischief in the land twice, and you will surely become excessively overbearing.'

* 6. So when the time for the first of the two warnings came, We sent against you *some* servants of Ours possessed of great might in war, and they penetrated the *innermost parts of your* houses, and it was a warning that was bound to be carried out.

7. Then We gave you back the power against them, and aided you with wealth and children, and made you larger in numbers.

* 8. *Now,* if you do well, you will do well for your own souls; and if you do evil, it will *only go* against them. So when the time for the latter warning came, *We raised a people against you* to cover your faces with grief, and to enter the Mosque as they entered it the first time, and to destroy all that they conquered with utter destruction.

9. It may be that your Lord will *now* have mercy on you; but if you return *to*

المنزل ۴ الجزء ۱۵

بِسْمِ اللّٰهِ الرَّحْمٰنِ الرَّحِيْمِ ①

سُبْحٰنَ الَّذِيْۤ اَسْرٰى بِعَبْدِهٖ لَيْلًا مِّنَ الْمَسْجِدِ
الْحَرَامِ اِلَى الْمَسْجِدِ الْاَقْصَا الَّذِيْ بٰرَكْنَا حَوْلَهٗ
لِنُرِيَهٗ مِنْ اٰيٰتِنَا ؕ اِنَّهٗ هُوَ السَّمِيْعُ الْبَصِيْرُ ②
وَ اٰتَيْنَا مُوْسَى الْكِتٰبَ وَ جَعَلْنٰهُ هُدًى لِّبَنِيْۤ
اِسْرَآءِيْلَ اَلَّا تَتَّخِذُوْا مِنْ دُوْنِيْ وَكِيْلًا ؕ ③
ذُرِّيَّةَ مَنْ حَمَلْنَا مَعَ نُوْحٍ ؕ اِنَّهٗ كَانَ عَبْدًا شَكُوْرًا ④
وَ قَضَيْنَاۤ اِلٰى بَنِيْۤ اِسْرَآءِيْلَ فِي الْكِتٰبِ لَتُفْسِدُنَّ
فِي الْاَرْضِ مَرَّتَيْنِ وَ لَتَعْلُنَّ عُلُوًّا كَبِيْرًا ⑤
فَاِذَا جَآءَ وَعْدُ اُوْلٰىهُمَا بَعَثْنَا عَلَيْكُمْ عِبَادًا لَّنَاۤ
اُولِيْ بَاْسٍ شَدِيْدٍ فَجَاسُوْا خِلٰلَ الدِّيَارِ ؕ وَ كَانَ وَعْدًا
مَّفْعُوْلًا ⑥
ثُمَّ رَدَدْنَا لَكُمُ الْكَرَّةَ عَلَيْهِمْ وَ اَمْدَدْنٰكُمْ بِاَمْوَالٍ
وَّ بَنِيْنَ وَ جَعَلْنٰكُمْ اَكْثَرَ نَفِيْرًا ⑦
اِنْ اَحْسَنْتُمْ اَحْسَنْتُمْ لِاَنْفُسِكُمْ ۟ وَ اِنْ اَسَاْتُمْ فَلَهَا ؕ
فَاِذَا جَآءَ وَعْدُ الْاٰخِرَةِ لِيَسُوْٓءٗا وُجُوْهَكُمْ وَ لِيَدْخُلُوا
الْمَسْجِدَ كَمَا دَخَلُوْهُ اَوَّلَ مَرَّةٍ وَّ لِيُتَبِّرُوْا مَا عَلَوْا
تَتْبِيْرًا ⑧
لازم عَسٰى رَبُّكُمْ اَنْ يَّرْحَمَكُمْ ۚ وَ اِنْ عُدْتُّمْ عُدْنَا ۘ وَ جَعَلْنَا

your previous state, We *too* will return, and We have made Hell a prison for the disbelievers.

جَهَنَّمَ لِلْكٰفِرِيْنَ حَصِيْرًا ۝٩

10. Surely, this Qur'ān guides to what is most right; and gives to the believers who do good deeds the glad tidings that they shall have a great reward.

إِنَّ هٰذَا الْقُرْاٰنَ يَهْدِيْ لِلَّتِيْ هِيَ أَقْوَمُ وَيُبَشِّرُ
الْمُؤْمِنِيْنَ الَّذِيْنَ يَعْمَلُوْنَ الصّٰلِحٰتِ أَنَّ لَهُمْ
أَجْرًا كَبِيْرًا ۝١٠

11. And that for those who do not believe in what is to come later We have prepared a grievous punishment.

وَّأَنَّ الَّذِيْنَ لَا يُؤْمِنُوْنَ بِالْاٰخِرَةِ أَعْتَدْنَا لَهُمْ عَذَابًا
أَلِيْمًا ۝١١ ع

R. 2.

* 12. And man asks for evil as he should ask for good; and man is hasty.

وَيَدْعُ الْإِنْسَانُ بِالشَّرِّ دُعَآءَهٗ بِالْخَيْرِ ۗ وَكَانَ الْإِنْسَانُ
عَجُوْلًا ۝١٢

* 13. And We have made the night and the day two Signs, and the Sign of night We have made dark, and the Sign of day We have made sight-giving, that you may seek bounty from your Lord, and that you may know the computation of years and *the science of* reckoning. And everything We have explained with a detailed explanation.

وَجَعَلْنَا الَّيْلَ وَالنَّهَارَ اٰيَتَيْنِ فَمَحَوْنَآ اٰيَةَ الَّيْلِ
وَجَعَلْنَآ اٰيَةَ النَّهَارِ مُبْصِرَةً لِّتَبْتَغُوْا فَضْلًا مِّنْ
رَّبِّكُمْ وَلِتَعْلَمُوْا عَدَدَ السِّنِيْنَ وَالْحِسَابَ ۭ وَكُلَّ
شَيْءٍ فَصَّلْنٰهُ تَفْصِيْلًا ۝١٣

* 14. And every man's works have We fastened to his neck; and on the Day of Resurrection We shall bring out for him a book which he will find wide open.

وَكُلَّ إِنْسَانٍ أَلْزَمْنٰهُ طٰٓئِرَهٗ فِيْ عُنُقِهٖ ۭ وَنُخْرِجُ
لَهٗ يَوْمَ الْقِيٰمَةِ كِتٰبًا يَّلْقٰىهُ مَنْشُوْرًا ۝١٤

15. 'Read thy book. Sufficient is thy own soul this day as reckoner against thee.'

اِقْرَأْ كِتٰبَكَ ۭ كَفٰى بِنَفْسِكَ الْيَوْمَ عَلَيْكَ حَسِيْبًا ۝١٥

16. He who follows the right way follows it only for *the good of* his *own* soul: and he who goes astray, goes astray only to his *own* loss. And no bearer of burden shall bear the burden of another. We never punish until We have sent a Messenger.

مَنِ اهْتَدٰى فَإِنَّمَا يَهْتَدِيْ لِنَفْسِهٖ ۚ وَمَنْ ضَلَّ
فَإِنَّمَا يَضِلُّ عَلَيْهَا ۭ وَلَا تَزِرُ وَازِرَةٌ وِّزْرَ أُخْرٰى ۭ
وَمَا كُنَّا مُعَذِّبِيْنَ حَتّٰى نَبْعَثَ رَسُوْلًا ۝١٦

* 17. And when We intend to destroy a township, We address Our commandment to its rebellious people, but they transgress therein; so the sentence *of punishment* becomes due against it, and We destroy it with utter destruction.

وَإِذَآ أَرَدْنَآ أَنْ نُّهْلِكَ قَرْيَةً أَمَرْنَا مُتْرَفِيْهَا
فَفَسَقُوْا فِيْهَا فَحَقَّ عَلَيْهَا الْقَوْلُ فَدَمَّرْنٰهَا تَدْمِيْرًا ۝١٧

18. How many generations have We destroyed after Noah! And thy Lord suffices as the Knower and Seer of the sins of His servants.

وَكَمْ أَهْلَكْنَا مِنَ الْقُرُوْنِ مِنْ بَعْدِ نُوْحٍ ۭ وَكَفٰى
بِرَبِّكَ بِذُنُوْبِ عِبَادِهٖ خَبِيْرًۢا بَصِيْرًا ۝١٨

19. Whoso desires the present life, We hasten for him therein what We will—for such *of them* as We please; then have We appointed Hell for him; he shall burn therein, condemned *and* rejected.

مَنْ كَانَ يُرِيْدُ الْعَاجِلَةَ عَجَّلْنَا لَهٗ فِيْهَا مَا نَشَآءُ لِمَنْ
نُّرِيْدُ ثُمَّ جَعَلْنَا لَهٗ جَهَنَّمَ ۚ يَصْلٰىهَا مَذْمُوْمًا
مَّدْحُوْرًا ﴿١٩﴾

20. And whoso desires the Hereafter and strives for it as it should be striven for, and he is a believer—these are the ones whose striving shall find favour *with God.*

وَمَنْ اَرَادَ الْاٰخِرَةَ وَسَعٰى لَهَا سَعْيَهَا وَهُوَ مُؤْمِنٌ
فَاُولٰٓئِكَ كَانَ سَعْيُهُمْ مَّشْكُوْرًا ﴿٢٠﴾

21. To all We render aid—both to these and those—a gift from thy Lord. And the gift of thy Lord is not restricted.

كُلًّا نُّمِدُّ هٰٓؤُلَآءِ وَهٰٓؤُلَآءِ مِنْ عَطَآءِ رَبِّكَ ۭ وَمَا
كَانَ عَطَآءُ رَبِّكَ مَحْظُوْرًا ﴿٢١﴾

22. Behold, how We have exalted some of them over others *in the present life;* and surely, the Hereafter shall be greater in degrees *of rank* and greater in excellence.

اُنْظُرْ كَيْفَ فَضَّلْنَا بَعْضَهُمْ عَلٰى بَعْضٍ ۭ وَلَلْاٰخِرَةُ اَكْبَرُ
دَرَجٰتٍ وَّاَكْبَرُ تَفْضِيْلًا ﴿٢٢﴾

23. Set not up with Allah another God lest thou sit down disgraced *and* forsaken.

لَا تَجْعَلْ مَعَ اللّٰهِ اِلٰهًا اٰخَرَ فَتَقْعُدَ مَذْمُوْمًا
مَّخْذُوْلًا ﴿٢٣﴾ ع ٢

R. 3.

* 24. Thy Lord has commanded, "Worship none but Him, and *show* kindness to parents. If one of them or both of them attain old age with thee, never say unto them any word expressive of disgust nor reproach them, but address them with excellent speech.

وَقَضٰى رَبُّكَ اَلَّا تَعْبُدُوْٓا اِلَّآ اِيَّاهُ وَبِالْوَالِدَيْنِ
اِحْسَانًا ۭ اِمَّا يَبْلُغَنَّ عِنْدَكَ الْكِبَرَ اَحَدُهُمَآ اَوْ
كِلٰهُمَا فَلَا تَقُلْ لَّهُمَآ اُفٍّ وَّلَا تَنْهَرْهُمَا وَقُلْ لَّهُمَا
قَوْلًا كَرِيْمًا ﴿٢٤﴾

25. "And lower to them the wing of humility out of tenderness. And say, 'My Lord, have mercy on them even as they nourished me in *my* childhood.'"

وَاخْفِضْ لَهُمَا جَنَاحَ الذُّلِّ مِنَ الرَّحْمَةِ وَقُلْ
رَّبِّ ارْحَمْهُمَا كَمَا رَبَّيٰنِيْ صَغِيْرًا ﴿٢٥﴾

26. Your Lord knows best what is in your minds; if you are righteous, then surely, He is Most Forgiving to those who turn *to Him* again and again.

رَبُّكُمْ اَعْلَمُ بِمَا فِيْ نُفُوْسِكُمْ ۭ اِنْ تَكُوْنُوْا صٰلِحِيْنَ
فَاِنَّهٗ كَانَ لِلْاَوَّابِيْنَ غَفُوْرًا ﴿٢٦﴾

27. And give thou to the kinsman his due, and to the poor and the wayfarer, and squander not *thy wealth* extravagantly.

وَاٰتِ ذَا الْقُرْبٰى حَقَّهٗ وَالْمِسْكِيْنَ وَابْنَ السَّبِيْلِ
وَلَا تُبَذِّرْ تَبْذِيْرًا ﴿٢٧﴾

28. Verily, the extravagant are brothers

اِنَّ الْمُبَذِّرِيْنَ كَانُوْٓا اِخْوَانَ الشَّيٰطِيْنِ ۭ وَكَانَ

of satans, and Satan is ungrateful to his Lord.

29. And if thou hast to turn away from them while seeking thy Lord's mercy for which thou hopest, *even then* speak to them a gentle word.

* 30. And keep not thy hand chained to thy neck, nor stretch it out an entire stretching, lest thou sit down blamed *or* exhausted.

31. Surely, thy Lord enlarges *His* provision for whom He pleases, and straitens *it for whom He pleases*. Verily, He knows *and* sees His servants full well.

R. 4.

32. Kill not your children for fear of poverty. It is We Who provide for them and for you. Surely, the killing of them is a great sin.

33. And come not near unto adultery; surely, it is a foul thing and an evil way.

34. And kill not the soul which Allah has forbidden save for just cause. And whoso is killed wrongfully, We have surely given his heir authority *to demand retaliation*, but let him not exceed the *prescribed* bounds in slaying; for *therein* he is helped *by law*.

35. And come not near the property of the orphan, except in the best way, until he attains his maturity, and fulfil the covenant; for the covenant shall be questioned about.

36. And give full measure when you measure, and weigh with a right balance; that is best and most commendable in the end.

37. And follow not that of which thou hast no knowledge. Verily, the ear and the eye and the heart—all these shall be called to account.

38. And walk not in the earth haughtily, for thou canst not rend the earth, nor canst thou reach the mountains in height.

39. The evil of all these is hateful in the sight of thy Lord.

الشَّيْطٰنُ لِرَبِّهٖ كَفُوْرًا ﴿٢٨﴾
وَإِمَّا تُعْرِضَنَّ عَنْهُمُ ابْتِغَآءَ رَحْمَةٍ مِّنْ رَّبِّكَ
تَرْجُوْهَا فَقُلْ لَّهُمْ قَوْلًا مَّيْسُوْرًا ﴿٢٩﴾
وَلَا تَجْعَلْ يَدَكَ مَغْلُوْلَةً إِلٰى عُنُقِكَ وَلَا تَبْسُطْهَا
كُلَّ الْبَسْطِ فَتَقْعُدَ مَلُوْمًا مَّحْسُوْرًا ﴿٣٠﴾
إِنَّ رَبَّكَ يَبْسُطُ الرِّزْقَ لِمَنْ يَّشَآءُ وَيَقْدِرُ ۚ إِنَّهٗ
كَانَ بِعِبَادِهٖ خَبِيْرًۢا بَصِيْرًا ﴿٣١﴾
وَلَا تَقْتُلُوْٓا أَوْلَادَكُمْ خَشْيَةَ إِمْلَاقٍ ۖ نَحْنُ نَرْزُقُهُمْ
وَإِيَّاكُمْ ۚ إِنَّ قَتْلَهُمْ كَانَ خِطْأً كَبِيْرًا ﴿٣٢﴾
وَلَا تَقْرَبُوا الزِّنٰٓى إِنَّهٗ كَانَ فَاحِشَةً ۗ وَسَآءَ سَبِيْلًا ﴿٣٣﴾
وَلَا تَقْتُلُوا النَّفْسَ الَّتِيْ حَرَّمَ اللّٰهُ إِلَّا بِالْحَقِّ ۗ وَمَنْ
قُتِلَ مَظْلُوْمًا فَقَدْ جَعَلْنَا لِوَلِيِّهٖ سُلْطٰنًا فَلَا يُسْرِفْ
فِّي الْقَتْلِ ۗ إِنَّهٗ كَانَ مَنْصُوْرًا ﴿٣٤﴾
وَلَا تَقْرَبُوْا مَالَ الْيَتِيْمِ إِلَّا بِالَّتِيْ هِيَ أَحْسَنُ حَتّٰى
يَبْلُغَ أَشُدَّهٗ ۖ وَأَوْفُوْا بِالْعَهْدِ ۚ إِنَّ الْعَهْدَ كَانَ مَسْئُوْلًا ﴿٣٥﴾
وَأَوْفُوا الْكَيْلَ إِذَا كِلْتُمْ وَزِنُوْا بِالْقِسْطَاسِ الْمُسْتَقِيْمِ ۚ
ذٰلِكَ خَيْرٌ وَّأَحْسَنُ تَأْوِيْلًا ﴿٣٦﴾
وَلَا تَقْفُ مَا لَيْسَ لَكَ بِهٖ عِلْمٌ ۚ إِنَّ السَّمْعَ وَالْبَصَرَ
وَالْفُؤَادَ كُلُّ أُولٰٓئِكَ كَانَ عَنْهُ مَسْئُوْلًا ﴿٣٧﴾
وَلَا تَمْشِ فِي الْأَرْضِ مَرَحًا ۚ إِنَّكَ لَنْ تَخْرِقَ الْأَرْضَ
وَلَنْ تَبْلُغَ الْجِبَالَ طُوْلًا ﴿٣٨﴾
كُلُّ ذٰلِكَ كَانَ سَيِّئُهٗ عِنْدَ رَبِّكَ مَكْرُوْهًا ﴿٣٩﴾

40. This is part of that wisdom which thy Lord has revealed to thee. And set not up with Allah any other God, lest thou be cast into Hell, condemned *and* rejected.

ذٰلِكَ مِمَّآ أَوْحٰٓى إِلَيْكَ رَبُّكَ مِنَ الْحِكْمَةِ ۗ وَلَا تَجْعَلْ
مَعَ اللّٰهِ إِلٰهًا اٰخَرَ فَتُلْقٰى فِيْ جَهَنَّمَ مَلُوْمًا مَّدْحُوْرًا ﴿٤٠﴾

41. Has, then, your Lord honoured you with sons, and taken for Himself females from among the angels? Surely, you say a grievous saying.

أَفَأَصْفٰكُمْ رَبُّكُمْ بِالْبَنِيْنَ وَاتَّخَذَ مِنَ الْمَلٰٓئِكَةِ
إِنَاثًا ۗ إِنَّكُمْ لَتَقُوْلُوْنَ قَوْلًا عَظِيْمًا ﴿٤١﴾

R. 5.

42. We have explained *the truth* in this Qur'ān in various ways that they may be admonished, but it only increases them in aversion.

وَلَقَدْ صَرَّفْنَا فِيْ هٰذَا الْقُرْاٰنِ لِيَذَّكَّرُوْا ۗ وَمَا يَزِيْدُهُمْ
إِلَّا نُفُوْرًا ﴿٤٢﴾

43. Say, had there been other gods with Him, as they say, then they (idolaters) would have surely sought out a way to the Owner of the Throne.

قُلْ لَّوْ كَانَ مَعَهٗٓ اٰلِهَةٌ كَمَا يَقُوْلُوْنَ إِذًا لَّابْتَغَوْا إِلٰى
ذِي الْعَرْشِ سَبِيْلًا ﴿٤٣﴾

44. Holy is He, and exalted far above that which they say.

سُبْحٰنَهٗ وَتَعٰلٰى عَمَّا يَقُوْلُوْنَ عُلُوًّا كَبِيْرًا ﴿٤٤﴾

45. The seven heavens and the earth and those that are therein extol His glory; and there is not a thing but glorifies Him with His praise; but you understand not their glorification. Verily, He is Forbearing, Most Forgiving.

تُسَبِّحُ لَهُ السَّمٰوٰتُ السَّبْعُ وَالْأَرْضُ وَمَنْ فِيْهِنَّ ۗ
وَإِنْ مِّنْ شَيْءٍ إِلَّا يُسَبِّحُ بِحَمْدِهٖ وَلٰكِنْ لَّا تَفْقَهُوْنَ
تَسْبِيْحَهُمْ ۗ إِنَّهٗ كَانَ حَلِيْمًا غَفُوْرًا ﴿٤٥﴾

46. And when thou recitest the Qur'ān, We put between thee and those who believe not in the Hereafter a hidden veil;

وَإِذَا قَرَأْتَ الْقُرْاٰنَ جَعَلْنَا بَيْنَكَ وَبَيْنَ الَّذِيْنَ
لَا يُؤْمِنُوْنَ بِالْاٰخِرَةِ حِجَابًا مَّسْتُوْرًا ﴿٤٦﴾

* 47. And We put coverings over their hearts lest they should understand it, and in their ears a deafness. And when thou makest mention in the Qur'ān of thy Lord alone, they turn their backs in aversion.

وَّجَعَلْنَا عَلٰى قُلُوْبِهِمْ أَكِنَّةً أَنْ يَّفْقَهُوْهُ وَفِيْٓ اٰذَانِهِمْ
وَقْرًا ۗ وَإِذَا ذَكَرْتَ رَبَّكَ فِي الْقُرْاٰنِ وَحْدَهٗ وَلَّوْا
عَلٰٓى أَدْبَارِهِمْ نُفُوْرًا ﴿٤٧﴾

48. We know best what they listen for, when they listen to thee, and when they confer in private, when the wrongdoers say, 'You follow none but a man who is a victim of deception.'

نَحْنُ أَعْلَمُ بِمَا يَسْتَمِعُوْنَ بِهٖٓ إِذْ يَسْتَمِعُوْنَ إِلَيْكَ وَإِذْ هُمْ نَجْوٰٓى
إِذْ يَقُوْلُ الظّٰلِمُوْنَ إِنْ تَتَّبِعُوْنَ إِلَّا رَجُلًا مَّسْحُوْرًا ﴿٤٨﴾

49. See, how they coin similitudes for thee, and have thus gone astray so that they cannot find a way.

اُنْظُرْ كَيْفَ ضَرَبُوْا لَكَ الْأَمْثَالَ فَضَلُّوْا فَلَا يَسْتَطِيْعُوْنَ
سَبِيْلًا ﴿٤٩﴾

50. And they say, 'When we shall have become bones and broken particles, shall

وَقَالُوْٓا ءَإِذَا كُنَّا عِظَامًا وَّرُفَاتًا ءَإِنَّا لَمَبْعُوْثُوْنَ

we be really raised up as a new creation?'

خَلْقًا جَدِيدًا ﴿٥٠﴾

51. Say, 'Be ye stones or iron,

قُلْ كُونُوا حِجَارَةً أَوْ حَدِيدًا ﴿٥١﴾

52. 'Or created matter of *any kind* which appears hardest in your minds, *even then shall you be raised up.*' Then will they ask, 'Who shall restore us to life?' Say, 'He Who created you the first time.' They will then shake their heads at thee and say, 'When will it be?' Say, 'Maybe it is nigh,

أَوْ خَلْقًا مِّمَّا يَكْبُرُ فِي صُدُورِكُمْ ۚ فَسَيَقُولُونَ
مَنْ يُّعِيدُنَا ۖ قُلِ الَّذِي فَطَرَكُمْ أَوَّلَ مَرَّةٍ ۚ
فَسَيُنْغِضُونَ إِلَيْكَ رُءُوسَهُمْ وَيَقُولُونَ مَتَىٰ
هُوَ ۖ قُلْ عَسَىٰ أَنْ يَّكُونَ قَرِيبًا ﴿٥٢﴾

53. '*It will be* on the day when He will call you; then will you respond praising Him and you will think that you have tarried but a little while.'

يَوْمَ يَدْعُوكُمْ فَتَسْتَجِيبُونَ بِحَمْدِهِ وَتَظُنُّونَ إِنْ
لَّبِثْتُمْ إِلَّا قَلِيلًا ﴿٥٣﴾ ع ١٢ ٥

R. 6.

54. And say to My servants that they should speak that which is best. Surely, Satan stirs up discord among them. Surely, Satan is an open enemy to man.

وَقُلْ لِّعِبَادِي يَقُولُوا الَّتِي هِيَ أَحْسَنُ ۚ إِنَّ الشَّيْطٰنَ
يَنْزَغُ بَيْنَهُمْ ۚ إِنَّ الشَّيْطٰنَ كَانَ لِلْإِنْسَانِ عَدُوًّا
مُّبِينًا ﴿٥٤﴾

55. Your Lord knows you best. If He please, He will have mercy on you; or if He please, He will punish you. And We have not sent thee to be a keeper over them.

رَبُّكُمْ أَعْلَمُ بِكُمْ ۖ إِنْ يَّشَأْ يَرْحَمْكُمْ أَوْ إِنْ يَّشَأْ
يُعَذِّبْكُمْ ۚ وَمَا أَرْسَلْنٰكَ عَلَيْهِمْ وَكِيلًا ﴿٥٥﴾

* 56. And thy Lord knows best those that are in the heavens and the earth. And We exalted some of the Prophets over the others, and to David We gave a Book.

وَرَبُّكَ أَعْلَمُ بِمَنْ فِي السَّمٰوٰتِ وَالْأَرْضِ ۗ وَلَقَدْ
فَضَّلْنَا بَعْضَ النَّبِيّٖنَ عَلَىٰ بَعْضٍ وَّاٰتَيْنَا دَاوٗدَ
زَبُورًا ﴿٥٦﴾

57. Say, 'Call on those whom you think *to be gods* beside Him; then *you will know that* they have no power to remove affliction from you or to avert *it*.

قُلِ ادْعُوا الَّذِينَ زَعَمْتُمْ مِّنْ دُونِهِ فَلَا يَمْلِكُونَ
كَشْفَ الضُّرِّ عَنْكُمْ وَلَا تَحْوِيلًا ﴿٥٧﴾

58. Those whom they call on *themselves* seek nearness to their Lord—*even* those of them who are nearest—and hope for His mercy, and fear His punishment. Surely, the punishment of thy Lord is a thing to be feared.

أُولٰٓئِكَ الَّذِينَ يَدْعُونَ يَبْتَغُونَ إِلَىٰ رَبِّهِمُ الْوَسِيلَةَ
أَيُّهُمْ أَقْرَبُ وَيَرْجُونَ رَحْمَتَهُ وَيَخَافُونَ عَذَابَهُ ۚ
إِنَّ عَذَابَ رَبِّكَ كَانَ مَحْذُورًا ﴿٥٨﴾

59. There is not a township but We shall destroy it before the Day of Resurrec-

وَإِنْ مِّنْ قَرْيَةٍ إِلَّا نَحْنُ مُهْلِكُوهَا قَبْلَ يَوْمِ الْقِيٰمَةِ

tion, or punish it with a severe punishment. That is written down in the Book.

أَوْ مُعَذِّبُوهَا عَذَابًا شَدِيدًا ۚ كَانَ ذَٰلِكَ فِي الْكِتَابِ
مَسْطُورًا ﴿٥٩﴾

60. And nothing could hinder Us from sending Signs, except that the former people rejected them, *but this is no hindrance.* And We gave Thamūd the she-camel as a clear Sign, but they unjustly rejected it. And We send not Signs but to warn.

وَمَا مَنَعَنَا أَنْ نُرْسِلَ بِالْآيَاتِ إِلَّا أَنْ كَذَّبَ بِهَا
الْأَوَّلُونَ ۚ وَآتَيْنَا ثَمُودَ النَّاقَةَ مُبْصِرَةً فَظَلَمُوا
بِهَا ۚ وَمَا نُرْسِلُ بِالْآيَاتِ إِلَّا تَخْوِيفًا ﴿٦٠﴾

61. And *remember the time* when We said to thee: 'Surely, thy Lord has encompassed the people.' And We made not the vision which We showed thee but as a trial for men, as also the tree cursed in the Qur'ān. And We warn them, but it only increases them in great transgression.

وَإِذْ قُلْنَا لَكَ إِنَّ رَبَّكَ أَحَاطَ بِالنَّاسِ ۚ وَمَا جَعَلْنَا
الرُّؤْيَا الَّتِي أَرَيْنَاكَ إِلَّا فِتْنَةً لِلنَّاسِ وَالشَّجَرَةَ
الْمَلْعُونَةَ فِي الْقُرْآنِ ۚ وَنُخَوِّفُهُمْ فَمَا يَزِيدُهُمْ
إِلَّا طُغْيَانًا كَبِيرًا ﴿٦١﴾ ع

R. 7.

62. And *remember the time* when We said to the angels, 'Submit to Adam,' and they *all* submitted, except Iblīs. He said, 'Shall I submit to one whom Thou hast created of clay?'

وَإِذْ قُلْنَا لِلْمَلَائِكَةِ اسْجُدُوا لِآدَمَ فَسَجَدُوا إِلَّا
إِبْلِيسَ قَالَ أَأَسْجُدُ لِمَنْ خَلَقْتَ طِينًا ﴿٦٢﴾

63. *And* he said, 'What thinkest Thou? *Can* this whom Thou hast honoured above me *be my superior?* If Thou wilt grant me respite till the Day of Resurrection, I will most surely bring his descendants under my sway except a few.'

قَالَ أَرَأَيْتَكَ هَٰذَا الَّذِي كَرَّمْتَ عَلَيَّ لَئِنْ أَخَّرْتَنِ
إِلَىٰ يَوْمِ الْقِيَامَةِ لَأَحْتَنِكَنَّ ذُرِّيَّتَهُ إِلَّا قَلِيلًا ﴿٦٣﴾

64. He said, 'Begone! and whoso shall follow thee from among them, Hell shall surely be the recompense of you all—an ample recompense.

قَالَ اذْهَبْ فَمَنْ تَبِعَكَ مِنْهُمْ فَإِنَّ جَهَنَّمَ جَزَاؤُكُمْ
جَزَاءً مَوْفُورًا ﴿٦٤﴾

65. 'And entice whomsoever of them thou canst, with thy voice, and urge against them thy horsemen and thy footmen and be their partner in wealth, and children, and make promises to them.' And Satan promises them naught but deceit.

وَاسْتَفْزِزْ مَنِ اسْتَطَعْتَ مِنْهُمْ بِصَوْتِكَ وَأَجْلِبْ
عَلَيْهِمْ بِخَيْلِكَ وَرَجِلِكَ وَشَارِكْهُمْ فِي الْأَمْوَالِ
وَالْأَوْلَادِ وَعِدْهُمْ ۚ وَمَا يَعِدُهُمُ الشَّيْطَانُ إِلَّا غُرُورًا ﴿٦٥﴾

66. *As to* My servants, thou shalt certainly have no power over them, and sufficient is thy Lord as a Guardian.

إِنَّ عِبَادِي لَيْسَ لَكَ عَلَيْهِمْ سُلْطَانٌ ۚ وَكَفَىٰ بِرَبِّكَ
وَكِيلًا ﴿٦٦﴾

67. Your Lord is He Who drives for you the ships in the sea, that you may seek of His bounty. Surely, He is merciful toward you.

رَبُّكُمُ الَّذِي يُزْجِي لَكُمُ الْفُلْكَ فِي الْبَحْرِ لِتَبْتَغُوا
مِنْ فَضْلِهِ ۚ إِنَّهُ كَانَ بِكُمْ رَحِيمًا ﴿٦٧﴾

68. And when harm touches you on the sea, *all* those whom you call upon, except Him, become lost *to you*. But when He brings you safe to land, you turn aside; and man is very ungrateful.

وَإِذَا مَسَّكُمُ الضُّرُّ فِي الْبَحْرِ ضَلَّ مَنْ تَدْعُونَ إِلَّا
إِيَّاهُ فَلَمَّا نَجَّاكُمْ إِلَى الْبَرِّ أَعْرَضْتُمْ وَكَانَ
الْإِنْسَانُ كَفُورًا ﴿٦٨﴾

69. Do you then feel secure that He will *not* cause you to sink in the side of the land or send against you a violent sandstorm *and* then you will find no guardian for yourselves?

أَفَأَمِنْتُمْ أَنْ يَخْسِفَ بِكُمْ جَانِبَ الْبَرِّ أَوْ يُرْسِلَ
عَلَيْكُمْ حَاصِبًا ثُمَّ لَا تَجِدُوا لَكُمْ وَكِيلًا ﴿٦٩﴾

70. Or, do you feel secure that He will *not* send you back therein a second time, *and* then send against you a storm-blast, and drown you because of your disbelief? You will then find therein no helper for yourselves against Us.

أَمْ أَمِنْتُمْ أَنْ يُعِيدَكُمْ فِيهِ تَارَةً أُخْرَىٰ فَيُرْسِلَ
عَلَيْكُمْ قَاصِفًا مِنَ الرِّيحِ فَيُغْرِقَكُمْ بِمَا كَفَرْتُمْ
ثُمَّ لَا تَجِدُوا لَكُمْ عَلَيْنَا بِهِ تَبِيعًا ﴿٧٠﴾

71. Indeed, We have honoured the children of Adam, and carried them by land and sea, and given them of good things and exalted them far above many of those whom We have created.

وَلَقَدْ كَرَّمْنَا بَنِي آدَمَ وَحَمَلْنَاهُمْ فِي الْبَرِّ وَالْبَحْرِ
وَرَزَقْنَاهُمْ مِنَ الطَّيِّبَاتِ وَفَضَّلْنَاهُمْ عَلَىٰ كَثِيرٍ مِمَّنْ
خَلَقْنَا تَفْضِيلًا ﴿٧١﴾ ع

R. 8.

72. *Remember* the day when We shall summon every people with their Leader. Then whoso shall be given his book in his right hand—such will read their book, and they will not be wronged a whit.

يَوْمَ نَدْعُو كُلَّ أُنَاسٍ بِإِمَامِهِمْ فَمَنْ أُوتِيَ كِتَابَهُ
بِيَمِينِهِ فَأُولَٰئِكَ يَقْرَءُونَ كِتَابَهُمْ وَلَا يُظْلَمُونَ فَتِيلًا ﴿٧٢﴾

73. But whoso is blind in this world will be blind in the Hereafter, and even more astray from the way.

وَمَنْ كَانَ فِي هَٰذِهِ أَعْمَىٰ فَهُوَ فِي الْآخِرَةِ أَعْمَىٰ وَأَضَلُّ
سَبِيلًا ﴿٧٣﴾

74. And they had well-nigh caused thee *severest* affliction on account of what We have revealed to thee, that thou mightest invent against Us something other than that; and then they would have certainly taken thee for a *special* friend.

وَإِنْ كَادُوا لَيَفْتِنُونَكَ عَنِ الَّذِي أَوْحَيْنَا إِلَيْكَ
لِتَفْتَرِيَ عَلَيْنَا غَيْرَهُ وَإِذًا لَاتَّخَذُوكَ خَلِيلًا ﴿٧٤﴾

75. And if We had not strengthened thee *with the Qur'ān*, thou mightest have inclined to them a little.

وَلَوْلَا أَنْ ثَبَّتْنَاكَ لَقَدْ كِدْتَ تَرْكَنُ إِلَيْهِمْ شَيْئًا
قَلِيلًا ﴿٧٥﴾

76. In that case We would have made thee taste similar *afflictions* of life and similar *afflictions* of death, *and* then thou wouldst not have found for thyself any helper against Us.

إِذًا لَأَذَقْنَاكَ ضِعْفَ الْحَيَاةِ وَضِعْفَ الْمَمَاتِ ثُمَّ لَا
تَجِدُ لَكَ عَلَيْنَا نَصِيرًا ﴿٧٦﴾

77. And indeed they are near to unsettling thee from the land that they

وَإِنْ كَادُوا لَيَسْتَفِزُّونَكَ مِنَ الْأَرْضِ لِيُخْرِجُوكَ

might expel thee therefrom; but in that case they *themselves* would not have stayed after thee save a little.

78. *This has been Our* way with Our Messengers whom We sent before thee; and thou wilt not find any change in Our way.

R. 9.

79. Observe Prayer at the declining and paling of the sun on to the darkness of the night, and the recitation *of the Qur'ān in Prayer* at dawn. Verily, the recitation *of the Qur'ān* at dawn is *specially* acceptable *to God*.

80. And wake up for it (the Qur'ān) in *the latter part of* the night as a supererogatory service for thee. It may be that thy Lord will raise thee to an exalted station.

81. And say, 'O my Lord, make my entry a good entry and *then* make me come forth with a good forthcoming. And grant me from Thyself a helping power.'

82. And say, 'Truth has come and falsehood has vanished away. Falsehood does indeed vanish away *fast*.'

83. And We are *gradually* revealing of the Qur'ān that which is a healing and a mercy to the believers; but it only adds to the loss of the wrongdoers.

84. And when We bestow favour on man, he turns away and goes aside; and when evil touches him, he gives *himself* up to despair.

85. Say, 'Everyone acts according to his own way, and your Lord knows full well who is best guided.'

R. 10.

86. And they ask thee concerning the soul. Say, 'The soul is by the command of my Lord; and of the knowledge *thereof* you have been given but a little.'

87. And if We pleased, We could certainly take away that which We have revealed to thee *and* then thou wouldst find in *the matter* no guardian for thee against Us,

88. Except mercy from thy Lord. Surely, His grace towards thee is great.

مِنْهَا وَإِذًا لَّا يَلْبَثُوْنَ خِلٰفَكَ إِلَّا قَلِيْلًا ﴿٧٧﴾
سُنَّةَ مَنْ قَدْ أَرْسَلْنَا قَبْلَكَ مِنْ رُّسُلِنَا وَلَا تَجِدُ
لِسُنَّتِنَا تَحْوِيْلًا ﴿٧٨﴾ ع ۸
أَقِمِ الصَّلٰوةَ لِدُلُوْكِ الشَّمْسِ إِلٰى غَسَقِ الَّيْلِ وَ
قُرْاٰنَ الْفَجْرِ إِنَّ قُرْاٰنَ الْفَجْرِ كَانَ مَشْهُوْدًا ﴿٧٩﴾
وَمِنَ الَّيْلِ فَتَهَجَّدْ بِهٖ نَافِلَةً لَّكَ عَسٰٓى أَنْ يَّبْعَثَكَ
رَبُّكَ مَقَامًا مَّحْمُوْدًا ﴿٨٠﴾
وَقُلْ رَّبِّ أَدْخِلْنِيْ مُدْخَلَ صِدْقٍ وَّأَخْرِجْنِيْ مُخْرَجَ
صِدْقٍ وَّاجْعَلْ لِّيْ مِنْ لَّدُنْكَ سُلْطٰنًا نَّصِيْرًا ﴿٨١﴾
وَقُلْ جَآءَ الْحَقُّ وَزَهَقَ الْبَاطِلُ إِنَّ الْبَاطِلَ كَانَ
زَهُوْقًا ﴿٨٢﴾
وَنُنَزِّلُ مِنَ الْقُرْاٰنِ مَا هُوَ شِفَآءٌ وَّرَحْمَةٌ
لِّلْمُؤْمِنِيْنَ وَلَا يَزِيْدُ الظّٰلِمِيْنَ إِلَّا خَسَارًا ﴿٨٣﴾
وَإِذَآ أَنْعَمْنَا عَلَى الْإِنْسَانِ أَعْرَضَ وَنَاٰ بِجَانِبِهٖ وَإِذَا
مَسَّهُ الشَّرُّ كَانَ يَـُٔوْسًا ﴿٨٤﴾
قُلْ كُلٌّ يَّعْمَلُ عَلٰى شَاكِلَتِهٖ فَرَبُّكُمْ أَعْلَمُ بِمَنْ هُوَ
أَهْدٰى سَبِيْلًا ﴿٨٥﴾ ع ۹
وَيَسْـَٔلُوْنَكَ عَنِ الرُّوْحِ قُلِ الرُّوْحُ مِنْ أَمْرِ رَبِّيْ
وَمَآ أُوْتِيْتُمْ مِّنَ الْعِلْمِ إِلَّا قَلِيْلًا ﴿٨٦﴾
وَلَئِنْ شِئْنَا لَنَذْهَبَنَّ بِالَّذِيْٓ أَوْحَيْنَآ إِلَيْكَ ثُمَّ
لَا تَجِدُ لَكَ بِهٖ عَلَيْنَا وَكِيْلًا ﴿٨٧﴾
إِلَّا رَحْمَةً مِّنْ رَّبِّكَ إِنَّ فَضْلَهٗ كَانَ عَلَيْكَ كَبِيْرًا ﴿٨٨﴾

89. Say, 'If mankind and the Jinn gathered together to produce the like of this Qur'ān, they could not produce the like thereof, even though they should help one another.'

قُلْ لَّئِنِ اجْتَمَعَتِ الْاِنْسُ وَالْجِنُّ عَلٰٓى اَنْ يَّاْتُوْا بِمِثْلِ
هٰذَا الْقُرْاٰنِ لَا يَاْتُوْنَ بِمِثْلِهٖ وَلَوْ كَانَ بَعْضُهُمْ لِبَعْضٍ
ظَهِيْرًا ﴿۸۹﴾

90. And surely, We have set forth for mankind in various ways all kinds of similitudes in this Qur'ān, but most men would reject everything but disbelief.

وَلَقَدْ صَرَّفْنَا لِلنَّاسِ فِيْ هٰذَا الْقُرْاٰنِ مِنْ كُلِّ مَثَلٍ
فَاَبٰٓى اَكْثَرُ النَّاسِ اِلَّا كُفُوْرًا ﴿۹۰﴾

91. And they say, 'We will never believe thee until thou cause a spring to gush forth for us from the earth;

وَقَالُوْا لَنْ نُّؤْمِنَ لَكَ حَتّٰى تَفْجُرَ لَنَا مِنَ الْاَرْضِ
يَنْۢبُوْعًا ﴿۹۱﴾

92. 'Or thou have a garden of date-palms and vines, and cause streams to gush forth in the midst thereof in abundance;

اَوْ تَكُوْنَ لَكَ جَنَّةٌ مِّنْ نَّخِيْلٍ وَّعِنَبٍ فَتُفَجِّرَ
الْاَنْهٰرَ خِلٰلَهَا تَفْجِيْرًا ﴿۹۲﴾

93. 'Or thou cause the heaven to fall upon us in pieces, as thou hast claimed, or thou bring Allah and the angels before us face to face;

اَوْ تُسْقِطَ السَّمَآءَ كَمَا زَعَمْتَ عَلَيْنَا كِسَفًا اَوْ تَاْتِيَ
بِاللّٰهِ وَالْمَلٰٓئِكَةِ قَبِيْلًا ﴿۹۳﴾

94. 'Or thou have a house of gold or thou ascend up into heaven; and we will not believe in thy ascension until thou send down to us a book that we can read.' Say, 'Holy is my Lord! I am not but a man *sent as a* Messenger.'

اَوْ يَكُوْنَ لَكَ بَيْتٌ مِّنْ زُخْرُفٍ اَوْ تَرْقٰى فِي السَّمَآءِ
وَلَنْ نُّؤْمِنَ لِرُقِيِّكَ حَتّٰى تُنَزِّلَ عَلَيْنَا كِتٰبًا نَّقْرَؤُهٗ
قُلْ سُبْحَانَ رَبِّيْ هَلْ كُنْتُ اِلَّا بَشَرًا رَّسُوْلًا ﴿۹۴﴾ ع

R. 11.

95. And nothing has prevented men from believing when the guidance came to them save that they said, 'Has Allah sent a man *as a* Messenger?'

وَمَا مَنَعَ النَّاسَ اَنْ يُّؤْمِنُوْٓا اِذْ جَآءَهُمُ الْهُدٰٓى
اِلَّآ اَنْ قَالُوْٓا اَبَعَثَ اللّٰهُ بَشَرًا رَّسُوْلًا ﴿۹۵﴾

96. Say, 'Had there been in the earth angels walking about in peace and quiet, We should have certainly sent down to them from heaven an angel *as a* Messenger.'

قُلْ لَّوْ كَانَ فِي الْاَرْضِ مَلٰٓئِكَةٌ يَّمْشُوْنَ مُطْمَئِنِّيْنَ
لَنَزَّلْنَا عَلَيْهِمْ مِّنَ السَّمَآءِ مَلَكًا رَّسُوْلًا ﴿۹۶﴾

97. Say, 'Sufficient is Allah for a Witness between me and you; surely, He knows and sees His servants full well.'

قُلْ كَفٰى بِاللّٰهِ شَهِيْدًاۢ بَيْنِيْ وَبَيْنَكُمْ اِنَّهٗ كَانَ
بِعِبَادِهٖ خَبِيْرًاۢ بَصِيْرًا ﴿۹۷﴾

98. And he whom Allah guides, is the *only* one rightly guided; but *as for* those whom He allows to perish, thou wilt find for them no helpers beside Him. And on the Day of Resurrection We shall gather

وَمَنْ يَّهْدِ اللّٰهُ فَهُوَ الْمُهْتَدِ وَمَنْ يُّضْلِلْ فَلَنْ
تَجِدَ لَهُمْ اَوْلِيَآءَ مِنْ دُوْنِهٖ وَنَحْشُرُهُمْ يَوْمَ

them together on their faces, blind, dumb and deaf. Their abode will be Hell; every time it abates, We shall increase for them the flame.

الْقِيٰمَةِ عَلٰى وُجُوْهِهِمْ عُمْيًا وَّ بُكْمًا وَّ صُمًّا ۚ مَاْوٰىهُمْ
جَهَنَّمُ ۚ كُلَّمَا خَبَتْ زِدْنٰهُمْ سَعِيْرًا ﴿۹۸﴾

99. That is their recompense, because they rejected Our Signs and said, 'What! when we are reduced to bones and broken particles, shall we really be raised up as a new creation?'

ذٰلِكَ جَزَآؤُهُمْ بِاَنَّهُمْ كَفَرُوْا بِاٰيٰتِنَا وَ قَالُوْٓا ءَاِذَا
كُنَّا عِظَامًا وَّ رُفَاتًا ءَاِنَّا لَمَبْعُوْثُوْنَ خَلْقًا جَدِيْدًا ﴿۹۹﴾

100. Have they not seen that Allah Who created the heavens and the earth has the power to create the like of them? And He has appointed for them a term; there is no doubt about it. But the wrongdoers would reject everything but disbelief.

اَوَلَمْ يَرَوْا اَنَّ اللّٰهَ الَّذِيْ خَلَقَ السَّمٰوٰتِ وَ الْاَرْضَ
قَادِرٌ عَلٰٓى اَنْ يَّخْلُقَ مِثْلَهُمْ وَ جَعَلَ لَهُمْ اَجَلًا لَّا
رَيْبَ فِيْهِ ؕ فَاَبَى الظّٰلِمُوْنَ اِلَّا كُفُوْرًا ﴿۱۰۰﴾

101. Say, 'Even if you possessed the treasures of the mercy of my Lord, you would surely hold them back for fear of spending, for man is niggardly.'

قُلْ لَّوْ اَنْتُمْ تَمْلِكُوْنَ خَزَآئِنَ رَحْمَةِ رَبِّيْٓ اِذًا لَّاَمْسَكْتُمْ
خَشْيَةَ الْاِنْفَاقِ ؕ وَ كَانَ الْاِنْسَانُ قَتُوْرًا ﴿۱۰۱﴾

R. 12.

102. And of a truth We gave Moses nine manifest Signs. So ask *then* the children of Israel. When he came to them, Pharaoh said to him, 'I do think thee, O Moses, to be a victim of deception.'

وَ لَقَدْ اٰتَيْنَا مُوْسٰى تِسْعَ اٰيٰتٍۭ بَيِّنٰتٍ فَسْـَٔلْ بَنِيْٓ اِسْرَآءِيْلَ
اِذْ جَآءَهُمْ فَقَالَ لَهٗ فِرْعَوْنُ اِنِّيْ لَاَظُنُّكَ يٰمُوْسٰى
مَسْحُوْرًا ﴿۱۰۲﴾

103. He said, 'Thou knowest well *that* none has sent down these *Signs* but the Lord of the heavens and the earth as *so many* evidences; and I certainly think thee, O Pharaoh, to be *a* ruined *man*.'

قَالَ لَقَدْ عَلِمْتَ مَآ اَنْزَلَ هٰٓؤُلَآءِ اِلَّا رَبُّ السَّمٰوٰتِ
وَ الْاَرْضِ بَصَآئِرَ ۚ وَ اِنِّيْ لَاَظُنُّكَ يٰفِرْعَوْنُ مَثْبُوْرًا ﴿۱۰۳﴾

104. So he resolved to remove them from the land; but We drowned him and those who were with him, all together.

فَاَرَادَ اَنْ يَّسْتَفِزَّهُمْ مِّنَ الْاَرْضِ فَاَغْرَقْنٰهُ وَ مَنْ
مَّعَهٗ جَمِيْعًا ﴿۱۰۴﴾

* 105. And after him We said to the children of Israel, 'Dwell ye in the land; and when *the time of* the promise of the latter days comes, We shall bring you together *out of various peoples*.'

وَّ قُلْنَا مِنْۢ بَعْدِهٖ لِبَنِيْٓ اِسْرَآءِيْلَ اسْكُنُوا الْاَرْضَ
فَاِذَا جَآءَ وَعْدُ الْاٰخِرَةِ جِئْنَا بِكُمْ لَفِيْفًا ﴿۱۰۵﴾

106. And in truth have We sent it down and with truth has it descended. And We have sent thee only as a bearer of good tidings and a Warner.

وَ بِالْحَقِّ اَنْزَلْنٰهُ وَ بِالْحَقِّ نَزَلَ ؕ وَ مَآ اَرْسَلْنٰكَ اِلَّا
مُبَشِّرًا وَّ نَذِيْرًا ﴿۱۰۶﴾

* 107. And the Qur'ān We have revealed in pieces that thou mayest read it to mankind at intervals, and We have sent it down piecemeal.

وَ قُرْاٰنًا فَرَقْنٰهُ لِتَقْرَاَهٗ عَلَى النَّاسِ عَلٰى مُكْثٍ
وَّ نَزَّلْنٰهُ تَنْزِيْلًا ﴿۱۰۷﴾

108. Say, "Whether you believe therein or believe not, those to whom knowledge has been given before it, do fall down prostrate on their faces when it is recited to them,

قُلْ اٰمِنُوْا بِهٖۤ اَوْ لَا تُؤْمِنُوْا ؕ اِنَّ الَّذِیْنَ اُوْتُوا الْعِلْمَ
مِنْ قَبْلِهٖۤ اِذَا یُتْلٰی عَلَیْهِمْ یَخِرُّوْنَ لِلْاَذْقَانِ
سُجَّدًا ۙ﴿۱۰۸﴾

109. "And say, 'Holy is our Lord. Surely, the promise of our Lord is bound to be fulfilled.'"

وَّ یَقُوْلُوْنَ سُبْحٰنَ رَبِّنَاۤ اِنْ كَانَ وَعْدُ رَبِّنَا لَمَفْعُوْلًا ﴿۱۰۹﴾

110. They fall down on their faces weeping, and it increases humility in them.

السجدة
وَ یَخِرُّوْنَ لِلْاَذْقَانِ یَبْكُوْنَ وَ یَزِیْدُهُمْ خُشُوْعًا ﴿۱۱۰﴾

* 111. Say, 'Call upon Allah or call upon Raḥmān; *by* whichever name you call on Him, His are the most beautiful names.' And utter not thy prayer aloud, nor utter it *too* low, but seek a way between.

قُلِ ادْعُوا اللّٰهَ اَوِ ادْعُوا الرَّحْمٰنَ ؕ اَیًّا مَّا تَدْعُوْا فَلَهُ الْاَسْمَآءُ
الْحُسْنٰی ۚ وَ لَا تَجْهَرْ بِصَلَاتِكَ وَ لَا تُخَافِتْ بِهَا وَ
ابْتَغِ بَیْنَ ذٰلِكَ سَبِیْلًا ﴿۱۱۱﴾

112. And say, 'All praise belongs to Allah Who has taken unto Himself no son, and Who has no partner in *His* Kingdom, nor has He anyone to help *Him* on account of weakness.' And extol His glory with all glorification.

وَ قُلِ الْحَمْدُ لِلّٰهِ الَّذِیْ لَمْ یَتَّخِذْ وَلَدًا وَّ لَمْ یَكُنْ
لَّهٗ شَرِیْكٌ فِی الْمُلْكِ وَ لَمْ یَكُنْ لَّهٗ وَلِیٌّ مِّنَ الذُّلِّ
وَ كَبِّرْهُ تَكْبِیْرًا ﴿۱۱۲﴾ ع ۱۲

سُوْرَةُ الْكَهْفِ مَكِّيَّةٌ

رکوعاتها ١٢ (١٨) آياتها ١١١

AL-KAHF

(Revealed before Hijra)

1\. In the name of Allah, the Gracious, the Merciful.

بِسْمِ اللّٰهِ الرَّحْمٰنِ الرَّحِيْمِ ﴿١﴾

* 2. All praise belongs to Allah Who has sent down the Book to His servant and has not put therein any crookedness.

اَلْحَمْدُ لِلّٰهِ الَّذِيْٓ اَنْزَلَ عَلٰى عَبْدِهِ الْكِتٰبَ وَلَمْ
يَجْعَلْ لَّهٗ عِوَجًا ۜ سكتة ﴿٢﴾

3\. *He has made it* a guardian, that it may give warning of a grievous chastisement from Him, and that it may give the believers who do good deeds the glad tidings that they shall have a good reward,

قَيِّمًا لِّيُنْذِرَ بَاْسًا شَدِيْدًا مِّنْ لَّدُنْهُ وَيُبَشِّرَ
الْمُؤْمِنِيْنَ الَّذِيْنَ يَعْمَلُوْنَ الصّٰلِحٰتِ اَنَّ لَهُمْ
اَجْرًا حَسَنًا ۙ ﴿٣﴾

4\. Wherein they shall abide for ever;

مّٰكِثِيْنَ فِيْهِ اَبَدًا ۙ ﴿٤﴾

5\. And that it may warn those who say, 'Allah has taken unto Himself a son.'

وَّيُنْذِرَ الَّذِيْنَ قَالُوا اتَّخَذَ اللّٰهُ وَلَدًا ۖ ﴿٥﴾

6\. No knowledge have they thereof, nor *had* their fathers. Grievous is the word that comes from their mouths. They speak naught but a lie.

مَا لَهُمْ بِهٖ مِنْ عِلْمٍ وَّلَا لِاٰبَآئِهِمْ ۭ كَبُرَتْ
كَلِمَةً تَخْرُجُ مِنْ اَفْوَاهِهِمْ ۭ اِنْ يَّقُوْلُوْنَ اِلَّا
كَذِبًا ﴿٦﴾

7\. So haply thou wilt grieve thyself to death for sorrow after them if they believe not in this discourse.

فَلَعَلَّكَ بَاخِعٌ نَّفْسَكَ عَلٰٓى اٰثَارِهِمْ اِنْ لَّمْ يُؤْمِنُوْا
بِهٰذَا الْحَدِيْثِ اَسَفًا ﴿٧﴾

8\. Verily, We have made all that is on the earth as an ornament for it, that We may try them as to which of them is best in conduct.

اِنَّا جَعَلْنَا مَا عَلَى الْاَرْضِ زِيْنَةً لَّهَا لِنَبْلُوَهُمْ
اَيُّهُمْ اَحْسَنُ عَمَلًا ﴿٨﴾

9\. And We shall make all that is thereon a barren soil.

وَاِنَّا لَجٰعِلُوْنَ مَا عَلَيْهَا صَعِيْدًا جُرُزًا ۭ ﴿٩﴾

10\. Dost thou think that the People of the Cave and the Inscription were a wonder among Our Signs?

اَمْ حَسِبْتَ اَنَّ اَصْحٰبَ الْكَهْفِ وَالرَّقِيْمِ ۙ كَانُوْا
مِنْ اٰيٰتِنَا عَجَبًا ﴿١٠﴾

11\. When the young men betook themselves for refuge to the Cave and said, 'Our

اِذْ اَوَى الْفِتْيَةُ اِلَى الْكَهْفِ فَقَالُوْا رَبَّنَآ اٰتِنَا

Lord, bestow on us mercy from Thyself, and provide for us right guidance in our affair.'

* 12. So We sealed up their ears in the Cave for a number of years.

13. Then We raised them up that We might know which of the two parties would better reckon the time that they had tarried.

R. 2.

14. We will relate to thee their story with truth: They were young men who believed in their Lord, and We increased them in guidance.

15. And We strengthened their hearts, when they stood up and said, 'Our Lord is the Lord of the heavens and the earth. Never shall we call upon any God beside Him; *if we did*, we should indeed have uttered an enormity.

16. 'These, our people, have taken *for worship other* gods beside Him. Wherefore do they not bring a clear authority for them? And who is more unjust than he who invents a lie concerning Allah?

17. 'And *now* when you have withdrawn from them and from that which they worship beside Allah, then seek refuge in the Cave; your Lord will unfold for you His mercy and will provide for you comfort in *this* affair of yours.'

* 18. And thou couldst see the sun, as it rose, move away from their Cave on the right, and when it set, turn away from them on the left; and they were in the spacious hollow thereof. This is among the Signs of Allah. He whom Allah guides is rightly guided; but he whom He adjudges astray, for him thou wilt find no helper *or* guide.

R. 3.

19. Thou mightest deem them awake, whilst they are asleep; and We shall cause them to turn over to the right and to the left, their dog stretching out his forelegs

مِن لَّدُنكَ رَحْمَةً وَهَيِّئْ لَنَا مِنْ أَمْرِنَا رَشَدًا ⑪
فَضَرَبْنَا عَلَىٰ آذَانِهِمْ فِي الْكَهْفِ سِنِينَ عَدَدًا ⑫
ثُمَّ بَعَثْنَاهُمْ لِنَعْلَمَ أَيُّ الْحِزْبَيْنِ أَحْصَىٰ لِمَا
لَبِثُوا أَمَدًا ⑬
نَحْنُ نَقُصُّ عَلَيْكَ نَبَأَهُم بِالْحَقِّ إِنَّهُمْ فِتْيَةٌ
آمَنُوا بِرَبِّهِمْ وَزِدْنَاهُمْ هُدًى ⑭
وَرَبَطْنَا عَلَىٰ قُلُوبِهِمْ إِذْ قَامُوا فَقَالُوا رَبُّنَا رَبُّ
السَّمَاوَاتِ وَالْأَرْضِ لَن نَّدْعُوَ مِن دُونِهِ إِلَٰهًا
لَّقَدْ قُلْنَا إِذًا شَطَطًا ⑮
هَٰؤُلَاءِ قَوْمُنَا اتَّخَذُوا مِن دُونِهِ آلِهَةً لَّوْلَا
يَأْتُونَ عَلَيْهِم بِسُلْطَانٍ بَيِّنٍ فَمَنْ أَظْلَمُ مِمَّنِ
افْتَرَىٰ عَلَى اللَّهِ كَذِبًا ⑯
وَإِذِ اعْتَزَلْتُمُوهُمْ وَمَا يَعْبُدُونَ إِلَّا اللَّهَ فَأْوُوا
إِلَى الْكَهْفِ يَنشُرْ لَكُمْ رَبُّكُم مِّن رَّحْمَتِهِ وَيُهَيِّئْ
لَكُم مِّنْ أَمْرِكُم مِّرْفَقًا ⑰
وَتَرَى الشَّمْسَ إِذَا طَلَعَت تَّزَاوَرُ عَن كَهْفِهِمْ
ذَاتَ الْيَمِينِ وَإِذَا غَرَبَت تَّقْرِضُهُمْ ذَاتَ
الشِّمَالِ وَهُمْ فِي فَجْوَةٍ مِّنْهُ ذَٰلِكَ مِنْ آيَاتِ
اللَّهِ مَن يَهْدِ اللَّهُ فَهُوَ الْمُهْتَدِ وَمَن يُضْلِلْ فَلَن
تَجِدَ لَهُ وَلِيًّا مُّرْشِدًا ⑱
وَتَحْسَبُهُمْ أَيْقَاظًا وَهُمْ رُقُودٌ وَنُقَلِّبُهُمْ
ذَاتَ الْيَمِينِ وَذَاتَ الشِّمَالِ وَكَلْبُهُم بَاسِطٌ

on the threshold. If thou hadst had a look at them, thou wouldst surely have turned away from them in fright, and wouldst surely have been filled with awe of them.

ذِرَاعَيْهِ بِالْوَصِيْدِ ۭ لَوِ اطَّلَعْتَ عَلَيْهِمْ لَوَلَّيْتَ مِنْهُمْ
فِرَارًا وَّلَمُلِئْتَ مِنْهُمْ رُعْبًا ﴿١٩﴾

20. And so We raised them up that they might question one another. One of them said, 'How long have you tarried?' They said, 'We have tarried a day or part of a day.' *Others* said, 'Your Lord knows best *the time* you have tarried. Now send one of you with these silver coins of yours to the city; and let him see which of its *inhabitants* has the purest food, and let him bring you provisions thereof. And let him be courteous and let him not inform anyone about you.'

وَكَذٰلِكَ بَعَثْنٰهُمْ لِيَتَسَاۗءَلُوْا بَيْنَهُمْ ۭ قَالَ قَاۗىِٕلٌ
مِّنْهُمْ كَمْ لَبِثْتُمْ ۭ قَالُوْا لَبِثْنَا يَوْمًا اَوْ بَعْضَ يَوْمٍ ۭ
قَالُوْا رَبُّكُمْ اَعْلَمُ بِمَا لَبِثْتُمْ ۭ فَابْعَثُوْٓا اَحَدَكُمْ
بِوَرِقِكُمْ هٰذِهٖٓ اِلَى الْمَدِيْنَةِ فَلْيَنْظُرْ اَيُّهَآ اَزْكٰى
طَعَامًا فَلْيَاْتِكُمْ بِرِزْقٍ مِّنْهُ وَلْيَتَلَطَّفْ
وَلَا يُشْعِرَنَّ بِكُمْ اَحَدًا ﴿٢٠﴾

* 21. 'For, if they should come to know of you, they would stone you or make you return to their religion and then will you never prosper.'

اِنَّهُمْ اِنْ يَّظْهَرُوْا عَلَيْكُمْ يَرْجُمُوْكُمْ اَوْ يُعِيْدُوْكُمْ
فِيْ مِلَّتِهِمْ وَلَنْ تُفْلِحُوْٓا اِذًا اَبَدًا ﴿٢١﴾

* 22. And thus did We disclose them *to the people* that they might know that the promise of Allah was true, and that, as to the Hour, there was no doubt about it. *And remember the time* when people disputed among themselves concerning them, and said, 'Build over them a building.' Their Lord knew them best. Those who won their point said, 'We will, surely, build a place of worship over them.'

وَكَذٰلِكَ اَعْثَرْنَا عَلَيْهِمْ لِيَعْلَمُوْٓا اَنَّ وَعْدَ اللّٰهِ
حَقٌّ وَّاَنَّ السَّاعَةَ لَا رَيْبَ فِيْهَا ۚ اِذْ يَتَنَازَعُوْنَ
بَيْنَهُمْ اَمْرَهُمْ فَقَالُوا ابْنُوْا عَلَيْهِمْ بُنْيَانًا ۭ رَبُّهُمْ
اَعْلَمُ بِهِمْ ۭ قَالَ الَّذِيْنَ غَلَبُوْا عَلٰٓي اَمْرِهِمْ لَنَتَّخِذَنَّ
عَلَيْهِمْ مَّسْجِدًا ﴿٢٢﴾

* 23. *Some* say, 'They were three, the fourth was their dog,' and *others* say, 'They were five, the sixth was their dog,' guessing at random. And *yet others* say, 'They were seven, the eighth was their dog.' Say, 'My Lord knows best their number. None knows them except a few.' So argue not concerning them except with arguing *that is* overpowering, nor seek information about them from any one of them.

سَيَقُوْلُوْنَ ثَلٰثَةٌ رَّابِعُهُمْ كَلْبُهُمْ ۚ وَيَقُوْلُوْنَ
خَمْسَةٌ سَادِسُهُمْ كَلْبُهُمْ رَجْمًۢا بِالْغَيْبِ ۚ وَ
يَقُوْلُوْنَ سَبْعَةٌ وَّثَامِنُهُمْ كَلْبُهُمْ ۭ قُلْ رَّبِّيْٓ اَعْلَمُ
بِعِدَّتِهِمْ مَّا يَعْلَمُهُمْ اِلَّا قَلِيْلٌ ڛ فَلَا تُمَارِ
فِيْهِمْ اِلَّا مِرَاۗءً ظَاهِرًا ۠ وَّلَا تَسْتَفْتِ فِيْهِمْ
مِّنْهُمْ اَحَدًا ﴿٢٣﴾

R. 4.

24. And say not of anything, 'I am going to do it tomorrow,'

وَلَا تَقُوْلَنَّ لِشَايْءٍ اِنِّىْ فَاعِلٌ ذٰلِكَ غَدًا ﴿٢٤﴾

25. Unless Allah should will. And remember thy Lord when thou forgettest, and say, 'I hope my Lord will guide me to what is even nearer than this to the right path.'

إِلَّآ أَن يَشَآءَ ٱللَّهُ وَٱذْكُر رَّبَّكَ إِذَا نَسِيتَ وَقُلْ
عَسَىٰٓ أَن يَهْدِيَنِ رَبِّى لِأَقْرَبَ مِنْ هَٰذَا رَشَدًا ﴿٢٥﴾

26. And they stayed in their Cave three hundred years, and added nine more.

وَلَبِثُوا۟ فِى كَهْفِهِمْ ثَلَٰثَ مِا۟ئَةٍ سِنِينَ وَ
ٱزْدَادُوا۟ تِسْعًا ﴿٢٦﴾

* 27. Say, 'Allah knows best how long they tarried.' To Him belong the secrets of the heavens and the earth. How Seeing is He! and how Hearing! They have no helper beside Him, and He does not let anyone share in His government.

قُلِ ٱللَّهُ أَعْلَمُ بِمَا لَبِثُوا۟ لَهُۥ غَيْبُ ٱلسَّمَٰوَٰتِ وَٱلْأَرْضِ
أَبْصِرْ بِهِۦ وَأَسْمِعْ مَا لَهُم مِّن دُونِهِۦ مِن وَلِىٍّ
وَلَا يُشْرِكُ فِى حُكْمِهِۦٓ أَحَدًا ﴿٢٧﴾

28. And recite what has been revealed to thee of the Book of thy Lord. There is none who can change His words, and thou wilt find no refuge beside Him.

وَٱتْلُ مَآ أُوحِىَ إِلَيْكَ مِن كِتَابِ رَبِّكَ لَا مُبَدِّلَ
لِكَلِمَٰتِهِۦ وَلَن تَجِدَ مِن دُونِهِۦ مُلْتَحَدًا ﴿٢٨﴾

29. And keep thyself attached to those who call on their Lord, morning and evening, seeking His pleasure; and let not thy eyes pass beyond them, seeking the adornment of the life of the world; and obey not him whose heart We have made heedless of Our remembrance and who follows his evil inclinations, and his case exceeds all bounds.

وَٱصْبِرْ نَفْسَكَ مَعَ ٱلَّذِينَ يَدْعُونَ رَبَّهُم بِٱلْغَدَوٰةِ
وَٱلْعَشِىِّ يُرِيدُونَ وَجْهَهُۥ وَلَا تَعْدُ عَيْنَاكَ عَنْهُمْ
تُرِيدُ زِينَةَ ٱلْحَيَوٰةِ ٱلدُّنْيَا وَلَا تُطِعْ مَنْ
أَغْفَلْنَا قَلْبَهُۥ عَن ذِكْرِنَا وَٱتَّبَعَ هَوَىٰهُ
وَكَانَ أَمْرُهُۥ فُرُطًا ﴿٢٩﴾

30. And say, '*It is* the truth from your Lord; wherefore let him who will, believe, and let him who will, disbelieve.' Verily, We have prepared for the wrongdoers a fire whose *flaming* canopy shall enclose them. And if they cry for help, they will be helped with water like molten lead which will burn the faces. How dreadful the drink, and how evil is *the Fire as* a resting place!

وَقُلِ ٱلْحَقُّ مِن رَّبِّكُمْ فَمَن شَآءَ فَلْيُؤْمِن
وَمَن شَآءَ فَلْيَكْفُرْ إِنَّآ أَعْتَدْنَا لِلظَّٰلِمِينَ نَارًا
أَحَاطَ بِهِمْ سُرَادِقُهَا وَإِن يَسْتَغِيثُوا۟ يُغَاثُوا۟ بِمَآءٍ
كَٱلْمُهْلِ يَشْوِى ٱلْوُجُوهَ بِئْسَ ٱلشَّرَابُ وَسَآءَتْ
مُرْتَفَقًا ﴿٣٠﴾

31. Verily, those who believe and do good works—surely, We suffer not the reward of those who do good works to be lost.

إِنَّ ٱلَّذِينَ ءَامَنُوا۟ وَعَمِلُوا۟ ٱلصَّٰلِحَٰتِ إِنَّا لَا نُضِيعُ
أَجْرَ مَنْ أَحْسَنَ عَمَلًا ﴿٣١﴾

32. It is these who will have Gardens of Eternity beneath which streams shall

أُو۟لَٰٓئِكَ لَهُمْ جَنَّٰتُ عَدْنٍ تَجْرِى مِن تَحْتِهِمُ

flow. They will be adorned therein with bracelets of gold and will wear green garments of fine silk and heavy brocade, reclining therein upon raised couches. How good the reward and how excellent the place of rest!

الْاَنْهٰرُ يُحَلَّوْنَ فِيْهَا مِنْ اَسَاوِرَ مِنْ ذَهَبٍ
وَّيَلْبَسُوْنَ ثِيَابًا خُضْرًا مِّنْ سُنْدُسٍ وَّ
اِسْتَبْرَقٍ مُّتَّكِـِٕيْنَ فِيْهَا عَلَى الْاَرَآئِكِ نِعْمَ
ع الثَّوَابُ وَحَسُنَتْ مُرْتَفَقًا ﴿۳۲﴾

R. 5.

33. And set forth to them the parable of two men: one of them We provided with two gardens of grapes, and surrounded them with date-palms, and between the two We placed corn-fields.

وَاضْرِبْ لَهُمْ مَّثَلًا رَّجُلَيْنِ جَعَلْنَا لِاَحَدِهِمَا
جَنَّتَيْنِ مِنْ اَعْنَابٍ وَّحَفَفْنٰهُمَا بِنَخْلٍ وَّجَعَلْنَا
بَيْنَهُمَا زَرْعًا ﴿۳۳﴾

34. Each of the gardens yielded its fruit *in abundance*, and failed not the least therein. And in between the two We caused a stream to flow.

كِلْتَا الْجَنَّتَيْنِ اٰتَتْ اُكُلَهَا وَلَمْ تَظْلِمْ مِّنْهُ شَيْـًٔا
وَّفَجَّرْنَا خِلٰلَهُمَا نَهَرًا ﴿۳۴﴾

35. And he had fruit *in abundance*. And he said to his companion, arguing *boastfully* with him, 'I am richer than thou in wealth and stronger in respect of men.'

وَّكَانَ لَهٗ ثَمَرٌ فَقَالَ لِصَاحِبِهٖ وَهُوَ يُحَاوِرُهٗۤ
اَنَا اَكْثَرُ مِنْكَ مَالًا وَّاَعَزُّ نَفَرًا ﴿۳۵﴾

36. And he entered his garden while he was wronging his soul. He said, 'I do not think this will ever perish;

وَدَخَلَ جَنَّتَهٗ وَهُوَ ظَالِمٌ لِّنَفْسِهٖ قَالَ مَاۤ
اَظُنُّ اَنْ تَبِيْدَ هٰذِهٖۤ اَبَدًا ﴿۳۶﴾

37. 'And I do not think the Hour will *ever* come. And even if I am ever brought back to my Lord, I shall, surely, find a better resort than this.'

وَّمَاۤ اَظُنُّ السَّاعَةَ قَآئِمَةً وَّلَئِنْ رُّدِدْتُّ اِلٰى
رَبِّيْ لَاَجِدَنَّ خَيْرًا مِّنْهَا مُنْقَلَبًا ﴿۳۷﴾

* 38. His companion said to him, while he was arguing with him, "Dost thou disbelieve in Him Who created thee from dust, then from a sperm-drop, then fashioned thee into a *perfect* man?

قَالَ لَهٗ صَاحِبُهٗ وَهُوَ يُحَاوِرُهٗۤ اَكَفَرْتَ بِالَّذِيْ
خَلَقَكَ مِنْ تُرَابٍ ثُمَّ مِنْ نُّطْفَةٍ ثُمَّ سَوّٰىكَ
رَجُلًا ﴿۳۸﴾

39. "But *as for me*, I *believe that* Allah alone is my Lord, and I will not associate anyone with my Lord.

لٰكِنَّا۠ هُوَ اللّٰهُ رَبِّيْ وَلَاۤ اُشْرِكُ بِرَبِّيْۤ اَحَدًا ﴿۳۹﴾

40. "And why didst thou not say when thou didst enter thy garden: '*Only* that which Allah wills *comes to pass*. There is no power save in Allah?' if thou seest me as less than thee in riches and offspring.

وَلَوْلَاۤ اِذْ دَخَلْتَ جَنَّتَكَ قُلْتَ مَا شَآءَ اللّٰهُ
لَا قُوَّةَ اِلَّا بِاللّٰهِ اِنْ تَرَنِ اَنَا اَقَلَّ مِنْكَ مَالًا
وَّوَلَدًا ﴿۴۰﴾

41. "Perhaps my Lord will give me something better than thy garden, and will send on it (thy garden) a thunderbolt from heaven so that it will become a bare slippery ground.

42. "Or its water will become sunk *in the earth* so that thou wilt not be able to find it."

43. And his fruit was *actually* destroyed, and he began to wring his hands for what he had spent on it, and it had *all* fallen down on its trellises. And he said, 'Would that I had not associated anyone with my Lord!'

44. And he had no party to help him against Allah, nor was he able to defend himself.

* 45. In such a case protection *comes only* from Allah, the True. He is the Best in respect of reward, and the Best in respect of consequence.

R. 6.

46. And set forth to them the similitude of the life of this world: it is like the water which We send down from the sky, and the vegetation of the earth is mingled with it, and then it becomes dry grass broken into pieces which the winds scatter. And Allah has power over everything.

* 47. Wealth and children are an ornament of the life of this world. But enduring good works are better in the sight of thy Lord in respect of *immediate* reward, and better in respect of *future* hope.

48. And *bethink of* the day when We shall remove the mountains, and thou wilt see the *nations of the* earth march forth *against one another* and We shall gather them together and shall not leave any one of them behind.

49. And they will be presented to thy Lord, *standing* in rows: 'Now have you come to Us as We created you at first. But you thought that We would fix no time for the fulfilment of *Our* promise to you.'

50. And the Book will be placed *before them*, and thou wilt see the guilty

فَعَسٰى رَبِّيْٓ اَنْ يُّؤْتِيَنِ خَيْرًا مِّنْ جَنَّتِكَ وَيُرْسِلَ
عَلَيْهَا حُسْبَانًا مِّنَ السَّمَآءِ فَتُصْبِحَ صَعِيْدًا
زَلَقًا ۙ﴿۴۱﴾
اَوْ يُصْبِحَ مَآؤُهَا غَوْرًا فَلَنْ تَسْتَطِيْعَ لَهٗ طَلَبًا ﴿۴۲﴾
وَاُحِيْطَ بِثَمَرِهٖ فَاَصْبَحَ يُقَلِّبُ كَفَّيْهِ عَلٰى مَآ اَنْفَقَ
فِيْهَا وَهِيَ خَاوِيَةٌ عَلٰى عُرُوْشِهَا وَيَقُوْلُ يٰلَيْتَنِيْ
لَمْ اُشْرِكْ بِرَبِّيْٓ اَحَدًا ﴿۴۳﴾
وَلَمْ تَكُنْ لَّهٗ فِئَةٌ يَّنْصُرُوْنَهٗ مِنْ دُوْنِ اللّٰهِ وَمَا
كَانَ مُنْتَصِرًا ؕ﴿۴۴﴾
هُنَالِكَ الْوَلَايَةُ لِلّٰهِ الْحَقِّ ؕ هُوَ خَيْرٌ ثَوَابًا وَّ
خَيْرٌ عُقْبًا ﴿۴۵﴾ ع
وَاضْرِبْ لَهُمْ مَّثَلَ الْحَيٰوةِ الدُّنْيَا كَمَآءٍ اَنْزَلْنٰهُ
مِنَ السَّمَآءِ فَاخْتَلَطَ بِهٖ نَبَاتُ الْاَرْضِ فَاَصْبَحَ
هَشِيْمًا تَذْرُوْهُ الرِّيٰحُ ؕ وَكَانَ اللّٰهُ عَلٰى كُلِّ
شَيْءٍ مُّقْتَدِرًا ﴿۴۶﴾
اَلْمَالُ وَالْبَنُوْنَ زِيْنَةُ الْحَيٰوةِ الدُّنْيَا ۚ وَالْبٰقِيٰتُ
الصّٰلِحٰتُ خَيْرٌ عِنْدَ رَبِّكَ ثَوَابًا وَّخَيْرٌ اَمَلًا ﴿۴۷﴾
وَيَوْمَ نُسَيِّرُ الْجِبَالَ وَتَرَى الْاَرْضَ بَارِزَةً ۙ وَّحَشَرْنٰهُمْ
فَلَمْ نُغَادِرْ مِنْهُمْ اَحَدًا ۚ﴿۴۸﴾
وَعُرِضُوْا عَلٰى رَبِّكَ صَفًّا ؕ لَقَدْ جِئْتُمُوْنَا كَمَا خَلَقْنٰكُمْ
اَوَّلَ مَرَّةٍ ۫ بَلْ زَعَمْتُمْ اَلَّنْ نَّجْعَلَ لَكُمْ مَّوْعِدًا ﴿۴۹﴾
وَوُضِعَ الْكِتٰبُ فَتَرَى الْمُجْرِمِيْنَ مُشْفِقِيْنَ مِمَّا

fearful of that which is therein; and they will say, 'O woe to us! What kind of a Book is this! It leaves out nothing small or great but has recorded it.' And they will find all that they did confronting *them*, and thy Lord does not wrong anyone.

R. 7.

* 51. And *remember the time* when We said to the angels, 'Submit to Adam,' and they *all* submitted, except Iblīs. He was *one* of the Jinn; and he disobeyed the command of his Lord. Will you then take him and his offspring for friends instead of Me while they are your enemies? Evil is the exchange for the wrongdoers.

52. I did not make them witness the creation of the heavens and the earth, nor their own creation; nor could I take as helpers those who lead *people* astray.

53. And *remember* the day when He will say, 'Call those whom you deemed to be My partners.' Then they will call on them, but they will not answer them; and We shall place a barrier between them.

54. And the guilty shall see the Fire and realize that they are going to fall therein; and they shall find no way of escape therefrom.

R. 8.

55. And, surely, We have explained in various ways in this Qur'ān, for *the good of* mankind, all *kinds of* similitudes, but of all things man is most contentious.

* 56. And nothing hinders people from believing when the guidance comes to them, and from asking forgiveness of their Lord, except *that they wait* that there should happen to them the precedent of the ancients or that punishment should come upon them face to face.

57. And We send not the Messengers but as bearers of glad tidings and as Warners. And those who disbelieve contend by means of falsehood so that they may rebut the truth thereby. And they take My Signs and what they are warned of *only* as a jest.

58. And who is more unjust than he who is reminded of the Signs of his Lord,

فِيهِ وَيَقُولُونَ يٰوَيْلَتَنَا مَالِ هٰذَا الْكِتٰبِ لَا يُغَادِرُ
صَغِيرَةً وَّلَا كَبِيرَةً إِلَّآ أَحْصٰهَا ۚ وَوَجَدُوا مَا
عَمِلُوا حَاضِرًا ۗ وَلَا يَظْلِمُ رَبُّكَ أَحَدًا ﴿٥٠﴾
وَإِذْ قُلْنَا لِلْمَلٰٓئِكَةِ اسْجُدُوا لِاٰدَمَ فَسَجَدُوٓا إِلَّآ
إِبْلِيسَ ۖ كَانَ مِنَ الْجِنِّ فَفَسَقَ عَنْ أَمْرِ رَبِّهٖ ۗ
أَفَتَتَّخِذُونَهٗ وَذُرِّيَّتَهٗٓ أَوْلِيَآءَ مِنْ دُونِي وَهُمْ
لَكُمْ عَدُوٌّ ۚ بِئْسَ لِلظّٰلِمِينَ بَدَلًا ﴿٥١﴾
مَآ أَشْهَدْتُّهُمْ خَلْقَ السَّمٰوٰتِ وَالْأَرْضِ وَلَا خَلْقَ
أَنْفُسِهِمْ ۖ وَمَا كُنْتُ مُتَّخِذَ الْمُضِلِّينَ عَضُدًا ﴿٥٢﴾
وَيَوْمَ يَقُولُ نَادُوا شُرَكَآءِيَ الَّذِينَ زَعَمْتُمْ فَدَعَوْهُمْ
فَلَمْ يَسْتَجِيبُوا لَهُمْ وَجَعَلْنَا بَيْنَهُمْ مَّوْبِقًا ﴿٥٣﴾
وَرَاَ الْمُجْرِمُونَ النَّارَ فَظَنُّوٓا أَنَّهُمْ مُّوَاقِعُوهَا وَ
لَمْ يَجِدُوا عَنْهَا مَصْرِفًا ﴿٥٤﴾
وَلَقَدْ صَرَّفْنَا فِي هٰذَا الْقُرْاٰنِ لِلنَّاسِ مِنْ كُلِّ
مَثَلٍ ۚ وَكَانَ الْإِنْسَانُ أَكْثَرَ شَيْءٍ جَدَلًا ﴿٥٥﴾
وَمَا مَنَعَ النَّاسَ أَنْ يُّؤْمِنُوٓا إِذْ جَآءَهُمُ الْهُدٰى
وَيَسْتَغْفِرُوا رَبَّهُمْ إِلَّآ أَنْ تَأْتِيَهُمْ سُنَّةُ الْأَوَّلِينَ
أَوْ يَأْتِيَهُمُ الْعَذَابُ قُبُلًا ﴿٥٦﴾
وَمَا نُرْسِلُ الْمُرْسَلِينَ إِلَّا مُبَشِّرِينَ وَمُنْذِرِينَ ۚ
وَيُجَادِلُ الَّذِينَ كَفَرُوا بِالْبَاطِلِ لِيُدْحِضُوا بِهِ
الْحَقَّ وَاتَّخَذُوٓا اٰيٰتِي وَمَآ أُنْذِرُوا هُزُوًا ﴿٥٧﴾
وَمَنْ أَظْلَمُ مِمَّنْ ذُكِّرَ بِاٰيٰتِ رَبِّهٖ فَأَعْرَضَ عَنْهَا

but turns away from them, and forgets what his hands have sent forward? Verily, We have placed veils over their hearts that they understand it not, and in their ears a deafness. And if thou call them to guidance, they will never accept it.

59. And thy Lord is Most Forgiving, full of mercy. If He were to seize them for what they have earned, then surely He would have hastened the punishment for them. But they have an appointed time from which they will find no refuge.

60. And these towns—We destroyed them when they committed iniquities. And We appointed a fixed time for their destruction.

R. 9.

61. And *remember the time* when Moses said to his young *companion*, 'I will not stop until I reach the junction of the two seas, or I will journey on for ages.'

* 62. But when they reached the place where the two *seas* met, they forgot their fish, and it made its way into the sea *going away* swiftly.

63. And when they had gone further, he said to his young *companion*: 'Bring us our morning meal. Surely, we have suffered much fatigue on account of this journey of ours.'

* 64. He replied, 'Didst thou see, when we betook ourselves to the rock for rest, and I forgot the fish—and none but Satan caused me to forget to mention it *to thee*—it took its way into the sea in a marvellous manner?'

65. He said, 'That is what we have been seeking.' So they both returned, retracing their footsteps.

66. Then found they one of Our servants upon whom We had bestowed Our mercy, and whom We had taught knowledge from Ourself.

67. Moses said to him, 'May I follow thee on condition that thou teach

وَنَسِيَ مَا قَدَّمَتْ يَدٰهُ ؕ اِنَّا جَعَلْنَا عَلٰى قُلُوْبِهِمْ
اَكِنَّةً اَنْ يَّفْقَهُوْهُ وَفِيْٓ اٰذَانِهِمْ وَقْرًا ؕ وَاِنْ
تَدْعُهُمْ اِلَى الْهُدٰى فَلَنْ يَّهْتَدُوْٓا اِذًا اَبَدًا ﴿٥٨﴾
وَرَبُّكَ الْغَفُوْرُ ذُو الرَّحْمَةِ ؕ لَوْ يُؤَاخِذُهُمْ بِمَا
كَسَبُوْا لَعَجَّلَ لَهُمُ الْعَذَابَ ؕ بَلْ لَّهُمْ مَّوْعِدٌ
لَّنْ يَّجِدُوْا مِنْ دُوْنِهٖ مَوْئِلًا ﴿٥٩﴾
وَتِلْكَ الْقُرٰٓى اَهْلَكْنٰهُمْ لَمَّا ظَلَمُوْا وَجَعَلْنَا
لِمَهْلِكِهِمْ مَّوْعِدًا ﴿٦٠﴾ ع
وَاِذْ قَالَ مُوْسٰى لِفَتٰىهُ لَآ اَبْرَحُ حَتّٰٓى اَبْلُغَ
مَجْمَعَ الْبَحْرَيْنِ اَوْ اَمْضِيَ حُقُبًا ﴿٦١﴾
فَلَمَّا بَلَغَا مَجْمَعَ بَيْنِهِمَا نَسِيَا حُوْتَهُمَا فَاتَّخَذَ
سَبِيْلَهٗ فِي الْبَحْرِ سَرَبًا ﴿٦٢﴾
فَلَمَّا جَاوَزَا قَالَ لِفَتٰىهُ اٰتِنَا غَدَآءَنَا ٘ لَقَدْ لَقِيْنَا
مِنْ سَفَرِنَا هٰذَا نَصَبًا ﴿٦٣﴾
قَالَ اَرَءَيْتَ اِذْ اَوَيْنَآ اِلَى الصَّخْرَةِ فَاِنِّيْ نَسِيْتُ
الْحُوْتَ ٘ وَمَآ اَنْسٰنِيْهُ اِلَّا الشَّيْطٰنُ اَنْ اَذْكُرَهٗ ۚ
وَاتَّخَذَ سَبِيْلَهٗ فِي الْبَحْرِ ۖ عَجَبًا ﴿٦٤﴾
قَالَ ذٰلِكَ مَا كُنَّا نَبْغِ ۖ فَارْتَدَّا عَلٰٓى اٰثَارِهِمَا
قَصَصًا ﴿٦٥﴾
فَوَجَدَا عَبْدًا مِّنْ عِبَادِنَآ اٰتَيْنٰهُ رَحْمَةً مِّنْ
عِنْدِنَا وَعَلَّمْنٰهُ مِنْ لَّدُنَّا عِلْمًا ﴿٦٦﴾
قَالَ لَهٗ مُوْسٰى هَلْ اَتَّبِعُكَ عَلٰٓى اَنْ تُعَلِّمَنِ

me of the guidance which thou hast been taught?'

68. He replied, 'Thou canst not keep company with me in patience.

69. 'And how canst thou be patient about things the knowledge of which thou comprehendest not?'

* 70. He said, 'Thou wilt find me, if Allah please, patient and I shall not disobey any command of thine.'

71. He said, 'Well, if thou wouldst follow me, then ask me no questions about anything till I myself speak to thee concerning it.'

R. 10.

72. So they both set out till, when they embarked in a boat, he staved it in. *Moses* said, 'Hast thou staved it in to drown those who are in it? Surely, thou hast done an evil thing.'

73. He replied, 'Did I not tell *thee* that thou wouldst not be able to keep company with me in patience?'

74. *Moses* said, 'Take me not to task at my forgetting and be not hard on me for this *lapse* of mine.'

75. So they journeyed on till, when they met a young boy, he slew him. *Moses* said, 'Hast thou slain an innocent person without *his having slain* any one? Surely, thou hast done a hideous thing!'

76. He replied, 'Did I not tell thee that thou wouldst not be able to keep company with me in patience?'

77. *Moses* said, 'If I ask thee concerning anything after this, keep me not in thy company, for *then* thou shalt have got sufficient excuse from me.'

78. So they went on till, when they came to the people of a town, they asked its people for food, but they refused to make them *their* guests. And they found therein a wall which was about to fall, and he repaired it. *Moses* said, 'If thou hadst desired, thou couldst have taken payment for it.'

مِمَّا عُلِّمْتَ رُشْدًا ﴿٦٧﴾
قَالَ إِنَّكَ لَنْ تَسْتَطِيعَ مَعِيَ صَبْرًا ﴿٦٨﴾
وَكَيْفَ تَصْبِرُ عَلَىٰ مَا لَمْ تُحِطْ بِهِ خُبْرًا ﴿٦٩﴾
قَالَ سَتَجِدُنِي إِنْ شَاءَ اللَّهُ صَابِرًا وَلَا أَعْصِي لَكَ
أَمْرًا ﴿٧٠﴾
قَالَ فَإِنِ اتَّبَعْتَنِي فَلَا تَسْأَلْنِي عَنْ شَيْءٍ حَتَّىٰ أُحْدِثَ
لَكَ مِنْهُ ذِكْرًا ﴿٧١﴾
فَانْطَلَقَا حَتَّىٰ إِذَا رَكِبَا فِي السَّفِينَةِ خَرَقَهَا قَالَ
أَخَرَقْتَهَا لِتُغْرِقَ أَهْلَهَا لَقَدْ جِئْتَ شَيْئًا إِمْرًا ﴿٧٢﴾
قَالَ أَلَمْ أَقُلْ إِنَّكَ لَنْ تَسْتَطِيعَ مَعِيَ صَبْرًا ﴿٧٣﴾
قَالَ لَا تُؤَاخِذْنِي بِمَا نَسِيتُ وَلَا تُرْهِقْنِي مِنْ
أَمْرِي عُسْرًا ﴿٧٤﴾
فَانْطَلَقَا حَتَّىٰ إِذَا لَقِيَا غُلَامًا فَقَتَلَهُ قَالَ أَقَتَلْتَ
نَفْسًا زَكِيَّةً بِغَيْرِ نَفْسٍ لَقَدْ جِئْتَ شَيْئًا
نُكْرًا ﴿٧٥﴾
قَالَ أَلَمْ أَقُلْ لَكَ إِنَّكَ لَنْ تَسْتَطِيعَ مَعِيَ صَبْرًا ﴿٧٦﴾
قَالَ إِنْ سَأَلْتُكَ عَنْ شَيْءٍ بَعْدَهَا فَلَا تُصَاحِبْنِي قَدْ
بَلَغْتَ مِنْ لَدُنِّي عُذْرًا ﴿٧٧﴾
فَانْطَلَقَا حَتَّىٰ إِذَا أَتَيَا أَهْلَ قَرْيَةٍ اسْتَطْعَمَا أَهْلَهَا
فَأَبَوْا أَنْ يُضَيِّفُوهُمَا فَوَجَدَا فِيهَا جِدَارًا يُرِيدُ
أَنْ يَنْقَضَّ فَأَقَامَهُ قَالَ لَوْ شِئْتَ لَتَّخَذْتَ
عَلَيْهِ أَجْرًا ﴿٧٨﴾

79. He said, 'This is the parting *of ways* between me and thee. I will now tell thee the meaning of that which thou wast not able to bear with patience:

قَالَ هٰذَا فِرَاقُ بَيْنِيْ وَ بَيْنِكَ ۚ سَاُنَبِّئُكَ بِتَاْوِيْلِ
مَا لَمْ تَسْتَطِعْ عَّلَيْهِ صَبْرًا ﴿٧٩﴾

80. 'As for the boat, it belonged to *certain* poor people who worked on the sea; and I desired to damage it, for there was behind them a king, who seized every boat by force.

اَمَّا السَّفِيْنَةُ فَكَانَتْ لِمَسٰكِيْنَ يَعْمَلُوْنَ فِي الْبَحْرِ
فَاَرَدْتُّ اَنْ اَعِيْبَهَا وَكَانَ وَرَآءَهُمْ مَّلِكٌ يَّاْخُذُ
كُلَّ سَفِيْنَةٍ غَصْبًا ﴿٨٠﴾

81. 'And as for the youth, his parents were believers, and we feared lest he should cause them trouble through rebellion and disbelief.

وَ اَمَّا الْغُلٰمُ فَكَانَ اَبَوٰهُ مُؤْمِنَيْنِ فَخَشِيْنَآ اَنْ
يُّرْهِقَهُمَا طُغْيَانًا وَّ كُفْرًا ۚ ﴿٨١﴾

82. 'So we desired that their Lord should give them in exchange *a child* better than him in purity and closer in *filial* affection.

فَاَرَدْنَآ اَنْ يُّبْدِلَهُمَا رَبُّهُمَا خَيْرًا مِّنْهُ زَكٰوةً
وَّ اَقْرَبَ رُحْمًا ﴿٨٢﴾

83. 'And as for the wall, it belonged to two orphan boys in the town, and beneath it was a treasure belonging to them, and their father had been *a* righteous *man*, so thy Lord desired that they should reach their *age of* full strength and take out their treasure, as a mercy from thy Lord; and I did it not of my own accord. This is the explanation of that which thou wast not able to bear with patience.'

وَ اَمَّا الْجِدَارُ فَكَانَ لِغُلٰمَيْنِ يَتِيْمَيْنِ فِي الْمَدِيْنَةِ
وَكَانَ تَحْتَهٗ كَنْزٌ لَّهُمَا وَكَانَ اَبُوْهُمَا صَالِحًا ۚ
فَاَرَادَ رَبُّكَ اَنْ يَّبْلُغَآ اَشُدَّهُمَا وَ يَسْتَخْرِجَا كَنْزَهُمَا ۖ
رَحْمَةً مِّنْ رَّبِّكَ ۚ وَ مَا فَعَلْتُهٗ عَنْ اَمْرِيْ ۭ ذٰلِكَ
تَاْوِيْلُ مَا لَمْ تَسْطِعْ عَّلَيْهِ صَبْرًا ﴿٨٣﴾ ع

R. 11.

84. And they ask thee about Dhu'l Qarnain. Say, 'I will certainly recite to you *something* of his story.'

وَ يَسْـَٔلُوْنَكَ عَنْ ذِي الْقَرْنَيْنِ ۭ قُلْ سَاَتْلُوْا عَلَيْكُمْ
مِّنْهُ ذِكْرًا ﴿٨٤﴾

85. We established him in the earth and gave him the means to *accomplish* everything.

اِنَّا مَكَّنَّا لَهٗ فِي الْاَرْضِ وَ اٰتَيْنٰهُ مِنْ كُلِّ شَيْءٍ
سَبَبًا ﴿٨٥﴾

86. Then he followed a *certain* way

فَاَتْبَعَ سَبَبًا ﴿٨٦﴾

87. Until, when he reached the setting of the sun, he found it setting in a pool of murky water, and near it he found a people. We said, 'O Dhu'l Qarnain, either

حَتّٰٓى اِذَا بَلَغَ مَغْرِبَ الشَّمْسِ وَجَدَهَا تَغْرُبُ فِيْ
عَيْنٍ حَمِئَةٍ وَّ وَجَدَ عِنْدَهَا قَوْمًا ۬ قُلْنَا يٰذَا
الْقَرْنَيْنِ اِمَّآ اَنْ تُعَذِّبَ وَ اِمَّآ اَنْ تَتَّخِذَ فِيْهِمْ

punish them, or treat them with kindness.'

حُسْنًا ﴿٨٧﴾

88. He said, 'As for him who does wrong, we shall certainly punish him; then shall he be brought back to his Lord, Who will punish him with a dreadful punishment.'

قَالَ اَمَّا مَنْ ظَلَمَ فَسَوْفَ نُعَذِّبُهٗ ثُمَّ يُرَدُّ اِلٰى
رَبِّهٖ فَيُعَذِّبُهٗ عَذَابًا نُّكْرًا ﴿٨٨﴾

89. But as for him who believes and acts righteously, he will have a good reward, and We shall speak to him easy *words* of Our command.

وَاَمَّا مَنْ اٰمَنَ وَعَمِلَ صَالِحًا فَلَهٗ جَزَآءَ ۨالْحُسْنٰى
وَسَنَقُوْلُ لَهٗ مِنْ اَمْرِنَا يُسْرًا ﴿٨٩﴾

90. Then *indeed* he followed *another* way

ثُمَّ اَتْبَعَ سَبَبًا ﴿٩٠﴾

91. Until, when he reached the rising of the sun, he found it rising on a people for whom We had made no shelter against it.

حَتّٰٓى اِذَا بَلَغَ مَطْلِعَ الشَّمْسِ وَجَدَهَا تَطْلُعُ عَلٰى
قَوْمٍ لَّمْ نَجْعَلْ لَّهُمْ مِّنْ دُوْنِهَا سِتْرًا ﴿٩١﴾

92. Thus *indeed it was*. Verily, We encompassed with Our knowledge *all* that was with him.

كَذٰلِكَ ۭ وَقَدْ اَحَطْنَا بِمَا لَدَيْهِ خُبْرًا ﴿٩٢﴾

93. Then he followed *another* way

ثُمَّ اَتْبَعَ سَبَبًا ﴿٩٣﴾

94. Until, when he reached the place between the two mountains, he found beneath them a people who would scarcely understand a word.

حَتّٰٓى اِذَا بَلَغَ بَيْنَ السَّدَّيْنِ وَجَدَ مِنْ دُوْنِهِمَا قَوْمًا ۙ
لَّا يَكَادُوْنَ يَفْقَهُوْنَ قَوْلًا ﴿٩٤﴾

95. They said, 'O Dhu'l Qarnain, verily, Gog and Magog are creating disorder in the earth; shall we then pay thee tribute on condition that thou set up a barrier between us and them?'

قَالُوْا يٰذَا الْقَرْنَيْنِ اِنَّ يَاْجُوْجَ وَمَاْجُوْجَ مُفْسِدُوْنَ
فِي الْاَرْضِ فَهَلْ نَجْعَلُ لَكَ خَرْجًا عَلٰٓى اَنْ تَجْعَلَ
بَيْنَنَا وَبَيْنَهُمْ سَدًّا ﴿٩٥﴾

96. He replied, 'The power with which my Lord has endowed me about this is better, but you may help me with physical strength; I will set up between you and them a rampart.

قَالَ مَا مَكَّنِّيْ فِيْهِ رَبِّيْ خَيْرٌ فَاَعِيْنُوْنِيْ بِقُوَّةٍ اَجْعَلْ
بَيْنَكُمْ وَبَيْنَهُمْ رَدْمًا ﴿٩٦﴾

97. 'Bring me blocks of iron.' *They did so* till, when he had levelled up the space between the two mountain sides, he said, '*Now* blow *with your bellows.*' *They blew* till, when he had made it *red as* fire, he said, 'Bring me molten copper that I may pour it thereon.'

اٰتُوْنِيْ زُبَرَ الْحَدِيْدِ ۭ حَتّٰٓى اِذَا سَاوٰى بَيْنَ الصَّدَفَيْنِ
قَالَ انْفُخُوْا ۭ حَتّٰٓى اِذَا جَعَلَهٗ نَارًا ۙ قَالَ اٰتُوْنِيْٓ اُفْرِغْ
عَلَيْهِ قِطْرًا ﴿٩٧﴾

98. So they (Gog and Magog) were not able to scale it, nor were they able to dig through it.

فَمَا اسْطَاعُوْٓا اَنْ يَّظْهَرُوْهُ وَمَا اسْتَطَاعُوْا لَهٗ
نَقْبًا ﴿٩٨﴾

99. *Thereupon* he said, 'This is a mercy from my Lord. But when the promise of my Lord shall come to pass, He will break it into pieces. And the promise of my Lord is *certainly* true.'

قَالَ هٰذَا رَحْمَةٌ مِّنْ رَّبِّيْ ۚ فَاِذَا جَآءَ وَعْدُ رَبِّيْ
جَعَلَهٗ دَكَّآءَ ۚ وَكَانَ وَعْدُ رَبِّيْ حَقًّا ﴿۹۹﴾

100. And on that day We shall leave some of them to surge against others, and the trumpet will be blown. Then shall We gather them all together.

وَتَرَكْنَا بَعْضَهُمْ يَوْمَئِذٍ يَّمُوْجُ فِيْ بَعْضٍ وَّنُفِخَ
فِي الصُّوْرِ فَجَمَعْنٰهُمْ جَمْعًا ﴿۱۰۰﴾

101. And on that day We shall present Hell, face to face, to the disbelievers —

وَّعَرَضْنَا جَهَنَّمَ يَوْمَئِذٍ لِّلْكٰفِرِيْنَ عَرْضًا ﴿۱۰۱﴾

102. Whose eyes were under a veil *so as not to heed* My warning, and they could not even hear.

الَّذِيْنَ كَانَتْ اَعْيُنُهُمْ فِيْ غِطَآءٍ عَنْ ذِكْرِيْ وَكَانُوْا
لَا يَسْتَطِيْعُوْنَ سَمْعًا ﴿۱۰۲﴾

R. 12.

103. Do the disbelievers think that they can take My servants as protectors instead of Me? Surely, We have prepared Hell as an entertainment for the disbelievers.

اَفَحَسِبَ الَّذِيْنَ كَفَرُوْٓا اَنْ يَّتَّخِذُوْا عِبَادِيْ مِنْ
دُوْنِيْٓ اَوْلِيَآءَ ۭ اِنَّآ اَعْتَدْنَا جَهَنَّمَ لِلْكٰفِرِيْنَ
نُزُلًا ﴿۱۰۳﴾

* 104. Say, 'Shall We tell you of those who are the greatest losers in respect of their works? —

قُلْ هَلْ نُنَبِّئُكُمْ بِالْاَخْسَرِيْنَ اَعْمَالًا ﴿۱۰۴﴾

105. 'Those whose labour is *all* lost in *search after things pertaining to* the life of this world, and they think that they are doing good works.'

اَلَّذِيْنَ ضَلَّ سَعْيُهُمْ فِي الْحَيٰوةِ الدُّنْيَا وَهُمْ
يَحْسَبُوْنَ اَنَّهُمْ يُحْسِنُوْنَ صُنْعًا ﴿۱۰۵﴾

106. Those are they who disbelieve in the Signs of their Lord and in the meeting with Him. So their works are vain, and on the Day of Resurrection We shall give them no weight.

اُولٰٓئِكَ الَّذِيْنَ كَفَرُوْا بِاٰيٰتِ رَبِّهِمْ وَلِقَآئِهٖ
فَحَبِطَتْ اَعْمَالُهُمْ فَلَا نُقِيْمُ لَهُمْ يَوْمَ الْقِيٰمَةِ
وَزْنًا ﴿۱۰۶﴾

107. That is their reward—Hell; because they disbelieved, and made a jest of My Signs and My Messengers.

ذٰلِكَ جَزَآؤُهُمْ جَهَنَّمُ بِمَا كَفَرُوْا وَاتَّخَذُوْٓا اٰيٰتِيْ
وَرُسُلِيْ هُزُوًا ﴿۱۰۷﴾

108. Surely, those who believe and do good deeds, will have Gardens of Paradise for an abode,

اِنَّ الَّذِيْنَ اٰمَنُوْا وَعَمِلُوا الصّٰلِحٰتِ كَانَتْ لَهُمْ
جَنّٰتُ الْفِرْدَوْسِ نُزُلًا ﴿۱۰۸﴾

109. Wherein they will abide; they will not desire any change therefrom.

خٰلِدِيْنَ فِيْهَا لَا يَبْغُوْنَ عَنْهَا حِوَلًا ﴿۱۰۹﴾

110. Say, 'If the ocean became ink for the words of my Lord, surely, the ocean

قُلْ لَّوْ كَانَ الْبَحْرُ مِدَادًا لِّكَلِمٰتِ رَبِّيْ لَنَفِدَ

would be exhausted before the words of my Lord came to an end, even though We brought the like thereof as *further* help.'

الْبَحْرُ قَبْلَ اَنْ تَنْفَدَ كَلِمٰتُ رَبِّيْ وَلَوْ جِئْنَا
بِمِثْلِهٖ مَدَدًا ﴿۱۱۰﴾

111. Say, 'I am only a man like yourselves; *but* I have received the revelation that your God is only One God. So let him who hopes to meet his Lord do good deeds, and let him join no one in the worship of his Lord.'

قُلْ اِنَّمَآ اَنَا بَشَرٌ مِّثْلُكُمْ يُوْحٰٓى اِلَيَّ اَنَّمَآ اِلٰهُكُمْ اِلٰهٌ
وَّاحِدٌ ۚ فَمَنْ كَانَ يَرْجُوْا لِقَآءَ رَبِّهٖ فَلْيَعْمَلْ عَمَلًا
صَالِحًا وَّلَا يُشْرِكْ بِعِبَادَةِ رَبِّهٖٓ اَحَدًا ﴿۱۱۱﴾ ع

ركوعاتها ٦ سُوۡرَةُ مَرۡيَمَ مَكِّيَّةٌ (١٩) اٰياتها ٩٩

MARYAM

(Revealed before Hijra)

1. In the name of Allah, the Gracious, the Merciful.

2. Kāf Hā Yā 'Ain Ṣād *.

3. *This is* an account of the mercy of thy Lord *shown* to His servant, Zachariah.

4. When he called upon his Lord, a secret calling,

5. He said, 'My Lord, the bones have indeed waxed feeble in me, and the head glistens with hoariness, but never, my Lord, have I been unblessed in my prayer to Thee.

6. 'And I fear my relations after me, and my wife is barren. Grant me, therefore, a successor from Thyself,

7. 'That he may be heir to me and to the House of Jacob. And make him, my Lord, well-pleasing to Thee.'

8. 'O Zachariah, We give thee glad tidings of a son whose name *shall* be Yaḥyā**. We have not made any one before him of that name.'

9. He said, 'My Lord, how shall I have a son when my wife is barren and I have reached *the* extreme *limit of* old age?'

10. He said, 'So it is.' But thy Lord says, 'It is easy for Me, and indeed I created thee before, when thou wast nothing.'

11. He said, 'My Lord, appoint for me a token.' *God* said, 'Thy token is that thou shalt not speak to anyone for three full *days and* nights.'

12. Then he came forth unto his people from the chamber and asked them by signs

بِسۡمِ اللّٰهِ الرَّحۡمٰنِ الرَّحِيۡمِ ﴿١﴾

كٓهٰيٰعٓصٓ ﴿٢﴾

ذِكۡرُ رَحۡمَتِ رَبِّكَ عَبۡدَهٗ زَكَرِيَّا ﴿٣﴾

اِذۡ نَادٰى رَبَّهٗ نِدَآءً خَفِيًّا ﴿٤﴾

قَالَ رَبِّ اِنِّىۡ وَهَنَ الۡعَظۡمُ مِنِّىۡ وَاشۡتَعَلَ الرَّاۡسُ
شَيۡبًا وَّلَمۡ اَكُنۡۢ بِدُعَآئِكَ رَبِّ شَقِيًّا ﴿٥﴾

وَاِنِّىۡ خِفۡتُ الۡمَوَالِىَ مِنۡ وَّرَآءِىۡ وَكَانَتِ امۡرَاَتِىۡ
عَاقِرًا فَهَبۡ لِىۡ مِنۡ لَّدُنۡكَ وَلِيًّا ﴿٦﴾

يَّرِثُنِىۡ وَيَرِثُ مِنۡ اٰلِ يَعۡقُوۡبَ وَاجۡعَلۡهُ رَبِّ
رَضِيًّا ﴿٧﴾

يٰزَكَرِيَّاۤ اِنَّا نُبَشِّرُكَ بِغُلٰمِ اۨسۡمُهٗ يَحۡيٰى لَمۡ نَجۡعَلۡ
لَّهٗ مِنۡ قَبۡلُ سَمِيًّا ﴿٨﴾

قَالَ رَبِّ اَنّٰى يَكُوۡنُ لِىۡ غُلٰمٌ وَّكَانَتِ امۡرَاَتِىۡ عَاقِرًا
وَّقَدۡ بَلَغۡتُ مِنَ الۡكِبَرِ عِتِيًّا ﴿٩﴾

قَالَ كَذٰلِكَ قَالَ رَبُّكَ هُوَ عَلَىَّ هَيِّنٌ وَّقَدۡ
خَلَقۡتُكَ مِنۡ قَبۡلُ وَلَمۡ تَكُ شَيۡـًٔا ﴿١٠﴾

قَالَ رَبِّ اجۡعَلۡ لِّىۡۤ اٰيَةً قَالَ اٰيَتُكَ اَلَّا تُكَلِّمَ
النَّاسَ ثَلٰثَ لَيَالٍ سَوِيًّا ﴿١١﴾

فَخَرَجَ عَلٰى قَوۡمِهٖ مِنَ الۡمِحۡرَابِ فَاَوۡحٰۤى اِلَيۡهِمۡ

* Thou art sufficient for all and Thou art the True Guide, O All-Knowing, Truthful God!

** John.

to glorify *God* in the morning and in the evening.

اَنْ سَبِّحُوْا بُكْرَةً وَّعَشِيًّا ﴿١٢﴾

13. 'O Yaḥyā, hold fast the Book.' And We gave him wisdom while yet a child,

يٰيَحْيٰى خُذِ الْكِتٰبَ بِقُوَّةٍ ۭ وَاٰتَيْنٰهُ الْحُكْمَ
صَبِيًّا ﴿١٣﴾

14. And tenderness *of heart* from Ourself, and purity. And he was pious

وَّحَنَانًا مِّنْ لَّدُنَّا وَزَكٰوةً ۭ وَكَانَ تَقِيًّا ﴿١٤﴾

15. And dutiful toward his parents. And he was not haughty *and* rebellious.

وَّبَرًّا بِوَالِدَيْهِ وَلَمْ يَكُنْ جَبَّارًا عَصِيًّا ﴿١٥﴾

16. And peace was on him the day he was born, and the day he died, and *peace there will be on him* the day he will be raised up to life *again*.

وَسَلٰمٌ عَلَيْهِ يَوْمَ وُلِدَ وَيَوْمَ يَمُوْتُ وَيَوْمَ يُبْعَثُ
حَيًّا ﴿١٦﴾

R. 2.

17. And relate *the story of* Mary *as mentioned* in the Book. When she withdrew from her people to a place to the east,

وَاذْكُرْ فِي الْكِتٰبِ مَرْيَمَ ۘ اِذِ انْتَبَذَتْ مِنْ اَهْلِهَا
مَكَانًا شَرْقِيًّا ﴿١٧﴾

18. And screened herself off from them, then We sent Our angel to her, and he appeared to her in the form of a perfect man.

فَاتَّخَذَتْ مِنْ دُوْنِهِمْ حِجَابًا ۫ فَاَرْسَلْنَآ اِلَيْهَا
رُوْحَنَا فَتَمَثَّلَ لَهَا بَشَرًا سَوِيًّا ﴿١٨﴾

19. She said, 'I seek refuge with the Gracious *God* from thee if indeed thou dost fear *Him*.'

قَالَتْ اِنِّيْٓ اَعُوْذُ بِالرَّحْمٰنِ مِنْكَ اِنْ كُنْتَ تَقِيًّا ﴿١٩﴾

20. He replied, 'I am only a Messenger of thy Lord, that I may bestow on thee a righteous son.'

قَالَ اِنَّمَآ اَنَا رَسُوْلُ رَبِّكِ ۖ لِاَهَبَ لَكِ غُلٰمًا
زَكِيًّا ﴿٢٠﴾

21. She said, 'How can I have a son when no man has touched me, neither have I been unchaste?'

قَالَتْ اَنّٰى يَكُوْنُ لِيْ غُلٰمٌ وَّلَمْ يَمْسَسْنِيْ بَشَرٌ وَّ
لَمْ اَكُ بَغِيًّا ﴿٢١﴾

22. He replied, 'Thus it is.' But says thy Lord, 'It is easy for Me; and *We shall do so* that We may make him a Sign unto men, and a mercy from Us, and it is a thing decreed.'

قَالَ كَذٰلِكِ ۚ قَالَ رَبُّكِ هُوَ عَلَيَّ هَيِّنٌ ۚ وَلِنَجْعَلَهٗٓ اٰيَةً
لِّلنَّاسِ وَرَحْمَةً مِّنَّا ۚ وَكَانَ اَمْرًا مَّقْضِيًّا ﴿٢٢﴾

23. So she conceived him, and withdrew with him to a remote place.

فَحَمَلَتْهُ فَانْتَبَذَتْ بِهٖ مَكَانًا قَصِيًّا ﴿٢٣﴾

*24. And the pains of childbirth drove her unto the trunk of a palm-tree. She said, 'O! would that I had died before this and had become a thing quite forgotten!'

فَاَجَآءَهَا الْمَخَاضُ اِلٰى جِذْعِ النَّخْلَةِ ۚ قَالَتْ
يٰلَيْتَنِيْ مِتُّ قَبْلَ هٰذَا وَكُنْتُ نَسْيًا مَّنْسِيًّا ﴿٢٤﴾

25. Then he called her from beneath her, *saying*, "Grieve not. Thy Lord has placed

فَنَادٰىهَا مِنْ تَحْتِهَآ اَلَّا تَحْزَنِيْ قَدْ جَعَلَ رَبُّكِ

a rivulet below thee;

تَحْتَكِ سَرِيًّا ﴿٢٥﴾

26. "And shake towards thyself the trunk of the palm-tree; it will cause fresh ripe dates to fall upon thee.

وَهُزِّيْٓ إِلَيْكِ بِجِذْعِ النَّخْلَةِ تُسٰقِطْ عَلَيْكِ رُطَبًا جَنِيًّا ﴿٢٦﴾

27. "So eat and drink, and cool *thy* eye. And if thou seest any man, say, 'I have vowed a fast to the Gracious *God;* I will therefore not speak this day to any human being.' "

فَكُلِيْ وَاشْرَبِيْ وَقَرِّيْ عَيْنًا ۚ فَإِمَّا تَرَيِنَّ مِنَ الْبَشَرِ أَحَدًا ۙ فَقُوْلِيْٓ إِنِّيْ نَذَرْتُ لِلرَّحْمٰنِ صَوْمًا فَلَنْ أُكَلِّمَ الْيَوْمَ إِنْسِيًّا ﴿٢٧﴾

28. Then she brought him to her people, carrying him. They said, 'O Mary, thou hast brought forth a strange thing.

فَأَتَتْ بِهٖ قَوْمَهَا تَحْمِلُهٗ ۖ قَالُوْا يٰمَرْيَمُ لَقَدْ جِئْتِ شَيْـًٔا فَرِيًّا ﴿٢٨﴾

29. 'O sister of Aaron, thy father was not a wicked man nor was thy mother an unchaste woman!'

يٰٓأُخْتَ هٰرُوْنَ مَا كَانَ أَبُوْكِ امْرَأَ سَوْءٍ وَّمَا كَانَتْ أُمُّكِ بَغِيًّا ﴿٢٩﴾

30. Then she pointed to him. They said, 'How can we talk to one who is a child in the cradle?'

فَأَشَارَتْ إِلَيْهِ ۖ قَالُوْا كَيْفَ نُكَلِّمُ مَنْ كَانَ فِي الْمَهْدِ صَبِيًّا ﴿٣٠﴾

31. He said, 'I am a servant of Allah. He has given me the Book, and made me a Prophet;

قَالَ إِنِّيْ عَبْدُ اللّٰهِ ۗ اٰتٰنِيَ الْكِتٰبَ وَجَعَلَنِيْ نَبِيًّا ﴿٣١﴾

32. 'And He has made me blessed wheresoever I may be, and has enjoined upon me Prayer and almsgiving so long as I live;

وَّجَعَلَنِيْ مُبٰرَكًا أَيْنَ مَا كُنْتُ ۖ وَأَوْصٰنِيْ بِالصَّلٰوةِ وَالزَّكٰوةِ مَا دُمْتُ حَيًّا ﴿٣٢﴾

33. 'And *He has made me* dutiful toward my mother, and He has not made me haughty *and* unblessed.

وَّبَرًّا بِوَالِدَتِيْ ۫ وَلَمْ يَجْعَلْنِيْ جَبَّارًا شَقِيًّا ﴿٣٣﴾

34. 'And peace was on me the day I was born, and *peace there will be on me* the day I shall die, and the day I shall be raised up to life *again*.'

وَالسَّلٰمُ عَلَيَّ يَوْمَ وُلِدْتُّ وَيَوْمَ أَمُوْتُ وَيَوْمَ أُبْعَثُ حَيًّا ﴿٣٤﴾

35. Such was Jesus, son of Mary. *This is* a statement of the truth about which they doubt.

ذٰلِكَ عِيْسَى ابْنُ مَرْيَمَ ۚ قَوْلَ الْحَقِّ الَّذِيْ فِيْهِ يَمْتَرُوْنَ ﴿٣٥﴾

36. It does not befit *the Majesty of* Allah to take unto Himself a son. Holy is He. When He decrees a thing, He says to it, 'Be!', and it is.

مَا كَانَ لِلّٰهِ أَنْ يَّتَّخِذَ مِنْ وَّلَدٍ ۙ سُبْحٰنَهٗ ۚ إِذَا قَضٰٓى أَمْرًا فَإِنَّمَا يَقُوْلُ لَهٗ كُنْ فَيَكُوْنُ ﴿٣٦﴾

37. *Said Jesus:* 'Surely, Allah is my Lord, and your Lord. So worship Him *alone;* this is the right path.'

وَإِنَّ اللّٰهَ رَبِّيْ وَرَبُّكُمْ فَاعْبُدُوْهُ ۗ هٰذَا صِرَاطٌ مُّسْتَقِيْمٌ ﴿٣٧﴾

38. But the parties differed among themselves; so woe to those who disbelieve because of the meeting of the great day.

فَاخْتَلَفَ الْأَحْزَابُ مِنْۢ بَيْنِهِمْ ۚ فَوَيْلٌ لِّلَّذِيْنَ كَفَرُوْا مِنْ مَّشْهَدِ يَوْمٍ عَظِيْمٍ ﴿٣٨﴾

39. How wonderful will their hearing and seeing be on the day when they will come to Us! But today the wrongdoers are in manifest error.

أَسْمِعْ بِهِمْ وَأَبْصِرْ ۙ يَوْمَ يَأْتُوْنَنَا لٰكِنِ الظّٰلِمُوْنَ الْيَوْمَ فِيْ ضَلٰلٍ مُّبِيْنٍ ﴿٣٩﴾

40. And warn them of the day of grief when the matter will be decided. But now they are in *a state of* carelessness, so they do not believe.

وَأَنْذِرْهُمْ يَوْمَ الْحَسْرَةِ إِذْ قُضِيَ الْأَمْرُ ۘ وَهُمْ فِيْ غَفْلَةٍ وَّهُمْ لَا يُؤْمِنُوْنَ ﴿٤٠﴾ وقف لازم

41. It is We Who will inherit the earth and *all* who are thereon; and to Us will they *all* be returned.

إِنَّا نَحْنُ نَرِثُ الْأَرْضَ وَمَنْ عَلَيْهَا وَإِلَيْنَا يُرْجَعُوْنَ ﴿٤١﴾ ع

R. 3.

42. And relate *the story of* Abraham *as mentioned* in the Book. He was *a* truthful *man and* a Prophet.

وَاذْكُرْ فِي الْكِتٰبِ إِبْرٰهِيْمَ ۥ إِنَّهٗ كَانَ صِدِّيْقًا نَّبِيًّا ﴿٤٢﴾

43. When he said to his father, 'O my father, why dost thou worship that which hears not, nor sees, nor can avail thee aught?

إِذْ قَالَ لِأَبِيْهِ يٰٓأَبَتِ لِمَ تَعْبُدُ مَا لَا يَسْمَعُ وَلَا يُبْصِرُ وَلَا يُغْنِيْ عَنْكَ شَيْئًا ﴿٤٣﴾

44. 'O my father, there has indeed come to me knowledge such as has not come to thee; so follow me, I will guide thee to an even path.

يٰٓأَبَتِ إِنِّيْ قَدْ جَآءَنِيْ مِنَ الْعِلْمِ مَا لَمْ يَأْتِكَ فَاتَّبِعْنِيْٓ أَهْدِكَ صِرَاطًا سَوِيًّا ﴿٤٤﴾

45. 'O my father, serve not Satan; surely, Satan is a rebel against the Gracious *God*.

يٰٓأَبَتِ لَا تَعْبُدِ الشَّيْطٰنَ ۖ إِنَّ الشَّيْطٰنَ كَانَ لِلرَّحْمٰنِ عَصِيًّا ﴿٤٥﴾

46. 'O my father, indeed, I fear lest a punishment from the Gracious *God* seize thee, and thou become a comrade of Satan.'

يٰٓأَبَتِ إِنِّيْٓ أَخَافُ أَنْ يَّمَسَّكَ عَذَابٌ مِّنَ الرَّحْمٰنِ فَتَكُوْنَ لِلشَّيْطٰنِ وَلِيًّا ﴿٤٦﴾

47. He replied, 'Dost thou turn away from my gods, O Abraham? If thou cease not, I shall surely cut off all relations with thee. Now leave me alone for a long while.'

قَالَ أَرَاغِبٌ أَنْتَ عَنْ اٰلِهَتِيْ يٰٓإِبْرٰهِيْمُ ۚ لَئِنْ لَّمْ تَنْتَهِ لَأَرْجُمَنَّكَ وَاهْجُرْنِيْ مَلِيًّا ﴿٤٧﴾

48. *Abraham* said, 'Peace be on thee. I will ask forgiveness of my Lord for thee. He is indeed gracious to me.

قَالَ سَلٰمٌ عَلَيْكَ سَاَسْتَغْفِرُ لَكَ رَبِّيْ اِنَّهٗ كَانَ بِيْ حَفِيًّا ﴿٤٨﴾

49. 'And I shall keep away from you and from that which you call upon beside Allah; and I will pray unto my Lord; it may be that, in praying to my Lord, I shall not be disappointed.'

وَاَعْتَزِلُكُمْ وَمَا تَدْعُوْنَ مِنْ دُوْنِ اللّٰهِ وَاَدْعُوْا رَبِّيْ عَسٰۤى اَلَّاۤ اَكُوْنَ بِدُعَآءِ رَبِّيْ شَقِيًّا ﴿٤٩﴾

50. So when he had separated himself from them and from that which they worshipped beside Allah, We bestowed on him Isaac and Jacob, and each *of them* We made a Prophet.

فَلَمَّا اعْتَزَلَهُمْ وَمَا يَعْبُدُوْنَ مِنْ دُوْنِ اللّٰهِ وَهَبْنَا لَهٗۤ اِسْحٰقَ وَيَعْقُوْبَ وَكُلًّا جَعَلْنَا نَبِيًّا ﴿٥٠﴾

51. And We granted them of Our mercy; and We bestowed on them a true renown.

وَوَهَبْنَا لَهُمْ مِّنْ رَّحْمَتِنَا وَجَعَلْنَا لَهُمْ لِسَانَ صِدْقٍ عَلِيًّا ﴿٥١﴾ ع ٣

R. 4.

52. And relate *the story of* Moses *as mentioned* in the Book. He was indeed a chosen one; and he was a Messenger, a Prophet.

وَاذْكُرْ فِي الْكِتٰبِ مُوْسٰۤى اِنَّهٗ كَانَ مُخْلَصًا وَّكَانَ رَسُوْلًا نَّبِيًّا ﴿٥٢﴾

53. And We called him from the right side of the Mount, and made him draw near *to Us* for *special* communion.

وَنَادَيْنٰهُ مِنْ جَانِبِ الطُّوْرِ الْاَيْمَنِ وَقَرَّبْنٰهُ نَجِيًّا ﴿٥٣﴾

54. And We bestowed upon him, out of Our mercy, his brother Aaron as a Prophet.

وَوَهَبْنَا لَهٗ مِنْ رَّحْمَتِنَاۤ اَخَاهُ هٰرُوْنَ نَبِيًّا ﴿٥٤﴾

55. And relate *the story of* Ishmael *as mentioned* in the Book. He was indeed strict in *keeping his* promise. And he was a Messenger, a Prophet.

وَاذْكُرْ فِي الْكِتٰبِ اِسْمٰعِيْلَ اِنَّهٗ كَانَ صَادِقَ الْوَعْدِ وَكَانَ رَسُوْلًا نَّبِيًّا ﴿٥٥﴾

56. He used to enjoin Prayer and almsgiving on his people, and he was well pleasing to his Lord.

وَكَانَ يَاْمُرُ اَهْلَهٗ بِالصَّلٰوةِ وَالزَّكٰوةِ وَكَانَ عِنْدَ رَبِّهٖ مَرْضِيًّا ﴿٥٦﴾

57. And relate *the story of* Idrīs *as mentioned* in the Book. He was *a* truthful *man and* a Prophet.

وَاذْكُرْ فِي الْكِتٰبِ اِدْرِيْسَ اِنَّهٗ كَانَ صِدِّيْقًا نَّبِيًّا ﴿٥٧﴾

58. And We exalted him to a lofty station.

وَّرَفَعْنٰهُ مَكَانًا عَلِيًّا ﴿٥٨﴾

59. These are the people on whom Allah bestowed His blessings from among the Prophets, of the posterity of Adam, and of *the posterity of* those whom We carried *in the Ark* with Noah, and of the posterity of

اُولٰٓئِكَ الَّذِيْنَ اَنْعَمَ اللّٰهُ عَلَيْهِمْ مِّنَ النَّبِيّٖنَ مِنْ ذُرِّيَّةِ اٰدَمَ وَمِمَّنْ حَمَلْنَا مَعَ نُوْحٍ وَّمِنْ ذُرِّيَّةِ

Abraham and Israel; and *they are* of those whom We guided and chose. When the Signs of the Gracious *God* were recited unto them, they fell down, prostrating themselves *before God* and weeping.

ابرهيم واسراءيل وممن هدينا واجتبينا
اذا تتلى عليهم ايت الرحمن خروا سجدا وبكيا ۩ ٥٩

60. Then there came after them descendants who neglected Prayer, and followed evil desires. So they will meet with destruction,

فخلف من بعدهم خلف اضاعوا الصلوة واتبعوا
الشهوت فسوف يلقون غيا ٦٠

61. Except those who repent and believe and do good deeds. These will enter Heaven, and they will not be wronged in the least—

الا من تاب وامن وعمل صالحا فاولئك يدخلون
الجنة ولا يظلمون شيئا ٦١

62. Gardens of Eternity, which the Gracious *God* has promised to His servants in the unseen. Surely, His promise must come to pass.

جنت عدن التي وعد الرحمن عباده بالغيب
انه كان وعده ماتيا ٦٢

63. They will not hear therein anything vain, but only *greetings of* Peace: and they will have their sustenance therein, morning and evening.

لا يسمعون فيها لغوا الا سلما ولهم رزقهم فيها
بكرة وعشيا ٦٣

64. Such is the Heaven which We give for an inheritance to those of Our servants who are righteous.

تلك الجنة التي نورث من عبادنا من كان
تقيا ٦٤

65. 'And we (angels) do not come down save by the command of thy Lord. To Him belongs all that is before us and all that is behind us and all that is between; and thy Lord is not forgetful.'

وما نتنزل الا بامر ربك له ما بين ايدينا وما
خلفنا وما بين ذلك وما كان ربك نسيا ٦٥

66. *He is* the Lord of the heavens and the earth and of all that is between the two. Serve Him, therefore, and be steadfast in His service. Dost thou know any equal of His?

رب السموت والارض وما بينهما فاعبده واصطبر
ع لعبادته هل تعلم له سميا ٦٦

R. 5.

67. And says man, 'What! when I am dead, shall I be brought forth alive?'

ويقول الانسان ءاذا ما مت لسوف اخرج حيا ٦٧

68. Does not man remember that We created him before, when he was naught?

اولا يذكر الانسان انا خلقنه من قبل ولم يك
شيئا ٦٨

69. And, by thy Lord, We shall assuredly gather them together, and the satans *too;* then shall We bring them on their knees around Hell.

فوربك لنحشرنهم والشيطين ثم لنحضرنهم
حول جهنم جثيا ٦٩

* 70. Then shall We certainly pick out, from every group, those of them who were

ثم لننزعن من كل شيعة ايهم اشد على الرحمن

most stubborn in rebellion against the Gracious *God*.

عِتِيًّا ﴿٧٠﴾

71. And surely, We know best those most deserving to be burned therein.

ثُمَّ لَنَحْنُ أَعْلَمُ بِالَّذِينَ هُمْ أَوْلَىٰ بِهَا صِلِيًّا ﴿٧١﴾

72. And there is not one of you but will come to it. This is a fixed decree with thy Lord.

وَإِنْ مِنْكُمْ إِلَّا وَارِدُهَا ۚ كَانَ عَلَىٰ رَبِّكَ حَتْمًا
مَقْضِيًّا ﴿٧٢﴾

73. Then We shall save the righteous and We shall leave the wrongdoers therein, on their knees.

ثُمَّ نُنَجِّي الَّذِينَ اتَّقَوْا وَنَذَرُ الظَّالِمِينَ فِيهَا
جِثِيًّا ﴿٧٣﴾

74. And when Our manifest Signs are recited unto them, the disbelievers say to the believers, 'Which of the two parties is better in *respect of* position and *makes* a more impressive assembly?'

وَإِذَا تُتْلَىٰ عَلَيْهِمْ آيَاتُنَا بَيِّنَاتٍ قَالَ الَّذِينَ كَفَرُوا
لِلَّذِينَ آمَنُوا أَيُّ الْفَرِيقَيْنِ خَيْرٌ مَقَامًا وَأَحْسَنُ
نَدِيًّا ﴿٧٤﴾

75. And how many generations have We destroyed before them, who were better off in wealth and better in outward show!

وَكَمْ أَهْلَكْنَا قَبْلَهُمْ مِنْ قَرْنٍ هُمْ أَحْسَنُ أَثَاثًا
وَرِئْيًا ﴿٧٥﴾

76. Say, 'The Gracious *God* does give those who are in error long respite until, when they will see that with which they are threatened—whether it be punishment or the Hour—they will realize who is worse in *respect of* position and who is weaker in forces.

قُلْ مَنْ كَانَ فِي الضَّلَالَةِ فَلْيَمْدُدْ لَهُ الرَّحْمَٰنُ مَدًّا ۚ
حَتَّىٰ إِذَا رَأَوْا مَا يُوعَدُونَ إِمَّا الْعَذَابَ وَإِمَّا السَّاعَةَ
فَسَيَعْلَمُونَ مَنْ هُوَ شَرٌّ مَكَانًا وَأَضْعَفُ جُنْدًا ﴿٧٦﴾

77. 'And Allah increases in guidance those who follow guidance. And the good works that endure are best in the sight of thy Lord as reward, and best as resort.'

وَيَزِيدُ اللَّهُ الَّذِينَ اهْتَدَوْا هُدًى ۗ وَالْبَاقِيَاتُ الصَّالِحَاتُ
خَيْرٌ عِنْدَ رَبِّكَ ثَوَابًا وَخَيْرٌ مَرَدًّا ﴿٧٧﴾

78. Hast thou then seen him who disbelieves in Our Signs, and says, 'I shall certainly be given wealth and children?'

أَفَرَأَيْتَ الَّذِي كَفَرَ بِآيَاتِنَا وَقَالَ لَأُوتَيَنَّ مَالًا
وَوَلَدًا ﴿٧٨﴾

79. Has he become acquainted with the unseen or has he taken a promise from the Gracious *God?*

أَطَّلَعَ الْغَيْبَ أَمِ اتَّخَذَ عِنْدَ الرَّحْمَٰنِ عَهْدًا ﴿٧٩﴾

80. Nay! We shall note down what he says and We shall greatly prolong for him the punishment.

كَلَّا ۚ سَنَكْتُبُ مَا يَقُولُ وَنَمُدُّ لَهُ مِنَ الْعَذَابِ مَدًّا ﴿٨٠﴾

81. And We shall inherit of him all that of which he talks, and he shall come to Us all alone.

وَنَرِثُهُ مَا يَقُولُ وَيَأْتِينَا فَرْدًا ﴿٨١﴾

82. And they have taken *other* gods beside Allah, that they may be *a source of* power for them.

وَاتَّخَذُوا مِنْ دُونِ اللَّهِ آلِهَةً لِيَكُونُوا لَهُمْ عِزًّا ﴿٨٢﴾

83. Not at all! They will reject their worship, and become their opponents.

كَلَّا ۚ سَيَكْفُرُونَ بِعِبَادَتِهِمْ وَيَكُونُونَ عَلَيْهِمْ ضِدًّا ﴿٨٣﴾

R. 6.

84. Seest thou not that We have sent satans against the disbelievers goading them on *to acts of disobedience?*

أَلَمْ تَرَ أَنَّا أَرْسَلْنَا الشَّيٰطِينَ عَلَى الْكٰفِرِينَ تَؤُزُّهُمْ أَزًّا ﴿٨٤﴾

85. So be not thou in haste with regard to them; We are keeping full account of their *doings*.

فَلَا تَعْجَلْ عَلَيْهِمْ ۖ إِنَّمَا نَعُدُّ لَهُمْ عَدًّا ﴿٨٥﴾

86. *Remember* the day when We shall gather the righteous before the Gracious *God* as *honoured* guests.

يَوْمَ نَحْشُرُ الْمُتَّقِينَ إِلَى الرَّحْمٰنِ وَفْدًا ﴿٨٦﴾

* 87. And We shall drive the guilty to Hell like a herd *of thirsty camels*.

وَنَسُوقُ الْمُجْرِمِينَ إِلٰى جَهَنَّمَ وِرْدًا ﴿٨٧﴾

88. None will have the power of intercession save he who has received a promise from the Gracious *God*.

لَا يَمْلِكُونَ الشَّفَاعَةَ إِلَّا مَنِ اتَّخَذَ عِنْدَ الرَّحْمٰنِ عَهْدًا ﴿٨٨﴾

89. And they say, 'The Gracious *God* has taken unto Himself a son.'

وَقَالُوا اتَّخَذَ الرَّحْمٰنُ وَلَدًا ﴿٨٩﴾

90. Assuredly, you have done a most monstrous thing!

لَقَدْ جِئْتُمْ شَيْئًا إِدًّا ﴿٩٠﴾

91. The heavens might well-nigh burst thereat, and the earth cleave asunder, and the mountains fall down in pieces,

تَكَادُ السَّمٰوٰتُ يَتَفَطَّرْنَ مِنْهُ وَتَنْشَقُّ الْأَرْضُ وَتَخِرُّ الْجِبَالُ هَدًّا ﴿٩١﴾

92. Because they ascribe a son to the Gracious *God*.

أَنْ دَعَوْا لِلرَّحْمٰنِ وَلَدًا ﴿٩٢﴾

93. Whereas it becomes not the Gracious *God* to take unto Himself a son.

وَمَا يَنْبَغِي لِلرَّحْمٰنِ أَنْ يَتَّخِذَ وَلَدًا ﴿٩٣﴾

94. There is none in the heavens and the earth but he shall come to the Gracious *God* as a bondman.

إِنْ كُلُّ مَنْ فِي السَّمٰوٰتِ وَالْأَرْضِ إِلَّا آتِي الرَّحْمٰنِ عَبْدًا ﴿٩٤﴾

95. Verily, He comprehends them *by His knowledge* and has numbered them all fully.

لَقَدْ أَحْصٰىهُمْ وَعَدَّهُمْ عَدًّا ﴿٩٥﴾

96. And each of them shall come to Him singly on the Day of Resurrection.

وَكُلُّهُمْ آتِيهِ يَوْمَ الْقِيٰمَةِ فَرْدًا ﴿٩٦﴾

97. Those who believe and do good deeds—the Gracious *God* will create love in their *hearts*.

إِنَّ الَّذِينَ آمَنُوا وَعَمِلُوا الصّٰلِحٰتِ سَيَجْعَلُ لَهُمُ الرَّحْمٰنُ وُدًّا ﴿٩٧﴾

98. So We have made it (the Qur'ān) easy in thy tongue that thou mayest give thereby good tidings to the righteous, and warn thereby a people given to contention.

فَإِنَّمَا يَسَّرْنٰهُ بِلِسَانِكَ لِتُبَشِّرَ بِهِ الْمُتَّقِينَ وَتُنْذِرَ بِهِ قَوْمًا لُدًّا ﴿٩٨﴾

99. And how many a generation have We destroyed before them! Canst thou see a single one of them, or hear *even* a whisper of them?

وَكَمْ اَهْلَكْنَا قَبْلَهُمْ مِّنْ قَرْنٍ هَلْ تُحِسُّ مِنْهُمْ
مِّنْ اَحَدٍ اَوْ تَسْمَعُ لَهُمْ رِكْزًا ﴿٩٩﴾

سُوْرَةُ طٰهٰ مَكِّيَّةٌ (٢٠)

ṬĀ HĀ

(Revealed before Hijra)

1. In the name of Allah, the Gracious, the Merciful.

بِسْمِ اللّٰهِ الرَّحْمٰنِ الرَّحِيْمِ ﴿١﴾

2. Ṭā Hā *.

طٰهٰ ﴿٢﴾

3. We have not sent down the Qur'ān to thee that thou shouldst be distressed,

مَآ اَنْزَلْنَا عَلَيْكَ الْقُرْاٰنَ لِتَشْقٰٓى ﴿٣﴾

4. But as an exhortation for him who fears *God*,

اِلَّا تَذْكِرَةً لِّمَنْ يَّخْشٰى ﴿٤﴾

5. *And* a revelation from Him Who created the earth and the high heavens.

تَنْزِيْلًا مِّمَّنْ خَلَقَ الْاَرْضَ وَالسَّمٰوٰتِ الْعُلٰى ﴿٥﴾

6. *He is* the Gracious *God Who* has settled Himself on the Throne.

اَلرَّحْمٰنُ عَلَى الْعَرْشِ اسْتَوٰى ﴿٦﴾

7. To Him belongs whatsoever is in the heavens and whatsoever is in the earth, and whatsoever is between them, and whatsoever is beneath the moist sub-soil.

لَهٗ مَا فِي السَّمٰوٰتِ وَمَا فِي الْاَرْضِ وَمَا بَيْنَهُمَا وَمَا
تَحْتَ الثَّرٰى ﴿٧﴾

8. And if thou speakest aloud, *it makes no difference*, for He knows the secret *thought* and *what is yet* more hidden.

وَاِنْ تَجْهَرْ بِالْقَوْلِ فَاِنَّهٗ يَعْلَمُ السِّرَّ وَاَخْفٰى ﴿٨﴾

9. Allah — there is no God but He. His are the most beautiful names.

اَللّٰهُ لَآ اِلٰهَ اِلَّا هُوَ لَهُ الْاَسْمَآءُ الْحُسْنٰى ﴿٩﴾

10. And has the story of Moses come to thee?

وَهَلْ اَتٰىكَ حَدِيْثُ مُوْسٰى ﴿١٠﴾

11. When he saw a fire, he said to his family, 'Tarry ye, I perceive a fire; perhaps I may bring you a brand therefrom or find guidance at the fire.'

اِذْ رَاٰ نَارًا فَقَالَ لِاَهْلِهِ امْكُثُوْٓا اِنِّيْٓ اٰنَسْتُ نَارًا
لَّعَلِّيْٓ اٰتِيْكُمْ مِّنْهَا بِقَبَسٍ اَوْ اَجِدُ عَلَى النَّارِ
هُدًى ﴿١١﴾

* 12. And when he came to it, he was called *by a voice*, 'O Moses,

فَلَمَّآ اَتٰىهَا نُوْدِيَ يٰمُوْسٰى ﴿١٢﴾

13. 'Verily, I am thy Lord. So take off thy shoes; for thou art in the sacred Valley of Ṭuwā.

اِنِّيْٓ اَنَا رَبُّكَ فَاخْلَعْ نَعْلَيْكَ اِنَّكَ بِالْوَادِ الْمُقَدَّسِ
طُوًى ﴿١٣﴾

14. 'And I have chosen thee; so hearken to what is revealed.

وَاَنَا اخْتَرْتُكَ فَاسْتَمِعْ لِمَا يُوْحٰى ﴿١٤﴾

15. 'Verily, I am Allah; there is no God beside Me. So serve Me, and observe Prayer for My remembrance.

اِنَّنِيْٓ اَنَا اللّٰهُ لَآ اِلٰهَ اِلَّآ اَنَا فَاعْبُدْنِيْ وَاَقِمِ
الصَّلٰوةَ لِذِكْرِيْ ﴿١٥﴾

* O Perfect Man!

* 16. 'Surely, the Hour is coming; I am going to manifest it, that every soul may be recompensed for its endeavour.

إِنَّ السَّاعَةَ آتِيَةٌ أَكَادُ أُخْفِيهَا لِتُجْزَىٰ كُلُّ نَفْسٍ
بِمَا تَسْعَىٰ ﴿١٦﴾

17. 'So let not him who believes not therein and follows his own evil inclinations, turn thee away therefrom, lest thou perish.

فَلَا يَصُدَّنَّكَ عَنْهَا مَنْ لَّا يُؤْمِنُ بِهَا وَاتَّبَعَ
هَوٰىهُ فَتَرْدٰى ﴿١٧﴾

18. 'And what is that in thy right hand, O Moses?'

وَمَا تِلْكَ بِيَمِينِكَ يٰمُوسٰى ﴿١٨﴾

19. He replied, 'This is my rod, I lean on it, and beat down therewith leaves for my sheep, and I have *also* other uses for it.'

قَالَ هِيَ عَصَايَ أَتَوَكَّؤُا عَلَيْهَا وَأَهُشُّ بِهَا
عَلٰى غَنَمِي وَلِيَ فِيهَا مَآرِبُ أُخْرٰى ﴿١٩﴾

20. He said, 'Cast it down, O Moses.'

قَالَ أَلْقِهَا يٰمُوسٰى ﴿٢٠﴾

21. So he cast it down, and behold! it was a serpent running.

فَأَلْقٰهَا فَإِذَا هِيَ حَيَّةٌ تَسْعٰى ﴿٢١﴾

22. *God* said, 'Catch hold of it, and fear not. We shall restore it to its former condition.

قَالَ خُذْهَا وَلَا تَخَفْ سَنُعِيدُهَا سِيرَتَهَا
الْأُولٰى ﴿٢٢﴾

* 23. 'And draw thy hand close under thy arm-pit. It shall come forth white, without any disease—another Sign,

وَاضْمُمْ يَدَكَ إِلٰى جَنَاحِكَ تَخْرُجْ بَيْضَاءَ مِنْ
غَيْرِ سُوءٍ آيَةً أُخْرٰى ﴿٢٣﴾

24. 'That We may show thee some of Our greater Signs.

لِنُرِيَكَ مِنْ آيٰتِنَا الْكُبْرٰى ﴿٢٤﴾

25. 'Go thou to Pharaoh; he has indeed exceeded *all* bounds.'

ع اِذْهَبْ إِلٰى فِرْعَوْنَ إِنَّهُ طَغٰى ﴿٢٥﴾

R. 2.

* 26. *Moses* said, 'My Lord, open out for me my breast,

قَالَ رَبِّ اشْرَحْ لِي صَدْرِي ﴿٢٦﴾

27. 'And ease for me my task,

وَيَسِّرْ لِي أَمْرِي ﴿٢٧﴾

* 28. 'And loose the knot of my tongue,

وَاحْلُلْ عُقْدَةً مِّنْ لِّسَانِي ﴿٢٨﴾

29. 'That they may understand my speech,

يَفْقَهُوا قَوْلِي ﴿٢٩﴾

30. 'And grant me a helper from my family—

وَاجْعَلْ لِّي وَزِيرًا مِّنْ أَهْلِي ﴿٣٠﴾

31. 'Aaron, my brother;

هٰرُونَ أَخِي ﴿٣١﴾

32. 'Increase my strength with him,

اشْدُدْ بِهٖ أَزْرِي ﴿٣٢﴾

33. 'And make him share my task,

وَاَشْرِكْهُ فِيْٓ اَمْرِيْ ۙ﴿۳۳﴾

34. 'That we may glorify Thee much,

كَيْ نُسَبِّحَكَ كَثِيْرًا ۙ﴿۳۴﴾

35. 'And remember Thee much.

وَّنَذْكُرَكَ كَثِيْرًا ؕ﴿۳۵﴾

36. 'Thou possessest full knowledge of us.'

اِنَّكَ كُنْتَ بِنَا بَصِيْرًا ﴿۳۶﴾

37. *God* said, "Granted is thy prayer, O Moses!

قَالَ قَدْ اُوْتِيْتَ سُؤْلَكَ يٰمُوْسٰى ﴿۳۷﴾

38. "And We did indeed confer a favour upon thee at another time *also*,

وَلَقَدْ مَنَنَّا عَلَيْكَ مَرَّةً اُخْرٰٓى ۙ﴿۳۸﴾

39. "When We revealed to thy mother what was an *important* revelation, *saying*,

اِذْ اَوْحَيْنَآ اِلٰٓى اُمِّكَ مَا يُوْحٰٓى ۙ﴿۳۹﴾

40. " 'Put him in the ark, and throw it into the river, then the river will cast it on to the bank, *and one who is* an enemy to Me and also an enemy to him will take him up.' And I wrapped thee with love from Me; and *this I did* that thou mightest be reared before My eye.

41. "When thy sister walked along and said, 'Shall I guide you to one who will take charge of him?' So We restored thee to thy mother that her eye might be cooled and she might not grieve. And thou didst kill a man, but We delivered thee from sorrow. Then We proved thee in various ways. And thou didst tarry several years among the people of Midian. Then thou camest up to the standard, O Moses.

اَنِ اقْذِفِيْهِ فِي التَّابُوْتِ فَاقْذِفِيْهِ فِي الْيَمِّ فَلْيُلْقِهِ
الْيَمُّ بِالسَّاحِلِ يَاْخُذْهُ عَدُوٌّ لِّيْ وَعَدُوٌّ لَّهٗ ؕ وَ
اَلْقَيْتُ عَلَيْكَ مَحَبَّةً مِّنِّيْ ۚ۬ وَلِتُصْنَعَ عَلٰى عَيْنِيْ ۘ﴿۴۰﴾ لازم
اِذْ تَمْشِيْٓ اُخْتُكَ فَتَقُوْلُ هَلْ اَدُلُّكُمْ عَلٰى مَنْ يَّكْفُلُهٗ ؕ
فَرَجَعْنٰكَ اِلٰٓى اُمِّكَ كَيْ تَقَرَّ عَيْنُهَا وَلَا تَحْزَنَ ؕ۬ وَقَتَلْتَ
نَفْسًا فَنَجَّيْنٰكَ مِنَ الْغَمِّ وَفَتَنّٰكَ فُتُوْنًا ۫ فَلَبِثْتَ
سِنِيْنَ فِيْٓ اَهْلِ مَدْيَنَ ۙ۬ ثُمَّ جِئْتَ عَلٰى قَدَرٍ يّٰمُوْسٰى ﴿۴۱﴾

42. "And I have chosen thee for Myself.

وَاصْطَنَعْتُكَ لِنَفْسِيْ ۚ﴿۴۲﴾

43. "Go, thou and thy brother, with My Signs, and slacken not in remembering Me.

اِذْهَبْ اَنْتَ وَاَخُوْكَ بِاٰيٰتِيْ وَلَا تَنِيَا فِيْ ذِكْرِيْ ۚ﴿۴۳﴾

44. "Go, both of you, to Pharaoh, for he has transgressed *all* bounds.

اِذْهَبَآ اِلٰى فِرْعَوْنَ اِنَّهٗ طَغٰى ۚ﴿۴۴﴾

* 45. "But speak to him a gentle speech that he might possibly heed or fear."

فَقُوْلَا لَهٗ قَوْلًا لَّيِّنًا لَّعَلَّهٗ يَتَذَكَّرُ اَوْ يَخْشٰى ﴿۴۵﴾

46. They replied, 'Our Lord, we fear lest he commit some excess against us, or exceed *all* bounds in transgression.'

قَالَا رَبَّنَآ اِنَّنَا نَخَافُ اَنْ يَّفْرُطَ عَلَيْنَآ اَوْ اَنْ
يَّطْغٰى ﴿۴۶﴾

47. *God* said, "Fear not; for I am with you both. I hear and I see.

قَالَ لَا تَخَافَآ اِنَّنِيْ مَعَكُمَآ اَسْمَعُ وَاَرٰى ﴿۴۷﴾

48. "So go ye both to him and say, 'We are the Messengers of thy Lord; so let the

فَاْتِيٰهُ فَقُوْلَآ اِنَّا رَسُوْلَا رَبِّكَ فَاَرْسِلْ مَعَنَا بَنِيْٓ

children of Israel go with us; and afflict them not. We have indeed brought thee a Sign from thy Lord; and peace shall be on him who follows the guidance;

إِسْرَآءِيلَ ۥ وَلَا تُعَذِّبْهُمْ قَدْ جِئْنَٰكَ بِـَٔايَةٍ مِّن رَّبِّكَ وَٱلسَّلَٰمُ عَلَىٰ مَنِ ٱتَّبَعَ ٱلْهُدَىٰ ﴿٤٨﴾

49. 'It has indeed been revealed to us that punishment shall come on him who rejects and turns away.' "

إِنَّا قَدْ أُوحِىَ إِلَيْنَآ أَنَّ ٱلْعَذَابَ عَلَىٰ مَن كَذَّبَ وَتَوَلَّىٰ ﴿٤٩﴾

50. *Pharaoh* said, 'Who then is the Lord of you two, O Moses?'

قَالَ فَمَن رَّبُّكُمَا يَٰمُوسَىٰ ﴿٥٠﴾

51. He said, 'Our Lord is He Who gave unto everything its *proper* form *and* then guided *it to its proper function.*'

قَالَ رَبُّنَا ٱلَّذِىٓ أَعْطَىٰ كُلَّ شَىْءٍ خَلْقَهُۥ ثُمَّ هَدَىٰ ﴿٥١﴾

52. *Pharaoh* said, 'What then will be the fate of the former generations?'

قَالَ فَمَا بَالُ ٱلْقُرُونِ ٱلْأُولَىٰ ﴿٥٢﴾

53. He said, 'The knowledge thereof is with my Lord *recorded* in a Book. My Lord neither errs nor forgets.'

قَالَ عِلْمُهَا عِندَ رَبِّى فِى كِتَٰبٍ ۖ لَّا يَضِلُّ رَبِّى وَلَا يَنسَى ﴿٥٣﴾

54. *It is He* Who has made the earth for you a cradle, and has caused pathways for you to run through it; and Who sends down rain from the sky, and thereby We bring forth various kinds of vegetation.

ٱلَّذِى جَعَلَ لَكُمُ ٱلْأَرْضَ مَهْدًا وَسَلَكَ لَكُمْ فِيهَا سُبُلًا وَأَنزَلَ مِنَ ٱلسَّمَآءِ مَآءً فَأَخْرَجْنَا بِهِۦٓ أَزْوَٰجًا مِّن نَّبَاتٍ شَتَّىٰ ﴿٥٤﴾

55. Eat ye and pasture your cattle. Verily, in this are Signs for those who are endued with reason.

كُلُوا۟ وَٱرْعَوْا۟ أَنْعَٰمَكُمْ ۗ إِنَّ فِى ذَٰلِكَ لَءَايَٰتٍ لِّأُو۟لِى ٱلنُّهَىٰ ﴿٥٥﴾ ع

R. 3.

56. From it have We created you, and into it shall We cause you to return, and from it shall We bring you forth once more.

مِنْهَا خَلَقْنَٰكُمْ وَفِيهَا نُعِيدُكُمْ وَمِنْهَا نُخْرِجُكُمْ تَارَةً أُخْرَىٰ ﴿٥٦﴾

57. And We did show him (Pharaoh) Our Signs, all of them; but he rejected *them* and refused *to believe.*

وَلَقَدْ أَرَيْنَٰهُ ءَايَٰتِنَا كُلَّهَا فَكَذَّبَ وَأَبَىٰ ﴿٥٧﴾

58. He said, 'Hast thou come to us, O Moses, to drive us out of our land by thy magic?

قَالَ أَجِئْتَنَا لِتُخْرِجَنَا مِنْ أَرْضِنَا بِسِحْرِكَ يَٰمُوسَىٰ ﴿٥٨﴾

59. 'But we shall assuredly bring thee magic the like thereof; so make an appointment between us and thyself which we shall not fail to keep—neither we nor thou—at a place alike *for us both.*'

فَلَنَأْتِيَنَّكَ بِسِحْرٍ مِّثْلِهِۦ فَٱجْعَلْ بَيْنَنَا وَبَيْنَكَ مَوْعِدًا لَّا نُخْلِفُهُۥ نَحْنُ وَلَآ أَنتَ مَكَانًا سُوًى ﴿٥٩﴾

60. Moses said, 'Your appointment shall be for the day of the Festival, and let the people be assembled when the sun is risen high.'

قَالَ مَوْعِدُكُمْ يَوْمُ الزِّيْنَةِ وَ اَنْ يُّحْشَرَ النَّاسُ
ضُحًى ﴿٦٠﴾

* 61. Then Pharaoh withdrew and concerted his plan and then came *to the place of appointment*.

فَتَوَلّٰى فِرْعَوْنُ فَجَمَعَ كَيْدَهٗ ثُمَّ اَتٰى ﴿٦١﴾

62. Moses said to them, 'Woe to you; forge not a lie against Allah, lest He destroy you by some punishment; and surely, he who forges a lie shall perish.'

قَالَ لَهُمْ مُّوْسٰى وَيْلَكُمْ لَا تَفْتَرُوْا عَلَى اللّٰهِ كَذِبًا
فَيُسْحِتَكُمْ بِعَذَابٍ ۚ وَ قَدْ خَابَ مَنِ افْتَرٰى ﴿٦٢﴾

63. Then they argued their affair among themselves and conferred in secret.

فَتَنَازَعُوْٓا اَمْرَهُمْ بَيْنَهُمْ وَ اَسَرُّوا النَّجْوٰى ﴿٦٣﴾

64. They said, 'Certainly these two are magicians, who desire to drive you out from your land by their magic and to destroy your best traditions.

قَالُوْٓا اِنْ هٰذٰنِ لَسٰحِرٰنِ يُرِيْدٰنِ اَنْ يُّخْرِجٰكُمْ
مِّنْ اَرْضِكُمْ بِسِحْرِهِمَا وَ يَذْهَبَا بِطَرِيْقَتِكُمُ الْمُثْلٰى ﴿٦٤﴾

65. 'Concert, therefore, your plan and then come forward arrayed. And, surely, he who gains ascendancy this day shall prosper.'

فَاَجْمِعُوْا كَيْدَكُمْ ثُمَّ ائْتُوْا صَفًّا ۚ وَ قَدْ اَفْلَحَ
الْيَوْمَ مَنِ اسْتَعْلٰى ﴿٦٥﴾

66. They said, 'O Moses, either do thou throw *first*, or we shall be the first to throw.'

قَالُوْا يٰمُوْسٰٓى اِمَّآ اَنْ تُلْقِيَ وَ اِمَّآ اَنْ نَّكُوْنَ اَوَّلَ
مَنْ اَلْقٰى ﴿٦٦﴾

67. He said, 'Nay, throw ye.' Then lo! their cords and their staves appeared to him, by their magic, as though they ran *about*.

قَالَ بَلْ اَلْقُوْا ۚ فَاِذَا حِبَالُهُمْ وَ عِصِيُّهُمْ يُخَيَّلُ
اِلَيْهِ مِنْ سِحْرِهِمْ اَنَّهَا تَسْعٰى ﴿٦٧﴾

68. And Moses conceived a fear in his mind.

فَاَوْجَسَ فِيْ نَفْسِهٖ خِيْفَةً مُّوْسٰى ﴿٦٨﴾

69. We said, 'Fear not, for thou wilt have the upper hand.

قُلْنَا لَا تَخَفْ اِنَّكَ اَنْتَ الْاَعْلٰى ﴿٦٩﴾

70. 'And throw that which is in thy right hand; it will swallow that which they have wrought, for that which they have wrought is only a magician's trick. And a magician shall not thrive, come where he may.'

وَ اَلْقِ مَا فِيْ يَمِيْنِكَ تَلْقَفْ مَا صَنَعُوْا ۚ اِنَّمَا صَنَعُوْا
كَيْدُ سٰحِرٍ ۚ وَ لَا يُفْلِحُ السَّاحِرُ حَيْثُ اَتٰى ﴿٧٠﴾

71. Then the magicians were made to fall down prostrate. They said, 'We believe in the Lord of Aaron and Moses.'

فَاُلْقِيَ السَّحَرَةُ سُجَّدًا قَالُوْٓا اٰمَنَّا بِرَبِّ هٰرُوْنَ
وَ مُوْسٰى ﴿٧١﴾

72. *Pharaoh* said, 'Do you believe in him before I give you leave? He must be your chief who has taught you magic. I will therefore surely cut off your hands and

قَالَ اٰمَنْتُمْ لَهٗ قَبْلَ اَنْ اٰذَنَ لَكُمْ ۚ اِنَّهٗ لَكَبِيْرُكُمُ
الَّذِيْ عَلَّمَكُمُ السِّحْرَ ۚ فَلَاُقَطِّعَنَّ اَيْدِيَكُمْ وَ

your feet alternately, and I will surely crucify you on the trunks of palm-trees; and you shall know which of us is severer and more abiding in punishment.'

أرجلكم من خلاف ولأصلبنكم في جذوع
النخل ولتعلمن أينا أشد عذابا وأبقى ﴿٧٢﴾

73. They said, 'We shall not prefer thee to the manifest Signs that have come to us, nor *shall we prefer thee* to Him Who has created us. So decree what thou wilt decree; thou canst only decree concerning this present life.

قالوا لن نؤثرك على ما جاءنا من البينت و
الذي فطرنا فاقض ما أنت قاض إنما تقضي
هذه الحيوة الدنيا ﴿٧٣﴾

74. 'Surely we have believed in our Lord that He may forgive us our sins and *forgive us* the magic which thou didst force us *to use*. And Allah is the Best and the Most Abiding.'

إنا آمنا بربنا ليغفر لنا خطينا وما أكرهتنا
عليه من السحر والله خير وأبقى ﴿٧٤﴾

75. Verily, he who comes to his Lord a sinner—for him is Hell; he shall neither die therein nor live.

إنه من يأت ربه مجرما فإن له جهنم لا
يموت فيها ولا يحيى ﴿٧٥﴾

76. But he who comes to Him as a believer having done good deeds, for such are the highest ranks—

ومن يأته مؤمنا قد عمل الصلحت فأولئك
لهم الدرجت العلى ﴿٧٦﴾

77. Gardens of Eternity, beneath which rivers flow; they will abide therein *for ever*. And that is the recompense of those who keep themselves pure.

جنت عدن تجري من تحتها الأنهر خلدين
فيها وذلك جزؤا من تزكى ﴿٧٧﴾

R. 4.

78. And We sent a revelation to Moses, *saying*, 'Take away My servants by night, and strike for them a dry path through the sea. Thou wilt not be afraid of being overtaken, nor wilt thou have *any other* fear.'

ولقد أوحينا إلى موسى أن أسر بعبادي فاضرب
لهم طريقا في البحر يبسا لا تخف دركا ولا
تخشى ﴿٧٨﴾

79. Then Pharaoh pursued them with his hosts, and there overwhelmed them of the waters of the sea that which overwhelmed them.

فأتبعهم فرعون بجنوده فغشيهم من اليم
ما غشيهم ﴿٧٩﴾

80. And Pharaoh led his people astray and did not guide them aright.

وأضل فرعون قومه وما هدى ﴿٨٠﴾

81. 'O children of Israel, We delivered you from your enemy, and We made a covenant with you on the right side of the Mount, and We sent down on you Manna and Salwā.

يبني إسراءيل قد أنجينكم من عدوكم و
وعدنكم جانب الطور الأيمن ونزلنا عليكم
المن والسلوى ﴿٨١﴾

82. 'Eat of the good things that We have provided for you, and transgress not therein, lest My wrath descend upon you; and he on whom My wrath descends shall perish;

كُلُوا مِن طَيِّبَٰتِ مَا رَزَقْنَٰكُمْ وَلَا تَطْغَوْا فِيهِ فَيَحِلَّ
عَلَيْكُمْ غَضَبِي ۚ وَمَن يَحْلِلْ عَلَيْهِ غَضَبِي فَقَدْ
هَوَىٰ ﴿٨٢﴾

83. 'But surely I am forgiving to those who repent and believe and do good deeds, and then stick to guidance.

وَإِنِّي لَغَفَّارٌ لِّمَن تَابَ وَءَامَنَ وَعَمِلَ صَٰلِحًا ثُمَّ
اهْتَدَىٰ ﴿٨٣﴾

84. 'And what has hastened thee away from thy people, O Moses?'

وَمَا أَعْجَلَكَ عَن قَوْمِكَ يَٰمُوسَىٰ ﴿٨٤﴾

* 85. He said, 'They are *closely following* in my footsteps and I have hastened to Thee, my Lord, that Thou mightest be pleased.'

قَالَ هُمْ أُولَاءِ عَلَىٰ أَثَرِي وَعَجِلْتُ إِلَيْكَ رَبِّ
لِتَرْضَىٰ ﴿٨٥﴾

86. *God* said, 'We have tried thy people in thy absence, and the Sāmirī has led them astray.'

قَالَ فَإِنَّا قَدْ فَتَنَّا قَوْمَكَ مِن بَعْدِكَ وَأَضَلَّهُمُ
السَّامِرِيُّ ﴿٨٦﴾

87. So Moses returned to his people indignant and sad. He said, 'O my people, did not your Lord promise you a gracious promise? Did, then, the appointed time appear too long to you, or did you desire that wrath should descend upon you from your Lord, that you broke *your* promise to me?'

فَرَجَعَ مُوسَىٰ إِلَىٰ قَوْمِهِ غَضْبَٰنَ أَسِفًا ۚ قَالَ
يَٰقَوْمِ أَلَمْ يَعِدْكُمْ رَبُّكُمْ وَعْدًا حَسَنًا ۚ أَفَطَالَ
عَلَيْكُمُ الْعَهْدُ أَمْ أَرَدتُّمْ أَن يَحِلَّ عَلَيْكُمْ غَضَبٌ
مِّن رَّبِّكُمْ فَأَخْلَفْتُم مَّوْعِدِي ﴿٨٧﴾

88. They said, 'We have not broken *our* promise to thee of our own accord; but we were laden with loads of people's ornaments and we threw them away, and likewise did the Sāmirī cast.'

قَالُوا مَا أَخْلَفْنَا مَوْعِدَكَ بِمَلْكِنَا وَلَٰكِنَّا حُمِّلْنَا
أَوْزَارًا مِّن زِينَةِ الْقَوْمِ فَقَذَفْنَٰهَا فَكَذَٰلِكَ أَلْقَى
السَّامِرِيُّ ﴿٨٨﴾

* 89. Then he produced for them a calf—an image producing a lowing sound. And they said, 'This is your God, and the God of Moses.' So he gave up *the religion of Moses*.

فَأَخْرَجَ لَهُمْ عِجْلًا جَسَدًا لَّهُ خُوَارٌ فَقَالُوا هَٰذَا إِلَٰهُكُمْ
وَإِلَٰهُ مُوسَىٰ فَنَسِيَ ﴿٨٩﴾

90. Could they not see that it returned to them no answer, and had no power to do them either harm or good?

أَفَلَا يَرَوْنَ أَلَّا يَرْجِعُ إِلَيْهِمْ قَوْلًا وَلَا يَمْلِكُ لَهُمْ
ضَرًّا وَلَا نَفْعًا ﴿٩٠﴾ ع ١٤

R. 5.

91. And Aaron had said to them before this, 'O my people, you have only been

وَلَقَدْ قَالَ لَهُمْ هَٰرُونُ مِن قَبْلُ يَٰقَوْمِ إِنَّمَا

tried by means of it (the calf). And surely, the Gracious *God* is your Lord; so follow me and obey my command.'

فُتِنْتُمْ بِهٖ ۚ وَاِنَّ رَبَّكُمُ الرَّحْمٰنُ فَاتَّبِعُوْنِيْ وَاَطِيْعُوْٓا
اَمْرِيْ ﴿٩١﴾

92. They replied, 'We shall not cease to worship it until Moses return to us.'

قَالُوْا لَنْ نَّبْرَحَ عَلَيْهِ عٰكِفِيْنَ حَتّٰى يَرْجِعَ اِلَيْنَا
مُوْسٰى ﴿٩٢﴾

93. *Moses* said, "O Aaron, what hindered thee, when thou didst see them gone astray,

قَالَ يٰهٰرُوْنُ مَا مَنَعَكَ اِذْ رَاَيْتَهُمْ ضَلُّوْٓا ﴿٩٣﴾

94. 'From following me? Hast thou then disobeyed my command?'

اَلَّا تَتَّبِعَنِ ۖ اَفَعَصَيْتَ اَمْرِيْ ﴿٩٤﴾

* 95. He answered, "O son of my mother, seize me not by my beard, nor by *the hair of* my head. I feared lest thou shouldst say, 'Thou hast caused a division among the children of Israel, and didst not wait for my word.' "

قَالَ يَبْنَؤُمَّ لَا تَاْخُذْ بِلِحْيَتِيْ وَلَا بِرَاْسِيْ ۚ اِنِّيْ
خَشِيْتُ اَنْ تَقُوْلَ فَرَّقْتَ بَيْنَ بَنِيْٓ اِسْرَآءِيْلَ
وَلَمْ تَرْقُبْ قَوْلِيْ ﴿٩٥﴾

96. *Moses* said, 'And what hast thou to say, O Sāmirī?'

قَالَ فَمَا خَطْبُكَ يٰسَامِرِيُّ ﴿٩٦﴾

97. He said, 'I perceived what they perceived not. I *only* partly received the impress of the Messenger, but that *too* I cast away. Thus it is that my mind commended to me.'

قَالَ بَصُرْتُ بِمَا لَمْ يَبْصُرُوْا بِهٖ فَقَبَضْتُ قَبْضَةً
مِّنْ اَثَرِ الرَّسُوْلِ فَنَبَذْتُهَا وَكَذٰلِكَ سَوَّلَتْ لِيْ نَفْسِيْ ﴿٩٧﴾

98. *Moses* said, "Go away. It shall be thine to say throughout thy life, 'Touch *me* not;' and there is a promise of *punishment* for thee which shall not fail to be fulfilled about thee. Now look at thy god of which thou hast become a devoted worshipper. We will certainly burn it and then scatter it away into the sea."

قَالَ فَاذْهَبْ فَاِنَّ لَكَ فِي الْحَيٰوةِ اَنْ تَقُوْلَ لَا
مِسَاسَ ۖ وَاِنَّ لَكَ مَوْعِدًا لَّنْ تُخْلَفَهٗ ۚ وَانْظُرْ
اِلٰٓى اِلٰهِكَ الَّذِيْ ظَلْتَ عَلَيْهِ عَاكِفًا ۖ لَنُحَرِّقَنَّهٗ ثُمَّ
لَنَنْسِفَنَّهٗ فِي الْيَمِّ نَسْفًا ﴿٩٨﴾

99. Your God is only Allah, beside Whom there is no God. He embraces all things in *His* knowledge.

اِنَّمَآ اِلٰهُكُمُ اللّٰهُ الَّذِيْ لَآ اِلٰهَ اِلَّا هُوَ ۚ وَسِعَ كُلَّ
شَيْءٍ عِلْمًا ﴿٩٩﴾

100. Thus do We relate to thee the tidings of what has happened before. And We have given thee from Us a Reminder.

كَذٰلِكَ نَقُصُّ عَلَيْكَ مِنْ اَنْۢبَآءِ مَا قَدْ سَبَقَ ۚ
وَقَدْ اٰتَيْنٰكَ مِنْ لَّدُنَّا ذِكْرًا ﴿١٠٠﴾

101. Whoso turns away from it will surely bear a *heavy* burden on the Day of Resurrection,

مَنْ اَعْرَضَ عَنْهُ فَاِنَّهٗ يَحْمِلُ يَوْمَ الْقِيٰمَةِ وِزْرًا ﴿١٠١﴾

102. Abiding thereunder; and evil will the burden be to them on the Day of Resurrection,

خٰلِدِيْنَ فِيْهِ ۖ وَسَآءَ لَهُمْ يَوْمَ الْقِيٰمَةِ حِمْلًا ﴿١٠٢﴾

103. The day when the trumpet will be blown. And on that day We shall gather the sinful together, blue-eyed.

يوم ينفخ في الصور ونحشر المجرمين يومئذ
زرقا ﴿١٠٣﴾

104. They will talk to one another in a low tone *saying:* 'You tarried only ten *days'*—

يتخافتون بينهم إن لبثتم إلا عشرا ﴿١٠٤﴾

105. We know best what they will say—when the one possessing the best way of life among them will say, 'You have tarried only a day.'

نحن أعلم بما يقولون إذ يقول أمثلهم طريقة
إن لبثتم إلا يوما ﴿١٠٥﴾

R. 6.

106. And they ask thee concerning the mountains. Say, 'My Lord will break them into pieces and scatter them as dust.

ويسألونك عن الجبال فقل ينسفها ربي نسفا ﴿١٠٦﴾

107. 'And He will leave them as a barren, level plain,

فيذرها قاعا صفصفا ﴿١٠٧﴾

108. 'Wherein thou wilt see no depression, or elevation.'

لا ترى فيها عوجا ولا أمتا ﴿١٠٨﴾

* 109. On that day they will follow the Caller *straight*, there being no deviation therefrom; and *all* voices shall be hushed before the Gracious *God* and thou shalt not hear but a subdued sound of footsteps.

يومئذ يتبعون الداعي لا عوج له وخشعت
الأصوات للرحمن فلا تسمع إلا همسا ﴿١٠٩﴾

110. On that day intercession shall not avail *any person* save him in whose case the Gracious *God* grants permission and with whose word *of faith* He is pleased.

يومئذ لا تنفع الشفاعة إلا من أذن له
الرحمن ورضي له قولا ﴿١١٠﴾

111. He knows *all* that is before them and *all* that is behind them, but they cannot compass it with *their* knowledge.

يعلم ما بين أيديهم وما خلفهم ولا
يحيطون به علما ﴿١١١﴾

112. And *all* faces shall humble themselves before the Living, the Self-Subsisting and All-Sustaining *God*. And he shall indeed perish who bears *the burden of* iniquity.

وعنت الوجوه للحي القيوم وقد خاب من حمل
ظلما ﴿١١٢﴾

113. But he who does good works, being a believer, will have no fear of injustice or loss.

ومن يعمل من الصالحات وهو مؤمن فلا يخاف
ظلما ولا هضما ﴿١١٣﴾

* 114. And thus have We sent it down—the Qur'ān in Arabic—and We have explained therein certain warnings, that they may fear God or that it may give birth to *divine* remembrance in them.

وكذلك أنزلناه قرآنا عربيا وصرفنا فيه من
الوعيد لعلهم يتقون أو يحدث لهم ذكرا ﴿١١٤﴾

115. Exalted then is Allah, the True King! And be not impatient for the Qur'ān ere its revelation is completed unto thee,

فتعالى الله الملك الحق ولا تعجل بالقرآن
من قبل أن يقضى إليك وحيه وقل رب زدني

but *only* say, 'O my Lord, increase me in knowledge.'

116. And verily, We had made a covenant with Adam beforehand, but he forgot, and We found in him no determination *to disobey*.

R. 7.

117. And when We said to the angels, 'Submit to Adam,' and they all submitted. But Iblīs *did not*. He refused.

118. Then We said, 'O Adam, this is an enemy to thee, and to thy wife; so let him not drive you both out of the garden, lest thou come to grief.

119. 'It is *provided* for thee that thou wilt not hunger therein, nor wilt thou be naked.

120. 'And that thou wilt not thirst therein, nor wilt thou be exposed to the sun.'

121. But Satan whispered evil suggestions to him; he said, 'O Adam, shall I lead thee to the tree of eternity and to a kingdom that never decays?'

* 122. Then they both ate thereof, so that their shame became manifest to them, and they began to stick the leaves of the garden together over themselves. And Adam observed not the commandment of his Lord, so his life became miserable.

123. Then his Lord chose him *for His grace*, and turned to him with mercy and guided *him*.

124. He said, 'Go forth, both of you, from here, some of you being enemies of others. And if there comes to you guidance from Me, then whoso will follow My guidance, he will not go astray, nor will he come to grief.

125. 'But whosoever will turn away from My Reminder, his will be a strait life, and on the Day of Resurrection We shall raise him up blind.'

126. He will say, 'My Lord, why hast Thou raised me up blind, while I possessed sight *before?*'

127. *God* will say, 'Thus *it was to be;* Our Signs came to thee and thou didst disregard them; and in like manner wilt thou be disregarded this day.'

عِلْمًا ﴿١١٥﴾

وَلَقَدْ عَهِدْنَآ إِلٰٓى اٰدَمَ مِنْ قَبْلُ فَنَسِيَ وَلَمْ نَجِدْ
لَهٗ عَزْمًا ﴿١١٦﴾

وَإِذْ قُلْنَا لِلْمَلٰٓئِكَةِ اسْجُدُوْا لِاٰدَمَ فَسَجَدُوْٓا إِلَّآ إِبْلِيْسَ
أَبٰى ﴿١١٧﴾

فَقُلْنَا يٰٓاٰدَمُ إِنَّ هٰذَا عَدُوٌّ لَّكَ وَلِزَوْجِكَ فَلَا
يُخْرِجَنَّكُمَا مِنَ الْجَنَّةِ فَتَشْقٰى ﴿١١٨﴾

إِنَّ لَكَ أَلَّا تَجُوْعَ فِيْهَا وَلَا تَعْرٰى ﴿١١٩﴾

وَأَنَّكَ لَا تَظْمَؤُا فِيْهَا وَلَا تَضْحٰى ﴿١٢٠﴾

فَوَسْوَسَ إِلَيْهِ الشَّيْطٰنُ قَالَ يٰٓاٰدَمُ هَلْ أَدُلُّكَ عَلٰى
شَجَرَةِ الْخُلْدِ وَمُلْكٍ لَّا يَبْلٰى ﴿١٢١﴾

فَأَكَلَا مِنْهَا فَبَدَتْ لَهُمَا سَوْاٰتُهُمَا وَطَفِقَا يَخْصِفٰنِ
عَلَيْهِمَا مِنْ وَّرَقِ الْجَنَّةِ وَعَصٰٓى اٰدَمُ رَبَّهٗ فَغَوٰى ﴿١٢٢﴾

ثُمَّ اجْتَبٰهُ رَبُّهٗ فَتَابَ عَلَيْهِ وَهَدٰى ﴿١٢٣﴾

قَالَ اهْبِطَا مِنْهَا جَمِيْعًا بَعْضُكُمْ لِبَعْضٍ عَدُوٌّ فَإِمَّا
يَأْتِيَنَّكُمْ مِّنِّيْ هُدًى فَمَنِ اتَّبَعَ هُدَايَ فَلَا
يَضِلُّ وَلَا يَشْقٰى ﴿١٢٤﴾

وَمَنْ أَعْرَضَ عَنْ ذِكْرِيْ فَإِنَّ لَهٗ مَعِيْشَةً ضَنْكًا
وَّنَحْشُرُهٗ يَوْمَ الْقِيٰمَةِ أَعْمٰى ﴿١٢٥﴾

قَالَ رَبِّ لِمَ حَشَرْتَنِيْٓ أَعْمٰى وَقَدْ كُنْتُ بَصِيْرًا ﴿١٢٦﴾

قَالَ كَذٰلِكَ أَتَتْكَ اٰيٰتُنَا فَنَسِيْتَهَا وَكَذٰلِكَ الْيَوْمَ
تُنْسٰى ﴿١٢٧﴾

128. And thus do We recompense him who is extravagant and believes not in the Signs of his Lord; and the punishment of the Hereafter is surely severer and more lasting.

وَكَذٰلِكَ نَجْزِيْ مَنْ اَسْرَفَ وَلَمْ يُؤْمِنْ بِاٰيٰتِ رَبِّهٖ
وَلَعَذَابُ الْاٰخِرَةِ اَشَدُّ وَاَبْقٰى ﴿١٢٨﴾

129. Does it not afford guidance to them how many generations We destroyed before them, in whose dwellings they *now* walk? Therein verily are Signs for those who are endued with reason.

اَفَلَمْ يَهْدِ لَهُمْ كَمْ اَهْلَكْنَا قَبْلَهُمْ مِّنَ الْقُرُوْنِ
يَمْشُوْنَ فِيْ مَسٰكِنِهِمْ اِنَّ فِيْ ذٰلِكَ لَاٰيٰتٍ لِّاُولِي
النُّهٰى ﴿١٢٩﴾ ع ٣/١٦

R. 8.

* 130. And had it not been for a word already gone forth from thy Lord, and a term *already* fixed, *immediate punishment* would have been inevitable.

وَلَوْلَا كَلِمَةٌ سَبَقَتْ مِنْ رَّبِّكَ لَكَانَ لِزَامًا وَّاَجَلٌ
مُّسَمًّى ﴿١٣٠﴾

131. Bear patiently then what they say, and glorify thy Lord with *His* praise before the rising of the sun and before its setting; and glorify *Him* in the hours of the night and at the sides of the day, that thou mayest find *true* happiness.

فَاصْبِرْ عَلٰى مَا يَقُوْلُوْنَ وَسَبِّحْ بِحَمْدِ رَبِّكَ قَبْلَ
طُلُوْعِ الشَّمْسِ وَقَبْلَ غُرُوْبِهَا وَمِنْ اٰنَآئِ الَّيْلِ
فَسَبِّحْ وَاَطْرَافَ النَّهَارِ لَعَلَّكَ تَرْضٰى ﴿١٣١﴾

132. And strain not thy eyes after what We have bestowed on some classes of them to enjoy *for a short time*—the splendour of the present world—that We may try them thereby. And the provision of thy Lord is better and more lasting.

وَلَا تَمُدَّنَّ عَيْنَيْكَ اِلٰى مَا مَتَّعْنَا بِهٖٓ اَزْوَاجًا مِّنْهُمْ
زَهْرَةَ الْحَيٰوةِ الدُّنْيَا لِنَفْتِنَهُمْ فِيْهِ وَرِزْقُ رَبِّكَ
خَيْرٌ وَّاَبْقٰى ﴿١٣٢﴾

133. And enjoin Prayer on thy people, and be constant therein. We ask thee not for provision; it is We that provide for thee. And the end is for righteousness.

وَاْمُرْ اَهْلَكَ بِالصَّلٰوةِ وَاصْطَبِرْ عَلَيْهَا لَا نَسْـَٔلُكَ
رِزْقًا نَحْنُ نَرْزُقُكَ وَالْعَاقِبَةُ لِلتَّقْوٰى ﴿١٣٣﴾

* 134. And they say, 'Why does he not bring us a Sign from his Lord?' Has there not come to them the clear evidence in what is *contained* in the former Books?

وَقَالُوْا لَوْلَا يَاْتِيْنَا بِاٰيَةٍ مِّنْ رَّبِّهٖ اَوَلَمْ تَاْتِهِمْ
بَيِّنَةُ مَا فِي الصُّحُفِ الْاُوْلٰى ﴿١٣٤﴾

135. And if We had destroyed them with a punishment before it they would have surely said, 'Our Lord, wherefore didst Thou not send to us a Messenger that we might have followed Thy commandments before we were humbled and disgraced?'

وَلَوْ اَنَّآ اَهْلَكْنٰهُمْ بِعَذَابٍ مِّنْ قَبْلِهٖ لَقَالُوْا رَبَّنَا
لَوْلَآ اَرْسَلْتَ اِلَيْنَا رَسُوْلًا فَنَتَّبِعَ اٰيٰتِكَ مِنْ قَبْلِ
اَنْ نَّذِلَّ وَنَخْزٰى ﴿١٣٥﴾

136. Say, 'Each one is waiting; wait ye, therefore, and you will know who are the people of the right path and who follow *true* guidance.'

قُلْ كُلٌّ مُّتَرَبِّصٌ فَتَرَبَّصُوْا فَسَتَعْلَمُوْنَ مَنْ اَصْحٰبُ
الصِّرَاطِ السَّوِيِّ وَمَنِ اهْتَدٰى ﴿١٣٦﴾ ع

سُوْرَةُ الْاَنْبِيَآءِ مَكِّيَّةٌ
(٢١) آياتها ١١٢ ركوعاتها ٧

AL-ANBIYĀ'

(Revealed before Hijra)

الجزء ١٧

1. In the name of Allah, the Gracious, the Merciful.

بِسْمِ اللّٰهِ الرَّحْمٰنِ الرَّحِيْمِ ﴿١﴾

2. Nigh has drawn for men their reckoning, yet they turn away in heedlessness.

اِقْتَرَبَ لِلنَّاسِ حِسَابُهُمْ وَ هُمْ فِيْ غَفْلَةٍ
مُّعْرِضُوْنَ ﴿٢﴾

3. There comes not to them any new admonition from their Lord, but they listen to it while they make sport *of it*.

مَا يَاْتِيْهِمْ مِّنْ ذِكْرٍ مِّنْ رَّبِّهِمْ مُّحْدَثٍ اِلَّا اسْتَمَعُوْهُ
وَ هُمْ يَلْعَبُوْنَ ﴿٣﴾

* 4. *And* their hearts are forgetful. And they keep their counsels secret—those who act wrongfully, *then say*, 'Is this *man* aught but a human being like ourselves? Will you then accede to magic while you see *it?*'

لَاهِيَةً قُلُوْبُهُمْ وَ اَسَرُّوا النَّجْوَى الَّذِيْنَ ظَلَمُوْا
هَلْ هٰذَآ اِلَّا بَشَرٌ مِّثْلُكُمْ اَفَتَاْتُوْنَ السِّحْرَ وَ اَنْتُمْ
تُبْصِرُوْنَ ﴿٤﴾

5. *God* said *to the Prophet*, "*Say*, 'My Lord knows what is spoken in the heaven and the earth. And He is the All-Hearing, the All-Knowing,' "

قٰلَ رَبِّيْ يَعْلَمُ الْقَوْلَ فِي السَّمَآءِ وَ الْاَرْضِ وَ هُوَ
السَّمِيْعُ الْعَلِيْمُ ﴿٥﴾

6. Nay, they say, '*These are but* confused dreams; nay, he has forged it; nay, he is *but* a poet. Let him then bring us a Sign just as the former *Prophets* were sent *with Signs*.'

بَلْ قَالُوْٓا اَضْغَاثُ اَحْلَامٍ بَلِ افْتَرٰىهُ بَلْ هُوَ شَاعِرٌ
فَلْيَاْتِنَا بِاٰيَةٍ كَمَآ اُرْسِلَ الْاَوَّلُوْنَ ﴿٦﴾

7. No township, before them, which We destroyed, ever believed. Would they then believe?

مَآ اٰمَنَتْ قَبْلَهُمْ مِّنْ قَرْيَةٍ اَهْلَكْنٰهَا اَفَهُمْ يُؤْمِنُوْنَ ﴿٧﴾

* 8. And We sent none *as Messengers* before thee but men to whom We sent revelations. So ask the people of the Reminder, if you know not.

وَ مَآ اَرْسَلْنَا قَبْلَكَ اِلَّا رِجَالًا نُّوْحِيْٓ اِلَيْهِمْ فَسْـَٔلُوْٓا
اَهْلَ الذِّكْرِ اِنْ كُنْتُمْ لَا تَعْلَمُوْنَ ﴿٨﴾

9. And We did not give them bodies that ate no food, nor were they to live for ever.

وَ مَا جَعَلْنٰهُمْ جَسَدًا لَّا يَاْكُلُوْنَ الطَّعَامَ وَ مَا
كَانُوْا خٰلِدِيْنَ ﴿٩﴾

10. Then We fulfilled to them *Our* promise; and We saved them and those whom We pleased; and We destroyed the transgressors.

ثُمَّ صَدَقْنٰهُمُ الْوَعْدَ فَاَنْجَيْنٰهُمْ وَ مَنْ نَّشَآءُ
وَ اَهْلَكْنَا الْمُسْرِفِيْنَ ﴿١٠﴾

* 11. We have now sent down to you a Book wherein lies your *glory and* eminence; will you not then understand?

R. 2.

12. And how many a township that acted wrongfully have We utterly destroyed, and raised up after it another people!

13. And when they felt Our punishment, lo, they began to flee from it.

* 14. 'Flee not, but return to the comforts in which you exulted, and to your dwellings that you might be *approached and* consulted *as before*.'

15. They said, 'Alas for us, we were indeed wrongdoers!'

16. And this ceased not to be their cry till We mowed them down, reduced to ashes.

17. And We created not the heaven and the earth and all that is between the two in play.

18. If We had wished to find a pastime, We would surely have found it in what is with Us if at all We were to do *such a thing*.

19. Nay, We hurl the truth at falsehood, and it breaks its head, and lo, it perishes. And woe be to you for that which you ascribe *to God*.

20. To Him belongs whosoever is in the heavens and the earth. And those who are in His presence do not disdain to worship Him, nor do they weary;

21. They glorify *Him* night and day; *and* they flag not.

22. Have they taken gods from the earth who raise the dead?

* 23. If there had been in them (the heavens and the earth) other gods beside Allah, then surely both would have gone to ruin. Glorified then be Allah, the Lord of the Throne, above what they attribute.

24. He cannot be questioned as to what He does, but they will be questioned.

25. Have they taken gods beside Him? Say, 'Bring forth your proof. Here is

ع لَقَدْ أَنْزَلْنَا إِلَيْكُمْ كِتٰبًا فِيهِ ذِكْرُكُمْ أَفَلَا تَعْقِلُونَ ﴿١١﴾
وَكَمْ قَصَمْنَا مِنْ قَرْيَةٍ كَانَتْ ظَالِمَةً وَأَنْشَأْنَا
بَعْدَهَا قَوْمًا اٰخَرِينَ ﴿١٢﴾
فَلَمَّا أَحَسُّوا بَأْسَنَا إِذَا هُمْ مِنْهَا يَرْكُضُونَ ﴿١٣﴾
لَا تَرْكُضُوا وَارْجِعُوا إِلَىٰ مَا أُتْرِفْتُمْ فِيهِ وَمَسٰكِنِكُمْ
لَعَلَّكُمْ تُسْأَلُونَ ﴿١٤﴾
قَالُوا يٰوَيْلَنَا إِنَّا كُنَّا ظٰلِمِينَ ﴿١٥﴾
فَمَا زَالَتْ تِلْكَ دَعْوٰىهُمْ حَتّٰى جَعَلْنٰهُمْ حَصِيدًا
خٰمِدِينَ ﴿١٦﴾
وَمَا خَلَقْنَا السَّمَاءَ وَالْأَرْضَ وَمَا بَيْنَهُمَا لٰعِبِينَ ﴿١٧﴾
لَوْ أَرَدْنَا أَنْ نَتَّخِذَ لَهْوًا لَاتَّخَذْنٰهُ مِنْ لَدُنَّا
إِنْ كُنَّا فٰعِلِينَ ﴿١٨﴾
بَلْ نَقْذِفُ بِالْحَقِّ عَلَى الْبَاطِلِ فَيَدْمَغُهُ فَإِذَا
هُوَ زَاهِقٌ وَلَكُمُ الْوَيْلُ مِمَّا تَصِفُونَ ﴿١٩﴾
وَلَهُ مَنْ فِي السَّمٰوٰتِ وَالْأَرْضِ وَمَنْ عِنْدَهُ
لَا يَسْتَكْبِرُونَ عَنْ عِبَادَتِهِ وَلَا يَسْتَحْسِرُونَ ﴿٢٠﴾
يُسَبِّحُونَ الَّيْلَ وَالنَّهَارَ لَا يَفْتُرُونَ ﴿٢١﴾
أَمِ اتَّخَذُوا اٰلِهَةً مِنَ الْأَرْضِ هُمْ يُنْشِرُونَ ﴿٢٢﴾
لَوْ كَانَ فِيهِمَا اٰلِهَةٌ إِلَّا اللّٰهُ لَفَسَدَتَا فَسُبْحٰنَ اللّٰهِ
رَبِّ الْعَرْشِ عَمَّا يَصِفُونَ ﴿٢٣﴾
لَا يُسْأَلُ عَمَّا يَفْعَلُ وَهُمْ يُسْأَلُونَ ﴿٢٤﴾
أَمِ اتَّخَذُوا مِنْ دُونِهِ اٰلِهَةً قُلْ هَاتُوا بُرْهَانَكُمْ

the Book of those with me, and the Book of those before me.' Nay, most of them know not the truth, and so they turn away.

هٰذَا ذِكْرُ مَنْ مَّعِيَ وَذِكْرُ مَنْ قَبْلِيْ ۭ بَلْ اَكْثَرُهُمْ
لَا يَعْلَمُوْنَ ۙ الْحَقَّ فَهُمْ مُّعْرِضُوْنَ ﴿۲۵﴾

26. And We sent no Messenger before thee but We revealed to him, *saying*, 'There is no God but I; so worship Me *alone*.'

وَمَآ اَرْسَلْنَا مِنْ قَبْلِكَ مِنْ رَّسُوْلٍ اِلَّا نُوْحِيْٓ اِلَيْهِ
اَنَّهٗ لَآ اِلٰهَ اِلَّآ اَنَا فَاعْبُدُوْنِ ﴿۲۶﴾

27. And they say, 'The Gracious *God* has taken to Himself a son.' Holy is He. Nay, they are *only* honoured servants.

وَقَالُوا اتَّخَذَ الرَّحْمٰنُ وَلَدًا سُبْحٰنَهٗ ۭ بَلْ عِبَادٌ
مُّكْرَمُوْنَ ﴿۲۷﴾

28. They speak not before He speaks, and they act *only* by His command.

لَا يَسْبِقُوْنَهٗ بِالْقَوْلِ وَهُمْ بِاَمْرِهٖ يَعْمَلُوْنَ ﴿۲۸﴾

29. He knows what is before them and what is behind them, and they intercede not except for him whom He approves, and they act cautiously for fear of Him.

يَعْلَمُ مَا بَيْنَ اَيْدِيْهِمْ وَمَا خَلْفَهُمْ وَلَا يَشْفَعُوْنَ ۙ
اِلَّا لِمَنِ ارْتَضٰى وَهُمْ مِّنْ خَشْيَتِهٖ مُشْفِقُوْنَ ﴿۲۹﴾

30. And whosoever of them should say, 'I am a God beside Him,' him shall We requite with Hell. Thus do We requite the wrongdoers.

وَمَنْ يَّقُلْ مِنْهُمْ اِنِّيْٓ اِلٰهٌ مِّنْ دُوْنِهٖ فَذٰلِكَ نَجْزِيْهِ
جَهَنَّمَ ۭ كَذٰلِكَ نَجْزِي الظّٰلِمِيْنَ ﴿۳۰﴾ ع

R. 3.

31. Do not the disbelievers see that the heavens and the earth were *a* closed-up *mass*, then We opened them out? And We made from water every living thing. Will they not then believe?

اَوَلَمْ يَرَ الَّذِيْنَ كَفَرُوْٓا اَنَّ السَّمٰوٰتِ وَالْاَرْضَ كَانَتَا
رَتْقًا فَفَتَقْنٰهُمَا ۭ وَجَعَلْنَا مِنَ الْمَآءِ كُلَّ شَيْءٍ حَيٍّ ۭ
اَفَلَا يُؤْمِنُوْنَ ﴿۳۱﴾

32. And We have made in the earth firm mountains lest it should quake with them; and We have made therein wide pathways, that they may be rightly guided.

وَجَعَلْنَا فِي الْاَرْضِ رَوَاسِيَ اَنْ تَمِيْدَ بِهِمْ ۠ وَجَعَلْنَا
فِيْهَا فِجَاجًا سُبُلًا لَّعَلَّهُمْ يَهْتَدُوْنَ ﴿۳۲﴾

33. And We have made the heaven a roof, well protected; yet they turn away from its Signs.

وَجَعَلْنَا السَّمَآءَ سَقْفًا مَّحْفُوْظًا ښ وَّهُمْ عَنْ
اٰيٰتِهَا مُعْرِضُوْنَ ﴿۳۳﴾

34. And He it is Who created the night and the day, and the sun and the moon, each gliding along in *its* orbit.

وَهُوَ الَّذِيْ خَلَقَ الَّيْلَ وَالنَّهَارَ وَالشَّمْسَ وَ
الْقَمَرَ ۭ كُلٌّ فِيْ فَلَكٍ يَّسْبَحُوْنَ ﴿۳۴﴾

35. We granted not everlasting life to any human being before thee. If then thou shouldst die, shall they live *here* for ever?

وَمَا جَعَلْنَا لِبَشَرٍ مِّنْ قَبْلِكَ الْخُلْدَ ۭ اَفَاۡىِٕنْ مِّتَّ
فَهُمُ الْخٰلِدُوْنَ ﴿۳۵﴾

36. Every soul shall taste of death; and We prove you with evil and good by way of trial. And to Us shall you be returned.

كل نفس ذآئقة الموت ؕ و نبلوكم بالشر و
الخير فتنة ؕ و الينا ترجعون ﴿٣٦﴾

37. And when the disbelievers see thee, they only make a jest of thee. *They say:* 'Is this the one who makes *an evil* mention of your gods?' while it is they themselves who reject *with disdain* the mention of the Gracious *God*.

و اذا راك الذين كفروا ان يتخذونك الا هزوا ؕ
اهذا الذي يذكر الهتكم ۚ و هم بذكر الرحمن
هم كفرون ﴿٣٧﴾

38. Man is made of haste. I will *certainly* show you My Signs but ask Me not to hasten.

خلق الانسان من عجل ؕ ساوريكم ايتي فلا
تستعجلون ﴿٣٨﴾

39. And they say, 'When will this promise *be fulfilled*, if you are truthful?'

و يقولون متى هذا الوعد ان كنتم صدقين ﴿٣٩﴾

40. If only the disbelievers knew the time when they will not be able to keep off the fire from their faces nor from their backs, and they will not be helped!

لو يعلم الذين كفروا حين لا يكفون عن وجوههم
النار و لا عن ظهورهم و لا هم ينصرون ﴿٤٠﴾

41. Nay, it will come upon them unawares so that it will utterly confound them; and they will not be able to repel it, nor will they be given respite.

بل تاتيهم بغتة فتبهتهم فلا يستطيعون ردها
و لا هم ينظرون ﴿٤١﴾

42. And Messengers have indeed been mocked at before thee, but that whereat they mocked encompassed those of them who scoffed.

و لقد استهزئ برسل من قبلك فحاق بالذين
سخروا منهم ما كانوا به يستهزءون ﴿٤٢﴾ ع

R. 4.

43. Say, 'Who can protect you by night and by day from the Gracious *God?*' Yet they turn away from the remembrance of their Lord.

قل من يكلؤكم باليل و النهار من الرحمن ؕ
بل هم عن ذكر ربهم معرضون ﴿٤٣﴾

44. Have they any gods that can protect them beside Us? They cannot help themselves, nor can they be befriended *by any one* against Us.

ام لهم الهة تمنعهم من دوننا ؕ لا يستطيعون
نصر انفسهم و لا هم منا يصحبون ﴿٤٤﴾

45. Nay, We provided those and their fathers *with the good things of this world* till life grew long for them. Do they not see that We are visiting the land, reducing it from its outlying borders? Can they even then be victors?

بل متعنا هؤلاء و اباءهم حتى طال عليهم
العمر ؕ افلا يرون انا ناتي الارض ننقصها
من اطرافها ؕ افهم الغلبون ﴿٤٥﴾

46. Say, 'I warn you not but according to *divine* revelation.' But the deaf cannot

قل انما انذركم بالوحي ۖ و لا يسمع الصم

hear the call when they are warned.

الدُّعَآءَ اِذَا مَا يُنْذَرُوْنَ ﴿٤٦﴾

47. And if even a breath of thy Lord's punishment touch them, they will surely cry out, 'Woe to us! we were indeed wrong-doers.'

وَلَئِنْ مَّسَّتْهُمْ نَفْحَةٌ مِّنْ عَذَابِ رَبِّكَ لَيَقُوْلُنَّ
يٰوَيْلَنَآ اِنَّا كُنَّا ظٰلِمِيْنَ ﴿٤٧﴾

48. And We shall set up *accurate* scales of justice for the Day of Resurrection so that no soul will be wronged in aught. And even if it were the weight of a grain of mustard seed, We would bring it forth. And sufficient are We as reckoners.

وَنَضَعُ الْمَوَازِيْنَ الْقِسْطَ لِيَوْمِ الْقِيٰمَةِ فَلَا تُظْلَمُ
نَفْسٌ شَيْـًٔا ۗ وَاِنْ كَانَ مِثْقَالَ حَبَّةٍ مِّنْ خَرْدَلٍ
اَتَيْنَا بِهَا ۗ وَكَفٰى بِنَا حٰسِبِيْنَ ﴿٤٨﴾

49. And We gave Moses and Aaron the Discrimination and a Light and a Reminder for the righteous,

وَلَقَدْ اٰتَيْنَا مُوْسٰى وَهٰرُوْنَ الْفُرْقَانَ وَضِيَآءً
وَّذِكْرًا لِّلْمُتَّقِيْنَ ﴿٤٩﴾

50. Those who fear their Lord in secret, and who dread the Hour *of Judgment*.

الَّذِيْنَ يَخْشَوْنَ رَبَّهُمْ بِالْغَيْبِ وَهُمْ مِّنَ السَّاعَةِ
مُشْفِقُوْنَ ﴿٥٠﴾

51. And this is a blessed Reminder that We have sent down; will you then reject it?

وَهٰذَا ذِكْرٌ مُّبٰرَكٌ اَنْزَلْنٰهُ ۚ اَفَاَنْتُمْ لَهٗ مُنْكِرُوْنَ ﴿٥١﴾

R. 5.

52. And before *this* We gave Abraham his guidance and We knew him well.

وَلَقَدْ اٰتَيْنَآ اِبْرٰهِيْمَ رُشْدَهٗ مِنْ قَبْلُ وَكُنَّا
بِهٖ عٰلِمِيْنَ ﴿٥٢﴾

53. When he said to his father and his people, 'What are these images to which you are so devoted?'

اِذْ قَالَ لِاَبِيْهِ وَقَوْمِهٖ مَا هٰذِهِ التَّمَاثِيْلُ الَّتِيْٓ
اَنْتُمْ لَهَا عٰكِفُوْنَ ﴿٥٣﴾

54. They replied, 'We found our fathers worshipping them.'

قَالُوْا وَجَدْنَآ اٰبَآءَنَا لَهَا عٰبِدِيْنَ ﴿٥٤﴾

55. He said, 'Indeed, you yourselves as well as your fathers have been in manifest error.'

قَالَ لَقَدْ كُنْتُمْ اَنْتُمْ وَاٰبَآؤُكُمْ فِيْ ضَلٰلٍ مُّبِيْنٍ ﴿٥٥﴾

56. They said, 'Is it *really* the truth that thou hast brought us, or art thou one of those who jest?'

قَالُوْٓا اَجِئْتَنَا بِالْحَقِّ اَمْ اَنْتَ مِنَ اللّٰعِبِيْنَ ﴿٥٦﴾

57. He replied, 'Nay, your Lord is the Lord of the heavens and the earth, He Who made them; and I am one of those who bear witness to that.

قَالَ بَلْ رَّبُّكُمْ رَبُّ السَّمٰوٰتِ وَالْاَرْضِ الَّذِيْ
فَطَرَهُنَّ ۖ وَاَنَا عَلٰى ذٰلِكُمْ مِّنَ الشّٰهِدِيْنَ ﴿٥٧﴾

58. 'And, by Allah, I will certainly plan against your idols after you have gone away *and* turned your backs.'

وَتَاللّٰهِ لَاَكِيْدَنَّ اَصْنَامَكُمْ بَعْدَ اَنْ تُوَلُّوْا
مُدْبِرِيْنَ ﴿٥٨﴾

59. So he broke them to pieces, *all* except the chief of them, that they might return to it *for enquiry*.

فَجَعَلَهُمْ جُذٰذًا اِلَّا كَبِيْرًا لَّهُمْ لَعَلَّهُمْ اِلَيْهِ يَرْجِعُوْنَ ﴿٥٩﴾

60. They said, 'Who has done this to our gods? Surely, he must be a wrongdoer.'

قَالُوْا مَنْ فَعَلَ هٰذَا بِاٰلِهَتِنَآ اِنَّهٗ لَمِنَ الظّٰلِمِيْنَ ﴿٦٠﴾

61. They said, 'We heard a young man speak *ill* of them; he is called Abraham.'

قَالُوْا سَمِعْنَا فَتًى يَّذْكُرُهُمْ يُقَالُ لَهٗٓ اِبْرٰهِيْمُ ﴿٦١﴾

62. They said, 'Then bring him before the eyes of the people, that they may bear witness.'

قَالُوْا فَاْتُوْا بِهٖ عَلٰٓى اَعْيُنِ النَّاسِ لَعَلَّهُمْ يَشْهَدُوْنَ ﴿٦٢﴾

63. Then they said *to Abraham*, 'Is it thou who hast done this to our gods, O Abraham?'

قَالُوْٓا ءَاَنْتَ فَعَلْتَ هٰذَا بِاٰلِهَتِنَا يٰٓاِبْرٰهِيْمُ ﴿٦٣﴾

* 64. He replied, 'Aye, somebody has surely done this. Here is their chief. But ask them if they can speak.'

قَالَ بَلْ فَعَلَهٗ ۖ كَبِيْرُهُمْ هٰذَا فَسْـَٔلُوْهُمْ اِنْ
كَانُوْا يَنْطِقُوْنَ ﴿٦٤﴾

65. Then they turned towards one another and said, 'You yourselves are surely in the wrong.'

فَرَجَعُوْٓا اِلٰٓى اَنْفُسِهِمْ فَقَالُوْٓا اِنَّكُمْ اَنْتُمُ الظّٰلِمُوْنَ ﴿٦٥﴾

66. And their heads were made to hang low *for shame and they said*, 'Certainly thou knowest well that these do not speak.'

ثُمَّ نُكِسُوْا عَلٰى رُءُوْسِهِمْ ۚ لَقَدْ عَلِمْتَ مَا هٰٓؤُلَآءِ
يَنْطِقُوْنَ ﴿٦٦﴾

67. He said, 'Do you then worship instead of Allah that which cannot profit you at all, nor harm you?

قَالَ اَفَتَعْبُدُوْنَ مِنْ دُوْنِ اللّٰهِ مَا لَا يَنْفَعُكُمْ
شَيْـًٔا وَّلَا يَضُرُّكُمْ ﴿٦٧﴾

68. 'Fie on you and on that which you worship instead of Allah! Will you not then understand?'

اُفٍّ لَّكُمْ وَلِمَا تَعْبُدُوْنَ مِنْ دُوْنِ اللّٰهِ ؕ اَفَلَا
تَعْقِلُوْنَ ﴿٦٨﴾

69. They said, 'Burn him and help your gods, if *at all* you *mean to* do *anything*.'

قَالُوْا حَرِّقُوْهُ وَانْصُرُوْٓا اٰلِهَتَكُمْ اِنْ كُنْتُمْ فٰعِلِيْنَ ﴿٦٩﴾

* 70. We said, 'O fire, be thou cold and a *means of* safety for Abraham!'

قُلْنَا يٰنَارُ كُوْنِيْ بَرْدًا وَّسَلٰمًا عَلٰٓى اِبْرٰهِيْمَ ﴿٧٠﴾

71. And they had sought to do evil to him, but We made them the worst losers.

وَاَرَادُوْا بِهٖ كَيْدًا فَجَعَلْنٰهُمُ الْاَخْسَرِيْنَ ﴿٧١﴾

72. And We saved him and Lot *and brought them* to the land which We blessed for the peoples.

وَنَجَّيْنٰهُ وَلُوْطًا اِلَى الْاَرْضِ الَّتِيْ بٰرَكْنَا فِيْهَا
لِلْعٰلَمِيْنَ ﴿٧٢﴾

73. And We bestowed upon him Isaac, and as a grandson, Jacob, and We made all *of them* righteous.

وَوَهَبْنَا لَهٗٓ اِسْحٰقَ ؕ وَيَعْقُوْبَ نَافِلَةً ؕ وَكُلًّا
جَعَلْنَا صٰلِحِيْنَ ﴿٧٣﴾

74. And We made them leaders who guided *people* by Our command, and We

وَجَعَلْنٰهُمْ اَئِمَّةً يَّهْدُوْنَ بِاَمْرِنَا وَاَوْحَيْنَآ

إِلَيْهِمْ فِعْلَ الْخَيْرٰتِ وَإِقَامَ الصَّلٰوةِ وَإِيتَآءَ
الزَّكٰوةِ ۚ وَكَانُوا لَنَا عٰبِدِينَ ﴿٧٤﴾

sent revelation to them *enjoining* the doing of good works, and the observing of Prayer, and the giving of alms. And they were worshippers of Us *alone*.

وَلُوطًا اٰتَيْنٰهُ حُكْمًا وَّعِلْمًا وَّنَجَّيْنٰهُ مِنَ الْقَرْيَةِ
الَّتِي كَانَتْ تَّعْمَلُ الْخَبٰٓئِثَ ۗ إِنَّهُمْ كَانُوا قَوْمَ سَوْءٍ
فٰسِقِينَ ﴿٧٥﴾

75. And to Lot We gave wisdom and knowledge. And We saved him from the city which practised abominations. They were indeed a wicked *and* rebellious people.

وَأَدْخَلْنٰهُ فِي رَحْمَتِنَا ۖ إِنَّهُ مِنَ الصّٰلِحِينَ ﴿٧٦﴾

76. And We admitted him to Our mercy; surely he was *one* of the righteous.

R. 6.

وَنُوحًا إِذْ نَادٰى مِنْ قَبْلُ فَاسْتَجَبْنَا لَهُ فَنَجَّيْنٰهُ
وَأَهْلَهُ مِنَ الْكَرْبِ الْعَظِيمِ ﴿٧٧﴾

77. And *remember* Noah when he cried *to Us* aforetime, and We heard his prayer and delivered him and his family from the great distress.

وَنَصَرْنٰهُ مِنَ الْقَوْمِ الَّذِينَ كَذَّبُوا بِاٰيٰتِنَا ۚ
إِنَّهُمْ كَانُوا قَوْمَ سَوْءٍ فَأَغْرَقْنٰهُمْ أَجْمَعِينَ ﴿٧٨﴾

78. And We helped him against the people who rejected Our Signs. They were surely a wicked people; so We drowned them all.

وَدَاوٗدَ وَسُلَيْمٰنَ إِذْ يَحْكُمٰنِ فِي الْحَرْثِ إِذْ
نَفَشَتْ فِيهِ غَنَمُ الْقَوْمِ ۚ وَكُنَّا لِحُكْمِهِمْ شٰهِدِينَ ﴿٧٩﴾

79. And *remember* David and Solomon when they exercised their *respective* judgments concerning the crop when the sheep of *certain* people strayed therein *by night;* and We were witness to their judgment.

فَفَهَّمْنٰهَا سُلَيْمٰنَ ۚ وَكُلًّا اٰتَيْنَا حُكْمًا وَّعِلْمًا ۫ وَّ
سَخَّرْنَا مَعَ دَاوٗدَ الْجِبَالَ يُسَبِّحْنَ وَالطَّيْرَ ۚ وَكُنَّا
فٰعِلِينَ ﴿٨٠﴾

80. We gave Solomon the *right* understanding of *the matter* and to each of them gave We wisdom and knowledge. And We subjected the mountains and the birds to celebrate *God's* praises with David. And it is We Who do *all such things*.

وَعَلَّمْنٰهُ صَنْعَةَ لَبُوسٍ لَّكُمْ لِتُحْصِنَكُمْ مِّنْۢ
بَأْسِكُمْ ۚ فَهَلْ أَنْتُمْ شٰكِرُونَ ﴿٨١﴾

81. And We taught him the making of coats of mail for you, that they might protect you from each other's violence. Will you then be thankful?

وَلِسُلَيْمٰنَ الرِّيحَ عَاصِفَةً تَجْرِي بِأَمْرِهٖٓ إِلَى
الْأَرْضِ الَّتِي بٰرَكْنَا فِيهَا ۚ وَكُنَّا بِكُلِّ شَيْءٍ
عٰلِمِينَ ﴿٨٢﴾

82. And *We subjected* to Solomon the violent wind. It blew, at his bidding, toward the land which We had blessed. And We have knowledge of all things.

وَمِنَ الشَّيٰطِينِ مَنْ يَّغُوصُونَ لَهُ وَيَعْمَلُونَ
عَمَلًا دُونَ ذٰلِكَ ۚ وَكُنَّا لَهُمْ حٰفِظِينَ ﴿٨٣﴾

83. And *We subjected to him* deep divers who dived for him, and did other work beside that; and it was We Who guarded them.

84. And *remember* Job when he cried to his Lord, *saying*, 'Affliction has touched me, and Thou art the Most Merciful of all who show mercy.'

وَ اَيُّوْبَ اِذْ نَادٰى رَبَّهٗۤ اَنِّيْ مَسَّنِيَ الضُّرُّ وَ اَنْتَ
اَرْحَمُ الرّٰحِمِيْنَ ﴿۸۴﴾

85. So We heard his prayer and removed the distress from which he suffered, and We gave him his family and the like thereof with them, as a mercy from Us, and as a reminder for the worshippers.

فَاسْتَجَبْنَا لَهٗ فَكَشَفْنَا مَا بِهٖ مِنْ ضُرٍّ وَّ اٰتَيْنٰهُ اَهْلَهٗ
وَ مِثْلَهُمْ مَّعَهُمْ رَحْمَةً مِّنْ عِنْدِنَا وَ ذِكْرٰى
لِلْعٰبِدِيْنَ ﴿۸۵﴾

86. And *remember* Ishmael, and Idris, and Dhu'l-Kifl. All were of the steadfast.

وَ اِسْمٰعِيْلَ وَ اِدْرِيْسَ وَ ذَا الْكِفْلِ ؕ كُلٌّ مِّنَ
الصّٰبِرِيْنَ ﴿۸۶﴾

87. And We admitted them to Our mercy. Surely, they were of the righteous.

وَ اَدْخَلْنٰهُمْ فِيْ رَحْمَتِنَا ؕ اِنَّهُمْ مِّنَ الصّٰلِحِيْنَ ﴿۸۷﴾

* 88. And *remember* Dhu'l-Nūn, when he went away in anger, and he thought that We would never cause him distress and he cried out in *depths of* darkness, *saying*, 'There is no God but Thou, Holy art Thou. I have indeed been of the wrongdoers.'

وَ ذَا النُّوْنِ اِذْ ذَّهَبَ مُغَاضِبًا فَظَنَّ اَنْ لَّنْ نَّقْدِرَ
عَلَيْهِ فَنَادٰى فِي الظُّلُمٰتِ اَنْ لَّاۤ اِلٰهَ اِلَّاۤ اَنْتَ
سُبْحٰنَكَ ۖ اِنِّيْ كُنْتُ مِنَ الظّٰلِمِيْنَ ﴿۸۸﴾

89. So We heard his prayer and delivered him from the distress. And thus do We deliver the believers.

فَاسْتَجَبْنَا لَهٗ ۙ وَ نَجَّيْنٰهُ مِنَ الْغَمِّ ؕ وَ كَذٰلِكَ
نُـْۨجِي الْمُؤْمِنِيْنَ ﴿۸۹﴾

90. And *remember* Zachariah when he cried to his Lord, *saying*, 'My Lord, leave me not childless, and Thou art the Best of inheritors.'

وَ زَكَرِيَّاۤ اِذْ نَادٰى رَبَّهٗ رَبِّ لَا تَذَرْنِيْ فَرْدًا
وَّ اَنْتَ خَيْرُ الْوٰرِثِيْنَ ﴿۹۰﴾

91. So We heard his prayer and bestowed upon him John and cured his wife for him. They used to vie with one another in good works and they called on Us in hope and in fear, and they humbled themselves before Us.

فَاسْتَجَبْنَا لَهٗ ۫ وَ وَهَبْنَا لَهٗ يَحْيٰى وَ اَصْلَحْنَا لَهٗ
زَوْجَهٗ ؕ اِنَّهُمْ كَانُوْا يُسٰرِعُوْنَ فِي الْخَيْرٰتِ وَ
يَدْعُوْنَنَا رَغَبًا وَّ رَهَبًا ؕ وَ كَانُوْا لَنَا خٰشِعِيْنَ ﴿۹۱﴾

* 92. And *remember* her who preserved her chastity; so We breathed into her of Our word and We made her and her son a Sign for peoples.

وَ الَّتِيْۤ اَحْصَنَتْ فَرْجَهَا فَنَفَخْنَا فِيْهَا مِنْ رُّوْحِنَا
وَ جَعَلْنٰهَا وَ ابْنَهَاۤ اٰيَةً لِّلْعٰلَمِيْنَ ﴿۹۲﴾

93. Verily, this is your people—one people; and I am your Lord, so worship Me.

اِنَّ هٰذِهٖۤ اُمَّتُكُمْ اُمَّةً وَّاحِدَةً ۫ۖ وَّ اَنَا رَبُّكُمْ
فَاعْبُدُوْنِ ﴿۹۳﴾

94. But they have become divided among themselves in their affair; and all will return to Us.

R. 7.

* 95. So Whoever does good works and is a believer, his effort will not be disregarded and We shall surely record it.

96. And it is an inviolable law for a township which We have destroyed that they shall not return.

97. *It shall be so* even when Gog and Magog are let loose and they shall hasten forth from every height.

98. And the true promise draws nigh; then behold, the eyes of those who disbelieve will fixedly stare *and they will say*, 'Alas for us! we were indeed heedless of this; nay, we were wrongdoers!'

99. 'Surely, you and that which you worship beside Allah are the fuel of Hell. To it shall you *all* come.'

100. If these had been gods, they would not have come to it; and all will abide therein.

101. Therein, groaning will be their *lot* and they will not hear therein *anything else*.

102. *But* as for those for whom *the promise of* a good reward has already gone forth from Us, these will be removed far from it.

103. They will not hear the slightest sound thereof; and they shall abide in that which their souls desire.

104. The Great Terror will not grieve them, and the angels will meet them, *saying*, 'This is your day which you were promised.'

105. *Remember* the day when We shall roll up the heavens like the rolling up of written scrolls by a scribe. As We began the first creation, so shall We repeat it—a promise *binding* upon Us; We shall cer-

ع وَتَقَطَّعُوْٓا اَمْرَهُمْ بَيْنَهُمْ ؕ كُلٌّ اِلَيْنَا رٰجِعُوْنَ ﴿۹۴﴾
فَمَنْ يَّعْمَلْ مِنَ الصّٰلِحٰتِ وَهُوَ مُؤْمِنٌ فَلَا
كُفْرَانَ لِسَعْيِهٖ ۚ وَاِنَّا لَهٗ كٰتِبُوْنَ ﴿۹۵﴾
وَحَرٰمٌ عَلٰى قَرْيَةٍ اَهْلَكْنٰهَآ اَنَّهُمْ لَا يَرْجِعُوْنَ ﴿۹۶﴾
حَتّٰٓى اِذَا فُتِحَتْ يَاْجُوْجُ وَمَاْجُوْجُ وَهُمْ مِّنْ كُلِّ
حَدَبٍ يَّنْسِلُوْنَ ﴿۹۷﴾
وَاقْتَرَبَ الْوَعْدُ الْحَقُّ فَاِذَا هِيَ شَاخِصَةٌ اَبْصَارُ
الَّذِيْنَ كَفَرُوْا ؕ يٰوَيْلَنَا قَدْ كُنَّا فِيْ غَفْلَةٍ مِّنْ هٰذَا
بَلْ كُنَّا ظٰلِمِيْنَ ﴿۹۸﴾
اِنَّكُمْ وَمَا تَعْبُدُوْنَ مِنْ دُوْنِ اللّٰهِ حَصَبُ جَهَنَّمَ ؕ
اَنْتُمْ لَهَا وٰرِدُوْنَ ﴿۹۹﴾
لَوْ كَانَ هٰٓؤُلَآءِ اٰلِهَةً مَّا وَرَدُوْهَا ؕ وَكُلٌّ فِيْهَا
خٰلِدُوْنَ ﴿۱۰۰﴾
لَهُمْ فِيْهَا زَفِيْرٌ وَّهُمْ فِيْهَا لَا يَسْمَعُوْنَ ﴿۱۰۱﴾
اِنَّ الَّذِيْنَ سَبَقَتْ لَهُمْ مِّنَّا الْحُسْنٰٓى ۙ اُولٰٓئِكَ
عَنْهَا مُبْعَدُوْنَ ۙ﴿۱۰۲﴾
لَا يَسْمَعُوْنَ حَسِيْسَهَا ۚ وَهُمْ فِيْ مَا اشْتَهَتْ
اَنْفُسُهُمْ خٰلِدُوْنَ ۚ﴿۱۰۳﴾
لَا يَحْزُنُهُمُ الْفَزَعُ الْاَكْبَرُ وَتَتَلَقّٰىهُمُ الْمَلٰٓئِكَةُ ؕ
هٰذَا يَوْمُكُمُ الَّذِيْ كُنْتُمْ تُوْعَدُوْنَ ﴿۱۰۴﴾
يَوْمَ نَطْوِي السَّمَآءَ كَطَيِّ السِّجِلِّ لِلْكُتُبِ ؕ كَمَا
بَدَاْنَآ اَوَّلَ خَلْقٍ نُّعِيْدُهٗ ؕ وَعْدًا عَلَيْنَا ؕ اِنَّا كُنَّا

tainly perform *it*.

فٰعِلِيْنَ ﴿١٠٥﴾

* 106. And already have We written in the Book *of David*, after the exhortation, that My righteous servants shall inherit the land.

وَلَقَدْ كَتَبْنَا فِي الزَّبُوْرِ مِنْ بَعْدِ الذِّكْرِ
أَنَّ الْاَرْضَ يَرِثُهَا عِبَادِيَ الصّٰلِحُوْنَ ﴿١٠٦﴾

* 107. Herein, surely, is a message for people who worship *God*.

إِنَّ فِيْ هٰذَا لَبَلٰغًا لِّقَوْمٍ عٰبِدِيْنَ ﴿١٠٧﴾

108. And We have sent thee not but as a mercy for all peoples.

وَمَآ اَرْسَلْنٰكَ إِلَّا رَحْمَةً لِّلْعٰلَمِيْنَ ﴿١٠٨﴾

109. Say, 'Surely it has been revealed to me that your God is but One God. Will you then submit?'

قُلْ إِنَّمَا يُوْحٰٓى إِلَيَّ اَنَّمَآ إِلٰهُكُمْ إِلٰهٌ وَّاحِدٌ
فَهَلْ اَنْتُمْ مُّسْلِمُوْنَ ﴿١٠٩﴾

110. But if they turn back, say, 'I have warned you all alike and I know not whether that which you are promised is near or distant.

فَإِنْ تَوَلَّوْا فَقُلْ اٰذَنْتُكُمْ عَلٰى سَوَآءٍ وَإِنْ اَدْرِيْٓ
اَقَرِيْبٌ اَمْ بَعِيْدٌ مَّا تُوْعَدُوْنَ ﴿١١٠﴾

111. 'Verily, He knows what is open in speech, and He knows that which you conceal.

إِنَّهٗ يَعْلَمُ الْجَهْرَ مِنَ الْقَوْلِ وَيَعْلَمُ مَا تَكْتُمُوْنَ ﴿١١١﴾

112. 'And I know not but that it may be a trial for you, and *only* an enjoyment for a while.'

وَإِنْ اَدْرِيْ لَعَلَّهٗ فِتْنَةٌ لَّكُمْ وَمَتَاعٌ إِلٰى
حِيْنٍ ﴿١١٢﴾

113. He *also* said, 'My Lord, judge Thou with truth. Our Lord is the Gracious *God* Whose help is to be sought against that which you assert.'

قٰلَ رَبِّ احْكُمْ بِالْحَقِّ وَرَبُّنَا الرَّحْمٰنُ الْمُسْتَعَانُ
عَلٰى مَا تَصِفُوْنَ ﴿١١٣﴾ ع ٩

ركوعاتها سُوْرَةُ الْحَجِّ مَدَنِيَّةٌ (٢٢) اٰياتها

AL-ḤAJJ

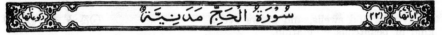

(Revealed after Hijra)

1. In the name of Allah, the Gracious, the Merciful.

بِسْمِ اللّٰهِ الرَّحْمٰنِ الرَّحِيْمِ ﴿١﴾

* 2. O people, fear your Lord; verily the earthquake of the Hour is a tremendous thing—

يٰۤاَيُّهَا النَّاسُ اتَّقُوْا رَبَّكُمْ ۚ اِنَّ زَلْزَلَةَ السَّاعَةِ
شَيْءٌ عَظِيْمٌ ﴿٢﴾

* 3. The day when you see it, every woman giving suck shall forget her suckling and every pregnant woman shall cast her burden; and thou shalt see men as drunken while they will not be drunken, but severe will indeed be the punishment of Allah.

يَوْمَ تَرَوْنَهَا تَذْهَلُ كُلُّ مُرْضِعَةٍ عَمَّاۤ اَرْضَعَتْ
وَتَضَعُ كُلُّ ذَاتِ حَمْلٍ حَمْلَهَا وَتَرَى النَّاسَ
سُكٰرٰى وَمَا هُمْ بِسُكٰرٰى وَلٰكِنَّ عَذَابَ اللّٰهِ
شَدِيْدٌ ﴿٣﴾

4. And among men there are some who dispute concerning Allah without knowledge, and follow every rebellious satan,

وَمِنَ النَّاسِ مَنْ يُّجَادِلُ فِي اللّٰهِ بِغَيْرِ عِلْمٍ وَّ
يَتَّبِعُ كُلَّ شَيْطٰنٍ مَّرِيْدٍ ﴿٤﴾

5. For whom it is decreed that whosoever makes friends with him, him he will lead astray and will guide him to the punishment of the Fire.

كُتِبَ عَلَيْهِ اَنَّهٗ مَنْ تَوَلَّاهُ فَاَنَّهٗ يُضِلُّهٗ وَيَهْدِيْهِ
اِلٰى عَذَابِ السَّعِيْرِ ﴿٥﴾

* 6. O people, if you are in doubt concerning the Resurrection, *then consider that* We have indeed created you from dust, then from a sperm-drop, then from clotted blood, then from a lump of flesh, partly formed and partly unformed, in order that We may make *Our power* manifest to you. And We cause what We will to remain in the wombs for an appointed term; then We bring you forth as babes; then *We rear you* that you may attain to your *age of* full strength. And there are some of you who are caused to die *prematurely*, and there are others among you who are driven to the worst part of life *with the result* that they know nothing after *having had* knowledge. And thou seest the earth lifeless, but when We send down water there-

يٰۤاَيُّهَا النَّاسُ اِنْ كُنْتُمْ فِيْ رَيْبٍ مِّنَ الْبَعْثِ فَاِنَّا
خَلَقْنٰكُمْ مِّنْ تُرَابٍ ثُمَّ مِنْ نُّطْفَةٍ ثُمَّ مِنْ عَلَقَةٍ
ثُمَّ مِنْ مُّضْغَةٍ مُّخَلَّقَةٍ وَّغَيْرِ مُخَلَّقَةٍ لِّنُبَيِّنَ
لَكُمْ ۗ وَنُقِرُّ فِي الْاَرْحَامِ مَا نَشَآءُ اِلٰۤى اَجَلٍ مُّسَمًّى
ثُمَّ نُخْرِجُكُمْ طِفْلًا ثُمَّ لِتَبْلُغُوْۤا اَشُدَّكُمْ ۚ وَمِنْكُمْ
مَّنْ يُّتَوَفّٰى وَمِنْكُمْ مَّنْ يُّرَدُّ اِلٰۤى اَرْذَلِ الْعُمُرِ لِكَيْلَا
يَعْلَمَ مِنْ بَعْدِ عِلْمٍ شَيْـًٔا ؕ وَتَرَى الْاَرْضَ هَامِدَةً
فَاِذَاۤ اَنْزَلْنَا عَلَيْهَا الْمَآءَ اهْتَزَّتْ وَرَبَتْ وَاَنْۢبَتَتْ

on, it stirs and swells, and grows every kind of beauteous vegetation.

مِنْ كُلِّ زَوْجٍ بَهِيْجٍ ﴿٦﴾

7. That is because Allah is the Truth, and that it is He Who brings the dead to life, and that He has power over all things;

ذٰلِكَ بِاَنَّ اللّٰهَ هُوَ الْحَقُّ وَاَنَّهٗ يُحْيِ الْمَوْتٰى وَ
اَنَّهٗ عَلٰى كُلِّ شَيْءٍ قَدِيْرٌ ﴿٧﴾

8. And because the Hour will *certainly* come, there is no doubt about it, and because Allah will raise up those who are in the graves.

وَّاَنَّ السَّاعَةَ اٰتِيَةٌ لَّا رَيْبَ فِيْهَا وَاَنَّ اللّٰهَ
يَبْعَثُ مَنْ فِي الْقُبُوْرِ ﴿٨﴾

9. And among men there is he who disputes concerning Allah without knowledge and without guidance and without an enlightening Book,

وَمِنَ النَّاسِ مَنْ يُّجَادِلُ فِي اللّٰهِ بِغَيْرِ عِلْمٍ وَّ
لَا هُدًى وَّلَا كِتٰبٍ مُّنِيْرٍ ﴿٩﴾

10. Turning his side *disdainfully*, that he may lead *men* astray from the way of Allah. For him is disgrace in this world; and on the Day of Resurrection We shall make him taste the punishment of burning.

ثَانِيَ عِطْفِهٖ لِيُضِلَّ عَنْ سَبِيْلِ اللّٰهِ لَهٗ فِي
الدُّنْيَا خِزْيٌ وَّنُذِيْقُهٗ يَوْمَ الْقِيٰمَةِ عَذَابَ
الْحَرِيْقِ ﴿١٠﴾

11. This is because of what thy hands have sent on before, and Allah is not unjust to *His* servants.

ذٰلِكَ بِمَا قَدَّمَتْ يَدٰكَ وَاَنَّ اللّٰهَ لَيْسَ بِظَلَّامٍ
لِّلْعَبِيْدِ ﴿١١﴾ ع

R. 2.

* 12. And among men there is he who serves Allah, *standing as it were* on the verge. Then if good befall him, he is content therewith; and if there befall him a trial, he returns to his *former* way. He loses in this world as well as in the Hereafter. That is an evident loss.

وَمِنَ النَّاسِ مَنْ يَّعْبُدُ اللّٰهَ عَلٰى حَرْفٍ فَاِنْ
اَصَابَهٗ خَيْرُ اِطْمَاَنَّ بِهٖ وَاِنْ اَصَابَتْهُ فِتْنَةُ
اِنْقَلَبَ عَلٰى وَجْهِهٖ خَسِرَ الدُّنْيَا وَالْاٰخِرَةَ
ذٰلِكَ هُوَ الْخُسْرَانُ الْمُبِيْنُ ﴿١٢﴾

13. He calls beside Allah on that which can neither harm him, nor benefit him. That is indeed straying far away.

يَدْعُوْا مِنْ دُوْنِ اللّٰهِ مَا لَا يَضُرُّهٗ وَمَا لَا
يَنْفَعُهٗ ذٰلِكَ هُوَ الضَّلٰلُ الْبَعِيْدُ ﴿١٣﴾

14. He calls on him whose harm is nearer than his benefit. Evil indeed is the patron, and evil indeed the associate.

يَدْعُوْا لَمَنْ ضَرُّهٗٓ اَقْرَبُ مِنْ نَّفْعِهٖ لَبِئْسَ
الْمَوْلٰى وَلَبِئْسَ الْعَشِيْرُ ﴿١٤﴾

15. Verily, Allah will cause those who believe and do good deeds to enter Gardens beneath which rivers flow; surely

اِنَّ اللّٰهَ يُدْخِلُ الَّذِيْنَ اٰمَنُوْا وَعَمِلُوا الصّٰلِحٰتِ
جَنّٰتٍ تَجْرِيْ مِنْ تَحْتِهَا الْاَنْهٰرُ اِنَّ اللّٰهَ يَفْعَلُ

Allah does what He will.

مَا يُرِيْدُ ⑮

16. Whoso thinks that Allah will not help him (the Prophet) in this world and the Hereafter, let him, *if he can*, find a way to heaven, and let him cut off *the divine help*. Then let him see if his device can remove that which enrages *him*.

مَنْ كَانَ يَظُنُّ اَنْ لَّنْ يَّنْصُرَهُ اللّٰهُ فِي الدُّنْيَا وَ
الْاٰخِرَةِ فَلْيَمْدُدْ بِسَبَبٍ اِلَى السَّمَآءِ ثُمَّ لْيَقْطَعْ
فَلْيَنْظُرْ هَلْ يُذْهِبَنَّ كَيْدُهٗ مَا يَغِيْظُ ⑯

17. And thus have We sent it (the Qur'ān) down as manifest Signs, and surely Allah guides whom He will.

وَكَذٰلِكَ اَنْزَلْنٰهُ اٰيٰتٍۭ بَيِّنٰتٍ وَّاَنَّ اللّٰهَ يَهْدِيْ مَنْ
يُّرِيْدُ ⑰

18. *As to* those who believe, and the Jews, and the Sabians, and the Christians, and the Magians and the idolaters, verily, Allah will judge between them on the Day of Resurrection; surely Allah is Witness over all things.

اِنَّ الَّذِيْنَ اٰمَنُوْا وَالَّذِيْنَ هَادُوْا وَالصّٰبِـِٕيْنَ وَ
النَّصٰرٰى وَالْمَجُوْسَ وَالَّذِيْنَ اَشْرَكُوْٓا ۖ اِنَّ اللّٰهَ
يَفْصِلُ بَيْنَهُمْ يَوْمَ الْقِيٰمَةِ ۭ اِنَّ اللّٰهَ عَلٰى كُلِّ
شَيْءٍ شَهِيْدٌ ⑱

19. Hast thou not seen that to Allah submits whosoever is in the heavens and whosoever is in the earth, and the sun, and the moon, and the stars, and the mountains, and the trees, and the beasts, and many of mankind? But there are many who become deserving of punishment. And whomsoever Allah disgraces, none can raise him to honour. Verily, Allah does what He pleases.

اَلَمْ تَرَ اَنَّ اللّٰهَ يَسْجُدُ لَهٗ مَنْ فِي السَّمٰوٰتِ وَمَنْ
فِي الْاَرْضِ وَالشَّمْسُ وَالْقَمَرُ وَالنُّجُوْمُ وَالْجِبَالُ
وَالشَّجَرُ وَالدَّوَآبُّ وَكَثِيْرٌ مِّنَ النَّاسِ ۭ وَكَثِيْرٌ
حَقَّ عَلَيْهِ الْعَذَابُ ۭ وَمَنْ يُّهِنِ اللّٰهُ فَمَا لَهٗ مِنْ
مُّكْرِمٍ ۭ اِنَّ اللّٰهَ يَفْعَلُ مَا يَشَآءُ ۩ ⑲

20. These two are two disputants who dispute concerning their Lord. As for those who disbelieve, garments of fire will be cut out for them; *and* boiling water will be poured down on their heads,

هٰذٰنِ خَصْمٰنِ اخْتَصَمُوْا فِيْ رَبِّهِمْ ۡ فَالَّذِيْنَ كَفَرُوْا
قُطِّعَتْ لَهُمْ ثِيَابٌ مِّنْ نَّارٍ ۭ يُصَبُّ مِنْ فَوْقِ
رُءُوْسِهِمُ الْحَمِيْمُ ⑳

21. Whereby that which is in their bellies, and *their* skins too, will be melted;

يُصْهَرُ بِهٖ مَا فِيْ بُطُوْنِهِمْ وَالْجُلُوْدُ ۭ ㉑

22. And for them there will be maces of iron *with which to punish them*.

وَلَهُمْ مَّقَامِعُ مِنْ حَدِيْدٍ ㉒

23. Whenever they will seek to get out of it from anguish, they will be turned back into it: and *it will be said to them*, 'Taste ye the punishment of burning!'

كُلَّمَآ اَرَادُوْٓا اَنْ يَّخْرُجُوْا مِنْهَا مِنْ غَمٍّ اُعِيْدُوْا
فِيْهَا ۗ وَذُوْقُوْا عَذَابَ الْحَرِيْقِ ㉓ ع

R. 3.

24. But Allah will cause those who believe and do good deeds to enter Gardens beneath which rivers flow. They will be adorned therein with bracelets of gold, and with pearls; and their raiment therein will be of silk.

اِنَّ اللّٰهَ يُدْخِلُ الَّذِيْنَ اٰمَنُوْا وَعَمِلُوا الصّٰلِحٰتِ
جَنّٰتٍ تَجْرِيْ مِنْ تَحْتِهَا الْاَنْهٰرُ يُحَلَّوْنَ فِيْهَا
مِنْ اَسَاوِرَ مِنْ ذَهَبٍ وَّلُؤْلُؤًا ۚ وَلِبَاسُهُمْ فِيْهَا
حَرِيْرٌ ﴿۲۴﴾

* 25. And they will be guided to pure speech, and they will be guided to the path of the Praiseworthy *God*.

وَهُدُوْٓا اِلَى الطَّيِّبِ مِنَ الْقَوْلِ ۚۖ وَهُدُوْٓا اِلٰى
صِرَاطِ الْحَمِيْدِ ﴿۲۵﴾

26. *As to* those who disbelieve, and hinder *men* from the way of Allah, and from the Sacred Mosque, which We have appointed equally for all men, be they dwellers therein or visitors from the desert, and whoso seeks wrongfully to deviate therein *from the right path*—We shall cause them to taste of a grievous punishment.

اِنَّ الَّذِيْنَ كَفَرُوْا وَيَصُدُّوْنَ عَنْ سَبِيْلِ اللّٰهِ
وَالْمَسْجِدِ الْحَرَامِ الَّذِيْ جَعَلْنٰهُ لِلنَّاسِ سَوَآءَ
اِلْعَاكِفُ فِيْهِ وَالْبَادِ ۚ وَمَنْ يُّرِدْ فِيْهِ بِاِلْحَادٍۭ
بِظُلْمٍ نُّذِقْهُ مِنْ عَذَابٍ اَلِيْمٍ ﴿۲۶﴾ ع

R. 4.

27. And *remember the time* when We assigned to Abraham the site of the House *and said*, 'Associate not anything with Me, and keep My House clean for those who perform the circuits, and those who stand up and those who bow down *and* fall prostrate *in Prayer;*

وَاِذْ بَوَّاْنَا لِاِبْرٰهِيْمَ مَكَانَ الْبَيْتِ اَنْ لَّا تُشْرِكْ
بِيْ شَيْـًٔا وَّطَهِّرْ بَيْتِيَ لِلطَّآئِفِيْنَ وَالْقَآئِمِيْنَ
وَالرُّكَّعِ السُّجُوْدِ ﴿۲۷﴾

28. 'And proclaim unto mankind the Pilgrimage. They will come to thee on foot, and on every lean camel, coming by every distant track,

وَاَذِّنْ فِي النَّاسِ بِالْحَجِّ يَاْتُوْكَ رِجَالًا وَّعَلٰى
كُلِّ ضَامِرٍ يَّاْتِيْنَ مِنْ كُلِّ فَجٍّ عَمِيْقٍ ۙ ﴿۲۸﴾

29. 'That they may witness *its* benefits for them and may mention the name of Allah, during the appointed days, over the quadrupeds of *the class of* cattle that He has provided for them. Then eat ye thereof and feed the distressed, the needy.

لِّيَشْهَدُوْا مَنَافِعَ لَهُمْ وَيَذْكُرُوا اسْمَ اللّٰهِ فِيْٓ
اَيَّامٍ مَّعْلُوْمٰتٍ عَلٰى مَا رَزَقَهُمْ مِّنْۢ بَهِيْمَةِ الْاَنْعَامِ ۚ
فَكُلُوْا مِنْهَا وَاَطْعِمُوا الْبَآئِسَ الْفَقِيْرَ ﴿۲۹﴾ ۫

* 30. 'Then let them accomplish their needful acts of cleansing, and fulfil their vows, and go around the Ancient House.'

ثُمَّ لْيَقْضُوْا تَفَثَهُمْ وَلْيُوْفُوْا نُذُوْرَهُمْ وَلْيَطَّوَّفُوْا
بِالْبَيْتِ الْعَتِيْقِ ﴿۳۰﴾

* 31. That is *God's commandment*. And whoso honours the sacred things of Allah, it will be good for him with his Lord. And cattle are made lawful to you but not that

ذٰلِكَ ۗ وَمَنْ يُّعَظِّمْ حُرُمٰتِ اللّٰهِ فَهُوَ خَيْرٌ لَّهٗ عِنْدَ
رَبِّهٖ ۗ وَاُحِلَّتْ لَكُمُ الْاَنْعَامُ اِلَّا مَا يُتْلٰى عَلَيْكُمْ

which has been announced to you. Shun therefore the abomination of idols, and shun all words of untruth,

فَاجْتَنِبُوا الرِّجْسَ مِنَ الْأَوْثَانِ وَاجْتَنِبُوا قَوْلَ الزُّورِ ﴿٣١﴾

32. Remaining ever inclined to Allah, not associating anything with Him. And whoso associates anything with Allah, falls, as it were, from a height, and the birds snatch him up, or the wind blows him away to a distant place.

حُنَفَاءَ لِلَّهِ غَيْرَ مُشْرِكِينَ بِهِ ۚ وَمَنْ يُشْرِكْ بِاللَّهِ فَكَأَنَّمَا خَرَّ مِنَ السَّمَاءِ فَتَخْطَفُهُ الطَّيْرُ أَوْ تَهْوِي بِهِ الرِّيحُ فِي مَكَانٍ سَحِيقٍ ﴿٣٢﴾

33. That *is so*. And whoso respects the sacred Signs of Allah—that indeed *proceeds* from the righteousness of hearts.

ذَٰلِكَ وَمَنْ يُعَظِّمْ شَعَائِرَ اللَّهِ فَإِنَّهَا مِنْ تَقْوَى الْقُلُوبِ ﴿٣٣﴾

34. In them (offerings) are benefits for you for an appointed term, then their place of sacrifice is at the Ancient House.

لَكُمْ فِيهَا مَنَافِعُ إِلَىٰ أَجَلٍ مُسَمًّى ثُمَّ مَحِلُّهَا إِلَى الْبَيْتِ الْعَتِيقِ ﴿٣٤﴾ ع

R. 5.

35. And to every people We appointed rites of sacrifice, that they might mention the name of Allah over the quadrupeds of *the class of* cattle that He has provided for them So your God is One God; therefore submit ye *all* to Him. And give thou glad tidings to the humble,

وَلِكُلِّ أُمَّةٍ جَعَلْنَا مَنْسَكًا لِيَذْكُرُوا اسْمَ اللَّهِ عَلَىٰ مَا رَزَقَهُمْ مِنْ بَهِيمَةِ الْأَنْعَامِ ۗ فَإِلَٰهُكُمْ إِلَٰهٌ وَاحِدٌ فَلَهُ أَسْلِمُوا ۗ وَبَشِّرِ الْمُخْبِتِينَ ﴿٣٥﴾

* 36. Whose hearts are filled with fear when Allah is mentioned, and who patiently endure whatever befalls them, and who observe Prayer, and spend out of what We have provided for them.

الَّذِينَ إِذَا ذُكِرَ اللَّهُ وَجِلَتْ قُلُوبُهُمْ وَالصَّابِرِينَ عَلَىٰ مَا أَصَابَهُمْ وَالْمُقِيمِي الصَّلَاةِ وَمِمَّا رَزَقْنَاهُمْ يُنْفِقُونَ ﴿٣٦﴾

37. And among the sacred Signs of Allah We have appointed for you the sacrificial camels. In them there is *much* good for you. So mention the name of Allah over them as they stand tied up in lines. And when they fall down *dead* on their sides, eat thereof and feed him who is *needy but* contented and him who supplicates. Thus have We subjected them to you, that you may be thankful.

وَالْبُدْنَ جَعَلْنَاهَا لَكُمْ مِنْ شَعَائِرِ اللَّهِ لَكُمْ فِيهَا خَيْرٌ ۖ فَاذْكُرُوا اسْمَ اللَّهِ عَلَيْهَا صَوَافَّ ۖ فَإِذَا وَجَبَتْ جُنُوبُهَا فَكُلُوا مِنْهَا وَأَطْعِمُوا الْقَانِعَ وَالْمُعْتَرَّ ۚ كَذَٰلِكَ سَخَّرْنَاهَا لَكُمْ لَعَلَّكُمْ تَشْكُرُونَ ﴿٣٧﴾

38. Their flesh reaches not Allah, nor does their blood, but it is your righteousness that reaches Him. Thus has He subjected them to you, that you may glorify Allah for His guiding you. And give glad tidings to those who do good.

لَنْ يَنَالَ اللَّهَ لُحُومُهَا وَلَا دِمَاؤُهَا وَلَٰكِنْ يَنَالُهُ التَّقْوَىٰ مِنْكُمْ ۚ كَذَٰلِكَ سَخَّرَهَا لَكُمْ لِتُكَبِّرُوا اللَّهَ عَلَىٰ مَا هَدَاكُمْ ۗ وَبَشِّرِ الْمُحْسِنِينَ ﴿٣٨﴾

39. Surely, Allah defends those who believe. Surely, Allah loves not any one who is perfidious *or* ungrateful.

اِنَّ اللّٰهَ يُدٰفِعُ عَنِ الَّذِيْنَ اٰمَنُوْا ۗ اِنَّ اللّٰهَ لَا يُحِبُّ
كُلَّ خَوَّانٍ كَفُوْرٍ ﴿٣٩﴾ ع ٥

R. 6.

40. Permission *to fight* is given to those against whom war is made, because they have been wronged—and Allah indeed has power to help them—

اُذِنَ لِلَّذِيْنَ يُقٰتَلُوْنَ بِاَنَّهُمْ ظُلِمُوْا ۗ وَاِنَّ اللّٰهَ عَلٰى
نَصْرِهِمْ لَقَدِيْرُ ﴿٤٠﴾

41. Those who have been driven out from their homes unjustly only because they said, 'Our Lord is Allah'—And if Allah did not repel some men by means of others, there would surely have been pulled down cloisters and churches and synagogues and mosques, wherein the name of Allah is oft commemorated. And Allah will surely help one who helps Him. Allah is indeed Powerful, Mighty—

الَّذِيْنَ اُخْرِجُوْا مِنْ دِيَارِهِمْ بِغَيْرِ حَقٍّ اِلَّآ اَنْ
يَّقُوْلُوْا رَبُّنَا اللّٰهُ ۗ وَلَوْلَا دَفْعُ اللّٰهِ النَّاسَ بَعْضَهُمْ
بِبَعْضٍ لَّهُدِّمَتْ صَوَامِعُ وَبِيَعٌ وَّصَلَوٰتٌ وَّ
مَسٰجِدُ يُذْكَرُ فِيْهَا اسْمُ اللّٰهِ كَثِيْرًا ۗ وَلَيَنْصُرَنَّ
اللّٰهُ مَنْ يَّنْصُرُهٗ ۗ اِنَّ اللّٰهَ لَقَوِيٌّ عَزِيْزٌ ﴿٤١﴾

42. Those who, if We establish them in the earth, will observe Prayer and pay the Zakāt and enjoin good and forbid evil. And with Allah rests the final issue of all affairs.

اَلَّذِيْنَ اِنْ مَّكَّنّٰهُمْ فِي الْاَرْضِ اَقَامُوا الصَّلٰوةَ
وَاٰتَوُا الزَّكٰوةَ وَاَمَرُوْا بِالْمَعْرُوْفِ وَنَهَوْا عَنِ
الْمُنْكَرِ ۗ وَلِلّٰهِ عَاقِبَةُ الْاُمُوْرِ ﴿٤٢﴾

43. And if they accuse thee of falsehood, even so, before them, the people of Noah and *the tribes of* 'Ād and Thamūd *also* accused *their Prophets* of falsehood.

وَاِنْ يُّكَذِّبُوْكَ فَقَدْ كَذَّبَتْ قَبْلَهُمْ قَوْمُ نُوْحٍ
وَّعَادٌ وَّثَمُوْدُ ﴿٤٣﴾

44. *So did* the people of Abraham and the people of Lot;

وَقَوْمُ اِبْرٰهِيْمَ وَقَوْمُ لُوْطٍ ﴿٤٤﴾

45. And the inhabitants of Midian. And Moses *too* was accused of falsehood. But I gave respite to the disbelievers; then I seized them, and how *terrible* was the change I *effected in them!*

وَّاَصْحٰبُ مَدْيَنَ ۚ وَكُذِّبَ مُوْسٰى فَاَمْلَيْتُ لِلْكٰفِرِيْنَ
ثُمَّ اَخَذْتُهُمْ ۚ فَكَيْفَ كَانَ نَكِيْرِ ﴿٤٥﴾

46. And how many a city have We destroyed, while it was given to wrong-doing, so that it is fallen down on its roofs; and *how many a* deserted well and lofty castle!

فَكَاَيِّنْ مِّنْ قَرْيَةٍ اَهْلَكْنٰهَا وَهِيَ ظَالِمَةٌ فَهِيَ
خَاوِيَةٌ عَلٰى عُرُوْشِهَا وَبِئْرٍ مُّعَطَّلَةٍ وَّقَصْرٍ
مَّشِيْدٍ ﴿٤٦﴾

47. Have they not travelled in the land, so that they may have hearts wherewith to understand, or ears wherewith to hear? But *the fact is that* it is not the eyes that are

اَفَلَمْ يَسِيْرُوْا فِي الْاَرْضِ فَتَكُوْنَ لَهُمْ قُلُوْبٌ
يَّعْقِلُوْنَ بِهَآ اَوْ اٰذَانٌ يَّسْمَعُوْنَ بِهَا ۚ فَاِنَّهَا لَا

blind, but it is the hearts which are in the breasts that are blind.

تَعْمَى الْأَبْصَارُ وَلَٰكِن تَعْمَى الْقُلُوبُ الَّتِي فِي
الصُّدُورِ ﴿٤٧﴾

48. And they ask thee to hasten on the punishment, but Allah will never break His promise. And verily, a day with thy Lord is as a thousand years of your reckoning.

وَيَسْتَعْجِلُونَكَ بِالْعَذَابِ وَلَن يُخْلِفَ اللَّهُ وَعْدَهُ
وَإِنَّ يَوْمًا عِندَ رَبِّكَ كَأَلْفِ سَنَةٍ مِّمَّا تَعُدُّونَ ﴿٤٨﴾

49. And how many a city there is to which I gave respite, while it was given to wrongdoing. Then I seized it, and unto Me is the return.

وَكَأَيِّن مِّن قَرْيَةٍ أَمْلَيْتُ لَهَا وَهِيَ ظَالِمَةٌ ثُمَّ
ع أَخَذْتُهَا وَإِلَيَّ الْمَصِيرُ ﴿٤٩﴾

R. 7.

50. Say, 'O mankind, I am but a plain Warner to you.'

قُلْ يَا أَيُّهَا النَّاسُ إِنَّمَا أَنَا لَكُمْ نَذِيرٌ مُّبِينٌ ﴿٥٠﴾

51. Those who believe and do good works, for them is forgiveness and an honourable provision.

فَالَّذِينَ آمَنُوا وَعَمِلُوا الصَّالِحَاتِ لَهُم مَّغْفِرَةٌ وَ
رِزْقٌ كَرِيمٌ ﴿٥١﴾

52. But those who strive against Our Signs, seeking to frustrate *Our purpose*—these shall be the inmates of the Fire.

وَالَّذِينَ سَعَوْا فِي آيَاتِنَا مُعَاجِزِينَ أُولَٰئِكَ أَصْحَابُ
الْجَحِيمِ ﴿٥٢﴾

53. Never sent We a Messenger or a Prophet before thee, but when he sought *to attain what he aimed at,* Satan put *obstacles* in *the way of* what he sought after. But Allah removes *the obstacles* that are placed by Satan. Then Allah firmly establishes His Signs. And Allah is All-Knowing, Wise.

وَمَا أَرْسَلْنَا مِن قَبْلِكَ مِن رَّسُولٍ وَلَا نَبِيٍّ إِلَّا
إِذَا تَمَنَّىٰ أَلْقَى الشَّيْطَانُ فِي أُمْنِيَّتِهِ فَيَنسَخُ اللَّهُ مَا
يُلْقِي الشَّيْطَانُ ثُمَّ يُحْكِمُ اللَّهُ آيَاتِهِ وَاللَّهُ عَلِيمٌ
حَكِيمٌ ﴿٥٣﴾

54. *He permits this* that He may make *the obstacles* which Satan puts *in the way of the Prophets* a trial for those in whose hearts is a disease and those whose hearts are hardened—and surely the wrongdoers are gone far *in error*—

لِّيَجْعَلَ مَا يُلْقِي الشَّيْطَانُ فِتْنَةً لِّلَّذِينَ فِي
قُلُوبِهِم مَّرَضٌ وَالْقَاسِيَةِ قُلُوبُهُمْ وَإِنَّ الظَّالِمِينَ
لَفِي شِقَاقٍ بَعِيدٍ ﴿٥٤﴾

55. And that those to whom knowledge has been given may know that it is the truth from thy Lord, so that they may believe therein and their hearts may become lowly unto Him. And surely Allah guides those who believe to the right path.

وَلِيَعْلَمَ الَّذِينَ أُوتُوا الْعِلْمَ أَنَّهُ الْحَقُّ مِن رَّبِّكَ
فَيُؤْمِنُوا بِهِ فَتُخْبِتَ لَهُ قُلُوبُهُمْ وَإِنَّ اللَّهَ
لَهَادِ الَّذِينَ آمَنُوا إِلَىٰ صِرَاطٍ مُّسْتَقِيمٍ ﴿٥٥﴾

56. And those who disbelieve will not cease to be in doubt about it until the

وَلَا يَزَالُ الَّذِينَ كَفَرُوا فِي مِرْيَةٍ مِّنْهُ حَتَّىٰ

Hour comes suddenly upon them or there comes to them the punishment of a destructive day.

تَأْتِيَهُمُ السَّاعَةُ بَغْتَةً أَوْ يَأْتِيَهُمْ عَذَابُ يَوْمٍ
عَقِيمٍ ٥٦

57. The kingdom on that day shall be Allah's. He will judge between them. So those who believe and do good deeds will be in Gardens of Delight.

الْمُلْكُ يَوْمَئِذٍ لِّلَّهِ يَحْكُمُ بَيْنَهُمْ فَالَّذِينَ آمَنُوا
وَعَمِلُوا الصَّالِحَاتِ فِي جَنَّاتِ النَّعِيمِ ٥٧

58. But those who disbelieve and reject Our Signs, will have an humiliating punishment.

وَالَّذِينَ كَفَرُوا وَكَذَّبُوا بِآيَاتِنَا فَأُولَٰئِكَ لَهُمْ
عَذَابٌ مُّهِينٌ ٥٨ ع

R. 8.

59. And those who leave their homes for the cause of Allah, and are then slain or die, Allah will surely provide for them a goodly provision. And surely Allah is the Best of providers.

وَالَّذِينَ هَاجَرُوا فِي سَبِيلِ اللَّهِ ثُمَّ قُتِلُوا أَوْ
مَاتُوا لَيَرْزُقَنَّهُمُ اللَّهُ رِزْقًا حَسَنًا وَإِنَّ اللَّهَ لَهُوَ
خَيْرُ الرَّازِقِينَ ٥٩

60. He will surely cause them to enter a place with which they will be well pleased. And Allah is indeed All-Knowing, Forbearing.

لَيُدْخِلَنَّهُم مُّدْخَلًا يَرْضَوْنَهُ وَإِنَّ اللَّهَ لَعَلِيمٌ
حَلِيمٌ ٦٠

61. That *shall be so*. And whoso retaliates with the like of that with which he has been afflicted and is then transgressed against, Allah will surely help him. Allah is indeed the Effacer of sins *and is* Forgiving.

ذَٰلِكَ وَمَنْ عَاقَبَ بِمِثْلِ مَا عُوقِبَ بِهِ ثُمَّ بُغِيَ
عَلَيْهِ لَيَنصُرَنَّهُ اللَّهُ إِنَّ اللَّهَ لَعَفُوٌّ غَفُورٌ ٦١

62. That is because Allah causes the night to enter into the day, and causes the day to enter into the night, and because Allah is All-Hearing, All-Seeing.

ذَٰلِكَ بِأَنَّ اللَّهَ يُولِجُ اللَّيْلَ فِي النَّهَارِ وَيُولِجُ
النَّهَارَ فِي اللَّيْلِ وَأَنَّ اللَّهَ سَمِيعٌ بَصِيرٌ ٦٢

63. That is because it is Allah Who is the Truth, and that which they call on beside Him is falsehood, and because Allah is the High, the Great.

ذَٰلِكَ بِأَنَّ اللَّهَ هُوَ الْحَقُّ وَأَنَّ مَا يَدْعُونَ مِن
دُونِهِ هُوَ الْبَاطِلُ وَأَنَّ اللَّهَ هُوَ الْعَلِيُّ الْكَبِيرُ ٦٣

* 64. Hast thou not seen that Allah sends down water from the sky and the earth becomes green? Allah is indeed the Knower of subtleties, the All-Aware.

أَلَمْ تَرَ أَنَّ اللَّهَ أَنزَلَ مِنَ السَّمَاءِ مَاءً فَتُصْبِحُ
الْأَرْضُ مُخْضَرَّةً إِنَّ اللَّهَ لَطِيفٌ خَبِيرٌ ٦٤

65. To Him belongs all that is in the heavens and all that is in the earth. And surely Allah is Self-Sufficient, Praiseworthy.

لَّهُ مَا فِي السَّمَاوَاتِ وَمَا فِي الْأَرْضِ وَإِنَّ اللَّهَ
لَهُوَ الْغَنِيُّ الْحَمِيدُ ٦٥ ع

R. 9.

* 66. Hast thou not seen that Allah has subjected to you whatever is in the earth,

أَلَمْ تَرَ أَنَّ اللَّهَ سَخَّرَ لَكُم مَّا فِي الْأَرْضِ وَالْفُلْكَ

and the ships that sail through the sea by His command? And He withholds the rain from falling on the earth save by His leave. Surely, Allah is Compassionate *and* Merciful to men.

تَجْرِيْ فِي الْبَحْرِ بِاَمْرِهٖ ۭ وَيُمْسِكُ السَّمَاۗءَ اَنْ تَقَعَ
عَلَى الْاَرْضِ اِلَّا بِاِذْنِهٖ ۭ اِنَّ اللّٰهَ بِالنَّاسِ لَرَءُوْفٌ
رَّحِيْمٌ ﴿٦٦﴾

67. And He it is Who gave you life, then He will cause you to die, then will He give you life *again*. Surely, man is most ungrateful.

وَهُوَ الَّذِيْٓ اَحْيَاكُمْ ۡ ثُمَّ يُمِيْتُكُمْ ثُمَّ يُحْيِيْكُمْ ۭ
اِنَّ الْاِنْسَانَ لَكَفُوْرٌ ﴿٦٧﴾

68. To every people have We appointed ways of worship which they observe; so let them not dispute with thee in the matter; and invite thou to thy Lord, for surely, thou followest the right guidance.

لِكُلِّ اُمَّةٍ جَعَلْنَا مَنْسَكًا هُمْ نَاسِكُوْهُ فَلَا يُنَازِعُنَّكَ
فِي الْاَمْرِ وَادْعُ اِلٰى رَبِّكَ ۭ اِنَّكَ لَعَلٰى هُدًى
مُّسْتَقِيْمٍ ﴿٦٨﴾

69. And if they contend with thee, say, 'Allah knows best what you do.

وَاِنْ جٰدَلُوْكَ فَقُلِ اللّٰهُ اَعْلَمُ بِمَا تَعْمَلُوْنَ ﴿٦٩﴾

70. 'Allah will judge between you on the Day of Resurrection concerning that about which you used to differ.'

اَللّٰهُ يَحْكُمُ بَيْنَكُمْ يَوْمَ الْقِيٰمَةِ فِيْمَا كُنْتُمْ فِيْهِ
تَخْتَلِفُوْنَ ﴿٧٠﴾

71. Dost thou not know that Allah knows whatsoever is in the heavens and the earth? Surely, it is *all preserved* in a Book, *and* that is easy for Allah.

اَلَمْ تَعْلَمْ اَنَّ اللّٰهَ يَعْلَمُ مَا فِي السَّمَاۗءِ وَالْاَرْضِ ۭ
اِنَّ ذٰلِكَ فِيْ كِتٰبٍ ۭ اِنَّ ذٰلِكَ عَلَى اللّٰهِ يَسِيْرٌ ﴿٧١﴾

72. And they worship beside Allah that for which He has sent down no authority, and that of which they have no knowledge. And for those that do wrong there is no helper.

وَيَعْبُدُوْنَ مِنْ دُوْنِ اللّٰهِ مَا لَمْ يُنَزِّلْ بِهٖ سُلْطٰنًا وَّ
مَا لَيْسَ لَهُمْ بِهٖ عِلْمٌ ۭ وَمَا لِلظّٰلِمِيْنَ مِنْ نَّصِيْرٍ ﴿٧٢﴾

73. And when Our clear Signs are recited unto them, thou wilt notice a denial on the faces of those who disbelieve. They would well-nigh attack those who recite Our Signs to them. Say, 'Shall I tell you of something worse than that? *It is* the Fire! Allah has promised it to those who disbelieve. And a vile destination it is!'

وَاِذَا تُتْلٰى عَلَيْهِمْ اٰيٰتُنَا بَيِّنٰتٍ تَعْرِفُ فِيْ وُجُوْهِ
الَّذِيْنَ كَفَرُوا الْمُنْكَرَ ۭ يَكَادُوْنَ يَسْطُوْنَ بِالَّذِيْنَ
يَتْلُوْنَ عَلَيْهِمْ اٰيٰتِنَا ۭ قُلْ اَفَاُنَبِّئُكُمْ بِشَرٍّ مِّنْ
ذٰلِكُمْ ۭ اَلنَّارُ ۭ وَعَدَهَا اللّٰهُ الَّذِيْنَ كَفَرُوْا ۭ وَبِئْسَ
الْمَصِيْرُ ﴿٧٣﴾ ع ٩ ٨ ١٦

R. 10.

74. O men, a similitude is set forth, so listen to it. Surely, those on whom you call instead of Allah cannot create *even* a fly, though they combine together for the

يٰٓاَيُّهَا النَّاسُ ضُرِبَ مَثَلٌ فَاسْتَمِعُوْا لَهٗ ۭ اِنَّ
الَّذِيْنَ تَدْعُوْنَ مِنْ دُوْنِ اللّٰهِ لَنْ يَّخْلُقُوْا ذُبَابًا

purpose. And if the fly should snatch away anything from them, they cannot recover it therefrom. Weak indeed are *both* the seeker and the sought.

وَّلَوِ اجْتَمَعُوْا لَهٗ ؕ وَاِنْ يَّسْلُبْهُمُ الذُّبَابُ شَيْـًٔا
لَّا يَسْتَنْقِذُوْهُ مِنْهُ ؕ ضَعُفَ الطَّالِبُ وَالْمَطْلُوْبُ ﴿۷۴﴾

75. They esteem not Allah with the estimation which is His due. Surely, Allah is Powerful, Mighty.

مَا قَدَرُوا اللّٰهَ حَقَّ قَدْرِهٖ ؕ اِنَّ اللّٰهَ لَقَوِيٌّ عَزِيْزٌ ﴿۷۵﴾

* 76. Allah chooses *His* Messengers from among angels, and from among men. Surely, Allah is All-Hearing, All-Seeing.

اَللّٰهُ يَصْطَفِيْ مِنَ الْمَلٰٓئِكَةِ رُسُلًا وَّمِنَ النَّاسِ ؕ
اِنَّ اللّٰهَ سَمِيْعٌۢ بَصِيْرٌ ﴿۷۶﴾ ج

* 77. He knows what is before them and what is behind them; and to Allah shall *all* affairs be returned *for decision*.

يَعْلَمُ مَا بَيْنَ اَيْدِيْهِمْ وَمَا خَلْفَهُمْ ؕ وَاِلَى اللّٰهِ تُرْجَعُ
الْاُمُوْرُ ﴿۷۷﴾

78. O ye who believe! bow down and prostrate yourselves in Prayer, and worship your Lord, and do good deeds that you may prosper.

يٰۤاَيُّهَا الَّذِيْنَ اٰمَنُوا ارْكَعُوْا وَاسْجُدُوْا وَاعْبُدُوْا
رَبَّكُمْ وَافْعَلُوا الْخَيْرَ لَعَلَّكُمْ تُفْلِحُوْنَ ﴿۷۸﴾ السجدة

79. And strive in the cause of Allah as it behoves you to strive for it. He has chosen you, and has laid no hardship upon you in religion; *so follow* the faith of your father Abraham; He named you Muslims *both* before and in this *Book*, so that the Messenger may be a witness over you, and that you may be witnesses over mankind. Therefore observe Prayer and pay the Zakāt, and hold fast to Allah. He is your Master. An excellent Master and an excellent Helper!

وَجَاهِدُوْا فِي اللّٰهِ حَقَّ جِهَادِهٖ ؕ هُوَ اجْتَبٰىكُمْ
وَمَا جَعَلَ عَلَيْكُمْ فِي الدِّيْنِ مِنْ حَرَجٍ ؕ مِلَّةَ
اَبِيْكُمْ اِبْرٰهِيْمَ ؕ هُوَ سَمّٰىكُمُ الْمُسْلِمِيْنَ ۙ۵ مِنْ
قَبْلُ وَفِيْ هٰذَا لِيَكُوْنَ الرَّسُوْلُ شَهِيْدًا عَلَيْكُمْ
وَتَكُوْنُوْا شُهَدَآءَ عَلَى النَّاسِ ۚۖ فَاَقِيْمُوا الصَّلٰوةَ
وَاٰتُوا الزَّكٰوةَ وَاعْتَصِمُوْا بِاللّٰهِ ؕ هُوَ مَوْلٰىكُمْ ۚ فَنِعْمَ
الْمَوْلٰى وَنِعْمَ النَّصِيْرُ ﴿۷۹﴾ ع

آياتها ١١٩ (٢٣) سُوۡرَةُ الۡمُؤۡمِنُوۡنَ مَكِّيَّةٌ ركوعاتها ٦

AL-MU'MINŪN

(Revealed before Hijra)

الجزء ١٨

1. In the name of Allah, the Gracious, the Merciful.

بِسۡمِ اللّٰهِ الرَّحۡمٰنِ الرَّحِيۡمِ ﴿١﴾

2. Surely, success does come to the believers,

قَدۡ اَفۡلَحَ الۡمُؤۡمِنُوۡنَ ﴿٢﴾

3. Who are humble in their Prayers,

الَّذِيۡنَ هُمۡ فِىۡ صَلَاتِهِمۡ خٰشِعُوۡنَ ﴿٣﴾

4. And who shun all that which is vain,

وَالَّذِيۡنَ هُمۡ عَنِ اللَّغۡوِ مُعۡرِضُوۡنَ ﴿٤﴾

5. And who are active in paying the Zakāt,

وَالَّذِيۡنَ هُمۡ لِلزَّكٰوةِ فٰعِلُوۡنَ ﴿٥﴾

6. And who guard their chastity—

وَالَّذِيۡنَ هُمۡ لِفُرُوۡجِهِمۡ حٰفِظُوۡنَ ﴿٦﴾

7. Except from their wives or what their right hands possess, for then they are not to be blamed;

اِلَّا عَلٰٓى اَزۡوَاجِهِمۡ اَوۡ مَا مَلَكَتۡ اَيۡمَانُهُمۡ فَاِنَّهُمۡ
غَيۡرُ مَلُوۡمِيۡنَ ﴿٧﴾

8. But those who seek *anything* beyond that are the transgressors—

فَمَنِ ابۡتَغٰى وَرَآءَ ذٰلِكَ فَاُولٰٓئِكَ هُمُ الۡعٰدُوۡنَ ﴿٨﴾

9. And who are watchful of their trusts and their covenants,

وَالَّذِيۡنَ هُمۡ لِاَمٰنٰتِهِمۡ وَعَهۡدِهِمۡ رٰعُوۡنَ ﴿٩﴾

* 10. And who are strict in the observance of their Prayers.

وَالَّذِيۡنَ هُمۡ عَلٰى صَلَوٰتِهِمۡ يُحَافِظُوۡنَ ﴿١٠﴾ وقف لازم

11. These are the heirs,

اُولٰٓئِكَ هُمُ الۡوٰرِثُوۡنَ ﴿١١﴾

12. Who will inherit Paradise. They will abide therein.

الَّذِيۡنَ يَرِثُوۡنَ الۡفِرۡدَوۡسَ هُمۡ فِيۡهَا خٰلِدُوۡنَ ﴿١٢﴾

13. Verily, We created man from an extract of clay;

وَلَقَدۡ خَلَقۡنَا الۡاِنۡسَانَ مِنۡ سُلٰلَةٍ مِّنۡ طِيۡنٍ ﴿١٣﴾

14. Then We placed him as a drop of sperm in a safe depository;

ثُمَّ جَعَلۡنٰهُ نُطۡفَةً فِىۡ قَرَارٍ مَّكِيۡنٍ ﴿١٤﴾

15. Then We fashioned the sperm into a clot; then We fashioned the clot into a *shapeless* lump; then We fashioned bones out of this *shapeless* lump; then We clothed the bones with flesh; then We developed it into another creation. So blessed be Allah, the Best of creators.

ثُمَّ خَلَقۡنَا النُّطۡفَةَ عَلَقَةً فَخَلَقۡنَا الۡعَلَقَةَ مُضۡغَةً فَخَلَقۡنَا الۡمُضۡغَةَ عِظٰمًا
فَكَسَوۡنَا الۡعِظٰمَ لَحۡمًا ثُمَّ اَنۡشَاۡنٰهُ خَلۡقًا اٰخَرَ
فَتَبٰرَكَ اللّٰهُ اَحۡسَنُ الۡخٰلِقِيۡنَ ﴿١٥﴾

16. Then after that you must surely die.

ثُمَّ اِنَّكُمۡ بَعۡدَ ذٰلِكَ لَمَيِّتُوۡنَ ﴿١٦﴾

17. Then on the Day of Resurrection will you be raised up.

18. And We have created above you seven *heavens* lying one above the other, and We are never neglectful of the creation.

19. And We sent down water from the sky according to measure, and We caused it to stay in the earth—and surely it is We Who determine its taking away—

20. And We produced for you thereby gardens of date-palms and vines; for you therein are abundant fruits; and of them you eat.

* 21. And a tree which springs forth from Mount Sinai; it produces oil and a sauce for those who eat.

22. And in the cattle *also* there is a lesson for you. We give you to drink of that which is in their bellies and you have in them many benefits, and of them you *also* eat;

23. And on them and on ships you are borne.

R. 2.

24. And We did send Noah to his people, and he said, 'O my people, serve Allah. You have no God other than Him. Will you not then be righteous?'

* 25. And the chiefs of his people, who disbelieved, said, 'He is only a man like yourselves; he seeks to make himself superior to you. And if Allah had so willed, He could have surely sent down angels *with him*. We have never heard of such *a thing* among our forefathers.

26. 'He is only a man *stricken* with madness; wait, therefore, concerning him for a while.'

27. He said, 'O my Lord, help me, for they have treated me as a liar.'

28. So We sent revelation to him, *saying*, "Make the Ark under Our eyes and *according to* Our revelation. And when Our command comes, and the fountains *of the earth* gush forth, take thou into it two of every kind, male and female, and

ثُمَّ إِنَّكُمْ يَوْمَ الْقِيٰمَةِ تُبْعَثُونَ ﴿١٧﴾

وَلَقَدْ خَلَقْنَا فَوْقَكُمْ سَبْعَ طَرَآئِقَ ۖ وَمَا كُنَّا عَنِ الْخَلْقِ
غٰفِلِينَ ﴿١٨﴾

وَأَنْزَلْنَا مِنَ السَّمَآءِ مَآءً بِقَدَرٍ فَأَسْكَنّٰهُ فِي الْأَرْضِ ۖ
وَإِنَّا عَلٰى ذَهَابٍ بِهٖ لَقٰدِرُونَ ﴿١٩﴾

وقف لازم

فَأَنْشَأْنَا لَكُمْ بِهٖ جَنّٰتٍ مِّنْ نَّخِيلٍ وَّأَعْنَابٍ لَكُمْ فِيهَا
فَوَاكِهُ كَثِيرَةٌ وَّمِنْهَا تَأْكُلُونَ ﴿٢٠﴾

وَشَجَرَةً تَخْرُجُ مِنْ طُورِ سَيْنَآءَ تَنْبُتُ بِالدُّهْنِ
وَصِبْغٍ لِّلْأٰكِلِينَ ﴿٢١﴾

وَإِنَّ لَكُمْ فِي الْأَنْعَامِ لَعِبْرَةً ۚ نُسْقِيكُمْ مِّمَّا فِي بُطُونِهَا
وَلَكُمْ فِيهَا مَنَافِعُ كَثِيرَةٌ وَّمِنْهَا تَأْكُلُونَ ﴿٢٢﴾

ع وَعَلَيْهَا وَعَلَى الْفُلْكِ تُحْمَلُونَ ﴿٢٣﴾

وَلَقَدْ أَرْسَلْنَا نُوحًا إِلٰى قَوْمِهٖ فَقَالَ يٰقَوْمِ اعْبُدُوا
اللّٰهَ مَا لَكُمْ مِّنْ إِلٰهٍ غَيْرُهٗ ۖ أَفَلَا تَتَّقُونَ ﴿٢٤﴾

فَقَالَ الْمَلَؤُا الَّذِينَ كَفَرُوا مِنْ قَوْمِهٖ مَا هٰذَا إِلَّا بَشَرٌ
مِّثْلُكُمْ يُرِيدُ أَنْ يَّتَفَضَّلَ عَلَيْكُمْ ۖ وَلَوْ شَآءَ اللّٰهُ لَأَنْزَلَ
مَلٰٓئِكَةً ۚ مَّا سَمِعْنَا بِهٰذَا فِي آبَآئِنَا الْأَوَّلِينَ ﴿٢٥﴾

إِنْ هُوَ إِلَّا رَجُلٌ بِهٖ جِنَّةٌ فَتَرَبَّصُوا بِهٖ حَتّٰى حِينٍ ﴿٢٦﴾

قَالَ رَبِّ انْصُرْنِي بِمَا كَذَّبُونِ ﴿٢٧﴾

فَأَوْحَيْنَآ إِلَيْهِ أَنِ اصْنَعِ الْفُلْكَ بِأَعْيُنِنَا وَوَحْيِنَا
فَإِذَا جَآءَ أَمْرُنَا وَفَارَ التَّنُّورُ ۙ فَاسْلُكْ فِيهَا مِنْ
كُلٍّ زَوْجَيْنِ اثْنَيْنِ وَأَهْلَكَ إِلَّا مَنْ سَبَقَ عَلَيْهِ

thy family, except those of them against whom the word has already gone forth. And address Me not concerning those who have done wrong; they shall be drowned.

الْقَوْلُ مِنْهُمْ ۚ وَلَا تُخَاطِبْنِي فِي الَّذِينَ ظَلَمُوا ۚ إِنَّهُمْ
مُّغْرَقُونَ ﴿٢٨﴾

29. "And when thou hast settled on the Ark—thou and those that are with thee—say, 'All praise belongs to Allah Who has saved us from the unjust people!'

فَإِذَا اسْتَوَيْتَ أَنْتَ وَمَنْ مَّعَكَ عَلَى الْفُلْكِ فَقُلِ
الْحَمْدُ لِلّٰهِ الَّذِي نَجّٰنَا مِنَ الْقَوْمِ الظّٰلِمِينَ ﴿٢٩﴾

30. "And say, 'My Lord, cause me to land a blessed landing, for Thou art the Best of those who bring *men* to land.' "

وَقُلْ رَّبِّ أَنْزِلْنِي مُنْزَلًا مُّبٰرَكًا وَّأَنْتَ خَيْرُ
الْمُنْزِلِينَ ﴿٣٠﴾

* 31. Verily, in this there are Signs. Surely, We did try *the people of Noah.*

إِنَّ فِي ذٰلِكَ لَاٰيٰتٍ وَّإِنْ كُنَّا لَمُبْتَلِينَ ﴿٣١﴾

32. Then We raised after them another generation.

ثُمَّ أَنْشَأْنَا مِنْ بَعْدِهِمْ قَرْنًا اٰخَرِينَ ﴿٣٢﴾

33. And We sent among them a Messenger from among themselves *who said*, 'Serve Allah. You have no God other than Him. Will you not then fear God?'

فَأَرْسَلْنَا فِيهِمْ رَسُولًا مِّنْهُمْ أَنِ اعْبُدُوا اللّٰهَ مَا لَكُمْ
مِّنْ إِلٰهٍ غَيْرُهُ ۚ أَفَلَا تَتَّقُونَ ﴿٣٣﴾ ع

R. 3.

34. And the chiefs of his people, who disbelieved and denied the meeting of the Hereafter and whom We had afforded ease and comfort in this life, said, 'This is but a man like yourselves. He eats of that of which you eat, and drinks of that of which you drink.

وَقَالَ الْمَلَأُ مِنْ قَوْمِهِ الَّذِينَ كَفَرُوا وَكَذَّبُوا بِلِقَاءِ
الْاٰخِرَةِ وَأَتْرَفْنٰهُمْ فِي الْحَيٰوةِ الدُّنْيَا ۙ مَا هٰذَا إِلَّا بَشَرٌ
مِّثْلُكُمْ ۙ يَأْكُلُ مِمَّا تَأْكُلُونَ مِنْهُ وَيَشْرَبُ مِمَّا
تَشْرَبُونَ ﴿٣٤﴾

35. 'And if you obey a man like yourselves, you will then be surely losers.

وَلَئِنْ أَطَعْتُمْ بَشَرًا مِّثْلَكُمْ إِنَّكُمْ إِذًا لَّخٰسِرُونَ ﴿٣٥﴾

36. 'Does he promise you that when you are dead and have become dust and bones, you will be brought forth *again?*

أَيَعِدُكُمْ أَنَّكُمْ إِذَا مِتُّمْ وَكُنْتُمْ تُرَابًا وَّعِظَامًا
أَنَّكُمْ مُّخْرَجُونَ ﴿٣٦﴾

37. 'Far, far *from truth* is that which you are promised.

هَيْهَاتَ هَيْهَاتَ لِمَا تُوعَدُونَ ﴿٣٧﴾

* 38. 'There is no life other than our present life; we were lifeless and *now* we live, but we shall not be raised up again.

إِنْ هِيَ إِلَّا حَيَاتُنَا الدُّنْيَا نَمُوتُ وَنَحْيَا وَمَا نَحْنُ
بِمَبْعُوثِينَ ﴿٣٨﴾

39. 'He is only a man who has forged a lie against Allah; and we are not going to believe him.'

إِنْ هُوَ إِلَّا رَجُلٌ افْتَرٰى عَلَى اللّٰهِ كَذِبًا وَّمَا نَحْنُ
لَهُ بِمُؤْمِنِينَ ﴿٣٩﴾

40. He said, 'My Lord, help me, for they have treated me as a liar.'

قَالَ رَبِّ انْصُرْنِيْ بِمَا كَذَّبُوْنِ ﴿٤٠﴾

41. *God* said, 'In a little while they will surely become repentant.'

قَالَ عَمَّا قَلِيْلٍ لَّيُصْبِحُنَّ نٰدِمِيْنَ ﴿٤١﴾

42. Then punishment overtook them rightfully, and We made them *as* rubbish. Cursed, then, be the people who do wrong!

فَاَخَذَتْهُمُ الصَّيْحَةُ بِالْحَقِّ فَجَعَلْنٰهُمْ غُثَآءً ۚ
فَبُعْدًا لِّلْقَوْمِ الظّٰلِمِيْنَ ﴿٤٢﴾

43. Then We raised after them other generations.

ثُمَّ اَنْشَاْنَا مِنْۢ بَعْدِهِمْ قُرُوْنًا اٰخَرِيْنَ ﴿٤٣﴾

44. No people can go ahead of their appointed time, nor can they remain behind *it*.

مَا تَسْبِقُ مِنْ اُمَّةٍ اَجَلَهَا وَمَا يَسْتَاْخِرُوْنَ ﴿٤٤﴾

45. Then We sent Our Messengers one after another. Every time there came to a people their Messenger, they treated him as a liar. So We made them follow one another *to destruction* and We made them mere tales. Cursed, then, be the people who believe not!

ثُمَّ اَرْسَلْنَا رُسُلَنَا تَتْرَا ؕ كُلَّمَا جَآءَ اُمَّةً رَّسُوْلُهَا
كَذَّبُوْهُ فَاَتْبَعْنَا بَعْضَهُمْ بَعْضًا وَّجَعَلْنٰهُمْ اَحَادِيْثَ ۚ
فَبُعْدًا لِّقَوْمٍ لَّا يُؤْمِنُوْنَ ﴿٤٥﴾

46. Then We sent Moses and his brother Aaron, with Our Signs and a clear authority,

ثُمَّ اَرْسَلْنَا مُوْسٰى وَاَخَاهُ هٰرُوْنَ ۙ بِاٰيٰتِنَا
وَسُلْطٰنٍ مُّبِيْنٍ ﴿٤٦﴾

47. To Pharaoh and his chiefs; but they behaved arrogantly and they were a haughty people.

اِلٰى فِرْعَوْنَ وَمَلَا۟ئِهٖ فَاسْتَكْبَرُوْا وَكَانُوْا قَوْمًا
عَالِيْنَ ﴿٤٧﴾

48. And they said, 'Shall we believe in two men like ourselves while their people are our servants?'

فَقَالُوْٓا اَنُؤْمِنُ لِبَشَرَيْنِ مِثْلِنَا وَقَوْمُهُمَا لَنَا
عٰبِدُوْنَ ﴿٤٨﴾

49. So they called them liars, and they were of those who were destroyed.

فَكَذَّبُوْهُمَا فَكَانُوْا مِنَ الْمُهْلَكِيْنَ ﴿٤٩﴾

50. And We gave Moses the Book, that they might be guided.

وَلَقَدْ اٰتَيْنَا مُوْسَى الْكِتٰبَ لَعَلَّهُمْ يَهْتَدُوْنَ ﴿٥٠﴾

* 51. And We made the son of Mary and his mother a Sign, and gave them refuge on an elevated land of *green* valleys and springs of running water.

وَجَعَلْنَا ابْنَ مَرْيَمَ وَاُمَّهٗٓ اٰيَةً وَّاٰوَيْنٰهُمَآ اِلٰى
رَبْوَةٍ ذَاتِ قَرَارٍ وَّمَعِيْنٍ ﴿٥١﴾ ع ٣/٣

R. 3.

52. O ye Messengers, eat of the things that are pure, and do good works. Verily, I am well aware of what you do.

يٰٓاَيُّهَا الرُّسُلُ كُلُوْا مِنَ الطَّيِّبٰتِ وَاعْمَلُوْا صَالِحًا ؕ
اِنِّيْ بِمَا تَعْمَلُوْنَ عَلِيْمٌ ﴿٥٢﴾

* 53. And *know* that this community of your is one community, and I am your

وَاِنَّ هٰذِهٖٓ اُمَّتُكُمْ اُمَّةً وَّاحِدَةً وَّاَنَا رَبُّكُمْ

Lord. So take Me as *your* Protector.

فَاتَّقُوْنِ ﴿٥٣﴾

* 54. But they (the people) have cut up their affairs among themselves *forming themselves into* parties, each group rejoicing in what they have.

فَتَقَطَّعُوْٓا اَمْرَهُمْ بَيْنَهُمْ زُبُرًا ؕ كُلُّ حِزْبٍۭ بِمَا لَدَيْهِمْ
فَرِحُوْنَ ﴿٥٤﴾

55. So leave them in their confusion for a time.

فَذَرْهُمْ فِيْ غَمْرَتِهِمْ حَتّٰى حِيْنٍ ﴿٥٥﴾

56. Do they think that by the wealth and children with which We help them,

اَيَحْسَبُوْنَ اَنَّمَا نُمِدُّهُمْ بِهٖ مِنْ مَّالٍ وَّ بَنِيْنَ ﴿٥٦﴾

57. We hasten to do them good? Nay, but they understand not.

نُسَارِعُ لَهُمْ فِي الْخَيْرٰتِ ؕ بَلْ لَّا يَشْعُرُوْنَ ﴿٥٧﴾

* 58. Verily, those who fear their Lord, *holding Him* in reverence,

اِنَّ الَّذِيْنَ هُمْ مِّنْ خَشْيَةِ رَبِّهِمْ مُّشْفِقُوْنَ ﴿٥٨﴾

59. And those who believe in the Signs of their Lord,

وَالَّذِيْنَ هُمْ بِاٰيٰتِ رَبِّهِمْ يُؤْمِنُوْنَ ﴿٥٩﴾

60. And those who ascribe not partners to their Lord,

وَالَّذِيْنَ هُمْ بِرَبِّهِمْ لَا يُشْرِكُوْنَ ﴿٦٠﴾

61. And those who give what they give while their hearts are full of fear because to their Lord they will return—

وَالَّذِيْنَ يُؤْتُوْنَ مَآ اٰتَوْا وَّ قُلُوْبُهُمْ وَجِلَةٌ اَنَّهُمْ
اِلٰى رَبِّهِمْ رٰجِعُوْنَ ﴿٦١﴾

62. These it is who hasten to do good works, and these it is who are foremost in them.

اُولٰٓئِكَ يُسٰرِعُوْنَ فِي الْخَيْرٰتِ وَهُمْ لَهَا سٰبِقُوْنَ ﴿٦٢﴾

63. And We burden not any soul beyond its capacity, and with Us is a Book that speaks the truth, and they will not be wronged.

وَلَا نُكَلِّفُ نَفْسًا اِلَّا وُسْعَهَا وَلَدَيْنَا كِتٰبٌ يَّنْطِقُ
بِالْحَقِّ وَهُمْ لَا يُظْلَمُوْنَ ﴿٦٣﴾

64. Nay, their hearts are utterly heedless of this *Book*, and besides that they have deeds in which they are engaged;

بَلْ قُلُوْبُهُمْ فِيْ غَمْرَةٍ مِّنْ هٰذَا وَلَهُمْ اَعْمَالٌ
مِّنْ دُوْنِ ذٰلِكَ هُمْ لَهَا عٰمِلُوْنَ ﴿٦٤﴾

65. Until, when We seize those of them who indulge in luxury with punishment, behold, they cry for help.

حَتّٰٓى اِذَآ اَخَذْنَا مُتْرَفِيْهِمْ بِالْعَذَابِ اِذَا هُمْ
يَجْـَٔرُوْنَ ﴿٦٥﴾

66. 'Cry not for help this day, surely you shall not be helped by Us.

لَا تَجْـَٔرُوا الْيَوْمَ ۟ اِنَّكُمْ مِّنَّا لَا تُنْصَرُوْنَ ﴿٦٦﴾

67. 'Verily, My Signs were recited unto you, but you used to turn back on your heels,

قَدْ كَانَتْ اٰيٰتِيْ تُتْلٰى عَلَيْكُمْ فَكُنْتُمْ عَلٰٓى اَعْقَابِكُمْ
تَنْكِصُوْنَ ﴿٦٧﴾

68. 'Big with pride, telling stories about it (the Qur'ān) by night, talking nonsense.'

مُسْتَكْبِرِيْنَ ۖۚ بِهٖ سٰمِرًا تَهْجُرُوْنَ ﴿٦٨﴾

69. Have they not, then, pondered over the *Divine* Word, or has that come unto them which came not to their fathers of old?

أَفَلَمْ يَدَّبَّرُوا الْقَوْلَ أَمْ جَاءَهُمْ مَا لَمْ يَأْتِ آبَاءَهُمُ الْأَوَّلِينَ ﴿٦٩﴾

70. Or do they not recognize their Messenger, that they *thus* deny him?

أَمْ لَمْ يَعْرِفُوا رَسُولَهُمْ فَهُمْ لَهُ مُنْكِرُونَ ﴿٧٠﴾

71. Or do they say, there is madness in him? Nay, he has brought them the truth, and most of them hate the truth.

أَمْ يَقُولُونَ بِهِ جِنَّةٌ ۚ بَلْ جَاءَهُمْ بِالْحَقِّ وَأَكْثَرُهُمْ لِلْحَقِّ كَارِهُونَ ﴿٧١﴾

* 72. And if the Truth had followed their desires, verily, the heavens and the earth and whosoever is therein would have been corrupted. Nay, We have brought them their admonition, but from their own admonition they *now* turn aside.

وَلَوِ اتَّبَعَ الْحَقُّ أَهْوَاءَهُمْ لَفَسَدَتِ السَّمَاوَاتُ وَالْأَرْضُ وَمَنْ فِيهِنَّ ۚ بَلْ أَتَيْنَاهُمْ بِذِكْرِهِمْ فَهُمْ عَنْ ذِكْرِهِمْ مُعْرِضُونَ ﴿٧٢﴾

73. Or dost thou ask of them any reward? But the reward of thy Lord is best; and He is the Best of providers.

أَمْ تَسْأَلُهُمْ خَرْجًا فَخَرَاجُ رَبِّكَ خَيْرٌ ۖ وَهُوَ خَيْرُ الرَّازِقِينَ ﴿٧٣﴾

74. And most surely thou invitest them to a right path.

وَإِنَّكَ لَتَدْعُوهُمْ إِلَىٰ صِرَاطٍ مُسْتَقِيمٍ ﴿٧٤﴾

75. And those who believe not in the Hereafter, are indeed deviating from that path.

وَإِنَّ الَّذِينَ لَا يُؤْمِنُونَ بِالْآخِرَةِ عَنِ الصِّرَاطِ لَنَاكِبُونَ ﴿٧٥﴾

76. And if We had mercy on them and relieved them of their affliction, they would still persist in their transgression, wandering blindly.

وَلَوْ رَحِمْنَاهُمْ وَكَشَفْنَا مَا بِهِمْ مِنْ ضُرٍّ لَلَجُّوا فِي طُغْيَانِهِمْ يَعْمَهُونَ ﴿٧٦﴾

77. We did seize them with punishment, but they humbled not themselves to their Lord, nor would they supplicate *in lowliness*.

وَلَقَدْ أَخَذْنَاهُمْ بِالْعَذَابِ فَمَا اسْتَكَانُوا لِرَبِّهِمْ وَمَا يَتَضَرَّعُونَ ﴿٧٧﴾

78. Until, when We open on them a gate of severe chastisement, behold, they are in despair thereat.

حَتَّىٰ إِذَا فَتَحْنَا عَلَيْهِمْ بَابًا ذَا عَذَابٍ شَدِيدٍ إِذَا هُمْ فِيهِ مُبْلِسُونَ ﴿٧٨﴾

R. 5.

79. And He it is Who has created for you ears, and eyes, and hearts; *but* little thanks do you give.

وَهُوَ الَّذِي أَنْشَأَ لَكُمُ السَّمْعَ وَالْأَبْصَارَ وَالْأَفْئِدَةَ ۚ قَلِيلًا مَا تَشْكُرُونَ ﴿٧٩﴾

80. And He it is Who has multiplied you in the earth, and unto Him shall you be gathered.

وَهُوَ الَّذِي ذَرَأَكُمْ فِي الْأَرْضِ وَإِلَيْهِ تُحْشَرُونَ ﴿٨٠﴾

81. And He it is Who gives life and causes death, and in His hands is the alternation of night and day. Will you not then understand?

وَهُوَ الَّذِيْ يُحْيٖ وَيُمِيْتُ وَلَهُ اخْتِلَافُ الَّيْلِ وَ
النَّهَارِ اَفَلَا تَعْقِلُوْنَ ﴿٨١﴾

82. But they say like what the former people said.

بَلْ قَالُوْا مِثْلَ مَا قَالَ الْاَوَّلُوْنَ ﴿٨٢﴾

83. They say, 'What! when we are dead and have become *mere* dust and bones, shall we indeed be raised up again?

قَالُوْٓا ءَاِذَا مِتْنَا وَكُنَّا تُرَابًا وَّعِظَامًا ءَاِنَّا
لَمَبْعُوْثُوْنَ ﴿٨٣﴾

84. 'This is what we have been promised before, we and our fathers. This is nothing but fables of the ancients.'

لَقَدْ وُعِدْنَا نَحْنُ وَاٰبَآؤُنَا هٰذَا مِنْ قَبْلُ اِنْ هٰذَآ
اِلَّآ اَسَاطِيْرُ الْاَوَّلِيْنَ ﴿٨٤﴾

85. Say, 'To whom belongs the earth and whosoever is therein, if you know?'

قُلْ لِّمَنِ الْاَرْضُ وَمَنْ فِيْهَآ اِنْ كُنْتُمْ تَعْلَمُوْنَ ﴿٨٥﴾

86. 'To Allah,' they will say. Say, 'Will you not then be admonished?'

سَيَقُوْلُوْنَ لِلّٰهِ قُلْ اَفَلَا تَذَكَّرُوْنَ ﴿٨٦﴾

87. Say, 'Who is the Lord of the seven heavens, and the Lord of the Great Throne?'

قُلْ مَنْ رَّبُّ السَّمٰوٰتِ السَّبْعِ وَرَبُّ الْعَرْشِ
الْعَظِيْمِ ﴿٨٧﴾

* 88. They will say, '*They are* Allah's.' Say, 'Will you not then take *Him* as *your* Protector?'

سَيَقُوْلُوْنَ لِلّٰهِ قُلْ اَفَلَا تَتَّقُوْنَ ﴿٨٨﴾

89. Say, 'In Whose hand is the dominion over all things and Who protects, but against Whom there is no protection, if you know?'

قُلْ مَنْۢ بِيَدِهٖ مَلَكُوْتُ كُلِّ شَيْءٍ وَّهُوَ يُجِيْرُ وَلَا
يُجَارُ عَلَيْهِ اِنْ كُنْتُمْ تَعْلَمُوْنَ ﴿٨٩﴾

90. They will say, '*All this belongs* to Allah.' Say, 'How then are you deluded?'

سَيَقُوْلُوْنَ لِلّٰهِ قُلْ فَاَنّٰى تُسْحَرُوْنَ ﴿٩٠﴾

91. Yea, We have brought them the truth, and they are certainly liars.

بَلْ اَتَيْنٰهُمْ بِالْحَقِّ وَاِنَّهُمْ لَكٰذِبُوْنَ ﴿٩١﴾

92. Allah has not taken unto Himself any son, nor is there any *other* God along with Him; in that case each god would have taken away what he had created, and some of them would surely have dominated over others. Glorified be Allah above all that which they attribute *to Him!*

مَا اتَّخَذَ اللّٰهُ مِنْ وَّلَدٍ وَّمَا كَانَ مَعَهٗ مِنْ
اِلٰهٍ اِذًا لَّذَهَبَ كُلُّ اِلٰهٍۢ بِمَا خَلَقَ وَلَعَلَا بَعْضُهُمْ
عَلٰى بَعْضٍ سُبْحٰنَ اللّٰهِ عَمَّا يَصِفُوْنَ ﴿٩٢﴾

93. Knower of the unseen and of the seen! Exalted therefore is He above *all* that which they associate *with Him!*

عٰلِمِ الْغَيْبِ وَالشَّهَادَةِ فَتَعٰلٰى عَمَّا يُشْرِكُوْنَ ﴿٩٣﴾

R. 6.

94. Say, 'My Lord, if Thou wilt show me that with which they are threatened.

قُلْ رَّبِّ اِمَّا تُرِيَنِّيْ مَا يُوْعَدُوْنَ ﴿٩٤﴾

95. 'My Lord, then place me not with the wrongdoing people.'

رَبِّ فَلَا تَجْعَلْنِيْ فِي الْقَوْمِ الظّٰلِمِيْنَ ﴿٩٥﴾

96. And certainly We have the power to show thee that with which We threaten them.

وَإِنَّا عَلَىٰٓ أَن نُّرِيَكَ مَا نَعِدُهُمْ لَقَٰدِرُونَ ﴿٩٦﴾

97. Repel evil with that which is best. We are well acquainted with *the things* they allege.

ٱدْفَعْ بِٱلَّتِى هِىَ أَحْسَنُ ٱلسَّيِّئَةَ ۚ نَحْنُ أَعْلَمُ بِمَا
يَصِفُونَ ﴿٩٧﴾

* 98. And say, 'My Lord, I seek refuge in Thee from the incitements of the evil ones.

وَقُل رَّبِّ أَعُوذُ بِكَ مِنْ هَمَزَٰتِ ٱلشَّيَٰطِينِ ﴿٩٨﴾

99. 'And I seek refuge in Thee, my Lord, lest they come near me.'

وَأَعُوذُ بِكَ رَبِّ أَن يَحْضُرُونِ ﴿٩٩﴾

100. Until, when death comes to one of them, he says *entreating*, 'My Lord, send me back,

حَتَّىٰٓ إِذَا جَآءَ أَحَدَهُمُ ٱلْمَوْتُ قَالَ رَبِّ ٱرْجِعُونِ ﴿١٠٠﴾

101. 'That I may do righteous *deeds* in *the life* that I have left *behind*.' Never, it is but a word that he utters. And behind them is a barrier until the day when they shall be raised again.

لَعَلِّىٓ أَعْمَلُ صَٰلِحًا فِيمَا تَرَكْتُ ۚ كَلَّآ ۚ إِنَّهَا كَلِمَةٌ
هُوَ قَآئِلُهَا ۖ وَمِن وَرَآئِهِم بَرْزَخٌ إِلَىٰ يَوْمِ
يُبْعَثُونَ ﴿١٠١﴾

102. And when the trumpet is blown, there will be no ties of relationship between them that day, nor will they ask after one another.

فَإِذَا نُفِخَ فِى ٱلصُّورِ فَلَآ أَنسَابَ بَيْنَهُمْ يَوْمَئِذٍ
وَلَا يَتَسَآءَلُونَ ﴿١٠٢﴾

* 103. Then those whose good works are heavy—these will be prosperous;

فَمَن ثَقُلَتْ مَوَٰزِينُهُۥ فَأُو۟لَٰٓئِكَ هُمُ ٱلْمُفْلِحُونَ ﴿١٠٣﴾

104. But those whose good works are light—these are they who ruin their souls; in Hell will they abide.

وَمَنْ خَفَّتْ مَوَٰزِينُهُۥ فَأُو۟لَٰٓئِكَ ٱلَّذِينَ خَسِرُوٓا۟
أَنفُسَهُمْ فِى جَهَنَّمَ خَٰلِدُونَ ﴿١٠٤﴾

* 105. The Fire will burn their faces and they will grin *with fear* therein.

تَلْفَحُ وُجُوهَهُمُ ٱلنَّارُ وَهُمْ فِيهَا كَٰلِحُونَ ﴿١٠٥﴾

106. 'Were not My Signs recited unto you, and you treated them as lies?'

أَلَمْ تَكُنْ ءَايَٰتِى تُتْلَىٰ عَلَيْكُمْ فَكُنتُم بِهَا
تُكَذِّبُونَ ﴿١٠٦﴾

107. They will say, 'Our Lord, our wickedness overcame us, and we were an erring people.

قَالُوا۟ رَبَّنَا غَلَبَتْ عَلَيْنَا شِقْوَتُنَا وَكُنَّا قَوْمًا
ضَآلِّينَ ﴿١٠٧﴾

108. 'Our Lord, take us out of this, then if we return *to disobedience*, we shall indeed be wrongdoers.'

رَبَّنَآ أَخْرِجْنَا مِنْهَا فَإِنْ عُدْنَا فَإِنَّا ظَٰلِمُونَ ﴿١٠٨﴾

* 109. *God* will say, "Away with you, despised therein, and speak not unto Me.

قَالَ ٱخْسَـُٔوا۟ فِيهَا وَلَا تُكَلِّمُونِ ﴿١٠٩﴾

110. "There was a party from among My servants who said, 'Our Lord, we believe;

إِنَّهُۥ كَانَ فَرِيقٌ مِّنْ عِبَادِى يَقُولُونَ رَبَّنَآ ءَامَنَّا

forgive us therefore *our sins*, and have mercy on us; for Thou art the Best of those who show mercy.'

فَاغْفِرْ لَنَا وَارْحَمْنَا وَاَنْتَ خَيْرُ الرّٰحِمِيْنَ ﴿١١٠﴾

111. "But you made them a laughing-stock until they became the cause of your forgetting My remembrance while you *continued* laughing at them.

فَاتَّخَذْتُمُوْهُمْ سِخْرِيًّا حَتّٰٓى اَنْسَوْكُمْ ذِكْرِيْ وَكُنْتُمْ
مِّنْهُمْ تَضْحَكُوْنَ ﴿١١١﴾

112. "I have rewarded them this day for their steadfastness so that they alone have triumphed."

اِنِّيْ جَزَيْتُهُمُ الْيَوْمَ بِمَا صَبَرُوْٓا اَنَّهُمْ هُمُ الْفَآئِزُوْنَ ﴿١١٢﴾

113. *God* will say, 'What number of years did you tarry in the earth?'

قٰلَ كَمْ لَبِثْتُمْ فِي الْاَرْضِ عَدَدَ سِنِيْنَ ﴿١١٣﴾

114. They will say, 'We tarried for a day or part of a day, but ask those who keep count.'

قَالُوْا لَبِثْنَا يَوْمًا اَوْ بَعْضَ يَوْمٍ فَسْـَٔلِ الْعَآدِّيْنَ ﴿١١٤﴾

115. He will say, 'You tarried but a little, if only you knew!

قٰلَ اِنْ لَّبِثْتُمْ اِلَّا قَلِيْلًا لَّوْ اَنَّكُمْ كُنْتُمْ تَعْلَمُوْنَ ﴿١١٥﴾

116. 'Did you then think that We had created you without purpose, and that you would not be brought back to Us?'

اَفَحَسِبْتُمْ اَنَّمَا خَلَقْنٰكُمْ عَبَثًا وَّاَنَّكُمْ اِلَيْنَا لَا
تُرْجَعُوْنَ ﴿١١٦﴾

* 117. Exalted then be Allah, the True King. There is no God but He, the Lord of the Glorious Throne.

فَتَعٰلَى اللّٰهُ الْمَلِكُ الْحَقُّ لَآ اِلٰهَ اِلَّا هُوَ رَبُّ الْعَرْشِ
الْكَرِيْمِ ﴿١١٧﴾

118. And he who calls on another God along with Allah, for which he has no proof, shall have to render an account to his Lord. Certainly the disbelievers will not prosper.

وَمَنْ يَّدْعُ مَعَ اللّٰهِ اِلٰهًا اٰخَرَ لَا بُرْهَانَ لَهٗ بِهٖ
فَاِنَّمَا حِسَابُهٗ عِنْدَ رَبِّهٖ اِنَّهٗ لَا يُفْلِحُ الْكٰفِرُوْنَ ﴿١١٨﴾

119. And say, 'My Lord, forgive and have mercy, and Thou art the Best of those who show mercy.'

وَقُلْ رَّبِّ اغْفِرْ وَارْحَمْ وَاَنْتَ خَيْرُ الرّٰحِمِيْنَ ﴿١١٩﴾

سُوْرَةُ النُّوْرِ مَدَنِيَّةٌ

AL-NŪR

(Revealed after Hijra)

1. In the name of Allah, the Gracious, the Merciful.

بِسْمِ اللّٰهِ الرَّحْمٰنِ الرَّحِيْمِ ①

2. *This is* a Sūra which We have revealed and which We have made obligatory; and We have revealed therein clear Signs, that you may take heed.

سُوْرَةٌ اَنْزَلْنٰهَا وَفَرَضْنٰهَا وَاَنْزَلْنَا فِيْهَآ اٰيٰتٍۭ بَيِّنٰتٍ
لَّعَلَّكُمْ تَذَكَّرُوْنَ ②

* 3. The adulteress and the adulterer (or the fornicatress and the fornicator)—flog each one of them with a hundred stripes. And let not pity for the twain take hold of you in *executing* the judgment of Allah, if you believe in Allah and the Last Day. And let a party of the believers witness their punishment.

اَلزَّانِيَةُ وَالزَّانِيْ فَاجْلِدُوْا كُلَّ وَاحِدٍ مِّنْهُمَا مِائَةَ
جَلْدَةٍ ۪ وَّلَا تَاْخُذْكُمْ بِهِمَا رَاْفَةٌ فِيْ دِيْنِ اللّٰهِ اِنْ
كُنْتُمْ تُؤْمِنُوْنَ بِاللّٰهِ وَالْيَوْمِ الْاٰخِرِ ۚ وَلْيَشْهَدْ عَذَابَهُمَا
طَآئِفَةٌ مِّنَ الْمُؤْمِنِيْنَ ③

4. The adulterer (or fornicator) shall not marry but an adulteress (or fornicatress) or an idolatrous woman, and an adulteress (or fornicatress) shall not marry but an adulterer (or fornicator) or an idolatrous man. That indeed is forbidden to the believers.

اَلزَّانِيْ لَا يَنْكِحُ اِلَّا زَانِيَةً اَوْ مُشْرِكَةً ۫ وَّالزَّانِيَةُ
لَا يَنْكِحُهَآ اِلَّا زَانٍ اَوْ مُشْرِكٌ ۚ وَحُرِّمَ ذٰلِكَ عَلَى
الْمُؤْمِنِيْنَ ④

5. And those who calumniate chaste women but bring not four witnesses—flog them with eighty stripes, and never admit their evidence *thereafter*, and it is they that are the transgressors,

وَالَّذِيْنَ يَرْمُوْنَ الْمُحْصَنٰتِ ثُمَّ لَمْ يَاْتُوْا بِاَرْبَعَةِ
شُهَدَآءَ فَاجْلِدُوْهُمْ ثَمٰنِيْنَ جَلْدَةً وَّلَا تَقْبَلُوْا
لَهُمْ شَهَادَةً اَبَدًا ۚ وَاُولٰٓئِكَ هُمُ الْفٰسِقُوْنَ ⑤

6. Except those who repent thereafter and make amends, for truly Allah is Most Forgiving, Merciful.

اِلَّا الَّذِيْنَ تَابُوْا مِنْۢ بَعْدِ ذٰلِكَ وَاَصْلَحُوْا ۚ فَاِنَّ اللّٰهَ
غَفُوْرٌ رَّحِيْمٌ ⑥

7. And as for those who calumniate their wives, and have no witnesses except themselves—the evidence of any one of such people *shall suffice* if he bears witness four times in the name of Allah *saying* that he is surely of those who speak the truth.

وَالَّذِيْنَ يَرْمُوْنَ اَزْوَاجَهُمْ وَلَمْ يَكُنْ لَّهُمْ شُهَدَآءُ
اِلَّآ اَنْفُسُهُمْ فَشَهَادَةُ اَحَدِهِمْ اَرْبَعُ شَهٰدٰتٍۭ
بِاللّٰهِ ۙ اِنَّهٗ لَمِنَ الصّٰدِقِيْنَ ⑦

8. And *his* fifth *oath shall be to say* that Allah's curse be upon him if he be of the

وَالْخَامِسَةُ اَنَّ لَعْنَتَ اللّٰهِ عَلَيْهِ اِنْ كَانَ مِنَ

liars.

الْكٰذِبِيْنَ ۝٨

9. But it shall avert the punishment from her if she bears witness four times in the name of Allah *saying* that he is of the liars.

وَيَدْرَؤُا عَنْهَا الْعَذَابَ اَنْ تَشْهَدَ اَرْبَعَ شَهٰدٰتٍۭ بِاللّٰهِ ۙ اِنَّهٗ لَمِنَ الْكٰذِبِيْنَ ۙ ۝٩

10. And *her* fifth *oath shall be to say* that the wrath of Allah be upon her if he speaks the truth.

وَالْخَامِسَةَ اَنَّ غَضَبَ اللّٰهِ عَلَيْهَاۤ اِنْ كَانَ مِنَ الصّٰدِقِيْنَ ۝١٠

11. And were it not for Allah's grace and His mercy upon you, and *the fact* that Allah is Compassionate *and* Wise, *you would have come to grief.*

وَلَوْلَا فَضْلُ اللّٰهِ عَلَيْكُمْ وَرَحْمَتُهٗ وَاَنَّ اللّٰهَ تَوَّابٌ حَكِيْمٌ ۝١١ ع

R. 2.

12. Verily, those who brought forth the lie are a party from among you. Think it not to be an evil for you; nay, it is good for you. Every one of them shall have *his share of* what he has earned of the sin; and he among them who took the chief part therein shall have a grievous punishment.

اِنَّ الَّذِيْنَ جَآءُوْ بِالْاِفْكِ عُصْبَةٌ مِّنْكُمْ ؕ لَا تَحْسَبُوْهُ شَرًّا لَّكُمْ ؕ بَلْ هُوَ خَيْرٌ لَّكُمْ ؕ لِكُلِّ امْرِئٍ مِّنْهُمْ مَّا اكْتَسَبَ مِنَ الْاِثْمِ ۚ وَالَّذِيْ تَوَلّٰى كِبْرَهٗ مِنْهُمْ لَهٗ عَذَابٌ عَظِيْمٌ ۝١٢

13. Why did not the believing men and believing women, when you heard of it, think well of their own people, and say, 'This is a manifest lie?'

لَوْلَاۤ اِذْ سَمِعْتُمُوْهُ ظَنَّ الْمُؤْمِنُوْنَ وَالْمُؤْمِنٰتُ بِاَنْفُسِهِمْ خَيْرًا ۙ وَّقَالُوْا هٰذَاۤ اِفْكٌ مُّبِيْنٌ ۝١٣

14. Why did they not bring four witnesses to *prove* it? Since they have not brought the *required* witnesses, they are indeed liars in the sight of Allah!

لَوْلَا جَآءُوْ عَلَيْهِ بِاَرْبَعَةِ شُهَدَآءَ ۚ فَاِذْ لَمْ يَاْتُوْا بِالشُّهَدَآءِ فَاُولٰٓئِكَ عِنْدَ اللّٰهِ هُمُ الْكٰذِبُوْنَ ۝١٤

15. Were it not for the grace of Allah and His mercy upon you, in this world and the Hereafter, a great punishment would have befallen you for *the slander* into which you plunged.

وَلَوْلَا فَضْلُ اللّٰهِ عَلَيْكُمْ وَرَحْمَتُهٗ فِی الدُّنْيَا وَالْاٰخِرَةِ لَمَسَّكُمْ فِیْ مَاۤ اَفَضْتُمْ فِيْهِ عَذَابٌ عَظِيْمٌ ۚۖ ۝١٥

* 16. When you received it *and then talked about it* with your tongues, and you uttered with your mouths that of which you had no knowledge, and you thought it to be a light matter, while in the sight of Allah it was *a* grievous *thing*.

اِذْ تَلَقَّوْنَهٗ بِاَلْسِنَتِكُمْ وَتَقُوْلُوْنَ بِاَفْوَاهِكُمْ مَّا لَيْسَ لَكُمْ بِهٖ عِلْمٌ وَّتَحْسَبُوْنَهٗ هَيِّنًا ۖۗ وَّهُوَ عِنْدَ اللّٰهِ عَظِيْمٌ ۝١٦

17. And wherefore did you not say, when you heard of it, 'It is not proper for us to talk about it. Holy art Thou, *O God*, this is a grievous calumny!'

وَلَوْلَاۤ اِذْ سَمِعْتُمُوْهُ قُلْتُمْ مَّا يَكُوْنُ لَنَاۤ اَنْ نَّتَكَلَّمَ بِهٰذَا ۖۗ سُبْحٰنَكَ هٰذَا بُهْتَانٌ عَظِيْمٌ ۝١٧

18. Allah admonishes you never to return to the like thereof, if you are believers.

يَعِظُكُمُ اللّٰهُ اَنْ تَعُوْدُوْا لِمِثْلِهٖۤ اَبَدًا اِنْ كُنْتُمْ مُّؤْمِنِيْنَ ﴿۱۸﴾

19. And Allah explains to you the commandments; and Allah is All-Knowing, Wise.

وَيُبَيِّنُ اللّٰهُ لَكُمُ الْاٰيٰتِ ۗ وَاللّٰهُ عَلِيْمٌ حَكِيْمٌ ﴿۱۹﴾

20. Those who love that immorality should spread among the believers, will have a painful punishment in this world and the Hereafter. And Allah knows, and you know not.

اِنَّ الَّذِيْنَ يُحِبُّوْنَ اَنْ تَشِيْعَ الْفَاحِشَةُ فِي الَّذِيْنَ اٰمَنُوْا لَهُمْ عَذَابٌ اَلِيْمٌ ۙ فِي الدُّنْيَا وَالْاٰخِرَةِ ۗ وَاللّٰهُ يَعْلَمُ وَاَنْتُمْ لَا تَعْلَمُوْنَ ﴿۲۰﴾

21. And but for the grace of Allah and His mercy upon you and *the fact* that Allah is Compassionate *and* Merciful, *you would have been ruined.*

وَلَوْلَا فَضْلُ اللّٰهِ عَلَيْكُمْ وَرَحْمَتُهٗ وَاَنَّ اللّٰهَ رَءُوْفٌ رَّحِيْمٌ ﴿۲۱﴾

R. 3.

22. O ye who believe! follow not the footsteps of Satan, and whoso follows the footsteps of Satan *should know that* he surely enjoins immorality and manifest evil. And but for the grace of Allah and His mercy upon you, not one of you would ever be pure; but Allah purifies whom He pleases. And Allah is All-Hearing, All-Knowing.

يٰۤاَيُّهَا الَّذِيْنَ اٰمَنُوْا لَا تَتَّبِعُوْا خُطُوٰتِ الشَّيْطٰنِ ۚ وَمَنْ يَّتَّبِعْ خُطُوٰتِ الشَّيْطٰنِ فَاِنَّهٗ يَاْمُرُ بِالْفَحْشَآءِ وَالْمُنْكَرِ ۚ وَلَوْلَا فَضْلُ اللّٰهِ عَلَيْكُمْ وَرَحْمَتُهٗ مَا زَكٰى مِنْكُمْ مِّنْ اَحَدٍ اَبَدًا ۙ وَّلٰكِنَّ اللّٰهَ يُزَكِّيْ مَنْ يَّشَآءُ ۗ وَاللّٰهُ سَمِيْعٌ عَلِيْمٌ ﴿۲۲﴾

* 23. And let not those who possess wealth and plenty among you swear not to give *aught* to the kindred and to the needy and to those who have left their homes in the cause of Allah. Let them forgive and pass over *the offence*. Do you not desire that Allah should forgive you? And Allah is Most Forgiving, Merciful.

وَلَا يَاْتَلِ اُولُوا الْفَضْلِ مِنْكُمْ وَالسَّعَةِ اَنْ يُّؤْتُوْۤا اُولِي الْقُرْبٰى وَالْمَسٰكِيْنَ وَالْمُهٰجِرِيْنَ فِيْ سَبِيْلِ اللّٰهِ ۖ وَلْيَعْفُوْا وَلْيَصْفَحُوْا ۗ اَلَا تُحِبُّوْنَ اَنْ يَّغْفِرَ اللّٰهُ لَكُمْ ۗ وَاللّٰهُ غَفُوْرٌ رَّحِيْمٌ ﴿۲۳﴾

24. Verily, those who accuse chaste, unwary, believing women are cursed in this world and the Hereafter. And for them is a grievous chastisement,

اِنَّ الَّذِيْنَ يَرْمُوْنَ الْمُحْصَنٰتِ الْغٰفِلٰتِ الْمُؤْمِنٰتِ لُعِنُوْا فِي الدُّنْيَا وَالْاٰخِرَةِ ۪ وَلَهُمْ عَذَابٌ عَظِيْمٌ ﴿۲۴﴾

25. On the day when their tongues and their hands and their feet will bear witness against them as to what they used to do.

يَّوْمَ تَشْهَدُ عَلَيْهِمْ اَلْسِنَتُهُمْ وَاَيْدِيْهِمْ وَاَرْجُلُهُمْ بِمَا كَانُوْا يَعْمَلُوْنَ ﴿۲۵﴾

26. On that day will Allah pay them their just due, and they will know that Allah alone is the Manifest Truth.

يَوْمَئِذٍ يُّوَفِّيْهِمُ اللّٰهُ دِيْنَهُمُ الْحَقَّ وَيَعْلَمُوْنَ اَنَّ
اللّٰهَ هُوَ الْحَقُّ الْمُبِيْنُ ﴿٢٦﴾

27. Bad things are for bad men, and bad men are for bad things. And good things are for good men, and good men are for good things; these are innocent of all that they (the calumniators) allege. For them is forgiveness and an honourable provision.

اَلْخَبِيْثٰتُ لِلْخَبِيْثِيْنَ وَالْخَبِيْثُوْنَ لِلْخَبِيْثٰتِ ۚ وَ
الطَّيِّبٰتُ لِلطَّيِّبِيْنَ وَالطَّيِّبُوْنَ لِلطَّيِّبٰتِ ۚ اُولٰٓئِكَ
مُبَرَّءُوْنَ مِمَّا يَقُوْلُوْنَ ۗ لَهُمْ مَّغْفِرَةٌ وَّرِزْقٌ
كَرِيْمٌ ﴿٢٧﴾ ع ٣ ٩

R. 4.

28. O ye who believe! enter not houses other than your own until you have asked leave and saluted the inmates thereof. That is better for you, that you may be heedful.

يٰٓاَيُّهَا الَّذِيْنَ اٰمَنُوْا لَا تَدْخُلُوْا بُيُوْتًا غَيْرَ بُيُوْتِكُمْ
حَتّٰى تَسْتَاْنِسُوْا وَتُسَلِّمُوْا عَلٰٓى اَهْلِهَا ۗ ذٰلِكُمْ خَيْرٌ لَّكُمْ
لَعَلَّكُمْ تَذَكَّرُوْنَ ﴿٢٨﴾

29. And if you find no one therein, do not enter them until you are given permission. And if it be said to you, 'Go back,' then go back; that is purer for you. And Allah knows well what you do.

فَاِنْ لَّمْ تَجِدُوْا فِيْهَآ اَحَدًا فَلَا تَدْخُلُوْهَا حَتّٰى يُؤْذَنَ
لَكُمْ ۚ وَاِنْ قِيْلَ لَكُمُ ارْجِعُوْا فَارْجِعُوْا هُوَ اَزْكٰى لَكُمْ ۗ
وَاللّٰهُ بِمَا تَعْمَلُوْنَ عَلِيْمٌ ﴿٢٩﴾

30. It is no sin on your part to enter uninhabited houses wherein are your goods. And Allah knows what you reveal and what you conceal.

لَيْسَ عَلَيْكُمْ جُنَاحٌ اَنْ تَدْخُلُوْا بُيُوْتًا غَيْرَ مَسْكُوْنَةٍ
فِيْهَا مَتَاعٌ لَّكُمْ ۗ وَاللّٰهُ يَعْلَمُ مَا تُبْدُوْنَ وَمَا تَكْتُمُوْنَ ﴿٣٠﴾

31. Say to the believing men that they restrain their eyes and guard their private parts. That is purer for them. Surely, Allah is well aware of what they do.

قُلْ لِّلْمُؤْمِنِيْنَ يَغُضُّوْا مِنْ اَبْصَارِهِمْ وَيَحْفَظُوْا فُرُوْجَهُمْ ۗ
ذٰلِكَ اَزْكٰى لَهُمْ ۗ اِنَّ اللّٰهَ خَبِيْرٌۢ بِمَا يَصْنَعُوْنَ ﴿٣١﴾

* 32. And say to the believing women that they restrain their eyes and guard their private parts, and that they disclose not their *natural and artificial* beauty except that which is apparent thereof, and that they draw their head-coverings over their bosoms, and that they disclose not their beauty save to their husbands, or to their fathers, or the fathers of their husbands or their sons or the sons of their husbands or their brothers, or the sons of their brothers, or the sons of their sisters, or their women,

وَقُلْ لِّلْمُؤْمِنٰتِ يَغْضُضْنَ مِنْ اَبْصَارِهِنَّ وَيَحْفَظْنَ
فُرُوْجَهُنَّ وَلَا يُبْدِيْنَ زِيْنَتَهُنَّ اِلَّا مَا ظَهَرَ مِنْهَا
وَلْيَضْرِبْنَ بِخُمُرِهِنَّ عَلٰى جُيُوْبِهِنَّ ۖ وَلَا يُبْدِيْنَ
زِيْنَتَهُنَّ اِلَّا لِبُعُوْلَتِهِنَّ اَوْ اٰبَآئِهِنَّ اَوْ اٰبَآءِ بُعُوْلَتِهِنَّ
اَوْ اَبْنَآئِهِنَّ اَوْ اَبْنَآءِ بُعُوْلَتِهِنَّ اَوْ اِخْوَانِهِنَّ اَوْ
بَنِيْٓ اِخْوَانِهِنَّ اَوْ بَنِيْٓ اَخَوٰتِهِنَّ اَوْ نِسَآئِهِنَّ اَوْ مَا

or what their right hands possess, or such of male attendants as have no sexual appetite, or young children who have no knowledge of the hidden parts of women. And they strike not their feet so that what they hide of their ornaments may become known. And turn ye to Allah all together, O believers, that you may succeed.

مَلَكَتْ اَيْمَانُهُنَّ اَوِ التّٰبِعِيْنَ غَيْرِ اُولِي الْاِرْبَةِ
مِنَ الرِّجَالِ اَوِ الطِّفْلِ الَّذِيْنَ لَمْ يَظْهَرُوْا عَلٰى عَوْرٰتِ
النِّسَآءِ ۪ وَلَا يَضْرِبْنَ بِاَرْجُلِهِنَّ لِيُعْلَمَ مَا يُخْفِيْنَ
مِنْ زِيْنَتِهِنَّ ؕ وَتُوْبُوْۤا اِلَى اللّٰهِ جَمِيْعًا اَيُّهَ الْمُؤْمِنُوْنَ
لَعَلَّكُمْ تُفْلِحُوْنَ ﴿۳۲﴾

33. And marry widows from among you, and your male slaves and female slaves who are fit *for marriage*. If they be poor, Allah will grant them means out of His bounty; and Allah is Bountiful, All-Knowing.

وَاَنْكِحُوا الْاَيَامٰى مِنْكُمْ وَالصّٰلِحِيْنَ مِنْ عِبَادِكُمْ
وَاِمَآئِكُمْ ؕ اِنْ يَّكُوْنُوْا فُقَرَآءَ يُغْنِهِمُ اللّٰهُ مِنْ فَضْلِهٖ ؕ
وَاللّٰهُ وَاسِعٌ عَلِيْمٌ ﴿۳۳﴾

* 34. And those who find no *means of* marriage should keep themselves chaste, until Allah grants them means out of His bounty. And such as desire *a deed of manumission in* writing from among those whom your right hands possess, write it for them if you know any good in them; and give them out of the wealth of Allah which He has bestowed upon you. And force not your maids to unchaste life *by keeping them unmarried* if they desire to keep chaste, in order that you may seek the gain of the present life. But if any one forces them, then after their compulsion Allah will be Forgiving *and* Merciful *to them*.

وَلْيَسْتَعْفِفِ الَّذِيْنَ لَا يَجِدُوْنَ نِكَاحًا حَتّٰى يُغْنِيَهُمُ
اللّٰهُ مِنْ فَضْلِهٖ ؕ وَالَّذِيْنَ يَبْتَغُوْنَ الْكِتٰبَ مِمَّا مَلَكَتْ
اَيْمَانُكُمْ فَكَاتِبُوْهُمْ اِنْ عَلِمْتُمْ فِيْهِمْ خَيْرًا ۖ وَّاٰتُوْهُمْ
مِّنْ مَّالِ اللّٰهِ الَّذِيْۤ اٰتٰىكُمْ ؕ وَلَا تُكْرِهُوْا فَتَيٰتِكُمْ
عَلَى الْبِغَآءِ اِنْ اَرَدْنَ تَحَصُّنًا لِّتَبْتَغُوْا عَرَضَ الْحَيٰوةِ
الدُّنْيَا ؕ وَمَنْ يُّكْرِهْهُّنَّ فَاِنَّ اللّٰهَ مِنْۢ بَعْدِ اِكْرَاهِهِنَّ
غَفُوْرٌ رَّحِيْمٌ ﴿۳۴﴾

35. And We have sent down to you manifest Signs, and the example of those who have passed away before you, and an exhortation to the God-fearing.

وَلَقَدْ اَنْزَلْنَاۤ اِلَيْكُمْ اٰيٰتٍ مُّبَيِّنٰتٍ وَّمَثَلًا مِّنَ الَّذِيْنَ
ع خَلَوْا مِنْ قَبْلِكُمْ وَمَوْعِظَةً لِّلْمُتَّقِيْنَ ﴿۳۵﴾

R. 5.

36. Allah is the Light of the heavens and the earth. The similitude of His light is as a *lustrous* niche, wherein is a lamp. The lamp is in a glass. The glass is as it were a glittering star. It is lit from a blessed tree—an olive—neither of the east nor of the west, whose oil would well-nigh glow forth even though fire touched it not. Light upon light! Allah guides to His light

اَللّٰهُ نُوْرُ السَّمٰوٰتِ وَالْاَرْضِ ؕ مَثَلُ نُوْرِهٖ كَمِشْكٰوةٍ فِيْهَا
مِصْبَاحٌ ؕ اَلْمِصْبَاحُ فِيْ زُجَاجَةٍ ؕ اَلزُّجَاجَةُ كَاَنَّهَا كَوْكَبٌ
دُرِّيٌّ يُّوْقَدُ مِنْ شَجَرَةٍ مُّبٰرَكَةٍ زَيْتُوْنَةٍ لَّا شَرْقِيَّةٍ
وَّلَا غَرْبِيَّةٍ ۙ يَّكَادُ زَيْتُهَا يُضِيْٓءُ وَلَوْ لَمْ تَمْسَسْهُ
نَارٌ ؕ نُوْرٌ عَلٰى نُوْرٍ ؕ يَهْدِي اللّٰهُ لِنُوْرِهٖ مَنْ يَّشَآءُ ؕ

whomsoever He will. And Allah sets forth parables to men, and Allah knows all things full well.

وَيَضْرِبُ اللّٰهُ الْاَمْثَالَ لِلنَّاسِ ؕ وَاللّٰهُ بِكُلِّ شَيْءٍ
عَلِيْمٌ ۙ ﴿۳۶﴾

* 37. *This light is now lit* in houses with regard to which Allah has ordained that they be exalted and that His name be remembered in them. Therein is He glorified in the mornings and the evenings

فِيْ بُيُوْتٍ اَذِنَ اللّٰهُ اَنْ تُرْفَعَ وَيُذْكَرَ فِيْهَا اسْمُهٗ ۙ
يُسَبِّحُ لَهٗ فِيْهَا بِالْغُدُوِّ وَالْاٰصَالِ ۙ ﴿۳۷﴾

* 38. *By* men, whom neither merchandise nor traffic diverts from the remembrance of Allah and the observance of Prayer, and the giving of the Zakāt. They fear a day in which hearts and eyes will be agitated,

رِجَالٌ ۙ لَّا تُلْهِيْهِمْ تِجَارَةٌ وَّلَا بَيْعٌ عَنْ ذِكْرِ اللّٰهِ
وَاِقَامِ الصَّلٰوةِ وَاِيْتَآءِ الزَّكٰوةِ ۙ يَخَافُوْنَ يَوْمًا
تَتَقَلَّبُ فِيْهِ الْقُلُوْبُ وَالْاَبْصَارُ ۙ ﴿۳۸﴾

39. So that Allah may give them the best reward of their deeds, and give them increase out of His bounty. And Allah does provide for whomsoever He pleases without measure.

لِيَجْزِيَهُمُ اللّٰهُ اَحْسَنَ مَا عَمِلُوْا وَيَزِيْدَهُمْ مِّنْ
فَضْلِهٖ ؕ وَاللّٰهُ يَرْزُقُ مَنْ يَّشَآءُ بِغَيْرِ حِسَابٍ ﴿۳۹﴾

* 40. And *as to* those who disbelieve, their deeds are like a mirage in a desert. The thirsty one thinks it to be water until, when he comes up to it, he finds it to be nothing. And he finds Allah near him, Who then fully pays him his account; and Allah is swift at reckoning.

وَالَّذِيْنَ كَفَرُوْٓا اَعْمَالُهُمْ كَسَرَابٍۭ بِقِيْعَةٍ يَّحْسَبُهُ
الظَّمْاٰنُ مَآءً ؕ حَتّٰٓى اِذَا جَآءَهٗ لَمْ يَجِدْهُ شَيْئًا وَّوَجَدَ
اللّٰهَ عِنْدَهٗ فَوَفّٰىهُ حِسَابَهٗ ؕ وَاللّٰهُ سَرِيْعُ الْحِسَابِ ۙ ﴿۴۰﴾

41. Or *their deeds are* like thick darkness in a vast and deep sea, which a wave covers, over which there is another wave, above which are clouds: layers of darkness, one upon another. When he holds out his hand, he can hardly see it; and he whom Allah gives no light—for him there is no light at all.

اَوْ كَظُلُمٰتٍ فِيْ بَحْرٍ لُّجِّيٍّ يَّغْشٰىهُ مَوْجٌ مِّنْ فَوْقِهٖ مَوْجٌ مِّنْ فَوْقِهٖ
سَحَابٌ ؕ ظُلُمٰتٌۢ بَعْضُهَا فَوْقَ بَعْضٍ ؕ اِذَآ اَخْرَجَ يَدَهٗ
لَمْ يَكَدْ يَرٰىهَا ؕ وَمَنْ لَّمْ يَجْعَلِ اللّٰهُ لَهٗ نُوْرًا فَمَا
لَهٗ مِنْ نُّوْرٍ ﴿۴۱﴾ ع

R. 6.

42. Hast thou not seen that it is Allah Whose praises all who are in the heavens and the earth celebrate, and *so do* the birds with their wings outspread? Each one knows his own *mode of* prayer and praise. And Allah knows well what they do.

اَلَمْ تَرَ اَنَّ اللّٰهَ يُسَبِّحُ لَهٗ مَنْ فِي السَّمٰوٰتِ وَالْاَرْضِ
وَالطَّيْرُ صٰٓفّٰتٍ ؕ كُلٌّ قَدْ عَلِمَ صَلَاتَهٗ وَتَسْبِيْحَهٗ ؕ
وَاللّٰهُ عَلِيْمٌۢ بِمَا يَفْعَلُوْنَ ﴿۴۲﴾

43. And to Allah belongs the kingdom of the heavens and the earth, and to Allah shall be the return.

وَلِلّٰهِ مُلْكُ السَّمٰوٰتِ وَالْاَرْضِ ۚ وَاِلَى اللّٰهِ الْمَصِيْرُ ﴿۴۳﴾

44. Hast thou not seen that Allah drives the clouds, then joins them together, then piles them up so that thou seest rain

اَلَمْ تَرَ اَنَّ اللّٰهَ يُزْجِيْ سَحَابًا ثُمَّ يُؤَلِّفُ بَيْنَهٗ ثُمَّ
يَجْعَلُهٗ رُكَامًا فَتَرَى الْوَدْقَ يَخْرُجُ مِنْ خِلٰلِهٖ ۚ وَ

issue forth from the midst thereof? And He sends down from the sky *clouds like* mountains wherein is hail, and He smites therewith whom He pleases, and turns it away from whom He pleases. The flash of its lightning may well-nigh take away the sight.

45. Allah alternates the night and the day. Therein surely is a lesson for those who have eyes.

* 46. And Allah has created every animal from water. Of them are *some* that go upon their bellies, and of them are *some* that go upon two feet, and among them are *some* that go upon four. Allah creates what He pleases. Surely, Allah has the power to do all that He pleases.

47. We have indeed sent down manifest Signs. And Allah guides whom He pleases to the right path.

48. And they say, 'We believe in Allah and in the Messenger, and we obey;' then after that some of them turn away. But such are not believers.

49. And when they are called to Allah and His Messenger that he may judge between them, lo! a party of them turn away.

50. And if *they consider* the right *to be* on their side, they come to him running in *all* submission.

51. Is it that there is a disease in their hearts? Or do they doubt, or do they fear that Allah and His Messenger will be unjust to them? Nay, it is they themselves who are the wrongdoers.

R. 7.

52. The response of the believers, when they are called to Allah and His Messenger in order that he may judge between them, is only that they say: 'We hear and we obey.' And it is they who will prosper.

53. And whoso obeys Allah and His Messenger, and fears Allah, and takes Him

يُنَزِّلُ مِنَ السَّمَآءِ مِنْ جِبَالٍ فِيْهَا مِنْۢ بَرَدٍ فَيُصِيْبُ
بِهٖ مَنْ يَّشَآءُ وَ يَصْرِفُهٗ عَنْ مَّنْ يَّشَآءُ ؕ يَكَادُ سَنَا
بَرْقِهٖ يَذْهَبُ بِالْاَبْصَارِ ﴿۴۴﴾
يُقَلِّبُ اللّٰهُ الَّيْلَ وَ النَّهَارَ ؕ اِنَّ فِیْ ذٰلِكَ لَعِبْرَةً
لِّاُولِی الْاَبْصَارِ ﴿۴۵﴾
وَ اللّٰهُ خَلَقَ كُلَّ دَآبَّةٍ مِّنْ مَّآءٍ ۚ فَمِنْهُمْ مَّنْ يَّمْشِیْ
عَلٰى بَطْنِهٖ ۚ وَ مِنْهُمْ مَّنْ يَّمْشِیْ عَلٰى رِجْلَيْنِ ۚ وَ مِنْهُمْ مَّنْ
يَّمْشِیْ عَلٰۤى اَرْبَعٍ ؕ يَخْلُقُ اللّٰهُ مَا يَشَآءُ ؕ اِنَّ اللّٰهَ عَلٰى كُلِّ
شَیْءٍ قَدِيْرٌ ﴿۴۶﴾
لَقَدْ اَنْزَلْنَاۤ اٰيٰتٍ مُّبَيِّنٰتٍ ؕ وَ اللّٰهُ يَهْدِیْ مَنْ يَّشَآءُ اِلٰى
صِرَاطٍ مُّسْتَقِيْمٍ ﴿۴۷﴾
وَ يَقُوْلُوْنَ اٰمَنَّا بِاللّٰهِ وَ بِالرَّسُوْلِ وَ اَطَعْنَا ثُمَّ يَتَوَلّٰى
فَرِيْقٌ مِّنْهُمْ مِّنْۢ بَعْدِ ذٰلِكَ ؕ وَ مَاۤ اُولٰٓئِكَ بِالْمُؤْمِنِيْنَ ﴿۴۸﴾
وَ اِذَا دُعُوْۤا اِلَى اللّٰهِ وَ رَسُوْلِهٖ لِيَحْكُمَ بَيْنَهُمْ اِذَا فَرِيْقٌ
مِّنْهُمْ مُّعْرِضُوْنَ ﴿۴۹﴾
وَ اِنْ يَّكُنْ لَّهُمُ الْحَقُّ يَاْتُوْۤا اِلَيْهِ مُذْعِنِيْنَ ﴿۵۰﴾
اَفِیْ قُلُوْبِهِمْ مَّرَضٌ اَمِ ارْتَابُوْۤا اَمْ يَخَافُوْنَ اَنْ يَّحِيْفَ
اللّٰهُ عَلَيْهِمْ وَ رَسُوْلُهٗ ؕ بَلْ اُولٰٓئِكَ هُمُ الظّٰلِمُوْنَ ﴿۵۱﴾ ع ٦ ١٣
اِنَّمَا كَانَ قَوْلَ الْمُؤْمِنِيْنَ اِذَا دُعُوْۤا اِلَى اللّٰهِ وَ رَسُوْلِهٖ
لِيَحْكُمَ بَيْنَهُمْ اَنْ يَّقُوْلُوْا سَمِعْنَا وَ اَطَعْنَا ؕ وَ اُولٰٓئِكَ
هُمُ الْمُفْلِحُوْنَ ﴿۵۲﴾
وَ مَنْ يُّطِعِ اللّٰهَ وَ رَسُوْلَهٗ وَ يَخْشَ اللّٰهَ وَ يَتَّقْهِ فَاُولٰٓئِكَ

as a shield *for protection*, it is they who will be successful.

هُمُ الْفَآئِزُوْنَ ۝٥٣

54. And they swear by Allah their strongest oaths that, if thou command them, they will surely go forth. Say, 'Swear not; *what is required is actual* obedience in what is right. Surely, Allah is well aware of what you do.'

وَاَقْسَمُوْا بِاللّٰهِ جَهْدَ اَيْمَانِهِمْ لَئِنْ اَمَرْتَهُمْ لَيَخْرُجُنَّ ؕ
قُلْ لَّا تُقْسِمُوْا ۚ طَاعَةٌ مَّعْرُوْفَةٌ ؕ اِنَّ اللّٰهَ خَبِيْرٌۢ بِمَا
تَعْمَلُوْنَ ۝٥٤

* 55. Say, 'Obey Allah, and obey the Messenger.' But if you turn away, then upon him is his burden, and upon you is your burden. And if you obey him, you will be rightly guided. And the Messenger is not responsible but for the plain delivery of the Message.

قُلْ اَطِيْعُوا اللّٰهَ وَاَطِيْعُوا الرَّسُوْلَ ۚ فَاِنْ تَوَلَّوْا فَاِنَّمَا
عَلَيْهِ مَا حُمِّلَ وَعَلَيْكُمْ مَّا حُمِّلْتُمْ ؕ وَاِنْ تُطِيْعُوْهُ
تَهْتَدُوْا ؕ وَمَا عَلَى الرَّسُوْلِ اِلَّا الْبَلٰغُ الْمُبِيْنُ ۝٥٥

56. Allah has promised to those among you who believe and do good works that He will surely make them Successors in the earth, as He made Successors *from among* those who were before them; and that He will surely establish for them their religion which He has chosen for them; and that He will surely give them in exchange security *and peace* after their fear: They will worship Me, *and* they will not associate anything with Me. Then whoso is ungrateful after that, they will be the rebellious.

وَعَدَ اللّٰهُ الَّذِيْنَ اٰمَنُوْا مِنْكُمْ وَعَمِلُوا الصّٰلِحٰتِ
لَيَسْتَخْلِفَنَّهُمْ فِي الْاَرْضِ كَمَا اسْتَخْلَفَ الَّذِيْنَ مِنْ
قَبْلِهِمْ ۪ وَلَيُمَكِّنَنَّ لَهُمْ دِيْنَهُمُ الَّذِي ارْتَضٰى لَهُمْ
وَلَيُبَدِّلَنَّهُمْ مِّنْۢ بَعْدِ خَوْفِهِمْ اَمْنًا ؕ يَعْبُدُوْنَنِيْ
لَا يُشْرِكُوْنَ بِيْ شَيْـًٔا ؕ وَمَنْ كَفَرَ بَعْدَ ذٰلِكَ فَاُولٰٓئِكَ
هُمُ الْفٰسِقُوْنَ ۝٥٦

57. And observe Prayer and give the Zakāt and obey the Messenger, that you may be shown mercy.

وَاَقِيْمُوا الصَّلٰوةَ وَاٰتُوا الزَّكٰوةَ وَاَطِيْعُوا الرَّسُوْلَ
لَعَلَّكُمْ تُرْحَمُوْنَ ۝٥٧

58. Think not that those who disbelieve can frustrate *Our plan* in the earth; their abode is Hell; and it is indeed an evil resort.

لَا تَحْسَبَنَّ الَّذِيْنَ كَفَرُوْا مُعْجِزِيْنَ فِي الْاَرْضِ ۚ
وَمَاْوٰىهُمُ النَّارُ ؕ وَلَبِئْسَ الْمَصِيْرُ ۝٥٨ ع

R. 8.

59. O ye who believe! let those whom your right hands possess, and those of you who have not attained to puberty, ask leave of you at three times *before coming into your presence:* before the morning Prayer, and when you take off your clothes at noon in summer, and after the night Prayer. *These are* three times of privacy for you. At *times* other than these there is no blame on you or on them, *for*

يٰٓاَيُّهَا الَّذِيْنَ اٰمَنُوْا لِيَسْتَاْذِنْكُمُ الَّذِيْنَ مَلَكَتْ
اَيْمَانُكُمْ وَالَّذِيْنَ لَمْ يَبْلُغُوا الْحُلُمَ مِنْكُمْ ثَلٰثَ
مَرّٰتٍ ؕ مِنْ قَبْلِ صَلٰوةِ الْفَجْرِ وَحِيْنَ تَضَعُوْنَ ثِيَابَكُمْ
مِّنَ الظَّهِيْرَةِ وَمِنْۢ بَعْدِ صَلٰوةِ الْعِشَآءِ ؕ ثَلٰثُ عَوْرٰتٍ
لَّكُمْ ؕ لَيْسَ عَلَيْكُمْ وَلَا عَلَيْهِمْ جُنَاحٌۢ بَعْدَهُنَّ ؕ

they have to move about *waiting upon* you, some of you *attending* upon others. Thus does Allah make plain to you the Signs; for Allah is All-Knowing, Wise.

60. And when the children among you attain to puberty, they *too* should ask permission, even as those *mentioned* before them asked permission. Thus does Allah make plain to you His commandments; and Allah is All-Knowing, Wise.

* 61. *As to* elderly women, who have no desire for marriage—there is no blame on them if they lay aside their *outer* clothing without displaying their beauty. But to abstain *from that even* is better for them. And Allah is All-Hearing, All-Knowing.

62. There is no harm for the blind and there is no harm for the lame, and there is no harm for the sick and none for yourselves, that you eat from your own houses, or the houses of your fathers, or the houses of your mothers or the houses of your brothers, or the houses of your sisters, or the houses of your fathers' brothers or the houses of your fathers' sisters, or the houses of your mothers' brothers, or the houses of your mothers' sisters, or *from* that of which the keys are in your possession, or *from the house of* a friend of yours. There is no harm for you whether you eat together or separately. But when you enter houses, salute your people—a greeting from your Lord, full of blessing and purity. Thus does Allah make plain to you the commandments, that you may understand.

R. 9.

* 63. Those only are *true* believers who believe in Allah and His Messenger, and who, when they are with him on some matter *of common importance* which has brought *them* together, go not away until they have asked leave of him. Surely those who ask leave of thee, it is they who *really*

طَوّٰفُوْنَ عَلَيْكُمْ بَعْضُكُمْ عَلٰى بَعْضٍ ۭ كَذٰلِكَ يُبَيِّنُ
اللّٰهُ لَكُمُ الْاٰيٰتِ ۭ وَاللّٰهُ عَلِيْمٌ حَكِيْمٌ ﴿٥٩﴾
وَاِذَا بَلَغَ الْاَطْفَالُ مِنْكُمُ الْحُلُمَ فَلْيَسْتَاْذِنُوْا كَمَا
اسْتَاْذَنَ الَّذِيْنَ مِنْ قَبْلِهِمْ ۭ كَذٰلِكَ يُبَيِّنُ اللّٰهُ لَكُمْ
اٰيٰتِهٖ ۭ وَاللّٰهُ عَلِيْمٌ حَكِيْمٌ ﴿٦٠﴾
وَالْقَوَاعِدُ مِنَ النِّسَاۗءِ الّٰتِيْ لَا يَرْجُوْنَ نِكَاحًا
فَلَيْسَ عَلَيْهِنَّ جُنَاحٌ اَنْ يَّضَعْنَ ثِيَابَهُنَّ غَيْرَ
مُتَبَرِّجٰتٍۢ بِزِيْنَةٍ ۭ وَاَنْ يَّسْتَعْفِفْنَ خَيْرٌ لَّهُنَّ ۭ
وَاللّٰهُ سَمِيْعٌ عَلِيْمٌ ﴿٦١﴾
لَيْسَ عَلَى الْاَعْمٰى حَرَجٌ وَّلَا عَلَى الْاَعْرَجِ حَرَجٌ وَّلَا
عَلَى الْمَرِيْضِ حَرَجٌ وَّلَا عَلٰٓى اَنْفُسِكُمْ اَنْ تَاْكُلُوْا مِنْ
بُيُوْتِكُمْ اَوْ بُيُوْتِ اٰبَاۗىِٕكُمْ اَوْ بُيُوْتِ اُمَّهٰتِكُمْ اَوْ
بُيُوْتِ اِخْوَانِكُمْ اَوْ بُيُوْتِ اَخَوٰتِكُمْ اَوْ بُيُوْتِ اَعْمَامِكُمْ
اَوْ بُيُوْتِ عَمّٰتِكُمْ اَوْ بُيُوْتِ اَخْوَالِكُمْ اَوْ بُيُوْتِ خٰلٰتِكُمْ
اَوْ مَا مَلَكْتُمْ مَّفَاتِحَهٗٓ اَوْ صَدِيْقِكُمْ ۭ لَيْسَ عَلَيْكُمْ
جُنَاحٌ اَنْ تَاْكُلُوْا جَمِيْعًا اَوْ اَشْتَاتًا ۭ فَاِذَا دَخَلْتُمْ
بُيُوْتًا فَسَلِّمُوْا عَلٰٓى اَنْفُسِكُمْ تَحِيَّةً مِّنْ عِنْدِ اللّٰهِ
مُبٰرَكَةً طَيِّبَةً ۭ كَذٰلِكَ يُبَيِّنُ اللّٰهُ لَكُمُ الْاٰيٰتِ لَعَلَّكُمْ
تَعْقِلُوْنَ ﴿٦٢﴾ ع
اِنَّمَا الْمُؤْمِنُوْنَ الَّذِيْنَ اٰمَنُوْا بِاللّٰهِ وَرَسُوْلِهٖ وَاِذَا
كَانُوْا مَعَهٗ عَلٰٓى اَمْرٍ جَامِعٍ لَّمْ يَذْهَبُوْا حَتّٰى يَسْتَاْذِنُوْهُ ۭ
اِنَّ الَّذِيْنَ يَسْتَاْذِنُوْنَكَ اُولٰۗىِٕكَ الَّذِيْنَ يُؤْمِنُوْنَ

believe in Allah and His Messenger. So, when they ask thy leave for some affair of theirs, give leave to those of them whom thou pleasest, and ask forgiveness for them of Allah. Surely, Allah is Most Forgiving, Merciful.

بِاللّٰهِ وَ رَسُوْلِهٖ ۚ فَاِذَا اسْتَاْذَنُوْكَ لِبَعْضِ شَاْنِهِمْ
فَاْذَنْ لِّمَنْ شِئْتَ مِنْهُمْ وَ اسْتَغْفِرْ لَهُمُ اللّٰهَ ؕ اِنَّ
اللّٰهَ غَفُوْرٌ رَّحِيْمٌ ﴿۶۳﴾

64. Treat not the calling of the Messenger among you like the calling of one of you to another. Allah does know those of you who steal away covertly. So let those who go against His command beware lest a trial afflict them or a grievous punishment overtake them.

لَا تَجْعَلُوْا دُعَآءَ الرَّسُوْلِ بَيْنَكُمْ كَدُعَآءِ بَعْضِكُمْ بَعْضًا ؕ
قَدْ يَعْلَمُ اللّٰهُ الَّذِيْنَ يَتَسَلَّلُوْنَ مِنْكُمْ لِوَاذًا ۚ فَلْيَحْذَرِ
الَّذِيْنَ يُخَالِفُوْنَ عَنْ اَمْرِهٖۤ اَنْ تُصِيْبَهُمْ فِتْنَةٌ اَوْ
يُصِيْبَهُمْ عَذَابٌ اَلِيْمٌ ﴿۶۴﴾

* 65. Hearken ye! To Allah belongs whatsoever is in the heavens and the earth. He does know in what condition you are. And on the day when they will be returned unto Him, He will inform them of what they did. And Allah knows everything full well.

اَلَآ اِنَّ لِلّٰهِ مَا فِي السَّمٰوٰتِ وَ الْاَرْضِ ؕ قَدْ يَعْلَمُ مَآ اَنْتُمْ
عَلَيْهِ ؕ وَ يَوْمَ يُرْجَعُوْنَ اِلَيْهِ فَيُنَبِّئُهُمْ بِمَا عَمِلُوْا ؕ وَ اللّٰهُ
بِكُلِّ شَيْءٍ عَلِيْمٌ ﴿۶۵﴾ ع

سُوْرَةُ الْفُرْقَانِ مَكِّيَّةٌ

AL-FURQĀN

(Revealed before Hijra)

1. In the name of Allah, the Gracious, the Merciful.

بِسْمِ اللّٰهِ الرَّحْمٰنِ الرَّحِيْمِ ﴿١﴾

2. Blessed is He Who has sent down the Discrimination to His servant, that he may be a Warner to *all* the worlds—

تَبٰرَكَ الَّذِيْ نَزَّلَ الْفُرْقَانَ عَلٰى عَبْدِهٖ لِيَكُوْنَ
لِلْعٰلَمِيْنَ نَذِيْرًا ﴿٢﴾

3. He to Whom belongs the kingdom of the heavens and the earth. And He has taken unto Himself no son, and has no partner in the kingdom, and has created everything, and has ordained for it *its* proper measure.

الَّذِيْ لَهٗ مُلْكُ السَّمٰوٰتِ وَالْاَرْضِ وَلَمْ يَتَّخِذْ وَلَدًا
وَّلَمْ يَكُنْ لَّهٗ شَرِيْكٌ فِي الْمُلْكِ وَخَلَقَ كُلَّ شَيْءٍ فَقَدَّرَهٗ
تَقْدِيْرًا ﴿٣﴾

4. Yet they have taken beside Him gods, who create nothing but are themselves created, and who have no power to harm or benefit themselves and they control not death nor life nor resurrection.

وَاتَّخَذُوْا مِنْ دُوْنِهٖۤ اٰلِهَةً لَّا يَخْلُقُوْنَ شَيْـًٔا وَّهُمْ
يُخْلَقُوْنَ وَلَا يَمْلِكُوْنَ لِاَنْفُسِهِمْ ضَرًّا وَّلَا نَفْعًا
وَّلَا يَمْلِكُوْنَ مَوْتًا وَّلَا حَيٰوةً وَّلَا نُشُوْرًا ﴿٤﴾

5. And those who disbelieve say, 'It is naught but a lie which he has forged, and other people have helped him with it.' Indeed, they have brought forth an injustice and an untruth.

وَقَالَ الَّذِيْنَ كَفَرُوْۤا اِنْ هٰذَاۤ اِلَّاۤ اِفْكُ ِۨافْتَرٰىهُ وَ
اَعَانَهٗ عَلَيْهِ قَوْمٌ اٰخَرُوْنَ ۚ فَقَدْ جَآءُوْ ظُلْمًا وَّ
زُوْرًا ﴿٥﴾

6. And they say, '*These are* fables of the ancients; *and* he has got them written down, and they are dictated to him morning and evening.'

وَقَالُوْۤا اَسَاطِيْرُ الْاَوَّلِيْنَ اكْتَتَبَهَا فَهِيَ تُمْلٰى عَلَيْهِ
بُكْرَةً وَّاَصِيْلًا ﴿٦﴾

7. Say, 'He Who knows *every* secret *that is* in the heavens and the earth has revealed it. Verily, He is Most Forgiving, Merciful.'

قُلْ اَنْزَلَهُ الَّذِيْ يَعْلَمُ السِّرَّ فِي السَّمٰوٰتِ وَالْاَرْضِ
اِنَّهٗ كَانَ غَفُوْرًا رَّحِيْمًا ﴿٧﴾

8. And they say, 'What is the matter with this Messenger that he eats food, and walks in the streets? Why has not an angel been sent down to him that he might be a warner with him?

وَقَالُوْا مَالِ هٰذَا الرَّسُوْلِ يَأْكُلُ الطَّعَامَ وَيَمْشِيْ
فِي الْاَسْوَاقِ لَوْلَاۤ اُنْزِلَ اِلَيْهِ مَلَكٌ فَيَكُوْنَ مَعَهٗ
نَذِيْرًا ﴿٨﴾

9. 'Or a treasure should have been thrown down to him, or he should have had a garden to eat therefrom.' And the wrongdoers say, 'You follow none but a man bewitched.'

أَوْ يُلْقَىٰ إِلَيْهِ كَنزٌ أَوْ تَكُونُ لَهُ جَنَّةٌ يَأْكُلُ مِنْهَا
وَقَالَ الظَّالِمُونَ إِن تَتَّبِعُونَ إِلَّا رَجُلًا مَّسْحُورًا ﴿٩﴾

10. See how they coin similitudes for thee! Thus they have gone astray and cannot find a way.

انظُرْ كَيْفَ ضَرَبُوا لَكَ الْأَمْثَالَ فَضَلُّوا فَلَا يَسْتَطِيعُونَ
سَبِيلًا ﴿١٠﴾ ع

R. 2.

11. Blessed is He Who, if He please, will assign thee better than all that—Gardens through which rivers flow—and will *also* assign thee palaces.

تَبَارَكَ الَّذِي إِن شَاءَ جَعَلَ لَكَ خَيْرًا مِّن ذَٰلِكَ
جَنَّاتٍ تَجْرِي مِن تَحْتِهَا الْأَنْهَارُ وَيَجْعَل لَّكَ
قُصُورًا ﴿١١﴾

12. Nay, they deny the Hour, and for those who deny the Hour We have prepared a blazing fire.

بَلْ كَذَّبُوا بِالسَّاعَةِ ۖ وَأَعْتَدْنَا لِمَن كَذَّبَ
بِالسَّاعَةِ سَعِيرًا ﴿١٢﴾

13. When it sees them from a place far off, they will hear its raging and roaring.

إِذَا رَأَتْهُم مِّن مَّكَانٍ بَعِيدٍ سَمِعُوا لَهَا تَغَيُّظًا
وَزَفِيرًا ﴿١٣﴾

14. And when they are thrown into a narrow place thereof, chained together, they will pray there for destruction.

وَإِذَا أُلْقُوا مِنْهَا مَكَانًا ضَيِّقًا مُّقَرَّنِينَ دَعَوْا هُنَالِكَ
ثُبُورًا ﴿١٤﴾

15. 'Pray not today for one destruction, but pray for many destructions.'

لَّا تَدْعُوا الْيَوْمَ ثُبُورًا وَاحِدًا وَادْعُوا ثُبُورًا كَثِيرًا ﴿١٥﴾

16. Say, 'Is that better or the Garden of Eternity, which is promised to the righteous? It will be their reward and resort.'

قُلْ أَذَٰلِكَ خَيْرٌ أَمْ جَنَّةُ الْخُلْدِ الَّتِي وُعِدَ الْمُتَّقُونَ
كَانَتْ لَهُمْ جَزَاءً وَمَصِيرًا ﴿١٦﴾

17. They will have therein whatsoever they desire, abiding *therein for ever*. It is a promise from thy Lord, to be *always* prayed for.

لَّهُمْ فِيهَا مَا يَشَاءُونَ خَالِدِينَ ۚ كَانَ عَلَىٰ رَبِّكَ وَعْدًا
مَّسْئُولًا ﴿١٧﴾

18. And the day when He will assemble them and those whom they worship beside Allah, He will ask, 'Was it you who led astray these My servants, or did they *themselves* stray away from the path?'

وَيَوْمَ يَحْشُرُهُمْ وَمَا يَعْبُدُونَ مِن دُونِ اللَّهِ
فَيَقُولُ أَأَنتُمْ أَضْلَلْتُمْ عِبَادِي هَٰؤُلَاءِ أَمْ هُمْ ضَلُّوا
السَّبِيلَ ﴿١٨﴾

19. They will say, 'Holy art Thou! It was not proper for us to take protectors

قَالُوا سُبْحَانَكَ مَا كَانَ يَنبَغِي لَنَا أَن نَّتَّخِذَ مِن

other than Thee; but Thou didst bestow on them and their fathers the good things *of this life* until they forgot the admonition and became a ruined people.'

دونك من أولياء ولكن متعتهم وآباءهم حتى نسوا الذكر وكانوا قوما بورا ١٩

20. *Then We shall say to the idolaters:* 'Now have they given you the lie regarding what you said, so you cannot avert *the punishment* or *get* help.' And whosoever among you does wrong, We shall make him taste a grievous punishment.

فقد كذبوكم بما تقولون فما تستطيعون صرفا ولا نصرا ومن يظلم منكم نذقه عذابا كبيرا ٢٠

21. And We never sent any Messengers before thee but surely they ate food and walked in the streets. And We make some of you a trial for others. Will you *then* be steadfast? And thy Lord is All-Seeing.

وما أرسلنا قبلك من المرسلين إلا إنهم ليأكلون الطعام ويمشون في الأسواق وجعلنا بعضكم لبعض فتنة أتصبرون وكان ربك بصيرا ٢١

R. 3. ع الجزء ١٩

22. And those who look not for a meeting with Us say: 'Why are angels not sent down to us? Or why do we not see our Lord?' Surely they are too proud of themselves and have greatly exceeded the bounds.

وقال الذين لا يرجون لقاءنا لولا أنزل علينا الملائكة أو نرى ربنا لقد استكبروا في أنفسهم وعتو عتوا كبيرا ٢٢

23. On the day when they see the angels—there will be no good tidings on that day for the guilty; and they will say: 'Would that there were a great barrier!'

يوم يرون الملائكة لا بشرى يومئذ للمجرمين ويقولون حجرا محجورا ٢٣

* 24. And We shall turn to the works they did and We shall scatter it into particles of dust.

وقدمنا إلى ما عملوا من عمل فجعلناه هباء منثورا ٢٤

25. The inmates of Heaven on that day will be better off as regards *their* abode, and better off in respect of *their* place of repose.

أصحاب الجنة يومئذ خير مستقرا وأحسن مقيلا ٢٥

26. And the day when the heaven shall be rent asunder with the clouds, and the angels shall be sent down in large numbers—

ويوم تشقق السماء بالغمام ونزل الملائكة تنزيلا ٢٦

27. The true kingdom shall that day belong to the Gracious *God;* and it shall be a hard day for the disbelievers.

الملك يومئذ الحق للرحمن وكان يوما على الكافرين عسيرا ٢٧

* 28. *Remember* the day when the wrongdoer will bite his hands; he will say, 'O, would that I had taken *the same* way with the Messenger!

وَيَوْمَ يَعَضُّ الظَّالِمُ عَلَىٰ يَدَيْهِ يَقُولُ يَا لَيْتَنِي اتَّخَذْتُ
مَعَ الرَّسُولِ سَبِيلًا ﴿٢٨﴾

29. 'Ah, woe is me! Would that I had never taken such a one for a friend!

يَا وَيْلَتَىٰ لَيْتَنِي لَمْ أَتَّخِذْ فُلَانًا خَلِيلًا ﴿٢٩﴾

30. 'He led me astray from the Reminder after it had come to me.' And Satan is man's great deserter.

لَقَدْ أَضَلَّنِي عَنِ الذِّكْرِ بَعْدَ إِذْ جَاءَنِي ۗ وَكَانَ
الشَّيْطَانُ لِلْإِنسَانِ خَذُولًا ﴿٣٠﴾

31. And the Messenger will say, 'O my Lord, my people indeed treated this Qur'ān as *a* discarded *thing*.'

وَقَالَ الرَّسُولُ يَا رَبِّ إِنَّ قَوْمِي اتَّخَذُوا هَٰذَا الْقُرْآنَ مَهْجُورًا ﴿٣١﴾

32. Thus did We make for every Prophet an enemy from among the sinners; and sufficient is thy Lord as a Guide and a Helper.

وَكَذَٰلِكَ جَعَلْنَا لِكُلِّ نَبِيٍّ عَدُوًّا مِّنَ الْمُجْرِمِينَ ۗ وَكَفَىٰ
بِرَبِّكَ هَادِيًا وَنَصِيرًا ﴿٣٢﴾

33. And those who disbelieve say, 'Why was not the Qur'ān revealed to him all at once?' *We have revealed it* thus that We may strengthen thy heart therewith. And We have arranged it in the best form.

وَقَالَ الَّذِينَ كَفَرُوا لَوْلَا نُزِّلَ عَلَيْهِ الْقُرْآنُ جُمْلَةً
وَاحِدَةً ۚ كَذَٰلِكَ لِنُثَبِّتَ بِهِ فُؤَادَكَ ۖ وَرَتَّلْنَاهُ
تَرْتِيلًا ﴿٣٣﴾

34. And they bring thee no similitude but We provide thee with the truth and an excellent explanation.

وَلَا يَأْتُونَكَ بِمَثَلٍ إِلَّا جِئْنَاكَ بِالْحَقِّ وَأَحْسَنَ
تَفْسِيرًا ﴿٣٤﴾

35. Those who will be gathered on their faces unto Hell—they will be the worst in plight and most astray from the *right* path.

الَّذِينَ يُحْشَرُونَ عَلَىٰ وُجُوهِهِمْ إِلَىٰ جَهَنَّمَ أُولَٰئِكَ
شَرٌّ مَّكَانًا وَأَضَلُّ سَبِيلًا ﴿٣٥﴾ ع ٣

R. 4.

36. We gave Moses the Book, and appointed with him his brother Aaron as *his* assistant.

وَلَقَدْ آتَيْنَا مُوسَى الْكِتَابَ وَجَعَلْنَا مَعَهُ أَخَاهُ هَارُونَ
وَزِيرًا ﴿٣٦﴾

37. And We said, 'Go both of you to the people who have rejected Our Signs;' then We destroyed them, an utter destruction.

فَقُلْنَا اذْهَبَا إِلَى الْقَوْمِ الَّذِينَ كَذَّبُوا بِآيَاتِنَا فَدَمَّرْنَاهُمْ
تَدْمِيرًا ﴿٣٧﴾

38. And *as to* the people of Noah when they rejected the Messengers, We drowned them, and We made them a Sign for mankind. And We have prepared a painful punishment for the wrongdoers.

وَقَوْمَ نُوحٍ لَّمَّا كَذَّبُوا الرُّسُلَ أَغْرَقْنَاهُمْ وَجَعَلْنَاهُمْ
لِلنَّاسِ آيَةً ۖ وَأَعْتَدْنَا لِلظَّالِمِينَ عَذَابًا أَلِيمًا ﴿٣٨﴾

39. And *We destroyed* 'Ād and Thamūd, and the People of the Well, and many a

وَعَادًا وَثَمُودَ وَأَصْحَابَ الرَّسِّ وَقُرُونًا بَيْنَ ذَٰلِكَ

generation between them.

كَثِيْرًا ﴿٣٩﴾

* 40. And to each one We set forth *clear* similitudes; and each one We completely destroyed.

وَكُلًّا ضَرَبْنَا لَهُ الْاَمْثَالَ وَكُلًّا تَبَّرْنَا تَتْبِيْرًا ﴿٤٠﴾

* 41. And these (Meccans) must have visited the town whereon was rained an evil rain. Have they not then seen it? Nay, they hope not to be raised *after death*.

وَلَقَدْ اَتَوْا عَلَى الْقَرْيَةِ الَّتِيْٓ اُمْطِرَتْ مَطَرَ السَّوْءِ
اَفَلَمْ يَكُوْنُوْا يَرَوْنَهَا بَلْ كَانُوْا لَا يَرْجُوْنَ نُشُوْرًا ﴿٤١﴾

42. And when they see thee, they only make a jest of thee: 'Is this he whom Allah has sent *as* a Messenger?

وَاِذَا رَاَوْكَ اِنْ يَّتَّخِذُوْنَكَ اِلَّا هُزُوًا اَهٰذَا الَّذِيْ
بَعَثَ اللّٰهُ رَسُوْلًا ﴿٤٢﴾

43. 'He indeed had well-nigh led us astray from our gods, had we not steadily adhered to them.' And they shall know, when they see the punishment, who is most astray from the *right* path.

اِنْ كَادَ لَيُضِلُّنَا عَنْ اٰلِهَتِنَا لَوْلَآ اَنْ صَبَرْنَا عَلَيْهَا
وَسَوْفَ يَعْلَمُوْنَ حِيْنَ يَرَوْنَ الْعَذَابَ مَنْ اَضَلُّ
سَبِيْلًا ﴿٤٣﴾

44. Hast thou seen him who takes his own evil desire for his god? Couldst thou then be a guardian over him?

اَرَءَيْتَ مَنِ اتَّخَذَ اِلٰهَهٗ هَوٰىهُ اَفَاَنْتَ تَكُوْنُ
عَلَيْهِ وَكِيْلًا ﴿٤٤﴾

45. Dost thou think that most of them hear or understand? They are only like cattle—nay, they are worst astray from the path.

اَمْ تَحْسَبُ اَنَّ اَكْثَرَهُمْ يَسْمَعُوْنَ اَوْ يَعْقِلُوْنَ اِنْ
هُمْ اِلَّا كَالْاَنْعَامِ بَلْ هُمْ اَضَلُّ سَبِيْلًا ﴿٤٥﴾ ع

R. 5.

46. Hast thou not seen how thy Lord lengthens the shade? And if He had pleased, He could have made it stationary. Then We make the sun a guide thereof.

اَلَمْ تَرَ اِلٰى رَبِّكَ كَيْفَ مَدَّ الظِّلَّ وَلَوْ شَآءَ لَجَعَلَهٗ
سَاكِنًا ثُمَّ جَعَلْنَا الشَّمْسَ عَلَيْهِ دَلِيْلًا ﴿٤٦﴾

47. Then We draw it in towards Ourself, an easy drawing in.

ثُمَّ قَبَضْنٰهُ اِلَيْنَا قَبْضًا يَّسِيْرًا ﴿٤٧﴾

48. And He it is Who has made the night a covering for you, and *Who has made* sleep for rest, and has made the day for rising up.

وَهُوَ الَّذِيْ جَعَلَ لَكُمُ الَّيْلَ لِبَاسًا وَّالنَّوْمَ سُبَاتًا
وَّجَعَلَ النَّهَارَ نُشُوْرًا ﴿٤٨﴾

49. And He it is Who sends the winds as glad tidings before His mercy, and We send down pure water from the sky,

وَهُوَ الَّذِيْٓ اَرْسَلَ الرِّيٰحَ بُشْرًا بَيْنَ يَدَيْ رَحْمَتِهٖ
وَاَنْزَلْنَا مِنَ السَّمَآءِ مَآءً طَهُوْرًا ﴿٤٩﴾

50. That We may thereby give life to a dead land, and give it for drink to Our creation—cattle and men in great numbers.

لِّنُحْيِۦَ بِهٖ بَلْدَةً مَّيْتًا وَّنُسْقِيَهٗ مِمَّا خَلَقْنَآ اَنْعَامًا
وَّاَنَاسِيَّ كَثِيْرًا ﴿٥٠﴾

51. And We have explained it to them in diverse ways that they may take heed, but most men would reject everything but disbelief.

وَلَقَدْ صَرَّفْنٰهُ بَيْنَهُمْ لِيَذَّكَّرُوْا فَاَبٰۤى اَكْثَرُ
النَّاسِ اِلَّا كُفُوْرًا ﴿٥١﴾

52. If We had pleased, We could have surely raised a Warner in every city.

وَلَوْ شِئْنَا لَبَعَثْنَا فِيْ كُلِّ قَرْيَةٍ نَّذِيْرًا ﴿٥٢﴾

* 53. So obey not the disbelievers and fight against them by means of it (the Qur'ān) a great fight.

فَلَا تُطِعِ الْكٰفِرِيْنَ وَجَاهِدْهُمْ بِهٖ جِهَادًا كَبِيْرًا ﴿٥٣﴾

54. And He it is Who has caused the two seas to flow, this palatable *and* sweet, and that saltish *and* bitter; and between them He has placed a barrier and a great partition.

وَهُوَ الَّذِيْ مَرَجَ الْبَحْرَيْنِ هٰذَا عَذْبٌ فُرَاتٌ وَّ
هٰذَا مِلْحٌ اُجَاجٌ ۚ وَجَعَلَ بَيْنَهُمَا بَرْزَخًا وَّحِجْرًا
مَّحْجُوْرًا ﴿٥٤﴾

55. And He it is Who has created man from water, and has made for him kindred by descent and kindred by marriage; and thy Lord is All-Powerful.

وَهُوَ الَّذِيْ خَلَقَ مِنَ الْمَآءِ بَشَرًا فَجَعَلَهٗ نَسَبًا
وَّصِهْرًا ۗ وَكَانَ رَبُّكَ قَدِيْرًا ﴿٥٥﴾

* 56. And they worship beside Allah that which can do them no good nor harm them. And the disbeliever is a helper of Satan against his Lord.

وَيَعْبُدُوْنَ مِنْ دُوْنِ اللّٰهِ مَا لَا يَنْفَعُهُمْ وَلَا
يَضُرُّهُمْ ۗ وَكَانَ الْكَافِرُ عَلٰى رَبِّهٖ ظَهِيْرًا ﴿٥٦﴾

57. And We have not sent thee but as a bearer of glad tidings and a Warner.

وَمَآ اَرْسَلْنٰكَ اِلَّا مُبَشِّرًا وَّنَذِيْرًا ﴿٥٧﴾

58. Say, 'I ask of you no recompense for it, save that whoso chooses may take a way unto his Lord.'

قُلْ مَآ اَسْـَٔلُكُمْ عَلَيْهِ مِنْ اَجْرٍ اِلَّا مَنْ شَآءَ اَنْ
يَّتَّخِذَ اِلٰى رَبِّهٖ سَبِيْلًا ﴿٥٨﴾

59. And trust thou in the Living One, Who dies not, and glorify *Him* with His praise. And sufficient is He as the Knower of the sins of His servants,

وَتَوَكَّلْ عَلَى الْحَيِّ الَّذِيْ لَا يَمُوْتُ وَسَبِّحْ بِحَمْدِهٖ ۗ
وَكَفٰى بِهٖ بِذُنُوْبِ عِبَادِهٖ خَبِيْرًا ﴿٥٩﴾

* 60. He Who created the heavens and the earth and all that is between them in six periods, then He settled Himself on the Throne. The Gracious *God!* Ask thou then concerning Him one who knows.

اۨلَّذِيْ خَلَقَ السَّمٰوٰتِ وَالْاَرْضَ وَمَا بَيْنَهُمَا فِيْ سِتَّةِ
اَيَّامٍ ثُمَّ اسْتَوٰى عَلَى الْعَرْشِ ۛۚ اَلرَّحْمٰنُ فَسْـَٔلْ بِهٖ
خَبِيْرًا ﴿٦٠﴾

61. And when it is said to them, 'Submit to the Gracious *God*,' they say, 'And who is the Gracious *God?* Shall we submit to whatever thou biddest us?' And it increases their aversion.

وَاِذَا قِيْلَ لَهُمُ اسْجُدُوْا لِلرَّحْمٰنِ قَالُوْا وَمَا الرَّحْمٰنُ ق
اَنَسْجُدُ لِمَا تَاْمُرُنَا وَزَادَهُمْ نُفُوْرًا ﴿٦١﴾ السجدة

R. 6.

* 62. Blessed is He Who has made mansions in the heaven and has placed there-

تَبٰرَكَ الَّذِيْ جَعَلَ فِي السَّمَآءِ بُرُوْجًا وَّجَعَلَ فِيْهَا

in a Lamp and a Moon giving light.

سِرٰجًا وَّقَمَرًا مُّنِيْرًا ﴿٦٢﴾

63. And He it is Who has made the night and the day, each following the other, for him who desires to remember, or desires to be grateful.

وَهُوَ الَّذِيْ جَعَلَ الَّيْلَ وَالنَّهَارَ خِلْفَةً لِّمَنْ اَرَادَ
اَنْ يَّذَّكَّرَ اَوْ اَرَادَ شُكُوْرًا ﴿٦٣﴾

64. And the servants of the Gracious *God* are those who walk on the earth in a dignified manner, and when the ignorant address them, they say, 'Peace!'

وَعِبَادُ الرَّحْمٰنِ الَّذِيْنَ يَمْشُوْنَ عَلَى الْاَرْضِ هَوْنًا
وَّاِذَا خَاطَبَهُمُ الْجٰهِلُوْنَ قَالُوْا سَلٰمًا ﴿٦٤﴾

65. And who spend the night before their Lord, prostrate and standing,

وَالَّذِيْنَ يَبِيْتُوْنَ لِرَبِّهِمْ سُجَّدًا وَّقِيَامًا ﴿٦٥﴾

66. And who say, 'Our Lord, avert from us the punishment of Hell; for the punishment thereof is a lasting torment.

وَالَّذِيْنَ يَقُوْلُوْنَ رَبَّنَا اصْرِفْ عَنَّا عَذَابَ جَهَنَّمَ
اِنَّ عَذَابَهَا كَانَ غَرَامًا ﴿٦٦﴾

67. 'It is indeed evil as a place of rest and as an abode;'

اِنَّهَا سَآءَتْ مُسْتَقَرًّا وَّمُقَامًا ﴿٦٧﴾

68. And those who, when they spend, are neither extravagant nor niggardly but moderate between the two;

وَالَّذِيْنَ اِذَآ اَنْفَقُوْا لَمْ يُسْرِفُوْا وَلَمْ يَقْتُرُوْا وَكَانَ
بَيْنَ ذٰلِكَ قَوَامًا ﴿٦٨﴾

* 69. And those who call not on any other God along with Allah, nor kill a person that Allah has forbidden except for just cause, nor commit adultery (or fornication), and he who does that shall meet with the punishment of sin.

وَالَّذِيْنَ لَا يَدْعُوْنَ مَعَ اللّٰهِ اِلٰهًا اٰخَرَ وَلَا يَقْتُلُوْنَ
النَّفْسَ الَّتِيْ حَرَّمَ اللّٰهُ اِلَّا بِالْحَقِّ وَلَا يَزْنُوْنَ
وَمَنْ يَّفْعَلْ ذٰلِكَ يَلْقَ اَثَامًا ﴿٦٩﴾

70. Doubled to him will be the punishment on the Day of Resurrection, and he will abide therein disgraced,

يُّضٰعَفْ لَهُ الْعَذَابُ يَوْمَ الْقِيٰمَةِ وَيَخْلُدْ فِيْهٖ
مُهَانًا ﴿٧٠﴾

71. Except those who repent, and believe and do good deeds; for as to these, Allah will change their evil deeds into good deeds; and Allah is Most Forgiving, Merciful;

اِلَّا مَنْ تَابَ وَاٰمَنَ وَعَمِلَ عَمَلًا صَالِحًا فَاُولٰٓئِكَ
يُبَدِّلُ اللّٰهُ سَيِّاٰتِهِمْ حَسَنٰتٍ وَكَانَ اللّٰهُ غَفُوْرًا
رَّحِيْمًا ﴿٧١﴾

72. And those who repent and do good *deeds*, indeed turn to Allah with *true* repentance;

وَمَنْ تَابَ وَعَمِلَ صَالِحًا فَاِنَّهٗ يَتُوْبُ اِلَى اللّٰهِ
مَتَابًا ﴿٧٢﴾

73. And those who bear not false witness, and when they pass by anything vain,

وَالَّذِيْنَ لَا يَشْهَدُوْنَ الزُّوْرَ وَاِذَا مَرُّوْا بِاللَّغْوِ

they pass on with dignity;

مَرُّوْا كِرَامًا ﴿٧٣﴾

74. And those who, when they are reminded of the Signs of their Lord, fall not deaf and blind thereat;

وَالَّذِيْنَ اِذَا ذُكِّرُوْا بِاٰيٰتِ رَبِّهِمْ لَمْ يَخِرُّوْا عَلَيْهَا
صُمًّا وَّعُمْيَانًا ﴿٧٤﴾

* 75. And those who say, 'Our Lord, grant us of our wives and children the delight of *our* eyes, and make us a model for the righteous.'

وَالَّذِيْنَ يَقُوْلُوْنَ رَبَّنَا هَبْ لَنَا مِنْ اَزْوَاجِنَا وَ
ذُرِّيّٰتِنَا قُرَّةَ اَعْيُنٍ وَّاجْعَلْنَا لِلْمُتَّقِيْنَ اِمَامًا ﴿٧٥﴾

* 76. It is such as will be rewarded a high place *in Paradise* because they were steadfast, and they will be received therein with greeting and peace,

اُولٰٓئِكَ يُجْزَوْنَ الْغُرْفَةَ بِمَا صَبَرُوْا وَيُلَقَّوْنَ فِيْهَا
تَحِيَّةً وَّسَلٰمًا ﴿٧٦﴾

77. Abiding therein. Excellent it is as a place of rest and as an abode.

خٰلِدِيْنَ فِيْهَا حَسُنَتْ مُسْتَقَرًّا وَّمُقَامًا ﴿٧٧﴾

78. Say *to the disbelievers:* 'But for your prayer *to Him* my Lord would not care for you. You have indeed rejected *the truth,* and *the punishment of your rejection* will now cleave *to you.*'

قُلْ مَا يَعْبَؤُا بِكُمْ رَبِّيْ لَوْلَا دُعَآؤُكُمْ فَقَدْ
كَذَّبْتُمْ فَسَوْفَ يَكُوْنُ لِزَامًا ﴿٧٨﴾

آياتها ٢٢٨ (٢٦) سُورَةُ الشُّعَرَآءِ مَكِّيَّةٌ ركوعاتها ١١

AL-SHU'ARĀ'

(Revealed before Hijra)

المنزل ٥

1. In the name of Allah, the Gracious, the Merciful.

بِسْمِ اللّٰهِ الرَّحْمٰنِ الرَّحِيْمِ ﴿١﴾

2. Ṭā Sīn Mīm *

طٰسٓمّٓ ﴿٢﴾

3. These are verses of the clear Book.

تِلْكَ اٰيٰتُ الْكِتٰبِ الْمُبِيْنِ ﴿٣﴾

4. Haply thou wilt grieve thyself to death because they believe not.

لَعَلَّكَ بَاخِعٌ نَّفْسَكَ اَلَّا يَكُوْنُوْا مُؤْمِنِيْنَ ﴿٤﴾

5. If We please, We can send down to them a Sign from the heaven, so that their necks will bow down before it.

اِنْ نَّشَاْ نُنَزِّلْ عَلَيْهِمْ مِّنَ السَّمَآءِ اٰيَةً فَظَلَّتْ
اَعْنَاقُهُمْ لَهَا خٰضِعِيْنَ ﴿٥﴾

6. And there comes not to them a new Reminder from the Gracious *God*, but they turn away from it.

وَ مَا يَاْتِيْهِمْ مِّنْ ذِكْرٍ مِّنَ الرَّحْمٰنِ مُحْدَثٍ اِلَّا
كَانُوْا عَنْهُ مُعْرِضِيْنَ ﴿٦﴾

7. They have, indeed, treated *it* as a lie, but soon there will come to them the tidings of that at which they mocked.

فَقَدْ كَذَّبُوْا فَسَيَاْتِيْهِمْ اَنْۢبٰٓؤُا مَا كَانُوْا بِهٖ يَسْتَهْزِءُوْنَ ﴿٧﴾

8. Have they not looked at the earth, how many of every noble species have We caused to grow therein?

اَوَلَمْ يَرَوْا اِلَى الْاَرْضِ كَمْ اَنْۢبَتْنَا فِيْهَا مِنْ كُلِّ زَوْجٍ
كَرِيْمٍ ﴿٨﴾

9. In that there is a Sign indeed; but most of these would not believe.

اِنَّ فِيْ ذٰلِكَ لَاٰيَةً ؕ وَمَا كَانَ اَكْثَرُهُمْ مُّؤْمِنِيْنَ ﴿٩﴾

10. And verily, thy Lord-He is the Mighty, the Merciful.

وَ اِنَّ رَبَّكَ لَهُوَ الْعَزِيْزُ الرَّحِيْمُ ﴿١٠﴾ ع

R. 2.

11. And *remember* when thy Lord called Moses, *saying*, 'Go to the wrongdoing people—

وَ اِذْ نَادٰى رَبُّكَ مُوْسٰۤى اَنِ ائْتِ الْقَوْمَ الظّٰلِمِيْنَ ﴿١١﴾

12. 'The people of Pharaoh. Will they not fear God?'

قَوْمَ فِرْعَوْنَ ؕ اَلَا يَتَّقُوْنَ ﴿١٢﴾

13. He said, 'My Lord, I fear that they will treat me as a liar;

قَالَ رَبِّ اِنِّيْۤ اَخَافُ اَنْ يُّكَذِّبُوْنِ ﴿١٣﴾

14. 'And my breast is straitened and my tongue is not fluent; therefore, send *word* to Aaron.

وَ يَضِيْقُ صَدْرِيْ وَ لَا يَنْطَلِقُ لِسَانِيْ فَاَرْسِلْ اِلٰى
هٰرُوْنَ ﴿١٤﴾

* 15. 'And they have a charge against me, so I fear that they may kill me.'

وَ لَهُمْ عَلَيَّ ذَنْۢبٌ فَاَخَافُ اَنْ يَّقْتُلُوْنِ ﴿١٥﴾

16. *God* said, "Not so, go then, both of you, with Our Signs; We are with you *and* We hear.

قَالَ كَلَّا ۚ فَاذْهَبَا بِاٰيٰتِنَاۤ اِنَّا مَعَكُمْ مُّسْتَمِعُوْنَ ﴿١٦﴾

* Benignant, All-Hearing, All-Knowing God!

17. "So go to Pharaoh, and say, 'We are the Messengers of the Lord of the worlds,

فَأْتِيَا فِرْعَوْنَ فَقُولَا إِنَّا رَسُولُ رَبِّ الْعٰلَمِينَ ﴿١٧﴾

18. '*To tell thee to* send the children of Israel with us.' "

أَنْ أَرْسِلْ مَعَنَا بَنِي إِسْرَاءِيلَ ﴿١٨﴾

19. *Pharaoh* said, 'Did we not bring thee up among us as a child? And thou didst stay among us *many* years of thy life.

قَالَ أَلَمْ نُرَبِّكَ فِينَا وَلِيدًا وَلَبِثْتَ فِينَا مِنْ
عُمُرِكَ سِنِينَ ﴿١٩﴾

20. 'And thou didst do thy deed which thou didst, and thou art of the ungrateful.'

وَفَعَلْتَ فَعْلَتَكَ الَّتِي فَعَلْتَ وَأَنْتَ مِنَ الْكٰفِرِينَ ﴿٢٠﴾

21. *Moses* said, 'I did do it then, and I was *one* of the erring.

قَالَ فَعَلْتُهَا إِذًا وَأَنَا مِنَ الضَّالِّينَ ﴿٢١﴾

* 22. 'So I fled from you when I feared you; then my Lord granted me *right* judgment and made me *one* of the Messengers.

فَفَرَرْتُ مِنْكُمْ لَمَّا خِفْتُكُمْ فَوَهَبَ لِي رَبِّي حُكْمًا
وَجَعَلَنِي مِنَ الْمُرْسَلِينَ ﴿٢٢﴾

23. 'And this is the favour for which thou tauntest me; that thou hast enslaved the children of Israel.'

وَتِلْكَ نِعْمَةٌ تَمُنُّهَا عَلَيَّ أَنْ عَبَّدْتَ بَنِي إِسْرَاءِيلَ ﴿٢٣﴾

24. Pharaoh said, 'And what is the Lord of the worlds?'

قَالَ فِرْعَوْنُ وَمَا رَبُّ الْعٰلَمِينَ ﴿٢٤﴾

25. *Moses* said, 'The Lord of the heavens and the earth and of all that is between the two, if you would be convinced.'

قَالَ رَبُّ السَّمٰوٰتِ وَالْأَرْضِ وَمَا بَيْنَهُمَا إِنْ كُنْتُمْ
مُوقِنِينَ ﴿٢٥﴾

26. *Pharaoh* said to those around him, 'Do you not hear?'

قَالَ لِمَنْ حَوْلَهُ أَلَا تَسْتَمِعُونَ ﴿٢٦﴾

27. *Moses* said, 'Your Lord, and the Lord of your fathers of yore.'

قَالَ رَبُّكُمْ وَرَبُّ آبَائِكُمُ الْأَوَّلِينَ ﴿٢٧﴾

28. *Pharaoh* said, 'Most surely this Messenger of yours who has been sent to you is a madman.'

قَالَ إِنَّ رَسُولَكُمُ الَّذِي أُرْسِلَ إِلَيْكُمْ لَمَجْنُونٌ ﴿٢٨﴾

29. *Moses* said, 'The Lord of the East and of the West, and of all that is between the two, if you did but understand.'

قَالَ رَبُّ الْمَشْرِقِ وَالْمَغْرِبِ وَمَا بَيْنَهُمَا إِنْ كُنْتُمْ
تَعْقِلُونَ ﴿٢٩﴾

30. *Pharaoh* said, 'If thou takest a God other than me, I will certainly put thee into prison.'

قَالَ لَئِنِ اتَّخَذْتَ إِلٰهًا غَيْرِي لَأَجْعَلَنَّكَ مِنَ
الْمَسْجُونِينَ ﴿٣٠﴾

31. *Moses* said, 'What, even though I bring thee something that is manifest!'

قَالَ أَوَلَوْ جِئْتُكَ بِشَيْءٍ مُبِينٍ ﴿٣١﴾

32. *Pharaoh* said, 'Bring it then, if thou speakest the truth.'

قَالَ فَأْتِ بِهِ إِنْ كُنْتَ مِنَ الصّٰدِقِينَ ﴿٣٢﴾

33. So he threw down his rod, and behold! it was a serpent plainly visible.

فَأَلْقَىٰ عَصَاهُ فَإِذَا هِيَ ثُعْبَانٌ مُبِينٌ ﴿٣٣﴾

34. And he drew forth his hand, and lo! it was white for the beholders.

وَنَزَعَ يَدَهٗ فَاِذَا هِيَ بَيْضَآءُ لِلنّٰظِرِيْنَ ۝٣٤

R. 3.

35. *Pharaoh* said to the chiefs around him, 'This is surely a skilful magician.

قَالَ لِلْمَلَاِ حَوْلَهٗٓ اِنَّ هٰذَا لَسٰحِرٌ عَلِيْمٌ ۝٣٥

36. 'He seeks to turn you out of your land by his magic. Now what do you advise?'

يُّرِيْدُ اَنْ يُّخْرِجَكُمْ مِّنْ اَرْضِكُمْ بِسِحْرِهٖ ۖ فَمَاذَا
تَاْمُرُوْنَ ۝٣٦

37. They said, 'Put him off and his brother *awhile* and send into the cities summoners,

قَالُوْٓا اَرْجِهْ وَاَخَاهُ وَابْعَثْ فِي الْمَدَآئِنِ حٰشِرِيْنَ ۝٣٧

38. 'Who should bring thee every skilful sorcerer.'

يَاْتُوْكَ بِكُلِّ سَحَّارٍ عَلِيْمٍ ۝٣٨

39. So the magicians were assembled together at the appointed time on a fixed day.

فَجُمِعَ السَّحَرَةُ لِمِيْقَاتِ يَوْمٍ مَّعْلُوْمٍ ۝٣٩

40. And it was said to the people, 'Will you *also* gather together,

وَّقِيْلَ لِلنَّاسِ هَلْ اَنْتُمْ مُّجْتَمِعُوْنَ ۝٤٠

41. 'So that we may follow the magicians if they are the winners?'

لَعَلَّنَا نَتَّبِعُ السَّحَرَةَ اِنْ كَانُوْا هُمُ الْغٰلِبِيْنَ ۝٤١

42. And, when the magicians came, they said to Pharaoh, 'Shall we have a reward if we are the winners?'

فَلَمَّا جَآءَ السَّحَرَةُ قَالُوْا لِفِرْعَوْنَ اَئِنَّ لَنَا لَاَجْرًا
اِنْ كُنَّا نَحْنُ الْغٰلِبِيْنَ ۝٤٢

* 43. He said, 'Yes, and surely then you will be among those who are near *my person*.'

قَالَ نَعَمْ وَاِنَّكُمْ اِذًا لَّمِنَ الْمُقَرَّبِيْنَ ۝٤٣

44. Moses said to them, '*Now* throw ye what you have to throw.'

قَالَ لَهُمْ مُّوْسٰٓى اَلْقُوْا مَآ اَنْتُمْ مُّلْقُوْنَ ۝٤٤

45. So they threw down their ropes and their rods, and said, 'By Pharaoh's honour, it is we who will surely win.'

فَاَلْقَوْا حِبَالَهُمْ وَعِصِيَّهُمْ وَقَالُوْا بِعِزَّةِ فِرْعَوْنَ
اِنَّا لَنَحْنُ الْغٰلِبُوْنَ ۝٤٥

46. Then Moses threw down his rod, and lo! it swallowed up that which they had fabricated.

فَاَلْقٰى مُوْسٰى عَصَاهُ فَاِذَا هِيَ تَلْقَفُ مَا يَاْفِكُوْنَ ۝٤٦

47. Thereupon the magicians were impelled to fall down prostrate.

فَاُلْقِيَ السَّحَرَةُ سٰجِدِيْنَ ۝٤٧

48. They said, 'We believe in the Lord of the worlds,

قَالُوْٓا اٰمَنَّا بِرَبِّ الْعٰلَمِيْنَ ۝٤٨

49. 'The Lord of Moses, and of Aaron.'

رَبِّ مُوْسٰى وَهٰرُوْنَ ۝٤٩

50. *Pharaoh* said, 'You have believed in him before I gave you leave? He is surely your chief who has taught you magic. But you shall know *the consequences thereof*. I will most surely cut off your hands and your feet on alternate sides,

قَالَ اٰمَنْتُمْ لَهٗ قَبْلَ اَنْ اٰذَنَ لَكُمْ ۚ اِنَّهٗ لَكَبِيْرُكُمُ
الَّذِيْ عَلَّمَكُمُ السِّحْرَ ۚ فَلَسَوْفَ تَعْلَمُوْنَ ۥ لَاُقَطِّعَنَّ
اَيْدِيَكُمْ وَاَرْجُلَكُمْ مِّنْ خِلَافٍ وَّلَاُوصَلِّبَنَّكُمْ

and I will most surely crucify you all.'

أَجْمَعِينَ ﴿٥٠﴾

51. They said, 'There is no harm; to our Lord shall we return.

قَالُوا لَا ضَيْرَ إِنَّا إِلَىٰ رَبِّنَا مُنْقَلِبُونَ ﴿٥١﴾

52. 'We do hope that our Lord will forgive us our sins, since we are the first among the believers.'

إِنَّا نَطْمَعُ أَنْ يَغْفِرَ لَنَا رَبُّنَا خَطَايَانَا أَنْ كُنَّا أَوَّلَ الْمُؤْمِنِينَ ﴿٥٢﴾

R. 4.

53. And We revealed to Moses, *saying*, 'Take away My servants by night, you will surely be pursued.'

وَأَوْحَيْنَا إِلَىٰ مُوسَىٰ أَنْ أَسْرِ بِعِبَادِي إِنَّكُمْ مُتَّبَعُونَ ﴿٥٣﴾

54. And Pharaoh sent summoners into the cities, *saying*,

فَأَرْسَلَ فِرْعَوْنُ فِي الْمَدَائِنِ حَاشِرِينَ ﴿٥٤﴾

55. 'These are a small party,

إِنَّ هَٰؤُلَاءِ لَشِرْذِمَةٌ قَلِيلُونَ ﴿٥٥﴾

56. 'And they have offended us;

وَإِنَّهُمْ لَنَا لَغَائِظُونَ ﴿٥٦﴾

57. 'And we are a multitude *fully prepared and* vigilant.'

وَإِنَّا لَجَمِيعٌ حَاذِرُونَ ﴿٥٧﴾

58. So We turned them out of gardens, and springs,

فَأَخْرَجْنَاهُمْ مِنْ جَنَّاتٍ وَعُيُونٍ ﴿٥٨﴾

59. And treasures, and an abode of honour.

وَكُنُوزٍ وَمَقَامٍ كَرِيمٍ ﴿٥٩﴾

60. Thus *indeed it was;* and We gave them as heritage to the children of Israel—

كَذَٰلِكَ وَأَوْرَثْنَاهَا بَنِي إِسْرَائِيلَ ﴿٦٠﴾

61. And they pursued and overtook them at sunrise.

فَأَتْبَعُوهُمْ مُشْرِقِينَ ﴿٦١﴾

62. And when the two hosts came in sight of each other the companions of Moses said, 'We are surely overtaken.'

فَلَمَّا تَرَاءَى الْجَمْعَانِ قَالَ أَصْحَابُ مُوسَىٰ إِنَّا لَمُدْرَكُونَ ﴿٦٢﴾

63. 'Nay, *speak not thus!*' said he, 'My Lord is with me. He will direct me aright.'

قَالَ كَلَّا إِنَّ مَعِيَ رَبِّي سَيَهْدِينِ ﴿٦٣﴾

64. Then We revealed to Moses, *saying*, 'Strike the sea with thy rod.' Thereupon it parted, and every part *looked* like a huge mountain.

فَأَوْحَيْنَا إِلَىٰ مُوسَىٰ أَنِ اضْرِبْ بِعَصَاكَ الْبَحْرَ
فَانْفَلَقَ فَكَانَ كُلُّ فِرْقٍ كَالطَّوْدِ الْعَظِيمِ ﴿٦٤﴾

* 65. And We made others approach that place.

وَأَزْلَفْنَا ثَمَّ الْآخَرِينَ ﴿٦٥﴾

66. And We saved Moses and those who were with him.

وَأَنْجَيْنَا مُوسَىٰ وَمَنْ مَعَهُ أَجْمَعِينَ ﴿٦٦﴾

67. Then We drowned the others.

ثُمَّ أَغْرَقْنَا الْآخَرِينَ ﴿٦٧﴾

68. In this, verily, there is a Sign; but most of these would not believe.

إِنَّ فِي ذَٰلِكَ لَآيَةً وَمَا كَانَ أَكْثَرُهُمْ مُؤْمِنِينَ ﴿٦٨﴾

69. And surely thy Lord—He is the Mighty, the Merciful.

وَإِنَّ رَبَّكَ لَهُوَ الْعَزِيزُ الرَّحِيمُ ﴿٦٩﴾

R. 5.

70. And recite unto them the story of Abraham.

وَاتْلُ عَلَيْهِمْ نَبَاَ اِبْرٰهِيْمَ ﴿٧٠﴾ لازم

71. When he said to his father and his people, 'What do you worship?'

اِذْ قَالَ لِاَبِيْهِ وَقَوْمِهٖ مَا تَعْبُدُوْنَ ﴿٧١﴾

72. They said, 'We worship idols, and we continue to be devoted to them.'

قَالُوْا نَعْبُدُ اَصْنَامًا فَنَظَلُّ لَهَا عٰكِفِيْنَ ﴿٧٢﴾

* 73. He said, 'Can they listen to you when you call *on them?*

قَالَ هَلْ يَسْمَعُوْنَكُمْ اِذْ تَدْعُوْنَ ﴿٧٣﴾

74. 'Or do you good or harm *you?*'

اَوْ يَنْفَعُوْنَكُمْ اَوْ يَضُرُّوْنَ ﴿٧٤﴾

75. They said, 'Nay, but we found our fathers doing likewise.'

قَالُوْا بَلْ وَجَدْنَآ اٰبَآءَنَا كَذٰلِكَ يَفْعَلُوْنَ ﴿٧٥﴾

76. He said, 'What think ye of that which you have been worshipping—

قَالَ اَفَرَءَيْتُمْ مَّا كُنْتُمْ تَعْبُدُوْنَ ﴿٧٦﴾

77. 'You and your fathers before *you.*

اَنْتُمْ وَاٰبَآؤُكُمُ الْاَقْدَمُوْنَ ﴿٧٧﴾

78. 'They are *all* enemies to me, except the Lord of the worlds;

فَاِنَّهُمْ عَدُوٌّ لِّيْٓ اِلَّا رَبَّ الْعٰلَمِيْنَ ﴿٧٨﴾

79. 'Who has created me, and it is He Who guides me;

الَّذِيْ خَلَقَنِيْ فَهُوَ يَهْدِيْنِ ﴿٧٩﴾

* 80. 'And Who gives me food and gives me drink;

وَالَّذِيْ هُوَ يُطْعِمُنِيْ وَيَسْقِيْنِ ﴿٨٠﴾

81. 'And when I am ill, it is He Who restores me to health;

وَاِذَا مَرِضْتُ فَهُوَ يَشْفِيْنِ ﴿٨١﴾

82. 'And Who will cause me to die, and then bring me to life *again*;

وَالَّذِيْ يُمِيْتُنِيْ ثُمَّ يُحْيِيْنِ ﴿٨٢﴾

83. 'And Who, I hope, will forgive me my faults on the Day of Judgment.

وَالَّذِيْٓ اَطْمَعُ اَنْ يَّغْفِرَ لِيْ خَطِيْٓئَتِيْ يَوْمَ الدِّيْنِ ﴿٨٣﴾

84. 'My Lord, bestow wisdom on me and join me with the righteous;

رَبِّ هَبْ لِيْ حُكْمًا وَّاَلْحِقْنِيْ بِالصّٰلِحِيْنَ ﴿٨٤﴾

85. 'And give me a true reputation among posterity;

وَاجْعَلْ لِّيْ لِسَانَ صِدْقٍ فِي الْاٰخِرِيْنَ ﴿٨٥﴾

86. 'And make me *one* of the inheritors of the Garden of Bliss;

وَاجْعَلْنِيْ مِنْ وَّرَثَةِ جَنَّةِ النَّعِيْمِ ﴿٨٦﴾

87. 'And forgive my father; for he is *one* of the erring;

وَاغْفِرْ لِاَبِيْٓ اِنَّهٗ كَانَ مِنَ الضَّآلِّيْنَ ﴿٨٧﴾

88. 'And disgrace me not on the day when they will be raised up,

وَلَا تُخْزِنِيْ يَوْمَ يُبْعَثُوْنَ ﴿٨٨﴾

89. 'The day when wealth and sons shall not avail;

يَوْمَ لَا يَنْفَعُ مَالٌ وَّلَا بَنُوْنَ ﴿٨٩﴾

* 90. 'But he *alone will be saved* who brings to Allah a sound heart;'

اِلَّا مَنْ اَتَى اللّٰهَ بِقَلْبٍ سَلِيْمٍ ﴿٩٠﴾

91. And Heaven shall be brought near to the righteous.

وَاُزْلِفَتِ الْجَنَّةُ لِلْمُتَّقِيْنَ ﴿٩١﴾

* 92. And Hell shall be opened to those who have gone astray.

وَبُرِّزَتِ الْجَحِيْمُ لِلْغٰوِيْنَ ﴿٩٢﴾

93. And it will be said to them, 'Where is that which you worshipped

وَقِيْلَ لَهُمْ اَيْنَمَا كُنْتُمْ تَعْبُدُوْنَ ﴿٩٣﴾

94. 'Beside Allah? Can they help you or get help *for themselves?*'

مِنْ دُوْنِ اللّٰهِ هَلْ يَنْصُرُوْنَكُمْ اَوْ يَنْتَصِرُوْنَ ﴿٩٤﴾

95. Then will they be thrown headlong therein, they and those who have gone astray,

فَكُبْكِبُوْا فِيْهَا هُمْ وَالْغَاوٗنَ ﴿٩٥﴾

96. And the hosts of Iblīs, all together.

وَجُنُوْدُ اِبْلِيْسَ اَجْمَعُوْنَ ﴿٩٦﴾

97. They will say, whilst they dispute between themselves therein:

قَالُوْا وَهُمْ فِيْهَا يَخْتَصِمُوْنَ ﴿٩٧﴾

98. 'By Allah, we were in manifest error,

تَاللّٰهِ اِنْ كُنَّا لَفِيْ ضَلٰلٍ مُّبِيْنٍ ﴿٩٨﴾

99. 'When we held you as equal with the Lord of the worlds;

اِذْ نُسَوِّيْكُمْ بِرَبِّ الْعٰلَمِيْنَ ﴿٩٩﴾

100. 'And none led us astray but the guilty ones.

وَمَآ اَضَلَّنَآ اِلَّا الْمُجْرِمُوْنَ ﴿١٠٠﴾

101. 'And now we have no intercessors,

فَمَا لَنَا مِنْ شَافِعِيْنَ ﴿١٠١﴾

102. 'Nor any loving friend.

وَلَا صَدِيْقٍ حَمِيْمٍ ﴿١٠٢﴾

103. 'Would that there were for us a return *to the world*, that we might be among the believers!'

فَلَوْ اَنَّ لَنَا كَرَّةً فَنَكُوْنَ مِنَ الْمُؤْمِنِيْنَ ﴿١٠٣﴾

104. In this, verily, there is a Sign, but most of these would not believe.

اِنَّ فِيْ ذٰلِكَ لَاٰيَةً ؕ وَمَا كَانَ اَكْثَرُهُمْ مُّؤْمِنِيْنَ ﴿١٠٤﴾

105. And verily thy Lord — He is the Mighty, the Merciful.

وَاِنَّ رَبَّكَ لَهُوَ الْعَزِيْزُ الرَّحِيْمُ ﴿١٠٥﴾ ع

R. 6.

106. The people of Noah treated the Messengers as liars,

كَذَّبَتْ قَوْمُ نُوْحِ ٟالْمُرْسَلِيْنَ ﴿١٠٦﴾

107. When their brother Noah said to them, 'Will you not be righteous?

اِذْ قَالَ لَهُمْ اَخُوْهُمْ نُوْحٌ اَلَا تَتَّقُوْنَ ﴿١٠٧﴾

108. 'Surely, I am unto you a Messenger, faithful to *my* trust.

اِنِّيْ لَكُمْ رَسُوْلٌ اَمِيْنٌ ﴿١٠٨﴾

109. 'So fear Allah, and obey me.

فَاتَّقُوا اللّٰهَ وَاَطِيْعُوْنِ ﴿١٠٩﴾

110. 'And I ask of you no reward for it. My reward is only with the Lord of the worlds.

وَمَآ اَسْـَٔلُكُمْ عَلَيْهِ مِنْ اَجْرٍ ۚ اِنْ اَجْرِيَ اِلَّا عَلٰى
رَبِّ الْعٰلَمِيْنَ ﴿١١٠﴾

111. 'So fear Allah, and obey me.'

فَاتَّقُوا اللّٰهَ وَاَطِيْعُوْنِ ﴿١١١﴾

112. They said, 'Shall we believe thee, when it is the meanest that follow thee?'

قَالُوْٓا اَنُؤْمِنُ لَكَ وَاتَّبَعَكَ الْاَرْذَلُوْنَ ﴿١١٢﴾

قَالَ وَمَا عِلۡمِیۡ بِمَا کَانُوۡا یَعۡمَلُوۡنَ ۚ﴿۱۱۳﴾

113. He said, 'And what knowledge have I as to what they have been doing?

اِنۡ حِسَابُهُمۡ اِلَّا عَلٰی رَبِّیۡ لَوۡ تَشۡعُرُوۡنَ ۚ﴿۱۱۴﴾

114. 'Their account is only with my Lord, if you only knew!

وَمَاۤ اَنَا بِطَارِدِ الۡمُؤۡمِنِیۡنَ ۚ﴿۱۱۵﴾

115. 'And I am not going to drive away the believers.

اِنۡ اَنَا اِلَّا نَذِیۡرٌ مُّبِیۡنٌ ؕ﴿۱۱۶﴾

116. 'I am only a plain Warner.'

قَالُوۡا لَئِنۡ لَّمۡ تَنۡتَهِ یٰنُوۡحُ لَتَکُوۡنَنَّ مِنَ الۡمَرۡجُوۡمِیۡنَ ؕ﴿۱۱۷﴾

117. They said, 'If thou desist not, O Noah, thou shalt surely be one of those who are stoned.'

قَالَ رَبِّ اِنَّ قَوۡمِیۡ کَذَّبُوۡنِ ۚۖ﴿۱۱۸﴾ النصف

118. He said, 'My Lord, my people have treated me as a liar.

فَافۡتَحۡ بَیۡنِیۡ وَبَیۡنَهُمۡ فَتۡحًا وَّنَجِّنِیۡ وَمَنۡ مَّعِیَ مِنَ
الۡمُؤۡمِنِیۡنَ ﴿۱۱۹﴾

119. 'Therefore judge Thou decisively between me and them; and save me and the believers that are with me.'

فَاَنۡجَیۡنٰهُ وَمَنۡ مَّعَهٗ فِی الۡفُلۡکِ الۡمَشۡحُوۡنِ ۚ﴿۱۲۰﴾

120. So We saved him, and those who were with him in the fully laden Ark.

ثُمَّ اَغۡرَقۡنَا بَعۡدُ الۡبٰقِیۡنَ ؕ﴿۱۲۱﴾

121. Then We drowned thereafter those who remained behind.

اِنَّ فِیۡ ذٰلِکَ لَاٰیَةً ؕ وَمَا کَانَ اَکۡثَرُهُمۡ مُّؤۡمِنِیۡنَ ﴿۱۲۲﴾

122. In this, verily, there is a Sign, but most of them would not believe.

وَاِنَّ رَبَّکَ لَهُوَ الۡعَزِیۡزُ الرَّحِیۡمُ ﴿۱۲۳﴾ ع

123. And verily thy Lord — He is the Mighty, the Merciful.

R. 7.

کَذَّبَتۡ عَادُ ۣالۡمُرۡسَلِیۡنَ ۚۖ﴿۱۲۴﴾

124. *The tribe of* 'Ād rejected the Messengers,

اِذۡ قَالَ لَهُمۡ اَخُوۡهُمۡ هُوۡدٌ اَلَا تَتَّقُوۡنَ ۚ﴿۱۲۵﴾

125. When their brother Hūd said to them, 'Will you not be righteous?

اِنِّیۡ لَکُمۡ رَسُوۡلٌ اَمِیۡنٌ ۙ﴿۱۲۶﴾

* 126. 'Surely, I am unto you a Messenger, faithful to *my* trust.

فَاتَّقُوا اللّٰهَ وَاَطِیۡعُوۡنِ ۚ﴿۱۲۷﴾

127. 'So fear Allah, and obey me.

وَمَاۤ اَسۡـَٔلُکُمۡ عَلَیۡهِ مِنۡ اَجۡرٍ ۚ اِنۡ اَجۡرِیَ اِلَّا عَلٰی
رَبِّ الۡعٰلَمِیۡنَ ؕ﴿۱۲۸﴾

128. 'And I ask of you no reward for it. My reward is only with the Lord of the worlds.

اَتَبۡنُوۡنَ بِکُلِّ رِیۡعٍ اٰیَةً تَعۡبَثُوۡنَ ۙ﴿۱۲۹﴾

129. 'Do you build monuments on every high place seeking vain glory,

وَتَتَّخِذُوۡنَ مَصَانِعَ لَعَلَّکُمۡ تَخۡلُدُوۡنَ ۚ﴿۱۳۰﴾

* 130. 'And do you erect palaces as though you will live for ever?

وَاِذَا بَطَشۡتُمۡ بَطَشۡتُمۡ جَبَّارِیۡنَ ۚ﴿۱۳۱﴾

131. 'And when you lay hands *upon any one*, you lay hands as tyrants.

فَاتَّقُوا اللّٰهَ وَاَطِیۡعُوۡنِ ۚ﴿۱۳۲﴾

132. 'So fear Allah, and obey me.

133. 'And fear Him Who has helped you with all that you know.

وَاتَّقُوا الَّذِيٓ اَمَدَّكُمْ بِمَا تَعْلَمُوْنَ ﴿۱۳۳﴾

134. 'He has helped you with cattle, and sons,

اَمَدَّكُمْ بِاَنْعَامٍ وَّبَنِيْنَ ﴿۱۳۴﴾

135. 'And gardens, and springs.

وَجَنّٰتٍ وَّعُيُوْنٍ ﴿۱۳۵﴾

* 136. 'Indeed, I fear for you the punishment of an awful day.'

اِنِّيْٓ اَخَافُ عَلَيْكُمْ عَذَابَ يَوْمٍ عَظِيْمٍ ﴿۱۳۶﴾

137. They said, 'It is the same to us whether thou admonish *us* or whether thou be not of those who admonish.'

قَالُوْا سَوَآءٌ عَلَيْنَآ اَوَعَظْتَ اَمْ لَمْ تَكُنْ مِّنَ الْوٰعِظِيْنَ ﴿۱۳۷﴾

138. 'This is nothing but a habit of the ancients,

اِنْ هٰذَآ اِلَّا خُلُقُ الْاَوَّلِيْنَ ﴿۱۳۸﴾

139. And we shall not be punished.'

وَمَا نَحْنُ بِمُعَذَّبِيْنَ ﴿۱۳۹﴾

140. So they rejected him, and We destroyed them. In that indeed there is a Sign, but most of these would not believe.

فَكَذَّبُوْهُ فَاَهْلَكْنٰهُمْ اِنَّ فِيْ ذٰلِكَ لَاٰيَةً وَمَا كَانَ اَكْثَرُهُمْ مُّؤْمِنِيْنَ ﴿۱۴۰﴾

141. And verily thy Lord — He is the Mighty, the Merciful.

وَاِنَّ رَبَّكَ لَهُوَ الْعَزِيْزُ الرَّحِيْمُ ﴿۱۴۱﴾

R. 8.

142. *The tribe of* Thamūd rejected the Messengers,

كَذَّبَتْ ثَمُوْدُ الْمُرْسَلِيْنَ ﴿۱۴۲﴾

143. When their brother Ṣāliḥ said to them, 'Will you not be righteous?

اِذْ قَالَ لَهُمْ اَخُوْهُمْ صٰلِحٌ اَلَا تَتَّقُوْنَ ﴿۱۴۳﴾

* 144. 'Surely, I am unto you a Messenger, faithful to *my* trust.

اِنِّيْ لَكُمْ رَسُوْلٌ اَمِيْنٌ ﴿۱۴۴﴾

145. 'So fear Allah, and obey me.

فَاتَّقُوا اللّٰهَ وَاَطِيْعُوْنِ ﴿۱۴۵﴾

146. 'And I ask of you no reward for it. My reward is only with the Lord of the worlds.

وَمَآ اَسْـَٔلُكُمْ عَلَيْهِ مِنْ اَجْرٍ اِنْ اَجْرِيَ اِلَّا عَلٰى رَبِّ الْعٰلَمِيْنَ ﴿۱۴۶﴾

147. 'Will you be left secure amid the things *that you have* here,

اَتُتْرَكُوْنَ فِيْ مَا هٰهُنَآ اٰمِنِيْنَ ﴿۱۴۷﴾

148. 'Amid gardens and springs,

فِيْ جَنّٰتٍ وَّعُيُوْنٍ ﴿۱۴۸﴾

* 149. 'And cornfields, and date-palms with *heavy* spathes near breaking?

وَّزُرُوْعٍ وَّنَخْلٍ طَلْعُهَا هَضِيْمٌ ﴿۱۴۹﴾

150. 'And you hew out houses in the mountains with great skill.

وَتَنْحِتُوْنَ مِنَ الْجِبَالِ بُيُوْتًا فٰرِهِيْنَ ﴿۱۵۰﴾

151. 'So fear Allah, and obey me.

فَاتَّقُوا اللّٰهَ وَاَطِيْعُوْنِ ﴿۱۵۱﴾

152. 'And obey not the bidding of those who exceed the bounds,

وَلَا تُطِيْعُوْٓا اَمْرَ الْمُسْرِفِيْنَ ﴿۱۵۲﴾

153. 'Who create disorder in the earth, and reform *it* not.'

الَّذِينَ يُفْسِدُونَ فِي الْأَرْضِ وَلَا يُصْلِحُونَ ﴿۱۵۳﴾

154. They said, 'Thou art but *one* of the bewitched;

قَالُوٓا إِنَّمَآ أَنْتَ مِنَ الْمُسَحَّرِينَ ﴿۱۵۴﴾

155. 'Thou art only a man like ourselves. So bring a Sign, if thou art *one* of the truthful.'

مَآ أَنْتَ إِلَّا بَشَرٌ مِّثْلُنَا ۚ فَأْتِ بِاٰيَةٍ إِنْ كُنْتَ
مِنَ الصّٰدِقِينَ ﴿۱۵۵﴾

156. He said, 'Here is a she-camel: she has *her* turn of drinking, and you have *your* turn of drinking on an appointed day.

قَالَ هٰذِهٖ نَاقَةٌ لَّهَا شِرْبٌ وَّلَكُمْ شِرْبُ يَوْمٍ
مَّعْلُومٍ ﴿۱۵۶﴾

* 157. 'And touch her not with evil lest there overtake you the punishment of an awful day.'

وَلَا تَمَسُّوهَا بِسُوٓءٍ فَيَأْخُذَكُمْ عَذَابُ يَوْمٍ عَظِيمٍ ﴿۱۵۷﴾

158. But they hamstrung her; and then they became regretful.

فَعَقَرُوهَا فَأَصْبَحُوا نٰدِمِينَ ﴿۱۵۸﴾

159. So the punishment overtook them. In that verily there is a Sign, but most of these would not believe.

فَأَخَذَهُمُ الْعَذَابُ ۗ إِنَّ فِي ذٰلِكَ لَاٰيَةً ۗ وَمَا كَانَ
أَكْثَرُهُمْ مُّؤْمِنِينَ ﴿۱۵۹﴾

160. And surely thy Lord — He is the Mighty, the Merciful.

وَإِنَّ رَبَّكَ لَهُوَ الْعَزِيزُ الرَّحِيمُ ﴿۱۶۰﴾ ع ۹ ۱۲

R. 9.

161. The people of Lot rejected the Messengers,

كَذَّبَتْ قَوْمُ لُوطِ ٱلْمُرْسَلِينَ ﴿۱۶۱﴾

162. When their brother Lot said to them, 'Will you not become righteous?

إِذْ قَالَ لَهُمْ أَخُوهُمْ لُوطٌ أَلَا تَتَّقُونَ ﴿۱۶۲﴾

* 163. 'Surely, I am unto you a Messenger, faithful to *my* trust.

إِنِّي لَكُمْ رَسُولٌ أَمِينٌ ﴿۱۶۳﴾

164. 'So fear Allah, and obey me.

فَاتَّقُوا اللّٰهَ وَأَطِيعُونِ ﴿۱۶۴﴾

165. 'And I ask of you no reward for it. My reward is only with the Lord of the worlds.

وَمَآ أَسْئَلُكُمْ عَلَيْهِ مِنْ أَجْرٍ ۚ إِنْ أَجْرِيَ إِلَّا عَلٰى
رَبِّ الْعٰلَمِينَ ﴿۱۶۵﴾

166. 'Do you, of all peoples, approach males,

أَتَأْتُونَ الذُّكْرَانَ مِنَ الْعٰلَمِينَ ﴿۱۶۶﴾

167. 'And leave your wives whom your Lord has created for you? Nay, you are a people who transgress.'

وَتَذَرُونَ مَا خَلَقَ لَكُمْ رَبُّكُمْ مِّنْ أَزْوَاجِكُمْ ۚ
بَلْ أَنْتُمْ قَوْمٌ عٰدُونَ ﴿۱۶۷﴾

168. They said, 'If thou desist not, O Lot, thou wilt surely be *one* of the banished ones.'

قَالُوا لَئِنْ لَّمْ تَنْتَهِ يٰلُوطُ لَتَكُونَنَّ مِنَ الْمُخْرَجِينَ ﴿۱۶۸﴾

* 169. He said, 'Certainly I hate your practice.

قَالَ إِنِّي لِعَمَلِكُمْ مِّنَ الْقَالِينَ ﴿۱۶۹﴾

170. 'My Lord, save me and my family from what they do.'

رَبِّ نَجِّنِي وَأَهْلِي مِمَّا يَعْمَلُونَ ﴿١٧٠﴾

171. So We saved him and his family, all *of them*,

فَنَجَّيْنٰهُ وَأَهْلَهُ أَجْمَعِينَ ﴿١٧١﴾

172. Save an old woman among those who stayed behind.

إِلَّا عَجُوزًا فِي الْغٰبِرِينَ ﴿١٧٢﴾

173. Then We destroyed the others.

ثُمَّ دَمَّرْنَا الْاٰخَرِينَ ﴿١٧٣﴾

* 174. And We rained upon them a rain; and evil was the rain for those who were warned.

وَأَمْطَرْنَا عَلَيْهِمْ مَطَرًا فَسَآءَ مَطَرُ الْمُنْذَرِينَ ﴿١٧٤﴾

175. In that verily there is a Sign, but most of these would not believe.

إِنَّ فِي ذٰلِكَ لَاٰيَةً وَمَا كَانَ أَكْثَرُهُمْ مُؤْمِنِينَ ﴿١٧٥﴾

176. And surely thy Lord—He is the Mighty, the Merciful.

وَإِنَّ رَبَّكَ لَهُوَ الْعَزِيزُ الرَّحِيمُ ﴿١٧٦﴾

R. 10.

177. The People of the Wood rejected the Messengers,

كَذَّبَ أَصْحٰبُ لْئَيْكَةِ الْمُرْسَلِينَ ﴿١٧٧﴾

178. When Shu'aib said to them, 'Will you not be righteous?

إِذْ قَالَ لَهُمْ شُعَيْبٌ أَلَا تَتَّقُونَ ﴿١٧٨﴾

* 179. 'Surely, I am unto you a Messenger, faithful to *my* trust.

إِنِّي لَكُمْ رَسُولٌ أَمِينٌ ﴿١٧٩﴾

180. 'So fear Allah, and obey me,

فَاتَّقُوا اللّٰهَ وَأَطِيعُونِ ﴿١٨٠﴾

181. 'And I ask of you no reward for it. My reward is only with the Lord of the worlds.

وَمَآ أَسْئَلُكُمْ عَلَيْهِ مِنْ أَجْرٍ إِنْ أَجْرِيَ إِلَّا عَلٰى
رَبِّ الْعٰلَمِينَ ﴿١٨١﴾

182. 'Give full measure, and be not of those who give less,

أَوْفُوا الْكَيْلَ وَلَا تَكُونُوا مِنَ الْمُخْسِرِينَ ﴿١٨٢﴾

* 183. 'And weigh with a true balance,

وَزِنُوا بِالْقِسْطَاسِ الْمُسْتَقِيمِ ﴿١٨٣﴾

* 184. 'And diminish not unto people their things, nor act corruptly in the earth, making mischief.

وَلَا تَبْخَسُوا النَّاسَ أَشْيَآءَهُمْ وَلَا تَعْثَوْا فِي الْأَرْضِ
مُفْسِدِينَ ﴿١٨٤﴾

* 185. 'And fear Him Who created you and the earlier peoples.'

وَاتَّقُوا الَّذِي خَلَقَكُمْ وَالْجِبِلَّةَ الْأَوَّلِينَ ﴿١٨٥﴾

186. They said, 'Thou art but *one* of the bewitched.

قَالُوٓا إِنَّمَآ أَنْتَ مِنَ الْمُسَحَّرِينَ ﴿١٨٦﴾

187. 'And thou art only a man like ourselves, and we believe thee to be *one* of the liars.

وَمَآ أَنْتَ إِلَّا بَشَرٌ مِثْلُنَا وَإِنْ نَظُنُّكَ لَمِنَ الْكٰذِبِينَ ﴿١٨٧﴾

188. 'So cause fragments of the sky to fall on us, if thou art *one* of the truthful.'

فَأَسْقِطْ عَلَيْنَا كِسَفًا مِنَ السَّمَآءِ إِنْ كُنْتَ مِنَ
الصّٰدِقِينَ ﴿١٨٨﴾

189. He said, 'My Lord knows best what you do.'

قَالَ رَبِّيْٓ اَعْلَمُ بِمَا تَعْمَلُوْنَ ﴿١٨٩﴾

190. So they declared him to be a liar. Then the punishment of the day of overshadowing gloom overtook them. That was indeed the punishment of a dreadful day.

فَكَذَّبُوْهُ فَاَخَذَهُمْ عَذَابُ يَوْمِ الظُّلَّةِ ۭ اِنَّهٗ كَانَ
عَذَابَ يَوْمٍ عَظِيْمٍ ﴿١٩٠﴾

191. In that verily there is a Sign, but most of these would not believe.

اِنَّ فِيْ ذٰلِكَ لَاٰيَةً ۭ وَمَا كَانَ اَكْثَرُهُمْ مُّؤْمِنِيْنَ ﴿١٩١﴾

192. And surely thy Lord-He is the Mighty, the Merciful.

وَاِنَّ رَبَّكَ لَهُوَ الْعَزِيْزُ الرَّحِيْمُ ﴿١٩٢﴾ ع

R. 11.

193. And verily this is a revelation from the Lord of the worlds.

وَاِنَّهٗ لَتَنْزِيْلُ رَبِّ الْعٰلَمِيْنَ ﴿١٩٣﴾

194. The Spirit, Faithful to the Trust, has descended with it

نَزَلَ بِهِ الرُّوْحُ الْاَمِيْنُ ﴿١٩٤﴾

195. On thy heart, that thou mayest be of the Warners,

عَلٰى قَلْبِكَ لِتَكُوْنَ مِنَ الْمُنْذِرِيْنَ ﴿١٩٥﴾

196. In plain and clear Arabic tongue.

بِلِسَانٍ عَرَبِيٍّ مُّبِيْنٍ ﴿١٩٦﴾

197. And it is surely *mentioned* in the Scriptures of the former peoples.

وَاِنَّهٗ لَفِيْ زُبُرِ الْاَوَّلِيْنَ ﴿١٩٧﴾

198. And is it not a Sign to them that the learned among the children of Israel know it?

اَوَلَمْ يَكُنْ لَّهُمْ اٰيَةً اَنْ يَّعْلَمَهٗ عُلَمٰٓؤُا بَنِيْٓ
اِسْرَآءِيْلَ ﴿١٩٨﴾

* 199. And if We had sent it down to one of the non-Arabs,

وَلَوْ نَزَّلْنٰهُ عَلٰى بَعْضِ الْاَعْجَمِيْنَ ﴿١٩٩﴾

* 200. And he had read it to them, *even then* they would never have believed in it.

فَقَرَاَهٗ عَلَيْهِمْ مَّا كَانُوْا بِهٖ مُؤْمِنِيْنَ ﴿٢٠٠﴾

201. Thus have We caused it (disbelief) to enter into the hearts of the sinful.

كَذٰلِكَ سَلَكْنٰهُ فِيْ قُلُوْبِ الْمُجْرِمِيْنَ ﴿٢٠١﴾

202. They will not believe in it until they see the grievous punishment.

لَا يُؤْمِنُوْنَ بِهٖ حَتّٰى يَرَوُا الْعَذَابَ الْاَلِيْمَ ﴿٢٠٢﴾

203. But it will come upon them suddenly, while they know not,

فَيَاْتِيَهُمْ بَغْتَةً وَّهُمْ لَا يَشْعُرُوْنَ ﴿٢٠٣﴾

204. And they will say, 'Shall we be given any respite?'

فَيَقُوْلُوْا هَلْ نَحْنُ مُنْظَرُوْنَ ﴿٢٠٤﴾

205. What! do they seek to hasten Our punishment?

اَفَبِعَذَابِنَا يَسْتَعْجِلُوْنَ ﴿٢٠٥﴾

206. What thinkest thou? If We let them enjoy *the good things of this world* for years;

اَفَرَءَيْتَ اِنْ مَّتَّعْنٰهُمْ سِنِيْنَ ﴿٢٠٦﴾

207. Then there comes to them that with which they are threatened.

ثُمَّ جَآءَهُمْ مَّا كَانُوْا يُوْعَدُوْنَ ﴿٢٠٧﴾

208. Of no avail shall be to them that which they were allowed to enjoy.

مَآ اَغْنٰى عَنْهُمْ مَّا كَانُوْا يُمَتَّعُوْنَ ﴿٢٠٨﴾

209. And never did We destroy any township but it had Warners.

وَمَا أَهْلَكْنَا مِن قَرْيَةٍ إِلَّا لَهَا مُنذِرُونَ ﴿٢٠٩﴾

210. *This is* an admonition; and We are not unjust.

ذِكْرَىٰ وَمَا كُنَّا ظَالِمِينَ ﴿٢١٠﴾

211. And the evil ones have not brought it down.

وَمَا تَنَزَّلَتْ بِهِ الشَّيَاطِينُ ﴿٢١١﴾

* 212. They are not fit for it, nor have they the power *to do so.*

وَمَا يَنبَغِي لَهُمْ وَمَا يَسْتَطِيعُونَ ﴿٢١٢﴾

213. Surely they are debarred from hearing.

إِنَّهُمْ عَنِ السَّمْعِ لَمَعْزُولُونَ ﴿٢١٣﴾

214. Call not, therefore, on any other God beside Allah, lest thou become one of those who are punished.

فَلَا تَدْعُ مَعَ اللَّهِ إِلَٰهًا آخَرَ فَتَكُونَ مِنَ الْمُعَذَّبِينَ ﴿٢١٤﴾

215. And warn thy nearest kinsmen,

وَأَنذِرْ عَشِيرَتَكَ الْأَقْرَبِينَ ﴿٢١٥﴾

216. And lower thy wing *of mercy* to the believers who follow thee.

وَاخْفِضْ جَنَاحَكَ لِمَنِ اتَّبَعَكَ مِنَ الْمُؤْمِنِينَ ﴿٢١٦﴾

217. Then if they disobey thee, say, 'I repudiate all connection with what you do.'

فَإِنْ عَصَوْكَ فَقُلْ إِنِّي بَرِيءٌ مِّمَّا تَعْمَلُونَ ﴿٢١٧﴾

218. And put thy trust in the Mighty, the Merciful,

وَتَوَكَّلْ عَلَى الْعَزِيزِ الرَّحِيمِ ﴿٢١٨﴾

219. Who sees thee when thou standest up *in Prayer*.

الَّذِي يَرَاكَ حِينَ تَقُومُ ﴿٢١٩﴾

220. And *Who sees* thy movements among those who prostrate themselves *before God.*

وَتَقَلُّبَكَ فِي السَّاجِدِينَ ﴿٢٢٠﴾

221. He is indeed the All-Hearing, the All-Knowing.

إِنَّهُ هُوَ السَّمِيعُ الْعَلِيمُ ﴿٢٢١﴾

222. Shall I inform you on whom the evil ones descend?

هَلْ أُنَبِّئُكُمْ عَلَىٰ مَن تَنَزَّلُ الشَّيَاطِينُ ﴿٢٢٢﴾

223. They descend on every great liar *and* sinner,

تَنَزَّلُ عَلَىٰ كُلِّ أَفَّاكٍ أَثِيمٍ ﴿٢٢٣﴾

224. Repeating what they hear, and most of them are liars.

يُلْقُونَ السَّمْعَ وَأَكْثَرُهُمْ كَاذِبُونَ ﴿٢٢٤﴾

225. And *as for* the poets—it is the erring ones who follow them.

وَالشُّعَرَاءُ يَتَّبِعُهُمُ الْغَاوُونَ ﴿٢٢٥﴾

226. Dost thou not see how they wander distracted in every valley,

أَلَمْ تَرَ أَنَّهُمْ فِي كُلِّ وَادٍ يَهِيمُونَ ﴿٢٢٦﴾

227. And that they say what they practise not?—

وَأَنَّهُمْ يَقُولُونَ مَا لَا يَفْعَلُونَ ﴿٢٢٧﴾

228. Save those who believe and do good works, and remember Allah much, and retaliate *only* after they are wronged. And the wrongdoers will soon know to what place of return they shall return.

إِلَّا الَّذِينَ آمَنُوا وَعَمِلُوا الصَّالِحَاتِ وَذَكَرُوا اللَّهَ
كَثِيرًا وَانتَصَرُوا مِن بَعْدِ مَا ظُلِمُوا ۗ وَسَيَعْلَمُ
ع ١٥ الَّذِينَ ظَلَمُوا أَيَّ مُنقَلَبٍ يَنقَلِبُونَ ﴿٢٢٨﴾

سُورَةُ النَّمْلِ مَكِّيَّةٌ (٢٧) آياتها ٩٤ ركوعاتها ٧

AL-NAML

(Revealed before Hijra)

1. In the name of Allah, the Gracious, the Merciful.

بِسْمِ اللّٰهِ الرَّحْمٰنِ الرَّحِيْمِ (١)

2. Ṭā Sīn *. These are verses of the Qur'ān, and of an illuminating Book,

طٰسٓ تِلْكَ اٰيٰتُ الْقُرْاٰنِ وَكِتَابٍ مُّبِيْنٍ (٢)

3. A guidance and good tidings to those who would believe,

هُدًى وَّبُشْرٰى لِلْمُؤْمِنِيْنَ (٣)

4. Who observe Prayer and pay the Zakāt, and have firm faith in the Hereafter.

الَّذِيْنَ يُقِيْمُوْنَ الصَّلٰوةَ وَيُؤْتُوْنَ الزَّكٰوةَ وَهُمْ
بِالْاٰخِرَةِ هُمْ يُوْقِنُوْنَ (٤)

5. *As to* those who believe not in the Hereafter, We have made their deeds *appear* beautiful to them, so they are wandering blindly.

اِنَّ الَّذِيْنَ لَا يُؤْمِنُوْنَ بِالْاٰخِرَةِ زَيَّنَّا لَهُمْ اَعْمَالَهُمْ
فَهُمْ يَعْمَهُوْنَ (٥)

6. It is they who shall have a grievous torment, and they alone it is who shall be the greatest losers in the Hereafter.

اُولٰٓئِكَ الَّذِيْنَ لَهُمْ سُوْٓءُ الْعَذَابِ وَهُمْ فِي الْاٰخِرَةِ
هُمُ الْاَخْسَرُوْنَ (٦)

7. Verily, thou hast been given the Qur'ān from the presence of One Wise, All-Knowing.

وَاِنَّكَ لَتُلَقَّى الْقُرْاٰنَ مِنْ لَّدُنْ حَكِيْمٍ عَلِيْمٍ (٧)

8. *Remember* when Moses said to his family, 'I perceive a fire. I will bring you from there some information, or I will bring you a flame, a *burning* brand, that you may warm yourselves.'

اِذْ قَالَ مُوْسٰى لِاَهْلِهٖٓ اِنِّيْٓ اٰنَسْتُ نَارًا ؕ سَاٰتِيْكُمْ
مِّنْهَا بِخَبَرٍ اَوْ اٰتِيْكُمْ بِشِهَابٍ قَبَسٍ لَّعَلَّكُمْ
تَصْطَلُوْنَ (٨)

9. So when he came to it, he was called *by a voice:* 'Blessed is he who is in the fire and *also* those around it; and glorified be Allah, the Lord of the worlds.

فَلَمَّا جَآءَهَا نُوْدِيَ اَنْۢ بُوْرِكَ مَنْ فِي النَّارِ وَ
مَنْ حَوْلَهَا ؕ وَسُبْحٰنَ اللّٰهِ رَبِّ الْعٰلَمِيْنَ (٩)

10. 'O Moses, verily I am Allah, the Mighty, the Wise.

يٰمُوْسٰٓى اِنَّهٗٓ اَنَا اللّٰهُ الْعَزِيْزُ الْحَكِيْمُ (١٠)

11. 'And throw down thy rod.' And when he saw it move as though it were a serpent, he turned back retreating and did not look back. 'O Moses, fear not. Verily I am *with thee;* the Messengers need have no fear in My presence.

وَاَلْقِ عَصَاكَ ؕ فَلَمَّا رَاٰهَا تَهْتَزُّ كَاَنَّهَا جَآنٌّ وَّلّٰى
مُدْبِرًا وَّلَمْ يُعَقِّبْ ؕ يٰمُوْسٰى لَا تَخَفْ اِنِّيْ لَا يَخَافُ
لَدَيَّ الْمُرْسَلُوْنَ (١١)

* Benignant, All-Hearing God!

12. 'As to those who do wrong and then substitute good for evil; *to them*, I am indeed Most Forgiving, Merciful.

إِلَّا مَنْ ظَلَمَ ثُمَّ بَدَّلَ حُسْنًا بَعْدَ سُوٓءٍ فَإِنِّي
غَفُورٌ رَّحِيمٌ ﴿١٢﴾

* 13. 'And put thy hand into thy bosom; it will come forth white without any disease. *This is* among the nine Signs unto Pharaoh and his people; for they are a rebellious people.'

وَأَدْخِلْ يَدَكَ فِي جَيْبِكَ تَخْرُجْ بَيْضَآءَ مِنْ غَيْرِ
سُوٓءٍ فِي تِسْعِ اٰيٰتٍ إِلٰى فِرْعَوْنَ وَقَوْمِهٖ إِنَّهُمْ
كَانُوا قَوْمًا فٰسِقِينَ ﴿١٣﴾

14. But when Our sight-giving Signs came to them, they said, 'This is plain magic.'

فَلَمَّا جَآءَتْهُمْ اٰيٰتُنَا مُبْصِرَةً قَالُوا هٰذَا سِحْرٌ مُّبِينٌ ﴿١٤﴾

15. And they rejected them wrongfully and arrogantly, while their souls were convinced of them. See then, how *evil* was the end of those who acted corruptly!

وَجَحَدُوا بِهَا وَاسْتَيْقَنَتْهَآ أَنْفُسُهُمْ ظُلْمًا وَّعُلُوًّا
فَانْظُرْ كَيْفَ كَانَ عَاقِبَةُ الْمُفْسِدِينَ ﴿١٥﴾ ع

R. 2.

16. And We gave knowledge to David and Solomon, and they said, 'All praise belongs to Allah, Who has exalted us above many of His believing servants.'

وَلَقَدْ اٰتَيْنَا دَاوٗدَ وَسُلَيْمٰنَ عِلْمًا ۚ وَقَالَا الْحَمْدُ
لِلّٰهِ الَّذِي فَضَّلَنَا عَلٰى كَثِيرٍ مِّنْ عِبَادِهِ
الْمُؤْمِنِينَ ﴿١٦﴾

17. And Solomon was heir to David. And he said, 'O ye people, we have been taught the language of birds; and we have had everything bestowed upon us. This indeed is *God's* manifest grace.'

وَوَرِثَ سُلَيْمٰنُ دَاوٗدَ وَقَالَ يٰٓأَيُّهَا النَّاسُ عُلِّمْنَا
مَنْطِقَ الطَّيْرِ وَأُوتِينَا مِنْ كُلِّ شَيْءٍ ۖ إِنَّ هٰذَا لَهُوَ
الْفَضْلُ الْمُبِينُ ﴿١٧﴾

18. And there were gathered together unto Solomon his hosts of Jinn and men and birds, and they were formed into *separate* divisions,

وَحُشِرَ لِسُلَيْمٰنَ جُنُودُهٗ مِنَ الْجِنِّ وَالْإِنْسِ
وَالطَّيْرِ فَهُمْ يُوزَعُونَ ﴿١٨﴾

* 19. Until when they came to the Valley of Al-Naml, one woman *of the tribe* of the Naml said, 'O ye Naml, enter your habitations, lest Solomon and his hosts crush you, while they know not.'

حَتّٰىٓ إِذَآ أَتَوْا عَلٰى وَادِ النَّمْلِ قَالَتْ نَمْلَةٌ يّٰٓأَيُّهَا
النَّمْلُ ادْخُلُوا مَسٰكِنَكُمْ ۚ لَا يَحْطِمَنَّكُمْ سُلَيْمٰنُ
وَجُنُودُهٗ وَهُمْ لَا يَشْعُرُونَ ﴿١٩﴾

* 20. Thereupon he smiled, laughing at her words, and said, 'My Lord, grant me *the will and power* to be grateful for Thy favour which Thou hast bestowed upon me and upon my parents, and to do *such* good works as would please Thee, and admit me, by Thy mercy, among Thy

فَتَبَسَّمَ ضَاحِكًا مِّنْ قَوْلِهَا وَقَالَ رَبِّ أَوْزِعْنِيٓ
أَنْ أَشْكُرَ نِعْمَتَكَ الَّتِيٓ أَنْعَمْتَ عَلَيَّ وَعَلٰى وَالِدَيَّ
وَأَنْ أَعْمَلَ صَالِحًا تَرْضٰىهُ وَأَدْخِلْنِي بِرَحْمَتِكَ

righteous servants.'

فِيْ عِبَادِكَ الصّٰلِحِيْنَ ﴿٢٠﴾

* 21. And he reviewed the birds, and said, 'How is it that I do not see Hudhud? Is he among the absentees?

وَتَفَقَّدَ الطَّيْرَ فَقَالَ مَا لِيَ لَآ اَرَى الْهُدْهُدَ ۖ
اَمْ كَانَ مِنَ الْغَآئِبِيْنَ ﴿٢١﴾

* 22. 'I will surely punish him with a severe punishment or I will slay him, unless he bring me a clear reason *for his absence*.'

لَاُعَذِّبَنَّهٗ عَذَابًا شَدِيْدًا اَوْ لَاَاذْبَحَنَّهٗٓ اَوْ
لَيَاْتِيَنِّيْ بِسُلْطٰنٍ مُّبِيْنٍ ﴿٢٢﴾

23. And he did not tarry long *before Hudhud came* and said, 'I have encompassed that which thou hast not encompassed; and I have come to thee from Saba' with sure tidings.

فَمَكَثَ غَيْرَ بَعِيْدٍ فَقَالَ اَحَطْتُّ بِمَا لَمْ تُحِطْ بِهٖ
وَجِئْتُكَ مِنْ سَبَاٍ بِنَبَاٍ يَّقِيْنٍ ﴿٢٣﴾

24. 'I found a woman ruling over them, and she has been given everything, and she has a mighty throne.

اِنِّيْ وَجَدْتُّ امْرَاَةً تَمْلِكُهُمْ وَاُوْتِيَتْ مِنْ كُلِّ
شَيْءٍ وَّلَهَا عَرْشٌ عَظِيْمٌ ﴿٢٤﴾

25. 'I found her and her people worshipping the sun instead of Allah; and Satan has made their works *look* beautiful to them, and has thus hindered them from the *right* way, so that they follow not guidance;

وَجَدْتُّهَا وَقَوْمَهَا يَسْجُدُوْنَ لِلشَّمْسِ مِنْ دُوْنِ
اللّٰهِ وَزَيَّنَ لَهُمُ الشَّيْطٰنُ اَعْمَالَهُمْ فَصَدَّهُمْ عَنِ
السَّبِيْلِ فَهُمْ لَا يَهْتَدُوْنَ ﴿٢٥﴾

26. '*And Satan has bidden them* not to worship Allah, Who brings to light that which is hidden in the heavens and the earth, and Who knows what you conceal and what you make known.

اَلَّا يَسْجُدُوْا لِلّٰهِ الَّذِيْ يُخْرِجُ الْخَبْءَ فِي السَّمٰوٰتِ
وَالْاَرْضِ وَيَعْلَمُ مَا تُخْفُوْنَ وَمَا تُعْلِنُوْنَ ﴿٢٦﴾

27. 'Allah! there is no God but He, the Lord of the Mighty Throne.'

السجدة
اَللّٰهُ لَآ اِلٰهَ اِلَّا هُوَ رَبُّ الْعَرْشِ الْعَظِيْمِ ﴿٢٧﴾

28. *Solomon* said, 'We shall see whether thou hast spoken the truth or whether thou art one of those who lie.

قَالَ سَنَنْظُرُ اَصَدَقْتَ اَمْ كُنْتَ مِنَ الْكٰذِبِيْنَ ﴿٢٨﴾

29. 'Go thou, with this letter of mine, and lay it before them; then withdraw from them and see what *answer* they return.'

اِذْهَبْ بِّكِتٰبِيْ هٰذَا فَاَلْقِهْ اِلَيْهِمْ ثُمَّ تَوَلَّ عَنْهُمْ
فَانْظُرْ مَاذَا يَرْجِعُوْنَ ﴿٢٩﴾

30. *The Queen* said, "Ye chiefs, there has been delivered to me a noble letter.

قَالَتْ يٰٓاَيُّهَا الْمَلَؤُا اِنِّيْٓ اُلْقِيَ اِلَيَّ كِتٰبٌ كَرِيْمٌ ﴿٣٠﴾

31. "It is from Solomon, and it is: 'In the name of Allah, the Gracious, the Merciful;

اِنَّهٗ مِنْ سُلَيْمٰنَ وَاِنَّهٗ بِسْمِ اللّٰهِ الرَّحْمٰنِ الرَّحِيْمِ ﴿٣١﴾

32. 'Behave not proudly towards me, but come to me in submission.' "

اَلَّا تَعْلُوْا عَلَيَّ وَاْتُوْنِيْ مُسْلِمِيْنَ ﴿٣٢﴾ ع

R. 3.

33. She said, 'Ye chiefs, advise me in the matter that is before me. I never decide

قَالَتْ يٰٓاَيُّهَا الْمَلَؤُا اَفْتُوْنِيْ فِيْٓ اَمْرِيْ ۚ مَا كُنْتُ

any matter until you are present with me *and give me your advice.'*

* 34. They replied, 'We possess power and we possess great prowess in war, but it is for thee to command; therefore consider thou what thou wilt command.'

35. She said, 'Surely, kings, when they enter a country, despoil it, and turn the highest of its people into the lowest. And thus will they do.

36. 'But I am going to send them a present and wait to see what *answer* the envoys bring back.'

37. So when *the Queen's ambassador* came to Solomon, he said, 'Do you mean to help me with *your* wealth? But that which Allah has given me is better than that which He has given you. Nay, but you rejoice in your gift.

38. 'Go back to them, for we shall surely come to them with hosts against which they will have no power, and we shall drive them out from there disgraced, and they will be humbled.'

* 39. He said, 'O nobles, which of you will bring me a throne for her before they come to me, submitting?'

40. Said a stalwart from among the Jinn: 'I will bring it to thee before thou rise from thy camp; and indeed I possess power therefor *and I am* trustworthy.'

* 41. Said one who had knowledge of the Book, 'I will bring it to thee before thy noble *messengers* return to thee.' And when he saw it set before him, he said, 'This is by the grace of my Lord, that He may try me whether I am grateful or ungrateful. And whosoever is grateful is grateful for the good of his *own* soul; but whosoever is ungrateful, truly my Lord is Self-Sufficient, Generous.'

* 42. He said, 'Make her throne unrecognizable to her, and let us see whether she follows the right way or whether she is *one* of those who follow not the right way.'

قَاطِعَةً أَمْرًا حَتّٰى تَشْهَدُوْنِ ﴿٣٣﴾
قَالُوْا نَحْنُ أُولُوْا قُوَّةٍ وَّأُولُوْا بَأْسٍ شَدِيْدٍ ۙ وَّ
الْأَمْرُ إِلَيْكِ فَانْظُرِيْ مَاذَا تَأْمُرِيْنَ ﴿٣٤﴾
قَالَتْ إِنَّ الْمُلُوْكَ إِذَا دَخَلُوْا قَرْيَةً أَفْسَدُوْهَا وَ
جَعَلُوْا أَعِزَّةَ أَهْلِهَا أَذِلَّةً ۚ وَكَذٰلِكَ يَفْعَلُوْنَ ﴿٣٥﴾
وَإِنِّيْ مُرْسِلَةٌ إِلَيْهِمْ بِهَدِيَّةٍ فَنٰظِرَةٌ بِمَ يَرْجِعُ
الْمُرْسَلُوْنَ ﴿٣٦﴾
فَلَمَّا جَآءَ سُلَيْمٰنَ قَالَ أَتُمِدُّوْنَنِ بِمَالٍ فَمَآ اٰتٰىنِۦَ
اللّٰهُ خَيْرٌ مِّمَّآ اٰتٰىكُمْ ۚ بَلْ أَنْتُمْ بِهَدِيَّتِكُمْ تَفْرَحُوْنَ ﴿٣٧﴾
اِرْجِعْ إِلَيْهِمْ فَلَنَأْتِيَنَّهُمْ بِجُنُوْدٍ لَّا قِبَلَ لَهُمْ بِهَا
وَلَنُخْرِجَنَّهُمْ مِّنْهَآ أَذِلَّةً وَّهُمْ صٰغِرُوْنَ ﴿٣٨﴾
قَالَ يٰٓأَيُّهَا الْمَلَؤُا أَيُّكُمْ يَأْتِيْنِيْ بِعَرْشِهَا قَبْلَ أَنْ
يَّأْتُوْنِيْ مُسْلِمِيْنَ ﴿٣٩﴾
قَالَ عِفْرِيْتٌ مِّنَ الْجِنِّ أَنَا اٰتِيْكَ بِهٖ قَبْلَ أَنْ
تَقُوْمَ مِنْ مَّقَامِكَ ۚ وَإِنِّيْ عَلَيْهِ لَقَوِيٌّ أَمِيْنٌ ﴿٤٠﴾
قَالَ الَّذِيْ عِنْدَهٗ عِلْمٌ مِّنَ الْكِتٰبِ أَنَا اٰتِيْكَ بِهٖ
قَبْلَ أَنْ يَّرْتَدَّ إِلَيْكَ طَرْفُكَ ۚ فَلَمَّا رَاٰهُ مُسْتَقِرًّا عِنْدَهٗ
قَالَ هٰذَا مِنْ فَضْلِ رَبِّيْ ۖ لِيَبْلُوَنِيْٓ ءَأَشْكُرُ أَمْ
أَكْفُرُ ۚ وَمَنْ شَكَرَ فَإِنَّمَا يَشْكُرُ لِنَفْسِهٖ ۚ وَمَنْ كَفَرَ
فَإِنَّ رَبِّيْ غَنِيٌّ كَرِيْمٌ ﴿٤١﴾
قَالَ نَكِّرُوْا لَهَا عَرْشَهَا نَنْظُرْ أَتَهْتَدِيْٓ أَمْ تَكُوْنُ
مِنَ الَّذِيْنَ لَا يَهْتَدُوْنَ ﴿٤٢﴾

43. And when she came, it was said, 'Is thy throne like this?' She replied, 'It is as though it were the same. And we had been given knowledge before this, and we have already submitted.'

فَلَمَّا جَآءَتْ قِيْلَ اَهٰكَذَا عَرْشُكِ ۭ قَالَتْ كَاَنَّهٗ هُوَ ۚ
وَاُوْتِيْنَا الْعِلْمَ مِنْ قَبْلِهَا وَكُنَّا مُسْلِمِيْنَ ﴿۴۳﴾

44. And that which she used to worship beside Allah had stopped her *from believing;* for she came of a disbelieving people.

وَصَدَّهَا مَا كَانَتْ تَّعْبُدُ مِنْ دُوْنِ اللّٰهِ ۭ اِنَّهَا
كَانَتْ مِنْ قَوْمٍ كٰفِرِيْنَ ﴿۴۴﴾

* 45. It was said to her, 'Enter the palace.' And when she saw it, she thought it to be a great expanse of water, and she uncovered her shanks. *Solomon* said, 'It is a palace paved smooth with slabs of glass.' She said, 'My Lord, I indeed wronged my soul; and I submit myself with Solomon to Allah, the Lord of the worlds.'

قِيْلَ لَهَا ادْخُلِي الصَّرْحَ ۚ فَلَمَّا رَاَتْهُ حَسِبَتْهُ لُجَّةً
وَّكَشَفَتْ عَنْ سَاقَيْهَا ۭ قَالَ اِنَّهٗ صَرْحٌ مُّمَرَّدٌ
مِّنْ قَوَارِيْرَ ۥ قَالَتْ رَبِّ اِنِّيْ ظَلَمْتُ نَفْسِيْ وَاَسْلَمْتُ
مَعَ سُلَيْمٰنَ لِلّٰهِ رَبِّ الْعٰلَمِيْنَ ﴿۴۵﴾ ع

R. 4.

46. And We sent to Thamūd their brother Ṣāliḥ, *who said,* 'Worship Allah.' But behold, they became two parties contending with each other.

وَلَقَدْ اَرْسَلْنَآ اِلٰى ثَمُوْدَ اَخَاهُمْ صٰلِحًا اَنِ اعْبُدُوا
اللّٰهَ فَاِذَا هُمْ فَرِيْقٰنِ يَخْتَصِمُوْنَ ﴿۴۶﴾

47. He said, 'O my people, why do you wish to hasten on the evil rather than the good? Wherefore do you not ask forgiveness of Allah that you may be shown mercy?'

قَالَ يٰقَوْمِ لِمَ تَسْتَعْجِلُوْنَ بِالسَّيِّئَةِ قَبْلَ الْحَسَنَةِ ۚ
لَوْلَا تَسْتَغْفِرُوْنَ اللّٰهَ لَعَلَّكُمْ تُرْحَمُوْنَ ﴿۴۷﴾

* 48. They said, 'We auger evil from thee and from those that are with thee.' He said, '*The cause of* your evil fortune is with Allah. Nay, but you are a people who are on trial.'

قَالُوا اطَّيَّرْنَا بِكَ وَبِمَنْ مَّعَكَ ۭ قَالَ طٰٓئِرُكُمْ عِنْدَ
اللّٰهِ بَلْ اَنْتُمْ قَوْمٌ تُفْتَنُوْنَ ﴿۴۸﴾

49. And there were in the city a party of nine *persons* who made mischief in the land, and would not reform.

وَكَانَ فِي الْمَدِيْنَةِ تِسْعَةُ رَهْطٍ يُّفْسِدُوْنَ فِي
الْاَرْضِ وَلَا يُصْلِحُوْنَ ﴿۴۹﴾

50. They said, "Swear to each other by Allah that we will surely attack him and his family by night, and then we will say to his heir, 'We witnessed not the destruction of his family, and most surely we are truthful.' "

قَالُوْا تَقَاسَمُوْا بِاللّٰهِ لَنُبَيِّتَنَّهٗ وَاَهْلَهٗ ثُمَّ لَنَقُوْلَنَّ
لِوَلِيِّهٖ مَا شَهِدْنَا مَهْلِكَ اَهْلِهٖ وَاِنَّا لَصٰدِقُوْنَ ﴿۵۰﴾

* 51. And they planned a plan, and We planned a plan, but they perceived *it* not.

وَمَكَرُوْا مَكْرًا وَّمَكَرْنَا مَكْرًا وَّهُمْ لَا يَشْعُرُوْنَ ﴿۵۱﴾

52. Then see how *evil* was the end of their plan! Verily, We utterly destroyed them and their people all together.

فَانْظُرْ كَيْفَ كَانَ عَاقِبَةُ مَكْرِهِمْ ۙ اَنَّا دَمَّرْنٰهُمْ
وَقَوْمَهُمْ اَجْمَعِيْنَ ﴿۵۲﴾

* 53. And yonder are their houses empty, because of their wrongdoing. In that,

فَتِلْكَ بُيُوْتُهُمْ خَاوِيَةًۢ بِمَا ظَلَمُوْا ۭ اِنَّ فِيْ ذٰلِكَ

verily, is a Sign for a people who possess knowledge.

لَاٰيَةً لِّقَوْمٍ يَّعْلَمُوْنَ ۝٥٣

54. And We saved those who believed and feared God.

وَاَنْجَيْنَا الَّذِيْنَ اٰمَنُوْا وَكَانُوْا يَتَّقُوْنَ ۝٥٤

55. And *remember* Lot, when he said to his people, 'Do you commit abomination while you see *the evil thereof?*

وَلُوْطًا اِذْ قَالَ لِقَوْمِهٖٓ اَتَاْتُوْنَ الْفَاحِشَةَ وَاَنْتُمْ
تُبْصِرُوْنَ ۝٥٥

* 56. 'What! do you approach men lustfully rather than women? Nay, you are indeed an ignorant people.'

اَئِنَّكُمْ لَتَاْتُوْنَ الرِّجَالَ شَهْوَةً مِّنْ دُوْنِ النِّسَآءِ ؕ
بَلْ اَنْتُمْ قَوْمٌ تَجْهَلُوْنَ ۝٥٦

* 57. But the answer of his people was naught save that they said, 'Drive out Lot's family from your city. They are a people who would keep clean.'

فَمَا كَانَ جَوَابَ قَوْمِهٖٓ اِلَّآ اَنْ قَالُوْٓا اَخْرِجُوْٓا اٰلَ
لُوْطٍ مِّنْ قَرْيَتِكُمْ ۚ اِنَّهُمْ اُنَاسٌ يَّتَطَهَّرُوْنَ ۝٥٧

58. So We saved him and his family, except his wife; her We decreed to be of those who stayed behind.

فَاَنْجَيْنٰهُ وَاَهْلَهٗٓ اِلَّا امْرَاَتَهٗ ۫ قَدَّرْنٰهَا مِنَ الْغٰبِرِيْنَ ۝٥٨

59. And We rained upon them a rain; and evil was the rain for those who were warned.

ع وَاَمْطَرْنَا عَلَيْهِمْ مَّطَرًا ۚ فَسَآءَ مَطَرُ الْمُنْذَرِيْنَ ۝٥٩

R. 5.

* 60. Say, 'All praise belongs to Allah, and peace be upon those servants of His whom He has chosen. Is Allah better or what they associate *with Him?*'

قُلِ الْحَمْدُ لِلّٰهِ وَسَلٰمٌ عَلٰى عِبَادِهِ الَّذِيْنَ اصْطَفٰى ؕ
آٰللّٰهُ خَيْرٌ اَمَّا يُشْرِكُوْنَ ۝٦٠

61. Or, Who created the heavens and the earth, and Who sent down water for you from the sky wherewith We cause to grow beautiful orchards? You could not cause their trees to grow. Is there a God besides Allah? Nay, they are a people who deviate *from the right path*.

الجزء ٢٠ اَمَّنْ خَلَقَ السَّمٰوٰتِ وَالْاَرْضَ وَاَنْزَلَ لَكُمْ مِّنَ
السَّمَآءِ مَآءً ۚ فَاَنْۢبَتْنَا بِهٖ حَدَآئِقَ ذَاتَ بَهْجَةٍ ۚ
مَا كَانَ لَكُمْ اَنْ تُنْۢبِتُوْا شَجَرَهَا ؕ ءَاِلٰهٌ مَّعَ اللّٰهِ ؕ
بَلْ هُمْ قَوْمٌ يَّعْدِلُوْنَ ۝٦١

62. Or, Who made the earth a place of rest, and placed rivers in its midst, and placed upon it firm mountains, and put a barrier between the two waters? Is there a God besides Allah? Nay, most of them know not.

اَمَّنْ جَعَلَ الْاَرْضَ قَرَارًا وَّجَعَلَ خِلٰلَهَآ اَنْهٰرًا
وَّجَعَلَ لَهَا رَوَاسِيَ وَجَعَلَ بَيْنَ الْبَحْرَيْنِ حَاجِزًا ؕ
ءَاِلٰهٌ مَّعَ اللّٰهِ ؕ بَلْ اَكْثَرُهُمْ لَا يَعْلَمُوْنَ ۝٦٢

63. Or, Who answers the distressed person when he calls upon Him, and removes the evil, and makes you successors in the earth? Is there a God besides Allah? Little is it that you reflect.

اَمَّنْ يُّجِيْبُ الْمُضْطَرَّ اِذَا دَعَاهُ وَيَكْشِفُ السُّوْٓءَ
وَيَجْعَلُكُمْ خُلَفَآءَ الْاَرْضِ ؕ ءَاِلٰهٌ مَّعَ اللّٰهِ ؕ قَلِيْلًا
مَّا تَذَكَّرُوْنَ ۝٦٣

64. Or, Who guides you in every *kind of* darkness of the land and of the sea, and Who sends the winds as glad tidings before His mercy? Is there a God besides Allah? Exalted is Allah above what they associate *with Him*.

أَمَّنْ يَّهْدِيْكُمْ فِيْ ظُلُمٰتِ الْبَرِّ وَالْبَحْرِ وَمَنْ يُّرْسِلُ
الرِّيٰحَ بُشْرًا بَيْنَ يَدَيْ رَحْمَتِهٖ ؕ ءَاِلٰهٌ مَّعَ اللّٰهِ ؕ
تَعٰلَى اللّٰهُ عَمَّا يُشْرِكُوْنَ ؕ ﴿٦٤﴾

65. Or, Who originates creation, *and* then repeats it and Who provides for you from the heaven and the earth? Is there a God besides Allah? Say, 'Bring forward your proof if you are truthful.'

أَمَّنْ يَّبْدَؤُا الْخَلْقَ ثُمَّ يُعِيْدُهٗ وَمَنْ يَّرْزُقُكُمْ
مِّنَ السَّمَآءِ وَالْاَرْضِ ؕ ءَاِلٰهٌ مَّعَ اللّٰهِ ؕ قُلْ هَاتُوْا بُرْهَانَكُمْ
اِنْ كُنْتُمْ صٰدِقِيْنَ ﴿٦٥﴾

66. Say, 'None in the heavens and the earth knows the unseen save Allah; and they do not know when they will be raised up.'

قُلْ لَّا يَعْلَمُ مَنْ فِي السَّمٰوٰتِ وَالْاَرْضِ الْغَيْبَ
اِلَّا اللّٰهُ ؕ وَمَا يَشْعُرُوْنَ اَيَّانَ يُبْعَثُوْنَ ﴿٦٦﴾

67. Nay, their knowledge has reached its end respecting the Hereafter; nay, they are *indeed* in doubt about it; nay, they are blind to it.

بَلِ ادّٰرَكَ عِلْمُهُمْ فِي الْاٰخِرَةِ ۫ بَلْ هُمْ فِيْ شَكٍّ
مِّنْهَا ۫ بَلْ هُمْ مِّنْهَا عَمُوْنَ ﴿٦٧﴾ ع

R. 6.

68. And those who disbelieve say, 'What! when we and our fathers have become dust, shall we indeed be brought forth *again*?

وَقَالَ الَّذِيْنَ كَفَرُوْٓا ءَاِذَا كُنَّا تُرٰبًا وَّاٰبَآؤُنَآ اَئِنَّا
لَمُخْرَجُوْنَ ﴿٦٨﴾

69. 'We were surely promised this before—we and our fathers; this is nothing but tales of the ancients.'

لَقَدْ وُعِدْنَا هٰذَا نَحْنُ وَاٰبَآؤُنَا مِنْ قَبْلُ ۙ اِنْ
هٰذَآ اِلَّآ اَسَاطِيْرُ الْاَوَّلِيْنَ ﴿٦٩﴾

70. Say, 'Travel in the earth and see how *evil* was the end of the sinful!'

قُلْ سِيْرُوْا فِي الْاَرْضِ فَانْظُرُوْا كَيْفَ كَانَ عَاقِبَةُ
الْمُجْرِمِيْنَ ﴿٧٠﴾

71. And grieve thou not for them, nor be thou in distress at what they plot.

وَلَا تَحْزَنْ عَلَيْهِمْ وَلَا تَكُنْ فِيْ ضَيْقٍ مِّمَّا يَمْكُرُوْنَ ﴿٧١﴾

72. And they say, 'When will this promise be *fulfilled*, if you are truthful?'

وَيَقُوْلُوْنَ مَتٰى هٰذَا الْوَعْدُ اِنْ كُنْتُمْ صٰدِقِيْنَ ﴿٧٢﴾

73. Say, 'It may be that a part of that which you would hasten on may be close behind you.'

قُلْ عَسٰٓى اَنْ يَّكُوْنَ رَدِفَ لَكُمْ بَعْضُ الَّذِيْ
تَسْتَعْجِلُوْنَ ﴿٧٣﴾

74. And, truly, thy Lord is gracious to mankind, but most of them are not grateful.

وَاِنَّ رَبَّكَ لَذُوْ فَضْلٍ عَلَى النَّاسِ وَلٰكِنَّ اَكْثَرَهُمْ
لَا يَشْكُرُوْنَ ﴿٧٤﴾

75. And, surely, thy Lord knows what their bosoms conceal and what they reveal.

وَإِنَّ رَبَّكَ لَيَعْلَمُ مَا تُكِنُّ صُدُورُهُمْ وَمَا يُعْلِنُونَ ﴿٧٥﴾

76. And there is nothing hidden in the heaven and the earth, but it is *recorded* in a clear Book.

وَمَا مِنْ غَائِبَةٍ فِي السَّمَاءِ وَالْأَرْضِ إِلَّا فِي كِتَابٍ
مُبِينٍ ﴿٧٦﴾

77. Verily, this Qur'ān explains to the children of Israel most of that concerning which they differ.

إِنَّ هٰذَا الْقُرْآنَ يَقُصُّ عَلٰى بَنِي إِسْرَائِيلَ أَكْثَرَ
الَّذِي هُمْ فِيهِ يَخْتَلِفُونَ ﴿٧٧﴾

78. And verily, it is a guidance and a mercy to the believers.

وَإِنَّهُ لَهُدًى وَرَحْمَةٌ لِلْمُؤْمِنِينَ ﴿٧٨﴾

79. Verily, thy Lord will decide between them by His judgment, and He is the Mighty, the All-Knowing.

إِنَّ رَبَّكَ يَقْضِي بَيْنَهُمْ بِحُكْمِهِ ۚ وَهُوَ الْعَزِيزُ
الْعَلِيمُ ﴿٧٩﴾

80. So put thy trust in Allah; surely, thou *standest* on manifest truth.

فَتَوَكَّلْ عَلَى اللّٰهِ ۖ إِنَّكَ عَلَى الْحَقِّ الْمُبِينِ ﴿٨٠﴾

81. Verily, thou canst not make the dead to hear, nor canst thou make the deaf to hear the call, when they turn back retreating.

إِنَّكَ لَا تُسْمِعُ الْمَوْتٰى وَلَا تُسْمِعُ الصُّمَّ الدُّعَاءَ إِذَا
وَلَّوْا مُدْبِرِينَ ﴿٨١﴾

* 82. And thou canst not guide the blind out of their error. Thou canst make only those to hear who believe in Our Signs, for they submit.

وَمَا أَنْتَ بِهَادِي الْعُمْيِ عَنْ ضَلَالَتِهِمْ ۖ إِنْ تُسْمِعُ
إِلَّا مَنْ يُؤْمِنُ بِآيَاتِنَا فَهُمْ مُسْلِمُونَ ﴿٨٢﴾

* 83. And when the sentence is passed against them, We shall bring forth for them a germ out of the earth, which shall wound them because people did not believe in Our Signs.

وَإِذَا وَقَعَ الْقَوْلُ عَلَيْهِمْ أَخْرَجْنَا لَهُمْ دَابَّةً مِنَ
الْأَرْضِ تُكَلِّمُهُمْ أَنَّ النَّاسَ كَانُوا بِآيَاتِنَا
لَا يُوقِنُونَ ﴿٨٣﴾

R. 7.

84. And *remind them of* the day when We shall gather together from every people a party from among those who rejected Our Signs, and they shall be placed in *separate* bands.

وَيَوْمَ نَحْشُرُ مِنْ كُلِّ أُمَّةٍ فَوْجًا مِمَّنْ يُكَذِّبُ بِآيَاتِنَا
فَهُمْ يُوزَعُونَ ﴿٨٤﴾

* 85. Till, when they come, He will say, 'Did you reject My Signs, while you did not embrace them in your knowledge? Or what was it that you were doing?'

حَتّٰى إِذَا جَاءُوا قَالَ أَكَذَّبْتُمْ بِآيَاتِي وَلَمْ تُحِيطُوا بِهَا
عِلْمًا أَمَّاذَا كُنْتُمْ تَعْمَلُونَ ﴿٨٥﴾

* 86. And the sentence shall fall upon them because they did wrong, and they will be speechless.

وَوَقَعَ الْقَوْلُ عَلَيْهِمْ بِمَا ظَلَمُوا فَهُمْ لَا يَنْطِقُونَ ﴿٨٦﴾

87. Have they not seen that We have made the night that they may rest therein,

أَلَمْ يَرَوْا أَنَّا جَعَلْنَا اللَّيْلَ لِيَسْكُنُوا فِيهِ وَالنَّهَارَ

and the day sight-giving? In that verily are Signs for a people who believe.

مُبْصِرًا ۚ إِنَّ فِي ذَٰلِكَ لَآيَاتٍ لِقَوْمٍ يُؤْمِنُونَ ﴿٨٧﴾

88. And on the day when the trumpet will be blown, whoever is in the heavens and whoever is in the earth will be struck with terror, save him whom Allah pleases. And all shall come unto Him, humbled.

وَيَوْمَ يُنْفَخُ فِي الصُّورِ فَفَزِعَ مَنْ فِي السَّمٰوٰتِ وَمَنْ فِي الْأَرْضِ إِلَّا مَنْ شَاءَ اللّٰهُ ۚ وَكُلٌّ أَتَوْهُ دٰخِرِينَ ﴿٨٨﴾

* 89. And thou seest the mountains which thou thinkest to be firmly fixed, but they shall pass away like the passing of the clouds—the work of Allah Who has made everything perfect. Verily, He knows full well what you do.

وَتَرَى الْجِبَالَ تَحْسَبُهَا جَامِدَةً وَهِيَ تَمُرُّ مَرَّ السَّحَابِ ۚ صُنْعَ اللّٰهِ الَّذِي أَتْقَنَ كُلَّ شَيْءٍ ۚ إِنَّهُ خَبِيرٌ بِمَا تَفْعَلُونَ ﴿٨٩﴾

90. Whoever does a good deed, shall have a better reward than that, and such will be secure from terror that day.

مَنْ جَاءَ بِالْحَسَنَةِ فَلَهُ خَيْرٌ مِنْهَا ۚ وَهُمْ مِنْ فَزَعٍ يَوْمَئِذٍ اٰمِنُونَ ﴿٩٠﴾

91. And those who do evil, shall be thrown down on their faces into the Fire: 'Are you not rewarded for what you have been doing?'

وَمَنْ جَاءَ بِالسَّيِّئَةِ فَكُبَّتْ وُجُوهُهُمْ فِي النَّارِ ۖ هَلْ تُجْزَوْنَ إِلَّا مَا كُنْتُمْ تَعْمَلُونَ ﴿٩١﴾

92. *Say*, 'I am commanded only to serve the Lord of this city which He has made sacred, and to Him belong all things; and I am commanded to be of those who submit *to God*;

إِنَّمَا أُمِرْتُ أَنْ أَعْبُدَ رَبَّ هٰذِهِ الْبَلْدَةِ الَّذِي حَرَّمَهَا وَلَهُ كُلُّ شَيْءٍ ۖ وَأُمِرْتُ أَنْ أَكُونَ مِنَ الْمُسْلِمِينَ ﴿٩٢﴾

93. 'And to recite the Qur'ān.' So whoever follows guidance, follows it only for *the good of* his own soul; and *as to him* who goes astray, say, 'I am only a warner.'

وَأَنْ أَتْلُوَ الْقُرْاٰنَ ۖ فَمَنِ اهْتَدٰى فَإِنَّمَا يَهْتَدِي لِنَفْسِهِ ۚ وَمَنْ ضَلَّ فَقُلْ إِنَّمَا أَنَا مِنَ الْمُنْذِرِينَ ﴿٩٣﴾

94. And say, 'All praise belongs to Allah; He will soon show you His Signs, and you will know them.' And thy Lord is not unaware of what you do.

وَقُلِ الْحَمْدُ لِلّٰهِ سَيُرِيكُمْ اٰيٰتِهِ فَتَعْرِفُونَهَا ۚ وَمَا رَبُّكَ بِغَافِلٍ عَمَّا تَعْمَلُونَ ﴿٩٤﴾ ع

سُوْرَةُ الْقَصَصِ مَكِّيَّةٌ (٢٨)

AL-QAṢAṢ

(Revealed before Hijra)

1. In the name of Allah, the Gracious, the Merciful.

بِسْمِ اللّٰهِ الرَّحْمٰنِ الرَّحِيْمِ (١)

2. Ṭā Sīn Mīm*.

طٰسٓمّٓ (٢)

3. These are verses of the clear Book.

تِلْكَ اٰيٰتُ الْكِتٰبِ الْمُبِيْنِ (٣)

* 4. We rehearse unto thee *a portion* of the story of Moses and Pharaoh with truth, for *the benefit of* a people who would believe.

نَتْلُوْا عَلَيْكَ مِنْ نَّبَاِ مُوْسٰى وَفِرْعَوْنَ بِالْحَقِّ
لِقَوْمٍ يُّؤْمِنُوْنَ (٤)

5. Verily, Pharaoh behaved arrogantly in the earth, and divided the people thereof into parties: he sought to weaken a party of them, slaying their sons, and sparing their women. Certainly, he was of the mischief-makers.

اِنَّ فِرْعَوْنَ عَلَا فِي الْاَرْضِ وَجَعَلَ اَهْلَهَا شِيَعًا
يَّسْتَضْعِفُ طَآئِفَةً مِّنْهُمْ يُذَبِّحُ اَبْنَآءَهُمْ وَيَسْتَحْيٖ
نِسَآءَهُمْ ؕ اِنَّهٗ كَانَ مِنَ الْمُفْسِدِيْنَ (٥)

6. And We desired to show favour unto those who had been considered weak in the earth, and to make them leaders and to make them inheritors *of Our favours*,

وَنُرِيْدُ اَنْ نَّمُنَّ عَلَى الَّذِيْنَ اسْتُضْعِفُوْا فِي الْاَرْضِ
وَنَجْعَلَهُمْ اَئِمَّةً وَّنَجْعَلَهُمُ الْوٰرِثِيْنَ (٦)

7. And to establish them in the earth, and to show Pharaoh and Hāmān and their hosts that which they feared from them.

وَنُمَكِّنَ لَهُمْ فِي الْاَرْضِ وَنُرِيَ فِرْعَوْنَ وَهَامٰنَ
وَجُنُوْدَهُمَا مِنْهُمْ مَّا كَانُوْا يَحْذَرُوْنَ (٧)

8. And We revealed to the mother of Moses *saying*, 'Suckle him; and when thou fearest for him, then cast him into the river and fear not, nor grieve; for We shall restore him to thee, and shall make him *one* of the Messengers.'

وَاَوْحَيْنَآ اِلٰٓى اُمِّ مُوْسٰٓى اَنْ اَرْضِعِيْهِ ۚ فَاِذَا خِفْتِ
عَلَيْهِ فَاَلْقِيْهِ فِي الْيَمِّ وَلَا تَخَافِيْ وَلَا تَحْزَنِيْ ۚ اِنَّا
رَآدُّوْهُ اِلَيْكِ وَجَاعِلُوْهُ مِنَ الْمُرْسَلِيْنَ (٨)

* 9. And the family of Pharaoh picked him up that he might become for them an enemy and a *source of* sorrow. Verily, Pharaoh and Hāmān and their hosts were wrongdoers.

فَالْتَقَطَهٗٓ اٰلُ فِرْعَوْنَ لِيَكُوْنَ لَهُمْ عَدُوًّا وَّحَزَنًا ؕ
اِنَّ فِرْعَوْنَ وَهَامٰنَ وَجُنُوْدَهُمَا كَانُوْا خٰطِـِٕيْنَ (٩)

10. And Pharaoh's wife said, '*He will be* a joy of the eye, for me and for thee. Kill him not. Haply he will be useful to us, or we may adopt him as a son.' And they

وَقَالَتِ امْرَاَتُ فِرْعَوْنَ قُرَّتُ عَيْنٍ لِّيْ وَلَكَ ؕ لَا
تَقْتُلُوْهُ ۖ عَسٰٓى اَنْ يَّنْفَعَنَآ اَوْ نَتَّخِذَهٗ وَلَدًا وَّهُمْ

---

* Benignant, All-Hearing, All-Knowing God!

perceived not *the consequences thereof.*

لَا يَشْعُرُونَ ﴿١٠﴾

* 11. And the heart of the mother of Moses became free *from anxiety.* She had almost disclosed *his identity,* were it not that We had strengthened her heart so that she might be of the *firm* believers.

وَاَصْبَحَ فُؤَادُ اُمِّ مُوْسٰى فٰرِغًا ۭ اِنْ كَادَتْ لَتُبْدِيْ
بِهٖ لَوْلَآ اَنْ رَّبَطْنَا عَلٰى قَلْبِهَا لِتَكُوْنَ مِنَ الْمُؤْمِنِيْنَ ﴿١١﴾

* 12. And she said to his sister, 'Follow him up.' So she observed him from afar; and they knew not *of her relationship.*

وَقَالَتْ لِاُخْتِهٖ قُصِّيْهِ ۡ فَبَصُرَتْ بِهٖ عَنْ جُنُبٍ وَّهُمْ
لَا يَشْعُرُوْنَ ﴿١٢﴾

* 13. And We had already ordained that he shall refuse the wet nurses; so she said, 'Shall I tell you of a household who will bring him up for you and will be his sincere well-wishers?'

وَحَرَّمْنَا عَلَيْهِ الْمَرَاضِعَ مِنْ قَبْلُ فَقَالَتْ هَلْ اَدُلُّكُمْ
عَلٰٓى اَهْلِ بَيْتٍ يَّكْفُلُوْنَهٗ لَكُمْ وَهُمْ لَهٗ نٰصِحُوْنَ ﴿١٣﴾

* 14. Thus did We restore him to his mother that her eye might be gladdened and that she might not grieve, and that she might know that the promise of Allah is true. But most of them know not.

فَرَدَدْنٰهُ اِلٰٓى اُمِّهٖ كَيْ تَقَرَّ عَيْنُهَا وَلَا تَحْزَنَ وَلِتَعْلَمَ
اَنَّ وَعْدَ اللّٰهِ حَقٌّ وَّلٰكِنَّ اَكْثَرَهُمْ لَا يَعْلَمُوْنَ ﴿١٤﴾

R. 2.

15. And when he reached his *age of* full strength and attained maturity, We gave him wisdom and knowledge; and thus do We reward those who do good.

وَلَمَّا بَلَغَ اَشُدَّهٗ وَاسْتَوٰٓى اٰتَيْنٰهُ حُكْمًا وَّعِلْمًا ۭ
وَكَذٰلِكَ نَجْزِي الْمُحْسِنِيْنَ ﴿١٥﴾

* 16. And he entered the city at a time when its inhabitants were in a state of heedlessness; and he found therein two men fighting—one of his own party, and the other of his enemies. And he who was of his party sought his help against him who was of his enemies. So Moses smote him with his fist; and *thereby* caused his death. He said, 'This is of Satan's doing; he is indeed an enemy, a manifest misleader.'

وَدَخَلَ الْمَدِيْنَةَ عَلٰى حِيْنِ غَفْلَةٍ مِّنْ اَهْلِهَا
فَوَجَدَ فِيْهَا رَجُلَيْنِ يَقْتَتِلٰنِ ۤ هٰذَا مِنْ شِيْعَتِهٖ
وَهٰذَا مِنْ عَدُوِّهٖ ۚ فَاسْتَغَاثَهُ الَّذِيْ مِنْ شِيْعَتِهٖ
عَلَى الَّذِيْ مِنْ عَدُوِّهٖ ۙ فَوَكَزَهٗ مُوْسٰى فَقَضٰى عَلَيْهِ ۤ
قَالَ هٰذَا مِنْ عَمَلِ الشَّيْطٰنِ ۭ اِنَّهٗ عَدُوٌّ مُّضِلٌّ مُّبِيْنٌ ﴿١٦﴾

17. He said, 'My Lord, I have wronged my soul, therefore forgive me.' So He forgave him; He is Most Forgiving, Merciful.

قَالَ رَبِّ اِنِّيْ ظَلَمْتُ نَفْسِيْ فَاغْفِرْ لِيْ فَغَفَرَ لَهٗ ۭ
اِنَّهٗ هُوَ الْغَفُوْرُ الرَّحِيْمُ ﴿١٧﴾

18. He said, 'My Lord, because Thou hast bestowed favour upon me, I will never be a helper of the guilty.'

قَالَ رَبِّ بِمَآ اَنْعَمْتَ عَلَيَّ فَلَنْ اَكُوْنَ ظَهِيْرًا
لِّلْمُجْرِمِيْنَ ﴿١٨﴾

* 19. And morning found him in the city, apprehensive, watchful; and lo! he who had sought his help the day before cried out to him *again* for help. Moses said to

فَاَصْبَحَ فِي الْمَدِيْنَةِ خَاۗىِٕفًا يَّتَرَقَّبُ فَاِذَا الَّذِي
اسْتَنْصَرَهٗ بِالْاَمْسِ يَسْتَصْرِخُهٗ ۭ قَالَ لَهٗ مُوْسٰٓى

him: 'Verily, thou art manifestly a misguided fellow.'

إِنَّكَ لَغَوِيٌّ مُّبِينٌ (19)

20. And when he made up his mind to lay hold of the man who was an enemy to both of them, he said, 'O Moses, dost thou intend to kill me as thou didst kill a man yesterday? Thou only intendest to become a tyrant in the land, and thou intendest not to be a peacemaker.'

فَلَمَّآ اَنْ اَرَادَ اَنْ يَّبْطِشَ بِالَّذِيْ هُوَ عَدُوٌّ لَّهُمَا
قَالَ يٰمُوْسٰٓى اَتُرِيْدُ اَنْ تَقْتُلَنِيْ كَمَا قَتَلْتَ نَفْسًا
بِالْاَمْسِ اِنْ تُرِيْدُ اِلَّآ اَنْ تَكُوْنَ جَبَّارًا فِي الْاَرْضِ
وَمَا تُرِيْدُ اَنْ تَكُوْنَ مِنَ الْمُصْلِحِيْنَ (20)

21. And there came a man from the far side of the city, running. He said, 'O Moses, of a truth, the chiefs are taking counsel together against thee to kill thee. Therefore get thee away; surely I am of thy well-wishers.'

وَجَآءَ رَجُلٌ مِّنْ اَقْصَا الْمَدِيْنَةِ يَسْعٰى قَالَ يٰمُوْسٰٓى
اِنَّ الْمَلَاَ يَاْتَمِرُوْنَ بِكَ لِيَقْتُلُوْكَ فَاخْرُجْ اِنِّيْ لَكَ
مِنَ النّٰصِحِيْنَ (21)

22. So he went forth therefrom, fearing, watchful. He said, 'My Lord, deliver me from the unjust people.'

فَخَرَجَ مِنْهَا خَآئِفًا يَّتَرَقَّبُ قَالَ رَبِّ نَجِّنِيْ مِنَ
الْقَوْمِ الظّٰلِمِيْنَ (22) ع

R. 3.

23. And when he turned his face towards Midian, he said, 'I hope, my Lord will guide me to the right way.'

وَلَمَّا تَوَجَّهَ تِلْقَآءَ مَدْيَنَ قَالَ عَسٰى رَبِّيْٓ اَنْ
يَّهْدِيَنِيْ سَوَآءَ السَّبِيْلِ (23)

24. And when he arrived at the water of Midian, he found there a party of men, watering *their flocks*. And he found beside them two women keeping back *their flocks*. He said, 'What is the matter with you?' They replied, 'We cannot water *our flocks* until the shepherds take away *their flocks*, and our father is a very old man.'

وَلَمَّا وَرَدَ مَآءَ مَدْيَنَ وَجَدَ عَلَيْهِ اُمَّةً مِّنَ
النَّاسِ يَسْقُوْنَ ۥ وَوَجَدَ مِنْ دُوْنِهِمُ امْرَاَتَيْنِ
تَذُوْدٰنِ قَالَ مَا خَطْبُكُمَا قَالَتَا لَا نَسْقِيْ حَتّٰى
يُصْدِرَ الرِّعَآءُ وَاَبُوْنَا شَيْخٌ كَبِيْرٌ (24)

* 25. So he watered *their flocks* for them. Then he turned aside into the shade, and said, 'My Lord, I am in need of whatever good Thou mayest send down to me.'

فَسَقٰى لَهُمَا ثُمَّ تَوَلّٰىٓ اِلَى الظِّلِّ فَقَالَ رَبِّ اِنِّيْ لِمَآ
اَنْزَلْتَ اِلَيَّ مِنْ خَيْرٍ فَقِيْرٌ (25)

26. And one of the two *women* came to him, walking bashfully. She said, 'My father calls thee that he may reward thee for thy having watered *our flocks* for us.' So when he came to him and told him the story, he said, 'Fear not; thou hast escaped from the unjust people.'

فَجَآءَتْهُ اِحْدٰىهُمَا تَمْشِيْ عَلَى اسْتِحْيَآءٍ قَالَتْ اِنَّ
اَبِيْ يَدْعُوْكَ لِيَجْزِيَكَ اَجْرَ مَا سَقَيْتَ لَنَا فَلَمَّا
جَآءَهٗ وَقَصَّ عَلَيْهِ الْقَصَصَ قَالَ لَا تَخَفْ نَجَوْتَ
مِنَ الْقَوْمِ الظّٰلِمِيْنَ (26)

27. One of the two *women* said, 'O my father, hire him; for the best man that thou canst hire is the one who is strong and trustworthy.'

قَالَتْ إِحْدٰىهُمَا يٰٓأَبَتِ اسْتَأْجِرْهُ إِنَّ خَيْرَ مَنِ
اسْتَأْجَرْتَ الْقَوِيُّ الْأَمِيْنُ ﴿٢٧﴾

28. He said, 'I intend to marry one of these two daughters of mine to thee on condition that thou serve me on hire for eight years. But if thou complete ten *years*, it will be of thine own accord. And I would not lay any hardship upon thee; thou wilt find me, if Allah wills, of the righteous.'

قَالَ إِنِّيْٓ أُرِيْدُ أَنْ أُنْكِحَكَ إِحْدَى ابْنَتَيَّ هٰتَيْنِ
عَلٰٓى أَنْ تَأْجُرَنِيْ ثَمٰنِيَ حِجَجٍ فَإِنْ أَتْمَمْتَ عَشْرًا
فَمِنْ عِنْدِكَ وَمَآ أُرِيْدُ أَنْ أَشُقَّ عَلَيْكَ سَتَجِدُنِيْٓ
إِنْ شَآءَ اللّٰهُ مِنَ الصّٰلِحِيْنَ ﴿٢٨﴾

* 29. He said, 'That is *settled* between me and thee. Whichever of the two terms I fulfil, there shall be no injustice to me; and Allah watches over what we say.'

قَالَ ذٰلِكَ بَيْنِيْ وَبَيْنَكَ أَيَّمَا الْأَجَلَيْنِ قَضَيْتُ فَلَا
عُدْوَانَ عَلَيَّ وَاللّٰهُ عَلٰى مَا نَقُوْلُ وَكِيْلٌ ﴿٢٩﴾

R. 4.

30. And when Moses had fulfilled the term, and journeyed with his family, he perceived a fire in the direction of the Mount. He said to his family, 'Wait, I perceive a fire; haply I may bring you some *useful* information therefrom, or a burning brand from the fire that you may warm yourselves.'

فَلَمَّا قَضٰى مُوْسَى الْأَجَلَ وَسَارَ بِأَهْلِهٖٓ اٰنَسَ مِنْ
جَانِبِ الطُّوْرِ نَارًا قَالَ لِأَهْلِهِ امْكُثُوْٓا إِنِّيْٓ اٰنَسْتُ
نَارًا لَّعَلِّيْٓ اٰتِيْكُمْ مِّنْهَا بِخَبَرٍ أَوْ جَذْوَةٍ مِّنَ النَّارِ
لَعَلَّكُمْ تَصْطَلُوْنَ ﴿٣٠﴾

* 31. And when he came to it, he was called *by a voice* from the right side of the Valley, in the blessed spot, out of the tree: 'O Moses, verily I am, I am Allah, the Lord of the worlds.'

فَلَمَّآ أَتٰىهَا نُوْدِيَ مِنْ شَاطِئِ الْوَادِ الْأَيْمَنِ فِي الْبُقْعَةِ
الْمُبٰرَكَةِ مِنَ الشَّجَرَةِ أَنْ يّٰمُوْسٰٓى إِنِّيْٓ أَنَا اللّٰهُ رَبُّ
الْعٰلَمِيْنَ ﴿٣١﴾

32. And *it also said:* 'Throw down thy rod.' And when he saw it move as though it were a serpent, he turned back retreating and did not wait. 'O Moses, come forward and fear not; surely thou art of those who are safe.

وَأَنْ أَلْقِ عَصَاكَ فَلَمَّا رَاٰهَا تَهْتَزُّ كَأَنَّهَا جَآنٌّ وَّلّٰى
مُدْبِرًا وَّلَمْ يُعَقِّبْ يٰمُوْسٰٓى أَقْبِلْ وَلَا تَخَفْ إِنَّكَ
مِنَ الْاٰمِنِيْنَ ﴿٣٢﴾

33. 'Insert thy hand into thy bosom; it will come forth white without evil *effect*, and draw back thy arm toward thyself *to be free* from fear. So these *shall be* two proofs from thy Lord to Pharaoh and his chiefs. Surely they are a rebellious people.'

اُسْلُكْ يَدَكَ فِيْ جَيْبِكَ تَخْرُجْ بَيْضَآءَ مِنْ غَيْرِ سُوْٓءٍ
وَّاضْمُمْ إِلَيْكَ جَنَاحَكَ مِنَ الرَّهْبِ فَذٰنِكَ بُرْهَانٰنِ
مِنْ رَّبِّكَ إِلٰى فِرْعَوْنَ وَمَلَا۠ئِهٖ إِنَّهُمْ كَانُوْا قَوْمًا
فٰسِقِيْنَ ﴿٣٣﴾

34. He said, 'My Lord, I killed a person from among them, and I fear that they will kill me.

قال رب إني قتلت منهم نفسا فأخاف أن
يقتلون ٣٤

35. 'And my brother Aaron—he is more eloquent in speech than I; send him therefore with me as a helper that he may bear witness to my truth. I fear that they will accuse me of falsehood.'

وأخي هرون هو أفصح مني لسانا فأرسله معي
ردا يصدقني إني أخاف أن يكذبون ٣٥

36. *God* said, 'We will strengthen thy arm with thy brother, and We will give power to you both so that they shall not be able to reach you. *Go* with Our Signs. You two and those who follow you will be the winners.'

قال سنشد عضدك بأخيك ونجعل لكما سلطنا
فلا يصلون إليكما بأيتنا أنتما ومن اتبعكما
الغلبون ٣٦

37. And when Moses came to them with Our clear Signs, they said, 'This is nothing but sorcery devised, and we never heard *the like* of this among our forefathers.'

فلما جاءهم موسى بأيتنا بينت قالوا ما هذا
إلا سحر مفترى وما سمعنا بهذا في آبائنا
الأولين ٣٧

38. Moses said, 'My Lord knows best who it is that has brought guidance from Him, and whose will be the reward of the *final* abode. Verily, the wrongdoers never prosper.'

وقال موسى ربي أعلم بمن جاء بالهدى من
عنده ومن تكون له عاقبة الدار إنه لا يفلح
الظلمون ٣٨

* 39. And Pharaoh said, 'O chiefs, I know of no God for you other than myself; so burn me *bricks of* clay, O Hāmān, and build me a tower, that I may have a look at the God of Moses, though I believe him to be one of the liars.'

وقال فرعون يأيها الملأ ما علمت لكم من
إله غيري فأوقد لي يهمن على الطين فاجعل
لي صرحا لعلي أطلع إلى إله موسى وإني لأظنه
من الكذبين ٣٩

40. And he and his hosts behaved arrogantly in the land without any justification. And they thought that they would never be brought back to Us.

واستكبر هو وجنوده في الأرض بغير الحق و
ظنوا أنهم إلينا لا يرجعون ٤٠

41. So We seized him and his hosts, and cast them into the sea. See, then, how *evil* was the end of the wrongdoers!

فأخذنه وجنوده فنبذنهم في اليم فانظر
كيف كان عاقبة الظلمين ٤١

42. And We made them leaders inviting *people* unto the Fire; and on the Day of

وجعلنهم أئمة يدعون إلى النار ويوم القيمة

Resurrection they will receive no help.

لَا يُنْصَرُوْنَ ﴿٤٢﴾

43. And We caused them to be followed by a curse in this world; and on the Day of Resurrection they will be among those deprived of *all* good.

وَاَتْبَعْنٰهُمْ فِيْ هٰذِهِ الدُّنْيَا لَعْنَةً ۚ وَيَوْمَ الْقِيٰمَةِ هُمْ
ع مِّنَ الْمَقْبُوْحِيْنَ ﴿٤٣﴾

R. 5.

44. And We gave the Book to Moses, after We had destroyed the earlier generations, as *a source of* enlightenment for men, and a guidance and a mercy, that they might reflect.

وَلَقَدْ اٰتَيْنَا مُوْسَى الْكِتٰبَ مِنْۢ بَعْدِ مَآ اَهْلَكْنَا الْقُرُوْنَ
الْاُوْلٰى بَصَآئِرَ لِلنَّاسِ وَهُدًى وَّرَحْمَةً لَّعَلَّهُمْ
يَتَذَكَّرُوْنَ ﴿٤٤﴾

45. And thou wast not on the western side *of the Mount* when We revealed the command to Moses, nor wast thou among the witnesses.

وَمَا كُنْتَ بِجَانِبِ الْغَرْبِيِّ اِذْ قَضَيْنَآ اِلٰى مُوْسَى
الْاَمْرَ وَمَا كُنْتَ مِنَ الشّٰهِدِيْنَ ﴿٤٥﴾

46. But We brought forth generations *after Moses*, and life became prolonged for them. And thou wast not a dweller among the people of Midian, rehearsing Our Signs unto them; but it is We Who sent Messengers.

وَلٰكِنَّآ اَنْشَاْنَا قُرُوْنًا فَتَطَاوَلَ عَلَيْهِمُ الْعُمُرُ ۚ وَمَا
كُنْتَ ثَاوِيًا فِيْٓ اَهْلِ مَدْيَنَ تَتْلُوْا عَلَيْهِمْ اٰيٰتِنَا ۙ
وَلٰكِنَّا كُنَّا مُرْسِلِيْنَ ﴿٤٦﴾

47. And thou wast not at the side of the Mount when We called. But *We have sent thee as* a mercy from thy Lord, that thou mayest warn a people to whom no Warner had come before thee, that they may reflect.

وَمَا كُنْتَ بِجَانِبِ الطُّوْرِ اِذْ نَادَيْنَا وَلٰكِنْ رَّحْمَةً
مِّنْ رَّبِّكَ لِتُنْذِرَ قَوْمًا مَّآ اَتٰىهُمْ مِّنْ نَّذِيْرٍ
مِّنْ قَبْلِكَ لَعَلَّهُمْ يَتَذَكَّرُوْنَ ﴿٤٧﴾

* 48. And had it not been *for the fact* that, if an affliction should befall them because of what their hands have sent before *them*, they would say, 'Our Lord, wherefore didst Thou not send a Messenger to us that we might have followed Thy Signs, and been of the believers?' *We should not have sent thee as a Messenger.*

وَلَوْلَآ اَنْ تُصِيْبَهُمْ مُّصِيْبَةٌۢ بِمَا قَدَّمَتْ اَيْدِيْهِمْ
فَيَقُوْلُوْا رَبَّنَا لَوْلَآ اَرْسَلْتَ اِلَيْنَا رَسُوْلًا فَنَتَّبِعَ اٰيٰتِكَ
وَنَكُوْنَ مِنَ الْمُؤْمِنِيْنَ ﴿٤٨﴾

* 49. But when the truth came to them from Us, they said, 'Why has he not been given the like of what was given to Moses?' Did they not reject that which was given to Moses before? They say, 'Two *works* of sorcery—*the Torah and the Qur'ān*—that back up each other.' And they say, 'We disbelieve in all.'

فَلَمَّا جَآءَهُمُ الْحَقُّ مِنْ عِنْدِنَا قَالُوْا لَوْلَآ اُوْتِيَ
مِثْلَ مَآ اُوْتِيَ مُوْسٰى ۗ اَوَلَمْ يَكْفُرُوْا بِمَآ اُوْتِيَ مُوْسٰى
مِنْ قَبْلُ ۚ قَالُوْا سِحْرٰنِ تَظٰهَرَا ۗ وَقَالُوْآ اِنَّا بِكُلٍّ
كٰفِرُوْنَ ﴿٤٩﴾

* 50. Say, 'Then bring a Book from Allah which is a better guide than *these* two, that

قُلْ فَاْتُوْا بِكِتٰبٍ مِّنْ عِنْدِ اللّٰهِ هُوَ اَهْدٰى مِنْهُمَآ

I may follow it, if you are truthful.'

51. But if they answer thee not, then know that they only follow their own evil inclinations. And who is more erring than he who follows his evil inclinations without any guidance from Allah? Verily Allah guides not the unjust people.

R. 6.

52. And We have, indeed, thoroughly conveyed to them the Word, that they may be admonished.

53. Those to whom We gave the Book before it—they believe in it;

54. And when it is recited unto them, they say, 'We believe in it. Verily, it is the truth from our Lord. Indeed, even before it we had submitted ourselves *to God*.'

55. These will be given their reward twice, for they have been steadfast and they repel evil with good, and spend out of what We have given them.

56. And when they hear vain talk, they turn away from it and say, 'Unto us our works and unto you your works. Peace be to you. We seek not the ignorant.'

57. Surely thou wilt not be able to guide *all* whom thou lovest; but Allah guides whomsoever He pleases; and He knows best those who would accept guidance.

58. And they say, 'If we were to follow the guidance with thee, we should be snatched away from our land.' Have We not established for them a safe sanctuary, to which are brought the fruits of all things, *as* a provision from Us? But most of them know not.

59. And how many a habitation have We destroyed which exulted in its *manner of* life! And these are their dwellings which have not been inhabited after them except a little. And it is We Who became the Inheritors.

60. And thy Lord would never destroy the towns until He has raised in the mother *town* thereof a Messenger, reciting unto them Our Signs; nor would We destroy the towns unless the people thereof are wrong-

اَتَّبِعْهُ اِنْ كُنْتُمْ صٰدِقِيْنَ ﴿۵۰﴾
فَاِنْ لَّمْ يَسْتَجِيْبُوْا لَكَ فَاعْلَمْ اَنَّمَا يَتَّبِعُوْنَ اَهْوَآءَهُمْ
وَمَنْ اَضَلُّ مِمَّنِ اتَّبَعَ هَوٰىهُ بِغَيْرِ هُدًى مِّنَ اللّٰهِ
اِنَّ اللّٰهَ لَا يَهْدِي الْقَوْمَ الظّٰلِمِيْنَ ﴿۵۱﴾ ع
وَلَقَدْ وَصَّلْنَا لَهُمُ الْقَوْلَ لَعَلَّهُمْ يَتَذَكَّرُوْنَ ﴿۵۲﴾
اَلَّذِيْنَ اٰتَيْنٰهُمُ الْكِتٰبَ مِنْ قَبْلِهٖ هُمْ بِهٖ يُؤْمِنُوْنَ ﴿۵۳﴾ النصف
وَاِذَا يُتْلٰى عَلَيْهِمْ قَالُوْٓا اٰمَنَّا بِهٖٓ اِنَّهُ الْحَقُّ مِنْ رَّبِّنَآ
اِنَّا كُنَّا مِنْ قَبْلِهٖ مُسْلِمِيْنَ ﴿۵۴﴾
اُولٰٓئِكَ يُؤْتَوْنَ اَجْرَهُمْ مَّرَّتَيْنِ بِمَا صَبَرُوْا وَ
يَدْرَءُوْنَ بِالْحَسَنَةِ السَّيِّئَةَ وَمِمَّا رَزَقْنٰهُمْ يُنْفِقُوْنَ ﴿۵۵﴾
وَاِذَا سَمِعُوا اللَّغْوَ اَعْرَضُوْا عَنْهُ وَقَالُوْا لَنَآ اَعْمَالُنَا
وَلَكُمْ اَعْمَالُكُمْ سَلٰمٌ عَلَيْكُمْ لَا نَبْتَغِي الْجٰهِلِيْنَ ﴿۵۶﴾
اِنَّكَ لَا تَهْدِيْ مَنْ اَحْبَبْتَ وَلٰكِنَّ اللّٰهَ يَهْدِيْ مَنْ
يَّشَآءُ وَهُوَ اَعْلَمُ بِالْمُهْتَدِيْنَ ﴿۵۷﴾
وَقَالُوْٓا اِنْ نَّتَّبِعِ الْهُدٰى مَعَكَ نُتَخَطَّفْ مِنْ اَرْضِنَا
اَوَلَمْ نُمَكِّنْ لَّهُمْ حَرَمًا اٰمِنًا يُّجْبٰٓى اِلَيْهِ ثَمَرٰتُ
كُلِّ شَيْءٍ رِّزْقًا مِّنْ لَّدُنَّا وَلٰكِنَّ اَكْثَرَهُمْ لَا يَعْلَمُوْنَ ﴿۵۸﴾
وَكَمْ اَهْلَكْنَا مِنْ قَرْيَةٍ بَطِرَتْ مَعِيْشَتَهَا فَتِلْكَ
مَسٰكِنُهُمْ لَمْ تُسْكَنْ مِّنْ بَعْدِهِمْ اِلَّا قَلِيْلًا وَ
كُنَّا نَحْنُ الْوٰرِثِيْنَ ﴿۵۹﴾
وَمَا كَانَ رَبُّكَ مُهْلِكَ الْقُرٰى حَتّٰى يَبْعَثَ فِيْٓ اُمِّهَا
رَسُوْلًا يَتْلُوْا عَلَيْهِمْ اٰيٰتِنَا وَمَا كُنَّا مُهْلِكِي الْقُرٰٓى

doers.

61. And whatever of the things *of this world* you are given is only a temporary enjoyment of the present life and an adornment thereof; and that which is with Allah is better and more lasting. Will you not then understand?

R. 7.

62. Is he, then, to whom We have promised a goodly promise *the fulfilment of* which he will meet, like the one whom We have provided with the good things of this life, and then on the Day of Resurrection he will be of those who will be brought *arraigned before God?*

63. And on that day He will call to them, and say, 'Where are My 'partners' that you so imagined?'

64. Those against whom the sentence will become due, will say, 'Our Lord, these are those whom we led astray. We led them astray, even as we had gone astray *ourselves*. We *now* dissociate ourselves *from them and turn* to Thee. It was not us that they worshipped.'

65. And it will be said, 'Call upon your partners.' And they will call upon them, but they will not answer them. And they will see the punishment. Would that they had followed the guidance!

66. And on that day He will call to them and say, 'What answer did you give to the Messengers?'

* 67. Then all excuses will become obscure to them on that day, and they shall not *even* ask each other.

68. But as for him who repents and believes and does righteous deeds, maybe he will be among the prosperous.

69. And thy Lord creates whatever He pleases and chooses *whomsoever He pleases*. It is not for them to choose. Glorified be Allah, and far is He above all that they associate *with Him*.

70. And thy Lord knows what their breasts conceal, and what they reveal.

71. And He is Allah; there is no God but He. To Him belongs all praise in the beginning and the Hereafter. His is the judgment, and to Him shall you be brought back.

* 72. Say, 'Tell me, if Allah make the

إِلَّا وَأَهْلُهَا ظَٰلِمُونَ ﴿٦٠﴾
وَمَآ أُوتِيتُم مِّن شَيْءٍ فَمَتَٰعُ الْحَيَوٰةِ الدُّنْيَا وَ
زِينَتُهَا وَمَا عِندَ اللَّهِ خَيْرٌ وَأَبْقَىٰ أَفَلَا تَعْقِلُونَ ﴿٦١﴾ ع
أَفَمَن وَعَدْنَٰهُ وَعْدًا حَسَنًا فَهُوَ لَٰقِيهِ كَمَن مَّتَّعْنَٰهُ
مَتَٰعَ الْحَيَوٰةِ الدُّنْيَا ثُمَّ هُوَ يَوْمَ الْقِيَٰمَةِ مِنَ الْمُحْضَرِينَ ﴿٦٢﴾
وَيَوْمَ يُنَادِيهِمْ فَيَقُولُ أَيْنَ شُرَكَآءِيَ الَّذِينَ
كُنتُمْ تَزْعُمُونَ ﴿٦٣﴾
قَالَ الَّذِينَ حَقَّ عَلَيْهِمُ الْقَوْلُ رَبَّنَا هَٰٓؤُلَآءِ الَّذِينَ
أَغْوَيْنَا ج أَغْوَيْنَٰهُمْ كَمَا غَوَيْنَا ج تَبَرَّأْنَآ إِلَيْكَ مَا
كَانُوٓا إِيَّانَا يَعْبُدُونَ ﴿٦٤﴾
وَقِيلَ ادْعُوا شُرَكَآءَكُمْ فَدَعَوْهُمْ فَلَمْ يَسْتَجِيبُوا
لَهُمْ وَرَأَوُا الْعَذَابَ لَوْ أَنَّهُمْ كَانُوا يَهْتَدُونَ ﴿٦٥﴾
وَيَوْمَ يُنَادِيهِمْ فَيَقُولُ مَاذَآ أَجَبْتُمُ الْمُرْسَلِينَ ﴿٦٦﴾
فَعَمِيَتْ عَلَيْهِمُ الْأَنۢبَآءُ يَوْمَئِذٍ فَهُمْ لَا يَتَسَآءَلُونَ ﴿٦٧﴾
فَأَمَّا مَن تَابَ وَءَامَنَ وَعَمِلَ صَٰلِحًا فَعَسَىٰٓ أَن يَكُونَ
مِنَ الْمُفْلِحِينَ ﴿٦٨﴾
وَرَبُّكَ يَخْلُقُ مَا يَشَآءُ وَيَخْتَارُ مَا كَانَ لَهُمُ الْخِيَرَةُ
سُبْحَٰنَ اللَّهِ وَتَعَٰلَىٰ عَمَّا يُشْرِكُونَ ﴿٦٩﴾
وَرَبُّكَ يَعْلَمُ مَا تُكِنُّ صُدُورُهُمْ وَمَا يُعْلِنُونَ ﴿٧٠﴾
وَهُوَ اللَّهُ لَآ إِلَٰهَ إِلَّا هُوَ لَهُ الْحَمْدُ فِي الْأُولَىٰ وَالْآخِرَةِ
وَلَهُ الْحُكْمُ وَإِلَيْهِ تُرْجَعُونَ ﴿٧١﴾
قُلْ أَرَءَيْتُمْ إِن جَعَلَ اللَّهُ عَلَيْكُمُ الَّيْلَ سَرْمَدًا

night continue over you till the Day of Resurrection, what God is there besides Allah who could bring you light? Will you not then hearken?'

إِلَىٰ يَوْمِ الْقِيَامَةِ مَنْ إِلَٰهٌ غَيْرُ اللَّهِ يَأْتِيكُمْ بِضِيَاءٍ ۖ
أَفَلَا تَسْمَعُونَ ﴿٧٢﴾

* 73. Say, 'Tell me, if Allah make the day continue over you till the Day of Resurrection, what God is there besides Allah who could bring you a night wherein you could rest? Will you not then see?'

قُلْ أَرَأَيْتُمْ إِنْ جَعَلَ اللَّهُ عَلَيْكُمُ النَّهَارَ سَرْمَدًا
إِلَىٰ يَوْمِ الْقِيَامَةِ مَنْ إِلَٰهٌ غَيْرُ اللَّهِ يَأْتِيكُمْ بِلَيْلٍ
تَسْكُنُونَ فِيهِ ۖ أَفَلَا تُبْصِرُونَ ﴿٧٣﴾

74. And of His mercy He has made for you the night and the day, that you may rest therein, and that you may seek of His bounty, and that you may be grateful.

وَمِنْ رَحْمَتِهِ جَعَلَ لَكُمُ اللَّيْلَ وَالنَّهَارَ لِتَسْكُنُوا
فِيهِ وَلِتَبْتَغُوا مِنْ فَضْلِهِ وَلَعَلَّكُمْ تَشْكُرُونَ ﴿٧٤﴾

75. And on that day He will call to them and say, "Where are My 'partners', whom you so imagined?"

وَيَوْمَ يُنَادِيهِمْ فَيَقُولُ أَيْنَ شُرَكَائِيَ الَّذِينَ كُنْتُمْ
تَزْعُمُونَ ﴿٧٥﴾

76. And We shall draw from every people a witness and We shall say, 'Bring your proof.' Then they will know that the truth belongs to Allah. And that which they used to forge will be lost unto them.

وَنَزَعْنَا مِنْ كُلِّ أُمَّةٍ شَهِيدًا فَقُلْنَا هَاتُوا بُرْهَانَكُمْ
ع فَعَلِمُوا أَنَّ الْحَقَّ لِلَّهِ وَضَلَّ عَنْهُمْ مَا كَانُوا يَفْتَرُونَ ﴿٧٦﴾

R. 8.

* 77. Verily, Korah was of the people of Moses, but he behaved arrogantly towards them. And We had given him of treasures so much that his hoardings would have weighed down a party of strong men. When his people said to him, 'Exult not, surely Allah loves not those who exult.

إِنَّ قَارُونَ كَانَ مِنْ قَوْمِ مُوسَىٰ فَبَغَىٰ عَلَيْهِمْ ۖ وَآتَيْنَاهُ
مِنَ الْكُنُوزِ مَا إِنَّ مَفَاتِحَهُ لَتَنُوءُ بِالْعُصْبَةِ أُولِي
الْقُوَّةِ إِذْ قَالَ لَهُ قَوْمُهُ لَا تَفْرَحْ ۖ إِنَّ اللَّهَ لَا يُحِبُّ
الْفَرِحِينَ ﴿٧٧﴾

78. 'And seek, in that which Allah has given thee, the Home of the Hereafter; and neglect not thy lot in this world; and do good *to others* as Allah has done good to thee; and seek not to make mischief in the earth, verily Allah loves not those who make mischief.'

وَابْتَغِ فِيمَا آتَاكَ اللَّهُ الدَّارَ الْآخِرَةَ ۖ وَلَا تَنْسَ
نَصِيبَكَ مِنَ الدُّنْيَا ۖ وَأَحْسِنْ كَمَا أَحْسَنَ اللَّهُ
إِلَيْكَ ۖ وَلَا تَبْغِ الْفَسَادَ فِي الْأَرْضِ ۖ إِنَّ اللَّهَ لَا يُحِبُّ
الْمُفْسِدِينَ ﴿٧٨﴾

79. He said, 'This has been given to me because of the knowledge I possess.' Did he not know that Allah had destroyed before him generations that were mightier than he and greater in riches? And the guilty shall not be asked *to offer an explanation*

قَالَ إِنَّمَا أُوتِيتُهُ عَلَىٰ عِلْمٍ عِنْدِي ۚ أَوَلَمْ يَعْلَمْ أَنَّ
اللَّهَ قَدْ أَهْلَكَ مِنْ قَبْلِهِ مِنَ الْقُرُونِ مَنْ هُوَ أَشَدُّ
مِنْهُ قُوَّةً وَأَكْثَرُ جَمْعًا ۚ وَلَا يُسْأَلُ عَنْ ذُنُوبِهِمُ

of their sins.

الْمُجْرِمُونَ ﴿٧٩﴾

80. So he went forth before his people in his pomp. Those who were desirous of the life of this world said, 'O would that we had the like of what Korah has been given! Truly, he is the master of great fortune.'

فَخَرَجَ عَلَىٰ قَوْمِهِ فِي زِينَتِهِ ۖ قَالَ الَّذِينَ يُرِيدُونَ الْحَيَاةَ الدُّنْيَا يَا لَيْتَ لَنَا مِثْلَ مَا أُوتِيَ قَارُونُ إِنَّهُ لَذُو حَظٍّ عَظِيمٍ ﴿٨٠﴾

81. But those who had been given knowledge said, 'Woe to you, Allah's reward is best for those who believe and do good works; and it shall be granted to none except those who are steadfast.'

وَقَالَ الَّذِينَ أُوتُوا الْعِلْمَ وَيْلَكُمْ ثَوَابُ اللَّهِ خَيْرٌ لِمَنْ آمَنَ وَعَمِلَ صَالِحًا وَلَا يُلَقَّاهَا إِلَّا الصَّابِرُونَ ﴿٨١﴾

* 82. Then We caused the earth to swallow him up and his dwelling; and he had no party to help him against Allah, nor was he of those who can defend themselves.

فَخَسَفْنَا بِهِ وَبِدَارِهِ الْأَرْضَ فَمَا كَانَ لَهُ مِنْ فِئَةٍ يَنْصُرُونَهُ مِنْ دُونِ اللَّهِ وَمَا كَانَ مِنَ الْمُنْتَصِرِينَ ﴿٨٢﴾

83. And those who had coveted his position the day before began to say, 'Ah! it is indeed Allah Who enlarges the provision for such of His servants as He pleases and straitens *it for whom He pleases*. Had not Allah been gracious to us, He would have caused it to swallow us up *also*. Ah! the ungrateful never prosper.'

وَأَصْبَحَ الَّذِينَ تَمَنَّوْا مَكَانَهُ بِالْأَمْسِ يَقُولُونَ وَيْكَأَنَّ اللَّهَ يَبْسُطُ الرِّزْقَ لِمَنْ يَشَاءُ مِنْ عِبَادِهِ وَيَقْدِرُ ۖ لَوْلَا أَنْ مَنَّ اللَّهُ عَلَيْنَا لَخَسَفَ بِنَا ۖ وَيْكَأَنَّهُ لَا يُفْلِحُ الْكَافِرُونَ ﴿٨٣﴾ ع

R. 9.

84. This is the Home of the Hereafter! We give it to those who desire not self-exaltation in the earth, nor corruption. And the end is for the righteous.

تِلْكَ الدَّارُ الْآخِرَةُ نَجْعَلُهَا لِلَّذِينَ لَا يُرِيدُونَ عُلُوًّا فِي الْأَرْضِ وَلَا فَسَادًا ۚ وَالْعَاقِبَةُ لِلْمُتَّقِينَ ﴿٨٤﴾

85. He who does a good deed shall have better reward than that; and *as for him* who does an evil deed—those who do evil deeds shall not be rewarded but *according to* what they did.

مَنْ جَاءَ بِالْحَسَنَةِ فَلَهُ خَيْرٌ مِنْهَا ۖ وَمَنْ جَاءَ بِالسَّيِّئَةِ فَلَا يُجْزَى الَّذِينَ عَمِلُوا السَّيِّئَاتِ إِلَّا مَا كَانُوا يَعْمَلُونَ ﴿٨٥﴾

86. Most surely He Who had made *the teaching of* the Qur'ān binding on thee will bring thee back to *thy* place of return. Say, 'My Lord knows best who brings the guidance, and who is in manifest error.'

إِنَّ الَّذِي فَرَضَ عَلَيْكَ الْقُرْآنَ لَرَادُّكَ إِلَىٰ مَعَادٍ ۚ قُلْ رَبِّي أَعْلَمُ مَنْ جَاءَ بِالْهُدَىٰ وَمَنْ هُوَ فِي ضَلَالٍ مُبِينٍ ﴿٨٦﴾

87. And thou didst never expect that the Book would be revealed to thee; but it is a mercy from thy Lord; so never be a helper of those who disbelieve.

وَمَا كُنْتَ تَرْجُو أَنْ يُلْقَىٰ إِلَيْكَ الْكِتَابُ إِلَّا رَحْمَةً مِنْ رَبِّكَ ۖ فَلَا تَكُونَنَّ ظَهِيرًا لِلْكَافِرِينَ ﴿٨٧﴾

88. And let them not turn thee away from the Signs of Allah, after they have

وَلَا يَصُدُّنَّكَ عَنْ آيَاتِ اللَّهِ بَعْدَ إِذْ أُنْزِلَتْ إِلَيْكَ

been sent down to thee; and call *mankind* to thy Lord, and be not of those who attribute partners *to Him*.

وَادْعُ إِلَىٰ رَبِّكَ وَلَا تَكُونَنَّ مِنَ الْمُشْرِكِينَ ﴿٨٨﴾

89. And call not on any other God beside Allah. There is no God but He. Everything will perish except Himself. His is the judgment, and to Him will you be brought back.

وَلَا تَدْعُ مَعَ اللّٰهِ إِلٰهًا اٰخَرَ لَا إِلٰهَ إِلَّا هُوَ كُلُّ
شَيْءٍ هَالِكٌ إِلَّا وَجْهَهُ لَهُ الْحُكْمُ وَإِلَيْهِ تُرْجَعُونَ ﴿٨٩﴾

سُوْرَةُ الْعَنْكَبُوْتِ مَكِّيَّةٌ

آياتها (٢٩) ركوعاتها

AL-'ANKABŪT

(Revealed before Hijra)

1. In the name of Allah, the Gracious, the Merciful.

بِسْمِ اللّٰهِ الرَّحْمٰنِ الرَّحِيْمِ ۝١

2. Alif Lām Mīm*.

الٓمّٓ ۝٢

* 3. Do men think that they will be left alone because they say, 'We believe,' and that they will not be tested?

اَحَسِبَ النَّاسُ اَنْ يُّتْرَكُوْٓا اَنْ يَّقُوْلُوْٓا اٰمَنَّا وَهُمْ
لَا يُفْتَنُوْنَ ۝٣

4. And We did test those who were before them. So Allah will surely distinguish those who are truthful and He will surely distinguish the liars *from the truthful*.

وَلَقَدْ فَتَنَّا الَّذِيْنَ مِنْ قَبْلِهِمْ فَلَيَعْلَمَنَّ اللّٰهُ الَّذِيْنَ
صَدَقُوْا وَلَيَعْلَمَنَّ الْكٰذِبِيْنَ ۝٤

5. Or do those who commit evil deeds think that they will escape Us? Evil is what they judge.

اَمْ حَسِبَ الَّذِيْنَ يَعْمَلُوْنَ السَّيِّاٰتِ اَنْ يَّسْبِقُوْنَا ؕ
سَآءَ مَا يَحْكُمُوْنَ ۝٥

6. Whoso hopes to meet Allah, *let him be prepared for it*, for Allah's appointed time is certainly coming. And He is the All-Hearing, the All-Knowing.

مَنْ كَانَ يَرْجُوْا لِقَآءَ اللّٰهِ فَاِنَّ اَجَلَ اللّٰهِ لَاٰتٍ ؕ
وَهُوَ السَّمِيْعُ الْعَلِيْمُ ۝٦

* 7. And whoso strives, strives only for his own soul; verily Allah is Independent of all creatures.

وَمَنْ جَاهَدَ فَاِنَّمَا يُجَاهِدُ لِنَفْسِهٖ ؕ اِنَّ اللّٰهَ لَغَنِيٌّ
عَنِ الْعٰلَمِيْنَ ۝٧

8. And *as to* those who believe and do good works, We shall surely remove from them their evils, and We shall surely give them the best reward of their works.

وَالَّذِيْنَ اٰمَنُوْا وَعَمِلُوا الصّٰلِحٰتِ لَنُكَفِّرَنَّ عَنْهُمْ
سَيِّاٰتِهِمْ وَلَنَجْزِيَنَّهُمْ اَحْسَنَ الَّذِيْ كَانُوْا يَعْمَلُوْنَ ۝٨

* 9. And We have enjoined on man kindness to his parents; but if they strive to make thee associate that with Me of which thou hast no knowledge, then obey them not. Unto Me is your return, and I shall inform you of what you did.

وَوَصَّيْنَا الْاِنْسَانَ بِوَالِدَيْهِ حُسْنًا ؕ وَاِنْ جَاهَدٰكَ
لِتُشْرِكَ بِيْ مَا لَيْسَ لَكَ بِهٖ عِلْمٌ فَلَا تُطِعْهُمَا ؕ اِلَيَّ
مَرْجِعُكُمْ فَاُنَبِّئُكُمْ بِمَا كُنْتُمْ تَعْمَلُوْنَ ۝٩

10. And those who believe and do good works—them We shall surely admit into *the company of* the righteous.

وَالَّذِيْنَ اٰمَنُوْا وَعَمِلُوا الصّٰلِحٰتِ لَنُدْخِلَنَّهُمْ فِي
الصّٰلِحِيْنَ ۝١٠

* I am Allah, the All-Knowing.

* 11. And of men there are *some* who say, 'We believe in Allah,' but when they are made to suffer in the cause of Allah, they regard the persecution of men to be like the punishment of Allah. And if help comes from thy Lord, they are sure to say, 'Certainly, we were with you.' Is not Allah best aware of what is in the bosom of *His* creatures?

12. And Allah will surely distinguish those who believe and He will surely distinguish the hypocrites *from the believers*.

13. And those who disbelieve say to those who believe, 'Follow our way, and we will surely bear your sins.' And they cannot bear aught of their sins. They are surely liars.

* 14. But they shall surely bear their own burdens, and *other* burdens along with their own burdens. And they will surely be questioned on the Day of Resurrection concerning that which they fabricated.

R. 2.

* 15. And We certainly sent Noah to his people, and he dwelt among them a thousand years save fifty years. Then the deluge overtook them, while they were wrongdoers.

16. But We saved him and those who were *with him* in the Ark; and We made it a Sign for all peoples.

* 17. And *remember* Abraham when he said to his people, 'Worship Allah and fear Him. That is better for you if you understand.

18. 'You only worship idols beside Allah, and you forge a lie. Those whom you worship beside Allah have no power to provide sustenance for you. Then seek sustenance from Allah, and worship Him, and be grateful to Him. Unto Him will you be brought back.

19. 'And if you reject, then generations before you *also* rejected. And the Messenger is only responsible for the clear conveying *of the Message*.

وَمِنَ النَّاسِ مَنْ يَّقُوْلُ اٰمَنَّا بِاللّٰهِ فَاِذَآ اُوْذِیَ فِی
اللّٰهِ جَعَلَ فِتْنَةَ النَّاسِ كَعَذَابِ اللّٰهِ ؕ وَلَئِنْ جَآءَ
نَصْرٌ مِّنْ رَّبِّكَ لَيَقُوْلُنَّ اِنَّا كُنَّا مَعَكُمْ ؕ اَوَلَيْسَ اللّٰهُ
بِاَعْلَمَ بِمَا فِیْ صُدُوْرِ الْعٰلَمِيْنَ ﴿۱۱﴾
وَلَيَعْلَمَنَّ اللّٰهُ الَّذِيْنَ اٰمَنُوْا وَلَيَعْلَمَنَّ الْمُنٰفِقِيْنَ ﴿۱۲﴾
وَقَالَ الَّذِيْنَ كَفَرُوْا لِلَّذِيْنَ اٰمَنُوا اتَّبِعُوْا سَبِيْلَنَا
وَلْنَحْمِلْ خَطٰيٰكُمْ ؕ وَمَا هُمْ بِحٰمِلِيْنَ مِنْ خَطٰيٰهُمْ
مِّنْ شَیْءٍ ؕ اِنَّهُمْ لَكٰذِبُوْنَ ﴿۱۳﴾
وَلَيَحْمِلُنَّ اَثْقَالَهُمْ وَاَثْقَالًا مَّعَ اَثْقَالِهِمْ ؗ وَلَيُسْئَلُنَّ
ع يَوْمَ الْقِيٰمَةِ عَمَّا كَانُوْا يَفْتَرُوْنَ ﴿۱۴﴾
وَلَقَدْ اَرْسَلْنَا نُوْحًا اِلٰى قَوْمِهٖ فَلَبِثَ فِيْهِمْ اَلْفَ
سَنَةٍ اِلَّا خَمْسِيْنَ عَامًا ؕ فَاَخَذَهُمُ الطُّوْفَانُ وَ
هُمْ ظٰلِمُوْنَ ﴿۱۵﴾
فَاَنْجَيْنٰهُ وَاَصْحٰبَ السَّفِيْنَةِ وَجَعَلْنٰهَآ اٰيَةً لِّلْعٰلَمِيْنَ ﴿۱۶﴾
وَاِبْرٰهِيْمَ اِذْ قَالَ لِقَوْمِهِ اعْبُدُوا اللّٰهَ وَاتَّقُوْهُ ؕ
ذٰلِكُمْ خَيْرٌ لَّكُمْ اِنْ كُنْتُمْ تَعْلَمُوْنَ ﴿۱۷﴾
اِنَّمَا تَعْبُدُوْنَ مِنْ دُوْنِ اللّٰهِ اَوْثَانًا وَّتَخْلُقُوْنَ
اِفْكًا ؕ اِنَّ الَّذِيْنَ تَعْبُدُوْنَ مِنْ دُوْنِ اللّٰهِ لَا يَمْلِكُوْنَ
لَكُمْ رِزْقًا فَابْتَغُوْا عِنْدَ اللّٰهِ الرِّزْقَ وَاعْبُدُوْهُ
وَاشْكُرُوْا لَهٗ ؕ اِلَيْهِ تُرْجَعُوْنَ ﴿۱۸﴾
وَاِنْ تُكَذِّبُوْا فَقَدْ كَذَّبَ اُمَمٌ مِّنْ قَبْلِكُمْ ؕ وَمَا
عَلَى الرَّسُوْلِ اِلَّا الْبَلٰغُ الْمُبِيْنُ ﴿۱۹﴾

20. See they not how Allah originates creation, then repeats it? That surely is easy for Allah.

اَوَلَمْ يَرَوْا كَيْفَ يُبْدِئُ اللّٰهُ الْخَلْقَ ثُمَّ يُعِيْدُهٗ ؕ
اِنَّ ذٰلِكَ عَلَى اللّٰهِ يَسِيْرٌ ﴿۲۰﴾

* 21. Say, 'Travel in the earth, and see how He originated the creation. Then will Allah provide the latter creation.' Surely, Allah has power over all things.

قُلْ سِيْرُوْا فِي الْاَرْضِ فَانْظُرُوْا كَيْفَ بَدَاَ الْخَلْقَ
ثُمَّ اللّٰهُ يُنْشِئُ النَّشْاَةَ الْاٰخِرَةَ ؕ اِنَّ اللّٰهَ عَلٰى كُلِّ
شَيْءٍ قَدِيْرٌ ﴿۲۱﴾

22. He punishes whom He pleases and shows mercy unto whom He pleases; and to Him will you be turned back.

يُعَذِّبُ مَنْ يَّشَآءُ وَيَرْحَمُ مَنْ يَّشَآءُ ۚ وَاِلَيْهِ تُقْلَبُوْنَ ﴿۲۲﴾

23. And you cannot frustrate *the designs of Allah* in the earth nor in the heaven; nor have you any friend or helper beside Allah.

وَمَآ اَنْتُمْ بِمُعْجِزِيْنَ فِي الْاَرْضِ وَلَا فِي السَّمَآءِ ۫ وَ
مَا لَكُمْ مِّنْ دُوْنِ اللّٰهِ مِنْ وَّلِيٍّ وَّلَا نَصِيْرٍ ﴿۲۳﴾

R. 3.

24. Those who disbelieve in the Signs of Allah and the meeting with Him—it is they who have despaired of My mercy. And they will have a grievous punishment.

وَالَّذِيْنَ كَفَرُوْا بِاٰيٰتِ اللّٰهِ وَلِقَآئِهٖٓ اُولٰٓئِكَ
يَئِسُوْا مِنْ رَّحْمَتِيْ وَاُولٰٓئِكَ لَهُمْ عَذَابٌ
اَلِيْمٌ ﴿۲۴﴾

25. And the only answer of his people was that they said, 'Slay him or burn him.' But Allah saved him from the fire. In that surely are Signs for a people who *would* believe.

فَمَا كَانَ جَوَابَ قَوْمِهٖٓ اِلَّآ اَنْ قَالُوا اقْتُلُوْهُ اَوْ حَرِّقُوْهُ
فَاَنْجٰىهُ اللّٰهُ مِنَ النَّارِ ؕ اِنَّ فِيْ ذٰلِكَ لَاٰيٰتٍ لِّقَوْمٍ
يُّؤْمِنُوْنَ ﴿۲۵﴾

26. And he said, 'Verily you have taken for yourselves idols beside Allah, out of love for each other in the present life. Then on the Day of Resurrection you will deny each other, and curse each other. And your abode will be the Fire; and you will have no helpers.'

وَقَالَ اِنَّمَا اتَّخَذْتُمْ مِّنْ دُوْنِ اللّٰهِ اَوْثَانًا ۙ مَّوَدَّةَ
بَيْنِكُمْ فِي الْحَيٰوةِ الدُّنْيَا ۚ ثُمَّ يَوْمَ الْقِيٰمَةِ يَكْفُرُ
بَعْضُكُمْ بِبَعْضٍ وَّيَلْعَنُ بَعْضُكُمْ بَعْضًا ۫ وَّمَاْوٰىكُمُ
النَّارُ وَمَا لَكُمْ مِّنْ نّٰصِرِيْنَ ﴿۲۶﴾

27. And Lot believed him; and *Abraham* said, 'I take refuge with my Lord; surely He is the Mighty, the Wise.'

فَاٰمَنَ لَهٗ لُوْطٌ ۘ وَقَالَ اِنِّيْ مُهَاجِرٌ اِلٰى رَبِّيْ ؕ اِنَّهٗ
هُوَ الْعَزِيْزُ الْحَكِيْمُ ﴿۲۷﴾

28. And We bestowed on him Isaac and Jacob, and We placed *the gift of* prophethood and the Book among his descendants, and We gave him his reward in this life,

وَوَهَبْنَا لَهٗٓ اِسْحٰقَ وَيَعْقُوْبَ وَجَعَلْنَا فِيْ ذُرِّيَّتِهِ
النُّبُوَّةَ وَالْكِتٰبَ وَاٰتَيْنٰهُ اَجْرَهٗ فِي الدُّنْيَا ۚ وَاِنَّهٗ فِي

and in the Hereafter he will surely be among the righteous.

الْاٰخِرَةِ لَمِنَ الصّٰلِحِيْنَ ﴿۲۸﴾

29. And *We sent* Lot; he said to his people, 'You commit an abomination which none among mankind has ever committed before you.

وَ لُوْطًا اِذْ قَالَ لِقَوْمِهٖۤ اِنَّكُمْ لَتَاْتُوْنَ الْفَاحِشَةَ ۫ مَا
سَبَقَكُمْ بِهَا مِنْ اَحَدٍ مِّنَ الْعٰلَمِيْنَ ﴿۲۹﴾

* 30. 'Do you indeed come *lustfully* to men and cut off the highway *for travellers?* And you commit abomination in your meetings!' But the only answer of his people was that they said, 'Bring upon us the punishment of Allah if thou speakest the truth.'

اَىِٕنَّكُمْ لَتَاْتُوْنَ الرِّجَالَ وَ تَقْطَعُوْنَ السَّبِيْلَ ۙ۬ وَ
تَاْتُوْنَ فِيْ نَادِيْكُمُ الْمُنْكَرَ ؕ فَمَا كَانَ جَوَابَ قَوْمِهٖۤ
اِلَّاۤ اَنْ قَالُوا ائْتِنَا بِعَذَابِ اللّٰهِ اِنْ كُنْتَ مِنَ
الصّٰدِقِيْنَ ﴿۳۰﴾

31. He said, 'Help me, my Lord, against the wicked people.'

قَالَ رَبِّ انْصُرْنِيْ عَلَى الْقَوْمِ الْمُفْسِدِيْنَ ﴿۳۱﴾

R. 4.

32. And when Our messengers brought Abraham the glad tidings, they said, 'We are going to destroy the people of this town; surely its people are wrongdoers.'

وَ لَمَّا جَآءَتْ رُسُلُنَاۤ اِبْرٰهِيْمَ بِالْبُشْرٰى ۙ قَالُوْۤا اِنَّا
مُهْلِكُوْۤا اَهْلِ هٰذِهِ الْقَرْيَةِ ۚ اِنَّ اَهْلَهَا كَانُوْا
ظٰلِمِيْنَ ﴿۳۲﴾

33. He said, 'But Lot is there.' They said, 'We know full well who is there. We will surely save him and his family, except his wife, who is of those who remain behind.'

قَالَ اِنَّ فِيْهَا لُوْطًا ؕ قَالُوْا نَحْنُ اَعْلَمُ بِمَنْ فِيْهَا ٝ
لَنُنَجِّيَنَّهٗ وَ اَهْلَهٗۤ اِلَّا امْرَاَتَهٗ ٭ كَانَتْ مِنَ
الْغٰبِرِيْنَ ﴿۳۳﴾

34. And when Our messengers came to Lot, he was distressed on account of them and felt powerless with regard to them. And they said, 'Fear not, nor grieve; we will surely save thee and thy family except thy wife, who is of those who remain behind.

وَ لَمَّاۤ اَنْ جَآءَتْ رُسُلُنَا لُوْطًا سِیْٓءَ بِهِمْ وَ ضَاقَ بِهِمْ
ذَرْعًا وَّ قَالُوْا لَا تَخَفْ وَ لَا تَحْزَنْ ٝ اِنَّا مُنَجُّوْكَ وَ اَهْلَكَ
اِلَّا امْرَاَتَكَ كَانَتْ مِنَ الْغٰبِرِيْنَ ﴿۳۴﴾

35. 'We are surely going to bring down on the people of this town a punishment from heaven, for they have been rebellious.'

اِنَّا مُنْزِلُوْنَ عَلٰۤى اَهْلِ هٰذِهِ الْقَرْيَةِ رِجْزًا مِّنَ السَّمَآءِ
بِمَا كَانُوْا يَفْسُقُوْنَ ﴿۳۵﴾

36. And We have left thereof a clear Sign for a people who would understand.

وَ لَقَدْ تَّرَكْنَا مِنْهَاۤ اٰيَةًۢ بَيِّنَةً لِّقَوْمٍ يَّعْقِلُوْنَ ﴿۳۶﴾

37. And to Midian *We sent* their brother Shu'aib who said, 'O my people, serve Allah, and fear the Last Day and commit not iniquity in the earth, creating disorder.'

وَ اِلٰى مَدْيَنَ اَخَاهُمْ شُعَيْبًا ۙ فَقَالَ يٰقَوْمِ اعْبُدُوا اللّٰهَ
وَ ارْجُوا الْيَوْمَ الْاٰخِرَ وَ لَا تَعْثَوْا فِي الْاَرْضِ مُفْسِدِيْنَ ﴿۳۷﴾

38. But they called him a liar. So a violent earthquake seized them, and in their homes they lay prostrate upon the ground.

فَكَذَّبُوهُ فَأَخَذَتْهُمُ الرَّجْفَةُ فَأَصْبَحُوا فِي دَارِهِمْ
جٰثِمِينَ ۝٣٨

* 39. And *We destroyed* 'Ād and Thamūd; and it is evident to you from their dwelling-places. And Satan made their deeds *appear* good to them, and thus turned them away from the path, sagacious though they were.

وَعَادًا وَثَمُودَا۟ وَقَد تَّبَيَّنَ لَكُم مِّن مَّسٰكِنِهِمْ وَزَيَّنَ
لَهُمُ الشَّيْطٰنُ أَعْمٰلَهُمْ فَصَدَّهُمْ عَنِ السَّبِيلِ وَ
كَانُوا مُسْتَبْصِرِينَ ۝٣٩

40. And *We destroyed* Korah and Pharaoh and Hāmān. And Moses did come to them with manifest Signs but they behaved proudly in the earth, yet they could not outstrip *Us*.

وَقٰرُونَ وَفِرْعَوْنَ وَهٰمٰنَ وَلَقَدْ جَآءَهُم مُّوسٰى
بِالْبَيِّنٰتِ فَاسْتَكْبَرُوا فِي الْأَرْضِ وَمَا كَانُوا سٰبِقِينَ ۝٤٠

41. So each one *of them* We seized in his sin; of them were those against whom We sent a violent sandstorm, and of them were those whom a roaring blast overtook, and of them were those whom We caused the earth to swallow up, and of them were those whom We drowned. And Allah would not wrong them, but they used to wrong their own souls.

فَكُلًّا أَخَذْنَا بِذَنۢبِهِۦ فَمِنْهُم مَّنْ أَرْسَلْنَا عَلَيْهِ حَاصِبًا
وَمِنْهُم مَّنْ أَخَذَتْهُ الصَّيْحَةُ وَمِنْهُم مَّنْ خَسَفْنَا
بِهِ الْأَرْضَ وَمِنْهُم مَّنْ أَغْرَقْنَا وَمَا كَانَ اللّٰهُ
لِيَظْلِمَهُمْ وَلٰكِن كَانُوا أَنفُسَهُمْ يَظْلِمُونَ ۝٤١

42. The case of those who take helpers beside Allah is like unto the case of the spider, who makes for herself a house; and surely the frailest of *all* houses is the house of the spider, if they but knew!

مَثَلُ الَّذِينَ اتَّخَذُوا مِن دُونِ اللّٰهِ أَوْلِيَآءَ كَمَثَلِ
الْعَنكَبُوتِ اتَّخَذَتْ بَيْتًا وَإِنَّ أَوْهَنَ الْبُيُوتِ لَبَيْتُ
الْعَنكَبُوتِ لَوْ كَانُوا يَعْلَمُونَ ۝٤٢ لازم

43. Verily, Allah knows whatever they call upon beside Him; and He is the Mighty, the Wise.

إِنَّ اللّٰهَ يَعْلَمُ مَا يَدْعُونَ مِن دُونِهِۦ مِن شَيْءٍ وَهُوَ
الْعَزِيزُ الْحَكِيمُ ۝٤٣

44. And these are similitudes which We set forth for mankind, but only those understand them who have knowledge.

وَتِلْكَ الْأَمْثٰلُ نَضْرِبُهَا لِلنَّاسِ وَمَا يَعْقِلُهَآ إِلَّا
الْعٰلِمُونَ ۝٤٤

* 45. Allah created the heavens and the earth in accordance with the requirements of wisdom. In that surely is a Sign for the believers.

خَلَقَ اللّٰهُ السَّمٰوٰتِ وَالْأَرْضَ بِالْحَقِّ إِنَّ فِي ذٰلِكَ
لَآيَةً لِّلْمُؤْمِنِينَ ۝٤٥ ع

R. 5.

46. Recite that which has been revealed to thee of the Book, and observe Prayer. Surely, Prayer restrains *one* from indecency and manifest evil, and remembrance of

اتْلُ مَآ أُوحِيَ إِلَيْكَ مِنَ الْكِتٰبِ وَأَقِمِ الصَّلٰوةَ إِنَّ الجزء ٢١
الصَّلٰوةَ تَنْهٰى عَنِ الْفَحْشَآءِ وَالْمُنكَرِ وَلَذِكْرُ اللّٰهِ

Allah indeed is the greatest *virtue*. And Allah knows what you do.

47. And argue not with the People of the Book except with what is best; but *argue not at all* with such of them as are unjust. And say, 'We believe in that which has been revealed to us and that which has been revealed to you; and our God and your God is one; and to Him we submit.'

48. And in like manner have We sent down the Book to thee, so those to whom We have given *true knowledge of* the Book believe in it (the Qur'ān); and of these *Meccans also* there are some who believe in it. And none but the ungrateful deny Our Signs.

49. And thou didst not recite any Book before it, nor didst thou write one with thy right hand; in that case the liars would have doubted.

50. Nay, it is *a collection of* clear Signs in the hearts of those who are given knowledge. And none but the wrongdoers deny Our Signs.

51. And they say, 'Why are not Signs sent down to him from his Lord?' Say, 'The Signs are with Allah, and certainly I am a clear Warner.'

52. Is it not enough for them that We have sent down to thee the Book which is recited to them? Verily, there is mercy in it and a reminder for a people who believe.

R. 6.

53. Say, 'Allah is sufficient as a Witness between me and you. He knows what is in the heavens and the earth. And *as for* those who believe in falsehood and disbelieve in Allah, they it is who are the losers.'

54. They ask thee to hasten on the punishment; and had there not been an appointed term, the punishment would have come upon them. And it shall surely overtake them unexpectedly, while they perceive not.

55. They ask thee to hasten on the punishment; but verily, Hell is *already* encompassing the disbelievers.

56. *Remember* the day when the punishment will overwhelm them from above

أَكْبَرُ ۗ وَاللَّهُ يَعْلَمُ مَا تَصْنَعُونَ ﴿٤٦﴾
وَلَا تُجَادِلُوٓا أَهْلَ الْكِتٰبِ إِلَّا بِالَّتِي هِيَ أَحْسَنُ ۖ إِلَّا الَّذِينَ
ظَلَمُوا مِنْهُمْ وَقُولُوٓا اٰمَنَّا بِالَّذِيٓ أُنْزِلَ إِلَيْنَا وَأُنْزِلَ
إِلَيْكُمْ وَإِلٰهُنَا وَإِلٰهُكُمْ وَاحِدٌ وَّنَحْنُ لَهُ مُسْلِمُونَ ﴿٤٧﴾
وَكَذٰلِكَ أَنْزَلْنَآ إِلَيْكَ الْكِتٰبَ ۚ فَالَّذِينَ اٰتَيْنٰهُمُ الْكِتٰبَ
يُؤْمِنُونَ بِهٖ ۚ وَمِنْ هٰٓؤُلَآءِ مَنْ يُّؤْمِنُ بِهٖ ۚ وَمَا يَجْحَدُ
بِاٰيٰتِنَآ إِلَّا الْكٰفِرُونَ ﴿٤٨﴾
وَمَا كُنْتَ تَتْلُوا مِنْ قَبْلِهٖ مِنْ كِتٰبٍ وَّلَا تَخُطُّهٗ بِيَمِينِكَ
إِذًا لَّارْتَابَ الْمُبْطِلُونَ ﴿٤٩﴾
بَلْ هُوَ اٰيٰتٌ بَيِّنٰتٌ فِي صُدُورِ الَّذِينَ أُوتُوا الْعِلْمَ ۚ
وَمَا يَجْحَدُ بِاٰيٰتِنَآ إِلَّا الظّٰلِمُونَ ﴿٥٠﴾
وَقَالُوا لَوْلَآ أُنْزِلَ عَلَيْهِ اٰيٰتٌ مِّنْ رَّبِّهٖ ۚ قُلْ إِنَّمَا
الْاٰيٰتُ عِنْدَ اللّٰهِ ۚ وَإِنَّمَآ أَنَا نَذِيرٌ مُّبِينٌ ﴿٥١﴾
أَوَلَمْ يَكْفِهِمْ أَنَّآ أَنْزَلْنَا عَلَيْكَ الْكِتٰبَ يُتْلٰى عَلَيْهِمْ ۚ
إِنَّ فِي ذٰلِكَ لَرَحْمَةً وَّذِكْرٰى لِقَوْمٍ يُّؤْمِنُونَ ﴿٥٢﴾ ع
قُلْ كَفٰى بِاللّٰهِ بَيْنِي وَبَيْنَكُمْ شَهِيدًا ۚ يَعْلَمُ مَا فِي
السَّمٰوٰتِ وَالْأَرْضِ ۗ وَالَّذِينَ اٰمَنُوا بِالْبَاطِلِ وَكَفَرُوا
بِاللّٰهِ ۙ أُولٰٓئِكَ هُمُ الْخٰسِرُونَ ﴿٥٣﴾
وَيَسْتَعْجِلُونَكَ بِالْعَذَابِ ۚ وَلَوْلَآ أَجَلٌ مُّسَمًّى لَّجَآءَهُمُ
الْعَذَابُ ۚ وَلَيَأْتِيَنَّهُمْ بَغْتَةً وَّهُمْ لَا يَشْعُرُونَ ﴿٥٤﴾
يَسْتَعْجِلُونَكَ بِالْعَذَابِ ۚ وَإِنَّ جَهَنَّمَ لَمُحِيطَةٌ ۢ بِالْكٰفِرِينَ ﴿٥٥﴾
يَوْمَ يَغْشٰىهُمُ الْعَذَابُ مِنْ فَوْقِهِمْ وَمِنْ تَحْتِ

them and from underneath their feet, and He will say, 'Taste ye *the fruit of* your actions.'

57. O My servants who believe! verily, vast is My earth, so worship Me alone.

58. Every soul shall taste of death; then to Us shall you be brought back.

59. And those who believe and do good works—them shall We surely house in lofty mansions of Paradise, beneath which rivers flow. They will abide therein. Excellent is the reward of those who work *good*,

60. Those who are steadfast, and put their trust in their Lord.

61. And how many an animal there is that carries not its own sustenance! Allah provides for it and for you. And He is the All-Hearing, the All-Knowing.

* 62. And if thou ask them, 'Who has created the heavens and the earth and pressed into service the sun and the moon?', they will surely say, 'Allah'. How then are they being turned away *from the truth?*

63. Allah enlarges *the means of* sustenance for such of His servants as He pleases, and straitens *them* for whom *He pleases*. Surely Allah has full knowledge of all things.

64. And if thou ask them, 'Who sends down water from the sky and therewith gives life to the earth after its death?', they will surely say, 'Allah'. Say, 'All praise belongs to Allah.' But most of them understand not.

R. 7.

65. And this life of the world is nothing but a pastime and a sport, and the Home of the Hereafter—that indeed is Life, if they but knew!

66. And when they go on board a ship, they call on Allah, with sincere and exclusive faith in Him. But when He brings them safe to land, behold, they associate partners *with Him;*

67. That they may deny that which We have bestowed on them, and that they may enjoy themselves *for a time*. But they will soon come to know.

أَرْجُلِهِمْ وَيَقُولُ ذُوقُوا مَا كُنْتُمْ تَعْمَلُونَ ﴿٥٦﴾
يٰعِبَادِيَ الَّذِينَ آمَنُوا إِنَّ أَرْضِي وَاسِعَةٌ فَإِيَّايَ
فَاعْبُدُونِ ﴿٥٧﴾
كُلُّ نَفْسٍ ذَائِقَةُ الْمَوْتِ ثُمَّ إِلَيْنَا تُرْجَعُونَ ﴿٥٨﴾
وَالَّذِينَ آمَنُوا وَعَمِلُوا الصّٰلِحٰتِ لَنُبَوِّئَنَّهُمْ مِنَ
الْجَنَّةِ غُرَفًا تَجْرِي مِنْ تَحْتِهَا الْأَنْهٰرُ خٰلِدِينَ فِيهَا
نِعْمَ أَجْرُ الْعٰمِلِينَ ﴿٥٩﴾
الَّذِينَ صَبَرُوا وَعَلٰى رَبِّهِمْ يَتَوَكَّلُونَ ﴿٦٠﴾
وَكَأَيِّنْ مِنْ دَابَّةٍ لَا تَحْمِلُ رِزْقَهَا اللّٰهُ يَرْزُقُهَا
وَإِيَّاكُمْ وَهُوَ السَّمِيعُ الْعَلِيمُ ﴿٦١﴾
وَلَئِنْ سَأَلْتَهُمْ مَنْ خَلَقَ السَّمٰوٰتِ وَالْأَرْضَ وَسَخَّرَ
الشَّمْسَ وَالْقَمَرَ لَيَقُولُنَّ اللّٰهُ فَأَنّٰى يُؤْفَكُونَ ﴿٦٢﴾
اللّٰهُ يَبْسُطُ الرِّزْقَ لِمَنْ يَشَاءُ مِنْ عِبَادِهِ وَيَقْدِرُ
لَهُ إِنَّ اللّٰهَ بِكُلِّ شَيْءٍ عَلِيمٌ ﴿٦٣﴾
وَلَئِنْ سَأَلْتَهُمْ مَنْ نَزَّلَ مِنَ السَّمَاءِ مَاءً فَأَحْيَا بِهِ
الْأَرْضَ مِنْ بَعْدِ مَوْتِهَا لَيَقُولُنَّ اللّٰهُ قُلِ الْحَمْدُ
لِلّٰهِ بَلْ أَكْثَرُهُمْ لَا يَعْقِلُونَ ﴿٦٤﴾ ع
وَمَا هٰذِهِ الْحَيٰوةُ الدُّنْيَا إِلَّا لَهْوٌ وَلَعِبٌ وَإِنَّ
الدَّارَ الْآخِرَةَ لَهِيَ الْحَيَوَانُ لَوْ كَانُوا يَعْلَمُونَ ﴿٦٥﴾
فَإِذَا رَكِبُوا فِي الْفُلْكِ دَعَوُا اللّٰهَ مُخْلِصِينَ لَهُ الدِّينَ
فَلَمَّا نَجّٰهُمْ إِلَى الْبَرِّ إِذَا هُمْ يُشْرِكُونَ ﴿٦٦﴾
لِيَكْفُرُوا بِمَا آتَيْنٰهُمْ وَلِيَتَمَتَّعُوا فَسَوْفَ يَعْلَمُونَ ﴿٦٧﴾

68. Have they not seen that We have made the sanctuary secure *for them*, while people are snatched away from all around them? Would they then believe in falsehood and deny the favour of Allah?

69. And who is more unjust than he who invents a lie concerning Allah, or rejects the truth when it comes to him? Is there not an abode in Hell for those who disbelieve?

70. And *as for* those who strive in Our path—We will surely guide them in Our ways. And verily Allah is with those who do good.

أَوَلَمْ يَرَوْا أَنَّا جَعَلْنَا حَرَمًا آمِنًا وَيُتَخَطَّفُ النَّاسُ مِنْ
حَوْلِهِمْ ۚ أَفَبِالْبَاطِلِ يُؤْمِنُونَ وَبِنِعْمَةِ اللَّهِ يَكْفُرُونَ ﴿٦٨﴾
وَمَنْ أَظْلَمُ مِمَّنِ افْتَرَىٰ عَلَى اللَّهِ كَذِبًا أَوْ كَذَّبَ
بِالْحَقِّ لَمَّا جَاءَهُ ۚ أَلَيْسَ فِي جَهَنَّمَ مَثْوًى لِلْكَافِرِينَ ﴿٦٩﴾
وَالَّذِينَ جَاهَدُوا فِينَا لَنَهْدِيَنَّهُمْ سُبُلَنَا ۚ وَإِنَّ اللَّهَ
لَمَعَ الْمُحْسِنِينَ ﴿٧٠﴾

ركوعاتها ٦ سُوْرَةُ الرُّوْمِ مَكِّيَّةٌ (٣٠) اٰياتها ٦١

AL-RŪM

(Revealed before Hijra)

1. In the name of Allah, the Gracious, the Merciful.

بِسْمِ اللّٰهِ الرَّحْمٰنِ الرَّحِيْمِ ﴿١﴾

2. Alif Lām Mīm *.

الٓمّٓ ﴿٢﴾

3. The Romans have been defeated,

غُلِبَتِ الرُّوْمُ ﴿٣﴾

4. In the land nearby, and they, after their defeat, will be victorious

فِيْٓ اَدْنَى الْاَرْضِ وَهُمْ مِّنْۢ بَعْدِ غَلَبِهِمْ سَيَغْلِبُوْنَ ﴿٤﴾

5. In a few years—Allah's is the command before and after *that*—and on that day the believers will rejoice,

فِيْ بِضْعِ سِنِيْنَ ۗ لِلّٰهِ الْاَمْرُ مِنْ قَبْلُ وَمِنْۢ بَعْدُ ؕ
وَيَوْمَئِذٍ يَّفْرَحُ الْمُؤْمِنُوْنَ ﴿٥﴾

6. With the help of Allah. He helps whom He pleases; and He is the Mighty, the Merciful.

بِنَصْرِ اللّٰهِ ؕ يَنْصُرُ مَنْ يَّشَآءُ ؕ وَهُوَ الْعَزِيْزُ الرَّحِيْمُ ﴿٦﴾

7. Allah *has made* this promise. Allah breaks not His promise, but most men know not.

وَعْدَ اللّٰهِ ؕ لَا يُخْلِفُ اللّٰهُ وَعْدَهٗ وَلٰكِنَّ اَكْثَرَ النَّاسِ
لَا يَعْلَمُوْنَ ﴿٧﴾

8. They know *only* the outer *aspect* of the life of this world, and of the Hereafter they are utterly unmindful.

يَعْلَمُوْنَ ظَاهِرًا مِّنَ الْحَيٰوةِ الدُّنْيَا ۚ وَهُمْ عَنِ
الْاٰخِرَةِ هُمْ غٰفِلُوْنَ ﴿٨﴾

9. Do they not reflect in their own minds? Allah has not created the heavens and the earth and all that is between the two but in accordance with the requirements of wisdom and for a fixed term. But many among men believe not in the meeting of their Lord.

اَوَلَمْ يَتَفَكَّرُوْا فِيْٓ اَنْفُسِهِمْ ۫ مَا خَلَقَ اللّٰهُ السَّمٰوٰتِ
وَالْاَرْضَ وَمَا بَيْنَهُمَآ اِلَّا بِالْحَقِّ وَاَجَلٍ مُّسَمًّى ؕ
وَاِنَّ كَثِيْرًا مِّنَ النَّاسِ بِلِقَآئِ رَبِّهِمْ لَكٰفِرُوْنَ ﴿٩﴾

10. Have they not travelled in the earth so that they might see how *evil* was the end of those who were before them? They were stronger than these in power, and they tilled the soil and populated it more *and better* than these have populated it. And their Messengers came to them with manifest Signs. And Allah would not wrong them, but they wronged their own souls.

اَوَلَمْ يَسِيْرُوْا فِي الْاَرْضِ فَيَنْظُرُوْا كَيْفَ كَانَ عَاقِبَةُ
الَّذِيْنَ مِنْ قَبْلِهِمْ ؕ كَانُوْٓا اَشَدَّ مِنْهُمْ قُوَّةً وَّاَثَارُوا
الْاَرْضَ وَعَمَرُوْهَآ اَكْثَرَ مِمَّا عَمَرُوْهَا وَجَآءَتْهُمْ
رُسُلُهُمْ بِالْبَيِّنٰتِ ؕ فَمَا كَانَ اللّٰهُ لِيَظْلِمَهُمْ وَلٰكِنْ
كَانُوْٓا اَنْفُسَهُمْ يَظْلِمُوْنَ ﴿١٠﴾

---

* I am Allah, the All-Knowing.

11. Then evil was the end of those who did evil, because they rejected the Signs of Allah, and mocked at them.

ثُمَّ كَانَ عَاقِبَةَ الَّذِينَ أَسَاءُوا السُّوٓأَىٰ أَنْ كَذَّبُوا
بِآيَاتِ اللَّهِ وَكَانُوا بِهَا يَسْتَهْزِئُونَ ﴿١١﴾ ع

R. 2.

12. Allah originates creation; then He repeats it; then to Him shall you be brought back.

اللَّهُ يَبْدَؤُا الْخَلْقَ ثُمَّ يُعِيدُهُ ثُمَّ إِلَيْهِ تُرْجَعُونَ ﴿١٢﴾

13. And on the day when the Hour will arrive the guilty shall be in despair.

وَيَوْمَ تَقُومُ السَّاعَةُ يُبْلِسُ الْمُجْرِمُونَ ﴿١٣﴾

14. And they shall have no intercessors from *among them* whom they associate *with God;* and they will deny *those* whom they associate *with Him*.

وَلَمْ يَكُنْ لَهُمْ مِنْ شُرَكَآئِهِمْ شُفَعَٰٓؤُا وَكَانُوا
بِشُرَكَآئِهِمْ كَٰفِرِينَ ﴿١٤﴾

15. And on the day when the Hour will arrive—on that day will they become separated *from one another*.

وَيَوْمَ تَقُومُ السَّاعَةُ يَوْمَئِذٍ يَتَفَرَّقُونَ ﴿١٥﴾

16. Then those who believed and did good works will be honoured and made happy in a garden.

فَأَمَّا الَّذِينَ آمَنُوا وَعَمِلُوا الصَّٰلِحَٰتِ فَهُمْ فِي رَوْضَةٍ
يُحْبَرُونَ ﴿١٦﴾

17. But as for those who disbelieved and rejected Our Signs and the meeting of the Hereafter, these will be brought forth in punishment.

وَأَمَّا الَّذِينَ كَفَرُوا وَكَذَّبُوا بِآيَاتِنَا وَلِقَآئِ الْآخِرَةِ
فَأُولَٰٓئِكَ فِي الْعَذَابِ مُحْضَرُونَ ﴿١٧﴾

18. So glorify Allah when you enter the evening and when you enter the morning—

فَسُبْحَٰنَ اللَّهِ حِينَ تُمْسُونَ وَحِينَ تُصْبِحُونَ ﴿١٨﴾

19. And to Him belongs all praise in the heavens and the earth—and *glorify Him* in the afternoon and when you enter upon the time of the decline of the sun.

وَلَهُ الْحَمْدُ فِي السَّمَٰوَٰتِ وَالْأَرْضِ وَعَشِيًّا وَحِينَ
تُظْهِرُونَ ﴿١٩﴾

20. He brings forth the living from the dead, and He brings forth the dead from the living; and He gives life to the earth after its death. And in like manner shall you be brought forth.

يُخْرِجُ الْحَيَّ مِنَ الْمَيِّتِ وَيُخْرِجُ الْمَيِّتَ مِنَ
الْحَيِّ وَيُحْيِ الْأَرْضَ بَعْدَ مَوْتِهَا ۚ وَكَذَٰلِكَ
تُخْرَجُونَ ﴿٢٠﴾ ع

R. 3.

21. And *one* of His Signs *is this*, that He created you from dust; then, behold, you are men who move about *on the face of the earth*.

وَمِنْ آيَاتِهِ أَنْ خَلَقَكُمْ مِنْ تُرَابٍ ثُمَّ إِذَا أَنْتُمْ
بَشَرٌ تَنْتَشِرُونَ ﴿٢١﴾

22. And *one* of His Signs *is this*, that He has created wives for you from among yourselves that you may find peace of mind in them, and He has put love and tenderness between you. In that surely are Signs for a people who reflect.

وَمِنْ آيَاتِهِ أَنْ خَلَقَ لَكُمْ مِنْ أَنْفُسِكُمْ أَزْوَاجًا
لِتَسْكُنُوا إِلَيْهَا وَجَعَلَ بَيْنَكُمْ مَوَدَّةً وَرَحْمَةً ۚ
إِنَّ فِي ذَٰلِكَ لَآيَاتٍ لِقَوْمٍ يَتَفَكَّرُونَ ﴿٢٢﴾

23. And among His Signs is the creation of the heavens and the earth, and the diversity of your tongues and colours. In that surely are Signs for those who possess knowledge.

وَمِنْ اٰيٰتِهٖ خَلْقُ السَّمٰوٰتِ وَالْاَرْضِ وَاخْتِلَافُ
اَلْسِنَتِكُمْ وَاَلْوَانِكُمْ ؕ اِنَّ فِيْ ذٰلِكَ لَاٰيٰتٍ لِّلْعٰلِمِيْنَ ﴿۲۳﴾

24. And among His Signs is your sleep by night and day, and your seeking of His bounty. In that surely are Signs for a people who hear.

وَمِنْ اٰيٰتِهٖ مَنَامُكُمْ بِالَّيْلِ وَالنَّهَارِ وَابْتِغَآؤُكُمْ
مِّنْ فَضْلِهٖ ؕ اِنَّ فِيْ ذٰلِكَ لَاٰيٰتٍ لِّقَوْمٍ يَّسْمَعُوْنَ ﴿۲۴﴾

25. And *one* of His Signs *is this*, that He shows you the lightning as *a source of* fear and hope, and He sends down water from the sky, and quickens therewith the earth after its death. In that surely are Signs for a people who understand.

وَمِنْ اٰيٰتِهٖ يُرِيْكُمُ الْبَرْقَ خَوْفًا وَّطَمَعًا وَّيُنَزِّلُ
مِنَ السَّمَآءِ مَآءً فَيُحْيٖ بِهِ الْاَرْضَ بَعْدَ مَوْتِهَا ؕ
اِنَّ فِيْ ذٰلِكَ لَاٰيٰتٍ لِّقَوْمٍ يَّعْقِلُوْنَ ﴿۲۵﴾

26. And among His Signs *is this*, that the heaven and the earth stand *firm* by His command. Then when He calls you by a call *coming* from the earth, behold, you will come forth.

وَمِنْ اٰيٰتِهٖ اَنْ تَقُوْمَ السَّمَآءُ وَالْاَرْضُ بِاَمْرِهٖ ؕ ثُمَّ
اِذَا دَعَاكُمْ دَعْوَةً ۖۗ مِّنَ الْاَرْضِ ۖۗ اِذَآ اَنْتُمْ
تَخْرُجُوْنَ ﴿۲۶﴾

27. And to Him belongs whosoever is in the heavens and the earth. All are obedient to Him.

وَلَهٗ مَنْ فِي السَّمٰوٰتِ وَالْاَرْضِ ؕ كُلٌّ لَّهٗ قٰنِتُوْنَ ﴿۲۷﴾

28. And He it is Who originates the creation, then repeats it, and it is most easy for Him. His is the most exalted state in the heavens and the earth; and He is the Mighty, the Wise.

وَهُوَ الَّذِيْ يَبْدَؤُا الْخَلْقَ ثُمَّ يُعِيْدُهٗ وَهُوَ اَهْوَنُ
عَلَيْهِ ؕ وَلَهُ الْمَثَلُ الْاَعْلٰى فِي السَّمٰوٰتِ وَالْاَرْضِ ۚ
وَهُوَ الْعَزِيْزُ الْحَكِيْمُ ﴿۲۸﴾ ع

R. 4.

29. He sets forth for you a parable concerning yourselves. Have you, among those whom your right hands possess, partners in what We have provided for you so that you become equal *sharers* therein *and* fear them as you fear each other? Thus do We explain the Signs to a people who understand.

ضَرَبَ لَكُمْ مَّثَلًا مِّنْ اَنْفُسِكُمْ ؕ هَلْ لَّكُمْ مِّنْ مَّا
مَلَكَتْ اَيْمَانُكُمْ مِّنْ شُرَكَآءَ فِيْ مَا رَزَقْنٰكُمْ فَاَنْتُمْ
فِيْهِ سَوَآءٌ تَخَافُوْنَهُمْ كَخِيْفَتِكُمْ اَنْفُسَكُمْ ؕ كَذٰلِكَ
نُفَصِّلُ الْاٰيٰتِ لِقَوْمٍ يَّعْقِلُوْنَ ﴿۲۹﴾

30. Nay, but those who are unjust follow their own low desires without any knowledge. Then who can guide him whom Allah has adjudged as lost? There will be no helpers for them.

بَلِ اتَّبَعَ الَّذِيْنَ ظَلَمُوْٓا اَهْوَآءَهُمْ بِغَيْرِ عِلْمٍ ۚ فَمَنْ
يَّهْدِيْ مَنْ اَضَلَّ اللّٰهُ ؕ وَمَا لَهُمْ مِّنْ نّٰصِرِيْنَ ﴿۳۰﴾

* 31. So set thy face to *the service of* religion as one devoted *to God. And follow* the nature made by Allah—the nature in which He has created mankind. There is no altering the creation of Allah. That is

فَاَقِمْ وَجْهَكَ لِلدِّيْنِ حَنِيْفًا ؕ فِطْرَتَ اللّٰهِ الَّتِيْ فَطَرَ
النَّاسَ عَلَيْهَا ؕ لَا تَبْدِيْلَ لِخَلْقِ اللّٰهِ ؕ ذٰلِكَ الدِّيْنُ

the right religion. But most men know not.

الْقَيِّمُ ۙ وَلٰكِنَّ اَكْثَرَ النَّاسِ لَا يَعْلَمُوْنَ ﴿٣١﴾

32. *Set your face to God*, turning to Him *in repentance*, and fear Him, and observe Prayer, and be not of those who associate partners *with God*—

مُنِيْبِيْنَ اِلَيْهِ وَاتَّقُوْهُ وَاَقِيْمُوا الصَّلٰوةَ وَلَا تَكُوْنُوْا
مِنَ الْمُشْرِكِيْنَ ﴿٣٢﴾

33. Of those who split up their religion and have become divided into sects; every party rejoicing in what they have.

مِنَ الَّذِيْنَ فَرَّقُوْا دِيْنَهُمْ وَكَانُوْا شِيَعًا ۭ كُلُّ حِزْبٍۢ
بِمَا لَدَيْهِمْ فَرِحُوْنَ ﴿٣٣﴾

34. And when an affliction befalls men, they cry unto their Lord, turning to Him *in repentance;* then, when He has made them taste of mercy from Him, lo! a section of them associate partners with their Lord,

وَاِذَا مَسَّ النَّاسَ ضُرٌّ دَعَوْا رَبَّهُمْ مُّنِيْبِيْنَ اِلَيْهِ
ثُمَّ اِذَآ اَذَاقَهُمْ مِّنْهُ رَحْمَةً اِذَا فَرِيْقٌ مِّنْهُمْ بِرَبِّهِمْ
يُشْرِكُوْنَ ﴿٣٤﴾

35. So as to be ungrateful for what We have given them. So enjoy yourselves *awhile*, but soon you will come to know.

لِيَكْفُرُوْا بِمَآ اٰتَيْنٰهُمْ ۭ فَتَمَتَّعُوْا ۣ فَسَوْفَ تَعْلَمُوْنَ ﴿٣٥﴾

36. Have We sent down to them any authority which speaks *in favour* of what they associate with Him?

اَمْ اَنْزَلْنَا عَلَيْهِمْ سُلْطٰنًا فَهُوَ يَتَكَلَّمُ بِمَا كَانُوْا بِهٖ
يُشْرِكُوْنَ ﴿٣٦﴾

* 37. And when We make mankind taste of mercy, they rejoice therein; but if an evil befall them because of that which their own hands have sent on, behold! they are in despair.

وَاِذَآ اَذَقْنَا النَّاسَ رَحْمَةً فَرِحُوْا بِهَا ۭ وَاِنْ تُصِبْهُمْ
سَيِّئَةٌۢ بِمَا قَدَّمَتْ اَيْدِيْهِمْ اِذَا هُمْ يَقْنَطُوْنَ ﴿٣٧﴾

38. Have they not seen that Allah enlarges the provision to whomsoever He pleases, and straitens *it to whomsoever He pleases?* In that truly are Signs for a people who believe.

اَوَلَمْ يَرَوْا اَنَّ اللّٰهَ يَبْسُطُ الرِّزْقَ لِمَنْ يَّشَآءُ وَ
يَقْدِرُ ۭ اِنَّ فِيْ ذٰلِكَ لَاٰيٰتٍ لِّقَوْمٍ يُّؤْمِنُوْنَ ﴿٣٨﴾

39. So give to the kinsman his due, and to the needy, and to the wayfarer. That is best for those who seek the favour of Allah, and it is they who will prosper.

فَاٰتِ ذَا الْقُرْبٰى حَقَّهٗ وَالْمِسْكِيْنَ وَابْنَ السَّبِيْلِ ۭ
ذٰلِكَ خَيْرٌ لِّلَّذِيْنَ يُرِيْدُوْنَ وَجْهَ اللّٰهِ ۡ وَاُولٰۗىِٕكَ
هُمُ الْمُفْلِحُوْنَ ﴿٣٩﴾

40. Whatever you pay as interest that it may increase the wealth of the people, it does not increase in the sight of Allah; but whatever you give in Zakāt seeking the favour of Allah—it is these who will increase *their wealth* manifold.

وَمَآ اٰتَيْتُمْ مِّنْ رِّبًا لِّيَرْبُوَا۟ فِيْٓ اَمْوَالِ النَّاسِ فَلَا
يَرْبُوْا عِنْدَ اللّٰهِ ۚ وَمَآ اٰتَيْتُمْ مِّنْ زَكٰوةٍ تُرِيْدُوْنَ
وَجْهَ اللّٰهِ فَاُولٰۗىِٕكَ هُمُ الْمُضْعِفُوْنَ ﴿٤٠﴾

41. It is Allah Who has created you, *and* then He has provided for you; then He will cause you to die, *and* then He will

اَللّٰهُ الَّذِيْ خَلَقَكُمْ ثُمَّ رَزَقَكُمْ ثُمَّ يُمِيْتُكُمْ ثُمَّ

bring you to life. Is there any of your 'partners' who can do any of these things? Glorified be He and exalted above that which they associate *with Him*.

يحييكم هل من شركائكم من يفعل من ذلكم
من شيء سبحنه وتعلى عما يشركون ﴿٤١﴾ ع

R. 5.

42. Corruption has appeared on land and sea because of what men's hands have wrought, that He may make them taste *the fruit* of some of their doings, so that they may turn back *from evil*.

ظهر الفساد في البر والبحر بما كسبت أيدي
الناس ليذيقهم بعض الذي عملوا لعلهم
يرجعون ﴿٤٢﴾

43. Say, 'Travel in the earth and see how *evil* was the end of those before *you*! Most of them were idolaters.'

قل سيروا في الأرض فانظروا كيف كان عاقبة
الذين من قبل كان أكثرهم مشركين ﴿٤٣﴾

* 44. So set thy face to *the service of* the right religion before there comes the day from Allah for which there will be no averting. On that day *mankind* will split up *into parts*.

فأقم وجهك للدين القيم من قبل أن يأتي
يوم لا مرد له من الله يومئذ يصدعون ﴿٤٤﴾

45. Those who disbelieve will bear *the consequences of* their disbelief; and those who do righteous deeds prepare *good* for themselves,

من كفر فعليه كفره ومن عمل صالحا فلأنفسهم
يمهدون ﴿٤٥﴾

46. That He, out of His bounty, may reward those who believe and do righteous deeds. Surely, He loves not the disbelievers.

ليجزي الذين امنوا وعملوا الصلحت من فضله
إنه لا يحب الكفرين ﴿٤٦﴾

47. And among His Signs *is this*, that He sends the winds as bearers of glad tidings and that He may make you taste of His mercy, and that the ships may sail at His command, and that you may seek of His bounty, and that you may be grateful.

ومن ايته أن يرسل الرياح مبشرت وليذيقكم
من رحمته ولتجري الفلك بأمره ولتبتغوا من
فضله ولعلكم تشكرون ﴿٤٧﴾

48. And surely We sent Messengers before thee to their own people, and they brought them clear Signs. Then We punished those who were guilty. And it was certainly due from Us to help the believers.

ولقد أرسلنا من قبلك رسلا إلى قومهم فجاءوهم
بالبينت فانتقمنا من الذين أجرموا وكان حقا
علينا نصر المؤمنين ﴿٤٨﴾

49. *It is* Allah Who sends the winds so that they raise a cloud. Then He spreads it in the sky as He pleases and places it layer upon layer and thou seest the rain issuing forth from its midst. And when He causes it to fall on whom He pleases of His

الله الذي يرسل الريح فتثير سحابا فيبسطه
في السماء كيف يشاء ويجعله كسفا فترى الودق
يخرج من خلله فإذا أصاب به من يشاء من

servants, behold! they rejoice;

عِبَادِهٖۤ اِذَا هُمۡ يَسۡتَبۡشِرُوۡنَ ﴿۴۹﴾

50. Though before that—before it was sent down upon them—they were in despair.

وَاِنۡ كَانُوۡا مِنۡ قَبۡلِ اَنۡ يُّنَزَّلَ عَلَيۡهِمۡ مِّنۡ قَبۡلِهٖ لَمُبۡلِسِيۡنَ ﴿۵۰﴾

51. Look, therefore, at the marks of Allah's mercy: how He quickens the earth after its death. Verily, the same *God* will quicken the dead; for He has power over all things.

فَانۡظُرۡ اِلٰۤى اَثَرِ رَحۡمَتِ اللّٰهِ كَيۡفَ يُحۡيِ الۡاَرۡضَ بَعۡدَ مَوۡتِهَا ؕ اِنَّ ذٰلِكَ لَمُحۡيِ الۡمَوۡتٰى ۚ وَهُوَ عَلٰى كُلِّ شَىۡءٍ قَدِيۡرٌ ﴿۵۱﴾

52. And if We sent a wind and they saw it (their harvest) turn yellow, they would certainly, thereafter, *begin to* deny *Our favours.*

وَلَئِنۡ اَرۡسَلۡنَا رِيۡحًا فَرَاَوۡهُ مُصۡفَرًّا لَّظَلُّوۡا مِنۡۢ بَعۡدِهٖ يَكۡفُرُوۡنَ ﴿۵۲﴾

53. And thou canst not make the dead to hear, nor canst thou make the deaf to hear the call, when they turn away showing their backs.

فَاِنَّكَ لَا تُسۡمِعُ الۡمَوۡتٰى وَلَا تُسۡمِعُ الصُّمَّ الدُّعَآءَ اِذَا وَلَّوۡا مُدۡبِرِيۡنَ ﴿۵۳﴾

54. Nor canst thou guide the blind out of their error. Thou canst make only those to hear who would believe in Our Signs and they submit.

وَمَاۤ اَنۡتَ بِهٰدِ الۡعُمۡىِ عَنۡ ضَلٰلَتِهِمۡ ؕ اِنۡ تُسۡمِعُ اِلَّا مَنۡ يُّؤۡمِنُ بِاٰيٰتِنَا فَهُمۡ مُّسۡلِمُوۡنَ ﴿۵۴﴾ ع

R. 6.

55. *It is* Allah Who created you in *a state of* weakness, and after weakness gave strength; then, after strength, caused weakness and old age. He creates what He pleases. He is the All-Knowing, the All-Powerful.

اَللّٰهُ الَّذِىۡ خَلَقَكُمۡ مِّنۡ ضُعۡفٍ ثُمَّ جَعَلَ مِنۡۢ بَعۡدِ ضُعۡفٍ قُوَّةً ثُمَّ جَعَلَ مِنۡۢ بَعۡدِ قُوَّةٍ ضُعۡفًا وَّشَيۡبَةً ؕ يَخۡلُقُ مَا يَشَآءُ ۚ وَهُوَ الۡعَلِيۡمُ الۡقَدِيۡرُ ﴿۵۵﴾

56. And on the day when the Hour shall arrive the guilty will swear that they tarried not save an hour—thus were they turned away *from the right path.*

وَيَوۡمَ تَقُوۡمُ السَّاعَةُ يُقۡسِمُ الۡمُجۡرِمُوۡنَ ۙ مَا لَبِثُوۡا غَيۡرَ سَاعَةٍ ؕ كَذٰلِكَ كَانُوۡا يُؤۡفَكُوۡنَ ﴿۵۶﴾

57. But those who are given knowledge and faith will say, 'You have indeed tarried according to the Book of Allah, till the Day of Resurrection. And this is the Day of Resurrection, but you did not *care to* know.'

وَقَالَ الَّذِيۡنَ اُوۡتُوا الۡعِلۡمَ وَالۡاِيۡمَانَ لَقَدۡ لَبِثۡتُمۡ فِىۡ كِتٰبِ اللّٰهِ اِلٰى يَوۡمِ الۡبَعۡثِ فَهٰذَا يَوۡمُ الۡبَعۡثِ وَلٰكِنَّكُمۡ كُنۡتُمۡ لَا تَعۡلَمُوۡنَ ﴿۵۷﴾

* 58. So on that day their excuses will not avail the wrongdoers; nor will they be allowed to make amends.

فَيَوۡمَئِذٍ لَّا يَنۡفَعُ الَّذِيۡنَ ظَلَمُوۡا مَعۡذِرَتُهُمۡ وَلَا هُمۡ يُسۡتَعۡتَبُوۡنَ ﴿۵۸﴾

59. And truly, We have set forth for men in this Qur'ān every kind of parable; and indeed, if thou bring them a Sign, those who disbelieve will surely say, 'You are but liars.'

وَلَقَدْ ضَرَبْنَا لِلنَّاسِ فِيْ هٰذَا الْقُرْاٰنِ مِنْ كُلِّ
مَثَلٍ ۭ وَلَئِنْ جِئْتَهُمْ بِاٰيَةٍ لَّيَقُوْلَنَّ الَّذِيْنَ كَفَرُوْٓا
اِنْ اَنْتُمْ اِلَّا مُبْطِلُوْنَ ﴿٥٩﴾

60. Thus does Allah seal the hearts of those who have no knowledge.

كَذٰلِكَ يَطْبَعُ اللّٰهُ عَلٰى قُلُوْبِ الَّذِيْنَ لَا يَعْلَمُوْنَ ﴿٦٠﴾

61. So be thou patient. Surely the promise of Allah is true; and let not those who have no certainty *of faith* make light of thee.

فَاصْبِرْ اِنَّ وَعْدَ اللّٰهِ حَقٌّ وَّلَا يَسْتَخِفَّنَّكَ الَّذِيْنَ
لَا يُوْقِنُوْنَ ﴿٦١﴾ ع

سُوْرَةُ لُقْمٰنَ مَكِّيَّةٌ (٣١)

LUQMĀN

(Revealed before Hijra)

1. In the name of Allah, the Gracious, the Merciful.

بِسْمِ اللّٰهِ الرَّحْمٰنِ الرَّحِيْمِ ﴿١﴾

2. Alif Lām Mīm*.

الٓمّٓ ﴿٢﴾

3. These are verses of the Book of Wisdom,

تِلْكَ اٰيٰتُ الْكِتٰبِ الْحَكِيْمِ ﴿٣﴾

4. A guidance and a mercy for those who do good,

هُدًى وَّ رَحْمَةً لِّلْمُحْسِنِيْنَ ﴿٤﴾

5. Those who observe Prayer and pay the Zakāt and who have firm faith in the Hereafter.

الَّذِيْنَ يُقِيْمُوْنَ الصَّلٰوةَ وَيُؤْتُوْنَ الزَّكٰوةَ وَ هُمْ
بِالْاٰخِرَةِ هُمْ يُوْقِنُوْنَ ﴿٥﴾

6. It is they who follow guidance from their Lord, and it is they who shall prosper.

اُولٰٓئِكَ عَلٰى هُدًى مِّنْ رَّبِّهِمْ وَ اُولٰٓئِكَ هُمُ
الْمُفْلِحُوْنَ ﴿٦﴾

7. And of men is he who takes idle tales in exchange *for guidance* to lead *men* astray from the path of Allah, without knowledge, and to make fun of it. For such there will be humiliating punishment.

وَ مِنَ النَّاسِ مَنْ يَّشْتَرِيْ لَهْوَ الْحَدِيْثِ لِيُضِلَّ
عَنْ سَبِيْلِ اللّٰهِ بِغَيْرِ عِلْمٍ ۖ وَّيَتَّخِذَهَا هُزُوًا ۗ
اُولٰٓئِكَ لَهُمْ عَذَابٌ مُّهِيْنٌ ﴿٧﴾

8. And when Our Signs are recited to him, he turns proudly away, as though he heard them not, as if there were a heaviness in both his ears. So announce to him a painful punishment.

وَاِذَا تُتْلٰى عَلَيْهِ اٰيٰتُنَا وَلّٰى مُسْتَكْبِرًا كَاَنْ لَّمْ يَسْمَعْهَا
كَاَنَّ فِيْٓ اُذُنَيْهِ وَقْرًا ۚ فَبَشِّرْهُ بِعَذَابٍ اَلِيْمٍ ﴿٨﴾

9. Surely those who believe and do good works—they will have Gardens of Delight,

اِنَّ الَّذِيْنَ اٰمَنُوْا وَعَمِلُوا الصّٰلِحٰتِ لَهُمْ جَنّٰتُ النَّعِيْمِ ﴿٩﴾

10. Wherein they will abide. Allah has *made* a true promise; and He is the Mighty, the Wise.

خٰلِدِيْنَ فِيْهَا ۗ وَعْدَ اللّٰهِ حَقًّا ۗ وَهُوَ الْعَزِيْزُ الْحَكِيْمُ ﴿١٠﴾

11. He has created the heavens without any pillars that you can see, and He has placed in the earth firm mountains that it may not quake with you, and He has scattered therein all kinds of creatures; and We have sent down water from the clouds, and caused to grow therein every noble species.

خَلَقَ السَّمٰوٰتِ بِغَيْرِ عَمَدٍ تَرَوْنَهَا وَاَلْقٰى فِي الْاَرْضِ
رَوَاسِيَ اَنْ تَمِيْدَ بِكُمْ وَبَثَّ فِيْهَا مِنْ كُلِّ دَآبَّةٍ ۗ
وَاَنْزَلْنَا مِنَ السَّمَآءِ مَآءً فَاَنْۢبَتْنَا فِيْهَا مِنْ كُلِّ زَوْجٍ
كَرِيْمٍ ﴿١١﴾

* I am Allah, the All-Knowing.

12. This is the creation of Allah. Now show me what others beside Him have created. Nay, but the wrongdoers are in manifest error.

هٰذَا خَلْقُ اللّٰهِ فَاَرُوْنِيْ مَاذَا خَلَقَ الَّذِيْنَ مِنْ دُوْنِهٖ
بَلِ الظّٰلِمُوْنَ فِيْ ضَلٰلٍ مُّبِيْنٍ (١٢)

R. 2.

13. And We bestowed wisdom on Luqmān, *saying*, 'Be grateful to Allah:' and whoso is grateful, is grateful only for *the good of* his own soul. And whoso is ungrateful, then surely Allah is Self-Sufficient, Praiseworthy.

وَلَقَدْ اٰتَيْنَا لُقْمٰنَ الْحِكْمَةَ اَنِ اشْكُرْ لِلّٰهِ ۚ وَمَنْ
يَّشْكُرْ فَاِنَّمَا يَشْكُرُ لِنَفْسِهٖ ۚ وَمَنْ كَفَرَ فَاِنَّ اللّٰهَ غَنِيٌّ
حَمِيْدٌ (١٣)

14. And *remember* when Luqmān said to his son while exhorting him, 'O my dear son! associate not partners with Allah. Surely, associating partners *with God* is a grievous wrong.'

وَاِذْ قَالَ لُقْمٰنُ لِابْنِهٖ وَهُوَ يَعِظُهٗ يٰبُنَيَّ لَا تُشْرِكْ
بِاللّٰهِ ۗ اِنَّ الشِّرْكَ لَظُلْمٌ عَظِيْمٌ (١٤)

15. And We have enjoined on man concerning his parents—his mother bears him in weakness upon weakness, and his weaning takes two years—'Give thanks to Me and to thy parents. Unto Me is the *final* return.

وَوَصَّيْنَا الْاِنْسَانَ بِوَالِدَيْهِ ۚ حَمَلَتْهُ اُمُّهٗ وَهْنًا
عَلٰى وَهْنٍ وَّفِصٰلُهٗ فِيْ عَامَيْنِ اَنِ اشْكُرْ لِيْ وَلِوَالِدَيْكَ ۗ
اِلَيَّ الْمَصِيْرُ (١٥)

16. 'And if they contend with thee to make thee set up equals with Me concerning which thou hast no knowledge, obey them not, but be a kind companion to them in *all* worldly affairs; and *in spiritual matters* follow the way of him who turns to Me. Then unto Me will be your return and I shall inform you of what you used to do.'

وَاِنْ جَاهَدٰكَ عَلٰٓى اَنْ تُشْرِكَ بِيْ مَا لَيْسَ لَكَ بِهٖ
عِلْمٌ ۙ فَلَا تُطِعْهُمَا وَصَاحِبْهُمَا فِي الدُّنْيَا مَعْرُوْفًا ۫
وَّاتَّبِعْ سَبِيْلَ مَنْ اَنَابَ اِلَيَّ ۚ ثُمَّ اِلَيَّ مَرْجِعُكُمْ
فَاُنَبِّئُكُمْ بِمَا كُنْتُمْ تَعْمَلُوْنَ (١٦)

17. 'O my dear son! even though it be the weight of a grain of mustard seed, and even though it be in a rock, or in the heavens, or in the earth, Allah will surely bring it out; verily Allah is the Knower of all subtleties, All-Aware.

يٰبُنَيَّ اِنَّهَآ اِنْ تَكُ مِثْقَالَ حَبَّةٍ مِّنْ خَرْدَلٍ فَتَكُنْ فِيْ
صَخْرَةٍ اَوْ فِي السَّمٰوٰتِ اَوْ فِي الْاَرْضِ يَاْتِ بِهَا اللّٰهُ ۗ
اِنَّ اللّٰهَ لَطِيْفٌ خَبِيْرٌ (١٧)

18. 'O my dear son! observe Prayer, and enjoin good, and forbid evil, and endure patiently whatever may befall thee. Surely, this is of those matters *which require* firm resolve.

يٰبُنَيَّ اَقِمِ الصَّلٰوةَ وَاْمُرْ بِالْمَعْرُوْفِ وَانْهَ عَنِ الْمُنْكَرِ
وَاصْبِرْ عَلٰى مَآ اَصَابَكَ ۗ اِنَّ ذٰلِكَ مِنْ عَزْمِ الْاُمُوْرِ (١٨)

19. 'And turn not thy cheek away from men in pride nor walk in the earth haughtily; surely, Allah loves not any arrogant boaster.

وَلَا تُصَعِّرْ خَدَّكَ لِلنَّاسِ وَلَا تَمْشِ فِي الْاَرْضِ مَرَحًا ۗ
اِنَّ اللّٰهَ لَا يُحِبُّ كُلَّ مُخْتَالٍ فَخُوْرٍ (١٩)

20. 'And walk thou at a moderate pace, and lower thy voice; verily, the most

وَاقْصِدْ فِيْ مَشْيِكَ وَاغْضُضْ مِنْ صَوْتِكَ ۗ اِنَّ

disagreeable of voices is the voice of the ass.'

ع أَنْكَرَ الْأَصْوَاتِ لَصَوْتُ الْحَمِيْرِ ٢٠

R. 3.

21. Have you not seen that Allah has pressed for you into service whatever is in the heavens and whatever is in the earth, and has completed His favours on you, *both* externally and internally? And among men there are some who dispute concerning Allah, without knowledge or guidance or an illuminating Book.

أَلَمْ تَرَوْا أَنَّ اللّٰهَ سَخَّرَ لَكُمْ مَّا فِي السَّمٰوٰتِ وَمَا فِي
الْأَرْضِ وَأَسْبَغَ عَلَيْكُمْ نِعَمَهٗ ظَاهِرَةً وَّبَاطِنَةً ۗ وَ
مِنَ النَّاسِ مَنْ يُّجَادِلُ فِي اللّٰهِ بِغَيْرِ عِلْمٍ وَّلَا هُدًى
وَّلَا كِتٰبٍ مُّنِيْرٍ ٢١

22. And when it is said to them, 'Follow that which Allah has revealed,' they say, 'Nay, we shall follow that which we found our fathers following.' What! even though Satan was inviting them to the punishment of the burning fire?

وَإِذَا قِيْلَ لَهُمُ اتَّبِعُوْا مَآ أَنْزَلَ اللّٰهُ قَالُوْا بَلْ نَتَّبِعُ
مَا وَجَدْنَا عَلَيْهِ آبَآءَنَا ۗ أَوَلَوْ كَانَ الشَّيْطٰنُ
يَدْعُوْهُمْ إِلٰى عَذَابِ السَّعِيْرِ ٢٢

23. And he who submits himself *completely* to Allah, and is a doer of good, he has surely grasped a strong handle. And with Allah *rests* the end of all affairs.

وَمَنْ يُّسْلِمْ وَجْهَهٗٓ إِلَى اللّٰهِ وَهُوَ مُحْسِنٌ فَقَدِ
اسْتَمْسَكَ بِالْعُرْوَةِ الْوُثْقٰى ۗ وَإِلَى اللّٰهِ عَاقِبَةُ
الْأُمُوْرِ ٢٣

24. And *as for* him who disbelieves, let not his disbelief grieve thee. Unto Us is their return and We shall tell them what they did; surely Allah knows full well what is in the breasts.

وَمَنْ كَفَرَ فَلَا يَحْزُنْكَ كُفْرُهٗ ۗ إِلَيْنَا مَرْجِعُهُمْ فَنُنَبِّئُهُمْ
بِمَا عَمِلُوْا ۗ إِنَّ اللّٰهَ عَلِيْمٌ ۢبِذَاتِ الصُّدُوْرِ ٢٤

25. We shall let them enjoy themselves a little; then We shall drive them to a severe torment.

نُمَتِّعُهُمْ قَلِيْلًا ثُمَّ نَضْطَرُّهُمْ إِلٰى عَذَابٍ غَلِيْظٍ ٢٥

26. And if thou ask them, 'Who created the heavens and the earth?' they will surely answer, 'Allah.' Say, 'All praise belongs to Allah.' But most of them know not.

وَلَئِنْ سَأَلْتَهُمْ مَّنْ خَلَقَ السَّمٰوٰتِ وَالْأَرْضَ لَيَقُوْلُنَّ
اللّٰهُ ۗ قُلِ الْحَمْدُ لِلّٰهِ ۗ بَلْ أَكْثَرُهُمْ لَا يَعْلَمُوْنَ ٢٦

27. To Allah belongs whatever is in the heavens and the earth. Verily, Allah is Self-Sufficient, Praiseworthy.

لِلّٰهِ مَا فِي السَّمٰوٰتِ وَالْأَرْضِ ۗ إِنَّ اللّٰهَ هُوَ الْغَنِيُّ
الْحَمِيْدُ ٢٧

28. And if all the trees that are in the earth were pens, and the ocean *were ink*, with seven oceans swelling it thereafter, the words of Allah would not be exhausted. Surely, Allah is Mighty, Wise.

وَلَوْ أَنَّ مَا فِي الْأَرْضِ مِنْ شَجَرَةٍ أَقْلَامٌ وَّالْبَحْرُ
يَمُدُّهٗ مِنْۢ بَعْدِهٖ سَبْعَةُ أَبْحُرٍ مَّا نَفِدَتْ كَلِمٰتُ
اللّٰهِ ۗ إِنَّ اللّٰهَ عَزِيْزٌ حَكِيْمٌ ٢٨

* 29. Your creation and your resurrection are only like *the creation and resurrection of* a single soul. Verily Allah is All-Hearing,

مَا خَلْقُكُمْ وَلَا بَعْثُكُمْ إِلَّا كَنَفْسٍ وَّاحِدَةٍ ۗ إِنَّ اللّٰهَ

All-Seeing.

سَمِيعٌ بَصِيرٌ ﴿٢٩﴾

30. Hast thou not seen that Allah makes the night pass into the day, and makes the day pass into the night, and He has pressed the sun and the moon into service; each pursuing its course till an appointed term, and that Allah is well aware of what you do?

أَلَمْ تَرَ أَنَّ اللّٰهَ يُولِجُ الَّيْلَ فِي النَّهَارِ وَيُولِجُ النَّهَارَ فِي الَّيْلِ وَسَخَّرَ الشَّمْسَ وَالْقَمَرَ كُلٌّ يَجْرِي إِلَىٰ أَجَلٍ مُّسَمًّى وَأَنَّ اللّٰهَ بِمَا تَعْمَلُونَ خَبِيرٌ ﴿٣٠﴾

31. That is because it is Allah alone Who is the True *God*, and whatever they call upon beside Him is falsehood, and because it is Allah alone Who is the Most High, the Incomparably Great.

ذٰلِكَ بِأَنَّ اللّٰهَ هُوَ الْحَقُّ وَأَنَّ مَا يَدْعُونَ مِن دُونِهِ الْبَاطِلُ وَأَنَّ اللّٰهَ هُوَ الْعَلِيُّ الْكَبِيرُ ﴿٣١﴾ ع

R. 4.

32. Dost thou not see that the ships sail on the sea by the favour of Allah, that He may show you of His Signs? Therein surely are Signs for everyone who is patient *and* grateful.

أَلَمْ تَرَ أَنَّ الْفُلْكَ تَجْرِي فِي الْبَحْرِ بِنِعْمَتِ اللّٰهِ لِيُرِيَكُم مِّنْ آيَاتِهِ إِنَّ فِي ذٰلِكَ لَآيَاتٍ لِّكُلِّ صَبَّارٍ شَكُورٍ ﴿٣٢﴾

33. And when waves engulf them like *so many* coverings, they call upon Allah, being sincere to Him in faith; but when He brings them safe to land, then some of them take the right course. And none denies Our Signs save every perfidious *and* ungrateful person.

وَإِذَا غَشِيَهُم مَّوْجٌ كَالظُّلَلِ دَعَوُا اللّٰهَ مُخْلِصِينَ لَهُ الدِّينَ فَلَمَّا نَجَّاهُمْ إِلَى الْبَرِّ فَمِنْهُم مُّقْتَصِدٌ وَمَا يَجْحَدُ بِآيَاتِنَا إِلَّا كُلُّ خَتَّارٍ كَفُورٍ ﴿٣٣﴾

34. O men, seek protection with your Lord and fear the day when the father will not be of any avail to his son, nor will the son at all be of any avail to his father. Allah's promise is surely true. So let not worldly life beguile you, nor let the Deceiver deceive you concerning Allah.

يَا أَيُّهَا النَّاسُ اتَّقُوا رَبَّكُمْ وَاخْشَوْا يَوْمًا لَّا يَجْزِي وَالِدٌ عَن وَلَدِهِ وَلَا مَوْلُودٌ هُوَ جَازٍ عَن وَالِدِهِ شَيْئًا إِنَّ وَعْدَ اللّٰهِ حَقٌّ فَلَا تَغُرَّنَّكُمُ الْحَيٰوةُ الدُّنْيَا وَلَا يَغُرَّنَّكُم بِاللّٰهِ الْغَرُورُ ﴿٣٤﴾

35. Verily, with Allah alone is the knowledge of the Hour. And He sends down the rain, and He knows what is in the wombs. And no soul knows what it will earn tomorrow, and no soul knows in what land it will die. Surely, Allah is All-Knowing, All-Aware.

إِنَّ اللّٰهَ عِندَهُ عِلْمُ السَّاعَةِ وَيُنَزِّلُ الْغَيْثَ وَيَعْلَمُ مَا فِي الْأَرْحَامِ وَمَا تَدْرِي نَفْسٌ مَّاذَا تَكْسِبُ غَدًا وَمَا تَدْرِي نَفْسٌ بِأَيِّ أَرْضٍ تَمُوتُ إِنَّ اللّٰهَ عَلِيمٌ خَبِيرٌ ﴿٣٥﴾ ع

سُوْرَةُ السَّجْدَةِ مَكِّيَّةٌ (٣٢)

AL-SAJDAH

(Revealed before Hijra)

1. In the name of Allah, the Gracious, the Merciful.

بِسْمِ اللّٰهِ الرَّحْمٰنِ الرَّحِيْمِ ﴿١﴾

2. Alif Lām Mīm*.

الٓمّٓ ﴿٢﴾

3. The revelation of the Book—there is no doubt about it—is from the Lord of the worlds.

تَنْزِيْلُ الْكِتٰبِ لَا رَيْبَ فِيْهِ مِنْ رَّبِّ الْعٰلَمِيْنَ ﴿٣﴾

4. Do they say, 'He has forged it?' Nay, it is the truth from thy Lord, that thou mayest warn a people to whom no Warner has come before thee, that haply they may follow guidance.

أَمْ يَقُوْلُوْنَ افْتَرٰىهُ ۚ بَلْ هُوَ الْحَقُّ مِنْ رَّبِّكَ لِتُنْذِرَ
قَوْمًا مَّآ أَتٰىهُمْ مِّنْ نَّذِيْرٍ مِّنْ قَبْلِكَ لَعَلَّهُمْ يَهْتَدُوْنَ ﴿٤﴾

5. Allah it is Who created the heavens and the earth, and that which is between them, in six periods; then He settled on the Throne. You have no helper or intercessor beside Him. Will you not then reflect?

اَللّٰهُ الَّذِيْ خَلَقَ السَّمٰوٰتِ وَالْأَرْضَ وَمَا بَيْنَهُمَا فِيْ
سِتَّةِ أَيَّامٍ ثُمَّ اسْتَوٰى عَلَى الْعَرْشِ ۗ مَا لَكُمْ مِّنْ دُوْنِهٖ
مِنْ وَّلِيٍّ وَّلَا شَفِيْعٍ ۗ أَفَلَا تَتَذَكَّرُوْنَ ﴿٥﴾

6. He will plan the *Divine* Ordinance from the heaven unto the earth, then shall it go up to Him in a day the duration of which is a thousand years according to what you reckon.

يُدَبِّرُ الْأَمْرَ مِنَ السَّمَآءِ إِلَى الْأَرْضِ ثُمَّ يَعْرُجُ إِلَيْهِ فِيْ يَوْمٍ
كَانَ مِقْدَارُهٗٓ أَلْفَ سَنَةٍ مِّمَّا تَعُدُّوْنَ ﴿٦﴾

7. Such is the Knower of the unseen and the seen, the Mighty, the Merciful,

ذٰلِكَ عٰلِمُ الْغَيْبِ وَالشَّهَادَةِ الْعَزِيْزُ الرَّحِيْمُ ﴿٧﴾

8. Who has made perfect everything He has created. And He began the creation of man from clay.

الَّذِيْٓ أَحْسَنَ كُلَّ شَيْءٍ خَلَقَهٗ وَبَدَأَ خَلْقَ الْإِنْسَانِ
مِنْ طِيْنٍ ﴿٨﴾

9. Then He made his progeny from an extract of an insignificant fluid.

ثُمَّ جَعَلَ نَسْلَهٗ مِنْ سُلٰلَةٍ مِّنْ مَّآءٍ مَّهِيْنٍ ﴿٩﴾

* 10. Then He fashioned him and breathed into him of His spirit. And He has given you ears, and eyes, and hearts. *But* little thanks do you give!

ثُمَّ سَوّٰىهُ وَنَفَخَ فِيْهِ مِنْ رُّوْحِهٖ وَجَعَلَ لَكُمُ السَّمْعَ
وَالْأَبْصَارَ وَالْأَفْئِدَةَ ۗ قَلِيْلًا مَّا تَشْكُرُوْنَ ﴿١٠﴾

11. And they say, 'What! when we are lost in the earth, shall we then become a new creation?' Nay, but they are disbelievers in the meeting of their Lord.

وَقَالُوْٓا ءَإِذَا ضَلَلْنَا فِي الْأَرْضِ ءَإِنَّا لَفِيْ خَلْقٍ جَدِيْدٍ ۚ
بَلْ هُمْ بِلِقَآءِ رَبِّهِمْ كٰفِرُوْنَ ﴿١١﴾

12. Say, 'The angel of death that has been put in charge of you will cause you

قُلْ يَتَوَفّٰىكُمْ مَّلَكُ الْمَوْتِ الَّذِيْ وُكِّلَ بِكُمْ ثُمَّ

---

* I am Allah, the All-Knowing.

to die; then to your Lord will you be brought back.'

إِلَىٰ رَبِّكُمْ تُرْجَعُونَ ﴿١٢﴾

R. 2

13. If only thou couldst see when the guilty will hang down their heads before their Lord, *and say*, 'Our Lord, we have seen and we have heard, so send us back that we may do good works; for *now* we are convinced.'

وَلَوْ تَرَىٰٓ إِذِ الْمُجْرِمُونَ نَاكِسُوا رُءُوسِهِمْ عِنْدَ رَبِّهِمْ
رَبَّنَآ أَبْصَرْنَا وَسَمِعْنَا فَارْجِعْنَا نَعْمَلْ صَالِحًا إِنَّا
مُوقِنُونَ ﴿١٣﴾

14. And if We had *enforced* Our will, We could have given every soul its guidance, but the word from Me has come true: 'I will fill Hell with Jinn and men all together.'

وَلَوْ شِئْنَا لَآتَيْنَا كُلَّ نَفْسٍ هُدَاهَا وَلَٰكِنْ حَقَّ الْقَوْلُ
مِنِّي لَأَمْلَأَنَّ جَهَنَّمَ مِنَ الْجِنَّةِ وَالنَّاسِ أَجْمَعِينَ ﴿١٤﴾

15. So taste ye *the punishment of your deeds* for you forgot the meeting of this day of yours. We *too* have forgotten you. And taste ye the lasting punishment because of that which you used to do.

فَذُوقُوا بِمَا نَسِيتُمْ لِقَآءَ يَوْمِكُمْ هَٰذَآ إِنَّا نَسِينَٰكُمْ
وَذُوقُوا عَذَابَ الْخُلْدِ بِمَا كُنْتُمْ تَعْمَلُونَ ﴿١٥﴾

16. Only they believe in Our Signs who, when they are reminded of them, fall down prostrate and celebrate the praises of their Lord, and they are not proud.

إِنَّمَا يُؤْمِنُ بِآيَٰتِنَا الَّذِينَ إِذَا ذُكِّرُوا بِهَا خَرُّوا سُجَّدًا
السجدة
وَسَبَّحُوا بِحَمْدِ رَبِّهِمْ وَهُمْ لَا يَسْتَكْبِرُونَ ﴿١٦﴾

17. Their sides keep away from their beds; *and* they call on their Lord in fear and hope, and spend out of what We have bestowed on them.

تَتَجَافَىٰ جُنُوبُهُمْ عَنِ الْمَضَاجِعِ يَدْعُونَ رَبَّهُمْ خَوْفًا
وَطَمَعًا وَمِمَّا رَزَقْنَٰهُمْ يُنْفِقُونَ ﴿١٧﴾

18. And no soul knows what joy of the eyes is kept hidden for them, as a reward for their good works.

فَلَا تَعْلَمُ نَفْسٌ مَّآ أُخْفِيَ لَهُمْ مِّنْ قُرَّةِ أَعْيُنٍ جَزَآءً
بِمَا كَانُوا يَعْمَلُونَ ﴿١٨﴾

19. Is he, then, who is a believer like one who is disobedient? They are not equal.

أَفَمَنْ كَانَ مُؤْمِنًا كَمَنْ كَانَ فَاسِقًا لَا يَسْتَوُونَ ﴿١٩﴾

20. As for those who believe and do good works, they will have Gardens of Eternal Abode, as an entertainment, for what they used to do.

أَمَّا الَّذِينَ آمَنُوا وَعَمِلُوا الصَّالِحَاتِ فَلَهُمْ جَنَّاتُ
الْمَأْوَىٰ نُزُلًا بِمَا كَانُوا يَعْمَلُونَ ﴿٢٠﴾

21. And as for those who are disobedient, their abode will be the Fire. Every time they desire to come forth therefrom, they will be turned back into it, and it will be said to them, 'Taste the punishment of the Fire which you used to deny.'

وَأَمَّا الَّذِينَ فَسَقُوا فَمَأْوَاهُمُ النَّارُ كُلَّمَا أَرَادُوا أَنْ
يَخْرُجُوا مِنْهَا أُعِيدُوا فِيهَا وَقِيلَ لَهُمْ ذُوقُوا عَذَابَ
النَّارِ الَّذِي كُنْتُمْ بِهِ تُكَذِّبُونَ ﴿٢١﴾

* 22. And most surely We will make them taste of the nearer punishment before the greater punishment, so that they may return *to Us with repentance*.

وَلَنُذِيقَنَّهُمْ مِنَ الْعَذَابِ الْأَدْنَىٰ دُونَ الْعَذَابِ
الْأَكْبَرِ لَعَلَّهُمْ يَرْجِعُونَ ﴿٢٢﴾

23. And who does greater wrong than he who is reminded of the Signs of his Lord and then turns away from them? We will surely punish the guilty.

وَمَنْ أَظْلَمُ مِمَّنْ ذُكِّرَ بِآيَاتِ رَبِّهِ ثُمَّ أَعْرَضَ عَنْهَا ۚ إِنَّا مِنَ الْمُجْرِمِينَ مُنْتَقِمُونَ ﴿٢٣﴾

R. 3.

24. And We did give Moses the Book—be not therefore in doubt as to the meeting with Him—and We made it a guidance for the children of Israel.

وَلَقَدْ آتَيْنَا مُوسَى الْكِتَابَ فَلَا تَكُنْ فِي مِرْيَةٍ مِنْ لِقَائِهِ ۖ وَجَعَلْنَاهُ هُدًى لِبَنِي إِسْرَائِيلَ ﴿٢٤﴾

25. And We made from among them leaders, who guided *the people* by Our command, whilst they *themselves* were steadfast and had firm faith in Our Signs.

وَجَعَلْنَا مِنْهُمْ أَئِمَّةً يَهْدُونَ بِأَمْرِنَا لَمَّا صَبَرُوا ۖ وَكَانُوا بِآيَاتِنَا يُوقِنُونَ ﴿٢٥﴾

26. Verily, thy Lord—He will judge between them on the Day of Resurrection concerning that in which they disagree.

إِنَّ رَبَّكَ هُوَ يَفْصِلُ بَيْنَهُمْ يَوْمَ الْقِيَامَةِ فِيمَا كَانُوا فِيهِ يَخْتَلِفُونَ ﴿٢٦﴾

27. Does it not guide them how many a generation We have destroyed before them, amid whose dwellings they *now* walk about? In that surely are Signs. Will they not then hearken?

أَوَلَمْ يَهْدِ لَهُمْ كَمْ أَهْلَكْنَا مِنْ قَبْلِهِمْ مِنَ الْقُرُونِ يَمْشُونَ فِي مَسَاكِنِهِمْ ۚ إِنَّ فِي ذَٰلِكَ لَآيَاتٍ ۖ أَفَلَا يَسْمَعُونَ ﴿٢٧﴾

28. Have they not seen that We drive the water to the dry land and produce thereby crops of which their cattle eat, and they themselves? Will they not then see?

أَوَلَمْ يَرَوْا أَنَّا نَسُوقُ الْمَاءَ إِلَى الْأَرْضِ الْجُرُزِ فَنُخْرِجُ بِهِ زَرْعًا تَأْكُلُ مِنْهُ أَنْعَامُهُمْ وَأَنْفُسُهُمْ ۖ أَفَلَا يُبْصِرُونَ ﴿٢٨﴾

29. And they say, 'When will this victory come, if you are truthful?'

وَيَقُولُونَ مَتَىٰ هَٰذَا الْفَتْحُ إِنْ كُنْتُمْ صَادِقِينَ ﴿٢٩﴾

30. Say, 'On the day of victory the believing of the disbelievers will not avail them, nor will they be granted respite.'

قُلْ يَوْمَ الْفَتْحِ لَا يَنْفَعُ الَّذِينَ كَفَرُوا إِيمَانُهُمْ وَلَا هُمْ يُنْظَرُونَ ﴿٣٠﴾

31. So turn away from them, and wait. They are also waiting.

فَأَعْرِضْ عَنْهُمْ وَانْتَظِرْ إِنَّهُمْ مُنْتَظِرُونَ ﴿٣١﴾

سُوْرَةُ الْاَحْزَابِ مَدَنِيَّةٌ

(٣٣) آياتها ٧٣ — ركوعاتها ٩

AL-AHZĀB

(Revealed after Hijra)

1. In the name of Allah, the Gracious, the Merciful.

بِسْمِ اللّٰهِ الرَّحْمٰنِ الرَّحِيْمِ ﴿١﴾

2. O thou Prophet, seek protection in Allah, and follow not *the wishes of* the disbelievers and the hypocrites. Verily, Allah is All-Knowing, Wise.

يٰۤاَيُّهَا النَّبِيُّ اتَّقِ اللّٰهَ وَلَا تُطِعِ الْكٰفِرِيْنَ وَالْمُنٰفِقِيْنَ ؕ
اِنَّ اللّٰهَ كَانَ عَلِيْمًا حَكِيْمًا ﴿٢﴾

3. And follow that which is revealed to thee from thy Lord. Verily Allah is well aware of what you do.

وَّاتَّبِعْ مَا يُوْحٰۤى اِلَيْكَ مِنْ رَّبِّكَ ؕ اِنَّ اللّٰهَ كَانَ بِمَا
تَعْمَلُوْنَ خَبِيْرًا ﴿٣﴾

4. And put thy trust in Allah, and Allah is sufficient as a Guardian.

وَّتَوَكَّلْ عَلَى اللّٰهِ ؕ وَكَفٰى بِاللّٰهِ وَكِيْلًا ﴿٤﴾

* 5. Allah has not made for any man two hearts in his breast; nor has He made those of your wives, from whom you keep away by calling them mothers, your *real* mothers, nor has He made your adopted sons your *real* sons. That is *merely* a word of your mouths; but Allah speaks the truth, and He guides to the *right* path.

مَا جَعَلَ اللّٰهُ لِرَجُلٍ مِّنْ قَلْبَيْنِ فِيْ جَوْفِهٖ ۚ وَمَا جَعَلَ
اَزْوَاجَكُمُ الّٰٓـِٔيْ تُظٰهِرُوْنَ مِنْهُنَّ اُمَّهٰتِكُمْ ۚ وَمَا جَعَلَ
اَدْعِيَآءَكُمْ اَبْنَآءَكُمْ ؕ ذٰلِكُمْ قَوْلُكُمْ بِاَفْوَاهِكُمْ ؕ وَاللّٰهُ
يَقُوْلُ الْحَقَّ وَهُوَ يَهْدِي السَّبِيْلَ ﴿٥﴾

* 6. Call them by *the names of* their fathers. That is more equitable in the sight of Allah. But if you know not their fathers, then they are your brothers in faith and your friends. And there is no blame on you in any mistake you may unintentionally make in this *matter*, but *what matters is* that which your hearts intend. And Allah is Most Forgiving, Merciful.

اُدْعُوْهُمْ لِاٰبَآئِهِمْ هُوَ اَقْسَطُ عِنْدَ اللّٰهِ ۚ فَاِنْ لَّمْ
تَعْلَمُوْۤا اٰبَآءَهُمْ فَاِخْوَانُكُمْ فِي الدِّيْنِ وَمَوَالِيْكُمْ ؕ
وَلَيْسَ عَلَيْكُمْ جُنَاحٌ فِيْمَاۤ اَخْطَاْتُمْ بِهٖ ۙ وَلٰكِنْ مَّا
تَعَمَّدَتْ قُلُوْبُكُمْ ؕ وَكَانَ اللّٰهُ غَفُوْرًا رَّحِيْمًا ﴿٦﴾

* 7. The Prophet is nearer to the believers than their own selves, and his wives are *as* mothers to them. And blood-relations are nearer to one another, according to the Book of Allah, than *the rest of* the believers *from among the Helpers* as well as the Emigrants, except that you show kindness to your friends. That *also* is written down in the Book.

اَلنَّبِيُّ اَوْلٰى بِالْمُؤْمِنِيْنَ مِنْ اَنْفُسِهِمْ وَاَزْوَاجُهٗۤ
اُمَّهٰتُهُمْ ؕ وَاُولُوا الْاَرْحَامِ بَعْضُهُمْ اَوْلٰى بِبَعْضٍ
فِيْ كِتٰبِ اللّٰهِ مِنَ الْمُؤْمِنِيْنَ وَالْمُهٰجِرِيْنَ اِلَّاۤ اَنْ
تَفْعَلُوْۤا اِلٰۤى اَوْلِيٰٓـئِكُمْ مَّعْرُوْفًا ؕ كَانَ ذٰلِكَ فِي الْكِتٰبِ
مَسْطُوْرًا ﴿٧﴾

8. And *remember* when We took from the Prophets their covenant, and from thee, and from Noah, and Abraham, and Moses, and Jesus, son of Mary, and We *indeed* took from them a solemn covenant;

وَإِذْ أَخَذْنَا مِنَ النَّبِيِّينَ مِيثَاقَهُمْ وَمِنْكَ وَمِنْ
نُوحٍ وَإِبْرَاهِيمَ وَمُوسَىٰ وَعِيسَى ابْنِ مَرْيَمَ
وَأَخَذْنَا مِنْهُمْ مِيثَاقًا غَلِيظًا ﴿٨﴾

9. That He may question the truthful about their truthfulness. And for the disbelievers He has prepared a painful punishment.

لِيَسْأَلَ الصَّادِقِينَ عَنْ صِدْقِهِمْ وَأَعَدَّ لِلْكَافِرِينَ
عَذَابًا أَلِيمًا ﴿٩﴾ ع

R. 2.

10. O ye who believe! remember the favour of Allah on you when there came down upon you hosts, and We sent against them a wind and hosts that you saw not. And Allah sees what you do.

يَا أَيُّهَا الَّذِينَ آمَنُوا اذْكُرُوا نِعْمَةَ اللَّهِ عَلَيْكُمْ إِذْ
جَاءَتْكُمْ جُنُودٌ فَأَرْسَلْنَا عَلَيْهِمْ رِيحًا وَجُنُودًا لَمْ
تَرَوْهَا وَكَانَ اللَّهُ بِمَا تَعْمَلُونَ بَصِيرًا ﴿١٠﴾

* 11. When they came upon you from above you, and from below you, and when *your* eyes became distracted, and *your* hearts reached to the throats, and you thought *diverse* thoughts about Allah.

إِذْ جَاءُوكُمْ مِنْ فَوْقِكُمْ وَمِنْ أَسْفَلَ مِنْكُمْ وَإِذْ
زَاغَتِ الْأَبْصَارُ وَبَلَغَتِ الْقُلُوبُ الْحَنَاجِرَ وَتَظُنُّونَ
بِاللَّهِ الظُّنُونَا ﴿١١﴾

12. There *and then* were the believers *sorely* tried, and they were shaken with a violent shaking.

هُنَالِكَ ابْتُلِيَ الْمُؤْمِنُونَ وَزُلْزِلُوا زِلْزَالًا شَدِيدًا ﴿١٢﴾

13. And when the hypocrites and those in whose hearts was a disease said, 'Allah and His Messenger promised us nothing but a delusion.'

وَإِذْ يَقُولُ الْمُنَافِقُونَ وَالَّذِينَ فِي قُلُوبِهِمْ مَرَضٌ
مَا وَعَدَنَا اللَّهُ وَرَسُولُهُ إِلَّا غُرُورًا ﴿١٣﴾

14. And when a party of them said, 'O people of Yathrib*, you have *possibly* no stand *against the enemy*, therefore turn back.' And a section of them *even* asked leave of the Prophet, saying, 'Our houses are exposed *and defenceless*.' And they were *in truth* not exposed. They only sought to flee away.

وَإِذْ قَالَتْ طَائِفَةٌ مِنْهُمْ يَا أَهْلَ يَثْرِبَ لَا مُقَامَ
لَكُمْ فَارْجِعُوا وَيَسْتَأْذِنُ فَرِيقٌ مِنْهُمُ النَّبِيَّ يَقُولُونَ
إِنَّ بُيُوتَنَا عَوْرَةٌ وَمَا هِيَ بِعَوْرَةٍ إِنْ يُرِيدُونَ
إِلَّا فِرَارًا ﴿١٤﴾

15. And if entry were effected against them *into the town* from its environs, and then they were asked *to join in* the disturbances, they would have *at once* done so, and would not have tarried in their houses save a little.

وَلَوْ دُخِلَتْ عَلَيْهِمْ مِنْ أَقْطَارِهَا ثُمَّ سُئِلُوا الْفِتْنَةَ
لَآتَوْهَا وَمَا تَلَبَّثُوا بِهَا إِلَّا يَسِيرًا ﴿١٥﴾

* 16. And truly they had already covenanted with Allah *that* they would not turn their backs. And a covenant with Allah will have to be answered for.

وَلَقَدْ كَانُوا عَاهَدُوا اللَّهَ مِنْ قَبْلُ لَا يُوَلُّونَ
الْأَدْبَارَ وَكَانَ عَهْدُ اللَّهِ مَسْئُولًا ﴿١٦﴾

* **Medina was known by this name before Hijra.**

17. Say, 'Flight shall not avail you if you flee from death or slaughter; and *even* then you will enjoy but a little.'

قُلْ لَّنْ يَّنْفَعَكُمُ الْفِرَارُ اِنْ فَرَرْتُمْ مِّنَ الْمَوْتِ اَوِ الْقَتْلِ وَاِذًا لَّا تُمَتَّعُوْنَ اِلَّا قَلِيْلًا ﴿۱۷﴾

18. Say, 'Who is it that can save you against Allah if it be His wish to do you harm or if it be His wish to show you mercy?' And they will not find for themselves any friend or helper other than Allah.

قُلْ مَنْ ذَا الَّذِيْ يَعْصِمُكُمْ مِّنَ اللّٰهِ اِنْ اَرَادَ بِكُمْ سُوْٓءًا اَوْ اَرَادَ بِكُمْ رَحْمَةً ؕ وَلَا يَجِدُوْنَ لَهُمْ مِّنْ دُوْنِ اللّٰهِ وَلِيًّا وَّلَا نَصِيْرًا ﴿۱۸﴾

19. Verily Allah knows those among you who hinder *men* and those who say to their brethren, 'Come to us;' and they come not to the fight but a little,

قَدْ يَعْلَمُ اللّٰهُ الْمُعَوِّقِيْنَ مِنْكُمْ وَالْقَآئِلِيْنَ لِاِخْوَانِهِمْ هَلُمَّ اِلَيْنَا ۚ وَلَا يَاْتُوْنَ الْبَاْسَ اِلَّا قَلِيْلًا ﴿۱۹﴾

20. Being niggardly with regard to you. But when danger comes, thou seest them looking towards thee, their eyes rolling like one who is fainting on account of death. But when the fear has passed away, they assail you with sharp tongues being greedy for wealth. These have never believed; so Allah has rendered their works null and void. And that is an easy thing for Allah.

اَشِحَّةً عَلَيْكُمْ ۚۖ فَاِذَا جَآءَ الْخَوْفُ رَاَيْتَهُمْ يَنْظُرُوْنَ اِلَيْكَ تَدُوْرُ اَعْيُنُهُمْ كَالَّذِيْ يُغْشٰى عَلَيْهِ مِنَ الْمَوْتِ ۚ فَاِذَا ذَهَبَ الْخَوْفُ سَلَقُوْكُمْ بِاَلْسِنَةٍ حِدَادٍ اَشِحَّةً عَلَى الْخَيْرِ ؕ اُولٰٓئِكَ لَمْ يُؤْمِنُوْا فَاَحْبَطَ اللّٰهُ اَعْمَالَهُمْ ؕ وَكَانَ ذٰلِكَ عَلَى اللّٰهِ يَسِيْرًا ﴿۲۰﴾

* **21.** They think that the confederates have not gone away; and if the confederates should come *again*, they would wish to be among the nomad Arabs in the desert, asking for news about you. And if they were among you they would not fight save a little.

يَحْسَبُوْنَ الْاَحْزَابَ لَمْ يَذْهَبُوْا ۚ وَاِنْ يَّاْتِ الْاَحْزَابُ يَوَدُّوْا لَوْ اَنَّهُمْ بَادُوْنَ فِي الْاَعْرَابِ يَسْاَلُوْنَ عَنْ اَنْۢبَآئِكُمْ ؕ وَلَوْ كَانُوْا فِيْكُمْ مَّا قٰتَلُوْٓا اِلَّا قَلِيْلًا ﴿۲۱﴾ ع ۲ ۱۸

R. 3.

22. Verily you have in the Prophet of Allah an excellent model, for him who fears Allah and the Last Day and who remembers Allah much.

لَقَدْ كَانَ لَكُمْ فِيْ رَسُوْلِ اللّٰهِ اُسْوَةٌ حَسَنَةٌ لِّمَنْ كَانَ يَرْجُوا اللّٰهَ وَالْيَوْمَ الْاٰخِرَ وَذَكَرَ اللّٰهَ كَثِيْرًا ﴿۲۲﴾

23. And when the believers saw the confederates, they said, 'This is what Allah and His Messenger promised us; and Allah and His Messenger spoke the truth.' And it only added to their faith and submission.

وَلَمَّا رَاَ الْمُؤْمِنُوْنَ الْاَحْزَابَ ۙ قَالُوْا هٰذَا مَا وَعَدَنَا اللّٰهُ وَرَسُوْلُهٗ وَصَدَقَ اللّٰهُ وَرَسُوْلُهٗ ۫ وَمَا زَادَهُمْ اِلَّآ اِيْمَانًا وَّتَسْلِيْمًا ﴿۲۳﴾

24. Among the believers are men who have been true to the covenant they made

مِنَ الْمُؤْمِنِيْنَ رِجَالٌ صَدَقُوْا مَا عَاهَدُوا اللّٰهَ عَلَيْهِ

with Allah. There are *some* of them who have fulfilled their vow, and *some* who *still* wait, and they have not changed *their condition* in the least;

فَمِنْهُمْ مَّنْ قَضٰى نَحْبَهٗ وَمِنْهُمْ مَّنْ يَّنْتَظِرُ ۖ وَمَا
بَدَّلُوْا تَبْدِيْلًا ﴿۲۴﴾

25. That Allah may reward the truthful for their truth, and punish the hypocrites if He so please, or turn to them in mercy. Verily Allah is Most Forgiving, Merciful.

لِّيَجْزِيَ اللّٰهُ الصّٰدِقِيْنَ بِصِدْقِهِمْ وَيُعَذِّبَ الْمُنٰفِقِيْنَ
إِنْ شَآءَ أَوْ يَتُوْبَ عَلَيْهِمْ ۭ إِنَّ اللّٰهَ كَانَ غَفُوْرًا
رَّحِيْمًا ﴿۲۵﴾

26. And Allah turned back the disbelievers in their rage; they gained no good. And Allah sufficed the believers in their fight. And Allah is Powerful, Mighty.

وَرَدَّ اللّٰهُ الَّذِيْنَ كَفَرُوْا بِغَيْظِهِمْ لَمْ يَنَالُوْا خَيْرًا ۭ
وَكَفَى اللّٰهُ الْمُؤْمِنِيْنَ الْقِتَالَ ۭ وَكَانَ اللّٰهُ قَوِيًّا
عَزِيْزًا ﴿۲۶﴾

27. And He brought those of the People of the Book who aided them down from their fortresses and cast terror into their hearts. Some you slew, and some you took captive.

وَأَنْزَلَ الَّذِيْنَ ظَاهَرُوْهُمْ مِّنْ أَهْلِ الْكِتٰبِ مِنْ
صَيَاصِيْهِمْ وَقَذَفَ فِيْ قُلُوْبِهِمُ الرُّعْبَ فَرِيْقًا
تَقْتُلُوْنَ وَتَأْسِرُوْنَ فَرِيْقًا ﴿۲۷﴾

28. And He made you inherit their land and their houses and their wealth, and a land on which you had never set foot. And Allah has power over all things.

وَأَوْرَثَكُمْ أَرْضَهُمْ وَدِيَارَهُمْ وَأَمْوَالَهُمْ وَأَرْضًا
لَّمْ تَطَئُوْهَا ۭ وَكَانَ اللّٰهُ عَلٰى كُلِّ شَيْءٍ قَدِيْرًا ﴿۲۸﴾

R. 4.

29. O Prophet! say to thy wives, 'If you desire the life of this world and its adornment, come then, I will provide for you and send you away in a handsome manner.

يٰٓأَيُّهَا النَّبِيُّ قُلْ لِّأَزْوَاجِكَ إِنْ كُنْتُنَّ تُرِدْنَ الْحَيٰوةَ
الدُّنْيَا وَزِيْنَتَهَا فَتَعَالَيْنَ أُمَتِّعْكُنَّ وَأُسَرِّحْكُنَّ
سَرَاحًا جَمِيْلًا ﴿۲۹﴾

30. 'But if you desire Allah and His Messenger and the Home of the Hereafter, then truly Allah has prepared for those of you who do good a great reward.'

وَإِنْ كُنْتُنَّ تُرِدْنَ اللّٰهَ وَرَسُوْلَهٗ وَالدَّارَ الْاٰخِرَةَ
فَإِنَّ اللّٰهَ أَعَدَّ لِلْمُحْسِنٰتِ مِنْكُنَّ أَجْرًا عَظِيْمًا ﴿۳۰﴾

31. O wives of the Prophet! if any of you be guilty of manifestly dishonourable conduct, the punishment will be doubled for her. And that is easy for Allah.

يٰنِسَآءَ النَّبِيِّ مَنْ يَّأْتِ مِنْكُنَّ بِفَاحِشَةٍ مُّبَيِّنَةٍ
يُّضٰعَفْ لَهَا الْعَذَابُ ضِعْفَيْنِ ۭ وَكَانَ ذٰلِكَ عَلَى
اللّٰهِ يَسِيْرًا ﴿۳۱﴾

32. But whoever of you is obedient to Allah and His Messenger and does good works, We shall give her her reward twice

وَمَنْ يَّقْنُتْ مِنْكُنَّ لِلّٰهِ وَرَسُوْلِهٖ وَتَعْمَلْ صَالِحًا

الجزء ۲۲

نُؤْتِهَآ أَجْرَهَا مَرَّتَيْنِ وَأَعْتَدْنَا لَهَا رِزْقًا كَرِيمًا ﴿٣٢﴾

over; and We have prepared for her an honourable provision.

يٰنِسَآءَ النَّبِيِّ لَسْتُنَّ كَأَحَدٍ مِّنَ النِّسَآءِ إِنِ اتَّقَيْتُنَّ
فَلَا تَخْضَعْنَ بِالْقَوْلِ فَيَطْمَعَ الَّذِي فِي قَلْبِهِ مَرَضٌ
وَّقُلْنَ قَوْلًا مَّعْرُوفًا ﴿٣٣﴾

33. O wives of the Prophet! you are not like any *other* women if you are righteous. So be not soft in speech, lest he in whose heart is a disease should feel tempted; and speak a decent speech.

وَقَرْنَ فِي بُيُوتِكُنَّ وَلَا تَبَرَّجْنَ تَبَرُّجَ الْجَاهِلِيَّةِ
الْأُولٰى وَأَقِمْنَ الصَّلٰوةَ وَاٰتِيْنَ الزَّكٰوةَ وَأَطِعْنَ
اللّٰهَ وَرَسُولَهٗ ۚ إِنَّمَا يُرِيدُ اللّٰهُ لِيُذْهِبَ عَنْكُمُ
الرِّجْسَ أَهْلَ الْبَيْتِ وَيُطَهِّرَكُمْ تَطْهِيرًا ﴿٣٤﴾

* 34. And stay in your houses *with dignity*, and do not show off yourselves like the showing off of the former days of ignorance, and observe Prayer, and pay the Zakāt, and obey Allah and His Messenger. Surely Allah desires to remove from you *all* uncleanness, O Members of the Household, and purify you completely.

وَاذْكُرْنَ مَا يُتْلٰى فِي بُيُوتِكُنَّ مِنْ اٰيٰتِ اللّٰهِ وَالْحِكْمَةِ
إِنَّ اللّٰهَ كَانَ لَطِيفًا خَبِيرًا ﴿٣٥﴾ ع

35. And remember what is rehearsed in your houses of the Signs of Allah and of wisdom. Verily Allah is the Knower of subtleties, All-Aware.

R. 5.

إِنَّ الْمُسْلِمِينَ وَالْمُسْلِمٰتِ وَالْمُؤْمِنِينَ وَالْمُؤْمِنٰتِ
وَالْقٰنِتِينَ وَالْقٰنِتٰتِ وَالصّٰدِقِينَ وَالصّٰدِقٰتِ وَ
الصّٰبِرِينَ وَالصّٰبِرٰتِ وَالْخٰشِعِينَ وَالْخٰشِعٰتِ
وَالْمُتَصَدِّقِينَ وَالْمُتَصَدِّقٰتِ وَالصَّآئِمِينَ وَالصّٰٓئِمٰتِ
وَالْحٰفِظِينَ فُرُوجَهُمْ وَالْحٰفِظٰتِ وَالذّٰكِرِينَ اللّٰهَ
كَثِيرًا وَّالذّٰكِرٰتِ أَعَدَّ اللّٰهُ لَهُمْ مَّغْفِرَةً وَّأَجْرًا
عَظِيمًا ﴿٣٦﴾

36. Surely, men who submit themselves *to God* and women who submit themselves *to Him*, and believing men and believing women, and obedient men and obedient women and truthful men and truthful women, and men steadfast *in their faith* and steadfast women, and men who are humble and women who are humble, and men who give alms and women who give alms, and men who fast and women who fast, and men who guard their chastity and women who guard their chastity, and men who remember Allah much and women who remember *Him*—Allah has prepared for *all of* them forgiveness and a great reward.

وَمَا كَانَ لِمُؤْمِنٍ وَّلَا مُؤْمِنَةٍ إِذَا قَضَى اللّٰهُ وَرَسُولُهٗٓ
أَمْرًا أَنْ يَّكُونَ لَهُمُ الْخِيَرَةُ مِنْ أَمْرِهِمْ ۗ وَمَنْ يَّعْصِ
اللّٰهَ وَرَسُولَهٗ فَقَدْ ضَلَّ ضَلٰلًا مُّبِينًا ﴿٣٧﴾

37. And it behoves not a believing man or a believing woman, when Allah and His Messenger have decided a matter, that there should be a choice for them in the matter concerning them. And whoso disobeys Allah and His Messenger. surely strays away in manifest error.

وَإِذْ تَقُولُ لِلَّذِيٓ أَنْعَمَ اللّٰهُ عَلَيْهِ وَأَنْعَمْتَ عَلَيْهِ
أَمْسِكْ عَلَيْكَ زَوْجَكَ وَاتَّقِ اللّٰهَ وَتُخْفِي فِي نَفْسِكَ

38. And *remember* when thou didst say to him on whom Allah had bestowed favours and on whom thou *also* hadst bestowed favours: 'Keep thy wife to thy-

self, and fear Allah.' And thou didst conceal in thy heart what Allah was going to bring to light, and thou wast afraid of the people, whereas Allah has better right that thou shouldst fear Him. Then, when Zaid had accomplished his want of her *so as to have no further need of her*, We joined her in marriage to thee, so that there may be no hindrance for the believers with regard to the wives of their adopted sons, when they have accomplished their want of them. And Allah's decree must be fulfilled.

39. There can be no hindrance for the Prophet with regard to that which Allah has made incumbent upon him. Such indeed was the way of Allah with those who have passed away before—and the command of Allah is a decree ordained—

40. Those who delivered the Messages of Allah and feared Him, and feared none but Allah. And sufficient is Allah as a Reckoner.

41. Muhammad is not the father of any of your men, but *he is* the Messenger of Allah and the Seal of the Prophets; and Allah has full knowledge of all things.

R. 6.

42. O ye who believe! remember Allah with much remembrance;

43. And glorify Him morning and evening.

44. He it is Who sends blessings on you, as *do* His angels, that He may bring you forth from all *kinds of* darkness into light. And He is Merciful to the believers.

45. Their greeting on the day when they meet Him will be, 'Peace'. And He has prepared for them an honourable reward.

46. O Prophet, truly We have sent thee as a Witness, and a Bearer of glad tidings, and a Warner,

* 47. And as a Summoner unto Allah by His command, and as a Lamp that gives *bright* light.

48. And announce to the believers the glad tidings that they will have great bounty from Allah.

* 49. And follow not the disbelievers and the hypocrites, and leave alone their

مَا اللّٰهُ مُبْدِيْهِ وَ تَخْشَى النَّاسَ ۚ وَاللّٰهُ اَحَقُّ اَنْ
تَخْشٰىهُ ؕ فَلَمَّا قَضٰى زَيْدٌ مِّنْهَا وَطَرًا زَوَّجْنٰكَهَا لِكَیْ
لَا يَكُوْنَ عَلَى الْمُؤْمِنِيْنَ حَرَجٌ فِيْۤ اَزْوَاجِ اَدْعِيَآئِهِمْ
اِذَا قَضَوْا مِنْهُنَّ وَطَرًا ؕ وَكَانَ اَمْرُ اللّٰهِ مَفْعُوْلًا ﴿۳۸﴾
مَا كَانَ عَلَى النَّبِيِّ مِنْ حَرَجٍ فِيْمَا فَرَضَ اللّٰهُ لَهٗ ؕ سُنَّةَ
اللّٰهِ فِي الَّذِيْنَ خَلَوْا مِنْ قَبْلُ ؕ وَكَانَ اَمْرُ اللّٰهِ قَدَرًا
مَّقْدُوْرَا ۙ﴿۳۹﴾
الَّذِيْنَ يُبَلِّغُوْنَ رِسٰلٰتِ اللّٰهِ وَيَخْشَوْنَهٗ وَلَا يَخْشَوْنَ
اَحَدًا اِلَّا اللّٰهَ ؕ وَكَفٰى بِاللّٰهِ حَسِيْبًا ﴿۴۰﴾
مَا كَانَ مُحَمَّدٌ اَبَآ اَحَدٍ مِّنْ رِّجَالِكُمْ وَلٰكِنْ رَّسُوْلَ
اللّٰهِ وَخَاتَمَ النَّبِيّٖنَ ؕ وَكَانَ اللّٰهُ بِكُلِّ شَیْءٍ عَلِيْمًا ﴿۴۱﴾ ع
يٰۤاَيُّهَا الَّذِيْنَ اٰمَنُوا اذْكُرُوا اللّٰهَ ذِكْرًا كَثِيْرًا ﴿۴۲﴾
وَّسَبِّحُوْهُ بُكْرَةً وَّاَصِيْلًا ﴿۴۳﴾
هُوَ الَّذِيْ يُصَلِّيْ عَلَيْكُمْ وَمَلٰٓئِكَتُهٗ لِيُخْرِجَكُمْ مِّنَ
الظُّلُمٰتِ اِلَى النُّوْرِ ؕ وَكَانَ بِالْمُؤْمِنِيْنَ رَحِيْمًا ﴿۴۴﴾
تَحِيَّتُهُمْ يَوْمَ يَلْقَوْنَهٗ سَلٰمٌ ۚۖ وَاَعَدَّ لَهُمْ اَجْرًا
كَرِيْمًا ﴿۴۵﴾
يٰۤاَيُّهَا النَّبِيُّ اِنَّاۤ اَرْسَلْنٰكَ شَاهِدًا وَّمُبَشِّرًا وَّ
نَذِيْرًا ۙ﴿۴۶﴾
وَّدَاعِيًا اِلَى اللّٰهِ بِاِذْنِهٖ وَسِرَاجًا مُّنِيْرًا ﴿۴۷﴾
وَبَشِّرِ الْمُؤْمِنِيْنَ بِاَنَّ لَهُمْ مِّنَ اللّٰهِ فَضْلًا كَبِيْرًا ﴿۴۸﴾
وَلَا تُطِعِ الْكٰفِرِيْنَ وَالْمُنٰفِقِيْنَ وَدَعْ اَذٰىهُمْ وَتَوَكَّلْ

annoyance, and put thy trust in Allah; for Allah is sufficient as a Guardian.

* 50. O ye who believe! when you marry believing women and then divorce them before you have touched them, then you have no right against them with regard to the period of waiting that you reckon. So make some provision for them and send them away in a handsome manner.

51. O Prophet, We have made lawful to thee thy wives whom thou hast paid their dowries, and those whom thy right hand possesses from among those whom Allah has given thee as gains of war, and the daughters of thy paternal uncle, and the daughters of thy paternal aunts, and the daughters of thy maternal uncle, and the daughters of thy maternal aunts who have emigrated with thee, and any *other* believing woman if she offers herself *for marriage* to the Prophet provided the Prophet desires to marry her: *this is* only for thee, as against *other* believers—We have already made known what We have enjoined on them concerning their wives and those whom their right hands possess—in order that there may be no difficulty for thee *in the discharge of thy work*. And Allah is Most Forgiving, Merciful.

* 52. Thou mayest defer *the marriage of* any of them that thou pleasest, and receive unto thyself whom thou pleasest; and if thou desirest *to take back* any of those whom thou hast put aside, there is no blame on thee. That is more likely that their eyes may be cooled, and that they may not grieve, and that they may all be pleased with that which thou hast given them. And Allah knows what is in your hearts; and Allah is All-Knowing, Forbearing.

53. It is not allowed to thee *to marry* women after that, nor to change them for *other* wives even though their goodness please thee, except any that thy right hand possesses. And Allah is Watchful over all things.

R. 7.

* 54. O ye who believe! enter not the houses of the Prophet unless leave is granted to

عَلَى اللّٰهِ ۚ وَكَفٰى بِاللّٰهِ وَكِيْلًا ﴿٤٩﴾
يٰٓاَيُّهَا الَّذِيْنَ اٰمَنُوْٓا اِذَا نَكَحْتُمُ الْمُؤْمِنٰتِ ثُمَّ طَلَّقْتُمُوْهُنَّ
مِنْ قَبْلِ اَنْ تَمَسُّوْهُنَّ فَمَا لَكُمْ عَلَيْهِنَّ مِنْ عِدَّةٍ
تَعْتَدُّوْنَهَا ۚ فَمَتِّعُوْهُنَّ وَسَرِّحُوْهُنَّ سَرَاحًا جَمِيْلًا ﴿٥٠﴾
يٰٓاَيُّهَا النَّبِيُّ اِنَّآ اَحْلَلْنَا لَكَ اَزْوَاجَكَ الّٰتِيْٓ اٰتَيْتَ
اُجُوْرَهُنَّ وَمَا مَلَكَتْ يَمِيْنُكَ مِمَّآ اَفَآءَ اللّٰهُ عَلَيْكَ
وَبَنٰتِ عَمِّكَ وَبَنٰتِ عَمّٰتِكَ وَبَنٰتِ خَالِكَ وَبَنٰتِ
خٰلٰتِكَ الّٰتِيْ هَاجَرْنَ مَعَكَ ۫ وَامْرَاَةً مُّؤْمِنَةً اِنْ
وَّهَبَتْ نَفْسَهَا لِلنَّبِيِّ اِنْ اَرَادَ النَّبِيُّ اَنْ يَّسْتَنْكِحَهَا ۗ
خَالِصَةً لَّكَ مِنْ دُوْنِ الْمُؤْمِنِيْنَ ۭ قَدْ عَلِمْنَا مَا
فَرَضْنَا عَلَيْهِمْ فِيْٓ اَزْوَاجِهِمْ وَمَا مَلَكَتْ اَيْمَانُهُمْ
لِكَيْلَا يَكُوْنَ عَلَيْكَ حَرَجٌ ۭ وَكَانَ اللّٰهُ غَفُوْرًا رَّحِيْمًا ﴿٥١﴾
تُرْجِيْ مَنْ تَشَآءُ مِنْهُنَّ وَتُـْٔوِيْٓ اِلَيْكَ مَنْ تَشَآءُ ۭ
وَمَنِ ابْتَغَيْتَ مِمَّنْ عَزَلْتَ فَلَا جُنَاحَ عَلَيْكَ ۭ ذٰلِكَ
اَدْنٰٓى اَنْ تَقَرَّ اَعْيُنُهُنَّ وَلَا يَحْزَنَّ وَيَرْضَيْنَ بِمَآ
اٰتَيْتَهُنَّ كُلُّهُنَّ ۭ وَاللّٰهُ يَعْلَمُ مَا فِيْ قُلُوْبِكُمْ ۭ وَكَانَ
اللّٰهُ عَلِيْمًا حَلِيْمًا ﴿٥٢﴾
لَا يَحِلُّ لَكَ النِّسَآءُ مِنْ بَعْدُ وَلَآ اَنْ تَبَدَّلَ بِهِنَّ
مِنْ اَزْوَاجٍ وَّلَوْ اَعْجَبَكَ حُسْنُهُنَّ اِلَّا مَا مَلَكَتْ
يَمِيْنُكَ ۭ وَكَانَ اللّٰهُ عَلٰى كُلِّ شَيْءٍ رَّقِيْبًا ﴿٥٣﴾ ع ٧/٤
يٰٓاَيُّهَا الَّذِيْنَ اٰمَنُوْا لَا تَدْخُلُوْا بُيُوْتَ النَّبِيِّ اِلَّآ اَنْ
يُّؤْذَنَ لَكُمْ اِلٰى طَعَامٍ غَيْرَ نٰظِرِيْنَ اِنٰىهُ ۙ وَلٰكِنْ

you for a meal without waiting for its *appointed* time. But enter when you are invited, and when you have finished eating, disperse, without seeking to engage in talk. That causes inconvenience to the Prophet, and he feels shy of *asking* you *to leave*. But Allah is not shy of *saying* what is true. And when you ask them (the wives of the Prophet) for anything, ask them from behind a curtain. That is purer for your hearts and their hearts. And it behoves you not to cause inconvenience to the Messenger of Allah, nor that you should ever marry his wives after him. Indeed that would be an enormity in the sight of Allah.

إِذَا دُعِيتُمْ فَادْخُلُوا فَإِذَا طَعِمْتُمْ فَانْتَشِرُوا وَ
لَا مُسْتَأْنِسِينَ لِحَدِيثٍ إِنَّ ذٰلِكُمْ كَانَ يُؤْذِي
النَّبِيَّ فَيَسْتَحْيِي مِنْكُمْ وَاللّٰهُ لَا يَسْتَحْيِي مِنَ الْحَقِّ
وَإِذَا سَأَلْتُمُوهُنَّ مَتَاعًا فَسْئَلُوهُنَّ مِنْ وَرَاءِ حِجَابٍ
ذٰلِكُمْ أَطْهَرُ لِقُلُوبِكُمْ وَقُلُوبِهِنَّ وَمَا كَانَ لَكُمْ
أَنْ تُؤْذُوا رَسُولَ اللّٰهِ وَلَا أَنْ تَنْكِحُوا أَزْوَاجَهُ مِنْ
بَعْدِهِ أَبَدًا إِنَّ ذٰلِكُمْ كَانَ عِنْدَ اللّٰهِ عَظِيمًا ﴿٥٤﴾

55. Whether you reveal a thing or conceal it, Allah knows all things full well.

إِنْ تُبْدُوا شَيْئًا أَوْ تُخْفُوهُ فَإِنَّ اللّٰهَ كَانَ بِكُلِّ شَيْءٍ
عَلِيمًا ﴿٥٥﴾

56. There is no blame on them *in this respect* with regard to their fathers or their sons or their brothers or the sons of their brothers or the sons of their sisters or their womenfolk or those whom their right hands possess. And fear Allah, *O wives of the Prophet*, verily, Allah is Witness over all things.

لَا جُنَاحَ عَلَيْهِنَّ فِي آبَائِهِنَّ وَلَا أَبْنَائِهِنَّ وَلَا
إِخْوَانِهِنَّ وَلَا أَبْنَاءِ إِخْوَانِهِنَّ وَلَا أَبْنَاءِ أَخَوَاتِهِنَّ
وَلَا نِسَائِهِنَّ وَلَا مَا مَلَكَتْ أَيْمَانُهُنَّ وَاتَّقِينَ
اللّٰهَ إِنَّ اللّٰهَ كَانَ عَلٰى كُلِّ شَيْءٍ شَهِيدًا ﴿٥٦﴾

57. Allah and His angels send blessings on the Prophet. O ye who believe! you *also* should invoke blessings on him and salute *him* with the salutation of peace.

إِنَّ اللّٰهَ وَمَلٰٓئِكَتَهُ يُصَلُّونَ عَلَى النَّبِيِّ يٰأَيُّهَا الَّذِينَ
آمَنُوا صَلُّوا عَلَيْهِ وَسَلِّمُوا تَسْلِيمًا ﴿٥٧﴾

* 58. Verily, those who malign Allah and His Messenger—Allah has cursed them in this world and in the Hereafter, and has prepared for them an abasing punishment.

إِنَّ الَّذِينَ يُؤْذُونَ اللّٰهَ وَرَسُولَهُ لَعَنَهُمُ اللّٰهُ فِي
الدُّنْيَا وَالْآخِرَةِ وَأَعَدَّ لَهُمْ عَذَابًا مُهِينًا ﴿٥٨﴾

59. And those who malign believing men and believing women for what they have not earned shall bear *the guilt of* a calumny and a manifest sin.

وَالَّذِينَ يُؤْذُونَ الْمُؤْمِنِينَ وَالْمُؤْمِنٰتِ بِغَيْرِ مَا
اكْتَسَبُوا فَقَدِ احْتَمَلُوا بُهْتَانًا وَإِثْمًا مُبِينًا ﴿٥٩﴾ ع

R. 8.

* 60. O Prophet! tell thy wives and thy daughters and the women of the believers that they should draw close to them portions of their *loose* outer coverings. That is nearer that they may *thus* be distinguished and not molested. And Allah is Most Forgiving, Merciful.

يٰأَيُّهَا النَّبِيُّ قُلْ لِأَزْوَاجِكَ وَبَنٰتِكَ وَنِسَاءِ الْمُؤْمِنِينَ
يُدْنِينَ عَلَيْهِنَّ مِنْ جَلَابِيبِهِنَّ ذٰلِكَ أَدْنٰى أَنْ
يُعْرَفْنَ فَلَا يُؤْذَيْنَ وَكَانَ اللّٰهُ غَفُورًا رَحِيمًا ﴿٦٠﴾

* 61. If the hypocrites, and those in whose heart is a disease, and those who cause agitation in the city, desist not, We shall surely give thee authority over them; then they will not dwell therein as thy neighbours, save for a little while.

لَئِنْ لَّمْ يَنْتَهِ الْمُنٰفِقُوْنَ وَالَّذِيْنَ فِيْ قُلُوْبِهِمْ مَّرَضٌ
وَّالْمُرْجِفُوْنَ فِي الْمَدِيْنَةِ لَنُغْرِيَنَّكَ بِهِمْ ثُمَّ لَا
يُجَاوِرُوْنَكَ فِيْهَآ اِلَّا قَلِيْلًا ﴿٦١﴾

62. *Then they will be* accursed. Whereever they are found, they will be seized, and cut into pieces.

مَّلْعُوْنِيْنَ ۚ اَيْنَمَا ثُقِفُوْٓا اُخِذُوْا وَقُتِّلُوْا تَقْتِيْلًا ﴿٦٢﴾

63. Such has been the way of Allah in *the case of* those who passed away before, and thou wilt never find a change in the way of Allah.

سُنَّةَ اللّٰهِ فِي الَّذِيْنَ خَلَوْا مِنْ قَبْلُ ۚ وَلَنْ تَجِدَ لِسُنَّةِ
اللّٰهِ تَبْدِيْلًا ﴿٦٣﴾ ع

64. Men ask thee concerning the Hour. Say, 'The knowledge of it is with Allah *alone*.' And what will make thee know that the Hour may be nigh?

يَسْـَٔلُكَ النَّاسُ عَنِ السَّاعَةِ ۗ قُلْ اِنَّمَا عِلْمُهَا عِنْدَ
اللّٰهِ ۗ وَمَا يُدْرِيْكَ لَعَلَّ السَّاعَةَ تَكُوْنُ قَرِيْبًا ﴿٦٤﴾

65. Allah has surely cursed the disbelievers, and has prepared for them a burning fire,

اِنَّ اللّٰهَ لَعَنَ الْكٰفِرِيْنَ وَاَعَدَّ لَهُمْ سَعِيْرًا ﴿٦٥﴾

66. Wherein they will abide for ever. They will find *therein* no friend nor helper.

خٰلِدِيْنَ فِيْهَآ اَبَدًا ۚ لَا يَجِدُوْنَ وَلِيًّا وَّلَا نَصِيْرًا ﴿٦٦﴾

67. On the day when their faces are turned over in the Fire, they will say, 'Oh, would that we had obeyed Allah and obeyed the Messenger!'

يَوْمَ تُقَلَّبُ وُجُوْهُهُمْ فِي النَّارِ يَقُوْلُوْنَ يٰلَيْتَنَآ
اَطَعْنَا اللّٰهَ وَاَطَعْنَا الرَّسُوْلَا ﴿٦٧﴾

68. And they will say, 'Our Lord, we obeyed our chiefs and our great ones and they led us astray from the way.

وَقَالُوْا رَبَّنَآ اِنَّآ اَطَعْنَا سَادَتَنَا وَكُبَرَآءَنَا فَاَضَلُّوْنَا
السَّبِيْلَا ﴿٦٨﴾

69. 'Our Lord, give them double punishment and curse them with a very great curse.'

رَبَّنَآ اٰتِهِمْ ضِعْفَيْنِ مِنَ الْعَذَابِ وَالْعَنْهُمْ لَعْنًا
كَبِيْرًا ﴿٦٩﴾ ٨ ع١٧ ٥

R. 9.

* 70. O ye who believe! be not like those who vexed and slandered Moses; but Allah cleared him of what they spoke *of him*. And he was honourable in the sight of Allah.

يٰٓاَيُّهَا الَّذِيْنَ اٰمَنُوْا لَا تَكُوْنُوْا كَالَّذِيْنَ اٰذَوْا مُوْسٰى
فَبَرَّاَهُ اللّٰهُ مِمَّا قَالُوْا ۗ وَكَانَ عِنْدَ اللّٰهِ وَجِيْهًا ﴿٧٠﴾

71. O ye who believe! fear Allah, and say the right word.

يٰٓاَيُّهَا الَّذِيْنَ اٰمَنُوا اتَّقُوا اللّٰهَ وَقُوْلُوْا قَوْلًا سَدِيْدًا ﴿٧١﴾

* 72. He will bless your works for you and forgive you your sins. And whoso obeys Allah and His Messenger, shall surely attain a mighty success.

يُّصْلِحْ لَكُمْ اَعْمَالَكُمْ وَيَغْفِرْ لَكُمْ ذُنُوْبَكُمْ ۗ وَمَنْ
يُّطِعِ اللّٰهَ وَرَسُوْلَهٗ فَقَدْ فَازَ فَوْزًا عَظِيْمًا ﴿٧٢﴾

* 73 Verily, We offered the Trust to the

اِنَّا عَرَضْنَا الْاَمَانَةَ عَلَى السَّمٰوٰتِ وَالْاَرْضِ وَ

heavens and the earth and the mountains, but they refused to bear it and were afraid of it. But man bore it. Indeed, he is *capable of being* unjust *to, and* neglectful *of, himself.*

الْجِبَالِ فَأَبَيْنَ أَنْ يَّحْمِلْنَهَا وَأَشْفَقْنَ مِنْهَا وَحَمَلَهَا
الْإِنْسَانُ ۖ إِنَّهُ كَانَ ظَلُوْمًا جَهُوْلًا ﴿٧٣﴾

74. *The result is* that Allah will punish hypocritical men and hypocritical women, and idolatrous men and idolatrous women; and Allah turns in mercy to believing men and believing women; and Allah is Most Forgiving, Merciful.

لِّيُعَذِّبَ اللّٰهُ الْمُنٰفِقِيْنَ وَالْمُنٰفِقٰتِ وَالْمُشْرِكِيْنَ
وَالْمُشْرِكٰتِ وَيَتُوْبَ اللّٰهُ عَلَى الْمُؤْمِنِيْنَ وَالْمُؤْمِنٰتِ ۗ
وَكَانَ اللّٰهُ غَفُوْرًا رَّحِيْمًا ﴿٧٤﴾ ع

سُوْرَةُ سَبَاٍ مَكِّيَّةٌ (٣٤) اٰيَاتُهَا ٥٥ رُكُوْعَاتُهَا ٦

AL-SABA'

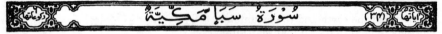

(Revealed before Hijra)

1. In the name of Allah, the Gracious, the Merciful.

بِسْمِ اللّٰهِ الرَّحْمٰنِ الرَّحِيْمِ ﴿١﴾

2. All praise is due to Allah, to Whom belongs whatever is in the heavens and whatever is in the earth. And His is all praise in the Hereafter; and He is the Wise, the All-Aware.

اَلْحَمْدُ لِلّٰهِ الَّذِيْ لَهٗ مَا فِي السَّمٰوٰتِ وَمَا فِي الْاَرْضِ
وَلَهُ الْحَمْدُ فِي الْاٰخِرَةِ ؕ وَهُوَ الْحَكِيْمُ الْخَبِيْرُ ﴿٢﴾

3. He knows whatever goes into the earth and whatever comes forth from it, and whatever descends from the heaven and whatever ascends into it; and He is Merciful, Most Forgiving.

يَعْلَمُ مَا يَلِجُ فِي الْاَرْضِ وَمَا يَخْرُجُ مِنْهَا وَمَا
يَنْزِلُ مِنَ السَّمَآءِ وَمَا يَعْرُجُ فِيْهَا ؕ وَهُوَ الرَّحِيْمُ
الْغَفُوْرُ ﴿٣﴾

4. And those who disbelieve say, 'The Hour will never come upon us.' Say, 'Yea, by my Lord Who knows the unseen, it will surely come upon you! Not an atom's weight in the heavens or in the earth or anything less than that or greater escapes Him, but *all is recorded* in a perspicuous Book,

وَقَالَ الَّذِيْنَ كَفَرُوْا لَا تَاْتِيْنَا السَّاعَةُ ؕ قُلْ بَلٰى وَ
رَبِّيْ لَتَاْتِيَنَّكُمْ عٰلِمِ الْغَيْبِ ۚ لَا يَعْزُبُ عَنْهُ مِثْقَالُ
ذَرَّةٍ فِي السَّمٰوٰتِ وَلَا فِي الْاَرْضِ وَلَاۤ اَصْغَرُ مِنْ
ذٰلِكَ وَلَاۤ اَكْبَرُ اِلَّا فِيْ كِتٰبٍ مُّبِيْنٍ ﴿٤﴾

5. 'That He may reward those who believe and do good works. It is these who will have forgiveness and an honourable provision.'

لِّيَجْزِيَ الَّذِيْنَ اٰمَنُوْا وَعَمِلُوا الصّٰلِحٰتِ ؕ اُولٰٓئِكَ لَهُمْ
مَّغْفِرَةٌ وَّرِزْقٌ كَرِيْمٌ ﴿٥﴾

6. But *as to* those who strive against Our Signs, seeking to frustrate *Our plans*, it is they for whom there will be the suffering of a painful punishment.

وَالَّذِيْنَ سَعَوْ فِيْۤ اٰيٰتِنَا مُعٰجِزِيْنَ اُولٰٓئِكَ لَهُمْ عَذَابٌ
مِّنْ رِّجْزٍ اَلِيْمٌ ﴿٦﴾

7. And those who are given knowledge see that whatever has been revealed to thee from thy Lord is the truth, and guides unto the path of the Mighty, the Praiseworthy.

وَيَرَى الَّذِيْنَ اُوْتُوا الْعِلْمَ الَّذِيْۤ اُنْزِلَ اِلَيْكَ مِنْ
رَّبِّكَ هُوَ الْحَقَّ ۙ وَيَهْدِيْۤ اِلٰى صِرَاطِ الْعَزِيْزِ
الْحَمِيْدِ ﴿٧﴾

8. And those who disbelieve say, 'Shall we show you a man who will tell you *that* when you are broken up into pieces, you shall be *raised as* a new creation?

وَقَالَ الَّذِيْنَ كَفَرُوْا هَلْ نَدُلُّكُمْ عَلٰى رَجُلٍ يُّنَبِّئُكُمْ
اِذَا مُزِّقْتُمْ كُلَّ مُمَزَّقٍ ۙ اِنَّكُمْ لَفِيْ خَلْقٍ جَدِيْدٍ ﴿٨﴾

9. 'Has he forged a lie against Allah or is he afflicted with madness?' Nay, but it is those who believe not in the Hereafter that are suffering from the punishment and are too far gone in error.

افترى على الله كذبا ام به جنة ط بل الذين لا يؤمنون
بالاخرة في العذاب والضلل البعيد ⑨

* 10. Do they not see what is before them and what is behind them of the heaven and the earth? If We please, We could cause the earth to sink with them, or cause pieces of the sky to fall upon them. In that verily is a Sign for every repentant servant.

افلم يروا الى ما بين ايديهم وما خلفهم من السماء
والارض ط ان نشا نخسف بهم الارض او نسقط
عليهم كسفا من السماء ط ان في ذلك لاية لكل عبد
منيب ⑩ ع

R. 2.

* 11. And certainly, We bestowed grace upon David from *Ourselves*: 'O ye mountains, repeat *the praises of Allah* with him, and O birds, *ye also*.' And We made the iron soft for him,

ولقد اتينا داود منا فضلا ط يجبال اوبي معه و
الطير ج والنا له الحديد ⑪

12. *Saying*, 'Make thou full-length coats of mail, and make the rings of a proper measure. And do righteous deeds, surely I see all that you do.'

ان اعمل سبغت وقدر في السرد واعملوا صالحا ط
اني بما تعملون بصير ⑫

13. And to Solomon *We subjected* the wind; its morning course was a month's *journey*, and its evening course was a month's *journey too*. And We caused a fount of molten copper to flow for him. And of the Jinn were *some* who worked under him, by the command of his Lord. And *We had told them that* if any of them turned away from Our command, We would make him taste the punishment of burning fire.

ولسليمن الريح غدوها شهر ورواحها شهر و
اسلنا له عين القطر ط ومن الجن من يعمل بين
يديه باذن ربه ط ومن يزغ منهم عن امرنا نذقه
من عذاب السعير ⑬

14. They made for him what he desired: palaces and statues, and basins like reservoirs, and large cooking vessels fixed in their places: 'Work ye, O House of David, gratefully;' but few of My servants are grateful.

يعملون له ما يشاء من محاريب وتماثيل وجفان
كالجواب وقدور رسيت ط اعملوا ال داود شكرا ط
وقليل من عبادي الشكور ⑭

* 15. And when We decreed his (Solomon's) death, nothing pointed out to them that he was dead save a worm of the earth that ate away his staff. So when he fell down, the Jinn plainly realized that if they had known the unseen, they would not have remained in a state of degrading torment.

فلما قضينا عليه الموت ما دلهم على موته الا
دابة الارض تاكل منساته ج فلما خر تبينت
الجن ان لو كانوا يعلمون الغيب ما لبثوا في
العذاب المهين ⑮

16. There was indeed a Sign for Saba' in their home-land: two gardens on the right

لقد كان لسبا في مسكنهم اية ج جنتن عن يمين

hand and on the left: 'Eat of the provision of your Lord and be grateful to Him. A good land and a Most Forgiving Lord!'

وَّشِمَالٍ ۥ كُلُوْا مِنْ رِّزْقِ رَبِّكُمْ وَاشْكُرُوْا لَهٗ ؕ بَلْدَةٌ
طَيِّبَةٌ وَّرَبٌّ غَفُوْرٌ ﴿۱۶﴾

* 17. But they turned away; so We sent against them a fierce flood. And We gave them, in lieu of their gardens, two gardens bearing bitter fruit and tamarisk and a few lote-trees.

فَاَعْرَضُوْا فَاَرْسَلْنَا عَلَيْهِمْ سَيْلَ الْعَرِمِ وَبَدَّلْنٰهُمْ
بِجَنَّتَيْهِمْ جَنَّتَيْنِ ذَوَاتَيْ اُكُلٍ خَمْطٍ وَّاَثْلٍ وَّشَيْءٍ
مِّنْ سِدْرٍ قَلِيْلٍ ﴿۱۷﴾

18. That We awarded them because of their ingratitude; and none do We requite *in this way* but the ungrateful.

ذٰلِكَ جَزَيْنٰهُمْ بِمَا كَفَرُوْا ؕ وَهَلْ نُجٰزِيْۤ اِلَّا الْكَفُوْرَ ﴿۱۸﴾

19. And We placed, between them and the towns which We had blessed, *other* towns that were prominently visible, and We fixed easy stages between them: 'Travel in them for nights and days in security.'

وَجَعَلْنَا بَيْنَهُمْ وَبَيْنَ الْقُرَى الَّتِيْ بٰرَكْنَا فِيْهَا
قُرًى ظَاهِرَةً وَّقَدَّرْنَا فِيْهَا السَّيْرَ ؕ سِيْرُوْا فِيْهَا
لَيَالِيَ وَاَيَّامًا اٰمِنِيْنَ ﴿۱۹﴾

20. But they said, 'Our Lord, place longer distances between *the stages of* our journeys.' And they wronged themselves; so We made them bywords and We broke them into pieces, a complete breaking up. In that verily are Signs for every steadfast and grateful person.

فَقَالُوْا رَبَّنَا بٰعِدْ بَيْنَ اَسْفَارِنَا وَظَلَمُوْۤا اَنْفُسَهُمْ
فَجَعَلْنٰهُمْ اَحَادِيْثَ وَمَزَّقْنٰهُمْ كُلَّ مُمَزَّقٍ ؕ اِنَّ فِيْ
ذٰلِكَ لَاٰيٰتٍ لِّكُلِّ صَبَّارٍ شَكُوْرٍ ﴿۲۰﴾

21. And Iblīs found that his judgment of them was true, so they followed him, *all* except a party of *true* believers.

وَلَقَدْ صَدَّقَ عَلَيْهِمْ اِبْلِيْسُ ظَنَّهٗ فَاتَّبَعُوْهُ اِلَّا
فَرِيْقًا مِّنَ الْمُؤْمِنِيْنَ ﴿۲۱﴾

22. And he had no power over them, but *it was so* that We might distinguish those who believed in the Hereafter from those who were in doubt about it. And thy Lord is Watchful over all things.

وَمَا كَانَ لَهٗ عَلَيْهِمْ مِّنْ سُلْطٰنٍ اِلَّا لِنَعْلَمَ مَنْ يُّؤْمِنُ
بِالْاٰخِرَةِ مِمَّنْ هُوَ مِنْهَا فِيْ شَكٍّ ؕ وَرَبُّكَ عَلٰى كُلِّ
شَيْءٍ حَفِيْظٌ ﴿۲۲﴾ ع

R. 3.

23. Say, 'Call upon those whom you assert *to be gods* beside Allah. They control not *even* the weight of an atom in the heavens or in the earth, nor have they any share in either, nor has He any helper among them.'

قُلِ ادْعُوا الَّذِيْنَ زَعَمْتُمْ مِّنْ دُوْنِ اللّٰهِ ۚ لَا يَمْلِكُوْنَ
مِثْقَالَ ذَرَّةٍ فِي السَّمٰوٰتِ وَلَا فِي الْاَرْضِ وَمَا لَهُمْ
فِيْهِمَا مِنْ شِرْكٍ وَّمَا لَهٗ مِنْهُمْ مِّنْ ظَهِيْرٍ ﴿۲۳﴾

24. No intercession avails with Him, except for him about whom He permits *it*, until when their hearts are relieved of fright they would say, 'What is it that your Lord said?' They (the Messengers)

وَلَا تَنْفَعُ الشَّفَاعَةُ عِنْدَهٗۤ اِلَّا لِمَنْ اَذِنَ لَهٗ ؕ حَتّٰۤى
اِذَا فُزِّعَ عَنْ قُلُوْبِهِمْ قَالُوْا مَاذَا ۙ قَالَ رَبُّكُمْ ؕ قَالُوْا

will answer, 'The truth.' And He is the High, the Great.

الحق وهو العلي الكبير ﴿٢٤﴾

25. Say, 'Who gives you sustenance from the heavens and the earth?' Say, 'Allah. Either we or you are on right guidance or in manifest error.'

قل من يرزقكم من السموت والارض قل الله
وانا او اياكم لعلى هدى او في ضلل مبين ﴿٢٥﴾

26. Say, 'You will not be questioned as to our sins, nor shall we be questioned as to what you do.'

قل لا تسئلون عما اجرمنا ولا نسئل عما تعملون ﴿٢٦﴾

27. Say, 'Our Lord will bring us all together; then He will judge between us with truth: and He is the Judge, the All-Knowing.'

قل يجمع بيننا ربنا ثم يفتح بيننا بالحق وهو
الفتاح العليم ﴿٢٧﴾

28. Say, 'Show me those whom you have joined with Him as partners. Nay! *You cannot do so,* for He is Allah, the Mighty, the Wise.'

قل اروني الذين الحقتم به شركاء كلا بل هو
الله العزيز الحكيم ﴿٢٨﴾

29. And We have not sent thee but as a bearer of glad tidings and a Warner, for all mankind, but most men know not.

وما ارسلنك الا كافة للناس بشيرا ونذيرا و
لكن اكثر الناس لا يعلمون ﴿٢٩﴾

30. And they say, 'When will this promise *be fulfilled,* if you are truthful?'

ويقولون متى هذا الوعد ان كنتم صدقين ﴿٣٠﴾

31. Say, 'For you is the promise of a day from which you cannot remain behind a single moment nor can you get ahead *of it.*'

قل لكم ميعاد يوم لا تستاخرون عنه ساعة
ولا تستقدمون ﴿٣١﴾ ع النصف

R. 4.

32. And those who disbelieve say, 'We will never believe in this Qur'ān, nor in what is before it;' and couldst thou see when the wrongdoers will be made to stand before their Lord, throwing back on one another the blame. Those who were considered weak will say to those who were proud, 'Had it not been for you, we should surely have been believers.'

وقال الذين كفروا لن نؤمن بهذا القران ولا
بالذي بين يديه ولو ترى اذ الظلمون موقوفون
عند ربهم يرجع بعضهم الى بعض القول
يقول الذين استضعفوا للذين استكبروا لولا انتم
لكنا مؤمنين ﴿٣٢﴾

33. Those who were proud will say to those who were considered weak, 'Was it we that kept you away from the guidance, after it had come to you? Nay, it was you yourselves who were guilty.'

قال الذين استكبروا للذين استضعفوا انحن
صددنكم عن الهدى بعد اذ جاءكم بل كنتم
مجرمين ﴿٣٣﴾

34. And those who were considered weak will say to those who were proud, 'Nay, but

وقال الذين استضعفوا للذين استكبروا بل مكر

it was *your* scheming night and day, when you bade us disbelieve in Allah and set up equals unto Him.' And they will conceal *their* remorse when they see the punishment; and We shall put chains round the necks of those who disbelieved. They will not be requited but for what they did.

الَّيْلِ وَالنَّهَارِ اِذْ تَاْمُرُوْنَنَآ اَنْ نَّكْفُرَ بِاللّٰهِ وَنَجْعَلَ
لَهٗٓ اَنْدَادًا ؕ وَاَسَرُّوا النَّدَامَةَ لَمَّا رَاَوُا الْعَذَابَ ؕ وَ
جَعَلْنَا الْاَغْلٰلَ فِيْٓ اَعْنَاقِ الَّذِيْنَ كَفَرُوْا ؕ هَلْ يُجْزَوْنَ
اِلَّا مَا كَانُوْا يَعْمَلُوْنَ ﴿۳۴﴾

* 35. And We never sent a Warner to any city but the wealthy ones thereof said, 'Surely, we disbelieve in what you have been sent with.'

وَمَآ اَرْسَلْنَا فِيْ قَرْيَةٍ مِّنْ نَّذِيْرٍ اِلَّا قَالَ مُتْرَفُوْهَآ ۙ
اِنَّا بِمَآ اُرْسِلْتُمْ بِهٖ كٰفِرُوْنَ ﴿۳۵﴾

36. And they say, 'We have more riches and children; and we are not going to be punished.'

وَقَالُوْا نَحْنُ اَكْثَرُ اَمْوَالًا وَّاَوْلَادًا ۙ وَّمَا نَحْنُ بِمُعَذَّبِيْنَ ﴿۳۶﴾

37. Say, 'Verily, my Lord enlarges the provision for whomsoever He pleases, and straitens *it for whomsoever He pleases;* but most men do not know.'

قُلْ اِنَّ رَبِّيْ يَبْسُطُ الرِّزْقَ لِمَنْ يَّشَآءُ وَيَقْدِرُ وَلٰكِنَّ
اَكْثَرَ النَّاسِ لَا يَعْلَمُوْنَ ﴿۳۷﴾ ع

R. 5.

38. And it is not your riches nor your children that will bring you near Us in rank, but those who believe and do good works, will have a double reward for what they did. And in lofty mansions will they be secure.

وَمَآ اَمْوَالُكُمْ وَلَآ اَوْلَادُكُمْ بِالَّتِيْ تُقَرِّبُكُمْ عِنْدَنَا
زُلْفٰٓى اِلَّا مَنْ اٰمَنَ وَعَمِلَ صَالِحًا ؗ فَاُولٰٓئِكَ لَهُمْ
جَزَآءُ الضِّعْفِ بِمَا عَمِلُوْا وَهُمْ فِي الْغُرُفٰتِ اٰمِنُوْنَ ﴿۳۸﴾

39. And *as to* those who strive to frustrate *the purpose of* Our Signs, it is they who will be brought face to face with punishment.

وَالَّذِيْنَ يَسْعَوْنَ فِيْٓ اٰيٰتِنَا مُعٰجِزِيْنَ اُولٰٓئِكَ فِي
الْعَذَابِ مُحْضَرُوْنَ ﴿۳۹﴾

40. Say, 'Surely, my Lord enlarges the provision for such of His servants as He pleases and straitens *it* for such of them as *He pleases*. And whatever you spend, He will replace it; and He is the Best of providers.'

قُلْ اِنَّ رَبِّيْ يَبْسُطُ الرِّزْقَ لِمَنْ يَّشَآءُ مِنْ عِبَادِهٖ وَ
يَقْدِرُ لَهٗ ؕ وَمَآ اَنْفَقْتُمْ مِّنْ شَيْءٍ فَهُوَ يُخْلِفُهٗ ۚ وَ
هُوَ خَيْرُ الرّٰزِقِيْنَ ﴿۴۰﴾

* 41. And *remember* the day, when He will gather them all together; then He will say to the angels: 'Was it you that they worshipped?'

وَيَوْمَ يَحْشُرُهُمْ جَمِيْعًا ثُمَّ يَقُوْلُ لِلْمَلٰٓئِكَةِ اَهٰٓؤُلَآءِ
اِيَّاكُمْ كَانُوْا يَعْبُدُوْنَ ﴿۴۱﴾

42. They will say, 'Holy art Thou. Thou art our Protector against them. Nay, but they worshipped the Jinn; it was in them that most of them believed.'

قَالُوْا سُبْحٰنَكَ اَنْتَ وَلِيُّنَا مِنْ دُوْنِهِمْ ۚ بَلْ كَانُوْا
يَعْبُدُوْنَ الْجِنَّ ۚ اَكْثَرُهُمْ بِهِمْ مُّؤْمِنُوْنَ ﴿۴۲﴾

43. 'So, this day, you will have no power either to profit or harm one another.' And

فَالْيَوْمَ لَا يَمْلِكُ بَعْضُكُمْ لِبَعْضٍ نَّفْعًا وَّلَا ضَرًّا

We shall say to those who did wrong: 'Taste ye the punishment of the Fire that you denied.'

وَنَقُولُ لِلَّذِينَ ظَلَمُوا ذُوقُوا عَذَابَ النَّارِ الَّتِي كُنتُم
بِهَا تُكَذِّبُونَ ﴿٤٣﴾

44. And when Our manifest Signs are recited to them, they say, 'This is but a man who seeks to turn you away from that which your fathers worshipped.' And they say, 'This is but a forged lie.' And those who disbelieve say about the truth when it comes to them, 'This is nothing but clear magic.'

وَإِذَا تُتْلَىٰ عَلَيْهِمْ آيَاتُنَا بَيِّنَاتٍ قَالُوا مَا هَٰذَا إِلَّا رَجُلٌ
يُرِيدُ أَن يَصُدَّكُمْ عَمَّا كَانَ يَعْبُدُ آبَاؤُكُمْ وَ
قَالُوا مَا هَٰذَا إِلَّا إِفْكٌ مُّفْتَرًى وَقَالَ الَّذِينَ كَفَرُوا
لِلْحَقِّ لَمَّا جَاءَهُمْ إِنْ هَٰذَا إِلَّا سِحْرٌ مُّبِينٌ ﴿٤٤﴾

45. And We gave them no books which they studied, nor did We send to them any Warner before thee.

وَمَا آتَيْنَاهُم مِّن كُتُبٍ يَدْرُسُونَهَا وَمَا أَرْسَلْنَا إِلَيْهِمْ
قَبْلَكَ مِن نَّذِيرٍ ﴿٤٥﴾

46. And those who were before them *also* rejected *the truth*—and these have not attained *even* to a tenth of that which We gave them, but they treated My Messengers as liars. So how *terrible* was the change I *brought about*!

وَكَذَّبَ الَّذِينَ مِن قَبْلِهِمْ وَمَا بَلَغُوا مِعْشَارَ
مَا آتَيْنَاهُمْ فَكَذَّبُوا رُسُلِي فَكَيْفَ كَانَ نَكِيرِ ﴿٤٦﴾

R. 6.

47. Say, 'I only exhort you *to do* one thing: that you stand up before Allah in twos and singly and then reflect. *You will then know that* there is no insanity in your companion; he is only a Warner to you of an impending severe punishment.'

قُلْ إِنَّمَا أَعِظُكُم بِوَاحِدَةٍ أَن تَقُومُوا لِلَّهِ مَثْنَىٰ
وَفُرَادَىٰ ثُمَّ تَتَفَكَّرُوا مَا بِصَاحِبِكُم مِّن جِنَّةٍ
إِنْ هُوَ إِلَّا نَذِيرٌ لَّكُم بَيْنَ يَدَيْ عَذَابٍ شَدِيدٍ ﴿٤٧﴾

48. Say, 'Whatever reward I might have asked of you—let it be yours. My reward is only with Allah; and He is Witness over all things.'

قُلْ مَا سَأَلْتُكُم مِّنْ أَجْرٍ فَهُوَ لَكُمْ إِنْ أَجْرِيَ إِلَّا
عَلَى اللَّهِ وَهُوَ عَلَىٰ كُلِّ شَيْءٍ شَهِيدٌ ﴿٤٨﴾

49. Say, 'Truly, my Lord hurls the Truth *at falsehood. He is* the Great Knower of the unseen.'

قُلْ إِنَّ رَبِّي يَقْذِفُ بِالْحَقِّ عَلَّامُ الْغُيُوبِ ﴿٤٩﴾

* 50. Say, 'The Truth has come, and falsehood could neither originate *any good* nor reproduce *it*.'

قُلْ جَاءَ الْحَقُّ وَمَا يُبْدِئُ الْبَاطِلُ وَمَا يُعِيدُ ﴿٥٠﴾

51. Say, 'If I err, I err only against myself; and if I am rightly guided, it is because of what my Lord has revealed to me. Verily, He is All-Hearing, Nigh.'

قُلْ إِن ضَلَلْتُ فَإِنَّمَا أَضِلُّ عَلَىٰ نَفْسِي وَإِنِ اهْتَدَيْتُ
فَبِمَا يُوحِي إِلَيَّ رَبِّي إِنَّهُ سَمِيعٌ قَرِيبٌ ﴿٥١﴾

52. Couldst thou but see when they will be smitten with fear! Then there will be no escape, and they will be seized from a place nearby.

وَلَوْ تَرَىٰ إِذْ فَزِعُوا فَلَا فَوْتَ وَأُخِذُوا مِن مَّكَانٍ
قَرِيبٍ ﴿٥٢﴾

* 53. And they will say, 'We *now* believe therein.' But how can the attaining *of*

وَقَالُوا آمَنَّا بِهِ وَأَنَّىٰ لَهُمُ التَّنَاوُشُ مِن مَّكَانٍ

faith be possible to them from a position *so* far off,

بَعِيْدٍ ۝٥٣

* 54. While they had disbelieved in it before? And they are uttering conjectures from a far-off place.

وَّقَدْ كَفَرُوْا بِهٖ مِنْ قَبْلُ ۚ وَيَقْذِفُوْنَ بِالْغَيْبِ مِنْ
مَّكَانٍۭ بَعِيْدٍ ۝٥٤

55. And a barrier will be placed between them and that which they long for, as was done with the likes of them before. They *too* were in disquieting doubt indeed.

وَحِيْلَ بَيْنَهُمْ وَبَيْنَ مَا يَشْتَهُوْنَ كَمَا فُعِلَ
ع بِاَشْيَاعِهِمْ مِّنْ قَبْلُ ۭ اِنَّهُمْ كَانُوْا فِيْ شَكٍّ مُّرِيْبٍ ۝٥٥

سُوْرَةُ فَاطِرٍ مَّكِّيَّةٌ (٣٥) آياتها ركوعاتها

FAṬIR

(Revealed before Hijra)

1. In the name of Allah, the Gracious, the Merciful.

بِسْمِ اللّٰهِ الرَّحْمٰنِ الرَّحِيْمِ ①

2. All praise belongs to Allah, the Maker of the heavens and the earth, Who employs the angels as messengers, having wings, two, three, and four. He adds to *His* creation whatever He pleases; for Allah has power over all things.

اَلْحَمْدُ لِلّٰهِ فَاطِرِ السَّمٰوٰتِ وَالْاَرْضِ جَاعِلِ
الْمَلٰٓئِكَةِ رُسُلًا اُولِيْٓ اَجْنِحَةٍ مَّثْنٰى وَ ثُلٰثَ وَرُبٰعَ ؕ
يَزِيْدُ فِي الْخَلْقِ مَا يَشَآءُ ؕ اِنَّ اللّٰهَ عَلٰى كُلِّ شَيْءٍ
قَدِيْرٌ ②

3. Whatever of mercy Allah grants to men—there is none to withhold it; and whatever He withholds, there is none who can release it after that; and He is the Mighty, the Wise.

مَا يَفْتَحِ اللّٰهُ لِلنَّاسِ مِنْ رَّحْمَةٍ فَلَا مُمْسِكَ لَهَا ۚ
وَمَا يُمْسِكْ ۙ فَلَا مُرْسِلَ لَهٗ مِنْۢ بَعْدِهٖ ؕ وَهُوَ الْعَزِيْزُ
الْحَكِيْمُ ③

4. O ye men, remember the favour of Allah towards you. Is there any Creator other than Allah *Who* provides for you from the heaven and the earth? There is none worthy of worship but He. Whither then are you turned away?

يٰٓاَيُّهَا النَّاسُ اذْكُرُوْا نِعْمَتَ اللّٰهِ عَلَيْكُمْ ؕ هَلْ
مِنْ خَالِقٍ غَيْرُ اللّٰهِ يَرْزُقُكُمْ مِّنَ السَّمَآءِ وَالْاَرْضِ ؕ
لَآ اِلٰهَ اِلَّا هُوَ ۖ فَاَنّٰى تُؤْفَكُوْنَ ④

5. And if they reject thee, verily, *God's* Messengers have been rejected before thee; and unto Allah *all* things are brought back *for decision*.

وَاِنْ يُّكَذِّبُوْكَ فَقَدْ كُذِّبَتْ رُسُلٌ مِّنْ قَبْلِكَ ؕ وَ
اِلَى اللّٰهِ تُرْجَعُ الْاُمُوْرُ ⑤

6. O ye men, assuredly the promise of Allah is true, so let not the present life deceive you, nor let the Deceiver deceive you with respect to Allah.

يٰٓاَيُّهَا النَّاسُ اِنَّ وَعْدَ اللّٰهِ حَقٌّ فَلَا تَغُرَّنَّكُمُ
الْحَيٰوةُ الدُّنْيَا ٚ وَلَا يَغُرَّنَّكُمْ بِاللّٰهِ الْغَرُوْرُ ⑥

7. Surely Satan is an enemy to you; so take him as an enemy. He calls his followers only that they may become inmates of the burning Fire.

اِنَّ الشَّيْطٰنَ لَكُمْ عَدُوٌّ فَاتَّخِذُوْهُ عَدُوًّا ؕ اِنَّمَا يَدْعُوْا
حِزْبَهٗ لِيَكُوْنُوْا مِنْ اَصْحٰبِ السَّعِيْرِ ؕ ⑦

8. For those who disbelieve there is a severe punishment. And for those who believe and do good works there is forgiveness and a great reward.

اَلَّذِيْنَ كَفَرُوْا لَهُمْ عَذَابٌ شَدِيْدٌ ؕ وَالَّذِيْنَ اٰمَنُوْا
وَعَمِلُوا الصّٰلِحٰتِ لَهُمْ مَّغْفِرَةٌ وَّاَجْرٌ كَبِيْرٌ ⑧ ع ١٣

R. 2.

* 9. Is he, then, to whom the evil of his deed is made *to appear* pleasing, so that he looks upon it as good, *like him who believes and does good deeds?* Surely, Allah adjudges astray whom He will and guides whom He will. So let not thy soul waste away in sighing for them. Surely Allah knows what they do.

أَفَمَنْ زُيِّنَ لَهٗ سُوْٓءُ عَمَلِهٖ فَرَاٰهُ حَسَنًا ؕ فَاِنَّ اللّٰهَ
يُضِلُّ مَنْ يَّشَآءُ وَيَهْدِيْ مَنْ يَّشَآءُ ۖ فَلَا تَذْهَبْ
نَفْسُكَ عَلَيْهِمْ حَسَرٰتٍ ؕ اِنَّ اللّٰهَ عَلِيْمٌۢ بِمَا يَصْنَعُوْنَ ﴿٩﴾

10. And Allah it is Who sends the winds which raise the clouds; then do We drive them to a lifeless tract of land, and quicken thereby the earth after its death. Likewise *shall* the Resurrection *be*.

وَاللّٰهُ الَّذِيْٓ اَرْسَلَ الرِّيٰحَ فَتُثِيْرُ سَحَابًا فَسُقْنٰهُ اِلٰى
بَلَدٍ مَّيِّتٍ فَاَحْيَيْنَا بِهِ الْاَرْضَ بَعْدَ مَوْتِهَا ؕ كَذٰلِكَ
النُّشُوْرُ ﴿١٠﴾

* 11. Whoso desires honour, then *let him know that* all honour belongs to Allah. Unto Him ascend good words, and righteous work does He exalt. And those who plot evils—for them is a severe punishment; and the plotting of such will perish.

مَنْ كَانَ يُرِيْدُ الْعِزَّةَ فَلِلّٰهِ الْعِزَّةُ جَمِيْعًا ؕ اِلَيْهِ
يَصْعَدُ الْكَلِمُ الطَّيِّبُ وَالْعَمَلُ الصَّالِحُ يَرْفَعُهٗ ؕ
وَالَّذِيْنَ يَمْكُرُوْنَ السَّيِّاٰتِ لَهُمْ عَذَابٌ شَدِيْدٌ ؕ
وَمَكْرُ اُولٰٓئِكَ هُوَ يَبُوْرُ ﴿١١﴾

12. And Allah created you from dust, then from a sperm-drop, then He made you pairs. And no female conceives, nor does she bring forth *a child* without His knowledge. And no one whose life is prolonged has *his* life prolonged, nor is anything diminished of his life, but *it is recorded* in a Book. That surely is easy for Allah.

وَاللّٰهُ خَلَقَكُمْ مِّنْ تُرَابٍ ثُمَّ مِنْ نُّطْفَةٍ ثُمَّ جَعَلَكُمْ
اَزْوَاجًا ؕ وَمَا تَحْمِلُ مِنْ اُنْثٰى وَلَا تَضَعُ اِلَّا بِعِلْمِهٖ ؕ
وَمَا يُعَمَّرُ مِنْ مُّعَمَّرٍ وَّلَا يُنْقَصُ مِنْ عُمُرِهٖٓ اِلَّا
فِيْ كِتٰبٍ ؕ اِنَّ ذٰلِكَ عَلَى اللّٰهِ يَسِيْرٌ ﴿١٢﴾

13. And the two seas are not alike: this one palatable, sweet *and* pleasant to drink, and the other, salt *and* bitter. And from each you eat fresh meat, and take forth ornaments which you wear. And thou seest the ships therein ploughing *the waves* that you may seek of His bounty, and that you may be grateful.

وَمَا يَسْتَوِي الْبَحْرٰنِ ۖ هٰذَا عَذْبٌ فُرَاتٌ سَآئِغٌ
شَرَابُهٗ وَهٰذَا مِلْحٌ اُجَاجٌ ؕ وَمِنْ كُلٍّ تَاْكُلُوْنَ
لَحْمًا طَرِيًّا وَّتَسْتَخْرِجُوْنَ حِلْيَةً تَلْبَسُوْنَهَا ۚ وَ
تَرَى الْفُلْكَ فِيْهِ مَوَاخِرَ لِتَبْتَغُوْا مِنْ فَضْلِهٖ وَ
لَعَلَّكُمْ تَشْكُرُوْنَ ﴿١٣﴾

14. He merges the night into the day, and He merges the day into the night. And He has pressed into service the sun and the moon; each one runs *its* course to an appointed term. Such is Allah, your Lord; His is the kingdom, and those whom you

يُوْلِجُ الَّيْلَ فِي النَّهَارِ وَيُوْلِجُ النَّهَارَ فِي الَّيْلِ ۙ
وَسَخَّرَ الشَّمْسَ وَالْقَمَرَ ۖ كُلٌّ يَّجْرِيْ لِاَجَلٍ
مُّسَمًّى ؕ ذٰلِكُمُ اللّٰهُ رَبُّكُمْ لَهُ الْمُلْكُ ؕ وَالَّذِيْنَ تَدْعُوْنَ

call upon beside Allah own not even a whit.

15. If you call on them, they will not hear your call; and even if they heard it, they could not answer you. And on the Day of Resurrection they will deny your having associated *them with God*. And none can inform thee like the *One Who is* All-Aware.

R. 3.

* 16. O ye men, it is you that stand in need of Allah, but Allah is He Who is Self-Sufficient, the Praiseworthy.

17. If He please, He could destroy you, and bring a new creation *instead*.

18. And that is not difficult for Allah.

19. And no burdened *soul* can bear the burden of another; and if a heavily laden *soul* call another to *bear* its load, naught of it shall be carried *by the other*, even though he be a kinsman. Thou canst warn only those who fear their Lord in secret and observe Prayer. And whoso purifies himself, purifies himself only to his own advantage; and to Allah shall be the return.

20. And the blind and the seeing are not alike,

21. Nor the darkness and light,

22. Nor the shade and heat.

23. Nor alike are the living and the dead. Surely, Allah causes him to hear whom He pleases; and thou canst not make those to hear who are in the graves.

24. Thou art only a Warner.

25. Verily, We have sent thee with the truth, *as* a bearer of glad tidings and *as* a Warner; and there is no people to whom a Warner has not been sent.

26. And if they treat thee as a liar, those who were before them *also* treated *their*

مِنْ دُوْنِهٖ مَا يَمْلِكُوْنَ مِنْ قِطْمِيْرٍ ﴿۱۴﴾

اِنْ تَدْعُوْهُمْ لَا يَسْمَعُوْا دُعَآءَكُمْ ۚ وَلَوْ سَمِعُوْا مَا
اسْتَجَابُوْا لَكُمْ ۚ وَيَوْمَ الْقِيٰمَةِ يَكْفُرُوْنَ بِشِرْكِكُمْ ؕ
وَلَا يُنَبِّئُكَ مِثْلُ خَبِيْرٍ ﴿۱۵﴾

يٰۤاَيُّهَا النَّاسُ اَنْتُمُ الْفُقَرَآءُ اِلَى اللّٰهِ ۚ وَاللّٰهُ هُوَ
الْغَنِيُّ الْحَمِيْدُ ﴿۱۶﴾

اِنْ يَّشَاْ يُذْهِبْكُمْ وَيَاْتِ بِخَلْقٍ جَدِيْدٍ ﴿۱۷﴾

وَمَا ذٰلِكَ عَلَى اللّٰهِ بِعَزِيْزٍ ﴿۱۸﴾

وَلَا تَزِرُ وَازِرَةٌ وِّزْرَ اُخْرٰى ؕ وَاِنْ تَدْعُ مُثْقَلَةٌ
اِلٰى حِمْلِهَا لَا يُحْمَلْ مِنْهُ شَيْءٌ وَّلَوْ كَانَ ذَا قُرْبٰى ؕ
اِنَّمَا تُنْذِرُ الَّذِيْنَ يَخْشَوْنَ رَبَّهُمْ بِالْغَيْبِ وَ
اَقَامُوا الصَّلٰوةَ ؕ وَمَنْ تَزَكّٰى فَاِنَّمَا يَتَزَكّٰى لِنَفْسِهٖ ؕ
وَاِلَى اللّٰهِ الْمَصِيْرُ ﴿۱۹﴾

وَمَا يَسْتَوِي الْاَعْمٰى وَالْبَصِيْرُ ﴿۲۰﴾

وَلَا الظُّلُمٰتُ وَلَا النُّوْرُ ﴿۲۱﴾

وَلَا الظِّلُّ وَلَا الْحَرُوْرُ ﴿۲۲﴾

وَمَا يَسْتَوِي الْاَحْيَآءُ وَلَا الْاَمْوَاتُ ؕ اِنَّ اللّٰهَ يُسْمِعُ
مَنْ يَّشَآءُ ۚ وَمَآ اَنْتَ بِمُسْمِعٍ مَّنْ فِي الْقُبُوْرِ ﴿۲۳﴾

اِنْ اَنْتَ اِلَّا نَذِيْرٌ ﴿۲۴﴾

اِنَّآ اَرْسَلْنٰكَ بِالْحَقِّ بَشِيْرًا وَّنَذِيْرًا ؕ وَاِنْ مِّنْ اُمَّةٍ
اِلَّا خَلَا فِيْهَا نَذِيْرٌ ﴿۲۵﴾

وَاِنْ يُّكَذِّبُوْكَ فَقَدْ كَذَّبَ الَّذِيْنَ مِنْ قَبْلِهِمْ ۚ

Prophets as liars. Their Messengers came to them with clear Signs, and with the Scriptures, and with the illuminating Book.

جَآءَتْهُمْ رُسُلُهُمْ بِالْبَيِّنٰتِ وَبِالزُّبُرِ وَبِالْكِتٰبِ
الْمُنِيْرِ ﴿٢٦﴾

27. Then I seized those who disbelieved and how *terrible* was the change I *brought about*!

ثُمَّ اَخَذْتُ الَّذِيْنَ كَفَرُوْا فَكَيْفَ كَانَ نَكِيْرِ ﴿٢٧﴾ ع ٣ ١٥

R. 4.

28. Dost thou not see that Allah sends down water from the sky, and We bring forth therewith fruits of different colours; and among the mountains are streaks, white and red, of diverse hues and others raven black;

اَلَمْ تَرَ اَنَّ اللّٰهَ اَنْزَلَ مِنَ السَّمَآءِ مَآءً ۚ فَاَخْرَجْنَا بِهٖ
ثَمَرٰتٍ مُّخْتَلِفًا اَلْوَانُهَا ۭ وَمِنَ الْجِبَالِ جُدَدٌۢ بِيْضٌ
وَّحُمْرٌ مُّخْتَلِفٌ اَلْوَانُهَا وَغَرَابِيْبُ سُوْدٌ ﴿٢٨﴾

29. And of men and beasts and cattle, in like manner, there are various colours? Only those of His servants who possess knowledge fear Allah. Verily, Allah is Mighty, Most Forgiving.

وَمِنَ النَّاسِ وَالدَّوَآبِّ وَالْاَنْعَامِ مُخْتَلِفٌ اَلْوَانُهٗ
كَذٰلِكَ ۭ اِنَّمَا يَخْشَى اللّٰهَ مِنْ عِبَادِهِ الْعُلَمٰٓؤُا ۭ اِنَّ
اللّٰهَ عَزِيْزٌ غَفُوْرٌ ﴿٢٩﴾

30. Surely, *only* those who follow the Book of Allah and observe Prayer and spend out of what We have provided for them, secretly and openly, hope for a bargain which will never fail;

اِنَّ الَّذِيْنَ يَتْلُوْنَ كِتٰبَ اللّٰهِ وَاَقَامُوا الصَّلٰوةَ وَ
اَنْفَقُوْا مِمَّا رَزَقْنٰهُمْ سِرًّا وَّعَلَانِيَةً يَّرْجُوْنَ تِجَارَةً
لَّنْ تَبُوْرَ ﴿٣٠﴾

31. In order that He may give them their full rewards, and *even* increase them out of His bounty. He is surely Most Forgiving, Most Appreciating.

لِيُوَفِّيَهُمْ اُجُوْرَهُمْ وَيَزِيْدَهُمْ مِّنْ فَضْلِهٖ ۭ اِنَّهٗ
غَفُوْرٌ شَكُوْرٌ ﴿٣١﴾

32. And the Book which We have revealed to thee is the truth *itself*, fulfilling that which is before it. Surely, Allah is All-Aware, All-Seeing with respect to His servants.

وَالَّذِيْٓ اَوْحَيْنَآ اِلَيْكَ مِنَ الْكِتٰبِ هُوَ الْحَقُّ مُصَدِّقًا
لِّمَا بَيْنَ يَدَيْهِ ۭ اِنَّ اللّٰهَ بِعِبَادِهٖ لَخَبِيْرٌۢ بَصِيْرٌ ﴿٣٢﴾

33. Then We gave the Book for an inheritance to those of Our servants whom We chose. And of them are *some* who are breaking down their own selves *by suppressing their desires*, and of them are *some* who keep to the right course, and of them are *some* who excel *others* in acts of goodness by Allah's leave. And that *indeed* is the great distinction.

ثُمَّ اَوْرَثْنَا الْكِتٰبَ الَّذِيْنَ اصْطَفَيْنَا مِنْ عِبَادِنَا ۚ
فَمِنْهُمْ ظَالِمٌ لِّنَفْسِهٖ ۚ وَمِنْهُمْ مُّقْتَصِدٌ ۚ وَمِنْهُمْ
سَابِقٌۢ بِالْخَيْرٰتِ بِاِذْنِ اللّٰهِ ۭ ذٰلِكَ هُوَ الْفَضْلُ
الْكَبِيْرُ ﴿٣٣﴾

34. Gardens of Eternity! They will enter them. They will be adorned therein with bracelets of gold, and pearls; and their garments therein will be of silk.

جَنّٰتُ عَدْنٍ يَّدْخُلُوْنَهَا يُحَلَّوْنَ فِيْهَا مِنْ اَسَاوِرَ
مِنْ ذَهَبٍ وَّلُؤْلُؤًا ۚ وَلِبَاسُهُمْ فِيْهَا حَرِيْرٌ ﴿٣٤﴾

35. And they will say, 'All praise belongs to Allah Who has removed grief from us. Surely, our Lord is Most Forgiving, Most Appreciating,

وَقَالُوا الْحَمْدُ لِلّٰهِ الَّذِيْٓ اَذْهَبَ عَنَّا الْحَزَنَ ۭ اِنَّ
رَبَّنَا لَغَفُوْرٌ شَكُوْرُ ۙ ﴿٣٥﴾

36. 'Who has, out of His bounty, settled us in the Abode of Eternity, where no toil will touch us, nor any *sense of* weariness affect us therein.'

الَّذِيْٓ اَحَلَّنَا دَارَ الْمُقَامَةِ مِنْ فَضْلِهٖ ۚ لَا يَمَسُّنَا
فِيْهَا نَصَبٌ وَّلَا يَمَسُّنَا فِيْهَا لُغُوْبٌ ﴿٣٦﴾

* 37. But *as for* those who disbelieve, for them is the fire of Hell. Death will not be decreed for them so that they may die; nor will the punishment thereof be lightened for them. Thus do We requite every ungrateful person.

وَالَّذِيْنَ كَفَرُوْا لَهُمْ نَارُ جَهَنَّمَ ۚ لَا يُقْضٰى عَلَيْهِمْ
فَيَمُوْتُوْا وَلَا يُخَفَّفُ عَنْهُمْ مِّنْ عَذَابِهَا ۭ كَذٰلِكَ
نَجْزِيْ كُلَّ كَفُوْرٍ ۚ ﴿٣٧﴾

38. And they will cry for help therein, 'O our Lord, take us out, we will do righteous works other than those we used to do.' 'Did We not give you a life *long enough* so that he who would reflect could reflect therein? And there came unto you a Warner *too*. So taste ye *the punishment;* for wrongdoers have no helper.'

وَهُمْ يَصْطَرِخُوْنَ فِيْهَا ۚ رَبَّنَآ اَخْرِجْنَا نَعْمَلْ صَالِحًا
غَيْرَ الَّذِيْ كُنَّا نَعْمَلُ ۭ اَوَلَمْ نُعَمِّرْكُمْ مَّا يَتَذَكَّرُ
فِيْهِ مَنْ تَذَكَّرَ وَجَاۗءَكُمُ النَّذِيْرُ ۭ فَذُوْقُوْا فَمَا
لِلظّٰلِمِيْنَ مِنْ نَّصِيْرٍ ﴿٣٨﴾ ع

R. 5

39. Verily, Allah knows the secrets of the heavens and of the earth. Verily, He knows full well all *that lies hidden* in the breasts.

اِنَّ اللّٰهَ عٰلِمُ غَيْبِ السَّمٰوٰتِ وَالْاَرْضِ ۭ اِنَّهٗ عَلِيْمٌۢ
بِذَاتِ الصُّدُوْرِ ﴿٣٩﴾

40. He it is Who made you vicegerents in the earth. So he who disbelieves, will *himself* suffer *the consequences of* his disbelief. And for the disbelievers their disbelief will only increase odium in the sight of their Lord, and their disbelief will increase for the disbelievers nothing but loss.

هُوَ الَّذِيْ جَعَلَكُمْ خَلٰۗىِٕفَ فِي الْاَرْضِ ۭ فَمَنْ كَفَرَ
فَعَلَيْهِ كُفْرُهٗ ۭ وَلَا يَزِيْدُ الْكٰفِرِيْنَ كُفْرُهُمْ عِنْدَ
رَبِّهِمْ اِلَّا مَقْتًا ۚ وَلَا يَزِيْدُ الْكٰفِرِيْنَ كُفْرُهُمْ اِلَّا
خَسَارًا ﴿٤٠﴾

41. Say, 'Have you seen your associate-gods whom you call on beside Allah? Show me *then* what they have created of the earth. Or have they a share in the creation of the heavens? Or have We given them a Book so that they have an evidence therefrom?' Nay, the wrongdoers promise one another nothing but deception.

قُلْ اَرَءَيْتُمْ شُرَكَاۗءَكُمُ الَّذِيْنَ تَدْعُوْنَ مِنْ دُوْنِ
اللّٰهِ ۭ اَرُوْنِيْ مَاذَا خَلَقُوْا مِنَ الْاَرْضِ اَمْ لَهُمْ شِرْكٌ
فِي السَّمٰوٰتِ ۚ اَمْ اٰتَيْنٰهُمْ كِتٰبًا فَهُمْ عَلٰي بَيِّنَتٍ مِّنْهُ ۚ
بَلْ اِنْ يَّعِدُ الظّٰلِمُوْنَ بَعْضُهُمْ بَعْضًا اِلَّا غُرُوْرًا ﴿٤١﴾

42. Surely, Allah holds the heavens and the earth lest they deviate *from their*

اِنَّ اللّٰهَ يُمْسِكُ السَّمٰوٰتِ وَالْاَرْضَ اَنْ تَزُوْلَا ڬ وَ

places. And if they did deviate, none can hold them after Him. Verily, He is Forbearing, Most Forgiving.

لَئِن زَالَتَآ إِنْ أَمْسَكَهُمَا مِنْ أَحَدٍ مِّنْ بَعْدِهِ ۚ إِنَّهُ
كَانَ حَلِيمًا غَفُورًا ﴿٤٢﴾

43. And they swore by Allah their strongest oaths, that if a Warner came to them, they would follow guidance better than any other people. But when a Warner did come to them, it only increased them in aversion,

وَأَقْسَمُوا بِاللهِ جَهْدَ أَيْمَانِهِمْ لَئِن جَآءَهُمْ نَذِيرٌ
لَّيَكُونُنَّ أَهْدٰى مِنْ إِحْدَى الْأُمَمِ ۚ فَلَمَّا جَآءَهُمْ
نَذِيرٌ مَّا زَادَهُمْ إِلَّا نُفُورًا ﴿٤٣﴾

44. Out of arrogance in the earth and evil plotting. But the evil plot encompasses none but the authors thereof. Do they then look for anything but *God's* way of *dealing with* the peoples of old? But thou wilt never find any change in the way of Allah; nor wilt thou ever find any alteration in the way of Allah.

اِسْتِكْبَارًا فِي الْأَرْضِ وَمَكْرَ السَّيِّئِ ۚ وَلَا يَحِيقُ
الْمَكْرُ السَّيِّئُ إِلَّا بِأَهْلِهِ ۚ فَهَلْ يَنْظُرُونَ إِلَّا سُنَّتَ
الْأَوَّلِينَ ۚ فَلَن تَجِدَ لِسُنَّتِ اللهِ تَبْدِيلًا ۚ وَلَن تَجِدَ
لِسُنَّتِ اللهِ تَحْوِيلًا ﴿٤٤﴾

45. Have they not travelled in the earth and seen how *evil* was the end of those who were before them? And they were stronger than they in power. And Allah is not such that anything in the heavens or the earth should frustrate His *plans*; verily, He is All-Knowing, All-Powerful.

أَوَلَمْ يَسِيرُوا فِي الْأَرْضِ فَيَنْظُرُوا كَيْفَ كَانَ عَاقِبَةُ
الَّذِينَ مِن قَبْلِهِمْ وَكَانُوا أَشَدَّ مِنْهُمْ قُوَّةً ۚ وَمَا
كَانَ اللهُ لِيُعْجِزَهُ مِن شَيْءٍ فِي السَّمٰوٰتِ وَلَا فِي
الْأَرْضِ ۚ إِنَّهُ كَانَ عَلِيمًا قَدِيرًا ﴿٤٥﴾

* 46. And if Allah were to punish people for what they do, He would not leave a living creature on the surface of *the earth;* but He grants them respite until an appointed term; and when their appointed time comes, then *they will know that* Allah has all His servants under *His* eyes.

وَلَوْ يُؤَاخِذُ اللهُ النَّاسَ بِمَا كَسَبُوا مَا تَرَكَ عَلٰى
ظَهْرِهَا مِن دَآبَّةٍ وَلٰكِن يُؤَخِّرُهُمْ إِلٰى أَجَلٍ
مُّسَمًّى ۚ فَإِذَا جَآءَ أَجَلُهُمْ فَإِنَّ اللهَ كَانَ بِعِبَادِهِ
بَصِيرًا ﴿٤٦﴾

سُورَةُ يٰسٓ مَكِّيَّةٌ (٣٦)

YĀ SĪN

(Revealed before Hijra)

1. In the name of Allah, the Gracious, the Merciful.

بِسْمِ اللّٰهِ الرَّحْمٰنِ الرَّحِيْمِ ﴿١﴾

2. Yā Sīn*.

يٰسٓ ﴿٢﴾

3. By the Qur'ān, full of wisdom,

وَالْقُرْاٰنِ الْحَكِيْمِ ﴿٣﴾

4. Thou art indeed *one* of the Messengers,

اِنَّكَ لَمِنَ الْمُرْسَلِيْنَ ﴿٤﴾

5. On a right path.

عَلٰى صِرَاطٍ مُّسْتَقِيْمٍ ﴿٥﴾

6. *This is* a revelation of the Mighty, the Merciful,

تَنْزِيْلَ الْعَزِيْزِ الرَّحِيْمِ ﴿٦﴾

7. That thou mayest warn a people whose fathers were not warned, and so they are heedless.

لِتُنْذِرَ قَوْمًا مَّآ اُنْذِرَ اٰبَآؤُهُمْ فَهُمْ غٰفِلُوْنَ ﴿٧﴾

8. Surely the word has proved true against most of them, for they believe not.

لَقَدْ حَقَّ الْقَوْلُ عَلٰٓى اَكْثَرِهِمْ فَهُمْ لَا يُؤْمِنُوْنَ ﴿٨﴾

* 9. We have put, round their necks, chains reaching unto the chins, so that their heads are forced up.

اِنَّا جَعَلْنَا فِيْٓ اَعْنَاقِهِمْ اَغْلٰلًا فَهِيَ اِلَى الْاَذْقَانِ فَهُمْ مُّقْمَحُوْنَ ﴿٩﴾

10. And We have set a barrier before them and a barrier behind them, and have covered them over, so that they cannot see.

وَجَعَلْنَا مِنْۢ بَيْنِ اَيْدِيْهِمْ سَدًّا وَّمِنْ خَلْفِهِمْ سَدًّا فَاَغْشَيْنٰهُمْ فَهُمْ لَا يُبْصِرُوْنَ ﴿١٠﴾

11. And it is equal to them whether thou warn them or warn them not: they will not believe.

وَسَوَآءٌ عَلَيْهِمْ ءَاَنْذَرْتَهُمْ اَمْ لَمْ تُنْذِرْهُمْ لَا يُؤْمِنُوْنَ ﴿١١﴾

12. Thou canst warn only him who would follow the Reminder and fear the Gracious *God* in secret. So give him the glad tidings of forgiveness and a noble reward.

اِنَّمَا تُنْذِرُ مَنِ اتَّبَعَ الذِّكْرَ وَخَشِيَ الرَّحْمٰنَ بِالْغَيْبِ ۚ فَبَشِّرْهُ بِمَغْفِرَةٍ وَّاَجْرٍ كَرِيْمٍ ﴿١٢﴾

13. Surely, We *alone* give life to the dead, and We record that which they send forward and that which they leave behind; and all things have We recorded in a clear Book.

اِنَّا نَحْنُ نُحْيِ الْمَوْتٰى وَنَكْتُبُ مَا قَدَّمُوْا وَاٰثَارَهُمْ ؕ وَكُلَّ شَيْءٍ اَحْصَيْنٰهُ فِيْٓ اِمَامٍ مُّبِيْنٍ ﴿١٣﴾

R. 2.

14. And set forth to them the parable of a people of the town, when the

وَاضْرِبْ لَهُمْ مَّثَلًا اَصْحٰبَ الْقَرْيَةِ ۘ اِذْ جَآءَهَا

* O Perfect Leader!

Messengers came to it.

الْمُرْسَلُونَ ﴿١٤﴾

15. When We sent to them two Messengers, and they rejected them both; so We strengthened *them* by a third, and they said, 'Verily we have been sent to you as Messengers.'

إِذْ أَرْسَلْنَا إِلَيْهِمُ اثْنَيْنِ فَكَذَّبُوهُمَا فَعَزَّزْنَا بِثَالِثٍ
فَقَالُوا إِنَّا إِلَيْكُم مُّرْسَلُونَ ﴿١٥﴾

16. They replied, 'You are but men like us and the Gracious *God* has not revealed anything. You only lie.'

قَالُوا مَا أَنتُمْ إِلَّا بَشَرٌ مِّثْلُنَا وَمَا أَنزَلَ الرَّحْمَٰنُ
مِن شَيْءٍ إِنْ أَنتُمْ إِلَّا تَكْذِبُونَ ﴿١٦﴾

17. They said, 'Our Lord knows that we are indeed *His* Messengers to you;

قَالُوا رَبُّنَا يَعْلَمُ إِنَّا إِلَيْكُمْ لَمُرْسَلُونَ ﴿١٧﴾

18. 'And on us lies only the plain delivery of the Message.'

وَمَا عَلَيْنَا إِلَّا الْبَلَاغُ الْمُبِينُ ﴿١٨﴾

19. They said, 'Surely we augur evil fortune from you; if you desist not, we will certainly stone you, and a painful punishment will surely befall you at our hands.'

قَالُوا إِنَّا تَطَيَّرْنَا بِكُمْ لَئِن لَّمْ تَنتَهُوا لَنَرْجُمَنَّكُمْ
وَلَيَمَسَّنَّكُم مِّنَّا عَذَابٌ أَلِيمٌ ﴿١٩﴾

20. They replied, 'Your evil fortune is with your own selves. Is it because you have been admonished? Nay, you are a people transgressing all bounds.'

قَالُوا طَائِرُكُم مَّعَكُمْ أَئِن ذُكِّرْتُم بَلْ أَنتُمْ قَوْمٌ
مُّسْرِفُونَ ﴿٢٠﴾

21. And from the farthest part of the town there came a man running. He said, 'O my people, follow the Messengers,

وَجَاءَ مِنْ أَقْصَى الْمَدِينَةِ رَجُلٌ يَسْعَىٰ قَالَ يَا قَوْمِ
اتَّبِعُوا الْمُرْسَلِينَ ﴿٢١﴾

22. 'Follow those who ask of you no reward, and who are rightly guided.

اتَّبِعُوا مَن لَّا يَسْأَلُكُمْ أَجْرًا وَهُم مُّهْتَدُونَ ﴿٢٢﴾

23. 'And what reason have I that I should not worship Him Who has created me, and unto Whom you will be brought back?

وَمَا لِيَ لَا أَعْبُدُ الَّذِي فَطَرَنِي وَإِلَيْهِ تُرْجَعُونَ ﴿٢٣﴾ الجزء ٢٣

24. 'Shall I take others beside Him as gods? If the Gracious *God* should intend me any harm, their intercession will avail me naught, nor can they rescue me.

أَأَتَّخِذُ مِن دُونِهِ آلِهَةً إِن يُرِدْنِ الرَّحْمَٰنُ بِضُرٍّ
لَّا تُغْنِ عَنِّي شَفَاعَتُهُمْ شَيْئًا وَلَا يُنقِذُونِ ﴿٢٤﴾

25. 'In that case I should indeed be in manifest error.

إِنِّي إِذًا لَّفِي ضَلَالٍ مُّبِينٍ ﴿٢٥﴾

26. 'I believe in your Lord; so listen to me.'

إِنِّي آمَنتُ بِرَبِّكُمْ فَاسْمَعُونِ ﴿٢٦﴾

27. It was said *to him,* 'Enter Paradise.' He said, 'O, would that my people knew,

قِيلَ ادْخُلِ الْجَنَّةَ قَالَ يَا لَيْتَ قَوْمِي يَعْلَمُونَ ﴿٢٧﴾

28. 'How *graciously* my Lord has granted me forgiveness and has made me of the honoured ones!'

بِمَا غَفَرَ لِي رَبِّي وَجَعَلَنِي مِنَ الْمُكْرَمِينَ ﴿٢٨﴾

29. And We sent not down against his

وَمَا أَنزَلْنَا عَلَىٰ قَوْمِهِ مِن بَعْدِهِ مِن جُندٍ مِّنَ

people, after him, any host from heaven, nor did We need to send down *any*.

السَّمَآءِ وَمَا كُنَّا مُنْزِلِيْنَ ﴿۲۹﴾

30. It was but a single blast and lo! they were extinct.

إِنْ كَانَتْ إِلَّا صَيْحَةً وَّاحِدَةً فَإِذَا هُمْ خٰمِدُوْنَ ﴿۳۰﴾

* 31. Alas for *My* servants! there comes not a Messenger to them but they mock at him.

يٰحَسْرَةً عَلَى الْعِبَادِ مَا يَأْتِيْهِمْ مِّنْ رَّسُوْلٍ إِلَّا
كَانُوْا بِهٖ يَسْتَهْزِءُوْنَ ﴿۳۱﴾

32. Have they not seen how many generations We have destroyed before them, *and* that they never return to them?

أَلَمْ يَرَوْا كَمْ أَهْلَكْنَا قَبْلَهُمْ مِّنَ الْقُرُوْنِ أَنَّهُمْ
إِلَيْهِمْ لَا يَرْجِعُوْنَ ﴿۳۲﴾

33. And all of them, gathered together, will certainly be brought before Us.

وَإِنْ كُلٌّ لَّمَّا جَمِيْعٌ لَّدَيْنَا مُحْضَرُوْنَ ﴿۳۳﴾ ع

R. 3.

34. And the dead earth is a Sign for them: We quicken it and bring forth therefrom grain, of which they eat.

وَاٰيَةٌ لَّهُمُ الْأَرْضُ الْمَيْتَةُ أَحْيَيْنٰهَا وَأَخْرَجْنَا
مِنْهَا حَبًّا فَمِنْهُ يَأْكُلُوْنَ ﴿۳۴﴾

35. And We have placed in it gardens of date-palms and grapes, and We have caused springs to gush forth therein,

وَجَعَلْنَا فِيْهَا جَنّٰتٍ مِّنْ نَّخِيْلٍ وَّأَعْنَابٍ وَّفَجَّرْنَا
فِيْهَا مِنَ الْعُيُوْنِ ﴿۳۵﴾

36. That they may eat of the fruit thereof, and it was not their hands that made them. Will they not then be grateful?

لِيَأْكُلُوْا مِنْ ثَمَرِهٖ وَمَا عَمِلَتْهُ أَيْدِيْهِمْ أَفَلَا
يَشْكُرُوْنَ ﴿۳۶﴾

37. Holy is He Who created all things in pairs, of what the earth grows, and of themselves, and of what they know not.

سُبْحٰنَ الَّذِيْ خَلَقَ الْأَزْوَاجَ كُلَّهَا مِمَّا تُنْبِتُ
الْأَرْضُ وَمِنْ أَنْفُسِهِمْ وَمِمَّا لَا يَعْلَمُوْنَ ﴿۳۷﴾

* 38. And a Sign for them is the night from which We strip off the day, and lo! they are in darkness.

وَاٰيَةٌ لَّهُمُ الَّيْلُ نَسْلَخُ مِنْهُ النَّهَارَ فَإِذَا هُمْ
مُّظْلِمُوْنَ ﴿۳۸﴾

* 39. And the sun is moving on the course *prescribed* for it. That is the decree of the Almighty, the All-Knowing *God*.

وَالشَّمْسُ تَجْرِيْ لِمُسْتَقَرٍّ لَّهَا ذٰلِكَ تَقْدِيْرُ
الْعَزِيْزِ الْعَلِيْمِ ﴿۳۹﴾

40. And for the moon We have appointed stages, till it becomes again like an old dry branch of a palm-tree.

وَالْقَمَرَ قَدَّرْنٰهُ مَنَازِلَ حَتّٰى عَادَ كَالْعُرْجُوْنِ
الْقَدِيْمِ ﴿۴۰﴾

41. It is not for the sun to overtake the moon, nor can the night outstrip the day.

لَا الشَّمْسُ يَنْۢبَغِيْ لَهَآ أَنْ تُدْرِكَ الْقَمَرَ وَلَا

All of them float in an orbit.

الَّيْلُ سَابِقُ النَّهَارِ ۗ وَكُلٌّ فِي فَلَكٍ يَسْبَحُونَ ﴿٤١﴾

42. And a Sign for them is that We carry their offspring in the laden ship,

وَآيَةٌ لَّهُمْ أَنَّا حَمَلْنَا ذُرِّيَّتَهُمْ فِي الْفُلْكِ الْمَشْحُونِ ﴿٤٢﴾

* 43. And We have created for them the like thereof whereon they ride.

وَخَلَقْنَا لَهُم مِّن مِّثْلِهِ مَا يَرْكَبُونَ ﴿٤٣﴾

44. And if We *so* willed, We could drown them; then they would have no one to succour *them*, nor would they be rescued,

وَإِن نَّشَأْ نُغْرِقْهُمْ فَلَا صَرِيخَ لَهُمْ وَلَا هُمْ
يُنقَذُونَ ﴿٤٤﴾

45. Except through mercy from Us and as a provision for a time.

إِلَّا رَحْمَةً مِّنَّا وَمَتَاعًا إِلَىٰ حِينٍ ﴿٤٥﴾

46. And when it is said to them, 'Guard yourselves against that which is before you and that which is behind you, in order that you may receive mercy,' *they turn away*.

وَإِذَا قِيلَ لَهُمُ اتَّقُوا مَا بَيْنَ أَيْدِيكُمْ وَمَا خَلْفَكُمْ
لَعَلَّكُمْ تُرْحَمُونَ ﴿٤٦﴾

47. And there comes not to them any Sign out of the Signs of their Lord, but they turn away from it.

وَمَا تَأْتِيهِم مِّنْ آيَةٍ مِّنْ آيَاتِ رَبِّهِمْ إِلَّا كَانُوا
عَنْهَا مُعْرِضِينَ ﴿٤٧﴾

48. And when it is said to them, 'Spend out of that with which Allah has provided you,' those who disbelieve say to those who believe, 'Shall we feed him whom Allah would have fed, if He had *so* willed? You are but in manifest error.'

وَإِذَا قِيلَ لَهُمْ أَنفِقُوا مِمَّا رَزَقَكُمُ اللَّهُ ۙ قَالَ
الَّذِينَ كَفَرُوا لِلَّذِينَ آمَنُوا أَنُطْعِمُ مَن لَّوْ يَشَاءُ
اللَّهُ أَطْعَمَهُ ۖ إِنْ أَنتُمْ إِلَّا فِي ضَلَالٍ مُّبِينٍ ﴿٤٨﴾

49. And they say, 'When will this promise *be fulfilled*, if *indeed* you are truthful?'

وَيَقُولُونَ مَتَىٰ هَٰذَا الْوَعْدُ إِن كُنتُمْ صَادِقِينَ ﴿٤٩﴾

50. They are waiting only for a single blast which will seize them while they are disputing.

مَا يَنظُرُونَ إِلَّا صَيْحَةً وَاحِدَةً تَأْخُذُهُمْ وَهُمْ
يَخِصِّمُونَ ﴿٥٠﴾

51. And they will not be able to make a will, nor will they return to their families.

فَلَا يَسْتَطِيعُونَ تَوْصِيَةً وَلَا إِلَىٰ أَهْلِهِمْ يَرْجِعُونَ ﴿٥١﴾

R. 4.

52. And the trumpet shall be blown, and lo! from the graves they will hasten on to their Lord.

وَنُفِخَ فِي الصُّورِ فَإِذَا هُم مِّنَ الْأَجْدَاثِ إِلَىٰ رَبِّهِمْ
يَنسِلُونَ ﴿٥٢﴾

53. They will say, 'O! woe to us! who has raised us up from our place of sleep? This is what the Gracious *God* had promised, and the Messengers spoke the truth.'

قَالُوا يَا وَيْلَنَا مَن بَعَثَنَا مِن مَّرْقَدِنَا ۜ هَٰذَا مَا
وَعَدَ الرَّحْمَٰنُ وَصَدَقَ الْمُرْسَلُونَ ﴿٥٣﴾

54. It will be but one blast and lo! they

إِن كَانَتْ إِلَّا صَيْحَةً وَاحِدَةً فَإِذَا هُمْ جَمِيعٌ لَّدَيْنَا

will all be brought before Us.

مُحْضَرُونَ ﴿٥٤﴾

55. And on that day, no soul will be wronged in aught; nor will you be rewarded but for what you used to do.

فَالْيَوْمَ لَا تُظْلَمُ نَفْسٌ شَيْئًا وَلَا تُجْزَوْنَ إِلَّا مَا
كُنتُمْ تَعْمَلُونَ ﴿٥٥﴾

* 56. Verily the inmates of Heaven will, on that day, be happy in *their* occupation.

إِنَّ أَصْحَابَ الْجَنَّةِ الْيَوْمَ فِي شُغُلٍ فَاكِهُونَ ﴿٥٦﴾

57. They and their wives will be in pleasant shades, reclining on raised couches.

هُمْ وَأَزْوَاجُهُمْ فِي ظِلَالٍ عَلَى الْأَرَائِكِ مُتَّكِئُونَ ﴿٥٧﴾

58. They will have fruits therein, and they will have whatever they call for.

لَهُمْ فِيهَا فَاكِهَةٌ وَلَهُم مَّا يَدَّعُونَ ﴿٥٨﴾

59. 'Peace *on you*'—a word *of greeting* from the Merciful Lord.

سَلَامٌ قَوْلًا مِّن رَّبٍّ رَّحِيمٍ ﴿٥٩﴾

60. And *God will say*, 'Separate yourselves *from the righteous* this day, O ye guilty ones!

وَامْتَازُوا الْيَوْمَ أَيُّهَا الْمُجْرِمُونَ ﴿٦٠﴾

61. 'Did I not enjoin on you, O ye sons of Adam, that you worship not Satan —for he is to you an open enemy—

أَلَمْ أَعْهَدْ إِلَيْكُمْ يَا بَنِي آدَمَ أَن لَّا تَعْبُدُوا الشَّيْطَانَ
إِنَّهُ لَكُمْ عَدُوٌّ مُّبِينٌ ﴿٦١﴾

62. 'And that you worship Me? This is the right path.

وَأَنِ اعْبُدُونِي هَٰذَا صِرَاطٌ مُّسْتَقِيمٌ ﴿٦٢﴾

63. 'And he did lead astray a great multitude of you. Why did you not then understand?

وَلَقَدْ أَضَلَّ مِنكُمْ جِبِلًّا كَثِيرًا أَفَلَمْ تَكُونُوا
تَعْقِلُونَ ﴿٦٣﴾

64. 'This is the Hell which you were promised.

هَٰذِهِ جَهَنَّمُ الَّتِي كُنتُمْ تُوعَدُونَ ﴿٦٤﴾

65. 'Enter it this day, because you disbelieved.'

اصْلَوْهَا الْيَوْمَ بِمَا كُنتُمْ تَكْفُرُونَ ﴿٦٥﴾

66. This day We shall put a seal on their mouths, and their hands will speak to Us, and their feet will bear witness to what they had earned.

الْيَوْمَ نَخْتِمُ عَلَىٰ أَفْوَاهِهِمْ وَتُكَلِّمُنَا أَيْدِيهِمْ
وَتَشْهَدُ أَرْجُلُهُم بِمَا كَانُوا يَكْسِبُونَ ﴿٦٦﴾

67. And if We had *so* willed, We could have put out their eyes, then they would have rushed to *find* the way. But how could they see?

وَلَوْ نَشَاءُ لَطَمَسْنَا عَلَىٰ أَعْيُنِهِمْ فَاسْتَبَقُوا الصِّرَاطَ
فَأَنَّىٰ يُبْصِرُونَ ﴿٦٧﴾

68. And if We had *so* willed, We could have transformed them *so as to transfix them* in their places, then they would not be able to move forward or turn back.

وَلَوْ نَشَاءُ لَمَسَخْنَاهُمْ عَلَىٰ مَكَانَتِهِمْ فَمَا اسْتَطَاعُوا
مُضِيًّا وَلَا يَرْجِعُونَ ﴿٦٨﴾

R. 5.

* 69. And him whom We grant long life—We revert him to a weak *condition of* creation. Will they not then understand?

وَمَن نُّعَمِّرْهُ نُنَكِّسْهُ فِي الْخَلْقِ أَفَلَا يَعْقِلُونَ ﴿٦٩﴾

* 70. And We have not taught him poetry, nor does that suit it (the Qur'ān). It is but a Reminder and a Qur'ān that makes *things* plain,

* 71. So that it may warn all who live, and that the word *of punishment* be justified against the disbelievers.

72. Do they not see that, among the things which Our hands have fashioned, We have created for them cattle of which they are masters?

73. And We have subjected the same to them, so that some of them they use for riding and some *others* they eat.

74. And in them they have *other* benefits and *also* drinks. Will they not then be grateful?

75. And they have taken *other* gods beside Allah, that they might be helped.

* 76. They are not able to help them, but they will be brought *before God* as their *allied* host.

77. So let not their speech grieve thee. Verily We know what they conceal and what they proclaim.

78. Does not man see that We have created him from a *mere* sperm-drop? Yet lo! he is an open quarreller!

79. And he coins similitudes for Us and forgets his own creation. He says, 'Who can quicken the bones when they are decayed?'

80. Say, 'He, Who created them the first time, will quicken them; and He knows every *kind of* creation full well,

81. 'He Who produces for you fire out of the green tree, and behold, you kindle from it.

82. 'Has not He Who created the heavens and the earth the power to create the like of them?' Yea, and He is indeed the Supreme Creator, the All-Knowing.

* 83. Verily His command, when He intends a thing, is *only* that He says to it, 'Be!', and it is.

وَمَا عَلَّمْنٰهُ الشِّعْرَ وَمَا يَنْۢبَغِيْ لَهٗ ؕ اِنْ هُوَ اِلَّا
ذِكْرٌ وَّقُرْاٰنٌ مُّبِيْنٌ ۙ﴿٧٠﴾
لِّيُنْذِرَ مَنْ كَانَ حَيًّا وَّيَحِقَّ الْقَوْلُ عَلَى الْكٰفِرِيْنَ ﴿٧١﴾
اَوَلَمْ يَرَوْا اَنَّا خَلَقْنَا لَهُمْ مِّمَّا عَمِلَتْ اَيْدِيْنَاۤ
اَنْعَامًا فَهُمْ لَهَا مٰلِكُوْنَ ﴿٧٢﴾
وَذَلَّلْنٰهَا لَهُمْ فَمِنْهَا رَكُوْبُهُمْ وَمِنْهَا يَاْكُلُوْنَ ﴿٧٣﴾
وَلَهُمْ فِيْهَا مَنَافِعُ وَمَشَارِبُ ؕ اَفَلَا يَشْكُرُوْنَ ﴿٧٤﴾
وَاتَّخَذُوْا مِنْ دُوْنِ اللّٰهِ اٰلِهَةً لَّعَلَّهُمْ يُنْصَرُوْنَ ﴿٧٥﴾
لَا يَسْتَطِيْعُوْنَ نَصْرَهُمْ ۙ وَهُمْ لَهُمْ جُنْدٌ مُّحْضَرُوْنَ ﴿٧٦﴾ وقف لازم
فَلَا يَحْزُنْكَ قَوْلُهُمْ ۘ اِنَّا نَعْلَمُ مَا يُسِرُّوْنَ وَمَا
يُعْلِنُوْنَ ﴿٧٧﴾
اَوَلَمْ يَرَ الْاِنْسَانُ اَنَّا خَلَقْنٰهُ مِنْ نُّطْفَةٍ فَاِذَا هُوَ
خَصِيْمٌ مُّبِيْنٌ ﴿٧٨﴾
وَضَرَبَ لَنَا مَثَلًا وَّنَسِيَ خَلْقَهٗ ؕ قَالَ مَنْ يُّحْيِ
الْعِظَامَ وَهِيَ رَمِيْمٌ ﴿٧٩﴾
قُلْ يُحْيِيْهَا الَّذِيْۤ اَنْشَاَهَاۤ اَوَّلَ مَرَّةٍ ؕ وَهُوَ بِكُلِّ
خَلْقٍ عَلِيْمُ ۙ﴿٨٠﴾
اِۨلَّذِيْ جَعَلَ لَكُمْ مِّنَ الشَّجَرِ الْاَخْضَرِ نَارًا فَاِذَاۤ
اَنْتُمْ مِّنْهُ تُوْقِدُوْنَ ﴿٨١﴾
اَوَلَيْسَ الَّذِيْ خَلَقَ السَّمٰوٰتِ وَالْاَرْضَ بِقٰدِرٍ
عَلٰۤى اَنْ يَّخْلُقَ مِثْلَهُمْ ؕ بَلٰى ۗ وَهُوَ الْخَلّٰقُ الْعَلِيْمُ ﴿٨٢﴾
اِنَّمَاۤ اَمْرُهٗۤ اِذَاۤ اَرَادَ شَيْـًٔا اَنْ يَّقُوْلَ لَهٗ كُنْ فَيَكُوْنُ ﴿٨٣﴾

84. So Holy is He, in Whose hand is the kingdom of all things. And to Him will you *all* be brought back.

فَسُبۡحٰنَ الَّذِیۡ بِیَدِهٖ مَلَکُوۡتُ کُلِّ شَیۡءٍ وَّ اِلَیۡهِ تُرۡجَعُوۡنَ ﴿۸۴﴾

آياتها ١٨٣ (٣٧) سُورَةُ الصّٰفّٰتِ مَكِّيَّةٌ ركوعاتها ٥

AL-ṢĀFFĀT

(Revealed before Hijra)

1. In the name of Allah, the Gracious, the Merciful.

بِسْمِ اللّٰهِ الرَّحْمٰنِ الرَّحِيْمِ ﴿١﴾

2. By those who range themselves in close ranks,

وَالصّٰفّٰتِ صَفًّا ﴿٢﴾

3. Then they drive away the enemy vigorously,

فَالزّٰجِرٰتِ زَجْرًا ﴿٣﴾

4. Then they recite the *Qur'ān as a* Reminder,

فَالتّٰلِيٰتِ ذِكْرًا ﴿٤﴾

5. Surely your God is One,

اِنَّ اِلٰهَكُمْ لَوَاحِدٌ ﴿٥﴾

6. Lord of the heavens and the earth and all that is between them and the Lord of the sun's risings.

رَبُّ السَّمٰوٰتِ وَالْاَرْضِ وَمَا بَيْنَهُمَا وَرَبُّ
الْمَشَارِقِ ﴿٦﴾

* 7. We have adorned the lowest heaven with an adornment—the planets;

اِنَّا زَيَّنَّا السَّمَآءَ الدُّنْيَا بِزِيْنَةِ ۨالْكَوَاكِبِ ﴿٧﴾

8. And have guarded it against all rebellious satans.

وَحِفْظًا مِّنْ كُلِّ شَيْطٰنٍ مَّارِدٍ ﴿٨﴾

* 9. They cannot hear *anything* from the exalted assembly *of angels*—and they are pelted from every side,

لَا يَسَّمَّعُوْنَ اِلَى الْمَلَاِ الْاَعْلٰى وَيُقْذَفُوْنَ مِنْ
كُلِّ جَانِبٍ ﴿٩﴾

10. Repulsed, and for them is a perpetual punishment—

دُحُوْرًا وَّلَهُمْ عَذَابٌ وَّاصِبٌ ﴿١٠﴾

11. Except him who snatches away *something* by stealth, and then there pursues him a piercing flame *of fire*.

اِلَّا مَنْ خَطِفَ الْخَطْفَةَ فَاَتْبَعَهٗ شِهَابٌ ثَاقِبٌ ﴿١١﴾

* 12. So ask them whether it is they who are harder to create, or *others* whom We have created? Them We have created of cohesive clay.

فَاسْتَفْتِهِمْ اَهُمْ اَشَدُّ خَلْقًا اَمْ مَّنْ خَلَقْنَا اِنَّا
خَلَقْنٰهُمْ مِّنْ طِيْنٍ لَّازِبٍ ﴿١٢﴾

13. Nay, thou dost wonder, and they ridicule.

بَلْ عَجِبْتَ وَيَسْخَرُوْنَ ﴿١٣﴾

14. And when they are admonished, they pay no heed.

وَاِذَا ذُكِّرُوْا لَا يَذْكُرُوْنَ ﴿١٤﴾

15. And when they see a Sign, they seek to ridicule it.

وَاِذَا رَاَوْا اٰيَةً يَّسْتَسْخِرُوْنَ ﴿١٥﴾

16. And they say, 'This is nothing but plain magic.

وَقَالُوْٓا اِنْ هٰذَآ اِلَّا سِحْرٌ مُّبِيْنٌ ﴿١٦﴾

17. 'What! when we are dead and have become dust and bones, shall we then be raised up *again?*

18. 'And our forefathers of yore *also?*'

19. Say, 'Yea; and you will *then* be abased.'

* 20. Then it will be but one shout of reproach, and behold, they will begin to see.

21. And they will say, 'Alas for us! this is the Day of Requital.

22. 'This is the Day of the *final* decision which you used to deny.'

R. 2.

23. *And it will be said to the angels,* 'Assemble those who acted wrongfully, along with their companions, and what they used to worship

24. 'Beside Allah; and lead them to the path of the Fire;

25. 'And stop them; for they must be questioned.'

26. 'What is the matter with you that you help not one another?'

27. Nay, on that day they will surrender themselves.

28. And some of them will address the others, questioning one another.

* 29. They will say, 'Verily, you used to come to us, swearing *that you were truthful.*'

30. They will answer, 'Nay, you yourselves were not believers.

31. 'And we had no power over you; but you yourselves were a transgressing people.

32. 'Now the word of our Lord has been justified against us that we shall surely *have to* taste *the punishment.*

33. 'And we caused you to go astray for we ourselves had gone astray.'

34. Truly, on that day they will *all* be sharers in the punishment.

35. Surely, thus do We deal with the guilty:

36. For when it was said to them, 'There is no God but Allah,' they turned away

ءَاِذَا مِتْنَا وَكُنَّا تُرَابًا وَّعِظَامًا ءَاِنَّا لَمَبْعُوْثُوْنَ ﴿١٧﴾

اَوَ اٰبَآؤُنَا الْاَوَّلُوْنَ ﴿١٨﴾

قُلْ نَعَمْ وَاَنْتُمْ دَاخِرُوْنَ ﴿١٩﴾

فَاِنَّمَا هِيَ زَجْرَةٌ وَّاحِدَةٌ فَاِذَا هُمْ يَنْظُرُوْنَ ﴿٢٠﴾

وَقَالُوْا يٰوَيْلَنَا هٰذَا يَوْمُ الدِّيْنِ ﴿٢١﴾

هٰذَا يَوْمُ الْفَصْلِ الَّذِيْ كُنْتُمْ بِهٖ تُكَذِّبُوْنَ ﴿٢٢﴾ ع ٢

اُحْشُرُوا الَّذِيْنَ ظَلَمُوْا وَاَزْوَاجَهُمْ وَمَا كَانُوْا
يَعْبُدُوْنَ ﴿٢٣﴾

مِنْ دُوْنِ اللّٰهِ فَاهْدُوْهُمْ اِلٰى صِرَاطِ الْجَحِيْمِ ﴿٢٤﴾ الربع

وَقِفُوْهُمْ اِنَّهُمْ مَّسْـُٔوْلُوْنَ ﴿٢٥﴾

مَا لَكُمْ لَا تَنَاصَرُوْنَ ﴿٢٦﴾

بَلْ هُمُ الْيَوْمَ مُسْتَسْلِمُوْنَ ﴿٢٧﴾

وَاَقْبَلَ بَعْضُهُمْ عَلٰى بَعْضٍ يَّتَسَآءَلُوْنَ ﴿٢٨﴾

قَالُوْٓا اِنَّكُمْ كُنْتُمْ تَاْتُوْنَنَا عَنِ الْيَمِيْنِ ﴿٢٩﴾

قَالُوْا بَلْ لَّمْ تَكُوْنُوْا مُؤْمِنِيْنَ ﴿٣٠﴾

وَمَا كَانَ لَنَا عَلَيْكُمْ مِّنْ سُلْطٰنٍ بَلْ كُنْتُمْ قَوْمًا
طٰغِيْنَ ﴿٣١﴾

فَحَقَّ عَلَيْنَا قَوْلُ رَبِّنَآ اِنَّا لَذَآئِقُوْنَ ﴿٣٢﴾

فَاَغْوَيْنٰكُمْ اِنَّا كُنَّا غٰوِيْنَ ﴿٣٣﴾

فَاِنَّهُمْ يَوْمَئِذٍ فِي الْعَذَابِ مُشْتَرِكُوْنَ ﴿٣٤﴾

اِنَّا كَذٰلِكَ نَفْعَلُ بِالْمُجْرِمِيْنَ ﴿٣٥﴾

اِنَّهُمْ كَانُوْٓا اِذَا قِيْلَ لَهُمْ لَآ اِلٰهَ اِلَّا اللّٰهُ

with disdain,

يَسْتَكْبِرُونَ ﴿٣٦﴾

37. And said, 'Shall we give up our gods for a mad poet?'

وَيَقُولُونَ أَئِنَّا لَتَارِكُوا آلِهَتِنَا لِشَاعِرٍ مَجْنُونٍ ﴿٣٧﴾

38. Nay, he has brought the truth and has testified to the truth of *all* the Messengers.

بَلْ جَاءَ بِالْحَقِّ وَصَدَّقَ الْمُرْسَلِينَ ﴿٣٨﴾

39. You shall surely taste the painful punishment.

إِنَّكُمْ لَذَائِقُو الْعَذَابِ الْأَلِيمِ ﴿٣٩﴾

40. And you will be rewarded only for what you have wrought—

وَمَا تُجْزَوْنَ إِلَّا مَا كُنْتُمْ تَعْمَلُونَ ﴿٤٠﴾

41. Save the chosen servants of Allah;

إِلَّا عِبَادَ اللَّهِ الْمُخْلَصِينَ ﴿٤١﴾

42. These will have a known provision:

أُولَٰئِكَ لَهُمْ رِزْقٌ مَعْلُومٌ ﴿٤٢﴾

43. Fruits; and they shall be honoured,

فَوَاكِهُ ۚ وَهُمْ مُكْرَمُونَ ﴿٤٣﴾

44. In the Gardens of Bliss,

فِي جَنَّاتِ النَّعِيمِ ﴿٤٤﴾

45. *Seated* on thrones, facing one another.

عَلَىٰ سُرُرٍ مُتَقَابِلِينَ ﴿٤٥﴾

46. They will be served round with a cup from a flowing fountain,

يُطَافُ عَلَيْهِمْ بِكَأْسٍ مِنْ مَعِينٍ ﴿٤٦﴾

47. *Sparkling* white, delicious to the drinkers,

بَيْضَاءَ لَذَّةٍ لِلشَّارِبِينَ ﴿٤٧﴾

48. Wherein there will be no intoxication, nor will they be exhausted thereby.

لَا فِيهَا غَوْلٌ وَلَا هُمْ عَنْهَا يُنْزَفُونَ ﴿٤٨﴾

49. And with them will be *chaste* women, with restrained looks *and* large beautiful eyes,

وَعِنْدَهُمْ قَاصِرَاتُ الطَّرْفِ عِينٌ ﴿٤٩﴾

50. As though they were sheltered eggs.

كَأَنَّهُنَّ بَيْضٌ مَكْنُونٌ ﴿٥٠﴾

51. Then some of them will address the others, questioning one another.

فَأَقْبَلَ بَعْضُهُمْ عَلَىٰ بَعْضٍ يَتَسَاءَلُونَ ﴿٥١﴾

52. A speaker from among them will say, "I had a companion,

قَالَ قَائِلٌ مِنْهُمْ إِنِّي كَانَ لِي قَرِينٌ ﴿٥٢﴾

53. "Who used to say, 'Art thou indeed among those who believe *it* to be true?

يَقُولُ أَئِنَّكَ لَمِنَ الْمُصَدِّقِينَ ﴿٥٣﴾

54. 'When we are dead, and have become dust and bones, shall we indeed be requited?' "

أَئِذَا مِتْنَا وَكُنَّا تُرَابًا وَعِظَامًا أَئِنَّا لَمَدِينُونَ ﴿٥٤﴾

55. He will ask, 'Will you have a look *at him?*'

قَالَ هَلْ أَنْتُمْ مُطَّلِعُونَ ﴿٥٥﴾

56. Then he will look and see him in the midst of the Fire.

فَاطَّلَعَ فَرَآهُ فِي سَوَاءِ الْجَحِيمِ ﴿٥٦﴾

57. He will say, 'By Allah, thou didst almost cause me to perish.

قَالَ تَاللَّهِ إِنْ كِدْتَ لَتُرْدِينِ ﴿٥٧﴾

58. 'And had it not been for the favour of my Lord, I should surely have been of those who are called up *before Him*.

وَلَوْلَا نِعْمَةُ رَبِّي لَكُنْتُ مِنَ الْمُحْضَرِيْنَ (٥٨)

59. 'Is it *not so that* we are not going to die *again*,

اَفَمَا نَحْنُ بِمَيِّتِيْنَ (٥٩)

60. 'Save our previous death, and that we are not to be punished?

اِلَّا مَوْتَتَنَا الْاُوْلٰى وَمَا نَحْنُ بِمُعَذَّبِيْنَ (٦٠)

61. 'Surely this is the supreme triumph.

اِنَّ هٰذَا لَهُوَ الْفَوْزُ الْعَظِيْمُ (٦١)

62. 'For the like of this, then, let the workers work.'

لِمِثْلِ هٰذَا فَلْيَعْمَلِ الْعٰمِلُوْنَ (٦٢)

63. Is that better as an entertainment, or the tree of Zaqqūm?

اَذٰلِكَ خَيْرٌ نُّزُلًا اَمْ شَجَرَةُ الزَّقُّوْمِ (٦٣)

64. Verily We have made it a trial for the wrongdoers.

اِنَّا جَعَلْنٰهَا فِتْنَةً لِّلظّٰلِمِيْنَ (٦٤)

65. It is a tree that springs forth in the bottom of Hell;

اِنَّهَا شَجَرَةٌ تَخْرُجُ فِيْٓ اَصْلِ الْجَحِيْمِ (٦٥)

66. The fruit thereof is as though it were the heads of serpents.

طَلْعُهَا كَاَنَّهٗ رُءُوْسُ الشَّيٰطِيْنِ (٦٦)

67. And they shall eat of it and fill *their* bellies therewith.

فَاِنَّهُمْ لَاٰكِلُوْنَ مِنْهَا فَمَالِـُٔوْنَ مِنْهَا الْبُطُوْنَ (٦٧)

68. Then will they have in addition to it a mixture of boiling water *as a drink*.

ثُمَّ اِنَّ لَهُمْ عَلَيْهَا لَشَوْبًا مِّنْ حَمِيْمٍ (٦٨)

69. Then surely their return shall be to Hell.

ثُمَّ اِنَّ مَرْجِعَهُمْ لَاِلَى الْجَحِيْمِ (٦٩)

70. They indeed found their fathers erring,

اِنَّهُمْ اَلْفَوْا اٰبَآءَهُمْ ضَآلِّيْنَ (٧٠)

71. And they hurried on in their footsteps.

فَهُمْ عَلٰٓى اٰثٰرِهِمْ يُهْرَعُوْنَ (٧١)

72. And most of the ancient peoples had erred before them,

وَلَقَدْ ضَلَّ قَبْلَهُمْ اَكْثَرُ الْاَوَّلِيْنَ (٧٢)

73. And We had sent Warners among them.

وَلَقَدْ اَرْسَلْنَا فِيْهِمْ مُّنْذِرِيْنَ (٧٣)

74. Behold, then, how *evil* was the end of those who were warned,

فَانْظُرْ كَيْفَ كَانَ عَاقِبَةُ الْمُنْذَرِيْنَ (٧٤)

75. Save the chosen servants of Allah.

اِلَّا عِبَادَ اللّٰهِ الْمُخْلَصِيْنَ (٧٥) ع

R. 3.

76. And Noah indeed did cry unto Us, and what an excellent answer did We give *to his prayer!*

وَلَقَدْ نَادٰىنَا نُوْحٌ فَلَنِعْمَ الْمُجِيْبُوْنَ (٧٦)

77. And We saved him and his family from the great distress;

وَنَجَّيْنٰهُ وَاَهْلَهٗ مِنَ الْكَرْبِ الْعَظِيْمِ (٧٧)

78. And We made his offspring the only survivors.

وَجَعَلْنَا ذُرِّيَّتَهٗ هُمُ الْبٰقِيْنَ (٧٨)

79. And We left for him *a good name* among the following generations—

وَتَرَكْنَا عَلَيْهِ فِي الْاٰخِرِيْنَ (٧٩)

* 80. 'Peace be upon Noah among the peoples!'
سَلٰمٌ عَلٰى نُوْحٍ فِي الْعٰلَمِيْنَ ﴿٨٠﴾

81. Thus indeed do We reward those who do good.
اِنَّا كَذٰلِكَ نَجْزِي الْمُحْسِنِيْنَ ﴿٨١﴾

82. He was surely *one* of Our believing servants.
اِنَّهٗ مِنْ عِبَادِنَا الْمُؤْمِنِيْنَ ﴿٨٢﴾

83. Then We drowned the others.
ثُمَّ اَغْرَقْنَا الْاٰخَرِيْنَ ﴿٨٣﴾

84. And verily of his party was Abraham;
وَاِنَّ مِنْ شِيْعَتِهٖ لَاِبْرٰهِيْمَ ﴿٨٤﴾

* 85. When he came to his Lord with a sound heart;
اِذْ جَآءَ رَبَّهٗ بِقَلْبٍ سَلِيْمٍ ﴿٨٥﴾

86. When he said to his father and to his people, 'What is it that you worship?
اِذْ قَالَ لِاَبِيْهِ وَقَوْمِهٖ مَاذَا تَعْبُدُوْنَ ﴿٨٦﴾

* 87. 'Do you falsely seek gods beside Allah?
اَئِفْكًا اٰلِهَةً دُوْنَ اللّٰهِ تُرِيْدُوْنَ ﴿٨٧﴾

88. 'So what is your idea about the Lord of the worlds?'
فَمَا ظَنُّكُمْ بِرَبِّ الْعٰلَمِيْنَ ﴿٨٨﴾

89. Then he cast a glance at the stars,
فَنَظَرَ نَظْرَةً فِي النُّجُوْمِ ﴿٨٩﴾

90. And said, 'I am indeed *feeling* unwell.'
فَقَالَ اِنِّيْ سَقِيْمٌ ﴿٩٠﴾

91. So they went away from him turning their backs.
فَتَوَلَّوْا عَنْهُ مُدْبِرِيْنَ ﴿٩١﴾

92. Then he went secretly to their gods and said, 'Will you not eat?
فَرَاغَ اِلٰٓى اٰلِهَتِهِمْ فَقَالَ اَلَا تَاْكُلُوْنَ ﴿٩٢﴾

93. 'What is the matter with you that you speak not?'
مَا لَكُمْ لَا تَنْطِقُوْنَ ﴿٩٣﴾

94. Then he began suddenly to strike them with the right hand.
فَرَاغَ عَلَيْهِمْ ضَرْبًا بِالْيَمِيْنِ ﴿٩٤﴾

95. Thereupon *the people* came towards him hastening.
فَاَقْبَلُوْٓا اِلَيْهِ يَزِفُّوْنَ ﴿٩٥﴾

96. He said, 'Do you worship that which you have *yourselves* carved out,
قَالَ اَتَعْبُدُوْنَ مَا تَنْحِتُوْنَ ﴿٩٦﴾

97. 'Whereas Allah has created you and your handiwork?'
وَاللّٰهُ خَلَقَكُمْ وَمَا تَعْمَلُوْنَ ﴿٩٧﴾

98. They said, 'Build for him a structure and cast him into the fire.'
قَالُوا ابْنُوْا لَهٗ بُنْيَانًا فَاَلْقُوْهُ فِي الْجَحِيْمِ ﴿٩٨﴾

99. Thus they intended an evil design against him, but We made them most humiliated.
فَاَرَادُوْا بِهٖ كَيْدًا فَجَعَلْنٰهُمُ الْاَسْفَلِيْنَ ﴿٩٩﴾

100. And he said, 'I am going to my Lord, Who will guide me.
وَقَالَ اِنِّيْ ذَاهِبٌ اِلٰى رَبِّيْ سَيَهْدِيْنِ ﴿١٠٠﴾

101. 'My Lord, grant me a righteous *son*.'
رَبِّ هَبْ لِيْ مِنَ الصّٰلِحِيْنَ ﴿١٠١﴾

102. So We gave him the glad tidings of a forbearing son.

فَبَشَّرْنٰهُ بِغُلٰمٍ حَلِيْمٍ ﴿١٠٢﴾

103. And when he was old enough to work with him, he said, 'O my dear son, I have seen in a dream that I am slaughtering thee. So consider, what thou thinkest *of it!*' He replied, 'O my father, do as thou art commanded; thou wilt find me, if Allah please, of those who are patient.'

فَلَمَّا بَلَغَ مَعَهُ السَّعْيَ قَالَ يٰبُنَيَّ اِنِّيْٓ اَرٰى فِي
الْمَنَامِ اَنِّيْٓ اَذْبَحُكَ فَانْظُرْ مَاذَا تَرٰى ؕ قَالَ
يٰٓاَبَتِ افْعَلْ مَا تُؤْمَرُ ؗ سَتَجِدُنِيْٓ اِنْ شَآءَ اللّٰهُ
مِنَ الصّٰبِرِيْنَ ﴿١٠٣﴾

* 104. And when they both submitted *to the will of God,* and he had thrown him down on his forehead,

فَلَمَّآ اَسْلَمَا وَتَلَّهٗ لِلْجَبِيْنِ ﴿١٠٤﴾

105. We called to him: 'O Abraham,

وَنَادَيْنٰهُ اَنْ يّٰٓاِبْرٰهِيْمُ ﴿١٠٥﴾

106. 'Thou hast indeed fulfilled the dream.' Thus indeed do We reward those who do good.

قَدْ صَدَّقْتَ الرُّءْيَا ۚ اِنَّا كَذٰلِكَ نَجْزِي الْمُحْسِنِيْنَ ﴿١٠٦﴾

107. That surely was a manifest trial.

اِنَّ هٰذَا لَهُوَ الْبَلٰٓؤُا الْمُبِيْنُ ﴿١٠٧﴾

108. And We ransomed him with a great sacrifice.

وَفَدَيْنٰهُ بِذِبْحٍ عَظِيْمٍ ﴿١٠٨﴾

109. And We left for him *a good name* among the following generations—

وَتَرَكْنَا عَلَيْهِ فِي الْاٰخِرِيْنَ ﴿١٠٩﴾

110. 'Peace be upon Abraham!'

سَلٰمٌ عَلٰٓى اِبْرٰهِيْمَ ﴿١١٠﴾

111. Thus do We reward those who do good.

كَذٰلِكَ نَجْزِي الْمُحْسِنِيْنَ ﴿١١١﴾

112. Surely, he was *one* of Our believing servants.

اِنَّهٗ مِنْ عِبَادِنَا الْمُؤْمِنِيْنَ ﴿١١٢﴾

113. And We gave him the glad tidings of Isaac, a Prophet, *and one* of the righteous.

وَبَشَّرْنٰهُ بِاِسْحٰقَ نَبِيًّا مِّنَ الصّٰلِحِيْنَ ﴿١١٣﴾

* 114. And We bestowed blessings on him and Isaac. And among their progeny are *some* who do good and others who clearly wrong themselves.

وَبٰرَكْنَا عَلَيْهِ وَعَلٰٓى اِسْحٰقَ ۭ وَمِنْ ذُرِّيَّتِهِمَا
مُحْسِنٌ وَّظَالِمٌ لِّنَفْسِهٖ مُبِيْنٌ ﴿١١٤﴾ ع

R. 4.

115. And, indeed, We bestowed favours on Moses and Aaron.

وَلَقَدْ مَنَنَّا عَلٰى مُوْسٰى وَهٰرُوْنَ ﴿١١٥﴾

116. And We saved them both and their people from the great distress;

وَنَجَّيْنٰهُمَا وَقَوْمَهُمَا مِنَ الْكَرْبِ الْعَظِيْمِ ﴿١١٦﴾

117. And We helped them, and it was they who were victorious.

وَنَصَرْنٰهُمْ فَكَانُوْا هُمُ الْغٰلِبِيْنَ ﴿١١٧﴾

* 118. And We gave them the Book that made *things* clear;

وَاٰتَيْنٰهُمَا الْكِتٰبَ الْمُسْتَبِيْنَ ﴿١١٨﴾

119. And We guided them to the right path.

وَهَدَيْنٰهُمَا الصِّرَاطَ الْمُسْتَقِيْمَ ﴿١١٩﴾

120. And We left for them *a good name* among the following generations—

وَتَرَكْنَا عَلَيْهِمَا فِي الْاٰخِرِيْنَ ﴿١٢٠﴾

121. 'Peace be on Moses and Aaron!'

سَلٰمٌ عَلٰى مُوْسٰى وَهٰرُوْنَ ﴿١٢١﴾

122. Thus indeed do We reward those who do good.

اِنَّا كَذٰلِكَ نَجْزِي الْمُحْسِنِيْنَ ﴿١٢٢﴾

123. Surely they were both among Our believing servants.

اِنَّهُمَا مِنْ عِبَادِنَا الْمُؤْمِنِيْنَ ﴿١٢٣﴾

124. And assuredly Elias *also* was *one* of the Messengers,

وَاِنَّ اِلْيَاسَ لَمِنَ الْمُرْسَلِيْنَ ﴿١٢٤﴾

125. When he said to his people, 'Will you not fear God?

اِذْ قَالَ لِقَوْمِهٖٓ اَلَا تَتَّقُوْنَ ﴿١٢٥﴾

126. 'Do you call on Ba'l, and forsake the Best of creators,

اَتَدْعُوْنَ بَعْلًا وَّتَذَرُوْنَ اَحْسَنَ الْخٰلِقِيْنَ ﴿١٢٦﴾

127. 'Allah, your Lord and the Lord of your forefathers of old?'

اللّٰهَ رَبَّكُمْ وَرَبَّ اٰبَآئِكُمُ الْاَوَّلِيْنَ ﴿١٢٧﴾

128. But they treated him as a liar, and they will surely be brought *before God to render an account;*

فَكَذَّبُوْهُ فَاِنَّهُمْ لَمُحْضَرُوْنَ ﴿١٢٨﴾

129. Except the chosen servants of Allah.

اِلَّا عِبَادَ اللّٰهِ الْمُخْلَصِيْنَ ﴿١٢٩﴾

130. And We left for him *a good name* among the following generations—

وَتَرَكْنَا عَلَيْهِ فِي الْاٰخِرِيْنَ ﴿١٣٠﴾

131. 'Peace be on Elias *and his people!*'

سَلٰمٌ عَلٰٓى اِلْ يَاسِيْنَ ﴿١٣١﴾

132. Thus indeed do We reward those who do good.

اِنَّا كَذٰلِكَ نَجْزِي الْمُحْسِنِيْنَ ﴿١٣٢﴾

133. Surely he was *one* of Our believing servants.

اِنَّهٗ مِنْ عِبَادِنَا الْمُؤْمِنِيْنَ ﴿١٣٣﴾

134. And assuredly Lot *too* was *one* of the Messengers,

وَاِنَّ لُوْطًا لَّمِنَ الْمُرْسَلِيْنَ ﴿١٣٤﴾

135. When We delivered him and all his family,

اِذْ نَجَّيْنٰهُ وَاَهْلَهٗٓ اَجْمَعِيْنَ ﴿١٣٥﴾

136. Except an old woman *who was* among those who stayed *behind*.

اِلَّا عَجُوْزًا فِي الْغٰبِرِيْنَ ﴿١٣٦﴾

137. Then We utterly destroyed the others.

ثُمَّ دَمَّرْنَا الْاٰخَرِيْنَ ﴿١٣٧﴾

138. And surely you pass by them in the morning,

وَاِنَّكُمْ لَتَمُرُّوْنَ عَلَيْهِمْ مُّصْبِحِيْنَ ﴿١٣٨﴾

139. And by night. Then why do you not understand?

وَبِالَّيْلِ اَفَلَا تَعْقِلُوْنَ ﴿١٣٩﴾ ع ٥ ٨

R. 5.

140. And surely Jonah *also* was *one* of the Messengers,

وَاِنَّ يُوْنُسَ لَمِنَ الْمُرْسَلِيْنَ ﴿١٤٠﴾

141. When he fled to the laden ship;

اِذْ اَبَقَ اِلَى الْفُلْكِ الْمَشْحُوْنِ ﴿١٤١﴾

* 142. And he cast lots *with the crew of the ship* and was of the losers.

فساهم فكان من المدحضين ﴿١٤٢﴾

143. And the fish swallowed him while he was blaming *himself*.

فالتقمه الحوت وهو مليم ﴿١٤٣﴾

144. And had he not been of those who glorify *God*,

فلولا انه كان من المسبحين ﴿١٤٤﴾

145. He would have surely tarried in its belly till the Day of Resurrection.

للبث في بطنه الى يوم يبعثون ﴿١٤٥﴾

146. Then We cast him on a bare tract of land, and he was sick;

فنبذنه بالعراء وهو سقيم ﴿١٤٦﴾

147. And We caused a plant of gourd to grow over him.

وانبتنا عليه شجرة من يقطين ﴿١٤٧﴾

148. And We sent him *as a Messenger* to a hundred thousand *people* or more,

وارسلنه الى مائة الف او يزيدون ﴿١٤٨﴾

149. And they believed; so We gave them provision for a while.

فامنوا فمتعنهم الى حين ﴿١٤٩﴾

150. Now ask them whether thy Lord has daughters whereas they have sons.

فاستفتهم الربك البنات ولهم البنون ﴿١٥٠﴾

151. Did We create the angels females while they were witnesses?

ام خلقنا الملئكة اناثا وهم شهدون ﴿١٥١﴾

* 152. Now, surely it is one of their fabrications that they say,

الا انهم من افكهم ليقولون ﴿١٥٢﴾

153. 'Allah has begotten *children*;' and they are certainly liars.

ولد الله وانهم لكذبون ﴿١٥٣﴾

154. Has He chosen daughters in preference to sons?

اصطفى البنات على البنين ﴿١٥٤﴾

155. What is the matter with you? How judge ye?

ما لكم كيف تحكمون ﴿١٥٥﴾

156. Will you not then reflect?

افلا تذكرون ﴿١٥٦﴾

157. Or have you a clear authority?

ام لكم سلطن مبين ﴿١٥٧﴾

158. Then produce your Book, if you are truthful.

فاتوا بكتبكم ان كنتم صدقين ﴿١٥٨﴾

* 159. And they assert a blood relationship between Him and the Jinn, while the Jinn *themselves* know that they will be brought *before God for judgment*.

وجعلوا بينه وبين الجنة نسبا ولقد علمت
الجنة انهم لمحضرون ﴿١٥٩﴾

160. Holy is Allah *and free* from what they attribute *to Him*.

سبحن الله عما يصفون ﴿١٦٠﴾

161. But the chosen servants of Allah *do not do so*.

الا عباد الله المخلصين ﴿١٦١﴾

162. Verily, you and what you worship—

فانكم وما تعبدون ﴿١٦٢﴾

163. None of you can mislead *anyone* against Him,

مَآ أَنۡتُمۡ عَلَيۡهِ بِفٰتِنِيۡنَ ﴿١٦٣﴾

164. Except him who shall burn in Hell.

إِلَّا مَنۡ هُوَ صَالِ الۡجَحِيۡمِ ﴿١٦٤﴾

165. *And the angels say:* 'And there is not one of us but has an appointed station.

وَمَا مِنَّآ إِلَّا لَهٗ مَقَامٌ مَّعۡلُوۡمٌ ﴿١٦٥﴾

166. 'And, verily, we are those who stand ranged in ranks.

وَّإِنَّا لَنَحۡنُ الصَّآفُّوۡنَ ﴿١٦٦﴾

167. 'And we are verily those who glorify *God*.'

وَإِنَّا لَنَحۡنُ الۡمُسَبِّحُوۡنَ ﴿١٦٧﴾

168. And surely they used to say,

وَإِنۡ كَانُوۡا لَيَقُوۡلُوۡنَ ﴿١٦٨﴾

169. 'If we had with us a Book *like that* of the people of old,

لَوۡ أَنَّ عِنۡدَنَا ذِكۡرًا مِّنَ الۡأَوَّلِيۡنَ ﴿١٦٩﴾

170. 'We would surely have been Allah's chosen servants.'

لَكُنَّا عِبَادَ اللّٰهِ الۡمُخۡلَصِيۡنَ ﴿١٧٠﴾

171. Yet *when it is come to them* they disbelieve therein, but they will soon come to know.

فَكَفَرُوۡا بِهٖ فَسَوۡفَ يَعۡلَمُوۡنَ ﴿١٧١﴾

172. And surely Our word has gone forth respecting Our servants, the Messengers,

وَلَقَدۡ سَبَقَتۡ كَلِمَتُنَا لِعِبَادِنَا الۡمُرۡسَلِيۡنَ ﴿١٧٢﴾

173. That it is certainly they who would be helped;

إِنَّهُمۡ لَهُمُ الۡمَنۡصُوۡرُوۡنَ ﴿١٧٣﴾

174. And that it is Our host that would certainly be victorious.

وَإِنَّ جُنۡدَنَا لَهُمُ الۡغٰلِبُوۡنَ ﴿١٧٤﴾

175. So turn thou away from them for a while.

فَتَوَلَّ عَنۡهُمۡ حَتّٰى حِيۡنٍ ﴿١٧٥﴾

176. And watch them, for they will soon see.

وَّأَبۡصِرۡهُمۡ فَسَوۡفَ يُبۡصِرُوۡنَ ﴿١٧٦﴾

177. Is it then Our punishment that they seek to hasten on?

أَفَبِعَذَابِنَا يَسۡتَعۡجِلُوۡنَ ﴿١٧٧﴾

178. But when it descends into their courtyard, it shall be an evil morning to those who were warned.

فَإِذَا نَزَلَ بِسَاحَتِهِمۡ فَسَآءَ صَبَاحُ الۡمُنۡذَرِيۡنَ ﴿١٧٨﴾

179. So turn thou away from them for a while.

وَتَوَلَّ عَنۡهُمۡ حَتّٰى حِيۡنٍ ﴿١٧٩﴾

180. And watch, for they will soon see.

وَّأَبۡصِرۡ فَسَوۡفَ يُبۡصِرُوۡنَ ﴿١٨٠﴾

181. Holy is thy Lord, the Lord of Honour *and Power*, far above that which they assert.

سُبۡحٰنَ رَبِّكَ رَبِّ الۡعِزَّةِ عَمَّا يَصِفُوۡنَ ﴿١٨١﴾

182. And peace be upon the Messengers!

وَسَلٰمٌ عَلَى الۡمُرۡسَلِيۡنَ ﴿١٨٢﴾

183. And all praise belongs to Allah, the Lord of the worlds.

وَالۡحَمۡدُ لِلّٰهِ رَبِّ الۡعٰلَمِيۡنَ ﴿١٨٣﴾ ع ٩

سُوْرَةُ صٓ مَكِّيَّةٌ (٣٨)

ṢĀD

(Revealed before Hijra)

1. In the name of Allah, the Gracious, the Merciful.

بِسْمِ اللّٰهِ الرَّحْمٰنِ الرَّحِيْمِ (١)

2. Ṣād*. By the Qur'ān, full of exhortation, *it is Our revealed word.*

صٓ وَالْقُرْاٰنِ ذِي الذِّكْرِ (٢)

3. But those who disbelieve are *steeped* in *false* pride and enmity.

بَلِ الَّذِيْنَ كَفَرُوْا فِيْ عِزَّةٍ وَّشِقَاقٍ (٣)

4. How many a generation before them have We destroyed! They cried out *for help*, but it was no longer the time for escape.

كَمْ اَهْلَكْنَا مِنْ قَبْلِهِمْ مِّنْ قَرْنٍ فَنَادَوْا وَّلَاتَ
حِيْنَ مَنَاصٍ (٤)

5. And they wonder that a Warner has come to them from among themselves; and the disbelievers say, 'This is a magician, a great liar.

وَعَجِبُوْٓا اَنْ جَآءَهُمْ مُّنْذِرٌ مِّنْهُمْ وَقَالَ الْكٰفِرُوْنَ
هٰذَا سٰحِرٌ كَذَّابٌ (٥)

* 6. 'Does he make the gods to be one God? This is indeed a strange thing.'

اَجَعَلَ الْاٰلِهَةَ اِلٰهًا وَّاحِدًا ۚ اِنَّ هٰذَا لَشَيْءٌ
عُجَابٌ (٦)

* 7. And the leaders among them spoke out, 'Go and stick to your gods. This is a thing designed.

وَانْطَلَقَ الْمَلَاُ مِنْهُمْ اَنِ امْشُوْا وَاصْبِرُوْا عَلٰٓى
اٰلِهَتِكُمْ ۚ اِنَّ هٰذَا لَشَيْءٌ يُّرَادُ (٧)

* 8. 'We have not heard of this *even* in the latest religion. This is nothing but a fabrication.

مَا سَمِعْنَا بِهٰذَا فِي الْمِلَّةِ الْاٰخِرَةِ ۚ اِنْ هٰذَآ اِلَّا
اخْتِلَاقٌ (٨)

* 9. 'Has the exhortation been sent down to him *in preference to all* of us?' Nay, they are in doubt concerning My exhortation. Nay, but they have not yet tasted My punishment.

ءَاُنْزِلَ عَلَيْهِ الذِّكْرُ مِنْ بَيْنِنَا ۭ بَلْ هُمْ فِيْ شَكٍّ
مِّنْ ذِكْرِيْ ۚ بَلْ لَّمَّا يَذُوْقُوْا عَذَابِ (٩)

10. Do they possess the treasures of the mercy of thy Lord, the Mighty, the Great Bestower?

اَمْ عِنْدَهُمْ خَزَآئِنُ رَحْمَةِ رَبِّكَ الْعَزِيْزِ الْوَهَّابِ (١٠)

11. Or is the kingdom of the heavens and the earth and all that is between them theirs? So let them ascend with the means *at their disposal.*

اَمْ لَهُمْ مُّلْكُ السَّمٰوٰتِ وَالْاَرْضِ وَمَا بَيْنَهُمَا ۣ
فَلْيَرْتَقُوْا فِي الْاَسْبَابِ (١١)

12. *They are* a host from among the confederates *which will be* routed here.

جُنْدٌ مَّا هُنَالِكَ مَهْزُوْمٌ مِّنَ الْاَحْزَابِ (١٢)

* Truthful God!

* 13. Before them *too* the people of Noah, and *the tribe of* 'Ād and Pharaoh, the lord of stakes, treated *the Messengers* as liars;

كَذَّبَتْ قَبْلَهُمْ قَوْمُ نُوحٍ وَّعَادٌ وَّفِرْعَوْنُ
ذُو الْأَوْتَادِ ﴿١٣﴾

* 14. And *the tribe of* Thamūd, and the people of Lot, and the dwellers of the Wood—these were the confederates.

وَثَمُودُ وَقَوْمُ لُوطٍ وَّأَصْحٰبُ لْـَٔيْكَةِ ۭ أُولٰٓئِكَ
الْأَحْزَابُ ﴿١٤﴾

* 15. There was not one *of them* but treated *their* Messengers as liars, so My punishment rightly overtook *them*.

ع إِنْ كُلٌّ إِلَّا كَذَّبَ الرُّسُلَ فَحَقَّ عِقَابِ ﴿١٥﴾

R. 2.

* 16. And these only wait for a single blast, and there shall be no delaying it.

وَمَا يَنْظُرُ هٰٓؤُلَآءِ إِلَّا صَيْحَةً وَّاحِدَةً مَّا لَهَا مِنْ فَوَاقٍ ﴿١٦﴾

17. They say, 'Our Lord, hasten to us our portion *of the punishment* before the Day of Reckoning.'

وَقَالُوْا رَبَّنَا عَجِّلْ لَّنَا قِطَّنَا قَبْلَ يَوْمِ الْحِسَابِ ﴿١٧﴾

* 18. Bear patiently what they say, and remember Our servant David, *man* of *strong* hands; surely he was always turning *to God*.

اِصْبِرْ عَلٰى مَا يَقُوْلُوْنَ وَاذْكُرْ عَبْدَنَا دَاوٗدَ ذَا الْأَيْدِ
إِنَّهٗٓ أَوَّابٌ ﴿١٨﴾

* 19. We subjected *to him* the mountains. They celebrated God's praises with him at nightfall and sunrise.

إِنَّا سَخَّرْنَا الْجِبَالَ مَعَهٗ يُسَبِّحْنَ بِالْعَشِيِّ وَ
الْإِشْرَاقِ ﴿١٩﴾

* 20. And *We subjected to him* the birds gathered together: all turned to him.

وَالطَّيْرَ مَحْشُوْرَةً ۭ كُلٌّ لَّهٗٓ أَوَّابٌ ﴿٢٠﴾

* 21. And We strengthened his kingdom, and gave him wisdom and decisive judgment.

وَشَدَدْنَا مُلْكَهٗ وَاٰتَيْنٰهُ الْحِكْمَةَ وَفَصْلَ
الْخِطَابِ ﴿٢١﴾

22. And has the story of the disputants reached thee when they climbed over the wall of *his* chamber?—

وَهَلْ أَتٰىكَ نَبَؤُا الْخَصْمِ إِذْ تَسَوَّرُوا الْمِحْرَابَ ﴿٢٢﴾

23. When they entered in upon David, and he was afraid of them. They said, "Fear not. *We are* two disputants; one of us has transgressed against the other; so judge between us with justice, and deviate not from the right course and guide us to the right way.

إِذْ دَخَلُوْا عَلٰى دَاوٗدَ فَفَزِعَ مِنْهُمْ قَالُوْا لَا تَخَفْ ۚ
خَصْمٰنِ بَغٰى بَعْضُنَا عَلٰى بَعْضٍ فَاحْكُمْ بَيْنَنَا
بِالْحَقِّ وَلَا تُشْطِطْ وَاهْدِنَآ إِلٰى سَوَآءِ الصِّرَاطِ ﴿٢٣﴾

24. "This is my brother; he has ninety-nine ewes, and I have one ewe. Yet he says, 'Give it to me,' and has been overbearing to me in his address."

إِنَّ هٰذَآ أَخِيْ لَهٗ تِسْعٌ وَّتِسْعُوْنَ نَعْجَةً وَّلِيَ
نَعْجَةٌ وَّاحِدَةٌ فَقَالَ أَكْفِلْنِيْهَا وَعَزَّنِيْ
فِي الْخِطَابِ ﴿٢٤﴾

25. *David* said, 'Surely, he has wronged thee in demanding thy ewe in addition to his own ewes.

قَالَ لَقَدْ ظَلَمَكَ بِسُؤَالِ نَعْجَتِكَ إِلٰى نِعَاجِهٖ ۭ

And certainly many partners transgress against one another, except those who believe *in God* and do good works; and these are but few.' And David perceived that We had tried him; so he asked forgiveness of his Lord, and fell down bowing in worship and turned *to Him.*

وَإِنَّ كَثِيرًا مِّنَ الْخُلَطَاءِ لَيَبْغِي بَعْضُهُمْ عَلَىٰ بَعْضٍ
إِلَّا الَّذِينَ آمَنُوا وَعَمِلُوا الصَّالِحَاتِ وَقَلِيلٌ مَّا هُمْ ۗ
وَظَنَّ دَاوُودُ أَنَّمَا فَتَنَّاهُ فَاسْتَغْفَرَ رَبَّهُ وَخَرَّ رَاكِعًا
السجدة
وَأَنَابَ ﴿٢٥﴾

26. So We forgave him that; and indeed, he had a position of nearness with Us and an excellent retreat.

فَغَفَرْنَا لَهُ ذَٰلِكَ ۖ وَإِنَّ لَهُ عِندَنَا لَزُلْفَىٰ وَحُسْنَ
مَآبٍ ﴿٢٦﴾

27. 'O David, We have made thee a vicegerent in the earth; so judge between men with justice, and follow not vain desire, lest it should lead thee astray from the way of Allah.' Surely those who go astray from the way of Allah will have a severe punishment, because they forgot the Day of Reckoning.

يَا دَاوُودُ إِنَّا جَعَلْنَاكَ خَلِيفَةً فِي الْأَرْضِ فَاحْكُم
بَيْنَ النَّاسِ بِالْحَقِّ وَلَا تَتَّبِعِ الْهَوَىٰ فَيُضِلَّكَ
عَن سَبِيلِ اللَّهِ ۚ إِنَّ الَّذِينَ يَضِلُّونَ عَن سَبِيلِ
اللَّهِ لَهُمْ عَذَابٌ شَدِيدٌ بِمَا نَسُوا يَوْمَ الْحِسَابِ ﴿٢٧﴾

R. 3.

28. And We have not created the heaven and the earth and all that is between them in vain. That is the view of those who disbelieve. Woe, then, to the disbelievers because of the Fire.

وَمَا خَلَقْنَا السَّمَاءَ وَالْأَرْضَ وَمَا بَيْنَهُمَا بَاطِلًا ۚ
ذَٰلِكَ ظَنُّ الَّذِينَ كَفَرُوا ۚ فَوَيْلٌ لِّلَّذِينَ كَفَرُوا
مِنَ النَّارِ ﴿٢٨﴾

29. Shall We treat those who believe and do good works like those who act corruptly in the earth? Shall We treat the righteous like the wicked?

أَمْ نَجْعَلُ الَّذِينَ آمَنُوا وَعَمِلُوا الصَّالِحَاتِ كَالْمُفْسِدِينَ
فِي الْأَرْضِ أَمْ نَجْعَلُ الْمُتَّقِينَ كَالْفُجَّارِ ﴿٢٩﴾

30. *This is* a Book which We have revealed to thee, full of blessings, that they may reflect over its verses, and that those gifted with understanding may take heed.

كِتَابٌ أَنزَلْنَاهُ إِلَيْكَ مُبَارَكٌ لِّيَدَّبَّرُوا آيَاتِهِ وَ
لِيَتَذَكَّرَ أُولُو الْأَلْبَابِ ﴿٣٠﴾

31. And We bestowed on David, Solomon who was an excellent servant. He was always turning *to Us.*

وَوَهَبْنَا لِدَاوُودَ سُلَيْمَانَ ۚ نِعْمَ الْعَبْدُ ۖ إِنَّهُ
أَوَّابٌ ﴿٣١﴾

32. When there were brought before him at eventide steeds of noblest breed and swift of foot,

إِذْ عُرِضَ عَلَيْهِ بِالْعَشِيِّ الصَّافِنَاتُ الْجِيَادُ ﴿٣٢﴾

* 33. He said, 'I love the love of horses because of the remembrance of my Lord.' *So great was his love of them that* when they were hidden behind the veil, *he said,*

فَقَالَ إِنِّي أَحْبَبْتُ حُبَّ الْخَيْرِ عَن ذِكْرِ رَبِّي
وقفة
حَتَّىٰ تَوَارَتْ بِالْحِجَابِ ﴿٣٣﴾

* 34. 'Bring them back to me.' Then he began to pass his hand over *their* legs and *their* necks.

ردوها علي فطفق مسحا بالسوق والاعناق ﴿٣٤﴾

35. And We did try Solomon and We placed on his throne a *mere* body. Then he turned *to God, seeking His mercy*.

ولقد فتنا سليمن والقينا على كرسيه جسدا ثم اناب ﴿٣٥﴾

* 36. He said, 'O my Lord, grant me forgiveness and bestow on me a kingdom that will not suit anyone after me; surely Thou art the Great Bestower.'

قال رب اغفر لي وهب لي ملكا لا ينبغي لاحد من بعدي انك انت الوهاب ﴿٣٦﴾

37. So We subjected to him the wind, blowing gently by his command whithersoever he desired to go,

فسخرنا له الريح تجري بامره رخاء حيث اصاب ﴿٣٧﴾

38. And the giants, all *sorts of* builders and divers,

والشيطين كل بناء وغواص ﴿٣٨﴾

39. And others bound in fetters.

واخرين مقرنين في الاصفاد ﴿٣٩﴾

40. 'This is Our gift—so give freely or withhold—without reckoning.'

هذا عطاؤنا فامنن او امسك بغير حساب ﴿٤٠﴾

41. And certainly he had a position of nearness with Us and an excellent retreat.

وان له عندنا لزلفى وحسن ماب ﴿٤١﴾

R. 4.

42. And remember Our servant Job, when he cried unto his Lord, *saying*, 'Satan has afflicted me with toil and torment.'

واذكر عبدنا ايوب اذ نادى ربه اني مسني الشيطن بنصب وعذاب ﴿٤٢﴾ لازم

* 43. 'Strike *and urge thy riding beast* with thy foot. Here is cool water to wash with and a drink.'

اركض برجلك هذا مغتسل بارد وشراب ﴿٤٣﴾

* 44. And We bestowed on him his family and as many more with them, *by way of* mercy from Us, and as a reminder to men of understanding.

ووهبنا له اهله ومثلهم معهم رحمة منا وذكرى لاولي الالباب ﴿٤٤﴾

45. And *We said to him*, 'Take in thy hand a handful of dry twigs and strike therewith, and break not thy oath.' Indeed, We found him steadfast. An excellent servant was he. Surely, he was always turning *to God*.

وخذ بيدك ضغثا فاضرب به ولا تحنث انا وجدنه صابرا نعم العبد انه اواب ﴿٤٥﴾

* 46. And remember Our servants Abraham, and Isaac, and Jacob, *men* of strong hands and *powerful* vision.

واذكر عبدنا ابرهيم واسحق ويعقوب اولي الايدي والابصار ﴿٤٦﴾

* 47. We chose them for a special *purpose* — reminding *people* of the abode *of the Hereafter*.

انا اخلصنهم بخالصة ذكرى الدار ﴿٤٧﴾

48. And truly, they are in Our sight among the elect *and* the best.

وانهم عندنا لمن المصطفين الاخيار ﴿٤٨﴾

49. And remember Ishmael and Elisha and Dhu'l-Kifl*; and all were of the best.

وَاذْكُرْ إِسْمٰعِيلَ وَالْيَسَعَ وَذَا الْكِفْلِ ۖ وَكُلٌّ مِّنَ الْأَخْيَارِ ﴿٤٩﴾

50. This is a reminder. And the righteous will surely have excellent retreat:

هٰذَا ذِكْرٌ ۚ وَإِنَّ لِلْمُتَّقِينَ لَحُسْنَ مَآبٍ ﴿٥٠﴾

51. Gardens of Eternity, with their gates thrown open to them,

جَنّٰتِ عَدْنٍ مُّفَتَّحَةً لَّهُمُ الْأَبْوَابُ ﴿٥١﴾

52. Reclining therein *on cushions;* they will therein call *at pleasure* for plenteous fruit and drink.

مُتَّكِئِينَ فِيهَا يَدْعُونَ فِيهَا بِفَاكِهَةٍ كَثِيرَةٍ وَّشَرَابٍ ﴿٥٢﴾

53. And with them will be *chaste women*, restraining their looks, companions of equal age.

وَعِنْدَهُمْ قٰصِرٰتُ الطَّرْفِ أَتْرَابٌ ﴿٥٣﴾

54. This is what you are promised for the Day of Reckoning.

هٰذَا مَا تُوعَدُونَ لِيَوْمِ الْحِسَابِ ﴿٥٤﴾

55. Verily, this is Our provision which will never be exhausted.

إِنَّ هٰذَا لَرِزْقُنَا مَا لَهُ مِنْ نَّفَادٍ ﴿٥٥﴾

56. This is *for the believers*. But for the rebellious there is an evil place of return—

هٰذَا ۚ وَإِنَّ لِلطّٰغِينَ لَشَرَّ مَآبٍ ﴿٥٦﴾

57. Hell, wherein they will burn. What an evil resting-place!

جَهَنَّمَ ۚ يَصْلَوْنَهَا ۚ فَبِئْسَ الْمِهَادُ ﴿٥٧﴾

58. This is *what they will have*. So let them taste it: a boiling fluid, and an intensely cold and stinking drink.

هٰذَا ۙ فَلْيَذُوقُوهُ حَمِيمٌ وَّغَسَّاقٌ ﴿٥٨﴾

59. And *various kinds of* other *torments* of a similar nature.

وَّآخَرُ مِنْ شَكْلِهِ أَزْوَاجٌ ﴿٥٩﴾

60. 'This is a host *of yours* rushing headlong with you, *O leaders of mischief.*' No welcome for them. They must burn in the Fire.

هٰذَا فَوْجٌ مُّقْتَحِمٌ مَّعَكُمْ ۚ لَا مَرْحَبًا بِهِمْ ۚ إِنَّهُمْ صَالُوا النَّارِ ﴿٦٠﴾

61. They will say, 'Nay, it is you. No welcome for you *in truth*. It is you who prepared this for us. So what an evil resting-place it is!'

قَالُوا بَلْ أَنْتُمْ ۖ لَا مَرْحَبًا بِكُمْ ۖ أَنْتُمْ قَدَّمْتُمُوهُ لَنَا ۖ فَبِئْسَ الْقَرَارُ ﴿٦١﴾

62. They will *also* say, 'Our Lord, whosoever prepared this for us—so add to him a double punishment in the Fire.'

قَالُوا رَبَّنَا مَنْ قَدَّمَ لَنَا هٰذَا فَزِدْهُ عَذَابًا ضِعْفًا فِي النَّارِ ﴿٦٢﴾

63. And they will say, 'What has happened to us that we see not the men whom we used to reckon among the wicked?

وَقَالُوا مَا لَنَا لَا نَرَىٰ رِجَالًا كُنَّا نَعُدُّهُمْ مِّنَ الْأَشْرَارِ ﴿٦٣﴾

64. 'Is it because we subjected them to ridicule *unjustly*, or have the eyes missed them?'

أَتَّخَذْنٰهُمْ سِخْرِيًّا أَمْ زَاغَتْ عَنْهُمُ الْأَبْصَارُ ﴿٦٤﴾

* Ezekiel.

* 65. Surely, this is a fact—the disputing together of the people of the Fire.

إِنَّ ذَٰلِكَ لَحَقٌّ تَخَاصُمُ أَهْلِ النَّارِ ﴿٦٥﴾

R. 5.

66. Say, 'I am only a Warner; and there is no God but Allah, the One, the Most Supreme;

قُلْ إِنَّمَا أَنَا مُنذِرٌ ۖ وَمَا مِنْ إِلَٰهٍ إِلَّا اللَّهُ الْوَاحِدُ الْقَهَّارُ ﴿٦٦﴾

67. 'The Lord of the heavens and the earth, and all that is between the two, the Mighty, the Great Forgiver.'

رَبُّ السَّمَٰوَٰتِ وَالْأَرْضِ وَمَا بَيْنَهُمَا الْعَزِيزُ الْغَفَّارُ ﴿٦٧﴾

68. Say, 'It is a big news,

قُلْ هُوَ نَبَؤٌا عَظِيمٌ ﴿٦٨﴾

69. 'From which you are turning away.

أَنتُمْ عَنْهُ مُعْرِضُونَ ﴿٦٩﴾

70. 'I had no knowledge of the exalted Assembly when they discussed *it* among themselves,

مَا كَانَ لِيَ مِنْ عِلْمٍ بِالْمَلَإِ الْأَعْلَىٰ إِذْ يَخْتَصِمُونَ ﴿٧٠﴾

71. 'But this that it has been revealed to me, that I am a plain Warner.'

إِن يُوحَىٰ إِلَيَّ إِلَّا أَنَّمَا أَنَا نَذِيرٌ مُّبِينٌ ﴿٧١﴾

72. When thy Lord said to the angels, 'I am about to create man from clay,

إِذْ قَالَ رَبُّكَ لِلْمَلَٰٓئِكَةِ إِنِّي خَالِقٌ بَشَرًا مِّن طِينٍ ﴿٧٢﴾

73. 'And so when I have fashioned him *in perfection*, and have breathed into him of My Spirit, fall ye down in submission to him.'

فَإِذَا سَوَّيْتُهُ وَنَفَخْتُ فِيهِ مِن رُّوحِي فَقَعُوا لَهُ سَٰجِدِينَ ﴿٧٣﴾

74. So the angels submitted, all of them together.

فَسَجَدَ الْمَلَٰٓئِكَةُ كُلُّهُمْ أَجْمَعُونَ ﴿٧٤﴾

75. But Iblīs *did not*. He behaved proudly, and was of those who disbelieved.

إِلَّا إِبْلِيسَ اسْتَكْبَرَ وَكَانَ مِنَ الْكَٰفِرِينَ ﴿٧٥﴾

* 76. *God* said, 'O Iblīs, what hindered thee from submitting to what I had created with My two hands? Is it that thou art *too* proud or art thou *really* of the exalted ones?'

قَالَ يَٰٓإِبْلِيسُ مَا مَنَعَكَ أَن تَسْجُدَ لِمَا خَلَقْتُ بِيَدَيَّ ۖ أَسْتَكْبَرْتَ أَمْ كُنتَ مِنَ الْعَالِينَ ﴿٧٦﴾

77. He said, 'I am better than he. Thou hast created me of fire and him hast Thou created of clay.'

قَالَ أَنَا خَيْرٌ مِّنْهُ ۖ خَلَقْتَنِي مِن نَّارٍ وَخَلَقْتَهُ مِن طِينٍ ﴿٧٧﴾

78. *God* said, 'Then get out hence, for, surely thou art rejected.

قَالَ فَاخْرُجْ مِنْهَا فَإِنَّكَ رَجِيمٌ ﴿٧٨﴾

79. 'And surely on thee shall be My curse till the Day of Judgment.'

وَإِنَّ عَلَيْكَ لَعْنَتِي إِلَىٰ يَوْمِ الدِّينِ ﴿٧٩﴾

80. He said, 'My Lord, then grant me respite till the day when they shall be raised.'

قَالَ رَبِّ فَأَنظِرْنِي إِلَىٰ يَوْمِ يُبْعَثُونَ ﴿٨٠﴾

81. *God* said, 'Certainly thou art of those that are granted respite,

قَالَ فَإِنَّكَ مِنَ الْمُنظَرِينَ ﴿٨١﴾

82. 'Till the day of the appointed time.'

83. He said, 'So by Thy might, I will surely lead them all astray,

84. 'Except Thy chosen servants from among them.'

85. *God* said, 'Then the truth is, and the truth I speak,

86. '*That* I will certainly fill Hell with thee and with those who follow thee, all together.'

87. Say, 'I ask not of you any reward for it, nor am I of those who are given to affectation.

88. 'It is nothing but a Reminder for *all* peoples.

* 89. 'And you shall surely know the truth of it after a while.'

إِلَىٰ يَوْمِ الْوَقْتِ الْمَعْلُومِ ﴿٨٢﴾

قَالَ فَبِعِزَّتِكَ لَأُغْوِيَنَّهُمْ أَجْمَعِينَ ﴿٨٣﴾

إِلَّا عِبَادَكَ مِنْهُمُ الْمُخْلَصِينَ ﴿٨٤﴾

قَالَ فَالْحَقُّ وَالْحَقَّ أَقُولُ ﴿٨٥﴾

لَأَمْلَأَنَّ جَهَنَّمَ مِنْكَ وَمِمَّنْ تَبِعَكَ مِنْهُمْ أَجْمَعِينَ ﴿٨٦﴾

قُلْ مَا أَسْأَلُكُمْ عَلَيْهِ مِنْ أَجْرٍ وَمَا أَنَا مِنَ الْمُتَكَلِّفِينَ ﴿٨٧﴾

إِنْ هُوَ إِلَّا ذِكْرٌ لِلْعَالَمِينَ ﴿٨٨﴾

وَلَتَعْلَمُنَّ نَبَأَهُ بَعْدَ حِينٍ ﴿٨٩﴾

ركوعاتها ٨ سُوْرَةُ الزُّمَرِ مَكِّيَّةٌ (٣٩) اٰياتها ٧٦

AL-ZUMAR

(Revealed before Hijra)

1. In the name of Allah, the Gracious, the Merciful.

بِسْمِ اللّٰهِ الرَّحْمٰنِ الرَّحِيْمِ ①

2. The revelation of this Book is from Allah, the Mighty, the Wise.

تَنْزِيْلُ الْكِتٰبِ مِنَ اللّٰهِ الْعَزِيْزِ الْحَكِيْمِ ②

* 3. Surely it is We Who have revealed the Book to thee with truth; so worship Allah, being sincere to Him in obedience.

اِنَّآ اَنْزَلْنَآ اِلَيْكَ الْكِتٰبَ بِالْحَقِّ فَاعْبُدِ اللّٰهَ مُخْلِصًا
لَّهُ الدِّيْنَ ③

4. Hearken, it is to Allah *alone* that sincere obedience is due. And those who take for protectors others beside Him *say*, 'We serve them only that they may bring us near to Allah in station.' Surely, Allah will judge between them concerning that wherein they differ. Surely, Allah guides not him who is an ungrateful liar.

اَلَا لِلّٰهِ الدِّيْنُ الْخَالِصُ ۚ وَالَّذِيْنَ اتَّخَذُوْا مِنْ
دُوْنِهٖٓ اَوْلِيَآءَ ۘ مَا نَعْبُدُهُمْ اِلَّا لِيُقَرِّبُوْنَآ اِلَى لازم
اللّٰهِ زُلْفٰى ۭ اِنَّ اللّٰهَ يَحْكُمُ بَيْنَهُمْ فِيْ مَا هُمْ فِيْهِ
يَخْتَلِفُوْنَ ۥ اِنَّ اللّٰهَ لَا يَهْدِيْ مَنْ هُوَ كٰذِبٌ
كَفَّارٌ ④

* 5. If Allah had desired to take to Himself a son, He could have chosen whom He pleased out of what He creates. Holy is He! He is Allah, the One, the Most Supreme.

لَوْ اَرَادَ اللّٰهُ اَنْ يَّتَّخِذَ وَلَدًا لَّاصْطَفٰى مِمَّا يَخْلُقُ
مَا يَشَآءُ ۙ سُبْحٰنَهٗ ۭ هُوَ اللّٰهُ الْوَاحِدُ الْقَهَّارُ ⑤

6. He created the heavens and the earth in accordance with the requirements of wisdom. He makes the night to cover the day, and He makes the day to cover the night; and He has pressed the sun and the moon into service; each pursues *its* course until an appointed time. Hearken, *it is* He *alone Who* is the Mighty, the Great Forgiver.

خَلَقَ السَّمٰوٰتِ وَالْاَرْضَ بِالْحَقِّ ۚ يُكَوِّرُ الَّيْلَ عَلَى
النَّهَارِ وَيُكَوِّرُ النَّهَارَ عَلَى الَّيْلِ وَسَخَّرَ الشَّمْسَ وَ
الْقَمَرَ ۭ كُلٌّ يَّجْرِيْ لِاَجَلٍ مُّسَمًّى ۭ اَلَا هُوَ الْعَزِيْزُ
الْغَفَّارُ ⑥

* 7. He created you from a single being; then from that He made its mate; and He has sent down for you eight *head* of cattle in pairs. He creates you in the wombs of your mothers, creation after creation, in threefold darkness. This is Allah, your Lord. His is the kingdom. There is no God

خَلَقَكُمْ مِّنْ نَّفْسٍ وَّاحِدَةٍ ثُمَّ جَعَلَ مِنْهَا زَوْجَهَا
وَاَنْزَلَ لَكُمْ مِّنَ الْاَنْعَامِ ثَمٰنِيَةَ اَزْوَاجٍ ۭ يَخْلُقُكُمْ
فِيْ بُطُوْنِ اُمَّهٰتِكُمْ خَلْقًا مِّنْ بَعْدِ خَلْقٍ فِيْ
ظُلُمٰتٍ ثَلٰثٍ ۭ ذٰلِكُمُ اللّٰهُ رَبُّكُمْ لَهُ الْمُلْكُ ۭ لَآ اِلٰهَ

but He. Whither then are you being turned away?

8. If you are ungrateful, surely Allah is Self-Sufficient *being independent* of you. And He is not pleased with ingratitude in His servants. But if you show gratefulness, He likes it in you. And no bearer of burden shall bear the burden of another. Then to your Lord is your return; and He will inform you of what you have been doing. Surely, He knows full well all that is hidden in the breasts.

9. And when an affliction befalls a man, he calls upon his Lord, turning *penitently* to Him. Then, when He confers upon him a favour from Himself, he forgets what he used to pray for before, and begins to assign rivals to Allah, that he may lead *men* astray from His way. Say, 'Benefit thyself with thy disbelief a little while; thou art surely of the inmates of the Fire.'

* 10. Is he who prays devoutly *to God* in the hours of the night, prostrating himself and standing, *and* fears the Hereafter and hopes for the mercy of his Lord, *like him who does not do so?* Say, 'Are those who know equal to those who know not?' Verily, only those endowed with understanding will take heed.

R. 2.

11. Say, 'O ye My servants who believe, fear your Lord. There is good for those who do good in this life. And Allah's earth is spacious Verily the steadfast will have their reward without measure.'

12. Say, 'Verily I am commanded to worship Allah, being sincere to Him in religion.

13. 'And I am commanded to be the first of those who submit *to Him*.'

14. Say, 'Indeed I fear, if I disobey my Lord, the punishment of the great day.'

15. Say, 'It is Allah I worship, being sincere to Him in my religion.

إِلَّا هُوَ ۚ فَأَنّٰى تُصْرَفُونَ ⑦
إِنْ تَكْفُرُوا فَإِنَّ اللّٰهَ غَنِيٌّ عَنْكُمْ ۟ وَلَا يَرْضٰى لِعِبَادِهِ
الْكُفْرَ ۚ وَإِنْ تَشْكُرُوا يَرْضَهُ لَكُمْ ۗ وَلَا تَزِرُ وَازِرَةٌ
وِزْرَ أُخْرٰى ۗ ثُمَّ إِلٰى رَبِّكُمْ مَّرْجِعُكُمْ فَيُنَبِّئُكُمْ
بِمَا كُنْتُمْ تَعْمَلُونَ ۗ إِنَّهُ عَلِيمٌ بِذَاتِ الصُّدُورِ ⑧
وَإِذَا مَسَّ الْإِنْسَانَ ضُرٌّ دَعَا رَبَّهُ مُنِيبًا إِلَيْهِ
ثُمَّ إِذَا خَوَّلَهُ نِعْمَةً مِّنْهُ نَسِيَ مَا كَانَ يَدْعُوا
إِلَيْهِ مِنْ قَبْلُ وَجَعَلَ لِلّٰهِ أَنْدَادًا لِّيُضِلَّ عَنْ
سَبِيلِهِ ۗ قُلْ تَمَتَّعْ بِكُفْرِكَ قَلِيلًا ۖ إِنَّكَ مِنْ أَصْحٰبِ
النَّارِ ⑨
أَمَّنْ هُوَ قَانِتٌ آنَاءَ اللَّيْلِ سَاجِدًا وَّقَائِمًا يَّحْذَرُ
الْآخِرَةَ وَيَرْجُوا رَحْمَةَ رَبِّهِ ۗ قُلْ هَلْ يَسْتَوِي
الَّذِينَ يَعْلَمُونَ وَالَّذِينَ لَا يَعْلَمُونَ ۗ إِنَّمَا يَتَذَكَّرُ
أُولُوا الْأَلْبَابِ ⑩ ع
قُلْ يٰعِبَادِ الَّذِينَ آمَنُوا اتَّقُوا رَبَّكُمْ ۗ لِلَّذِينَ أَحْسَنُوا
فِي هٰذِهِ الدُّنْيَا حَسَنَةٌ ۗ وَأَرْضُ اللّٰهِ وَاسِعَةٌ ۗ
إِنَّمَا يُوَفَّى الصّٰبِرُونَ أَجْرَهُمْ بِغَيْرِ حِسَابٍ ⑪
قُلْ إِنِّي أُمِرْتُ أَنْ أَعْبُدَ اللّٰهَ مُخْلِصًا لَّهُ الدِّينَ ⑫
وَأُمِرْتُ لِأَنْ أَكُونَ أَوَّلَ الْمُسْلِمِينَ ⑬
قُلْ إِنِّي أَخَافُ إِنْ عَصَيْتُ رَبِّي عَذَابَ يَوْمٍ
عَظِيمٍ ⑭
قُلِ اللّٰهَ أَعْبُدُ مُخْلِصًا لَّهُ دِينِي ⑮

16. 'So worship what you like beside Him.' Say, 'Surely the losers will be those who ruin their souls and *ruin* their families on the Day of Resurrection.' Beware! that will surely be the manifest loss.

فَاعْبُدُوْا مَا شِئْتُمْ مِّنْ دُوْنِهٖ ۗ قُلْ اِنَّ الْخٰسِرِيْنَ
الَّذِيْنَ خَسِرُوْٓا اَنْفُسَهُمْ وَاَهْلِيْهِمْ يَوْمَ الْقِيٰمَةِ ۗ
اَلَا ذٰلِكَ هُوَ الْخُسْرَانُ الْمُبِيْنُ ﴿١٦﴾

* 17. They will have over them coverings of fire, and beneath them *similar* coverings. It is this against which Allah warns His servants. 'O My servants, take Me, then, for your Protector.'

لَهُمْ مِّنْ فَوْقِهِمْ ظُلَلٌ مِّنَ النَّارِ وَمِنْ تَحْتِهِمْ
ظُلَلٌ ۗ ذٰلِكَ يُخَوِّفُ اللّٰهُ بِهٖ عِبَادَهٗ ۗ يٰعِبَادِ فَاتَّقُوْنِ ﴿١٧﴾

18. And those who shun false gods lest they worship them and turn to Allah—for them is glad tidings. So give glad tidings to My servants,

وَالَّذِيْنَ اجْتَنَبُوا الطَّاغُوْتَ اَنْ يَّعْبُدُوْهَا وَاَنَابُوْٓا
اِلَى اللّٰهِ لَهُمُ الْبُشْرٰى ۚ فَبَشِّرْ عِبَادِ ﴿١٨﴾

19. Who listen to the Word and follow the best thereof. It is they whom Allah has guided, and it is they who are men of understanding.

الَّذِيْنَ يَسْتَمِعُوْنَ الْقَوْلَ فَيَتَّبِعُوْنَ اَحْسَنَهٗ ۗ اُولٰٓئِكَ
الَّذِيْنَ هَدٰىهُمُ اللّٰهُ وَاُولٰٓئِكَ هُمْ اُولُوا الْاَلْبَابِ ﴿١٩﴾

20. Is he, then, against whom the sentence of punishment has become due *fit to be rescued?* Canst thou rescue him who is in the Fire?

اَفَمَنْ حَقَّ عَلَيْهِ كَلِمَةُ الْعَذَابِ ۗ اَفَاَنْتَ تُنْقِذُ
مَنْ فِى النَّارِ ﴿٢٠﴾

21. But for them who fear their Lord there are lofty mansions built over lofty mansions, beneath which rivers flow. Allah has made that promise; *and* Allah breaks not *His* promise.

لٰكِنِ الَّذِيْنَ اتَّقَوْا رَبَّهُمْ لَهُمْ غُرَفٌ مِّنْ فَوْقِهَا
غُرَفٌ مَّبْنِيَّةٌ ۙ تَجْرِىْ مِنْ تَحْتِهَا الْاَنْهٰرُ ۗ وَعْدَ
اللّٰهِ ۗ لَا يُخْلِفُ اللّٰهُ الْمِيْعَادَ ﴿٢١﴾

22. Hast thou not seen that Allah sends down water from the sky, and causes it to flow in *the form of* streamlets in the earth and then brings forth thereby herbage, varying in its colours? Then it dries up and thou seest it turn yellow; then He reduces it to broken straw. In that verily is a reminder for men of understanding.

اَلَمْ تَرَ اَنَّ اللّٰهَ اَنْزَلَ مِنَ السَّمَآءِ مَآءً فَسَلَكَهٗ
يَنَابِيْعَ فِى الْاَرْضِ ثُمَّ يُخْرِجُ بِهٖ زَرْعًا مُّخْتَلِفًا
اَلْوَانُهٗ ثُمَّ يَهِيْجُ فَتَرٰىهُ مُصْفَرًّا ثُمَّ يَجْعَلُهٗ
حُطَامًا ۗ اِنَّ فِىْ ذٰلِكَ لَذِكْرٰى لِاُولِى الْاَلْبَابِ ﴿٢٢﴾ ع

R. 3.

23. Is he then whose bosom Allah has opened for *the acceptance of* Islam, so that he possesses a light from his Lord, *like him who is groping in the darkness of disbelief?* Woe, then, to those whose hearts are hardened against the remembrance of Allah! They are in manifest error.

اَفَمَنْ شَرَحَ اللّٰهُ صَدْرَهٗ لِلْاِسْلَامِ فَهُوَ عَلٰى نُوْرٍ
مِّنْ رَّبِّهٖ ۗ فَوَيْلٌ لِّلْقٰسِيَةِ قُلُوْبُهُمْ مِّنْ ذِكْرِ اللّٰهِ ۗ
اُولٰٓئِكَ فِىْ ضَلٰلٍ مُّبِيْنٍ ﴿٢٣﴾

24. Allah has sent down the best Message *in the form of* a Book, *whose verses are*

اَللّٰهُ نَزَّلَ اَحْسَنَ الْحَدِيْثِ كِتٰبًا مُّتَشَابِهًا مَّثَانِىَ

mutually supporting *and* repeated *in diverse forms* at which do creep the skins of those who fear their Lord; then their skins and their hearts soften to the remembrance of Allah. Such is the guidance of Allah; He guides therewith whom He pleases. And he whom Allah adjudges astray—he shall have no guide.

تَقْشَعِرُّ مِنْهُ جُلُوْدُ الَّذِيْنَ يَخْشَوْنَ رَبَّهُمْ ۚ ثُمَّ تَلِيْنُ
جُلُوْدُهُمْ وَقُلُوْبُهُمْ اِلٰى ذِكْرِ اللّٰهِ ۭ ذٰلِكَ هُدَى
اللّٰهِ يَهْدِيْ بِهٖ مَنْ يَّشَآءُ ۭ وَمَنْ يُّضْلِلِ اللّٰهُ
فَمَا لَهٗ مِنْ هَادٍ ﴿٢٤﴾

25. Is he, then, who has nothing but his own face to protect him with from the evil punishment on the Day of Resurrection *like him who is secure?* And it will be said to the wrongdoers, 'Taste ye what you used to earn.'

اَفَمَنْ يَّتَّقِيْ بِوَجْهِهٖ سُوْٓءَ الْعَذَابِ يَوْمَ الْقِيٰمَةِ ۭ
وَقِيْلَ لِلظّٰلِمِيْنَ ذُوْقُوْا مَا كُنْتُمْ تَكْسِبُوْنَ ﴿٢٥﴾

26. Those who were before them rejected *Our Messengers*, so the punishment came upon them whence they knew not.

كَذَّبَ الَّذِيْنَ مِنْ قَبْلِهِمْ فَاَتٰىهُمُ الْعَذَابُ
مِنْ حَيْثُ لَا يَشْعُرُوْنَ ﴿٢٦﴾

27. So Allah made them taste humiliation in the present life and the punishment of the Hereafter will certainly be greater, if they but knew!

فَاَذَاقَهُمُ اللّٰهُ الْخِزْيَ فِي الْحَيٰوةِ الدُّنْيَا ۚ وَ
لَعَذَابُ الْاٰخِرَةِ اَكْبَرُ ۘ لَوْ كَانُوْا يَعْلَمُوْنَ ﴿٢٧﴾ وقف لازم

28. And, indeed, We have set forth to men all kinds of parables in this Qur'ān that they may take heed.

وَلَقَدْ ضَرَبْنَا لِلنَّاسِ فِيْ هٰذَا الْقُرْاٰنِ مِنْ
كُلِّ مَثَلٍ لَّعَلَّهُمْ يَتَذَكَّرُوْنَ ﴿٢٨﴾ ۚ

* 29. *We have revealed* the Qur'ān in Arabic wherein there is no deviation from rectitude, that they may become righteous.

قُرْاٰنًا عَرَبِيًّا غَيْرَ ذِيْ عِوَجٍ لَّعَلَّهُمْ يَتَّقُوْنَ ﴿٢٩﴾

* 30. Allah sets forth a parable: a man belonging to several partners, disagreeing with one another, and a man belonging wholly to one man. Are they both equal in condition? All praise belongs to Allah. But most of them know not.

ضَرَبَ اللّٰهُ مَثَلًا رَّجُلًا فِيْهِ شُرَكَآءُ مُتَشٰكِسُوْنَ
وَرَجُلًا سَلَمًا لِّرَجُلٍ ۭ هَلْ يَسْتَوِيٰنِ مَثَلًا ۭ اَلْحَمْدُ
لِلّٰهِ ۚ بَلْ اَكْثَرُهُمْ لَا يَعْلَمُوْنَ ﴿٣٠﴾

31. Surely thou wilt die, and surely they *too* will die.

اِنَّكَ مَيِّتٌ وَّاِنَّهُمْ مَّيِّتُوْنَ ﴿٣١﴾

32. Then surely on the Day of Resurrection you will dispute with one another before your Lord.

ثُمَّ اِنَّكُمْ يَوْمَ الْقِيٰمَةِ عِنْدَ رَبِّكُمْ تَخْتَصِمُوْنَ ﴿٣٢﴾ الجزء ٢٤

R. 4.

33. Who, then, is more unjust than he who lies against Allah or he who rejects the truth when it comes to him? Is there not in Hell an abode for the disbelievers?

فَمَنْ اَظْلَمُ مِمَّنْ كَذَبَ عَلَى اللّٰهِ وَكَذَّبَ
بِالصِّدْقِ اِذْ جَآءَهٗ ۭ اَلَيْسَ فِيْ جَهَنَّمَ مَثْوًى
لِّلْكٰفِرِيْنَ ﴿٣٣﴾

34. But he who has brought the truth, and *he who* testifies to it *as such*—these it is

وَالَّذِيْ جَآءَ بِالصِّدْقِ وَصَدَّقَ بِهٖٓ اُولٰٓئِكَ هُمُ

who are the righteous.

الْمُتَّقُوْنَ ﴿٣٤﴾

35. They will have with their Lord whatever they desire; that is the reward of those who do good.

لَهُمْ مَّا يَشَآءُوْنَ عِنْدَ رَبِّهِمْ ؕ ذٰلِكَ جَزٰٓؤُا
الْمُحْسِنِيْنَ ﴿٣٥﴾ ۚۖ

36. So that Allah will remove from them the evil *consequences* of what they did, and will give them their reward according to the best of their actions.

لِيُكَفِّرَ اللّٰهُ عَنْهُمْ اَسْوَاَ الَّذِيْ عَمِلُوْا وَيَجْزِيَهُمْ
اَجْرَهُمْ بِاَحْسَنِ الَّذِيْ كَانُوْا يَعْمَلُوْنَ ﴿٣٦﴾

37. Is not Allah sufficient for His servant? And yet they would frighten thee with those beside Him. And he whom Allah adjudges astray—for him there is no guide.

اَلَيْسَ اللّٰهُ بِكَافٍ عَبْدَهٗ ؕ وَيُخَوِّفُوْنَكَ بِالَّذِيْنَ
مِنْ دُوْنِهٖ ؕ وَمَنْ يُّضْلِلِ اللّٰهُ فَمَا لَهٗ مِنْ هَادٍ ﴿٣٧﴾ ۚ

38. And he whom Allah guides—there is none to lead him astray. Is not Allah the Mighty, the Lord of retribution?

وَمَنْ يَّهْدِ اللّٰهُ فَمَا لَهٗ مِنْ مُّضِلٍّ ؕ اَلَيْسَ
اللّٰهُ بِعَزِيْزٍ ذِي انْتِقَامٍ ﴿٣٨﴾

39. And if thou ask them, 'Who created the heavens and the earth?' they will surely say, 'Allah'. Say, 'What think ye, if Allah intends to do me an injury, will those whom you call upon beside Allah be able to remove the injury inflicted by Him? Or if He wills to show me mercy, could they withhold His mercy?' Say, 'Allah is sufficient for me. In Him trust those who would trust.'

وَلَئِنْ سَاَلْتَهُمْ مَّنْ خَلَقَ السَّمٰوٰتِ وَالْاَرْضَ
لَيَقُوْلُنَّ اللّٰهُ ؕ قُلْ اَفَرَءَيْتُمْ مَّا تَدْعُوْنَ مِنْ دُوْنِ
اللّٰهِ اِنْ اَرَادَنِيَ اللّٰهُ بِضُرٍّ هَلْ هُنَّ كٰشِفٰتُ
ضُرِّهٖٓ اَوْ اَرَادَنِيْ بِرَحْمَةٍ هَلْ هُنَّ مُمْسِكٰتُ رَحْمَتِهٖ ؕ
قُلْ حَسْبِيَ اللّٰهُ ؕ عَلَيْهِ يَتَوَكَّلُ الْمُتَوَكِّلُوْنَ ﴿٣٩﴾

40. Say, 'O my people, act as *best* you can; I *too* am acting; soon shall you know,

قُلْ يٰقَوْمِ اعْمَلُوْا عَلٰى مَكَانَتِكُمْ اِنِّيْ عَامِلٌ ۚ فَسَوْفَ
تَعْلَمُوْنَ ﴿٤٠﴾ لا

41. 'Who it is unto whom comes a punishment that will disgrace him, and on whom there descends an abiding punishment.'

مَنْ يَّاْتِيْهِ عَذَابٌ يُّخْزِيْهِ وَيَحِلُّ عَلَيْهِ عَذَابٌ
مُّقِيْمٌ ﴿٤١﴾

42. Verily, We have revealed to thee the Book with truth for *the good of* mankind. So whoever follows guidance, *follows it* for the benefit of his own soul; and whoever goes astray, goes astray only to its detriment. And thou art not a guardian over them.

اِنَّآ اَنْزَلْنَا عَلَيْكَ الْكِتٰبَ لِلنَّاسِ بِالْحَقِّ ۚ فَمَنِ
اهْتَدٰى فَلِنَفْسِهٖ ۚ وَمَنْ ضَلَّ فَاِنَّمَا يَضِلُّ عَلَيْهَا ۚ
وَمَآ اَنْتَ عَلَيْهِمْ بِوَكِيْلٍ ﴿٤٢﴾ ع

R. 5.

* 43. Allah takes away the souls of human beings at the time of their death; and

اَللّٰهُ يَتَوَفَّى الْاَنْفُسَ حِيْنَ مَوْتِهَا وَالَّتِيْ لَمْ تَمُتْ

during their sleep of those *also* that are not *yet* dead. And then He retains those against which He has decreed death, and sends *back* the others till an appointed term. In that surely are Signs for a people who reflect.

فِي مَنَامِهَا ۚ فَيُمْسِكُ الَّتِي قَضَىٰ عَلَيْهَا الْمَوْتَ
وَيُرْسِلُ الْأُخْرَىٰ إِلَىٰ أَجَلٍ مُسَمًّى ۚ إِنَّ فِي ذَٰلِكَ
لَآيَاتٍ لِقَوْمٍ يَتَفَكَّرُونَ ﴿٤٣﴾

44. Have they taken intercessors beside Allah? Say, 'Even if they have no power over anything and no intelligence?'

أَمِ اتَّخَذُوا مِنْ دُونِ اللَّهِ شُفَعَاءَ ۚ قُلْ أَوَلَوْ كَانُوا
لَا يَمْلِكُونَ شَيْئًا وَلَا يَعْقِلُونَ ﴿٤٤﴾

45. Say, 'All intercession rests with Allah. To Him belongs the kingdom of the heavens and the earth. And to Him then shall you be brought back.'

قُلْ لِلَّهِ الشَّفَاعَةُ جَمِيعًا ۖ لَهُ مُلْكُ السَّمَاوَاتِ وَ
الْأَرْضِ ۖ ثُمَّ إِلَيْهِ تُرْجَعُونَ ﴿٤٥﴾

* 46. And when Allah alone is mentioned the hearts of those who believe not in the Hereafter shrink with aversion; but when those beside Him are mentioned, behold, they begin to rejoice.

وَإِذَا ذُكِرَ اللَّهُ وَحْدَهُ اشْمَأَزَّتْ قُلُوبُ الَّذِينَ
لَا يُؤْمِنُونَ بِالْآخِرَةِ ۖ وَإِذَا ذُكِرَ الَّذِينَ مِنْ دُونِهِ
إِذَا هُمْ يَسْتَبْشِرُونَ ﴿٤٦﴾

47. Say, 'O Allah! Originator of the heavens and the earth; Knower of the unseen and the seen; Thou *alone* wilt judge between Thy servants concerning that in which they differed.'

قُلِ اللَّهُمَّ فَاطِرَ السَّمَاوَاتِ وَالْأَرْضِ عَالِمَ الْغَيْبِ
وَالشَّهَادَةِ أَنْتَ تَحْكُمُ بَيْنَ عِبَادِكَ فِي مَا كَانُوا
فِيهِ يَخْتَلِفُونَ ﴿٤٧﴾

48. And even if the wrongdoers possessed all that is in the earth, and the like thereof in addition to it, they would surely *seek to* ransom themselves with it from the evil punishment on the Day of Resurrection; but there shall appear unto them, from Allah, that which they never thought of.

وَلَوْ أَنَّ لِلَّذِينَ ظَلَمُوا مَا فِي الْأَرْضِ جَمِيعًا وَمِثْلَهُ
مَعَهُ لَافْتَدَوْا بِهِ مِنْ سُوءِ الْعَذَابِ يَوْمَ الْقِيَامَةِ ۚ
وَبَدَا لَهُمْ مِنَ اللَّهِ مَا لَمْ يَكُونُوا يَحْتَسِبُونَ ﴿٤٨﴾

49. And the evil *consequences* of what they had earned will become apparent to them and that which they used to mock at will encompass them.

وَبَدَا لَهُمْ سَيِّئَاتُ مَا كَسَبُوا وَحَاقَ بِهِمْ مَا
كَانُوا بِهِ يَسْتَهْزِئُونَ ﴿٤٩﴾

50. And when trouble touches man, he cries unto Us. But when We bestow on him a favour from Us, he says, 'This has been given to me on account of *my own* knowledge.' Nay, it is only a trial; but most of them know not.

فَإِذَا مَسَّ الْإِنْسَانَ ضُرٌّ دَعَانَا ثُمَّ إِذَا خَوَّلْنَاهُ
نِعْمَةً مِنَّا قَالَ إِنَّمَا أُوتِيتُهُ عَلَىٰ عِلْمٍ ۚ بَلْ
هِيَ فِتْنَةٌ وَلَٰكِنَّ أَكْثَرَهُمْ لَا يَعْلَمُونَ ﴿٥٠﴾

51. Those who were before them said the same thing, yet all that they had

قَدْ قَالَهَا الَّذِينَ مِنْ قَبْلِهِمْ فَمَا أَغْنَىٰ عَنْهُمْ مَا

earned availed them not;

52. So the evil *consequences* of what they had earned overtook them; and those who do wrong from among these *disbelievers*—the evil *consequences* of what they earned shall also overtake them. They cannot escape.

53. Know they not that Allah enlarges the provision for whomsoever He pleases, and straitens *it for whomsoever He pleases?* Verily, in that are Signs for a people who believe.

R. 6.

54. Say, "O My servants who have committed excesses against their own souls! despair not of the mercy of Allah, surely Allah forgives all sins. Verily He is Most Forgiving, Merciful.

55. "And turn ye to your Lord, and submit yourselves to Him, before there comes unto you the punishment; *for* then you shall not be helped.

56. "And follow the best *teaching* that has been revealed to you from your Lord, before the punishment comes upon you unawares, while you perceive not;

* 57. "Lest a soul should say, 'O my grief for my remissness *in my duty* in respect of Allah! and surely I was among those who scoffed;'

58. "Or lest it should say, 'If Allah had guided me, I should certainly have been among the righteous;'

59. "Or lest it should say, when it sees the punishment, 'Would that there were for me a return *to the world*, I would then be among those who do good!'"

60. *God will answer*, 'Aye, there came to thee My Signs, but thou didst treat them as lies, and thou wast arrogant, and thou wast of the disbelievers.'

61. And on the Day of Resurrection, thou wilt see those who lied against Allah with their faces blackened. Is there not in Hell an abode for the proud?

* 62. And Allah will deliver the righteous *and lead them* to a place of security and

كانوا يكسبون ﴿٥١﴾
فأصابهم سيئات ما كسبوا والذين ظلموا من
هؤلاء سيصيبهم سيئات ما كسبوا وما هم بمعجزين ﴿٥٢﴾
أولم يعلموا أن الله يبسط الرزق لمن يشاء ويقدر
إن في ذلك لآيات لقوم يؤمنون ﴿٥٣﴾ ع
قل يعبادي الذين أسرفوا على أنفسهم لا تقنطوا
من رحمة الله إن الله يغفر الذنوب جميعا
إنه هو الغفور الرحيم ﴿٥٤﴾
وأنيبوا إلى ربكم وأسلموا له من قبل أن يأتيكم
العذاب ثم لا تنصرون ﴿٥٥﴾
واتبعوا أحسن ما أنزل إليكم من ربكم من
قبل أن يأتيكم العذاب بغتة وأنتم لا تشعرون ﴿٥٦﴾
أن تقول نفس يحسرتى على ما فرطت في جنب
الله وإن كنت لمن السخرين ﴿٥٧﴾
أو تقول لو أن الله هدىني لكنت من المتقين ﴿٥٨﴾
أو تقول حين ترى العذاب لو أن لي كرة فأكون
من المحسنين ﴿٥٩﴾
بلى قد جاءتك آيتي فكذبت بها واستكبرت
وكنت من الكفرين ﴿٦٠﴾
ويوم القيمة ترى الذين كذبوا على الله وجوههم
مسودة أليس في جهنم مثوى للمتكبرين ﴿٦١﴾
وينجي الله الذين اتقوا بمفازتهم لا يمسهم

success; evil shall not touch them, nor shall they grieve.

63. Allah is the Creator of all things, and He is Guardian over all things.

64. To Him belong the keys of the heavens and the earth; and as for those who disbelieve in the Signs of Allah, these it is who are the losers.

R. 7.

65. Say, 'Is it other *gods* than Allah that you bid me worship, O ye ignorant ones?'

66. And verily it has been revealed to thee as unto those before thee: 'If thou attribute partners *to God*, thy work shall surely go vain and thou shalt certainly be of the losers.'

67. Aye, worship Allah and be among the thankful.

* 68. And they do not esteem Allah, with the esteem that is due to Him. And the whole earth will be *but* His handful on the Day of Resurrection, and the heavens will be rolled up in His right hand. Glory to Him and exalted is He above that which they associate *with Him*.

69. And the trumpet will be blown, and *all* who are in the heavens and *all* who are in the earth will *fall down in a* swoon, except those whom Allah will please *to exempt*. Then will it be blown a second time, and lo! they will be standing, awaiting.

70. And the earth will shine with the light of her Lord, and the Book will be laid *open before them*, and the Prophets and the witnesses will be brought, and judgment will be given between them with justice, and they will not be wronged.

71. And every soul will be fully rewarded for what it did. And He knows full well what they do.

R. 8.

72. And those who disbelieve will be driven to Hell in troops until, when they reach it, its gates will be opened, and its Keepers will say to them: 'Did not Messengers from among yourselves come to you, reciting unto you the Signs of your Lord, and warning you of the meeting of this Day of yours?' They will say, 'Yea, but the sentence of punishment has become

السُّوْٓءُ وَلَا هُمْ يَحْزَنُوْنَ ﴿٦٢﴾
اَللّٰهُ خَالِقُ كُلِّ شَيْءٍ وَّ هُوَ عَلٰى كُلِّ شَيْءٍ وَّكِيْلٌ ﴿٦٣﴾
لَهٗ مَقَالِيْدُ السَّمٰوٰتِ وَالْاَرْضِ وَالَّذِيْنَ كَفَرُوْا
بِاٰيٰتِ اللّٰهِ اُولٰٓئِكَ هُمُ الْخٰسِرُوْنَ ﴿٦٤﴾ ع
قُلْ اَفَغَيْرَ اللّٰهِ تَاْمُرُوْٓنِّيْٓ اَعْبُدُ اَيُّهَا الْجٰهِلُوْنَ ﴿٦٥﴾
وَلَقَدْ اُوْحِيَ اِلَيْكَ وَاِلَى الَّذِيْنَ مِنْ قَبْلِكَ لَئِنْ
اَشْرَكْتَ لَيَحْبَطَنَّ عَمَلُكَ وَلَتَكُوْنَنَّ مِنَ الْخٰسِرِيْنَ ﴿٦٦﴾
بَلِ اللّٰهَ فَاعْبُدْ وَكُنْ مِّنَ الشّٰكِرِيْنَ ﴿٦٧﴾
وَمَا قَدَرُوا اللّٰهَ حَقَّ قَدْرِهٖ وَالْاَرْضُ جَمِيْعًا
قَبْضَتُهٗ يَوْمَ الْقِيٰمَةِ وَالسَّمٰوٰتُ مَطْوِيّٰتٌۢ بِيَمِيْنِهٖ
سُبْحٰنَهٗ وَتَعٰلٰى عَمَّا يُشْرِكُوْنَ ﴿٦٨﴾
وَنُفِخَ فِي الصُّوْرِ فَصَعِقَ مَنْ فِي السَّمٰوٰتِ وَمَنْ
فِي الْاَرْضِ اِلَّا مَنْ شَآءَ اللّٰهُ ثُمَّ نُفِخَ فِيْهِ اُخْرٰى
فَاِذَا هُمْ قِيَامٌ يَّنْظُرُوْنَ ﴿٦٩﴾
وَاَشْرَقَتِ الْاَرْضُ بِنُوْرِ رَبِّهَا وَوُضِعَ الْكِتٰبُ وَ
جِايْٓءَ بِالنَّبِيّٖنَ وَالشُّهَدَآءِ وَقُضِيَ بَيْنَهُمْ بِالْحَقِّ وَهُمْ لَا
يُظْلَمُوْنَ ﴿٧٠﴾
وَوُفِّيَتْ كُلُّ نَفْسٍ مَّا عَمِلَتْ وَهُوَ اَعْلَمُ بِمَا يَفْعَلُوْنَ ﴿٧١﴾ ع
وَسِيْقَ الَّذِيْنَ كَفَرُوْٓا اِلٰى جَهَنَّمَ زُمَرًا حَتّٰٓى اِذَا
جَآءُوْهَا فُتِحَتْ اَبْوَابُهَا وَقَالَ لَهُمْ خَزَنَتُهَآ اَلَمْ
يَاْتِكُمْ رُسُلٌ مِّنْكُمْ يَتْلُوْنَ عَلَيْكُمْ اٰيٰتِ رَبِّكُمْ
وَيُنْذِرُوْنَكُمْ لِقَآءَ يَوْمِكُمْ هٰذَا قَالُوْا بَلٰى وَلٰكِنْ

justly due against the disbelievers.'

حَقَّتْ كَلِمَةُ الْعَذَابِ عَلَى الْكٰفِرِيْنَ ﴿٧٢﴾

73. It will be said, 'Enter ye the gates of Hell, abiding therein. And evil is the abode of the arrogant.'

قِيْلَ ادْخُلُوْٓا اَبْوَابَ جَهَنَّمَ خٰلِدِيْنَ فِيْهَا ۚ فَبِئْسَ
مَثْوَى الْمُتَكَبِّرِيْنَ ﴿٧٣﴾

74. And those who feared their Lord will be conducted to Heaven in groups until, when they reach it, and its gates are opened, and its Keepers say to them, 'Peace be upon you! be ye happy, and enter it abiding *therein;*'

وَسِيْقَ الَّذِيْنَ اتَّقَوْا رَبَّهُمْ اِلَى الْجَنَّةِ زُمَرًا ۭ
حَتّٰٓى اِذَا جَآءُوْهَا وَفُتِحَتْ اَبْوَابُهَا وَقَالَ لَهُمْ
خَزَنَتُهَا سَلٰمٌ عَلَيْكُمْ طِبْتُمْ فَادْخُلُوْهَا خٰلِدِيْنَ ﴿٧٤﴾

75. And they will say, 'All praise belongs to Allah Who has fulfilled His promise to us, and has given us the land for an inheritance, making our abode in the Garden wherever we please.' How excellent then is the reward of the *righteous* workers!

وَقَالُوا الْحَمْدُ لِلّٰهِ الَّذِيْ صَدَقَنَا وَعْدَهٗ وَاَوْرَثَنَا
الْاَرْضَ نَتَبَوَّاُ مِنَ الْجَنَّةِ حَيْثُ نَشَآءُ ۚ فَنِعْمَ
اَجْرُ الْعٰمِلِيْنَ ﴿٧٥﴾

76. And thou wilt see the angels going round the Throne, glorifying their Lord with *His* praise. And it will be judged between them with justice. And it will be said: 'All praise belongs to Allah, the Lord of the worlds.'

وَتَرَى الْمَلٰٓئِكَةَ حَآفِّيْنَ مِنْ حَوْلِ الْعَرْشِ يُسَبِّحُوْنَ
بِحَمْدِ رَبِّهِمْ ۚ وَقُضِيَ بَيْنَهُمْ بِالْحَقِّ وَقِيْلَ
الْحَمْدُ لِلّٰهِ رَبِّ الْعٰلَمِيْنَ ﴿٧٦﴾

سُورَةُ الْمُؤْمِنِ مَكِّيَّةٌ

آياتها ٨٦ (٤٠) ركوعاتها ٩

AL-MU'MIN

(Revealed before Hijra)

1. In the name of Allah, the Gracious, the Merciful.

بِسْمِ اللّٰهِ الرَّحْمٰنِ الرَّحِيْمِ ①

2. Ḥā Mīm*.

حٰمٓ ②

3. The revelation of the Book is from Allah, the Mighty, the All-Knowing,

تَنْزِيْلُ الْكِتٰبِ مِنَ اللّٰهِ الْعَزِيْزِ الْعَلِيْمِ ③

4. The Forgiver of sin and the Acceptor of repentance, Severe in punishment, the Possessor of bounty. There is no God but He. Towards Him is the final return.

غَافِرِ الذَّنْبِ وَ قَابِلِ التَّوْبِ شَدِيْدِ الْعِقَابِ ۙ
ذِى الطَّوْلِ ۭ لَآ اِلٰهَ اِلَّا هُوَ ۭ اِلَيْهِ الْمَصِيْرُ ④

5. None disputes about the Signs of Allah except those who disbelieve. Let not, then, their going about in the land deceive thee.

مَا يُجَادِلُ فِيْٓ اٰيٰتِ اللّٰهِ اِلَّا الَّذِيْنَ كَفَرُوْا فَلَا يَغْرُرْكَ
تَقَلُّبُهُمْ فِى الْبِلَادِ ⑤

6. The people of Noah and *other* groups after them denied *Our Signs* before these *people*, and every nation strove to seize their Messenger, and disputed by means of false *arguments* that they might rebut the truth thereby. Then I seized them, and how *terrible* was My retribution!

كَذَّبَتْ قَبْلَهُمْ قَوْمُ نُوْحٍ وَّ الْاَحْزَابُ مِنْۢ بَعْدِهِمْ ۠
وَهَمَّتْ كُلُّ اُمَّةٍۢ بِرَسُوْلِهِمْ لِيَاْخُذُوْهُ وَجٰدَلُوْا
بِالْبَاطِلِ لِيُدْحِضُوْا بِهِ الْحَقَّ فَاَخَذْتُهُمْ ۣ فَكَيْفَ
كَانَ عِقَابِ ⑥

7. Thus was the word of thy Lord proved true against the disbelievers: that they are the inmates of the Fire.

وَكَذٰلِكَ حَقَّتْ كَلِمَتُ رَبِّكَ عَلَى الَّذِيْنَ كَفَرُوْٓا
اَنَّهُمْ اَصْحٰبُ النَّارِ ⑦ ۘ

وقف لازم
وقف النبي
صلى الله عليه وسلم

8. Those who bear the Throne, and those who are around it, glorify their Lord with *His* praise, and believe in Him, and ask forgiveness for those who believe, *saying:* 'Our Lord, Thou dost comprehend all things in *Thy* mercy and knowledge. So forgive those who repent and follow Thy way; and protect them from the punishment of Hell.

اَلَّذِيْنَ يَحْمِلُوْنَ الْعَرْشَ وَمَنْ حَوْلَهٗ يُسَبِّحُوْنَ بِحَمْدِ
رَبِّهِمْ وَيُؤْمِنُوْنَ بِهٖ وَيَسْتَغْفِرُوْنَ لِلَّذِيْنَ
اٰمَنُوْا ۚ رَبَّنَا وَسِعْتَ كُلَّ شَيْءٍ رَّحْمَةً وَّعِلْمًا
فَاغْفِرْ لِلَّذِيْنَ تَابُوْا وَاتَّبَعُوْا سَبِيْلَكَ وَقِهِمْ
عَذَابَ الْجَحِيْمِ ⑧

9. 'And make them, our Lord, enter the Gardens of Eternity which Thou hast

رَبَّنَا وَاَدْخِلْهُمْ جَنّٰتِ عَدْنِ ۣ الَّتِيْ وَعَدْتَّهُمْ

* The Praiseworthy, the Lord of Honour.

promised them, as well as such of their fathers and their wives and their children as are virtuous. Surely Thou art the Mighty, the Wise.

وَمَنْ صَلَحَ مِنْ آبَائِهِمْ وَأَزْوَاجِهِمْ وَذُرِّيَّاتِهِمْ
إِنَّكَ أَنْتَ الْعَزِيزُ الْحَكِيمُ ⑨

10. 'And protect them from evils; and he whom Thou dost protect from evils on that day—him hast Thou surely shown mercy. And that *indeed* is the supreme triumph.'

وَقِهِمُ السَّيِّئَاتِ ۚ وَمَنْ تَقِ السَّيِّئَاتِ يَوْمَئِذٍ
فَقَدْ رَحِمْتَهُ ۚ وَذَٰلِكَ هُوَ الْفَوْزُ الْعَظِيمُ ⑩ ع

R. 2.

* 11. An announcement will be made to those who disbelieve *in the words:* 'Greater was the abhorrence of Allah when you were called to the faith and you disbelieved than your *own* abhorrence of yourselves *today*.'

إِنَّ الَّذِينَ كَفَرُوا يُنَادَوْنَ لَمَقْتُ اللَّهِ أَكْبَرُ
مِنْ مَقْتِكُمْ أَنْفُسَكُمْ إِذْ تُدْعَوْنَ إِلَى الْإِيمَانِ
فَتَكْفُرُونَ ⑪

12. They will say, 'Our Lord, Thou hast caused us to die twice, and Thou hast given us life twice, and now we confess our sins. Is then there a way out?'

قَالُوا رَبَّنَا أَمَتَّنَا اثْنَتَيْنِ وَأَحْيَيْتَنَا اثْنَتَيْنِ
فَاعْتَرَفْنَا بِذُنُوبِنَا فَهَلْ إِلَىٰ خُرُوجٍ مِنْ
سَبِيلٍ ⑫

* 13. *It will be said to them*, 'This is because, when Allah was proclaimed as One, you disbelieved, but when partners were associated with Him, you believed. The decision *now* belongs only to Allah, the High, the Incomparably Great.'

ذَٰلِكُمْ بِأَنَّهُ إِذَا دُعِيَ اللَّهُ وَحْدَهُ كَفَرْتُمْ ۖ
وَإِنْ يُشْرَكْ بِهِ تُؤْمِنُوا ۚ فَالْحُكْمُ لِلَّهِ الْعَلِيِّ
الْكَبِيرِ ⑬

14. He it is Who shows you His Signs, and sends down provision for you from heaven; but none pays heed save he who turns *to God.*

هُوَ الَّذِي يُرِيكُمْ آيَاتِهِ وَيُنَزِّلُ لَكُمْ مِنَ
السَّمَاءِ رِزْقًا ۚ وَمَا يَتَذَكَّرُ إِلَّا مَنْ يُنِيبُ ⑭

* 15. Call ye then on Allah, being sincere to Him in religion, though the disbelievers may be averse.

فَادْعُوا اللَّهَ مُخْلِصِينَ لَهُ الدِّينَ وَلَوْ كَرِهَ
الْكَافِرُونَ ⑮

* 16. *He is* of most exalted attributes, Lord of the Throne. He sends the Word by His command to whomsoever of His servants He pleases, that He may give warning of the Day of Meeting,

رَفِيعُ الدَّرَجَاتِ ذُو الْعَرْشِ يُلْقِي الرُّوحَ مِنْ
أَمْرِهِ عَلَىٰ مَنْ يَشَاءُ مِنْ عِبَادِهِ لِيُنْذِرَ يَوْمَ
التَّلَاقِ ⑯

* 17. The day when they will *all* come forth; nothing concerning them will be hidden from Allah. 'Whose is the kingdom this day?' '*It is* Allah's, the One, the Most Supreme.

يَوْمَ هُمْ بَارِزُونَ ۚ لَا يَخْفَىٰ عَلَى اللَّهِ مِنْهُمْ
شَيْءٌ ۚ لِمَنِ الْمُلْكُ الْيَوْمَ ۖ لِلَّهِ الْوَاحِدِ الْقَهَّارِ ⑰

18. 'This day will every soul be requited for that which it has earned. No injustice this day. Surely, Allah is Swift at reckoning.'

اَلْيَوْمَ تُجْزٰى كُلُّ نَفْسٍۢ بِمَا كَسَبَتْ ۗ لَا ظُلْمَ
اَلْيَوْمَ ۗ اِنَّ اللّٰهَ سَرِيْعُ الْحِسَابِ ﴿۱۸﴾

19. And warn them of the Approaching Day, when the hearts will reach to the throats while they will be full of suppressed grief. The wrongdoers will have no loving friend, nor any intercessor whose *intercession* will be complied with.

وَاَنْذِرْهُمْ يَوْمَ الْاٰزِفَةِ اِذِ الْقُلُوْبُ لَدَى
الْحَنَاجِرِ كٰظِمِيْنَ ۬ؕ مَا لِلظّٰلِمِيْنَ مِنْ حَمِيْمٍ
وَّلَا شَفِيْعٍ يُّطَاعُ ﴿۱۹﴾

20. He knows the treachery of the eyes and what the breasts conceal.

يَعْلَمُ خَآئِنَةَ الْاَعْيُنِ وَمَا تُخْفِي الصُّدُوْرُ ﴿۲۰﴾

* 21. And Allah judges with truth, but those on whom they call beside Him cannot judge at all. Surely, Allah is the All-Hearing, the All-Seeing.

وَاللّٰهُ يَقْضِيْ بِالْحَقِّ ؕ وَالَّذِيْنَ يَدْعُوْنَ مِنْ
دُوْنِهٖ لَا يَقْضُوْنَ بِشَيْءٍ ؕ اِنَّ اللّٰهَ هُوَ السَّمِيْعُ
الْبَصِيْرُ ﴿۲۱﴾ ع

R. 3.

* 22. Have they not travelled in the earth and seen what was the end of those before them? They were mightier than these in power and *in* the marks *they left* in the earth. But Allah seized them for their sins, and they had no protector against Allah.

اَوَلَمْ يَسِيْرُوْا فِي الْاَرْضِ فَيَنْظُرُوْا كَيْفَ
كَانَ عَاقِبَةُ الَّذِيْنَ كَانُوْا مِنْ قَبْلِهِمْ ؕ كَانُوْا هُمْ اَشَدَّ
مِنْهُمْ قُوَّةً وَّاٰثَارًا فِي الْاَرْضِ فَاَخَذَهُمُ اللّٰهُ بِذُنُوْبِهِمْ ؕ
وَمَا كَانَ لَهُمْ مِّنَ اللّٰهِ مِنْ وَّاقٍ ﴿۲۲﴾

23. That was because their Messengers came to them with manifest Signs, but they disbelieved; so Allah seized them. Surely He is Powerful, Severe in punishment.

ذٰلِكَ بِاَنَّهُمْ كَانَتْ تَّاْتِيْهِمْ رُسُلُهُمْ بِالْبَيِّنٰتِ فَكَفَرُوْا
فَاَخَذَهُمُ اللّٰهُ ؕ اِنَّهٗ قَوِيٌّ شَدِيْدُ الْعِقَابِ ﴿۲۳﴾

24. And We did send Moses, with Our Signs and manifest authority,

وَلَقَدْ اَرْسَلْنَا مُوْسٰى بِاٰيٰتِنَا وَسُلْطٰنٍ مُّبِيْنٍ ﴿۲۴﴾

25. Unto Pharaoh and Hāmān and Korah; but they said, '*He is* a magician and an impostor.'

اِلٰى فِرْعَوْنَ وَهَامٰنَ وَقَارُوْنَ فَقَالُوْا سٰحِرٌ كَذَّابٌ ﴿۲۵﴾

* 26. And when he came to them with truth from Us, they said: 'Slay the sons of those who have believed with him, and let their women live.' But the design of the disbelievers is but a thing wasted.

فَلَمَّا جَآءَهُمْ بِالْحَقِّ مِنْ عِنْدِنَا قَالُوا اقْتُلُوْٓا اَبْنَآءَ
الَّذِيْنَ اٰمَنُوْا مَعَهٗ وَاسْتَحْيُوْا نِسَآءَهُمْ ؕ وَمَا كَيْدُ
الْكٰفِرِيْنَ اِلَّا فِيْ ضَلٰلٍ ﴿۲۶﴾

* 27. And Pharaoh said: 'Leave me *alone* that I may kill Moses; and let him call on his Lord. I fear lest he should change your

وَقَالَ فِرْعَوْنُ ذَرُوْنِيْٓ اَقْتُلْ مُوْسٰى وَلْيَدْعُ
رَبَّهٗ ؕ اِنِّيْٓ اَخَافُ اَنْ يُّبَدِّلَ دِيْنَكُمْ اَوْ اَنْ يُّظْهِرَ

فِي الْأَرْضِ الْفَسَادَ ﴿٢٧﴾

religion or cause disorder to show itself in the land.'

وَقَالَ مُوسَىٰ إِنِّي عُذْتُ بِرَبِّي وَرَبِّكُم مِّن كُلِّ مُتَكَبِّرٍ لَّا يُؤْمِنُ بِيَوْمِ الْحِسَابِ ﴿٢٨﴾

28. And Moses said, 'I take refuge with my Lord and your Lord from every arrogant *person* who believes not in the Day of Reckoning.'

R. 4.

وَقَالَ رَجُلٌ مُّؤْمِنٌ مِّنْ آلِ فِرْعَوْنَ يَكْتُمُ إِيمَانَهُ أَتَقْتُلُونَ رَجُلًا أَن يَقُولَ رَبِّيَ اللَّهُ وَقَدْ جَاءَكُم بِالْبَيِّنَاتِ مِن رَّبِّكُمْ ۖ وَإِن يَكُ كَاذِبًا فَعَلَيْهِ كَذِبُهُ ۖ وَإِن يَكُ صَادِقًا يُصِبْكُم بَعْضُ الَّذِي يَعِدُكُمْ ۖ إِنَّ اللَّهَ لَا يَهْدِي مَنْ هُوَ مُسْرِفٌ كَذَّابٌ ﴿٢٩﴾

29. And a believing man from among the people of Pharaoh, who concealed his faith, said, "Will you slay a man because he says, 'My Lord is Allah,' while he has brought you clear proofs from your Lord? And if he be a liar, on him will be *the sin of* his lie; but if he is truthful, then some of that which he threatens you with will *surely* befall you. Certainly Allah guides not one who is a transgressor, *and* a liar.

يَا قَوْمِ لَكُمُ الْمُلْكُ الْيَوْمَ ظَاهِرِينَ فِي الْأَرْضِ فَمَن يَنصُرُنَا مِن بَأْسِ اللَّهِ إِن جَاءَنَا ۚ قَالَ فِرْعَوْنُ مَا أُرِيكُمْ إِلَّا مَا أَرَىٰ وَمَا أَهْدِيكُمْ إِلَّا سَبِيلَ الرَّشَادِ ﴿٣٠﴾

30. "O my people, yours is the sovereignty this day, you being dominant in the land. But who will help us *and protect us* from the punishment of Allah if it comes upon us?" Pharaoh said: 'I only point out to you that which I see myself, and I guide you only to the path of rectitude.'

وَقَالَ الَّذِي آمَنَ يَا قَوْمِ إِنِّي أَخَافُ عَلَيْكُم مِّثْلَ يَوْمِ الْأَحْزَابِ ﴿٣١﴾

* 31. And he who believed said: "O my people, I fear for you *something* like the day of the parties,

مِثْلَ دَأْبِ قَوْمِ نُوحٍ وَعَادٍ وَثَمُودَ وَالَّذِينَ مِن بَعْدِهِمْ ۚ وَمَا اللَّهُ يُرِيدُ ظُلْمًا لِّلْعِبَادِ ﴿٣٢﴾

32. "Like the case of the people of Noah, and 'Ād and Thamūd and those after them. And Allah intends no injustice to *His* servants.

وَيَا قَوْمِ إِنِّي أَخَافُ عَلَيْكُمْ يَوْمَ التَّنَادِ ﴿٣٣﴾

* 33. "And O my people, I fear for you the day of mutual calling *and wailing*,

يَوْمَ تُوَلُّونَ مُدْبِرِينَ مَا لَكُم مِّنَ اللَّهِ مِنْ عَاصِمٍ ۗ وَمَن يُضْلِلِ اللَّهُ فَمَا لَهُ مِنْ هَادٍ ﴿٣٤﴾

34. "A day when you shall turn your backs fleeing. No defender shall you have against Allah. And for him whom Allah adjudges astray shall be no guide.

وَلَقَدْ جَاءَكُمْ يُوسُفُ مِن قَبْلُ بِالْبَيِّنَاتِ فَمَا زِلْتُمْ فِي شَكٍّ مِّمَّا جَاءَكُم بِهِ ۖ حَتَّىٰ إِذَا هَلَكَ قُلْتُمْ

35. "And Joseph did come to you before with clear proofs, but you ceased not to be in doubt concerning that with which he came to you till, when he died, you said:

'Allah will never raise up a Messenger after him.' Thus does Allah adjudge as lost those who transgress, *and* are doubters,

لَنْ يَّبْعَثَ اللّٰهُ مِنْۢ بَعْدِهٖ رَسُوْلًا ؕ كَذٰلِكَ يُضِلُّ
اللّٰهُ مَنْ هُوَ مُسْرِفٌ مُّرْتَابٌ ۚ ۳۵

36. "Those who dispute concerning the Signs of Allah without any authority having come to them. Grievously hateful is this in the sight of Allah and in the sight of those who believe. Thus does Allah seal up the heart of every arrogant, haughty *person*."

الَّذِيْنَ يُجَادِلُوْنَ فِيْۤ اٰيٰتِ اللّٰهِ بِغَيْرِ سُلْطٰنٍ اَتٰىهُمْ ؕ
كَبُرَ مَقْتًا عِنْدَ اللّٰهِ وَعِنْدَ الَّذِيْنَ اٰمَنُوْا ؕ كَذٰلِكَ
يَطْبَعُ اللّٰهُ عَلٰى كُلِّ قَلْبِ مُتَكَبِّرٍ جَبَّارٍ ۳۶

* 37. And Pharaoh said: 'O Hāmān, build thou for me a lofty building that I may attain to the means of approach,

وَقَالَ فِرْعَوْنُ يٰهَامٰنُ ابْنِ لِيْ صَرْحًا لَّعَلِّيْۤ
اَبْلُغُ الْاَسْبَابَ ۳۷

* 38. 'The means of approach to the heavens, so that I may have a look at the God of Moses, and I surely think him to be a liar.' And thus the evil of his doing was made *to look* fair in the eyes of Pharaoh, and he was turned away from the *right* path; and the design of Pharaoh ended in nothing but ruin.

اَسْبَابَ السَّمٰوٰتِ فَاَطَّلِعَ اِلٰۤى اِلٰهِ مُوْسٰى وَاِنِّيْ
لَاَظُنُّهٗ كَاذِبًا ؕ وَكَذٰلِكَ زُيِّنَ لِفِرْعَوْنَ سُوْٓءُ عَمَلِهٖ
وَصُدَّ عَنِ السَّبِيْلِ ؕ وَمَا كَيْدُ فِرْعَوْنَ اِلَّا فِيْ
تَبَابٍ ۳۸ ع

R. 5.

39. And he who believed said: 'O my people, follow me. I will guide you to the path of rectitude.

وَقَالَ الَّذِيْۤ اٰمَنَ يٰقَوْمِ اتَّبِعُوْنِ اَهْدِكُمْ سَبِيْلَ
الرَّشَادِ ۳۹

40. 'O my people, this life of the world is but a *temporary* provision; and the Hereafter is certainly the home for permanent stay.

يٰقَوْمِ اِنَّمَا هٰذِهِ الْحَيٰوةُ الدُّنْيَا مَتَاعٌ ؗ وَّاِنَّ الْاٰخِرَةَ
هِيَ دَارُ الْقَرَارِ ۴۰

41. 'Whoso does evil will be requited only with the like of it; but whoso does good, whether male or female, and is a believer—these will enter the Garden; they will be provided therein without measure.

مَنْ عَمِلَ سَيِّئَةً فَلَا يُجْزٰۤى اِلَّا مِثْلَهَا ۚ وَمَنْ
عَمِلَ صَالِحًا مِّنْ ذَكَرٍ اَوْ اُنْثٰى وَهُوَ مُؤْمِنٌ فَاُولٰٓئِكَ
يَدْخُلُوْنَ الْجَنَّةَ يُرْزَقُوْنَ فِيْهَا بِغَيْرِ حِسَابٍ ۴۱

42. 'And O my people, how *strange* it is that I call you to salvation, and you call me to the Fire.

وَيٰقَوْمِ مَا لِيْۤ اَدْعُوْكُمْ اِلَى النَّجٰوةِ وَتَدْعُوْنَنِيْۤ
اِلَى النَّارِ ؕ ۴۲ النصف

43. 'You invite me to disbelieve in Allah and to associate with Him that of which I have no knowledge, while I invite you to the Mighty, the Great Forgiver.

تَدْعُوْنَنِيْ لِاَكْفُرَ بِاللّٰهِ وَاُشْرِكَ بِهٖ مَا لَيْسَ
لِيْ بِهٖ عِلْمٌ ؗ وَّاَنَا اَدْعُوْكُمْ اِلَى الْعَزِيْزِ الْغَفَّارِ ۴۳

44. 'Surely that to which you call me has no *title* to be called upon in this world or in the Hereafter; and that our return is certainly to Allah and that the transgressors will be the inmates of the Fire.

لَا جَرَمَ أَنَّمَا تَدْعُوْنَنِيْٓ إِلَيْهِ لَيْسَ لَهُ دَعْوَةٌ فِي
الدُّنْيَا وَلَا فِي الْاٰخِرَةِ وَأَنَّ مَرَدَّنَآ إِلَى اللّٰهِ وَأَنَّ
الْمُسْرِفِيْنَ هُمْ أَصْحٰبُ النَّارِ ﴿٤٤﴾

45. 'So you will soon remember what I say to you. And I entrust my cause to Allah. Verily, Allah sees *all His* servants.'

فَسَتَذْكُرُوْنَ مَآ أَقُوْلُ لَكُمْ ۚ وَأُفَوِّضُ أَمْرِيْٓ إِلَى
اللّٰهِ ۚ إِنَّ اللّٰهَ بَصِيْرٌۢ بِالْعِبَادِ ﴿٤٥﴾

46. The result was that Allah preserved him from the evils of whatever they plotted, and a grievous punishment encompassed the people of Pharaoh—

فَوَقٰىهُ اللّٰهُ سَيِّاٰتِ مَا مَكَرُوْا وَحَاقَ بِاٰلِ فِرْعَوْنَ
سُوْٓءُ الْعَذَابِ ﴿٤٦﴾

47. The Fire. They are exposed to it morning and evening. And on the day when the Hour will come, *it will be said:* 'Cast Pharaoh's people into the severest punishment.'

اَلنَّارُ يُعْرَضُوْنَ عَلَيْهَا غُدُوًّا وَّعَشِيًّا ۚ وَيَوْمَ
تَقُوْمُ السَّاعَةُ ۗ أَدْخِلُوْٓا اٰلَ فِرْعَوْنَ أَشَدَّ
الْعَذَابِ ﴿٤٧﴾

48. And when they will dispute with one another in the Fire, the weak will say to those who were proud, 'Verily, we were your followers; will you then relieve us of a portion of the Fire?'

وَإِذْ يَتَحَآجُّوْنَ فِي النَّارِ فَيَقُوْلُ الضُّعَفٰٓؤُا لِلَّذِيْنَ
اسْتَكْبَرُوْٓا إِنَّا كُنَّا لَكُمْ تَبَعًا فَهَلْ أَنْتُمْ مُّغْنُوْنَ
عَنَّا نَصِيْبًا مِّنَ النَّارِ ﴿٤٨﴾

49. Those, who were proud, will say: 'We are all in it. Allah has already judged between *His* servants.'

قَالَ الَّذِيْنَ اسْتَكْبَرُوْٓا إِنَّا كُلٌّ فِيْهَآ ۙ إِنَّ اللّٰهَ قَدْ
حَكَمَ بَيْنَ الْعِبَادِ ﴿٤٩﴾

50. And those in the Fire will say to the Keepers of Hell, 'Pray to your Lord that He may lighten for us the punishment for a *single* day.'

وَقَالَ الَّذِيْنَ فِي النَّارِ لِخَزَنَةِ جَهَنَّمَ ادْعُوْا
رَبَّكُمْ يُخَفِّفْ عَنَّا يَوْمًا مِّنَ الْعَذَابِ ﴿٥٠﴾

51. They will say: 'Did not your Messengers come to you with manifest Signs?' They will say: 'Yea'. *The Keepers* will say, 'Then pray on.' But the prayer of disbelievers is of no avail.

قَالُوْٓا أَوَلَمْ تَكُ تَأْتِيْكُمْ رُسُلُكُمْ بِالْبَيِّنٰتِ ۗ قَالُوْا
بَلٰى ۗ قَالُوْا فَادْعُوْا ۚ وَمَا دُعٰٓؤُا الْكٰفِرِيْنَ إِلَّا فِيْ
ع ٥ ١٣ ضَلٰلٍ ﴿٥١﴾

R. 6.

52. Most surely We help Our Messengers and those who believe, *both* in the present life and on the day when the witnesses will stand forth,

إِنَّا لَنَنْصُرُ رُسُلَنَا وَالَّذِيْنَ اٰمَنُوْا فِي الْحَيٰوةِ الدُّنْيَا
وَيَوْمَ يَقُوْمُ الْأَشْهَادُ ﴿٥٢﴾

53. The day when their excuses will not profit the wrongdoers, and theirs will be the curse and theirs the evil abode.

يَوْمَ لَا يَنْفَعُ الظّٰلِمِيْنَ مَعْذِرَتُهُمْ وَلَهُمُ اللَّعْنَةُ
وَلَهُمْ سُوْٓءُ الدَّارِ ﴿٥٣﴾

54. And indeed We gave Moses the guidance, and made the children of Israel the inheritors of the Book—

وَلَقَدْ اٰتَيْنَا مُوْسَى الْهُدٰى وَاَوْرَثْنَا بَنِيْٓ
اِسْرَآءِيْلَ الْكِتٰبَ ﴿٥٤﴾

55. A guidance and a reminder for men of understanding.

هُدًى وَّذِكْرٰى لِاُولِي الْاَلْبَابِ ﴿٥٥﴾

56. So have patience. Surely the promise of Allah is true. And ask forgiveness for thy frailty, and glorify thy Lord with His praise in the evening and in the morning.

فَاصْبِرْ اِنَّ وَعْدَ اللّٰهِ حَقٌّ وَّاسْتَغْفِرْ لِذَنْۢبِكَ وَ
سَبِّحْ بِحَمْدِ رَبِّكَ بِالْعَشِيِّ وَالْاِبْكَارِ ﴿٥٦﴾

* 57. Those who dispute concerning the Signs of Allah without any authority having come to them—there is nothing in their breasts but *a feeling of* greatness which they will never attain. So seek refuge in Allah. Surely He is the All-Hearing, the All-Seeing.

اِنَّ الَّذِيْنَ يُجَادِلُوْنَ فِيْٓ اٰيٰتِ اللّٰهِ بِغَيْرِ سُلْطٰنٍ
اَتٰىهُمْ اِنْ فِيْ صُدُوْرِهِمْ اِلَّا كِبْرٌ مَّا هُمْ بِبَالِغِيْهِ
فَاسْتَعِذْ بِاللّٰهِ اِنَّهٗ هُوَ السَّمِيْعُ الْبَصِيْرُ ﴿٥٧﴾

58. Certainly, the creation of the heavens and the earth is greater than the creation of mankind; but most men know not.

لَخَلْقُ السَّمٰوٰتِ وَالْاَرْضِ اَكْبَرُ مِنْ خَلْقِ النَّاسِ
وَلٰكِنَّ اَكْثَرَ النَّاسِ لَا يَعْلَمُوْنَ ﴿٥٨﴾

59. And the blind and the seeing are not equal; neither are those who believe and do good deeds *equal to* those who do evil. Little do you reflect.

وَمَا يَسْتَوِي الْاَعْمٰى وَالْبَصِيْرُ وَالَّذِيْنَ اٰمَنُوْا
وَعَمِلُوا الصّٰلِحٰتِ وَلَا الْمُسِيْٓءُ قَلِيْلًا مَّا
تَتَذَكَّرُوْنَ ﴿٥٩﴾

60. The Hour will surely come; there is no doubt about it; yet most men believe not.

اِنَّ السَّاعَةَ لَاٰتِيَةٌ لَّا رَيْبَ فِيْهَا وَلٰكِنَّ اَكْثَرَ
النَّاسِ لَا يُؤْمِنُوْنَ ﴿٦٠﴾

61. And your Lord says: 'Pray unto Me; I will answer your *prayer*. But those who are too proud to worship Me will surely enter Hell, despised.'

وَقَالَ رَبُّكُمُ ادْعُوْنِيْٓ اَسْتَجِبْ لَكُمْ اِنَّ الَّذِيْنَ
يَسْتَكْبِرُوْنَ عَنْ عِبَادَتِيْ سَيَدْخُلُوْنَ جَهَنَّمَ دٰخِرِيْنَ ﴿٦١﴾ ع

R. 7.

62. It is Allah Who has made the night for you that you may rest therein, and the day *to enable you* to see. Verily, Allah is the Lord of bounty for mankind, yet most men are ungrateful.

اَللّٰهُ الَّذِيْ جَعَلَ لَكُمُ الَّيْلَ لِتَسْكُنُوْا فِيْهِ وَالنَّهَارَ
مُبْصِرًا اِنَّ اللّٰهَ لَذُوْ فَضْلٍ عَلَى النَّاسِ وَلٰكِنَّ
اَكْثَرَ النَّاسِ لَا يَشْكُرُوْنَ ﴿٦٢﴾

63. Such is Allah, your Lord, the Creator of all things. There is no God but He. How then are you turned away?

ذٰلِكُمُ اللّٰهُ رَبُّكُمْ خَالِقُ كُلِّ شَيْءٍ ۘ لَآ اِلٰهَ اِلَّا هُوَ ۖ
فَاَنّٰى تُؤْفَكُوْنَ ﴿۶۳﴾

64. Thus indeed are turned away those who deny the Signs of Allah.

كَذٰلِكَ يُؤْفَكُ الَّذِيْنَ كَانُوْا بِاٰيٰتِ اللّٰهِ يَجْحَدُوْنَ ﴿۶۴﴾

* 65. Allah it is Who has made for you the earth a resting-place, and the heaven a canopy, and has given you shape and made your shapes perfect, and has provided you with good things. Such is Allah, your Lord. So blessed is Allah, the Lord of the worlds.

اَللّٰهُ الَّذِيْ جَعَلَ لَكُمُ الْاَرْضَ قَرَارًا وَّ السَّمَآءَ
بِنَآءً وَّ صَوَّرَكُمْ فَاَحْسَنَ صُوَرَكُمْ وَ رَزَقَكُمْ
مِّنَ الطَّيِّبٰتِ ؕ ذٰلِكُمُ اللّٰهُ رَبُّكُمْ ۚۖ فَتَبٰرَكَ اللّٰهُ
رَبُّ الْعٰلَمِيْنَ ﴿۶۵﴾

66. He is the Living *God*. There is no God but He. So pray unto Him, being sincere to Him in religion. All praise belongs to Allah, the Lord of the worlds.

هُوَ الْحَيُّ لَآ اِلٰهَ اِلَّا هُوَ فَادْعُوْهُ مُخْلِصِيْنَ لَهُ
الدِّيْنَ ؕ اَلْحَمْدُ لِلّٰهِ رَبِّ الْعٰلَمِيْنَ ﴿۶۶﴾

67. Say, 'I have been forbidden to worship those whom you call upon beside Allah since there have come unto me clear proofs from my Lord; and I have been commanded to submit myself to the Lord of the worlds.'

قُلْ اِنِّيْ نُهِيْتُ اَنْ اَعْبُدَ الَّذِيْنَ تَدْعُوْنَ مِنْ
دُوْنِ اللّٰهِ لَمَّا جَآءَنِيَ الْبَيِّنٰتُ مِنْ رَّبِّيْ وَ اُمِرْتُ
اَنْ اُسْلِمَ لِرَبِّ الْعٰلَمِيْنَ ﴿۶۷﴾

68. He it is Who created you from dust, then from a sperm-drop, then from a clot; then He brings you forth as a child; then *He lets you grow* that you may attain your full strength; then *He lets* you become old—though some among you are caused to die before—and *He lets you live* that you may reach a term appointed, and that you may learn wisdom.

هُوَ الَّذِيْ خَلَقَكُمْ مِّنْ تُرَابٍ ثُمَّ مِنْ نُّطْفَةٍ
ثُمَّ مِنْ عَلَقَةٍ ثُمَّ يُخْرِجُكُمْ طِفْلًا ثُمَّ لِتَبْلُغُوْٓا
اَشُدَّكُمْ ثُمَّ لِتَكُوْنُوْا شُيُوْخًا ۚ وَ مِنْكُمْ مَّنْ يُّتَوَفّٰى
مِنْ قَبْلُ وَ لِتَبْلُغُوْٓا اَجَلًا مُّسَمًّى وَّ لَعَلَّكُمْ
تَعْقِلُوْنَ ﴿۶۸﴾

69. He it is Who gives life and causes death. And when He decrees a thing, He says to it only, 'Be!', and it is.

هُوَ الَّذِيْ يُحْيٖ وَ يُمِيْتُ ۚ فَاِذَا قَضٰٓى اَمْرًا فَاِنَّمَا
يَقُوْلُ لَهٗ كُنْ فَيَكُوْنُ ﴿۶۹﴾

R. 8.

70. Hast thou not seen those who dispute concerning the Signs of Allah? How they are being turned away *from the truth!*

اَلَمْ تَرَ اِلَى الَّذِيْنَ يُجَادِلُوْنَ فِيْٓ اٰيٰتِ اللّٰهِ ؕ اَنّٰى
يُصْرَفُوْنَ ﴿۷۰﴾

71. Those who reject the Book and that with which We sent Our Messengers. But

الَّذِيْنَ كَذَّبُوْا بِالْكِتٰبِ وَ بِمَآ اَرْسَلْنَا بِهٖ رُسُلَنَا

soon will they come to know,

72. When the iron-collars will be round their necks, and chains *too*. They will be dragged

73. Into boiling water; then in the Fire will they be burnt.

74. Then it will be said to them, 'Where are those whom you associated *with God*

75. 'Beside Allah?' They will say, 'They have vanished away from us. Nay, we never prayed to anything before.' Thus will Allah confound the disbelievers.

76. 'That is because you exulted in the earth without justification, and because you behaved insolently.

77. 'Enter ye the gates of Hell, to abide therein. And evil is the abode of the proud.'

78. Then have patience. Surely, the promise of Allah is true. And whether We show thee part of what We have promised them, or whether We cause thee to die *before the fulfilment of Our promise*, to Us *in any case* will they be brought back.

79. And We did send Messengers before thee; of them are some whom We have mentioned to thee, and of them there are some whom We have not mentioned to thee; and it is not possible for any Messenger to bring a Sign except by the leave of Allah. But when Allah's decree came, the matter was decided with truth, and then there perished those who uttered falsehoods.

R. 9.

80. It is Allah Who has made cattle for you, that you may ride on some of them, and eat of some of them—

81. And you have *other* advantages in them—and that, by means of them, you may satisfy any desire *that there may be* in your breasts. And on them and on ships are you borne.

82. And He shows you His Signs; which then of the Signs of Allah will you deny?

فَسَوْفَ يَعْلَمُوْنَ ﴿٧١﴾

إِذِ الْاَغْلٰلُ فِيْٓ اَعْنَاقِهِمْ وَالسَّلٰسِلُ يُسْحَبُوْنَ ﴿٧٢﴾

فِي الْحَمِيْمِ ۙ ثُمَّ فِي النَّارِ يُسْجَرُوْنَ ﴿٧٣﴾

ثُمَّ قِيْلَ لَهُمْ اَيْنَ مَا كُنْتُمْ تُشْرِكُوْنَ ﴿٧٤﴾

مِنْ دُوْنِ اللّٰهِ ۭ قَالُوْا ضَلُّوْا عَنَّا بَلْ لَّمْ نَكُنْ

نَّدْعُوْا مِنْ قَبْلُ شَيْـًٔا ۭ كَذٰلِكَ يُضِلُّ اللّٰهُ

الْكٰفِرِيْنَ ﴿٧٥﴾

ذٰلِكُمْ بِمَا كُنْتُمْ تَفْرَحُوْنَ فِي الْاَرْضِ بِغَيْرِ

الْحَقِّ وَبِمَا كُنْتُمْ تَمْرَحُوْنَ ﴿٧٦﴾

اُدْخُلُوْٓا اَبْوَابَ جَهَنَّمَ خٰلِدِيْنَ فِيْهَا ۚ فَبِئْسَ

مَثْوَى الْمُتَكَبِّرِيْنَ ﴿٧٧﴾

فَاصْبِرْ اِنَّ وَعْدَ اللّٰهِ حَقٌّ ۚ فَاِمَّا نُرِيَنَّكَ بَعْضَ

الَّذِيْ نَعِدُهُمْ اَوْ نَتَوَفَّيَنَّكَ فَاِلَيْنَا يُرْجَعُوْنَ ﴿٧٨﴾

وَلَقَدْ اَرْسَلْنَا رُسُلًا مِّنْ قَبْلِكَ مِنْهُمْ مَّنْ قَصَصْنَا

عَلَيْكَ وَمِنْهُمْ مَّنْ لَّمْ نَقْصُصْ عَلَيْكَ ۭ وَمَا كَانَ

لِرَسُوْلٍ اَنْ يَّاْتِيَ بِاٰيَةٍ اِلَّا بِاِذْنِ اللّٰهِ ۚ فَاِذَا جَآءَ

اَمْرُ اللّٰهِ قُضِيَ بِالْحَقِّ وَخَسِرَ هُنَالِكَ الْمُبْطِلُوْنَ ﴿٧٩﴾ ع ١٣

اَللّٰهُ الَّذِيْ جَعَلَ لَكُمُ الْاَنْعَامَ لِتَرْكَبُوْا مِنْهَا وَمِنْهَا

تَاْكُلُوْنَ ﴿٨٠﴾

وَلَكُمْ فِيْهَا مَنَافِعُ وَلِتَبْلُغُوْا عَلَيْهَا حَاجَةً فِيْ

صُدُوْرِكُمْ وَعَلَيْهَا وَعَلَى الْفُلْكِ تُحْمَلُوْنَ ﴿٨١﴾

وَيُرِيْكُمْ اٰيٰتِهٖ ۖ فَاَيَّ اٰيٰتِ اللّٰهِ تُنْكِرُوْنَ ﴿٨٢﴾

83. Have they not travelled in the earth that they might see what was the end of those who were before them? They were more numerous than these, and mightier in power and *in* the marks *they left behind them* in the earth. But all that which they earned was of no avail to them.

أَفَلَمْ يَسِيرُوا فِي الْأَرْضِ فَيَنْظُرُوا كَيْفَ كَانَ
عَاقِبَةُ الَّذِينَ مِنْ قَبْلِهِمْ ۚ كَانُوا أَكْثَرَ مِنْهُمْ وَأَشَدَّ
قُوَّةً وَآثَارًا فِي الْأَرْضِ فَمَا أَغْنَىٰ عَنْهُمْ مَا كَانُوا
يَكْسِبُونَ ﴿٨٣﴾

84. And when their Messengers came to them with manifest Signs, they exulted in the knowledge which they possessed. And that at which they mocked encompassed them.

فَلَمَّا جَاءَتْهُمْ رُسُلُهُمْ بِالْبَيِّنَاتِ فَرِحُوا بِمَا عِنْدَهُمْ
مِنَ الْعِلْمِ وَحَاقَ بِهِمْ مَا كَانُوا بِهِ يَسْتَهْزِئُونَ ﴿٨٤﴾

85. And when they saw Our punishment, they said: 'We believe in Allah alone and we reject all that which we used to associate with Him.'

فَلَمَّا رَأَوْا بَأْسَنَا قَالُوا آمَنَّا بِاللَّهِ وَحْدَهُ وَكَفَرْنَا بِمَا
كُنَّا بِهِ مُشْرِكِينَ ﴿٨٥﴾

86. But their faith could not profit them *at the time* when they saw Our punishment. This is Allah's law that has *ever* been in operation in respect of His servants. And thus have perished those who disbelieved.

فَلَمْ يَكُ يَنْفَعُهُمْ إِيمَانُهُمْ لَمَّا رَأَوْا بَأْسَنَا ۖ
سُنَّتَ اللَّهِ الَّتِي قَدْ خَلَتْ فِي عِبَادِهِ ۖ وَخَسِرَ
هُنَالِكَ الْكَافِرُونَ ﴿٨٦﴾ ع

سُوۡرَۃُ حٰمٓ السَّجۡدَۃِ مَکِّیَّۃٌ

ḤĀ MĪM SAJDAH

(Revealed before Hijra)

1. In the name of Allah, the Gracious, the Merciful.

بِسۡمِ اللّٰہِ الرَّحۡمٰنِ الرَّحِیۡمِ ﴿۱﴾

2. Ḥā Mīm*.

حٰمٓ ﴿۲﴾

3. *This is* a revelation from the Gracious, the Merciful.

تَنۡزِیۡلٌ مِّنَ الرَّحۡمٰنِ الرَّحِیۡمِ ﴿۳﴾

* 4. A Book, the verses of which have been expounded in detail—the Qur'ān in clear, eloquent language—for a people who have knowledge,

کِتٰبٌ فُصِّلَتۡ اٰیٰتُہٗ قُرۡاٰنًا عَرَبِیًّا لِّقَوۡمٍ یَّعۡلَمُوۡنَ ﴿۴﴾

5. A bringer of glad tidings and a warner. But most of them turn away and they hear not.

بَشِیۡرًا وَّ نَذِیۡرًا ۚ فَاَعۡرَضَ اَکۡثَرُہُمۡ فَہُمۡ لَا
یَسۡمَعُوۡنَ ﴿۵﴾

* 6. And they say: 'Our hearts are under covers *and are protected* against that to which thou callest us, and in our ears there is a deafness, and between us and thee there is a screen. So carry on thy work; we *too* are working.'

وَ قَالُوۡا قُلُوۡبُنَا فِیۡۤ اَکِنَّۃٍ مِّمَّا تَدۡعُوۡنَاۤ اِلَیۡہِ
وَ فِیۡۤ اٰذَانِنَا وَقۡرٌ وَّ مِنۡۢ بَیۡنِنَا وَ بَیۡنِکَ حِجَابٌ
فَاعۡمَلۡ اِنَّنَا عٰمِلُوۡنَ ﴿۶﴾

7. Say, 'I am only a man like you. It is revealed to me that your God is One God; so go ye straight to Him *without deviating*, and ask forgiveness of Him.' And woe to the idolaters,

قُلۡ اِنَّمَاۤ اَنَا بَشَرٌ مِّثۡلُکُمۡ یُوۡحٰۤی اِلَیَّ اَنَّمَاۤ اِلٰـہُکُمۡ
اِلٰہٌ وَّاحِدٌ فَاسۡتَقِیۡمُوۡۤا اِلَیۡہِ وَ اسۡتَغۡفِرُوۡہُ ؕ وَ وَیۡلٌ
لِّلۡمُشۡرِکِیۡنَ ﴿۷﴾

8. Who give not the Zakāt, and they it is who deny the Hereafter.

الَّذِیۡنَ لَا یُؤۡتُوۡنَ الزَّکٰوۃَ وَ ہُمۡ بِالۡاٰخِرَۃِ ہُمۡ کٰفِرُوۡنَ ﴿۸﴾

9. *As to* those who believe and do good works, they will surely have a reward that will never end.

اِنَّ الَّذِیۡنَ اٰمَنُوۡا وَ عَمِلُوا الصّٰلِحٰتِ لَہُمۡ اَجۡرٌ غَیۡرُ
مَمۡنُوۡنٍ ﴿۹﴾

R. 2.

* 10. Say: 'Do you really disbelieve in Him Who created the earth in two days? And do you set up equals to Him?' That is the Lord of the worlds.

قُلۡ اَئِنَّکُمۡ لَتَکۡفُرُوۡنَ بِالَّذِیۡ خَلَقَ الۡاَرۡضَ فِیۡ
یَوۡمَیۡنِ وَ تَجۡعَلُوۡنَ لَہٗۤ اَنۡدَادًا ؕ ذٰلِکَ رَبُّ
الۡعٰلَمِیۡنَ ﴿۱۰﴾

* 11. He placed therein firm mountains rising above its *surface*, and blessed it *with*

وَ جَعَلَ فِیۡہَا رَوَاسِیَ مِنۡ فَوۡقِہَا وَ بٰرَکَ فِیۡہَا

* The Praiseworthy, the Lord of Honour.

abundance, and provided therein its foods in proper measure in four days—alike for *all* seekers.

وَقَدَّرَ فِيهَا أَقْوَاتَهَا فِي أَرْبَعَةِ أَيَّامٍ سَوَاءً
لِلسَّائِلِينَ ﴿١١﴾

12. Then He turned to the heaven while it was *something like* smoke, and said to it and to the earth: 'Come ye both of you, willingly or unwillingly.' They said, 'We come willingly.'

ثُمَّ اسْتَوَىٰ إِلَى السَّمَاءِ وَهِيَ دُخَانٌ فَقَالَ لَهَا
وَلِلْأَرْضِ ائْتِيَا طَوْعًا أَوْ كَرْهًا قَالَتَا أَتَيْنَا
طَائِعِينَ ﴿١٢﴾

13. So He completed them into seven heavens in two days, and He revealed to each heaven its function. And We adorned the lowest heaven with lamps *for light* and for protection. That is the decree of the Mighty, the All-Knowing.

فَقَضَاهُنَّ سَبْعَ سَمَاوَاتٍ فِي يَوْمَيْنِ وَأَوْحَىٰ
فِي كُلِّ سَمَاءٍ أَمْرَهَا وَزَيَّنَّا السَّمَاءَ الدُّنْيَا
بِمَصَابِيحَ وَحِفْظًا ذَٰلِكَ تَقْدِيرُ الْعَزِيزِ
الْعَلِيمِ ﴿١٣﴾

14. But if they turn away, then say: 'I warn you of a destructive punishment like the punishment which *overtook* 'Ād and Thamūd.'

فَإِنْ أَعْرَضُوا فَقُلْ أَنْذَرْتُكُمْ صَاعِقَةً مِثْلَ
صَاعِقَةِ عَادٍ وَثَمُودَ ﴿١٤﴾

15. When their Messengers came to them from before them and behind them, *saying*: 'Worship none but Allah,' they said: 'If our Lord had *so* willed, He would have certainly sent down angels. So we do disbelieve in that with which you have been sent.'

إِذْ جَاءَتْهُمُ الرُّسُلُ مِنْ بَيْنِ أَيْدِيهِمْ وَمِنْ
خَلْفِهِمْ أَلَّا تَعْبُدُوا إِلَّا اللَّهَ قَالُوا لَوْ شَاءَ رَبُّنَا
لَأَنْزَلَ مَلَائِكَةً فَإِنَّا بِمَا أُرْسِلْتُمْ بِهِ كَافِرُونَ ﴿١٥﴾

16. As for 'Ād, they behaved arrogantly in the earth without any justification and said, 'Who is mightier than we in power?' Do they not see that Allah, Who created them, is mightier than they in power? Still they continued to deny Our Signs.

فَأَمَّا عَادٌ فَاسْتَكْبَرُوا فِي الْأَرْضِ بِغَيْرِ الْحَقِّ وَ
قَالُوا مَنْ أَشَدُّ مِنَّا قُوَّةً أَوَلَمْ يَرَوْا أَنَّ اللَّهَ
الَّذِي خَلَقَهُمْ هُوَ أَشَدُّ مِنْهُمْ قُوَّةً وَكَانُوا
بِآيَاتِنَا يَجْحَدُونَ ﴿١٦﴾

17. So We sent upon them a furious wind for several ominous days, that We might make them taste the punishment of humiliation in this life. And the punishment of the Hereafter will surely be more humiliating, and they will not be helped.

فَأَرْسَلْنَا عَلَيْهِمْ رِيحًا صَرْصَرًا فِي أَيَّامٍ نَحِسَاتٍ
لِنُذِيقَهُمْ عَذَابَ الْخِزْيِ فِي الْحَيَاةِ الدُّنْيَا
وَلَعَذَابُ الْآخِرَةِ أَخْزَىٰ وَهُمْ لَا يُنْصَرُونَ ﴿١٧﴾

18. And as for Thamūd, We gave them guidance, but they preferred blindness to

وَأَمَّا ثَمُودُ فَهَدَيْنَاهُمْ فَاسْتَحَبُّوا الْعَمَىٰ عَلَى

guidance, so the calamity of a humiliating punishment seized them, on account of what they had earned.

الْهُدٰى فَاَخَذَتْهُمْ صٰعِقَةُ الْعَذَابِ الْهُوْنِ
بِمَا كَانُوْا يَكْسِبُوْنَ ﴿١٨﴾

19. And We saved those who believed and acted righteously.

وَنَجَّيْنَا الَّذِيْنَ اٰمَنُوْا وَكَانُوْا يَتَّقُوْنَ ﴿١٩﴾

R. 3.

* 20. And on the day when the enemies of Allah will be gathered together and driven to the Fire, they will be goaded on.

وَيَوْمَ يُحْشَرُ اَعْدَآءُ اللّٰهِ اِلَى النَّارِ فَهُمْ
يُوْزَعُوْنَ ﴿٢٠﴾

21. Till, when they reach it, their ears and their eyes and their skins will bear witness against them as to what they had been doing.

حَتّٰٓى اِذَا مَا جَآءُوْهَا شَهِدَ عَلَيْهِمْ سَمْعُهُمْ وَ
اَبْصَارُهُمْ وَجُلُوْدُهُمْ بِمَا كَانُوْا يَعْمَلُوْنَ ﴿٢١﴾

22. And they will say to their skins: 'Why bear ye witness against us?' They will say: 'Allah has made us to speak as He has made everything *else* to speak. And He it is Who created you the first time, and unto Him have you been brought back.

وَقَالُوْا لِجُلُوْدِهِمْ لِمَ شَهِدْتُّمْ عَلَيْنَا ؕ قَالُوْٓا
اَنْطَقَنَا اللّٰهُ الَّذِيْٓ اَنْطَقَ كُلَّ شَيْءٍ وَّهُوَ خَلَقَكُمْ
اَوَّلَ مَرَّةٍ وَّاِلَيْهِ تُرْجَعُوْنَ ﴿٢٢﴾

23. 'And you did not fear *while committing sins* that your ears and your eyes and your skins would bear witness against you, nay, you thought that *even* Allah did not know much of what you used to do.

وَمَا كُنْتُمْ تَسْتَتِرُوْنَ اَنْ يَّشْهَدَ عَلَيْكُمْ سَمْعُكُمْ
وَلَآ اَبْصَارُكُمْ وَلَا جُلُوْدُكُمْ وَلٰكِنْ ظَنَنْتُمْ اَنَّ
اللّٰهَ لَا يَعْلَمُ كَثِيْرًا مِّمَّا تَعْمَلُوْنَ ﴿٢٣﴾

24. 'And that thought of yours, which you entertained concerning your Lord, has ruined you. So *now* you have become of those who are lost.'

وَذٰلِكُمْ ظَنُّكُمُ الَّذِيْ ظَنَنْتُمْ بِرَبِّكُمْ اَرْدٰىكُمْ
فَاَصْبَحْتُمْ مِّنَ الْخٰسِرِيْنَ ﴿٢٤﴾

* 25. Now if they can endure, the Fire is their abode; and if they ask for forgiveness, they are not of those whom forgiveness can be shown.

فَاِنْ يَّصْبِرُوْا فَالنَّارُ مَثْوًى لَّهُمْ ۚ وَاِنْ يَّسْتَعْتِبُوْا
فَمَا هُمْ مِّنَ الْمُعْتَبِيْنَ ﴿٢٥﴾

* 26. And We had assigned for them companions who made *to appear* attractive to them what was before them and what was behind them; and the sentence became due against them along with the communities of Jinn and mankind that had gone before them. Surely, they were *the* losers.

وَقَيَّضْنَا لَهُمْ قُرَنَآءَ فَزَيَّنُوْا لَهُمْ مَّا بَيْنَ
اَيْدِيْهِمْ وَمَا خَلْفَهُمْ وَحَقَّ عَلَيْهِمُ الْقَوْلُ
فِيْٓ اُمَمٍ قَدْ خَلَتْ مِنْ قَبْلِهِمْ مِّنَ الْجِنِّ وَالْاِنْسِ ۚ
اِنَّهُمْ كَانُوْا خٰسِرِيْنَ ﴿٢٦﴾

R. 4.

27. And those who disbelieve say: 'Listen not to this Qur'ān, but make

وَقَالَ الَّذِيْنَ كَفَرُوْا لَا تَسْمَعُوْا لِهٰذَا الْقُرْاٰنِ

noise during its *recital* that you may have the upper hand.'

وَالْغَوْا فِيهِ لَعَلَّكُمْ تَغْلِبُونَ ﴿٢٧﴾

28. And most certainly We will make those who disbelieve taste a severe punishment, and, most certainly, We will requite them for the worst of their deeds.

فَلَنُذِيقَنَّ الَّذِينَ كَفَرُوا عَذَابًا شَدِيدًا وَّ
لَنَجْزِيَنَّهُمْ أَسْوَأَ الَّذِي كَانُوا يَعْمَلُونَ ﴿٢٨﴾

29. That is the reward of the enemies of Allah—the Fire. For them there will be an abiding home therein as a requital because they used to deny Our Signs.

ذٰلِكَ جَزَآءُ أَعْدَآءِ اللّٰهِ النَّارُ لَهُمْ فِيهَا دَارُ
الْخُلْدِ جَزَآءً بِمَا كَانُوا بِاٰيٰتِنَا يَجْحَدُونَ ﴿٢٩﴾

30. And those who disbelieve will say, 'Our Lord, show us those who led us astray from among both the Jinn and men, that we may put them under our feet so that both of them may become of the lowest.'

وَقَالَ الَّذِينَ كَفَرُوا رَبَّنَآ أَرِنَا الَّذَيْنِ أَضَلّٰنَا
مِنَ الْجِنِّ وَالْإِنْسِ نَجْعَلْهُمَا تَحْتَ أَقْدَامِنَا
لِيَكُونَا مِنَ الْأَسْفَلِينَ ﴿٣٠﴾

31. *As for* those who say, 'Our Lord is Allah,' and then remain steadfast, the angels descend on them, *saying:* 'Fear ye not, nor grieve; and rejoice in the Garden that you were promised.

إِنَّ الَّذِينَ قَالُوا رَبُّنَا اللّٰهُ ثُمَّ اسْتَقَامُوا تَتَنَزَّلُ
عَلَيْهِمُ الْمَلٰٓئِكَةُ أَلَّا تَخَافُوا وَلَا تَحْزَنُوا وَأَبْشِرُوا
بِالْجَنَّةِ الَّتِي كُنْتُمْ تُوعَدُونَ ﴿٣١﴾

32. 'We are your friends in this life and in the Hereafter. Therein you will have all that your souls will desire, and therein you will have all that you will ask for—

نَحْنُ أَوْلِيٰٓؤُكُمْ فِي الْحَيٰوةِ الدُّنْيَا وَفِي الْاٰخِرَةِ
وَلَكُمْ فِيهَا مَا تَشْتَهِيٓ أَنْفُسُكُمْ وَلَكُمْ فِيهَا مَا
تَدَّعُونَ ﴿٣٢﴾

33. 'An entertainment from the Most Forgiving, the Merciful.'

نُزُلًا مِّنْ غَفُورٍ رَّحِيمٍ ﴿٣٣﴾

R. 5.

34. And who is better in speech than he who invites *men* to Allah and does good works and says, 'I am surely of those who submit?'

وَمَنْ أَحْسَنُ قَوْلًا مِّمَّنْ دَعَآ إِلَى اللّٰهِ وَعَمِلَ
صَالِحًا وَّقَالَ إِنَّنِي مِنَ الْمُسْلِمِينَ ﴿٣٤﴾

35. And good and evil are not alike. Repel *evil* with that which is best. And lo, he between whom and thyself was enmity will become as though he were a warm friend.

وَلَا تَسْتَوِي الْحَسَنَةُ وَلَا السَّيِّئَةُ ادْفَعْ بِالَّتِي
هِيَ أَحْسَنُ فَإِذَا الَّذِي بَيْنَكَ وَبَيْنَهُ عَدَاوَةٌ
كَأَنَّهُ وَلِيٌّ حَمِيمٌ ﴿٣٥﴾

* 36. But none is granted it save those who are steadfast; and none is granted it save those who possess a large share of good.

وَمَا يُلَقّٰىهَآ إِلَّا الَّذِينَ صَبَرُوا وَمَا يُلَقّٰىهَآ
إِلَّا ذُو حَظٍّ عَظِيمٍ ﴿٣٦﴾

37. And if an incitement from Satan incite thee, then seek refuge in Allah. Surely He is the All-Hearing, the All-Knowing.

وَاِمَّا يَنْزَغَنَّكَ مِنَ الشَّيْطٰنِ نَزْغٌ فَاسْتَعِذْ
بِاللّٰهِ ؕ اِنَّهٗ هُوَ السَّمِيْعُ الْعَلِيْمُ ﴿۳۷﴾

38. And among His Signs are the night and the day and the sun and the moon. Prostrate not yourselves before the sun, nor before the moon, but prostrate yourselves before Allah, Who created them, if it is Him Whom you *really* worship.

وَمِنْ اٰيٰتِهِ الَّيْلُ وَالنَّهَارُ وَالشَّمْسُ وَالْقَمَرُ ؕ
لَا تَسْجُدُوْا لِلشَّمْسِ وَلَا لِلْقَمَرِ وَاسْجُدُوْا لِلّٰهِ الَّذِيْ
خَلَقَهُنَّ اِنْ كُنْتُمْ اِيَّاهُ تَعْبُدُوْنَ ﴿۳۸﴾

39. But if they turn away with disdain *they do it to their own detriment*, while those who are with thy Lord glorify Him night and day, and they are never wearied.

فَاِنِ اسْتَكْبَرُوْا فَالَّذِيْنَ عِنْدَ رَبِّكَ يُسَبِّحُوْنَ لَهٗ
بِالَّيْلِ وَالنَّهَارِ وَهُمْ لَا يَسْـَٔمُوْنَ ۩ ﴿۳۹﴾ السجدة

* 40. And among His Signs is *this:* that thou seest the earth *lying* withered, but when We send down water on it, it stirs and swells *with verdure*. Surely, He Who quickened it can quicken the dead. Verily He has power over all things.

وَمِنْ اٰيٰتِهٖۤ اَنَّكَ تَرَى الْاَرْضَ خَاشِعَةً فَاِذَاۤ اَنْزَلْنَا
عَلَيْهَا الْمَآءَ اهْتَزَّتْ وَرَبَتْ ؕ اِنَّ الَّذِيْۤ اَحْيَاهَا
لَمُحْيِ الْمَوْتٰى ؕ اِنَّهٗ عَلٰى كُلِّ شَيْءٍ قَدِيْرٌ ﴿۴۰﴾

* 41. Surely, those who deviate *from the right path* with respect to Our Signs are not hidden from Us. Is he, then, who is cast into the Fire better or he who comes out safe on the Day of Resurrection? Do what you will. Surely He sees all that you do.

اِنَّ الَّذِيْنَ يُلْحِدُوْنَ فِيْۤ اٰيٰتِنَا لَا يَخْفَوْنَ عَلَيْنَا ؕ
اَفَمَنْ يُّلْقٰى فِي النَّارِ خَيْرٌ اَمْ مَّنْ يَّاْتِيْۤ اٰمِنًا يَّوْمَ
الْقِيٰمَةِ ؕ اِعْمَلُوْا مَا شِئْتُمْ ۙ اِنَّهٗ بِمَا تَعْمَلُوْنَ بَصِيْرٌ ﴿۴۱﴾

42. Those who disbelieve in the Reminder when it comes to them *are the losers*. And, truly, it is a mighty Book.

اِنَّ الَّذِيْنَ كَفَرُوْا بِالذِّكْرِ لَمَّا جَآءَهُمْ ۚ وَاِنَّهٗ لَكِتٰبٌ
عَزِيْزٌ ﴿۴۲﴾

43. Falsehood cannot approach it *either* from before or from behind it. *It is* a revelation from the Wise, the Praiseworthy.

لَّا يَاْتِيْهِ الْبَاطِلُ مِنْ بَيْنِ يَدَيْهِ وَلَا مِنْ خَلْفِهٖ ؕ
تَنْزِيْلٌ مِّنْ حَكِيْمٍ حَمِيْدٍ ﴿۴۳﴾

44. Nothing is said to thee but what was said to the Messengers before thee. Thy Lord is indeed the Master of forgiveness; and *also* the Master of painful chastisement.

مَا يُقَالُ لَكَ اِلَّا مَا قَدْ قِيْلَ لِلرُّسُلِ مِنْ قَبْلِكَ ؕ
اِنَّ رَبَّكَ لَذُوْ مَغْفِرَةٍ وَّذُوْ عِقَابٍ اَلِيْمٍ ﴿۴۴﴾

45. And if We had made it a Qur'ān in a foreign tongue, they surely would have said, 'Why have not its verses been made clear? What! a foreign tongue and an Arab?' Say, 'It is a guidance and a healing for those who believe.' But *as to those* who believe not, there is a deafness in their

وَلَوْ جَعَلْنٰهُ قُرْاٰنًا اَعْجَمِيًّا لَّقَالُوْا لَوْلَا فُصِّلَتْ اٰيٰتُهٗ ؕ
ءَاَعْجَمِيٌّ وَّعَرَبِيٌّ ؕ قُلْ هُوَ لِلَّذِيْنَ اٰمَنُوْا هُدًى
وَّشِفَآءٌ ؕ وَالَّذِيْنَ لَا يُؤْمِنُوْنَ فِيْۤ اٰذَانِهِمْ وَقْرٌ

ears, and it is blindness for them. They are, *as it were*, being called to from a far off place.

وَهُوَ عَلَيْهِمْ عَمًى أُولَٰئِكَ يُنَادَوْنَ مِنْ مَكَانٍ بَعِيدٍ ٤٥

R. 6.

46. And We did give Moses the Book, but differences were created concerning it; and had it not been for a word that had gone before from thy Lord, *the matter* would have been decided between them; and certainly they are in a disquieting doubt about it.

وَلَقَدْ آتَيْنَا مُوسَى الْكِتَابَ فَاخْتُلِفَ فِيهِ وَلَوْلَا كَلِمَةٌ سَبَقَتْ مِنْ رَبِّكَ لَقُضِيَ بَيْنَهُمْ وَإِنَّهُمْ لَفِي شَكٍّ مِنْهُ مُرِيبٍ ٤٦

47. Whoso does right, it is for his own soul; and whoso does evil, it will *only go* against it. And thy Lord is not at all unjust to *His* servants.

مَنْ عَمِلَ صَالِحًا فَلِنَفْسِهِ وَمَنْ أَسَاءَ فَعَلَيْهَا وَمَا رَبُّكَ بِظَلَّامٍ لِلْعَبِيدِ ٤٧

* 48. To Him *alone* is referred the knowledge of the Hour. And no fruits come forth from their spathes, nor does any female bear *a child*, nor does she give birth *to it*, but with His knowledge. And on the day when He will call unto them, *saying*, "Where are My 'partners'?" they will say, 'We declare unto Thee, not one of us is a witness *thereto*.'

إِلَيْهِ يُرَدُّ عِلْمُ السَّاعَةِ وَمَا تَخْرُجُ مِنْ ثَمَرَاتٍ مِنْ أَكْمَامِهَا وَمَا تَحْمِلُ مِنْ أُنْثَىٰ وَلَا تَضَعُ إِلَّا بِعِلْمِهِ وَيَوْمَ يُنَادِيهِمْ أَيْنَ شُرَكَائِي قَالُوا آذَنَّاكَ مَا مِنَّا مِنْ شَهِيدٍ ٤٨

* 49. And all that they used to call upon before will be lost to them, and they will know for certain that they have no place of escape.

وَضَلَّ عَنْهُمْ مَا كَانُوا يَدْعُونَ مِنْ قَبْلُ وَظَنُّوا مَا لَهُمْ مِنْ مَحِيصٍ ٤٩

50. Man does not tire of praying for good; but if evil touch him, he despairs, *and* gives up *all* hope.

لَا يَسْأَمُ الْإِنْسَانُ مِنْ دُعَاءِ الْخَيْرِ وَإِنْ مَسَّهُ الشَّرُّ فَيَئُوسٌ قَنُوطٌ ٥٠

51. And if We make him taste of mercy from Ourself, after *some* affliction that has befallen him, he will surely say, 'This is my due; and I do not think the Hour will *ever* come. But if I am returned to my Lord, I shall surely have with Him the very best.' Then We will surely tell the disbelievers all that they did, and We will certainly make them taste hard punishment.

وَلَئِنْ أَذَقْنَاهُ رَحْمَةً مِنَّا مِنْ بَعْدِ ضَرَّاءَ مَسَّتْهُ لَيَقُولَنَّ هَٰذَا لِي وَمَا أَظُنُّ السَّاعَةَ قَائِمَةً وَلَئِنْ رُجِعْتُ إِلَىٰ رَبِّي إِنَّ لِي عِنْدَهُ لَلْحُسْنَىٰ فَلَنُنَبِّئَنَّ الَّذِينَ كَفَرُوا بِمَا عَمِلُوا وَلَنُذِيقَنَّهُمْ مِنْ عَذَابٍ غَلِيظٍ ٥١

* 52. And when We bestow a favour on man, he goes away, turning aside; but when evil touches him, lo! he *starts* offering long prayers.

وَإِذَا أَنْعَمْنَا عَلَى الْإِنْسَانِ أَعْرَضَ وَنَأَىٰ بِجَانِبِهِ وَإِذَا مَسَّهُ الشَّرُّ فَذُو دُعَاءٍ عَرِيضٍ ٥٢

53. Say, 'Tell me: if it is from Allah but you disbelieve in it—who is more astray than one who has drifted away *from Allah?*'

قُلْ اَرَءَيْتُمْ اِنْ كَانَ مِنْ عِنْدِ اللّٰهِ ثُمَّ كَفَرْتُمْ
بِهٖ مَنْ اَضَلُّ مِمَّنْ هُوَ فِيْ شِقَاقٍۭ بَعِيْدٍ ﴿٥٣﴾

* 54. Soon We will show them Our Signs in all parts *of the earth*, and among their own people until it becomes manifest to them that it is the truth. Is it not enough that thy Lord is Witness over all things?

سَنُرِيْهِمْ اٰيٰتِنَا فِي الْاٰفَاقِ وَفِيْٓ اَنْفُسِهِمْ حَتّٰى
يَتَبَيَّنَ لَهُمْ اَنَّهُ الْحَقُّ ۭ اَوَلَمْ يَكْفِ بِرَبِّكَ اَنَّهٗ
عَلٰى كُلِّ شَيْءٍ شَهِيْدٌ ﴿٥٤﴾

55. Aye, they are surely in doubt concerning the meeting with their Lord. Aye, He certainly encompasses all things.

اَلَآ اِنَّهُمْ فِيْ مِرْيَةٍ مِّنْ لِّقَاۗءِ رَبِّهِمْ ۭ اَلَآ اِنَّهٗ
بِكُلِّ شَيْءٍ مُّحِيْطٌ ﴿٥٥﴾ ع

سُوْرَةُ الشُّوْرٰى مَكِّيَّةٌ (٤٢)

AL-SHŪRĀ

(Revealed before Hijra)

1. In the name of Allah, the Gracious, the Merciful.

بِسْمِ اللّٰهِ الرَّحْمٰنِ الرَّحِيْمِ ﴿١﴾

2. Ḥā Mīm*.

حٰمٓ ﴿٢﴾

3. 'Ain Sīn Qāf**.

عٓسٓقٓ ﴿٣﴾

* 4. Thus has Allah, the Mighty, the Wise, been revealing to thee and to those that preceded thee.

كَذٰلِكَ يُوْحِيْٓ اِلَيْكَ وَاِلَى الَّذِيْنَ مِنْ قَبْلِكَ ۙ
اللّٰهُ الْعَزِيْزُ الْحَكِيْمُ ﴿٤﴾

5. To Him belongs whatever is in the heavens and whatever is in the earth, and He is the High, the Great.

لَهٗ مَا فِي السَّمٰوٰتِ وَمَا فِي الْاَرْضِ ۭ وَهُوَ الْعَلِيُّ
الْعَظِيْمُ ﴿٥﴾

* 6. The heavens may well-nigh rend asunder from above them; and the angels glorify their Lord with His praise and ask forgiveness for those on the earth. Behold! it is surely Allah Who is the Most Forgiving, the Merciful.

تَكَادُ السَّمٰوٰتُ يَتَفَطَّرْنَ مِنْ فَوْقِهِنَّ وَالْمَلٰٓئِكَةُ
يُسَبِّحُوْنَ بِحَمْدِ رَبِّهِمْ وَيَسْتَغْفِرُوْنَ لِمَنْ فِي
الْاَرْضِ ۭ اَلَآ اِنَّ اللّٰهَ هُوَ الْغَفُوْرُ الرَّحِيْمُ ﴿٦﴾

7. And *as for* those who take *for themselves* protectors beside Him, Allah watches over them; and thou art not a guardian over them.

وَالَّذِيْنَ اتَّخَذُوْا مِنْ دُوْنِهٖٓ اَوْلِيَاۗءَ اللّٰهُ حَفِيْظٌ
عَلَيْهِمْ ښ وَمَآ اَنْتَ عَلَيْهِمْ بِوَكِيْلٍ ﴿٧﴾

* 8. Thus have We revealed to thee the Qur'ān in Arabic, that thou mayest warn the Mother of towns, and all around it; and *that* thou mayest warn *them* of the Day of Gathering whereof there is no doubt: A party *will be* in the Garden, and a party in the blazing Fire.

وَكَذٰلِكَ اَوْحَيْنَآ اِلَيْكَ قُرْاٰنًا عَرَبِيًّا لِّتُنْذِرَ اُمَّ
الْقُرٰى وَمَنْ حَوْلَهَا وَتُنْذِرَ يَوْمَ الْجَمْعِ لَا رَيْبَ
فِيْهِ ۭ فَرِيْقٌ فِي الْجَنَّةِ وَفَرِيْقٌ فِي السَّعِيْرِ ﴿٨﴾

9. And if Allah had *so* pleased, He could have made them one people; but He admits into His mercy whomsoever He pleases. And *as for* the wrongdoers, they will have no protector and no helper.

وَلَوْ شَاۗءَ اللّٰهُ لَجَعَلَهُمْ اُمَّةً وَّاحِدَةً وَّلٰكِنْ
يُّدْخِلُ مَنْ يَّشَاۗءُ فِيْ رَحْمَتِهٖ ۭ وَالظّٰلِمُوْنَ مَا لَهُمْ
مِّنْ وَّلِيٍّ وَّلَا نَصِيْرٍ ﴿٩﴾

10. Have they taken *for themselves* protectors other than Him? But it is Allah Who is the *real* Protector. And He

اَمِ اتَّخَذُوْا مِنْ دُوْنِهٖٓ اَوْلِيَاۗءَ ۚ فَاللّٰهُ هُوَ الْوَلِيُّ

* The Praiseworthy, the Lord of Honour.

** The All-Knowing, the All-Hearing, the Possessor of Power.

quickens the dead, and He has power over all things.

R. 2.

11. And in whatsoever you differ, the decision thereof *rests* with Allah. *Say:* 'Such is Allah, my Lord; in Him I put my trust, and to Him I *always* turn.'

* 12. *He is* the Maker of the heavens and the earth. He has made for you pairs of your own selves, andof the cattle *also He has made* pairs. He multiplies you therein. There is nothing whatever like unto Him; and He is the All-Hearing, the All-Seeing.

13. To Him belong the keys of the heavens and the earth. He enlarges the provision for whomsoever He pleases and straitens *it for whomsoever He pleases*. Surely, He knows all things full well.

14. He has prescribed for you the religion which He enjoined on Noah, and which We have revealed to thee, and which We enjoined on Abraham and Moses and Jesus, *saying*, 'Remain steadfast in obedience, and be not divided therein. Hard upon the idolaters is that to which thou callest them. Allah chooses for Himself whom He pleases, and guides to Himself him who turns *to Him*.'

* 15. And they did not become divided but after knowledge had come to them, through jealousy among themselves. And had it not been for a word that had already gone forth from thy Lord for an appointed term, *the matter* would surely have been decided between them. And surely those who were made to inherit the Book after them are in a disquieting doubt concerning it.

16. To this, then, do thou invite *mankind*. And be thou steadfast as thou art commanded, and follow not their evil inclinations, but say, 'I believe in whatever Book Allah has sent down, and I am commanded to judge justly between you. Allah is our Lord and your Lord. For us is the reward of our works, and for you the reward of your works. There is no quarrel between us and you. Allah will gather us together, and to Him is the return.'

وَهُوَ يُحْيِ الْمَوْتٰى وَهُوَ عَلٰى كُلِّ شَيْءٍ قَدِيْرٌ ﴿١٠﴾ ع
وَمَا اخْتَلَفْتُمْ فِيْهِ مِنْ شَيْءٍ فَحُكْمُهٗٓ اِلَى اللّٰهِ ؕ
ذٰلِكُمُ اللّٰهُ رَبِّيْ عَلَيْهِ تَوَكَّلْتُ ۖۚ وَاِلَيْهِ اُنِيْبُ ﴿١١﴾
فَاطِرُ السَّمٰوٰتِ وَالْاَرْضِ ؕ جَعَلَ لَكُمْ مِّنْ اَنْفُسِكُمْ
اَزْوَاجًا وَّمِنَ الْاَنْعَامِ اَزْوَاجًا ۚ يَذْرَؤُكُمْ فِيْهِ ؕ
لَيْسَ كَمِثْلِهٖ شَيْءٌ ۚ وَهُوَ السَّمِيْعُ الْبَصِيْرُ ﴿١٢﴾
لَهٗ مَقَالِيْدُ السَّمٰوٰتِ وَالْاَرْضِ ۚ يَبْسُطُ الرِّزْقَ
لِمَنْ يَّشَآءُ وَيَقْدِرُ ؕ اِنَّهٗ بِكُلِّ شَيْءٍ عَلِيْمٌ ﴿١٣﴾
شَرَعَ لَكُمْ مِّنَ الدِّيْنِ مَا وَصّٰى بِهٖ نُوْحًا وَّالَّذِيْٓ
اَوْحَيْنَآ اِلَيْكَ وَمَا وَصَّيْنَا بِهٖٓ اِبْرٰهِيْمَ وَمُوْسٰى
وَعِيْسٰٓى اَنْ اَقِيْمُوا الدِّيْنَ وَلَا تَتَفَرَّقُوْا فِيْهِ ؕ كَبُرَ
عَلَى الْمُشْرِكِيْنَ مَا تَدْعُوْهُمْ اِلَيْهِ ؕ اَللّٰهُ يَجْتَبِيْٓ
اِلَيْهِ مَنْ يَّشَآءُ وَيَهْدِيْٓ اِلَيْهِ مَنْ يُّنِيْبُ ﴿١٤﴾
وَمَا تَفَرَّقُوْٓا اِلَّا مِنْۢ بَعْدِ مَا جَآءَهُمُ الْعِلْمُ
بَغْيًۢا بَيْنَهُمْ ؕ وَلَوْلَا كَلِمَةٌ سَبَقَتْ مِنْ رَّبِّكَ
اِلٰٓى اَجَلٍ مُّسَمًّى لَّقُضِيَ بَيْنَهُمْ ؕ وَاِنَّ الَّذِيْنَ
اُوْرِثُوا الْكِتٰبَ مِنْۢ بَعْدِهِمْ لَفِيْ شَكٍّ مِّنْهُ مُرِيْبٍ ﴿١٥﴾
فَلِذٰلِكَ فَادْعُ ۚ وَاسْتَقِمْ كَمَآ اُمِرْتَ ۚ وَلَا تَتَّبِعْ
اَهْوَآءَهُمْ ۚ وَقُلْ اٰمَنْتُ بِمَآ اَنْزَلَ اللّٰهُ مِنْ كِتٰبٍ ۚ
وَاُمِرْتُ لِاَعْدِلَ بَيْنَكُمْ ؕ اَللّٰهُ رَبُّنَا وَرَبُّكُمْ ؕ
لَنَآ اَعْمَالُنَا وَلَكُمْ اَعْمَالُكُمْ ؕ لَا حُجَّةَ بَيْنَنَا وَ
بَيْنَكُمْ ؕ اَللّٰهُ يَجْمَعُ بَيْنَنَا ۚ وَاِلَيْهِ الْمَصِيْرُ ﴿١٦﴾

17. And those who dispute concerning Allah after He has been accepted—their dispute is futile in the sight of their Lord; and on them is *God's* wrath and for them will be a severe punishment.

وَالَّذِيْنَ يُحَاجُّوْنَ فِي اللّٰهِ مِنْۢ بَعْدِ مَا اسْتُجِيْبَ
لَهٗ حُجَّتُهُمْ دَاحِضَةٌ عِنْدَ رَبِّهِمْ وَعَلَيْهِمْ
غَضَبٌ وَّلَهُمْ عَذَابٌ شَدِيْدٌ ﴿١٧﴾

18. Allah it is Who has sent down the Book with truth and *also* the Balance. And what will make thee know that the Hour may be near at hand?

اَللّٰهُ الَّذِيْٓ اَنْزَلَ الْكِتٰبَ بِالْحَقِّ وَالْمِيْزَانَ ۭ وَمَا
يُدْرِيْكَ لَعَلَّ السَّاعَةَ قَرِيْبٌ ﴿١٨﴾

19. Those who believe not therein seek to hasten it; but those who believe are fearful of it, and know that it is the truth. Beware! those who dispute concerning the Hour are in error, far gone.

يَسْتَعْجِلُ بِهَا الَّذِيْنَ لَا يُؤْمِنُوْنَ بِهَا ۚ وَالَّذِيْنَ
اٰمَنُوْا مُشْفِقُوْنَ مِنْهَا ۙ وَيَعْلَمُوْنَ اَنَّهَا الْحَقُّ ۭ
اَلَآ اِنَّ الَّذِيْنَ يُمَارُوْنَ فِي السَّاعَةِ لَفِيْ ضَلٰلٍۢ
بَعِيْدٍ ﴿١٩﴾

* 20. Allah is Benignant to His servants. He provides for whom He pleases. And He is the Powerful, the Mighty.

اَللّٰهُ لَطِيْفٌۢ بِعِبَادِهٖ يَرْزُقُ مَنْ يَّشَاۗءُ ۚ وَهُوَ
ع الْقَوِيُّ الْعَزِيْزُ ﴿٢٠﴾

R. 3.

21. Whoso desires the harvest of the Hereafter, We give him increase in his harvest; and whoso desires the harvest of this world, We give him *thereof*, but in the Hereafter he will have no share.

مَنْ كَانَ يُرِيْدُ حَرْثَ الْاٰخِرَةِ نَزِدْ لَهٗ فِيْ حَرْثِهٖ ۚ
وَمَنْ كَانَ يُرِيْدُ حَرْثَ الدُّنْيَا نُؤْتِهٖ مِنْهَا وَ
مَا لَهٗ فِي الْاٰخِرَةِ مِنْ نَّصِيْبٍ ﴿٢١﴾

22. Have they *such* associates *of Allah* as have made lawful for them in religion that which Allah has not allowed? And but for *Our* word about the final judgment, *the matter* would have been decided *by now* between them. And surely the wrongdoers will have a grievous punishment.

اَمْ لَهُمْ شُرَكٰۗؤُا شَرَعُوْا لَهُمْ مِّنَ الدِّيْنِ مَا لَمْ يَاْذَنْۢ
بِهِ اللّٰهُ ۭ وَلَوْلَا كَلِمَةُ الْفَصْلِ لَقُضِيَ بَيْنَهُمْ ۭ وَ
اِنَّ الظّٰلِمِيْنَ لَهُمْ عَذَابٌ اَلِيْمٌ ﴿٢٢﴾

23. Thou wilt see the wrongdoers in fear on account of that which they have earned, and it is sure to befall them. But those who believe and do good works will be in the meadows of the Gardens. They shall have with their Lord whatever they will desire. That is the great bounty *of God*.

تَرَى الظّٰلِمِيْنَ مُشْفِقِيْنَ مِمَّا كَسَبُوْا وَهُوَ وَاقِعٌۢ
بِهِمْ ۭ وَالَّذِيْنَ اٰمَنُوْا وَعَمِلُوا الصّٰلِحٰتِ فِيْ رَوْضٰتِ
الْجَنّٰتِ ۚ لَهُمْ مَّا يَشَاۗءُوْنَ عِنْدَ رَبِّهِمْ ۭ ذٰلِكَ هُوَ
الْفَضْلُ الْكَبِيْرُ ﴿٢٣﴾

* 24. This it is whereof Allah gives the glad tidings to His servants who believe

ذٰلِكَ الَّذِيْ يُبَشِّرُ اللّٰهُ عِبَادَهُ الَّذِيْنَ اٰمَنُوْا وَعَمِلُوا

and do good works. Say: 'I ask of you no reward for it, except *that I am inviting you to God because of* love of kinship.' And whoso earns a good deed, We give him increase of good therein. Surely, Allah is Most Forgiving, Most Appreciating.

الصّٰلِحٰتِ ۭ قُلْ لَّآ اَسْـَٔلُكُمْ عَلَيْهِ اَجْرًا اِلَّا الْمَوَدَّةَ
فِي الْقُرْبٰى ۭ وَمَنْ يَّقْتَرِفْ حَسَنَةً نَّزِدْ لَهٗ فِيْهَا
حُسْنًا ۭ اِنَّ اللّٰهَ غَفُوْرٌ شَكُوْرٌ ﴿٢٤﴾

* 25. Do they say, 'He has forged a lie against Allah?' If Allah had *so* willed, He could seal thy heart *as He has sealed the hearts of thy enemies*. But Allah is blotting out falsehood *through thee* and is establishing the truth by His words. Surely, He knows full well what is in the breasts.

اَمْ يَقُوْلُوْنَ افْتَرٰى عَلَى اللّٰهِ كَذِبًا ۚ فَاِنْ يَّشَاِ اللّٰهُ
يَخْتِمْ عَلٰى قَلْبِكَ ۭ وَيَمْحُ اللّٰهُ الْبَاطِلَ وَيُحِقُّ الْحَقَّ
بِكَلِمٰتِهٖ ۭ اِنَّهٗ عَلِيْمٌۢ بِذَاتِ الصُّدُوْرِ ﴿٢٥﴾

26. And He it is Who accepts repentance from His servants, and forgives sins. And He knows what you do.

وَهُوَ الَّذِيْ يَقْبَلُ التَّوْبَةَ عَنْ عِبَادِهٖ وَيَعْفُوْا
عَنِ السَّيِّاٰتِ وَيَعْلَمُ مَا تَفْعَلُوْنَ ﴿٢٦﴾

27. And He accepts *the prayers of* those who believe and do good works, and gives them more out of His grace; and *as for* the disbelievers, they will have a severe punishment.

وَيَسْتَجِيْبُ الَّذِيْنَ اٰمَنُوْا وَعَمِلُوا الصّٰلِحٰتِ وَيَزِيْدُهُمْ
مِّنْ فَضْلِهٖ ۭ وَالْكٰفِرُوْنَ لَهُمْ عَذَابٌ شَدِيْدٌ ﴿٢٧﴾

28. And if Allah should enlarge the provision for His servants, they would rebel in the earth; but He sends down according to a *proper* measure as He pleases. Indeed, He is All-Aware and All-Seeing with regard to His servants.

وَلَوْ بَسَطَ اللّٰهُ الرِّزْقَ لِعِبَادِهٖ لَبَغَوْا فِي الْاَرْضِ
وَلٰكِنْ يُّنَزِّلُ بِقَدَرٍ مَّا يَشَاۗءُ ۭ اِنَّهٗ بِعِبَادِهٖ خَبِيْرٌۢ
بَصِيْرٌ ﴿٢٨﴾

29. And He it is Who sends down rain after they have despaired, and spreads out His mercy. And He is the Protector, the Praiseworthy.

وَهُوَ الَّذِيْ يُنَزِّلُ الْغَيْثَ مِنْ بَعْدِ مَا قَنَطُوْا
وَيَنْشُرُ رَحْمَتَهٗ ۭ وَهُوَ الْوَلِيُّ الْحَمِيْدُ ﴿٢٩﴾

30. And among His Signs is the creation of the heavens and the earth, and *of* whatever living creatures He has spread forth in both. And He has the power to gather them together when He pleases.

وَمِنْ اٰيٰتِهٖ خَلْقُ السَّمٰوٰتِ وَالْاَرْضِ وَمَا بَثَّ
فِيْهِمَا مِنْ دَاۗبَّةٍ ۭ وَهُوَ عَلٰي جَمْعِهِمْ اِذَا يَشَاۗءُ
قَدِيْرٌ ﴿٣٠﴾ ع

R. 4.

31. And whatever misfortune befalls you, is due to what your own hands have wrought. And He forgives many *of your sins*.

وَمَآ اَصَابَكُمْ مِّنْ مُّصِيْبَةٍ فَبِمَا كَسَبَتْ اَيْدِيْكُمْ
وَيَعْفُوْا عَنْ كَثِيْرٍ ﴿٣١﴾

32. And you cannot frustrate *God's plan* in the earth; nor have you any friend or helper beside Allah.

وَمَآ اَنْتُمْ بِمُعْجِزِيْنَ فِي الْاَرْضِ ښ وَمَا لَكُمْ
مِّنْ دُوْنِ اللّٰهِ مِنْ وَّلِيٍّ وَّلَا نَصِيْرٍ ﴿٣٢﴾

33. And of His Signs are the sailing-ships on the sea like mountain tops:

وَمِنْ اٰيٰتِهِ الْجَوَارِ فِي الْبَحْرِ كَالْاَعْلَامِ ﴿٣٣﴾

34. If He *so* will, He can cause the wind to become still so that they become motionless upon the surface thereof—in that, surely, are Signs for every person who is most patient and grateful—

اِنْ يَّشَاْ يُسْكِنِ الرِّيْحَ فَيَظْلَلْنَ رَوَاكِدَ عَلٰى ظَهْرِهٖ ؕ اِنَّ فِيْ ذٰلِكَ لَاٰيٰتٍ لِّكُلِّ صَبَّارٍ شَكُوْرٍ ﴿٣٤﴾

35. Or He can destroy them because of that which they (the men) have earned—but He forgives many *of their sins*—

اَوْ يُوْبِقْهُنَّ بِمَا كَسَبُوْا وَيَعْفُ عَنْ كَثِيْرٍ ﴿٣٥﴾

36. And *He destroys them so that* those who dispute about the Signs of Allah may know *that* they have no refuge.

وَّيَعْلَمَ الَّذِيْنَ يُجَادِلُوْنَ فِيْۤ اٰيٰتِنَا ؕ مَا لَهُمْ مِّنْ مَّحِيْصٍ ﴿٣٦﴾

37. And whatever you have been given is only a temporary provision of this life, but that which is with Allah is better and more lasting for those who believe and put their trust in their Lord,

فَمَاۤ اُوْتِيْتُمْ مِّنْ شَيْءٍ فَمَتَاعُ الْحَيٰوةِ الدُّنْيَا ۚ وَمَا عِنْدَ اللّٰهِ خَيْرٌ وَّاَبْقٰى لِلَّذِيْنَ اٰمَنُوْا وَعَلٰى رَبِّهِمْ يَتَوَكَّلُوْنَ ﴿٣٧﴾

38. And who eschew the more grievous sins and indecencies, and, when they are wroth, they forgive,

وَالَّذِيْنَ يَجْتَنِبُوْنَ كَبٰٓئِرَ الْاِثْمِ وَالْفَوَاحِشَ وَاِذَا مَا غَضِبُوْا هُمْ يَغْفِرُوْنَ ﴿٣٨﴾

39. And those who hearken to their Lord, and observe Prayer, and whose affairs are *decided* by mutual consultation, and who spend out of what We have provided for them,

وَالَّذِيْنَ اسْتَجَابُوْا لِرَبِّهِمْ وَاَقَامُوا الصَّلٰوةَ ۪ وَاَمْرُهُمْ شُوْرٰى بَيْنَهُمْ ۪ وَمِمَّا رَزَقْنٰهُمْ يُنْفِقُوْنَ ﴿٣٩﴾

40. And those who, when a wrong is done to them, defend themselves.

وَالَّذِيْنَ اِذَاۤ اَصَابَهُمُ الْبَغْيُ هُمْ يَنْتَصِرُوْنَ ﴿٤٠﴾

41. And the recompense of an injury is an injury the like thereof; but whoso forgives and *his act* brings about reformation, his reward is with Allah. Surely, He loves not the wrongdoers.

وَجَزٰٓؤُا سَيِّئَةٍ سَيِّئَةٌ مِّثْلُهَا ۚ فَمَنْ عَفَا وَاَصْلَحَ فَاَجْرُهٗ عَلَى اللّٰهِ ؕ اِنَّهٗ لَا يُحِبُّ الظّٰلِمِيْنَ ﴿٤١﴾

42. But there is no blame on those who defend themselves after they have been wronged.

وَلَمَنِ انْتَصَرَ بَعْدَ ظُلْمِهٖ فَاُولٰٓئِكَ مَا عَلَيْهِمْ مِّنْ سَبِيْلٍ ﴿٤٢﴾

43. The blame is only on those who wrong men and transgress in the earth without justification. Such will have a grievous punishment.

اِنَّمَا السَّبِيْلُ عَلَى الَّذِيْنَ يَظْلِمُوْنَ النَّاسَ وَيَبْغُوْنَ فِي الْاَرْضِ بِغَيْرِ الْحَقِّ ؕ اُولٰٓئِكَ لَهُمْ عَذَابٌ اَلِيْمٌ ﴿٤٣﴾

44. And he who is patient and forgives—that surely is a matter of strong determination.

وَلَمَنْ صَبَرَ وَغَفَرَ اِنَّ ذٰلِكَ لَمِنْ عَزْمِ الْاُمُوْرِ ﴿٤٤﴾

R. 5.

45. And he whom Allah adjudges astray

وَمَنْ يُّضْلِلِ اللّٰهُ فَمَا لَهٗ مِنْ وَّلِيٍّ مِّنْۢ بَعْدِهٖ ؕ

—there is no protector for him thereafter. And thou wilt find the wrongdoers, when they see the punishment, saying: 'Is there any way of return?'

وَتَرَى الظّٰلِمِيْنَ لَمَّا رَاَوُا الْعَذَابَ يَقُوْلُوْنَ هَلْ
اِلٰى مَرَدٍّ مِّنْ سَبِيْلٍ ﴿۴۵﴾

46. And thou wilt see them brought before it (the Fire), casting down *their eyes* on account of disgrace, looking *thereat* with a stealthy glance. And those who believe will say, 'The losers indeed are those who ruin themselves and their families on the Day of Resurrection.' Behold! the wrongdoers are *to remain* in a lasting punishment.

وَتَرٰىهُمْ يُعْرَضُوْنَ عَلَيْهَا خٰشِعِيْنَ مِنَ الذُّلِّ
يَنْظُرُوْنَ مِنْ طَرْفٍ خَفِيٍّ ؕ وَقَالَ الَّذِيْنَ اٰمَنُوْٓا
اِنَّ الْخٰسِرِيْنَ الَّذِيْنَ خَسِرُوْٓا اَنْفُسَهُمْ وَاَهْلِيْهِمْ
يَوْمَ الْقِيٰمَةِ ؕ اَلَآ اِنَّ الظّٰلِمِيْنَ فِيْ عَذَابٍ مُّقِيْمٍ ﴿۴۶﴾

47. And they have no helpers to help them other than Allah. And for him whom Allah adjudges astray there is no way *at all*.

وَمَا كَانَ لَهُمْ مِّنْ اَوْلِيَآءَ يَنْصُرُوْنَهُمْ مِّنْ دُوْنِ
اللّٰهِ ؕ وَمَنْ يُّضْلِلِ اللّٰهُ فَمَا لَهٗ مِنْ سَبِيْلٍ ؕ ﴿۴۷﴾

48. Hearken ye to your Lord before there comes a day for which there will be no averting in opposition to *the decree of* Allah. There will be no refuge for you on that day, nor will there be for you any *possibility of* denial.

اِسْتَجِيْبُوْا لِرَبِّكُمْ مِّنْ قَبْلِ اَنْ يَّاْتِيَ يَوْمٌ لَّا مَرَدَّ
لَهٗ مِنَ اللّٰهِ ؕ مَا لَكُمْ مِّنْ مَّلْجَاٍ يَّوْمَئِذٍ وَّمَا لَكُمْ
مِّنْ نَّكِيْرٍ ﴿۴۸﴾

49. But if they turn away, We have not sent thee as a guardian over them. Thy duty is only to convey *the Message*. And truly when We cause man to taste of mercy from Us, he rejoices therein. But if an evil befalls them because of what their hands have sent forth, then lo! man is ungrateful.

فَاِنْ اَعْرَضُوْا فَمَآ اَرْسَلْنٰكَ عَلَيْهِمْ حَفِيْظًا ؕ اِنْ عَلَيْكَ
اِلَّا الْبَلٰغُ ؕ وَاِنَّآ اِذَآ اَذَقْنَا الْاِنْسَانَ مِنَّا رَحْمَةً فَرِحَ
بِهَا ۚ وَاِنْ تُصِبْهُمْ سَيِّئَةٌ ۢ بِمَا قَدَّمَتْ اَيْدِيْهِمْ
فَاِنَّ الْاِنْسَانَ كَفُوْرٌ ﴿۴۹﴾

50. To Allah belongs the kingdom of the heavens and the earth. He creates what He pleases. He bestows daughters upon whom He pleases, and He bestows sons upon whom He pleases;

لِلّٰهِ مُلْكُ السَّمٰوٰتِ وَالْاَرْضِ ؕ يَخْلُقُ مَا يَشَآءُ ؕ
يَهَبُ لِمَنْ يَّشَآءُ اِنَاثًا وَّيَهَبُ لِمَنْ يَّشَآءُ
الذُّكُوْرَ ۙ ﴿۵۰﴾

51. Or He mixes them, males and females; and He makes whom He pleases barren. Surely, He is All-Knowing, Powerful.

اَوْ يُزَوِّجُهُمْ ذُكْرَانًا وَّاِنَاثًا ۚ وَيَجْعَلُ مَنْ يَّشَآءُ
عَقِيْمًا ؕ اِنَّهٗ عَلِيْمٌ قَدِيْرٌ ﴿۵۱﴾

52. And it is not for a man that Allah should speak to him except by revelation or from behind a veil or by sending a messenger to reveal by His command what

وَمَا كَانَ لِبَشَرٍ اَنْ يُّكَلِّمَهُ اللّٰهُ اِلَّا وَحْيًا اَوْ مِنْ
وَّرَآئِ حِجَابٍ اَوْ يُرْسِلَ رَسُوْلًا فَيُوْحِيَ بِاِذْنِهٖ

He pleases. Surely, He is High, Wise.

مَا يَشَآءُ ۭ اِنَّهٗ عَلِيٌّ حَكِيْمٌ ﴿۵۲﴾

53. And thus have We revealed to thee the Word by Our command. Thou didst not know what the Book was, nor what the faith. But We have made it (the revelation) a light, whereby We guide such of Our servants as We please. And truly, thou guidest *mankind* to the right path,

وَكَذٰلِكَ اَوْحَيْنَآ اِلَيْكَ رُوْحًا مِّنْ اَمْرِنَا ۭ مَا كُنْتَ
تَدْرِيْ مَا الْكِتٰبُ وَلَا الْاِيْمَانُ وَلٰكِنْ جَعَلْنٰهُ
نُوْرًا نَّهْدِيْ بِهٖ مَنْ نَّشَآءُ مِنْ عِبَادِنَا ۭ وَاِنَّكَ
لَتَهْدِيْٓ اِلٰى صِرَاطٍ مُّسْتَقِيْمٍ ﴿۵۳﴾

54. The path of Allah, to Whom belongs whatever is in the heavens and whatever is in the earth. Behold! to Allah do all things return.

صِرَاطِ اللّٰهِ الَّذِيْ لَهٗ مَا فِي السَّمٰوٰتِ وَمَا فِي الْاَرْضِ
اَلَآ اِلَى اللّٰهِ تَصِيْرُ الْاُمُوْرُ ﴿۵۴﴾ ع

سُوْرَةُ الزُّخْرُفِ مَكِّيَّةٌ (٤٣)

AL-ZUKHRUF

(Revealed before Hijra)

1. In the name of Allah, the Gracious, the Merciful.

2. Ḥā Mīm*.

3. By this perspicuous Book,

4. We have made it a Qur'ān in clear, eloquent language that you may understand.

* 5. And surely, it is *safe* with Us in the Mother of the Book, exalted *and* full of wisdom.

6. Shall We then take away the Reminder from you, neglecting *you* because you are an extravagant people?

7. And how many a Prophet did We send among the earlier peoples!

8. But there never came to them a Prophet but they mocked at him.

* 9. And We destroyed *those* who were stronger in power than these, and the example of the earlier peoples has gone before.

10. And if thou ask them, 'Who created the heavens and the earth?' they will surely say, 'The Mighty, the All-Knowing *God* created them.'

11. *He*, Who has made the earth for you a cradle, and has made pathways, for you therein, that you may follow the right way;

12. And Who sends down water from the sky in proper measure, and We thereby quicken a dead land;—even so will you be raised;—

13. And Who has created all the pairs, and has made for you ships and cattle whereon you ride,

* 14. That you may sit firmly upon their backs, *and* then, when you are firmly seated thereon, you may remember the favour of your Lord, and say, 'Holy is He

بِسْمِ اللّٰهِ الرَّحْمٰنِ الرَّحِيْمِ ①

حٰمٓ ②

وَالْكِتٰبِ الْمُبِيْنِ ③

إِنَّا جَعَلْنٰهُ قُرْءٰنًا عَرَبِيًّا لَّعَلَّكُمْ تَعْقِلُوْنَ ④

وَإِنَّهٗ فِيْٓ أُمِّ الْكِتٰبِ لَدَيْنَا لَعَلِيٌّ حَكِيْمٌ ⑤

أَفَنَضْرِبُ عَنْكُمُ الذِّكْرَ صَفْحًا أَنْ كُنْتُمْ قَوْمًا مُّسْرِفِيْنَ ⑥

وَكَمْ أَرْسَلْنَا مِنْ نَّبِيٍّ فِي الْأَوَّلِيْنَ ⑦

وَمَا يَأْتِيْهِمْ مِّنْ نَّبِيٍّ إِلَّا كَانُوْا بِهٖ يَسْتَهْزِءُوْنَ ⑧

فَأَهْلَكْنَآ أَشَدَّ مِنْهُمْ بَطْشًا وَّمَضٰى مَثَلُ الْأَوَّلِيْنَ ⑨

وَلَئِنْ سَأَلْتَهُمْ مَّنْ خَلَقَ السَّمٰوٰتِ وَالْأَرْضَ
لَيَقُوْلُنَّ خَلَقَهُنَّ الْعَزِيْزُ الْعَلِيْمُ ⑩

الَّذِيْ جَعَلَ لَكُمُ الْأَرْضَ مَهْدًا وَّجَعَلَ لَكُمْ
فِيْهَا سُبُلًا لَّعَلَّكُمْ تَهْتَدُوْنَ ⑪

وَالَّذِيْ نَزَّلَ مِنَ السَّمَآءِ مَآءً بِقَدَرٍ فَأَنْشَرْنَا
بِهٖ بَلْدَةً مَّيْتًا كَذٰلِكَ تُخْرَجُوْنَ ⑫

وَالَّذِيْ خَلَقَ الْأَزْوَاجَ كُلَّهَا وَجَعَلَ لَكُمْ مِّنَ
الْفُلْكِ وَالْأَنْعَامِ مَا تَرْكَبُوْنَ ⑬

لِتَسْتَوٗا عَلٰى ظُهُوْرِهٖ ثُمَّ تَذْكُرُوْا نِعْمَةَ رَبِّكُمْ
إِذَا اسْتَوَيْتُمْ عَلَيْهِ وَتَقُوْلُوْا سُبْحٰنَ الَّذِيْ سَخَّرَ

* The Praiseworthy, the Lord of Honour.

Who has subjected this to us, and we had not the strength to subdue it *ourselves*.

15. 'And to our Lord surely shall we return.'

* 16. And a portion of His servants they assert to be His *children*. Indeed man is clearly ungrateful.

R. 2.

17. Has He taken daughters from what He has created, and honoured you with sons?

18. Yet when tidings are given to one of them of that the like of which he ascribes to the Gracious *God*, his face becomes darkened and he is choked with grief.

19. *Do you ascribe to God* one who is reared among ornaments, and who is not clear in disputation?

20. And they describe the angels, who are the servants of the Gracious *God*, as females. Did they witness their creation? Then their testimony will be recorded, and they shall be questioned.

21. And they say, 'If the Gracious *God* had *so* willed, we should not have worshipped them.' They have no knowledge whatsoever of that. They do nothing but conjecture.

22. Have We given them a Scripture before this, so that they are holding fast to it?

23. Nay, they say, 'We found our fathers following a *certain* course, and we are guided by their footsteps.'

* 24. And thus *has it always been* that We never sent any Warner before thee to any township but the evil leaders thereof said: 'We found our fathers following a *certain* course, and we are following in their footsteps.'

25. *Their Warner* said: 'What! even though I bring you a better guidance than that which you found your fathers following?' They said: 'Certainly we disbelieve in that which you are sent with.'

* 26. So We punished them. Behold then

لَنَا هٰذَا وَمَا كُنَّا لَهٗ مُقْرِنِيْنَ ﴿١٤﴾

وَاِنَّآ اِلٰى رَبِّنَا لَمُنْقَلِبُوْنَ ﴿١٥﴾

وَجَعَلُوْا لَهٗ مِنْ عِبَادِهٖ جُزْءًا ۭ اِنَّ الْاِنْسَانَ لَكَفُوْرٌ

مُّبِيْنٌ ﴿١٦﴾ ع

اَمِ اتَّخَذَ مِمَّا يَخْلُقُ بَنٰتٍ وَّاَصْفٰكُمْ بِالْبَنِيْنَ ﴿١٧﴾

وَاِذَا بُشِّرَ اَحَدُهُمْ بِمَا ضَرَبَ لِلرَّحْمٰنِ مَثَلًا

ظَلَّ وَجْهُهٗ مُسْوَدًّا وَّهُوَ كَظِيْمٌ ﴿١٨﴾

اَوَمَنْ يُّنَشَّؤُا فِي الْحِلْيَةِ وَهُوَ فِي الْخِصَامِ غَيْرُ

مُبِيْنٍ ﴿١٩﴾

وَجَعَلُوا الْمَلٰٓئِكَةَ الَّذِيْنَ هُمْ عِبٰدُ الرَّحْمٰنِ اِنَاثًا ۭ

اَشَهِدُوْا خَلْقَهُمْ ۭ سَتُكْتَبُ شَهَادَتُهُمْ وَيُسْئَلُوْنَ ﴿٢٠﴾

وَقَالُوْا لَوْ شَآءَ الرَّحْمٰنُ مَا عَبَدْنٰهُمْ ۭ مَا لَهُمْ

بِذٰلِكَ مِنْ عِلْمٍ ۤ اِنْ هُمْ اِلَّا يَخْرُصُوْنَ ﴿٢١﴾

اَمْ اٰتَيْنٰهُمْ كِتٰبًا مِّنْ قَبْلِهٖ فَهُمْ بِهٖ مُسْتَمْسِكُوْنَ ﴿٢٢﴾

بَلْ قَالُوْٓا اِنَّا وَجَدْنَآ اٰبَآءَنَا عَلٰٓى اُمَّةٍ وَّاِنَّا عَلٰٓى اٰثٰرِهِمْ

مُّهْتَدُوْنَ ﴿٢٣﴾

وَكَذٰلِكَ مَآ اَرْسَلْنَا مِنْ قَبْلِكَ فِيْ قَرْيَةٍ مِّنْ نَّذِيْرٍ

اِلَّا قَالَ مُتْرَفُوْهَآ ۙ اِنَّا وَجَدْنَآ اٰبَآءَنَا عَلٰٓى اُمَّةٍ وَّ

اِنَّا عَلٰٓى اٰثٰرِهِمْ مُّقْتَدُوْنَ ﴿٢٤﴾

قٰلَ اَوَلَوْ جِئْتُكُمْ بِاَهْدٰى مِمَّا وَجَدْتُّمْ عَلَيْهِ

اٰبَآءَكُمْ ۭ قَالُوْٓا اِنَّا بِمَآ اُرْسِلْتُمْ بِهٖ كٰفِرُوْنَ ﴿٢٥﴾

فَانْتَقَمْنَا مِنْهُمْ فَانْظُرْ كَيْفَ كَانَ عَاقِبَةُ

what was the end of those who rejected *the Prophets!*

الْمُكَذِّبِينَ ﴿٢٦﴾

R. 3.

27. And *remember* when Abraham said to his father and his people: 'I *positively* disown what you worship,

وَإِذْ قَالَ إِبْرٰهِيمُ لِأَبِيهِ وَقَوْمِهِٓ إِنَّنِي بَرَآءٌ مِّمَّا تَعْبُدُونَ ﴿٢٧﴾

28. 'Except Him Who created me, and He will surely guide me.'

إِلَّا الَّذِي فَطَرَنِي فَإِنَّهُ سَيَهْدِينِ ﴿٢٨﴾

29. And He made it a byword to last among his posterity, that they might turn *to God*.

وَجَعَلَهَا كَلِمَةًۢ بَاقِيَةً فِي عَقِبِهِ لَعَلَّهُمْ يَرْجِعُونَ ﴿٢٩﴾

30. Nay, but I allowed them and their fathers *temporary* enjoyment until there came to them the truth and a Messenger who makes *his Message* clear.

بَلْ مَتَّعْتُ هٰٓؤُلَآءِ وَآبَآءَهُمْ حَتّٰى جَآءَهُمُ الْحَقُّ وَرَسُولٌ مُّبِينٌ ﴿٣٠﴾

31. But when the truth came to them they said, 'This is magic, and we do reject it.'

وَلَمَّا جَآءَهُمُ الْحَقُّ قَالُوا هٰذَا سِحْرٌ وَّإِنَّا بِهِ كٰفِرُونَ ﴿٣١﴾

32. And they say, 'Why has not this Qur'ān been sent to some great man of the two towns?'

وَقَالُوا لَوْلَا نُزِّلَ هٰذَا الْقُرْآنُ عَلٰى رَجُلٍ مِّنَ الْقَرْيَتَيْنِ عَظِيمٍ ﴿٣٢﴾

* 33. Is it they who would distribute the mercy of thy Lord? It is We Who distribute among them their livelihood in the present life, and We exalt some of them above others in degrees *of rank*, so that some of them may make others subservient *to themselves*. And the mercy of thy Lord is better than that which they amass.

أَهُمْ يَقْسِمُونَ رَحْمَتَ رَبِّكَ نَحْنُ قَسَمْنَا بَيْنَهُم مَّعِيشَتَهُمْ فِي الْحَيٰوةِ الدُّنْيَا وَرَفَعْنَا بَعْضَهُمْ فَوْقَ بَعْضٍ دَرَجٰتٍ لِّيَتَّخِذَ بَعْضُهُم بَعْضًا سُخْرِيًّا وَرَحْمَتُ رَبِّكَ خَيْرٌ مِّمَّا يَجْمَعُونَ ﴿٣٣﴾

34. And were it not that mankind would have *all* become one *type of* people, We would have given to those who disbelieve in the Gracious *God*, roofs of silver for their houses, and *silver* stairways by which they could go up;

وَلَوْلَآ أَن يَكُونَ النَّاسُ أُمَّةً وَّاحِدَةً لَّجَعَلْنَا لِمَن يَكْفُرُ بِالرَّحْمٰنِ لِبُيُوتِهِمْ سُقُفًا مِّن فِضَّةٍ وَّمَعَارِجَ عَلَيْهَا يَظْهَرُونَ ﴿٣٤﴾

35. And doors *of silver* to their houses, and couches *of silver*, on which they could recline,

وَلِبُيُوتِهِمْ أَبْوَابًا وَّسُرُرًا عَلَيْهَا يَتَّكِـُٔونَ ﴿٣٥﴾

36. And *other articles of* embellishment. But all that is nothing but a *temporary* provision of the present life. And the Hereafter with thy Lord is for the righteous.

وَزُخْرُفًا وَإِن كُلُّ ذٰلِكَ لَمَّا مَتَاعُ الْحَيٰوةِ الدُّنْيَا وَالْآخِرَةُ عِندَ رَبِّكَ لِلْمُتَّقِينَ ﴿٣٦﴾

R. 4.

37. And he who turns away from the remembrance of the Gracious *God*, We

وَمَن يَعْشُ عَن ذِكْرِ الرَّحْمٰنِ نُقَيِّضْ لَهُ شَيْطٰنًا

appoint for him a satan, who becomes his companion.

فَهُوَ لَهٗ قَرِيۡنٌ ﴿٣٧﴾

38. And surely they hinder them from the way *of God*, but they think that they are rightly guided;

وَ اِنَّهُمۡ لَيَصُدُّوۡنَهُمۡ عَنِ السَّبِيۡلِ وَ يَحۡسَبُوۡنَ اَنَّهُمۡ
مُّهۡتَدُوۡنَ ﴿٣٨﴾

39. Till, when such a one comes to Us, he says *to his companion*, 'Would that between me and thee were the distance of the East and the West!' What an evil companion is he!

حَتّٰۤى اِذَا جَآءَنَا قَالَ يٰلَيۡتَ بَيۡنِىۡ وَ بَيۡنَكَ بُعۡدَ
الۡمَشۡرِقَيۡنِ فَبِئۡسَ الۡقَرِيۡنُ ﴿٣٩﴾

* 40. 'And *the fact* that you are partners in punishment will not profit you this day for you have acted wrongfully.'

وَ لَنۡ يَّنۡفَعَكُمُ الۡيَوۡمَ اِذۡ ظَّلَمۡتُمۡ اَنَّكُمۡ فِى الۡعَذَابِ
مُشۡتَرِكُوۡنَ ﴿٤٠﴾

41. Canst thou, then, make the deaf hear, or guide the blind and him who is in manifest error?

اَفَاَنۡتَ تُسۡمِعُ الصُّمَّ اَوۡ تَهۡدِى الۡعُمۡىَ وَ مَنۡ كَانَ
فِىۡ ضَلٰلٍ مُّبِيۡنٍ ﴿٤١﴾

42. And if We take thee away, We shall surely exact retribution from them,

فَاِمَّا نَذۡهَبَنَّ بِكَ فَاِنَّا مِنۡهُمۡ مُّنۡتَقِمُوۡنَ ﴿٤٢﴾

43. Or We shall show thee that which We have promised them; for surely We have complete power over them.

اَوۡ نُرِيَنَّكَ الَّذِىۡ وَعَدۡنٰهُمۡ فَاِنَّا عَلَيۡهِمۡ مُّقۡتَدِرُوۡنَ ﴿٤٣﴾

44. So hold thou fast to that which has been revealed to thee; for thou art on the right path.

فَاسۡتَمۡسِكۡ بِالَّذِىۡۤ اُوۡحِىَ اِلَيۡكَ ۚ اِنَّكَ عَلٰى صِرَاطٍ
مُّسۡتَقِيۡمٍ ﴿٤٤﴾

* 45. And, truly, it is *a source of* eminence for thee and for thy people; and you will be inquired about.

وَ اِنَّهٗ لَذِكۡرٌ لَّكَ وَ لِقَوۡمِكَ ۚ وَ سَوۡفَ تُسۡـَٔلُوۡنَ ﴿٤٥﴾

46. And ask those of Our Messengers whom We sent before thee, 'Did We appoint any deities beside the Gracious *God*, to be worshipped?'

وَ سۡـَٔلۡ مَنۡ اَرۡسَلۡنَا مِنۡ قَبۡلِكَ مِنۡ رُّسُلِنَاۤ اَجَعَلۡنَا
مِنۡ دُوۡنِ الرَّحۡمٰنِ اٰلِهَةً يُّعۡبَدُوۡنَ ﴿٤٦﴾ ع

R. 5.

47. And We did send Moses with Our Signs to Pharaoh and his chiefs, and he said, 'I am truly a Messenger of the Lord of the worlds.'

وَ لَقَدۡ اَرۡسَلۡنَا مُوۡسٰى بِاٰيٰتِنَاۤ اِلٰى فِرۡعَوۡنَ وَ مَلَا۟ئِهٖ
فَقَالَ اِنِّىۡ رَسُوۡلُ رَبِّ الۡعٰلَمِيۡنَ ﴿٤٧﴾

48. But when he came to them with Our Signs, lo! they laughed at them.

فَلَمَّا جَآءَهُمۡ بِاٰيٰتِنَاۤ اِذَا هُمۡ مِّنۡهَا يَضۡحَكُوۡنَ ﴿٤٨﴾

49. And We showed them no Sign but it was greater than its *preceding* sister, and We seized them with punishment, that they might turn *to Us*.

وَ مَا نُرِيۡهِمۡ مِّنۡ اٰيَةٍ اِلَّا هِىَ اَكۡبَرُ مِنۡ اُخۡتِهَا ۫ وَ
اَخَذۡنٰهُمۡ بِالۡعَذَابِ لَعَلَّهُمۡ يَرۡجِعُوۡنَ ﴿٤٩﴾

50. And they said, 'O thou magician, pray for us to thy Lord, according to the covenant He has made with thee: for, then

وَ قَالُوۡا يٰۤاَيُّهَ السّٰحِرُ ادۡعُ لَنَا رَبَّكَ بِمَا عَهِدَ عِنۡدَكَ

we will surely accept guidance.'

إِنَّنَا لَمُهْتَدُونَ ٥٠

51. But when We removed the punishment from them, behold! they broke their word.

فَلَمَّا كَشَفْنَا عَنْهُمُ الْعَذَابَ إِذَا هُمْ يَنْكُثُونَ ٥١

52. And Pharaoh proclaimed among his people, *saying*, 'O my people! does not the kingdom of Egypt belong to me and these streams flowing under me? Do you not then see?

وَنَادَىٰ فِرْعَوْنُ فِي قَوْمِهِ قَالَ يَٰقَوْمِ أَلَيْسَ لِي
مُلْكُ مِصْرَ وَهَٰذِهِ الْأَنْهَٰرُ تَجْرِي مِنْ تَحْتِي أَفَلَا
تُبْصِرُونَ ٥٢

53. 'Nay, I am better than this *fellow* who is despicable and can scarcely express *himself* clearly.

أَمْ أَنَا خَيْرٌ مِنْ هَٰذَا الَّذِي هُوَ مَهِينٌ وَلَا يَكَادُ
يُبِينُ ٥٣

54. 'And why have not bracelets of gold been bestowed on him, or angels accompanied him in serried ranks?'

فَلَوْلَا أُلْقِيَ عَلَيْهِ أَسْوِرَةٌ مِنْ ذَهَبٍ أَوْ جَاءَ مَعَهُ
الْمَلَٰئِكَةُ مُقْتَرِنِينَ ٥٤

55. Thus did he make light of his people, and they obeyed him. Indeed they were a wicked people.

فَاسْتَخَفَّ قَوْمَهُ فَأَطَاعُوهُ إِنَّهُمْ كَانُوا قَوْمًا فَٰسِقِينَ ٥٥

56. So, when they excited Our anger, We exacted retribution from them, and drowned them all.

فَلَمَّا آسَفُونَا انْتَقَمْنَا مِنْهُمْ فَأَغْرَقْنَٰهُمْ أَجْمَعِينَ ٥٦

57. And We made them a precedent, and an example for the coming generations.

فَجَعَلْنَٰهُمْ سَلَفًا وَمَثَلًا لِلْآخِرِينَ ٥٧ ع

R. 6.

* 58. And when the son of Mary is mentioned as an instance, lo! thy people raise a clamour thereat;

وَلَمَّا ضُرِبَ ابْنُ مَرْيَمَ مَثَلًا إِذَا قَوْمُكَ مِنْهُ
يَصِدُّونَ ٥٨

59. And they say, 'Are our gods better, or he?' They mention not this to thee but for *the sake of* disputation. Nay, but they are a contentious people.

وَقَالُوا ءَأَٰلِهَتُنَا خَيْرٌ أَمْ هُوَ مَا ضَرَبُوهُ لَكَ إِلَّا جَدَلًا
بَلْ هُمْ قَوْمٌ خَصِمُونَ ٥٩

60. He was only Our servant on whom We bestowed Our favour, and We made him an example for the children of Israel.

إِنْ هُوَ إِلَّا عَبْدٌ أَنْعَمْنَا عَلَيْهِ وَجَعَلْنَٰهُ مَثَلًا لِبَنِي
إِسْرَاءِيلَ ٦٠

61. And if We *so* willed, We could make from among you angels in the earth to be successors *therein*.

وَلَوْ نَشَاءُ لَجَعَلْنَا مِنْكُمْ مَلَٰئِكَةً فِي الْأَرْضِ
يَخْلُفُونَ ٦١

* 62. But verily, he was a sign of the Hour. So have no doubt about it, but follow me. This is the right path.

وَإِنَّهُ لَعِلْمٌ لِلسَّاعَةِ فَلَا تَمْتَرُنَّ بِهَا وَاتَّبِعُونِ
هَٰذَا صِرَٰطٌ مُسْتَقِيمٌ ٦٢

63. And let not Satan hinder you. Surely, he is to you an open enemy.

ولا يصدنكم الشيطن انه لكم عدو مبين ﴿٦٣﴾

64. And when Jesus came with clear proofs, he said, 'Truly I am come to you with wisdom, and to make clear to you some of that about which you differ. So fear Allah and obey me.

ولما جاء عيسى بالبينت قال قد جئتكم بالحكمة ولابين لكم بعض الذي تختلفون فيه فاتقوا الله واطيعون ﴿٦٤﴾

65. 'Verily Allah—He is my Lord and your Lord. So worship Him. This is the right path.'

ان الله هو ربي وربكم فاعبدوه هذا صراط مستقيم ﴿٦٥﴾

66. But the parties differed among themselves. So woe to the wrongdoers because of the punishment of a grievous day.

فاختلف الاحزاب من بينهم فويل للذين ظلموا من عذاب يوم اليم ﴿٦٦﴾

67. They wait not but for the Hour to come suddenly upon them, while they perceive *it* not.

هل ينظرون الا الساعة ان تاتيهم بغتة وهم لا يشعرون ﴿٦٧﴾

68. Friends on that day will be foes to each other, except the righteous.

الاخلاء يومئذ بعضهم لبعض عدو الا المتقين ﴿٦٨﴾

R. 7.

69. 'O My servants, there is no fear for you this day, nor shall you grieve;

يعباد لا خوف عليكم اليوم ولا انتم تحزنون ﴿٦٩﴾

* 70. '*You* who believed in Our Signs and submitted,

الذين امنوا بايتنا وكانوا مسلمين ﴿٧٠﴾

* 71. 'Enter ye the Garden, you and your wives, honoured and happy.'

ادخلوا الجنة انتم وازواجكم تحبرون ﴿٧١﴾

72. To them will be passed round dishes of gold and cups, and therein will be all that the souls desire and *in which* the eyes delight. 'And therein will you abide.

يطاف عليهم بصحاف من ذهب واكواب وفيها ما تشتهيه الانفس وتلذ الاعين وانتم فيها خلدون ﴿٧٢﴾

73. 'And this is the Garden to which you have been made heirs because of what you have been doing.

وتلك الجنة التي اورثتموها بما كنتم تعملون ﴿٧٣﴾

74. 'Therein for you is fruit in abundance, which you will eat.'

لكم فيها فاكهة كثيرة منها تاكلون ﴿٧٤﴾

75. The guilty will certainly abide in the punishment of Hell.

ان المجرمين في عذاب جهنم خلدون ﴿٧٥﴾

76. It will not be mitigated to them, and they will be seized therein with despair.

لا يفتر عنهم وهم فيه مبلسون ﴿٧٦﴾

77. And We wronged them not, but it was they themselves who were the wrong-doers.

* 78. And they will cry: 'O master! let thy Lord finish with us.' He will say, 'You must remain.'

79. *God will say:* 'We certainly brought you the truth; but most of you were averse to the truth.'

80. Have they determined upon a course? Then We *too* are determined.

81. Do they think that We hear not their secrets and their private counsels? Yea! And Our messengers remain with them recording *everything*.

82. Say, 'If there had been a son to the Gracious *God*, I would have been the first of worshippers.'

83. Holy is *Allah*, the Lord of the heavens and the earth, the Lord of the Throne, *and He is free* from all that which they attribute *to Him*.

84. So leave them alone to indulge in vain discourse and amuse themselves until they meet that Day of theirs which they have been promised.

85. And He it is Who is God in heaven, and God on earth; and He is the Wise, the All-Knowing.

86. And blessed is He to Whom belongs the kingdom of the heavens and the earth and all that is between them, and with Him is the knowledge of the Hour, and to Him shall you be brought back.

87. And those on whom they call beside Him possess no power of intercession but he who bears witness to the truth, and they know *him*.

88. And if thou ask them, 'Who created them?', they will surely say, 'Allah'. How then are they being turned away?

89. *I swear* by his *repeated* cry 'O my Lord!' that these are a people who will not believe.

90. Therefore, turn aside from them, and say, 'Peace'; and soon shall they know.

وَمَا ظَلَمْنٰهُمْ وَلٰكِنْ كَانُوْا هُمُ الظّٰلِمِيْنَ ﴿٧٧﴾
وَنَادَوْا يٰمٰلِكُ لِيَقْضِ عَلَيْنَا رَبُّكَ ۭ قَالَ اِنَّكُمْ مّٰكِثُوْنَ ﴿٧٨﴾
لَقَدْ جِئْنٰكُمْ بِالْحَقِّ وَلٰكِنَّ اَكْثَرَكُمْ لِلْحَقِّ كٰرِهُوْنَ ﴿٧٩﴾
اَمْ اَبْرَمُوْٓا اَمْرًا فَاِنَّا مُبْرِمُوْنَ ﴿٨٠﴾
اَمْ يَحْسَبُوْنَ اَنَّا لَا نَسْمَعُ سِرَّهُمْ وَنَجْوٰىهُمْ ۭ بَلٰى وَرُسُلُنَا لَدَيْهِمْ يَكْتُبُوْنَ ﴿٨١﴾
قُلْ اِنْ كَانَ لِلرَّحْمٰنِ وَلَدٌ ڰ فَاَنَا اَوَّلُ الْعٰبِدِيْنَ ﴿٨٢﴾
سُبْحٰنَ رَبِّ السَّمٰوٰتِ وَالْاَرْضِ رَبِّ الْعَرْشِ عَمَّا يَصِفُوْنَ ﴿٨٣﴾
فَذَرْهُمْ يَخُوْضُوْا وَيَلْعَبُوْا حَتّٰى يُلٰقُوْا يَوْمَهُمُ الَّذِيْ يُوْعَدُوْنَ ﴿٨٤﴾
وَهُوَ الَّذِيْ فِي السَّمَاۗءِ اِلٰهٌ وَّفِي الْاَرْضِ اِلٰهٌ ۭ وَهُوَ الْحَكِيْمُ الْعَلِيْمُ ﴿٨٥﴾
وَتَبٰرَكَ الَّذِيْ لَهٗ مُلْكُ السَّمٰوٰتِ وَالْاَرْضِ وَمَا بَيْنَهُمَا ۚ وَعِنْدَهٗ عِلْمُ السَّاعَةِ ۚ وَاِلَيْهِ تُرْجَعُوْنَ ﴿٨٦﴾
وَلَا يَمْلِكُ الَّذِيْنَ يَدْعُوْنَ مِنْ دُوْنِهِ الشَّفَاعَةَ اِلَّا مَنْ شَهِدَ بِالْحَقِّ وَهُمْ يَعْلَمُوْنَ ﴿٨٧﴾
وَلَىِٕنْ سَاَلْتَهُمْ مَّنْ خَلَقَهُمْ لَيَقُوْلُنَّ اللّٰهُ فَاَنّٰى يُؤْفَكُوْنَ ﴿٨٨﴾
وَقِيْلِهٖ يٰرَبِّ اِنَّ هٰٓؤُلَاۗءِ قَوْمٌ لَّا يُؤْمِنُوْنَ ﴿٨٩﴾
فَاصْفَحْ عَنْهُمْ وَقُلْ سَلٰمٌ ۭ فَسَوْفَ يَعْلَمُوْنَ ﴿٩٠﴾

سُوْرَةُ الدُّخَانِ مَكِّيَّةٌ (٤٤)

AL-DUKHĀN

(Revealed before Hijra)

1. In the name of Allah, the Gracious, the Merciful.

2. Ḥā Mīm*.

3. By this perspicuous Book.

4. Truly, We revealed it in a blessed Night. Truly, We have *ever* been warning *against evil*.

5. In it all wise things are decided,

6. *By* Our *own* command. Verily, We have ever been sending *Messengers*,

7. As a mercy from thy Lord. Verily, He is the All-Hearing, the All-Knowing,

8. The Lord of the heavens and the earth and all that is between them, if you would *only* have faith.

9. There is no God but He. He gives life and He causes death. He is your Lord, and the Lord of your forefathers.

10. Yet they play about in doubt.

11. But watch thou for the day when the sky will bring forth a visible smoke,

12. That will envelop the people. This will be a painful torment.

13. *Then will the people cry:* 'Our Lord, remove from us the torment; truly, we are believers.'

14. How can they benefit by admonition, when there has already come to them a Messenger, explaining things clearly,

15. And yet they turned away from him and said: 'He is tutored, a man possessed?'

16. We shall remove the punishment for a little while, *but* you will certainly revert *to disbelief*.

17. On the day when We shall seize *you* with the great seizure, then certainly We will exact retribution.

بِسْمِ اللّٰهِ الرَّحْمٰنِ الرَّحِيْمِ (١)

حٰمٓ (٢)

وَالْكِتٰبِ الْمُبِيْنِ (٣)

اِنَّآ اَنْزَلْنٰهُ فِيْ لَيْلَةٍ مُّبٰرَكَةٍ اِنَّا كُنَّا مُنْذِرِيْنَ (٤)

فِيْهَا يُفْرَقُ كُلُّ اَمْرٍ حَكِيْمٍ (٥)

اَمْرًا مِّنْ عِنْدِنَا ۭ اِنَّا كُنَّا مُرْسِلِيْنَ (٦)

رَحْمَةً مِّنْ رَّبِّكَ ۭ اِنَّهٗ هُوَ السَّمِيْعُ الْعَلِيْمُ (٧)

رَبِّ السَّمٰوٰتِ وَالْاَرْضِ وَمَا بَيْنَهُمَا ۘ اِنْ كُنْتُمْ مُّوْقِنِيْنَ (٨)

لَآ اِلٰهَ اِلَّا هُوَ يُحْيٖ وَيُمِيْتُ ۭ رَبُّكُمْ وَرَبُّ اٰبَآىِٕكُمُ الْاَوَّلِيْنَ (٩)

بَلْ هُمْ فِيْ شَكٍّ يَّلْعَبُوْنَ (١٠)

فَارْتَقِبْ يَوْمَ تَاْتِي السَّمَآءُ بِدُخَانٍ مُّبِيْنٍ (١١)

يَّغْشَى النَّاسَ ۭ هٰذَا عَذَابٌ اَلِيْمٌ (١٢)

رَبَّنَا اكْشِفْ عَنَّا الْعَذَابَ اِنَّا مُؤْمِنُوْنَ (١٣)

اَنّٰى لَهُمُ الذِّكْرٰى وَقَدْ جَآءَهُمْ رَسُوْلٌ مُّبِيْنٌ (١٤)

ثُمَّ تَوَلَّوْا عَنْهُ وَقَالُوْا مُعَلَّمٌ مَّجْنُوْنٌ (١٥)

اِنَّا كَاشِفُوا الْعَذَابِ قَلِيْلًا اِنَّكُمْ عَآىِٕدُوْنَ (١٦)

يَوْمَ نَبْطِشُ الْبَطْشَةَ الْكُبْرٰى ۚ اِنَّا مُنْتَقِمُوْنَ (١٧)

---

* The Praiseworthy, the Lord of Honour.

18. And We tried the people of Pharaoh before them, and there came to them a noble Messenger,

وَلَقَدْ فَتَنَّا قَبْلَهُمْ قَوْمَ فِرْعَوْنَ وَجَآءَهُمْ رَسُولٌ
كَرِيمٌ ﴿١٨﴾

19. *Saying*, 'Deliver to me the servants of Allah. Truly, I am to you a Messenger, faithful to *my* trust;

أَنْ أَدُّوٓا إِلَيَّ عِبَادَ اللّٰهِ ۖ إِنِّي لَكُمْ رَسُولٌ أَمِينٌ ﴿١٩﴾

20. 'And exalt not yourselves in defiance of Allah. Surely, I come to you with a clear authority.

وَأَن لَّا تَعْلُوا عَلَى اللّٰهِ ۖ إِنِّيٓ اٰتِيكُم بِسُلْطٰنٍ مُّبِينٍ ﴿٢٠﴾

21. 'And I seek refuge in my Lord and your Lord, lest you stone me.

وَإِنِّي عُذْتُ بِرَبِّي وَرَبِّكُمْ أَن تَرْجُمُونِ ﴿٢١﴾

22. 'And if you believe me not, then keep yourselves away from me.'

وَإِن لَّمْ تُؤْمِنُوا لِي فَاعْتَزِلُونِ ﴿٢٢﴾

23. Then he prayed unto his Lord, *saying*, 'These are indeed a sinful people.'

فَدَعَا رَبَّهٗٓ أَنَّ هٰٓؤُلَآءِ قَوْمٌ مُّجْرِمُونَ ﴿٢٣﴾ الثلثة

24. *God said*, 'Take My servants away by night; for you will surely be pursued.

فَأَسْرِ بِعِبَادِي لَيْلًا إِنَّكُم مُّتَّبَعُونَ ﴿٢٤﴾

25. 'And leave thou the sea *at a time when it is* motionless. Surely, they are a host that are doomed to be drowned.'

وَاتْرُكِ الْبَحْرَ رَهْوًا ۖ إِنَّهُمْ جُندٌ مُّغْرَقُونَ ﴿٢٥﴾

26. How many were the gardens and the springs that they left behind!

كَمْ تَرَكُوا مِن جَنّٰتٍ وَّعُيُونٍ ﴿٢٦﴾

27. And the cornfields and the noble places!

وَّزُرُوعٍ وَّمَقَامٍ كَرِيمٍ ﴿٢٧﴾

28. And the comforts wherein they took delight!

وَّنَعْمَةٍ كَانُوا فِيهَا فٰكِهِينَ ﴿٢٨﴾

29. Thus *it was destined to be*. And We made another people inherit these things.

كَذٰلِكَ ۖ وَأَوْرَثْنٰهَا قَوْمًا اٰخَرِينَ ﴿٢٩﴾

30. And the heaven and the earth wept not for them, nor were they given a respite.

فَمَا بَكَتْ عَلَيْهِمُ السَّمَآءُ وَالْأَرْضُ وَمَا كَانُوا
مُنظَرِينَ ﴿٣٠﴾ ع

R. 2.

31. And We delivered the children of Israel from the abasing torment

وَلَقَدْ نَجَّيْنَا بَنِيٓ إِسْرَآءِيلَ مِنَ الْعَذَابِ الْمُهِينِ ﴿٣١﴾

32. *Inflicted* by Pharaoh; he was surely haughty *even* among the extravagant.

مِن فِرْعَوْنَ ۚ إِنَّهٗ كَانَ عَالِيًا مِّنَ الْمُسْرِفِينَ ﴿٣٢﴾

33. And We chose them knowingly above the peoples *of their time*.

وَلَقَدِ اخْتَرْنٰهُمْ عَلٰى عِلْمٍ عَلَى الْعٰلَمِينَ ﴿٣٣﴾

34. And We gave them some Signs wherein was a clear trial.

وَاٰتَيْنٰهُم مِّنَ الْاٰيٰتِ مَا فِيهِ بَلٰٓؤٌا مُّبِينٌ ﴿٣٤﴾

35. These *people* do say:

إِنَّ هٰٓؤُلَآءِ لَيَقُولُونَ ﴿٣٥﴾

36. 'It is but our first *and only* death, *after which there is no life* and we shall not be raised again.

إِنْ هِيَ إِلَّا مَوْتَتُنَا الْأُولٰى وَمَا نَحْنُ بِمُنشَرِينَ ﴿٣٦﴾

37. 'So bring *back* our fathers, if you speak the truth.'

فَأْتُوا بِاٰبَآئِنَآ إِن كُنتُمْ صٰدِقِينَ ﴿٣٧﴾

38. Are they better or the people of Tubba‘ and those before them? We destroyed them because they were sinful.

39. And We created not the heavens and the earth, and all that is between them, in sport.

40. We created them not but with the requirements of truth *and justice,* but most of them understand not.

41. Verily, the Day of Decision is the appointed time for all of them,

42. The Day when a friend shall not avail a friend at all, nor shall they be helped,

43. Save those to whom Allah shows mercy. Surely, He is the Mighty, the Merciful.

R. 3.

44. Verily, the tree of Zaqqūm

45. Will be the food of the sinful,

46. Like molten copper, it will boil in *their* bellies,

47. Like the boiling of scalding water.

48. ‘Seize him and drag him into the midst of the blazing Fire;

49. ‘Then pour upon his head the torment of boiling water.’

50. ‘Taste *it!* Thou *didst consider* thyself the mighty, the honourable.

51. ‘This indeed is what you did doubt.’

52. Verily, the righteous will be in a place of security,

53. Amid gardens and springs,

54. Attired in fine silk and heavy brocade, facing one another.

55. Thus *will it be.* And We shall consort them with fair maidens, having wide, *beautiful* eyes.

56. They will call therein for every *kind of* fruit, in *peace and* security.

57. They will not taste death therein, other than the first death. And He will save them from the punishment of the blazing Fire,

أَهُمْ خَيْرٌ أَمْ قَوْمُ تُبَّعٍ وَّالَّذِيْنَ مِنْ قَبْلِهِمْ أَهْلَكْنٰهُمْ
إِنَّهُمْ كَانُوْا مُجْرِمِيْنَ ﴿٣٨﴾
وَمَا خَلَقْنَا السَّمٰوٰتِ وَالْأَرْضَ وَمَا بَيْنَهُمَا لٰعِبِيْنَ ﴿٣٩﴾
مَا خَلَقْنٰهُمَآ إِلَّا بِالْحَقِّ وَلٰكِنَّ أَكْثَرَهُمْ لَا يَعْلَمُوْنَ ﴿٤٠﴾
إِنَّ يَوْمَ الْفَصْلِ مِيْقَاتُهُمْ أَجْمَعِيْنَ ﴿٤١﴾
يَوْمَ لَا يُغْنِيْ مَوْلًى عَنْ مَّوْلًى شَيْـًٔا وَّلَا هُمْ يُنْصَرُوْنَ ﴿٤٢﴾
إِلَّا مَنْ رَّحِمَ اللّٰهُ إِنَّهٗ هُوَ الْعَزِيْزُ الرَّحِيْمُ ﴿٤٣﴾
إِنَّ شَجَرَتَ الزَّقُّوْمِ ﴿٤٤﴾
طَعَامُ الْأَثِيْمِ ﴿٤٥﴾
كَالْمُهْلِ يَغْلِيْ فِي الْبُطُوْنِ ﴿٤٦﴾
كَغَلْيِ الْحَمِيْمِ ﴿٤٧﴾
خُذُوْهُ فَاعْتِلُوْهُ إِلٰى سَوَآءِ الْجَحِيْمِ ﴿٤٨﴾
ثُمَّ صُبُّوْا فَوْقَ رَأْسِهٖ مِنْ عَذَابِ الْحَمِيْمِ ﴿٤٩﴾
ذُقْ إِنَّكَ أَنْتَ الْعَزِيْزُ الْكَرِيْمُ ﴿٥٠﴾
إِنَّ هٰذَا مَا كُنْتُمْ بِهٖ تَمْتَرُوْنَ ﴿٥١﴾
إِنَّ الْمُتَّقِيْنَ فِيْ مَقَامٍ أَمِيْنٍ ﴿٥٢﴾
فِيْ جَنّٰتٍ وَّعُيُوْنٍ ﴿٥٣﴾
يَّلْبَسُوْنَ مِنْ سُنْدُسٍ وَّإِسْتَبْرَقٍ مُّتَقٰبِلِيْنَ ﴿٥٤﴾
كَذٰلِكَ وَزَوَّجْنٰهُمْ بِحُوْرٍ عِيْنٍ ﴿٥٥﴾
يَدْعُوْنَ فِيْهَا بِكُلِّ فَاكِهَةٍ أٰمِنِيْنَ ﴿٥٦﴾
لَا يَذُوْقُوْنَ فِيْهَا الْمَوْتَ إِلَّا الْمَوْتَةَ الْأُوْلٰى وَ
وَقٰهُمْ عَذَابَ الْجَحِيْمِ ﴿٥٧﴾

58. *As an act of* grace from thy Lord. That is the supreme triumph.

فضلا من ربك ذلك هو الفوز العظيم ﴿٥٨﴾

59. And We have made it (the Qur'ān) easy in thy tongue that they may give heed.

فإنما يسرنه بلسانك لعلهم يتذكرون ﴿٥٩﴾

60. So wait thou; they *too* are waiting.

فارتقب إنهم مرتقبون ﴿٦٠﴾

سورة الجاثية مكية (٤٥) آياتها ٣٨ ركوعاتها ٤

Part 25 AL-JĀTHIYAH Chapter 45

(Revealed before Hijra)

1. In the name of Allah, the Gracious, the Merciful.

بسم الله الرحمن الرحيم ﴿١﴾

2. Ḥā Mīm*.

حم ﴿٢﴾

3. The revelation of this Book is from Allah, the Mighty, the Wise.

تنزيل الكتب من الله العزيز الحكيم ﴿٣﴾

4. Verily in the heavens and the earth are Signs for those who believe.

إن في السموت والأرض لأيت للمؤمنين ﴿٤﴾

5. And in your own creation and *in* that of all the creatures which He scatters *in the earth* are Signs for a people who possess firm faith.

وفي خلقكم وما يبث من دابة أيت لقوم
يوقنون ﴿٥﴾

6. And *in* the alternation of night and day, and the provision that Allah sends down from the sky, whereby He quickens the earth after its death, and *in* the change of the winds, are Signs for a people who *try to* understand.

واختلاف اليل والنهار وما أنزل الله من السماء
من رزق فأحيا به الأرض بعد موتها وتصريف
الريح أيت لقوم يعقلون ﴿٦﴾

7. These are the Signs of Allah which We rehearse unto thee with truth. In what word, then, after *rejecting that of* Allah and His Signs will they believe?

تلك أيت الله نتلوها عليك بالحق فبأي حديث
بعد الله وأيته يؤمنون ﴿٧﴾

8. Woe to every sinful liar,

ويل لكل أفاك أثيم ﴿٨﴾

9. Who hears the Signs of Allah recited unto him, and then proudly persists *in his disbelief*, as though he heard them not. So give him the tidings of a painful punishment.

يسمع أيت الله تتلى عليه ثم يصر مستكبرا كأن
لم يسمعها فبشره بعذاب أليم ﴿٩﴾

10. And when he learns something of

وإذا علم من أيتنا شيئا اتخذها هزوا أولئك

* The Praiseworthy, the Lord of Honour.

Our Signs, he makes a jest of them. For such there is an abasing punishment.

لَهُمْ عَذَابٌ مُّهِينٌ ﴿١٠﴾

11. Before them is Hell; and that which they have earned shall not avail them aught, nor shall those whom they have taken for protectors beside Allah. And they will have a great punishment.

مِن وَرَآئِهِمْ جَهَنَّمُ وَلَا يُغْنِي عَنْهُم مَّا كَسَبُوا شَيْئًا وَلَا مَا اتَّخَذُوا مِن دُونِ اللَّهِ أَوْلِيَاءَ وَلَهُمْ عَذَابٌ عَظِيمٌ ﴿١١﴾

12. This is guidance. And for those who disbelieve in the Signs of their Lord is the torture of a painful punishment.

هَٰذَا هُدًى وَالَّذِينَ كَفَرُوا بِآيَاتِ رَبِّهِمْ لَهُمْ عَذَابٌ مِّن رِّجْزٍ أَلِيمٌ ﴿١٢﴾

R. 2.

13. Allah it is Who has subjected the sea to you that ships may sail thereon by His command, and that you may seek of His bounty, and that you may be grateful.

اللَّهُ الَّذِي سَخَّرَ لَكُمُ الْبَحْرَ لِتَجْرِيَ الْفُلْكُ فِيهِ بِأَمْرِهِ وَلِتَبْتَغُوا مِن فَضْلِهِ وَلَعَلَّكُمْ تَشْكُرُونَ ﴿١٣﴾

14. And He has subjected to you whatsoever is in the heavens and whatsoever is in the earth; all *this is* from Him. In that surely are Signs for a people who reflect.

وَسَخَّرَ لَكُم مَّا فِي السَّمَاوَاتِ وَمَا فِي الْأَرْضِ جَمِيعًا مِّنْهُ إِنَّ فِي ذَٰلِكَ لَآيَاتٍ لِّقَوْمٍ يَتَفَكَّرُونَ ﴿١٤﴾

* 15. Tell those who believe to forgive those who *persecute them and* fear not the Days of Allah, that He may requite a people for what they earn.

قُل لِّلَّذِينَ آمَنُوا يَغْفِرُوا لِلَّذِينَ لَا يَرْجُونَ أَيَّامَ اللَّهِ لِيَجْزِيَ قَوْمًا بِمَا كَانُوا يَكْسِبُونَ ﴿١٥﴾

16. Whoso does right, does it for his own soul; and whoso does wrong, does so to its detriment. Then to your Lord will you *all* be brought back.

مَنْ عَمِلَ صَالِحًا فَلِنَفْسِهِ وَمَنْ أَسَاءَ فَعَلَيْهَا ثُمَّ إِلَىٰ رَبِّكُمْ تُرْجَعُونَ ﴿١٦﴾

17. And verily, We gave the children of Israel the Book, and sovereignty, and prophethood; and We provided them with *good and* pure things, and We exalted them over the peoples *of the time*.

وَلَقَدْ آتَيْنَا بَنِي إِسْرَائِيلَ الْكِتَابَ وَالْحُكْمَ وَالنُّبُوَّةَ وَرَزَقْنَاهُم مِّنَ الطَّيِّبَاتِ وَفَضَّلْنَاهُمْ عَلَى الْعَالَمِينَ ﴿١٧﴾

* 18. And We gave them clear Signs regarding this affair. And they did not differ but after *true* knowledge had come to them, through mutual envy. Verily, thy Lord will judge between them on the Day of Resurrection concerning that wherein they differed.

وَآتَيْنَاهُم بَيِّنَاتٍ مِّنَ الْأَمْرِ فَمَا اخْتَلَفُوا إِلَّا مِن بَعْدِ مَا جَاءَهُمُ الْعِلْمُ بَغْيًا بَيْنَهُمْ إِنَّ رَبَّكَ يَقْضِي بَيْنَهُمْ يَوْمَ الْقِيَامَةِ فِيمَا كَانُوا فِيهِ يَخْتَلِفُونَ ﴿١٨﴾

* 19. Then We set thee on a clear path in the matter *of religion;* so follow it, and follow not the evil inclinations of those who know not.

ثُمَّ جَعَلْنَاكَ عَلَىٰ شَرِيعَةٍ مِّنَ الْأَمْرِ فَاتَّبِعْهَا وَلَا تَتَّبِعْ أَهْوَاءَ الَّذِينَ لَا يَعْلَمُونَ ﴿١٩﴾

20. Verily, they will not avail thee aught against Allah. And as for the wrongdoers, some of them are friends of others; but Allah is the Friend of the righteous.

اِنَّهُمْ لَنْ يُّغْنُوْا عَنْكَ مِنَ اللّٰهِ شَيْـًٔا ؕ وَاِنَّ الظّٰلِمِيْنَ
بَعْضُهُمْ اَوْلِيَآءُ بَعْضٍ ۚ وَاللّٰهُ وَلِيُّ الْمُتَّقِيْنَ ﴿۲۰﴾

21. This *Book contains* clear evidences for mankind and is a guidance and a mercy for a people who possess firm faith.

هٰذَا بَصَآئِرُ لِلنَّاسِ وَهُدًى وَّرَحْمَةٌ لِّقَوْمٍ
يُّوْقِنُوْنَ ﴿۲۱﴾

22. Do those who commit evil deeds think that We shall make them like those who believe and do good works, so that their life and their death shall be equal? Evil *indeed* is what they judge.

اَمْ حَسِبَ الَّذِيْنَ اجْتَرَحُوا السَّيِّاٰتِ اَنْ نَّجْعَلَهُمْ
كَالَّذِيْنَ اٰمَنُوْا وَعَمِلُوا الصّٰلِحٰتِ ۙ سَوَآءً مَّحْيَاهُمْ
وَمَمَاتُهُمْ ؕ سَآءَ مَا يَحْكُمُوْنَ ﴿۲۲﴾ ع ۲ / ۱۸

R. 3.

23. And Allah has created the heavens and the earth with truth and that every soul may be requited for that which it earns; and they shall not be wronged.

وَخَلَقَ اللّٰهُ السَّمٰوٰتِ وَالْاَرْضَ بِالْحَقِّ وَلِتُجْزٰى
كُلُّ نَفْسٍۭ بِمَا كَسَبَتْ وَهُمْ لَا يُظْلَمُوْنَ ﴿۲۳﴾

* 24. Hast thou seen him who conceives of his god according to his own fancy, and whom Allah has adjudged astray on the basis of *His* knowledge, and whose ears and whose heart He has sealed up, and on whose eyes He has put a covering? Who, then, will guide him after Allah *has condemned him?* Will you not then heed?

اَفَرَءَيْتَ مَنِ اتَّخَذَ اِلٰهَهٗ هَوٰىهُ وَاَضَلَّهُ اللّٰهُ
عَلٰى عِلْمٍ وَّخَتَمَ عَلٰى سَمْعِهٖ وَقَلْبِهٖ وَجَعَلَ عَلٰى
بَصَرِهٖ غِشٰوَةً ؕ فَمَنْ يَّهْدِيْهِ مِنْۢ بَعْدِ اللّٰهِ ؕ
اَفَلَا تَذَكَّرُوْنَ ﴿۲۴﴾

25. And they say, 'There is nothing but this our present life; we die and we live *here;* and nothing but Time destroys us.' But they have no knowledge of that; they do but conjecture.

وَقَالُوْا مَا هِيَ اِلَّا حَيَاتُنَا الدُّنْيَا نَمُوْتُ وَنَحْيَا
وَمَا يُهْلِكُنَآ اِلَّا الدَّهْرُ ۚ وَمَا لَهُمْ بِذٰلِكَ مِنْ
عِلْمٍ ۚ اِنْ هُمْ اِلَّا يَظُنُّوْنَ ﴿۲۵﴾

26. And when Our clear Signs are recited unto them, their only contention is that they say, 'Bring *back* our fathers, if you are truthful.'

وَاِذَا تُتْلٰى عَلَيْهِمْ اٰيٰتُنَا بَيِّنٰتٍ مَّا كَانَ حُجَّتَهُمْ
اِلَّآ اَنْ قَالُوا ائْتُوْا بِاٰبَآئِنَآ اِنْ كُنْتُمْ صٰدِقِيْنَ ﴿۲۶﴾

27. Say, '*It is* Allah *Who* gives you life, then causes you to die; then He will gather you together unto the Day of Resurrection about which there is no doubt. But most men know not.'

قُلِ اللّٰهُ يُحْيِيْكُمْ ثُمَّ يُمِيْتُكُمْ ثُمَّ يَجْمَعُكُمْ اِلٰى
يَوْمِ الْقِيٰمَةِ لَا رَيْبَ فِيْهِ وَلٰكِنَّ اَكْثَرَ النَّاسِ
لَا يَعْلَمُوْنَ ﴿۲۷﴾ ع ۳ / ۱۹

R. 4.

* 28. To Allah belongs the kingdom of the heavens and the earth; and on the day when the Hour shall come, on that day

وَلِلّٰهِ مُلْكُ السَّمٰوٰتِ وَالْاَرْضِ ؕ وَيَوْمَ تَقُوْمُ السَّاعَةُ

يَوْمَئِذٍ يَّخْسَرُ الْمُبْطِلُوْنَ ﴿٢٨﴾

those who follow falsehood will be the losers.

وَتَرٰى كُلَّ اُمَّةٍ جَاثِيَةً كُلُّ اُمَّةٍ تُدْعٰٓى اِلٰى
كِتٰبِهَا اَلْيَوْمَ تُجْزَوْنَ مَا كُنْتُمْ تَعْمَلُوْنَ ﴿٢٩﴾

29. And thou wilt see every people on *their* knees. Every people will be summoned to their record, *and it shall be said to them*, 'This day shall you be requited for that which you did.

هٰذَا كِتٰبُنَا يَنْطِقُ عَلَيْكُمْ بِالْحَقِّ اِنَّا كُنَّا نَسْتَنْسِخُ
مَا كُنْتُمْ تَعْمَلُوْنَ ﴿٣٠﴾

30. 'This is Our Book; it speaks against you with truth. We caused *all* that you did to be *fully* recorded.'

فَاَمَّا الَّذِيْنَ اٰمَنُوْا وَعَمِلُوا الصّٰلِحٰتِ فَيُدْخِلُهُمْ
رَبُّهُمْ فِيْ رَحْمَتِهٖ ذٰلِكَ هُوَ الْفَوْزُ الْمُبِيْنُ ﴿٣١﴾

31. Now as for those who believed and did good works, their Lord will admit them into His mercy. That is the clear achievement.

وَاَمَّا الَّذِيْنَ كَفَرُوْا اَفَلَمْ تَكُنْ اٰيٰتِيْ تُتْلٰى عَلَيْكُمْ
فَاسْتَكْبَرْتُمْ وَكُنْتُمْ قَوْمًا مُّجْرِمِيْنَ ﴿٣٢﴾

32. But as to those who disbelieved: "Were not My Signs recited unto you? But you were arrogant, and were a guilty people.

وَاِذَا قِيْلَ اِنَّ وَعْدَ اللّٰهِ حَقٌّ وَّالسَّاعَةُ لَا رَيْبَ
فِيْهَا قُلْتُمْ مَّا نَدْرِيْ مَا السَّاعَةُ اِنْ نَّظُنُّ اِلَّا ظَنًّا
وَّمَا نَحْنُ بِمُسْتَيْقِنِيْنَ ﴿٣٣﴾

33. "And when it was said, 'The promise of Allah is certainly true, and *as to* the Hour, there is no doubt about its *coming*,' you said, 'We know not what the Hour is; we think it to be nothing but a conjecture, and we are not convinced.' "

وَبَدَا لَهُمْ سَيِّاٰتُ مَا عَمِلُوْا وَحَاقَ بِهِمْ مَّا كَانُوْا
بِهٖ يَسْتَهْزِءُوْنَ ﴿٣٤﴾

34. And the evil *consequences* of their deeds will become apparent to them, and that which they used to mock at shall encompass them.

وَقِيْلَ الْيَوْمَ نَنْسٰىكُمْ كَمَا نَسِيْتُمْ لِقَآءَ يَوْمِكُمْ هٰذَا
وَمَاْوٰىكُمُ النَّارُ وَمَا لَكُمْ مِّنْ نّٰصِرِيْنَ ﴿٣٥﴾

35. And it will be said *to them*, 'This day shall We forget you, as you forgot the meeting of this day of yours. And your resort is the Fire, and you will have no helpers.

ذٰلِكُمْ بِاَنَّكُمُ اتَّخَذْتُمْ اٰيٰتِ اللّٰهِ هُزُوًا وَّغَرَّتْكُمُ
الْحَيٰوةُ الدُّنْيَا فَالْيَوْمَ لَا يُخْرَجُوْنَ مِنْهَا وَلَا هُمْ
يُسْتَعْتَبُوْنَ ﴿٣٦﴾

* 36. 'This *is so*, because you made a jest of the Signs of Allah, and the life of the world deceived you.' Therefore, that day they will not be taken out from thence, nor will they be taken back into favour.

فَلِلّٰهِ الْحَمْدُ رَبِّ السَّمٰوٰتِ وَرَبِّ الْاَرْضِ رَبِّ
الْعٰلَمِيْنَ ﴿٣٧﴾

37. All praise, then, belongs to Allah, Lord of the heavens, and Lord of the earth, the Lord of *all* the worlds.

وَلَهُ الْكِبْرِيَآءُ فِي السَّمٰوٰتِ وَالْاَرْضِ وَهُوَ الْعَزِيْزُ

38. And His is the majesty in the heavens and the earth; and He is the

Mighty, the Wise.

الْحَكِيْمُ ﴿٣٨﴾ ع

آياتها (٣٦) سُوْرَةُ الْاَحْقَافِ مَكِّيَّةٌ ركوعاتها

AL-AḤQĀF

(Revealed before Hijra)

1. In the name of Allah, the Gracious, the Merciful.

بِسْمِ اللّٰهِ الرَّحْمٰنِ الرَّحِيْمِ ﴿١﴾

2. Ḥā Mīm*.

حٰمٓ ﴿٢﴾

3. The revelation of this Book is from Allah, the Mighty, the Wise.

تَنْزِيْلُ الْكِتٰبِ مِنَ اللّٰهِ الْعَزِيْزِ الْحَكِيْمِ ﴿٣﴾

4. We have not created the heavens and the earth, and all that is between them, but with truth, and for an appointed term; but those who disbelieve turn away from that of which they have been warned.

مَا خَلَقْنَا السَّمٰوٰتِ وَالْاَرْضَ وَمَا بَيْنَهُمَآ اِلَّا
بِالْحَقِّ وَاَجَلٍ مُّسَمًّى ۗ وَالَّذِيْنَ كَفَرُوْا عَمَّآ اُنْذِرُوْا
مُعْرِضُوْنَ ﴿٤﴾

5. Say, 'Do you know what it is you call on beside Allah? Show me what they have created of the earth. Or have they a share in the *creation of the* heavens? Bring me a Book *revealed* before this or some vestige of knowledge *in your support*, if you *indeed* speak the truth.'

قُلْ اَرَءَيْتُمْ مَّا تَدْعُوْنَ مِنْ دُوْنِ اللّٰهِ اَرُوْنِيْ
مَاذَا خَلَقُوْا مِنَ الْاَرْضِ اَمْ لَهُمْ شِرْكٌ فِي السَّمٰوٰتِ ۭ
اِيْتُوْنِيْ بِكِتٰبٍ مِّنْ قَبْلِ هٰذَآ اَوْ اَثٰرَةٍ مِّنْ عِلْمٍ
اِنْ كُنْتُمْ صٰدِقِيْنَ ﴿٥﴾

6. And who is more astray than those who, instead of Allah, pray unto such as will not answer them till the Day of Resurrection, and they are even unconscious of their prayer?

وَمَنْ اَضَلُّ مِمَّنْ يَّدْعُوْا مِنْ دُوْنِ اللّٰهِ مَنْ
لَّا يَسْتَجِيْبُ لَهٗٓ اِلٰى يَوْمِ الْقِيٰمَةِ وَهُمْ عَنْ دُعَآئِهِمْ
غٰفِلُوْنَ ﴿٦﴾

7. And when mankind are gathered together they will become enemies to them, and will deny their worship.

وَاِذَا حُشِرَ النَّاسُ كَانُوْا لَهُمْ اَعْدَآءً وَّكَانُوْا
بِعِبَادَتِهِمْ كٰفِرِيْنَ ﴿٧﴾

8. And when Our clear Signs are recited unto them, those who disbelieve say of the truth when it comes to them, 'This is manifest sorcery.'

وَاِذَا تُتْلٰى عَلَيْهِمْ اٰيٰتُنَا بَيِّنٰتٍ قَالَ الَّذِيْنَ كَفَرُوْا
لِلْحَقِّ لَمَّا جَآءَهُمْ ۙ هٰذَا سِحْرٌ مُّبِيْنٌ ﴿٨﴾

* The Praiseworthy, the Lord of Honour.

9. Do they say, 'He has forged it?' Say, 'If I have forged it, you cannot avail me aught against Allah. He knows best what *mischievous* talk you indulge in. Sufficient is He for a Witness between me and you. And He is the Most Forgiving, the Merciful.'

أَمْ يَقُولُونَ افْتَرَاهُ ۖ قُلْ إِنِ افْتَرَيْتُهُ فَلَا تَمْلِكُونَ
لِي مِنَ اللَّهِ شَيْئًا ۖ هُوَ أَعْلَمُ بِمَا تُفِيضُونَ فِيهِ ۖ
كَفَىٰ بِهِ شَهِيدًا بَيْنِي وَبَيْنَكُمْ ۖ وَهُوَ الْغَفُورُ
الرَّحِيمُ (9)

10. Say, 'I am no new Messenger, nor do I know what will be done with me or with you *in this life*. I do but follow what is revealed to me; and I am but a plain Warner.'

قُلْ مَا كُنتُ بِدْعًا مِّنَ الرُّسُلِ وَمَا أَدْرِي مَا يُفْعَلُ
بِي وَلَا بِكُمْ ۖ إِنْ أَتَّبِعُ إِلَّا مَا يُوحَىٰ إِلَيَّ وَمَا أَنَا
إِلَّا نَذِيرٌ مُّبِينٌ (10)

11. Say, 'Tell me, if this is from Allah and you disbelieve therein, and a witness from among the children of Israel bears witness to *the advent of* one like him, and he believed, but you are too proud, *how should you fare?*' Verily, Allah guides not the wrongdoing people.

قُلْ أَرَأَيْتُمْ إِن كَانَ مِنْ عِندِ اللَّهِ وَكَفَرْتُم بِهِ
وَشَهِدَ شَاهِدٌ مِّن بَنِي إِسْرَائِيلَ عَلَىٰ مِثْلِهِ
فَآمَنَ وَاسْتَكْبَرْتُمْ ۖ إِنَّ اللَّهَ لَا يَهْدِي الْقَوْمَ الظَّالِمِينَ (11)

R. 2.

12. And those who disbelieve say of those who believe: 'If it were any good, they could not have been ahead of us in attaining it.' And since they have not been guided thereby, they will say, 'This is an old lie.'

وَقَالَ الَّذِينَ كَفَرُوا لِلَّذِينَ آمَنُوا لَوْ كَانَ خَيْرًا مَّا
سَبَقُونَا إِلَيْهِ ۚ وَإِذْ لَمْ يَهْتَدُوا بِهِ فَسَيَقُولُونَ
هَٰذَا إِفْكٌ قَدِيمٌ (12)

13. And before it there was the Book of Moses, a guide and a mercy; and this is a Book in the Arabic language fulfilling *previous prophecies*, that it may warn those who do wrong; and as glad tidings to those who do good.

وَمِن قَبْلِهِ كِتَابُ مُوسَىٰ إِمَامًا وَرَحْمَةً ۚ وَهَٰذَا
كِتَابٌ مُّصَدِّقٌ لِّسَانًا عَرَبِيًّا لِّيُنذِرَ الَّذِينَ ظَلَمُوا
وَبُشْرَىٰ لِلْمُحْسِنِينَ (13)

14. Verily, those who say, 'Our Lord is Allah,' *and* then remain steadfast—no fear *shall come* upon them, nor shall they grieve.

إِنَّ الَّذِينَ قَالُوا رَبُّنَا اللَّهُ ثُمَّ اسْتَقَامُوا فَلَا خَوْفٌ
عَلَيْهِمْ وَلَا هُمْ يَحْزَنُونَ (14)

15. These are the dwellers of the Garden; they shall abide therein—a recompense for what they did.

أُولَٰئِكَ أَصْحَابُ الْجَنَّةِ خَالِدِينَ فِيهَا جَزَاءً بِمَا كَانُوا
يَعْمَلُونَ (15)

16. And We have enjoined on man to be good to his parents. His mother bears him with pain, and brings him forth with pain. And the bearing of him and his weaning

وَوَصَّيْنَا الْإِنسَانَ بِوَالِدَيْهِ إِحْسَانًا ۖ حَمَلَتْهُ
أُمُّهُ كُرْهًا وَوَضَعَتْهُ كُرْهًا ۖ وَحَمْلُهُ وَفِصَالُهُ

takes thirty months, till, when he attains his full maturity and reaches *the age of* forty years, he says, 'My Lord, grant me *the power* that I may be grateful for Thy favour which Thou hast bestowed upon me and upon my parents, and that I may do such good works as may please Thee. And make my seed righteous for me. I do turn to Thee; and, truly, I am of those who submit *to Thee*.'

ثَلٰثُوْنَ شَهْرًا ۭ حَتّٰٓى اِذَا بَلَغَ اَشُدَّهٗ وَبَلَغَ اَرْبَعِيْنَ
سَنَةً ۙ قَالَ رَبِّ اَوْزِعْنِيْٓ اَنْ اَشْكُرَ نِعْمَتَكَ الَّتِيْٓ
اَنْعَمْتَ عَلَيَّ وَعَلٰى وَالِدَيَّ وَاَنْ اَعْمَلَ صَالِحًا
تَرْضٰىهُ وَاَصْلِحْ لِيْ فِيْ ذُرِّيَّتِيْ ۚ اِنِّيْ تُبْتُ اِلَيْكَ
وَاِنِّيْ مِنَ الْمُسْلِمِيْنَ ﴿١٦﴾

17. Those are they from whom We accept their good works and overlook their ill deeds. *They shall be* among the inmates of the Garden, *in fulfilment of* the true promise which was made to them.

اُولٰٓئِكَ الَّذِيْنَ نَتَقَبَّلُ عَنْهُمْ اَحْسَنَ مَا عَمِلُوْا وَ
نَتَجَاوَزُ عَنْ سَيِّاٰتِهِمْ فِيْٓ اَصْحٰبِ الْجَنَّةِ ۭ وَعْدَ
الصِّدْقِ الَّذِيْ كَانُوْا يُوْعَدُوْنَ ﴿١٧﴾

18. But the one who says to his parents, 'Fie on you both! do you threaten me that I shall be brought forth *again*, when generations have already passed away before me?' And they both cry unto Allah for help *and say to him:* 'Woe unto thee! believe; for the promise of Allah is true.' But he says, 'This is nothing but the fables of the ancients.'

وَالَّذِيْ قَالَ لِوَالِدَيْهِ اُفٍّ لَّكُمَآ اَتَعِدٰنِنِيْٓ اَنْ
اُخْرَجَ وَقَدْ خَلَتِ الْقُرُوْنُ مِنْ قَبْلِيْ ۚ وَهُمَا
يَسْتَغِيْثٰنِ اللّٰهَ وَيْلَكَ اٰمِنْ ۖ اِنَّ وَعْدَ اللّٰهِ حَقٌّ ۚ
فَيَقُوْلُ مَا هٰذَآ اِلَّآ اَسَاطِيْرُ الْاَوَّلِيْنَ ﴿١٨﴾

19. These are they against whom the sentence *of punishment* became due, along with the communities of the Jinn and mankind that had gone before them. Indeed, they were the losers.

اُولٰٓئِكَ الَّذِيْنَ حَقَّ عَلَيْهِمُ الْقَوْلُ فِيْٓ اُمَمٍ قَدْ
خَلَتْ مِنْ قَبْلِهِمْ مِّنَ الْجِنِّ وَالْاِنْسِ ۭ اِنَّهُمْ
كَانُوْا خٰسِرِيْنَ ﴿١٩﴾

20. And for all are degrees *of rank* according to what they did, and that Allah may fully repay them for their deeds; and they shall not be wronged.

وَلِكُلٍّ دَرَجٰتٌ مِّمَّا عَمِلُوْا ۚ وَلِيُوَفِّيَهُمْ اَعْمَالَهُمْ
وَهُمْ لَا يُظْلَمُوْنَ ﴿٢٠﴾

21. And on the day when those who disbelieve will be brought before the Fire, *it will be said to them*, 'You exhausted your good things in the life of the world, and you *fully* enjoyed them. Now this day you shall be requited with ignominious punishment because you were arrogant in the earth without justification, and because you acted rebelliously.'

وَيَوْمَ يُعْرَضُ الَّذِيْنَ كَفَرُوْا عَلَى النَّارِ ۭ اَذْهَبْتُمْ
طَيِّبٰتِكُمْ فِيْ حَيَاتِكُمُ الدُّنْيَا وَاسْتَمْتَعْتُمْ بِهَا ۚ
فَالْيَوْمَ تُجْزَوْنَ عَذَابَ الْهُوْنِ بِمَا كُنْتُمْ تَسْتَكْبِرُوْنَ
فِي الْاَرْضِ بِغَيْرِ الْحَقِّ وَبِمَا كُنْتُمْ تَفْسُقُوْنَ ﴿٢١﴾ ع

R. 3.

22. And make mention of the brother of 'Ād, when he warned his people among

وَاذْكُرْ اَخَا عَادٍ ۭ اِذْ اَنْذَرَ قَوْمَهٗ بِالْاَحْقَافِ وَ

the sand-hills—and Warners there have been before him and after him—*saying*, 'Worship none but Allah, I fear for you the punishment of a great day.'

قَدْ خَلَتِ النُّذُرُ مِنْ بَيْنِ يَدَيْهِ وَمِنْ خَلْفِهٖٓ
اَلَّا تَعْبُدُوْٓا اِلَّا اللّٰهَ ۭ اِنِّيْٓ اَخَافُ عَلَيْكُمْ عَذَابَ
يَوْمٍ عَظِيْمٍ ﴿٢٢﴾

23. They said, 'Hast thou come to us to turn us away from our gods? Bring us then that with which thou dost threaten us, if *indeed* thou art of the truthful.'

قَالُوْٓا اَجِئْتَنَا لِتَاْفِكَنَا عَنْ اٰلِهَتِنَا ۚ فَاْتِنَا بِمَا
تَعِدُنَآ اِنْ كُنْتَ مِنَ الصّٰدِقِيْنَ ﴿٢٣﴾

24. He said, 'The knowledge *thereof* is only with Allah. And I convey to you what I have been sent with, but I see you to be a *very* ignorant people.'

قَالَ اِنَّمَا الْعِلْمُ عِنْدَ اللّٰهِ ۡ وَاُبَلِّغُكُمْ مَّآ اُرْسِلْتُ
بِهٖ وَلٰكِنِّيْٓ اَرٰىكُمْ قَوْمًا تَجْهَلُوْنَ ﴿٢٤﴾

25. Then, when they saw it coming towards their valleys as a cloud, they said, 'This is a cloud which will give us rain.' 'Nay, but it is that which you sought to hasten—a wind wherein is a grievous punishment.

فَلَمَّا رَاَوْهُ عَارِضًا مُّسْتَقْبِلَ اَوْدِيَتِهِمْ ۙ قَالُوْا هٰذَا
عَارِضٌ مُّمْطِرُنَا ۭ بَلْ هُوَ مَا اسْتَعْجَلْتُمْ بِهٖ ۭ رِيْحٌ
فِيْهَا عَذَابٌ اَلِيْمٌ ﴿٢٥﴾

26. 'It will destroy everything by the command of its Lord.' And they became such that there was nothing left to be seen, except their dwellings. Thus do We requite the guilty people.

تُدَمِّرُ كُلَّ شَيْءٍۢ بِاَمْرِ رَبِّهَا فَاَصْبَحُوْا لَا يُرٰٓى
اِلَّا مَسٰكِنُهُمْ ۭ كَذٰلِكَ نَجْزِي الْقَوْمَ الْمُجْرِمِيْنَ ﴿٢٦﴾

27. And We had established them in what We have established you not; and We gave them ears and eyes and hearts. But their ears and their eyes and their hearts availed them naught si ce they denied the Signs of Allah; and that at which they used to mock encompassed them.

وَلَقَدْ مَكَّنّٰهُمْ فِيْمَآ اِنْ مَّكَّنّٰكُمْ فِيْهِ وَجَعَلْنَا
لَهُمْ سَمْعًا وَّاَبْصَارًا وَّاَفْـِٕدَةً ڮ فَمَآ اَغْنٰى عَنْهُمْ
سَمْعُهُمْ وَلَآ اَبْصَارُهُمْ وَلَآ اَفْـِٕدَتُهُمْ مِّنْ شَيْءٍ
اِذْ كَانُوْا يَجْحَدُوْنَ بِاٰيٰتِ اللّٰهِ وَحَاقَ بِهِمْ مَّا كَانُوْا
بِهٖ يَسْتَهْزِءُوْنَ ﴿٢٧﴾ ع

R. 4.

* 28. And We did destroy townships round about you; and We have varied the Signs, that they might turn *to Us*.

وَلَقَدْ اَهْلَكْنَا مَا حَوْلَكُمْ مِّنَ الْقُرٰى وَصَرَّفْنَا
الْاٰيٰتِ لَعَلَّهُمْ يَرْجِعُوْنَ ﴿٢٨﴾

29. Why, then, did not those help them whom they had taken for gods beside Allah, seeking *His* nearness *through them*? Nay, they were lost to them. That was *the result of* their lie, and of what they fabricated.

فَلَوْلَا نَصَرَهُمُ الَّذِيْنَ اتَّخَذُوْا مِنْ دُوْنِ اللّٰهِ قُرْبَانًا
اٰلِهَةً ۭ بَلْ ضَلُّوْا عَنْهُمْ ۚ وَذٰلِكَ اِفْكُهُمْ وَمَا كَانُوْا
يَفْتَرُوْنَ ﴿٢٩﴾

30. And *remember* when We turned towards thee a party of the Jinn who wished to hear the Qur'ān and, when they were present at its *recitation*, they said *to one another*, 'Be silent *and listen*,' and, when it was finished, they went back to their people, warning *them*.

وَإِذْ صَرَفْنَآ إِلَيْكَ نَفَرًا مِّنَ الْجِنِّ يَسْتَمِعُونَ الْقُرْآنَ
فَلَمَّا حَضَرُوهُ قَالُوٓا أَنصِتُوا فَلَمَّا قُضِيَ وَلَّوْا إِلَىٰ
قَوْمِهِم مُّنذِرِينَ ﴿٣٠﴾

31. They said, 'O our people, we have heard a Book, which has been sent down after Moses, fulfilling that which is before it; it guides to the truth, and to the right path.

قَالُوا يَٰقَوْمَنَآ إِنَّا سَمِعْنَا كِتَٰبًا أُنزِلَ مِنۢ بَعْدِ مُوسَىٰ
مُصَدِّقًا لِّمَا بَيْنَ يَدَيْهِ يَهْدِيٓ إِلَى الْحَقِّ وَإِلَىٰ
طَرِيقٍ مُّسْتَقِيمٍ ﴿٣١﴾

32. 'O our people, respond to Allah's Summoner and believe in Him. He will forgive you your sins, and protect you from a painful punishment.

يَٰقَوْمَنَآ أَجِيبُوا دَاعِيَ اللَّهِ وَآمِنُوا بِهِۦ يَغْفِرْ لَكُم
مِّن ذُنُوبِكُمْ وَيُجِرْكُم مِّنْ عَذَابٍ أَلِيمٍ ﴿٣٢﴾

33. 'And whoso does not respond to Allah's Summoner, he cannot escape *Him* in the earth, nor can he have any protector beside Him. Such are in manifest error.'

وَمَن لَّا يُجِبْ دَاعِيَ اللَّهِ فَلَيْسَ بِمُعْجِزٍ فِي الْأَرْضِ
وَلَيْسَ لَهُۥ مِن دُونِهِۦٓ أَوْلِيَآءُ أُولَٰٓئِكَ فِي ضَلَٰلٍ مُّبِينٍ ﴿٣٣﴾

34. Have they not seen that Allah, Who created the heavens and the earth and was not wearied by their creation, has the power to give life to the dead? Yea, verily, He has power over all things.

أَوَلَمْ يَرَوْا أَنَّ اللَّهَ الَّذِي خَلَقَ السَّمَٰوَٰتِ وَالْأَرْضَ
وَلَمْ يَعْيَ بِخَلْقِهِنَّ بِقَٰدِرٍ عَلَىٰٓ أَن يُحْـِۧيَ الْمَوْتَىٰ
بَلَىٰٓ إِنَّهُۥ عَلَىٰ كُلِّ شَيْءٍ قَدِيرٌ ﴿٣٤﴾

35. And on the day when those who disbelieve will be brought before the Fire, *it will be said to them*, 'Is not this the truth?' They will say, 'Aye, by our Lord.' He will say, 'Then taste the punishment, because you disbelieved.'

وَيَوْمَ يُعْرَضُ الَّذِينَ كَفَرُوا عَلَى النَّارِ أَلَيْسَ هَٰذَا
بِالْحَقِّ قَالُوا بَلَىٰ وَرَبِّنَا قَالَ فَذُوقُوا الْعَذَابَ
بِمَا كُنتُمْ تَكْفُرُونَ ﴿٣٥﴾

36. Have patience, then, as had the Messengers of strong determination; and be in no haste about them. On the day when they see that with which they are threatened, it will appear to them as though they had not tarried save for an hour of a day. *This warning* has been conveyed; and none but the disobedient people shall be destroyed.

فَاصْبِرْ كَمَا صَبَرَ أُولُوا الْعَزْمِ مِنَ الرُّسُلِ وَلَا
تَسْتَعْجِل لَّهُمْ كَأَنَّهُمْ يَوْمَ يَرَوْنَ مَا يُوعَدُونَ
لَمْ يَلْبَثُوٓا إِلَّا سَاعَةً مِّن نَّهَارٍ بَلَٰغٌ فَهَلْ يُهْلَكُ
إِلَّا الْقَوْمُ الْفَٰسِقُونَ ﴿٣٦﴾ الربع

سُوْرَةُ مُحَمَّدٍ مَدَنِيَّةٌ (٤٧)

MUḤAMMAD

(Revealed after Hijra)

1\. In the name of Allah, the Gracious, the Merciful.

بِسْمِ اللّٰهِ الرَّحْمٰنِ الرَّحِيْمِ ﴿١﴾

2\. Those who disbelieve and hinder *men* from the way of Allah—He renders their works vain.

اَلَّذِيْنَ كَفَرُوْا وَصَدُّوْا عَنْ سَبِيْلِ اللّٰهِ اَضَلَّ اَعْمَالَهُمْ ﴿٢﴾

* 3. But *as for* those who believe and do good works and believe in that which has been revealed to Muḥammad—and it is the truth from their Lord—He removes from them their sins and improves their condition.

وَالَّذِيْنَ اٰمَنُوْا وَعَمِلُوا الصّٰلِحٰتِ وَاٰمَنُوْا بِمَا نُزِّلَ عَلٰى مُحَمَّدٍ وَّهُوَ الْحَقُّ مِنْ رَّبِّهِمْ ۙ كَفَّرَ عَنْهُمْ سَيِّاٰتِهِمْ وَاَصْلَحَ بَالَهُمْ ﴿٣﴾

4\. That is because those who disbelieve follow falsehood while those who believe follow the truth from their Lord. Thus does Allah set forth for men their similitudes.

ذٰلِكَ بِاَنَّ الَّذِيْنَ كَفَرُوا اتَّبَعُوا الْبَاطِلَ وَاَنَّ الَّذِيْنَ اٰمَنُوا اتَّبَعُوا الْحَقَّ مِنْ رَّبِّهِمْ ؕ كَذٰلِكَ يَضْرِبُ اللّٰهُ لِلنَّاسِ اَمْثَالَهُمْ ﴿٤﴾

* 5. And when you meet *in regular battle* those who disbelieve, smite *their* necks; and, when you have overcome them, bind fast the fetters—then afterwards either *release them as a* favour or *by taking* ransom—until the war lays down its burdens. That *is the ordinance*. And if Allah had *so* pleased, He could have punished them *Himself*, but *He has willed* that He may try some of you by others. And those who are killed in the way of Allah—He will never render their works vain.

فَاِذَا لَقِيْتُمُ الَّذِيْنَ كَفَرُوْا فَضَرْبَ الرِّقَابِ ؕ حَتّٰۤى اِذَاۤ اَثْخَنْتُمُوْهُمْ فَشُدُّوا الْوَثَاقَ ۙ فَاِمَّا مَنًّاۢ بَعْدُ وَاِمَّا فِدَآءً حَتّٰى تَضَعَ الْحَرْبُ اَوْزَارَهَا ۛ ذٰلِكَ ؕ وَلَوْ يَشَآءُ اللّٰهُ لَانْتَصَرَ مِنْهُمْ وَلٰكِنْ لِّيَبْلُوَا بَعْضَكُمْ بِبَعْضٍ ؕ وَالَّذِيْنَ قُتِلُوْا فِيْ سَبِيْلِ اللّٰهِ فَلَنْ يُّضِلَّ اَعْمَالَهُمْ ﴿٥﴾

6\. He will guide them and improve their condition,

سَيَهْدِيْهِمْ وَيُصْلِحُ بَالَهُمْ ﴿٦﴾

* 7. And admit them into the Garden which He has made known to them.

وَيُدْخِلُهُمُ الْجَنَّةَ عَرَّفَهَا لَهُمْ ﴿٧﴾

8\. O ye who believe! if you help *the cause of* Allah, He will help you and will make your steps firm.

يٰۤاَيُّهَا الَّذِيْنَ اٰمَنُوْۤا اِنْ تَنْصُرُوا اللّٰهَ يَنْصُرْكُمْ وَيُثَبِّتْ اَقْدَامَكُمْ ﴿٨﴾

9\. But *as for* those who disbelieve, perdition is their *lot*; and He will make their works vain.

وَالَّذِيْنَ كَفَرُوْا فَتَعْسًا لَّهُمْ وَاَضَلَّ اَعْمَالَهُمْ ﴿٩﴾

10. That is because they hate what Allah has revealed; so He has made their works futile.

ذٰلِكَ بِاَنَّهُمۡ كَرِهُوۡا مَاۤ اَنۡزَلَ اللّٰهُ فَاَحۡبَطَ اَعۡمَالَهُمۡ ﴿۱۰﴾

11. Have they not travelled in the earth and seen what was the end of those who were before them? Allah *utterly* destroyed them, and for the disbelievers there will be the like thereof.

اَفَلَمۡ يَسِيۡرُوۡا فِى الۡاَرۡضِ فَيَنۡظُرُوۡا كَيۡفَ كَانَ
عَاقِبَةُ الَّذِيۡنَ مِنۡ قَبۡلِهِمۡ ؕ دَمَّرَ اللّٰهُ عَلَيۡهِمۡ ۫ وَ
لِلۡكٰفِرِيۡنَ اَمۡثَالُهَا ﴿۱۱﴾

12. That is because Allah is the Protector of those who believe, and as for the disbelievers, there is no protector for them.

ذٰلِكَ بِاَنَّ اللّٰهَ مَوۡلَى الَّذِيۡنَ اٰمَنُوۡا وَاَنَّ الۡكٰفِرِيۡنَ
لَا مَوۡلٰى لَهُمۡ ﴿۱۲﴾ ع

R. 2.

13. Verily, Allah will make those who believe and do good works enter the Gardens underneath which rivers flow; while those who disbelieve enjoy themselves and eat even as the cattle eat, and the Fire will be their resort.

اِنَّ اللّٰهَ يُدۡخِلُ الَّذِيۡنَ اٰمَنُوۡا وَعَمِلُوا الصّٰلِحٰتِ
جَنّٰتٍ تَجۡرِىۡ مِنۡ تَحۡتِهَا الۡاَنۡهٰرُ ؕ وَالَّذِيۡنَ كَفَرُوۡا
يَتَمَتَّعُوۡنَ وَيَاۡكُلُوۡنَ كَمَا تَاۡكُلُ الۡاَنۡعَامُ وَالنَّارُ
مَثۡوًى لَّهُمۡ ﴿۱۳﴾

14. And how many a township, more powerful than thy town which has driven thee out, have We destroyed, and they had no helper!

وَكَاَيِّنۡ مِّنۡ قَرۡيَةٍ هِىَ اَشَدُّ قُوَّةً مِّنۡ قَرۡيَتِكَ
الَّتِىۡۤ اَخۡرَجَتۡكَ ۚ اَهۡلَكۡنٰهُمۡ فَلَا نَاصِرَ لَهُمۡ ﴿۱۴﴾

15. Is he then who stands upon a clear proof from his Lord like those to whom the evil of their deeds is made *to look* beautiful and who follow their evil inclinations?

اَفَمَنۡ كَانَ عَلٰى بَيِّنَةٍ مِّنۡ رَّبِّهٖ كَمَنۡ زُيِّنَ لَهٗ سُوۡٓءُ
عَمَلِهٖ وَاتَّبَعُوۡۤا اَهۡوَآءَهُمۡ ﴿۱۵﴾

16. A description of the Garden promised to the righteous: therein are rivers of water which corrupts not; and rivers of milk of which the taste changes not; and rivers of wine, a delight to those who drink, and rivers of clarified honey. And in it will they have all *kinds of* fruit, and forgiveness from their Lord. Can *those who enjoy such bliss* be like those who abide in the Fire and who are given boiling water to drink so that it tears their bowels?

مَثَلُ الۡجَنَّةِ الَّتِىۡ وُعِدَ الۡمُتَّقُوۡنَ ؕ فِيۡهَاۤ اَنۡهٰرٌ
مِّنۡ مَّآءٍ غَيۡرِ اٰسِنٍ ۚ وَاَنۡهٰرٌ مِّنۡ لَّبَنٍ لَّمۡ يَتَغَيَّرۡ
طَعۡمُهٗ ۚ وَاَنۡهٰرٌ مِّنۡ خَمۡرٍ لَّذَّةٍ لِّلشّٰرِبِيۡنَ ۬ۚ وَاَنۡهٰرٌ
مِّنۡ عَسَلٍ مُّصَفًّى ؕ وَلَهُمۡ فِيۡهَا مِنۡ كُلِّ الثَّمَرٰتِ
وَمَغۡفِرَةٌ مِّنۡ رَّبِّهِمۡ ؕ كَمَنۡ هُوَ خَالِدٌ فِى النَّارِ
وَسُقُوۡا مَآءً حَمِيۡمًا فَقَطَّعَ اَمۡعَآءَهُمۡ ﴿۱۶﴾

17. And among them are some who listen to thee till, when they go forth from thy presence, they say to those who have been given knowledge, 'What has he been

وَمِنۡهُمۡ مَّنۡ يَّسۡتَمِعُ اِلَيۡكَ ۚ حَتّٰۤى اِذَا خَرَجُوۡا مِنۡ
عِنۡدِكَ قَالُوۡا لِلَّذِيۡنَ اُوۡتُوا الۡعِلۡمَ مَاذَا قَالَ اٰنِفًا ۟

talking about just now?' These are they whose hearts Allah has sealed, and who follow their own evil inclinations.

أُولٰٓئِكَ الَّذِينَ طَبَعَ اللّٰهُ عَلٰى قُلُوبِهِمْ وَاتَّبَعُوٓا
أَهْوَآءَهُمْ ﴿١٧﴾

18. But *as for* those who follow guidance, He adds to their guidance, and bestows on them their righteousness.

وَالَّذِينَ اهْتَدَوْا زَادَهُمْ هُدًى وَّاٰتٰهُمْ
تَقْوٰىهُمْ ﴿١٨﴾

19. They wait not but for the Hour, that it should come upon them suddenly. The signs thereof have already come. But *of* what *avail* will their admonition be to them when it has *actually* come upon them?

فَهَلْ يَنْظُرُونَ إِلَّا السَّاعَةَ أَنْ تَأْتِيَهُمْ بَغْتَةً
فَقَدْ جَآءَ أَشْرَاطُهَا ۚ فَأَنّٰى لَهُمْ إِذَا جَآءَتْهُمْ
ذِكْرٰىهُمْ ﴿١٩﴾

20. Know, therefore, that there is no God other than Allah, and ask forgiveness for thy frailties, and for believing men and believing women. And Allah knows the place where you move about and the place where you stay.

فَاعْلَمْ أَنَّهُ لَآ إِلٰهَ إِلَّا اللّٰهُ وَاسْتَغْفِرْ لِذَنْبِكَ وَ
لِلْمُؤْمِنِينَ وَالْمُؤْمِنٰتِ ۗ وَاللّٰهُ يَعْلَمُ مُتَقَلَّبَكُمْ وَ
مَثْوٰىكُمْ ﴿٢٠﴾ ع ٢ ٤

R. 3.

* 21. And those who believe say, 'Why is not a Sūra revealed?' But when a decisive Sūra is revealed and fighting is mentioned therein, thou seest those in whose hearts is a disease looking towards thee with the look of one who is fainting on account of *approaching* death. So ruin seize them!

وَيَقُولُ الَّذِينَ اٰمَنُوا لَوْلَا نُزِّلَتْ سُورَةٌ ۚ فَإِذَآ
أُنْزِلَتْ سُورَةٌ مُّحْكَمَةٌ وَّذُكِرَ فِيهَا الْقِتَالُ ۙ رَأَيْتَ
الَّذِينَ فِي قُلُوبِهِمْ مَّرَضٌ يَّنْظُرُونَ إِلَيْكَ نَظَرَ
الْمَغْشِيِّ عَلَيْهِ مِنَ الْمَوْتِ ۗ فَأَوْلٰى لَهُمْ ﴿٢١﴾

22. Obedience and a kind word *is better for them*. And when the matter is determined upon, it is good for them if they were true to Allah.

طَاعَةٌ وَّقَوْلٌ مَّعْرُوفٌ ۫ فَإِذَا عَزَمَ الْأَمْرُ ۫ فَلَوْ
صَدَقُوا اللّٰهَ لَكَانَ خَيْرًا لَّهُمْ ﴿٢٢﴾

23. Would you then, if you are placed in authority, create disorder in the land and sever your ties of kinship?

فَهَلْ عَسَيْتُمْ إِنْ تَوَلَّيْتُمْ أَنْ تُفْسِدُوا فِي الْأَرْضِ
وَتُقَطِّعُوٓا أَرْحَامَكُمْ ﴿٢٣﴾

24. It is these whom Allah curses so that He makes them deaf and makes their eyes blind.

أُولٰٓئِكَ الَّذِينَ لَعَنَهُمُ اللّٰهُ فَأَصَمَّهُمْ وَأَعْمٰٓى
أَبْصَارَهُمْ ﴿٢٤﴾

* 25. Will they not, then, ponder over the Qur'ān, or is it that on the hearts are their locks?

أَفَلَا يَتَدَبَّرُونَ الْقُرْاٰنَ أَمْ عَلٰى قُلُوبٍ أَقْفَالُهَا ﴿٢٥﴾

26. Surely, those who turn their backs

إِنَّ الَّذِينَ ارْتَدُّوا عَلٰٓى أَدْبَارِهِمْ مِّنْ بَعْدِ مَا

after guidance has become manifest to them, Satan has seduced them, and holds out to them false hopes.

تَبَيَّنَ لَهُمُ الْهُدَى الشَّيْطٰنُ سَوَّلَ لَهُمْ وَأَمْلٰى
لَهُمْ ﴿٢٦﴾

27. That is because they said to those who hate what Allah has revealed, 'We will obey you in some matters;' and Allah knows their secrets.

ذٰلِكَ بِأَنَّهُمْ قَالُوا لِلَّذِينَ كَرِهُوا مَا نَزَّلَ اللّٰهُ
سَنُطِيعُكُمْ فِي بَعْضِ الْأَمْرِ ۚ وَاللّٰهُ يَعْلَمُ
إِسْرَارَهُمْ ﴿٢٧﴾

28. But how *will they fare* when the angels will cause them to die, smiting their faces and their backs?

فَكَيْفَ إِذَا تَوَفَّتْهُمُ الْمَلٰٓئِكَةُ يَضْرِبُونَ وُجُوهَهُمْ
وَأَدْبَارَهُمْ ﴿٢٨﴾

29. This is because they followed that which displeased Allah, and hated that which pleased Him. So He rendered their works vain.

ذٰلِكَ بِأَنَّهُمُ اتَّبَعُوا مَا أَسْخَطَ اللّٰهَ وَكَرِهُوا
رِضْوَانَهُ فَأَحْبَطَ أَعْمَالَهُمْ ﴿٢٩﴾ ع ٤

R. 4.

30. Do those in whose hearts is a disease suppose that Allah will not bring to light their malice?

أَمْ حَسِبَ الَّذِينَ فِي قُلُوبِهِمْ مَرَضٌ أَنْ لَنْ يُخْرِجَ
اللّٰهُ أَضْغَانَهُمْ ﴿٣٠﴾

31. And if We pleased, We could show them to thee so that thou shouldst know them by their marks. And thou shalt surely recognize them by the tone of *their* speech. And Allah knows your deeds.

وَلَوْ نَشَآءُ لَأَرَيْنٰكَهُمْ فَلَعَرَفْتَهُمْ بِسِيمٰهُمْ ۚ وَ
لَتَعْرِفَنَّهُمْ فِي لَحْنِ الْقَوْلِ ۚ وَاللّٰهُ يَعْلَمُ أَعْمَالَكُمْ ﴿٣١﴾

* 32. And We will surely try you until We distinguish those among you who strive *for the cause of God* and those who are steadfast. And We will make known the facts about you.

وَلَنَبْلُوَنَّكُمْ حَتّٰى نَعْلَمَ الْمُجٰهِدِينَ مِنْكُمْ وَ
الصّٰبِرِينَ ۙ وَنَبْلُوَا أَخْبَارَكُمْ ﴿٣٢﴾

33. Those who disbelieve and hinder *men* from the way of Allah and oppose the Messenger after guidance has become manifest to them, shall not harm Allah in the least; and He will make their works fruitless.

إِنَّ الَّذِينَ كَفَرُوا وَصَدُّوا عَنْ سَبِيلِ اللّٰهِ وَ
شَآقُّوا الرَّسُولَ مِنْ بَعْدِ مَا تَبَيَّنَ لَهُمُ الْهُدٰى ۙ
لَنْ يَضُرُّوا اللّٰهَ شَيْئًا ۚ وَسَيُحْبِطُ أَعْمَالَهُمْ ﴿٣٣﴾

34. O ye who believe! obey Allah and obey the Messenger and let not your works go vain.

يٰٓأَيُّهَا الَّذِينَ آمَنُوٓا أَطِيعُوا اللّٰهَ وَأَطِيعُوا الرَّسُولَ
وَلَا تُبْطِلُوٓا أَعْمَالَكُمْ ﴿٣٤﴾

35. Verily, those who disbelieve and hinder *men* from the way of Allah, *and* then die while they are disbelievers—Allah certainly will not forgive them.

إِنَّ الَّذِينَ كَفَرُوا وَصَدُّوا عَنْ سَبِيلِ اللّٰهِ ثُمَّ
مَاتُوا وَهُمْ كُفَّارٌ فَلَنْ يَغْفِرَ اللّٰهُ لَهُمْ ﴿٣٥﴾

* 36. So be not slack and sue not for peace; for you will *certainly* have the upper hand. And Allah is with you, and He will not deprive you of *the reward of* your actions.

فَلَا تَهِنُوا وَتَدْعُوا إِلَى السَّلْمِ ۖ وَأَنْتُمُ الْأَعْلَوْنَ ۖ
وَاللّٰهُ مَعَكُمْ وَلَنْ يَتِرَكُمْ أَعْمَالَكُمْ ﴿۳۶﴾

37. The life of *this* world is but a sport and a pastime, and if you believe and be righteous, He will give you your rewards, and will not ask of you your possessions.

إِنَّمَا الْحَيٰوةُ الدُّنْيَا لَعِبٌ وَلَهْوٌ ۚ وَإِنْ تُؤْمِنُوا
وَتَتَّقُوا يُؤْتِكُمْ أُجُورَكُمْ وَلَا يَسْـَٔلْكُمْ أَمْوَالَكُمْ ﴿۳۷﴾

38. If He ask them of you, and press you, you would be niggardly, and He would bring to light your malice.

إِنْ يَسْـَٔلْكُمُوهَا فَيُحْفِكُمْ تَبْخَلُوا وَيُخْرِجْ
أَضْغَانَكُمْ ﴿۳۸﴾

39. Behold, you are those who are called upon to spend in the way of Allah; but of you there are some who are niggardly. And whoso is niggardly, is niggardly only against his own soul. And Allah is Self-Sufficient, and it is you that are needy. And if you turn your backs, He will bring in your stead a people other than you, then they will not be like you.

هٰٓأَنْتُمْ هٰٓؤُلَآءِ تُدْعَوْنَ لِتُنْفِقُوا فِي سَبِيلِ اللّٰهِ ۚ
فَمِنْكُمْ مَنْ يَبْخَلُ ۚ وَمَنْ يَبْخَلْ فَإِنَّمَا يَبْخَلُ عَنْ
نَفْسِهِ ۚ وَاللّٰهُ الْغَنِيُّ وَأَنْتُمُ الْفُقَرَآءُ ۚ وَإِنْ تَتَوَلَّوْا
ع يَسْتَبْدِلْ قَوْمًا غَيْرَكُمْ ثُمَّ لَا يَكُونُوا أَمْثَالَكُمْ ﴿۳۹﴾

آیاتها ۳۰ (۴۸) سُورَةُ الْفَتْحِ مَدَنِيَّةٌ رکوعاتها ۴

Chapter 48 AL-FATḤ Part 26

(Revealed after Hijra)

1. In the name of Allah, the Gracious, the Merciful.

بِسْمِ اللّٰهِ الرَّحْمٰنِ الرَّحِيمِ ﴿۱﴾

2. Verily, We have granted thee a clear victory,

إِنَّا فَتَحْنَا لَكَ فَتْحًا مُبِينًا ﴿۲﴾

3. That Allah may cover up for thee thy shortcomings, past and future, and that He may complete His favour upon thee, and may guide thee on a right path;

لِيَغْفِرَ لَكَ اللّٰهُ مَا تَقَدَّمَ مِنْ ذَنْبِكَ وَمَا تَأَخَّرَ
وَيُتِمَّ نِعْمَتَهُ عَلَيْكَ وَيَهْدِيَكَ صِرَاطًا مُسْتَقِيمًا ﴿۳﴾

4. And that Allah may help thee with a mighty help.

وَيَنْصُرَكَ اللّٰهُ نَصْرًا عَزِيزًا ﴿۴﴾

5. He it is Who sent down tranquillity into the hearts of the believers that they might add faith to their faith—and to Allah belong the hosts of the heavens and the earth, and Allah is All-Knowing, Wise—

هُوَ الَّذِيٓ أَنْزَلَ السَّكِينَةَ فِي قُلُوبِ الْمُؤْمِنِينَ
لِيَزْدَادُوٓا إِيمَانًا مَعَ إِيمَانِهِمْ ۗ وَلِلّٰهِ جُنُودُ
السَّمٰوٰتِ وَالْأَرْضِ ۚ وَكَانَ اللّٰهُ عَلِيمًا حَكِيمًا ﴿۵﴾

6. That He may make the believing men and the believing women enter the Gardens beneath which streams flow, wherein they will abide, and *that* He may remove their evils from them—and that, in the sight of Allah, is the supreme triumph—

لِيُدْخِلَ الْمُؤْمِنِيْنَ وَ الْمُؤْمِنٰتِ جَنّٰتٍ تَجْرِيْ
مِنْ تَحْتِهَا الْاَنْهٰرُ خٰلِدِيْنَ فِيْهَا وَ يُكَفِّرَ عَنْهُمْ
سَيِّاٰتِهِمْ ؕ وَ كَانَ ذٰلِكَ عِنْدَ اللّٰهِ فَوْزًا عَظِيْمًا ۙ﴿۶﴾

* 7. And *that* He may punish the hypocritical men and the hypocritical women, and the idolatrous men and the idolatrous women, who entertain evil thoughts concerning Allah. On them *shall fall* an evil calamity; and the wrath of Allah is upon them. And He has cursed them, and has prepared Hell for them. And that indeed is an evil destination.

وَّ يُعَذِّبَ الْمُنٰفِقِيْنَ وَ الْمُنٰفِقٰتِ وَ الْمُشْرِكِيْنَ وَ
الْمُشْرِكٰتِ الظَّآنِّيْنَ بِاللّٰهِ ظَنَّ السَّوْءِ ؕ عَلَيْهِمْ دَآئِرَةُ
السَّوْءِ ۚ وَ غَضِبَ اللّٰهُ عَلَيْهِمْ وَ لَعَنَهُمْ وَ اَعَدَّ لَهُمْ
جَهَنَّمَ ؕ وَ سَآءَتْ مَصِيْرًا ﴿۷﴾

8. And to Allah belong the hosts of the heavens and the earth; and Allah is Mighty, Wise.

وَ لِلّٰهِ جُنُوْدُ السَّمٰوٰتِ وَ الْاَرْضِ ؕ وَ كَانَ اللّٰهُ عَزِيْزًا
حَكِيْمًا ﴿۸﴾

9. We have sent thee as a Witness and a bearer of glad tidings and a Warner,

اِنَّاۤ اَرْسَلْنٰكَ شَاهِدًا وَّ مُبَشِّرًا وَّ نَذِيْرًا ۙ﴿۹﴾

10. That you should believe in Allah and His Messenger, and may help him, and honour him, and *that* you may glorify Him morning and evening.

لِّتُؤْمِنُوْا بِاللّٰهِ وَ رَسُوْلِهٖ وَ تُعَزِّرُوْهُ وَ تُوَقِّرُوْهُ ؕ وَ
تُسَبِّحُوْهُ بُكْرَةً وَّ اَصِيْلًا ﴿۱۰﴾

11. Verily, those who swear allegiance to thee indeed swear allegiance to Allah. The hand of Allah is over their hands. So whoever breaks *his oath*, breaks *it* to his own loss; and whoever fulfils the covenant that he has made with Allah, He will surely give him a great reward.

اِنَّ الَّذِيْنَ يُبَايِعُوْنَكَ اِنَّمَا يُبَايِعُوْنَ اللّٰهَ ؕ يَدُ اللّٰهِ
فَوْقَ اَيْدِيْهِمْ ۚ فَمَنْ نَّكَثَ فَاِنَّمَا يَنْكُثُ عَلٰى
نَفْسِهٖ ۚ وَ مَنْ اَوْفٰى بِمَا عٰهَدَ عَلَيْهُ اللّٰهَ فَسَيُؤْتِيْهِ
اَجْرًا عَظِيْمًا ﴿۱۱﴾ ع

R. 2.

12. Those of the desert Arabs, who were left behind, will say to thee, 'Our possessions and our families kept us occupied, so ask forgiveness for us.' They say with their tongues that which is not in their hearts. Say, 'Who can avail you aught against Allah, if He intends you some harm, or if He intends you some benefit? Nay, Allah is Well-Aware of what you do.

سَيَقُوْلُ لَكَ الْمُخَلَّفُوْنَ مِنَ الْاَعْرَابِ شَغَلَتْنَاۤ
اَمْوَالُنَا وَ اَهْلُوْنَا فَاسْتَغْفِرْ لَنَا ۚ يَقُوْلُوْنَ بِاَلْسِنَتِهِمْ
مَّا لَيْسَ فِيْ قُلُوْبِهِمْ ؕ قُلْ فَمَنْ يَّمْلِكُ لَكُمْ مِّنَ اللّٰهِ
شَيْـًٔا اِنْ اَرَادَ بِكُمْ ضَرًّا اَوْ اَرَادَ بِكُمْ نَفْعًا ؕ بَلْ
كَانَ اللّٰهُ بِمَا تَعْمَلُوْنَ خَبِيْرًا ﴿۱۲﴾

* 13. 'Nay, you thought that the Messenger and the believers would never come

بَلْ ظَنَنْتُمْ اَنْ لَّنْ يَّنْقَلِبَ الرَّسُوْلُ وَ الْمُؤْمِنُوْنَ

back to their families, and that was made *to appear* pleasing to your hearts, and you thought an evil thought, and you were a ruined people.'

إِلَىٰ أَهْلِيهِمْ أَبَدًا وَزُيِّنَ ذَٰلِكَ فِي قُلُوبِكُمْ وَ
ظَنَنتُمْ ظَنَّ السَّوْءِ وَكُنتُمْ قَوْمًا بُورًا ﴿١٣﴾

14. And *as for* those who believe not in Allah and His Messenger— We have surely prepared for the disbelievers a blazing fire.

وَمَن لَّمْ يُؤْمِن بِاللَّهِ وَرَسُولِهِ فَإِنَّا أَعْتَدْنَا
لِلْكَافِرِينَ سَعِيرًا ﴿١٤﴾

15. And to Allah belongs the kingdom of the heavens and the earth. He forgives whom He pleases, and punishes whom He pleases. And Allah is Most Forgiving, Merciful.

وَلِلَّهِ مُلْكُ السَّمَاوَاتِ وَالْأَرْضِ يَغْفِرُ لِمَن يَشَاءُ
وَيُعَذِّبُ مَن يَشَاءُ وَكَانَ اللَّهُ غَفُورًا رَّحِيمًا ﴿١٥﴾

16. Those *who had managed to be* left behind will say, when you go forth to the spoils that you may get them, 'Let us follow you.' They seek to change the decree of Allah. Say, 'You shall not follow us. Thus has Allah said beforehand.' Then they will say, 'Nay, but you envy us.' Not so, but they understand not except a little.

سَيَقُولُ الْمُخَلَّفُونَ إِذَا انطَلَقْتُمْ إِلَىٰ مَغَانِمَ
لِتَأْخُذُوهَا ذَرُونَا نَتَّبِعْكُمْ يُرِيدُونَ أَن
يُبَدِّلُوا كَلَامَ اللَّهِ قُل لَّن تَتَّبِعُونَا كَذَٰلِكُمْ قَالَ
اللَّهُ مِن قَبْلُ فَسَيَقُولُونَ بَلْ تَحْسُدُونَنَا بَلْ
كَانُوا لَا يَفْقَهُونَ إِلَّا قَلِيلًا ﴿١٦﴾

17. Say to the desert Arabs who were left behind, 'You shall be called *to fight* against a people of mighty valour; you shall fight them until they surrender. Then, if you obey, Allah will give you a good reward, but if you turn your backs, as you turned your backs before, He will punish you with a painful punishment.'

قُل لِّلْمُخَلَّفِينَ مِنَ الْأَعْرَابِ سَتُدْعَوْنَ إِلَىٰ
قَوْمٍ أُولِي بَأْسٍ شَدِيدٍ تُقَاتِلُونَهُمْ أَوْ يُسْلِمُونَ
فَإِن تُطِيعُوا يُؤْتِكُمُ اللَّهُ أَجْرًا حَسَنًا وَإِن
تَتَوَلَّوْا كَمَا تَوَلَّيْتُم مِّن قَبْلُ يُعَذِّبْكُمْ عَذَابًا
أَلِيمًا ﴿١٧﴾

18. There is no blame on the blind, nor is there blame on the lame, nor is there blame on the sick, *if they go not forth for fight*. And whoso obeys Allah and His Messenger, He will make him enter the Gardens beneath which streams flow; but whoso turns his back, him will He punish with a grievous punishment.

لَّيْسَ عَلَى الْأَعْمَىٰ حَرَجٌ وَلَا عَلَى الْأَعْرَجِ حَرَجٌ
وَلَا عَلَى الْمَرِيضِ حَرَجٌ وَمَن يُطِعِ اللَّهَ وَ
رَسُولَهُ يُدْخِلْهُ جَنَّاتٍ تَجْرِي مِن تَحْتِهَا
الْأَنْهَارُ وَمَن يَتَوَلَّ يُعَذِّبْهُ عَذَابًا أَلِيمًا ﴿١٨﴾ ع

R. 3.

19. Surely, Allah was well pleased with the believers when they were swearing allegiance to thee under the Tree, and He knew what was in their hearts, and He

لَّقَدْ رَضِيَ اللَّهُ عَنِ الْمُؤْمِنِينَ إِذْ يُبَايِعُونَكَ تَحْتَ
الشَّجَرَةِ فَعَلِمَ مَا فِي قُلُوبِهِمْ فَأَنزَلَ السَّكِينَةَ

sent down tranquillity on them, and He rewarded them with a victory near at hand;

20. And great spoils that they will take. And Allah is Mighty, Wise.

21. Allah has promised you great spoils that you will take, and He has given you this in advance, and has restrained the hands of men from you, that it may be a Sign for the believers, and that He may guide you on a right path.

22. And *He has promised you* another *victory*, which you have not yet been able to achieve, *but* Allah has surely compassed it. And Allah has power over all things.

23. And if those who disbelieve should fight you, they would certainly turn their backs; then they would find neither protector nor helper.

* 24. Such is the law of Allah that has been *in operation* before; and thou shalt not find any change in the law of Allah.

25. And He it is Who withheld their hands from you and your hands from them in the valley of Mecca, after He had given you victory over them. And Allah sees all that you do.

26. It is they who disbelieved and hindered you from the Sacred Mosque and the offering which was prevented from reaching its place of sacrifice. And had it not been for believing men and believing women whom you knew not and whom you might have trampled down so that harm might have come to you on their account unknowingly, *He would have permitted you to fight, but He did not do so* that He might admit into His mercy whom He will. If they had been separated *from the disbelievers*, We would have surely punished those of them who disbelieved with a grievous punishment.

* 27. When those who disbelieved harboured in their hearts prideful

عَلَيْهِمْ وَأَثَابَهُمْ فَتْحًا قَرِيبًا ﴿١٩﴾
وَمَغَانِمَ كَثِيرَةً يَأْخُذُونَهَا ۗ وَكَانَ اللَّهُ عَزِيزًا
حَكِيمًا ﴿٢٠﴾
وَعَدَكُمُ اللَّهُ مَغَانِمَ كَثِيرَةً تَأْخُذُونَهَا فَعَجَّلَ
لَكُمْ هَٰذِهِ وَكَفَّ أَيْدِيَ النَّاسِ عَنْكُمْ ۚ وَلِتَكُونَ
آيَةً لِلْمُؤْمِنِينَ وَيَهْدِيَكُمْ صِرَاطًا مُسْتَقِيمًا ﴿٢١﴾
وَأُخْرَىٰ لَمْ تَقْدِرُوا عَلَيْهَا قَدْ أَحَاطَ اللَّهُ بِهَا ۚ
وَكَانَ اللَّهُ عَلَىٰ كُلِّ شَيْءٍ قَدِيرًا ﴿٢٢﴾
وَلَوْ قَاتَلَكُمُ الَّذِينَ كَفَرُوا لَوَلَّوُا الْأَدْبَارَ ثُمَّ لَا
يَجِدُونَ وَلِيًّا وَلَا نَصِيرًا ﴿٢٣﴾
سُنَّةَ اللَّهِ الَّتِي قَدْ خَلَتْ مِنْ قَبْلُ ۖ وَلَنْ تَجِدَ
لِسُنَّةِ اللَّهِ تَبْدِيلًا ﴿٢٤﴾
وَهُوَ الَّذِي كَفَّ أَيْدِيَهُمْ عَنْكُمْ وَأَيْدِيَكُمْ
عَنْهُمْ بِبَطْنِ مَكَّةَ مِنْ بَعْدِ أَنْ أَظْفَرَكُمْ عَلَيْهِمْ ۚ
وَكَانَ اللَّهُ بِمَا تَعْمَلُونَ بَصِيرًا ﴿٢٥﴾
هُمُ الَّذِينَ كَفَرُوا وَصَدُّوكُمْ عَنِ الْمَسْجِدِ الْحَرَامِ
وَالْهَدْيَ مَعْكُوفًا أَنْ يَبْلُغَ مَحِلَّهُ ۚ وَلَوْلَا رِجَالٌ
مُؤْمِنُونَ وَنِسَاءٌ مُؤْمِنَاتٌ لَمْ تَعْلَمُوهُمْ أَنْ
تَطَئُوهُمْ فَتُصِيبَكُمْ مِنْهُمْ مَعَرَّةٌ بِغَيْرِ عِلْمٍ ۖ
لِيُدْخِلَ اللَّهُ فِي رَحْمَتِهِ مَنْ يَشَاءُ ۚ لَوْ تَزَيَّلُوا
لَعَذَّبْنَا الَّذِينَ كَفَرُوا مِنْهُمْ عَذَابًا أَلِيمًا ﴿٢٦﴾
إِذْ جَعَلَ الَّذِينَ كَفَرُوا فِي قُلُوبِهِمُ الْحَمِيَّةَ حَمِيَّةَ

indignation, the indignation *of the Days* of Ignorance, Allah sent down His tranquillity on His Messenger and on the believers, and made them cleave to the principle of righteousness, and they were better entitled to it and more worthy of it. And Allah knows everything full well.

R. 4.

28. Surely has Allah in truth fulfilled for His Messenger the Vision. You will certainly enter the Sacred Mosque, if Allah will, in security, *some* having *their* heads shaven, and *others* having *their* hair cut short; *and* you will have no fear. But He knew what you knew not. He has in fact ordained for you, besides that, a victory near at hand.

29. He it is Who has sent His Messenger, with guidance and the Religion of truth, that He may make it prevail over *all other* religions. And sufficient is Allah as a Witness.

* 30. Muhammad is the Messenger of Allah. And those who are with him are hard against the disbelievers, tender among themselves. Thou seest them bowing *and* prostrating themselves *in Prayer*, seeking grace from Allah and *His* pleasure. Their mark is upon their faces, being the traces of prostrations. This is their description in the Torah. And their description in the Gospel is like unto a seed-produce that sends forth its sprout, then makes it strong; it then becomes thick, and stands firm on its stem, delighting the sowers —that He may cause the disbelievers to burn with rage *at the sight* of them. Allah has promised, unto those of them who believe and do good works, forgiveness and a great reward.

الْجَاهِلِيَّةِ فَأَنْزَلَ اللّٰهُ سَكِيْنَتَهٗ عَلٰى رَسُوْلِهٖ وَ
عَلَى الْمُؤْمِنِيْنَ وَ اَلْزَمَهُمْ كَلِمَةَ التَّقْوٰى وَكَانُوْٓا
ع اَحَقَّ بِهَا وَ اَهْلَهَا ۭ وَكَانَ اللّٰهُ بِكُلِّ شَيْءٍ عَلِيْمًا ﴿۲۷﴾
لَقَدْ صَدَقَ اللّٰهُ رَسُوْلَهُ الرُّءْيَا بِالْحَقِّ ۚ لَتَدْخُلُنَّ
الْمَسْجِدَ الْحَرَامَ اِنْ شَآءَ اللّٰهُ اٰمِنِيْنَ ۙ مُحَلِّقِيْنَ
رُءُوْسَكُمْ وَ مُقَصِّرِيْنَ ۙ لَا تَخَافُوْنَ ۭ فَعَلِمَ مَا لَمْ
تَعْلَمُوْا فَجَعَلَ مِنْ دُوْنِ ذٰلِكَ فَتْحًا قَرِيْبًا ﴿۲۸﴾
هُوَ الَّذِيْٓ اَرْسَلَ رَسُوْلَهٗ بِالْهُدٰى وَدِيْنِ الْحَقِّ
لِيُظْهِرَهٗ عَلَى الدِّيْنِ كُلِّهٖ ۭ وَكَفٰى بِاللّٰهِ شَهِيْدًا ﴿۲۹﴾
مُحَمَّدٌ رَّسُوْلُ اللّٰهِ ۭ وَالَّذِيْنَ مَعَهٗٓ اَشِدَّاۗءُ عَلَى الْكُفَّارِ
رُحَمَاۗءُ بَيْنَهُمْ تَرٰىهُمْ رُكَّعًا سُجَّدًا يَّبْتَغُوْنَ فَضْلًا
مِّنَ اللّٰهِ وَ رِضْوَانًا ۡ سِيْمَاهُمْ فِيْ وُجُوْهِهِمْ مِّنْ
اَثَرِ السُّجُوْدِ ۭ ذٰلِكَ مَثَلُهُمْ فِي التَّوْرٰىةِ ۚ وَمَثَلُهُمْ
فِي الْاِنْجِيْلِ ۚ كَزَرْعٍ اَخْرَجَ شَطْــَٔهٗ فَاٰزَرَهٗ فَاسْتَغْلَظَ
فَاسْتَوٰى عَلٰى سُوْقِهٖ يُعْجِبُ الزُّرَّاعَ لِيَغِيْظَ بِهِمُ
الْكُفَّارَ ۭ وَعَدَ اللّٰهُ الَّذِيْنَ اٰمَنُوْا وَعَمِلُوا الصّٰلِحٰتِ
ع مِنْهُمْ مَّغْفِرَةً وَّ اَجْرًا عَظِيْمًا ﴿۳۰﴾

سُوۡرَةُ الۡحُجُرٰتِ مَدَنِيَّةٌ (۴۹)

آیَاتُهَا ۱۹ — رُکُوۡعَاتُهَا ۲

AL-ḤUJURĀT

(Revealed after Hijra)

1. In the name of Allah, the Gracious, the Merciful.

بِسۡمِ اللّٰهِ الرَّحۡمٰنِ الرَّحِيۡمِ (۱)

* 2. O ye who believe! be not forward in the presence of Allah and His Messenger, but fear Allah. Verily, Allah is All-Hearing, All-Knowing.

يٰۤاَيُّهَا الَّذِيۡنَ اٰمَنُوۡا لَا تُقَدِّمُوۡا بَيۡنَ يَدَىِ اللّٰهِ
وَرَسُوۡلِهٖ وَاتَّقُوا اللّٰهَ ؕ اِنَّ اللّٰهَ سَمِيۡعٌ عَلِيۡمٌ (۲)

3. O ye who believe! raise not your voices above the voice of the Prophet, and speak not aloud to him, as you speak aloud to one another, lest your works become vain while you perceive not.

يٰۤاَيُّهَا الَّذِيۡنَ اٰمَنُوۡا لَا تَرۡفَعُوۡۤا اَصۡوَاتَكُمۡ فَوۡقَ
صَوۡتِ النَّبِىِّ وَلَا تَجۡهَرُوۡا لَهٗ بِالۡقَوۡلِ كَجَهۡرِ
بَعۡضِكُمۡ لِبَعۡضٍ اَنۡ تَحۡبَطَ اَعۡمَالُكُمۡ وَاَنۡتُمۡ
لَا تَشۡعُرُوۡنَ (۳)

* 4. Verily those who lower their voices in the presence of the Messenger of Allah are the ones whose hearts Allah has purified for righteousness. For them is forgiveness and a great reward.

اِنَّ الَّذِيۡنَ يَغُضُّوۡنَ اَصۡوَاتَهُمۡ عِنۡدَ رَسُوۡلِ اللّٰهِ
اُولٰٓـئِكَ الَّذِيۡنَ امۡتَحَنَ اللّٰهُ قُلُوۡبَهُمۡ لِلتَّقۡوٰى ؕ
لَهُمۡ مَّغۡفِرَةٌ وَّاَجۡرٌ عَظِيۡمٌ (۴)

* 5. Those who shout out to thee from without *thy private* apartments—most of them lack understanding.

اِنَّ الَّذِيۡنَ يُنَادُوۡنَكَ مِنۡ وَّرَآءِ الۡحُجُرٰتِ
اَكۡثَرُهُمۡ لَا يَعۡقِلُوۡنَ (۵)

6. And if they had waited patiently until thou came out to them, it would be better for them. But Allah is Most Forgiving, Merciful.

وَلَوۡ اَنَّهُمۡ صَبَرُوۡا حَتّٰى تَخۡرُجَ اِلَيۡهِمۡ لَكَانَ
خَيۡرًا لَّهُمۡ ؕ وَاللّٰهُ غَفُوۡرٌ رَّحِيۡمٌ (۶)

7. O ye who believe! if an unrighteous person brings you any news, ascertain *the correctness of the report* fully, lest you harm a people in ignorance, and then become repentant for what you have done.

يٰۤاَيُّهَا الَّذِيۡنَ اٰمَنُوۡۤا اِنۡ جَآءَكُمۡ فَاسِقٌۢ بِنَبَاٍ
فَتَبَيَّنُوۡۤا اَنۡ تُصِيۡبُوۡا قَوۡمًۢا بِجَهَالَةٍ فَتُصۡبِحُوۡا
عَلٰى مَا فَعَلۡتُمۡ نٰدِمِيۡنَ (۷)

8. And know that among you is the Messenger of Allah; if he were to comply with your wishes in most of the matters, you would surely come to trouble; but Allah has endeared the faith to you and

وَاعۡلَمُوۡۤا اَنَّ فِيۡكُمۡ رَسُوۡلَ اللّٰهِ ؕ لَوۡ يُطِيۡعُكُمۡ فِىۡ
كَثِيۡرٍ مِّنَ الۡاَمۡرِ لَعَنِتُّمۡ وَلٰـكِنَّ اللّٰهَ حَبَّبَ اِلَيۡكُمُ

has made it *look* beautiful to your hearts, and He has made disbelief, wickedness and disobedience hateful to you. Such indeed are those who follow the right course,

الْإِيْمَانَ وَزَيَّنَهٗ فِيْ قُلُوْبِكُمْ وَكَرَّهَ إِلَيْكُمُ الْكُفْرَ
وَالْفُسُوْقَ وَالْعِصْيَانَ ۭ أُولٰٓئِكَ هُمُ الرّٰشِدُوْنَ ﴿٨﴾

9. Through the grace and favour of Allah. And Allah is All-Knowing, Wise.

فَضْلًا مِّنَ اللّٰهِ وَنِعْمَةً ۭ وَاللّٰهُ عَلِيْمٌ حَكِيْمٌ ﴿٩﴾

10. And if two parties of believers fight *against each other*, make peace between them; then if *after that* one of them transgresses against the other, fight the party that transgresses until it returns to the command of Allah. Then if it returns, make peace between them with equity, and act justly. Verily, Allah loves the just.

وَإِنْ طَآئِفَتٰنِ مِنَ الْمُؤْمِنِيْنَ اقْتَتَلُوْا فَأَصْلِحُوْا
بَيْنَهُمَا ۚ فَإِنْۢ بَغَتْ إِحْدٰىهُمَا عَلَى الْأُخْرٰى فَقَاتِلُوا
الَّتِيْ تَبْغِيْ حَتّٰى تَفِيْٓءَ إِلٰٓى أَمْرِ اللّٰهِ ۚ فَإِنْ فَآءَتْ
فَأَصْلِحُوْا بَيْنَهُمَا بِالْعَدْلِ وَأَقْسِطُوْا ۭ إِنَّ اللّٰهَ
يُحِبُّ الْمُقْسِطِيْنَ ﴿١٠﴾

11. Surely *all* believers are brothers. So make peace between brothers, and fear Allah that mercy may be shown to you.

إِنَّمَا الْمُؤْمِنُوْنَ إِخْوَةٌ فَأَصْلِحُوْا بَيْنَ أَخَوَيْكُمْ
وَاتَّقُوا اللّٰهَ لَعَلَّكُمْ تُرْحَمُوْنَ ﴿١١﴾

R. 2.

* 12. O ye who believe! let not one people deride *another* people, who may be better than they, nor let women *deride other* women, who may be better than they. And defame not your own people, nor call *one another* by nick-names. Bad *indeed* is evil reputation after *the profession of* belief; and those who repent not are the wrong-doers.

يٰٓأَيُّهَا الَّذِيْنَ اٰمَنُوْا لَا يَسْخَرْ قَوْمٌ مِّنْ قَوْمٍ عَسٰٓى
أَنْ يَّكُوْنُوْا خَيْرًا مِّنْهُمْ وَلَا نِسَآءٌ مِّنْ نِّسَآءٍ عَسٰٓى
أَنْ يَّكُنَّ خَيْرًا مِّنْهُنَّ ۚ وَلَا تَلْمِزُوْٓا أَنْفُسَكُمْ وَلَا
تَنَابَزُوْا بِالْأَلْقَابِ ۭ بِئْسَ الِاسْمُ الْفُسُوْقُ بَعْدَ
الْإِيْمَانِ ۚ وَمَنْ لَّمْ يَتُبْ فَأُولٰٓئِكَ هُمُ الظّٰلِمُوْنَ ﴿١٢﴾

* 13. O ye who believe! avoid most of suspicions; for suspicion in some cases is a sin. And spy not, nor back-bite one another. Would any of you like to eat the flesh of his brother who is dead? Certainly you would loathe it. And fear Allah, surely, Allah is Oft-Returning *with compassion and is* Merciful.

يٰٓأَيُّهَا الَّذِيْنَ اٰمَنُوا اجْتَنِبُوْا كَثِيْرًا مِّنَ الظَّنِّ إِنَّ
بَعْضَ الظَّنِّ إِثْمٌ وَّلَا تَجَسَّسُوْا وَلَا يَغْتَبْ
بَّعْضُكُمْ بَعْضًا ۭ أَيُحِبُّ أَحَدُكُمْ أَنْ يَّأْكُلَ لَحْمَ
أَخِيْهِ مَيْتًا فَكَرِهْتُمُوْهُ ۭ وَاتَّقُوا اللّٰهَ ۭ إِنَّ اللّٰهَ
تَوَّابٌ رَّحِيْمٌ ﴿١٣﴾

* 14. O mankind, We have created you from a male and a female; and We have made you into tribes and sub-tribes that you may recognize one another. Verily, the

يٰٓأَيُّهَا النَّاسُ إِنَّا خَلَقْنٰكُمْ مِّنْ ذَكَرٍ وَّأُنْثٰى
وَجَعَلْنٰكُمْ شُعُوْبًا وَّقَبَآئِلَ لِتَعَارَفُوْا ۭ إِنَّ

most honourable among you, in the sight of Allah, is he who is the most righteous among you. Surely, Allah is All-Knowing, All-Aware.

أَكْرَمَكُمْ عِنْدَ اللّٰهِ أَتْقٰكُمْ ۭ إِنَّ اللّٰهَ عَلِيْمٌ
خَبِيْرٌ ﴿١٤﴾

15. The Arabs of the desert say, 'We believe.' Say, "You have not believed *yet*; but rather say, 'We have accepted Islam,' for the *true* belief has not yet entered into your hearts." But if you obey Allah and His Messenger, He will not detract anything from your deeds. Surely, Allah is Most Forgiving, Merciful.

قَالَتِ الْأَعْرَابُ اٰمَنَّا ۭ قُلْ لَّمْ تُؤْمِنُوْا وَلٰكِنْ
قُوْلُوْٓا أَسْلَمْنَا وَلَمَّا يَدْخُلِ الْإِيْمَانُ فِيْ قُلُوْبِكُمْ ۭ
وَإِنْ تُطِيْعُوا اللّٰهَ وَرَسُوْلَهٗ لَا يَلِتْكُمْ مِّنْ أَعْمَالِكُمْ
شَيْـًٔا ۭ إِنَّ اللّٰهَ غَفُوْرٌ رَّحِيْمٌ ﴿١٥﴾

16. The believers are only those who *truly* believe in Allah and His Messenger, and then doubt not, but strive with their possessions and their persons in the cause of Allah. It is they who are truthful.

إِنَّمَا الْمُؤْمِنُوْنَ الَّذِيْنَ اٰمَنُوْا بِاللّٰهِ وَرَسُوْلِهٖ ثُمَّ
لَمْ يَرْتَابُوْا وَجٰهَدُوْا بِأَمْوَالِهِمْ وَأَنْفُسِهِمْ فِيْ
سَبِيْلِ اللّٰهِ ۭ أُولٰٓئِكَ هُمُ الصّٰدِقُوْنَ ﴿١٦﴾

17. Say, 'Will you acquaint Allah with your faith, while Allah knows whatever is in the heavens and whatever is in the earth, and Allah knows all things full well?'

قُلْ أَتُعَلِّمُوْنَ اللّٰهَ بِدِيْنِكُمْ ۭ وَاللّٰهُ يَعْلَمُ مَا فِي
السَّمٰوٰتِ وَمَا فِي الْأَرْضِ ۭ وَاللّٰهُ بِكُلِّ شَيْءٍ
عَلِيْمٌ ﴿١٧﴾

* 18. They think they have done thee a favour by their embracing Islam. Say, 'Deem not your embracing Islam a favour unto me. On the contrary, Allah has bestowed a favour upon you in that He has guided you to the *true* Faith, if you are truthful.'

يَمُنُّوْنَ عَلَيْكَ أَنْ أَسْلَمُوْا ۭ قُلْ لَّا تَمُنُّوْا عَلَيَّ إِسْلَامَكُمْ ۚ
بَلِ اللّٰهُ يَمُنُّ عَلَيْكُمْ أَنْ هَدٰىكُمْ لِلْإِيْمَانِ إِنْ
كُنْتُمْ صٰدِقِيْنَ ﴿١٨﴾

19. Verily, Allah knows the secrets of the heavens and the earth. And Allah sees all that you do.

إِنَّ اللّٰهَ يَعْلَمُ غَيْبَ السَّمٰوٰتِ وَالْأَرْضِ ۭ وَاللّٰهُ
بَصِيْرٌ بِمَا تَعْمَلُوْنَ ﴿١٩﴾

رکوعاتها سُوْرَةُ قٓ مَكِّيَّةٌ (٥٠) اٰیاتها

QĀF

(Revealed before Hijra)

1. In the name of Allah, the Gracious, the Merciful.

بِسْمِ اللّٰهِ الرَّحْمٰنِ الرَّحِيْمِ ﴿١﴾

2. Qāf*. By the glorious Qur'ān, *thou art a Messenger of God.*

قٓ ۚ وَالْقُرْاٰنِ الْمَجِيْدِ ﴿٢﴾

3. But they wonder that there has come to them a Warner from among themselves. And the disbelievers say, 'This is a strange thing!

بَلْ عَجِبُوْٓا اَنْ جَآءَهُمْ مُّنْذِرٌ مِّنْهُمْ فَقَالَ الْكٰفِرُوْنَ
هٰذَا شَيْءٌ عَجِيْبٌ ﴿٣﴾

4. 'What! when we are dead and have become dust, *shall we be raised to life again?* That is a return far *from possible.*'

ءَاِذَا مِتْنَا وَكُنَّا تُرَابًا ۚ ذٰلِكَ رَجْعٌۢ بَعِيْدٌ ﴿٤﴾

5. We know how much the earth diminishes of them and with Us is a Book that preserves *everything.*

قَدْ عَلِمْنَا مَا تَنْقُصُ الْاَرْضُ مِنْهُمْ ۚ وَعِنْدَنَا
كِتٰبٌ حَفِيْظٌ ﴿٥﴾

6. Nay, they rejected the truth when it came to them, and so they are in a state of confusion.

بَلْ كَذَّبُوْا بِالْحَقِّ لَمَّا جَآءَهُمْ فَهُمْ فِيْٓ اَمْرٍ
مَّرِيْجٍ ﴿٦﴾

7. Have they not looked at the sky above them, how We have made it and adorned it, and there are no flaws in it?

اَفَلَمْ يَنْظُرُوْٓا اِلَى السَّمَآءِ فَوْقَهُمْ كَيْفَ بَنَيْنٰهَا
وَزَيَّنّٰهَا وَمَا لَهَا مِنْ فُرُوْجٍ ﴿٧﴾

8. And the earth—We have spread it out, and placed therein firm mountains; and We have made to grow therein every *kind of* beautiful species,

وَالْاَرْضَ مَدَدْنٰهَا وَاَلْقَيْنَا فِيْهَا رَوَاسِيَ وَاَنْۢبَتْنَا
فِيْهَا مِنْ كُلِّ زَوْجٍۢ بَهِيْجٍ ﴿٨﴾

9. As *a means of* enlightenment and as a reminder to every servant that turns *to God.*

تَبْصِرَةً وَّذِكْرٰى لِكُلِّ عَبْدٍ مُّنِيْبٍ ﴿٩﴾

10. And We send down from the sky water which is full of blessings, and We produce therewith gardens and grain harvests,

وَنَزَّلْنَا مِنَ السَّمَآءِ مَآءً مُّبٰرَكًا فَاَنْۢبَتْنَا بِهٖ جَنّٰتٍ
وَّحَبَّ الْحَصِيْدِ ﴿١٠﴾

11. And tall palm-trees, with spathes piled one above the other,

وَالنَّخْلَ بٰسِقٰتٍ لَّهَا طَلْعٌ نَّضِيْدٌ ﴿١١﴾

12. As a provision for *Our* servants; and We quicken thereby a dead land. Even so shall be the Resurrection.

رِّزْقًا لِّلْعِبَادِ ۙ وَاَحْيَيْنَا بِهٖ بَلْدَةً مَّيْتًا ۚ كَذٰلِكَ
الْخُرُوْجُ ﴿١٢﴾

المنزل

* The Possessor of Power!

13. The people of Noah rejected *the truth* before them and *so did* the People of the Well*, and Thamūd,

14. And 'Ād, and Pharaoh and the brethren of Lot,

15. And the Dwellers of the Wood*, and the people of Tubba'*. All *of them* rejected the Messengers with the result that My threatened punishment befell *them*.

16. Have We then become weary with the first creation? Nay, but they are in confusion about the new creation.

R. 2.

* 17. And assuredly, We have created man and We know what his *physical* self whispers *to him*, and We are nearer to him than *even his* jugular vein.

18. When the two Recording *angels* record *the deeds of men*, *one* sitting on the right and *the other* on the left,

19. He utters not a word but there is by him a guardian *angel* ready *to record it*.

20. And the stupor of death certainly comes. 'This is what thou wast trying to run from.'

21. And the trumpet shall be blown: 'This is the Day of Promise.'

22. And every soul shall come forth *and* along with it there will be an *angel* to drive and an *angel* to bear witness.

23. 'Thou wast heedless of this; now We have removed from thee thy veil, and sharp is thy sight this day.'

24. And his companion will say, 'This is what I have *of the record* ready.

25. 'Cast ye twain into Hell every ungrateful enemy *of truth*,

26. 'Hinderer of good, transgressor, doubter,

27. 'Who sets up another God beside Allah. So do ye twain cast him into the dreadful torment.'

كَذَّبَتْ قَبْلَهُمْ قَوْمُ نُوْحٍ وَّاَصْحٰبُ الرَّسِّ وَثَمُوْدُ ﴿۱۳﴾
وَعَادٌ وَّفِرْعَوْنُ وَاِخْوَانُ لُوْطٍ ﴿۱۴﴾
وَّاَصْحٰبُ الْاَيْكَةِ وَقَوْمُ تُبَّعٍ ؕ كُلٌّ كَذَّبَ الرُّسُلَ
فَحَقَّ وَعِيْدِ ﴿۱۵﴾
اَفَعَيِيْنَا بِالْخَلْقِ الْاَوَّلِ ؕ بَلْ هُمْ فِيْ لَبْسٍ مِّنْ
خَلْقٍ جَدِيْدٍ ﴿۱۶﴾ ع ۱۵
وَلَقَدْ خَلَقْنَا الْاِنْسَانَ وَنَعْلَمُ مَا تُوَسْوِسُ بِهٖ
نَفْسُهٗ ۚۖ وَنَحْنُ اَقْرَبُ اِلَيْهِ مِنْ حَبْلِ الْوَرِيْدِ ﴿۱۷﴾
اِذْ يَتَلَقَّى الْمُتَلَقِّيٰنِ عَنِ الْيَمِيْنِ وَعَنِ الشِّمَالِ
قَعِيْدٌ ﴿۱۸﴾
مَا يَلْفِظُ مِنْ قَوْلٍ اِلَّا لَدَيْهِ رَقِيْبٌ عَتِيْدٌ ﴿۱۹﴾
وَجَآءَتْ سَكْرَةُ الْمَوْتِ بِالْحَقِّ ؕ ذٰلِكَ مَا كُنْتَ
مِنْهُ تَحِيْدُ ﴿۲۰﴾
وَنُفِخَ فِي الصُّوْرِ ؕ ذٰلِكَ يَوْمُ الْوَعِيْدِ ﴿۲۱﴾
وَجَآءَتْ كُلُّ نَفْسٍ مَّعَهَا سَآئِقٌ وَّشَهِيْدٌ ﴿۲۲﴾
لَقَدْ كُنْتَ فِيْ غَفْلَةٍ مِّنْ هٰذَا فَكَشَفْنَا عَنْكَ
غِطَآءَكَ فَبَصَرُكَ الْيَوْمَ حَدِيْدٌ ﴿۲۳﴾
وَقَالَ قَرِيْنُهٗ هٰذَا مَا لَدَيَّ عَتِيْدٌ ؕ ﴿۲۴﴾
اَلْقِيَا فِيْ جَهَنَّمَ كُلَّ كَفَّارٍ عَنِيْدٍ ﴿۲۵﴾
مَّنَّاعٍ لِّلْخَيْرِ مُعْتَدٍ مُّرِيْبِ ﴿۲۶﴾
اِلَّذِيْ جَعَلَ مَعَ اللّٰهِ اِلٰهًا اٰخَرَ فَاَلْقِيٰهُ فِي الْعَذَابِ
الشَّدِيْدِ ﴿۲۷﴾

* Ancient Arab tribes.

28. His associate will say, 'O our Lord, I did not cause him to rebel; but he *himself* was too far gone in error.'

قَالَ قَرِيْنُهٗ رَبَّنَا مَآ اَطْغَيْتُهٗ وَلٰكِنْ كَانَ فِيْ
ضَلٰلٍۭ بَعِيْدٍ ﴿۲۸﴾

29. *God* will say, 'Quarrel not in My presence, I gave you the warning beforehand.

قَالَ لَا تَخْتَصِمُوْا لَدَيَّ وَقَدْ قَدَّمْتُ اِلَيْكُمْ
بِالْوَعِيْدِ ﴿۲۹﴾

30. 'The sentence *passed* by Me cannot be changed, and I am not at all unjust to *My* servants.'

مَا يُبَدَّلُ الْقَوْلُ لَدَيَّ وَمَآ اَنَا بِظَلَّامٍ لِّلْعَبِيْدِ ﴿۳۰﴾

R. 3.

31. On that day We will say to Hell, 'Art thou filled up?' and it will answer, 'Is there more?'

يَوْمَ نَقُوْلُ لِجَهَنَّمَ هَلِ امْتَلَاْتِ وَتَقُوْلُ هَلْ
مِنْ مَّزِيْدٍ ﴿۳۱﴾

32. And Heaven will be brought near to the righteous, no longer remote.

وَاُزْلِفَتِ الْجَنَّةُ لِلْمُتَّقِيْنَ غَيْرَ بَعِيْدٍ ﴿۳۲﴾

33. 'This is what was promised to you—to everyone who always turned *to God* and was watchful *of his actions*,

هٰذَا مَا تُوْعَدُوْنَ لِكُلِّ اَوَّابٍ حَفِيْظٍ ﴿۳۳﴾

34. 'Who feared the Gracious *God* in private and came *to Him* with a penitent heart.

مَنْ خَشِيَ الرَّحْمٰنَ بِالْغَيْبِ وَجَآءَ بِقَلْبٍ مُّنِيْبِ ﴿۳۴﴾

35. 'Enter ye therein in peace. This is the Day of Eternity.'

اِۨدْخُلُوْهَا بِسَلٰمٍ ذٰلِكَ يَوْمُ الْخُلُوْدِ ﴿۳۵﴾

36. They will have therein whatever they desire, and with Us is *a good deal* more.

لَهُمْ مَّا يَشَآءُوْنَ فِيْهَا وَلَدَيْنَا مَزِيْدٌ ﴿۳۶﴾

37. And how many a generation who were greater than they in power have We destroyed before them! *But when the punishment came*, they went about the lands. Was there any place of refuge *for them?*

وَكَمْ اَهْلَكْنَا قَبْلَهُمْ مِّنْ قَرْنٍ هُمْ اَشَدُّ مِنْهُمْ
بَطْشًا فَنَقَّبُوْا فِي الْبِلَادِ هَلْ مِنْ مَّحِيْصٍ ﴿۳۷﴾

38. Therein, verily, is a reminder for him who has a heart, or who gives ear, and is attentive.

اِنَّ فِيْ ذٰلِكَ لَذِكْرٰى لِمَنْ كَانَ لَهٗ قَلْبٌ اَوْ اَلْقَى
السَّمْعَ وَهُوَ شَهِيْدٌ ﴿۳۸﴾

39. And verily, We created the heavens and the earth and all that is between them in six periods, and no weariness touched Us.

وَلَقَدْ خَلَقْنَا السَّمٰوٰتِ وَالْاَرْضَ وَمَا بَيْنَهُمَا فِيْ
سِتَّةِ اَيَّامٍ وَّمَا مَسَّنَا مِنْ لُّغُوْبٍ ﴿۳۹﴾

40. So bear with patience what they say, and glorify thy Lord with *His* praise, before the rising of the sun and before *its* setting;

فَاصْبِرْ عَلٰى مَا يَقُوْلُوْنَ وَسَبِّحْ بِحَمْدِ رَبِّكَ قَبْلَ
طُلُوْعِ الشَّمْسِ وَقَبْلَ الْغُرُوْبِ ﴿۴۰﴾

41. And in *a part of* the night *also* do thou glorify Him, and after *prescribed* prostrations.

وَمِنَ الَّيْلِ فَسَبِّحْهُ وَاَدْبَارَ السُّجُوْدِ ﴿۴۱﴾

42. And listen! The day when the crier will cry from a place nearby,

وَاسْتَمِعْ يَوْمَ يُنَادِ الْمُنَادِ مِنْ مَّكَانٍ قَرِيْبٍ ﴿۴۲﴾

* 43. The day when they will hear the blast in truth; that will be the day of coming forth *from the graves*.

يَوْمَ يَسْمَعُونَ الصَّيْحَةَ بِالْحَقِّ ذٰلِكَ يَوْمُ الْخُرُوجِ ﴿٤٣﴾

44. Verily, it is We Who give life and cause death, and to Us is the *final* return.

إِنَّا نَحْنُ نُحْيِي وَنُمِيتُ وَإِلَيْنَا الْمَصِيرُ ﴿٤٤﴾

45. *On* the day when the earth will cleave asunder from over them *and they will come forth* hastening—that will be a gathering together, quite easy for Us.

يَوْمَ تَشَقَّقُ الْأَرْضُ عَنْهُمْ سِرَاعًا ذٰلِكَ حَشْرٌ عَلَيْنَا يَسِيرٌ ﴿٤٥﴾

46. We know best what they say; and thou hast not been *appointed* to compel them *in any way*. So admonish, by means of the Qur'ān, him who fears My warning.

نَحْنُ أَعْلَمُ بِمَا يَقُولُونَ وَمَا أَنْتَ عَلَيْهِمْ بِجَبَّارٍ فَذَكِّرْ بِالْقُرْآنِ مَنْ يَخَافُ وَعِيدِ ﴿٤٦﴾

سُورَةُ الذّٰرِيٰتِ مَكِّيَّةٌ (٥١)

(Revealed before Hijra)

1. In the name of Allah, the Gracious, the Merciful.

بِسْمِ اللّٰهِ الرَّحْمٰنِ الرَّحِيْمِ ﴿١﴾

* 2. By *the winds* that scatter *seeds with a true* scattering,

وَالذّٰرِيٰتِ ذَرْوًا ﴿٢﴾

* 3. Then by *the clouds* that carry the load *of moisture*,

فَالْحٰمِلٰتِ وِقْرًا ﴿٣﴾

* 4. Then by *the rivers* that flow gently,

فَالْجٰرِيٰتِ يُسْرًا ﴿٤﴾

* 5. *And* then by *the angels* that finally administer and execute affairs,

فَالْمُقَسِّمٰتِ أَمْرًا ﴿٥﴾

6. Surely, that which you are promised is true;

إِنَّمَا تُوْعَدُوْنَ لَصَادِقٌ ﴿٦﴾

7. And the Judgment will surely come to pass.

وَإِنَّ الدِّيْنَ لَوَاقِعٌ ﴿٧﴾

8. And by the heaven *full* of tracks,

وَالسَّمَآءِ ذَاتِ الْحُبُكِ ﴿٨﴾

* 9. Truly you are discordant in *your* utterances.

إِنَّكُمْ لَفِيْ قَوْلٍ مُّخْتَلِفٍ ﴿٩﴾

* 10. He *alone* is turned away from *the truth* who is *destined to be thus* turned away.

يُّؤْفَكُ عَنْهُ مَنْ أُفِكَ ﴿١٠﴾

* 11. Cursed be the liars,

قُتِلَ الْخَرّٰصُوْنَ ﴿١١﴾

* 12. Who are heedless in the depth *of ignorance*.

الَّذِيْنَ هُمْ فِيْ غَمْرَةٍ سَاهُوْنَ ﴿١٢﴾

13. They ask: 'When will be the Day of Judgment?'

يَسْـَٔلُوْنَ اَيَّانَ يَوْمُ الدِّيْنِ ﴿۱۳﴾

14. *It will be* the day when they will be tormented at the Fire.

يَوْمَ هُمْ عَلَى النَّارِ يُفْتَنُوْنَ ﴿۱۴﴾

* 15. 'Taste ye your torment. This is what you would hasten.'

ذُوْقُوْا فِتْنَتَكُمْ ۭ هٰذَا الَّذِيْ كُنْتُمْ بِهٖ تَسْتَعْجِلُوْنَ ﴿۱۵﴾

16. *But* surely the righteous will be in the midst of gardens and springs,

اِنَّ الْمُتَّقِيْنَ فِيْ جَنّٰتٍ وَّعُيُوْنٍ ﴿۱۶﴾

17. Receiving what their Lord will give them; for they used to do good before that.

اٰخِذِيْنَ مَآ اٰتٰىهُمْ رَبُّهُمْ ۭ اِنَّهُمْ كَانُوْا قَبْلَ ذٰلِكَ مُحْسِنِيْنَ ﴿۱۷﴾

18. They used to sleep but a little of the night;

كَانُوْا قَلِيْلًا مِّنَ الَّيْلِ مَا يَهْجَعُوْنَ ﴿۱۸﴾

19. And at the dawn of the day they sought forgiveness;

وَبِالْاَسْحَارِ هُمْ يَسْتَغْفِرُوْنَ ﴿۱۹﴾

* 20. And in their wealth was a share for one who asked for help and *for* one who could not.

وَفِيْٓ اَمْوَالِهِمْ حَقٌّ لِّلسَّآئِلِ وَالْمَحْرُوْمِ ﴿۲۰﴾

21. And in the earth are Signs for those who have certainty of faith,

وَفِي الْاَرْضِ اٰيٰتٌ لِّلْمُوْقِنِيْنَ ﴿۲۱﴾

22. And *also* in your own selves. Will you not then see?

وَفِيْٓ اَنْفُسِكُمْ ۭ اَفَلَا تُبْصِرُوْنَ ﴿۲۲﴾

23. And in heaven is your sustenance, and *also* that which you are promised.

وَفِي السَّمَآءِ رِزْقُكُمْ وَمَا تُوْعَدُوْنَ ﴿۲۳﴾

24. And by the Lord of the heaven and the earth, it is certainly the truth, even as *it is true that* you speak.

فَوَرَبِّ السَّمَآءِ وَالْاَرْضِ اِنَّهٗ لَحَقٌّ مِّثْلَ مَآ اَنَّكُمْ
ع ۱۸ تَنْطِقُوْنَ ﴿۲۴﴾

R. 2.

25. Has the story of Abraham's honoured guests reached thee?

لازم هَلْ اَتٰىكَ حَدِيْثُ ضَيْفِ اِبْرٰهِيْمَ الْمُكْرَمِيْنَ ﴿۲۵﴾

26. When they entered upon him and said, 'Peace!' he said, 'Peace!' *They were* all strangers.

اِذْ دَخَلُوْا عَلَيْهِ فَقَالُوْا سَلٰمًا ۭ قَالَ سَلٰمٌ ۚ قَوْمٌ مُّنْكَرُوْنَ ﴿۲۶﴾

27. And he went quietly to his household, and brought a fatted calf,

فَرَاغَ اِلٰٓى اَهْلِهٖ فَجَآءَ بِعِجْلٍ سَمِيْنٍ ﴿۲۷﴾

28. And he placed it before them. He said, 'Will you not eat?'

فَقَرَّبَهٗٓ اِلَيْهِمْ قَالَ اَلَا تَاْكُلُوْنَ ﴿۲۸﴾

* 29. And he felt a fear on account of them. They said, 'Fear not.' And they gave him glad tidings of *the birth of* a son possessing knowledge.

فَاَوْجَسَ مِنْهُمْ خِيْفَةً ۭ قَالُوْا لَا تَخَفْ ۭ وَبَشَّرُوْهُ بِغُلٰمٍ عَلِيْمٍ ﴿۲۹﴾

30. Then his wife came forward crying and smote her face and said, 'A barren

فَاَقْبَلَتِ امْرَاَتُهٗ فِيْ صَرَّةٍ فَصَكَّتْ وَجْهَهَا وَ

old woman!'

قَالَتْ عَجُوزٌ عَقِيمٌ ﴿٣٠﴾

31. They said, 'Even so has thy Lord said. Surely, He is the Wise, the All-Knowing.'

قَالُوا كَذٰلِكِ قَالَ رَبُّكِ إِنَّهُ هُوَ الْحَكِيمُ الْعَلِيمُ ﴿٣١﴾

32. *Abraham* said, 'Now what is your errand, O ye messengers?'

قَالَ فَمَا خَطْبُكُمْ أَيُّهَا الْمُرْسَلُونَ ﴿٣٢﴾

33. They said, 'We have been sent to a sinful people,

قَالُوا إِنَّا أُرْسِلْنَا إِلَىٰ قَوْمٍ مُّجْرِمِينَ ﴿٣٣﴾

34. 'That we may send down upon them stones of clay,

لِنُرْسِلَ عَلَيْهِمْ حِجَارَةً مِّنْ طِينٍ ﴿٣٤﴾

35. 'Marked, with thy Lord, for those guilty of excesses.'

مُّسَوَّمَةً عِنْدَ رَبِّكَ لِلْمُسْرِفِينَ ﴿٣٥﴾

36. And We brought forth therefrom such of the believers as were there,

فَأَخْرَجْنَا مَنْ كَانَ فِيهَا مِنَ الْمُؤْمِنِينَ ﴿٣٦﴾

37. And We found not there except only one house of Muslims.

فَمَا وَجَدْنَا فِيهَا غَيْرَ بَيْتٍ مِّنَ الْمُسْلِمِينَ ﴿٣٧﴾

38. And We left therein a Sign for those who fear the painful punishment.

وَتَرَكْنَا فِيهَا آيَةً لِّلَّذِينَ يَخَافُونَ الْعَذَابَ الْأَلِيمَ ﴿٣٨﴾

39. And *We left another Sign* in Moses when We sent him to Pharaoh with clear authority,

وَفِي مُوسَىٰ إِذْ أَرْسَلْنَاهُ إِلَىٰ فِرْعَوْنَ بِسُلْطَانٍ مُّبِينٍ ﴿٣٩﴾

* 40. But he turned away *from Moses* in his *pride of* power, and said, 'A sorcerer, or a madman.'

فَتَوَلَّىٰ بِرُكْنِهِ وَقَالَ سَاحِرٌ أَوْ مَجْنُونٌ ﴿٤٠﴾

41. So We seized him and his hosts and threw them into the sea; and he *himself* was to blame.

فَأَخَذْنَاهُ وَجُنُودَهُ فَنَبَذْنَاهُمْ فِي الْيَمِّ وَهُوَ مُلِيمٌ ﴿٤١﴾

42. And *there was a Sign* in *the tribe of* 'Ād, when We sent against them the destructive wind.

وَفِي عَادٍ إِذْ أَرْسَلْنَا عَلَيْهِمُ الرِّيحَ الْعَقِيمَ ﴿٤٢﴾

43. It left nothing whatever that it visited, but made it like a rotten bone.

مَا تَذَرُ مِنْ شَيْءٍ أَتَتْ عَلَيْهِ إِلَّا جَعَلَتْهُ كَالرَّمِيمِ ﴿٤٣﴾

44. And *a Sign there was* in *the tribe of* Thamūd when it was said to them, 'Enjoy yourselves for a while.'

وَفِي ثَمُودَ إِذْ قِيلَ لَهُمْ تَمَتَّعُوا حَتَّىٰ حِينٍ ﴿٤٤﴾

45. But they rebelled against the command of their Lord. So the thunderbolt overtook them while they gazed;

فَعَتَوْا عَنْ أَمْرِ رَبِّهِمْ فَأَخَذَتْهُمُ الصَّاعِقَةُ وَهُمْ يَنْظُرُونَ ﴿٤٥﴾

46. And they were not able to rise *again*, nor could they defend themselves.

فَمَا اسْتَطَاعُوا مِنْ قِيَامٍ وَّمَا كَانُوا مُنْتَصِرِينَ ﴿٤٦﴾

47. And *We destroyed* the people of Noah before *them;* they were a disobedient people.

وَقَوْمَ نُوحٍ مِّنْ قَبْلُ إِنَّهُمْ كَانُوا قَوْمًا فَاسِقِينَ ﴿٤٧﴾

R. 3.

* 48. And We have built the heaven with *Our own* hands, and verily We have vast powers.

وَالسَّمَآءَ بَنَيْنٰهَا بِاَيْىدٍ وَّاِنَّا لَمُوْسِعُوْنَ ﴿۴۸﴾

49. And the earth We have spread out, and *how* excellently do We prepare *things!*

وَالْاَرْضَ فَرَشْنٰهَا فَنِعْمَ الْمٰهِدُوْنَ ﴿۴۹﴾

50. And of everything have We created pairs, that you may reflect.

وَمِنْ كُلِّ شَيْءٍ خَلَقْنَا زَوْجَيْنِ لَعَلَّكُمْ تَذَكَّرُوْنَ ﴿۵۰﴾

51. Flee ye therefore unto Allah. Surely, I am a plain Warner unto you from Him.

فَفِرُّوْٓا اِلَى اللّٰهِ ؕ اِنِّيْ لَكُمْ مِّنْهُ نَذِيْرٌ مُّبِيْنٌ ﴿۵۱﴾

52. And do not set up another God along with Allah. Surely, I am a plain Warner unto you from Him.

وَلَا تَجْعَلُوْا مَعَ اللّٰهِ اِلٰهًا اٰخَرَ ؕ اِنِّيْ لَكُمْ مِّنْهُ نَذِيْرٌ مُّبِيْنٌ ﴿۵۲﴾

53. Even so there came no Messenger to those before them, but they said, 'A sorcerer, or a madman!'

كَذٰلِكَ مَآ اَتَى الَّذِيْنَ مِنْ قَبْلِهِمْ مِّنْ رَّسُوْلٍ اِلَّا قَالُوْا سَاحِرٌ اَوْ مَجْنُوْنٌ ﴿۵۳﴾

54. Have they made it a legacy to one another? Nay, they are *all* a rebellious people.

اَتَوَاصَوْا بِهٖ ۚ بَلْ هُمْ قَوْمٌ طَاغُوْنَ ﴿۵۴﴾

55. So turn away from them; and there will be no blame on thee.

فَتَوَلَّ عَنْهُمْ فَمَآ اَنْتَ بِمَلُوْمٍ ﴿۵۵﴾

* 56. And keep on exhorting; for verily, exhortation benefits those who would believe.

وَّذَكِّرْ فَاِنَّ الذِّكْرٰى تَنْفَعُ الْمُؤْمِنِيْنَ ﴿۵۶﴾

57. And I have not created the Jinn and the men but that they may worship Me.

وَمَا خَلَقْتُ الْجِنَّ وَالْاِنْسَ اِلَّا لِيَعْبُدُوْنِ ﴿۵۷﴾

58. I desire no sustenance from them, nor do I desire that they should feed Me.

مَآ اُرِيْدُ مِنْهُمْ مِّنْ رِّزْقٍ وَّمَآ اُرِيْدُ اَنْ يُّطْعِمُوْنِ ﴿۵۸﴾

59. Surely, it is Allah *Himself* Who is the Great Sustainer, the Powerful, the Strong.

اِنَّ اللّٰهَ هُوَ الرَّزَّاقُ ذُو الْقُوَّةِ الْمَتِيْنُ ﴿۵۹﴾

* 60. And for those who do wrong there is a share *of comfort* like the share *enjoyed by* their fellows *of the earlier times;* so let them not ask Me to hasten on *the punishment.*

فَاِنَّ لِلَّذِيْنَ ظَلَمُوْا ذَنُوْبًا مِّثْلَ ذَنُوْبِ اَصْحٰبِهِمْ فَلَا يَسْتَعْجِلُوْنِ ﴿۶۰﴾

61. Woe, then, to those who disbelieve, because of that day of theirs which they have been promised!

فَوَيْلٌ لِّلَّذِيْنَ كَفَرُوْا مِنْ يَّوْمِهِمُ الَّذِيْ يُوْعَدُوْنَ ﴿۶۱﴾

رُكُوْعَاتُهَا ۲ سُوْرَةُ الطُّوْرِ مَكِّيَّةٌ (۵۲) اٰيَاتُهَا ۵۰

AL-ṬŪR

(Revealed before Hijra)

1. In the name of Allah, the Gracious, the Merciful.

بِسْمِ اللّٰهِ الرَّحْمٰنِ الرَّحِيْمِ ﴿١﴾

2. By the Mount;

وَالطُّوْرِ ﴿٢﴾

3. And *by* the Book inscribed

وَكِتٰبٍ مَّسْطُوْرٍ ﴿٣﴾

4. On parchment unfolded;

فِيْ رَقٍّ مَّنْشُوْرٍ ﴿٤﴾

5. And *by* the frequented House;

وَّالْبَيْتِ الْمَعْمُوْرِ ﴿٥﴾

6. And *by* the elevated Roof;

وَالسَّقْفِ الْمَرْفُوْعِ ﴿٦﴾

7. And *by* the swollen sea;

وَالْبَحْرِ الْمَسْجُوْرِ ﴿٧﴾

8. The punishment of thy Lord shall certainly come to pass;

اِنَّ عَذَابَ رَبِّكَ لَوَاقِعٌ ﴿٨﴾

9. There is none that can avert it.

مَّا لَهٗ مِنْ دَافِعٍ ﴿٩﴾

* 10. On the day when the heaven will heave *with awful* heaving,

يَّوْمَ تَمُوْرُ السَّمَآءُ مَوْرًا ﴿١٠﴾

* 11. And the mountains will move, *with terrible* moving,

وَّتَسِيْرُ الْجِبَالُ سَيْرًا ﴿١١﴾

12. Then woe that day to those who reject the truth,

فَوَيْلٌ يَّوْمَئِذٍ لِّلْمُكَذِّبِيْنَ ﴿١٢﴾

13. Who sportingly indulge in idle talk.

الَّذِيْنَ هُمْ فِيْ خَوْضٍ يَّلْعَبُوْنَ ﴿١٣﴾ وقف لازم

14. The day when they shall be thrust into the fire of Hell *with* a *violent* thrust.

يَوْمَ يُدَعُّوْنَ اِلٰى نَارِ جَهَنَّمَ دَعًّا ﴿١٤﴾

15. 'This is the Fire which you treated as a lie.

هٰذِهِ النَّارُ الَّتِيْ كُنْتُمْ بِهَا تُكَذِّبُوْنَ ﴿١٥﴾

16. 'Is this then magic, or do you not see?

اَفَسِحْرٌ هٰذَآ اَمْ اَنْتُمْ لَا تُبْصِرُوْنَ ﴿١٦﴾

17. 'Burn ye therein; and whether you show patience or you show *it* not, it will be the same for you. You are requited *only* for what you used to do.'

اِصْلَوْهَا فَاصْبِرُوْٓا اَوْ لَا تَصْبِرُوْا سَوَآءٌ عَلَيْكُمْ
اِنَّمَا تُجْزَوْنَ مَا كُنْتُمْ تَعْمَلُوْنَ ﴿١٧﴾

18. Verily, the righteous are in Gardens and in bliss,

اِنَّ الْمُتَّقِيْنَ فِيْ جَنّٰتٍ وَّنَعِيْمٍ ﴿١٨﴾

19. Enjoying what their Lord has bestowed on them; and their Lord has saved them from the torment of the Fire.

فَكِهِيْنَ بِمَآ اٰتٰهُمْ رَبُّهُمْ ۚ وَوَقٰهُمْ رَبُّهُمْ عَذَابَ الْجَحِيْمِ ﴿١٩﴾

* 20. 'Eat and drink in happiness because of what you used to do,

كُلُوْا وَاشْرَبُوْا هَنِيْٓـًٔا بِمَا كُنْتُمْ تَعْمَلُوْنَ ﴿٢٠﴾

21. 'Reclining on couches arranged in rows.' And We shall consort them with fair maidens having wide, *beautiful* eyes.

مُتَّكِـِٕيْنَ عَلٰى سُرُرٍ مَّصْفُوْفَةٍ ۚ وَزَوَّجْنٰهُمْ بِحُوْرٍ عِيْنٍ ﴿٢١﴾

22. And those who believe and whose children follow them in faith—with them shall We join their children. And We will not diminish anything from *the reward of* their works. Every man stands pledged for what he has earned.

وَالَّذِيْنَ اٰمَنُوْا وَاتَّبَعَتْهُمْ ذُرِّيَّتُهُمْ بِاِيْمَانٍ اَلْحَقْنَا بِهِمْ ذُرِّيَّتَهُمْ وَمَآ اَلَتْنٰهُمْ مِّنْ عَمَلِهِمْ مِّنْ شَيْءٍ ۚ كُلُّ امْرِئٍۢ بِمَا كَسَبَ رَهِيْنٌ ﴿٢٢﴾

23. And We shall bestow upon them *an abundance of* fruit and meat such as they will wish for.

وَاَمْدَدْنٰهُمْ بِفَاكِهَةٍ وَّلَحْمٍ مِّمَّا يَشْتَهُوْنَ ﴿٢٣﴾

24. There they will pass from one to another a cup wherein is neither levity nor sin.

يَتَنَازَعُوْنَ فِيْهَا كَاْسًا لَّا لَغْوٌ فِيْهَا وَلَا تَاْثِيْمٌ ﴿٢٤﴾

25. And there will wait upon them youths of their own, as though they were pearls well-preserved.

وَيَطُوْفُ عَلَيْهِمْ غِلْمَانٌ لَّهُمْ كَاَنَّهُمْ لُؤْلُؤٌ مَّكْنُوْنٌ ﴿٢٥﴾

26. And they will turn to one another, asking mutual questions.

وَاَقْبَلَ بَعْضُهُمْ عَلٰى بَعْضٍ يَّتَسَآءَلُوْنَ ﴿٢٦﴾

27. They will say, 'Before this, when *we were* among our family, we were very much afraid *of God's displeasure;*

قَالُوْٓا اِنَّا كُنَّا قَبْلُ فِيْٓ اَهْلِنَا مُشْفِقِيْنَ ﴿٢٧﴾

28. 'But Allah has been gracious unto us and has saved us from the torment of the burning blast.

فَمَنَّ اللّٰهُ عَلَيْنَا وَوَقٰىنَا عَذَابَ السَّمُوْمِ ﴿٢٨﴾

29. 'We used to pray to Him before. Surely, He is the Beneficent, the Merciful.'

اِنَّا كُنَّا مِنْ قَبْلُ نَدْعُوْهُ ۗ اِنَّهٗ هُوَ الْبَرُّ الرَّحِيْمُ ﴿٢٩﴾ ع

R. 2.

30. Admonish then. By the grace of thy Lord, thou art neither a soothsayer, nor a madman.

فَذَكِّرْ فَمَآ اَنْتَ بِنِعْمَتِ رَبِّكَ بِكَاهِنٍ وَّلَا مَجْنُوْنٍ ﴿٣٠﴾

31. Do they say, '*He is* a poet; we are waiting for some calamity which time will bring upon him?'

اَمْ يَقُوْلُوْنَ شَاعِرٌ نَّتَرَبَّصُ بِهٖ رَيْبَ الْمَنُوْنِ ﴿٣١﴾

32. Say, 'Await ye then! I *too* am with you among those who are waiting.'

قُلْ تَرَبَّصُوْا فَاِنِّيْ مَعَكُمْ مِّنَ الْمُتَرَبِّصِيْنَ ﴿٣٢﴾

33. Do their intellect *and reason* enjoin this upon them or are they a rebellious people?

اَمْ تَاْمُرُهُمْ اَحْلَامُهُمْ بِهٰذَآ اَمْ هُمْ قَوْمٌ طَاغُوْنَ ﴿٣٣﴾

34. Do they say, 'He has fabricated it?' Nay, but they would not believe.

اَمْ يَقُوْلُوْنَ تَقَوَّلَهٗ ۚ بَلْ لَّا يُؤْمِنُوْنَ ﴿٣٤﴾

* 35. Let them, then, bring forth an announcement like this, if they speak the truth!

فَلْيَأْتُوا بِحَدِيثٍ مِّثْلِهِ إِن كَانُوا صَادِقِينَ ﴿٣٥﴾

* 36. Have they been created for nothing, or are they themselves the creators?

أَمْ خُلِقُوا مِنْ غَيْرِ شَيْءٍ أَمْ هُمُ الْخَالِقُونَ ﴿٣٦﴾

37. Did they create the heavens and the earth? Nay, but they have no faith.

أَمْ خَلَقُوا السَّمَاوَاتِ وَالْأَرْضَ بَل لَّا يُوقِنُونَ ﴿٣٧﴾

38. Do they own the treasures of thy Lord, or are they the guardians *thereof?*

أَمْ عِندَهُمْ خَزَائِنُ رَبِّكَ أَمْ هُمُ الْمُصَيْطِرُونَ ﴿٣٨﴾

39. Have they a ladder *unto heaven* by means of which they can overhear? Then let their listener bring a manifest authority.

أَمْ لَهُمْ سُلَّمٌ يَسْتَمِعُونَ فِيهِ فَلْيَأْتِ مُسْتَمِعُهُم بِسُلْطَانٍ مُّبِينٍ ﴿٣٩﴾

40. Has He daughters and you have sons?

أَمْ لَهُ الْبَنَاتُ وَلَكُمُ الْبَنُونَ ﴿٤٠﴾

41. Dost thou ask a reward from them, so that they are weighed down with a load of debt?

أَمْ تَسْأَلُهُمْ أَجْرًا فَهُم مِّن مَّغْرَمٍ مُّثْقَلُونَ ﴿٤١﴾

42. Do they possess *knowledge of* the unseen, so that they write *it* down?

أَمْ عِندَهُمُ الْغَيْبُ فَهُمْ يَكْتُبُونَ ﴿٤٢﴾

43. Do they intend a plot? But it is those who disbelieve that will be caught in the plot.

أَمْ يُرِيدُونَ كَيْدًا فَالَّذِينَ كَفَرُوا هُمُ الْمَكِيدُونَ ﴿٤٣﴾

44. Have they a God other than Allah? Exalted is Allah above *all* that which they associate *with Him!*

أَمْ لَهُمْ إِلَٰهٌ غَيْرُ اللَّهِ سُبْحَانَ اللَّهِ عَمَّا يُشْرِكُونَ ﴿٤٤﴾

* 45. And if they should see a piece of the cloud falling down, they would say, 'Clouds piled up.'

وَإِن يَرَوْا كِسْفًا مِّنَ السَّمَاءِ سَاقِطًا يَقُولُوا سَحَابٌ مَّرْكُومٌ ﴿٤٥﴾

* 46. So leave them until they meet that day of theirs, on which they will be overtaken by a thunderbolt,

فَذَرْهُمْ حَتَّىٰ يُلَاقُوا يَوْمَهُمُ الَّذِي فِيهِ يُصْعَقُونَ ﴿٤٦﴾

47. The day when their plotting will not avail them aught, nor shall they be helped.

يَوْمَ لَا يُغْنِي عَنْهُمْ كَيْدُهُمْ شَيْئًا وَلَا هُمْ يُنصَرُونَ ﴿٤٧﴾

48. And verily, for those who do wrong there is a punishment besides that. But most of them know not.

وَإِنَّ لِلَّذِينَ ظَلَمُوا عَذَابًا دُونَ ذَٰلِكَ وَلَٰكِنَّ أَكْثَرَهُمْ لَا يَعْلَمُونَ ﴿٤٨﴾

49. So wait patiently for the judgment of thy Lord; for assuredly thou art before Our eyes; and glorify thy Lord with *His* praise when thou risest up *from sleep;*

وَاصْبِرْ لِحُكْمِ رَبِّكَ فَإِنَّكَ بِأَعْيُنِنَا وَسَبِّحْ بِحَمْدِ رَبِّكَ حِينَ تَقُومُ ﴿٤٩﴾

50. And for part of the night *also* do thou glorify Him and at the setting of the stars.

وَمِنَ اللَّيْلِ فَسَبِّحْهُ وَإِدْبَارَ النُّجُومِ ﴿٥٠﴾

(٥٣) سُوْرَةُ النَّجْمِ مَكِّيَّةٌ

AL-NAJM

(Revealed before Hijra)

1. In the name of Allah, the Gracious, the Merciful.

بِسْمِ اللّٰهِ الرَّحْمٰنِ الرَّحِيْمِ ①

* 2. By the stemless plant when it falls,

وَالنَّجْمِ اِذَا هَوٰى ②

3. Your companion has neither erred, nor has he gone astray,

مَا ضَلَّ صَاحِبُكُمْ وَمَا غَوٰى ③

4. Nor does he speak out of *his own* desire.

وَمَا يَنْطِقُ عَنِ الْهَوٰى ④

5. It is nothing but *pure* revelation *that has been* revealed *by God*.

اِنْ هُوَ اِلَّا وَحْيٌ يُّوْحٰى ⑤

6. *The Lord* of mighty powers has taught him,

عَلَّمَهٗ شَدِيْدُ الْقُوٰى ⑥

* 7. *The One* Possessor of strength. So He manifested His ascendance *over everything*,

ذُوْ مِرَّةٍ فَاسْتَوٰى ⑦

* 8. And *He revealed His Word* when he was on the uppermost horizon,

وَهُوَ بِالْاُفُقِ الْاَعْلٰى ⑧

9. Then he drew nearer *to God;* then he came down *to mankind*,

ثُمَّ دَنَا فَتَدَلّٰى ⑨

10. So that he became, *as it were*, one chord to two bows or closer still.

فَكَانَ قَابَ قَوْسَيْنِ اَوْ اَدْنٰى ⑩

11. Then He revealed to His servant that which He revealed.

فَاَوْحٰٓى اِلٰى عَبْدِهٖ مَآ اَوْحٰى ⑪

* 12. The heart *of the Prophet* was not untrue to that which he saw.

مَا كَذَبَ الْفُؤَادُ مَا رَاٰى ⑫

13. Will you then dispute with him about what he saw?

اَفَتُمٰرُوْنَهٗ عَلٰى مَا يَرٰى ⑬

14. And certainly, he saw Him a second time *also*,

وَلَقَدْ رَاٰهُ نَزْلَةً اُخْرٰى ⑭

15. Near the farthest Lote-tree,

عِنْدَ سِدْرَةِ الْمُنْتَهٰى ⑮

16. Near which is the Garden of Eternal Abode.

عِنْدَهَا جَنَّةُ الْمَاْوٰى ⑯

17. *This was* when that which covers covered the Lote-tree.

اِذْ يَغْشَى السِّدْرَةَ مَا يَغْشٰى ⑰

18. The eye deviated not, nor did *it* wander.

مَا زَاغَ الْبَصَرُ وَمَا طَغٰى ⑱

19. Surely, he saw the greatest of the Signs of his Lord.

لَقَدْ رَاٰى مِنْ اٰيٰتِ رَبِّهِ الْكُبْرٰى ⑲

20. Now tell *me* about Lāt* and 'Uzzā*,

أَفَرَءَيْتُمُ اللّٰتَ وَالْعُزّٰى ﴿٢٠﴾

21. And Manāt*, the third one, another *goddess!*

وَمَنٰوةَ الثَّالِثَةَ الْاُخْرٰى ﴿٢١﴾

22. 'What! for you the males and for Him the females!'

اَلَكُمُ الذَّكَرُ وَلَهُ الْاُنْثٰى ﴿٢٢﴾

23. That indeed is an unfair division.

تِلْكَ اِذًا قِسْمَةٌ ضِيْزٰى ﴿٢٣﴾

24. 'These are but names which you have named—you and your fathers—for which Allah has sent down no authority.' They follow naught but conjecture and what their souls desire, while there has already come to them guidance from their Lord.

اِنْ هِيَ اِلَّآ اَسْمَآءٌ سَمَّيْتُمُوْهَآ اَنْتُمْ وَاٰبَآؤُكُمْ
مَّآ اَنْزَلَ اللّٰهُ بِهَا مِنْ سُلْطٰنٍ اِنْ يَّتَّبِعُوْنَ اِلَّا
الظَّنَّ وَمَا تَهْوَى الْاَنْفُسُ وَلَقَدْ جَآءَهُمْ مِّنْ
رَّبِّهِمُ الْهُدٰى ﴿٢٤﴾

* 25. Can man have whatever he desires?

اَمْ لِلْاِنْسَانِ مَا تَمَنّٰى ﴿٢٥﴾

* 26. Nay, to Allah belong the Hereafter and this *world.*

فَلِلّٰهِ الْاٰخِرَةُ وَالْاُوْلٰى ﴿٢٦﴾

R. 2.

27. And how many an angel is there in the heavens, but their intercession shall be of no avail, except after Allah has given permission to whomsoever He wills and pleases.

وَكَمْ مِّنْ مَّلَكٍ فِي السَّمٰوٰتِ لَا تُغْنِيْ شَفَاعَتُهُمْ
شَيْـًٔا اِلَّا مِنْۢ بَعْدِ اَنْ يَّاْذَنَ اللّٰهُ لِمَنْ يَّشَآءُ وَ
يَرْضٰى ﴿٢٧﴾

28. Those who believe not in the Hereafter name the angels with names of females;

اِنَّ الَّذِيْنَ لَا يُؤْمِنُوْنَ بِالْاٰخِرَةِ لَيُسَمُّوْنَ الْمَلٰٓئِكَةَ
تَسْمِيَةَ الْاُنْثٰى ﴿٢٨﴾

29. But they have no knowledge thereof. They follow nothing but conjecture; and conjecture avails naught against truth.

وَمَا لَهُمْ بِهٖ مِنْ عِلْمٍ اِنْ يَّتَّبِعُوْنَ اِلَّا الظَّنَّ وَ
اِنَّ الظَّنَّ لَا يُغْنِيْ مِنَ الْحَقِّ شَيْـًٔا ﴿٢٩﴾

30. So turn aside from him who turns away from Our remembrance, and seeks nothing but the life of this world.

فَاَعْرِضْ عَنْ مَّنْ تَوَلّٰى عَنْ ذِكْرِنَا وَلَمْ يُرِدْ اِلَّا
الْحَيٰوةَ الدُّنْيَا ﴿٣٠﴾

* 31. That is the utmost limit of their knowledge. Verily, thy Lord knows him best who strays from His way, and He knows him best who follows guidance.

ذٰلِكَ مَبْلَغُهُمْ مِّنَ الْعِلْمِ اِنَّ رَبَّكَ هُوَ اَعْلَمُ
بِمَنْ ضَلَّ عَنْ سَبِيْلِهٖ وَهُوَ اَعْلَمُ بِمَنِ اهْتَدٰى ﴿٣١﴾

32. And to Allah belongs whatever is in the heavens and whatever is in the

وَلِلّٰهِ مَا فِي السَّمٰوٰتِ وَمَا فِي الْاَرْضِ لِيَجْزِيَ

* Favourite idols of the Quraish of Mecca.

earth, that He may requite those who do evil for what they have wrought, and that He may reward with what is best those who do good.

الَّذِيْنَ اَسَآءُوْا بِمَا عَمِلُوْا وَيَجْزِيَ الَّذِيْنَ اَحْسَنُوْا بِالْحُسْنٰى ﴿٣٢﴾

* 33. Those who shun the grave sins and immoral actions except minor faults—verily, thy Lord is very liberal in forgiving. He knows you full well *from the time* when He created you from the earth, and when you were embryos in the bellies of your mothers. So ascribe not purity to yourselves. He knows him best who is *truly* righteous.

اَلَّذِيْنَ يَجْتَنِبُوْنَ كَبٰٓئِرَ الْاِثْمِ وَالْفَوَاحِشَ اِلَّا اللَّمَمَ ۭ اِنَّ رَبَّكَ وَاسِعُ الْمَغْفِرَةِ ۭ هُوَ اَعْلَمُ بِكُمْ اِذْ اَنْشَاَكُمْ مِّنَ الْاَرْضِ وَاِذْ اَنْتُمْ اَجِنَّةٌ فِيْ بُطُوْنِ اُمَّهٰتِكُمْ ۚ فَلَا تُزَكُّوْٓا اَنْفُسَكُمْ ۭ هُوَ اَعْلَمُ بِمَنِ اتَّقٰى ﴿٣٣﴾

R. 3.

34. Dost thou see him who turns away,

اَفَرَءَيْتَ الَّذِيْ تَوَلّٰى ﴿٣٤﴾

35. And gives a little, and does it grudgingly?

وَاَعْطٰى قَلِيْلًا وَّاَكْدٰى ﴿٣٥﴾

36. Has he the knowledge of the unseen so that he can see?

اَعِنْدَهٗ عِلْمُ الْغَيْبِ فَهُوَ يَرٰى ﴿٣٦﴾

37. Has he not been informed of what is in the Scriptures of Moses

اَمْ لَمْ يُنَبَّاْ بِمَا فِيْ صُحُفِ مُوْسٰى ﴿٣٧﴾

38. And *of* Abraham who fulfilled *the commandments?*—

وَاِبْرٰهِيْمَ الَّذِيْ وَفّٰٓى ﴿٣٨﴾

39. That no bearer of burden shall bear the burden of another;

اَلَّا تَزِرُ وَازِرَةٌ وِّزْرَ اُخْرٰى ﴿٣٩﴾

* 40. And that man will have nothing but what he strives for;

وَاَنْ لَّيْسَ لِلْاِنْسَانِ اِلَّا مَا سَعٰى ﴿٤٠﴾

* 41. And that his striving shall soon be seen;

وَاَنَّ سَعْيَهٗ سَوْفَ يُرٰى ﴿٤١﴾

42. Then will he be rewarded for it with the fullest reward;

ثُمَّ يُجْزٰىهُ الْجَزَآءَ الْاَوْفٰى ﴿٤٢﴾

43. And that to thy Lord do *all things* ultimately go;

وَاَنَّ اِلٰى رَبِّكَ الْمُنْتَهٰى ﴿٤٣﴾

44. And that it is He Who makes *men* laugh and makes *them* weep;

وَاَنَّهٗ هُوَ اَضْحَكَ وَاَبْكٰى ﴿٤٤﴾

45. And that it is He Who causes death and gives life;

وَاَنَّهٗ هُوَ اَمَاتَ وَاَحْيَا ﴿٤٥﴾

46. And that He creates the pairs, male and female,

وَاَنَّهٗ خَلَقَ الزَّوْجَيْنِ الذَّكَرَ وَالْاُنْثٰى ﴿٤٦﴾

47. From a sperm-drop when it is poured forth;

مِنْ نُّطْفَةٍ اِذَا تُمْنٰى ﴿٤٧﴾

48. And that it is for Him to bring forth the second creation;

وَاَنَّ عَلَيْهِ النَّشْاَةَ الْاُخْرٰى ﴿٤٨﴾

49. And that it is He Who enriches and grants wealth to *one's* satisfaction;

وَاَنَّهٗ هُوَ اَغْنٰى وَاَقْنٰى ﴿۴۹﴾

50. And that He is the Lord of Sirius;

وَاَنَّهٗ هُوَ رَبُّ الشِّعْرٰى ﴿۵۰﴾

51. And that He destroyed the first *tribe of* 'Ād,

وَاَنَّهٗۤ اَهْلَكَ عَادًا الْاُوْلٰى ﴿۵۱﴾

52. And *the tribe of* Thamūd, and He spared not *any of them*,

وَثَمُوْدَاۡ فَمَاۤ اَبْقٰى ﴿۵۲﴾

53. And *He destroyed* the people of Noah before *them*—verily, they were most unjust and most rebellious—

وَقَوْمَ نُوْحٍ مِّنْ قَبْلُ ؕ اِنَّهُمْ كَانُوْا هُمْ اَظْلَمَ وَاَطْغٰى ﴿۵۳﴾

* 54. And He overthrew the subverted cities *of the people of Lot*,

وَالْمُؤْتَفِكَةَ اَهْوٰى ﴿۵۴﴾

* 55. So that there covered them that which was to cover.

فَغَشّٰىهَا مَا غَشّٰى ﴿۵۵﴾

56. Which then, *O man*, of the bounties of thy Lord wilt thou dispute?

فَبِاَيِّ اٰلَآءِ رَبِّكَ تَتَمَارٰى ﴿۵۶﴾

57. This is a Warner from among the *class of the* Warners of old.

هٰذَا نَذِيْرٌ مِّنَ النُّذُرِ الْاُوْلٰى ﴿۵۷﴾

58. *The Hour* that was to come has come nigh,

اَزِفَتِ الْاٰزِفَةُ ﴿۵۸﴾

59. None but Allah can avert it.

لَيْسَ لَهَا مِنْ دُوْنِ اللّٰهِ كَاشِفَةٌ ﴿۵۹﴾

60. Do you then wonder at this announcement?

اَفَمِنْ هٰذَا الْحَدِيْثِ تَعْجَبُوْنَ ﴿۶۰﴾

61. And do you laugh, and weep not?

وَتَضْحَكُوْنَ وَلَا تَبْكُوْنَ ﴿۶۱﴾

62. And will you remain proudly heedless?

وَاَنْتُمْ سٰمِدُوْنَ ﴿۶۲﴾

63. So prostrate yourselves before Allah, and worship *Him*.

السجدة

فَاسْجُدُوْا لِلّٰهِ وَاعْبُدُوْا ﴿۶۳﴾ ع

اٰیَاتُهَا ۵۶ (۵۴) سُوْرَةُ الْقَمَرِ مَکِّیَّةٌ رُکُوْعَاتُهَا ۳

Part 27 AL-QAMAR Chapter 54

(Revealed before Hijra)

1. In the name of Allah, the Gracious, the Merciful.

بِسْمِ اللّٰهِ الرَّحْمٰنِ الرَّحِيْمِ ﴿۱﴾

2. The Hour has drawn nigh, and the moon is rent asunder.

اِقْتَرَبَتِ السَّاعَةُ وَانْشَقَّ الْقَمَرُ ﴿۲﴾

3. And if they see s Sign, they turn

وَاِنْ يَّرَوْا اٰيَةً يُّعْرِضُوْا وَيَقُوْلُوْا سِحْرٌ

away and say, 'A passing *feat of* magic.'

4. They reject *the truth* and follow their own fancies. But every decree *of God* shall certainly come to pass.

5. And there has already come to them the great news wherein is a warning—

6. Consummate wisdom; but the warnings profit them not.

7. Therefore turn thou away from them. The day when the Summoner will summon *them* to a disagreeable thing,

8. While their eyes will be cast down and they will come forth from *their* graves as though they were locusts scattered about,

9. Hastening towards the Summoner. The disbelievers will say, 'This is a hard day.'

10. The people of Noah rejected *the truth* before them; aye, they rejected Our servant and said, 'A madman and one who is spurned.'

11. He therefore prayed to his Lord *saying*, 'I am overcome, so *come* Thou *to my* help!'

12. Thereupon We opened the gates of heaven, with water pouring down;

13. And We caused the earth to burst forth with springs, so the *two* waters met for a purpose that was decreed.

14. And We carried him upon that *which was made* of planks and nails.

15. It floated on under Our eyes: a reward for him who had been rejected.

16. And We left it as a Sign *for the coming generations;* but is there anyone who would receive admonition?

17. How *terrible* then was My punishment and My warning!

18. And indeed We have made the Qur'ān easy *to understand and* to remember. But is there anyone who would receive admonition?

19. *The tribe of* 'Ād rejected *the truth*. How *terrible* then was My punishment and My warning!

20. We sent against them a furious

مُّسْتَمِرٌّ ﴿٣﴾

وَكَذَّبُوا وَاتَّبَعُوا أَهْوَاءَهُمْ وَكُلُّ أَمْرٍ مُّسْتَقِرٌّ ﴿٤﴾

وَلَقَدْ جَاءَهُم مِّنَ الْأَنبَاءِ مَا فِيهِ مُزْدَجَرٌ ﴿٥﴾

حِكْمَةٌ بَالِغَةٌ فَمَا تُغْنِ النُّذُرُ ﴿٦﴾

فَتَوَلَّ عَنْهُمْ يَوْمَ يَدْعُ الدَّاعِ إِلَىٰ شَيْءٍ نُّكُرٍ ﴿٧﴾

خُشَّعًا أَبْصَارُهُمْ يَخْرُجُونَ مِنَ الْأَجْدَاثِ كَأَنَّهُمْ
جَرَادٌ مُّنتَشِرٌ ﴿٨﴾

مُّهْطِعِينَ إِلَى الدَّاعِ يَقُولُ الْكَافِرُونَ هَٰذَا
يَوْمٌ عَسِرٌ ﴿٩﴾

كَذَّبَتْ قَبْلَهُمْ قَوْمُ نُوحٍ فَكَذَّبُوا عَبْدَنَا وَقَالُوا
مَجْنُونٌ وَازْدُجِرَ ﴿١٠﴾

فَدَعَا رَبَّهُ أَنِّي مَغْلُوبٌ فَانتَصِرْ ﴿١١﴾

فَفَتَحْنَا أَبْوَابَ السَّمَاءِ بِمَاءٍ مُّنْهَمِرٍ ﴿١٢﴾

وَفَجَّرْنَا الْأَرْضَ عُيُونًا فَالْتَقَى الْمَاءُ عَلَىٰ أَمْرٍ
قَدْ قُدِرَ ﴿١٣﴾

وَحَمَلْنَاهُ عَلَىٰ ذَاتِ أَلْوَاحٍ وَدُسُرٍ ﴿١٤﴾

تَجْرِي بِأَعْيُنِنَا جَزَاءً لِّمَن كَانَ كُفِرَ ﴿١٥﴾

وَلَقَد تَّرَكْنَاهَا آيَةً فَهَلْ مِن مُّدَّكِرٍ ﴿١٦﴾

فَكَيْفَ كَانَ عَذَابِي وَنُذُرِ ﴿١٧﴾

وَلَقَدْ يَسَّرْنَا الْقُرْآنَ لِلذِّكْرِ فَهَلْ مِن مُّدَّكِرٍ ﴿١٨﴾

كَذَّبَتْ عَادٌ فَكَيْفَ كَانَ عَذَابِي وَنُذُرِ ﴿١٩﴾

إِنَّا أَرْسَلْنَا عَلَيْهِمْ رِيحًا صَرْصَرًا فِي يَوْمِ نَحْسٍ

wind on a day of unending ill luck,

مُّسْتَمِرٍّ ﴿٢٠﴾

21. Tearing people away as though they were the trunks of uprooted palm-trees.

تَنزِعُ النَّاسَ كَأَنَّهُمْ أَعْجَازُ نَخْلٍ مُّنقَعِرٍ ﴿٢١﴾

22. How *terrible* then was My punishment and My warning!

فَكَيْفَ كَانَ عَذَابِي وَنُذُرِ ﴿٢٢﴾

23. And indeed We have made the Qur'ān easy *to understand and* to remember. But is there anyone who would receive admonition?

ع ٢ ٣ وَلَقَدْ يَسَّرْنَا الْقُرْآنَ لِلذِّكْرِ فَهَلْ مِن مُّدَّكِرٍ ﴿٢٣﴾

R. 2.

24. *The tribe of* Thamūd *also* rejected the Warners.

كَذَّبَتْ ثَمُودُ بِالنُّذُرِ ﴿٢٤﴾

* 25. And they said, 'What! a man, from among ourselves, a single individual! Shall we follow him? Then indeed we would be in manifest error, and *would be* mad.

فَقَالُوا أَبَشَرًا مِّنَّا وَاحِدًا نَّتَّبِعُهُ إِنَّا إِذًا لَّفِي ضَلَالٍ وَسُعُرٍ ﴿٢٥﴾

26. 'Has the Reminder been revealed to him *alone* of all of us? Nay, he is a boastful liar.'

أَأُلْقِيَ الذِّكْرُ عَلَيْهِ مِن بَيْنِنَا بَلْ هُوَ كَذَّابٌ أَشِرٌ ﴿٢٦﴾

27. 'Tomorrow will they know who is the boastful liar!

سَيَعْلَمُونَ غَدًا مَّنِ الْكَذَّابُ الْأَشِرُ ﴿٢٧﴾

28. 'We will send the she-camel as a trial for them. So watch them, *O Ṣāliḥ*, and have patience.

إِنَّا مُرْسِلُو النَّاقَةِ فِتْنَةً لَّهُمْ فَارْتَقِبْهُمْ وَاصْطَبِرْ ﴿٢٨﴾

* 29. 'And tell them that the water is shared *only* between them, *but as for the she-camel* every drinking time may be attended *by her*.'

وَنَبِّئْهُمْ أَنَّ الْمَاءَ قِسْمَةٌ بَيْنَهُمْ كُلُّ شِرْبٍ مُّحْتَضَرٌ ﴿٢٩﴾

* 30. But they called their comrade, and he seized *a sword* and hamstrung *her*.

فَنَادَوْا صَاحِبَهُمْ فَتَعَاطَىٰ فَعَقَرَ ﴿٣٠﴾

31. How *terrible* then was My punishment and My warning!

فَكَيْفَ كَانَ عَذَابِي وَنُذُرِ ﴿٣١﴾

32. We sent against them a single blast, and they became like the dry stubble, trampled upon.

إِنَّا أَرْسَلْنَا عَلَيْهِمْ صَيْحَةً وَاحِدَةً فَكَانُوا كَهَشِيمِ الْمُحْتَظِرِ ﴿٣٢﴾

33. And indeed We have made the Qur'ān easy *to understand and* to remember. But is there anyone who would receive admonition?

وَلَقَدْ يَسَّرْنَا الْقُرْآنَ لِلذِّكْرِ فَهَلْ مِن مُّدَّكِرٍ ﴿٣٣﴾

34. Lot's people *also* rejected the Warners.

كَذَّبَتْ قَوْمُ لُوطٍ بِالنُّذُرِ ﴿٣٤﴾

35. We sent a storm of stones upon them except the family of Lot, whom We delivered by early dawn,

إِنَّا أَرْسَلْنَا عَلَيْهِمْ حَاصِبًا إِلَّا آلَ لُوطٍ نَّجَّيْنَاهُم بِسَحَرٍ ﴿٣٥﴾

36. As a favour from Us. Thus do We reward him who is grateful.

37. And he indeed had warned them of Our punishment, but they doubted the warning.

38. And they *deceitfully* sought to turn him away from his guests. So We blinded their eyes, *and said,* 'Taste ye now My punishment and My warning.'

39. And there came upon them early in the morning a lasting punishment.

40. 'Now taste ye My punishment and My warning.'

41. And, indeed, We have made the Qur'ān easy *to understand and* to remember. But is there anyone who would receive admonition?

R. 3.

42. And surely to the people of Pharaoh *also* came Warners.

43. They rejected all Our Signs. So We seized them like the seizing of One Who is Mighty *and* Omnipotent.

44. Are your disbelievers better than those? Or have you an exemption in the Scriptures?

45. Do they say, 'We are a victorious host?'

46. The hosts shall soon be routed and will turn their backs *in flight.*

47. Aye, the Hour is their appointed time; and the Hour will be most calamitous and most bitter.

48. Surely, the guilty are in *manifest* error and gone mad.

49. On the day when they will be dragged into the Fire on their faces, *and it will be said to them,* 'Taste ye the touch of Hell.'

50. Verily, We have created everything in *due* measure.

51. And Our command is *carried out by* only one *word,* like the twinkling of an eye.

52. And indeed We have destroyed people *before you who were* like unto you. But is there anyone who would receive admonition?

53. And everything they have done is *recorded* in the Books.

54. And every matter, small and great, is written down.

نِعْمَةً مِّنْ عِنْدِنَا ۭ كَذٰلِكَ نَجْزِيْ مَنْ شَكَرَ ﴿٣٦﴾

وَلَقَدْ اَنْذَرَهُمْ بَطْشَتَنَا فَتَمَارَوْا بِالنُّذُرِ ﴿٣٧﴾

وَلَقَدْ رَاوَدُوْهُ عَنْ ضَيْفِهٖ فَطَمَسْنَآ اَعْيُنَهُمْ

فَذُوْقُوْا عَذَابِيْ وَنُذُرِ ﴿٣٨﴾

وَلَقَدْ صَبَّحَهُمْ بُكْرَةً عَذَابٌ مُّسْتَقِرٌّ ﴿٣٩﴾

فَذُوْقُوْا عَذَابِيْ وَنُذُرِ ﴿٤٠﴾

وَلَقَدْ يَسَّرْنَا الْقُرْاٰنَ لِلذِّكْرِ فَهَلْ مِنْ مُّدَّكِرٍ ﴿٤١﴾ ع ٢ ١٤ ٩

وَلَقَدْ جَآءَ اٰلَ فِرْعَوْنَ النُّذُرُ ﴿٤٢﴾

كَذَّبُوْا بِاٰيٰتِنَا كُلِّهَا فَاَخَذْنٰهُمْ اَخْذَ عَزِيْزٍ مُّقْتَدِرٍ ﴿٤٣﴾

اَكُفَّارُكُمْ خَيْرٌ مِّنْ اُولٰٓئِكُمْ اَمْ لَكُمْ بَرَآءَةٌ فِي

الزُّبُرِ ﴿٤٤﴾

اَمْ يَقُوْلُوْنَ نَحْنُ جَمِيْعٌ مُّنْتَصِرٌ ﴿٤٥﴾

سَيُهْزَمُ الْجَمْعُ وَيُوَلُّوْنَ الدُّبُرَ ﴿٤٦﴾

بَلِ السَّاعَةُ مَوْعِدُهُمْ وَالسَّاعَةُ اَدْهٰى وَاَمَرُّ ﴿٤٧﴾

اِنَّ الْمُجْرِمِيْنَ فِيْ ضَلٰلٍ وَّسُعُرٍ ﴿٤٨﴾ وقف لازم

يَوْمَ يُسْحَبُوْنَ فِي النَّارِ عَلٰى وُجُوْهِهِمْ ۭ ذُوْقُوْا

مَسَّ سَقَرَ ﴿٤٩﴾

اِنَّا كُلَّ شَيْءٍ خَلَقْنٰهُ بِقَدَرٍ ﴿٥٠﴾

وَمَآ اَمْرُنَآ اِلَّا وَاحِدَةٌ كَلَمْحٍ بِالْبَصَرِ ﴿٥١﴾

وَلَقَدْ اَهْلَكْنَآ اَشْيَاعَكُمْ فَهَلْ مِنْ مُّدَّكِرٍ ﴿٥٢﴾

وَكُلُّ شَيْءٍ فَعَلُوْهُ فِي الزُّبُرِ ﴿٥٣﴾

وَكُلُّ صَغِيْرٍ وَّكَبِيْرٍ مُّسْتَطَرٌ ﴿٥٤﴾

55. Verily, the righteous will be in the midst of Gardens and streams,

إِنَّ الْمُتَّقِيْنَ فِيْ جَنّٰتٍ وَّنَهَرٍ ﴿٥٥﴾

56. In the seat of truth with an Omnipotent King.

فِيْ مَقْعَدِ صِدْقٍ عِنْدَ مَلِيْكٍ مُّقْتَدِرٍ ﴿٥٦﴾

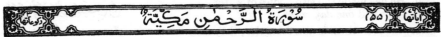

سُوْرَةُ الرَّحْمٰنِ مَكِّيَّةٌ

اٰيَاتُهَا ٧٩ (٥٥) رُكُوْعَاتُهَا ٣

Part 27 AL-RAHMĀN Chapter 55

(Revealed before Hijra)

1. In the name of Allah, the Gracious, the Merciful.

بِسْمِ اللّٰهِ الرَّحْمٰنِ الرَّحِيْمِ ﴿١﴾

2. *It is God*, the Gracious

اَلرَّحْمٰنُ ﴿٢﴾

3. Who has taught the Qur'ān.

عَلَّمَ الْقُرْاٰنَ ﴿٣﴾

4. He has created man.

خَلَقَ الْاِنْسَانَ ﴿٤﴾

* 5. He has taught him plain speech.

عَلَّمَهُ الْبَيَانَ ﴿٥﴾

6. The sun and the moon *run their courses* according to a fixed reckoning.

اَلشَّمْسُ وَالْقَمَرُ بِحُسْبَانٍ ﴿٦﴾

7. And the stemless plants and the trees *humbly* submit *to His will*.

وَّالنَّجْمُ وَالشَّجَرُ يَسْجُدٰنِ ﴿٧﴾

8. And the heaven He has raised high and set up a measure,

وَالسَّمَآءَ رَفَعَهَا وَوَضَعَ الْمِيْزَانَ ﴿٨﴾

9. That you may not transgress the measure.

اَلَّا تَطْغَوْا فِي الْمِيْزَانِ ﴿٩﴾

10. So weigh all things in justice and fall not short of the measure.

وَاَقِيْمُوا الْوَزْنَ بِالْقِسْطِ وَلَا تُخْسِرُوا الْمِيْزَانَ ﴿١٠﴾

11. And He has set the earth for *His* creatures;

وَالْاَرْضَ وَضَعَهَا لِلْاَنَامِ ﴿١١﴾

12. Therein are *all kinds of* fruit and palm-trees with sheaths,

فِيْهَا فَاكِهَةٌ وَّالنَّخْلُ ذَاتُ الْاَكْمَامِ ﴿١٢﴾

13. And grain with *its* husk and fragrant plants.

وَالْحَبُّ ذُو الْعَصْفِ وَالرَّيْحَانُ ﴿١٣﴾

14. Which, then, of the favours of your Lord will you twain deny, *O men and Jinn*?

فَبِاَيِّ اٰلَآءِ رَبِّكُمَا تُكَذِّبٰنِ ﴿١٤﴾

15. He created man from dry ringing clay *which is* like baked pottery.

خَلَقَ الْاِنْسَانَ مِنْ صَلْصَالٍ كَالْفَخَّارِ ﴿١٥﴾

16. And the Jinn He created from the flame of fire.

وَخَلَقَ الْجَآنَّ مِنْ مَّارِجٍ مِّنْ نَّارٍ ﴿١٦﴾

17. Which, then, of the favours of your Lord will you twain deny?

فَبِاَيِّ اٰلَآءِ رَبِّكُمَا تُكَذِّبٰنِ ﴿١٧﴾

18. The Lord of the two Easts and the Lord of the two Wests!

رَبُّ الْمَشْرِقَيْنِ وَرَبُّ الْمَغْرِبَيْنِ ﴿١٨﴾

19. Which, then, of the favours of your Lord will you twain deny?

فَبِاَيِّ اٰلَآءِ رَبِّكُمَا تُكَذِّبٰنِ ﴿١٩﴾

* 20. He has made the two bodies of water flow. They will *one day* meet.

مَرَجَ الْبَحْرَيْنِ يَلْتَقِيٰنِ ﴿٢٠﴾

21. Between them is *now* a barrier; they encroach not *one upon the other*.

بَيْنَهُمَا بَرْزَخٌ لَّا يَبْغِيٰنِ ﴿٢١﴾

22. Which, then, of the favours of your Lord will you twain deny?

فَبِاَيِّ اٰلَآءِ رَبِّكُمَا تُكَذِّبٰنِ ﴿٢٢﴾

23. There come out from them pearls and coral.

يَخْرُجُ مِنْهُمَا اللُّؤْلُؤُ وَالْمَرْجَانُ ﴿٢٣﴾

24. Which, then, of the favours of your Lord will you twain deny?

فَبِاَيِّ اٰلَآءِ رَبِّكُمَا تُكَذِّبٰنِ ﴿٢٤﴾

25. And His are the lofty ships reared aloft on the sea like mountains.

وَلَهُ الْجَوَارِ الْمُنْشَـٰٔتُ فِي الْبَحْرِ كَالْاَعْلَامِ ﴿٢٥﴾

26. Which, then, of the favours of your Lord will you twain deny?

فَبِاَيِّ اٰلَآءِ رَبِّكُمَا تُكَذِّبٰنِ ﴿٢٦﴾

R. 2.

27. All that is on it (earth) will pass away.

كُلُّ مَنْ عَلَيْهَا فَانٍ ﴿٢٧﴾

28. And there will remain *only* the Person of thy Lord, Master of Glory and Honour.

وَّيَبْقٰى وَجْهُ رَبِّكَ ذُو الْجَلٰلِ وَالْاِكْرَامِ ﴿٢٨﴾

29. Which, then, of the favours of your Lord will you twain deny?

فَبِاَيِّ اٰلَآءِ رَبِّكُمَا تُكَذِّبٰنِ ﴿٢٩﴾

30. Of Him do beg all that are in the heavens and the earth. Every day He *reveals Himself* in a different state.

يَسْـَٔلُهٗ مَنْ فِي السَّمٰوٰتِ وَالْاَرْضِ كُلَّ يَوْمٍ هُوَ فِيْ شَاْنٍ ﴿٣٠﴾

31. Which, then, of the favours of your Lord will you twain deny?

فَبِاَيِّ اٰلَآءِ رَبِّكُمَا تُكَذِّبٰنِ ﴿٣١﴾

* 32. Soon shall We attend to you, O ye two big groups!

سَنَفْرُغُ لَكُمْ اَيُّهَ الثَّقَلٰنِ ﴿٣٢﴾

33. Which, then, of the favours of your Lord will you twain deny?

فَبِاَيِّ اٰلَآءِ رَبِّكُمَا تُكَذِّبٰنِ ﴿٣٣﴾

34. O company of Jinn and men! if you have power to go beyond the confines of the heavens and the earth, then do go. But you cannot go save with authority.

يٰمَعْشَرَ الْجِنِّ وَالْاِنْسِ اِنِ اسْتَطَعْتُمْ اَنْ تَنْفُذُوْا مِنْ اَقْطَارِ السَّمٰوٰتِ وَالْاَرْضِ فَانْفُذُوْا لَا تَنْفُذُوْنَ اِلَّا بِسُلْطٰنٍ ﴿٣٤﴾

35. Which, then, of the favours of your Lord will you twain deny?

فَبِاَيِّ اٰلَآءِ رَبِّكُمَا تُكَذِّبٰنِ ﴿٣٥﴾

* 36. There shall be sent against you a flame of fire, and smoke; and you shall not be able to help yourselves.

يُرْسَلُ عَلَيْكُمَا شُوَاظٌ مِّنْ نَّارٍ وَّ نُحَاسٌ فَلَا تَنْتَصِرٰنِ ﴿٣٦﴾

37. Which, then, of the favours of your Lord will you twain deny?

فَبِاَيِّ اٰلَآءِ رَبِّكُمَا تُكَذِّبٰنِ ﴿٣٧﴾

38. And when the heaven is rent asunder, and becomes red like red hide—

فَاِذَا انْشَقَّتِ السَّمَآءُ فَكَانَتْ وَرْدَةً كَالدِّهَانِ ﴿٣٨﴾

39. Which, then, of the favours of your Lord will you twain deny?—

فَبِاَيِّ اٰلَآءِ رَبِّكُمَا تُكَذِّبٰنِ ﴿٣٩﴾

40. On that day neither man nor Jinn will be asked about his sin.

فَيَوْمَئِذٍ لَّا يُسْئَلُ عَنْ ذَنْۢبِهٖٓ اِنْسٌ وَّ لَا جَآنٌّ ﴿٤٠﴾

41. Which, then, of the favours of your Lord will you twain deny?

فَبِاَيِّ اٰلَآءِ رَبِّكُمَا تُكَذِّبٰنِ ﴿٤١﴾

42. The guilty will be known by their marks, and they will be seized by the forelocks and the feet.

يُعْرَفُ الْمُجْرِمُوْنَ بِسِيْمٰهُمْ فَيُؤْخَذُ بِالنَّوَاصِيْ وَ الْاَقْدَامِ ﴿٤٢﴾

43. Which, then, of the favours of your Lord will you twain deny?

فَبِاَيِّ اٰلَآءِ رَبِّكُمَا تُكَذِّبٰنِ ﴿٤٣﴾

44. This is the Hell which the guilty deny,

هٰذِهٖ جَهَنَّمُ الَّتِيْ يُكَذِّبُ بِهَا الْمُجْرِمُوْنَ ﴿٤٤﴾

45. Between it and fierce boiling water will they go round.

يَطُوْفُوْنَ بَيْنَهَا وَ بَيْنَ حَمِيْمٍ اٰنٍ ﴿٤٥﴾

46. Which, then, of the favours of your Lord will you twain deny?

فَبِاَيِّ اٰلَآءِ رَبِّكُمَا تُكَذِّبٰنِ ﴿٤٦﴾

R. 3.

* 47. But for him who fears to stand before his Lord there are two Gardens—

وَلِمَنْ خَافَ مَقَامَ رَبِّهٖ جَنَّتٰنِ ﴿٤٧﴾

48. Which, then, of the favours of your Lord will you twain deny?—

فَبِاَيِّ اٰلَآءِ رَبِّكُمَا تُكَذِّبٰنِ ﴿٤٨﴾

* 49. Having many varieties *of trees*.

ذَوَاتَآ اَفْنَانٍ ﴿٤٩﴾

50. Which, then, of the favours of your Lord will you twain deny?

فَبِاَيِّ اٰلَآءِ رَبِّكُمَا تُكَذِّبٰنِ ﴿٥٠﴾

51. In both of them there are two fountains flowing *free*.

فِيْهِمَا عَيْنٰنِ تَجْرِيٰنِ ﴿٥١﴾

52. Which, then, of the favours of your Lord will you twain deny?

فَبِاَيِّ اٰلَآءِ رَبِّكُمَا تُكَذِّبٰنِ ﴿٥٢﴾

53. Therein will be every *kind of* fruit in pairs.

فِيْهِمَا مِنْ كُلِّ فَاكِهَةٍ زَوْجٰنِ ﴿٥٣﴾

54. Which, then, of the favours of your Lord will you twain deny?

فَبِاَيِّ اٰلَآءِ رَبِّكُمَا تُكَذِّبٰنِ ﴿٥٤﴾

55. *They will* recline *on couches* above carpets, the linings of which will be of thick

مُتَّكِـِٕيْنَ عَلٰى فُرُشٍۢ بَطَآئِنُهَا مِنْ اِسْتَبْرَقٍ ؕ وَ

brocade. And the ripe fruit of the two Gardens will be within easy reach.

جَنَا الْجَنَّتَيْنِ دَانٍ ۝٥٥

56. Which, then, of the favours of your Lord will you twain deny?

فَبِأَيِّ آلَاءِ رَبِّكُمَا تُكَذِّبَانِ ۝٥٦

57. Therein will *also* be *chaste maidens* of modest gaze, whom neither man nor Jinn will have touched before them—

فِيهِنَّ قَاصِرَاتُ الطَّرْفِ لَمْ يَطْمِثْهُنَّ إِنْسٌ قَبْلَهُمْ
وَلَا جَانٌّ ۝٥٧

58. Which, then, of the favours of your Lord will you twain deny?—

فَبِأَيِّ آلَاءِ رَبِّكُمَا تُكَذِّبَانِ ۝٥٨

59. As if they were rubies and small pearls.

كَأَنَّهُنَّ الْيَاقُوتُ وَالْمَرْجَانُ ۝٥٩

60. Which, then, of the favours of your Lord will you twain deny?

فَبِأَيِّ آلَاءِ رَبِّكُمَا تُكَذِّبَانِ ۝٦٠

61. The reward of goodness is nothing but goodness.

هَلْ جَزَاءُ الْإِحْسَانِ إِلَّا الْإِحْسَانُ ۝٦١

62. Which, then, of the favours of your Lord will you twain deny?

فَبِأَيِّ آلَاءِ رَبِّكُمَا تُكَذِّبَانِ ۝٦٢

63. And besides these two, there are two *other* Gardens—

وَمِنْ دُونِهِمَا جَنَّتَانِ ۝٦٣

64. Which, then, of the favours of your Lord will you twain deny?—

فَبِأَيِّ آلَاءِ رَبِّكُمَا تُكَذِّبَانِ ۝٦٤

65. Dark green with foliage.

مُدْهَامَّتَانِ ۝٦٥

66. Which, then, of the favours of your Lord will you twain deny?

فَبِأَيِّ آلَاءِ رَبِّكُمَا تُكَذِّبَانِ ۝٦٦

67. Therein *also* will be two springs gushing forth with water.

فِيهِمَا عَيْنَانِ نَضَّاخَتَانِ ۝٦٧

68. Which, then, of the favours of your Lord will you twain deny?

فَبِأَيِّ آلَاءِ رَبِّكُمَا تُكَذِّبَانِ ۝٦٨

69. In both of them there will be *all kinds of* fruit, and dates and pomegranates.

فِيهِمَا فَاكِهَةٌ وَنَخْلٌ وَرُمَّانٌ ۝٦٩

70. Which, then, of the favours of your Lord will you twain deny?

فَبِأَيِّ آلَاءِ رَبِّكُمَا تُكَذِّبَانِ ۝٧٠

71. Therein will be *maidens*, good *and* beautiful—

فِيهِنَّ خَيْرَاتٌ حِسَانٌ ۝٧١

72. Which then, of the favours of your Lord will you twain deny?—

فَبِأَيِّ آلَاءِ رَبِّكُمَا تُكَذِّبَانِ ۝٧٢

73. Fair maidens with lovely black eyes, well-guarded in pavilions—

حُورٌ مَقْصُورَاتٌ فِي الْخِيَامِ ۝٧٣

74. Which, then, of the favours of your Lord will you twain deny?—

فَبِأَيِّ آلَاءِ رَبِّكُمَا تُكَذِّبَانِ ۝٧٤

75. Whom neither man nor Jinn will have touched before them—

لَمْ يَطْمِثْهُنَّ إِنْسٌ قَبْلَهُمْ وَلَا جَانٌّ ۝٧٥

76. Which, then, of the favours of your Lord will you twain deny?—

فَبِأَيِّ آلَاءِ رَبِّكُمَا تُكَذِّبَانِ ﴿٧٦﴾

77. Reclining on green cushions and beautiful carpets.

مُتَّكِئِينَ عَلَىٰ رَفْرَفٍ خُضْرٍ وَعَبْقَرِيٍّ حِسَانٍ ﴿٧٧﴾

78. Which, then, of the favours of your Lord will you twain deny?

فَبِأَيِّ آلَاءِ رَبِّكُمَا تُكَذِّبَانِ ﴿٧٨﴾

79. Blessed is the name of thy Lord, Master of Glory and Honour.

تَبَارَكَ اسْمُ رَبِّكَ ذِي الْجَلَالِ وَالْإِكْرَامِ ﴿٧٩﴾

سُورَةُ الْوَاقِعَةِ مَكِّيَّةٌ

آياتها ٩٧ (٥٦) ركوعاتها ٣

AL-WĀQI'AH

Part 27 Chapter 56

(Revealed before Hijra)

1. In the name of Allah, the Gracious, the Merciful.

بِسْمِ اللّٰهِ الرَّحْمٰنِ الرَّحِيْمِ ﴿١﴾

2. When the Event comes to pass—

إِذَا وَقَعَتِ الْوَاقِعَةُ ﴿٢﴾

* 3. None can say that its coming to pass is a lie—

لَيْسَ لِوَقْعَتِهَا كَاذِبَةٌ ﴿٣﴾

* 4. *Some* it will bring low, *others* it will exalt.

خَافِضَةٌ رَّافِعَةٌ ﴿٤﴾

5. When the earth will be shaken *with a terrible* shaking,

إِذَا رُجَّتِ الْأَرْضُ رَجًّا ﴿٥﴾

6. And the mountains will be shattered —a *complete* shattering.

وَبُسَّتِ الْجِبَالُ بَسًّا ﴿٦﴾

7. They shall *all* become like dust particles scattered about,

فَكَانَتْ هَبَاءً مُّنْبَثًّا ﴿٧﴾

8. And you shall be *divided into* three groups:

وَكُنْتُمْ أَزْوَاجًا ثَلٰثَةً ﴿٨﴾

* 9. *First*, those on the right hand—how *lucky* are those on the right hand!—

فَأَصْحٰبُ الْمَيْمَنَةِ مَا أَصْحٰبُ الْمَيْمَنَةِ ﴿٩﴾

* 10. *Second*, those on the left hand—how *unlucky* are those on the left hand!—

وَأَصْحٰبُ الْمَشْئَمَةِ مَا أَصْحٰبُ الْمَشْئَمَةِ ﴿١٠﴾

11. *Third*, the foremost; they are the foremost;

وَالسّٰبِقُوْنَ السّٰبِقُوْنَ ﴿١١﴾

12. They will have achieved nearness *to God*.

أُولٰٓئِكَ الْمُقَرَّبُوْنَ ﴿١٢﴾

13. *They will be* in the Gardens of Bliss—

فِيْ جَنّٰتِ النَّعِيْمِ ﴿١٣﴾

* 14. A large party from among the early *Muslims*,

ثُلَّةٌ مِّنَ الْأَوَّلِيْنَ ﴿١٤﴾

* 15. And a few from the later ones,

وَقَلِيْلٌ مِّنَ الْاٰخِرِيْنَ ﴿١٥﴾

16. *Seated* on couches inwrought *with gold and jewels,*

عَلٰى سُرُرٍ مَّوْضُوْنَةٍ ﴿١٦﴾

17. Reclining thereon facing each other.

مُّتَّكِـِٕيْنَ عَلَيْهَا مُتَقٰبِلِيْنَ ﴿١٧﴾

18. There will wait on them youths, who will not age,

يَطُوْفُ عَلَيْهِمْ وِلْدَانٌ مُّخَلَّدُوْنَ ﴿١٨﴾

19. Carrying goblets and ewers and cups *filled* out of a flowing spring—

بِاَكْوَابٍ وَّاَبَارِيْقَ ۙ وَكَاْسٍ مِّنْ مَّعِيْنٍ ﴿١٩﴾

20. No headache will they get therefrom, nor will they be intoxicated—

لَّا يُصَدَّعُوْنَ عَنْهَا وَلَا يُنْزِفُوْنَ ﴿٢٠﴾

21. And *carrying* such fruits as they choose,

وَفَاكِهَةٍ مِّمَّا يَتَخَيَّرُوْنَ ﴿٢١﴾

22. And flesh of birds as they may desire.

وَلَحْمِ طَيْرٍ مِّمَّا يَشْتَهُوْنَ ﴿٢٢﴾

23. And *there will be* fair maidens with wide, lovely eyes,

وَحُوْرٌ عِيْنٌ ﴿٢٣﴾

* 24. Like pearls, well preserved,

كَاَمْثَالِ اللُّؤْلُؤِ الْمَكْنُوْنِ ﴿٢٤﴾

25. As a reward for what they did.

جَزَآءًۢ بِمَا كَانُوْا يَعْمَلُوْنَ ﴿٢٥﴾

26. They will not hear therein any vain or sinful talk,

لَا يَسْمَعُوْنَ فِيْهَا لَغْوًا وَّلَا تَاْثِيْمًا ﴿٢٦﴾

27. Except *only* the word *of salutation,* 'Peace, peace.'

اِلَّا قِيْلًا سَلٰمًا سَلٰمًا ﴿٢٧﴾

* 28. And *as for* those on the right hand—how *lucky* are those on the right hand!—

وَاَصْحٰبُ الْيَمِيْنِ ۙ مَآ اَصْحٰبُ الْيَمِيْنِ ﴿٢٨﴾

29. *They* will be amidst thornless lote-trees,

فِيْ سِدْرٍ مَّخْضُوْدٍ ﴿٢٩﴾

30. And clustered bananas,

وَّطَلْحٍ مَّنْضُوْدٍ ﴿٣٠﴾

31. And extended shade,

وَّظِلٍّ مَّمْدُوْدٍ ﴿٣١﴾

32. And flowing water,

وَّمَآءٍ مَّسْكُوْبٍ ﴿٣٢﴾

33. And abundant fruit,

وَّفَاكِهَةٍ كَثِيْرَةٍ ﴿٣٣﴾

34. Neither failing, nor forbidden,

لَّا مَقْطُوْعَةٍ وَّلَا مَمْنُوْعَةٍ ﴿٣٤﴾

35. And *they will have* noble spouses—

وَّفُرُشٍ مَّرْفُوْعَةٍ ﴿٣٥﴾

36. Verily, We have created them a *good* creation,

اِنَّآ اَنْشَاْنٰهُنَّ اِنْشَآءً ﴿٣٦﴾

37. And made them virgins,

فَجَعَلْنٰهُنَّ اَبْكَارًا ﴿٣٧﴾

38. Loving, of equal age

عُرُبًا اَتْرَابًا ﴿٣٨﴾

* 39. With those on the right hand:

لِّاَصْحٰبِ الْيَمِيْنِ ﴿٣٩﴾

R. 2.

40. A large party from among the early *Muslims*,

ثُلَّةٌ مِّنَ الْاَوَّلِيْنَ ﴿٤٠﴾

41. And a large party from the later ones.

وَثُلَّةٌ مِّنَ الْاٰخِرِيْنَ ﴿٤١﴾

* 42. But *as for* those on the left hand—how *unlucky* are those on the left hand!—

وَاَصْحٰبُ الشِّمَالِ ۙ۬ مَآ اَصْحٰبُ الشِّمَالِ ﴿٤٢﴾

43. *They will be* in the midst of scorching winds and scalding water,

فِيْ سَمُوْمٍ وَّحَمِيْمٍ ﴿٤٣﴾

44. And under the shadow of black smoke,

وَّظِلٍّ مِّنْ يَّحْمُوْمٍ ﴿٤٤﴾

45. Neither cool nor of any good.

لَّا بَارِدٍ وَّلَا كَرِيْمٍ ﴿٤٥﴾

46. Before this they lived a life of ease and plenty

اِنَّهُمْ كَانُوْا قَبْلَ ذٰلِكَ مُتْرَفِيْنَ ﴿٤٦﴾

47. And used to persist in extreme sinfulness.

وَكَانُوْا يُصِرُّوْنَ عَلَى الْحِنْثِ الْعَظِيْمِ ﴿٤٧﴾

48. And they were wont to say, 'What! when we are dead and have become dust and bones, shall we indeed be raised again,

وَكَانُوْا يَقُوْلُوْنَ ۙ۬ اَئِذَا مِتْنَا وَكُنَّا تُرَابًا وَّ
عِظَامًا ءَاِنَّا لَمَبْعُوْثُوْنَ ﴿٤٨﴾

49. 'And our fathers of yore too?'

اَوَ اٰبَآؤُنَا الْاَوَّلُوْنَ ﴿٤٩﴾

50. Say, '*Yes*, the earlier ones and the later ones

قُلْ اِنَّ الْاَوَّلِيْنَ وَالْاٰخِرِيْنَ ﴿٥٠﴾

51. 'Will *all* be gathered together unto the fixed time of an appointed day.

لَمَجْمُوْعُوْنَ ۙ۬ اِلٰى مِيْقَاتِ يَوْمٍ مَّعْلُوْمٍ ﴿٥١﴾

52. 'Then, O ye that have gone astray and have rejected *the truth*,

ثُمَّ اِنَّكُمْ اَيُّهَا الضَّآلُّوْنَ الْمُكَذِّبُوْنَ ﴿٥٢﴾

53. 'You will surely eat of the tree of Zaqqūm,

لَاٰكِلُوْنَ مِنْ شَجَرٍ مِّنْ زَقُّوْمٍ ﴿٥٣﴾

54. 'And will fill *your* bellies therewith,

فَمَالِـُٔوْنَ مِنْهَا الْبُطُوْنَ ﴿٥٤﴾

55. 'And will drink thereon of boiling water,

فَشٰرِبُوْنَ عَلَيْهِ مِنَ الْحَمِيْمِ ﴿٥٥﴾

* 56. 'Drinking like the drinking of the camels that suffer from an insatiable thirst.'

فَشٰرِبُوْنَ شُرْبَ الْهِيْمِ ﴿٥٦﴾

57. This will be their entertainment on the Day of Judgment.

هٰذَا نُزُلُهُمْ يَوْمَ الدِّيْنِ ﴿٥٧﴾

* 58. We have created you. Why, then, do you not accept *the truth?*

نَحْنُ خَلَقْنٰكُمْ فَلَوْلَا تُصَدِّقُوْنَ ﴿۵۸﴾

59. What think ye *of the sperm-drop* that you emit?

اَفَرَءَيْتُمْ مَّا تُمْنُوْنَ ﴿۵۹﴾

60. Is it you who have created it or are We the Creator?

ءَاَنْتُمْ تَخْلُقُوْنَهٗۤ اَمْ نَحْنُ الْخٰلِقُوْنَ ﴿۶۰﴾

61. We have ordained death for *all of* you; and We cannot be prevented

نَحْنُ قَدَّرْنَا بَيْنَكُمُ الْمَوْتَ وَمَا نَحْنُ بِمَسْبُوْقِيْنَ ﴿۶۱﴾

* 62. From bringing in your place others like you, and *from* developing you into a form which *at present* you know not.

عَلٰۤى اَنْ نُّبَدِّلَ اَمْثَالَكُمْ وَنُنْشِئَكُمْ فِيْ مَا
لَا تَعْلَمُوْنَ ﴿۶۲﴾

63. And you have certainly known the first creation. Why, then, do you not reflect?

وَلَقَدْ عَلِمْتُمُ النَّشْاَةَ الْاُوْلٰى فَلَوْلَا تَذَكَّرُوْنَ ﴿۶۳﴾

64. Do you see what you sow?

اَفَرَءَيْتُمْ مَّا تَحْرُثُوْنَ ﴿۶۴﴾

65. Is it you who grow it or are We the Grower?

ءَاَنْتُمْ تَزْرَعُوْنَهٗۤ اَمْ نَحْنُ الزّٰرِعُوْنَ ﴿۶۵﴾

* 66. If We *so* pleased, We could reduce it all to broken pieces, then you would keep lamenting:

لَوْ نَشَآءُ لَجَعَلْنٰهُ حُطَامًا فَظَلْتُمْ تَفَكَّهُوْنَ ﴿۶۶﴾

67. 'We are ruined!

اِنَّا لَمُغْرَمُوْنَ ﴿۶۷﴾

68. 'Nay, we are deprived *of everything.*'

بَلْ نَحْنُ مَحْرُوْمُوْنَ ﴿۶۸﴾

69. Do you see the water which you drink?

اَفَرَءَيْتُمُ الْمَآءَ الَّذِيْ تَشْرَبُوْنَ ﴿۶۹﴾

70. Is it you who send it down from the clouds, or are We the Sender?

ءَاَنْتُمْ اَنْزَلْتُمُوْهُ مِنَ الْمُزْنِ اَمْ نَحْنُ الْمُنْزِلُوْنَ ﴿۷۰﴾

71. If We *so* pleased, We could make it bitter. Why, then, are you not grateful?

لَوْ نَشَآءُ جَعَلْنٰهُ اُجَاجًا فَلَوْلَا تَشْكُرُوْنَ ﴿۷۱﴾

72. Do you see the fire which you kindle?

اَفَرَءَيْتُمُ النَّارَ الَّتِيْ تُوْرُوْنَ ﴿۷۲﴾

73. Is it you who produce the tree for it, or are We the Producer?

ءَاَنْتُمْ اَنْشَاْتُمْ شَجَرَتَهَاۤ اَمْ نَحْنُ الْمُنْشِـُٔوْنَ ﴿۷۳﴾

74. We have made it a reminder and a benefit for the wayfarers.

نَحْنُ جَعَلْنٰهَا تَذْكِرَةً وَّمَتَاعًا لِّلْمُقْوِيْنَ ﴿۷۴﴾

75. So glorify the name of thy Lord, the Great.

فَسَبِّحْ بِاسْمِ رَبِّكَ الْعَظِيْمِ ﴿۷۵﴾

R. 3.

* 76. Nay, I swear by the shooting of the stars—

فَلَاۤ اُقْسِمُ بِمَوٰقِعِ النُّجُوْمِ ﴿۷۶﴾

77. And, indeed, that is a grand oath, if you only knew—

وَاِنَّهٗ لَقَسَمٌ لَّوْ تَعْلَمُوْنَ عَظِيْمٌ ﴿۷۷﴾

78. That this is indeed a noble Qur'ān,

اِنَّهٗ لَقُرْاٰنٌ كَرِيْمٌ ﴿۷۸﴾

79. In a well-preserved Book,

فِي كِتَٰبٍ مَّكْنُونٍ ﴿٧٩﴾

80. Which none shall touch except those who are purified.

لَّا يَمَسُّهُۥٓ إِلَّا ٱلْمُطَهَّرُونَ ﴿٨٠﴾

81. *It is* a revelation from the Lord of the worlds.

تَنزِيلٌ مِّن رَّبِّ ٱلْعَٰلَمِينَ ﴿٨١﴾

* 82. Is it this *Divine* discourse that you would reject?

أَفَبِهَٰذَا ٱلْحَدِيثِ أَنتُم مُّدْهِنُونَ ﴿٨٢﴾

83. And do you make the denial thereof your *means of* livelihood?

وَتَجْعَلُونَ رِزْقَكُمْ أَنَّكُمْ تُكَذِّبُونَ ﴿٨٣﴾

84. Why, then, when *the soul of the dying man* reaches the throat,

فَلَوْلَآ إِذَا بَلَغَتِ ٱلْحُلْقُومَ ﴿٨٤﴾

85. And you are at that moment looking on—

وَأَنتُمْ حِينَئِذٍ تَنظُرُونَ ﴿٨٥﴾

86. And We are nearer to him than you, but you see not—

وَنَحْنُ أَقْرَبُ إِلَيْهِ مِنكُمْ وَلَٰكِن لَّا تُبْصِرُونَ ﴿٨٦﴾

87. Why, then, if you are not to be called to account,

فَلَوْلَآ إِن كُنتُمْ غَيْرَ مَدِينِينَ ﴿٨٧﴾

88. You cannot bring it back, if you are truthful?

تَرْجِعُونَهَآ إِن كُنتُمْ صَٰدِقِينَ ﴿٨٨﴾

89. Now if he be of those who have attained nearness *to God*,

فَأَمَّآ إِن كَانَ مِنَ ٱلْمُقَرَّبِينَ ﴿٨٩﴾

90. Then *for him* is comfort and fragrance *of happiness* and a Garden of Bliss;

فَرَوْحٌ وَرَيْحَانٌ وَجَنَّتُ نَعِيمٍ ﴿٩٠﴾

91. And if he be of those who are on the right hand,

وَأَمَّآ إِن كَانَ مِنْ أَصْحَٰبِ ٱلْيَمِينِ ﴿٩١﴾

92. Then 'Peace be on thee, *who is* from those on the right hand.'

فَسَلَٰمٌ لَّكَ مِنْ أَصْحَٰبِ ٱلْيَمِينِ ﴿٩٢﴾

93. But if he be of those who reject *the truth* and are in error,

وَأَمَّآ إِن كَانَ مِنَ ٱلْمُكَذِّبِينَ ٱلضَّآلِّينَ ﴿٩٣﴾

94. Then *for him will be* an entertainment of boiling water,

فَنُزُلٌ مِّنْ حَمِيمٍ ﴿٩٤﴾

95. And burning in Hell.

وَتَصْلِيَةُ جَحِيمٍ ﴿٩٥﴾

96. Verily, this is the certain truth.

إِنَّ هَٰذَا لَهُوَ حَقُّ ٱلْيَقِينِ ﴿٩٦﴾

97. So glorify the name of thy Lord, the Great.

فَسَبِّحْ بِٱسْمِ رَبِّكَ ٱلْعَظِيمِ ﴿٩٧﴾

سُوْرَةُ الْحَدِيْدِ مَدَنِيَّةٌ (٥٧)

آیاتها ٣٠ — رکوعاتها ٤

AL-ḤADĪD

(Revealed after Hijra)

1. In the name of Allah, the Gracious, the Merciful.

بِسْمِ اللّٰهِ الرَّحْمٰنِ الرَّحِيْمِ ﴿١﴾

2. Whatever is in the heavens and the earth glorifies Allah; and He is the Mighty, the Wise.

سَبَّحَ لِلّٰهِ مَا فِي السَّمٰوٰتِ وَالْاَرْضِ ۚ وَهُوَ الْعَزِيْزُ الْحَكِيْمُ ﴿٢﴾

3. His is the kingdom of the heavens and the earth; He gives life and He causes death; and He has power over all things.

لَهٗ مُلْكُ السَّمٰوٰتِ وَالْاَرْضِ ۚ يُحْيٖ وَيُمِيْتُ ۚ وَهُوَ عَلٰى كُلِّ شَيْءٍ قَدِيْرٌ ﴿٣﴾

4. He is the First and the Last, and the Manifest and the Hidden, and He knows all things full well.

هُوَ الْاَوَّلُ وَالْاٰخِرُ وَالظَّاهِرُ وَالْبَاطِنُ ۚ وَهُوَ بِكُلِّ شَيْءٍ عَلِيْمٌ ﴿٤﴾

5. He it is Who created the heavens and the earth in six periods, then He settled Himself on the Throne. He knows what enters the earth and what comes out of it, and what comes down from heaven and what goes up into it. And He is with you wheresoever you may be. And Allah sees all that you do.

هُوَ الَّذِيْ خَلَقَ السَّمٰوٰتِ وَالْاَرْضَ فِيْ سِتَّةِ اَيَّامٍ ثُمَّ اسْتَوٰى عَلَى الْعَرْشِ ۗ يَعْلَمُ مَا يَلِجُ فِي الْاَرْضِ وَمَا يَخْرُجُ مِنْهَا وَمَا يَنْزِلُ مِنَ السَّمَآءِ وَمَا يَعْرُجُ فِيْهَا ۗ وَهُوَ مَعَكُمْ اَيْنَ مَا كُنْتُمْ ۗ وَاللّٰهُ بِمَا تَعْمَلُوْنَ بَصِيْرٌ ﴿٥﴾

6. His is the kingdom of the heavens and the earth; and to Allah are all affairs referred.

لَهٗ مُلْكُ السَّمٰوٰتِ وَالْاَرْضِ ۗ وَاِلَى اللّٰهِ تُرْجَعُ الْاُمُوْرُ ﴿٦﴾

7. He causes the night to pass into the day and causes the day to pass into the night; and He knows full well all that is in the breasts.

يُوْلِجُ الَّيْلَ فِي النَّهَارِ وَيُوْلِجُ النَّهَارَ فِي الَّيْلِ ۗ وَهُوَ عَلِيْمٌ ۢ بِذَاتِ الصُّدُوْرِ ﴿٧﴾

8. Believe in Allah and His Messenger, and spend *in the way of Allah* out of that to which He has made you heirs. And those of you who believe and spend will have a great reward.

اٰمِنُوْا بِاللّٰهِ وَرَسُوْلِهٖ وَاَنْفِقُوْا مِمَّا جَعَلَكُمْ مُّسْتَخْلَفِيْنَ فِيْهِ ۗ فَالَّذِيْنَ اٰمَنُوْا مِنْكُمْ وَاَنْفَقُوْا لَهُمْ اَجْرٌ كَبِيْرٌ ﴿٨﴾

9. Why is it that you believe not in Allah, while the Messenger calls you to believe in your Lord, and He has already taken a covenant from you, if indeed you are believers?

وَمَا لَكُمْ لَا تُؤْمِنُوْنَ بِاللّٰهِ ۚ وَالرَّسُوْلُ يَدْعُوْكُمْ
لِتُؤْمِنُوْا بِرَبِّكُمْ وَقَدْ اَخَذَ مِيْثَاقَكُمْ اِنْ كُنْتُمْ
مُّؤْمِنِيْنَ ﴿٩﴾

10. He it is Who sends down clear Signs to His servant, that He may bring you out of every *kind of* darkness into the light. And verily, Allah is Compassionate *and* Merciful to you.

هُوَ الَّذِيْ يُنَزِّلُ عَلٰى عَبْدِهٖٓ اٰيٰتٍۭ بَيِّنٰتٍ لِّيُخْرِجَكُمْ
مِّنَ الظُّلُمٰتِ اِلَى النُّوْرِ ۭ وَاِنَّ اللّٰهَ بِكُمْ لَرَءُوْفٌ
رَّحِيْمٌ ﴿١٠﴾

11. And why is it that you spend not in the way of Allah, while to Allah belongs the heritage of the heavens and the earth? Those of you who spent and fought before the Victory are not equal *to those who did so later*. They are greater in rank than those who spent and fought afterwards. And to all has Allah promised good. And Allah is Well-Aware of what you do.

وَمَا لَكُمْ اَلَّا تُنْفِقُوْا فِيْ سَبِيْلِ اللّٰهِ وَلِلّٰهِ مِيْرَاثُ
السَّمٰوٰتِ وَالْاَرْضِ ۭ لَا يَسْتَوِيْ مِنْكُمْ مَّنْ اَنْفَقَ
مِنْ قَبْلِ الْفَتْحِ وَقٰتَلَ ۭ اُولٰۗىِٕكَ اَعْظَمُ دَرَجَةً مِّنَ
الَّذِيْنَ اَنْفَقُوْا مِنْۢ بَعْدُ وَقٰتَلُوْا ۭ وَكُلًّا وَّعَدَ اللّٰهُ
الْحُسْنٰى ۭ وَاللّٰهُ بِمَا تَعْمَلُوْنَ خَبِيْرٌ ﴿١١﴾ ع

R. 2.

12. Who is he that will lend to Allah a goodly loan? So He will increase it manifold for him, and he will have a generous reward.

مَنْ ذَا الَّذِيْ يُقْرِضُ اللّٰهَ قَرْضًا حَسَنًا فَيُضٰعِفَهٗ
لَهٗ وَلَهٗٓ اَجْرٌ كَرِيْمٌ ﴿١٢﴾

13. And *think of* the day when thou wilt see the believing men and the believing women, their light running before them and on their right hands, *and it will be said to them*, 'Glad tidings for you this day! Gardens through which streams flow, wherein you will abide. That is the supreme triumph.'

يَوْمَ تَرَى الْمُؤْمِنِيْنَ وَالْمُؤْمِنٰتِ يَسْعٰى نُوْرُهُمْ
بَيْنَ اَيْدِيْهِمْ وَبِاَيْمَانِهِمْ بُشْرٰىكُمُ الْيَوْمَ
جَنّٰتٌ تَجْرِيْ مِنْ تَحْتِهَا الْاَنْهٰرُ خٰلِدِيْنَ فِيْهَا ۭ
ذٰلِكَ هُوَ الْفَوْزُ الْعَظِيْمُ ﴿١٣﴾

14. *On* the day when the hypocritical men and the hypocritical women will say to those who believe, 'Wait *a while* for us that we may take light from your light,' it will be said *to them*, 'Go ye back *if you can*, and seek for light.' Then there will be set up between them a wall with a door in it. The inside of it will be *all* mercy and in front, outside it, will be torment.

يَوْمَ يَقُوْلُ الْمُنٰفِقُوْنَ وَالْمُنٰفِقٰتُ لِلَّذِيْنَ اٰمَنُوا
انْظُرُوْنَا نَقْتَبِسْ مِنْ نُّوْرِكُمْ ۚ قِيْلَ ارْجِعُوْا
وَرَاۗءَكُمْ فَالْتَمِسُوْا نُوْرًا ۭ فَضُرِبَ بَيْنَهُمْ بِسُوْرٍ
لَّهٗ بَابٌ ۭ بَاطِنُهٗ فِيْهِ الرَّحْمَةُ وَظَاهِرُهٗ مِنْ قِبَلِهِ
الْعَذَابُ ﴿١٤﴾

15. They will call out to them, *saying*, 'Were we not with you?' They will answer, 'Yea, but you led yourselves into temptation and you hesitated and doubted and your vain desires deceived you till the decree of Allah came to pass. And the Deceiver deceived you in respect of Allah.

يُنَادُونَهُمْ أَلَمْ نَكُن مَّعَكُمْ قَالُوا بَلَىٰ وَلَٰكِنَّكُمْ
فَتَنتُمْ أَنفُسَكُمْ وَتَرَبَّصْتُمْ وَارْتَبْتُمْ وَغَرَّتْكُمُ
الْأَمَانِيُّ حَتَّىٰ جَاءَ أَمْرُ اللَّهِ وَغَرَّكُم بِاللَّهِ الْغَرُورُ ﴿١٥﴾

16. 'So this day no ransom shall be accepted from you, nor from those who disbelieved. Your final abode is the Fire; that is your friend; and a very evil destination it is.'

فَالْيَوْمَ لَا يُؤْخَذُ مِنكُمْ فِدْيَةٌ وَلَا مِنَ الَّذِينَ
كَفَرُوا مَأْوَاكُمُ النَّارُ هِيَ مَوْلَاكُمْ وَبِئْسَ
الْمَصِيرُ ﴿١٦﴾

17. Has not the time arrived for those who believe that their hearts should feel humbled at the remembrance of Allah and at the truth which has come down *to them*, and that they should not become like those who were given the Book before them and the term was prolonged for them, but their hearts were hardened, and many of them are wicked?

أَلَمْ يَأْنِ لِلَّذِينَ آمَنُوا أَن تَخْشَعَ قُلُوبُهُمْ لِذِكْرِ
اللَّهِ وَمَا نَزَلَ مِنَ الْحَقِّ وَلَا يَكُونُوا كَالَّذِينَ أُوتُوا
الْكِتَابَ مِن قَبْلُ فَطَالَ عَلَيْهِمُ الْأَمَدُ فَقَسَتْ
قُلُوبُهُمْ وَكَثِيرٌ مِّنْهُمْ فَاسِقُونَ ﴿١٧﴾

* 18. Know that Allah is *now* quickening the earth after its death. We have made the Signs manifest to you, that you may understand.

اعْلَمُوا أَنَّ اللَّهَ يُحْيِي الْأَرْضَ بَعْدَ مَوْتِهَا قَدْ
بَيَّنَّا لَكُمُ الْآيَاتِ لَعَلَّكُمْ تَعْقِلُونَ ﴿١٨﴾

19. *As to* the men that give alms, and the women that give alms, and those who lend to Allah a goodly loan—it will be increased manifold for them, and theirs will *also* be an honourable reward—

إِنَّ الْمُصَّدِّقِينَ وَالْمُصَّدِّقَاتِ وَأَقْرَضُوا اللَّهَ
قَرْضًا حَسَنًا يُضَاعَفُ لَهُمْ وَلَهُمْ أَجْرٌ كَرِيمٌ ﴿١٩﴾

20. And those who believe in Allah and His Messengers *and* they are the Truthful and the Witnesses in the sight of their Lord, they will have their reward and their light. But *as for* those who disbelieve and reject Our Signs, these are the inmates of Hell.

وَالَّذِينَ آمَنُوا بِاللَّهِ وَرُسُلِهِ أُولَٰئِكَ هُمُ الصِّدِّيقُونَ
وَالشُّهَدَاءُ عِندَ رَبِّهِمْ لَهُمْ أَجْرُهُمْ وَنُورُهُمْ
وَالَّذِينَ كَفَرُوا وَكَذَّبُوا بِآيَاتِنَا أُولَٰئِكَ أَصْحَابُ
الْجَحِيمِ ﴿٢٠﴾ ٢ ع ١٨

R. 3.

21. Know that the life of this world is only a sport and a pastime, and an adornment, and *a source of* boasting among yourselves, and *of* rivalry in multiplying riches and children. *This life is* like the rain the vegetation produced whereby rejoices the tillers. Then it dries up and thou seest it turn yellow; then it becomes broken pieces

اعْلَمُوا أَنَّمَا الْحَيَاةُ الدُّنْيَا لَعِبٌ وَلَهْوٌ وَزِينَةٌ
وَتَفَاخُرٌ بَيْنَكُمْ وَتَكَاثُرٌ فِي الْأَمْوَالِ وَالْأَوْلَادِ
كَمَثَلِ غَيْثٍ أَعْجَبَ الْكُفَّارَ نَبَاتُهُ ثُمَّ يَهِيجُ
فَتَرَاهُ مُصْفَرًّا ثُمَّ يَكُونُ حُطَامًا وَفِي الْآخِرَةِ

of straw. And in the Hereafter there is severe punishment, and *also* forgiveness from Allah, and *His* pleasure. And the life of this world is nothing but *temporary* enjoyment of deceitful things.

عَذَابٌ شَدِيدٌ وَمَغْفِرَةٌ مِّنَ اللّٰهِ وَرِضْوَانٌ
وَمَا الْحَيٰوةُ الدُّنْيَآ اِلَّا مَتَاعُ الْغُرُوْرِ ﴿٢١﴾

* 22. Vie with one another in seeking forgiveness from your Lord and for a Garden the value whereof is equal to the value of the heaven and the earth; it has been prepared for those who believe in Allah and His Messenger. That is Allah's grace; He bestows it upon whomsoever He pleases, and Allah is the Lord of immense grace.

سَابِقُوْٓا اِلٰى مَغْفِرَةٍ مِّنْ رَّبِّكُمْ وَجَنَّةٍ عَرْضُهَا
كَعَرْضِ السَّمَآءِ وَالْاَرْضِ اُعِدَّتْ لِلَّذِيْنَ اٰمَنُوْا
بِاللّٰهِ وَرُسُلِهٖ ذٰلِكَ فَضْلُ اللّٰهِ يُؤْتِيْهِ مَنْ يَّشَآءُ
وَاللّٰهُ ذُو الْفَضْلِ الْعَظِيْمِ ﴿٢٢﴾

23. There befalls not any calamity either in the earth or in your *own* persons, but it is *recorded* in a Book before We bring it into being—surely, that is easy for Allah—

مَآ اَصَابَ مِنْ مُّصِيْبَةٍ فِى الْاَرْضِ وَلَا فِيْٓ اَنْفُسِكُمْ
اِلَّا فِيْ كِتٰبٍ مِّنْ قَبْلِ اَنْ نَّبْرَاَهَا اِنَّ ذٰلِكَ عَلَى
اللّٰهِ يَسِيْرٌ ﴿٢٣﴾

24. That you may not grieve over what is lost to you nor exult because of that which He has given to you. And Allah loves not any self-conceited boaster,

لِّكَيْلَا تَاْسَوْا عَلٰى مَا فَاتَكُمْ وَلَا تَفْرَحُوْا بِمَآ اٰتٰىكُمْ
وَاللّٰهُ لَا يُحِبُّ كُلَّ مُخْتَالٍ فَخُوْرِ ﴿٢٤﴾

25. Such as are niggardly and *also* enjoin upon men to be niggardly. And whoso turns his back, then surely Allah is Self-Sufficient, Worthy of all praise.

الَّذِيْنَ يَبْخَلُوْنَ وَيَاْمُرُوْنَ النَّاسَ بِالْبُخْلِ وَمَنْ
يَّتَوَلَّ فَاِنَّ اللّٰهَ هُوَ الْغَنِيُّ الْحَمِيْدُ ﴿٢٥﴾

* 26. Verily, We sent Our Messengers with manifest Signs and sent down with them the Book and the Balance that people may act with justice; and We sent down iron, wherein is *material for* violent warfare and *many* benefits for mankind, and that Allah may distinguish those who help Him and His Messengers without having seen *Him*. Surely, Allah is Powerful, Mighty.

لَقَدْ اَرْسَلْنَا رُسُلَنَا بِالْبَيِّنٰتِ وَاَنْزَلْنَا مَعَهُمُ
الْكِتٰبَ وَالْمِيْزَانَ لِيَقُوْمَ النَّاسُ بِالْقِسْطِ وَاَنْزَلْنَا
الْحَدِيْدَ فِيْهِ بَاْسٌ شَدِيْدٌ وَّمَنَافِعُ لِلنَّاسِ
وَلِيَعْلَمَ اللّٰهُ مَنْ يَّنْصُرُهٗ وَرُسُلَهٗ بِالْغَيْبِ اِنَّ
اللّٰهَ قَوِيٌّ عَزِيْزٌ ﴿٢٦﴾ ٣ ع ١٩

R. 4.

27. And We did send Noah and Abraham, and We placed among their seed prophethood and the Book. So some of them followed the guidance, but many of them were rebellious.

وَلَقَدْ اَرْسَلْنَا نُوْحًا وَّاِبْرٰهِيْمَ وَجَعَلْنَا فِيْ
ذُرِّيَّتِهِمَا النُّبُوَّةَ وَالْكِتٰبَ فَمِنْهُمْ مُّهْتَدٍ وَ
كَثِيْرٌ مِّنْهُمْ فٰسِقُوْنَ ﴿٢٧﴾

* 28. Then We caused Our Messengers to follow in their footsteps; and We caused

ثُمَّ قَفَّيْنَا عَلٰٓى اٰثَارِهِمْ بِرُسُلِنَا وَقَفَّيْنَا بِعِيْسَى

Jesus, son of Mary, to follow *them*, and We gave him the Gospel. And We placed in the hearts of those who accepted him compassion and mercy. But monasticism which they invented for themselves—We did not prescribe it for them—for the seeking of Allah's pleasure; but they did not observe it with due observance. Yet We gave those of them who believed their *due* reward, but many of them are rebellious.

ابْنِ مَرْيَمَ وَاٰتَيْنٰهُ الْاِنْجِيْلَ ۙ وَجَعَلْنَا فِيْ
قُلُوْبِ الَّذِيْنَ اتَّبَعُوْهُ رَاْفَةً وَّرَحْمَةً ۭ وَرَهْبَانِيَّةَ
ابْتَدَعُوْهَا مَا كَتَبْنٰهَا عَلَيْهِمْ اِلَّا ابْتِغَاۗءَ
رِضْوَانِ اللّٰهِ فَمَا رَعَوْهَا حَقَّ رِعَايَتِهَا ۚ فَاٰتَيْنَا
الَّذِيْنَ اٰمَنُوْا مِنْهُمْ اَجْرَهُمْ ۚ وَكَثِيْرٌ مِّنْهُمْ
فٰسِقُوْنَ ﴿٢٨﴾

29. O ye who believe! fear Allah and believe in His Messenger; He will give you a double share of His mercy, and will provide for you a light wherein you will walk, and will grant you forgiveness —and verily Allah is Most Forgiving, Merciful—

يٰٓاَيُّهَا الَّذِيْنَ اٰمَنُوا اتَّقُوا اللّٰهَ وَاٰمِنُوْا بِرَسُوْلِهٖ
يُؤْتِكُمْ كِفْلَيْنِ مِنْ رَّحْمَتِهٖ وَيَجْعَلْ لَّكُمْ
نُوْرًا تَمْشُوْنَ بِهٖ وَيَغْفِرْ لَكُمْ ۭ وَاللّٰهُ غَفُوْرٌ
رَّحِيْمٌ ﴿٢٩﴾

30. That the People of the Book may not think that they (the Muslims) have no power to attain aught of the grace of Allah; whereas grace is *entirely* in the hands of Allah. He gives it to whomsoever He pleases. And Allah is the Master of immense grace.

لِّئَلَّا يَعْلَمَ اَهْلُ الْكِتٰبِ اَلَّا يَقْدِرُوْنَ عَلٰي شَيْءٍ
مِّنْ فَضْلِ اللّٰهِ وَاَنَّ الْفَضْلَ بِيَدِ اللّٰهِ يُؤْتِيْهِ
مَنْ يَّشَاۗءُ ۭ وَاللّٰهُ ذُو الْفَضْلِ الْعَظِيْمِ ﴿٣٠﴾ ع

سُوْرَةُ الْمُجَادَلَةِ مَدَنِيَّةٌ

آياتها ٢٢ (٥٨) ركوعاتها ٣

Chapter 58 AL-MUJĀDILAH Part 28

(Revealed after Hijra)

الجزء ٢٨

1. In the name of Allah, the Gracious, the Merciful.

بِسْمِ اللّٰهِ الرَّحْمٰنِ الرَّحِيْمِ ﴿١﴾

2. Allah has indeed heard the speech of her who pleads with thee concerning her husband, and complains unto Allah. And Allah has heard your dialogue. Verily, Allah is All-Hearing, All-Seeing.

قَدْ سَمِعَ اللّٰهُ قَوْلَ الَّتِيْ تُجَادِلُكَ فِيْ زَوْجِهَا وَ
تَشْتَكِيْٓ اِلَى اللّٰهِ ڰ وَاللّٰهُ يَسْمَعُ تَحَاوُرَكُمَا ۭ اِنَّ اللّٰهَ
سَمِيْعٌۢ بَصِيْرٌ ﴿٢﴾

3. Those among you who put away their wives by calling them mothers—they

اَلَّذِيْنَ يُظٰهِرُوْنَ مِنْكُمْ مِّنْ نِّسَاۗىِٕهِمْ مَّا هُنَّ

do not become their mothers; their mothers are only those who gave them birth; and they certainly utter words that are manifestly evil and untrue; but surely Allah is the Effacer of sins, Most Forgiving.

4. *As to* those who call their wives mothers, and then would go back on what they have said, *the penalty for it* is the freeing of a slave before they touch each other. This is what you are admonished with. And Allah is Well-Aware of what you do.

5. But whoso does not find *one*, he must fast for two successive months, before they touch each other. And whoso is not able to do so, should feed sixty poor people. This *is so*, that you may *truly* believe in Allah and His Messenger. And these are the limits *prescribed* by Allah; and for the disbelievers is a painful punishment.

6. Those who oppose Allah and His Messenger will surely be abased even as those before them were abased; and We have already sent down clear Signs. And the disbelievers will have an humiliating punishment.

7. *On* the day when Allah will raise them all together, He will inform them of what they did. Allah has kept account of it, while they forgot it. And Allah is Witness over all things.

R. 2.

8. Dost thou not see that Allah knows all that is in the heavens and all that is in the earth? There is no secret counsel of three, but He is their fourth, nor of five, but He is their sixth, nor of less than that, nor of more, but He is with them wheresoever they may be. Then on the Day of Resurrection He will inform them of what they did. Surely, Allah knows all things full well.

9. Hast thou not seen those who were forbidden *to hold* secret counsels and again

أُمَّهٰتِهِمْ ۖ إِنْ أُمَّهٰتُهُمْ إِلَّا الّٰٓئِىْ وَلَدْنَهُمْ ۖ وَ
إِنَّهُمْ لَيَقُوْلُوْنَ مُنْكَرًا مِّنَ الْقَوْلِ وَ زُوْرًا ۖ
وَإِنَّ اللّٰهَ لَعَفُوٌّ غَفُوْرٌ ﴿٣﴾
وَ الَّذِيْنَ يُظٰهِرُوْنَ مِنْ نِّسَآئِهِمْ ثُمَّ يَعُوْدُوْنَ
لِمَا قَالُوْا فَتَحْرِيْرُ رَقَبَةٍ مِّنْ قَبْلِ أَنْ يَّتَمَآسَّا ۖ
ذٰلِكُمْ تُوْعَظُوْنَ بِهٖ ۖ وَاللّٰهُ بِمَا تَعْمَلُوْنَ خَبِيْرٌ ﴿٤﴾
فَمَنْ لَّمْ يَجِدْ فَصِيَامُ شَهْرَيْنِ مُتَتَابِعَيْنِ مِنْ
قَبْلِ أَنْ يَّتَمَآسَّا ۚ فَمَنْ لَّمْ يَسْتَطِعْ فَإِطْعَامُ
سِتِّيْنَ مِسْكِيْنًا ۖ ذٰلِكَ لِتُؤْمِنُوْا بِاللّٰهِ وَرَسُوْلِهٖ ۖ
وَ تِلْكَ حُدُوْدُ اللّٰهِ ۖ وَلِلْكٰفِرِيْنَ عَذَابٌ أَلِيْمٌ ﴿٥﴾
إِنَّ الَّذِيْنَ يُحَآدُّوْنَ اللّٰهَ وَ رَسُوْلَهٗ كُبِتُوْا كَمَا كُبِتَ
الَّذِيْنَ مِنْ قَبْلِهِمْ وَقَدْ أَنْزَلْنَآ اٰيٰتٍ بَيِّنٰتٍ ۖ
وَ لِلْكٰفِرِيْنَ عَذَابٌ مُّهِيْنٌ ﴿٦﴾
يَوْمَ يَبْعَثُهُمُ اللّٰهُ جَمِيْعًا فَيُنَبِّئُهُمْ بِمَا عَمِلُوْا ۖ
أَحْصٰهُ اللّٰهُ وَ نَسُوْهُ ۖ وَاللّٰهُ عَلٰى كُلِّ شَيْءٍ شَهِيْدٌ ﴿٧﴾ ع
أَلَمْ تَرَ أَنَّ اللّٰهَ يَعْلَمُ مَا فِي السَّمٰوٰتِ وَمَا فِي الْأَرْضِ ۖ
مَا يَكُوْنُ مِنْ نَّجْوٰى ثَلٰثَةٍ إِلَّا هُوَ رَابِعُهُمْ وَلَا
خَمْسَةٍ إِلَّا هُوَ سَادِسُهُمْ وَلَآ أَدْنٰى مِنْ ذٰلِكَ
وَلَآ أَكْثَرَ إِلَّا هُوَ مَعَهُمْ أَيْنَ مَا كَانُوْا ۚ ثُمَّ
يُنَبِّئُهُمْ بِمَا عَمِلُوْا يَوْمَ الْقِيٰمَةِ ۖ إِنَّ اللّٰهَ بِكُلِّ
شَيْءٍ عَلِيْمٌ ﴿٨﴾
أَلَمْ تَرَ إِلَى الَّذِيْنَ نُهُوْا عَنِ النَّجْوٰى ثُمَّ يَعُوْدُوْنَ

return to what they were forbidden, and confer secretly for sin and transgression and disobedience to the Messenger? And when they come to thee, they greet thee with *a greeting with* which Allah has not greeted thee; but among themselves they say, 'Why does not Allah punish us for what we say?' Sufficient for them is Hell, wherein they will burn; and a most evil destination it is!

لِمَا نُهُوْا عَنْهُ وَيَتَنٰجَوْنَ بِالْاِثْمِ وَالْعُدْوَانِ
وَمَعْصِيَتِ الرَّسُوْلِ وَاِذَا جَآءُوْكَ حَيَّوْكَ بِمَا
لَمْ يُحَيِّكَ بِهِ اللّٰهُ ۙ وَيَقُوْلُوْنَ فِيْٓ اَنْفُسِهِمْ لَوْلَا
يُعَذِّبُنَا اللّٰهُ بِمَا نَقُوْلُ ۭ حَسْبُهُمْ جَهَنَّمُ ۚ يَصْلَوْنَهَا
فَبِئْسَ الْمَصِيْرُ ﴿٩﴾

10. O ye who believe! when you confer together in secret, confer not for *the commission of* sin and transgression and disobedience to the Messenger, but confer for *the attainment of* virtue and righteousness, and fear Allah unto Whom you shall *all* be gathered.

يٰٓاَيُّهَا الَّذِيْنَ اٰمَنُوْٓا اِذَا تَنَاجَيْتُمْ فَلَا تَتَنَاجَوْا
بِالْاِثْمِ وَالْعُدْوَانِ وَمَعْصِيَتِ الرَّسُوْلِ وَتَنَاجَوْا
بِالْبِرِّ وَالتَّقْوٰى ۭ وَاتَّقُوا اللّٰهَ الَّذِيْٓ اِلَيْهِ تُحْشَرُوْنَ ﴿١٠﴾

11. *Holding of* secret counsels *for evil purposes* is only of Satan, that he may cause grief to those who believe; but it cannot harm them in the least, except by Allah's leave. And in Allah should the believers put their trust.

اِنَّمَا النَّجْوٰى مِنَ الشَّيْطٰنِ لِيَحْزُنَ الَّذِيْنَ اٰمَنُوْا
وَلَيْسَ بِضَآرِّهِمْ شَيْـًٔا اِلَّا بِاِذْنِ اللّٰهِ ۭ وَعَلَى اللّٰهِ
فَلْيَتَوَكَّلِ الْمُؤْمِنُوْنَ ﴿١١﴾

12. O ye who believe! when it is said to you, 'Make room!' in *your* assemblies, then do make room; Allah will make ample room for you. And when it is said, 'Rise up!' then rise up; Allah will raise those who believe from among you, and those to whom knowledge is given, to degrees *of rank*. And Allah is Well-Aware of what you do.

يٰٓاَيُّهَا الَّذِيْنَ اٰمَنُوْٓا اِذَا قِيْلَ لَكُمْ تَفَسَّحُوْا فِي
الْمَجٰلِسِ فَافْسَحُوْا يَفْسَحِ اللّٰهُ لَكُمْ ۚ وَاِذَا قِيْلَ
انْشُزُوْا فَانْشُزُوْا يَرْفَعِ اللّٰهُ الَّذِيْنَ اٰمَنُوْا مِنْكُمْ ۙ
وَالَّذِيْنَ اُوْتُوا الْعِلْمَ دَرَجٰتٍ ۭ وَاللّٰهُ بِمَا تَعْمَلُوْنَ
خَبِيْرٌ ﴿١٢﴾

* 13. O ye who believe! when you consult the Messenger in private, give alms before your consultation. That is better for you and purer. But if you find not *anything to give*, then Allah is Most Forgiving, Merciful.

يٰٓاَيُّهَا الَّذِيْنَ اٰمَنُوْٓا اِذَا نَاجَيْتُمُ الرَّسُوْلَ فَقَدِّمُوْا
بَيْنَ يَدَيْ نَجْوٰىكُمْ صَدَقَةً ۭ ذٰلِكَ خَيْرٌ لَّكُمْ
وَاَطْهَرُ ۭ فَاِنْ لَّمْ تَجِدُوْا فَاِنَّ اللّٰهَ غَفُوْرٌ رَّحِيْمٌ ﴿١٣﴾

* 14. Are you afraid of giving alms before your consultation? So, when you do not do so and Allah has been merciful to you, then observe Prayer and pay the Zakāt and obey Allah and His Messenger. And

ءَاَشْفَقْتُمْ اَنْ تُقَدِّمُوْا بَيْنَ يَدَيْ نَجْوٰىكُمْ
صَدَقٰتٍ ۭ فَاِذْ لَمْ تَفْعَلُوْا وَتَابَ اللّٰهُ عَلَيْكُمْ
فَاَقِيْمُوا الصَّلٰوةَ وَاٰتُوا الزَّكٰوةَ وَاَطِيْعُوا اللّٰهَ وَ

Allah is Well-Aware of what you do.

ع رَسُولَهٗ ۚ وَاللّٰهُ خَبِيرٌۢ بِمَا تَعْمَلُونَ ﴿١٤﴾

R. 3.

15. Hast thou not seen those who make friends with a people with whom Allah is wroth? They are neither of you nor of them, and they swear to falsehood knowingly.

أَلَمْ تَرَ إِلَى الَّذِينَ تَوَلَّوْا قَوْمًا غَضِبَ اللّٰهُ عَلَيْهِمْ ۗ
مَا هُمْ مِّنكُمْ وَلَا مِنْهُمْ ۙ وَيَحْلِفُونَ عَلَى الْكَذِبِ
وَهُمْ يَعْلَمُونَ ﴿١٥﴾

16. Allah has prepared for them a severe punishment. Evil indeed is that which they used to do.

أَعَدَّ اللّٰهُ لَهُمْ عَذَابًا شَدِيدًا ۗ إِنَّهُمْ سَآءَ مَا
كَانُوا يَعْمَلُونَ ﴿١٦﴾

17. They have made their oaths a screen *for their misdeeds*, and they turn *men* away from the path of Allah; for them, therefore, will be an humiliating punishment.

اتَّخَذُوٓا أَيْمَانَهُمْ جُنَّةً فَصَدُّوا عَن سَبِيلِ
اللّٰهِ فَلَهُمْ عَذَابٌ مُّهِينٌ ﴿١٧﴾

18. Neither their riches nor their children will avail them aught against Allah. They are the inmates of the Fire wherein they will abide.

لَن تُغْنِيَ عَنْهُمْ أَمْوَالُهُمْ وَلَآ أَوْلَادُهُم مِّنَ
اللّٰهِ شَيْـًٔا ۗ أُولٰٓئِكَ أَصْحٰبُ النَّارِ ۖ هُمْ فِيهَا خٰلِدُونَ ﴿١٨﴾

19. *On* the day when Allah will raise them all together, they will swear to Him even as they swear to you, and they will think that they have something *to stand upon*. Now surely it is they who are the liars.

يَوْمَ يَبْعَثُهُمُ اللّٰهُ جَمِيعًا فَيَحْلِفُونَ لَهٗ كَمَا
يَحْلِفُونَ لَكُمْ وَيَحْسَبُونَ أَنَّهُمْ عَلٰى شَيْءٍ ۗ أَلَآ
إِنَّهُمْ هُمُ الْكٰذِبُونَ ﴿١٩﴾

20. Satan has gained mastery over them, and has made them forget the remembrance of Allah. They are Satan's party. Now surely it is Satan's party that are the losers.

اسْتَحْوَذَ عَلَيْهِمُ الشَّيْطٰنُ فَأَنسٰىهُمْ ذِكْرَ اللّٰهِ ۗ
أُولٰٓئِكَ حِزْبُ الشَّيْطٰنِ ۗ أَلَآ إِنَّ حِزْبَ الشَّيْطٰنِ
هُمُ الْخٰسِرُونَ ﴿٢٠﴾

21. Certainly those who oppose Allah and His Messenger will be among the lowest.

إِنَّ الَّذِينَ يُحَآدُّونَ اللّٰهَ وَرَسُولَهٗٓ أُولٰٓئِكَ فِي
الْأَذَلِّينَ ﴿٢١﴾

22. Allah has decreed: 'Most surely I will prevail, I and My Messengers.' Verily, Allah is Powerful, Mighty.

كَتَبَ اللّٰهُ لَأَغْلِبَنَّ أَنَا وَرُسُلِي ۗ إِنَّ اللّٰهَ قَوِيٌّ
عَزِيزٌ ﴿٢٢﴾

23. Thou wilt not find any people who believe in Allah and the Last Day loving those who oppose Allah and His Messenger, even though they be their fathers,

لَا تَجِدُ قَوْمًا يُؤْمِنُونَ بِاللّٰهِ وَالْيَوْمِ الْآخِرِ
يُوَآدُّونَ مَنْ حَآدَّ اللّٰهَ وَرَسُولَهٗ وَلَوْ كَانُوٓا آبَآءَهُمْ

or their sons or their brethren, or their kindred. These are they in whose hearts Allah has inscribed *true* faith and whom He has strengthened with inspiration from Himself. And He will make them enter Gardens through which streams flow. Therein will thay abide. Allah is well pleased with them, and they are well pleased with Him. They are Allah's party. Hearken ye *O people!* it is Allah's party who will be successful.

أَوْ أَبْنَآءَهُمْ أَوْ إِخْوَانَهُمْ أَوْ عَشِيرَتَهُمْ ۚ أُولٰٓئِكَ
كَتَبَ فِي قُلُوبِهِمُ الْإِيمَانَ وَأَيَّدَهُمْ بِرُوحٍ
مِّنْهُ ۖ وَيُدْخِلُهُمْ جَنّٰتٍ تَجْرِي مِنْ تَحْتِهَا
الْأَنْهٰرُ خٰلِدِينَ فِيهَا ۚ رَضِيَ اللّٰهُ عَنْهُمْ وَرَضُوا
عَنْهُ ۚ أُولٰٓئِكَ حِزْبُ اللّٰهِ ۚ أَلَآ إِنَّ حِزْبَ اللّٰهِ هُمُ
الْمُفْلِحُونَ ﴿٢٣﴾ ع

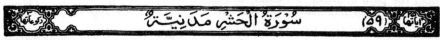

رکوعاتها ٣ سُورَةُ الْحَشْرِ مَدَنِيَّةٌ (٥٩) اٰياتها ٢٥

Chapter 59 AL-ḤASHR Part 28

(Revealed after Hijra)

1. In the name of Allah, the Gracious, the Merciful.

بِسْمِ اللّٰهِ الرَّحْمٰنِ الرَّحِيمِ ﴿١﴾

2. All that is in the heavens and all that is in the earth glorifies Allah; and He is the Mighty, the Wise.

سَبَّحَ لِلّٰهِ مَا فِي السَّمٰوٰتِ وَمَا فِي الْأَرْضِ ۚ وَهُوَ
الْعَزِيزُ الْحَكِيمُ ﴿٢﴾

3. He it is Who turned out the disbelievers among the People of the Book from their homes at *the time of* the first banishment. You did not think that they would go forth, and they thought that their fortresses would defend them against Allah. But Allah came upon them whence they did not expect, and cast terror into their hearts, so that they destroyed their houses with their own hands and the hands of the believers. So take a lesson, O ye who have eyes!

هُوَ الَّذِيٓ أَخْرَجَ الَّذِينَ كَفَرُوا مِنْ أَهْلِ الْكِتٰبِ
مِنْ دِيٰرِهِمْ لِأَوَّلِ الْحَشْرِ ۚ مَا ظَنَنْتُمْ أَنْ يَّخْرُجُوا
وَظَنُّوٓا أَنَّهُمْ مَّانِعَتُهُمْ حُصُونُهُمْ مِّنَ اللّٰهِ فَأَتٰىهُمُ
اللّٰهُ مِنْ حَيْثُ لَمْ يَحْتَسِبُوا ۖ وَقَذَفَ فِي قُلُوبِهِمُ
الرُّعْبَ يُخْرِبُونَ بُيُوتَهُمْ بِأَيْدِيهِمْ وَأَيْدِي
الْمُؤْمِنِينَ ۖ فَاعْتَبِرُوا يٰٓأُولِي الْأَبْصٰرِ ﴿٣﴾

4. And had it not been that Allah had decreed exile for them, He would have surely punished them *otherwise* in this world. And in the Hereafter they will certainly have the punishment of the Fire.

وَلَوْلَآ أَنْ كَتَبَ اللّٰهُ عَلَيْهِمُ الْجَلَآءَ لَعَذَّبَهُمْ فِي
الدُّنْيَا ۖ وَلَهُمْ فِي الْاٰخِرَةِ عَذَابُ النَّارِ ﴿٤﴾

5. That is because they opposed Allah and His Messenger; and whoso opposes

ذٰلِكَ بِأَنَّهُمْ شَآقُّوا اللّٰهَ وَرَسُولَهُ ۚ وَمَنْ يُّشَآقِّ

Allah—then surely Allah is Severe in retribution.

اللّٰهَ فَاِنَّ اللّٰهَ شَدِيْدُ الْعِقَابِ ﴿٥﴾

6. Whatever palm-trees you cut down or left standing on their roots, it was by Allah's leave, and that He might disgrace the transgressors.

مَا قَطَعْتُمْ مِّنْ لِّيْنَةٍ اَوْ تَرَكْتُمُوْهَا قَآئِمَةً عَلٰٓى
اُصُوْلِهَا فَبِاِذْنِ اللّٰهِ وَلِيُخْزِيَ الْفٰسِقِيْنَ ﴿٦﴾

* 7. And whatever Allah has given to His Messenger as spoils from them, you urged neither horse nor camel for that; but Allah grants power to His Messenger over whomsoever He pleases; and Allah has power over all things.

وَمَآ اَفَآءَ اللّٰهُ عَلٰى رَسُوْلِهٖ مِنْهُمْ فَمَآ اَوْجَفْتُمْ
عَلَيْهِ مِنْ خَيْلٍ وَّلَا رِكَابٍ وَّلٰكِنَّ اللّٰهَ يُسَلِّطُ
رُسُلَهٗ عَلٰى مَنْ يَّشَآءُ ۗ وَاللّٰهُ عَلٰى كُلِّ شَيْءٍ قَدِيْرٌ ﴿٧﴾

8. Whatever Allah has given to His Messenger as spoils from the people of the towns is for Allah and for the Messenger and for the near of kin and the orphans and the needy and the wayfarer, that it may not circulate *only* among those of you who are rich. And whatsoever the Messenger gives you, take it; and whatsoever he forbids you, abstain from *that*. And fear Allah; surely, Allah is Severe in retribution.

مَآ اَفَآءَ اللّٰهُ عَلٰى رَسُوْلِهٖ مِنْ اَهْلِ الْقُرٰى فَلِلّٰهِ
وَلِلرَّسُوْلِ وَلِذِى الْقُرْبٰى وَالْيَتٰمٰى وَالْمَسٰكِيْنِ
وَابْنِ السَّبِيْلِ كَيْ لَا يَكُوْنَ دُوْلَةًۢ بَيْنَ الْاَغْنِيَآءِ
مِنْكُمْ ۗ وَمَآ اٰتٰىكُمُ الرَّسُوْلُ فَخُذُوْهُ ۗ وَمَا نَهٰىكُمْ
عَنْهُ فَانْتَهُوْا ۚ وَاتَّقُوا اللّٰهَ ۗ اِنَّ اللّٰهَ شَدِيْدُ الْعِقَابِ ﴿٨﴾

9. *These spoils are* for the poor Refugees who have been driven out from their homes and their possessions while seeking grace from Allah and *His* pleasure, and helping Allah and His Messenger. These it is who are true *in their faith*.

لِلْفُقَرَآءِ الْمُهٰجِرِيْنَ الَّذِيْنَ اُخْرِجُوْا مِنْ دِيَارِهِمْ
وَاَمْوَالِهِمْ يَبْتَغُوْنَ فَضْلًا مِّنَ اللّٰهِ وَرِضْوَانًا
وَّيَنْصُرُوْنَ اللّٰهَ وَرَسُوْلَهٗ ۗ اُولٰٓئِكَ هُمُ الصّٰدِقُوْنَ ﴿٩﴾

* 10. And those who had established *their* home *in this city* before them and *had accepted* faith, love those who came to them for refuge, and find not in their breasts any desire for that which is given them (Refugees), but prefer *the Refugees* to themselves, even though poverty be their *own lot*. And whoso is rid of the covetousness of his own soul—it is these who will be successful.

وَالَّذِيْنَ تَبَوَّؤُ الدَّارَ وَالْاِيْمَانَ مِنْ قَبْلِهِمْ يُحِبُّوْنَ
مَنْ هَاجَرَ اِلَيْهِمْ وَلَا يَجِدُوْنَ فِيْ صُدُوْرِهِمْ
حَاجَةً مِّمَّآ اُوْتُوْا وَيُؤْثِرُوْنَ عَلٰٓى اَنْفُسِهِمْ وَلَوْ
كَانَ بِهِمْ خَصَاصَةٌ ۗ وَمَنْ يُّوْقَ شُحَّ نَفْسِهٖ
فَاُولٰٓئِكَ هُمُ الْمُفْلِحُوْنَ ﴿١٠﴾

11. And *the spoils are also for* those who came after them. They say, 'Our Lord, forgive us and our brothers who preceded us in the faith, and leave not in our hearts any rancour against those who believe.

وَالَّذِيْنَ جَآءُوْ مِنْۢ بَعْدِهِمْ يَقُوْلُوْنَ رَبَّنَا اغْفِرْ
لَنَا وَلِاِخْوَانِنَا الَّذِيْنَ سَبَقُوْنَا بِالْاِيْمَانِ وَلَا
تَجْعَلْ فِيْ قُلُوْبِنَا غِلًّا لِّلَّذِيْنَ اٰمَنُوْا رَبَّنَآ اِنَّكَ

Our Lord! Thou art indeed Compassionate, Merciful.'

رءوف رحيم ⑪

R. 2.

12. Hast thou not seen those who are hypocrites? They say to their brethren who disbelieve among the People of the Book, 'If you are turned out, we will surely go out with you, and we will never obey anyone against you: and if you are fought against, we will certainly help you.' But Allah bears witness that surely they are liars.

الم تر الى الذين نافقوا يقولون لاخوانهم الذين
كفروا من اهل الكتب لئن اخرجتم لنخرجن
معكم ولا نطيع فيكم احدا ابدا وان قوتلتم
لننصرنكم والله يشهد انهم لكذبون ⑫

13. If they are turned out, they will never go out with them; and if they are fought against they will never help them. And even if they help them, they will assuredly turn *their* backs; and then they shall not be helped.

لئن اخرجوا لا يخرجون معهم ولئن قوتلوا
لا ينصرونهم ولئن نصروهم ليولن الادبار
ثم لا ينصرون ⑬

14. Of a truth, they have greater fear of you in their hearts than of Allah. That is because they are a people who are devoid of *all* reason.

لانتم اشد رهبة في صدورهم من الله ذلك
بانهم قوم لا يفقهون ⑭

15. They will not fight you in a body except in fortified towns or from behind walls. Their fighting among themselves is severe. Thou thinkest them to be united, but their hearts are divided. That is because they are a people who have no sense.

لا يقاتلونكم جميعا الا في قرى محصنة او
من وراء جدر باسهم بينهم شديد تحسبهم
جميعا وقلوبهم شتى ذلك بانهم قوم لا يعقلون ⑮

16. *Their case is* like *the case of* those who have, a short time before them, tasted the evil consequences of their doings. And for them is a painful punishment.

كمثل الذين من قبلهم قريبا ذاقوا وبال امرهم
ولهم عذاب اليم ⑯

17. *It is* like *that of* Satan, when he says to man, 'Disbelieve;' but when he disbelieves, he says, 'I have nothing to do with thee; I fear Allah, the Lord of the worlds.'

كمثل الشيطن اذ قال للانسان اكفر فلما كفر
قال اني بريء منك اني اخاف الله رب العلمين ⑰

18. And the end of both will be that they will both be in the Fire, abiding therein. Such is the reward of the wrongdoers.

فكان عاقبتهما انهما في النار خالدين فيها و
ذلك جزؤا الظلمين ⑱

R. 3.

19. O ye who believe! fear Allah; and let *every* soul look to what it sends forth for the morrow. And fear Allah; verily Allah is Well-Aware of what you do.

يايها الذين امنوا اتقوا الله ولتنظر نفس ما قدمت
لغد واتقوا الله ان الله خبير بما تعملون ⑲

* 20. And be not like those who forgot Allah, and whom He has *consequently*

ولا تكونوا كالذين نسوا الله فانسهم انفسهم

caused to forget their own souls. It is they that are the rebellious.

أُولٰٓئِكَ هُمُ الْفٰسِقُوْنَ ﴿٢٠﴾

21. The inmates of the Fire and the inmates of the Garden are not equal. It is the inmates of the Garden that will triumph.

لَا يَسْتَوِيْٓ اَصْحٰبُ النَّارِ وَاَصْحٰبُ الْجَنَّةِ ۭ اَصْحٰبُ
الْجَنَّةِ هُمُ الْفَآئِزُوْنَ ﴿٢١﴾

22. If We had sent down this Qur'ān on a mountain, thou wouldst certainly have seen it humbled and rent asunder for fear of Allah. And these are similitudes that We set forth for mankind that they may reflect.

لَوْ اَنْزَلْنَا هٰذَا الْقُرْاٰنَ عَلٰى جَبَلٍ لَّرَاَيْتَهٗ خَاشِعًا
مُّتَصَدِّعًا مِّنْ خَشْيَةِ اللّٰهِ ۭ وَتِلْكَ الْاَمْثَالُ
نَضْرِبُهَا لِلنَّاسِ لَعَلَّهُمْ يَتَفَكَّرُوْنَ ﴿٢٢﴾

* 23. He is Allah, and there is no God beside Him, the Knower of the unseen and the seen. He is the Gracious, the Merciful.

هُوَ اللّٰهُ الَّذِيْ لَآ اِلٰهَ اِلَّا هُوَ ۚ عٰلِمُ الْغَيْبِ وَالشَّهَادَةِ ۚ
هُوَ الرَّحْمٰنُ الرَّحِيْمُ ﴿٢٣﴾

* 24. He is Allah, and there is no God beside Him, the Sovereign, the Holy One, the Source of Peace, the Bestower of Security, the Protector, the Mighty, the Subduer, the Exalted. Holy is Allah *far* above that which they associate *with Him.*

هُوَ اللّٰهُ الَّذِيْ لَآ اِلٰهَ اِلَّا هُوَ ۚ اَلْمَلِكُ الْقُدُّوْسُ
السَّلٰمُ الْمُؤْمِنُ الْمُهَيْمِنُ الْعَزِيْزُ الْجَبَّارُ الْمُتَكَبِّرُ ۭ
سُبْحٰنَ اللّٰهِ عَمَّا يُشْرِكُوْنَ ﴿٢٤﴾

25. He is Allah, the Creator, the Maker, the Fashioner. His are the most beautiful names. All that is in the heavens and the earth glorifies Him, and He is the Mighty, the Wise.

هُوَ اللّٰهُ الْخَالِقُ الْبَارِئُ الْمُصَوِّرُ لَهُ الْاَسْمَآءُ الْحُسْنٰى ۭ
يُسَبِّحُ لَهٗ مَا فِي السَّمٰوٰتِ وَالْاَرْضِ ۚ وَهُوَ الْعَزِيْزُ
الْحَكِيْمُ ﴿٢٥﴾ ع

سُوْرَةُ الْمُمْتَحِنَةِ مَدَنِيَّةٌ (٦٠)

Part 28 — AL-MUMTAḤANAH — Chapter 60

(Revealed after Hijra)

1. In the name of Allah, the Gracious, the Merciful.

بِسْمِ اللّٰهِ الرَّحْمٰنِ الرَّحِيْمِ ﴿١﴾

2. O ye who believe! take not My enemy and your enemy for friends, offering them love, while they disbelieve in the truth which has come to you *and* drive out the Messenger and yourselves *from your homes*

يٰٓاَيُّهَا الَّذِيْنَ اٰمَنُوْا لَا تَتَّخِذُوْا عَدُوِّيْ وَعَدُوَّكُمْ
اَوْلِيَآءَ تُلْقُوْنَ اِلَيْهِمْ بِالْمَوَدَّةِ وَقَدْ كَفَرُوْا بِمَا
جَآءَكُمْ مِّنَ الْحَقِّ ۚ يُخْرِجُوْنَ الرَّسُوْلَ وَاِيَّاكُمْ اَنْ

merely because you believe in Allah, your Lord. If you go forth, to strive in My cause and seek My pleasure, *take them not for friends*, sending them *messages of* love in secret, while I know best what you conceal and what you reveal. And whoever of you does so, has, surely, lost the right path.

تُؤْمِنُوْا بِاللّٰهِ رَبِّكُمْ ۭ اِنْ كُنْتُمْ خَرَجْتُمْ جِهَادًا فِيْ سَبِيْلِيْ وَابْتِغَآءَ مَرْضَاتِيْ ۖ تُسِرُّوْنَ اِلَيْهِمْ بِالْمَوَدَّةِ ۖ وَاَنَا اَعْلَمُ بِمَآ اَخْفَيْتُمْ وَمَآ اَعْلَنْتُمْ ۭ وَمَنْ يَّفْعَلْهُ مِنْكُمْ فَقَدْ ضَلَّ سَوَآءَ السَّبِيْلِ ﴿۲﴾

* 3. If they get the upper hand of you, they show themselves to be your *active* enemies, and will stretch forth their hands and their tongues towards you with evil *intent;* and they ardently desire that you should become disbelievers.

اِنْ يَّثْقَفُوْكُمْ يَكُوْنُوْا لَكُمْ اَعْدَآءً وَّيَبْسُطُوْٓا اِلَيْكُمْ اَيْدِيَهُمْ وَاَلْسِنَتَهُمْ بِالسُّوْٓءِ وَوَدُّوْا لَوْ تَكْفُرُوْنَ ﴿۳﴾

4. Neither your ties of kindred nor your children will avail you aught on the Day of Resurrection. He will decide between you. And Allah sees all that you do.

لَنْ تَنْفَعَكُمْ اَرْحَامُكُمْ وَلَآ اَوْلَادُكُمْ ۚ يَوْمَ الْقِيٰمَةِ ۚ يَفْصِلُ بَيْنَكُمْ ۭ وَاللّٰهُ بِمَا تَعْمَلُوْنَ بَصِيْرٌ ﴿۴﴾

5. There is a good model for you in Abraham and those with him, when they said to their people, 'We have nothing to do with you and with that which you worship beside Allah. We disbelieve all that you *believe*. There has arisen enmity and hatred between us and you for ever, until you believe in Allah alone'—with the exception of *this* saying of Abraham to his father, 'I will surely ask forgiveness for thee, though I have no power *to prevail* upon Allah in favour of thee.' *They prayed to God saying*, 'Our Lord, in Thee do we put our trust and to Thee do we turn *repentant*, and towards Thee is the *final* return.

قَدْ كَانَتْ لَكُمْ اُسْوَةٌ حَسَنَةٌ فِيْٓ اِبْرٰهِيْمَ وَالَّذِيْنَ مَعَهٗ ۚ اِذْ قَالُوْا لِقَوْمِهِمْ اِنَّا بُرَءٰٓؤُا مِنْكُمْ وَمِمَّا تَعْبُدُوْنَ مِنْ دُوْنِ اللّٰهِ ۡ كَفَرْنَا بِكُمْ وَبَدَا بَيْنَنَا وَبَيْنَكُمُ الْعَدَاوَةُ وَالْبَغْضَآءُ اَبَدًا حَتّٰى تُؤْمِنُوْا بِاللّٰهِ وَحْدَهٗٓ اِلَّا قَوْلَ اِبْرٰهِيْمَ لِاَبِيْهِ لَاَسْتَغْفِرَنَّ لَكَ وَمَآ اَمْلِكُ لَكَ مِنَ اللّٰهِ مِنْ شَيْءٍ ۭ رَبَّنَا عَلَيْكَ تَوَكَّلْنَا وَاِلَيْكَ اَنَبْنَا وَاِلَيْكَ الْمَصِيْرُ ﴿۵﴾

6. 'Our Lord, make us not a trial for those who disbelieve, and forgive us, our Lord; for Thou alone art the Mighty, the Wise.'

رَبَّنَا لَا تَجْعَلْنَا فِتْنَةً لِّلَّذِيْنَ كَفَرُوْا وَاغْفِرْ لَنَا رَبَّنَا ۚ اِنَّكَ اَنْتَ الْعَزِيْزُ الْحَكِيْمُ ﴿۶﴾

7. Surely, there is a good example in them for you—for *all* who have hope in Allah and the Last Day. And whosoever turns away—truly, Allah is Self-Sufficient, Worthy of all praise.

لَقَدْ كَانَ لَكُمْ فِيْهِمْ اُسْوَةٌ حَسَنَةٌ لِّمَنْ كَانَ يَرْجُوا اللّٰهَ وَالْيَوْمَ الْاٰخِرَ ۭ وَمَنْ يَّتَوَلَّ فَاِنَّ اللّٰهَ هُوَ الْغَنِيُّ الْحَمِيْدُ ﴿۷﴾ ع

R. 2.

8. It may be that Allah will bring about love between you and those of them with

عَسَى اللّٰهُ اَنْ يَّجْعَلَ بَيْنَكُمْ وَبَيْنَ الَّذِيْنَ عَادَيْتُمْ

whom you are *now* at enmity; and Allah is All-Powerful; and Allah is Most Forgiving, Merciful.

9. Allah forbids you not, respecting those who have not fought against you on account of *your* religion, and who have not driven you forth from your homes, that you be kind to them and act equitably towards them; surely Allah loves those who are equitable.

10. Allah only forbids you, respecting those who have fought against you on account of *your* religion, and have driven you out of your homes, and have helped *others* in driving you out, that you make friends of them, and whosoever makes friends of them—it is these that are the transgressors.

11. O ye who believe! when believing women come to you as Refugees, examine them. Allah knows best their faith. Then, if you find them *true* believers, send them not back to the disbelievers. These *women* are not lawful for them, nor are they lawful for these *women*. But give *their disbelieving husbands* what they have spent *on them*. And it is no sin for you to marry them, when you have given them their dowries. And hold not to *your* matrimonial ties with the disbelieving women; but demand *the return of* that which you have spent; and let *the disbelievers* demand that which they have spent. That is the judgment of Allah. He judges between you. And Allah is All-Knowing, Wise.

12. And if any of your wives goes away from you to the disbelievers, then when you retaliate *and get some spoils from the disbelievers*, give to those believers whose wives have gone away the like of that which they had spent *on their wives*. And fear Allah in Whom you believe.

13. O Prophet! when believing women come to thee, taking the oath of allegiance *at thy hands* that they will not associate anything with Allah, and that they will not steal, and will not commit adultery, nor kill their children, nor bring forth a scandalous charge which they themselves have deliberately forged, nor disobey thee

مِّنْهُم مَّوَدَّةً ۚ وَاللَّهُ قَدِيرٌ ۚ وَاللَّهُ غَفُورٌ رَّحِيمٌ ﴿٨﴾
لَا يَنْهَاكُمُ اللَّهُ عَنِ الَّذِينَ لَمْ يُقَاتِلُوكُمْ فِي
الدِّينِ وَلَمْ يُخْرِجُوكُم مِّن دِيَارِكُمْ أَن تَبَرُّوهُمْ
وَتُقْسِطُوا إِلَيْهِمْ ۚ إِنَّ اللَّهَ يُحِبُّ الْمُقْسِطِينَ ﴿٩﴾
إِنَّمَا يَنْهَاكُمُ اللَّهُ عَنِ الَّذِينَ قَاتَلُوكُمْ فِي الدِّينِ
وَأَخْرَجُوكُم مِّن دِيَارِكُمْ وَظَاهَرُوا عَلَىٰ إِخْرَاجِكُمْ
أَن تَوَلَّوْهُمْ ۚ وَمَن يَتَوَلَّهُمْ فَأُولَٰئِكَ هُمُ الظَّالِمُونَ ﴿١٠﴾
يَا أَيُّهَا الَّذِينَ آمَنُوا إِذَا جَاءَكُمُ الْمُؤْمِنَاتُ مُهَاجِرَاتٍ
فَامْتَحِنُوهُنَّ ۖ اللَّهُ أَعْلَمُ بِإِيمَانِهِنَّ ۖ فَإِنْ عَلِمْتُمُوهُنَّ
مُؤْمِنَاتٍ فَلَا تَرْجِعُوهُنَّ إِلَى الْكُفَّارِ ۖ لَا هُنَّ حِلٌّ
لَّهُمْ وَلَا هُمْ يَحِلُّونَ لَهُنَّ ۖ وَآتُوهُم مَّا أَنفَقُوا
وَلَا جُنَاحَ عَلَيْكُمْ أَن تَنكِحُوهُنَّ إِذَا آتَيْتُمُوهُنَّ
أُجُورَهُنَّ ۚ وَلَا تُمْسِكُوا بِعِصَمِ الْكَوَافِرِ وَاسْأَلُوا
مَا أَنفَقْتُمْ وَلْيَسْأَلُوا مَا أَنفَقُوا ۚ ذَٰلِكُمْ حُكْمُ اللَّهِ ۖ
يَحْكُمُ بَيْنَكُمْ ۚ وَاللَّهُ عَلِيمٌ حَكِيمٌ ﴿١١﴾
وَإِن فَاتَكُمْ شَيْءٌ مِّنْ أَزْوَاجِكُمْ إِلَى الْكُفَّارِ
فَعَاقَبْتُمْ فَآتُوا الَّذِينَ ذَهَبَتْ أَزْوَاجُهُم مِّثْلَ
مَا أَنفَقُوا ۚ وَاتَّقُوا اللَّهَ الَّذِي أَنتُم بِهِ مُؤْمِنُونَ ﴿١٢﴾
يَا أَيُّهَا النَّبِيُّ إِذَا جَاءَكَ الْمُؤْمِنَاتُ يُبَايِعْنَكَ عَلَىٰ
أَن لَّا يُشْرِكْنَ بِاللَّهِ شَيْئًا وَلَا يَسْرِقْنَ وَلَا يَزْنِينَ
وَلَا يَقْتُلْنَ أَوْلَادَهُنَّ وَلَا يَأْتِينَ بِبُهْتَانٍ يَفْتَرِينَهُ
بَيْنَ أَيْدِيهِنَّ وَأَرْجُلِهِنَّ وَلَا يَعْصِينَكَ فِي مَعْرُوفٍ

in what is right, then accept their allegiance and ask Allah to forgive them. Verily, Allah is Most Forgiving, Merciful.

فَبَايِعْهُنَّ وَاسْتَغْفِرْ لَهُنَّ اللّٰهَ ۭ إِنَّ اللّٰهَ غَفُوْرٌ
رَّحِيْمٌ ﴿١٣﴾

14. O ye who believe! make not friends of a people with whom Allah is wroth; they have indeed despaired of the Hereafter just as have the disbelievers despaired of those who are in the graves.

يٰٓأَيُّهَا الَّذِيْنَ اٰمَنُوْا لَا تَتَوَلَّوْا قَوْمًا غَضِبَ اللّٰهُ عَلَيْهِمْ
قَدْ يَئِسُوْا مِنَ الْاٰخِرَةِ كَمَا يَئِسَ الْكُفَّارُ مِنْ أَصْحٰبِ الْقُبُوْرِ ﴿١٤﴾ ع ٢ النصف

ركوعاتها ٢ سُوْرَةُ الصَّفِّ مَدَنِيَّةٌ (٦١) اٰياتها ١٥

Chapter 61 AL-ṢAFF Part 28

(Revealed after Hijra)

1. In the name of Allah, the Gracious, the Merciful.

بِسْمِ اللّٰهِ الرَّحْمٰنِ الرَّحِيْمِ ﴿١﴾

2. Whatever is in the heavens and whatever is in the earth glorifies Allah; and He is the Mighty, the Wise.

سَبَّحَ لِلّٰهِ مَا فِي السَّمٰوٰتِ وَمَا فِي الْأَرْضِ ۚ وَهُوَ
الْعَزِيْزُ الْحَكِيْمُ ﴿٢﴾

3. O ye who believe! why do you say what you do not do?

يٰٓأَيُّهَا الَّذِيْنَ اٰمَنُوْا لِمَ تَقُوْلُوْنَ مَا لَا تَفْعَلُوْنَ ﴿٣﴾

4. Most hateful is it in the sight of Allah that you say what you do not do.

كَبُرَ مَقْتًا عِنْدَ اللّٰهِ أَنْ تَقُوْلُوْا مَا لَا تَفْعَلُوْنَ ﴿٤﴾

5. Verily, Allah loves those who fight in His cause arrayed in *solid* ranks, as though they were a *strong* structure cemented with *molten* lead.

إِنَّ اللّٰهَ يُحِبُّ الَّذِيْنَ يُقَاتِلُوْنَ فِيْ سَبِيْلِهٖ صَفًّا
كَأَنَّهُمْ بُنْيَانٌ مَّرْصُوْصٌ ﴿٥﴾

* 6. And *remember* when Moses said to his people, 'O my people, why do you vex and slander me and you know that I am Allah's Messenger unto you?' So when they deviated *from the right course*, Allah caused their hearts to deviate, for Allah guides not the rebellious people.

وَإِذْ قَالَ مُوْسٰى لِقَوْمِهٖ يٰقَوْمِ لِمَ تُؤْذُوْنَنِيْ وَقَدْ
تَعْلَمُوْنَ أَنِّيْ رَسُوْلُ اللّٰهِ إِلَيْكُمْ ۭ فَلَمَّا زَاغُوْٓا أَزَاغَ
اللّٰهُ قُلُوْبَهُمْ ۭ وَاللّٰهُ لَا يَهْدِي الْقَوْمَ الْفٰسِقِيْنَ ﴿٦﴾

7. And *remember* when Jesus, son of Mary, said, 'O children of Israel, surely I am Allah's Messenger unto you, fulfilling that which is before me of the Torah, and giving glad tidings of a Messenger who will come after me. His name will be Aḥmad.' And when he came to them

وَإِذْ قَالَ عِيْسَى ابْنُ مَرْيَمَ يٰبَنِيْٓ إِسْرَآءِيْلَ إِنِّيْ
رَسُوْلُ اللّٰهِ إِلَيْكُمْ مُّصَدِّقًا لِّمَا بَيْنَ يَدَيَّ مِنَ
التَّوْرٰىةِ وَمُبَشِّرًا ۢ بِرَسُوْلٍ يَّأْتِيْ مِنْ ۢ بَعْدِي
اسْمُهٗٓ أَحْمَدُ ۭ فَلَمَّا جَآءَهُمْ بِالْبَيِّنٰتِ قَالُوْا هٰذَا

with clear proofs, they said, 'This is clear enchantment.'

سِحْرٌ مُّبِيْنٌ ۝٧

8. But who could do greater wrong than one who forges the lie against Allah while he is called to Islam? Allah guides not the wrongdoing people.

وَمَنْ اَظْلَمُ مِمَّنِ افْتَرٰى عَلَى اللّٰهِ الْكَذِبَ وَهُوَ
يُدْعٰۤى اِلَى الْاِسْلَامِ ۭ وَاللّٰهُ لَا يَهْدِي الْقَوْمَ
الظّٰلِمِيْنَ ۝٨

9. They desire to extinguish the light of Allah with *the breath of* their mouths, but Allah will perfect His light, even if the disbelievers hate *it*.

يُرِيْدُوْنَ لِيُطْفِـُٔوْا نُوْرَ اللّٰهِ بِاَفْوَاهِهِمْ وَاللّٰهُ مُتِمُّ
نُوْرِهٖ وَلَوْ كَرِهَ الْكٰفِرُوْنَ ۝٩

10. He it is Who has sent His Messenger with the guidance and the Religion of truth, that He may cause it to prevail over all religions, even if those who associate partners *with God* hate *it*.

هُوَ الَّذِيْٓ اَرْسَلَ رَسُوْلَهٗ بِالْهُدٰى وَدِيْنِ الْحَقِّ
لِيُظْهِرَهٗ عَلَى الدِّيْنِ كُلِّهٖ وَلَوْ كَرِهَ الْمُشْرِكُوْنَ ۝١٠

R. 2.

11. O ye who believe! shall I point out to you a bargain that will save you from a painful punishment?

يٰٓاَيُّهَا الَّذِيْنَ اٰمَنُوْا هَلْ اَدُلُّكُمْ عَلٰى تِجَارَةٍ تُنْجِيْكُمْ
مِّنْ عَذَابٍ اَلِيْمٍ ۝١١

12. That you believe in Allah and His Messenger, and strive in the cause of Allah with your wealth and your persons. That is better for you, if you did but know.

تُؤْمِنُوْنَ بِاللّٰهِ وَرَسُوْلِهٖ وَتُجَاهِدُوْنَ فِيْ سَبِيْلِ اللّٰهِ
بِاَمْوَالِكُمْ وَاَنْفُسِكُمْ ۭ ذٰلِكُمْ خَيْرٌ لَّكُمْ اِنْ كُنْتُمْ
تَعْلَمُوْنَ ۝١٢

13. He will forgive you your sins, and make you enter the Gardens through which streams flow, and pure and pleasant dwellings in Gardens of Eternity. That is the supreme triumph.

يَغْفِرْ لَكُمْ ذُنُوْبَكُمْ وَيُدْخِلْكُمْ جَنّٰتٍ تَجْرِيْ
مِنْ تَحْتِهَا الْاَنْهٰرُ وَمَسٰكِنَ طَيِّبَةً فِيْ جَنّٰتِ
عَدْنٍ ۭ ذٰلِكَ الْفَوْزُ الْعَظِيْمُ ۝١٣

14. And *He will bestow* another *favour* which you love: help from Allah and a near victory. So give glad tidings to the believers.

وَاُخْرٰى تُحِبُّوْنَهَا ۭ نَصْرٌ مِّنَ اللّٰهِ وَفَتْحٌ قَرِيْبٌ ۭ
وَبَشِّرِ الْمُؤْمِنِيْنَ ۝١٤

* 15. O ye who believe! be helpers of Allah, as said Jesus, son of Mary, to *his* disciples, 'Who are my helpers in *the cause of* Allah?' The disciples said, 'We are helpers of Allah.' So a party of the children of Israel believed, while a party disbelieved.

يٰٓاَيُّهَا الَّذِيْنَ اٰمَنُوْا كُوْنُوْٓا اَنْصَارَ اللّٰهِ كَمَا قَالَ
عِيْسَى ابْنُ مَرْيَمَ لِلْحَوَارِيّٖنَ مَنْ اَنْصَارِيْٓ اِلَى
اللّٰهِ ۭ قَالَ الْحَوَارِيُّوْنَ نَحْنُ اَنْصَارُ اللّٰهِ فَاٰمَنَتْ
طَّاۗىِٕفَةٌ مِّنْ بَنِيْٓ اِسْرَاۗءِيْلَ وَكَفَرَتْ طَّاۗىِٕفَةٌ

Then We gave power to those who believed against their enemy, and they became victorious.

فَاَيَّدْنَا الَّذِيْنَ اٰمَنُوْا عَلٰى عَدُوِّهِمْ فَاَصْبَحُوْا ظٰهِرِيْنَ (١٥) ع

سُوْرَةُ الْجُمُعَةِ مَدَنِيَّةٌ — اٰيَاتُهَا ١٢ — رُكُوْعَاتُهَا ٢ — (٦٢)

Chapter 62 AL-JUMU'AH Part 28

(Revealed after Hijra)

1. In the name of Allah, the Gracious, the Merciful.

بِسْمِ اللّٰهِ الرَّحْمٰنِ الرَّحِيْمِ (١)

2. Whatever is in the heavens and whatever is in the earth glorifies Allah, the Sovereign, the Holy, the Mighty, the Wise.

يُسَبِّحُ لِلّٰهِ مَا فِي السَّمٰوٰتِ وَمَا فِي الْاَرْضِ الْمَلِكِ الْقُدُّوْسِ الْعَزِيْزِ الْحَكِيْمِ (٢)

3. He it is Who has raised among the Unlettered *people* a Messenger from among themselves who recites unto them His Signs, and purifies them, and teaches them the Book and wisdom, although they had been, before, in manifest misguidance;

هُوَ الَّذِيْ بَعَثَ فِي الْاُمِّيّٖنَ رَسُوْلًا مِّنْهُمْ يَتْلُوْا عَلَيْهِمْ اٰيٰتِهٖ وَيُزَكِّيْهِمْ وَيُعَلِّمُهُمُ الْكِتٰبَ وَالْحِكْمَةَ ۗ وَاِنْ كَانُوْا مِنْ قَبْلُ لَفِيْ ضَلٰلٍ مُّبِيْنٍ (٣)

4. And *among* others from among them who have not yet joined them. He is the Mighty, the Wise.

وَّاٰخَرِيْنَ مِنْهُمْ لَمَّا يَلْحَقُوْا بِهِمْ ۗ وَهُوَ الْعَزِيْزُ الْحَكِيْمُ (٤)

5. That is Allah's grace; He bestows it on whom He pleases; and Allah is the Master of immense grace.

ذٰلِكَ فَضْلُ اللّٰهِ يُؤْتِيْهِ مَنْ يَّشَآءُ ۗ وَاللّٰهُ ذُو الْفَضْلِ الْعَظِيْمِ (٥)

6. The likeness of those who were made to bear the *law of* Torah, but would not bear it, is as the likeness of an ass carrying *a load of* books. Evil is the likeness of the people who reject the Signs of Allah. And Allah guides not the wrongdoing people.

مَثَلُ الَّذِيْنَ حُمِّلُوا التَّوْرٰىةَ ثُمَّ لَمْ يَحْمِلُوْهَا كَمَثَلِ الْحِمَارِ يَحْمِلُ اَسْفَارًا ۗ بِئْسَ مَثَلُ الْقَوْمِ الَّذِيْنَ كَذَّبُوْا بِاٰيٰتِ اللّٰهِ ۗ وَاللّٰهُ لَا يَهْدِي الْقَوْمَ الظّٰلِمِيْنَ (٦)

7. Say, 'O ye who are Jews, if you think you are the friends of Allah to the exclu-

قُلْ يٰٓاَيُّهَا الَّذِيْنَ هَادُوْٓا اِنْ زَعَمْتُمْ اَنَّكُمْ اَوْلِيَآءُ

sion of *all* other people, then wish for Death, if *indeed* you are truthful.'

لِلّٰهِ مِنْ دُوْنِ النَّاسِ فَتَمَنَّوُا الْمَوْتَ اِنْ كُنْتُمْ
صٰدِقِيْنَ ۝٧

8. But they will never wish for it, because of that which their hands have sent on *before them*. And Allah knows full well those who do wrong.

وَلَا يَتَمَنَّوْنَهٗٓ اَبَدًاۢ بِمَا قَدَّمَتْ اَيْدِيْهِمْ ۭ وَ
اللّٰهُ عَلِيْمٌۢ بِالظّٰلِمِيْنَ ۝٨

9. Say, 'The Death from which you flee will surely meet you. Then will you be returned unto Him Who knows the unseen and the seen, and He will inform you of what you had been doing.'

قُلْ اِنَّ الْمَوْتَ الَّذِيْ تَفِرُّوْنَ مِنْهُ فَاِنَّهٗ مُلٰقِيْكُمْ
ثُمَّ تُرَدُّوْنَ اِلٰى عٰلِمِ الْغَيْبِ وَالشَّهَادَةِ فَيُنَبِّئُكُمْ
بِمَا كُنْتُمْ تَعْمَلُوْنَ ۝٩ ع

R. 2.

10. O ye who believe! when the call is made for Prayer on Friday, hasten to the remembrance of Allah, and leave off *all* business. That is better for you, if you only knew.

يٰٓاَيُّهَا الَّذِيْنَ اٰمَنُوْٓا اِذَا نُوْدِيَ لِلصَّلٰوةِ مِنْ يَّوْمِ
الْجُمُعَةِ فَاسْعَوْا اِلٰى ذِكْرِ اللّٰهِ وَذَرُوا الْبَيْعَ ۭ ذٰلِكُمْ
خَيْرٌ لَّكُمْ اِنْ كُنْتُمْ تَعْلَمُوْنَ ۝١٠

11. And when the Prayer is finished, then disperse in the land and seek of Allah's grace, and remember Allah much, that you may prosper.

فَاِذَا قُضِيَتِ الصَّلٰوةُ فَانْتَشِرُوْا فِي الْاَرْضِ
وَابْتَغُوْا مِنْ فَضْلِ اللّٰهِ وَاذْكُرُوا اللّٰهَ كَثِيْرًا
لَّعَلَّكُمْ تُفْلِحُوْنَ ۝١١

12. But when they see some merchandise or some amusement, they break up for it, and leave thee standing. Say, 'That which is with Allah is better than amusement and merchandise, and Allah is the Best Provider.'

وَاِذَا رَاَوْا تِجَارَةً اَوْ لَهْوَا ا ۨنْفَضُّوْٓا اِلَيْهَا وَتَرَكُوْكَ
قَاۗىِٕمًا ۭ قُلْ مَا عِنْدَ اللّٰهِ خَيْرٌ مِّنَ اللَّهْوِ وَمِنَ
التِّجَارَةِ ۭ وَاللّٰهُ خَيْرُ الرّٰزِقِيْنَ ۝١٢ ع

ركوعاتها سُوْرَةُ الْمُنٰفِقُوْنَ مَدَنِيَّةٌ (٦٣) اٰياتها

AL-MUNĀFIQŪN

Part 28 Chapter 63

(Revealed after Hijra)

1. In the name of Allah, the Gracious, the Merciful.

بِسْمِ اللّٰهِ الرَّحْمٰنِ الرَّحِيْمِ ۝١

2. When the hypocrites come to thee, they say, 'We bear witness that thou art

اِذَا جَاۗءَكَ الْمُنٰفِقُوْنَ قَالُوْا نَشْهَدُ اِنَّكَ لَرَسُوْلُ

indeed the Messenger of Allah.' And Allah knows that thou art indeed His Messenger, but Allah bears witness that the hypocrites are surely liars.

اللّٰهِ وَاللّٰهُ يَعْلَمُ اِنَّكَ لَرَسُوْلُهٗ وَاللّٰهُ يَشْهَدُ
اِنَّ الْمُنٰفِقِيْنَ لَكٰذِبُوْنَ ۝٢

3. They have made their oaths a shield; thus they turn *men* away from the way of Allah. Evil surely is that which they have been doing.

اِتَّخَذُوْٓا اَيْمَانَهُمْ جُنَّةً فَصَدُّوْا عَنْ سَبِيْلِ اللّٰهِ
اِنَّهُمْ سَآءَ مَا كَانُوْا يَعْمَلُوْنَ ۝٣

4. That is because they *first* believed, then disbelieved. So a seal was set upon their hearts and *consequently* they understand not.

ذٰلِكَ بِاَنَّهُمْ اٰمَنُوْا ثُمَّ كَفَرُوْا فَطُبِعَ عَلٰى قُلُوْبِهِمْ
فَهُمْ لَا يَفْقَهُوْنَ ۝٤

* 5. And when thou seest them, their figures please thee; and if they speak, thou listenest to their speech. *They are* as though they were *blocks of* wood propped up. They think that every cry is against them. They are the enemy, so beware of them. Allah's curse be upon them! How are they being turned away!

وَاِذَا رَاَيْتَهُمْ تُعْجِبُكَ اَجْسَامُهُمْ وَاِنْ يَّقُوْلُوْا
تَسْمَعْ لِقَوْلِهِمْ كَاَنَّهُمْ خُشُبٌ مُّسَنَّدَةٌ يَحْسَبُوْنَ
كُلَّ صَيْحَةٍ عَلَيْهِمْ هُمُ الْعَدُوُّ فَاحْذَرْهُمْ قٰتَلَهُمُ
اللّٰهُ اَنّٰى يُؤْفَكُوْنَ ۝٥

6. And when it is said to them, 'Come, that the Messenger of Allah may ask forgiveness for you,' they turn their heads aside, and thou seest them keeping back while they are full of pride.

وَاِذَا قِيْلَ لَهُمْ تَعَالَوْا يَسْتَغْفِرْ لَكُمْ رَسُوْلُ اللّٰهِ
لَوَّوْا رُءُوْسَهُمْ وَرَاَيْتَهُمْ يَصُدُّوْنَ وَهُمْ
مُّسْتَكْبِرُوْنَ ۝٦

7. It is equal to them whether thou ask forgiveness for them or ask not forgiveness for them, Allah will never forgive them. Surely Allah guides not the rebellious people.

سَوَآءٌ عَلَيْهِمْ اَسْتَغْفَرْتَ لَهُمْ اَمْ لَمْ تَسْتَغْفِرْ
لَهُمْ لَنْ يَّغْفِرَ اللّٰهُ لَهُمْ اِنَّ اللّٰهَ لَا يَهْدِي
الْقَوْمَ الْفٰسِقِيْنَ ۝٧

* 8. They it is who say, 'Spend not on those who are with the Messenger of Allah that they may disperse *and leave him;*' while to Allah belong the treasures of the heavens and the earth; but the hypocrites understand not.

هُمُ الَّذِيْنَ يَقُوْلُوْنَ لَا تُنْفِقُوْا عَلٰى مَنْ عِنْدَ رَسُوْلِ
اللّٰهِ حَتّٰى يَنْفَضُّوْا وَلِلّٰهِ خَزَآئِنُ السَّمٰوٰتِ وَالْاَرْضِ
وَلٰكِنَّ الْمُنٰفِقِيْنَ لَا يَفْقَهُوْنَ ۝٨

9. They say, 'If we return to Medina, the one most honourable will surely drive out therefrom the one most mean;' while *true* honour belongs to Allah and to His Messenger and the believers; but the hypocrites know not.

يَقُوْلُوْنَ لَئِنْ رَّجَعْنَآ اِلَى الْمَدِيْنَةِ لَيُخْرِجَنَّ الْاَعَزُّ
مِنْهَا الْاَذَلَّ وَلِلّٰهِ الْعِزَّةُ وَلِرَسُوْلِهٖ وَلِلْمُؤْمِنِيْنَ
وَلٰكِنَّ الْمُنٰفِقِيْنَ لَا يَعْلَمُوْنَ ۝٩

R. 2.

10. O ye who believe! let not your wealth and your children divert you from the remembrance of Allah. And whoever does so—it is they who are the losers.

يٰٓاَيُّهَا الَّذِيْنَ اٰمَنُوْا لَا تُلْهِكُمْ اَمْوَالُكُمْ وَلَآ اَوْلَادُكُمْ
عَنْ ذِكْرِ اللّٰهِ ۚ وَمَنْ يَّفْعَلْ ذٰلِكَ فَاُولٰٓئِكَ هُمُ
الْخٰسِرُوْنَ ⑩

11. And spend out of that with which We have provided you before death comes upon one of you and he says, 'My Lord! if only Thou wouldst grant me respite for a little while, then I would give alms and be among the righteous.'

وَاَنْفِقُوْا مِنْ مَّا رَزَقْنٰكُمْ مِّنْ قَبْلِ اَنْ يَّاْتِيَ اَحَدَكُمُ
الْمَوْتُ فَيَقُوْلَ رَبِّ لَوْلَآ اَخَّرْتَنِيْٓ اِلٰٓى اَجَلٍ
قَرِيْبٍ ۙ فَاَصَّدَّقَ وَاَكُنْ مِّنَ الصّٰلِحِيْنَ ⑪

12. And Allah will not grant respite to a soul when its appointed time has come; and Allah is Well-Aware of what you do.

وَلَنْ يُّؤَخِّرَ اللّٰهُ نَفْسًا اِذَا جَآءَ اَجَلُهَا ۚ وَاللّٰهُ
خَبِيْرٌۢ بِمَا تَعْمَلُوْنَ ⑫ ع ٢

سُوْرَةُ التَّغَابُنِ مَدَنِيَّةٌ

اٰيَاتُهَا ١٩ (٦٤) رُكُوْعَاتُهَا ٢

Part 28 AL-TAGHĀBUN Chapter 64

(Revealed after Hijra)

1. In the name of Allah, the Gracious, the Merciful.

بِسْمِ اللّٰهِ الرَّحْمٰنِ الرَّحِيْمِ ①

2. Whatever is in the heavens and whatever is in the earth glorifies Allah; His is the kingdom and His the praise, and He has power over all things.

يُسَبِّحُ لِلّٰهِ مَا فِي السَّمٰوٰتِ وَمَا فِي الْاَرْضِ ۚ لَهُ الْمُلْكُ
وَلَهُ الْحَمْدُ ۫ وَهُوَ عَلٰى كُلِّ شَيْءٍ قَدِيْرٌ ②

* 3. It is He Who has created you, but *some* of you are disbelievers and *some* of you are believers; and Allah sees what you do.

هُوَ الَّذِيْ خَلَقَكُمْ فَمِنْكُمْ كَافِرٌ وَّمِنْكُمْ مُّؤْمِنٌ ۚ
وَاللّٰهُ بِمَا تَعْمَلُوْنَ بَصِيْرٌ ③

* 4. He created the heavens and the earth with truth, and He shaped you and made your shapes beautiful, and to Him is the *ultimate* return.

خَلَقَ السَّمٰوٰتِ وَالْاَرْضَ بِالْحَقِّ وَصَوَّرَكُمْ فَاَحْسَنَ
صُوَرَكُمْ ۚ وَاِلَيْهِ الْمَصِيْرُ ④

5. He knows whatever is in the heavens and the earth, and He knows what you conceal and what you disclose; and Allah knows full well *all* that is in the breasts.

يَعْلَمُ مَا فِي السَّمٰوٰتِ وَالْاَرْضِ وَيَعْلَمُ مَا تُسِرُّوْنَ
وَمَا تُعْلِنُوْنَ ۭ وَاللّٰهُ عَلِيْمٌۢ بِذَاتِ الصُّدُوْرِ ⑤

6. Has not the news reached you of those who disbelieved before? So they

اَلَمْ يَاْتِكُمْ نَبَؤُا الَّذِيْنَ كَفَرُوْا مِنْ قَبْلُ ۡ فَذَاقُوْا

tasted the evil consequences of their conduct, and they had a painful punishment.

وبال امرهم ولهم عذاب اليم ۶

* 7. That was because their Messengers came to them with manifest Signs, but they said, 'Shall mortals guide us?' So they disbelieved and turned away, but Allah had never any need *of them*; and Allah is Self-Sufficient, Worthy of all praise.

ذلك بانه كانت تاتيهم رسلهم بالبينت
فقالوا ابشر يهدوننا فكفروا وتولوا و
استغنى الله والله غني حميد ۷

8. Those who disbelieve assert that they will not be raised up. Say, 'Yea, by my Lord, you shall surely be raised up; then shall you surely be informed of what you did. And that is easy for Allah.'

زعم الذين كفروا ان لن يبعثوا قل بلى وربي
لتبعثن ثم لتنبؤن بما عملتم وذلك على
الله يسير ۸

9. Believe, therefore, in Allah and His Messenger, and in the Light which We have sent down. And Allah is Well-Aware of all that you do.

فامنوا بالله ورسوله والنور الذي انزلنا والله
بما تعملون خبير ۹

10. The day when He shall gather you, on the Day of Gathering, that will be the day of mutual loss *and gain*. And whoso believes in Allah and does good deeds—He will remove from them the evil *consequences* of their deeds and He will make them enter Gardens through which streams flow, to abide therein for ever. That is the supreme triumph.

يوم يجمعكم ليوم الجمع ذلك يوم التغابن
ومن يؤمن بالله ويعمل صالحا يكفر عنه
سياته ويدخله جنت تجري من تحتها الانهر
خلدين فيها ابدا ذلك الفوز العظيم ۱۰

11. But *as to* those who disbelieve and reject Our Signs, these shall be the inmates of the Fire, wherein they shall abide; and an evil destination it is!

والذين كفروا وكذبوا بايتنا اولئك اصحب النار
خلدين فيها وبئس المصير ۱۱

R. 2.

12. There befalls not any affliction but by the leave of Allah. And whosoever believes in Allah—He guides his heart *aright*. And Allah knows all things full well.

ما اصاب من مصيبة الا باذن الله ومن
يؤمن بالله يهد قلبه والله بكل شيء
عليم ۱۲

13. And obey Allah and obey the Messenger. But if you turn away, then Our Messenger is responsible only for the clear conveying *of the Message*.

واطيعوا الله واطيعوا الرسول فان توليتم فانما
على رسولنا البلغ المبين ۱۳

14. Allah! there is no God but He; so in Allah let the believers put their trust.

الله لا اله الا هو وعلى الله فليتوكل المؤمنون ۱۴

15. O ye who believe! surely among your wives and your children are *some*

يايها الذين امنوا ان من ازواجكم واولادكم

that are really your enemies, so beware of them. And if you overlook and forgive and pardon, then surely, Allah is Most Forgiving, Merciful.

عَدُوًّا لَّكُمْ فَاحْذَرُوهُمْ ۚ وَإِن تَعْفُوا وَتَصْفَحُوا
وَتَغْفِرُوا فَإِنَّ اللَّهَ غَفُورٌ رَّحِيمٌ ﴿١٥﴾

16. Verily, your wealth and your children are a trial; but with Allah is an immense reward.

إِنَّمَا أَمْوَالُكُمْ وَأَوْلَادُكُمْ فِتْنَةٌ ۚ وَاللَّهُ عِندَهُ
أَجْرٌ عَظِيمٌ ﴿١٦﴾

* 17. So fear Allah as best you can, and listen, and obey, and spend *in His cause;* it will be good for yourselves. And whoso is rid of the covetousness of his own soul—it is such who shall be successful.

فَاتَّقُوا اللَّهَ مَا اسْتَطَعْتُمْ وَاسْمَعُوا وَأَطِيعُوا وَ
أَنفِقُوا خَيْرًا لِّأَنفُسِكُمْ ۗ وَمَن يُوقَ شُحَّ نَفْسِهِ
فَأُولَٰئِكَ هُمُ الْمُفْلِحُونَ ﴿١٧﴾

18. If you lend to Allah a good loan, He will multiply it for you, and will forgive you; and Allah is Most Appreciating, Forbearing,

إِن تُقْرِضُوا اللَّهَ قَرْضًا حَسَنًا يُضَاعِفْهُ لَكُمْ وَ
يَغْفِرْ لَكُمْ ۚ وَاللَّهُ شَكُورٌ حَلِيمٌ ﴿١٨﴾

19. The Knower of the unseen and the seen, the Mighty, the Wise.

عَالِمُ الْغَيْبِ وَالشَّهَادَةِ الْعَزِيزُ الْحَكِيمُ ﴿١٩﴾ ع

سُورَةُ الطَّلَاقِ مَدَنِيَّةٌ (٦٥)

آياتها ١٣ — ركوعاتها ٢

Part 28 — AL-ṬALĀQ — Chapter 65

(Revealed after Hijra)

1. In the name of Allah, the Gracious, the Merciful.

بِسْمِ اللَّهِ الرَّحْمَٰنِ الرَّحِيمِ ﴿١﴾

* 2. O Prophet! when you divorce women, divorce them for the *prescribed* period, and reckon the period; and fear Allah. Turn them not out of their houses, nor should they *themselves* leave unless they commit an act which is manifestly foul. And these are the limits *set* by Allah; and whoso transgresses the limits of Allah, he indeed wrongs his own soul. Thou knowest not; it may be that thereafter Allah will bring something new to pass.

يَا أَيُّهَا النَّبِيُّ إِذَا طَلَّقْتُمُ النِّسَاءَ فَطَلِّقُوهُنَّ
لِعِدَّتِهِنَّ وَأَحْصُوا الْعِدَّةَ ۖ وَاتَّقُوا اللَّهَ رَبَّكُمْ ۖ
لَا تُخْرِجُوهُنَّ مِن بُيُوتِهِنَّ وَلَا يَخْرُجْنَ إِلَّا أَن
يَأْتِينَ بِفَاحِشَةٍ مُّبَيِّنَةٍ ۚ وَتِلْكَ حُدُودُ اللَّهِ ۚ وَ
مَن يَتَعَدَّ حُدُودَ اللَّهِ فَقَدْ ظَلَمَ نَفْسَهُ ۚ لَا تَدْرِي
لَعَلَّ اللَّهَ يُحْدِثُ بَعْدَ ذَٰلِكَ أَمْرًا ﴿٢﴾

3. Then, when they are about to reach their *prescribed* term, keep them with

فَإِذَا بَلَغْنَ أَجَلَهُنَّ فَأَمْسِكُوهُنَّ بِمَعْرُوفٍ أَوْ

kindness, or put them away with kindness, and call to witness two just persons from among you; and bear *true* witness for Allah. This is by which is admonished he who believes in Allah and the Last Day. And he who fears Allah—He will make for him a way out,

4. And will provide for him from where he expects not. And he who puts his trust in Allah—He is sufficient for him. Verily, Allah will accomplish His purpose. For everything has Allah appointed a measure.

* 5. And if you are in doubt *as to* such of your women as despair of monthly courses, then *know that* the prescribed period for them is three months, and *the same is for* such as have not had their monthly courses *yet*. And *as for those* who are with child, their period shall be until they are delivered of their burden. And whoso fears Allah, He will provide facilities for him in his affair.

6. That is the command of Allah which He has revealed to you. And whoso fears Allah—He will remove the evil *consequences* of his deeds and will enlarge his reward.

* 7. Lodge them *during the prescribed period* in the houses wherein you dwell, according to *the best of* your means; and harass them not that you may create hardships for them. And if they be with child, spend on them until they are delivered of their burden. And if they give suck *to the child* for you, give them their recompense, and consult with one another in kindness; but if you meet with difficulty from each other, then another *woman shall* suckle *the child* for him (the father).

8. Let him who has abundance of means spend out of his abundance. And let him whose means of subsistence are straitened spend out of what Allah has given him. Allah burdens not any soul beyond that which He has given it. Allah will soon bring about ease after hardship.

R. 2.

9. How many a city rebelled against the command of its Lord and His

فَارِقُوْهُنَّ بِمَعْرُوْفٍ وَّاَشْهِدُوْا ذَوَيْ عَدْلٍ
مِّنْكُمْ وَاَقِيْمُوا الشَّهَادَةَ لِلّٰهِ ذٰلِكُمْ يُوْعَظُ بِهٖ مَنْ
كَانَ يُؤْمِنُ بِاللّٰهِ وَالْيَوْمِ الْاٰخِرِ وَمَنْ يَّتَّقِ اللّٰهَ
يَجْعَلْ لَّهٗ مَخْرَجًا ﴿٣﴾
وَّيَرْزُقْهُ مِنْ حَيْثُ لَا يَحْتَسِبُ وَمَنْ يَّتَوَكَّلْ عَلَى
اللّٰهِ فَهُوَ حَسْبُهٗ اِنَّ اللّٰهَ بَالِغُ اَمْرِهٖ قَدْ جَعَلَ
اللّٰهُ لِكُلِّ شَيْءٍ قَدْرًا ﴿٤﴾
وَالّٰٓـِٔيْ يَئِسْنَ مِنَ الْمَحِيْضِ مِنْ نِّسَآئِكُمْ اِنِ ارْتَبْتُمْ
فَعِدَّتُهُنَّ ثَلٰثَةُ اَشْهُرٍ وَّالّٰٓـِٔيْ لَمْ يَحِضْنَ وَاُولَاتُ
الْاَحْمَالِ اَجَلُهُنَّ اَنْ يَّضَعْنَ حَمْلَهُنَّ وَمَنْ يَّتَّقِ
اللّٰهَ يَجْعَلْ لَّهٗ مِنْ اَمْرِهٖ يُسْرًا ﴿٥﴾
ذٰلِكَ اَمْرُ اللّٰهِ اَنْزَلَهٗٓ اِلَيْكُمْ وَمَنْ يَّتَّقِ اللّٰهَ يُكَفِّرْ
عَنْهُ سَيِّاٰتِهٖ وَيُعْظِمْ لَهٗٓ اَجْرًا ﴿٦﴾
اَسْكِنُوْهُنَّ مِنْ حَيْثُ سَكَنْتُمْ مِّنْ وُّجْدِكُمْ وَ
لَا تُضَآرُّوْهُنَّ لِتُضَيِّقُوْا عَلَيْهِنَّ وَاِنْ كُنَّ اُولَاتِ
حَمْلٍ فَاَنْفِقُوْا عَلَيْهِنَّ حَتّٰى يَضَعْنَ حَمْلَهُنَّ فَاِنْ
اَرْضَعْنَ لَكُمْ فَاٰتُوْهُنَّ اُجُوْرَهُنَّ وَاْتَمِرُوْا بَيْنَكُمْ
بِمَعْرُوْفٍ وَاِنْ تَعَاسَرْتُمْ فَسَتُرْضِعُ لَهٗٓ اُخْرٰى ﴿٧﴾
لِيُنْفِقْ ذُوْ سَعَةٍ مِّنْ سَعَتِهٖ وَمَنْ قُدِرَ عَلَيْهِ
رِزْقُهٗ فَلْيُنْفِقْ مِمَّآ اٰتٰىهُ اللّٰهُ لَا يُكَلِّفُ اللّٰهُ نَفْسًا
اِلَّا مَآ اٰتٰىهَا سَيَجْعَلُ اللّٰهُ بَعْدَ عُسْرٍ يُّسْرًا ﴿٨﴾ ع
وَكَاَيِّنْ مِّنْ قَرْيَةٍ عَتَتْ عَنْ اَمْرِ رَبِّهَا وَرُسُلِهٖ

Messengers, and We called it to severe account, and punished it with dire punishment!

فَحَاسَبْنٰهَا حِسَابًا شَدِيْدًا ۙ وَّعَذَّبْنٰهَا عَذَابًا نُّكْرًا ﴿٩﴾

10. So it tasted the evil consequences of its conduct, and the end of its affair was ruin.

فَذَاقَتْ وَبَالَ اَمْرِهَا وَكَانَ عَاقِبَةُ اَمْرِهَا
خُسْرًا ﴿١٠﴾

11. Allah has prepared for them a severe punishment; so fear Allah, O ye men of understanding, who have believed. Allah has indeed sent down to you a Reminder—

اَعَدَّ اللّٰهُ لَهُمْ عَذَابًا شَدِيْدًا ۙ فَاتَّقُوا اللّٰهَ يٰۤاُولِي
الْاَلْبَابِ ۚ الَّذِيْنَ اٰمَنُوْا ۚ قَدْ اَنْزَلَ اللّٰهُ اِلَيْكُمْ
ذِكْرًا ﴿١١﴾

12. A Messenger, who recites unto you the clear Signs of Allah, that he may bring those who believe and do good deeds out of every *kind of* darkness into light. And whoso believes in Allah and does good deeds—He will make him enter Gardens, through which rivers flow, to abide therein for ever. Allah has indeed made excellent provision for him.

رَّسُوْلًا يَّتْلُوْا عَلَيْكُمْ اٰيٰتِ اللّٰهِ مُبَيِّنٰتٍ لِّيُخْرِجَ
الَّذِيْنَ اٰمَنُوْا وَعَمِلُوا الصّٰلِحٰتِ مِنَ الظُّلُمٰتِ اِلَى
النُّوْرِ ۗ وَمَنْ يُّؤْمِنْ بِاللّٰهِ وَيَعْمَلْ صَالِحًا يُّدْخِلْهُ
جَنّٰتٍ تَجْرِيْ مِنْ تَحْتِهَا الْاَنْهٰرُ خٰلِدِيْنَ فِيْهَاۤ اَبَدًا ۗ
قَدْ اَحْسَنَ اللّٰهُ لَهٗ رِزْقًا ﴿١٢﴾

13. Allah is He Who created seven heavens, and of the earth the like thereof. The *divine* command comes down in their midst, that you may know that Allah has power over all things, and that Allah encompasses all things in *His* knowledge.

اَللّٰهُ الَّذِيْ خَلَقَ سَبْعَ سَمٰوٰتٍ وَّمِنَ الْاَرْضِ مِثْلَهُنَّ ۗ
يَتَنَزَّلُ الْاَمْرُ بَيْنَهُنَّ لِتَعْلَمُوْۤا اَنَّ اللّٰهَ عَلٰى كُلِّ
شَيْءٍ قَدِيْرٌ ۙ وَّاَنَّ اللّٰهَ قَدْ اَحَاطَ بِكُلِّ شَيْءٍ عِلْمًا ﴿١٣﴾ ع

سُوْرَةُ التَّحْرِيْمِ مَدَنِيَّةٌ (٦٦)

اٰيَاتُهَا ١٣ — رُكُوْعَاتُهَا ٢

Part 28 AL-TAḤRĪM Chapter 66

(Revealed after Hijra)

1. In the name of Allah, the Gracious, the Merciful.

بِسْمِ اللّٰهِ الرَّحْمٰنِ الرَّحِيْمِ ﴿١﴾

2. O Prophet! why dost thou forbid *thyself* that which Allah has made lawful to thee, seeking the pleasure of thy wives? And Allah is Most Forgiving, Merciful.

يٰۤاَيُّهَا النَّبِيُّ لِمَ تُحَرِّمُ مَاۤ اَحَلَّ اللّٰهُ لَكَ ۚ تَبْتَغِيْ
مَرْضَاتَ اَزْوَاجِكَ ۗ وَاللّٰهُ غَفُوْرٌ رَّحِيْمٌ ﴿٢﴾

* 3. Allah has indeed allowed to you the dissolution of your oaths, and Allah is

قَدْ فَرَضَ اللّٰهُ لَكُمْ تَحِلَّةَ اَيْمَانِكُمْ ۚ وَاللّٰهُ مَوْلٰىكُمْ

وَهُوَ الْعَلِيمُ الْحَكِيمُ ﴿٣﴾

your Friend; and He is All-Knowing, Wise.

وَإِذْ أَسَرَّ النَّبِيُّ إِلَىٰ بَعْضِ أَزْوَاجِهِ حَدِيثًا ۚ فَلَمَّا
نَبَّأَتْ بِهِ وَأَظْهَرَهُ اللَّهُ عَلَيْهِ عَرَّفَ بَعْضَهُ وَ
أَعْرَضَ عَنْ بَعْضٍ ۖ فَلَمَّا نَبَّأَهَا بِهِ قَالَتْ مَنْ
أَنْبَأَكَ هَٰذَا ۖ قَالَ نَبَّأَنِيَ الْعَلِيمُ الْخَبِيرُ ﴿٤﴾

4. And when the Prophet confided a matter unto one of his wives and she then divulged it, and Allah informed him of it, he made known *to her* part thereof, and avoided *mentioning* part *of it*. And when he informed her of it, she said, 'Who has informed thee of it?' He said, 'The All-Knowing, the All-Aware *God* has informed me.'

إِنْ تَتُوبَا إِلَى اللَّهِ فَقَدْ صَغَتْ قُلُوبُكُمَا ۖ وَإِنْ
تَظَاهَرَا عَلَيْهِ فَإِنَّ اللَّهَ هُوَ مَوْلَاهُ وَجِبْرِيلُ وَ
صَالِحُ الْمُؤْمِنِينَ ۖ وَالْمَلَائِكَةُ بَعْدَ ذَٰلِكَ ظَهِيرٌ ﴿٥﴾

5. *Now* if you two turn unto Allah repentant, *it will be better for you*, and your hearts are *already so* inclined. But if you back up each other against him, surely Allah is his Helper and Gabriel and the righteous among the believers; and furthermore, *all other* angels *too* are *his* helpers.

عَسَىٰ رَبُّهُ إِنْ طَلَّقَكُنَّ أَنْ يُبْدِلَهُ أَزْوَاجًا خَيْرًا
مِنْكُنَّ مُسْلِمَاتٍ مُؤْمِنَاتٍ قَانِتَاتٍ تَائِبَاتٍ عَابِدَاتٍ
سَائِحَاتٍ ثَيِّبَاتٍ وَأَبْكَارًا ﴿٦﴾

6. It may be that, if he divorce you, his Lord will give him instead wives better than you—resigned, believing, obedient, always turning to God, devout in worship, given to fasting, *both* widows and virgins.

يَا أَيُّهَا الَّذِينَ آمَنُوا قُوا أَنْفُسَكُمْ وَأَهْلِيكُمْ نَارًا
وَقُودُهَا النَّاسُ وَالْحِجَارَةُ عَلَيْهَا مَلَائِكَةٌ غِلَاظٌ
شِدَادٌ لَا يَعْصُونَ اللَّهَ مَا أَمَرَهُمْ وَيَفْعَلُونَ
مَا يُؤْمَرُونَ ﴿٧﴾

7. O ye who believe! save yourselves and your families from a Fire whose fuel is men and stones, over which are appointed angels, stern *and* severe, who disobey not Allah in what He commands them and do as they are commanded.

يَا أَيُّهَا الَّذِينَ كَفَرُوا لَا تَعْتَذِرُوا الْيَوْمَ ۖ إِنَّمَا
ع ١٩ تُجْزَوْنَ مَا كُنْتُمْ تَعْمَلُونَ ﴿٨﴾

8. O ye who disbelieve! make no excuses this day. You are requited for what you did.

R. 2.

يَا أَيُّهَا الَّذِينَ آمَنُوا تُوبُوا إِلَى اللَّهِ تَوْبَةً نَصُوحًا
عَسَىٰ رَبُّكُمْ أَنْ يُكَفِّرَ عَنْكُمْ سَيِّئَاتِكُمْ وَيُدْخِلَكُمْ
جَنَّاتٍ تَجْرِي مِنْ تَحْتِهَا الْأَنْهَارُ يَوْمَ لَا يُخْزِي
اللَّهُ النَّبِيَّ وَالَّذِينَ آمَنُوا مَعَهُ ۖ نُورُهُمْ يَسْعَىٰ
بَيْنَ أَيْدِيهِمْ وَبِأَيْمَانِهِمْ يَقُولُونَ رَبَّنَا أَتْمِمْ

9. O ye who believe! turn to Allah in sincere repentance. It may be that your Lord will remove the evil *consequences* of your deeds and make you enter Gardens through which rivers flow, on the day when Allah will not abase the Prophet nor those who have believed with him. Their light will run before them and on their right hands. They will say, 'Our Lord,

perfect our light for us and forgive us; surely Thou hast power over all things.'

لنا نورنا واغفر لنا ۚ إنك على كل شيء قدير ⑨

* 10. O Prophet! strive hard against the disbelievers and the hypocrites; and be strict against them. Their home is Hell, and an evil destination it is!

يا أيها النبي جاهد الكفار والمنافقين واغلظ
عليهم ۚ ومأواهم جهنم ۖ وبئس المصير ⑩

11. Allah sets forth for those who disbelieve the example of the wife of Noah and the wife of Lot. They were under two righteous servants of Ours, but they acted unfaithfully towards them. So they availed them naught against Allah, and it was said *to them*, 'Enter the Fire, ye twain, along with those who enter.'

ضرب الله مثلا للذين كفروا امرأت نوح و
امرأت لوط ۖ كانتا تحت عبدين من عبادنا
صالحين فخانتاهما فلم يغنيا عنهما من الله
شيئا وقيل ادخلا النار مع الداخلين ⑪

12. And Allah sets forth for those who believe the example of the wife of Pharaoh when she said, 'My Lord! build for me a house with Thee in the Garden; and deliver me from Pharaoh and his work, and deliver me from the wrongdoing people;'

وضرب الله مثلا للذين آمنوا امرأت فرعون (وقف لازم)
إذ قالت رب ابن لي عندك بيتا في الجنة و
نجني من فرعون وعمله ونجني من القوم
الظالمين ⑫

13. And *the example of* Mary, the daughter of 'Imrān, who guarded her private parts—so We breathed into him of Our Spirit—and she fulfilled *in her person* the words of her Lord and His Books and was one of the obedient.

ومريم ابنت عمران التي أحصنت فرجها
فنفخنا فيه من روحنا وصدقت بكلمات ربها
وكتبه وكانت من القانتين ⑬ ع

آياتها ٣١ (٦٧) سورة الملك مكية ركوعاتها ٢

(Revealed before Hijra)

الجزء ٢٩

1. In the name of Allah, the Gracious, the Merciful.

بسم الله الرحمن الرحيم ①

2. Blessed is He in Whose hand is the kingdom, and He has power over all things;

تبارك الذي بيده الملك وهو على كل شيء
قدير ②

3. Who has created death and life that He might try you—which of you is best in

الذي خلق الموت والحياة ليبلوكم أيكم

deeds; and He is the Mighty, the Most Forgiving.

أَحْسَنُ عَمَلًا ۚ وَهُوَ الْعَزِيزُ الْغَفُورُ ﴿٣﴾

4. Who has created seven heavens in harmony. No incongruity canst thou see in the creation of the Gracious *God*. Then look again: Seest thou any flaw?

الَّذِي خَلَقَ سَبْعَ سَمٰوٰتٍ طِبَاقًا ۖ مَا تَرٰى فِي
خَلْقِ الرَّحْمٰنِ مِنْ تَفٰوُتٍ ۖ فَارْجِعِ الْبَصَرَ هَلْ
تَرٰى مِنْ فُطُورٍ ﴿٤﴾

* 5. Aye, look again, and yet again, thy sight will *only* return unto thee confused and fatigued.

ثُمَّ ارْجِعِ الْبَصَرَ كَرَّتَيْنِ يَنْقَلِبْ إِلَيْكَ الْبَصَرُ
خَاسِئًا وَهُوَ حَسِيرٌ ﴿٥﴾

6. And verily, We have adorned the lowest heaven with lamps, and We have made them for driving away satans, and We have prepared for them the punishment of the blazing Fire.

وَلَقَدْ زَيَّنَّا السَّمَاءَ الدُّنْيَا بِمَصَابِيحَ وَجَعَلْنٰهَا
رُجُومًا لِلشَّيٰطِينِ وَأَعْتَدْنَا لَهُمْ عَذَابَ السَّعِيرِ ﴿٦﴾

7. And for those who disbelieve in their Lord there is the punishment of Hell, and an evil resort it is!

وَلِلَّذِينَ كَفَرُوا بِرَبِّهِمْ عَذَابُ جَهَنَّمَ ۖ وَبِئْسَ
الْمَصِيرُ ﴿٧﴾

8. When they are cast therein, they will hear it roaring as it boils up.

إِذَا أُلْقُوا فِيهَا سَمِعُوا لَهَا شَهِيقًا وَهِيَ تَفُورُ ﴿٨﴾

9. It would almost burst with fury. Whenever a host *of disbelievers* is cast into it the wardens thereof will ask them, 'Did no Warner come to you?'

تَكَادُ تَمَيَّزُ مِنَ الْغَيْظِ ۖ كُلَّمَا أُلْقِيَ فِيهَا فَوْجٌ
سَأَلَهُمْ خَزَنَتُهَا أَلَمْ يَأْتِكُمْ نَذِيرٌ ﴿٩﴾

10. They will say, "Yea, verily, a Warner did come to us, but we treated *him* as a liar, and we said: 'Allah has not revealed anything; you are but in great error.' "

قَالُوا بَلٰى قَدْ جَاءَنَا نَذِيرٌ ۙ فَكَذَّبْنَا وَقُلْنَا مَا
نَزَّلَ اللّٰهُ مِنْ شَيْءٍ ۖ إِنْ أَنْتُمْ إِلَّا فِي ضَلٰلٍ
كَبِيرٍ ﴿١٠﴾

11. And they will say, 'If we had but listened or possessed sense, we should not have been among the inmates of the blazing Fire.'

وَقَالُوا لَوْ كُنَّا نَسْمَعُ أَوْ نَعْقِلُ مَا كُنَّا فِي أَصْحٰبِ
السَّعِيرِ ﴿١١﴾

* 12. Then will they confess their sins; but far away are the inmates of the blazing Fire *from God's mercy*.

فَاعْتَرَفُوا بِذَنْبِهِمْ ۚ فَسُحْقًا لِأَصْحٰبِ السَّعِيرِ ﴿١٢﴾

* 13. Verily, those who fear their Lord in secret—for them is forgiveness and a great reward.

إِنَّ الَّذِينَ يَخْشَوْنَ رَبَّهُمْ بِالْغَيْبِ لَهُمْ مَغْفِرَةٌ
وَأَجْرٌ كَبِيرٌ ﴿١٣﴾

14. And whether you conceal what you say or make it public, He knows full well

وَأَسِرُّوا قَوْلَكُمْ أَوِ اجْهَرُوا بِهِ ۖ إِنَّهُ عَلِيمٌ بِذَاتِ

what is in *your* breasts.

15. Does He Who has created *you* not know *it?* He is the Knower of all subtleties, the All-Aware.

R. 2.

16. He it is Who has made the earth even and smooth for you; so traverse through its sides, and eat of His provision. And unto Him will be the resurrection.

17. Do you feel secure from Him Who is in the heaven that He will not cause the earth to sink with you when lo! it begins to shake?

18. Do you feel secure from Him Who is in the heaven that He will not send against you a sand-storm? Then will you know how *terrible* was My warning.

19. And indeed those before them also treated *My Messengers* as liars; then how *grievous* was My punishment!

20. Have they not seen the birds above them, spreading out their wings without moving *them* and then drawing *them* in *to swoop down upon the prey?* None withholds them but the Gracious *God*. Verily He sees all things.

21. Or who is he that can be an army for you to help you against the Gracious *God?* The disbelievers are only in deception.

22. Or who is he that will provide for you, if He should withhold His provision? Nay, but they obstinately persist in rebellion and aversion.

23. What! is he who walks grovelling upon his face better guided or he who walks upright on the straight path?

24. Say, 'He it is Who brought you into being, and made for you ears and eyes and hearts; *but* little thanks do you give.'

25. Say, 'He it is Who multiplied you in the earth, and unto Him will you be gathered.'

26. And they say, 'When will this promise *come to pass*, if *indeed* you are truthful?'

27. Say, 'The knowledge *of it* is with

الصُّدُوْرِ ﴿١٤﴾

ع أَلَا يَعْلَمُ مَنْ خَلَقَ ۖ وَهُوَ اللَّطِيْفُ الْخَبِيْرُ ﴿١٥﴾

هُوَ الَّذِيْ جَعَلَ لَكُمُ الْأَرْضَ ذَلُوْلًا فَامْشُوْا فِيْ

مَنَاكِبِهَا وَكُلُوْا مِنْ رِّزْقِهٖ ۖ وَإِلَيْهِ النُّشُوْرُ ﴿١٦﴾

ءَأَمِنْتُمْ مَّنْ فِي السَّمَآءِ أَنْ يَّخْسِفَ بِكُمُ الْأَرْضَ

فَإِذَا هِيَ تَمُوْرُ ﴿١٧﴾

أَمْ أَمِنْتُمْ مَّنْ فِي السَّمَآءِ أَنْ يُّرْسِلَ عَلَيْكُمْ حَاصِبًا ۖ

فَسَتَعْلَمُوْنَ كَيْفَ نَذِيْرِ ﴿١٨﴾

وَلَقَدْ كَذَّبَ الَّذِيْنَ مِنْ قَبْلِهِمْ فَكَيْفَ كَانَ نَكِيْرِ ﴿١٩﴾

أَوَلَمْ يَرَوْا إِلَى الطَّيْرِ فَوْقَهُمْ صٰٓفّٰتٍ وَّيَقْبِضْنَ ۚ

مَا يُمْسِكُهُنَّ إِلَّا الرَّحْمٰنُ ۗ إِنَّهٗ بِكُلِّ شَيْءٍۭ بَصِيْرٌ ﴿٢٠﴾

أَمَّنْ هٰذَا الَّذِيْ هُوَ جُنْدٌ لَّكُمْ يَنْصُرُكُمْ مِّنْ

دُوْنِ الرَّحْمٰنِ ۗ إِنِ الْكٰفِرُوْنَ إِلَّا فِيْ غُرُوْرٍ ﴿٢١﴾

أَمَّنْ هٰذَا الَّذِيْ يَرْزُقُكُمْ إِنْ أَمْسَكَ رِزْقَهٗ ۚ

بَلْ لَّجُّوْا فِيْ عُتُوٍّ وَّنُفُوْرٍ ﴿٢٢﴾

أَفَمَنْ يَّمْشِيْ مُكِبًّا عَلٰى وَجْهِهٖٓ أَهْدٰٓى أَمَّنْ يَّمْشِيْ

سَوِيًّا عَلٰى صِرَاطٍ مُّسْتَقِيْمٍ ﴿٢٣﴾

قُلْ هُوَ الَّذِيْٓ أَنْشَأَكُمْ وَجَعَلَ لَكُمُ السَّمْعَ

وَالْأَبْصَارَ وَالْأَفْئِدَةَ ۗ قَلِيْلًا مَّا تَشْكُرُوْنَ ﴿٢٤﴾

قُلْ هُوَ الَّذِيْ ذَرَأَكُمْ فِي الْأَرْضِ وَإِلَيْهِ تُحْشَرُوْنَ ﴿٢٥﴾

وَيَقُوْلُوْنَ مَتٰى هٰذَا الْوَعْدُ إِنْ كُنْتُمْ صٰدِقِيْنَ ﴿٢٦﴾

قُلْ إِنَّمَا الْعِلْمُ عِنْدَ اللّٰهِ ۖ وَإِنَّمَآ أَنَا نَذِيْرٌ

Allah, and I am only a plain Warner.'

مُّبِينٌ ﴿٢٧﴾

28. But when they see it near, the faces of those who disbelieve will become grief-stricken, and it will be said, 'This is what you used to ask for.'

فَلَمَّا رَأَوْهُ زُلْفَةً سِيٓـَٔتْ وُجُوهُ الَّذِينَ كَفَرُوا
وَقِيلَ هَٰذَا الَّذِي كُنتُم بِهِ تَدَّعُونَ ﴿٢٨﴾

29. Say, 'Tell me, if Allah should destroy me and those who are with me, or have mercy on us, who will protect the disbelievers from a painful punishment?'

قُلْ أَرَءَيْتُمْ إِنْ أَهْلَكَنِيَ اللَّهُ وَمَن مَّعِيَ أَوْ
رَحِمَنَا فَمَن يُجِيرُ الْكَافِرِينَ مِنْ عَذَابٍ أَلِيمٍ ﴿٢٩﴾

30. Say, 'He is the Gracious *God;* in Him have we believed and in Him have we put our trust. And you will soon know who is in manifest error.'

قُلْ هُوَ الرَّحْمَٰنُ آمَنَّا بِهِ وَعَلَيْهِ تَوَكَّلْنَا فَسَتَعْلَمُونَ
مَنْ هُوَ فِي ضَلَالٍ مُّبِينٍ ﴿٣٠﴾

* 31. Say, 'Tell me, if *all* your water were to disappear *in the earth,* who then will bring you *clear* flowing water?'

قُلْ أَرَءَيْتُمْ إِنْ أَصْبَحَ مَاؤُكُمْ غَوْرًا فَمَن
يَأْتِيكُم بِمَاءٍ مَّعِينٍ ﴿٣١﴾
ع

سُورَةُ الْقَلَمِ مَكِّيَّةٌ (٦٨)

آياتها ٥٣ — ركوعاتها ٢

(Revealed before Hijra)

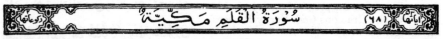

1. In the name of Allah, the Gracious, the Merciful.

بِسْمِ اللَّهِ الرَّحْمَٰنِ الرَّحِيمِ ﴿١﴾

2. By the inkstand and *by* the pen and *by* that which they write,

نٓ وَالْقَلَمِ وَمَا يَسْطُرُونَ ﴿٢﴾

3. Thou art not, by the grace of thy Lord, a madman.

مَآ أَنتَ بِنِعْمَةِ رَبِّكَ بِمَجْنُونٍ ﴿٣﴾

4. And for thee, most surely, there is an unending reward.

وَإِنَّ لَكَ لَأَجْرًا غَيْرَ مَمْنُونٍ ﴿٤﴾

5. And thou dost surely possess high moral excellences.

وَإِنَّكَ لَعَلَىٰ خُلُقٍ عَظِيمٍ ﴿٥﴾

6. And thou wilt soon see and they *too* will see

فَسَتُبْصِرُ وَيُبْصِرُونَ ﴿٦﴾

7. Which of you is afflicted *with madness.*

بِأَييِّكُمُ الْمَفْتُونُ ﴿٧﴾

8. Surely, thy Lord knows best those who go astray from His way, and He knows best those who follow guidance.

إِنَّ رَبَّكَ هُوَ أَعْلَمُ بِمَن ضَلَّ عَن سَبِيلِهِ وَهُوَ
أَعْلَمُ بِالْمُهْتَدِينَ ﴿٨﴾

9. So comply not with the wishes of those who reject *the truth*.

فلا تطع المكذبين ﴿٩﴾

10. They wish that thou shouldst be pliant so that they may *also* be pliant.

ودوا لو تدهن فيدهنون ﴿١٠﴾

11. And yield not to any mean swearer,

ولا تطع كل حلاف مهين ﴿١١﴾

12. Backbiter, one who goes about slandering,

هماز مشاء بنميم ﴿١٢﴾

13. Forbidder of good, transgressor, sinful,

مناع للخير معتد أثيم ﴿١٣﴾

14. Ill-mannered and, in addition to that, of doubtful birth.

عتل بعد ذلك زنيم ﴿١٤﴾

15. This is because he possesses riches and children.

أن كان ذا مال وبنين ﴿١٥﴾

16. When Our Signs are recited unto him, he says, 'Stories of the ancients!'

إذا تتلى عليه آياتنا قال أساطير الأولين ﴿١٦﴾

17. We will brand him on the snout.

سنسمه على الخرطوم ﴿١٧﴾

18. We will surely try them as We tried the owners of the garden when they vowed that they would certainly pluck *all* its *fruit* in the morning,

إنا بلوناهم كما بلونا أصحاب الجنة إذ أقسموا
ليصرمنها مصبحين ﴿١٨﴾

19. And they made no exception *and did not say, 'If God please.'*

ولا يستثنون ﴿١٩﴾

20. Then a visitation from thy Lord visited it while they were asleep;

فطاف عليها طائف من ربك وهم نائمون ﴿٢٠﴾

21. And the morning found it like *a garden* cut down *overnight*.

فأصبحت كالصريم ﴿٢١﴾

22. So they called to one another at *the break of* dawn,

فتنادوا مصبحين ﴿٢٢﴾

* 23. Saying, 'Go forth early in the morning to your field, if you would gather the fruit.'

أن اغدوا على حرثكم إن كنتم صارمين ﴿٢٣﴾

24. And they set out, talking to one another in low tones,

فانطلقوا وهم يتخافتون ﴿٢٤﴾

* 25. Saying, 'Let no poor man today enter it against you.'

أن لا يدخلنها اليوم عليكم مسكين ﴿٢٥﴾

* 26. And they went forth early in the morning, determined to *achieve their* purpose.

وغدوا على حرد قادرين ﴿٢٦﴾

27. But when they saw it, they said, 'Surely, we have lost *our way!*

فلما رأوها قالوا إنا لضالون ﴿٢٧﴾

28. 'Nay, we have been deprived of everything.'

بل نحن محرومون ﴿٢٨﴾

29. The best among them said, "Did I not say to you, 'Why do you not glorify *God?*' "

قال أوسطهم ألم أقل لكم لولا تسبحون ﴿٢٩﴾

30. *Now* they said, 'Glory be to our Lord. Surely, we have been wrongdoers.'

قَالُوْا سُبْحٰنَ رَبِّنَآ اِنَّا كُنَّا ظٰلِمِيْنَ ﴿۳۰﴾

31. Then some of them turned to the others, reproaching one another.

فَاَقْبَلَ بَعْضُهُمْ عَلٰى بَعْضٍ يَّتَلَاوَمُوْنَ ﴿۳۱﴾

* 32. They said, 'Woe to us! We were indeed rebellious *against God*.

قَالُوْا يٰوَيْلَنَآ اِنَّا كُنَّا طٰغِيْنَ ﴿۳۲﴾

33. 'Maybe our Lord will give us instead *a* better *garden* than this; we do humbly entreat our Lord.'

عَسٰى رَبُّنَآ اَنْ يُّبْدِلَنَا خَيْرًا مِّنْهَآ اِنَّآ اِلٰى رَبِّنَا رٰغِبُوْنَ ﴿۳۳﴾

34. Such is the punishment *of this world*. And surely the punishment of the Hereafter is greater. Did they but know!

وقف لازم كَذٰلِكَ الْعَذَابُ ۗ وَلَعَذَابُ الْاٰخِرَةِ اَكْبَرُ ۘ لَوْ كَانُوْا يَعْلَمُوْنَ ﴿۳۴﴾ ع

R. 2.

35. For the righteous, indeed, there are Gardens of Bliss with their Lord.

اِنَّ لِلْمُتَّقِيْنَ عِنْدَ رَبِّهِمْ جَنّٰتِ النَّعِيْمِ ﴿۳۵﴾

36. Shall We then treat those who submit *to Us* as *We treat* the guilty?

اَفَنَجْعَلُ الْمُسْلِمِيْنَ كَالْمُجْرِمِيْنَ ﴿۳۶﴾

37. What is the matter with you? How judge ye!

مَا لَكُمْ ۫ كَيْفَ تَحْكُمُوْنَ ﴿۳۷﴾

38. Have you a Book wherein you read,

اَمْ لَكُمْ كِتٰبٌ فِيْهِ تَدْرُسُوْنَ ﴿۳۸﴾

39. That you shall surely have in it whatever you choose?

اِنَّ لَكُمْ فِيْهِ لَمَا تَخَيَّرُوْنَ ﴿۳۹﴾

40. Or have you any covenant binding on Us till the Day of Resurrection that you shall surely have all that you order?

اَمْ لَكُمْ اَيْمَانٌ عَلَيْنَا بَالِغَةٌ اِلٰى يَوْمِ الْقِيٰمَةِ ۙ اِنَّ لَكُمْ لَمَا تَحْكُمُوْنَ ﴿۴۰﴾

41. Ask them which of them will vouch for that.

سَلْهُمْ اَيُّهُمْ بِذٰلِكَ زَعِيْمٌ ﴿۴۱﴾

42. Or have they any 'partners' *of God?* Let them, then, produce *those* 'partners' of theirs, if they speak the truth.

اَمْ لَهُمْ شُرَكَآءُ ۚ فَلْيَاْتُوْا بِشُرَكَآئِهِمْ اِنْ كَانُوْا صٰدِقِيْنَ ﴿۴۲﴾

43. On the day when the truth shall be laid bare and they will be called upon to prostrate themselves, they will not be able *to do so;*

يَوْمَ يُكْشَفُ عَنْ سَاقٍ وَّيُدْعَوْنَ اِلَى السُّجُوْدِ فَلَا يَسْتَطِيْعُوْنَ ﴿۴۳﴾

44. Their eyes will be cast down, *and* humiliation will cover them; and they were indeed called upon to prostrate themselves when they were safe and sound, *but they obeyed not*.

خَاشِعَةً اَبْصَارُهُمْ تَرْهَقُهُمْ ذِلَّةٌ ۗ وَقَدْ كَانُوْا يُدْعَوْنَ اِلَى السُّجُوْدِ وَهُمْ سٰلِمُوْنَ ﴿۴۴﴾

45. So leave Me *alone* with those who reject this word *of Ours*. We shall draw them *near to destruction* step by step from

فَذَرْنِيْ وَمَنْ يُّكَذِّبُ بِهٰذَا الْحَدِيْثِ ۗ سَنَسْتَدْرِجُهُمْ

whence they know not.

مِنْ حَيْثُ لَا يَعْلَمُونَ ﴿٤٥﴾

46. And I give them respite; for My plan is strong.

وَأُمْلِي لَهُمْ إِنَّ كَيْدِي مَتِينٌ ﴿٤٦﴾

47. Dost thou ask a reward of them that they are *as if* being weighed down with a *heavy* tax?

أَمْ تَسْأَلُهُمْ أَجْرًا فَهُمْ مِنْ مَغْرَمٍ مُثْقَلُونَ ﴿٤٧﴾

48. Is the unseen with them so that they write *it* down?

أَمْ عِنْدَهُمُ الْغَيْبُ فَهُمْ يَكْتُبُونَ ﴿٤٨﴾

49. So be thou steadfast in *carrying out* the command of thy Lord, and be not like the Man of the Fish when he called *to his Lord* and he was full of grief.

فَاصْبِرْ لِحُكْمِ رَبِّكَ وَلَا تَكُنْ كَصَاحِبِ الْحُوتِ إِذْ نَادَىٰ وَهُوَ مَكْظُومٌ ﴿٤٩﴾

50. Had not a favour from his Lord reached him, he would have surely been cast upon a bare tract of land, while he would have been blamed *by his people*.

لَوْلَا أَنْ تَدَارَكَهُ نِعْمَةٌ مِنْ رَبِّهِ لَنُبِذَ بِالْعَرَاءِ وَهُوَ مَذْمُومٌ ﴿٥٠﴾

51. But his Lord chose him and made him *one* of the righteous.

فَاجْتَبَاهُ رَبُّهُ فَجَعَلَهُ مِنَ الصَّالِحِينَ ﴿٥١﴾

52. And those who disbelieve would fain dislodge thee *from thy God-given station* with their *angry* looks when they hear the Reminder; and they say, 'He is certainly mad.'

وَإِنْ يَكَادُ الَّذِينَ كَفَرُوا لَيُزْلِقُونَكَ بِأَبْصَارِهِمْ لَمَّا سَمِعُوا الذِّكْرَ وَيَقُولُونَ إِنَّهُ لَمَجْنُونٌ ﴿٥٢﴾

* 53. Nay, it is naught but *a source of* honour for all the worlds.

وَمَا هُوَ إِلَّا ذِكْرٌ لِلْعَالَمِينَ ﴿٥٣﴾

سُورَةُ الْحَاقَّةِ مَكِّيَّةٌ

آياتها ٥٣ (٦٩) ركوعاتها ٢

Part 29 **AL-ḤĀQQAH** Chapter 69

(Revealed before Hijra)

1. In the name of Allah, the Gracious, the Merciful.

بِسْمِ اللَّهِ الرَّحْمَٰنِ الرَّحِيمِ ﴿١﴾

2. The Inevitable!

الْحَاقَّةُ ﴿٢﴾

3. What is the Inevitable?

مَا الْحَاقَّةُ ﴿٣﴾

4. And what should make thee know what the Inevitable is?

وَمَا أَدْرَاكَ مَا الْحَاقَّةُ ﴿٤﴾

* 5. *The tribe of* Thamūd and *the tribe of* 'Ād treated as a lie the *sudden* calamity.

كَذَّبَتْ ثَمُودُ وَعَادٌ بِالْقَارِعَةِ ﴿٥﴾

6. Then, as for Thamūd, they were destroyed with a violent blast.

فَأَمَّا ثَمُودُ فَأُهْلِكُوا بِالطَّاغِيَةِ ﴿٦﴾

7. And as for 'Ād, they were destroyed by a fierce roaring wind,

وَأَمَّا عَادٌ فَأُهْلِكُوا بِرِيحٍ صَرْصَرٍ عَاتِيَةٍ ۝٧

8. Which He caused to blow against them for seven nights and eight days consecutively, so that thou mightest have seen the people therein lying prostrate, as though they were trunks of palm-trees fallen down.

سَخَّرَهَا عَلَيْهِمْ سَبْعَ لَيَالٍ وَثَمٰنِيَةَ أَيَّامٍ
حُسُومًا فَتَرَى الْقَوْمَ فِيهَا صَرْعٰى كَأَنَّهُمْ أَعْجَازُ
نَخْلٍ خَاوِيَةٍ ۝٨

9. Dost thou see any remnant of them?

فَهَلْ تَرٰى لَهُمْ مِّنْ بَاقِيَةٍ ۝٩

10. And Pharaoh, and those who were before him, and the overthrown cities *persistently* committed sins.

وَجَآءَ فِرْعَوْنُ وَمَنْ قَبْلَهُ وَالْمُؤْتَفِكٰتُ بِالْخَاطِئَةِ ۝١٠

* 11. And they disobeyed the Messenger of their Lord, therefore He seized them—a severe seizing.

فَعَصَوْا رَسُولَ رَبِّهِمْ فَأَخَذَهُمْ أَخْذَةً رَّابِيَةً ۝١١

12. Verily, when the waters rose high, We bore you in the boat,

إِنَّا لَمَّا طَغَا الْمَآءُ حَمَلْنٰكُمْ فِي الْجَارِيَةِ ۝١٢

13. That We might make it a reminder for you, and that retaining ears might retain it.

لِنَجْعَلَهَا لَكُمْ تَذْكِرَةً وَّتَعِيَهَآ أُذُنٌ وَّاعِيَةٌ ۝١٣

14. And when a single blast is sounded on the trumpet,

فَإِذَا نُفِخَ فِي الصُّورِ نَفْخَةٌ وَّاحِدَةٌ ۝١٤

15. And the earth and the mountains are heaved up and then crushed in a single crash,

وَّحُمِلَتِ الْأَرْضُ وَالْجِبَالُ فَدُكَّتَا دَكَّةً وَّاحِدَةً ۝١٥

16. On that day will the *great* Event come to pass.

فَيَوْمَئِذٍ وَّقَعَتِ الْوَاقِعَةُ ۝١٦

17. And the heaven will cleave asunder, and it will become frail that day.

وَانْشَقَّتِ السَّمَآءُ فَهِيَ يَوْمَئِذٍ وَّاهِيَةٌ ۝١٧

* 18. And the angels will be *standing* on the sides thereof, and above them on that day eight *angels* will bear the throne of thy Lord.

وَّالْمَلَكُ عَلٰٓى أَرْجَآئِهَا ۚ وَيَحْمِلُ عَرْشَ رَبِّكَ فَوْقَهُمْ
يَوْمَئِذٍ ثَمٰنِيَةٌ ۝١٨

19. On that day you will be presented *before God; and* none of your secrets will remain hidden.

يَوْمَئِذٍ تُعْرَضُونَ لَا تَخْفٰى مِنْكُمْ خَافِيَةٌ ۝١٩

20. Then, as for him who is given his record in his right hand, he will say, 'Come, read my record.

فَأَمَّا مَنْ أُوتِيَ كِتٰبَهُ بِيَمِينِهِ فَيَقُولُ هَآؤُمُ اقْرَءُوا
كِتٰبِيَهْ ۝٢٠

21. 'Surely, I knew that I would meet my reckoning.'

إِنِّي ظَنَنْتُ أَنِّي مُلٰقٍ حِسَابِيَهْ ۝٢١

22. So he will have a delightful life,

فَهُوَ فِي عِيشَةٍ رَّاضِيَةٍ ۝٢٢

23. In a lofty Garden,

فِي جَنَّةٍ عَالِيَةٍ ۝٢٣

24. Whereof clusters of fruit will be within easy reach.

قُطُوفُهَا دَانِيَةٌ ۝٢٤

25. 'Eat and drink joyfully because of the *good* deeds you did in days gone by.'

كُلُوا وَاشْرَبُوا هَنِيْٓـًٔا بِمَآ أَسْلَفْتُمْ فِي الْأَيَّامِ الْخَالِيَةِ ﴿٢٥﴾

26. But as for him who is given his record in his left hand, he will say, 'O would that I had not been given my record!

وَأَمَّا مَنْ أُوتِيَ كِتٰبَهُ بِشِمَالِهِ فَيَقُولُ يٰلَيْتَنِي لَمْ أُوتَ كِتٰبِيَهْ ﴿٢٦﴾

27. 'Nor known what my reckoning was!

وَلَمْ أَدْرِ مَا حِسَابِيَهْ ﴿٢٧﴾

* 28. 'O would that *death* had made an end *of me*!

يٰلَيْتَهَا كَانَتِ الْقَاضِيَةَ ﴿٢٨﴾

29. 'My wealth has been of no avail to me.

مَآ أَغْنٰى عَنِّي مَالِيَهْ ﴿٢٩﴾

30. 'My power has perished from me.'

هَلَكَ عَنِّي سُلْطٰنِيَهْ ﴿٣٠﴾

31. 'Seize him and fetter him,

خُذُوهُ فَغُلُّوهُ ﴿٣١﴾

32. 'Then cast him into Hell.

ثُمَّ الْجَحِيمَ صَلُّوهُ ﴿٣٢﴾

33. 'Then put him into a chain the length of which is seventy cubits;

ثُمَّ فِي سِلْسِلَةٍ ذَرْعُهَا سَبْعُونَ ذِرَاعًا فَاسْلُكُوهُ ﴿٣٣﴾

34. 'Verily, he did not believe in Allah, the Great,

إِنَّهُ كَانَ لَا يُؤْمِنُ بِاللّٰهِ الْعَظِيمِ ﴿٣٤﴾

35. 'And he did not urge the feeding of the poor.

وَلَا يَحُضُّ عَلٰى طَعَامِ الْمِسْكِينِ ﴿٣٥﴾

36. 'No friend, therefore, has he here this day;

فَلَيْسَ لَهُ الْيَوْمَ هٰهُنَا حَمِيمٌ ﴿٣٦﴾

* 37. 'Nor any food save blood mixed with water,

وَلَا طَعَامٌ إِلَّا مِنْ غِسْلِينٍ ﴿٣٧﴾

38. 'Which none but the sinners eat.'

لَا يَأْكُلُهُ إِلَّا الْخٰطِـُٔونَ ﴿٣٨﴾ ع

R. 2.

39. But nay, I swear by all that you see,

فَلَآ أُقْسِمُ بِمَا تُبْصِرُونَ ﴿٣٩﴾

40. And by all that you see not,

وَمَا لَا تُبْصِرُونَ ﴿٤٠﴾

41. That it is surely the word *brought* by a noble Messenger;

إِنَّهُ لَقَوْلُ رَسُولٍ كَرِيمٍ ﴿٤١﴾

42. And it is not the word of a poet; little is it that you believe!

وَمَا هُوَ بِقَوْلِ شَاعِرٍ قَلِيلًا مَّا تُؤْمِنُونَ ﴿٤٢﴾

43. Nor is it the word of a soothsayer; little is it that you heed!

وَلَا بِقَوْلِ كَاهِنٍ قَلِيلًا مَّا تَذَكَّرُونَ ﴿٤٣﴾

44. *It is* a revelation from the Lord of the worlds.

تَنْزِيلٌ مِّنْ رَّبِّ الْعٰلَمِينَ ﴿٤٤﴾

* 45. And if he had forged *and attributed* any sayings to Us,

وَلَوْ تَقَوَّلَ عَلَيْنَا بَعْضَ الْأَقَاوِيلِ ﴿٤٥﴾

46. We would surely have seized him by the right hand,

لَأَخَذْنَا مِنْهُ بِالْيَمِينِ ﴿٤٦﴾

* 47. And then surely We would have severed his life-artery,

ثُمَّ لَقَطَعْنَا مِنْهُ الْوَتِينَ ﴿٤٧﴾

* 48. And not one of you could have held *Us* off from him.

فَمَا مِنْكُمْ مِنْ أَحَدٍ عَنْهُ حَاجِزِينَ ﴿٤٨﴾

49. And verily it is a reminder for the righteous.

وَإِنَّهُ لَتَذْكِرَةٌ لِلْمُتَّقِينَ ﴿٤٩﴾

50. And, surely, We know that there are some among you who reject *Our Signs*.

وَإِنَّا لَنَعْلَمُ أَنَّ مِنْكُمْ مُكَذِّبِينَ ﴿٥٠﴾

51. And, verily, it will be a *source of* regret for the disbelievers.

وَإِنَّهُ لَحَسْرَةٌ عَلَى الْكَافِرِينَ ﴿٥١﴾

52. And surely, it is the true certainty.

وَإِنَّهُ لَحَقُّ الْيَقِينِ ﴿٥٢﴾

53. So glorify the name of thy Lord, the Great.

ع فَسَبِّحْ بِاسْمِ رَبِّكَ الْعَظِيمِ ﴿٥٣﴾

سُورَةُ الْمَعَارِجِ مَكِّيَّةٌ

آياتها ٤٥ (٧٠) ركوعاتها ٢

Chapter 70 AL-MA'ĀRIJ Part 29

(Revealed before Hijra)

1. In the name of Allah, the Gracious, the Merciful.

بِسْمِ اللَّهِ الرَّحْمَٰنِ الرَّحِيمِ ﴿١﴾

2. An inquirer inquires concerning the punishment about to fall

سَأَلَ سَائِلٌ بِعَذَابٍ وَاقِعٍ ﴿٢﴾

3. Upon the disbelievers, which none can repel.

لِلْكَافِرِينَ لَيْسَ لَهُ دَافِعٌ ﴿٣﴾

4. *It is* from Allah, Lord of *great* ascents.

مِنَ اللَّهِ ذِي الْمَعَارِجِ ﴿٤﴾

5. The angels and the Spirit ascend to Him in a day the measure of which is fifty thousand years.

تَعْرُجُ الْمَلَائِكَةُ وَالرُّوحُ إِلَيْهِ فِي يَوْمٍ كَانَ مِقْدَارُهُ خَمْسِينَ أَلْفَ سَنَةٍ ﴿٥﴾

6. So be patient with admirable patience.

فَاصْبِرْ صَبْرًا جَمِيلًا ﴿٦﴾

7. They see it to be far off,

إِنَّهُمْ يَرَوْنَهُ بَعِيدًا ﴿٧﴾

8. But We see it to be nigh.

وَنَرَاهُ قَرِيبًا ﴿٨﴾

9. The day when the heaven will become like molten copper,

يَوْمَ تَكُونُ السَّمَآءُ كَالْمُهْلِ ﴿٩﴾

10. And the mountains will become like flakes of wool,

وَتَكُونُ الْجِبَالُ كَالْعِهْنِ ﴿١٠﴾

11. And a friend will not inquire after a friend.

وَلَا يَسْـَٔلُ حَمِيمٌ حَمِيمًا ﴿١١﴾

12. They will be placed in sight of one another, and the guilty one would fain ransom himself from the punishment of that day by *offering* his children,

يُبَصَّرُونَهُمْ يَوَدُّ الْمُجْرِمُ لَوْ يَفْتَدِي مِنْ عَذَابِ
يَوْمِئِذٍ بِبَنِيهِ ﴿١٢﴾

13. And his wife and his brother,

وَصَاحِبَتِهِ وَأَخِيهِ ﴿١٣﴾

14. And his kinsfolk who sheltered him,

وَفَصِيلَتِهِ الَّتِي تُـْٔوِيهِ ﴿١٤﴾

15. And *by offering all* those who are on the earth, if *only* thus he might save himself.

وَمَنْ فِي الْأَرْضِ جَمِيعًا ثُمَّ يُنْجِيهِ ﴿١٥﴾

16. But no! surely it is a flame of Fire,

كَلَّا إِنَّهَا لَظَىٰ ﴿١٦﴾

17. Stripping off the skin *even* to the extremities *of the body*.

نَزَّاعَةً لِلشَّوَىٰ ﴿١٧﴾

18. It will call him who turned his back and retreated

تَدْعُوا مَنْ أَدْبَرَ وَتَوَلَّىٰ ﴿١٨﴾

19. And hoarded *wealth*, and withheld *it*.

وَجَمَعَ فَأَوْعَىٰ ﴿١٩﴾

20. Verily, man is born impatient and miserly.

إِنَّ الْإِنْسَانَ خُلِقَ هَلُوعًا ﴿٢٠﴾

21. When evil touches him, he is full of lamentation,

إِذَا مَسَّهُ الشَّرُّ جَزُوعًا ﴿٢١﴾

22. But when good falls to his *lot*, he is niggardly.

وَإِذَا مَسَّهُ الْخَيْرُ مَنُوعًا ﴿٢٢﴾

23. But not those who pray.

إِلَّا الْمُصَلِّينَ ﴿٢٣﴾

24. Those who are constant in their Prayer,

الَّذِينَ هُمْ عَلَىٰ صَلَاتِهِمْ دَائِمُونَ ﴿٢٤﴾

25. And those in whose wealth there is a recognized right

وَالَّذِينَ فِي أَمْوَالِهِمْ حَقٌّ مَعْلُومٌ ﴿٢٥﴾

* 26. For one who asks *for help* and *for one* who does not.

لِلسَّائِلِ وَالْمَحْرُومِ ﴿٢٦﴾

27. And those who believe the Day of Judgment to be a reality,

وَالَّذِينَ يُصَدِّقُونَ بِيَوْمِ الدِّينِ ﴿٢٧﴾

28. And those who are fearful of the punishment of their Lord—

وَالَّذِينَ هُمْ مِنْ عَذَابِ رَبِّهِمْ مُشْفِقُونَ ﴿٢٨﴾

* 29. Verily the punishment of their Lord is not *a thing* to feel secure from—

إِنَّ عَذَابَ رَبِّهِمْ غَيْرُ مَأْمُونٍ ﴿٢٩﴾

30. And those who guard their private parts—

وَالَّذِيْنَ هُمْ لِفُرُوْجِهِمْ حٰفِظُوْنَ ۝٣٠

31. Except from their wives and *from* those whom their right hands possess; such indeed are not to blame;

اِلَّا عَلٰٓى اَزْوَاجِهِمْ اَوْ مَا مَلَكَتْ اَيْمَانُهُمْ فَاِنَّهُمْ
غَيْرُ مَلُوْمِيْنَ ۝٣١

32. But those who seek to go beyond that, it is these who are transgressors—

فَمَنِ ابْتَغٰى وَرَآءَ ذٰلِكَ فَاُولٰٓئِكَ هُمُ الْعٰدُوْنَ ۝٣٢

33. And those who are watchful of their trusts and their covenants,

وَالَّذِيْنَ هُمْ لِاَمٰنٰتِهِمْ وَعَهْدِهِمْ رٰعُوْنَ ۝٣٣

34. And those who are upright in their testimonies,

وَالَّذِيْنَ هُمْ بِشَهٰدٰتِهِمْ قَآئِمُوْنَ ۝٣٤

* 35. And those who are strict in the observance of their Prayer.

وَالَّذِيْنَ هُمْ عَلٰى صَلَاتِهِمْ يُحَافِظُوْنَ ۝٣٥

36. These will be in the Gardens, duly honoured.

ع اُولٰٓئِكَ فِيْ جَنّٰتٍ مُّكْرَمُوْنَ ۝٣٦

R. 2.

37. But what is the matter with those who disbelieve, that they come hastening towards thee,

فَمَالِ الَّذِيْنَ كَفَرُوْا قِبَلَكَ مُهْطِعِيْنَ ۝٣٧

38. From the right hand and from the left, in different parties?

عَنِ الْيَمِيْنِ وَعَنِ الشِّمَالِ عِزِيْنَ ۝٣٨

39. Does every man among them hope to enter the Garden of Bliss?

اَيَطْمَعُ كُلُّ امْرِئٍ مِّنْهُمْ اَنْ يُّدْخَلَ جَنَّةَ نَعِيْمٍ ۝٣٩

40. Never! We have created them of that which they know.

كَلَّا ؕ اِنَّا خَلَقْنٰهُمْ مِّمَّا يَعْلَمُوْنَ ۝٤٠

41. But nay! I swear by the Lord of the easts and of the wests, that We have the power

فَلَآ اُقْسِمُ بِرَبِّ الْمَشٰرِقِ وَالْمَغٰرِبِ اِنَّا لَقٰدِرُوْنَ ۝٤١

42. To bring in their place others better than they, and We cannot be frustrated *in Our plans.*

عَلٰٓى اَنْ نُّبَدِّلَ خَيْرًا مِّنْهُمْ وَمَا نَحْنُ بِمَسْبُوْقِيْنَ ۝٤٢

43. So leave them alone to indulge in idle talk and play until they meet that day of theirs which they are promised,

فَذَرْهُمْ يَخُوْضُوْا وَيَلْعَبُوْا حَتّٰى يُلٰقُوْا يَوْمَهُمُ
الَّذِيْ يُوْعَدُوْنَ ۝٤٣

* 44. The day when they will come forth from their graves hastening, as though they were racing to a target,

يَوْمَ يَخْرُجُوْنَ مِنَ الْاَجْدَاثِ سِرَاعًا كَاَنَّهُمْ اِلٰى
نُصُبٍ يُّوْفِضُوْنَ ۝٤٤

45. *With* their eyes cast down; and disgrace will cover them. Such is the day which they are promised.

خَاشِعَةً اَبْصَارُهُمْ تَرْهَقُهُمْ ذِلَّةٌ ؕ ذٰلِكَ الْيَوْمُ
ع الَّذِيْ كَانُوْا يُوْعَدُوْنَ ۝٤٥

سُوْرَةُ نُوْحٍ مَكِّيَّةٌ (٧١) آياتها ٢٩ ركوعاتها ٢

NŪḤ

(Revealed before Hijra)

1. In the name of Allah, the Gracious, the Merciful.

بِسْمِ اللّٰهِ الرَّحْمٰنِ الرَّحِيْمِ ۝١

2. We sent Noah to his people, *saying*, 'Warn thy people before there comes upon them a grievous punishment.'

إِنَّآ أَرْسَلْنَا نُوْحًا إِلٰى قَوْمِهٖٓ أَنْ أَنْذِرْ قَوْمَكَ مِنْ
قَبْلِ أَنْ يَّأْتِيَهُمْ عَذَابٌ أَلِيْمٌ ۝٢

3. He said, 'O my people! surely I am a plain Warner unto you,

قَالَ يٰقَوْمِ إِنِّيْ لَكُمْ نَذِيْرٌ مُّبِيْنٌ ۝٣

4. 'That you serve Allah and fear Him and obey me.

أَنِ اعْبُدُوا اللّٰهَ وَاتَّقُوْهُ وَأَطِيْعُوْنِ ۝٤

5. 'He will forgive you your sins and grant you respite till an appointed time. Verily the time appointed by Allah cannot be put back when it comes, if only you knew!'

يَغْفِرْ لَكُمْ مِّنْ ذُنُوْبِكُمْ وَيُؤَخِّرْكُمْ إِلٰٓى أَجَلٍ
مُّسَمًّى ۚ إِنَّ أَجَلَ اللّٰهِ إِذَا جَآءَ لَا يُؤَخَّرُ ۘ لَوْ كُنْتُمْ وقف لازم
تَعْلَمُوْنَ ۝٥

6. He said, "My Lord, I have called my people night and day,

قَالَ رَبِّ إِنِّيْ دَعَوْتُ قَوْمِيْ لَيْلًا وَّنَهَارًا ۝٦

7. "But my calling *them* has only made them flee *from me* all the more.

فَلَمْ يَزِدْهُمْ دُعَآءِيْٓ إِلَّا فِرَارًا ۝٧

* 8. "And every time I called them that Thou mightest forgive them, they put their fingers into their ears, and covered up their hearts, and persisted *in their iniquity*, and were disdainfully proud.

وَإِنِّيْ كُلَّمَا دَعَوْتُهُمْ لِتَغْفِرَ لَهُمْ جَعَلُوْٓا أَصَابِعَهُمْ
فِيْٓ اٰذَانِهِمْ وَاسْتَغْشَوْا ثِيَابَهُمْ وَأَصَرُّوْا وَاسْتَكْبَرُوا
اسْتِكْبَارًا ۝٨

* 9. "Then, I called them *to righteousness* openly.

ثُمَّ إِنِّيْ دَعَوْتُهُمْ جِهَارًا ۝٩

10. "Then I preached to them in public, and *also* spoke to them in private.

ثُمَّ إِنِّيْٓ أَعْلَنْتُ لَهُمْ وَأَسْرَرْتُ لَهُمْ إِسْرَارًا ۝١٠

* 11. "And I said, 'Seek forgiveness of your Lord; for He is the Great Forgiver.

فَقُلْتُ اسْتَغْفِرُوْا رَبَّكُمْ إِنَّهٗ كَانَ غَفَّارًا ۝١١

12. 'He will send down rain for you in abundance,

يُّرْسِلِ السَّمَآءَ عَلَيْكُمْ مِّدْرَارًا ۝١٢

13. 'And He will strengthen you with wealth and *with* children, and He will give you gardens and He will give you rivers.

وَّيُمْدِدْكُمْ بِأَمْوَالٍ وَّبَنِيْنَ وَيَجْعَلْ لَّكُمْ جَنّٰتٍ
وَّيَجْعَلْ لَّكُمْ أَنْهٰرًا ۝١٣

* 14. 'What is the matter with you that you expect not wisdom and staidness from Allah?

مَا لَكُمْ لَا تَرْجُوْنَ لِلّٰهِ وَقَارًا ﴿١٤﴾

* 15. 'And He has created you in *different* forms and *different* conditions.

وَقَدْ خَلَقَكُمْ اَطْوَارًا ﴿١٥﴾

* 16. 'Have you not seen how Allah has created seven heavens in *perfect* harmony,

اَلَمْ تَرَوْا كَيْفَ خَلَقَ اللّٰهُ سَبْعَ سَمٰوٰتٍ طِبَاقًا ﴿١٦﴾

17. 'And has placed the moon therein as a light, and made the sun as a lamp?

وَّجَعَلَ الْقَمَرَ فِيْهِنَّ نُوْرًا وَّجَعَلَ الشَّمْسَ سِرَاجًا ﴿١٧﴾

* 18. 'And Allah has caused you to grow as a *good* growth from the earth,

وَاللّٰهُ اَنْۢبَتَكُمْ مِّنَ الْاَرْضِ نَبَاتًا ﴿١٨﴾

* 19. 'Then will He cause you to return thereto, and He will bring you forth *a new* bringing forth.

ثُمَّ يُعِيْدُكُمْ فِيْهَا وَيُخْرِجُكُمْ اِخْرَاجًا ﴿١٩﴾

20. 'And Allah has made the earth for you a wide expanse

وَاللّٰهُ جَعَلَ لَكُمُ الْاَرْضَ بِسَاطًا ﴿٢٠﴾

21. 'That you may traverse the open ways thereof.' "

لِّتَسْلُكُوْا مِنْهَا سُبُلًا فِجَاجًا ﴿٢١﴾ ع

R. 2.

22. Noah said, "My Lord, they have disobeyed me, and followed one whose wealth and children have only added to his ruin.

قَالَ نُوْحٌ رَّبِّ اِنَّهُمْ عَصَوْنِيْ وَاتَّبَعُوْا مَنْ لَّمْ يَزِدْهُ مَالُهٗ وَوَلَدُهٗۤ اِلَّا خَسَارًا ﴿٢٢﴾

23. "And they have planned a mighty plan.

وَمَكَرُوْا مَكْرًا كُبَّارًا ﴿٢٣﴾

24. "And they say *to one another*, 'Forsake not your gods *under any circumstances*. And forsake neither Wadd*, nor Suwā'*, nor Yaghūth* and Ya'ūq* and Nasr*.'

وَقَالُوْا لَا تَذَرُنَّ اٰلِهَتَكُمْ وَلَا تَذَرُنَّ وَدًّا وَّلَا سُوَاعًا ۙ وَّلَا يَغُوْثَ وَيَعُوْقَ وَنَسْرًا ﴿٢٤﴾

25. "And they have led many astray; so increase Thou not the wrongdoers but in error."

وَقَدْ اَضَلُّوْا كَثِيْرًا ۚ وَلَا تَزِدِ الظّٰلِمِيْنَ اِلَّا ضَلٰلًا ﴿٢٥﴾

26. Because of their sins they were drowned and made to enter Fire. And they found no helpers for themselves against Allah.

مِمَّا خَطِيْٓـٰٔتِهِمْ اُغْرِقُوْا فَاُدْخِلُوْا نَارًا ۙ فَلَمْ يَجِدُوْا لَهُمْ مِّنْ دُوْنِ اللّٰهِ اَنْصَارًا ﴿٢٦﴾

* 27. And Noah said, 'My Lord, leave not in the land a single one of the disbelievers;

وَقَالَ نُوْحٌ رَّبِّ لَا تَذَرْ عَلَى الْاَرْضِ مِنَ الْكٰفِرِيْنَ دَيَّارًا ﴿٢٧﴾

28. 'For, if Thou dost leave them, they will *only* lead astray Thy servants and will not give birth but to a sinner *and* a disbeliever.

اِنَّكَ اِنْ تَذَرْهُمْ يُضِلُّوْا عِبَادَكَ وَلَا يَلِدُوْۤا اِلَّا فَاجِرًا كَفَّارًا ﴿٢٨﴾

* Idols of pagan Arabs.

29. 'My Lord, forgive me and my parents, and him who enters my house as a believer, and the believing men and the believing women; and increase Thou not the wrongdoers but in perdition.'

رَبِّ اغْفِرْ لِيْ وَلِوَالِدَيَّ وَلِمَنْ دَخَلَ بَيْتِيَ مُؤْمِنًا وَّلِلْمُؤْمِنِيْنَ وَالْمُؤْمِنٰتِ ۚ وَلَا تَزِدِ الظّٰلِمِيْنَ إِلَّا تَبَارًا ٢٩

سُوْرَةُ الْجِنِّ مَكِّيَّةٌ (٧٢)

Part 29 AL-JINN Chapter 72

(Revealed before Hijra)

1. In the name of Allah, the Gracious, the Merciful.

بِسْمِ اللّٰهِ الرَّحْمٰنِ الرَّحِيْمِ ١

2. Say, "It has been revealed to me that a company of the Jinn listened, and they said: 'Truly we have heard a Qur'ān that is wonderful,

قُلْ أُوْحِيَ إِلَيَّ أَنَّهُ اسْتَمَعَ نَفَرٌ مِّنَ الْجِنِّ فَقَالُوْٓا إِنَّا سَمِعْنَا قُرْاٰنًا عَجَبًا ٢

3. 'It guides to the right way; so we have believed in it, and we will not associate any one with our Lord.

يَّهْدِيْٓ إِلَى الرُّشْدِ فَاٰمَنَّا بِهٖ ۚ وَلَنْ نُّشْرِكَ بِرَبِّنَآ أَحَدًا ٣

4. 'And *we believe* that the majesty of our Lord is exalted. He has taken neither wife nor son unto Himself.

وَّأَنَّهُ تَعٰلٰى جَدُّ رَبِّنَا مَا اتَّخَذَ صَاحِبَةً وَّلَا وَلَدًا ٤

5. 'And *it is true* that the foolish amongst us used to utter extravagant lies concerning Allah.

وَّأَنَّهُ كَانَ يَقُوْلُ سَفِيْهُنَا عَلَى اللّٰهِ شَطَطًا ٥

6. 'And we thought that men and Jinn would never speak a lie concerning Allah.

وَّأَنَّا ظَنَنَّآ أَنْ لَّنْ تَقُوْلَ الْإِنْسُ وَالْجِنُّ عَلَى اللّٰهِ كَذِبًا ٦

7. 'And indeed some men from among the common folk used to seek the protection of some men from among the Jinn, and they *thus* increased *the latter in* their pride;

وَّأَنَّهُ كَانَ رِجَالٌ مِّنَ الْإِنْسِ يَعُوْذُوْنَ بِرِجَالٍ مِّنَ الْجِنِّ فَزَادُوْهُمْ رَهَقًا ٧

8. 'And indeed they thought, even as you think, that Allah would never raise any *Messenger*.

وَّأَنَّهُمْ ظَنُّوْا كَمَا ظَنَنْتُمْ أَنْ لَّنْ يَّبْعَثَ اللّٰهُ أَحَدًا ٨

9. 'And we sought to reach heaven, but we found it filled with strong guards and shooting stars.

وَّأَنَّا لَمَسْنَا السَّمَآءَ فَوَجَدْنٰهَا مُلِئَتْ حَرَسًا شَدِيْدًا وَّشُهُبًا ٩

10. 'And we used to sit on some of its seats to listen. But whoso listens now, finds a shooting star in ambush for him.

وَّأَنَّا كُنَّا نَقْعُدُ مِنْهَا مَقَاعِدَ لِلسَّمْعِ ۖ فَمَنْ يَّسْتَمِعِ الْاٰنَ يَجِدْ لَهٗ شِهَابًا رَّصَدًا ١٠

11. 'And we know not whether evil is intended for those who are in the earth or whether their Lord intends *something* good for them.

وَّاَنَّا لَا نَدْرِيْٓ اَشَرٌّ اُرِيْدَ بِمَنْ فِي الْاَرْضِ اَمْ اَرَادَ
بِهِمْ رَبُّهُمْ رَشَدًا ﴿١١﴾

12. 'And some of us are righteous and some of us are otherwise; and we are sects holding different views.

وَّاَنَّا مِنَّا الصّٰلِحُوْنَ وَمِنَّا دُوْنَ ذٰلِكَ كُنَّا طَرَآئِقَ
قِدَدًا ﴿١٢﴾

13. 'And we know that we cannot frustrate *the plan of* Allah in the earth, nor can we escape Him by flight.

وَّاَنَّا ظَنَنَّآ اَنْ لَّنْ نُّعْجِزَ اللّٰهَ فِي الْاَرْضِ وَلَنْ نُّعْجِزَهٗ
هَرَبًا ﴿١٣﴾

14. 'And when we heard the *call to* guidance, we believed in it. And he who believes in his Lord has no fear of loss or injustice.

وَّاَنَّا لَمَّا سَمِعْنَا الْهُدٰٓى اٰمَنَّا بِهٖ ۭ فَمَنْ يُّؤْمِنْۢ
بِرَبِّهٖ فَلَا يَخَافُ بَخْسًا وَّلَا رَهَقًا ﴿١٤﴾

15. 'And some of us submit *to God* and some of us have deviated *from the right course.*'" And those who submit *to God*—it is these who seek the right course.

وَّاَنَّا مِنَّا الْمُسْلِمُوْنَ وَمِنَّا الْقٰسِطُوْنَ ۭ فَمَنْ اَسْلَمَ
فَاُولٰٓئِكَ تَحَرَّوْا رَشَدًا ﴿١٥﴾

16. And as for those who deviate *from the right course*, they are the fuel of Hell.

وَاَمَّا الْقٰسِطُوْنَ فَكَانُوْا لِجَهَنَّمَ حَطَبًا ﴿١٦﴾

17. And if they keep to the *right* path, We shall certainly provide them with abundant water to drink,

وَّاَنْ لَّوِ اسْتَقَامُوْا عَلَى الطَّرِيْقَةِ لَاَسْقَيْنٰهُمْ مَّآءً
غَدَقًا ﴿١٧﴾

18. That We may try them thereby. And whoso turns away from the remembrance of his Lord—He will push him into an overwhelmingly severe punishment.

لِّنَفْتِنَهُمْ فِيْهِ ۭ وَمَنْ يُّعْرِضْ عَنْ ذِكْرِ رَبِّهٖ يَسْلُكْهُ
عَذَابًا صَعَدًا ﴿١٨﴾

19. And *all* places of worship belong to Allah; so call not on any one beside Allah.

وَّاَنَّ الْمَسٰجِدَ لِلّٰهِ فَلَا تَدْعُوْا مَعَ اللّٰهِ اَحَدًا ﴿١٩﴾

20. And when the Servant of Allah stands up praying to Him, they crowd upon him, well nigh suffocating him.

وَّاَنَّهٗ لَمَّا قَامَ عَبْدُ اللّٰهِ يَدْعُوْهُ كَادُوْا يَكُوْنُوْنَ
عَلَيْهِ لِبَدًا ﴿٢٠﴾ ع

R. 2.

21. Say, 'I pray to my Lord only, and I associate no one with Him.'

قُلْ اِنَّمَآ اَدْعُوْا رَبِّيْ وَلَآ اُشْرِكُ بِهٖٓ اَحَدًا ﴿٢١﴾

22. Say, 'I have no power to do you either harm or good.'

قُلْ اِنِّيْ لَآ اَمْلِكُ لَكُمْ ضَرًّا وَّلَا رَشَدًا ﴿٢٢﴾

23. Say, 'Surely none can protect me against Allah, nor can I find any place of refuge beside Him.

قُلْ اِنِّيْ لَنْ يُّجِيْرَنِيْ مِنَ اللّٰهِ اَحَدٌ ۬ وَّلَنْ اَجِدَ
مِنْ دُوْنِهٖ مُلْتَحَدًا ﴿٢٣﴾

24. '*My responsibility is* only to convey *the revelation* from Allah, and His Messages.' And for those who disobey Allah and His Messenger there is the fire of Hell, wherein they will abide for a long, long period.

25. *They will continue to disbelieve* until they see that which they are promised, and soon they will know who is weaker in helpers and fewer in numbers.

26. Say, 'I know not whether that which you are promised is nigh or whether my Lord has fixed for it a distant term.'

* 27. *He is the* Knower of the unseen; and He reveals not His secrets to any one,

* 28. Except to him whom He chooses, namely a Messenger *of His*. And then He causes an escort *of guarding angels* to go before him and behind him,

29. That He may know that they (His Messengers) have delivered the Messages of their Lord. And He encompasses *all* that is with them and He keeps count of all things.

اِلَّا بَلٰغًا مِّنَ اللّٰهِ وَرِسٰلٰتِهٖ ۚ وَمَنْ يَّعْصِ اللّٰهَ وَ
رَسُوْلَهٗ فَاِنَّ لَهٗ نَارَ جَهَنَّمَ خٰلِدِيْنَ فِيْهَآ اَبَدًا ﴿٢٤﴾
حَتّٰٓى اِذَا رَاَوْا مَا يُوْعَدُوْنَ فَسَيَعْلَمُوْنَ مَنْ
اَضْعَفُ نَاصِرًا وَّاَقَلُّ عَدَدًا ﴿٢٥﴾
قُلْ اِنْ اَدْرِيْٓ اَقَرِيْبٌ مَّا تُوْعَدُوْنَ اَمْ يَجْعَلُ لَهٗ
رَبِّيْٓ اَمَدًا ﴿٢٦﴾
عٰلِمُ الْغَيْبِ فَلَا يُظْهِرُ عَلٰى غَيْبِهٖٓ اَحَدًا ﴿٢٧﴾
اِلَّا مَنِ ارْتَضٰى مِنْ رَّسُوْلٍ فَاِنَّهٗ يَسْلُكُ مِنْ بَيْنِ
يَدَيْهِ وَمِنْ خَلْفِهٖ رَصَدًا ﴿٢٨﴾
لِّيَعْلَمَ اَنْ قَدْ اَبْلَغُوْا رِسٰلٰتِ رَبِّهِمْ وَاَحَاطَ بِمَا
ع لَدَيْهِمْ وَاَحْصٰى كُلَّ شَيْءٍ عَدَدًا ﴿٢٩﴾

سُوْرَةُ الْمُزَّمِّلِ مَكِّيَّةٌ

(٧٣) اٰيَاتُهَا ٢١ — رُكُوْعَاتُهَا ٢

Part 29 AL-MUZZAMMIL Chapter 73

(Revealed before Hijra)

1. In the name of Allah, the Gracious, the Merciful.

* 2. O thou who art bearing *a heavy responsibility,*

3. Stand up *in Prayer* at night except a small portion thereof—

4. Half of it, or make it a little less than that

5. Or make it a little more than that—and recite the Qur'ān slowly and thoughtfully.

6. Verily, We are charging thee with a weighty Word.

7. Verily, getting up at night is the most potent means of subduing *the self* and most effective in respect of words *of prayer*.

بِسْمِ اللّٰهِ الرَّحْمٰنِ الرَّحِيْمِ ﴿١﴾
يٰٓاَيُّهَا الْمُزَّمِّلُ ﴿٢﴾
قُمِ الَّيْلَ اِلَّا قَلِيْلًا ﴿٣﴾
نِّصْفَهٗٓ اَوِ انْقُصْ مِنْهُ قَلِيْلًا ﴿٤﴾
اَوْ زِدْ عَلَيْهِ وَرَتِّلِ الْقُرْاٰنَ تَرْتِيْلًا ﴿٥﴾
اِنَّا سَنُلْقِيْ عَلَيْكَ قَوْلًا ثَقِيْلًا ﴿٦﴾
اِنَّ نَاشِئَةَ الَّيْلِ هِيَ اَشَدُّ وَطْاً وَّاَقْوَمُ قِيْلًا ﴿٧﴾

8. Thou hast indeed, during the day, *a* long *chain of* engagements.

إِنَّ لَكَ فِي النَّهَارِ سَبْحًا طَوِيلًا ۝٨

9. So remember the name of thy Lord, and devote *thyself* to Him with full devotion.

وَاذْكُرِ اسْمَ رَبِّكَ وَتَبَتَّلْ إِلَيْهِ تَبْتِيلًا ۝٩

10. *He is the* Lord of the East and the West; there is no God but He; so take Him as *thy* Guardian.

رَبُّ الْمَشْرِقِ وَالْمَغْرِبِ لَا إِلٰهَ إِلَّا هُوَ فَاتَّخِذْهُ
وَكِيلًا ۝١٠

11. And bear patiently all that they say; and part with them in a decent manner.

وَاصْبِرْ عَلَىٰ مَا يَقُولُونَ وَاهْجُرْهُمْ هَجْرًا جَمِيلًا ۝١١

12. And leave Me alone with those who reject *the truth*, possessors of ease and plenty; and give them a little respite.

وَذَرْنِي وَالْمُكَذِّبِينَ أُولِي النَّعْمَةِ وَمَهِّلْهُمْ قَلِيلًا ۝١٢

13. Surely, with Us are *heavy* fetters and a *raging* fire,

إِنَّ لَدَيْنَا أَنْكَالًا وَجَحِيمًا ۝١٣

14. And food that chokes, and a painful punishment —

وَطَعَامًا ذَا غُصَّةٍ وَعَذَابًا أَلِيمًا ۝١٤

15. On the day when the earth and the mountains shall quake, and the mountains will become like crumbling sandhills.

يَوْمَ تَرْجُفُ الْأَرْضُ وَالْجِبَالُ وَكَانَتِ الْجِبَالُ
كَثِيبًا مَهِيلًا ۝١٥

16. Verily, We have sent to you a Messenger, who is a witness over you, even as We sent a Messenger to Pharaoh.

إِنَّا أَرْسَلْنَا إِلَيْكُمْ رَسُولًا شَاهِدًا عَلَيْكُمْ كَمَا
أَرْسَلْنَا إِلَىٰ فِرْعَوْنَ رَسُولًا ۝١٦

17. But Pharaoh disobeyed the Messenger, so We seized him with a terrible seizing.

فَعَصَىٰ فِرْعَوْنُ الرَّسُولَ فَأَخَذْنَاهُ أَخْذًا وَبِيلًا ۝١٧

* 18. How will you then, if you disbelieve, guard yourselves against a day which will turn children grey-headed?

فَكَيْفَ تَتَّقُونَ إِنْ كَفَرْتُمْ يَوْمًا يَجْعَلُ الْوِلْدَانَ
شِيبًا ۝١٨

19. *On that day* the heaven will be rent asunder *and* His promise will be fulfilled.

السَّمَاءُ مُنْفَطِرٌ بِهِ ۚ كَانَ وَعْدُهُ مَفْعُولًا ۝١٩

20. This, surely, is a reminder. So let him, who will, take a way unto his Lord.

ع إِنَّ هَٰذِهِ تَذْكِرَةٌ ۖ فَمَنْ شَاءَ اتَّخَذَ إِلَىٰ رَبِّهِ سَبِيلًا ۝٢٠

R. 2.

21. Surely, thy Lord knows that thou standest up *praying* for nearly two-thirds of the night, and *sometimes* half or a third thereof, and also a party of those who are with thee. And Allah determines the measure of the night and the day. He knows that you cannot keep its *measure*, so He has turned to you in mercy. Recite, then, as much of the Qur'ān as is easy *for you*. He knows that there will be some among you who may be sick and others

إِنَّ رَبَّكَ يَعْلَمُ أَنَّكَ تَقُومُ أَدْنَىٰ مِنْ ثُلُثَيِ اللَّيْلِ
وَنِصْفَهُ وَثُلُثَهُ وَطَائِفَةٌ مِنَ الَّذِينَ مَعَكَ ۚ
وَاللَّهُ يُقَدِّرُ اللَّيْلَ وَالنَّهَارَ ۚ عَلِمَ أَنْ لَنْ تُحْصُوهُ
فَتَابَ عَلَيْكُمْ ۖ فَاقْرَءُوا مَا تَيَسَّرَ مِنَ الْقُرْآنِ ۚ
عَلِمَ أَنْ سَيَكُونُ مِنْكُمْ مَرْضَىٰ ۙ وَآخَرُونَ يَضْرِبُونَ

who may travel in the land seeking Allah's bounty, and others who may fight in the cause of Allah. So recite of it that which is easy *for you*, and observe Prayer, and pay the Zakāt, and lend to Allah a goodly loan. And whatever good you send on before you for your souls, you will find it with Allah. It *will be* better and greater in reward. And seek forgiveness of Allah. Surely, Allah is Most Forgiving, Merciful.

فِي الْاَرْضِ يَبْتَغُوْنَ مِنْ فَضْلِ اللّٰهِ ۙ وَاٰخَرُوْنَ
يُقَاتِلُوْنَ فِيْ سَبِيْلِ اللّٰهِ ۖ فَاقْرَءُوْا مَا تَيَسَّرَ مِنْهُ ۙ وَ
اَقِيْمُوا الصَّلٰوةَ وَاٰتُوا الزَّكٰوةَ وَاَقْرِضُوا اللّٰهَ قَرْضًا
حَسَنًا ۭ وَمَا تُقَدِّمُوْا لِاَنْفُسِكُمْ مِّنْ خَيْرٍ تَجِدُوْهُ
عِنْدَ اللّٰهِ هُوَ خَيْرًا وَّاَعْظَمَ اَجْرًا ۭ وَاسْتَغْفِرُوا
اللّٰهَ ۭ اِنَّ اللّٰهَ غَفُوْرٌ رَّحِيْمٌ ﴿۲۱﴾

سُوْرَةُ الْمُدَّثِّرِ مَكِّيَّةٌ

AL-MUDDATHTHIR

(Revealed before Hijra)

Part 29 — Chapter 74

1. In the name of Allah, the Gracious, the Merciful.

بِسْمِ اللّٰهِ الرَّحْمٰنِ الرَّحِيْمِ ﴿۱﴾

2. O thou that has wrapped *thyself with thy mantle*!

يٰۤاَيُّهَا الْمُدَّثِّرُ ﴿۲﴾

3. Arise and warn.

قُمْ فَاَنْذِرْ ﴿۳﴾

* 4. And thy Lord do thou magnify.

وَرَبَّكَ فَكَبِّرْ ﴿۴﴾

* 5. And thy heart do thou purify,

وَثِيَابَكَ فَطَهِّرْ ﴿۵﴾

6. And uncleanliness do thou shun,

وَالرُّجْزَ فَاهْجُرْ ﴿۶﴾

7. And bestow not favours seeking to get more *in return*,

وَلَا تَمْنُنْ تَسْتَكْثِرُ ﴿۷﴾

8. And for the sake of thy Lord do thou endure patiently.

وَلِرَبِّكَ فَاصْبِرْ ﴿۸﴾

9. And when the trumpet is sounded,

فَاِذَا نُقِرَ فِي النَّاقُوْرِ ﴿۹﴾

10. That day will be a distressful day.

فَذٰلِكَ يَوْمَئِذٍ يَّوْمٌ عَسِيْرٌ ﴿۱۰﴾

11. For the disbelievers it will be anything but easy.

عَلَى الْكٰفِرِيْنَ غَيْرُ يَسِيْرٍ ﴿۱۱﴾

12. Leave Me to deal with him whom I created alone,

ذَرْنِيْ وَمَنْ خَلَقْتُ وَحِيْدًا ﴿۱۲﴾

13. And *then* I gave him abundant wealth,

وَّجَعَلْتُ لَهٗ مَالًا مَّمْدُوْدًا ﴿١٣﴾

14. And sons, abiding in *his* presence,

وَّبَنِيْنَ شُهُوْدًا ﴿١٤﴾

15. And I prepared for him all necessary things.

وَّمَهَّدْتُّ لَهٗ تَمْهِيْدًا ﴿١٥﴾

16. Yet he desires that I should give *him* more.

ثُمَّ يَطْمَعُ اَنْ اَزِيْدَ ﴿١٦﴾

17. Certainly not! for he has been hostile to Our Signs.

كَلَّا ۗ اِنَّهٗ كَانَ لِاٰيٰتِنَا عَنِيْدًا ﴿١٧﴾

18. I shall soon inflict on him an overwhelming hardship.

سَاُرْهِقُهٗ صَعُوْدًا ﴿١٨﴾

19. Lo! he reflected and calculated!

اِنَّهٗ فَكَّرَ وَقَدَّرَ ﴿١٩﴾

20. Ruin seize him! how he calculated!

فَقُتِلَ كَيْفَ قَدَّرَ ﴿٢٠﴾

21. Ruin seize him again! how he calculated!

ثُمَّ قُتِلَ كَيْفَ قَدَّرَ ﴿٢١﴾

22. Then he looked,

ثُمَّ نَظَرَ ﴿٢٢﴾

23. Then he frowned and scowled,

ثُمَّ عَبَسَ وَبَسَرَ ﴿٢٣﴾

24. Then he turned away and was disdainful,

ثُمَّ اَدْبَرَ وَاسْتَكْبَرَ ﴿٢٤﴾

25. And said, 'This is nothing but magic handed down;

فَقَالَ اِنْ هٰذَآ اِلَّا سِحْرٌ يُّؤْثَرُ ﴿٢٥﴾

26. 'This is nothing but the word of man.'

اِنْ هٰذَآ اِلَّا قَوْلُ الْبَشَرِ ﴿٢٦﴾

* 27. Soon shall I cast him into the fire of Hell.

سَاُصْلِيْهِ سَقَرَ ﴿٢٧﴾

* 28. And what makes thee know what Hell-fire is?

وَمَآ اَدْرٰىكَ مَا سَقَرُ ﴿٢٨﴾

* 29. It spares not and it leaves naught.

لَا تُبْقِيْ وَلَا تَذَرُ ﴿٢٩﴾

* 30. It scorches the face.

لَوَّاحَةٌ لِّلْبَشَرِ ﴿٣٠﴾

31. Over it are nineteen *angels*.

عَلَيْهَا تِسْعَةَ عَشَرَ ﴿٣١﴾

32. And none but angels have We made wardens of the Fire. And We have not fixed their number except as a trial for those who disbelieve, so that those who have been given the Book may attain to certainty, and those who believe may in-

وَمَا جَعَلْنَآ اَصْحٰبَ النَّارِ اِلَّا مَلٰٓئِكَةً ۙ وَّمَا جَعَلْنَا
عِدَّتَهُمْ اِلَّا فِتْنَةً لِّلَّذِيْنَ كَفَرُوْا ۙ لِيَسْتَيْقِنَ الَّذِيْنَ
اُوْتُوا الْكِتٰبَ وَيَزْدَادَ الَّذِيْنَ اٰمَنُوْٓا اِيْمَانًا وَّلَا يَرْتَابَ

crease in faith, and those who have been given the Book as well as the believers may not doubt, and that those in whose hearts is disease and the disbelievers may say, 'What does Allah mean by such an illustration?' Thus does Allah adjudge astray whom He pleases and guide whom He pleases. And none knows the hosts of thy Lord but He. And this is nothing but a Reminder for man.

الَّذِينَ أُوتُوا الْكِتٰبَ وَالْمُؤْمِنُونَ وَلِيَقُولَ الَّذِينَ فِي
قُلُوبِهِمْ مَّرَضٌ وَّالْكٰفِرُونَ مَاذَآ أَرَادَ اللّٰهُ بِهٰذَا
مَثَلًا كَذٰلِكَ يُضِلُّ اللّٰهُ مَنْ يَّشَآءُ وَيَهْدِي مَنْ
يَّشَآءُ وَمَا يَعْلَمُ جُنُودَ رَبِّكَ إِلَّا هُوَ وَمَا هِيَ إِلَّا
ذِكْرٰى لِلْبَشَرِ

R. 2.

33. Nay, by the moon,

كَلَّا وَالْقَمَرِ

34. And *by* the night when it retreats,

وَالَّيْلِ إِذْ أَدْبَرَ

35. And *by* the dawn when it shines forth,

وَالصُّبْحِ إِذَآ أَسْفَرَ

36. Verily, it is one of the greatest *calamities*.

إِنَّهَا لَإِحْدَى الْكُبَرِ

37. A warning to man,

نَذِيرًا لِّلْبَشَرِ

38. To him among you who wishes to advance or hang back.

لِمَنْ شَآءَ مِنْكُمْ أَنْ يَّتَقَدَّمَ أَوْ يَتَأَخَّرَ

39. Every soul is pledged for what it has earned;

كُلُّ نَفْسٍ بِمَا كَسَبَتْ رَهِينَةٌ

40. Except those on the right hand.

إِلَّآ أَصْحٰبَ الْيَمِينِ

41. *They will be* in Gardens asking one another

فِي جَنّٰتٍ يَتَسَآءَلُونَ

42. Concerning the guilty ones.

عَنِ الْمُجْرِمِينَ

* 43. 'What has brought you into the Fire of Hell?'

مَا سَلَكَكُمْ فِي سَقَرَ

44. They will say, 'We were not of those who offered Prayers,

قَالُوا لَمْ نَكُ مِنَ الْمُصَلِّينَ

45. 'Nor did we feed the poor.

وَلَمْ نَكُ نُطْعِمُ الْمِسْكِينَ

46. 'And we indulged in objectionable talk with those who indulge therein.

وَكُنَّا نَخُوضُ مَعَ الْخَآئِضِينَ

47. 'And we used to deny the Day of Judgment,

وَكُنَّا نُكَذِّبُ بِيَوْمِ الدِّينِ

48. 'Until death overtook us.'

حَتّٰى أَتٰىنَا الْيَقِينُ

49. So the intercession of intercessors will not avail them.

فَمَا تَنْفَعُهُمْ شَفَاعَةُ الشّٰفِعِينَ

50. Now what is the matter with them that they are turning away from the exhortation,

فَمَا لَهُمْ عَنِ التَّذْكِرَةِ مُعْرِضِيْنَ ﴿٥٠﴾

51. As if they were frightened asses

كَاَنَّهُمْ حُمُرٌ مُّسْتَنْفِرَةٌ ﴿٥١﴾

52. Fleeing from a lion?

فَرَّتْ مِنْ قَسْوَرَةٍ ﴿٥٢﴾

53. Nay, every man among them desires to have open sheets *of revelation* given to him.

بَلْ يُرِيْدُ كُلُّ امْرِئٍ مِّنْهُمْ اَنْ يُّؤْتٰى صُحُفًا مُّنَشَّرَةً ﴿٥٣﴾

54. Never! verily they fear not the Hereafter.

كَلَّا بَلْ لَّا يَخَافُوْنَ الْاٰخِرَةَ ﴿٥٤﴾

55. Never! verily this is an exhortation.

كَلَّآ اِنَّهٗ تَذْكِرَةٌ ﴿٥٥﴾

56. Let him, then, who will, remember it.

فَمَنْ شَآءَ ذَكَرَهٗ ﴿٥٦﴾

57. And they will not remember unless Allah *so* please. He *alone* is worthy to be feared and He *alone* is worthy to forgive.

وَمَا يَذْكُرُوْنَ اِلَّآ اَنْ يَّشَآءَ اللّٰهُ هُوَ اَهْلُ التَّقْوٰى وَاَهْلُ الْمَغْفِرَةِ ﴿٥٧﴾

سُوْرَةُ الْقِيٰمَةِ مَكِّيَّةٌ (٧٥)

Chapter 75

AL-QIYĀMAH

(Revealed before Hijra)

Part 29

1. In the name of Allah, the Gracious, the Merciful.

بِسْمِ اللّٰهِ الرَّحْمٰنِ الرَّحِيْمِ ﴿١﴾

2. Nay! I call to witness the Day of Resurrection.

لَآ اُقْسِمُ بِيَوْمِ الْقِيٰمَةِ ﴿٢﴾

* 3. And I do call to witness the self-accusing soul, *that the Day of Judgment is a certainty*.

وَلَآ اُقْسِمُ بِالنَّفْسِ اللَّوَّامَةِ ﴿٣﴾

4. Does man think that We shall not assemble his bones?

اَيَحْسَبُ الْاِنْسَانُ اَلَّنْ نَّجْمَعَ عِظَامَهٗ ﴿٤﴾

5. Yea, We have the power to restore his very finger-tips.

بَلٰى قٰدِرِيْنَ عَلٰٓى اَنْ نُّسَوِّيَ بَنَانَهٗ ﴿٥﴾

* 6. But man desires to continue to send forth evil deeds in front of him.

بَلْ يُرِيْدُ الْاِنْسَانُ لِيَفْجُرَ اَمَامَهٗ ﴿٦﴾

7. He asks, 'When will be the Day of Resurrection?'

يَسْـَٔلُ اَيَّانَ يَوْمُ الْقِيٰمَةِ ﴿٧﴾

8. When the eye is dazzled,

فَاِذَا بَرِقَ الْبَصَرُ ﴿٨﴾

9. And the moon is eclipsed,

وَخَسَفَ الْقَمَرُ ﴿٩﴾

10. And the sun and the moon are brought together,

وَجُمِعَ الشَّمْسُ وَالْقَمَرُ ﴿١٠﴾

11. On that day man will say, 'Whither to escape?'

يَقُولُ الْإِنْسَانُ يَوْمَئِذٍ أَيْنَ الْمَفَرُّ ﴿١١﴾

12. Nay! There is no refuge!

كَلَّا لَا وَزَرَ ﴿١٢﴾

13. With thy Lord *alone* will be the place of rest that day.

إِلَىٰ رَبِّكَ يَوْمَئِذٍ الْمُسْتَقَرُّ ﴿١٣﴾

14. That day will man be informed of that which he has sent forward and left behind.

يُنَبَّأُ الْإِنْسَانُ يَوْمَئِذٍ بِمَا قَدَّمَ وَأَخَّرَ ﴿١٤﴾

* 15. Nay, man is a witness against himself;

بَلِ الْإِنْسَانُ عَلَىٰ نَفْسِهِ بَصِيرَةٌ ﴿١٥﴾

16. Even though he puts forward his excuses.

وَلَوْ أَلْقَىٰ مَعَاذِيرَهُ ﴿١٦﴾

17. Move not thy tongue with this *revelation* that thou mayest hasten *to preserve* it.

لَا تُحَرِّكْ بِهِ لِسَانَكَ لِتَعْجَلَ بِهِ ﴿١٧﴾

18. Surely upon Us *rests* its collection and its recital.

إِنَّ عَلَيْنَا جَمْعَهُ وَقُرْآنَهُ ﴿١٨﴾

19. So when We recite it, then follow thou its recital.

فَإِذَا قَرَأْنَاهُ فَاتَّبِعْ قُرْآنَهُ ﴿١٩﴾

20. Then upon Us *rests* the expounding thereof.

ثُمَّ إِنَّ عَلَيْنَا بَيَانَهُ ﴿٢٠﴾

* 21. Nay, but you love the present life;

كَلَّا بَلْ تُحِبُّونَ الْعَاجِلَةَ ﴿٢١﴾

* 22. And you neglect the Hereafter.

وَتَذَرُونَ الْآخِرَةَ ﴿٢٢﴾

23. Some faces on that day will be bright,

وُجُوهٌ يَوْمَئِذٍ نَاضِرَةٌ ﴿٢٣﴾

24. Looking *eagerly* towards their Lord;

إِلَىٰ رَبِّهَا نَاظِرَةٌ ﴿٢٤﴾

25. And some faces on that day will be dismal,

وَوُجُوهٌ يَوْمَئِذٍ بَاسِرَةٌ ﴿٢٥﴾

26. Thinking that a back-breaking calamity is about to befall them.

تَظُنُّ أَنْ يُفْعَلَ بِهَا فَاقِرَةٌ ﴿٢٦﴾

27. Aye! when *the soul of the dying man* comes up to the throat,

كَلَّا إِذَا بَلَغَتِ التَّرَاقِيَ ﴿٢٧﴾

28. And it is said, 'Who is the wizard *to save him?*'

وَقِيلَ مَنْ رَاقٍ ﴿٢٨﴾

29. And he is sure that it is the *hour of* parting;

وَظَنَّ أَنَّهُ الْفِرَاقُ ﴿٢٩﴾

30. And one shank rubs against another shank *in agony;*

وَالْتَفَّتِ السَّاقُ بِالسَّاقِ ﴿٣٠﴾

31. Unto thy Lord that day will be the driving.

إِلَىٰ رَبِّكَ يَوْمَئِذٍ الْمَسَاقُ ﴿٣١﴾

R. 2.

32. For he neither accepted *the truth*, nor offered Prayers;

فَلَا صَدَّقَ وَلَا صَلَّىٰ ﴿٣٢﴾

33. But he rejected *the truth* and turned his back;

وَلَٰكِن كَذَّبَ وَتَوَلَّىٰ ﴿٣٣﴾

34. Then he went to his kinsfolk, strutting along.

ثُمَّ ذَهَبَ إِلَىٰ أَهْلِهِ يَتَمَطَّىٰ ﴿٣٤﴾

35. 'Woe unto thee! and woe again!

أَوْلَىٰ لَكَ فَأَوْلَىٰ ﴿٣٥﴾

36. 'Then woe unto thee! and woe again!'

ثُمَّ أَوْلَىٰ لَكَ فَأَوْلَىٰ ﴿٣٦﴾

* 37. Does man think that he is to be left *to himself* uncontrolled?

أَيَحْسَبُ الْإِنسَانُ أَن يُتْرَكَ سُدًى ﴿٣٧﴾

38. Was he not a drop of fluid, emitted forth?

أَلَمْ يَكُ نُطْفَةً مِّن مَّنِيٍّ يُمْنَىٰ ﴿٣٨﴾

39. Then he became a clot, then He shaped and perfected *him*.

ثُمَّ كَانَ عَلَقَةً فَخَلَقَ فَسَوَّىٰ ﴿٣٩﴾

40. Then He made of him a pair, the male and female.

فَجَعَلَ مِنْهُ الزَّوْجَيْنِ الذَّكَرَ وَالْأُنثَىٰ ﴿٤٠﴾

41. Has not such a One the power to raise the dead to life?

أَلَيْسَ ذَٰلِكَ بِقَادِرٍ عَلَىٰ أَن يُحْيِيَ الْمَوْتَىٰ ﴿٤١﴾

سُورَةُ الدَّهْرِ مَكِّيَّةٌ

آياتها ٣٢ (٧٦) ركوعاتها ٢

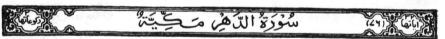

Chapter 76 **AL-DAHR** Part 29

(Revealed before Hijra)

1. In the name of Allah, the Gracious, the Merciful.

بِسْمِ اللَّهِ الرَّحْمَٰنِ الرَّحِيمِ ﴿١﴾

2. There has certainly come upon man a period of time when he was not a thing spoken of.

هَلْ أَتَىٰ عَلَى الْإِنسَانِ حِينٌ مِّنَ الدَّهْرِ لَمْ يَكُن شَيْئًا مَّذْكُورًا ﴿٢﴾

* 3. We have created man from a mingled sperm-drop that We might try him; so We made him hearing, seeing.

إِنَّا خَلَقْنَا الْإِنسَانَ مِن نُّطْفَةٍ أَمْشَاجٍ نَّبْتَلِيهِ فَجَعَلْنَاهُ سَمِيعًا بَصِيرًا ﴿٣﴾

4. We have shown him the Way, whether he be grateful or ungrateful.

إِنَّا هَدَيْنَاهُ السَّبِيلَ إِمَّا شَاكِرًا وَإِمَّا كَفُورًا ﴿٤﴾

5. Verily, We have prepared for the disbelievers chains and iron-collars and a blazing Fire.

إِنَّا أَعْتَدْنَا لِلْكَافِرِينَ سَلَاسِلَ وَأَغْلَالًا وَسَعِيرًا ﴿٥﴾

6. But the virtuous drink of a cup, tempered with camphor—

إِنَّ الْأَبْرَارَ يَشْرَبُونَ مِنْ كَأْسٍ كَانَ مِزَاجُهَا كَافُورًا ﴿٦﴾

7. A spring wherefrom the servants of Allah drink. They make it gush forth—a forceful gushing forth.

عَيْنًا يَشْرَبُ بِهَا عِبَادُ اللّٰهِ يُفَجِّرُونَهَا تَفْجِيرًا ﴿٧﴾

8. They fulfil *their* vow, and fear a day the evil of which is widespread.

يُوفُونَ بِالنَّذْرِ وَيَخَافُونَ يَوْمًا كَانَ شَرُّهُ مُسْتَطِيرًا ﴿٨﴾

9. And they feed, for love of Him, the poor, the orphan, and the prisoner,

وَيُطْعِمُونَ الطَّعَامَ عَلٰى حُبِّهِ مِسْكِينًا وَّيَتِيمًا وَّأَسِيرًا ﴿٩﴾

10. *Saying*, 'We feed you for Allah's pleasure *only*. We desire no reward nor thanks from you.

إِنَّمَا نُطْعِمُكُمْ لِوَجْهِ اللّٰهِ لَا نُرِيدُ مِنْكُمْ جَزَآءً وَّلَا شُكُورًا ﴿١٠﴾

11. 'Verily, we fear from our Lord a frowning and distressful day.'

إِنَّا نَخَافُ مِنْ رَّبِّنَا يَوْمًا عَبُوسًا قَمْطَرِيرًا ﴿١١﴾

12. So Allah will save them from the evil of that day, and will grant them cheerfulness and happiness.

فَوَقٰهُمُ اللّٰهُ شَرَّ ذٰلِكَ الْيَوْمِ وَلَقّٰهُمْ نَضْرَةً وَّسُرُورًا ﴿١٢﴾

13. And He will reward them, for their steadfastness, with a Garden and *a raiment of* silk,

وَجَزٰهُمْ بِمَا صَبَرُوا جَنَّةً وَّحَرِيرًا ﴿١٣﴾

14. Reclining therein upon couches, they will find there neither excessive heat nor excessive cold.

مُّتَّكِـِٔينَ فِيهَا عَلَى الْأَرَآئِكِ لَا يَرَوْنَ فِيهَا شَمْسًا وَّلَا زَمْهَرِيرًا ﴿١٤﴾

15. And its shades will be close over them, and its clustered fruits will be brought within easy reach.

وَدَانِيَةً عَلَيْهِمْ ظِلٰلُهَا وَذُلِّلَتْ قُطُوفُهَا تَذْلِيلًا ﴿١٥﴾

16. And vessels of silver will be passed round among them, and *also* goblets of glass,

وَيُطَافُ عَلَيْهِمْ بِاٰنِيَةٍ مِّنْ فِضَّةٍ وَّأَكْوَابٍ كَانَتْ قَوَارِيرَا۠ ﴿١٦﴾

* 17. *Bright as* glass *but made* of silver, which they will measure according to *their own* measure.

قَوَارِيرَا۠ مِنْ فِضَّةٍ قَدَّرُوهَا تَقْدِيرًا ﴿١٧﴾

18. And therein will they be given to drink a cup tempered with ginger,

وَيُسْقَوْنَ فِيهَا كَأْسًا كَانَ مِزَاجُهَا زَنْجَبِيلًا ﴿١٨﴾

19. *From* a spring therein named Salsabīl.

عَيْنًا فِيهَا تُسَمّٰى سَلْسَبِيلًا ﴿١٩﴾

20. And there will wait upon them youths who will not age. When thou seest

وَيَطُوفُ عَلَيْهِمْ وِلْدَانٌ مُّخَلَّدُونَ ۚ إِذَا رَأَيْتَهُمْ

them, thou thinkest them to be pearls scattered about.

حَسِبْتَهُمْ لُؤْلُؤًا مَّنْثُوْرًا ﴿٢٠﴾

21. And when thou seest thou wilt see there a bliss and a great kingdom.

وَإِذَا رَأَيْتَ ثَمَّ رَأَيْتَ نَعِيْمًا وَّمُلْكًا كَبِيْرًا ﴿٢١﴾

* 22. On them will be garments of fine green silk and thick brocade. And they will be made to wear bracelets of silver. And their Lord will give them to drink a pure beverage.

عٰلِيَهُمْ ثِيَابُ سُنْدُسٍ خُضْرٌ وَّإِسْتَبْرَقٌ وَّحُلُّوْٓا أَسَاوِرَ مِنْ فِضَّةٍ ۚ وَسَقٰهُمْ رَبُّهُمْ شَرَابًا طَهُوْرًا ﴿٢٢﴾

23. 'This is your reward, and your labour has been appreciated.'

ع إِنَّ هٰذَا كَانَ لَكُمْ جَزَآءً وَّكَانَ سَعْيُكُمْ مَّشْكُوْرًا ﴿٢٣﴾

R. 2.

24. Surely, We have revealed unto thee the Qur'ān piecemeal.

إِنَّا نَحْنُ نَزَّلْنَا عَلَيْكَ الْقُرْاٰنَ تَنْزِيْلًا ﴿٢٤﴾

25. So wait patiently for the judgment of thy Lord, and yield not to any one among them *who is* sinful or ungrateful.

فَاصْبِرْ لِحُكْمِ رَبِّكَ وَلَا تُطِعْ مِنْهُمْ اٰثِمًا أَوْ كَفُوْرًا ﴿٢٥﴾

26. And remember the name of thy Lord morning and evening.

وَاذْكُرِ اسْمَ رَبِّكَ بُكْرَةً وَّأَصِيْلًا ﴿٢٦﴾

27. And during the night prostrate thyself before Him, and extol His glory for *a* long *part of the* night.

وَمِنَ الَّيْلِ فَاسْجُدْ لَهٗ وَسَبِّحْهُ لَيْلًا طَوِيْلًا ﴿٢٧﴾

28. Verily, these *people* love the present life, and they neglect the hard day *that is* before them.

إِنَّ هٰٓؤُلَآءِ يُحِبُّوْنَ الْعَاجِلَةَ وَيَذَرُوْنَ وَرَآءَهُمْ يَوْمًا ثَقِيْلًا ﴿٢٨﴾

29. We have created them and strengthened their make; and when We will, We can replace them by others like them.

نَحْنُ خَلَقْنٰهُمْ وَشَدَدْنَآ أَسْرَهُمْ ۚ وَإِذَا شِئْنَا بَدَّلْنَآ أَمْثَالَهُمْ تَبْدِيْلًا ﴿٢٩﴾

30. Verily, this is a Reminder. So whoever wishes, may take a way unto his Lord.

إِنَّ هٰذِهٖ تَذْكِرَةٌ ۚ فَمَنْ شَآءَ اتَّخَذَ إِلٰى رَبِّهٖ سَبِيْلًا ﴿٣٠﴾

* 31. And you exercise your will because Allah has *so* willed. Verily, Allah is All-Knowing, Wise.

وَمَا تَشَآءُوْنَ إِلَّآ أَنْ يَّشَآءَ اللّٰهُ ۚ إِنَّ اللّٰهَ كَانَ عَلِيْمًا حَكِيْمًا ﴿٣١﴾

32. He causes whom He pleases to enter His mercy, and for the wrongdoers He has prepared a painful punishment.

ع يُّدْخِلُ مَنْ يَّشَآءُ فِيْ رَحْمَتِهٖ ۚ وَالظّٰلِمِيْنَ أَعَدَّ لَهُمْ عَذَابًا أَلِيْمًا ﴿٣٢﴾

سُوْرَةُ الْمُرْسَلٰتِ مَكِّيَّةٌ (٧٧)

AL-MURSALĀT

(Revealed before Hijra)

1. In the name of Allah, the Gracious, the Merciful.

بِسْمِ اللّٰهِ الرَّحْمٰنِ الرَّحِيْمِ ۝١

* 2. By *the angels* who are sent forth with goodness,

وَالْمُرْسَلٰتِ عُرْفًا ۝٢

* 3. *And* then they push on with a forceful pushing,

فَالْعٰصِفٰتِ عَصْفًا ۝٣

* 4. And by *the forces* that spread *the truth*, a good spreading,

وَّالنّٰشِرٰتِ نَشْرًا ۝٤

* 5. *And* then they distinguish fully *between good and evil.*

فَالْفٰرِقٰتِ فَرْقًا ۝٥

* 6. Then they carry the exhortation *far and wide*

فَالْمُلْقِيٰتِ ذِكْرًا ۝٦

* 7. To excuse *some* and warn *others*.

عُذْرًا اَوْ نُذْرًا ۝٧

8. Verily, that which you are promised must come to pass.

اِنَّمَا تُوْعَدُوْنَ لَوَاقِعٌ ۝٨

9. So when the stars are made to lose *their* light,

فَاِذَا النُّجُوْمُ طُمِسَتْ ۝٩

10. And when the heaven is rent asunder,

وَاِذَا السَّمَآءُ فُرِجَتْ ۝١٠

11. And when the mountains are blown away,

وَاِذَا الْجِبَالُ نُسِفَتْ ۝١١

12. And when the Messengers are made to appear at the appointed time—

وَاِذَا الرُّسُلُ اُقِّتَتْ ۝١٢

13. For what day has the time *of these happenings* been appointed?

لِاَيِّ يَوْمٍ اُجِّلَتْ ۝١٣

14. For the Day of Decision.

لِيَوْمِ الْفَصْلِ ۝١٤

15. And what should make thee know what the Day of Decision is!—

وَمَآ اَدْرٰىكَ مَا يَوْمُ الْفَصْلِ ۝١٥

16. Woe on that day unto those who reject *the truth*!

وَيْلٌ يَّوْمَئِذٍ لِّلْمُكَذِّبِيْنَ ۝١٦

17. Did We not destroy the earlier peoples?

اَلَمْ نُهْلِكِ الْاَوَّلِيْنَ ۝١٧

18. We will now cause the later ones to follow them.

ثُمَّ نُتْبِعُهُمُ الْاٰخِرِيْنَ ۝١٨

19. Thus do We deal with the guilty.

كَذٰلِكَ نَفْعَلُ بِالْمُجْرِمِيْنَ ۝١٩

20. Woe on that day unto those who reject *the truth!*

وَيْلٌ يَّوْمَئِذٍ لِّلْمُكَذِّبِيْنَ ۝٢٠

21. Did We not create you from an insignificant fluid,

اَلَمْ نَخْلُقْكُّمْ مِّنْ مَّآءٍ مَّهِيْنٍ ۝٢١

22. And We placed it in a safe place,

فَجَعَلْنٰهُ فِيْ قَرَارٍ مَّكِيْنٍ ۝٢٢

23. For a known measure *of time?*

اِلٰى قَدَرٍ مَّعْلُوْمٍ ۝٢٣

24. Thus did We measure, and how excellently do We measure!

فَقَدَرْنَا ۖ فَنِعْمَ الْقٰدِرُوْنَ ۝٢٤

25. Woe on that day unto those who reject *the truth!*

وَيْلٌ يَّوْمَئِذٍ لِّلْمُكَذِّبِيْنَ ۝٢٥

26. Have We not made the earth so as to hold

اَلَمْ نَجْعَلِ الْاَرْضَ كِفَاتًا ۝٢٦

27. The living and the dead?

اَحْيَآءً وَّاَمْوَاتًا ۝٢٧

28. And We placed thereon high mountains, and gave you sweet water to drink.

وَّجَعَلْنَا فِيْهَا رَوَاسِيَ شٰمِخٰتٍ وَّاَسْقَيْنٰكُمْ مَّآءً فُرَاتًا ۝٢٨

29. Woe on that day unto those who reject *the truth!*

وَيْلٌ يَّوْمَئِذٍ لِّلْمُكَذِّبِيْنَ ۝٢٩

30. 'Now move on towards that which you treated as a lie,

اِنْطَلِقُوْٓا اِلٰى مَا كُنْتُمْ بِهٖ تُكَذِّبُوْنَ ۝٣٠

31. '*Aye*, move on towards a shadow which has three sections,

اِنْطَلِقُوْٓا اِلٰى ظِلٍّ ذِيْ ثَلٰثِ شُعَبٍ ۝٣١

32. 'Neither affording shade, nor protecting from the flame.'

لَّا ظَلِيْلٍ وَّلَا يُغْنِيْ مِنَ اللَّهَبِ ۝٣٢

* 33. It throws up sparks like *huge* castles,

اِنَّهَا تَرْمِيْ بِشَرَرٍ كَالْقَصْرِ ۝٣٣

* 34. As if they were camels of dim colour.

كَاَنَّهٗ جِمٰلَتٌ صُفْرٌ ۝٣٤

35. Woe on that day unto those who reject *the truth!*

وَيْلٌ يَّوْمَئِذٍ لِّلْمُكَذِّبِيْنَ ۝٣٥

36. This is a day when they shall not *be able to* speak;

هٰذَا يَوْمُ لَا يَنْطِقُوْنَ ۝٣٦

37. Nor shall they be permitted to offer excuses.

وَلَا يُؤْذَنُ لَهُمْ فَيَعْتَذِرُوْنَ ۝٣٧

38. Woe on that day unto those who reject *the truth!*

وَيْلٌ يَّوْمَئِذٍ لِّلْمُكَذِّبِيْنَ ۝٣٨

39. 'This is the Day of Decision; We have gathered you and all the earlier peoples together.

هٰذَا يَوْمُ الْفَصْلِ ۚ جَمَعْنٰكُمْ وَالْاَوَّلِيْنَ ۝٣٩

40. 'If now you have any stratagem, use it against Me.'

فَاِنْ كَانَ لَكُمْ كَيْدٌ فَكِيْدُوْنِ ۝٤٠

41. Woe on that day unto those who reject *the truth!*

وَيْلٌ يَّوْمَئِذٍ لِّلْمُكَذِّبِيْنَ ﴿٤١﴾

R. 2.

42. The righteous will be in *the midst of* shades and springs,

إِنَّ الْمُتَّقِيْنَ فِيْ ظِلٰلٍ وَّعُيُوْنٍ ﴿٤٢﴾

43. And fruits, such as they will desire.

وَّفَوَاكِهَ مِمَّا يَشْتَهُوْنَ ﴿٤٣﴾

44. 'Eat and drink pleasantly as a reward for what you did.'

كُلُوْا وَاشْرَبُوْا هَنِيْٓـًٔا بِمَا كُنْتُمْ تَعْمَلُوْنَ ﴿٤٤﴾

45. Thus surely do We reward those who do good.

إِنَّا كَذٰلِكَ نَجْزِي الْمُحْسِنِيْنَ ﴿٤٥﴾

46. Woe on that day unto those who reject *the truth!*

وَيْلٌ يَّوْمَئِذٍ لِّلْمُكَذِّبِيْنَ ﴿٤٦﴾

47. 'Eat and enjoy yourselves a little while *in this world, O rejectors of truth*; surely you are the guilty ones.'

كُلُوْا وَتَمَتَّعُوْا قَلِيْلًا إِنَّكُمْ مُّجْرِمُوْنَ ﴿٤٧﴾

48. Woe on that day unto those who reject *the truth!*

وَيْلٌ يَّوْمَئِذٍ لِّلْمُكَذِّبِيْنَ ﴿٤٨﴾

49. And when it is said unto them, 'Bow down,' they do not bow down.

وَإِذَا قِيْلَ لَهُمُ ارْكَعُوْا لَا يَرْكَعُوْنَ ﴿٤٩﴾

50. Woe on that day unto those who reject *the truth!*

وَيْلٌ يَّوْمَئِذٍ لِّلْمُكَذِّبِيْنَ ﴿٥٠﴾

51. In which word then, after this, will they believe?

فَبِأَيِّ حَدِيْثٍ بَعْدَهٗ يُؤْمِنُوْنَ ﴿٥١﴾

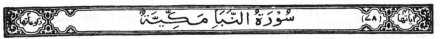

سُوْرَةُ النَّبَإِ مَكِّيَّةٌ

آياتها ٤١ (٧٨) ركوعاتها ٢

Part 30 AL-NABA' Chapter 78

(Revealed before Hijra)

1. In the name of Allah, the Gracious, the Merciful.

بِسْمِ اللّٰهِ الرَّحْمٰنِ الرَّحِيْمِ ﴿١﴾

2. About what do they question one another?

عَمَّ يَتَسَآءَلُوْنَ ﴿٢﴾

* 3. About the great Event,

عَنِ النَّبَإِ الْعَظِيْمِ ﴿٣﴾

4. Concerning which they differ.

الَّذِيْ هُمْ فِيْهِ مُخْتَلِفُوْنَ ﴿٤﴾

5. Nay, soon they will come to know.

كَلَّا سَيَعْلَمُوْنَ ﴿٥﴾

6. Nay, *We say it* again, they will soon come to know.

ثُمَّ كَلَّا سَيَعْلَمُوْنَ ﴿٦﴾

7. Have We not made the earth a bed,

أَلَمْ نَجْعَلِ الْأَرْضَ مِهٰدًا ﴿٧﴾

8. And the mountains as pegs?

وَالْجِبَالَ أَوْتَادًا ﴿٨﴾

9. And We have created you in pairs,

وَخَلَقْنَاكُمْ أَزْوَاجًا ﴿٩﴾

10. And We have made your sleep for rest,

وَجَعَلْنَا نَوْمَكُمْ سُبَاتًا ﴿١٠﴾

11. And We have made the night as a covering,

وَجَعَلْنَا اللَّيْلَ لِبَاسًا ﴿١١﴾

* 12. And We have made the day for the activities of life.

وَجَعَلْنَا النَّهَارَ مَعَاشًا ﴿١٢﴾

13. And We have built over you seven strong *heavens;*

وَبَنَيْنَا فَوْقَكُمْ سَبْعًا شِدَادًا ﴿١٣﴾

14. And We have made *the sun* a bright lamp.

وَجَعَلْنَا سِرَاجًا وَهَّاجًا ﴿١٤﴾

15. And We send down from the dripping clouds water pouring forth abundantly,

وَأَنزَلْنَا مِنَ الْمُعْصِرَاتِ مَاءً ثَجَّاجًا ﴿١٥﴾

16. That We may bring forth thereby grain and vegetation,

لِّنُخْرِجَ بِهِ حَبًّا وَنَبَاتًا ﴿١٦﴾

17. And gardens of luxuriant growth.

وَجَنَّاتٍ أَلْفَافًا ﴿١٧﴾

18. Surely, the Day of Decision has an appointed time:

إِنَّ يَوْمَ الْفَصْلِ كَانَ مِيقَاتًا ﴿١٨﴾

* 19. The day when the trumpet will be blown; and you will come in large groups;

يَوْمَ يُنفَخُ فِي الصُّورِ فَتَأْتُونَ أَفْوَاجًا ﴿١٩﴾

20. And the heaven shall be opened and shall become *all* doors;

وَفُتِحَتِ السَّمَاءُ فَكَانَتْ أَبْوَابًا ﴿٢٠﴾

21. And the mountains shall be made to move and shall become *as if they were* a mirage.

وَسُيِّرَتِ الْجِبَالُ فَكَانَتْ سَرَابًا ﴿٢١﴾

22. Surely Hell lies in ambush,

إِنَّ جَهَنَّمَ كَانَتْ مِرْصَادًا ﴿٢٢﴾

23. A home for the rebellious,

لِّلطَّاغِينَ مَآبًا ﴿٢٣﴾

24. Who will tarry therein for ages.

لَّابِثِينَ فِيهَا أَحْقَابًا ﴿٢٤﴾

* 25. They will taste therein neither sleep nor drink,

لَّا يَذُوقُونَ فِيهَا بَرْدًا وَلَا شَرَابًا ﴿٢٥﴾

* 26. Save boiling water and a stinking fluid —

إِلَّا حَمِيمًا وَغَسَّاقًا ﴿٢٦﴾

* 27. A meet requital.

جَزَاءً وِفَاقًا ﴿٢٧﴾

28. Verily, they feared not the reckoning,

إِنَّهُمْ كَانُوا لَا يَرْجُونَ حِسَابًا ﴿٢٨﴾

29. And rejected Our Signs totally.

وَكَذَّبُوا بِآيَاتِنَا كِذَّابًا ﴿٢٩﴾

30. And every thing have We recorded in a Book.

وَكُلَّ شَيْءٍ أَحْصَيْنَٰهُ كِتَٰبًا ﴿٣٠﴾

31. 'Taste ye therefore *the punishment:* We will give you no increase except in torment.'

ع فَذُوقُوا فَلَن نَّزِيدَكُمْ إِلَّا عَذَابًا ﴿٣١﴾

R. 2.

32. Verily, for the righteous is a triumph:

إِنَّ لِلْمُتَّقِينَ مَفَازًا ﴿٣٢﴾

33. Walled gardens and grape-vines,

حَدَآئِقَ وَأَعْنَٰبًا ﴿٣٣﴾

34. And young maidens of equal age,

وَكَوَاعِبَ أَتْرَابًا ﴿٣٤﴾

35. And overflowing cups.

وَكَأْسًا دِهَاقًا ﴿٣٥﴾

36. Therein they will hear no idle talk nor lying:

لَّا يَسْمَعُونَ فِيهَا لَغْوًا وَلَا كِذَّٰبًا ﴿٣٦﴾

37. A recompense from thy Lord—a gift in proportion *to their works*—

جَزَآءً مِّن رَّبِّكَ عَطَآءً حِسَابًا ﴿٣٧﴾

* 38. Lord of the heavens and the earth and all that is between them, the Gracious. They shall not have the power to address Him.

رَّبِّ السَّمَٰوَٰتِ وَالْأَرْضِ وَمَا بَيْنَهُمَا الرَّحْمَٰنِ
لَا يَمْلِكُونَ مِنْهُ خِطَابًا ﴿٣٨﴾

39. On the day when the Spirit and the angels will stand in rows, they shall not speak, except he whom the Gracious *God* will permit and who will speak only what is right.

يَوْمَ يَقُومُ الرُّوحُ وَالْمَلَٰٓئِكَةُ صَفًّا لَّا يَتَكَلَّمُونَ
إِلَّا مَنْ أَذِنَ لَهُ الرَّحْمَٰنُ وَقَالَ صَوَابًا ﴿٣٩﴾

40. That day is sure to come. So let him, who will, seek recourse unto his Lord.

ذَٰلِكَ الْيَوْمُ الْحَقُّ فَمَن شَآءَ اتَّخَذَ إِلَىٰ رَبِّهِ
مَـَٔابًا ﴿٤٠﴾

41. Verily, We have warned you of a punishment which is near at hand: a day when man will see what his hands have sent on before, and the disbeliever will say, 'Would that I were mere dust!'

إِنَّآ أَنذَرْنَٰكُمْ عَذَابًا قَرِيبًا يَوْمَ يَنظُرُ الْمَرْءُ
ع مَا قَدَّمَتْ يَدَاهُ وَيَقُولُ الْكَافِرُ يَٰلَيْتَنِي كُنتُ تُرَٰبًا ﴿٤١﴾

آياتها ٤٧ سُورَةُ النَّازِعَاتِ مَكِّيَّةٌ (٧٩) ركوعاتها ٢

Part 30 AL-NĀZI'ĀT Chapter 79

(Revealed before Hijra)

1. In the name of Allah, the Gracious, the Merciful.

بِسْمِ اللَّهِ الرَّحْمَٰنِ الرَّحِيمِ ﴿١﴾

* 2. By those beings who draw *people to true faith* vigorously,

وَالنَّٰزِعَٰتِ غَرْقًا ﴿٢﴾

* 3. And *by* those who tie *their* knots firmly,	وَّالنّٰشِطٰتِ نَشۡطًا ﴿٣﴾	
* 4. And *by* those who glide along swiftly,	وَّالسّٰبِحٰتِ سَبۡحًا ﴿٤﴾	
* 5. Then they *advance* and greatly excel *others*,	فَالسّٰبِقٰتِ سَبۡقًا ﴿٥﴾	
* 6. Then they manage the affair *entrusted to them*.	فَالۡمُدَبِّرٰتِ اَمۡرًا ﴿٦﴾	لازم
7. *This will happen* on the day when the quaking *earth* shall quake,	يَوۡمَ تَرۡجُفُ الرَّاجِفَةُ ﴿٧﴾	
8. And a second *quaking* shall follow it.	تَتۡبَعُهَا الرَّادِفَةُ ﴿٨﴾	
9. On that day hearts will tremble,	قُلُوۡبٌ يَّوۡمَئِذٍ وَّاجِفَةٌ ﴿٩﴾	
10. *And* their eyes will be cast down—	اَبۡصَارُهَا خَاشِعَةٌ ﴿١٠﴾	لازم
11. They say, 'Shall we *really* be restored to our former state?	يَقُوۡلُوۡنَ ءَاِنَّا لَمَرۡدُوۡدُوۡنَ فِى الۡحَافِرَةِ ﴿١١﴾	
12. 'What! even when we are rotten bones?'	ءَاِذَا كُنَّا عِظَامًا نَّخِرَةً ﴿١٢﴾	
13. They say, 'Then that indeed would be a losing return.'	قَالُوۡا تِلۡكَ اِذًا كَرَّةٌ خَاسِرَةٌ ﴿١٣﴾	لازم
14. It will only be a single cry,	فَاِنَّمَا هِىَ زَجۡرَةٌ وَّاحِدَةٌ ﴿١٤﴾	
15. And behold! they will *all come out* in the open.	فَاِذَا هُمۡ بِالسَّاهِرَةِ ﴿١٥﴾	
16. Has the story of Moses reached thee?	هَلۡ اَتٰٮكَ حَدِيۡثُ مُوۡسٰى ﴿١٦﴾	لازم
17. When his Lord called him in the holy Valley of Ṭuwā, *saying*,	اِذۡ نَادٰٮهُ رَبُّهٗ بِالۡوَادِ الۡمُقَدَّسِ طُوًى ﴿١٧﴾	
18. "Go thou to Pharaoh; he has rebelled.	اِذۡهَبۡ اِلٰى فِرۡعَوۡنَ اِنَّهٗ طَغٰى ﴿١٨﴾	
19. "And say *to him*, 'Wouldst thou *like to* be purified?	فَقُلۡ هَلۡ لَّكَ اِلٰٓى اَنۡ تَزَكّٰى ﴿١٩﴾	
20. 'And I will guide thee to thy Lord so that thou mayest fear Him.' "	وَاَهۡدِيَكَ اِلٰى رَبِّكَ فَتَخۡشٰى ﴿٢٠﴾	
21. So he showed him the great Sign,	فَاَرٰٮهُ الۡاٰيَةَ الۡكُبۡرٰى ﴿٢١﴾	
22. But he rejected *him* and disobeyed.	فَكَذَّبَ وَعَصٰى ﴿٢٢﴾	
23. Then he turned away *from Moses*, striving *against him*.	ثُمَّ اَدۡبَرَ يَسۡعٰى ﴿٢٣﴾	
24. And he gathered *his people* and proclaimed,	فَحَشَرَ فَنَادٰى ﴿٢٤﴾	

25. Saying, 'I am your Lord, the most high.'

فَقَالَ أَنَا رَبُّكُمُ الْأَعْلَىٰ ﴿٢٥﴾

26. So Allah seized him for the punishment of the Hereafter and the present world.

فَأَخَذَهُ اللَّهُ نَكَالَ الْآخِرَةِ وَالْأُولَىٰ ﴿٢٦﴾

27. Therein surely is a lesson for him who fears.

إِنَّ فِي ذَٰلِكَ لَعِبْرَةً لِّمَن يَخْشَىٰ ﴿٢٧﴾

R. 2.

28. Are you harder to create or the heaven that He has built?

ءَأَنتُمْ أَشَدُّ خَلْقًا أَمِ السَّمَاءُ ۚ بَنَاهَا ﴿٢٨﴾

29. He has raised the height thereof and made it perfect.

رَفَعَ سَمْكَهَا فَسَوَّاهَا ﴿٢٩﴾

30. And He has made its night dark, and has brought forth the morn thereof;

وَأَغْطَشَ لَيْلَهَا وَأَخْرَجَ ضُحَاهَا ﴿٣٠﴾

31. And the earth, along with it, He spread forth.

وَالْأَرْضَ بَعْدَ ذَٰلِكَ دَحَاهَا ﴿٣١﴾

32. He produced therefrom its water and its pasture,

أَخْرَجَ مِنْهَا مَاءَهَا وَمَرْعَاهَا ﴿٣٢﴾

33. And the mountains, He made them firm.

وَالْجِبَالَ أَرْسَاهَا ﴿٣٣﴾

34. *All this is* a provision for you and for your cattle.

مَتَاعًا لَّكُمْ وَلِأَنْعَامِكُمْ ﴿٣٤﴾

35. But when the great disaster comes,

فَإِذَا جَاءَتِ الطَّامَّةُ الْكُبْرَىٰ ﴿٣٥﴾

36. The day when man will call to mind *all* that he strove for,

يَوْمَ يَتَذَكَّرُ الْإِنسَانُ مَا سَعَىٰ ﴿٣٦﴾

37. And Hell will be made manifest to him who sees.

وَبُرِّزَتِ الْجَحِيمُ لِمَن يَرَىٰ ﴿٣٧﴾

38. Then, as for him who rebels,

فَأَمَّا مَن طَغَىٰ ﴿٣٨﴾

39. And who chooses the life of this world,

وَآثَرَ الْحَيَاةَ الدُّنْيَا ﴿٣٩﴾

40. The Fire of Hell shall surely be *his* home.

فَإِنَّ الْجَحِيمَ هِيَ الْمَأْوَىٰ ﴿٤٠﴾

41. But as for him who fears to stand before his Lord, and restrains his soul from evil desires,

وَأَمَّا مَنْ خَافَ مَقَامَ رَبِّهِ وَنَهَى النَّفْسَ عَنِ
الْهَوَىٰ ﴿٤١﴾

42. The Garden shall surely be *his* home.

فَإِنَّ الْجَنَّةَ هِيَ الْمَأْوَىٰ ﴿٤٢﴾

43. They ask thee concerning the Hour: 'When will it come?'

يَسْأَلُونَكَ عَنِ السَّاعَةِ أَيَّانَ مُرْسَاهَا ﴿٤٣﴾

44. But what hast thou to do with the mentioning thereof?

فِيمَ أَنتَ مِن ذِكْرَاهَا ﴿٤٤﴾

45. The ultimate knowledge of it *rests* with thy Lord.

إِلَىٰ رَبِّكَ مُنتَهَاهَا ﴿٤٥﴾

46. Thou art only a Warner unto him who fears it.

إِنَّمَآ أَنْتَ مُنْذِرُ مَنْ يَّخْشٰهَا ﴿٤٦﴾

47. On the day when they see it, *they will feel* as if they had not tarried *in the world* but an evening or a morn thereof.

كَأَنَّهُمْ يَوْمَ يَرَوْنَهَا لَمْ يَلْبَثُوٓا إِلَّا عَشِيَّةً أَوْ ضُحٰهَا ﴿٤٧﴾ ع

سُوْرَةُ عَبَسَ مَكِّيَّةٌ

اٰيَاتُهَا ٤٢ (٨٠) رُكُوْعُهَا ١

(Revealed before Hijra)

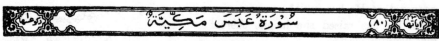

1. In the name of Allah, the Gracious, the Merciful.

بِسْمِ اللّٰهِ الرَّحْمٰنِ الرَّحِيْمِ ﴿١﴾

2. He frowned and turned aside,

عَبَسَ وَتَوَلّٰىٓ ﴿٢﴾

3. Because there came to him the blind man.

أَنْ جَآءَهُ الْأَعْمٰى ﴿٣﴾

4. And what makes thee know that he may be seeking to purify himself,

وَمَا يُدْرِيْكَ لَعَلَّهٗ يَزَّكّٰىٓ ﴿٤﴾

5. Or he may take heed and the Reminder may benefit him?

أَوْ يَذَّكَّرُ فَتَنْفَعَهُ الذِّكْرٰى ﴿٥﴾

6. As for him who is disdainfully indifferent,

أَمَّا مَنِ اسْتَغْنٰى ﴿٦﴾

7. Unto him thou dost pay attention,

فَأَنْتَ لَهٗ تَصَدّٰى ﴿٧﴾

8. Though thou art not responsible if he does not become purified.

وَمَا عَلَيْكَ أَلَّا يَزَّكّٰى ﴿٨﴾

9. But he who comes to thee hastening,

وَأَمَّا مَنْ جَآءَكَ يَسْعٰى ﴿٩﴾

10. And he fears *God*,

وَهُوَ يَخْشٰى ﴿١٠﴾

11. Him dost thou neglect.

فَأَنْتَ عَنْهُ تَلَهّٰى ﴿١١﴾

12. Nay! surely it is a Reminder—

كَلَّآ إِنَّهَا تَذْكِرَةٌ ﴿١٢﴾

13. So let him who desires pay heed to it—

فَمَنْ شَآءَ ذَكَرَهٗ ﴿١٣﴾ وقف لازم

14. On honoured sheets,

فِيْ صُحُفٍ مُّكَرَّمَةٍ ﴿١٤﴾

15. Exalted, purified,

مَّرْفُوْعَةٍ مُّطَهَّرَةٍ ﴿١٥﴾

16. In the hands of writers,

بِأَيْدِي سَفَرَةٍ ﴿١٦﴾

17. Noble *and* virtuous.

كِرَامٍ بَرَرَةٍ ﴿١٧﴾

18. Ruin seize the man! how ungrateful he is!

قُتِلَ الْإِنْسَانُ مَا أَكْفَرَهُ ﴿١٨﴾

19. Of what does He create him?

مِنْ أَيِّ شَيْءٍ خَلَقَهُ ﴿١٩﴾

20. Of a sperm-drop! He creates him and proportions him;

مِنْ نُطْفَةٍ خَلَقَهُ فَقَدَّرَهُ ﴿٢٠﴾

21. Then He makes the Way easy for him,

ثُمَّ السَّبِيلَ يَسَّرَهُ ﴿٢١﴾

22. Then He causes him to die and assigns a grave to him;

ثُمَّ أَمَاتَهُ فَأَقْبَرَهُ ﴿٢٢﴾

23. Then, when He pleases, He will raise him up again.

ثُمَّ إِذَا شَاءَ أَنْشَرَهُ ﴿٢٣﴾

24. Nay! he has not yet done what He commanded him *to do*.

كَلَّا لَمَّا يَقْضِ مَا أَمَرَهُ ﴿٢٤﴾

25. Now let man look at his food:

فَلْيَنْظُرِ الْإِنْسَانُ إِلَىٰ طَعَامِهِ ﴿٢٥﴾

26. How We pour down water in abundance,

أَنَّا صَبَبْنَا الْمَاءَ صَبًّا ﴿٢٦﴾

27. Then We cleave the earth—a proper cleaving—

ثُمَّ شَقَقْنَا الْأَرْضَ شَقًّا ﴿٢٧﴾

28. Then We cause to grow therein grain,

فَأَنْبَتْنَا فِيهَا حَبًّا ﴿٢٨﴾

29. And grapes and vegetables,

وَعِنَبًا وَقَضْبًا ﴿٢٩﴾

30. And the olive and the date-palm.

وَزَيْتُونًا وَنَخْلًا ﴿٣٠﴾

31. And walled gardens thickly planted,

وَحَدَائِقَ غُلْبًا ﴿٣١﴾

32. And fruits and herbage,

وَفَاكِهَةً وَأَبًّا ﴿٣٢﴾

33. Provision for you and your cattle.

مَتَاعًا لَكُمْ وَلِأَنْعَامِكُمْ ﴿٣٣﴾

34. But when the deafening shout comes,

فَإِذَا جَاءَتِ الصَّاخَّةُ ﴿٣٤﴾

35. On the day when a man flees from his brother,

يَوْمَ يَفِرُّ الْمَرْءُ مِنْ أَخِيهِ ﴿٣٥﴾

36. And *from* his mother and his father,

وَأُمِّهِ وَأَبِيهِ ﴿٣٦﴾

37. And *from* his wife and his sons,

وَصَاحِبَتِهِ وَبَنِيهِ ﴿٣٧﴾

38. Every man among them that day will have concern enough to make him indifferent *to others.*

لِكُلِّ امْرِئٍ مِّنْهُمْ يَوْمَئِذٍ شَأْنٌ يُّغْنِيهِ ۝٣٨

39. On that day some faces will be bright,

وُجُوهٌ يَّوْمَئِذٍ مُّسْفِرَةٌ ۝٣٩

40. Laughing, joyous!

ضَاحِكَةٌ مُّسْتَبْشِرَةٌ ۝٤٠

41. And some faces, on that day, will have dust upon them,

وَوُجُوهٌ يَّوْمَئِذٍ عَلَيْهَا غَبَرَةٌ ۝٤١

42. Darkness will cover them.

تَرْهَقُهَا قَتَرَةٌ ۝٤٢

43. Those are the ones that disbelieved *and* were wicked.

أُولَٰئِكَ هُمُ الْكَفَرَةُ الْفَجَرَةُ ۝٤٣ ع

سُوْرَةُ التَّكْوِيرِ مَكِّيَّةٌ

آياتها ٣٠ (٨١) ركوعها ١

Chapter 81 AL-TAKWĪR Part 30

(Revealed before Hijra)

1. In the name of Allah, the Gracious, the Merciful.

بِسْمِ اللّٰهِ الرَّحْمٰنِ الرَّحِيْمِ ۝١

2. When the sun is wrapped up,

إِذَا الشَّمْسُ كُوِّرَتْ ۝٢

3. And when the stars are obscured,

وَإِذَا النُّجُومُ انْكَدَرَتْ ۝٣

4. And when the mountains are made to move,

وَإِذَا الْجِبَالُ سُيِّرَتْ ۝٤

5. And when the she-camels, ten-month pregnant, are abandoned,

وَإِذَا الْعِشَارُ عُطِّلَتْ ۝٥

6. And when the beasts are gathered together,

وَإِذَا الْوُحُوشُ حُشِرَتْ ۝٦

7. And when the seas are made to flow forth *one into the other,*

وَإِذَا الْبِحَارُ سُجِّرَتْ ۝٧

8. And when people are brought together,

وَإِذَا النُّفُوسُ زُوِّجَتْ ۝٨

9. And when the girl-child buried alive is questioned about,

وَإِذَا الْمَوْءُدَةُ سُئِلَتْ ۝٩

10. 'For what crime was she killed?'

بِأَيِّ ذَنْبٍ قُتِلَتْ ۝١٠

11. And when books are spread abroad,

وَإِذَا الصُّحُفُ نُشِرَتْ ۝١١

12. And when the heaven is laid bare,

وَإِذَا السَّمَاءُ كُشِطَتْ ۝١٢

13. And when the Fire is caused to blaze up,

وَإِذَا الْجَحِيمُ سُعِّرَتْ ﴿١٣﴾

14. And when the Garden is brought nigh,

وَإِذَا الْجَنَّةُ أُزْلِفَتْ ﴿١٤﴾

15. Then every soul will know what it has brought forward.

عَلِمَتْ نَفْسٌ مَّا أَحْضَرَتْ ﴿١٥﴾

16. Nay! I call to witness the planets that recede,

فَلَا أُقْسِمُ بِالْخُنَّسِ ﴿١٦﴾

17. Go ahead *and then* hide.

الْجَوَارِ الْكُنَّسِ ﴿١٧﴾

18. And *I call to witness* the night as it passes away,

وَاللَّيْلِ إِذَا عَسْعَسَ ﴿١٨﴾

19. And the dawn as it begins to breathe,

وَالصُّبْحِ إِذَا تَنَفَّسَ ﴿١٩﴾

20. That this is surely the *revealed* word of a noble Messenger,

إِنَّهُ لَقَوْلُ رَسُولٍ كَرِيمٍ ﴿٢٠﴾

21. Possessor of power, established in the presence of the Lord of the Throne,

ذِي قُوَّةٍ عِنْدَ ذِي الْعَرْشِ مَكِينٍ ﴿٢١﴾

22. Obeyed there, *and* faithful to *his* trust.

مُطَاعٍ ثَمَّ أَمِينٍ ﴿٢٢﴾

23. And your companion is not mad.

وَمَا صَاحِبُكُمْ بِمَجْنُونٍ ﴿٢٣﴾

24. And he assuredly saw Him on the clear horizon.

وَلَقَدْ رَآهُ بِالْأُفُقِ الْمُبِينِ ﴿٢٤﴾

25. And he is not niggardly with respect to the unseen.

وَمَا هُوَ عَلَى الْغَيْبِ بِضَنِينٍ ﴿٢٥﴾

26. Nor is this the word of Satan, the rejected.

وَمَا هُوَ بِقَوْلِ شَيْطَانٍ رَجِيمٍ ﴿٢٦﴾

27. Whither, then, are you going?

فَأَيْنَ تَذْهَبُونَ ﴿٢٧﴾

28. It is nothing but a Reminder unto all the worlds,

إِنْ هُوَ إِلَّا ذِكْرٌ لِلْعَالَمِينَ ﴿٢٨﴾

29. Unto such among you as desire to go straight,

لِمَنْ شَاءَ مِنْكُمْ أَنْ يَسْتَقِيمَ ﴿٢٩﴾

30. While you desire not *a thing* except that Allah, the Lord of the worlds, desires *it*.

وَمَا تَشَاءُونَ إِلَّا أَنْ يَشَاءَ اللَّهُ رَبُّ
الْعَالَمِينَ ﴿٣٠﴾ ع

سُوْرَةُ الْاِنْفِطَارِ مَكِّيَّةٌ

اٰيَاتُهَا ٢٠ (٨٢) رُكُوْعُهَا ١

AL-INFIṬĀR

(Revealed before Hijra)

1. In the name of Allah, the Gracious, the Merciful.	بِسْمِ اللّٰهِ الرَّحْمٰنِ الرَّحِيْمِ ﴿١﴾
2. When the heaven is cleft asunder,	إِذَا السَّمَآءُ انْفَطَرَتْ ﴿٢﴾
3. And when the stars are scattered,	وَإِذَا الْكَوَاكِبُ انْتَثَرَتْ ﴿٣﴾
4. And when the rivers are made to flow forth *into canals*,	وَإِذَا الْبِحَارُ فُجِّرَتْ ﴿٤﴾
5. And when the graves are laid open,	وَإِذَا الْقُبُوْرُ بُعْثِرَتْ ﴿٥﴾
6. Each soul shall *then* know what it has sent forth and what it has held back.	عَلِمَتْ نَفْسٌ مَّا قَدَّمَتْ وَأَخَّرَتْ ﴿٦﴾
7. O man, what has emboldened thee against thy Gracious Lord,	يٰٓأَيُّهَا الْإِنْسَانُ مَا غَرَّكَ بِرَبِّكَ الْكَرِيْمِ ﴿٧﴾
8. Who created thee, then perfected thee, then proportioned thee aright?	الَّذِيْ خَلَقَكَ فَسَوّٰىكَ فَعَدَلَكَ ﴿٨﴾
9. In whatever form He pleased, He fashioned thee.	فِيْٓ أَيِّ صُوْرَةٍ مَّا شَآءَ رَكَّبَكَ ﴿٩﴾
10. Nay, but you deny the Judgment.	كَلَّا بَلْ تُكَذِّبُوْنَ بِالدِّيْنِ ﴿١٠﴾
11. But there are guardians over you	وَإِنَّ عَلَيْكُمْ لَحٰفِظِيْنَ ﴿١١﴾
12. Honoured recorders,	كِرَامًا كَاتِبِيْنَ ﴿١٢﴾
13. Who know *all* that you do.	يَعْلَمُوْنَ مَا تَفْعَلُوْنَ ﴿١٣﴾
14. Verily, the virtuous will be in bliss;	إِنَّ الْأَبْرَارَ لَفِيْ نَعِيْمٍ ﴿١٤﴾
15. And the wicked will be in Hell;	وَإِنَّ الْفُجَّارَ لَفِيْ جَحِيْمٍ ﴿١٥﴾
16. They will burn therein on the Day of Judgment;	يَّصْلَوْنَهَا يَوْمَ الدِّيْنِ ﴿١٦﴾
17. And they will not *be able to* escape therefrom.	وَمَا هُمْ عَنْهَا بِغَآئِبِيْنَ ﴿١٧﴾
18. And what should make thee know what the Day of Judgment is!	وَمَآ أَدْرٰىكَ مَا يَوْمُ الدِّيْنِ ﴿١٨﴾
19. Again, what should make thee know what the Day of Judgment is!	ثُمَّ مَآ أَدْرٰىكَ مَا يَوْمُ الدِّيْنِ ﴿١٩﴾

20. The day when a soul shall have no power to do aught for another soul! And the command on that day will be Allah's.

يَوْمَ لَا تَمْلِكُ نَفْسٌ لِّنَفْسٍ شَيْـًٔا ۖ وَالْأَمْرُ يَوْمَئِذٍ لِّلّٰهِ ﴿٢٠﴾

سُورَةُ التَّطْفِيفِ مَكِّيَّةٌ (٨٣)

(Revealed before Hijra)

1. In the name of Allah, the Gracious, the Merciful.

بِسْمِ اللّٰهِ الرَّحْمٰنِ الرَّحِيْمِ ﴿١﴾

2. Woe unto those who give short measure;

وَيْلٌ لِّلْمُطَفِّفِيْنَ ﴿٢﴾

3. Those who, when they take by measure from other people, take it full;

الَّذِيْنَ إِذَا اكْتَالُوْا عَلَى النَّاسِ يَسْتَوْفُوْنَ ﴿٣﴾

4. But when they give by measure to others or weigh to them, they give *them* less.

وَإِذَا كَالُوْهُمْ أَوْ وَّزَنُوْهُمْ يُخْسِرُوْنَ ﴿٤﴾

5. Do not such *people* know that they will be raised again

أَلَا يَظُنُّ أُولٰٓئِكَ أَنَّهُمْ مَّبْعُوْثُوْنَ ﴿٥﴾

6. Unto a terrible day,

لِيَوْمٍ عَظِيْمٍ ﴿٦﴾

7. The day when mankind will stand before the Lord of the worlds?

يَّوْمَ يَقُوْمُ النَّاسُ لِرَبِّ الْعٰلَمِيْنَ ﴿٧﴾

8. Nay! the record of the wicked is in Sijjīn.

كَلَّآ إِنَّ كِتٰبَ الْفُجَّارِ لَفِيْ سِجِّيْنٍ ﴿٨﴾

9. And what should make thee know what Sijjīn is?

وَمَآ أَدْرٰىكَ مَا سِجِّيْنٌ ﴿٩﴾

10. *It is* a Book written *comprehensively*.

كِتٰبٌ مَّرْقُوْمٌ ﴿١٠﴾

11. Woe, on that day, unto those who reject,

وَيْلٌ يَّوْمَئِذٍ لِّلْمُكَذِّبِيْنَ ﴿١١﴾

12. Who deny the Day of Judgment.

الَّذِيْنَ يُكَذِّبُوْنَ بِيَوْمِ الدِّيْنِ ﴿١٢﴾

13. And none denies it save every sinful transgressor,

وَمَا يُكَذِّبُ بِهٖٓ إِلَّا كُلُّ مُعْتَدٍ أَثِيْمٍ ﴿١٣﴾

14. *Who*, when Our Signs are recited unto him, says: 'Fables of the ancients!'

إِذَا تُتْلٰى عَلَيْهِ اٰيٰتُنَا قَالَ أَسَاطِيْرُ الْأَوَّلِيْنَ ﴿١٤﴾

15. Nay, but that which they have earned has rusted their hearts.

كَلَّا بَلْ ۜ رَانَ عَلٰى قُلُوْبِهِمْ مَّا كَانُوْا يَكْسِبُوْنَ ﴿١٥﴾

16. Nay, they will surely be debarred from *seeing* their Lord on that day.

كَلَّآ إِنَّهُمْ عَنْ رَّبِّهِمْ يَوْمَئِذٍ لَّمَحْجُوْبُوْنَ ﴿١٦﴾

17. Then, verily, they will burn in Hell,

ثُمَّ إِنَّهُمْ لَصَالُوا الْجَحِيمِ ﴿١٧﴾

18. Then it will be said *to them*, 'This is what you used to reject.'

ثُمَّ يُقَالُ هَٰذَا الَّذِي كُنتُم بِهِ تُكَذِّبُونَ ﴿١٨﴾

19. Nay! but the record of the virtuous is surely in 'Illīyyīn.

كَلَّا إِنَّ كِتَابَ الْأَبْرَارِ لَفِي عِلِّيِّينَ ﴿١٩﴾

20. And what should make thee know what 'Illīyyūn is ?

وَمَا أَدْرَاكَ مَا عِلِّيُّونَ ﴿٢٠﴾

21. *It is* a Book written *comprehensively*.

كِتَابٌ مَّرْقُومٌ ﴿٢١﴾

22. The chosen ones *of God* will witness it.

يَشْهَدُهُ الْمُقَرَّبُونَ ﴿٢٢﴾

23. Surely the virtuous *will be* in bliss,

إِنَّ الْأَبْرَارَ لَفِي نَعِيمٍ ﴿٢٣﴾

24. *Seated* on couches, gazing.

عَلَى الْأَرَائِكِ يَنظُرُونَ ﴿٢٤﴾

25. Thou wilt find in their faces the freshness of bliss.

تَعْرِفُ فِي وُجُوهِهِمْ نَضْرَةَ النَّعِيمِ ﴿٢٥﴾

26. They will be given to drink of a pure sealed beverage,

يُسْقَوْنَ مِن رَّحِيقٍ مَّخْتُومٍ ﴿٢٦﴾

27. The sealing of it will be *with* musk—for this let the aspirants aspire—

خِتَامُهُ مِسْكٌ وَفِي ذَٰلِكَ فَلْيَتَنَافَسِ الْمُتَنَافِسُونَ ﴿٢٧﴾

28. And it will be tempered with *the water of* Tasnīm,

وَمِزَاجُهُ مِن تَسْنِيمٍ ﴿٢٨﴾

29. A spring of which the chosen ones will drink.

عَيْنًا يَشْرَبُ بِهَا الْمُقَرَّبُونَ ﴿٢٩﴾

30. Those who were guilty used to laugh at those who believed;

إِنَّ الَّذِينَ أَجْرَمُوا كَانُوا مِنَ الَّذِينَ آمَنُوا يَضْحَكُونَ ﴿٣٠﴾

31. And when they passed by them, they winked at one another.

وَإِذَا مَرُّوا بِهِمْ يَتَغَامَزُونَ ﴿٣١﴾

32. And when they returned to their families they returned exulting;

وَإِذَا انقَلَبُوا إِلَىٰ أَهْلِهِمُ انقَلَبُوا فَكِهِينَ ﴿٣٢﴾

33. And when they saw them they said, 'These indeed are the lost ones!'

وَإِذَا رَأَوْهُمْ قَالُوا إِنَّ هَٰؤُلَاءِ لَضَالُّونَ ﴿٣٣﴾

34. But they were not sent as keepers over them.

وَمَا أُرْسِلُوا عَلَيْهِمْ حَافِظِينَ ﴿٣٤﴾

35. This day, therefore, it is the believers who will laugh at the disbelievers,

فَالْيَوْمَ الَّذِينَ آمَنُوا مِنَ الْكُفَّارِ يَضْحَكُونَ ﴿٣٥﴾

36. *Seated* on couches, gazing.

عَلَى الْأَرَائِكِ يَنظُرُونَ ﴿٣٦﴾

37. Are *not* the disbelievers *duly* paid for what they did?

هَلْ ثُوِّبَ الْكُفَّارُ مَا كَانُوا يَفْعَلُونَ ﴿٣٧﴾

اٰيَاتُهَا ٢٦ ﴿سُوْرَةُ الْاِنْشِقَاقِ مَكِّيَّةٌ﴾ (٨٤) رُكُوْعُهَا ١

AL-INSHIQĀQ

(Revealed before Hijra)

1. In the name of Allah, the Gracious, the Merciful.

بِسْمِ اللّٰهِ الرَّحْمٰنِ الرَّحِيْمِ ۝١

2. When the heaven bursts asunder,

اِذَا السَّمَآءُ انْشَقَّتْ ۝٢

3. And gives ear to her Lord—and *this* is incumbent upon her—

وَاَذِنَتْ لِرَبِّهَا وَحُقَّتْ ۝٣

4. And when the earth is spread out,

وَاِذَا الْاَرْضُ مُدَّتْ ۝٤

5. And casts out *all* that is in her, and becomes empty;

وَاَلْقَتْ مَا فِيْهَا وَتَخَلَّتْ ۝٥

6. And gives ear to her Lord—and *this* is incumbent upon her—

وَاَذِنَتْ لِرَبِّهَا وَحُقَّتْ ۝٦

7. Thou, O man, art verily labouring towards thy Lord, a hard labouring; then thou art going to meet Him.

يٰۤاَيُّهَا الْاِنْسَانُ اِنَّكَ كَادِحٌ اِلٰى رَبِّكَ كَدْحًا
فَمُلٰقِيْهِ ۝٧

8. Then as for him who is given his book *of record* in his right hand,

فَاَمَّا مَنْ اُوْتِيَ كِتٰبَهٗ بِيَمِيْنِهٖ ۝٨

9. He will soon have an easy reckoning,

فَسَوْفَ يُحَاسَبُ حِسَابًا يَّسِيْرًا ۝٩

10. And he will return to his household, rejoicing.

وَّيَنْقَلِبُ اِلٰۤى اَهْلِهٖ مَسْرُوْرًا ۝١٠

11. But as for him who will have his book *of record* given to him behind his back,

وَاَمَّا مَنْ اُوْتِيَ كِتٰبَهٗ وَرَآءَ ظَهْرِهٖ ۝١١

12. He will soon call for destruction,

فَسَوْفَ يَدْعُوْا ثُبُوْرًا ۝١٢

13. And he will burn in a blazing Fire.

وَّيَصْلٰى سَعِيْرًا ۝١٣

14. Verily, *before this* he lived joyfully among his family.

اِنَّهٗ كَانَ فِيْۤ اَهْلِهٖ مَسْرُوْرًا ۝١٤

15. He indeed thought that he would never return *to God*.

اِنَّهٗ ظَنَّ اَنْ لَّنْ يَّحُوْرَ ۝١٥

16. Yea! surely, his Lord sees him full well.

بَلٰۤى ۚ اِنَّ رَبَّهٗ كَانَ بِهٖ بَصِيْرًا ۝١٦

17. But nay! I call to witness the evening twilight,

فَلَاۤ اُقْسِمُ بِالشَّفَقِ ۝١٧

18. And the night and *all* that it envelops,

وَالَّيْلِ وَمَا وَسَقَ ۝١٨

19. And the moon when it becomes full,

وَالْقَمَرِ اِذَا اتَّسَقَ ﴿١٩﴾

20. That you shall assuredly pass on from one stage to another.

لَتَرْكَبُنَّ طَبَقًا عَنْ طَبَقٍ ﴿٢٠﴾

21. So what is the matter with them that they believe not,

فَمَا لَهُمْ لَا يُؤْمِنُوْنَ ﴿٢١﴾

22. And when the Qur'ān is recited unto them, they do not bow down in submission;

وَاِذَا قُرِئَ عَلَيْهِمُ الْقُرْاٰنُ لَا يَسْجُدُوْنَ ﴿٢٢﴾ السجدة

23. On the contrary, those who disbelieve reject *it*.

بَلِ الَّذِيْنَ كَفَرُوْا يُكَذِّبُوْنَ ﴿٢٣﴾

24. And Allah knows best what they keep hidden *in their hearts*.

وَاللّٰهُ اَعْلَمُ بِمَا يُوْعُوْنَ ﴿٢٤﴾

25. So give them tidings of a painful punishment.

فَبَشِّرْهُمْ بِعَذَابٍ اَلِيْمٍ ﴿٢٥﴾

26. But *as to* those who believe and do good works, theirs is an unending reward.

اِلَّا الَّذِيْنَ اٰمَنُوْا وَعَمِلُوا الصّٰلِحٰتِ لَهُمْ
اَجْرٌ غَيْرُ مَمْنُوْنٍ ﴿٢٦﴾ ع

سُوْرَةُ الْبُرُوْجِ مَكِّيَّةٌ (٨٥)

اٰيَاتُهَا ٢٣ — رُكُوْعَاتُهَا ١

Chapter 85 AL-BURŪJ Part 30

(Revealed before Hijra)

1. In the name of Allah, the Gracious, the Merciful.

بِسْمِ اللّٰهِ الرَّحْمٰنِ الرَّحِيْمِ ﴿١﴾

2. By the heaven having mansions *of stars*,

وَالسَّمَآءِ ذَاتِ الْبُرُوْجِ ﴿٢﴾

3. And *by* the Promised Day,

وَالْيَوْمِ الْمَوْعُوْدِ ﴿٣﴾

* 4. And *by* the Witness and that about whom witness has been borne,

وَشَاهِدٍ وَّمَشْهُوْدٍ ﴿٤﴾

* 5. Cursed be the Fellows of the Trench—

قُتِلَ اَصْحٰبُ الْاُخْدُوْدِ ﴿٥﴾

6. The fire *fed* with fuel—

النَّارِ ذَاتِ الْوَقُوْدِ ﴿٦﴾

7. As they sat by it,

اِذْ هُمْ عَلَيْهَا قُعُوْدٌ ﴿٧﴾

8. And they witnessed what they did to the believers.

وَّهُمْ عَلٰى مَا يَفْعَلُوْنَ بِالْمُؤْمِنِيْنَ شُهُوْدٌ ﴿٨﴾

9. And they hated them not but because they believed in Allah, the Almighty,

وَمَا نَقَمُوْا مِنْهُمْ اِلَّا اَنْ يُّؤْمِنُوْا بِاللّٰهِ الْعَزِيْزِ

the Praiseworthy,

الْحَمِيْدِ ۝٩

10. To Whom belongs the kingdom of the heavens and the earth; and Allah is Witness over all things.

الَّذِيْ لَهٗ مُلْكُ السَّمٰوٰتِ وَالْاَرْضِ ؕ وَاللّٰهُ عَلٰى كُلِّ
شَيْءٍ شَهِيْدٌ ۝١٠

11. Those who persecute the believing men and the believing women and then repent not, for them is surely the punishment of Hell, and for them is the punishment of burning.

اِنَّ الَّذِيْنَ فَتَنُوا الْمُؤْمِنِيْنَ وَالْمُؤْمِنٰتِ ثُمَّ لَمْ
يَتُوْبُوْا فَلَهُمْ عَذَابُ جَهَنَّمَ وَلَهُمْ عَذَابُ الْحَرِيْقِ ۝١١

12. But those who believe and do good works, for them are Gardens through which streams flow. That is the great triumph.

اِنَّ الَّذِيْنَ اٰمَنُوْا وَعَمِلُوا الصّٰلِحٰتِ لَهُمْ جَنّٰتٌ
تَجْرِيْ مِنْ تَحْتِهَا الْاَنْهٰرُ ؕ ذٰلِكَ الْفَوْزُ الْكَبِيْرُ ۝١٢

13. Surely the seizing of thy Lord is severe.

اِنَّ بَطْشَ رَبِّكَ لَشَدِيْدٌ ۝١٣

* 14. He it is Who originates and reproduces;

اِنَّهٗ هُوَ يُبْدِئُ وَيُعِيْدُ ۝١٤

15. And He is the Most Forgiving, the Loving;

وَهُوَ الْغَفُوْرُ الْوَدُوْدُ ۝١٥

16. The Lord of the Throne, the Lord of honour;

ذُو الْعَرْشِ الْمَجِيْدُ ۝١٦

* 17. Doer of whatever He wills.

فَعَّالٌ لِّمَا يُرِيْدُ ۝١٧

18. Has *not* the story of the hosts come to thee?

هَلْ اَتٰىكَ حَدِيْثُ الْجُنُوْدِ ۝١٨

19. Of Pharaoh and Thamūd?

فِرْعَوْنَ وَثَمُوْدَ ۝١٩

20. Nay, but those who disbelieve *persist* in rejecting *the truth.*

بَلِ الَّذِيْنَ كَفَرُوْا فِيْ تَكْذِيْبٍ ۝٢٠

* 21. And Allah encompasses *them* from before them and from behind them.

وَّاللّٰهُ مِنْ وَّرَآئِهِمْ مُّحِيْطٌ ۝٢١

22. Nay, but it is a glorious Qur'ān,

بَلْ هُوَ قُرْاٰنٌ مَّجِيْدٌ ۝٢٢

23. In a *well* guarded tablet.

فِيْ لَوْحٍ مَّحْفُوْظٍ ۝٢٣

سُوْرَةُ الطَّارِقِ مَكِّيَّةٌ (٨٦)

AL-ṬĀRIQ

(Revealed before Hijra)

1. In the name of Allah, the Gracious, the Merciful.

بِسۡمِ اللّٰهِ الرَّحۡمٰنِ الرَّحِيۡمِ ۝١

2. By the heaven and the Morning Star—

وَالسَّمَآءِ وَالطَّارِقِ ۝٢

3. And what should make thee know what the Morning Star is?

وَمَآ اَدۡرٰىكَ مَا الطَّارِقُ ۝٣

4. *It is* the star of piercing brightness—

النَّجۡمُ الثَّاقِبُ ۝٤

5. There is no soul but has a guardian over it.

اِنۡ كُلُّ نَفۡسٍ لَّمَّا عَلَيۡهَا حَافِظٌ ۝٥

6. So let man consider from what he is created.

فَلۡيَنۡظُرِ الۡاِنۡسَانُ مِمَّ خُلِقَ ۝٦

7. He is created from a gushing fluid,

خُلِقَ مِنۡ مَّآءٍ دَافِقٍ ۝٧

8. Which issues forth from between the loins and the breast-bones.

يَّخۡرُجُ مِنۡۢ بَيۡنِ الصُّلۡبِ وَالتَّرَآئِبِ ۝٨

9. Surely, He has the power to bring him back *to life*

اِنَّهٗ عَلٰى رَجۡعِهٖ لَقَادِرٌ ۝٩

10. *On* the day when secrets shall be disclosed.

يَوۡمَ تُبۡلَى السَّرَآئِرُ ۝١٠

11. Then he will have no strength and no helper.

فَمَا لَهٗ مِنۡ قُوَّةٍ وَّلَا نَاصِرٍ ۝١١

* 12. By the cloud which gives rain after rain,

وَالسَّمَآءِ ذَاتِ الرَّجۡعِ ۝١٢

13. And *by* the earth which opens out *with herbage*,

وَالۡاَرۡضِ ذَاتِ الصَّدۡعِ ۝١٣

14. It is surely a decisive word,

اِنَّهٗ لَقَوۡلٌ فَصۡلٌ ۝١٤

15. And it is not a useless talk.

وَّمَا هُوَ بِالۡهَزۡلِ ۝١٥

* 16. Surely they plan a plan,

اِنَّهُمۡ يَكِيۡدُوۡنَ كَيۡدًا ۝١٦

* 17. And I *also* plan a plan.

وَّاَكِيۡدُ كَيۡدًا ۝١٧

18. So give time to the disbelievers. *Aye*, give them time for a little while.

فَمَهِّلِ الۡكٰفِرِيۡنَ اَمۡهِلۡهُمۡ رُوَيۡدًا ۝١٨

سُورَةُ الْأَعْلٰى مَكِّيَّةٌ (٨٧) آياتها ٢٠ ركوعها ١

AL-A'LĀ

(Revealed before Hijra)

1. In the name of Allah, the Gracious, the Merciful.

بِسْمِ اللّٰهِ الرَّحْمٰنِ الرَّحِيْمِ ①

2. Glorify the name of thy Lord, the Most High,

سَبِّحِ اسْمَ رَبِّكَ الْأَعْلَى ②

3. Who creates and perfects,

الَّذِيْ خَلَقَ فَسَوّٰى ③

4. And Who designs and guides,

وَالَّذِيْ قَدَّرَ فَهَدٰى ④

5. And Who brings forth the pasturage,

وَالَّذِيْ أَخْرَجَ الْمَرْعٰى ⑤

6. Then turns it black, rotten rubbish.

فَجَعَلَهُ غُثَاءً أَحْوٰى ⑥

7. We shall teach thee *the Qur'ān*, and thou shalt forget *it* not,

سَنُقْرِئُكَ فَلَا تَنْسٰى ⑦

8. Except as Allah wills. Surely, He knows *what is* open and what is hidden.

إِلَّا مَا شَاءَ اللّٰهُ إِنَّهُ يَعْلَمُ الْجَهْرَ وَمَا يَخْفٰى ⑧

9. And We shall facilitate for thee *every* facility.

وَنُيَسِّرُكَ لِلْيُسْرٰى ⑨

10. So go on reminding; surely, reminding is profitable.

فَذَكِّرْ إِنْ نَفَعَتِ الذِّكْرٰى ⑩

11. He who fears will soon heed;

سَيَذَّكَّرُ مَنْ يَخْشٰى ⑪

12. But the reprobate will turn aside from it,

وَيَتَجَنَّبُهَا الْأَشْقَى ⑫

13. He who is to enter the great Fire.

الَّذِيْ يَصْلَى النَّارَ الْكُبْرٰى ⑬

14. Then he will neither die therein nor live.

ثُمَّ لَا يَمُوْتُ فِيْهَا وَلَا يَحْيٰى ⑭

15. Verily, he *truly* prospers who purifies himself,

قَدْ أَفْلَحَ مَنْ تَزَكّٰى ⑮

16. And remembers the name of his Lord and offers Prayers.

وَذَكَرَ اسْمَ رَبِّهِ فَصَلّٰى ⑯

17. But you prefer the life of this world,

بَلْ تُؤْثِرُوْنَ الْحَيٰوةَ الدُّنْيَا ⑰

18. Whereas the Hereafter is better and more lasting.

وَالْاٰخِرَةُ خَيْرٌ وَّأَبْقٰى ⑱

19. This indeed is *what is taught* in the former Scriptures—

إِنَّ هٰذَا لَفِي الصُّحُفِ الْأُوْلٰى ⑲

20. The Scriptures of Abraham and Moses.

صُحُفِ اِبْرٰهِيْمَ وَ مُوْسٰى ۲۰ ع ١٣

سُوْرَةُ الْغَاشِيَةِ مَكِّيَّةٌ

اٰيَاتُهَا ٢٦ (٨٨) رُكُوْعُهَا ١

Chapter 88 — AL-GHĀSHIYAH — art 30

(Revealed before Hijra)

1. In the name of Allah, the Gracious, the Merciful.

بِسْمِ اللّٰهِ الرَّحْمٰنِ الرَّحِيْمِ ١

2. Has there come to thee the news of the overwhelming *calamity?*

هَلْ اَتٰىكَ حَدِيْثُ الْغَاشِيَةِ ٢

3. *Some* faces on that day will be downcast;

وُجُوْهٌ يَّوْمَئِذٍ خَاشِعَةٌ ٣

4. Toiling, weary.

عَامِلَةٌ نَّاصِبَةٌ ٤

5. *They* shall enter a burning Fire;

تَصْلٰى نَارًا حَامِيَةً ٥

6. *And* will be made to drink from a boiling spring;

تُسْقٰى مِنْ عَيْنٍ اٰنِيَةٍ ٦

7. They will have no food save that of dry, bitter and thorny herbage,

لَيْسَ لَهُمْ طَعَامٌ اِلَّا مِنْ ضَرِيْعٍ ٧

8. Which will neither fatten, nor satisfy hunger.

لَّا يُسْمِنُ وَ لَا يُغْنِيْ مِنْ جُوْعٍ ٨

9. *And some* faces on that day will be joyful,

وُجُوْهٌ يَّوْمَئِذٍ نَّاعِمَةٌ ٩

10. Well pleased with their labour,

لِّسَعْيِهَا رَاضِيَةٌ ١٠

11. In a lofty Garden,

فِيْ جَنَّةٍ عَالِيَةٍ ١١

12. Wherein thou wilt hear no idle talk;

لَّا تَسْمَعُ فِيْهَا لَاغِيَةً ١٢

13. Therein is a running spring,

فِيْهَا عَيْنٌ جَارِيَةٌ ١٣ وقف لازم

14. Therein are raised couches,

فِيْهَا سُرُرٌ مَّرْفُوْعَةٌ ١٤

15. And goblets properly placed,

وَّ اَكْوَابٌ مَّوْضُوْعَةٌ ١٥

16. And cushions *beautifully* ranged,

وَّ نَمَارِقُ مَصْفُوْفَةٌ ١٦

17. And carpets *tastefully* spread.

وَّ زَرَابِيُّ مَبْثُوْثَةٌ ١٧

18. Do they not then look at the camel, how it is created?
أَفَلَا يَنظُرُونَ إِلَى الْإِبِلِ كَيْفَ خُلِقَتْ ﴿١٨﴾

19. And at the heaven, how it is raised high?
وَإِلَى السَّمَاءِ كَيْفَ رُفِعَتْ ﴿١٩﴾

* 20. And at the mountains, how they are set up?
وَإِلَى الْجِبَالِ كَيْفَ نُصِبَتْ ﴿٢٠﴾

21. And at the earth, how it is spread out?
وَإِلَى الْأَرْضِ كَيْفَ سُطِحَتْ ﴿٢١﴾

22. Admonish, therefore, for thou art but an admonisher;
فَذَكِّرْ إِنَّمَا أَنتَ مُذَكِّرٌ ﴿٢٢﴾

* 23. Thou hast no authority to *compel* them.
لَسْتَ عَلَيْهِم بِمُصَيْطِرٍ ﴿٢٣﴾

24. But whoever turns away and disbelieves,
إِلَّا مَن تَوَلَّىٰ وَكَفَرَ ﴿٢٤﴾

25. Allah will punish him with the greatest punishment.
فَيُعَذِّبُهُ اللَّهُ الْعَذَابَ الْأَكْبَرَ ﴿٢٥﴾

26. Unto Us surely is their return,
إِنَّ إِلَيْنَا إِيَابَهُمْ ﴿٢٦﴾

27. Then, surely, it is for Us to call them to account.
ثُمَّ إِنَّ عَلَيْنَا حِسَابَهُم ﴿٢٧﴾ ع ١٣ النصف

سُورَةُ الْفَجْرِ مَكِّيَّةٌ (٨٩)

اٰياتها ٣١ — ركوعها ١

(Revealed before Hijra)

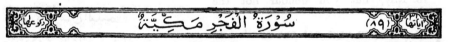

1. In the name of Allah, the Gracious, the Merciful.
بِسْمِ اللَّهِ الرَّحْمَٰنِ الرَّحِيمِ ﴿١﴾

2. By the Dawn,
وَالْفَجْرِ ﴿٢﴾

3. And the Ten Nights,
وَلَيَالٍ عَشْرٍ ﴿٣﴾

4. And the Even and the Odd,
وَالشَّفْعِ وَالْوَتْرِ ﴿٤﴾

5. And the Night when it moves on *to its end*,
وَاللَّيْلِ إِذَا يَسْرِ ﴿٥﴾

6. Is there *not* in it a strong evidence for a man of understanding?
هَلْ فِي ذَٰلِكَ قَسَمٌ لِّذِي حِجْرٍ ﴿٦﴾

7. Hast thou not seen how thy Lord dealt with 'Ād—
أَلَمْ تَرَ كَيْفَ فَعَلَ رَبُّكَ بِعَادٍ ﴿٧﴾

8. *The tribe of* Iram, possessors of lofty buildings,
إِرَمَ ذَاتِ الْعِمَادِ ﴿٨﴾

* 9. The like of whom have not been created in *these* parts—

الَّتِي لَمْ يُخْلَقْ مِثْلُهَا فِي الْبِلَادِ ﴿٩﴾

10. And *with* Thamūd who hewed out rocks in the valley,

وَثَمُودَ الَّذِينَ جَابُوا الصَّخْرَ بِالْوَادِ ﴿١٠﴾

11. And *with* Pharaoh, lord of vast camps?

وَفِرْعَوْنَ ذِي الْأَوْتَادِ ﴿١١﴾

* 12. Who transgressed in the cities,

الَّذِينَ طَغَوْا فِي الْبِلَادِ ﴿١٢﴾

13. And wrought much corruption therein.

فَأَكْثَرُوا فِيهَا الْفَسَادَ ﴿١٣﴾

14. Thy Lord then let fall on them the whip of punishment.

فَصَبَّ عَلَيْهِمْ رَبُّكَ سَوْطَ عَذَابٍ ﴿١٤﴾

15. Surely thy Lord is on the watch

إِنَّ رَبَّكَ لَبِالْمِرْصَادِ ﴿١٥﴾

16. As for man, when his Lord tries him and honours him and bestows favours on him, he says, 'My Lord has honoured me.'

فَأَمَّا الْإِنْسَانُ إِذَا مَا ابْتَلَاهُ رَبُّهُ فَأَكْرَمَهُ وَنَعَّمَهُ فَيَقُولُ رَبِّي أَكْرَمَنِ ﴿١٦﴾

17. But when He tries him and straitens for him his *means of* subsistence, he says, 'My Lord has disgraced me.'

وَأَمَّا إِذَا مَا ابْتَلَاهُ فَقَدَرَ عَلَيْهِ رِزْقَهُ فَيَقُولُ رَبِّي أَهَانَنِ ﴿١٧﴾

18. Nay, but you honour not the orphan,

كَلَّا بَلْ لَا تُكْرِمُونَ الْيَتِيمَ ﴿١٨﴾

19. And you urge not one another to feed the poor,

وَلَا تَحُضُّونَ عَلَى طَعَامِ الْمِسْكِينِ ﴿١٩﴾

20. And you devour the heritage *of other people* wholly,

وَتَأْكُلُونَ التُّرَاثَ أَكْلًا لَمًّا ﴿٢٠﴾

21. And you love wealth with exceeding love.

وَتُحِبُّونَ الْمَالَ حُبًّا جَمًّا ﴿٢١﴾

* 22. Nay, when the earth is completely broken into pieces and made level;

كَلَّا إِذَا دُكَّتِ الْأَرْضُ دَكًّا دَكًّا ﴿٢٢﴾

23. And thy Lord comes and *also* the angels ranged in rows after rows;

وَجَاءَ رَبُّكَ وَالْمَلَكُ صَفًّا صَفًّا ﴿٢٣﴾

24. And Hell is brought near that day; on that day man will remember, but of what avail shall be his remembrance?

وَجِيءَ يَوْمَئِذٍ بِجَهَنَّمَ يَوْمَئِذٍ يَتَذَكَّرُ الْإِنْسَانُ وَأَنَّى لَهُ الذِّكْرَى ﴿٢٤﴾

25. He will say, 'O would that I had sent on *some good works* for my life *here!*'

يَقُولُ يَا لَيْتَنِي قَدَّمْتُ لِحَيَاتِي ﴿٢٥﴾

26. So on that day none can punish like unto His punishment,

فَيَوْمَئِذٍ لَا يُعَذِّبُ عَذَابَهُ أَحَدٌ ﴿٢٦﴾

27. And none can bind like unto His binding;

وَلَا يُوثِقُ وَثَاقَهُ أَحَدٌ ﴿٢٧﴾

28. *And* thou, O soul at peace!

يٰۤاَيَّتُهَا النَّفۡسُ الۡمُطۡمَئِنَّةُ ﴿٢٨﴾

29. Return to thy Lord well pleased *with Him and* He well pleased *with thee.*

ارۡجِعِىۡۤ اِلٰى رَبِّكِ رَاضِيَةً مَّرۡضِيَّةً ﴿٢٩﴾

30. So enter thou among My chosen servants,

فَادۡخُلِىۡ فِىۡ عِبٰدِىۙ ﴿٣٠﴾

31. And enter thou My Garden.

وَادۡخُلِىۡ جَنَّتِىۡ ﴿٣١﴾

ركوعها ١ سُوۡرَةُ الۡبَلَدِ مَكِّيَّةٌ (٩٠) اٰياتها ٢١

Part 30 AL-BALAD Chapter 90

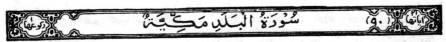

(Revealed before Hijra)

1. In the name of Allah, the Gracious, the Merciful.

بِسۡمِ اللّٰهِ الرَّحۡمٰنِ الرَّحِيۡمِ ﴿١﴾

2. Nay, but I do swear by this city—

لَاۤ اُقۡسِمُ بِهٰذَا الۡبَلَدِ ﴿٢﴾

3. And thou art dwelling in this city—

وَاَنۡتَ حِلٌّ ۢ بِهٰذَا الۡبَلَدِ ﴿٣﴾

4. And *I swear by* the begetter and whom he begot,

وَوَالِدٍ وَّمَا وَلَدَ ﴿٤﴾

5. We have surely created man to *face* hardships.

لَقَدۡ خَلَقۡنَا الۡاِنۡسَانَ فِىۡ كَبَدٍ ﴿٥﴾

6. Does he think that no one has power over him?

اَيَحۡسَبُ اَنۡ لَّنۡ يَّقۡدِرَ عَلَيۡهِ اَحَدٌ ﴿٦﴾

7. He says, 'I have spent enormous wealth.'

يَقُوۡلُ اَهۡلَكۡتُ مَالًا لُّبَدًا ﴿٧﴾

8. Does he think that no one sees him?

اَيَحۡسَبُ اَنۡ لَّمۡ يَرَهٗۤ اَحَدٌ ﴿٨﴾

9. Have We not given him two eyes,

اَلَمۡ نَجۡعَلۡ لَّهٗ عَيۡنَيۡنِ ﴿٩﴾

10. And a tongue and two lips?

وَلِسَانًا وَّشَفَتَيۡنِ ﴿١٠﴾

* 11. And We have pointed out to him the two highways *of good and evil.*

وَهَدَيۡنٰهُ النَّجۡدَيۡنِ ﴿١١﴾

* 12. But he attempted not the ascent *courageously.*

فَلَا اقۡتَحَمَ الۡعَقَبَةَ ﴿١٢﴾

* 13. And what should make thee know what the ascent is?

وَمَاۤ اَدۡرٰىكَ مَا الۡعَقَبَةُ ﴿١٣﴾

14. *It is* the freeing of a slave.

فَكُّ رَقَبَةٍ ﴿١٤﴾

15. Or feeding in a day of hunger

أَوْ إِطْعَامٌ فِي يَوْمٍ ذِي مَسْغَبَةٍ (١٥)

16. An orphan near of kin,

يَتِيمًا ذَا مَقْرَبَةٍ (١٦)

17. Or a poor man *lying* in the dust.

أَوْ مِسْكِينًا ذَا مَتْرَبَةٍ (١٧)

18. Again, he should have been of those who believe and exhort one another to perseverance and exhort one another to mercy.

ثُمَّ كَانَ مِنَ الَّذِينَ آمَنُوا وَتَوَاصَوْا بِالصَّبْرِ وَتَوَاصَوْا بِالْمَرْحَمَةِ (١٨)

19. These are the people of the right hand.

أُولَٰئِكَ أَصْحَابُ الْمَيْمَنَةِ (١٩)

20. But those who disbelieve Our Signs, they are the people of the left hand.

وَالَّذِينَ كَفَرُوا بِآيَاتِنَا هُمْ أَصْحَابُ الْمَشْأَمَةِ (٢٠)

* 21. Around them will be a fire closed over.

عَلَيْهِمْ نَارٌ مُؤْصَدَةٌ (٢١) ع

سُورَةُ الشَّمْسِ مَكِّيَّةٌ (٩١)

Chapter 91 AL-SHAMS Part 30

(Revealed before Hijra)

1. In the name of Allah, the Gracious, the Merciful.

بِسْمِ اللَّهِ الرَّحْمَٰنِ الرَّحِيمِ (١)

* 2. By the sun and its growing brightness,

وَالشَّمْسِ وَضُحَاهَا (٢)

3. And *by* the moon when it follows it (the sun),

وَالْقَمَرِ إِذَا تَلَاهَا (٣)

4. And *by* the day when it reveals its glory,

وَالنَّهَارِ إِذَا جَلَّاهَا (٤)

5. And *by* the night when it draws a veil over it,

وَاللَّيْلِ إِذَا يَغْشَاهَا (٥)

6. And *by* the heaven and its making,

وَالسَّمَاءِ وَمَا بَنَاهَا (٦)

7. And *by* the earth and its spreading out,

وَالْأَرْضِ وَمَا طَحَاهَا (٧)

8. And *by* the soul and its perfection—

وَنَفْسٍ وَمَا سَوَّاهَا (٨)

9. And He revealed to it what is wrong for it and what is right for it—

فَأَلْهَمَهَا فُجُورَهَا وَتَقْوَاهَا (٩)

* 10. He indeed *truly* prospers who purifies it,

قَدْ أَفْلَحَ مَنْ زَكَّاهَا (١٠)

11. And he who corrupts it is ruined.

وَقَدْ خَابَ مَنْ دَسَّاهَا (١١)

12. *The tribe of* Thamūd denied *the truth* because of their rebelliousness.

كَذَّبَتْ ثَمُوْدُ بِطَغْوٰىهَآ ﴿١٢﴾

13. When the most wretched among them got up,

إِذِ انْبَعَثَ أَشْقٰىهَا ﴿١٣﴾

14. Then the Messenger of Allah said, '*Leave alone* the she-camel of Allah, and *let* her drink.'

فَقَالَ لَهُمْ رَسُوْلُ اللّٰهِ نَاقَةَ اللّٰهِ وَسُقْيٰهَا ﴿١٤﴾

* 15. But they rejected him and hamstrung her, so their Lord destroyed them completely because of their sin, and made it (destruction) *overtake all of them* alike.

فَكَذَّبُوْهُ فَعَقَرُوْهَا فَدَمْدَمَ عَلَيْهِمْ رَبُّهُمْ بِذَنْۢبِهِمْ فَسَوّٰىهَا ﴿١٥﴾

16. And He cared not for the consequences thereof.

وَلَا يَخَافُ عُقْبٰهَا ﴿١٦﴾

سُوْرَةُ الَّيْلِ مَكِّيَّةٌ (٩٢) آياتها ٢٢ ركوعها ١

Part 30 AL-LAIL Chapter 92

(Revealed before Hijra)

1. In the name of Allah, the Gracious, the Merciful.

بِسْمِ اللّٰهِ الرَّحْمٰنِ الرَّحِيْمِ ﴿١﴾

2. By the night when it covers up!

وَالَّيْلِ إِذَا يَغْشٰى ﴿٢﴾

3. And *by* the day when it brightens up,

وَالنَّهَارِ إِذَا تَجَلّٰى ﴿٣﴾

4. And *by* the creating of the male and the female,

وَمَا خَلَقَ الذَّكَرَ وَالْأُنْثٰى ﴿٤﴾

5. Surely, your strivings are diverse.

إِنَّ سَعْيَكُمْ لَشَتّٰى ﴿٥﴾

6. Then as for him who gives and is righteous,

فَأَمَّا مَنْ أَعْطٰى وَاتَّقٰى ﴿٦﴾

* 7. And testifies to *the truth of* what is right,

وَصَدَّقَ بِالْحُسْنٰى ﴿٧﴾

8. We will facilitate for him *every* facility.

فَسَنُيَسِّرُهٗ لِلْيُسْرٰى ﴿٨﴾

9. But as for him who is niggardly and is *disdainfully* indifferent,

وَأَمَّا مَنْۢ بَخِلَ وَاسْتَغْنٰى ﴿٩﴾

10. And rejects what is right,

وَكَذَّبَ بِالْحُسْنٰى ﴿١٠﴾

11. We will make easy for him the path to distress.

فَسَنُيَسِّرُهٗ لِلْعُسْرٰى ﴿١١﴾

12. And his wealth shall not avail him when he perishes.

وَمَا يُغْنِيْ عَنْهُ مَالُهٗٓ إِذَا تَرَدّٰى ﴿١٢﴾

13. Surely it is for Us to guide;

إِنَّ عَلَيْنَا لَلْهُدٰى ﴿١٣﴾

14. And to Us belongs the Hereafter as well as the present world.	وَإِنَّ لَنَا لَلْآخِرَةَ وَالْأُولَىٰ ﴿١٤﴾
15. So I warn you of a flaming Fire.	فَأَنذَرْتُكُمْ نَارًا تَلَظَّىٰ ﴿١٥﴾
16. None shall enter it but the most wicked one,	لَا يَصْلَاهَا إِلَّا الْأَشْقَى ﴿١٦﴾
17. Who rejects *the truth* and turns *his* back.	الَّذِي كَذَّبَ وَتَوَلَّىٰ ﴿١٧﴾
18. But the righteous *one* shall be kept away from it,	وَسَيُجَنَّبُهَا الْأَتْقَى ﴿١٨﴾
19. Who gives his wealth to become purified.	الَّذِي يُؤْتِي مَالَهُ يَتَزَكَّىٰ ﴿١٩﴾
20. And he owes no favour to anyone, which is to be repaid,	وَمَا لِأَحَدٍ عِندَهُ مِن نِّعْمَةٍ تُجْزَىٰ ﴿٢٠﴾
21. Except *that he gives his wealth* to seek the pleasure of his Lord, the Most High.	إِلَّا ابْتِغَاءَ وَجْهِ رَبِّهِ الْأَعْلَىٰ ﴿٢١﴾
22. And soon will He be well pleased *with him*.	وَلَسَوْفَ يَرْضَىٰ ﴿٢٢﴾

سُورَةُ الضُّحَىٰ مَكِّيَّةٌ (٩٣)

آياتها ١٢ — ركوعها ١

Chapter 93 — **AL-ḌUḤĀ** — Part 30

(Revealed before Hijra)

1. In the name of Allah, the Gracious, the Merciful.	بِسْمِ اللَّهِ الرَّحْمَٰنِ الرَّحِيمِ ﴿١﴾
2. By the growing brightness of the forenoon,	وَالضُّحَىٰ ﴿٢﴾
3. And *by* the night when it becomes still,	وَاللَّيْلِ إِذَا سَجَىٰ ﴿٣﴾
4. Thy Lord has not forsaken thee, nor is He displeased *with thee*.	مَا وَدَّعَكَ رَبُّكَ وَمَا قَلَىٰ ﴿٤﴾
5. Surely *every hour* that follows is better for thee than *the one* that precedes.	وَلَلْآخِرَةُ خَيْرٌ لَّكَ مِنَ الْأُولَىٰ ﴿٥﴾
6. And thy Lord will soon give thee and thou wilt be well pleased.	وَلَسَوْفَ يُعْطِيكَ رَبُّكَ فَتَرْضَىٰ ﴿٦﴾
7. Did He not find thee an orphan and give *thee* shelter?	أَلَمْ يَجِدْكَ يَتِيمًا فَآوَىٰ ﴿٧﴾
8. And He found thee wandering in search *for Him* and guided thee *unto Himself*.	وَوَجَدَكَ ضَالًّا فَهَدَىٰ ﴿٨﴾
9. And He found thee in want and enriched *thee*.	وَوَجَدَكَ عَائِلًا فَأَغْنَىٰ ﴿٩﴾

10. So the orphan, oppress not,

فَاَمَّا الْيَتِيْمَ فَلَا تَقْهَرْ ⑩

* 11. And him who seeks *thy help,* chide not,

وَاَمَّا السَّآئِلَ فَلَا تَنْهَرْ ⑪

* 12. And the bounty of thy Lord, proclaim.

وَاَمَّا بِنِعْمَةِ رَبِّكَ فَحَدِّثْ ⑫ ع ١٨

سُوْرَةُ الْاِنْشِرَاحِ مَكِّيَّةٌ (٩٤) — اٰیاتها ٩ — رکوعها ١

Part 30 **AL-INSHIRĀḤ** Chapter 94

(Revealed before Hijra)

1. In the name of Allah, the Gracious, the Merciful.

بِسْمِ اللّٰهِ الرَّحْمٰنِ الرَّحِيْمِ ①

2. Have We not opened for thee thy bosom,

اَلَمْ نَشْرَحْ لَكَ صَدْرَكَ ②

3. And removed from thee thy burden

وَوَضَعْنَا عَنْكَ وِزْرَكَ ③

4. Which had *well nigh* broken thy back,

الَّذِيْٓ اَنْقَضَ ظَهْرَكَ ④

5. And We exalted thy name?

وَرَفَعْنَا لَكَ ذِكْرَكَ ⑤

6. Surely there is ease after hardship.

فَاِنَّ مَعَ الْعُسْرِ يُسْرًا ⑥

7. *Aye,* surely there is ease after hardship.

اِنَّ مَعَ الْعُسْرِ يُسْرًا ⑦

8. So when thou art free, strive hard,

فَاِذَا فَرَغْتَ فَانْصَبْ ⑧

* 9. And to thy Lord do thou attend *whole-heartedly.*

وَاِلٰى رَبِّكَ فَارْغَبْ ⑨ ع ١٩

سُوْرَةُ التِّيْنِ مَكِّيَّةٌ (٩٥) — اٰیاتها ٩ — رکوعها ١

Part 30 **AL-TĪN** Chapter 95

(Revealed before Hijra)

1. In the name of Allah, the Gracious, the Merciful.

بِسْمِ اللّٰهِ الرَّحْمٰنِ الرَّحِيْمِ ①

2. By the Fig and the Olive,

وَالتِّيْنِ وَالزَّيْتُوْنِ ②

3. And *by* Mount Sinai,

وَطُوْرِ سِيْنِيْنَ ۝٣

* 4. And *by* this Town of Security,

وَهٰذَا الْبَلَدِ الْاَمِيْنِ ۝٤

* 5. Surely, We have created man in the best make;

لَقَدْ خَلَقْنَا الْاِنْسَانَ فِيْٓ اَحْسَنِ تَقْوِيْمٍ ۝٥

* 6. Then, *if he works iniquity*, We reject him as the lowest of the low,

ثُمَّ رَدَدْنٰهُ اَسْفَلَ سٰفِلِيْنَ ۝٦

7. Except those who believe and do good works; so for them is an unending reward.

اِلَّا الَّذِيْنَ اٰمَنُوْا وَعَمِلُوا الصّٰلِحٰتِ فَلَهُمْ اَجْرٌ غَيْرُ مَمْنُوْنٍ ۝٧

8. Then what is there to give the lie to thee after *this* with regard to the Judgment?

فَمَا يُكَذِّبُكَ بَعْدُ بِالدِّيْنِ ۝٨

9. Is not Allah the Best of judges?

اَلَيْسَ اللّٰهُ بِاَحْكَمِ الْحٰكِمِيْنَ ۝٩ ع

ركوعها ١ سُوْرَةُ الْعَلَقِ مَكِّيَّةٌ (٩٦) اياتها ٢٠

Chapter 96 AL-'ALAQ Part 30

(Revealed before Hijra)

1. In the name of Allah, the Gracious, the Merciful.

بِسْمِ اللّٰهِ الرَّحْمٰنِ الرَّحِيْمِ ۝١

* 2. Convey thou in the name of thy Lord Who created,

اِقْرَاْ بِاسْمِ رَبِّكَ الَّذِيْ خَلَقَ ۝٢

* 3. Created man from a clot of blood.

خَلَقَ الْاِنْسَانَ مِنْ عَلَقٍ ۝٣

* 4. Convey! And thy Lord is Most Generous,

اِقْرَاْ وَرَبُّكَ الْاَكْرَمُ ۝٤

* 5. Who taught *man* by the pen,

الَّذِيْ عَلَّمَ بِالْقَلَمِ ۝٥

6. Taught man what he knew not.

عَلَّمَ الْاِنْسَانَ مَا لَمْ يَعْلَمْ ۝٦

7. Nay! man does indeed transgress,

كَلَّآ اِنَّ الْاِنْسَانَ لَيَطْغٰٓى ۝٧

8. Because he thinks himself to be independent.

اَنْ رَّاٰهُ اسْتَغْنٰى ۝٨

9. Surely, unto thy Lord is the return.

اِنَّ اِلٰى رَبِّكَ الرُّجْعٰى ۝٩

10. Hast thou seen him who forbids

اَرَءَيْتَ الَّذِيْ يَنْهٰى ۝١٠

11. A servant *of Ours* when he prays?

عبدا إذا صلى ﴿١١﴾

* 12. Tell me if he (Our servant) follows the guidance

أرءيت إن كان على الهدى ﴿١٢﴾

* 13. Or enjoins righteousness, *what will be the end of the forbidder?*

أو أمر بالتقوى ﴿١٣﴾

* 14. Tell me if he (the forbidder) rejects and turns his back,

أرءيت إن كذب وتولى ﴿١٤﴾

* 15. Does he not know that Allah sees *him?*

ألم يعلم بأن الله يرى ﴿١٥﴾

* 16. Nay, if he desist not, We will assuredly *seize and* drag him by the forelock,

كلا لئن لم ينته لنسفعا بالناصية ﴿١٦﴾

* 17. A forelock lying, sinful.

ناصية كاذبة خاطئة ﴿١٧﴾

* 18. Then let him call his associates,

فليدع ناديه ﴿١٨﴾

19. We *too* will call *Our* angels *of punishment who will thrust him into Hell.*

سندع الزبانية ﴿١٩﴾

20. Nay, yield not thou to him, but prostrate thyself and draw near *to God.*

كلا لا تطعه واسجد واقترب ﴿٢٠﴾

سورة القدر مكية

آياتها ٦ (٩٧) ركوعها ١

(Revealed before Hijra)

1. In the name of Allah, the Gracious, the Merciful.

بسم الله الرحمن الرحيم ﴿١﴾

2. Surely, We sent it down on the Night of Destiny.

إنا أنزلنه في ليلة القدر ﴿٢﴾

3. And what should make thee know what the Night of Destiny is?

وما أدرىك ما ليلة القدر ﴿٣﴾

4. The Night of Destiny is better than a thousand months.

ليلة القدر خير من ألف شهر ﴿٤﴾

* 5. Therein descend angels and the Spirit by the command of their Lord—with every matter.

تنزل الملئكة والروح فيها بإذن ربهم من كل أمر ﴿٥﴾

* 6. *It is all* peace till the rising of the dawn.

سلم هي حتى مطلع الفجر ﴿٦﴾

رکوعها ١ سُوْرَةُ الْبَيِّنَةِ مَدَنِيَّةٌ (٩٨) اٰياتها ٩

AL-BAYYINAH

(Revealed after Hijra)

1. In the name of Allah, the Gracious, the Merciful.

بِسْمِ اللّٰهِ الرَّحْمٰنِ الرَّحِيْمِ ①

2. Those who disbelieve from among the People of the Book and the idolaters would not desist *from disbelief* until there came to them the clear evidence—

لَمْ يَكُنِ الَّذِيْنَ كَفَرُوْا مِنْ اَهْلِ الْكِتٰبِ وَالْمُشْرِكِيْنَ
مُنْفَكِّيْنَ حَتّٰى تَاْتِيَهُمُ الْبَيِّنَةُ ②

* 3. A Messenger from Allah, reciting *unto them the* pure Scriptures.

رَسُوْلٌ مِّنَ اللّٰهِ يَتْلُوْا صُحُفًا مُّطَهَّرَةً ③

* 4. Therein are lasting commandments.

فِيْهَا كُتُبٌ قَيِّمَةٌ ④

5. And those to whom the Book was given did not become divided until after clear evidence had come to them.

وَمَا تَفَرَّقَ الَّذِيْنَ اُوْتُوا الْكِتٰبَ اِلَّا مِنْۢ بَعْدِ مَا
جَآءَتْهُمُ الْبَيِّنَةُ ⑤

6. And they were not commanded but to serve Allah, being sincere to Him in obedience, *and* being upright, and to observe Prayer, and pay the Zakāt. And that is the religion *of the people* of the right path.

وَمَآ اُمِرُوْٓا اِلَّا لِيَعْبُدُوا اللّٰهَ مُخْلِصِيْنَ لَهُ
الدِّيْنَ ۙ حُنَفَآءَ وَيُقِيْمُوا الصَّلٰوةَ وَيُؤْتُوا الزَّكٰوةَ
وَذٰلِكَ دِيْنُ الْقَيِّمَةِ ⑥

7. Verily, those who disbelieve from among the People of the Book and the idolaters will be in the Fire of Hell, abiding therein. They are the worst of creatures.

اِنَّ الَّذِيْنَ كَفَرُوْا مِنْ اَهْلِ الْكِتٰبِ وَالْمُشْرِكِيْنَ
فِيْ نَارِ جَهَنَّمَ خٰلِدِيْنَ فِيْهَا ؕ اُولٰٓئِكَ هُمْ شَرُّ
الْبَرِيَّةِ ⑦

8. Verily, those who believe and do good works—they are the best of creatures.

اِنَّ الَّذِيْنَ اٰمَنُوْا وَعَمِلُوا الصّٰلِحٰتِ ۙ اُولٰٓئِكَ هُمْ
خَيْرُ الْبَرِيَّةِ ⑧

9. Their reward is with their Lord—Gardens of Eternity, through which streams flow; they will abide therein for ever. Allah is well pleased with them, and they are well pleased with Him. That is for him who fears his Lord.

جَزَآؤُهُمْ عِنْدَ رَبِّهِمْ جَنّٰتُ عَدْنٍ تَجْرِيْ مِنْ
تَحْتِهَا الْاَنْهٰرُ خٰلِدِيْنَ فِيْهَآ اَبَدًا ؕ رَضِيَ اللّٰهُ
ع ١ عَنْهُمْ وَرَضُوْا عَنْهُ ؕ ذٰلِكَ لِمَنْ خَشِيَ رَبَّهٗ ⑨
٩ ٢٣

سُوْرَةُ الزِّلْزَالِ مَكِّيَّةٌ (٩٩)

آياتها ٩ — ركوعها ١

AL-ZILZĀL

(Revealed before Hijra)

1. In the name of Allah, the Gracious, the Merciful.

بِسْمِ اللّٰهِ الرَّحْمٰنِ الرَّحِيْمِ ﴿١﴾

2. When the earth is shaken with her *violent* shaking,

إِذَا زُلْزِلَتِ الْأَرْضُ زِلْزَالَهَا ﴿٢﴾

3. And the earth brings forth her burdens,

وَأَخْرَجَتِ الْأَرْضُ أَثْقَالَهَا ﴿٣﴾

4. And man says, 'What is the matter with her?'

وَقَالَ الْإِنْسَانُ مَا لَهَا ﴿٤﴾

5. That day will she tell her news,

يَوْمَئِذٍ تُحَدِّثُ أَخْبَارَهَا ﴿٥﴾

* 6. For thy Lord will have revealed about her.

بِأَنَّ رَبَّكَ أَوْحٰى لَهَا ﴿٦﴾

7. On that day will men come forth in scattered groups that they may be shown *the results of* their works.

يَوْمَئِذٍ يَّصْدُرُ النَّاسُ أَشْتَاتًا لِّيُرَوْا أَعْمَالَهُمْ ﴿٧﴾

8. Then whoso does an atom's weight of good will see it,

فَمَنْ يَّعْمَلْ مِثْقَالَ ذَرَّةٍ خَيْرًا يَّرَهٗ ﴿٨﴾

9. And whoso does an atom's weight of evil will *also* see it.

وَمَنْ يَّعْمَلْ مِثْقَالَ ذَرَّةٍ شَرًّا يَّرَهٗ ﴿٩﴾

سُوْرَةُ الْعٰدِيٰتِ مَكِّيَّةٌ (١٠٠)

آياتها ١٢ — ركوعها ١

AL-ʿĀDIYĀT

(Revealed before Hijra)

1. In the name of Allah, the Gracious, the Merciful.

بِسْمِ اللّٰهِ الرَّحْمٰنِ الرَّحِيْمِ ﴿١﴾

2. By the snorting chargers *of the warriors*,

وَالْعٰدِيٰتِ ضَبْحًا ﴿٢﴾

3. Striking sparks of fire,

فَالْمُوْرِيٰتِ قَدْحًا ﴿٣﴾

4. And making raids at dawn,

فَالْمُغِيْرٰتِ صُبْحًا ﴿٤﴾

5. And raising clouds of dust thereby,

فَأَثَرْنَ بِهٖ نَقْعًا ﴿٥﴾

* 6. And penetrating thereby into the centre of *the enemy* forces,

فَوَسَطْنَ بِهٖ جَمْعًا ﴿٦﴾

7. Surely, man is ungrateful to his Lord;

إِنَّ الْإِنْسَانَ لِرَبِّهِ لَكَنُودٌ ۝٧

8. And surely, he is a witness unto that;

وَإِنَّهُ عَلَىٰ ذَٰلِكَ لَشَهِيدٌ ۝٨

9. And surely, he is very keen for the love of wealth.

وَإِنَّهُ لِحُبِّ الْخَيْرِ لَشَدِيدٌ ۝٩

10. Does not such a one know that when those in the graves are raised,

أَفَلَا يَعْلَمُ إِذَا بُعْثِرَ مَا فِي الْقُبُورِ ۝١٠

11. And that which is in the breasts is brought forth,

وَحُصِّلَ مَا فِي الصُّدُورِ ۝١١

12. Surely their Lord will, on that day, be fully Aware of them.

إِنَّ رَبَّهُمْ بِهِمْ يَوْمَئِذٍ لَخَبِيرٌ ۝١٢

سُورَةُ الْقَارِعَةِ مَكِّيَّةٌ

آياتها ١٢ (١٠١) ركوعها ١

Chapter 101 AL-QĀRI'AH Part 30

(Revealed before Hijra)

1. In the name of Allah, the Gracious, the Merciful.

بِسْمِ اللَّهِ الرَّحْمَٰنِ الرَّحِيمِ ۝١

2. The great Calamity!

الْقَارِعَةُ ۝٢

3. What is the great Calamity?

مَا الْقَارِعَةُ ۝٣

4. And what should make thee know what the great Calamity is?

وَمَا أَدْرَاكَ مَا الْقَارِعَةُ ۝٤

5. The day when mankind will be like scattered moths,

يَوْمَ يَكُونُ النَّاسُ كَالْفَرَاشِ الْمَبْثُوثِ ۝٥

6. And the mountains will be like carded wool.

وَتَكُونُ الْجِبَالُ كَالْعِهْنِ الْمَنْفُوشِ ۝٦

7. Then, as for him whose scales are heavy,

فَأَمَّا مَنْ ثَقُلَتْ مَوَازِينُهُ ۝٧

8. He will have a pleasant life.

فَهُوَ فِي عِيشَةٍ رَاضِيَةٍ ۝٨

9. But as for him whose scales are light,

وَأَمَّا مَنْ خَفَّتْ مَوَازِينُهُ ۝٩

* 10. Hell will be his *nursing* mother.

فَأُمُّهُ هَاوِيَةٌ ۝١٠

11. And what should make thee know what that is?

وَمَا أَدْرَاكَ مَا هِيَهْ ۝١١

12. *It is* a burning Fire.

نَارٌ حَامِيَةٌ ۝١٢

سُوْرَةُ التَّكَاثُرِ مَكِّيَّةٌ (١٠٢)

AL-TAKĀTHUR

(Revealed before Hijra)

1. In the name of Allah, the Gracious, the Merciful.

بِسْمِ اللّٰهِ الرَّحْمٰنِ الرَّحِيْمِ ①

* 2. Mutual rivalry in *seeking worldly* increase diverts you *from God*

اَلْهٰكُمُ التَّكَاثُرُ ②

* 3. Till you reach the graves.

حَتّٰى زُرْتُمُ الْمَقَابِرَ ③

4. Nay! you will soon come to know.

كَلَّا سَوْفَ تَعْلَمُوْنَ ④

5. Nay again! you will soon come to know.

ثُمَّ كَلَّا سَوْفَ تَعْلَمُوْنَ ⑤

* 6. Nay! if you only knew with certain knowledge,

كَلَّا لَوْ تَعْلَمُوْنَ عِلْمَ الْيَقِيْنِ ⑥

7. You will surely see Hell *in this very life.*

لَتَرَوُنَّ الْجَحِيْمَ ⑦

8. Aye, you will surely see it with the eye of certainty.

ثُمَّ لَتَرَوُنَّهَا عَيْنَ الْيَقِيْنِ ⑧

9. Then, on that day you shall be called to account about the *worldly* favours.

ثُمَّ لَتُسْـَٔلُنَّ يَوْمَئِذٍ عَنِ النَّعِيْمِ ⑨ ع

سُوْرَةُ الْعَصْرِ مَكِّيَّةٌ (١٠٣)

AL-'AṢR

(Revealed before Hijra)

1. In the name of Allah, the Gracious the Merciful.

بِسْمِ اللّٰهِ الرَّحْمٰنِ الرَّحِيْمِ ①

* 2. By the *fleeting* Time,

وَالْعَصْرِ ②

3. Surely, man is in *a state of* loss,

اِنَّ الْاِنْسَانَ لَفِيْ خُسْرٍ ③

4. Except those who believe and do good works, and exhort one another to *accept* truth, and exhort one another to be steadfast.

اِلَّا الَّذِيْنَ اٰمَنُوْا وَعَمِلُوا الصّٰلِحٰتِ وَتَوَاصَوْا بِالْحَقِّ ۙ وَتَوَاصَوْا بِالصَّبْرِ ④ ع

رُكُوۡعُهَا ۱ سُوۡرَةُ الۡهُمَزَةِ مَكِّيَّةٌ (۱۰۴) اٰيَاتُهَا ۱۰

AL-HUMAZAH

(Revealed before Hijra)

1. In the name of Allah, the Gracious, the Merciful.

بِسۡمِ اللّٰهِ الرَّحۡمٰنِ الرَّحِيۡمِ ﴿۱﴾

2. Woe to every backbiter, slanderer,

وَيۡلٌ لِّكُلِّ هُمَزَةٍ لُّمَزَةِ ﴿۲﴾

3. Who amasses wealth and counts it time after time.

الَّذِىۡ جَمَعَ مَالًا وَّعَدَّدَهٗ ﴿۳﴾

4. He thinks that his wealth will make him immortal.

يَحۡسَبُ اَنَّ مَالَهٗۤ اَخۡلَدَهٗ ﴿۴﴾

* 5. Nay! he shall surely be cast into the crushing punishment.

كَلَّا لَيُنۡۢبَذَنَّ فِى الۡحُطَمَةِ ﴿۵﴾

* 6. And what should make thee know what the crushing punishment is?

وَمَاۤ اَدۡرٰٮكَ مَا الۡحُطَمَةُ ﴿۶﴾

7. *It is* Allah's kindled fire,

نَارُ اللّٰهِ الۡمُوۡقَدَةُ ﴿۷﴾

* 8. Which rises over the hearts.

الَّتِىۡ تَطَّلِعُ عَلَى الۡاَفۡـِٕدَةِ ﴿۸﴾

* 9. It will be closed in on them

اِنَّهَا عَلَيۡهِمۡ مُّؤۡصَدَةٌ ﴿۹﴾

* 10. In *the form of* extended columns.

فِىۡ عَمَدٍ مُّمَدَّدَةٍ ﴿۱۰﴾ ع ۲۹

رُكُوۡعُهَا ۱ سُوۡرَةُ الۡفِيۡلِ مَكِّيَّةٌ (۱۰۵) اٰيَاتُهَا ۶

Chapter 105 Part 30

AL-FĪL

(Revealed before Hijra)

1. In the name of Allah, the Gracious, the Merciful.

بِسۡمِ اللّٰهِ الرَّحۡمٰنِ الرَّحِيۡمِ ﴿۱﴾

2. Hast thou not seen how thy Lord dealt with the People of the Elephant*?

اَلَمۡ تَرَ كَيۡفَ فَعَلَ رَبُّكَ بِاَصۡحٰبِ الۡفِيۡلِ ﴿۲﴾

3. Did He not cause their plan to miscarry?

اَلَمۡ يَجۡعَلۡ كَيۡدَهُمۡ فِىۡ تَضۡلِيۡلٍ ﴿۳﴾

4. And He sent against them swarms of birds,

وَّاَرۡسَلَ عَلَيۡهِمۡ طَيۡرًا اَبَابِيۡلَ ﴿۴﴾

5. *Which ate their carrion*, striking them against stones of clay.

تَرۡمِيۡهِمۡ بِحِجَارَةٍ مِّنۡ سِجِّيۡلٍ ﴿۵﴾

6. And *thus* made them like broken straw, eaten up.

فَجَعَلَهُمۡ كَعَصۡفٍ مَّاۡكُوۡلٍ ﴿۶﴾ ع ۳۰

* Abraha, the Christian viceroy in Yaman of the King of Abyssinia.

ركوعها ١ سُوْرَةُ الْقُرَيْشِ مَكِّيَّةٌ (١٠٦) اٰياتها ٥

AL-QURAISH

(Revealed before Hijra)

1. In the name of Allah, the Gracious, the Merciful.

بِسْمِ اللّٰهِ الرَّحْمٰنِ الرَّحِيْمِ ①

* 2. Because of the attachment of the Quraish—

لِاِيْلٰفِ قُرَيْشٍ ②

* 3. *His* making them attached to *their* journey in winter and summer—

اٖلٰفِهِمْ رِحْلَةَ الشِّتَآءِ وَالصَّيْفِ ③

* 4. They should worship the Lord of this House,

فَلْيَعْبُدُوْا رَبَّ هٰذَا الْبَيْتِ ④

5. Who has fed them against hunger, and has given them security against fear.

الَّذِيْٓ اَطْعَمَهُمْ مِّنْ جُوْعٍ ۙ وَّاٰمَنَهُمْ مِّنْ خَوْفٍ ⑤ ع ٣١

ركوعها ١ سُوْرَةُ الْمَاعُوْنِ مَكِّيَّةٌ (١٠٧) اٰياتها ٨

Part 30 Chapter 107

AL-MĀ'ŪN

(Revealed before Hijra)

1. In the name of Allah, the Gracious, the Merciful.

بِسْمِ اللّٰهِ الرَّحْمٰنِ الرَّحِيْمِ ①

2. Hast thou seen him who rejects religion?

اَرَءَيْتَ الَّذِيْ يُكَذِّبُ بِالدِّيْنِ ②

3. That is the one who drives away the orphan,

فَذٰلِكَ الَّذِيْ يَدُعُّ الْيَتِيْمَ ③

4. And urges not the feeding of the poor.

وَلَا يَحُضُّ عَلٰى طَعَامِ الْمِسْكِيْنِ ④

5. So woe to those who pray,

فَوَيْلٌ لِّلْمُصَلِّيْنَ ⑤

6. But are unmindful of their Prayer.

الَّذِيْنَ هُمْ عَنْ صَلَاتِهِمْ سَاهُوْنَ ⑥

* 7. They like to be seen *of men*,

الَّذِيْنَ هُمْ يُرَآءُوْنَ ⑦

* 8. And withhold *legal* alms.

وَيَمْنَعُوْنَ الْمَاعُوْنَ ⑧ ع ٣٢

سُورَةُ الْكَوْثَرِ مَكِّيَّةٌ (١٠٨)

AL-KAUTHAR

(Revealed before Hijra)

1. In the name of Allah, the Gracious, the Merciful.

بِسْمِ اللّٰهِ الرَّحْمٰنِ الرَّحِيْمِ ﴿١﴾

2. Surely We have given thee abundance *of good;*

اِنَّآ اَعْطَيْنٰكَ الْكَوْثَرَ ﴿٢﴾

3. So pray to thy Lord, and offer sacrifice.

فَصَلِّ لِرَبِّكَ وَانْحَرْ ﴿٣﴾

4. Surely, it is thy enemy who is without issue.

اِنَّ شَانِئَكَ هُوَ الْاَبْتَرُ ﴿٤﴾

سُورَةُ الْكٰفِرُوْنَ مَكِّيَّةٌ (١٠٩)

Chapter 109 Part 30

AL-KĀFIRŪN

(Revealed before Hijra)

1. In the name of Allah, the Gracious, the Merciful.

بِسْمِ اللّٰهِ الرَّحْمٰنِ الرَّحِيْمِ ﴿١﴾

2. Say, 'O ye disbelievers!

قُلْ يٰٓاَيُّهَا الْكٰفِرُوْنَ ﴿٢﴾

3. 'I worship not that which you worship;

لَآ اَعْبُدُ مَا تَعْبُدُوْنَ ﴿٣﴾

4. 'Nor worship you what I worship.

وَلَآ اَنْتُمْ عٰبِدُوْنَ مَآ اَعْبُدُ ﴿٤﴾

5. 'And I am not *going* to worship that which you worship;

وَلَآ اَنَا عَابِدٌ مَّا عَبَدْتُّمْ ﴿٥﴾

6. 'Nor will you worship what I worship.

وَلَآ اَنْتُمْ عٰبِدُوْنَ مَآ اَعْبُدُ ﴿٦﴾

7. 'For you your religion, and for me my religion.'

لَكُمْ دِيْنُكُمْ وَلِيَ دِيْنِ ﴿٧﴾

سُورَةُ النَّصْرِ مَدَنِيَّةٌ

(١١٠)

AL-NAṢR

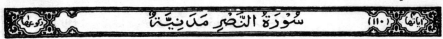

(Revealed after Hijra)

1 In the name of Allah, the Gracious, the Merciful.

بِسْمِ اللّٰهِ الرَّحْمٰنِ الرَّحِيْمِ (١)

2. When the help of Allah comes, and the victory,

إِذَا جَآءَ نَصْرُ اللّٰهِ وَالْفَتْحُ (٢)

3. And thou seest men entering the religion of Allah in troops,

وَرَأَيْتَ النَّاسَ يَدْخُلُوْنَ فِيْ دِيْنِ اللّٰهِ أَفْوَاجًا (٣)

4. Glorify thy Lord, with *His* praise, and seek forgiveness of Him. Surely He is Oft-Returning *with compassion*.

فَسَبِّحْ بِحَمْدِ رَبِّكَ وَاسْتَغْفِرْهُ إِنَّهُ كَانَ تَوَّابًا (٤) ع

وقف النبي صلى الله عليه وسلم

سُورَةُ اللَّهَبِ مَكِّيَّةٌ

(١١١) اٰياتها ٦

AL-LAHAB

(Revealed before Hijra)

1. In the name of Allah, the Gracious, the Merciful.

بِسْمِ اللّٰهِ الرَّحْمٰنِ الرَّحِيْمِ (١)

* 2. Perished be the two hands of Abū Lahab, and he will perish.

تَبَّتْ يَدَآ أَبِيْ لَهَبٍ وَّتَبَّ (٢)

3. His wealth and what he has earned shall avail him not.

مَآ أَغْنٰى عَنْهُ مَالُهُ وَمَا كَسَبَ (٣)

4. Soon shall he enter into a blazing fire;

سَيَصْلٰى نَارًا ذَاتَ لَهَبٍ (٤)

* 5. And his wife *too*, who goes about slandering.

وَّامْرَأَتُهُ حَمَّالَةَ الْحَطَبِ (٥)

6. Round her neck shall be a halter of twisted palm-fibre.

فِيْ جِيْدِهَا حَبْلٌ مِّنْ مَّسَدٍ (٦) ع

سُوْرَةُ الْإِخْلَاصِ مَكِّيَّةٌ (١١٢)

AL-IKHLĀṢ

(Revealed before Hijra)

1. In the name of Allah, the Gracious, the Merciful.	بِسْمِ اللّٰهِ الرَّحْمٰنِ الرَّحِيْمِ ﴿١﴾
2. Say, 'He is Allah, the One;	قُلْ هُوَ اللّٰهُ اَحَدٌ ﴿٢﴾
3. 'Allah, the Independent and Besought of all.	اَللّٰهُ الصَّمَدُ ﴿٣﴾
4. 'He begets not, nor is He begotten;	لَمْ يَلِدْ ۙ وَلَمْ يُوْلَدْ ﴿٤﴾
5. 'And there is none like unto Him.'	وَلَمْ يَكُنْ لَّهٗ كُفُوًا اَحَدٌ ﴿٥﴾ ع

سُوْرَةُ الْفَلَقِ مَدَنِيَّةٌ (١١٣)

Chapter 113 Part 30

AL-FALAQ

(Revealed after Hijra)

1. In the name of Allah, the Gracious, the Merciful.	بِسْمِ اللّٰهِ الرَّحْمٰنِ الرَّحِيْمِ ﴿١﴾
* 2. Say, 'I seek refuge in the Lord of the dawn,	قُلْ اَعُوْذُ بِرَبِّ الْفَلَقِ ﴿٢﴾
3. 'From the evil of that which He has created,	مِنْ شَرِّ مَا خَلَقَ ﴿٣﴾
4. 'And from the evil of the night when it overspreads,	وَمِنْ شَرِّ غَاسِقٍ اِذَا وَقَبَ ﴿٤﴾
5. 'And from the evil of those who blow into knots *to undo them*,	وَمِنْ شَرِّ النَّفّٰثٰتِ فِي الْعُقَدِ ﴿٥﴾
6. 'And from the evil of the envier when he envies.'	وَمِنْ شَرِّ حَاسِدٍ اِذَا حَسَدَ ﴿٦﴾ ع

سُوْرَةُ النَّاسِ مَدَنِيَّةٌ (١١٤)

AL-NĀS

(Revealed after Hijra)

1. In the name of Allah, the Gracious, the Merciful.

بِسْمِ اللّٰهِ الرَّحْمٰنِ الرَّحِيْمِ ﴿١﴾

2. Say, 'I seek refuge in the Lord of mankind,

قُلْ اَعُوْذُ بِرَبِّ النَّاسِ ﴿٢﴾

3. 'The King of mankind,

مَلِكِ النَّاسِ ﴿٣﴾

4. 'The God of mankind,

اِلٰهِ النَّاسِ ﴿٤﴾

5. 'From the evil of the sneaking whisperer,

مِنْ شَرِّ الْوَسْوَاسِ ۙ الْخَنَّاسِ ﴿٥﴾

6. 'Who whispers into the hearts of men,

الَّذِيْ يُوَسْوِسُ فِيْ صُدُوْرِ النَّاسِ ﴿٦﴾

7. 'From among the Jinn and mankind.'

مِنَ الْجِنَّةِ وَالنَّاسِ ﴿٧﴾

SOME ARABIC WORDS EXPLAINED

Abū Lahb: His real name was Abd al-'Uzza and he was an uncle of the Holy Prophet.

Al-Jūdī: is one of those mountains which divide Armenia on the south from Mesopotamia and that part of Assyria which is inhabited by the Curds, from whom the mountain took the name of Cardū or Gardu but the Greeks turned it into Gordyaei. The remains of the ark were to be seen on the Gordyaen mountains, and Emperor Heraclius is said to have gone from the town of Thamanin up to the mountain al-Jūdī and saw the place of the ark. There was also formerly a famous monastery on one of these mountains called *the monastery of the ark.*

Allah: The proper name of God.

Al-Safā wal Marwa: Two hills near the Ka'ba in Mecca which Arabian history and the traditions of Islam connect with the story of Hagar and Ishmael. Abraham left them in the wilderness near these hills. They stand as a monument to Hagar's travail when she ran between them seven times in search of water for Ishmael, and seven circuits between these hills constitute one of the rites of the Pilgrimage.

'Arafāt: The name given to a plain or valley near Mecca where pilgrims halt in the latter portion of the ninth day of Dhū'l-Ḥijja. It is nine miles from Mecca and the halt of the pilgrims at this place forms one of the principal ceremonies of the Pilgrimage.

Badr: Literally meaning 'full moon,' is the name of a place on the route between Mecca and Medina. Here the first regular battle took place between Muslims and the Quraish of Mecca in which the Quraishite power received a severe shaking.

Bahīra: A name given by pagan Arabs to a she-camel (according to some also an ewe or a she-goat) which they let loose to feed, after slitting its ears. It was dedicated to some god and its milk was not used, nor its back.

Ba'l: The name of a god, probably the sun-god.

Becca: is the name given to the valley of Mecca. The word is also considered by some to be the same as Mecca, its *meem* having been changed into *bay.*

Dhū'l-Nun or *Sāhib al-Hūt:* The Prophet Jonah.

Dhū'l-Qarnain: Dhū'l Qarnain mentioned in the Qur'ān refers to King Cyrus, the founder of the Medo-Persian empire which represented the two horns of the ram of Daniel's famous dream.

Hajj: Pilgrimage to the Ka'ba.

Hām or *Hāmī:* A camel forbidden to be used by the Arabs for riding or carrying burdens. The she-camel was neither ridden nor shorn of her hair and was not debarred from pasture or water.

Hunain: Scene of an important battle between the Holy Prophet and certain pagan tribes of Arabia in 8 A. H. The place lies to the south-east of Mecca, about 15 miles from it.

Iblīs: is a being who contains little of good and much of evil and who, on account of his having despaired of God's mercy, owing to his disobedience, is left perplexed and confounded. *Iblīs* may be said to represent the powers of evil as distinguished from the powers of good.

Idrīs: Enoch of the Bible.

Jālūt: In the Bible the parallel name is Goliath (I Sam. 17 : 4) which means, running, ravaging and destroying spirits or 'a leader' or 'a giant'.

Jinn: This word has been applied in the Qur'ān to the following:

(a) Evil spirits which inspire evil thoughts in the minds of men. They are the agents of Satan;
(b) Some imaginary beings whom the infidels worshipped but who existed nowhere in the world;
(c) The inhabitants of northern hilly tracts of Europe, of white and red colour, whom other peoples looked upon as beings separate from other human beings and who lived detached from the civilized peoples of Asia but who were destined to make great material progress in the latter days and to lead a great revolt against religion;
(d) Peoples belonging to alien religions and nationalities; and
(e) Wild and savage peoples who in pre-historic times, before man had developed enough morally to be given a revealed code of laws, lived in caves and hollows of the earth and were subject to no rules of conduct.

Ka'ba: The sacred House at Mecca to which Muslims turn their faces while praying.

Manna: The root meaning of this word is: (1) a favour; (2) anything obtained without trouble or difficulty; (3) honey-dew.

Mash'ar al-Harām: is the name given to a small hill in Muzdalifah which lies between Mecca and 'Arafāt. It is about six miles from Mecca. Here the pilgrims stop for the night after their return from 'Arafāt on the evening of the ninth day of the month of Ḥajj.

Qiblah: Literally meaning direction to which a person turns while praying, refers to the Ka'ba at Mecca.

Quraish: A famous tribe of Mecca to which the Holy Prophet belonged.

Rā'inā: The word means, 'look to us', but with a little change of the accent the word means, a foolish or conceited person.

Sā'ibah: A she-camel set free by the Arabs to go wherever she pleased, generally as an offering to the gods. Often a she-camel having given birth to ten female young ones was let loose to pasture where she would, and she was not ridden nor was her milk drunk except by her young.

Salwā: A whitish bird resembling a quail found in some parts of Arabia and the neighbouring countries. The root meaning of this word is: (1) whatever renders a person contented and happy; (2) honey.

Shahr Ramadān: The Islamic month of fasting.

Tālūt: In the Bible the parallel name is Saul (I Sam. 10 : 23).

Tuwā: The name of the valley where the first manifestation of God to Moses took place.

'Umra: Lesser Pilgrimage in which some of the rites of the Pilgrimage are left out.

Unzurnā: Ihe word means, 'have regard for us'.

Wādī al-Naml: The name of a valley which is situated between Jibrun and 'Asqalān, and Namlah is the name of a tribe.

Wasīlah: A she-camel that was let loose by the Arabs in the name of a god after she had given birth to seven female ones consecutively. If, at the seventh birth, she bore a pair, male and female, these were also le loose.

Zaid: A freed-slave of the Holy Prophet to whom was married (and afterwards divorced by him) Zainab, the daughter of the Holy Prophet's aunt.

Zakāt: Literally meaning increase, purification; technically signifies the obligatory alms prescribed by Islam.

Zaqqūm: It is a dust-coloured tree, having small round leaves without thorns. It has a pungent odour and is bitter. The word also means, any deadly food.

INDEX

Effacer of Sins, (Al-'Afuww) 4: 150; 22: 61; 58: 3.
Enlarger of the means of subsistence; (Al-Basit) 17: 31; 30: 38; 42: 13.
Equitable, (Al-Muqsit) 60: 9.
Exalted, (Al-Mutakabbir) 59: 24.
Exalter, (Al-Rafi) 40: 16.

Fashioner, (Al-Musawwir) 59: 25.
First, (Al-Awwal) 57: 4.
Forbearing, (Al-Halim) 2: 226; 22: 60; 33: 52; 64: 18.
Forgiver; The Great (Al-Ghaffar) 22: 61; 38: 67; 64: 15.
Forgiver of Sin, (Ghafer-izambe) 40: 4.
Forgiving; Liberal in (Wasse-ul-Maghferate) 53: 33.
Forgiving; The Most (Al-Ghafur) 4: 25, 44, 57; 22: 61; 58: 3, 60: 13; 64: 15.
Friend; (Al-Waliyy) 4: 46; 12: 102; 42: 10, 29.

Gatherer; Assembler of mankind on the Day of Judgement; (Al-Jami') 3: 10; 34: 27.
Generous; The Most (Al-Akra'm) 96: 4.
Glorious; (Al-Majid) 85: 16.
Gracious; (Al-Rahman) 1: 3.
Great; (Al-Azim) 42: 5; 56: 97.
Great; Incomparably (Al-Kabir) 4: 35; 22: 63; 31: 31; 34: 24.
Gaurdian; (Al-Hafiz) 34: 22.
Guardian; (Al-Vakil) 4: 172.
Guide; (Al-Hadi) 22: 55.

Healer; (Al-Shafi) 17: 83; 41: 45.
Helper; (Al-Naseer) 4: 46.
Hidden; One through whom hidden reality of everything is revealed; (al-Batin) 57: 4.
High; (Al-Aliyy) 4: 35; 22: 63; 31: 31; 42: 5; 43: 52.
High; The Most (Al-Muta'ali) 13: 10; 42: 5; 87: 2; 92: 21.
Holy One; (Al:Quddus) 59: 24.

Incomprehensible; The knower of all subtleties; The Benignant; (Al-Latif) 6: 104; 12: 101; 22: 64; 31: 17; 42: 20.
Indulgent; The Most (Al-Afuww) 4: 44.
Inheritor; (Al-Warith) 15: 24; 21: 90; 28: 59.

Judge; (Al-Fallah) 34: 27.
Judges; The Best of (Khair-ul-Ha'kemeen) 10: 110; 95: 9.
Judge; The Wise. 35: 3.

King of Mankind; (Malik-inna's) 114: 3.
Knower of the unseen and the seen; 59: 23.

Last; (Al-Akhir) 57: 4.
Life-giver; (Al-Muhyi) 21: 51; 40: 69.
Light; (Al-Nur) 24: 36.
Living; (Al-Hayy) 2: 256; 3: 3.
Lord; (Al-Rabb) 1: 2; 5: 28.
Lord of Great Ascents; (Dhil Mua'rij) 70: 4.
Lord of Honour; (Al-Majid) 85: 16.
Lord of Majesty; (Al-Jalil) 55: 28.
Lord of Retribution; (dhu-Intiquam) 39: 38.
Lord of Sovereignty; (Malik-al-Mulk) 62: 2.
Lord of the Throne; (dhul Arsh) 21: 21; 40: 16; 85: 16.
Loving; (Al-Wadud) 11: 91; 85: 15.

Maker; (Al-Bari) 59: 25.
Manifest Truth; (Haqq-ul-Mobeen) 24: 26.
Manifest; He to whose existence every created thing clearly points. (Al-Zahir) 57: 4.
Master of the Day of Judgement; (M'alike Yaum-ud-Din) 1: 4.
Master; The Excellent (Namul-Maula') 22: 79.
Merciful; (Al-Rahim) 1: 3; 4: 24, 57, 97.
Mighty; (Al-Aziz) 4: 57: 22: 75; 59: 24; 64: 19.

Nigh; The Nearest One; (Al-Qureeb) 34: 51.
Noble; (Al-Karim) 27: 41.

Oft-returning with Compassion; The Acceptor of Repentance; (Al; Tuwwab) 2: 55; 4: 65; 24: 11; 49: 13; 110: 4.
Omnipotent; (Al-Muqtadir) 54: 43, 56.
One; The (Al-Wahid) 13: 17; 38: 66; 39: 5.
Opener of doors of success for mankind; (Al-Fattah) 34: 27.
Originator; The Author of Life; (Al-Badi) 2: 118; 30: 28; 85: 14.

Peace; The Source of (Al-Salam) 59: 24.
Possessor of Power and Authority; (Al-Qadir) 16: 71; 30: 55; 64: 2.

Powerful; (Al-Qawiyy) 22: 75; 33: 26; 40: 23; 51: 59.
Praiseworthy; (Al-Hamid) 22: 65; 31: 27; 41: 43; 42: 29; 60: 7.
Preserver; He who preserves the faculties of all living things; The powerful; (Al-Muqit) 4: 86.
Protector; (Al-Muhaimin) 59: 24.
Provider; Best (Khairul-Ra'zequin) 22: 59; 34: 40; 62: 12.
Punishment; Severe in (Shadeed-il-Aquab) 40: 4.

Reckoner; (Al-Hasib) 4: 7, 87.
Reckoning; Swift at (Saree-ul-Hisab) 13: 42.
Repeater; Reproducer of life; (Al-Mu'id) 30: 28; 85: 14.
Repentance; Acceptor of (Qabil-e-Taub) 40: 4.
Requite; Possessor of the Power to (Dhun-teqa'm) 3: 5.
Ruler; (Al-Wali) 42: 5.

Self-subsisting and All-sustaining; (Al-Quyyum) 40: 4.
Self-sufficient; (Al-Ghaniyy) 2: 268; 22: 65; 27: 41; 31: 27; 60: 7; 64: 7.
Sovereign; (Al-Malik) 59: 29.
Strong; (Al-Matin) 51: 59.
Subduer or Reformer; (Al-Jabbar) 59: 24.
Sufficient (Al-Kafi) 39: 37.
Supreme; The Most (Al-Qahhar) 12: 40; 38: 66; 39: 5.
Sustainer; The Great (Al-Razzaq) 22: 59; 51: 59; 62: 12.
Swift to take Account; (Sari-ul-Hisab) 3: 200.

True; The (Al-Haqq) 10: 33.

Unique; The Lord of Unity; (Al-Ahad) 112: 2.

Watchful; (Al-Raqib) 33: 53.
Wise; The (Al-Hakim) 4: 57; 59: 25; 64: 19.
Witness; The Observer; (Al-Shahid) 4: 80; 33: 56; 34: 48.

(iii) *ALLAH, FAVOURS OF*
— are countless. 14: 35; 16: 19.
Allah is gracious to mankind. 27: 74.

(iv) *ALLAH, FRIENDSHIP WITH*
— is for those who are mindful of their duty. 45: 20.
— is for those who believe. 2: 258.
— is sufficient. 4: 46.
Allah is the guardian friend. 42: 10.

(v) *ALLAH, GLORIFICATION OF; WITH HIS PRAISE*
Everything glorifies Allah. 17: 45; 24: 42; 59: 2; 62: 2.
Allah enjoins all to glorify Him with His praise. 33: 43; 40: 56; 87: 2.
Glorify Allah before sunrise and at sunset and at night. 50: 40, 41.
Glorify Allah at the setting of the stars. 52: 50.
Glorify Allah during the greater part of the night. 76: 27.
Angels glorify Allah. 2: 31; 40: 8.
Thunder glorifies Allah with His praise. 13: 14.
Birds (i.e. spiritually exalted people) and the mountains (i.e. the chiefs) glorify Allah. 38: 19, 20.
Mountains and birds (i.e. righteous people) celebrated Allah's praise with David. 21: 80; 34: 11.

(vi) *ALLAH, KNOWLEDGE OF*
— extends over heavens and earth. 2: 256.
— of what troubles the mind of man. 50: 17.
— about the Hour and all that is in the wombs. 41: 48.
— concerning the secret and hidden. 20: 8.
— of secret thoughts and open words. 6: 4.
— of every falling leaf. 6: 60.
— of secret counsels. 58: 8.

(vii) *ALLAH, LOVE OF*
— for those who trust in Him. 3: 160.
— gains one His blessings. 27: 9.
— secured by turning to Him. 2: 223
— for the steadfast. 3: 147.
— those who fulfil their duty. 3: 77; 9: 4, 7.
— for those who judge equitably. 5: 43.
— for those who do good to others. 2: 196; 3: 135, 149.
— can be won by all who strive for it. 29: 70.

(viii) *ALLAH, MEETING WITH*
Those who do not believe in — are arrogant. 16: 23; 25: 22.
In — wordly desires fall off. 26: 46—52.

(ix) *ALLAH, MERCY OF*
Sinners can obtain —. 39: 54.
— embraces every thing. 6: 148; 7: 157; 40: 8.

APPENDIX

PREVIOUS TRANSLATION

PROPOSED TRANSLATION/NOTES

AL-FATEHA

7.
Those who have not incurred *Thy* displeasure,

غَيْرِ الْمَغْضُوبِ عَلَيْهِمْ

those who have not incurred displeasure

Note: The reader should not be misled by the word *Thy* in italics to believe that the word 'maghzoob' (مغضوب) is confined only to the wrath of God incurred by the Jews. This expression is open and covers not only the wrath of God but also the wrath of people which they may incur.

AL BAQARA

7. Those who have disbelieved---it being equal to them whether thou warn them or warn them not– they will not believe.

إِنَّ الَّذِينَ كَفَرُوا سَوَاءٌ عَلَيْهِمْ ءَأَنْذَرْتَهُمْ أَمْ لَمْ تُنْذِرْهُمْ لَا يُؤْمِنُونَ ⑦

7. Those who have disbelieved --- it is equal to them whether you warn them or warn them not ---they will not believe.

11. In their hearts was a disease, and Allah has increased their disease to them; and for them is a grievous punishment because they lied.

فِي قُلُوبِهِمْ مَرَضٌ فَزَادَهُمُ اللَّهُ مَرَضًا ۚ وَلَهُمْ عَذَابٌ أَلِيمٌ ۙ بِمَا كَانُوا يَكْذِبُونَ ⑪

11. In their hearts was a disease, and Allah has increased their disease to them; and for them is a grievous punishment, because **they used to lie.**

19. *They are* deaf, dumb *and* blind; so they will not return.

صُمٌّ بُكْمٌ عُمْيٌ فَهُمْ لَا يَرْجِعُونَ ﴿١٩﴾

Note: This verse may apply to the category of hypocrites who are described as deaf, dumb and blind because of their resolve not to listen to truth, not to speak truth nor to see truth. So they have wilfully denied their faculties and locked themselves in.

26. they will say: 'This is what was given us before,' and gifts mutually resembling shall be brought to them.

قَالُوا هَٰذَا الَّذِي رُزِقْنَا مِن قَبْلُ وَأُتُوا بِهِ مُتَشَابِهًا

26. they will say: 'This is what was given us before,' **Whereas only similar things** shall be brought to them.

31. And when thy Lord said to the angels: 'I am about to place a vicegerent in the earth,'

وَإِذْ قَالَ رَبُّكَ لِلْمَلَائِكَةِ إِنِّي جَاعِلٌ فِي الْأَرْضِ خَلِيفَةً

31. And when thy Lord said to the angels: 'I am about to **appoint** a vicegerent in the earth,'

35. And *remember the time* when We said to the angels: 'Submit to Adam,' and they *all* submitted. But Iblīs *did not*. He refused and was too proud; and he was of the disbelievers.

وَإِذْ قُلْنَا لِلْمَلَائِكَةِ اسْجُدُوا لِآدَمَ فَسَجَدُوا إِلَّا إِبْلِيسَ أَبَىٰ وَاسْتَكْبَرَ وَكَانَ مِنَ الْكَافِرِينَ ﴿٣٥﴾

35. And remember the time, when We said to the angels: 'Submit to Adam,' and they all submitted **except Iblis**. He refused and **acted with arrogance**; and he was of the disbelievers.

76. Do you expect that they will believe you when a party of them hear the word of Allah, then pervert it after they have understood it, and they know *the consequences thereof?*

أَفَتَطْمَعُونَ أَن يُؤْمِنُوا لَكُمْ وَقَدْ كَانَ فَرِيقٌ مِّنْهُمْ يَسْمَعُونَ كَلَامَ اللَّهِ ثُمَّ يُحَرِّفُونَهُ مِن بَعْدِ مَا عَقَلُوهُ وَهُمْ يَعْلَمُونَ ﴿٧٦﴾

76. Do you **entertain hope that they will believe in you while a party from**

among them has been *wilfully* perverting the word of Allah after they had heard it and understood it and knew it full well.

113. Nay, whoever submits himself completely to Allah, and is the doer of good, shall have his reward with his Lord.

بَلٰى مَنْ اَسْلَمَ وَجْهَهٗ لِلّٰهِ وَهُوَ مُحْسِنٌ فَلَهٗۤ اَجْرُهٗ
عِنْدَ رَبِّهٖ

113. Nay, whoever submits himself completely to Allah, **while he is excellent in conduct**, shall have his reward with his Lord.

139. *Say*, '*We will adopt* the religion of Allah; and who is better than Allah in *teaching* religion, and Him alone do we worship.'

صِبْغَةَ اللّٰهِ ۚ وَمَنْ اَحْسَنُ مِنَ اللّٰهِ صِبْغَةً ۫ وَّنَحْنُ
لَهٗ عٰبِدُوْنَ ﴿۱۳۹﴾

Note: Religion of Allah does not mean that God follows any religion. It only means a religion revealed by God.

147. Those to whom We have given the Book recognize it even as they recognize their sons, but surely some of them conceal the truth knowingly.

اَلَّذِيْنَ اٰتَيْنٰهُمُ الْكِتٰبَ يَعْرِفُوْنَهٗ كَمَا يَعْرِفُوْنَ اَبْنَآءَهُمْ ؕ
وَاِنَّ فَرِيْقًا مِّنْهُمْ لَيَكْتُمُوْنَ الْحَقَّ وَهُمْ يَعْلَمُوْنَ ﴿۱۴۷﴾

147. Those to whom We have given the Book recognise it ***as the truth*** even as they recognise their sons, but surely some of them conceal the truth knowingly.

Note: The word *it* primarily refers to the signs of the truth which they witness in the conduct of the Holy Prophet, peace be on him. It is evident that he is a godly person because he displays God's attributes. As they recognize their sons from the signs and imprints of their own character upon them and know them thereby to truly belong to them, so a man of God has to be recognised by the attributes of God which are displayed in his conduct and way of life.

167. *Aye, they would certainly realize if they could see the time* when those who were followed shall disown their followers and

اِذْ تَبَرَّاَ الَّذِيْنَ اتُّبِعُوْا مِنَ الَّذِيْنَ اتَّبَعُوْا وَرَاَوُا الْعَذَابَ

shall see the punishment, and all their ties shall be cut asunder.

وَتَقَطَّعَتۡ بِهِمُ الۡاَسۡبَابُ ﴿۱۶۷﴾

167. ***Truly**, they would certainly realise if they could see the time* when those who were followed shall disown their followers and shall see the punishment, and all **the means of escape** shall be cut asunder.

169. O ye men! eat of what is lawful *and* good in the earth;

یٰۤاَیُّهَا النَّاسُ کُلُوۡا مِمَّا فِی الۡاَرۡضِ حَلٰلًا طَیِّبًا

169. O ye **people**! eat of what is lawful *and* **wholesome** in the earth;

Note: The word 'tayyib' (طيب) may apply to personal choice as well as to the wholesome condition of that which has been declared lawful. In the first case the same food being lawful could be wholesome for one and unwholesome for others because of differences of choice, taste and circumstance. In the second case it may refer to the condition of food indicating that the believers prefer to eat food which is not only lawful but also found in a good, healthy and wholesome condition.

179. But if one is granted any remission by one's brother, then pursuing *the matter for the realization of the blood-money* shall be done with fairness and *the murderer* shall pay him the blood-money in a handsome manner.

فَمَنۡ عُفِیَ لَهٗ مِنۡ اَخِیۡهِ شَیۡءٌ فَاتِّبَاعٌۢ بِالۡمَعۡرُوۡفِ وَ
اَدَآءٌ اِلَیۡهِ بِاِحۡسَانٍ

Note: Meaning that the blood money should be fairly and handsomely assessed and paid to the relatives of the murdered person.

188. and eat and drink until the white thread becomes distinct to you from the black thread of the dawn.

وَکُلُوۡا وَاشۡرَبُوۡا حَتّٰی یَتَبَیَّنَ لَکُمُ الۡخَیۡطُ الۡاَبۡیَضُ
مِنَ الۡخَیۡطِ الۡاَسۡوَدِ مِنَ الۡفَجۡرِ

Note: In fact, white thread is associated with dawn; as such, the meaning would be: . . . . . . until the white thread of dawn is distinguishable from the dark thread of night.

189. And do not devour your wealth among yourselves through falsehood, and offer it not *as bribe* to the authorities that you may knowingly devour a part of the wealth of *other* people with injustice.

وَلَا تَأْكُلُوْٓا اَمْوَالَكُمْ بَيْنَكُمْ بِالْبَاطِلِ وَتُدْلُوْا بِهَآ اِلَى الْحُكَّامِ لِتَاْكُلُوْا فَرِيْقًا مِّنْ اَمْوَالِ النَّاسِ بِالْاِثْمِ وَاَنْتُمْ تَعْلَمُوْنَ ﴿۱۸۹﴾

Note: Here the word *'other'* seems to be unnecessary since this verse seems to apply primarily to the public money or national wealth.

223. And they ask thee concerning menstruation. Say: 'It is a harmful thing, so keep away from women during menstruation,

وَيَسْـَٔلُوْنَكَ عَنِ الْمَحِيْضِ قُلْ هُوَ اَذًى فَاعْتَزِلُوا النِّسَآءَ فِي الْمَحِيْضِ

223. And they ask thee concerning menstruation. Say: **'It is indisposition,** so keep away from women during menstruation,

Note: The word *harmful* does not seem to do justice to the Arabic word *'aza'* (اذى) in this context. The word *'aza'* should be understood in the sense of indisposition and temporary discomfort. Otherwise it would reflect on God to have created something which is harmful for women, which is not correct.

254. These Messengers have We exalted, some of them above others: among them there are those to whom Allah spoke*; and some of them He exalted by degrees of rank.

تِلْكَ الرُّسُلُ فَضَّلْنَا بَعْضَهُمْ عَلٰى بَعْضٍ مِنْهُمْ مَّنْ كَلَّمَ اللّٰهُ وَرَفَعَ بَعْضَهُمْ دَرَجٰتٍ

Note: This verse can be translated by placing a pause after the word 'min hum' (منهم) and not before it. In this case the translation is more easily readable and understandable and would run as follows: These Messengers of whom We have exalted some above others. Allah spoke to them and exalted some of them in degrees of rank.

256. His knowledge extends over the heavens and the earth;

وَسِعَ كُرْسِيُّهُ السَّمٰوٰتِ وَالْاَرْضَ

256. His **throne** extends over the heavens and the earth. . . . .

Note: The word 'kursi' (کرسی) primarily means seat of power or throne. This meaning of the word has wider application and covers not only knowledge but also other requisites of government.

268.
and seek not what is bad to spend out of it when you would not take it yourselves except that you connive at it.

وَلَا تَيَمَّمُوا الْخَبِيثَ
مِنْهُ تُنْفِقُونَ وَلَسْتُمْ بِآخِذِيهِ إِلَّا أَنْ تُغْمِضُوا فِيهِ

268. and seek not what is bad to spend out of it, when you would not take it yourselves except **with eyes downcast with shame.**

277. Allah will abolish interest and will cause charity to increase. And Allah loves not anyone who is a confirmed disbeliever and an arch-sinner.

يَمْحَقُ اللَّهُ الرِّبٰوا وَيُرْبِي الصَّدَقٰتِ ۗ وَاللَّهُ لَا يُحِبُّ
كُلَّ كَفَّارٍ أَثِيمٍ ﴿٢٧٧﴾

Note: This verse gives a clear-cut verdict that economies based on interest and usury are bound to perish whereas economies where charity is emphasized will prosper.

287. Allah burdens not any soul beyond its capacity. It shall have *the reward* it earns, and it shall get *the punishment* it incurs. Our Lord, do not punish us, if we forget or fall into error; and our Lord, lay not on us a responsibility as Thou didst lay upon those before us. Our Lord, burden us not with what we have not the strength to bear; and efface our *sins*, and grant us forgiveness and have mercy on us; Thou art our Master; so help us Thou against the disbelieving people.

لَا يُكَلِّفُ اللَّهُ نَفْسًا إِلَّا وُسْعَهَا ۚ لَهَا مَا كَسَبَتْ وَعَلَيْهَا
مَا اكْتَسَبَتْ ۗ رَبَّنَا لَا تُؤَاخِذْنَا إِنْ نَسِينَا أَوْ أَخْطَأْنَا ۚ
رَبَّنَا وَلَا تَحْمِلْ عَلَيْنَا إِصْرًا كَمَا حَمَلْتَهُ عَلَى الَّذِينَ
مِنْ قَبْلِنَا ۚ رَبَّنَا وَلَا تُحَمِّلْنَا مَا لَا طَاقَةَ لَنَا بِهِ ۚ
وَاعْفُ عَنَّا ۟ وَاغْفِرْ لَنَا ۟ وَارْحَمْنَا ۟ أَنْتَ مَوْلٰنَا
فَانْصُرْنَا عَلَى الْقَوْمِ الْكٰفِرِينَ ﴿٢٨٧﴾

Note: This refers to earlier peoples who were entrusted with religious responsibilities but treated them with disrespect and deemed them to be a burden. As such professional clergy from the lower ranks of society were made to carry that burden on their shoulders and a religious clergy came to be born which monopolised the knowledge of religion while they were incapable of doing full justice to it. This process ultimately led to the creation of a religious clergy which was narrow-minded, arrogant and intolerant and few among them understood the philosophy and the magnanimity of the word of God. Such religious leadership is likened to donkeys in 62:6 (Al-Jumu'ah) whose backs are loaded with religious books for transportation but the donkeys understand little of what they carry. So the word *'Isran'* (اِصْرًا) should be understood in this context because any responsibility laid down by God cannot be treated as a burden from which true believers seek escape.

AL-'IMRAN

4 & 5. He has sent down to thee the Book containing the truth *and* fulfilling that which precedes it; and He sent down the Torah and the Gospel before *this*, as a guidance to the people; and He has sent down the Discrimination.

نَزَّلَ عَلَيْكَ الْكِتٰبَ بِالْحَقِّ مُصَدِّقًا لِّمَا بَيْنَ يَدَيْهِ
وَاَنْزَلَ التَّوْرٰىةَ وَالْاِنْجِيْلَ ۝
مِنْ قَبْلُ هُدًى لِّلنَّاسِ وَاَنْزَلَ الْفُرْقَانَ ۝

4 & 5. He has sent down to thee the Book containing the truth *and* **confirming that** which precedes it; and He sent down the Torah and the Gospel before *this*, as a guidance to the people; and He has sent down the Discrimination.

Note: The word *'musaddiqan'* (مُصَدِّقًا) has a wider application than the expression 'fulfilling' used in the original translation. It means confirming the truth of previous revelations as well as fulfilment and realization of the prophecies contained therein. In the light of this perhaps it would be more appropriate to translate the verse under study as above.
'Al-Furqan' means incortrovertible truth as well as anything which clearly distinguishes something from another; as such it works as a criterion.

16. For those who fear God, there are Gardens with their Lord, beneath which rivers flow; therein shall

لِلَّذِيْنَ اتَّقَوْا عِنْدَ
رَبِّهِمْ جَنّٰتٌ تَجْرِيْ مِنْ تَحْتِهَا الْاَنْهٰرُ خٰلِدِيْنَ فِيْهَا

they abide; and pure spouses and Allah's pleasure. And Allah is Mindful of *His* servants,

وَأَزْوَاجٌ مُّطَهَّرَةٌ وَرِضْوَانٌ مِّنَ اللَّهِ ۗ وَاللَّهُ بَصِيرٌۢ
بِالْعِبَادِ ۚ ﴿١٦﴾

16. For those who fear God, there are Gardens with their Lord, beneath which rivers flow; therein shall they abide; ***there are* also spouses purified *by Allah*** and Allah's pleasure. And Allah is Mindful of *His* servants.

19. Allah bears witness that there is no God but He—and *also do* the angels and those possessed of knowledge—Maintainer of justice; there is no God but He, the Mighty, the Wise.

شَهِدَ اللَّهُ أَنَّهُ لَا إِلَٰهَ إِلَّا هُوَ وَالْمَلَائِكَةُ وَأُولُو الْعِلْمِ
قَائِمًا بِالْقِسْطِ ۚ لَا إِلَٰهَ إِلَّا هُوَ الْعَزِيزُ الْحَكِيمُ ﴿١٩﴾

Note: In fact the Arabic expression *'Qaiman bil qist'* (قائما بالقسط) is much stronger than the translation 'maintainer of justice' indicates. 'Always standing guard over justice' would be a better translation.

29. Let not the believers take disbelievers for friends in preference to believers —and whoever does that has no connection with Allah—except that you cautiously guard against them. And Allah cautions you against His punishment; and to Allah is the returning.

لَا يَتَّخِذِ الْمُؤْمِنُونَ الْكَافِرِينَ أَوْلِيَاءَ مِن دُونِ
الْمُؤْمِنِينَ ۖ وَمَن يَفْعَلْ ذَٰلِكَ فَلَيْسَ مِنَ اللَّهِ
فِي شَيْءٍ إِلَّا أَن تَتَّقُوا مِنْهُمْ تُقَاةً ۗ وَيُحَذِّرُكُمُ
اللَّهُ نَفْسَهُ ۗ وَإِلَى اللَّهِ الْمَصِيرُ ﴿٢٩﴾

Note: The Arabic word *'yuhazziro kumullaho nafsahu'* (يحذركم الله نفسه) literally means that 'Allah cautions you against Himself', which means that He cautions you against taking liberties regarding His commands and dictates.

37. But when she was delivered of it, she said, 'My Lord, I am delivered of a female'—and Allah knew best what she had brought forth and the male *she was thinking of* was not like the female *she had brought forth*—

فَلَمَّا وَضَعَتْهَا قَالَتْ رَبِّ إِنِّي وَضَعْتُهَا أُنثَىٰ وَاللَّهُ
أَعْلَمُ بِمَا وَضَعَتْ وَلَيْسَ الذَّكَرُ كَالْأُنثَىٰ ۖ

37. But when she was delivered of it, she said 'My Lord, I am delivered of a female' --- **while Allah knows best what**

she had delivered and the male *she was thinking of* was not like the female *she had brought forth* ---

48. She said, 'My Lord, how shall I have a son, when no man has touched me?' He said, "Such is *the way of* Allah, He creates what He pleases. When He decrees a thing, He says to it, 'Be!' and it is.

قَالَتْ رَبِّ اَنّٰى يَكُوْنُ لِيْ وَلَدٌ وَّلَمْ يَمْسَسْنِيْ بَشَرٌ ؕ
قَالَ كَذٰلِكِ اللّٰهُ يَخْلُقُ مَا يَشَآءُ ؕ اِذَا قَضٰۤى اَمْرًا فَاِنَّمَا
يَقُوْلُ لَهٗ كُنْ فَيَكُوْنُ ۝٤٨

Note: The expression " 'Be!' and it is" does not indicate spontaneous transformation into existence from nothingness. It mean that the moment God wills, His will begins to take shape and ultimately is done as He desires.

74. 'And obey none but him who follows your religion;' – Say, 'Surely, the *true* guidance, the guidance of Allah, is that one may be given the like of that which has been given to you'—'or they would dispute with you before your Lord.'

وَلَا تُؤْمِنُوْۤا اِلَّا لِمَنْ تَبِعَ دِيْنَكُمْ ؕ قُلْ اِنَّ الْهُدٰى
هُدَى اللّٰهِ ۙ اَنْ يُّؤْتٰۤى اَحَدٌ مِّثْلَ مَاۤ اُوْتِيْتُمْ اَوْ
يُحَآجُّوْكُمْ عِنْدَ رَبِّكُمْ ؕ

74. 'And obey none but him who follows your religion'; --- **Say, *O Prophet,* Verily the guidance is the guidance from Allah *whatever He please.* What is essential is that everyone should be bestowed *with a teaching* like you were bestowed earlier. Otherwise they would have a right to argue against you in the presence of your Lord. . . .**

Note: This indicates that it was not the Jews who had a case to argue against the Holy Prophet (peace and blessings of Allah be upon him) merely because the teachings granted to him were not exactly the same as theirs. On the contrary, it would rather be the right of the people of Islam to argue against them had they been deprived of a Divine teaching altogether indicating the partiality of God in favour of the people of the Book. The difference in teaching against which the Jews were taking exception is totally irrelevant.

80. It is not *possible* for a man that Allah should give him the Book and dominion and prophethood, *and* then he should say to men: 'Be servants to me and not to Allah;' but *he would say*: 'Be solely devoted to the Lord because you teach the Book and because you study *it*.'

مَا كَانَ لِبَشَرٍ اَنْ يُّؤْتِيَهُ اللّٰهُ الْكِتٰبَ وَالْحُكْمَ وَ
النُّبُوَّةَ ثُمَّ يَقُوْلَ لِلنَّاسِ كُوْنُوْا عِبَادًا لِّيْ مِنْ دُوْنِ
اللّٰهِ وَلٰكِنْ كُوْنُوْا رَبّٰنِيّٖنَ بِمَا كُنْتُمْ تُعَلِّمُوْنَ الْكِتٰبَ
وَبِمَا كُنْتُمْ تَدْرُسُوْنَ ﴿٨٠﴾

80. It is not *possible* for a man that Allah should give him the Book and **wisdom** and prophethood, *and* then he should say to men: 'Be servants to me and not to Allah;' but *he would say:* 'Be solely devoted to the Lord because you teach the Book and because you study it.'

114. Among the People of the Book there is a party who stand *by their covenant*; they recite the word of Allah in the hours of night and prostrate themselves *before Him*.

مِنْ اَهْلِ الْكِتٰبِ اُمَّةٌ قَآئِمَةٌ يَّتْلُوْنَ
اٰيٰتِ اللّٰهِ اٰنَآءَ الَّيْلِ وَهُمْ يَسْجُدُوْنَ ﴿١١٤﴾

114. Among the People of the Book there is a party who **stand firm** *by their covenant;* they recite the word of Allah in the hours of night and prostrate themselves *before Him.*

131. O ye who believe! devour not interest involving diverse additions;

يٰٓاَيُّهَا الَّذِيْنَ اٰمَنُوْا لَا تَاْكُلُوا الرِّبٰٓوا اَضْعَافًا مُّضٰعَفَةً

131. O ye who believe! Devour not interest involving **multiple** additions;

139. This (the Qur'ān) is a clear demonstration to men, and a guidance and an admonition to the God-fearing.

هٰذَا بَيَانٌ لِّلنَّاسِ وَهُدًى وَّمَوْعِظَةٌ لِّلْمُتَّقِيْنَ ﴿١٣٩﴾

139. This, *the Qur'an,* is a clear **pronouncement** to men, and a guidance and an admonition to the God-fearing.

144. And you used to wish for this death before you met it; now you have seen it while you were *actually* looking for *it*.

وَلَقَدْ كُنْتُمْ تَمَنَّوْنَ الْمَوْتَ مِنْ قَبْلِ اَنْ تَلْقَوْهُ
فَقَدْ رَاَيْتُمُوْهُ وَاَنْتُمْ تَنْظُرُوْنَ ﴿١٤٤﴾

144. And you used to wish for this death before you met it, **now that you have seen it at last, you stand watching** ***as if transfixed.***

147. And many a Prophet there has been beside whom fought numerous companies *of their followers*. They slackened not for aught that befell them in the way of Allah, nor did they weaken, nor did they humiliate themselves *before the enemy*. And Allah loves the steadfast.

وَكَأَيِّن مِّن نَّبِيٍّ قَٰتَلَ مَعَهُۥ رِبِّيُّونَ كَثِيرٌ فَمَا
وَهَنُوا۟ لِمَآ أَصَابَهُمْ فِى سَبِيلِ ٱللَّهِ وَمَا ضَعُفُوا۟
وَمَا ٱسْتَكَانُوا۟ وَٱللَّهُ يُحِبُّ ٱلصَّٰبِرِينَ ﴿١٤٦﴾

Note: The word *'Ribbiyun'* (ربيون) has been merely translated as 'companies (of their followers)' --- without the essential connotation of godliness which is implied in the word (ربيون). We suggest the following alternative translation : "Beside whom fought **a large number of godly people.".**

153. And Allah had surely made good to you His promise when you were slaying and destroying them by His leave, until, when you became lax and disagreed among yourselves concerning the order and you disobeyed after He had shown you that which you loved, *He withdrew His help*. Among you were those who desired the present world, and among you were those who desired the next. Then He turned you away from them, that He might try you —and He has surely pardoned you, and Allah is Gracious to the believers.—

وَلَقَدْ صَدَقَكُمُ ٱللَّهُ وَعْدَهُۥٓ إِذْ تَحُسُّونَهُم بِإِذْنِهِۦ
حَتَّىٰٓ إِذَا فَشِلْتُمْ وَتَنَٰزَعْتُمْ فِى ٱلْأَمْرِ وَعَصَيْتُم مِّنۢ
بَعْدِ مَآ أَرَىٰكُم مَّا تُحِبُّونَ مِنكُم مَّن يُرِيدُ ٱلدُّنْيَا
وَمِنكُم مَّن يُرِيدُ ٱلْءَاخِرَةَ ثُمَّ صَرَفَكُمْ عَنْهُمْ
لِيَبْتَلِيَكُمْ وَلَقَدْ عَفَا عَنكُمْ وَٱللَّهُ ذُو فَضْلٍ
عَلَى ٱلْمُؤْمِنِينَ ﴿١٥٢﴾

153. And Allah had surely made good to you His promise when you were slaying and destroying them by His leave, **until, when you faltered** ***concerning obedience to the Holy Prophet, peace be upon him*** **and started arguing among yourselves regarding the true intent of the order and disobeyed after He had granted you your heart's desire** ***in the form of***

victory, He *withdrew His help.* Among you were those who desired the present world, and among you were those who desired the next. Then He turned you away from them, that He might try you -- - and He has surely pardoned you, and Allah is Gracious to the believers.

154. When you were running away and looked not back at anyone while the Messenger was calling out to you from your rear, then He gave you a sorrow in recompense for a sorrow, that you might not grieve for what escaped you, nor for what befell you. And Allah is well aware of what you do.

إِذْ تُصْعِدُونَ وَلَا تَلْوُنَ عَلَىٰٓ أَحَدٍ وَالرَّسُولُ يَدْعُوكُمْ فِىٓ أُخْرَىٰكُمْ فَأَثَٰبَكُمْ غَمًّۢا بِغَمٍّ لِّكَيْلَا تَحْزَنُوا عَلَىٰ مَا فَاتَكُمْ وَلَا مَآ أَصَٰبَكُمْ وَاللَّهُ خَبِيرٌۢ بِمَا تَعْمَلُونَ ۝١٥٤

Note: Sometimes the threat of a bigger loss does away with the pain of comparatively minor losses incurred earlier. A similar situation prevailed during the battle of Uhud when the rumour of the death of the Holy Prophet, may peace be on him, completely dispelled consideration of all personal sufferings and losses the Muslim combatants had experienced. Then the news of his survival turned the sense of loss into a sense of deep content and thanksgiving.

160. and consult them in matters *of administration*;

وَشَاوِرْهُمْ فِى الْأَمْرِ

160. and consult them in matters of **importance**

170. Nay, they are living, in the presence of their Lord, *and* are granted gifts *from Him,*

بَلْ أَحْيَآءٌ عِندَ رَبِّهِمْ يُرْزَقُونَ ۝١٧٠

170. Nay, they are living, in the presence of their Lord, **being well provided.**

185. And if they accuse thee of lying, even so were accused of lying Messengers before thee who came with clear Signs and books of wisdom and the shining Book.

فَإِن كَذَّبُوكَ فَقَدْ كُذِّبَ رُسُلٌ مِّن قَبْلِكَ جَآءُو بِالْبَيِّنَٰتِ وَالزُّبُرِ وَالْكِتَٰبِ الْمُنِيرِ ۝١٨٥

185. And if they accuse you of lying, even so were accused of lying Messengers before you who came with clear Signs and books of wisdom and **the illuminating Book.**

194. **Our Lord,** forgive us, therefore, our errors **and remove** from us our evils, and in **death number** us with the righteous.

رَبَّنَا فَاغْفِرْ لَنَا ذُنُوْبَنَا وَكَفِّرْ عَنَّا
سَيِّاٰتِنَا وَتَوَفَّنَا مَعَ الْاَبْرَارِ ﴿١٩٤﴾

194. Our Lord, forgive us, therefore, our **sins** and remove from us our evils, and in death **join us** with the righteous.

AL-NISA

2. O ye people! fear your Lord, Who created you from a single soul and created therefrom its mate, and from them twain spread many men and women; and fear Allah, in Whose name you appeal to one another, and *fear Him particularly respecting* ties of relationship. Verily, Allah watches over you.

يٰۤاَيُّهَا النَّاسُ اتَّقُوْا رَبَّكُمُ الَّذِيْ خَلَقَكُمْ مِّنْ نَّفْسٍ
وَّاحِدَةٍ وَّخَلَقَ مِنْهَا زَوْجَهَا وَبَثَّ مِنْهُمَا رِجَالًا كَثِيْرًا
وَّنِسَآءً ۚ وَاتَّقُوا اللّٰهَ الَّذِيْ تَسَآءَلُوْنَ بِهٖ وَالْاَرْحَامَ ؕ
اِنَّ اللّٰهَ كَانَ عَلَيْكُمْ رَقِيْبًا ﴿٢﴾

2. O ye people! Fear your Lord, Who created you from a single **being** and created therefrom its mate, and from **the two** spread many men and women; and fear Allah, in Whose name you appeal to one another, and *fear Him particularly respecting* ties of relationship. Verily, Allah watches over you.

4. And if you fear that you will not be fair in dealing with the orphans, then marry of women as may be agreeable to you, two, or three, or four; and if you fear you will not deal justly, then *marry only* one or what your right hands possess. That is the nearest *way* for you to avoid injustice.

وَاِنْ خِفْتُمْ اَلَّا تُقْسِطُوْا فِي الْيَتٰمٰى فَانْكِحُوْا مَا طَابَ
لَكُمْ مِّنَ النِّسَآءِ مَثْنٰى وَثُلٰثَ وَرُبٰعَ ۚ فَاِنْ خِفْتُمْ
اَلَّا تَعْدِلُوْا فَوَاحِدَةً اَوْ مَا مَلَكَتْ اَيْمَانُكُمْ ؕ ذٰلِكَ
اَدْنٰۤى اَلَّا تَعُوْلُوْا ﴿٤﴾

4. And if you fear that you *the society* **may fail to do justice in matters concerning orphans** ***in the aftermath of war*** **then marry women of your choice two or three or four.** And if you fear you will not deal justly, then *marry only* one or what your right hands possess. That is the nearest *way* for you to avoid injustice.

6. And give not to the foolish your property which Allah has made for you a means of support; but feed them therewith and clothe them and speak to them words of kind advice.

وَلَا تُؤْتُوا السُّفَهَآءَ اَمْوَالَكُمُ الَّتِىْ جَعَلَ اللّٰهُ لَكُمْ قِيٰمًا وَّارْزُقُوْهُمْ فِيْهَا وَاكْسُوْهُمْ وَقُوْلُوْا لَهُمْ قَوْلًا مَّعْرُوْفًا ⑥

6. **Do not hand over the charge of property belonging to you which Allah has made for you as a means of support, to those who are mentally incapable of managing it properly. So feed them and clothe them properly and speak kindly to them.**

Note: Here the society is addressed as a whole while the property in question is not national property but belongs to the orphans whose number grows exceedingly large during wars. Obviously a considerable part of national wealth will be involved in such exceptional circumstances. If a nation as a whole does not take care of such property and leaves it entirely to the care of children inexperienced and incapable of handling their wealth sensibly, this is bound to adversely influence the entire national economy. To resolve this problem the nation is addressed as a whole and made responsible for the proper care of the property in question as if it belonged to them. It does not mean however that such orphans will be disinherited or dispossessed of their individual rights permanently.

The following verse and the verse 11 make the real import of this verse abundantly clear.

7. And prove the orphans until they attain *the age of* marriage;

وَابْتَلُوا الْيَتٰمٰى حَتّٰۤى اِذَا بَلَغُوا النِّكَاحَ

7. And **test *the understanding of*** the orphans until they attain *the age of* marriage;

13. But **if** they be more than that, then they shall be *equal* sharers in one-third, after *the payment of* any bequests which may have been bequeathed or of debt, without prejudice *to the debt. This is* an injunction from Allah, and Allah is All-Knowing, Forbearing.

فَاِنْ
كَانُوْٓا اَكْثَرَ مِنْ ذٰلِكَ فَهُمْ شُرَكَآءُ فِي الثُّلُثِ مِنْۢ
بَعْدِ وَصِيَّةٍ يُّوْصٰى بِهَآ اَوْ دَيْنٍ غَيْرَ مُضَآرٍّ ۚ وَصِيَّةً
مِّنَ اللّٰهِ ؕ وَاللّٰهُ عَلِيْمٌ حَلِيْمٌ ﴿۱۳﴾

13. But if they be more than that, then they shall be *equal* share holders in one-third, after *the payment of* any bequests which may have been bequeathed or of debt, **without *intent to cause* suffering to anyone.** *This is* an injunction from Allah, and Allah is All-Knowing, Forbearing.

36. And if you fear a breach between them, then appoint an arbiter from his folk and an arbiter from her folk. If they (the arbiters) desire reconciliation, Allah will effect it between them. Surely, Allah is All-Knowing, All-Aware.

وَاِنْ خِفْتُمْ شِقَاقَ بَيْنِهِمَا فَابْعَثُوْا حَكَمًا مِّنْ
اَهْلِهٖ وَحَكَمًا مِّنْ اَهْلِهَا ۚ اِنْ يُّرِيْدَآ اِصْلَاحًا يُّوَفِّقِ
اللّٰهُ بَيْنَهُمَا ؕ اِنَّ اللّٰهَ كَانَ عَلِيْمًا خَبِيْرًا ﴿۳۶﴾

36. And if you fear a breach between them, then appoint an arbiter from his folk and an arbiter from her folk. If they desire reconciliation, Allah will effect it between them. Surely, Allah is All-Knowing, All-Aware.

Note: We consider the word "the arbiters" unnecessary because the pronoun 'they' may also refer to the parties concerned.

44. O ye who believe! approach not Prayer when you are not in *full* possession

يٰٓاَيُّهَا الَّذِيْنَ اٰمَنُوْا لَا تَقْرَبُوا الصَّلٰوةَ وَاَنْتُمْ سُكٰرٰى

of your senses, until you know what you say, nor when you are unclean,

حَتّٰى تَعْلَمُوْا مَا تَقُوْلُوْنَ وَلَا جُنُبًا

44. O ye who believe! Approach not Prayer **while you are mentally dazed till you clearly** know what you say, nor when you are unclean,

Note: The expression "unclean" is questionable. The Arabic word *'Junuban'* (جنبًا) is applicable to a person after intercourse or after ejaculation even without intercourse. In such cases having a bath is essential before offering prayers.

47. There are some among the Jews who pervert words from their *proper* places. And they say, 'We hear and we disobey,' and 'hear *thou* without being heard,' and 'Rā'inā,' screening with their tongues *what is in their minds* and *seeking* to injure the Faith. And if they had said, 'We hear and we obey,' and 'hear *thou*,' and 'Unẓurnā,' it would have been better for them and more upright. But Allah has cursed them for their disbelief; so they believe but little.

مِنَ الَّذِيْنَ هَادُوْا يُحَرِّفُوْنَ الْكَلِمَ عَنْ مَّوَاضِعِهٖ
وَيَقُوْلُوْنَ سَمِعْنَا وَعَصَيْنَا وَاسْمَعْ غَيْرَ مُسْمَعٍ وَّ
رَاعِنَا لَيًّا بِاَلْسِنَتِهِمْ وَطَعْنًا فِي الدِّيْنِ ۭ وَلَوْ اَنَّهُمْ
قَالُوْا سَمِعْنَا وَاَطَعْنَا وَاسْمَعْ وَانْظُرْنَا لَكَانَ خَيْرًا
لَّهُمْ وَاَقْوَمَ ۙ وَلٰكِنْ لَّعَنَهُمُ اللّٰهُ بِكُفْرِهِمْ فَلَا
يُؤْمِنُوْنَ اِلَّا قَلِيْلًا ۝٤٧

Note: Justice cannot be done to the real import of this part of the verse by mere translation because here the hypocrites are described as intentionally mispronouncing some commonly used phrases to give them a twist with intention to insult the Holy Prophet. The believers used the phrase *'Same'na wa at'ana'* (سمعنا, اطعنا) which means we heard and we obeyed. Instead of saying *'At'ana'* (اطعنا) the hypocrites said *'Asai'na'* (عصينا) (the word used in the actual text of the verse) meaning thereby that we heard and disobeyed. Yet they pronounced it with slur intending to mislead the hearer into believing that they had said *'at'ana'* instead of *'Asai'na'* (عصينا). A keen hearer however could not miss the intended mischief and implied insult.
Again they uttered the word *'Rai'na'* (راعنا) with a twist of tongue to make it sound half way between *'Rai'na'* (راعنا) and *'Raeena'* (راعينا). *'Rai'na'* (راعنا) means be lenient to us while *Raeena'* (راعينا) means 'O our tender of sheeps. This again was an attempt to insult the Holy Prophet under the cover of pronunciation.

48. O ye People of the Book! believe in what We have sent down, fulfilling that which is with you, before We destroy *some of* the leaders and turn them on their backs or curse them as We cursed the People of the Sabbath. And the decree of Allah is *bound* to be carried out.

يٰٓاَيُّهَا الَّذِيْنَ اُوْتُوا الْكِتٰبَ اٰمِنُوْا بِمَا نَزَّلْنَا مُصَدِّقًا
لِّمَا مَعَكُمْ مِّنْ قَبْلِ اَنْ نَّطْمِسَ وُجُوْهًا فَنَرُدَّهَا عَلٰٓى
اَدْبَارِهَآ اَوْ نَلْعَنَهُمْ كَمَا لَعَنَّآ اَصْحٰبَ السَّبْتِ ۭ وَكَانَ
اَمْرُ اللّٰهِ مَفْعُوْلًا ﴿٤٨﴾

48. O ye People of the Book! Believe in what We have sent down, fulfilling that which is with you, before **We inflict humiliation upon some *of your* leaders causing them to turn their backs and take to their heels,** or curse them as We cursed the People of the Sabbath. And the decree of Allah is bound to be carried out.

58. therein shall they have pure spouses;

لَهُمْ فِيْهَآ اَزْوَاجٌ مُّطَهَّرَةٌ

58. therein shall they have **spouses purified *by Us;***

60. O ye who believe! obey Allah, and obey *His* Messenger and those who are in authority among you.

يٰٓاَيُّهَا الَّذِيْنَ اٰمَنُوْٓا اَطِيْعُوا اللّٰهَ وَاَطِيْعُوا الرَّسُوْلَ وَ
اُولِي الْاَمْرِ مِنْكُمْ

60. O ye who believe! obey Allah, and obey *His* Messenger and those who are in authority **over you.**

Note: The Arabic construction of the phrase *'Oulil amre minkum'* (اولی الامر منکم) (who are in authority over you) has not been properly understood by some. Of particular interest is the word (منکم) which in fact is composed of two propositions joined together that is (من) and (کم). (من) means 'from' and (کم) means 'you'. Literally translating this phrase some translators understand it to mean 'from among yourselves'. That is to say you should obey only that authority which happens to be from among yourselves, meaning Muslim authority alone. In this particular instance the proposition (من) only plays a role of linking the proposition (کم) with the word (اولی الامر) in a possesive relationship and the translation should be 'Those who are in authority over you'.

63. Then how is it that when an affliction befalls them because of what their hands have sent on before them, they come to thee swearing by Allah, *saying*, 'We meant nothing but the doing of good and reconciliation?'

فَكَيْفَ إِذَآ أَصَابَتْهُم مُّصِيبَةٌۢ بِمَا قَدَّمَتْ أَيْدِيهِمْ ثُمَّ جَآءُوكَ يَحْلِفُونَ بِاللّٰهِ إِنْ أَرَدْنَآ إِلَّآ إِحْسَانًا وَتَوْفِيقًا ﴿٦٣﴾

63. Then how is it that when an affliction befalls them because of what their hands have sent on before them, they come to thee swearing by Allah, *saying*, 'We meant nothing **but an act of kindness and conciliation'.**

67. And if We had commanded them, 'Kill your people or leave your homes,' they would not have done it except a few of them; and if they had done what they are exhorted to do, it would surely have been better for them and conducive to greater strength.

وَلَوْ أَنَّا كَتَبْنَا عَلَيْهِمْ أَنِ اقْتُلُوٓا أَنفُسَكُمْ أَوِ اخْرُجُوا مِن دِيَارِكُم مَّا فَعَلُوهُ إِلَّا قَلِيلٌ مِّنْهُمْ ۖ وَلَوْ أَنَّهُمْ فَعَلُوا مَا يُوعَظُونَ بِهِۦ لَكَانَ خَيْرًا لَّهُمْ وَأَشَدَّ تَثْبِيتًا ﴿٦٧﴾

Note: The expression 'kill your people' can be misunderstood. The correct translation should have been slay yourselves. This certainly does not mean that they were told to commit suicide but is merely an expression exhorting them to kill their egos and submit themselves completely to the will of God.

83. Will they not, then, meditate upon the Qur'ān? Had it been from anyone other than Allah, they would surely have found therein much disagreement.

أَفَلَا يَتَدَبَّرُونَ الْقُرْاٰنَ ۚ وَلَوْ كَانَ مِنْ عِندِ غَيْرِ اللّٰهِ لَوَجَدُوا فِيهِ اخْتِلَافًا كَثِيرًا ﴿٨٣﴾

Note: The Qur'anic expression *'Ikhtilafan Katheeran'* (اختلافا كثيرا), (much disagreement) in fact indicates contradiction, meaning thereby that if anyone other than Allah had been the author of the Holy Qur'an the people would have certainly found many contradictions in it. A similar expression concerning the creation of universe is found in 67:4 (Al-Mulk) declaring that it is impossible to find a flaw or contradiction in the work of God.

84. And when there comes to them any tidings *whether* of peace or of fear, they spread it about; whereas if they had referred it to the Messenger and to those in

وَإِذَا جَآءَهُمْ أَمْرٌ مِّنَ الْأَمْنِ أَوِ الْخَوْفِ أَذَاعُوا بِهِۦ ۖ وَلَوْ رَدُّوهُ إِلَى الرَّسُولِ وَإِلَىٰٓ أُولِي الْأَمْرِ مِنْهُمْ

authority among them, surely those of them, who can elicit *the truth from* it, would have understood it. And had it not been for the grace of Allah upon you and His mercy, you would have followed Satan, save a few.

لَعَلِمَهُ الَّذِينَ يَسْتَنْبِطُونَهُ مِنْهُمْ ۗ وَلَوْلَا فَضْلُ اللَّهِ عَلَيْكُمْ وَرَحْمَتُهُ لَاتَّبَعْتُمُ الشَّيْطَانَ إِلَّا قَلِيلًا ﴿٨٣﴾

Note: This translation implies that the Messenger and the persons of authority among them were not all capable of drawing right conclusion. Only those among them who had the faculty of sound judgement could have discovered the reality. We propose an alternative translation as follows which does not leave this flaw and indicates that each among them had the capability of discovering the truth if he had contemplated and examined the report: "When they conceive (rumours concerning) a matter of peace or alarm they spread it about. Whereas if they had referred to the Messenger and those in authority among them surely of them those who had critically examined the matter could know the truth".

86. Whoso makes a righteous intercession shall have a share thereof, and whoso makes an evil intercession, shall have a like portion thereof; and Allah is Powerful over everything.

مَنْ يَشْفَعْ شَفَاعَةً حَسَنَةً يَكُنْ لَهُ نَصِيبٌ مِنْهَا ۖ وَمَنْ يَشْفَعْ شَفَاعَةً سَيِّئَةً يَكُنْ لَهُ كِفْلٌ مِنْهَا ۗ وَكَانَ اللَّهُ عَلَىٰ كُلِّ شَيْءٍ مُقِيتًا ﴿٨٦﴾

86. Whoso makes a righteous intercession shall have a share thereof, and whoso makes an evil intercession, shall have a like portion ***of evil consequences*** thereof; and Allah is Powerful over everything.

87. And when you are greeted with a prayer, greet ye with a better prayer or *at least* return it. Surely, Allah takes account of all things.

وَإِذَا حُيِّيتُمْ بِتَحِيَّةٍ فَحَيُّوا بِأَحْسَنَ مِنْهَا أَوْ رُدُّوهَا ۗ إِنَّ اللَّهَ كَانَ عَلَىٰ كُلِّ شَيْءٍ حَسِيبًا ﴿٨٧﴾

Note: This translation narrows down the application of the verse to only verbal expressions of goodwill while the admonition contained therein has much wider application. In fact, it covers not only verbal greetings but also intends gifts of all kinds to be responded to more generously or at least in the same measure.

93. But whoso finds not *one*, then he shall fast for two consecutive months—a

فَمَنْ لَمْ يَجِدْ فَصِيَامُ شَهْرَيْنِ مُتَتَابِعَيْنِ تَوْبَةً

mercy from Allah. And Allah is All-Knowing, Wise.

مِّنَ اللّٰهِ وَكَانَ اللّٰهُ عَلِيْمًا حَكِيْمًا ﴿٩٢﴾

93. But whoso finds not *one*, then he shall fast for two consecutive months --- **a means of seeking forgiveness prescribed by Allah.** And Allah is All-knowing, Wise.

101. And whoso emigrates from his country in the cause of Allah will find in the earth an abundant place of refuge and plentifulness.

وَمَنْ يُّهَاجِرْ فِيْ سَبِيْلِ اللّٰهِ يَجِدْ فِي الْاَرْضِ مُرٰغَمًا
كَثِيْرًا وَّسَعَةً

Note: The Arabic words *'Fee sabeelillah'* (فی سبیل اللہ) mean for the sake of Allah or in the cause of Allah.

104. verily Prayer is enjoined on the believers *to be performed* at fixed hours.

اِنَّ الصَّلٰوةَ كَانَتْ عَلَى الْمُؤْمِنِيْنَ كِتٰبًا مَّوْقُوْتًا ﴿١٠٣﴾

104. Verily Prayer is enjoined on the believers *to be performed at* **prescribed times.**

106. And be not thou a disputer for the faithless;

وَلَا تَكُنْ لِّلْخَآئِنِيْنَ خَصِيْمًا ﴿١٠٦﴾

106. **And do not plead the cause of those who betray the trust.**

114. And but for the grace of Allah upon thee and His mercy, a party of them had resolved to bring about thy ruin. And they ruin none but themselves and they cannot harm thee at all.

وَلَوْلَا فَضْلُ اللّٰهِ عَلَيْكَ وَرَحْمَتُهٗ لَهَمَّتْ طَّآئِفَةٌ
مِّنْهُمْ اَنْ يُّضِلُّوْكَ وَمَا يُضِلُّوْنَ اِلَّآ اَنْفُسَهُمْ وَمَا
يَضُرُّوْنَكَ مِنْ شَيْءٍ

114. And but for the grace of Allah upon you and His mercy a party of them had resolved **to lead you astray *but He frustrated their designs.* In fact they lead none but themselves astray** and they cannot harm you at all.

115. There is no good in many of their conferences except *the conferences of* such as enjoin charity, or goodness, or the making of peace among men.

لَا خَيْرَ فِي كَثِيرٍ مِّن نَّجْوٰىهُمْ إِلَّا مَنْ أَمَرَ بِصَدَقَةٍ
أَوْ مَعْرُوفٍ أَوْ إِصْلَاحٍ بَيْنَ النَّاسِ

115. No good comes out of their secret consultations except when they decide to spend in the cause of the poor or to do works of public welfare or to effect reconciliation and reformation among people.

118. They invoke beside Him none but lifeless objects; and they invoke none but Satan, the rebellious,

إِن يَدْعُونَ مِن دُونِهِ إِلَّا إِنٰثًا وَإِن يَدْعُونَ إِلَّا شَيْطٰنًا مَّرِيدًا ﴿١١٨﴾

118. They invoke besides Him none but **false goddesses, while *in truth*** they invoke none but Satan, the rebellious,

120. and assuredly I will incite them and they will cut the ears of cattle; and assuredly I will incite them and they will alter Allah's creation.'

وَلَآمُرَنَّهُمْ فَلَيُبَتِّكُنَّ
آذَانَ الْأَنْعَامِ وَلَآمُرَنَّهُمْ فَلَيُغَيِّرُنَّ خَلْقَ اللّٰهِ

120. 'And assuredly **I will command them so that they will incise the ears of camels** ***and other cattle*** **and assuredly I will bid them and they will alter Allah's creations'.**

130. And you cannot keep *perfect* balance between wives, however much you may desire it. But incline not wholly *to one* so that you leave the other like a thing suspended.

وَلَن تَسْتَطِيعُوٓا أَن تَعْدِلُوا بَيْنَ النِّسَآءِ وَلَوْ حَرَصْتُمْ
فَلَا تَمِيلُوا كُلَّ الْمَيْلِ فَتَذَرُوهَا كَالْمُعَلَّقَةِ

130. And you cannot keep perfect balance between wives, **despite your best intentions, So incline not entirely to one lest the other should be left suspended, unattended and uncared for.**

136. O ye who believe! be strict in observing justice, *and be* witnesses for Allah, even though it be against yourselves

يَٰٓأَيُّهَا الَّذِينَ آمَنُوا كُونُوا قَوَّٰمِينَ بِالْقِسْطِ شُهَدَآءَ
لِلَّهِ وَلَوْ عَلَىٰٓ أَنفُسِكُمْ

136. O ye who believe! Be strict in observing justice, **being witnesses for the sake of Allah,** even though it be against yourselves . . . . .

143. The hypocrites seek to deceive Allah, but He will punish them for their deception.

إِنَّ الْمُنَٰفِقِينَ يُخَٰدِعُونَ اللَّهَ وَهُوَ خَٰدِعُهُمْ

143. The hypocrites seek to deceive Allah, but He will **cause them to be deceived themselves.**

154.
And We gave Moses manifest authority.

وَآتَيْنَا مُوسَىٰ سُلْطَٰنًا مُّبِينًا ﴿١٥٤﴾

154. And We gave Moses **clear overwhelming argument.**

158. And their saying, 'We did kill the Messiah, Jesus, son of Mary, the Messenger of Allah;' whereas they slew him not, nor crucified * him, but he was made to appear to them like *one crucified*; and those who differ therein are certainly in *a state of* doubt about it; they have no *definite* knowledge thereof, but only follow a conjecture; and they did not convert this *conjecture* into a certainty;

وَقَوْلِهِمْ إِنَّا قَتَلْنَا الْمَسِيحَ عِيسَى ابْنَ مَرْيَمَ
رَسُولَ اللَّهِ ۚ وَمَا قَتَلُوهُ وَمَا صَلَبُوهُ وَلَٰكِن شُبِّهَ
لَهُمْ ۚ وَإِنَّ الَّذِينَ اخْتَلَفُوا فِيهِ لَفِي شَكٍّ مِّنْهُ ۚ
مَا لَهُم بِهِ مِنْ عِلْمٍ إِلَّا اتِّبَاعَ الظَّنِّ ۚ وَمَا قَتَلُوهُ
يَقِينًا ﴿١٥٨﴾

Note: The emphasis is upon their failure to murder Jesus by any means. The reader is reminded that the very beginning of the verse refers to the Jewish boast that they had succeeded in murdering Jesus.

This Jewish claim is firmly rejected by the Holy Qur'an. That is why by the end of the verse, the conclusive declaration is that whatever may have happened they certainly failed to kill him. This implies that it is not the act of crucifixion which is denied. What is denied is death by crucifixion.

Wa la kin shubbiha lahum , ولكن شبّه لهم

The word *'shubbiha'* (شُبِّهَ) in the text must be carefully studied. The context of the preceding text would not permit the implied reference to any other than Jesus or alternatively it could refer to the incident in general. In conformity with the rules of grammer the implied pronoun in the word *'Shubbiha'* (شُبِّهَ) can refer to none other than Jesus Christ himself. This means that it was he who was obscured and made to appear to them similar to someone else. Hence as Jesus was hung upon the cross he hung in the likeness of someone else. Evidently the denial is not that of crucifixion or apparent death thereupon but the denial is death by crucifixion. There certainly was great confusion as to what actually had happened. So the verse continues to build the scenario of the confusion and doubt. All else is nothing but conjecture. That is the final conclusion.

If the word *'shubbiha'* refers to the incident as such, this would point to the divergent claims of the two disputing parties as to what had happened. Neither of the parties were certain of the validity of their claims. For instance the Christian belief of Jesus' death by crucifixion and later resurrection was not based on any tangible grounds but was merely conjectural. Likewise the Jewish claim of Jesus' death upon the cross was no less conjectural. Hence their appeal to Pilate for the possession of Jesus's body. In fact they clearly expressed their doubts regarding the entire episode of his so-called death and warned Pilate that in the likelihood of his survival he might reappear in public claiming that he had risen from the dead. (Matthew 27:63-64)

It is to this that the last part of the verse under study refers, when it says *'Wa innallazeena'* (وإنّ الّذين). Certainly those who differ about it (or about him as to what actually befell him) were themselves in doubt.

'Bal Rafa'a hullaho Ilaihi' بل رفعه الله اليه.

The majority of orthodox Muslims infer from this part of the verse that the connotation of 'bull' refers to the act of crucifixion i.e., instead of letting him die upon the cross, God rescued him by raising him bodily to somewhere in the heavens. As such he should be living somewhere in space in the same corporal form that he possessed prior to the attempt of his crucifixion. This interpretation raises many difficult questions, mainly:

(a) If Jesus was not crucified at all, is the entire history of crucifixion emphatically denied and the whole episode just a fiction or delusion suffered by the Jews, the Christians and the Romans alike?

(b) Where in the verse is the claim that Jesus was raised bodily to heavens? All that is mentioned simply is that Allah exalted him to Himself.

As to the first question the orthodox build a fantastic scenario according to which the fact of crucifixion itself is not denied but it is claimed that the person who was crucified was not Jesus but someone else who was given the likeness of Jesus by some angels at the command of God. Hence the doubts and conjectures were about the identity of the person who was crucified. Evedently this explanation creates only more problems than it solves. Moreover, the entire tale is absolutely without foundation. No scriptural evidence or evidence based on the traditions of the Holy Prophet (sas) is ever presented to support this bizarre claim which simply adds more conjectural confusion.

It is as if this explanation of the verse dawned only upon the medieval scholars while the Messenger of God peace be upon him, remained himself completely unaware of it.

As to the second question the weakness of the claim is apparent from the wording of the Holy Qur'an. The word *'Rafa'a'* (رفع) means elevated. Whenever Allah elevates a person the elevation always refers to the status of the person, never to his body. In fact it is impossible to translate this verse in any other way other than the said meaning i.e., the elevation of spiritual station.

The verse declares that Allah elevated Jesus to Himself. Evidently no point in space of Heaven is mentioned to which Allah raised him. He raised him to Himself while He was present there where Jesus was. No place in Heaven or earth is empty of Allah's presence. So when someone is said to be raised to Him, a bodily movement is impossible and inconceivable. According to Ahmadiyya understanding of this verse, the connotation of 'contrary' refers to the Jewish claim of the accursed death of Jesus. Obviously the opposite of curse is nearness to God.

160. And there is none among the People of the Book but will believe in it before his death; and on the Day of Resurrection, he (Jesus) shall be a witness against them—

وَإِنْ مِّنْ أَهْلِ الْكِتٰبِ إِلَّا لَيُؤْمِنَنَّ بِهٖ قَبْلَ مَوْتِهٖ ۚ وَيَوْمَ الْقِيٰمَةِ يَكُوْنُ عَلَيْهِمْ شَهِيْدًا ﴿١٦٠﴾

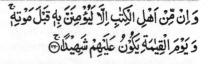

Note: This verse has been the subject of controversy regarding its real import. Some scholars believe that it refers to a remote future in relation to the time of crucifixion indicating that all Jews without exception will one day have faith in Jesus Christ and accept him as a true Prophet of God. They claim that it is also mentioned in this verse that this miracle would take place in the lifetime of Jesus Christ. This they infer from the words *'qable mautehi'* (قبل موته) which means before his death.

As the Jews have not yet accepted him, therefore, according to such scholars Jesus must be still alive.

Another commonly held view is that the expression 'before his death' refers to every member of the Jewish faith of the time of Jesus Christ. In this case this would mean that every Jew would believe in Jesus Christ before his death - a claim which can only be verified by God.

Unfortunately many problems and difficulties stand in the way of accepting these propositions in toto.

We propose a completely different and new solution to the problem. The verse under study is translated as such "There is no *one* among the people of the Book but will certainly believe in him before his death.".

The word in italics i.e., 'one' is not literally mentioned in the verse but is only implied. If it were mentioned the verse would mean as follows.

وان **احد** من اهل الكتاب

The word in bold letters is the implied word. We suggest that instead of *'Ahad'* being implied we should consider the word *'fareeq'* (فريق) as the implied word. In that case the translation would be : 'There is no sect or group from among the people of the Book but will have faith in him (Jesus Christ) before his death."

This requires that Jesus must have migrated to the lands occupied by the lost tribes of Israel and in doing so he fulfilled his mission of delivering his message to all the twelve flocks of the house of Israel. This view is further powerfully supported by a prophecy of Jesus Christ wherein he claimed that he would go in search of the lost sheep of the house of Israel. (Matthew 15:24)

164. **and We gave David a Book.** وَاٰتَيۡنَا دَاوٗدَ زَبُوۡرًا ۚ

Note: The word *'a Book'* is an attempted translation of the word 'Zaboora' (زبور) which refers to the Psalms.

165.
- and Allah spoke to Moses particularly— وَكَلَّمَ اللّٰهُ مُوۡسٰى تَكۡلِيۡمًا ۚ

Note: According to Arabic grammar when the root of a word is repeated as (تكليما) is repeated in this verse, it is done with an intention to indicate intensity or repetition or high quality or to clarify an ambiguity. All these connotations can be applicable simultaneously.

AL-MA'IDAH

يَاأَيُّهَا الَّذِينَ آمَنُوا لَا تُحِلُّوا شَعَائِرَ اللَّهِ

3. O ye who believe! profane not the Signs of Allah,

3. O ye who believe! Profane **none of the things sanctified by Allah.**

Note: The sanctified things may include certain specific periods of time, places or living beings.

وَلَقَدْ أَخَذَ اللَّهُ مِيثَاقَ بَنِي إِسْرَائِيلَ وَبَعَثْنَا مِنْهُمُ اثْنَيْ عَشَرَ نَقِيبًا

13. And indeed Allah did take a covenant from the children of Israel; and We raised among them twelve leaders.

Note: Perhaps there is no single word which can adequately do justice to the word *'naqeeb'*. It does not only mean 'a leader' but also means a proclaimer, the one who has the authority to read the proclamation or pronounce judgement on behalf of a sovereign or other higher authorities.

فَاعْفُ عَنْهُمْ وَاصْفَحْ

14. So pardon them and turn away *from them.*

14. So pardon them and **show forbearance.**

Note: Turning away indicates an act of forbearance and overlooking the faults of others with kindness.

فَأَغْرَيْنَا بَيْنَهُمُ الْعَدَاوَةَ وَالْبَغْضَاءَ إِلَى يَوْمِ الْقِيَامَةِ

15. So We have caused enmity and hatred among them till the Day of Resurrection.

Note: The Arabic word *Aghraina* (اغرينا) has the basic meaning to make something stick fast to another so that it becomes an inseparable part of it. Hence the translation we prefer is: **So we made mutual enmity and hatred their lot till the Day of Resurrection.**

وَآتَاكُمْ مَا لَمْ يُؤْتِ أَحَدًا مِنَ الْعَالَمِينَ ﴿٢١﴾

21. and gave you what He gave not to any other among the peoples.

21. and gave you what He gave not to **anyone else in the whole world.**

Note: The expression *whole world* applies to the people of that age.

42. And among the Jews *too* are those who would fondly listen to ***any*** lie–

وَمِنَ الَّذِيْنَ هَادُوْا ۛ سَمّٰعُوْنَ لِلْكَذِبِ

42. And among the Jews *too* are those who **are overeager to listen to lies**

56. Your friend is only Allah and His Messenger and the believers who observe Prayer and pay the Zakāt and worship God alone.

اِنَّمَا وَلِيُّكُمُ اللّٰهُ وَرَسُوْلُهٗ وَالَّذِيْنَ اٰمَنُوا الَّذِيْنَ يُقِيْمُوْنَ الصَّلٰوةَ وَيُؤْتُوْنَ الزَّكٰوةَ وَهُمْ رٰكِعُوْنَ ﴿۵۶﴾

56. Your friend is only Allah and His Messenger and the believers who observe Prayer and pay the Zakat **bowing to Him *with absolute sincerity.***

65. And the Jews say, 'The hand of Allah is tied up.' Their *own* hands shall be tied up and they shall be cursed for what they say.

وَقَالَتِ الْيَهُوْدُ يَدُ اللّٰهِ مَغْلُوْلَةٌ ؕ غُلَّتْ اَيْدِيْهِمْ وَلُعِنُوْا بِمَا قَالُوْا

65. And the Jews say, 'The hand of Allah is tied up'. **It is their *own* hands which are tied up** and they shall be cursed for what they say

67. Among them are a people who are moderate; but many of them—evil indeed is that which they do.

مِنْهُمْ اُمَّةٌ مُّقْتَصِدَةٌ ؕ وَكَثِيْرٌ مِّنْهُمْ سَآءَ مَا يَعْمَلُوْنَ ﴿۶۷﴾

67. Among them **there is a body of people** who are moderate; but **evil indeed is that which the majority of them do.**

74. They are surely disbelievers who say, 'Allah is the third of three;'

لَقَدْ كَفَرَ الَّذِيْنَ قَالُوْٓا اِنَّ اللّٰهَ ثَالِثُ ثَلٰثَةٍ

74. They are surely disbelievers who say, 'Allah is **one of the three;'** . . . . .

76. The Messiah, son of Mary, **was only a Messenger; surely,** Messengers *like unto him* had indeed passed away before him. And his mother was a truthful woman. They both used to eat food.

مَا الْمَسِيحُ ابْنُ مَرْيَمَ إِلَّا رَسُولٌ قَدْ خَلَتْ مِنْ
قَبْلِهِ الرُّسُلُ وَأُمُّهُ صِدِّيقَةٌ كَانَا يَأْكُلَانِ الطَّعَامَ

76. The Messiah, son of Mary, **was no more than a Messenger. All Messengers before him have passed away. And his mother was righteous. Both of them used to eat food**

80. They did not prohibit one another from the iniquity which they committed. Evil indeed was that which they used to do.

كَانُوا لَا يَتَنَاهَوْنَ عَنْ مُنْكَرٍ فَعَلُوهُ لَبِئْسَ مَا كَانُوا
يَفْعَلُونَ ۝

80. **They would not prohibit one another from offensive conduct which they practised.** Evil indeed was that which they used to do.

91. O ye who believe! wine and the game of hazard and idols and divining

يَا أَيُّهَا الَّذِينَ آمَنُوا إِنَّمَا الْخَمْرُ وَالْمَيْسِرُ وَالْأَنْصَابُ

91. O ye who believe! **Intoxicants and games of chance** and idols and divining. . . .

92. Satan desires only to create enmity and hatred among you by means of wine and the game of hazard,

إِنَّمَا يُرِيدُ الشَّيْطَانُ أَنْ يُوقِعَ بَيْنَكُمُ الْعَدَاوَةَ
وَالْبَغْضَاءَ فِي الْخَمْرِ وَالْمَيْسِرِ

92. Satan desires only to create enmity and hatred among you by means of **intoxicants and games of chance,**

102. Allah has left them out.

عَفَا اللَّهُ عَنْهَا

102. Allah has left them out ***out of kindness.***

Note: No course of action prescribed by God for the believers can be intended to cause them trouble. Yet out of His Mercy God does not want to give instructions in minute detail lest they should be difficult for some to follow and cause unnecessary discomfort.

104. Allah has not ordained any 'Baḥīra' or 'Sā'iba' or 'Waṣīla' or 'Ḥāmī'; but those who disbelieve forge a lie against Allah, and most of them do not make use of their understanding.

مَا جَعَلَ اللّٰهُ مِنْۢ بَحِيْرَةٍ وَّلَا سَآئِبَةٍ وَّلَا وَصِيْلَةٍ وَّلَا حَامٍ ۙ وَّلٰكِنَّ الَّذِيْنَ كَفَرُوْا يَفْتَرُوْنَ عَلَى اللّٰهِ الْكَذِبَ ۗ وَاَكْثَرُهُمْ لَا يَعْقِلُوْنَ ۝

Note: *'Bahirah'* (بحيرة) is a name given by pagan Arabs to a she-camel which had given birth to seven young ones and was then let loose to feed freely after its ear were slit. It was dedicated to some god and its milk was not used nor its back.

'Saibah' (سائبة) is a she-camel let loose to water and pasture after giving birth to five young ones.

'Wasilah' (وصيلة) is a she-camel (or an ewe or she-goat) let loose in the name of a god after she had given birth to seven female young ones consecutively. If at the seventh birth she bore a pair, male and female, these were also let loose.

'Hami' (حام) is a camel which had fathered seven young ones. It was let loose and was not used for riding or carrying. It was free to pasture and water.

After having stated that minor matters and details have been left to man to legislate as he thinks proper, the verse fittingly draws attention to the fact that such freedom and discretion are not allowed in fundamentals, because in fundamentals unanimity is essential and divergence of opinion may prove immensely harmful. The verse gives an illustration to show that human intellect cannot be trusted with the making of the laws on fundamental matters. The Arabs used to let loose the animals mentioned in the verse in honour of their idols. Besides being based on disbelief and superstition, the practice was also highly foolish. The animals thus let loose wrought great havoc wherever they went. The Qur'an refers to this evil practice as an example of man-made laws and warns Christians who question the wisdom of a revealed Law to learn a lesson from the morally degrading practices to which the pagan Arabs had resorted because they had no revealed Law to guide them.

106. O ye who believe! be heedful of your own selves.

يَآيُّهَا الَّذِيْنَ اٰمَنُوْا عَلَيْكُمْ اَنْفُسَكُمْ

106. O ye who believe! **Stand guard over yourselves.**

108. But if it be discovered that the two *witnesses* are guilty of sin, then two others shall take their place from among those against whom the *former* two *witnesses*—who were in a better position *to give true evidence—sinfully* deposed, and the two *latter witnesses* shall swear by Allah, *saying*, 'Surely, our testimony is truer than the testimony of the *former* two, and we have not been unfair *in any way;* for then, indeed, we should be of the unjust.'

فَاِنْ عُثِرَ عَلٰٓى اَنَّهُمَا اسْتَحَقَّآ اِثْمًا فَاٰخَرٰنِ يَقُوْمٰنِ
مَقَامَهُمَا مِنَ الَّذِيْنَ اسْتَحَقَّ عَلَيْهِمُ الْاَوْلَيٰنِ فَيُقْسِمٰنِ
بِاللّٰهِ لَشَهَادَتُنَآ اَحَقُّ مِنْ شَهَادَتِهِمَا وَمَا اعْتَدَيْنَآ
اِنَّآ اِذًا لَّمِنَ الظّٰلِمِيْنَ ﴿١٠٨﴾

108. **But if it becomes evident that they have committed the sin *of perjury* then the other two from among those against whose interest they had witnessed should stand in their place. Then having taken oath in the name of Allah give testimony against the former two affirming, 'Our testimony is truer than the testimony of the former two and we have not transgressed. In case we are false we should be counted amongst the transgressors *in the sight of Allah.'***

Note: This verse portrays the scenario of all the witnesses being present and the preference of bearing testimony is given to the first two more closely related. This is apparent from the preceding verse 107.

109. Thus it is more likely that they will give evidence according to facts or that they will fear that other oaths will be taken after their oaths.

ذٰلِكَ اَدْنٰۤى اَنْ يَّاْتُوْا بِالشَّهَادَةِ عَلٰى وَجْهِهَاۤ اَوْ يَخَافُوْۤا اَنْ تُرَدَّ اَيْمَانٌۢ بَعْدَ اَيْمَانِهِمْ

109. thus it is more likely ***that pressure will be put upon them so*** **that they will remain factual in their testimony fearing that other testimonies could also be entertained after their testimony.**

110. it is only Thou Who art the Knower of hidden things.'

اِنَّكَ اَنْتَ عَلَّامُ الْغُيُوْبِ ﴿۱۱۰﴾

110. it is only you **Who are the Best Knower** of hidden things.'

111. When Allah will say, "O Jesus, son of Mary, remember My favour upon thee and upon thy mother; when I strengthened thee with the Spirit of holiness *so that* thou didst speak to the people in the cradle and in middle age; and when I taught thee the Book and Wisdom and the Torah and the Gospel; and when thou didst fashion *a creation* out of clay, in the likeness of a bird, by My command; then thou didst breathe into it *a new spirit* and it became a soaring being by My command;

اِذْ قَالَ اللّٰهُ يٰعِيْسَى ابْنَ مَرْيَمَ اذْكُرْ نِعْمَتِيْ عَلَيْكَ
وَعَلٰى وَالِدَتِكَ ۘ اِذْ اَيَّدْتُّكَ بِرُوْحِ الْقُدُسِ ۟ تُكَلِّمُ
النَّاسَ فِي الْمَهْدِ وَكَهْلًا ۚ وَاِذْ عَلَّمْتُكَ الْكِتٰبَ وَ
الْحِكْمَةَ وَالتَّوْرٰىةَ وَالْاِنْجِيْلَ ۚ وَاِذْ تَخْلُقُ مِنَ الطِّيْنِ
كَهَيْـَٔةِ الطَّيْرِ بِاِذْنِيْ فَتَنْفُخُ فِيْهَا فَتَكُوْنُ طَيْرًۢا بِاِذْنِيْ
وَتُبْرِئُ الْاَكْمَهَ وَالْاَبْرَصَ بِاِذْنِيْ ۚ وَاِذْ تُخْرِجُ الْمَوْتٰى
بِاِذْنِيْ ۚ

Note: This is an expression indicating that Jesus spoke words of wisdom and godliness from his early childhood and continued to do so right up to his advanced years. The word *'kahlan'* (كَهْلًا) indicates the time when a person's hair begin to turn grey and from then on to advanced age.

This verse is a metaphorical expression of the spiritual revolution brought about by the prophets of God. This is a special tribute to the qualities of Jesus who out of all the Prophets of God was chosen as a model for bringing about such miraculous transformations.

AL-ANAAM

4. He knows your inside and your outside. And He knows what you earn.

يَعْلَمُ سِرَّكُمْ وَجَهْرَكُمْ وَيَعْلَمُ مَا تَكْسِبُونَ ﴿٣﴾

4. He knows **your secrets and also that which is apparent.** And He knows what you earn.

7. See they not how many a generation We have destroyed before them? We had established them in the earth as We have established you not, and We sent the clouds over them, pouring down abundant rain; and We caused streams to flow beneath them; then did We destroy them because of their sins and raised up after them another generation.

أَلَمْ يَرَوْا كَمْ أَهْلَكْنَا مِن قَبْلِهِم مِّن قَرْنٍ مَّكَّنَّاهُمْ
فِي الْأَرْضِ مَا لَمْ نُمَكِّن لَّكُمْ وَأَرْسَلْنَا السَّمَاءَ عَلَيْهِم
مِّدْرَارًا وَجَعَلْنَا الْأَنْهَارَ تَجْرِي مِن تَحْتِهِمْ فَأَهْلَكْنَاهُم
بِذُنُوبِهِمْ وَأَنشَأْنَا مِن بَعْدِهِمْ قَرْنًا آخَرِينَ ﴿٦﴾

7. See they not how many **ages** have We destroyed before them? We had established them in the earth as We have established you not, and We sent the clouds over them, pouring down abundant rain; and We caused streams to flow beneath them; then did We destroy them because of their sins and raised up after them another **people.**

13. Those who ruin their souls will not believe.

الَّذِينَ خَسِرُوا أَنفُسَهُمْ فَهُمْ لَا يُؤْمِنُونَ ﴿١٢﴾

13. **Those who have ruined themselves** will not believe.

16. Say, 'Of a truth, I fear, if I disobey my Lord, the punishment of an awful day.'

قُلْ إِنِّي أَخَافُ إِنْ عَصَيْتُ رَبِّي عَذَابَ يَوْمٍ عَظِيمٍ ﴿١٥﴾

Note: We propose the translation be changed from 'awful day' to 'an enormous day' which has all the connotation of the word '*azeem*' (عظيم) in this context.

18. and if He touch thee with happiness, then He has power to do all that He wills.

وَإِن يَمۡسَسۡكَ بِخَيۡرٖ فَهُوَ عَلَىٰ كُلِّ شَيۡءٖ قَدِيرٞ ١٨

18. and if He **bestows upon you good *fortune*** then He has power to do all that He wills.

19. And He is Supreme over His servants; and He is the Wise, the All-Aware.

وَهُوَ ٱلۡقَاهِرُ فَوۡقَ عِبَادِهِۦۚ وَهُوَ ٱلۡحَكِيمُ ٱلۡخَبِيرُ ١٩

19. And He is **All Powerful** over His **creatures --- the humankind;** and He is the Wise, the All-Aware.

20. Say, 'He is the One God, and certainly I am far removed from that which you associate *with Him*.'

قُلۡ إِنَّمَا هُوَ إِلَٰهٞ وَٰحِدٞ وَإِنَّنِي بَرِيٓءٞ مِّمَّا تُشۡرِكُونَ ٢٠

20. Say, 'He is the One God, and **I am completely absolved of what you associate** *with Him'*.

25. See how they lie against themselves. And that which they fabricated has failed them.

ٱنظُرۡ كَيۡفَ كَذَبُواْ عَلَىٰٓ أَنفُسِهِمۡۚ وَضَلَّ عَنۡهُم مَّا كَانُواْ يَفۡتَرُونَ ٢٥

25. See how they lie against themselves. **And what they fabricated was of no avail to them.**

37. Only those can accept who listen.

إِنَّمَا يَسۡتَجِيبُ ٱلَّذِينَ يَسۡمَعُونَۘ

37. Only those **who listen sincerely respond.**

40. Those who have rejected Our Signs are deaf and dumb, in utter darkness. Whom Allah wills He allows to perish and whom He wills He places on the right path.

وَٱلَّذِينَ كَذَّبُواْ بِـَٔايَٰتِنَا صُمّٞ وَبُكۡمٞ فِي ٱلظُّلُمَٰتِۗ مَن يَشَإِ ٱللَّهُ يُضۡلِلۡهُ وَمَن يَشَأۡ يَجۡعَلۡهُ عَلَىٰ صِرَٰطٖ مُّسۡتَقِيمٖ ٣٩

40. those who have rejected Our Signs are deaf and dumb, --- in utter darkness. About whomever Allah so adjudges He permits him to go astray. And about whomever He decides, He leads him to the straight path.

41. Say, 'What think ye? If the punishment of Allah come upon you or there come upon you the Hour, will you call upon any other than Allah, if you are truthful?'

قُلْ أَرَءَيْتَكُمْ إِنْ أَتَىٰكُمْ عَذَابُ ٱللَّهِ أَوْ أَتَتْكُمُ ٱلسَّاعَةُ أَغَيْرَ ٱللَّهِ تَدْعُونَ إِن كُنتُمْ صَٰدِقِينَ ﴿٤١﴾

41. Say, **What do you think *your response will be*** if the punishment of Allah comes upon you or there comes upon you the ***destined*** Hour, will you call upon any other than Allah, if you are truthful?

46. So the last remnant of the people who did wrong was cut off; and all praise belongs to Allah, the Lord of all the worlds.

فَقُطِعَ دَابِرُ ٱلْقَوْمِ ٱلَّذِينَ ظَلَمُوا۟ ۚ وَٱلْحَمْدُ لِلَّهِ رَبِّ ٱلْعَٰلَمِينَ ﴿٤٦﴾

46. So **the very roots of the people who did wrong were cut off;** and all praise belongs to Allah

50. And those who reject Our Signs, punishment will touch them, because they disobeyed.

وَٱلَّذِينَ كَذَّبُوا۟ بِـَٔايَٰتِنَا يَمَسُّهُمُ ٱلْعَذَابُ بِمَا كَانُوا۟ يَفْسُقُونَ ﴿٥٠﴾

50. And those who reject Our Signs, punishment will **befall them,** because they disobeyed.

57.
Say: 'I will not follow your evil inclinations.

قُل لَّآ أَتَّبِعُ أَهْوَآءَكُمْ

57. Say: 'I will not follow your **vain desires.**

66. Say, 'He has power to send punishment upon you from above you or from beneath your feet, or to confound you by *splitting you into* sects and make you taste the violence of one another.' See how We expound the Signs in various ways that they may understand!

قُلْ هُوَ الْقَادِرُ عَلٰٓى اَنْ يَّبْعَثَ عَلَيْكُمْ عَذَابًا مِّنْ
فَوْقِكُمْ اَوْ مِنْ تَحْتِ اَرْجُلِكُمْ اَوْ يَلْبِسَكُمْ شِيَعًا
وَّيُذِيْقَ بَعْضَكُمْ بَاْسَ بَعْضٍ ؕ اُنْظُرْ كَيْفَ نُصَرِّفُ
الْاٰيٰتِ لَعَلَّهُمْ يَفْقَهُوْنَ ﴿٦٦﴾

66. Say, 'He has power to send punishment upon you from above you or from beneath your feet, or **make it your lot to split into *mutually hostile* sects** and make you taste the violence of one another.' See how We expound the Signs in various ways that they may understand!

Note: The expression *'Yalbisakum'* (يلبسكم) invokes the image of a calamity which permanently sticks and becomes a part of the body like clothes. So a faithful translation demands the use of some expression of permanence.

69. And when thou seest those who engage in *vain discourse concerning* Our Signs,

وَاِذَا رَاَيْتَ الَّذِيْنَ يَخُوْضُوْنَ فِيْٓ اٰيٰتِنَا

69. And when you see those who **trifle with** Our Signs,

74. And He it is Who created the heavens and the earth in accordance with the requirements of wisdom; and the day He says, 'Be!,' it will be.

وَهُوَ الَّذِيْ خَلَقَ السَّمٰوٰتِ وَالْاَرْضَ بِالْحَقِّ ؕ وَيَوْمَ
يَقُوْلُ كُنْ فَيَكُوْنُ ؕ

74. And He it is Who created the heavens and the earth **the right way;** and the day when He will say, "'Be!' And it is".

Note: The expression " 'Be!' and it is" *'Kunn Fayakoon'* (كن فيكون) does not indicate spontaneous transformation into existence from nothingness. It means that the moment God wills, His will begins to take shape and ultimately is done as He desires.

90. It is these to whom We gave the Book and dominion and prophethood.

أُولَٰٓئِكَ الَّذِينَ آتَيْنَٰهُمُ الْكِتَٰبَ وَالْحُكْمَ وَالنُّبُوَّةَ

90. It is these to whom We gave the Book and **the faculty of judgement** and prophethood.

92. And they do not make a just estimate of Allah, when they say: 'Allah has not revealed anything to any man.'

وَمَا قَدَرُوا اللَّهَ حَقَّ قَدْرِهِۦٓ إِذْ قَالُوا مَآ أَنزَلَ اللَّهُ
عَلَىٰ بَشَرٍ مِّن شَيْءٍ

92. And they **failed to respect Allah as He should be respected when they said:** 'Allah has not revealed anything to any man.'

111. And We shall confound their hearts and their eyes, as they believed not therein at the first time, and We shall leave them in their transgression to wander in distraction.

وَنُقَلِّبُ أَفْـِٔدَتَهُمْ وَأَبْصَٰرَهُمْ كَمَا لَمْ يُؤْمِنُوا بِهِۦٓ أَوَّلَ
مَرَّةٍ وَنَذَرُهُمْ فِي طُغْيَٰنِهِمْ يَعْمَهُونَ ﴿١١١﴾

111. And We shall **cause their hearts and faculties of sight to revert to the same state as when they initially rejected Our Signs,** and We shall leave them in their transgression to wander in distraction.

117. And if thou obey the majority of those on earth, they will lead thee astray from Allah's way. They follow nothing but *mere* conjecture, and they do nothing but lie.

وَإِن تُطِعْ أَكْثَرَ مَن فِي الْأَرْضِ يُضِلُّوكَ عَن
سَبِيلِ اللَّهِ ۚ إِن يَتَّبِعُونَ إِلَّا الظَّنَّ وَإِنْ هُمْ
إِلَّا يَخْرُصُونَ ﴿١١٧﴾

Note: Here the word 'lie' is not sufficient to do justice to the fuller meaning of the word *'Yakhrosoon'* (يخرصون) which covers wider connotations like fabrication or professing to be able to predict the future while they only indulge in wild guesses.

121. And eschew open sins as well as secret ones.

وَذَرُوا ظَٰهِرَ الْإِثْمِ وَبَاطِنَهُۥٓ

121. And eschew **sin be it apparent or hidden.**

124. And thus have We made in every town the great ones from among its sinners *such as are in utter darkness* with the result that they plot therein;

> 124. And thus **We allowed the leaders of the sinners in every township to plot therein *against the truth;***

وَكَذٰلِكَ جَعَلْنَا فِيْ كُلِّ قَرْيَةٍ اَكٰبِرَ مُجْرِمِيْهَا لِيَمْكُرُوْا
فِيْهَا ؕ

> **Note:** The expression *'Akabera Mujremeeha'* اکابر مجرمیها literally means 'the great among the sinful of that township'. The word 'great' here may mean those who have the larger share of sin and as such they stand out among them as leaders or it may mean the great and influential members of a sinful society.

126. So, whomsoever Allah wishes to guide, He expands his bosom for *the acceptance of* Islam; and as to him whom He wishes to *let* go astray, He makes his bosom narrow *and* close, as though he were mounting up into the skies.

> 126. So whomever Allah wishes to guide, **He opens his heart** for *the acceptance of* Islam; *and as to him whom* **He wishes to let go astray, He constricts his heart as if he were climbing a steep height.** Thus does Allah inflict punishment on those who do not believe.

فَمَنْ يُّرِدِ اللّٰهُ اَنْ يَّهْدِيَهٗ يَشْرَحْ صَدْرَهٗ لِلْاِسْلَامِ
وَمَنْ يُّرِدْ اَنْ يُّضِلَّهٗ يَجْعَلْ صَدْرَهٗ ضَيِّقًا حَرَجًا
كَاَنَّمَا يَصَّعَّدُ فِي السَّمَآءِ ؕ

> **Note:** The word صدر can be translated as heart. (See Al-Munjid.)

137. **Evil is what they judge.**

> 137. Evil is what they **conclude.**

سَآءَ مَا يَحْكُمُوْنَ ﴿۱۳۶﴾

138. And in like manner have their associate-gods made the killing of their children

> 138. And in like manner have their **associates** made the killing of their children.

وَكَذٰلِكَ زَيَّنَ لِكَثِيْرٍ مِّنَ الْمُشْرِكِيْنَ قَتْلَ اَوْلَادِهِمْ

140.
He will reward them for their **assertion**.

سَيَجْزِيهِمْ وَصْفَهُمْ

140. He will **requite them** for their assertion.

144. *And of the cattle He has created* eight mates: of the sheep two, and of the goats two;–

ثَمٰنِيَةَ أَزْوٰجٍ مِّنَ الضَّأْنِ اثْنَيْنِ وَمِنَ الْمَعْزِ اثْنَيْنِ

144. *He has created* **eight mates altogether** *consisting* **of** the sheep two, and of the goats two; ---

146.
But whoso is driven by necessity, being neither disobedient nor exceeding *the limit*, then surely thy Lord is Most Forgiving, Merciful.'

فَمَنِ اضْطُرَّ غَيْرَ بَاغٍ وَّلَا عَادٍ فَإِنَّ رَبَّكَ غَفُورٌ رَّحِيمٌ

Note: Here the word *Izturra* (اضطر) means compelled by starvation and famished beyond one's capacity to withstand the pressure.

149. Those who join gods *with God* will say,

سَيَقُولُ الَّذِينَ أَشْرَكُوا

149. **Those who associate partners** *with Allah will say,*

150. Say, 'Allah's is the argument that reaches *home*.

قُلْ فَلِلّٰهِ الْحُجَّةُ الْبٰلِغَةُ

150. Say, **'To Allah belongs the conclusive argument.**

152. Say, 'Come, I will rehearse to you what your Lord has forbidden: that you associate not anything as partner with Him and *that you do* good to parents,

قُلْ تَعَالَوْا أَتْلُ مَا حَرَّمَ رَبُّكُمْ عَلَيْكُمْ أَلَّا تُشْرِكُوا بِهِ شَيْـًٔا وَّبِالْوٰلِدَيْنِ إِحْسٰنًا

152. Say, 'come, I will rehearse to you what your Lord has **made inviolable for you: that you may not associate anything with Him as a partner and that you must treat parents with exceeding kindness,**

155. Again, We gave Moses the Book —completing the favour upon him who did good, and an explanation of all *necessary* things, and a guidance and a mercy — that they might believe in the meeting with their Lord.

ثُمَّ اٰتَيۡنَا مُوۡسَى الۡكِتٰبَ تَمَامًا عَلَى الَّذِىۡۤ اَحۡسَنَ وَ
تَفۡصِيۡلًا لِّكُلِّ شَىۡءٍ وَّ هُدًى وَّ رَحۡمَةً لَّعَلَّهُمۡ بِلِقَآءِ
رَبِّهِمۡ يُؤۡمِنُوۡنَ ﴿۱۵۵﴾

155. Again, We gave Moses the Book **which completely fulfils the requirements of one who is excellent in conduct and explains everything to the last detail and is a guidance and blessing so that they come to believe in the** meeting with their Lord.

162.
religion, the religion of Abraham, the upright. And he was not of those who join gods *with God.'*

مِلَّةَ اِبۡرٰهِيۡمَ حَنِيۡفًا ۚ وَ مَا كَانَ مِنَ الۡمُشۡرِكِيۡنَ ﴿۱۶۲﴾

162. religion, the religion of Abraham **who was always inclined to the right path.** And he was not of those who associate partners *with God.*

165.
And no soul acts but only against itself; nor does any bearer of burden bear the burden of another. Then to your Lord will be your return,

وَ لَا تَزِرُ وَازِرَةٌ وِّزۡرَ اُخۡرٰى ۚ ثُمَّ اِلٰى رَبِّكُمۡ مَّرۡجِعُكُمۡ

165. And no soul **earns aught** *of evil* **but carries its burden against itself. And no bearer shall carry the burden of another.** Then to your Lord will be your return . . . . . .

166.
Lord is quick in punishment; and surely He is Most Forgiving, Merciful.

اِنَّ رَبَّكَ سَرِيۡعُ الۡعِقَابِ ۖ وَ اِنَّهٗ لَغَفُوۡرٌ رَّحِيۡمٌ ﴿۱۶۶﴾

166. Surely, **your** Lord is **swift in punishment;** and surely He is Most Forgiving, Merciful.

AL-A'ARAF

5. or while they slept at noon. اَوْهُمْ قَآئِلُوْنَ ﴿٥﴾

5. or while **they were resting at noon.**

21. But Satan whispered *evil suggestions* to them so that he might make known to them what was hidden from them of their shame, and said, 'Your Lord has only forbidden you this tree, lest you should become angels or such *beings* as live for ever.'

فَوَسْوَسَ لَهُمَا الشَّيْطٰنُ لِيُبْدِيَ لَهُمَا مَا وٗرِيَ عَنْهُمَا مِنْ سَوْاٰتِهِمَا وَقَالَ مَا نَهٰكُمَا رَبُّكُمَا عَنْ هٰذِهِ الشَّجَرَةِ اِلَّآ اَنْ تَكُوْنَا مَلَكَيْنِ اَوْ تَكُوْنَا مِنَ الْخٰلِدِيْنَ ﴿٢١﴾

21. But Satan whispered *suggestions* to them **so that he might reveal to them their shortcomings which had remained concealed in them** of their shame, and said, 'Your Lord has only forbidden you this tree, lest you should become angels or such *beings* as live for ever.'

38.
They will answer, 'We cannot find them;' قَالُوْا ضَلُّوْا عَنَّا

38. They will answer, 'To us they are entirely lost;'

41.
gates of the *spiritual* firmament will not be opened for them, لَا تُفَتَّحُ لَهُمْ اَبْوَابُ السَّمَآءِ

41. **gates of heaven** will not be opened for them,

79. So the earthquake seized them and in their homes they lay prostrate upon the ground. فَاَخَذَتْهُمُ الرَّجْفَةُ فَاَصْبَحُوْا فِيْ دَارِهِمْ جٰثِمِيْنَ ﴿٧٩﴾

79. **Then** the earthquake seized them so **that they turned into corpses lying**

prone in their houses.

وَلَا تَبْخَسُوا النَّاسَ أَشْيَاءَهُمْ

86. and diminish not unto people their things,

86. and do not give people less than what rightfully belongs to them,

وَسِعَ رَبُّنَا كُلَّ شَيْءٍ عِلْمًا

90. Our Lord comprehends all things in *His* knowledge.

90. **In knowledge our Lord comprehends all things.**

وَمَا وَجَدْنَا لِأَكْثَرِهِم مِّنْ عَهْدٍ ۖ وَإِن وَجَدْنَا أَكْثَرَهُمْ لَفَاسِقِينَ ﴿١٠٢﴾

103. And We found not in most of them any *observance of* covenant and surely We found most of them to be evil-doers.

103. And We found not in most of them any **regard for** *observance of* covenant and surely We found most of them to be evil-doers.

الَّذِينَ يَتَّبِعُونَ الرَّسُولَ النَّبِيَّ الْأُمِّيَّ

158. 'Those who follow the Messenger, the Prophet, the Immaculate one,

158. Those who follow the Messenger, the Prophet, **the unlettered one,**

أُمَّةٌ يَهْدُونَ بِالْحَقِّ

160. a party that exhorts *people* to truth

160. a party **that guides with truth**

قَالُوا مَعْذِرَةً إِلَىٰ رَبِّكُمْ وَلَعَلَّهُمْ يَتَّقُونَ ﴿١٦٤﴾

165. They said, 'As an excuse before your Lord, and that they may become righteous.'

165. They said, **'In order to be absolved in the sight of your Lord and perchance they fear *Allah*.**

166. because they were rebellious.

بِمَا كَانُوا يَفْسُقُونَ ﴿١٦٦﴾

166. because of the sins they used to commit.

172. And when We shook the mountain over them as though it were a covering, and they thought it was going to fall on them,

وَإِذْ نَتَقْنَا الْجَبَلَ فَوْقَهُمْ كَأَنَّهُ ظُلَّةٌ وَظَنُّوا أَنَّهُ
وَاقِعٌ بِهِمْ

172. And when **We caused the mountain to lean over them as though it were a canopy** and they thought it **was about to fall upon them,**

177. And if We had pleased, We could have exalted him thereby; but he inclined to the earth and followed his evil inclination. His case therefore is like the case of a *thirsty* dog; if thou drive him away, he hangs out his tongue; and if thou leave him, he hangs out his tongue. Such is the case of the people who disbelieve in Our Signs. So give *them* the description that they may ponder.

وَلَوْ شِئْنَا لَرَفَعْنَاهُ بِهَا وَلَٰكِنَّهُ أَخْلَدَ إِلَى الْأَرْضِ
وَاتَّبَعَ هَوَاهُ ۚ فَمَثَلُهُ كَمَثَلِ الْكَلْبِ إِنْ تَحْمِلْ عَلَيْهِ
يَلْهَثْ أَوْ تَتْرُكْهُ يَلْهَثْ ۚ ذَٰلِكَ مَثَلُ الْقَوْمِ الَّذِينَ
كَذَّبُوا بِآيَاتِنَا ۚ فَاقْصُصِ الْقَصَصَ لَعَلَّهُمْ يَتَفَكَّرُونَ ﴿١٧٧﴾

177. And if We had so **desired,** We could have exalted him thereby; but he inclined to the earth and followed his evil inclination. **His case is like that of a dog that hangs out his tongue in exhaustion *while barking at you* regardless of whether you make a motion of casting a stone at him or leave him alone,** he hangs out his tongue. Such is the case of the people who disbelieve in Our Signs. So **narrate episodes *from history* so that they may ponder *to draw lessons from them.***

190. He it is Who has created you from a single soul, and made therefrom its mate, that he might find comfort in her. And when he knows her, she bears a light

هُوَ الَّذِي خَلَقَكُمْ مِنْ نَفْسٍ وَاحِدَةٍ وَجَعَلَ مِنْهَا
زَوْجَهَا لِيَسْكُنَ إِلَيْهَا ۖ فَلَمَّا تَغَشَّاهَا حَمَلَتْ حَمْلًا

خَفِيفًا فَمَرَّتْ بِهِۦ ۖ فَلَمَّآ أَثْقَلَت دَّعَوَا ٱللَّهَ رَبَّهُمَا
لَئِنْ ءَاتَيْتَنَا صَٰلِحًا لَّنَكُونَنَّ مِنَ ٱلشَّٰكِرِينَ ﴿١٩٠﴾

burden, and goes about with it. And when she grows heavy, they both pray to Allah, their Lord, *saying:* 'If Thou give us a good *child*, we will surely be of the thankful.'

190. He it is Who has created you from a **single being** and made **from that** its mate, that he might find comfort in her. And when **he covered her she conceived and carried a light burden and walked about with it. And when she grew heavy, they both prayed to Allah: 'If you give us a healthy righteous child we shall surely be of those who are grateful.'**

هَٰذَا بَصَآئِرُ مِن رَّبِّكُمْ
وَهُدًى وَرَحْمَةٌ لِّقَوْمٍ يُؤْمِنُونَ ﴿٢٠٤﴾

204. These are evidences from your Lord, and guidance and mercy for a people that believe.'

204. **These are illuminating Signs from your Lord and a guidance and** blessing for a people that believe.'

AL-ANFĀL

وَلِيُبْلِىَ ٱلْمُؤْمِنِينَ مِنْهُ
بَلَآءً حَسَنًا ۚ إِنَّ ٱللَّهَ سَمِيعٌ عَلِيمٌ ﴿١٨﴾

18. and that He might confer on the believers a great favour from Himself. Surely, Allah is All-Hearing, All-Knowing.

18. and that He might confer on the believers **a trial** from Himself **— a goodly trial —** Surely Allah is All-Hearing, All-Knowing.

يَٰٓأَيُّهَا ٱلَّذِينَ ءَامَنُوا۟ لَا تَخُونُوا۟ ٱللَّهَ وَٱلرَّسُولَ وَتَخُونُوٓا۟
أَمَٰنَٰتِكُمْ وَأَنتُمْ تَعْلَمُونَ ﴿٢٨﴾

28. O ye who believe! prove not false to Allah and the Messenger, nor prove false to your trusts knowingly.

28. O ye who believe! **Do not betray Allah and the Messenger while you *so often* betray your trusts and you know it.**

إِنَّ الَّذِينَ كَفَرُوا يُنْفِقُونَ أَمْوَالَهُمْ لِيَصُدُّوا عَنْ
سَبِيلِ اللَّهِ ۚ فَسَيُنْفِقُونَهَا ثُمَّ تَكُونُ عَلَيْهِمْ حَسْرَةً
ثُمَّ يُغْلَبُونَ ۗ

37. Surely, those who disbelieve spend their wealth to turn *men* away from the way of Allah. They will surely continue to spend it; *but* then shall it become a *source of* regret for them, *and* then shall they be overcome.

37. Surely, those who disbelieve spend their wealth to turn **people** away from the way of Allah. They will surely continue to spend it, but then **it will result for them in *nothing but* lament *and mourning at their utter failure* and then shall they be *roundly* defeated.**

وَلَوْ تَوَاعَدْتُمْ لَاخْتَلَفْتُمْ فِي
الْمِيعَادِ ۙ وَلَٰكِنْ لِيَقْضِيَ اللَّهُ أَمْرًا كَانَ مَفْعُولًا ۙ لِيَهْلِكَ
مَنْ هَلَكَ عَنْ بَيِّنَةٍ وَيَحْيَىٰ مَنْ حَيَّ عَنْ بَيِّنَةٍ ۗ

43. And if you had to make a mutual appointment, you would have certainly differed with regard to the appointment. But *the encounter was brought about* that Allah might accomplish the thing that was decreed; so that he who had *already* perished through a clear Sign might perish, and he who had *already* come to life through a clear Sign might live.

43. And if you, ***both the belligerent parties,*** **were to decide the time of encounter, you would have differed regarding the time *to suit your own interests.* But it was destined that Allah would decide *the time* to accomplish that which had already been decreed so that they may perish who are doomed to perish by manifest justification, and they may survive who deserve to survive on the strength of manifest justification.**

48. And be not like those who came forth from their homes boastfully, and to be seen of men, and who turn *men* away from the path of Allah, and Allah encompasses all that they do.

وَلَا تَكُونُوا كَالَّذِينَ خَرَجُوا مِن دِيَارِهِم بَطَرًا وَّ
رِئَاءَ النَّاسِ وَيَصُدُّونَ عَن سَبِيلِ اللَّهِ ۚ وَاللَّهُ
بِمَا يَعْمَلُونَ مُحِيطٌ ﴿٤٨﴾

48. And be not like those who came forth from their homes **to boast *of their deeds* and to make a display to the people and they prevent *people* from reaching the path of Allah,** and Allah encompasses all that they do.

56. Surely, the worst of beasts in the sight of Allah are those who are ungrateful. So they will not believe,

إِنَّ شَرَّ الدَّوَابِّ عِندَ اللَّهِ الَّذِينَ كَفَرُوا فَهُمْ لَا
يُؤْمِنُونَ ﴿٥٦﴾

56. Surely, the worst of **creatures** in the sight of Allah are those who are ungrateful. So they will not believe,

72. And if they intend to deal treacherously with thee, they have already dealt treacherously with Allah before, but He gave *thee* power over them. And Allah is All-Knowing, Wise.

وَإِن يُرِيدُوا خِيَانَتَكَ فَقَدْ خَانُوا اللَّهَ مِن قَبْلُ
فَأَمْكَنَ مِنْهُمْ ۗ وَاللَّهُ عَلِيمٌ حَكِيمٌ ﴿٧٢﴾

72. **And if they intend to betray your trust, they have already betrayed the trust of Allah before. So He rendered them powerless.** And Allah is All-Knowing, Wise.

73. Surely, those who have believed and fled from their homes and striven with their property and their persons for the cause of Allah, and those who have given *them* shelter and help—these are friends one of another. But as for those who have believed

إِنَّ الَّذِينَ آمَنُوا وَهَاجَرُوا وَجَاهَدُوا بِأَمْوَالِهِمْ وَ
أَنفُسِهِمْ فِي سَبِيلِ اللَّهِ وَالَّذِينَ آوَوا وَّنَصَرُوا
أُولَٰئِكَ بَعْضُهُمْ أَوْلِيَاءُ بَعْضٍ ۚ وَالَّذِينَ آمَنُوا وَ

73. Surely, those who have believed and **left their homes** and striven with their property and their persons for the cause of Allah, and those who have given

them shelter and help — **are indeed mutual friends.** But as for those who have believed.

AL-TAUBA

3. Allah is clear of the idolaters, and so is His Messenger.

اَنَّ اللّٰهَ بَرِيْٓءٌ مِّنَ الْمُشْرِكِيْنَ ۙ وَرَسُوْلُهٗ

3. That Allah is **absolved** of the idolaters, and so is His Messenger.

4. who have not *subsequently* failed you in anything nor aided anyone against you. So fulfil to these the treaty *you have* made with them till their term. Surely, Allah loves those who are righteous.

لَمْ يَنْقُصُوْكُمْ

شَيْـًٔا وَّ لَمْ يُظَاهِرُوْا عَلَيْكُمْ اَحَدًا فَاَتِمُّوْٓا اِلَيْهِمْ عَهْدَهُمْ اِلٰى مُدَّتِهِمْ ؕ اِنَّ اللّٰهَ يُحِبُّ الْمُتَّقِيْنَ ۝

4. who have not **fallen short of fulfilling their obligations to you** nor aided anyone against you. So fulfil to these the treaty *you have* made with them till their term. Surely, Allah loves those who are righteous.

5. And when the forbidden months have passed,

فَاِذَا انْسَلَخَ الْاَشْهُرُ الْحُرُمُ

5. And when the **consecrated** months have passed,

12. and attack your religion,

وَطَعَنُوْا فِيْ دِيْنِكُمْ

12. and **revile** your religion,

17. The idolaters cannot keep the Mosques of Allah in a good and flourishing condition while they bear witness against themselves to disbelief.

مَا كَانَ لِلْمُشْرِكِيْنَ اَنْ يَّعْمُرُوْا مَسٰجِدَ اللّٰهِ شٰهِدِيْنَ عَلٰٓى اَنْفُسِهِمْ بِالْكُفْرِ ؕ

17. It is not for the idolaters to do justice to the purposes for which the mosques are built for Allah and to maintain them accordingly while they stand witness to their own disbelief. It

إِنَّمَا يَعْمُرُ مَسٰجِدَ اللّٰهِ مَنْ اٰمَنَ بِاللّٰهِ وَالْيَوْمِ الْاٰخِرِ
وَاَقَامَ الصَّلٰوةَ وَاٰتَى الزَّكٰوةَ وَلَمْ يَخْشَ اِلَّا اللّٰهَ فَعَسٰٓى
اُولٰٓئِكَ اَنْ يَّكُوْنُوْا مِنَ الْمُهْتَدِيْنَ ﴿١٨﴾

18. He alone can keep the Mosques of Allah in a good and flourishing condition who believes in Allah, and the Last Day, and observes Prayer, and pays the Zakāt, and fears none but Allah; so these it is who may be among those who reach the goal.

18. **Verily, he alone is worthy of maintaining the Mosques of Allah who** believes in Allah, and the Last Day, and observes Prayer, and pays Zakat, and fears none but Allah; so these it is who **are far more likely to be *counted* among the guided.**

ثُمَّ اَنْزَلَ اللّٰهُ سَكِيْنَتَهٗ عَلٰى رَسُوْلِهٖ وَعَلَى الْمُؤْمِنِيْنَ

26. Then Allah sent down His peace upon His Messenger and upon the believers,

26. Then Allah **caused tranquillity to descend upon** His Messenger and upon the believers,

حَتّٰى يُعْطُوا الْجِزْيَةَ عَنْ يَّدٍ وَّهُمْ صٰغِرُوْنَ ﴿٢٩﴾

29. until they pay the tax with *their own* hand and acknowledge their subjection.

29. until they pay the tax with *their own* hand ***submissively*** and acknowledge their subjection.

ذٰلِكَ قَوْلُهُمْ بِاَفْوَاهِهِمْ

30. that is what they say with their mouths.

30. they are but a word of their mouths.

36. That is the right creed.

ذٰلِكَ الدِّيْنُ الْقَيِّمُ

36. This is the religion that stays.

38. But the enjoyment of the present life is but little, as compared with the Hereafter.

فَمَا مَتَاعُ الْحَيٰوةِ الدُّنْيَا فِي الْاٰخِرَةِ اِلَّا قَلِيْلٌ ﴿۳۸﴾

38. The gains of the present life will but seem small and insignificant in the Hereafter.

47. **And there are among you those who would listen to them.**

وَفِيْكُمْ سَمّٰعُوْنَ لَهُمْ

47. And there are among you those who **are wont to** listen to them.

59. 'Sufficient for us is Allah; Allah will give us of His bounty, and so will His Messenger;

حَسْبُنَا اللّٰهُ سَيُؤْتِيْنَا اللّٰهُ مِنْ فَضْلِهٖ وَرَسُوْلُهٗٓ

59. 'Sufficient for us is Allah — and His Messenger; Surely Allah will bestow on us of His bounty;

61. And among them are those who annoy the Prophet and say, 'He *gives* ear *to all*.' Say, '*His giving* ear *to all* is good for you; he believes in Allah and believes the Faithful, and is a mercy for those of you who believe.'

وَمِنْهُمُ الَّذِيْنَ يُؤْذُوْنَ النَّبِيَّ وَيَقُوْلُوْنَ هُوَ اُذُنٌ
قُلْ اُذُنُ خَيْرٍ لَّكُمْ يُؤْمِنُ بِاللّٰهِ وَيُؤْمِنُ لِلْمُؤْمِنِيْنَ
وَرَحْمَةٌ لِّلَّذِيْنَ اٰمَنُوْا مِنْكُمْ

61. And among them are those who **hurt the Prophet and say, 'He is all ears'. Say, 'His disposition to listen *to all* is good for you;** he believes in Allah and **has trust in the believers,** and is a mercy for those of you who believe'.

74. And they meditated that which they could not attain. And they cherished hatred only because Allah and His Messenger had enriched them

وَمَا
نَقَمُوْٓا اِلَّآ اَنْ اَغْنٰهُمُ اللّٰهُ وَرَسُوْلُهٗ مِنْ فَضْلِهٖ

out of His bounty. So if they repent, it will be better for them; but if they turn away, Allah will punish them with a grievous punishment in this world and the Hereafter, and they shall have neither friend nor helper in the earth.

فَإِنْ يَتُوبُوا يَكُ خَيْرًا لَّهُمْ ۚ وَإِنْ يَتَوَلَّوْا يُعَذِّبْهُمُ اللهُ
عَذَابًا أَلِيمًا فِي الدُّنْيَا وَالْآخِرَةِ ۚ وَمَا لَهُمْ فِي الْأَرْضِ
مِنْ وَّلِيٍّ وَّلَا نَصِيرٍ ﴿٧٤﴾

74. And they meditated **upon** that which they ***subsequently*** **failed to attain.** And they **nourished** hatred only because Allah and His Messenger had enriched them out of His bounty. So if they repent, **it would** be better for them; but if they turn away, Allah will punish them with a grievous punishment in this world and the Hereafter, and they shall have neither friend nor helper in the earth.

78. Know they not that Allah knows their secrets as well as their private counsels and that Allah is the Best Knower of all unseen things?

أَلَمْ يَعْلَمُوا أَنَّ اللهَ يَعْلَمُ سِرَّهُمْ وَنَجْوٰىهُمْ وَأَنَّ
اللهَ عَلَّامُ الْغُيُوبِ ﴿٧٨﴾

78. Know they not that Allah knows their secrets **and covert deliberations** and that Allah is the Best Knower of the unseen things?

81. Those who were left behind rejoiced in their sitting *at home* behind *the back of* the Messenger of Allah, and were averse to striving with their property and their persons in the cause of Allah.

فَرِحَ الْمُخَلَّفُونَ بِمَقْعَدِهِمْ خِلٰفَ رَسُولِ اللهِ وَ
كَرِهُوا أَنْ يُّجَاهِدُوا بِأَمْوَالِهِمْ وَأَنْفُسِهِمْ فِي سَبِيلِ
اللهِ

81. **Those *who contrived to be* left behind rejoiced at their staying back in contradiction to the Messenger of Allah,** and were averse to striving with their property and their persons in the cause of Allah.

84. And never pray thou for any of them that dies, nor stand by his grave; for they disbelieved in Allah and His Messenger and died while they were disobedient.

وَلَا تُصَلِّ عَلٰٓى اَحَدٍ مِّنْهُمْ مَّاتَ اَبَدًا وَّلَا تَقُمْ عَلٰى قَبْرِهٖ ۭ اِنَّهُمْ كَفَرُوْا بِاللّٰهِ وَرَسُوْلِهٖ وَمَاتُوْا وَهُمْ فٰسِقُوْنَ ﴿۸۴﴾

84. **Never say prayer over any of them when he dies, nor stand by his grave** *to pray;* for they disbelieved in Allah and His Messenger and died while they were disobedient.

95. Surely, they are an abomination,

اِنَّهُمْ رِجْسٌ

95. Surely, they are **foul,**

98. And among the Arabs of the desert are those who regard that which they spend *for God* as a fine and they wait for calamities to *befall* you. On themselves shall fall an evil calamity.

وَمِنَ الْاَعْرَابِ مَنْ يَّتَّخِذُ مَا يُنْفِقُ مَغْرَمًا وَّيَتَرَبَّصُ بِكُمُ الدَّوَاۗىِٕرَ ۭ عَلَيْهِمْ دَاۗىِٕرَةُ السَّوْءِ ۭ

98. And among the Bedouin there are those who consider what they spend ***in the cause of Allah*** **a penalty and** ***wishfully*** **await calamities to befall you. Let evil befall them instead.**

100. and those who followed them in the best possible manner, Allah is well pleased with them and they are well pleased with Him;

وَالَّذِيْنَ اتَّبَعُوْهُمْ بِاِحْسَانٍ ۙ رَّضِيَ اللّٰهُ عَنْهُمْ وَرَضُوْا عَنْهُ

100. them **excellently,** Allah is well pleased with them and they are well pleased with Him;

104. takes alms, and that Allah is He Who is Oft-Returning *with compassion, and is* Merciful?

يَاْخُذُ الصَّدَقٰتِ وَاَنَّ اللّٰهَ هُوَ التَّوَّابُ الرَّحِيْمُ ﴿۱۰۴﴾

104. **acknowledges alms,** and that Allah is He Who is Oft-Returning *with compassion, and is* Merciful.

وَقُلِ اعْمَلُوْا فَسَيَرَى اللّٰهُ عَمَلَكُمْ وَرَسُوْلُهٗ وَالْمُؤْمِنُوْنَ
وَسَتُرَدُّوْنَ اِلٰى عٰلِمِ الْغَيْبِ وَالشَّهَادَةِ فَيُنَبِّئُكُمْ بِمَا
كُنْتُمْ تَعْمَلُوْنَ ﴿١٠٥﴾

105. And say, 'Work, and Allah will surely see your work and *also* His Messenger and the believers. And you shall be brought back to Him Who knows the unseen and the seen; then He will tell you what you used to do.'

105. And say, **'Do what you may, surely, Allah will watch your acts, so also will His Messenger and the believers. And you shall be made to return to the Knower of the unseen and the seen;** then He will tell you what you used to do.'

وَاٰخَرُوْنَ مُرْجَوْنَ لِاَمْرِ اللّٰهِ اِمَّا يُعَذِّبُهُمْ وَاِمَّا يَتُوْبُ
عَلَيْهِمْ

106. And *there are* others *whose* case has been postponed for the decree of Allah. He may punish them or He may turn to them with compassion.

106. And *there are* others **who are kept awaiting** the decree of Allah. He **may decide to** punish them or He may turn to them with compassion.

وَالَّذِيْنَ اتَّخَذُوْا مَسْجِدًا ضِرَارًا وَّكُفْرًا وَّتَفْرِيْقًا
بَيْنَ الْمُؤْمِنِيْنَ وَاِرْصَادًا لِّمَنْ حَارَبَ اللّٰهَ وَرَسُوْلَهٗ
مِنْ قَبْلُ

107. And *among the hypocrites are* those who have built a mosque in order to injure *Islam* and *help* disbelief and cause a division among the believers, and prepare an ambush for him who warred against Allah and His Messenger before *this*.

107. And *among the hypocrites are* those who have built a mosque in order to injure *Islam* and *help* disbelief and **cause division among the believers, and to provide a place of hiding for those who have already waged war against Allah and His Messenger.**

اَفَمَنْ اَسَّسَ بُنْيَانَهٗ عَلٰى تَقْوٰى مِنَ اللّٰهِ وَرِضْوَانٍ
خَيْرٌ اَمْ مَّنْ اَسَّسَ بُنْيَانَهٗ عَلٰى شَفَا جُرُفٍ هَارٍ

109. Is he, then, who founded his building on fear of Allah and His pleasure better or he who founded his building

on the brink of a tottering water-worn bank which tumbled down with him into the fire of Hell? And Allah guides not the wrongdoing people.

فَانْهَارَ بِهٖ فِيْ نَارِ جَهَنَّمَ ؕ وَاللّٰهُ لَا يَهْدِي الْقَوْمَ
الظّٰلِمِيْنَ ﴿۱۰۹﴾

109. Is he, then, **who laid his foundation on fear of Allah and His pleasure better or he who laid his foundation** on the brink of a tottering water-worn bank which tumbled down with him into the fire of Hell? And Allah **does not guide a people who transgress.**

110. *This* building of theirs, which they have built, will ever continue to be a *source of* disquiet in their hearts, unless their hearts be torn to pieces. And Allah is All-Knowing, Wise.

لَا يَزَالُ بُنْيَانُهُمُ الَّذِيْ بَنَوْا رِيْبَةً فِيْ قُلُوْبِهِمْ
اِلَّآ اَنْ تَقَطَّعَ قُلُوْبُهُمْ ؕ وَاللّٰهُ عَلِيْمٌ حَكِيْمٌ ﴿۱۱۰﴾

110. **This building of theirs, they have raised, will ever be a source of disquiet and uncertainty in their hearts, until their hearts split and are torn to pieces.** And Allah is All-Knowing, Wise.

118. And *He has turned with mercy* to the three whose *case* was deferred, until the earth became too strait for them with *all* its vastness,

وَّعَلَى الثَّلٰثَةِ الَّذِيْنَ خُلِّفُوْا ؕ حَتّٰٓى اِذَا ضَاقَتْ عَلَيْهِمُ الْاَرْضُ بِمَا
رَحُبَتْ

118. **And the three *who remained* behind, until the earth seemed too narrow for them despite *all* its vastness,**

120. nor do they cause an enemy any injury whatsoever,

لَا يَنَالُوْنَ مِنْ عَدُوٍّ نَّيْلًا

120. nor do they **gain an advantage over the enemy,**

122. that they may become' well versed in religion,

لِيَتَفَقَّهُوْا فِي الدِّيْنِ

122. that they **may gain better understanding of religion,**

123. let them find hardness in you;

وَلْيَجِدُوا فِيكُمْ غِلْظَةً

123. let them find **uncompromising firmness** in you;

126. Do they not see that they are tried every year once or twice?

أَوَلَا يَرَوْنَ أَنَّهُمْ يُفْتَنُونَ فِي كُلِّ عَامٍ مَّرَّةً أَوْ
مَرَّتَيْنِ

126. Do they not see that they are **put to trial** every year, once or twice?

YŪNUS

3. Is it a *matter of* wonder for men that We have inspired a man from among them, *saying*, 'Warn mankind and give glad tidings to those who believe that they have a true rank *of honour* with their Lord?' The disbelievers say, 'Surely, this is a manifest enchanter.'

أَكَانَ لِلنَّاسِ عَجَبًا أَنْ أَوْحَيْنَا إِلَىٰ رَجُلٍ مِّنْهُمْ أَنْ
أَنذِرِ النَّاسَ وَبَشِّرِ الَّذِينَ آمَنُوا أَنَّ لَهُمْ قَدَمَ
صِدْقٍ عِندَ رَبِّهِمْ ۗ قَالَ الْكَافِرُونَ إِنَّ هَٰذَا لَسَاحِرٌ
مُّبِينٌ ③

3. Is it a *matter of* wonder for **people** that We have sent down revelation to a man from among them *saying*, 'Warn mankind and give glad tidings to those who believe that **for them there is a station of truth** with their Lord.' The disbelievers say, 'Surely, this is a manifest enchanter.'

4. **He governs everything.**

يُدَبِّرُ الْأَمْرَ

4. **He regulates** everything.

6. He it is Who made the sun *radiate* a brilliant light and the moon *reflect* a lustre,

هُوَ الَّذِي جَعَلَ الشَّمْسَ ضِيَاءً وَالْقَمَرَ نُورًا

6. He it is Who made the sun **radiant and the moon lambent**

13. And when trouble befalls a man, he calls on Us, lying on his side, or sitting, or standing; but when We have removed his trouble from him, he goes his way as though he had never called on Us for the *removal of the* trouble that befell him.

وَإِذَا مَسَّ الْإِنسَانَ الضُّرُّ دَعَانَا لِجَنبِهِ أَوْ قَاعِدًا
أَوْ قَائِمًا فَلَمَّا كَشَفْنَا عَنْهُ ضُرَّهُ مَرَّ كَأَن لَّمْ يَدْعُنَا
إِلَىٰ ضُرٍّ مَّسَّهُ

13. And when **affliction** befalls a man, he calls on Us, lying on his side, or sitting, or standing; but when **We relieve him of his distress, he walks away as if he had never beseeched Us to attend to the misery afflicting him.**

14. And We destroyed the generations before you when they did wrong; and there came to them their Messengers with clear Signs, but they would not believe.

وَلَقَدْ أَهْلَكْنَا الْقُرُونَ مِن قَبْلِكُمْ لَمَّا ظَلَمُوا
وَجَاءَتْهُمْ رُسُلُهُم بِالْبَيِّنَاتِ وَمَا كَانُوا لِيُؤْمِنُوا

14. And We destroyed **many a generation before you when they transgressed, while Messengers had come to them *before that* with manifest Signs,** but they would not believe.

16. punishment of an awful day.'

عَذَابَ يَوْمٍ عَظِيمٍ ﴿١٦﴾

16. punishment of an **Enormous** Day.

18. Who is then more unjust than he who forges a lie against Allah or *he* who treats His Signs as lies?

فَمَنْ أَظْلَمُ مِمَّنِ افْتَرَىٰ عَلَى اللَّهِ كَذِبًا أَوْ كَذَّبَ بِآيَاتِهِ

18. Who **violates justice more blatantly than the one** who forges a lie against Allah or *he* who treats His Signs as lies?

19. Holy is He, and high exalted above *all* that which they associate *with Him.*

سُبْحَانَهُ وَتَعَالَىٰ عَمَّا يُشْرِكُونَ ﴿١٩﴾

19. Glorious is He, exalted far above that which they associate *with Him.*

20. And mankind were but one community, then they differed *among themselves;* and had it not been for a word that had gone before from thy Lord, it would have *already* been judged between them concerning that in which they differed.

وَمَا كَانَ النَّاسُ إِلَّآ أُمَّةً وَّاحِدَةً فَاخْتَلَفُوْا ۭ وَلَوْلَا
كَلِمَةٌ سَبَقَتْ مِنْ رَّبِّكَ لَقُضِيَ بَيْنَهُمْ فِيْمَا فِيْهِ
يَخْتَلِفُوْنَ ﴿٢٠﴾

20. And mankind were but one community, then **they differed; and had it not been for a word gone before from your Lord, their fate would have been sealed in accordance with all they differed therein.**

21.
Say, 'The unseen belongs only to Allah. So wait; I am with you among those who wait.'

فَقُلْ إِنَّمَا
الْغَيْبُ لِلّٰهِ فَانْتَظِرُوْٓا ۚ إِنِّيْ مَعَكُمْ مِّنَ الْمُنْتَظِرِيْنَ ﴿٢١﴾

21. Say, **To Allah belongs the unseen. Wait therefore;** I am with you among those who wait.'

22. And when We make people taste of mercy after adversity has touched them, behold, they begin to plan against Our Signs. Say, 'Allah is swifter in planning.' Surely, Our messengers write down all that you plan.

وَإِذَآ أَذَقْنَا النَّاسَ رَحْمَةً مِّنْ بَعْدِ ضَرَّآءَ مَسَّتْهُمْ
إِذَا لَهُمْ مَّكْرٌ فِيْٓ اٰيَاتِنَا ۭ قُلِ اللّٰهُ أَسْرَعُ مَكْرًا ۭ إِنَّ
رُسُلَنَا يَكْتُبُوْنَ مَا تَمْكُرُوْنَ ﴿٢٢﴾

22. The moment We give a taste of mercy to a people stricken by calamity, they begin to plot against Our Signs forthwith. Say, 'Swifter is Allah in planning.' Surely, Our Messengers maintain a record of what you plan.

23.
there overtakes them (the ships) a violent wind and the waves come on them from every side and they think they are encompassed, *then* they call upon Allah, purifying *their* religion for Him, *saying*, 'If Thou deliver us from this, we will surely be of the thankful.'

جَآءَتْهَا رِيْحٌ عَاصِفٌ وَّجَآءَهُمُ الْمَوْجُ مِنْ كُلِّ
مَكَانٍ وَّظَنُّوْٓا أَنَّهُمْ أُحِيْطَ بِهِمْ ۙ دَعَوُا اللّٰهَ مُخْلِصِيْنَ
لَهُ الدِّيْنَ ۚ لَئِنْ أَنْجَيْتَنَا مِنْ هٰذِهٖ لَنَكُوْنَنَّ مِنَ
الشّٰكِرِيْنَ ﴿٢٣﴾

23. there overtakes them **a ferocious wind** and the waves come on them from every side and they think they are encompassed, *then* they call upon Allah, **promising sincerity of faith for Him,** *saying;* 'If Thou deliver us from this, we will surely be of the thankful.'

24. O ye men, your excesses are only against your own selves. *Have* the enjoyment of the present life. Then to Us shall be your return; and We will inform you of what you used to do.

يَاَيُّهَا النَّاسُ اِنَّمَا بَغْيُكُمْ عَلٰٓى اَنْفُسِكُمْ مَّتَاعَ الْحَيٰوةِ
الدُّنْيَا ز ثُمَّ اِلَيْنَا مَرْجِعُكُمْ فَنُنَبِّئُكُمْ بِمَا كُنْتُمْ
تَعْمَلُوْنَ ﴿٢٤﴾

24. O ye men, your excesses are only against your own selves **— a mere enjoyment of the present life.** Then to Us shall be your return; and We will inform you of what you used to do.

25. The likeness of the present life is only as water which We send down from the clouds, then there mingles with it the produce of the earth, of which men and cattle eat till, when the earth receives its ornature and looks beautiful and its owners think that they have power over it, there comes to it Our command by night or by day and We render it a field that is mown down, as if nothing had existed there the day before. Thus do We expound the Signs for a people who reflect.

اِنَّمَا مَثَلُ الْحَيٰوةِ الدُّنْيَا كَمَآءٍ اَنْزَلْنٰهُ مِنَ السَّمَآءِ
فَاخْتَلَطَ بِهٖ نَبَاتُ الْاَرْضِ مِمَّا يَاْكُلُ النَّاسُ وَ
الْاَنْعَامُ ؕ حَتّٰٓى اِذَآ اَخَذَتِ الْاَرْضُ زُخْرُفَهَا وَ
ازَّيَّنَتْ وَظَنَّ اَهْلُهَآ اَنَّهُمْ قٰدِرُوْنَ عَلَيْهَآ ۙ اَتٰهَآ
اَمْرُنَا لَيْلًا اَوْ نَهَارًا فَجَعَلْنٰهَا حَصِيْدًا كَاَنْ لَّمْ تَغْنَ
بِالْاَمْسِ ؕ كَذٰلِكَ نُفَصِّلُ الْاٰيٰتِ لِقَوْمٍ يَّتَفَكَّرُوْنَ ﴿٢٥﴾

25. **The example of life on earth is like that of water that We cause to descend from heaven. Then with it mingles the vegetation of the earth of which both the people and the cattle partake. It continues to be so until the earth blossoms forth in full bloom and ripens into loveliness — then those who possess it deem themselves supreme over it, there suddenly**

descends Our decree at night or during the day. Then We render it a field that is mown down as if it had not existed the day before. Thus do We expound the Signs for a people who reflect.

29. **And *remember* the day when We shall gather them all together, then shall We say to those who ascribed partners *to God*, "*Stand back in* your places, you and your 'partners". Then We shall separate them widely, one from another, and their 'partners' will say: 'It was not us that you worshipped.**

وَيَوْمَ نَحْشُرُهُمْ جَمِيعًا ثُمَّ نَقُولُ لِلَّذِينَ أَشْرَكُوا
مَكَانَكُمْ أَنتُمْ وَشُرَكَاؤُكُمْ ۚ فَزَيَّلْنَا بَيْنَهُمْ ۖ وَقَالَ
شُرَكَاؤُهُم مَّا كُنتُمْ إِيَّانَا تَعْبُدُونَ ﴿٢٩﴾

29. Beware of the day when We shall gather them all together, then shall We say to those who ascribed partners *to God,* 'Stay put where you are — you and your associate gods'. Then shall We separate them; and those whom they had considered partners will say, 'It is not we whom you worshipped'.

30. **'So Allah is *now* sufficient as a Witness between us and you. We were certainly unaware of your worship.'**

فَكَفَىٰ بِاللَّهِ شَهِيدًا بَيْنَنَا وَبَيْنَكُمْ إِن كُنَّا عَنْ
عِبَادَتِكُمْ لَغَافِلِينَ ﴿٣٠﴾

30. 'So Allah is sufficient Witness between you and us. We were absolutely unaware of your devotion'.

32. . **Then say, 'Will you not then seek *His* protection?'**

فَقُلْ أَفَلَا تَتَّقُونَ ﴿٣٢﴾

32. Then say, 'Will you not then desist *from your wrong pursuits?'*

33. **Such is Allah, your true Lord. So what *would you have* after *discarding* the truth except error? How then are you being turned away *from the truth?***

فَذَٰلِكُمُ اللَّهُ رَبُّكُمُ الْحَقُّ ۖ فَمَاذَا بَعْدَ الْحَقِّ إِلَّا
الضَّلَالُ ۖ فَأَنَّىٰ تُصْرَفُونَ ﴿٣٣﴾

33. Such is Allah, your true Lord, So **what is left after truth but manifest error?** How then are you being turned away *from the truth?*

35. Say, 'Is there any of your associate-gods who originates creation and then reproduces it?' Say, 'It is Allah *alone* Who originates creation and then reproduces it. Whither then are you turned away?'

قُلْ هَلْ مِنْ شُرَكَآئِكُمْ مَّنْ يَّبْدَؤُا الْخَلْقَ ثُمَّ
يُعِيْدُهٗ قُلِ اللّٰهُ يَبْدَؤُا الْخَلْقَ ثُمَّ يُعِيْدُهٗ فَاَنّٰى
تُؤْفَكُوْنَ ﴿٣٥﴾

35. Say, 'Is there one among your associates who originates creation then repeats it?' Say, 'It is Allah *alone* Who initiates creation and then repeats it. How could you then be led astray?'

37. Surely, conjecture avails nothing against truth.

إِنَّ الظَّنَّ لَا يُغْنِيْ مِنَ الْحَقِّ شَيْـًٔا

37. Surely, **conjecture cannot substitute truth in the least.**

41. thy Lord well knows those who act corruptly.

رَبُّكَ اَعْلَمُ بِالْمُفْسِدِيْنَ ﴿٤١﴾

41. your Lord knows best those who provoke disorder.

42. And if they accuse thee of lying, say, 'For me is my work and for you is your work.

وَاِنْ كَذَّبُوْكَ فَقُلْ لِّيْ عَمَلِيْ وَلَكُمْ عَمَلُكُمْ

42. And if they **accuse you of lying, say, 'I am accountable for my actions and you for yours.**

46. and would not follow guidance.

وَمَا كَانُوْا مُهْتَدِيْنَ ﴿٤٦﴾

46. and would **not be guided.**

47. And if We show thee ***in thy lifetime the fulfilment of*** **some of the things with which We have threatened them,** ***thou wilt know it;*** **or if We cause thee to die** ***before that,*** **then to Us is their return,** ***and thou wilt see the fulfilment in the next world;*** **and Allah is Witness to all that they do.**

وَإِمَّا نُرِيَنَّكَ بَعْضَ الَّذِي نَعِدُهُمْ أَوْ نَتَوَفَّيَنَّكَ فَإِلَيْنَا
مَرْجِعُهُمْ ثُمَّ اللَّهُ شَهِيدٌ عَلَىٰ مَا يَفْعَلُونَ ﴿٤٧﴾
وَلِكُلِّ أُمَّةٍ رَّسُولٌ ۖ فَإِذَا جَاءَ رَسُولُهُمْ قُضِيَ بَيْنَهُم

47. **And if We make you witness a part of what We promised them or cause you to die** ***before that,*** to Us **shall be** their return; then will Allah stand witness against what they do.

51.
how will the guilty run away from it?

مَّاذَا يَسْتَعْجِلُ مِنْهُ الْمُجْرِمُونَ ﴿٥١﴾

51. how **could the guilty escape it however hastily?**

56. Know ye! to Allah, surely, belongs whatever is in the heavens and the earth. Know ye, that Allah's promise is surely true! But most of them understand not.

أَلَا إِنَّ لِلَّهِ مَا فِي السَّمَاوَاتِ وَالْأَرْضِ ۗ أَلَا إِنَّ وَعْدَ
اللَّهِ حَقٌّ وَلَٰكِنَّ أَكْثَرَهُمْ لَا يَعْلَمُونَ ﴿٥٦﴾

56. **Lo!** To Allah, surely, belongs whatever is in the heavens and the earth. **Lo! Verily, the promise of Allah is true. But most of them know not.**

62. And thou art not engaged in anything, and thou recitest not from Him any portion of the Qur'ān, and you do no work, but We are witnesses of you when you are engrossed therein. And there is not hidden from thy Lord even an atom's weight in the earth or in heaven. And there is nothing smaller than that or greater, but it is *recorded* in a clear Book.

وَمَا تَكُونُ فِي شَأْنٍ وَمَا تَتْلُو مِنْهُ مِن قُرْآنٍ وَ
لَا تَعْمَلُونَ مِنْ عَمَلٍ إِلَّا كُنَّا عَلَيْكُمْ شُهُودًا إِذْ تُفِيضُونَ
فِيهِ ۚ وَمَا يَعْزُبُ عَن رَّبِّكَ مِن مِّثْقَالِ ذَرَّةٍ فِي الْأَرْضِ
وَلَا فِي السَّمَاءِ وَلَا أَصْغَرَ مِن ذَٰلِكَ وَلَا أَكْبَرَ إِلَّا
فِي كِتَابٍ مُّبِينٍ ﴿٦٢﴾

62. And **you are** not engaged in anything, and **you recite** not from Him any portion of the Qur'an, and **you** do not do **anything but We watch you** when you are engrossed therein. **And nothing is hidden from the view of**

your Lord — even that which weighs no more than a particle or less thereof, or greater than that in the earth or in the heavens — but it is *recorded* in a clear Book.

64. Those who believed and kept to righteousness—

الَّذِينَ آمَنُوا وَكَانُوا يَتَّقُونَ ﴿٦٤﴾

64. Those who believed and **acted ever righteously.**

66. And let not their words grieve thee. Surely, all power belongs to Allah. He is the All-Hearing, the All-Knowing.

وَلَا يَحْزُنْكَ قَوْلُهُمْ إِنَّ الْعِزَّةَ لِلَّهِ جَمِيعًا هُوَ السَّمِيعُ
الْعَلِيمُ ﴿٦٦﴾

66. And let not their words grieve **you. Surely, all majesty** belongs to Allah. He is the All-Hearing, the All-Knowing.

67. Behold! whoever is in the heavens and whoever is in the earth is Allah's. Those who call on others than Allah do not *really* follow *these* 'partners'; they follow only a conjecture, and they do nothing but guess.

أَلَا إِنَّ لِلَّهِ مَنْ فِي السَّمَاوَاتِ وَمَنْ فِي الْأَرْضِ وَمَا
يَتَّبِعُ الَّذِينَ يَدْعُونَ مِنْ دُونِ اللَّهِ شُرَكَاءَ إِنْ
يَتَّبِعُونَ إِلَّا الظَّنَّ وَإِنْ هُمْ إِلَّا يَخْرُصُونَ ﴿٦٧﴾

67. **Lo! To Allah belongs whatever is in the heavens and whatever is in the earth.** Those who **pray to partners beside Allah** do not *really* follow **them. They follow nothing but fancy and indulge not but in conjectures.**

68. He it is Who has made for you the night *dark* that you may rest therein, and the day full of light.

هُوَ الَّذِي جَعَلَ لَكُمُ اللَّيْلَ لِتَسْكُنُوا فِيهِ وَالنَّهَارَ
مُبْصِرًا

68. He it is Who has made for you the night **that you may rest therein, and the day illuminating.**

مَتَاعٌ فِي الدُّنْيَا ثُمَّ إِلَيْنَا مَرْجِعُهُمْ ثُمَّ نُذِيقُهُمُ
الْعَذَابَ الشَّدِيدَ بِمَا كَانُوا يَكْفُرُونَ ﴿٧١﴾

71. *They will have some* enjoyment in this world. Then to Us is their return. Then shall We make them taste a severe punishment, because they used to disbelieve.

71. ***They will have*** **a small transient gain in this world.** Then to Us is their return. Then shall We make them taste a severe punishment, **because they would not believe.**

وَأُمِرْتُ أَنْ أَكُونَ مِنَ الْمُسْلِمِينَ ﴿٧٣﴾

73. and I have been commanded to be of those who are resigned *to Him.*'

73. and I have been commanded to be of those who **have submitted.'**

وَجَعَلْنَاهُمْ خَلَائِفَ وَأَغْرَقْنَا الَّذِينَ كَذَّبُوا بِآيَاتِنَا

74. And We made them inheritors *of Our favours*, while We drowned those who rejected Our Signs.

74. And We made them inheritors ***of the land,*** while We drowned those who rejected Our Signs.

فَمَا آمَنَ لِمُوسَىٰ إِلَّا ذُرِّيَّةٌ مِنْ قَوْمِهِ عَلَىٰ خَوْفٍ
مِنْ فِرْعَوْنَ وَمَلَئِهِمْ أَنْ يَفْتِنَهُمْ وَإِنَّ فِرْعَوْنَ
لَعَالٍ فِي الْأَرْضِ وَإِنَّهُ لَمِنَ الْمُسْرِفِينَ ﴿٨٤﴾

84. And none obeyed Moses save some youths from among his people, because of the fear of Pharaoh and their chiefs, lest he should persecute them. And of a truth, Pharaoh was a tyrant in the land and surely he was of the transgressors.

84. And none obeyed Moses **except a generation** from among his people, because of the fear of Pharaoh and their chiefs, lest he should persecute them. And verily, Pharaoh was a tyrant in the land, and **certainly** he was of the transgressors.

وَأَوْحَيْنَا إِلَىٰ مُوسَىٰ وَأَخِيهِ أَنْ تَبَوَّآ لِقَوْمِكُمَا

88. And We spoke to Moses and his brother, *saying*, 'Take, ye twain, *some* houses for your people in *the* town, and

make your houses so as to face one another, and observe Prayer. And give glad tidings to the believers.'

بِمِصْرَ بُيُوْتًا وَّ اجْعَلُوْا بُيُوْتَكُمْ قِبْلَةً وَّ اَقِيْمُوا الصَّلٰوةَ ؕ وَ بَشِّرِ الْمُؤْمِنِيْنَ ﴿۸۸﴾

88. And We spoke to Moses and his brother, **saying, 'Build houses for your people in the city and make your houses facing in the same direction,** and observe Prayer. And give glad tidings to the believers.

Note: The Arabic words *waj'aloo boyootakum qiblatan* واجعلوا بيوتكم قبلة in this verse may mean: facing the Qiblah i.e., the point or place to which the worship is oriented or facing each other or facing in the same direction.

As for the first meaning it is difficult to adopt this because there was no definite Qiblah prescribed for the Children of Israel before the building of the Temple of Solomon.

If the second meaning is preferred then the scenario will be that of houses built facing each other for the purpose of security.

We prefer the third option, meaning: build your houses facing the same direction. This has the advantage of enabling all the dwellers of the houses to worship in the same direction which creates a sense of unity and discipline among them.

Immediately after this instruction the believers are admonished to observe prayer which further strengthens our view. Because the Arabic word *Aqeemu as-Salata* اقيموا الصلوة does not merely enjoin performance of individual prayer but emphasises the performance of prayer in congregation.

89. And Moses said, 'Our Lord, Thou hast bestowed upon Pharaoh and his chiefs embellishment and wealth in the present life, with the result, our Lord, that they are leading *men* astray from Thy path. Our Lord! destroy their riches and attack their hearts—and they are not going to believe until they see the grievous punishment.'

وَ قَالَ مُوْسٰى رَبَّنَاۤ اِنَّكَ اٰتَيْتَ فِرْعَوْنَ وَ مَلَاَهٗ زِيْنَةً وَّ اَمْوَالًا فِي الْحَيٰوةِ الدُّنْيَا ۙ رَبَّنَا لِيُضِلُّوْا عَنْ سَبِيْلِكَ ۚ رَبَّنَا اطْمِسْ عَلٰۤى اَمْوَالِهِمْ وَ اشْدُدْ عَلٰى قُلُوْبِهِمْ فَلَا يُؤْمِنُوْا حَتّٰى يَرَوُا الْعَذَابَ الْاَلِيْمَ ﴿۸۹﴾

89. **And Moses said, 'Our Lord, you have bestowed upon Pharaoh and his chiefs ornaments and wealth in this life. Our Lord, it results only in their**

leading *people* astray from your path. Our Lord, obliterate their riches and be severe on their hearts, because *it seems* they would not believe until they see a grievous punishment'.

91. And We brought the children of Israel across the sea; and Pharaoh and his hosts pursued them wrongfully and aggressively,

وَجٰوَزْنَا بِبَنِيٓ اِسْرَآءِيْلَ الْبَحْرَ فَاَتْبَعَهُمْ فِرْعَوْنُ وَجُنُوْدُهٗ بَغْيًا وَّعَدْوًا

91. And We brought the children of Israel across the sea; and Pharaoh and his hosts pursued them **with evil intent and enmity.**

92. What! Now! while thou wast disobedient before *this* and wast of those who create disorder.

آٰلْئٰنَ وَ قَدْ عَصَيْتَ قَبْلُ وَكُنْتَ مِنَ الْمُفْسِدِيْنَ ﴿۹۲﴾

92. What! Now! **While you have been disobedient before and were of those who do mischief.**

HUD

2. Alif Lām Rā*. *This is* a Book whose verses have been made unchangeable *and* then they have been expounded in detail. *It is* from One Wise, *and* All-Aware.

الٓرٰ كِتٰبٌ اُحْكِمَتْ اٰيٰتُهٗ ثُمَّ فُصِّلَتْ مِنْ لَّدُنْ حَكِيْمٍ خَبِيْرٍ ﴿۲﴾

2. ALIF LĀM RĀ. This is a book whose verses **are fortified and made flawless and then** they have been expounded in detail. It *is* from One Wise, *and* All-Aware.

4.
And if you turn away, then surely, I fear for you the punishment of a dreadful day.

وَاِنْ تَوَلَّوْا فَاِنِّيْٓ اَخَافُ عَلَيْكُمْ عَذَابَ يَوْمٍ كَبِيْرٍ ﴿۴﴾

4. And if you turn away, then surely, I fear for you the punishment of a **colossal day.**

7. And He knows its lodging and its home. All *this* is *recorded* in a clear Book.

وَيَعْلَمُ مُسْتَقَرَّهَا وَمُسْتَوْدَعَهَا ۚ كُلٌّ فِي كِتَابٍ مُّبِينٍ ﴿٧﴾

7. And He knows its **place of temporary settlement and permanent abode.** All *this is recorded* in a clear Book.

18. Can he, then, who possesses a clear proof from his Lord, and *to testify to whose truth* a witness from Him shall follow him, and who was preceded by the Book of Moses, a guide and a mercy, *be an impostor?* Those *who consider these matters* believe therein, and whoever of the *opposing* parties disbelieves in it, Fire shall be his promised place. So be not thou in doubt about it. Surely, it is the truth from thy Lord; but most men do not believe.

أَفَمَن كَانَ عَلَىٰ بَيِّنَةٍ مِّن رَّبِّهِ وَيَتْلُوهُ شَاهِدٌ مِّنْهُ وَمِن قَبْلِهِ كِتَابُ مُوسَىٰ إِمَامًا وَرَحْمَةً ۚ أُولَٰئِكَ يُؤْمِنُونَ بِهِ ۚ وَمَن يَكْفُرْ بِهِ مِنَ الْأَحْزَابِ فَالنَّارُ مَوْعِدُهُ ۚ فَلَا تَكُ فِي مِرْيَةٍ مِّنْهُ ۚ إِنَّهُ الْحَقُّ مِن رَّبِّكَ وَلَٰكِنَّ أَكْثَرَ النَّاسِ لَا يُؤْمِنُونَ ﴿١٨﴾

18. **Can he, then, *be an impostor,* who *possesses* a clear proof from his Lord, and *to testify to whose truth* a witness from Him shall follow him, and who was preceded by the Book of Moses, a guide and a mercy? They believe in him; and whoever from among the different sects rejects him, Fire shall be his promised abode. So be not in doubt about it. Surely, it is the truth from your Lord; but most people do not believe.**

Note: It is very important to determine to whom the pronoun 'they' refers. The only two persons mentioned in this verse are the Holy Prophet (may peace and blessings of Allah be upon him) and the Divine witness who is to follow him. As far as Moses is concerned, it is not he but his Book to which reference is made because Books do not believe. It leaves us with the only option that a body of people is implied in the verse. The pronoun refers not only to the Prophet himself but also to his subordinate witness and some others.

The above verse should be understood in the same context that not only the Prophet and his witness believe in the truth of the Prophet and testify to it, but also the large number of their followers do the same.

It should be remembered that sometimes great Prophets are mentioned in the singular as one person but they have the potential to multiply and spread out. They are referred to as 'Ummah' (أُمَّة), a large body of people in themselves. For reference see chapter 16 verse 121.

Some have understood the pronoun 'they' (أُولَٰئِكَ) to refer to Moses and his people.

وَلَا يَنفَعُكُمْ نُصْحِىٓ إِنْ أَرَدتُّ أَنْ أَنصَحَ لَكُمْ إِن كَانَ ٱللَّهُ يُرِيدُ أَن يُغْوِيَكُمْ ۚ هُوَ رَبُّكُمْ وَإِلَيْهِ تُرْجَعُونَ ٣٥

35. 'And my advice will profit you not if I desire to advise you, if Allah intends to destroy you. He is your Lord and to Him shall you be made to return.'

35. 'And my **admonishment** will profit you not **however much** I desire to **admonish** you, if Allah intends to destroy you. He is your Lord and to Him shall you be made to return'.

وَأَخَذَ ٱلَّذِينَ ظَلَمُوا ٱلصَّيْحَةُ فَأَصْبَحُوا فِى دِيَٰرِهِمْ جَٰثِمِينَ ٦٨

68. And punishment overtook those who had done wrong, and they lay prostrate in their houses,

68. and **a thunderous blast** overtook those who had done wrong, **and as the morning broke they lay prostrate in their homes.**

فَلَمَّا رَءَآ أَيْدِيَهُمْ لَا تَصِلُ إِلَيْهِ نَكِرَهُمْ وَأَوْجَسَ مِنْهُمْ خِيفَةً ۚ قَالُوا لَا تَخَفْ إِنَّآ أُرْسِلْنَآ إِلَىٰ قَوْمِ لُوطٍ ٧١

71. But when he saw their hands not reaching thereto, he knew not what they were, and conceived a fear of them. They said, 'Fear not, for we have been sent to the people of Lot.'

71. But when he saw their hands not reaching thereto, **he took them as** ***unfriendly*** **strangers,** and conceived a fear of them. They said, 'Fear not, for we have been sent to the people of Lot'.

72. And his wife was standing *by*, and she *too* was frightened, whereupon We gave her glad tidings of the birth of Isaac and, after Isaac, of Jacob.

وَامْرَاَتُهٗ قَآئِمَةٌ فَضَحِكَتْ فَبَشَّرْنٰهَا بِاِسْحٰقَ ۙ وَ
مِنْ وَّرَآءِ اِسْحٰقَ يَعْقُوْبَ ﴿۷۲﴾

72. And his wife was standing *by*, **she chuckled,** whereupon We gave her glad tidings of the birth of Isaac and, after Isaac, of Jacob.

79.
He said, 'O my people, these are my daughters; they are purer for you. So fear Allah and disgrace me not in the presence of my guests. Is there not among you any right-minded man?'

قَالَ يٰقَوْمِ هٰٓؤُلَآءِ بَنَاتِيْ هُنَّ
اَطْهَرُ لَكُمْ فَاتَّقُوا اللّٰهَ وَ لَا تُخْزُوْنِ فِيْ ضَيْفِيْ ؕ اَلَيْسَ
مِنْكُمْ رَجُلٌ رَّشِيْدٌ ﴿۷۹﴾

79. He said, 'O my people, these are my daughters. **They are most chaste for you.** So fear Allah and **do not disgrace me concerning my guests.** Is there not among you any right-minded man?'

Note: It was a most apt and disarming retort to a people who were not interested in the charms of the opposite sex. Virtually women were chaste for them. It is to this that the expression 'most chaste' refers. However the wicked gave this reply a perverted twist and posed as if Lot had offered them his own daughters so that the honour of his guests could be protected at their cost. As if he were inviting them to abuse their innocence. Evidently this reply was a reflective of their perverted nature.

82. *The messengers* said, 'O Lot, we are the messengers of thy Lord. They shall by no means reach thee. So depart with thy family in a part of the night, and let none of you look back, but thy wife. Surely, what is going to befall them shall *also* befall her. Verily, their appointed time is the morning. Is not the morning nigh?'

قَالُوْا يٰلُوْطُ اِنَّا رُسُلُ رَبِّكَ لَنْ يَّصِلُوْٓا اِلَيْكَ فَاَسْرِ
بِاَهْلِكَ بِقِطْعٍ مِّنَ الَّيْلِ وَ لَا يَلْتَفِتْ مِنْكُمْ اَحَدٌ
اِلَّا امْرَاَتَكَ ؕ اِنَّهٗ مُصِيْبُهَا مَآ اَصَابَهُمْ ؕ اِنَّ مَوْعِدَهُمُ
الصُّبْحُ ؕ اَلَيْسَ الصُّبْحُ بِقَرِيْبٍ ﴿۸۲﴾

Note: This advice of the visiting messengers indicates that the dialogue between Lot and his people took place in camera and that so far they had no direct access to him or to anyone else in the house. Having failed in their attempt they might have intended to revisit Lot better prepared for forcing their entry into the house. This was denied then by the advice of the messengers to depart from the home with all his family members except his wife during the later part of the night.

وَيٰقَوْمِ اَوْفُوا الْمِكْيَالَ وَالْمِيْزَانَ بِالْقِسْطِ وَلَا
تَبْخَسُوا النَّاسَ اَشْيَآءَهُمْ وَلَا تَعْثَوْا فِى الْاَرْضِ
مُفْسِدِيْنَ ﴿٨٦﴾

86. 'And O my people, give full measure and full weight with equity, and defraud not people of their things and commit not iniquity in the earth, causing disorder.

86. 'And O my people, give full measure and full weight with equity, and **do not deprive people of things which *by right* belong to them** and commit not iniquity in the earth, causing disorder.

وَمَآ اَنْتَ عَلَيْنَا بِعَزِيْزٍ ﴿٩٢﴾

92. And thou holdest no strong position among us.'

92. **As for you, you hold no power over us'.**

يَقْدُمُ قَوْمَهٗ يَوْمَ الْقِيٰمَةِ فَاَوْرَدَهُمُ النَّارَ وَبِئْسَ
الْوِرْدُ الْمَوْرُوْدُ ﴿٩٩﴾

99. He will go before his people on the Day of Resurrection and will bring them down into the Fire, *even as cattle are brought to a watering-place*. And evil is the watering-place arrived at.

99. **He will walk in front of his people on the Day of Resurrection and will lead them on to the *pit of* Fire *even as cattle are brought to a watering-place.* Evil is the watering place and those who are led to it.**

وَاُتْبِعُوْا فِىْ هٰذِهٖ لَعْنَةً وَّيَوْمَ الْقِيٰمَةِ بِئْسَ الرِّفْدُ
الْمَرْفُوْدُ ﴿١٠٠﴾

100. And a curse was made to follow them in this *life* and on the Day of Resurrection. Evil is the gift which shall be given *them.*

100. They are chased by a curse in this *life* and on the Day of Resurrection. Evil is the gift and those given such a gift.

115. And observe Prayer at the two ends of the day, and in the hours of the **night** *that are nearer the day*. Surely, good **works drive away evil works. This is a reminder for those who would remember.**

وَاَقِمِ الصَّلٰوةَ طَرَفَيِ النَّهَارِ وَزُلَفًا مِّنَ الَّيْلِ ؕ اِنَّ الْحَسَنٰتِ يُذْهِبْنَ السَّيِّاٰتِ ؕ ذٰلِكَ ذِكْرٰى لِلذّٰكِرِيْنَ ۚ﴿۱۱۵﴾

115. And observe prayer at the two ends of the day, **and parts of the night close to the day. Surely virtues drive away evils.** This is a reminder for those who would remember.

YUSUF

3. We have revealed it—the Qur'ān in Arabic—that you may understand.

اِنَّاۤ اَنْزَلْنٰهُ قُرْءٰنًا عَرَبِيًّا لَّعَلَّكُمْ تَعْقِلُوْنَ ﴿۳﴾

3. We have revealed it — the Qur'an ***an oft recited Book*** — in Arabic ***a clear eloquent language*** — that you may understand.

4. We narrate unto thee the most beautiful narration by revealing to thee this Qur'ān, though thou wast, before this, of those not possessed of *requisite* knowledge.

نَحْنُ نَقُصُّ عَلَيْكَ اَحْسَنَ الْقَصَصِ بِمَاۤ اَوْحَيْنَاۤ اِلَيْكَ هٰذَا الْقُرْاٰنَ ۖۗ وَاِنْ كُنْتَ مِنْ قَبْلِهٖ لَمِنَ الْغٰفِلِيْنَ ﴿۴﴾

4. We narrate unto you the most beautiful narration by revealing to you this Qur'an, **while before this, you were of those who were unaware.**

7. 'And thus *shall it bè as thou hast seen*, thy Lord will choose thee and teach thee the interpretation of things and perfect His favour upon thee and upon the family of Jacob as He perfected it upon two of thy forefathers—Abraham and Isaac. Verily, thy Lord is All-Knowing, Wise.'

وَكَذٰلِكَ يَجْتَبِيْكَ رَبُّكَ وَيُعَلِّمُكَ مِنْ تَاْوِيْلِ الْاَحَادِيْثِ وَيُتِمُّ نِعْمَتَهٗ عَلَيْكَ وَعَلٰۤى اٰلِ يَعْقُوْبَ كَمَاۤ اَتَمَّهَا عَلٰۤى اَبَوَيْكَ مِنْ قَبْلُ اِبْرٰهِيْمَ وَاِسْحٰقَ ؕ اِنَّ رَبَّكَ عَلِيْمٌ حَكِيْمٌ ﴿۷﴾

7. 'And thus *shall it be as* **you have** *seen,* **your** Lord will choose **you** and teach **you the interpretation of**

narrated matters and perfect His favour upon **you** and upon the family of Jacob as He perfected it upon two of **your** forefathers — Abraham and Isaac. Verily, **your** Lord is All-Knowing, Wise.

16. So, when they took him away, and agreed to put him into the bottom of a deep well, *they had their malicious design carried out;* and We sent a revelation to him, *saying,* 'Thou shalt surely *one day* tell them of this affair of theirs and they shall not know.'

فَلَمَّا ذَهَبُوا بِهٖ وَ اَجْمَعُوْٓا اَنْ يَّجْعَلُوْهُ فِيْ غَيٰبَتِ الْجُبِّ وَاَوْحَيْنَآ اِلَيْهِ لَتُنَبِّئَنَّهُمْ بِاَمْرِهِمْ هٰذَا وَهُمْ لَا يَشْعُرُوْنَ ﴿۱۶﴾

16. So, when they took him away, and agreed to put him into the bottom of a deep well, We sent a revelation to him, saying 'Thou shalt surely *one day* tell them of this affair of theirs while **they will be unaware *of your identity*'.**

19. He said, 'Nay, but your souls have made a *great* thing appear light in your eyes. So *now* comely patience *is good for me.*

قَالَ بَلْ سَوَّلَتْ لَكُمْ اَنْفُسُكُمْ اَمْرًا فَصَبْرٌ جَمِيْلٌ

19. He said, 'Nay, **but your minds have made this *sinful* deed appear attractive to you.** So *now* dignified patience *is good for me.*

21. And they sold him for a paltry price, a few dirhems, and they were not desirous of it.

وَ شَرَوْهُ بِثَمَنٍۭ بَخْسٍ دَرَاهِمَ مَعْدُوْدَةٍ وَكَانُوْا فِيْهِ مِنَ الزَّاهِدِيْنَ ﴿۲۱﴾

21. And they sold him for a paltry price, a few dirhams, **and they were not keen to profit from him.**

22. We might *also* teach him the interpretation of things.

لِنُعَلِّمَهٗ مِنْ تَاْوِيْلِ الْاَحَادِيْثِ

22. We might *also* teach him the **interpretation of narrated matters.**

23. And when he attained his *age of* full strength, We granted him judgment and knowledge.

وَلَمَّا بَلَغَ اَشُدَّهٗۤ اٰتَيْنٰهُ حُكْمًا وَّعِلْمًا ؕ

23. And when he **reached the age of maturity,** We granted him judgement and knowledge.

25. And she made up her mind with regard to him, and he made up his mind with regard to her. If he had not seen a manifest Sign of his Lord, *he could not have shown such determination.*

وَلَقَدْ هَمَّتْ بِهٖ ۚ وَهَمَّ بِهَا لَوْلَاۤ اَنْ رَّاٰ بُرْهَانَ رَبِّهٖ ؕ

25. **And she fell for him and he *too* would have fallen for her, had he not seen the sign of his Lord.**

32. And when she heard of their *crafty* design, she sent for them and prepared for them a repast, and gave every one of them a knife and *then* said *to Joseph*, 'Come forth to them.' And when they saw him they thought much of him and cut their hands, and said, 'Allah be glorified! This is not a human being; this is but a noble angel.'

فَلَمَّا سَمِعَتْ بِمَكْرِهِنَّ اَرْسَلَتْ اِلَيْهِنَّ وَاَعْتَدَتْ
لَهُنَّ مُتَّكَاً وَّاٰتَتْ كُلَّ وَاحِدَةٍ مِّنْهُنَّ سِكِّيْنًا وَّ
قَالَتِ اخْرُجْ عَلَيْهِنَّ ۚ فَلَمَّا رَاَيْنَهٗۤ اَكْبَرْنَهٗ وَقَطَّعْنَ
اَيْدِيَهُنَّ وَقُلْنَ حَاشَ لِلّٰهِ مَا هٰذَا بَشَرًا ؕ اِنْ هٰذَاۤ
اِلَّا مَلَكٌ كَرِيْمٌ ﴿۳۲﴾

Note: The words *Qatt'ana aidiyahunna* قطعن ایدیهن (cut their hands) can be understood to apply literally or metaphorically as Hadhrat Imam Raghib has mentioned both usages with reference to the use of this word in the Holy Qur'an.

Here the literal meaning of قطعن ایدیهن would be to sever one's hand with some sharp instrument. This obviously is not meant by the Holy Qur'an and is inconceivable in this context. As an alternative, some scholars have attempted to attribute a minimised action of cutting, indicating just a few minor cuts, but the Arabic usage does not approve of it because the force and the intensity of the root meaning (in the measure of قطّع) does not permit this mild connotation. The only choice therefore is between the literal and metaphorical meaning and we believe that this expression in the given context can only be rightly understood metaphorically meaning that they accepted defeat by considering him inaccessible and beyond the reach of their hands.

41. 'You worship nothing beside Allah, but *mere* names that you have named, you and your fathers; Allah has sent down no authority for that. The decision rests with Allah alone. He has commanded that you shall not worship anything save Him. That is the right religion, but most men know *it* not.

مَا تَعْبُدُونَ مِنْ دُونِهِ إِلَّا أَسْمَاءً سَمَّيْتُمُوهَا
أَنْتُمْ وَآبَاؤُكُمْ مَا أَنْزَلَ اللَّهُ بِهَا مِنْ سُلْطَانٍ إِنِ
الْحُكْمُ إِلَّا لِلَّهِ أَمَرَ أَلَّا تَعْبُدُوا إِلَّا إِيَّاهُ ذَٰلِكَ
الدِّينُ الْقَيِّمُ وَلَٰكِنَّ أَكْثَرَ النَّاسِ لَا يَعْلَمُونَ ﴿٤١﴾

Note: The word *Qayyim* (قيّم) according to the usage of the Holy Qur'an has a connotation of being strong, powerful, right and possessing staying and power. It also signifies the ability to straighten and correct. Hence the fundamental, unchangeable constituents of faith common to all religions are referred to in the Holy Qur'an as *Deenul-Qayyimah* دين القيّمة . see 98:6 (Al-Bayyinah).

44. And the King said, 'I see *in a dream* seven fat kine which seven lean ones eat up, and seven green ears of corn and *seven* others withered.

وَقَالَ الْمَلِكُ إِنِّي أَرَىٰ سَبْعَ بَقَرَاتٍ سِمَانٍ يَأْكُلُهُنَّ
سَبْعٌ عِجَافٌ وَسَبْعَ سُنْبُلَاتٍ خُضْرٍ وَأُخَرَ يَابِسَاتٍ

44. The king said, 'I see *in a dream* seven fat cows whom seven lean cows are eating, and seven green ears of corn and *seven* others dried up.

50. 'Then there shall come after that a year in which people shall be relieved and in which they shall give presents *to each other*.'

ثُمَّ يَأْتِي مِنْ بَعْدِ ذَٰلِكَ عَامٌ فِيهِ يُغَاثُ النَّاسُ
وَفِيهِ يَعْصِرُونَ ﴿٥٠﴾

50. 'Then a year will follow when people will be granted abundant rain and therein they will *have plenty of fruits and oil seeds to* press *for juices and oils'*.

51. And the King said, 'Bring him to me.' But when the messenger came to him, he said, 'Go back to thy lord and ask him how fare the women who cut their hands: for, my Lord well knows their crafty design.'

وَقَالَ الْمَلِكُ ائْتُونِي بِهِ فَلَمَّا جَاءَهُ الرَّسُولُ قَالَ
ارْجِعْ إِلَىٰ رَبِّكَ فَاسْأَلْهُ مَا بَالُ النِّسْوَةِ اللَّاتِي قَطَّعْنَ
أَيْدِيَهُنَّ إِنَّ رَبِّي بِكَيْدِهِنَّ عَلِيمٌ ﴿٥١﴾

See Note verse 32.

52. They said, 'He kept away *from sin* for fear of Allah—we have known no evil against him.'

قُلْنَ حَاشَ لِلّٰهِ مَا عَلِمْنَا عَلَيْهِ مِنْ سُوْٓءٍ

52. They said, **'Allah be glorified for creating such a man —** we have known no evil against him.'

53. *Joseph said, 'I asked for that enquiry to be made* so that he (the 'Azīz) might know that I was not unfaithful to him in *his* absence and that Allah suffers not the device of the unfaithful to succeed.

ذٰلِكَ لِيَعْلَمَ اَنِّيْ لَمْ اَخُنْهُ بِالْغَيْبِ وَاَنَّ اللّٰهَ لَا يَهْدِيْ كَيْدَ الْخَآئِنِيْنَ ﴿۵۳﴾

53. *Joseph said, 'I asked for that enquiry to be made* so that he (the 'Aziz) might **learn that I did not betray his trust in his absence and *also that it should become known* that Allah does not permit the guile of dishonest people to succeed.**

54. 'And I do not hold my own self to be free from weakness; for, the soul is surely prone to enjoin evil, save that whereon my Lord has mercy. Surely, my Lord is Most Forgiving, Merciful.'

وَمَآ اُبَرِّئُ نَفْسِيْ اِنَّ النَّفْسَ لَاَمَّارَةٌ بِالسُّوْٓءِ اِلَّا مَا رَحِمَ رَبِّيْ اِنَّ رَبِّيْ غَفُوْرٌ رَّحِيْمٌ ﴿۵۴﴾

54. 'And I do not **absolve myself of** weakness; for, the soul is surely prone to enjoin evil, save that whereon my Lord has mercy. Surely, my Lord is Most Forgiving, Merciful.'

59. And Joseph's brethren came and entered in unto him; and he knew them, but they knew him not.

وَجَآءَ اِخْوَةُ يُوْسُفَ فَدَخَلُوْا عَلَيْهِ فَعَرَفَهُمْ وَهُمْ لَهٗ مُنْكِرُوْنَ ﴿۵۹﴾

59. And Joseph's brethren came and appeared before him, **and he recognised them but they took him as stranger.**

60. And when he had provided them with their provision, he said, 'Bring me your brother on your father's side. Do you not see that I give you full measure *of corn*

وَلَمَّا جَهَّزَهُمْ بِجَهَازِهِمْ قَالَ ائْتُوْنِيْ بِاَخٍ لَّكُمْ مِّنْ اَبِيْكُمْ اَلَا تَرَوْنَ اَنِّيْٓ اُوْفِي الْكَيْلَ وَاَنَا خَيْرُ

and that I am the best of hosts?

الْمُنْزِلِينَ ﴿٦٠﴾

60. And when he had provided them with their provision, he said, 'Bring me your brother on your father's side. Do you not see that I give you full measure and that I am the best of hosts?

69. And when they entered in the manner their father had commanded them, it could not avail them anything against Allah, except that there was a desire in Jacob's mind which he *thus* satisfied; and he was surely possessed of *great* knowledge because We **had taught** him, but most men know not.

وَلَمَّا دَخَلُوا مِنْ حَيْثُ أَمَرَهُمْ أَبُوهُمْ مَا كَانَ يُغْنِي
عَنْهُمْ مِنَ اللَّهِ مِنْ شَيْءٍ إِلَّا حَاجَةً فِي نَفْسِ يَعْقُوبَ
قَضَاهَا وَإِنَّهُ لَذُو عِلْمٍ لِمَا عَلَّمْنَاهُ وَلَٰكِنَّ أَكْثَرَ
النَّاسِ لَا يَعْلَمُونَ ﴿٦٩﴾

69. And when they entered in the manner their father had commanded them, it could not avail them anything against Allah, except that **Jacob had an intuitive urge within him which he so fulfilled;** and he was surely possessed of *great* knowledge because We had taught him, but most men know not.

81. And when they despaired of him, they retired, conferring together in private. Their leader said, "Know ye not that your father has taken from you a solemn promise in the name of Allah and how, before this, you failed in your duty with respect to Joseph? I will, therefore, not leave the land until my father permits me or Allah decides for me. And He is the Best of judges.

فَلَمَّا اسْتَيْأَسُوا مِنْهُ خَلَصُوا نَجِيًّا قَالَ كَبِيرُهُمْ أَلَمْ
تَعْلَمُوا أَنَّ أَبَاكُمْ قَدْ أَخَذَ عَلَيْكُمْ مَوْثِقًا مِنَ اللَّهِ
وَمِنْ قَبْلُ مَا فَرَّطْتُمْ فِي يُوسُفَ فَلَنْ أَبْرَحَ الْأَرْضَ
حَتَّىٰ يَأْذَنَ لِي أَبِي أَوْ يَحْكُمَ اللَّهُ لِي وَهُوَ خَيْرُ الْحَاكِمِينَ ﴿٨١﴾

81. And when they despaired of him, they retired, conferring together in private. Their **elder *brother*** said, 'Know you not that your father **had** taken from you a solemn promise in the name of Allah and **remember the injustice you did to Joseph.** I will, therefore, not leave

the land until my father permits me or Allah decides for me. And He is the Best of judges.

84. He replied, 'Nay, but your souls have embellished to you this thing. So *now* comely patience *is good for me.*

قَالَ بَلْ سَوَّلَتْ لَكُمْ أَنْفُسُكُمْ أَمْرًا ۖ
فَصَبْرٌ جَمِيلٌ ۖ

84. He replied, 'Nay, but your **minds have deceived you in presenting it to you as something good.** So ***I turn to*** **dignified patience.**

85. And he turned away from them and said, 'O my grief for Joseph!' And his eyes became white because of grief, and he was suppressing *his sorrow.*

وَتَوَلَّىٰ عَنْهُمْ وَقَالَ يَا أَسَفَىٰ عَلَىٰ يُوسُفَ وَابْيَضَّتْ
عَيْنَاهُ مِنَ الْحُزْنِ فَهُوَ كَظِيمٌ ﴿٨٥﴾

85. And he turned away from them and said, 'O my grief for Joseph!' And his eyes **were filled with tears** because of grief, and he was suppressing *his sorrow.*

86. They said, 'By Allah, thou wilt not cease talking of Joseph until thou art wasted away or thou art of those who perish.'

قَالُوا تَاللَّهِ تَفْتَأُ تَذْكُرُ يُوسُفَ حَتَّىٰ تَكُونَ حَرَضًا
أَوْ تَكُونَ مِنَ الْهَالِكِينَ ﴿٨٦﴾

86. They said, 'By Allah, **you will not cease talking of Joseph until you fall ill or even die.**

91. They replied, 'Art thou Joseph?' He said, '*Yes*, I am Joseph and this is my brother. Allah has indeed been gracious to us. Verily, whoso is righteous and is steadfast—Allah will never suffer the reward of the good to be lost.'

قَالُوا أَإِنَّكَ لَأَنْتَ يُوسُفُ ۖ قَالَ أَنَا يُوسُفُ وَهَٰذَا
أَخِي ۖ قَدْ مَنَّ اللَّهُ عَلَيْنَا ۖ إِنَّهُ مَنْ يَتَّقِ وَيَصْبِرْ
فَإِنَّ اللَّهَ لَا يُضِيعُ أَجْرَ الْمُحْسِنِينَ ﴿٩١﴾

91. They replied, **'Is it really you who is Joseph?'** He said, 'Yes, I am Joseph and this is my brother. Allah has indeed been gracious to us ***both.*** Verily

whoever is righteous and is steadfast — Allah **does not permit the reward of those who do good deeds to be lost.**

102. 'O my Lord, Thou hast bestowed power upon me and taught me the interpretation of dreams. O Maker of the heavens and the earth,

رَبِّ قَدْ اٰتَيْتَنِيْ مِنَ الْمُلْكِ وَعَلَّمْتَنِيْ مِنْ تَاْوِيْلِ
الْاَحَادِيْثِ فَاطِرَ السَّمٰوٰتِ وَالْاَرْضِ

102. 'O my Lord **you have blessed me with a share of sovereignty** and taught me the interpretation of **things.** O Maker of the heavens and the earth,

105. And thou dost not ask of them any reward for it. *On the contrary,* it is but *a source of* honour for all mankind.

وَمَا تَسْـَٔلُهُمْ عَلَيْهِ مِنْ اَجْرٍ اِنْ هُوَ اِلَّا ذِكْرٌ لِّلْعٰلَمِيْنَ ﴿١٠٥﴾

105. **And you do not ask of them any reward for it. It is only an admonishment** for all mankind.

109. Say, 'This is my way: I call unto Allah on sure knowledge, I and those who follow me.

قُلْ هٰذِهٖ سَبِيْلِيْٓ اَدْعُوْٓا اِلَى اللّٰهِ عَلٰى بَصِيْرَةٍ اَنَا وَمَنِ
اتَّبَعَنِيْ

109. Say, 'This is my way: I call unto Allah. **I occupy a position of manifest knowledge, so also those** who follow me.

111. Till, when the Messengers despaired *of the disbelievers* and they (the disbelievers) thought that they had been told a lie, Our help came to them, then was saved he whom We pleased.

حَتّٰٓى اِذَا اسْتَيْـَٔسَ الرُّسُلُ وَظَنُّوْٓا اَنَّهُمْ قَدْ كُذِبُوْا
جَآءَهُمْ نَصْرُنَا فَنُجِّيَ مَنْ نَّشَآءُ

111. **Until the time, when the Messengers despaired and perceived themselves to have been *taken* as liars, suddenly there came Our help to them and** then was saved he whom We pleased.

AL-RA'D

4. And He it is Who spread out the earth and made therein mountains and rivers. And fruits of every kind He made therein in two sexes.

وَهُوَ الَّذِيْ مَدَّ الْاَرْضَ وَجَعَلَ فِيْهَا رَوَاسِيَ وَ
اَنْهٰرًا ؕ وَمِنْ كُلِّ الثَّمَرٰتِ جَعَلَ فِيْهَا زَوْجَيْنِ اثْنَيْنِ

4. And He it is Who spread out the earth and made therein mountains and rivers. **And of the fruits He has made them in pairs, male and female.**

5. And in the earth are *diverse* tracts, adjoining one another, and gardens of vines, and corn-fields, and date-palms, growing together from one root and *others* not so growing;

وَفِي الْاَرْضِ قِطَعٌ مُّتَجٰوِرٰتٌ وَّجَنّٰتٌ مِّنْ اَعْنَابٍ وَّ
زَرْعٌ وَّ نَخِيْلٌ صِنْوَانٌ وَّغَيْرُ صِنْوَانٍ

5. And in the earth are *diverse* tracts, adjoining one another, and gardens of vines, and **fields of grain,** and date-palms, growing together from one root and *others* not so growing;

7. And they want thee to hasten on the punishment in preference to good, whereas exemplary punishments have *already* occurred before them.

وَيَسْتَعْجِلُوْنَكَ بِالسَّيِّئَةِ قَبْلَ الْحَسَنَةِ وَقَدْ خَلَتْ
مِنْ قَبْلِهِمُ الْمَثُلٰتُ

7. **And they are eager to demand from you that you may have evil brought upon them rather than good,** whereas exemplary punishments have *already* occurred before them.

15. Unto Him is the true prayer.

لَهٗ دَعْوَةُ الْحَقِّ

15. **To Him alone is addressed true prayer.**

40. Allah effaces what He wills and establishes *what He wills*, and with Him is the source of *all* commandments.

يَمْحُوا اللّٰهُ مَا يَشَآءُ وَ يُثْبِتُ ۚۖ وَعِنْدَهٗۤ اُمُّ الْكِتٰبِ ﴿۴۰﴾

40. Allah effaces what He wills, and establishes *what* He *wills,* **and with Him is the source of *all* decrees.**

IBRAHIM

10. Their Messengers came to them with clear Signs, but they turned their hands to their mouths, and said, 'We disbelieve in that with which you have been sent and surely, we are in disquieting doubt concerning that to which you call us.'

جَآءَتْهُمْ رُسُلُهُمْ بِالْبَيِّنٰتِ فَرَدُّوْٓا اَيْدِيَهُمْ فِيْٓ اَفْوَاهِهِمْ وَقَالُوْٓا اِنَّا كَفَرْنَا بِمَآ اُرْسِلْتُمْ بِهٖ وَاِنَّا لَفِيْ شَكٍّ مِّمَّا تَدْعُوْنَنَآ اِلَيْهِ مُرِيْبٍ ۝١٠

Note: The Qur'anic expression *Faraddoo aidiyahum fi afwahihim* فردوا ايديهم فى افواههم (they turned their hands to their mouths) paints a picture of somebody putting his hand to his mouth indicating blockade. Before explaining this special expression one has also to determine as to who is referred to in this verse. Evidently this act is attributed to non-believers; so it has two possibilities of interpretation. It can be translated as they, the non-believers, thrust their hands into their own mouths. This means that they refused to have any dialogue with the Messengers and their followers. This stage is reached when a person is ultimately nonplussed and is left with no arguments. So he acquires this posture of boycott, indicating that he has nothing more to say.

In the second reading the reference may be to the mouths of the Messengers. It also indicates the same break in dialogue but in a different way. Hence the message would be that the non-believers finally stop Messengers from further preaching telling them to shut their mouths. This alternative is further supported by the remaining part of the verse where the non-believers continue to develop the theme by saying further: 'We have rejected the message with which you were sent and verily we are in manifold doubt regarding that to which you call us.'

15. 'And We will, surely, make you dwell in the land after them. This is for him who fears to stand before My Tribunal and fears My warning.'

وَلَنُسْكِنَنَّكُمُ الْاَرْضَ مِنْۢ بَعْدِهِمْ ۗ ذٰلِكَ لِمَنْ خَافَ مَقَامِيْ وَخَافَ وَعِيْدِ ۝١٥

15. 'And We will, surely, make you dwell in the land after them. **That is for him who stands in awe of My station and takes heed of My warning.**

18. He shall sip it and shall not be able to swallow it easily. And death shall come to him from every quarter, *yet* he shall not die. And besides that there shall be *for him* a severe chastisement.

يَتَجَرَّعُهُ وَلَا يَكَادُ يُسِيغُهُ وَيَأْتِيهِ الْمَوْتُ مِنْ
كُلِّ مَكَانٍ وَمَا هُوَ بِمَيِّتٍ ۖ وَمِنْ وَرَائِهِ عَذَابٌ
غَلِيظٌ ﴿١٨﴾

18. **He will drink it sip by sip, reluctantly, being unable to quaff it.** And death shall come to him from every quarter, *yet* he shall not die. And besides that there shall be *for him* a severe chastisement.

19. They shall have no power over what they earned. That, indeed, is extreme ruin.

لَا يَقْدِرُونَ
مِمَّا كَسَبُوا عَلَىٰ شَيْءٍ ۚ ذَٰلِكَ هُوَ الضَّلَالُ الْبَعِيدُ ﴿١٩﴾

19. They shall have no power over what they earned. That, indeed, is **utter destruction.**

20. Dost thou not see that Allah created the heavens and the earth in accordance with the requirements of wisdom? If He please, He can do away with you, and bring a new creation.

أَلَمْ تَرَ أَنَّ اللَّهَ خَلَقَ السَّمَاوَاتِ وَالْأَرْضَ بِالْحَقِّ ۚ
إِنْ يَشَأْ يُذْهِبْكُمْ وَيَأْتِ بِخَلْقٍ جَدِيدٍ ﴿٢٠﴾

20. **Do you not see that Allah created the heavens and the earth with Truth.** If He so pleases, He can do away with you, and bring a new creation.

34. And He has *also* subjected to you the sun and the moon, both performing their work constantly. And He has subjected to you the night as well as the day.

وَسَخَّرَ لَكُمُ الشَّمْسَ وَالْقَمَرَ دَائِبَيْنِ ۖ وَسَخَّرَ
لَكُمُ اللَّيْلَ وَالنَّهَارَ ﴿٣٤﴾

34. **And He has pressed into your service the sun and the moon moving constantly. Also He has subjected the night and the day to serve you.**

41. 'My Lord, make me observe Prayer, and my children *too*. Our Lord! *bestow Thy grace on me* and accept my prayer.

رَبِّ اجْعَلْنِي مُقِيمَ الصَّلَاةِ وَمِنْ ذُرِّيَّتِي ۚ رَبَّنَا
وَتَقَبَّلْ دُعَاءِ ﴿٤١﴾

41. 'My Lord, make me observe Prayer, and my children *too.* **Our Lord! Do accept my prayer.**

47. And they have already made their designs; but their designs are with Allah. And even though their designs be such as to make the mountains move, *they cannot succeed.*

وَقَدْ مَكَرُوا مَكْرَهُمْ وَعِنْدَ اللّٰهِ مَكْرُهُمْ وَإِنْ
كَانَ مَكْرُهُمْ لِتَزُولَ مِنْهُ الْجِبَالُ ﴿٤٧﴾

47. **And they employed whatever deceit they could but *the outcome of* their deceit lies with Allah, even if their deceit were powerful enough to move mountains.**

53. This is a sufficient admonition for mankind *that they may benefit by it,* and that they may be warned thereby, and that they may know that He is the only One God, and that those possessed of understanding may ponder.

هٰذَا بَلٰغٌ لِلنَّاسِ وَلِيُنْذَرُوا بِهٖ وَلِيَعْلَمُوٓا أَنَّمَا هُوَ
إِلٰهٌ وَاحِدٌ وَلِيَذَّكَّرَ أُولُوا الْأَلْبَابِ ﴿٥٣﴾

53. **This is a message manifestly delivered for the benefit of mankind** that they may be warned thereby, and they may know that He is the only One God, and that those possessed of understanding may ponder.

AL-HIJR

11. And We sent *Messengers* before thee among parties of ancient peoples.

وَلَقَدْ أَرْسَلْنَا مِنْ قَبْلِكَ فِي شِيَعِ الْأَوَّلِينَ ﴿١١﴾

11. And We sent Messengers **before you among various denominations of earlier people.**

17. And We have, indeed, made mansions *of stars* in the heaven and have adorned it for beholders.

وَلَقَدْ جَعَلْنَا فِي السَّمَآءِ بُرُوجًا وَزَيَّنّٰهَا لِلنّٰظِرِينَ ﴿١٧﴾

17. **Verily, in the heavens We have** made **constellations** and adorned **them** for **those who behold.**

27. And, surely, We created man from dry ringing clay, from black mud wrought into shape.

وَلَقَدْ خَلَقْنَا الْإِنْسَانَ مِنْ صَلْصَالٍ مِّنْ حَمَإٍ مَّسْنُونٍ ﴿٢٧﴾

27. And, surely, We created man from dry ringing clay, ***fashioned out*** of **stagnant mud.**

28. And the Jinn We had created before from the fire of hot wind.

وَالْجَآنَّ خَلَقْنٰهُ مِنْ قَبْلُ مِنْ نَّارِ السَّمُوْمِ ﴿٢٨﴾

28. And the Jinn We had created **earlier from the fire of blazing winds.**

48. A d We shall remove whatever of rancour may be in their breasts *so that they will become* as brothers *seated* on thrones, facing one another.

وَنَزَعْنَا مَا فِيْ صُدُوْرِهِمْ مِّنْ غِلٍّ إِخْوَانًا عَلٰى سُرُرٍ مُّتَقٰبِلِيْنَ ﴿٤٨﴾

48. And We shall remove whatever of rancour may be in their breasts *so that they will become* as brothers **reclining on couches,** facing one another.

56. They said, 'We have, indeed, given thee glad tidings in truth; be not therefore of those who despair.'

قَالُوْا بَشَّرْنٰكَ بِالْحَقِّ فَلَا تَكُنْ مِّنَ الْقٰنِطِيْنَ ﴿٥٦﴾

56. They said, **'We have but given you glad tidings based on truth;** be not therefore of those who despair.'

72. He said, 'These are my daughters if you must do something.'

قَالَ هٰٓؤُلَآءِ بَنٰتِيْٓ إِنْ كُنْتُمْ فٰعِلِيْنَ ﴿٧٢﴾

72. He said, **'My daughters are *also standing* here. *Be mindful of this* if you are bent upon doing anything.'**

80. So We chastised them *also*. And they both lie on a manifest way.

فَانْتَقَمْنَا مِنْهُمْ ۘ وَإِنَّهُمَا لَبِإِمَامٍ مُّبِينٍ ﴿٨٠﴾

80. So We chastised them. **And they both lie *buried* by a prominent highway.**

86. And We have not created the heavens and the earth and all that is between the two but in accordance with the requirements of wisdom; and the Hour is sure to come. So turn away *from them* in a comely manner.

وَمَا خَلَقْنَا السَّمٰوٰتِ وَالْأَرْضَ وَمَا بَيْنَهُمَآ إِلَّا بِالْحَقِّ ۗ وَإِنَّ السَّاعَةَ لَاٰتِيَةٌ فَاصْفَحِ الصَّفْحَ الْجَمِيلَ ﴿٨٦﴾

86. And We have not created the heavens and the earth and that **which lies** between the **two but with truth;** and the Hour is sure to come. So turn away *from them,* **a turning away with grace.**

89. Stretch not thy eyes towards what We have bestowed on some classes of them to enjoy for a short time, and grieve not over them; and lower thy wing *of mercy* for the believers.

لَا تَمُدَّنَّ عَيْنَيْكَ إِلٰى مَا مَتَّعْنَا بِهٖٓ أَزْوَاجًا مِّنْهُمْ وَلَا تَحْزَنْ عَلَيْهِمْ وَاخْفِضْ جَنَاحَكَ لِلْمُؤْمِنِينَ ﴿٨٩﴾

89. **Stretch not your eyes *with greed* towards the transient pleasure We have bestowed upon some sections from among them,** and grieve not over them; and lower your wing *of mercy* for the believers.

90. And say, 'I am, indeed, a plain Warner.'

وَقُلْ إِنِّيٓ أَنَا النَّذِيرُ الْمُبِينُ ﴿٩٠﴾

90. And say, **'I am a plain Warner indeed'.**

91. Because We *have decided to* send down *punishment* on those who have formed themselves into groups *against thee;*

كَمَآ أَنْزَلْنَا عَلَى الْمُقْتَسِمِينَ ﴿٩١﴾

91. **Like always 'We shall send down punishment upon those who become split into sects,**

92. Who have pronounced the Qur'ān to be *so many* lies;

الَّذِيْنَ جَعَلُوا الْقُرْاٰنَ عِضِيْنَ ﴿۹۲﴾

92. *And* who would split the Qur'an into segments.

Note: We prefer to translate these verses in the future tense rather than the past because we consider them to possess a grave warning to Muslims. There is no wonder why the past tense is used to indicate future, because most of such prophecies as are inevitably bound to be fulfilled are expressed in the past tense in the Holy Qur'an. The past is unchangeable. Prophecies in the past tense emphasise certainty. Thus the translation should run as follows:

"And We have, indeed given thee the seven oft repeated *verses* and the great Qur'an. Do not stretch your eyes *with greed* towards the transient pleasure we have bestowed upon various groups among them, and grieve not over them; and lower your wing *of mercy* for the believers. And say, I am a plain Warner indeed. Like always, We shall send down punishment upon those who become split into sects, and who would split the Qur'an into segments."

This translation becomes evidently more appropriate when we bring into view the context of these verses and discover that the preceding verses begin with a dramatic introduction of the Holy Qur'an as a great Book. So all those who, despite claiming subservience to the Qur'an, disregard its most central message of unity, and get split into sects and to prove their own interpretation to be right, end up by practically splitting the Qur'an into segments: each group sticking to some verses interpreting them to their own advantage as against others who stick to some other verses interpreting them to their own advantage. This split is described to be so sharp and final that there is left no possibility of compromise between different warring factions. This causes people of the same *ummah* to split into sects and in the same process to divide the Qur'an into segments.

AL-NAHL

3. He sends down the angels with revelation by His command on whomsoever of His servants He pleases *saying*, 'Warn *people* that there is no God but I, so take Me *alone* for your Protector.'

يُنَزِّلُ الْمَلٰٓئِكَةَ بِالرُّوْحِ مِنْ اَمْرِهٖ عَلٰى مَنْ يَّشَآءُ مِنْ عِبَادِهٖٓ اَنْ اَنْذِرُوْٓا اَنَّهٗ لَآ اِلٰهَ اِلَّآ اَنَا فَاتَّقُوْنِ ﴿۳﴾

3. He sends down the angels with revelation by His command on whomsoever of His servants He pleases saying, 'Warn people that there is no God but I; **so fear Me alone.'**

6. And the cattle too He has created; you find in them warmth and *other* uses; and some of them you eat.

وَالْاَنْعَامَ خَلَقَهَا ۚ لَكُمْ فِيْهَا دِفْءٌ وَّمَنَافِعُ وَمِنْهَا تَاْكُلُوْنَ ۝٦

6. And the cattle too He has created; you find in them warmth **and many other benefits;** and some of them you eat.

12. Therewith He grows corn for you, and the olive and the date-palm, and the grapes, and all kinds of fruits. Surely, in that is a Sign for a people who reflect.

يُنْۢبِتُ لَكُمْ بِهِ الزَّرْعَ وَالزَّيْتُوْنَ وَالنَّخِيْلَ وَالْاَعْنَابَ وَمِنْ كُلِّ الثَّمَرٰتِ ۗ اِنَّ فِيْ ذٰلِكَ لَاٰيَةً لِّقَوْمٍ يَّتَفَكَّرُوْنَ ۝١٣

12. Therewith He grows **crops *of all kinds*** for you, and the olive and the date-palm, and the grapes, and all sorts of fruits. Surely, in that is a Sign for a people who reflect.

16. And He has placed in the earth firm mountains lest it quake with you, and rivers and routes that you may take the right way.

وَاَلْقٰى فِي الْاَرْضِ رَوَاسِيَ اَنْ تَمِيْدَ بِكُمْ وَاَنْهٰرًا وَّسُبُلًا لَّعَلَّكُمْ تَهْتَدُوْنَ ۝١٦

16. And He has placed in the earth firm mountains **to sustain you,** and rivers and **paths so** that you **keep to the right path.**

Note: Many scholars have translated the word *an tameeda bikum* ان تميد بكم as 'quake' which if accepted would mean that God is counting His bounties upon mankind by reminding them that We have created mountains to cause great earthquakes spelling destructions far and wide. Unfortunately, it has been ignored that the word *tameeda* تميد is derived from *maada* ماد which means to provide food. The word *maaidah* مائدہ used in the Holy Qur'an is from the same infinitive. With this meaning in view the entire understanding of this verse will be transformed. It will remind mankind that God has created mountains which are essential for providing food to all living beings. The water is constantly lifted from lakes, seas and oceans by evaporation carried by higher altitude to get condensed into thicker particles. The existence of mountains is essential for turning the vapour into water again, thus producing wide-spread rains which are channelled back to earth to create immense food chains. This translation is the only one which fits into the context and is in perfect agreement with the remaining part of the verse. The correct meaning, therefore, would be: 'He has entrenched mountains over the earth so that they may provide you with food, and rivers and tracks so that you may be guided.'

The relation of water and food is obvious. In the history of civilisation it was rivers which played the most important role in making the mountainous terrains possible and paths were carved along the courses of rivers.

44. And We sent not *as Messengers* before thee but men to whom We sent revelation, so ask those who possess the Reminder, if you know not.

وَمَآ أَرْسَلْنَا مِن قَبْلِكَ إِلَّا رِجَالًا نُّوحِىٓ إِلَيْهِمْ فَسْـَٔلُوٓا
أَهْلَ ٱلذِّكْرِ إِن كُنتُمْ لَا تَعْلَمُونَ ﴿٤٤﴾

44. And We sent not *as Messengers* before thee but men to whom We sent revelation **so ask those who are the custodians of divine scriptures,** if you know not.

45. *We sent Our Messengers* with clear Signs and Scriptures. And We have sent down to thee the Reminder that thou mayest explain to mankind that which has been sent down to them, and that they may reflect.

بِٱلْبَيِّنَٰتِ وَٱلزُّبُرِ وَأَنزَلْنَآ إِلَيْكَ ٱلذِّكْرَ لِتُبَيِّنَ
لِلنَّاسِ مَا نُزِّلَ إِلَيْهِمْ وَلَعَلَّهُمْ يَتَفَكَّرُونَ ﴿٤٥﴾

45. **We sent them with clear Signs and Scriptures.** And We have sent down to **you** the reminder that **you may** explain to mankind that which has been sent down to them, and that they may reflect.

53. And to Him belongs whatsoever is in the heavens and the earth and to Him is due obedience for ever. Will you then fear any other than Allah?

وَلَهُۥ مَا فِى ٱلسَّمَٰوَٰتِ وَٱلْأَرْضِ وَلَهُ ٱلدِّينُ وَاصِبًا
أَفَغَيْرَ ٱللَّهِ تَتَّقُونَ ﴿٥٣﴾

53. And to Him belongs whatsoever is in the heavens and the earth **and to Him eternally belongs *the right to determine* the path.** Will you then fear any other than Allah?

61. The state of those who do not believe in the Hereafter is evil, while Allah's attribute is sublime and He is the Mighty, the Wise.

لِلَّذِينَ لَا يُؤْمِنُونَ بِالْآخِرَةِ مَثَلُ السَّوْءِ ۖ وَلِلَّهِ الْمَثَلُ الْأَعْلَىٰ ۚ وَهُوَ الْعَزِيزُ الْحَكِيمُ ﴿٦١﴾

61. **Those who do not believe in the Hereafter to them applies the worst similitude; while to Allah belongs that which is the loftiest and** He is the Mighty, the Wise.

70. 'Then eat of every *kind of* fruit, and follow the ways of thy Lord *that have been* made easy *for thee*.' There comes forth from their bellies a drink of varying hues. Therein is cure for men. Surely, in that is a Sign for a people who reflect.

ثُمَّ كُلِي مِن كُلِّ الثَّمَرَاتِ فَاسْلُكِي سُبُلَ رَبِّكِ ذُلُلًا ۚ يَخْرُجُ مِن بُطُونِهَا شَرَابٌ مُّخْتَلِفٌ أَلْوَانُهُ فِيهِ شِفَاءٌ لِّلنَّاسِ ۗ إِنَّ فِي ذَٰلِكَ لَآيَةً لِّقَوْمٍ يَتَفَكَّرُونَ ﴿٧٠﴾

70. 'then eat of every *kind of* fruit, **and then pursue submissively the paths prescribed by your Lord'.** There comes forth from their bellies a drink of varying hues. Therein is cure for men. Surely, in that is a Sign for a people who reflect.

71. And Allah creates you, then He causes you to die; and there are *some* among you who are driven to the worst part of life, with the result that they know nothing after *having had* knowledge. Surely, Allah is All-Knowing, Powerful.

وَاللَّهُ خَلَقَكُمْ ثُمَّ يَتَوَفَّاكُمْ ۚ وَمِنكُم مَّن يُرَدُّ إِلَىٰ أَرْذَلِ الْعُمُرِ لِكَيْ لَا يَعْلَمَ بَعْدَ عِلْمٍ شَيْئًا ۚ إِنَّ اللَّهَ عَلِيمٌ قَدِيرٌ ﴿٧١﴾

71. And Allah creates you, then He causes you to die; and there are *some* among you **who reach the age of senility *with the result* that they loose all knowledge after having gained it.** Surely Allah is All-Knowing, Powerful.

80. Do they not see the birds held under subjection in the vault of heaven? None keeps them back save Allah. Verily, in that are Signs for a people who believe.

أَلَمْ يَرَوْا إِلَى الطَّيْرِ مُسَخَّرٰتٍ فِي جَوِّ السَّمَآءِ ۖ مَا يُمْسِكُهُنَّ إِلَّا اللّٰهُ ۗ إِنَّ فِي ذٰلِكَ لَاٰيٰتٍ لِّقَوْمٍ يُّؤْمِنُوْنَ ﴿٨٠﴾

80. **Do they not observe the birds held *aloft* in mid-heaven. None keeps them held *aloft* but Allah.** Verily in that are Signs for a people who believe.

84. They recognize the favour of Allah, yet they deny it; and most of them are *confirmed* disbelievers.

يَعْرِفُوْنَ نِعْمَتَ اللّٰهِ ثُمَّ يُنْكِرُوْنَهَا وَاَكْثَرُهُمُ الْكٰفِرُوْنَ ﴿٨٤﴾

84. They **know full well Allah's grace *as they see it*** yet they deny it; and most of them are **ingrate.**

85. And *remember* the day when We shall raise up a witness from every people, then those who disbelieve shall not be permitted *to make amends*, nor shall they be allowed to solicit *God's* favour.

وَيَوْمَ نَبْعَثُ مِنْ كُلِّ اُمَّةٍ شَهِيْدًا ثُمَّ لَا يُؤْذَنُ لِلَّذِيْنَ كَفَرُوْا وَلَا هُمْ يُسْتَعْتَبُوْنَ ﴿٨٥﴾

85. And *remember* the day when We shall raise up a witness from every people, then those who disbelieve shall not be **permitted *to plead* nor shall their plea be accepted.**

91. Verily, Allah enjoins justice, and the doing of good to others; and giving like kindred; and forbids indecency, and manifest evil, and wrongful transgression. He admonishes you that you may take heed.

إِنَّ اللّٰهَ يَأْمُرُ بِالْعَدْلِ وَالْإِحْسَانِ وَإِيْتَآئِ ذِي الْقُرْبٰى وَيَنْهٰى عَنِ الْفَحْشَآءِ وَالْمُنْكَرِ وَالْبَغْيِ ۚ يَعِظُكُمْ لَعَلَّكُمْ تَذَكَّرُوْنَ ﴿٩١﴾

91. Verily, Allah **requires you to abide by justice, and to treat with grace, and give like the giving of kin to kin;** and forbids indecency, **and manifest evil, and transgression.** He admonishes you that you may take heed.

97. That which you have shall pass away, but that which is with Allah is lasting. And We will certainly give those who are steadfast their reward according to the best of their works.

مَا عِندَكُمْ يَنفَدُ وَمَا عِندَ اللَّهِ بَاقٍ وَلَنَجْزِيَنَّ
الَّذِينَ صَبَرُوا أَجْرَهُم بِأَحْسَنِ مَا كَانُوا
يَعْمَلُونَ ﴿٩٧﴾

97. That which you have shall come to naught and whatever is with Allah will last ***forever.*** And We will certainly give those who are steadfast their reward according to the best of their works.

107. Whoso disbelieves in Allah after he has believed—save him who is forced *thereto* while his heart finds peace in the faith—but such as open their breasts to disbelief, on them is Allah's wrath; and they shall have a severe punishment.

مَن كَفَرَ بِاللَّهِ مِن بَعْدِ إِيمَانِهِ إِلَّا مَنْ أُكْرِهَ وَ
قَلْبُهُ مُطْمَئِنٌّ بِالْإِيمَانِ وَلَٰكِن مَّن شَرَحَ بِالْكُفْرِ
صَدْرًا فَعَلَيْهِمْ غَضَبٌ مِّنَ اللَّهِ وَلَهُمْ عَذَابٌ عَظِيمٌ ﴿١٠٧﴾

107. Whoever disbelieves in Allah after having believed except the one who is coerced *beyond the limit of his tolerance* while his heart remains firm in faith. But those whose hearts are content with rejection, upon them will fall the wrath of Allah and for them shall be a great chastisement.

113. And Allah sets forth *for you* the parable of a city which enjoyed security and peace; its provisions came to it in plenty from every quarter; but it denied the favours of Allah, so Allah made it taste hunger and fear *which clothed it like* a garment because of what they used to do.

وَضَرَبَ اللَّهُ مَثَلًا قَرْيَةً كَانَتْ آمِنَةً مُّطْمَئِنَّةً
يَأْتِيهَا رِزْقُهَا رَغَدًا مِّن كُلِّ مَكَانٍ فَكَفَرَتْ
بِأَنْعُمِ اللَّهِ فَأَذَاقَهَا اللَّهُ لِبَاسَ الْجُوعِ وَالْخَوْفِ
بِمَا كَانُوا يَصْنَعُونَ ﴿١١٣﴾

113. **Allah sets forth the parable of a township which enjoyed security and peace; its provisions came to it in plenty from every quarter; but it denied the favours of Allah, So Allah made its dwellers taste a life wrapped**

in hunger and fear as a consequence of what they used to do.

116. He has made unlawful for you only that which dies of itself and blood and the flesh of swine and that on which the name of any other than Allah has been invoked. But he who is driven by necessity, being neither disobedient nor exceeding the limit, then surely, Allah is Most Forgiving, Merciful.

إِنَّمَا حَرَّمَ عَلَيْكُمُ الْمَيْتَةَ وَالدَّمَ وَلَحْمَ الْخِنْزِيرِ وَمَا أُهِلَّ لِغَيْرِ اللَّهِ بِهِ فَمَنِ اضْطُرَّ غَيْرَ بَاغٍ وَلَا عَادٍ فَإِنَّ اللَّهَ غَفُورٌ رَّحِيمٌ ﴿١١٦﴾

116. He has only made unlawful for you to partake of the flesh of such animals as have died a natural death and of blood and the flesh of swine and that on which the name of any other than Allah has been invoked. But who is driven by extreme compulsion without relish or intent to transgress, then surely, Allah is Most Forgiving, Merciful.

118. *It is* a brief enjoyment, and *then* they shall have a grievous punishment.

مَتَاعٌ قَلِيلٌ وَلَهُمْ عَذَابٌ أَلِيمٌ ﴿١١٨﴾

118. *After a* small gain. For them there is a grievous punishment.

121. Abraham was indeed a paragon of virtue, obedient to Allah, ever inclined *to Him*, and he was not of those who set up equals *to God;*

إِنَّ إِبْرَاهِيمَ كَانَ أُمَّةً قَانِتًا لِلَّهِ حَنِيفًا وَلَمْ يَكُ مِنَ الْمُشْرِكِينَ ﴿١٢١﴾

121. Abraham was a nation unto himself, always obedient to Allah, *to Him* ever inclined; certainly not belonging to the idolaters.'

Note: Abraham was a nation unto himself means that he had the seed and the potential of a great nation promised unto him.

شَاكِرًا لِّأَنۡعُمِهِ ۚ اجۡتَبٰهُ وَهَدٰهُ اِلٰى صِرَاطٍ مُّسۡتَقِيۡمٍ ﴿۱۲۲﴾

122. Grateful for His favours; He chose him and guided him to a straight path.

122. **Ever** grateful for His favours; He chose him and guided him to a straight path.

اِنَّمَا جُعِلَ السَّبۡتُ عَلَى الَّذِيۡنَ اخۡتَلَفُوۡا فِيۡهِ ؕ وَ اِنَّ رَبَّكَ لَيَحۡكُمُ بَيۡنَهُمۡ يَوۡمَ الۡقِيٰمَةِ فِيۡمَا كَانُوۡا فِيۡهِ يَخۡتَلِفُوۡنَ ﴿۱۲۵﴾

125. The *punishment for profaning the* Sabbath was imposed only on those who had differed about it, and thy Lord will surely judge between them on the Day of Resurrection about that in which they differed.

125. **The Sabbath was imposed upon those who differed regarding him** ***Abraham and his religion*** **and your** Lord will surely judge between them on the Day of Resurrection about that in which they differed.

Note: The context is clear. Nothing but Abraham and his unshakable devotion and dedication to the Oneness of God is being discussed. Hence the reference has to be to Abraham and the differences the Israelites had among themselves regarding his true faith and conduct. Many among them had fallen prey to different forms of idolatry and it is quite likely that to justify their practices they might have attributed them also to Abraham. The Sabbath in this context appears to be not only a day of rest but also a day of purification and penance.

BANI ISRAEL

سُبۡحٰنَ الَّذِيۡۤ اَسۡرٰى بِعَبۡدِهٖ لَيۡلًا مِّنَ الۡمَسۡجِدِ الۡحَـرَامِ اِلَى الۡمَسۡجِدِ الۡاَقۡصَا الَّذِىۡ بٰرَكۡنَا حَوۡلَهٗ لِنُرِيَهٗ مِنۡ اٰيٰتِنَا ؕ اِنَّهٗ هُوَ السَّمِيۡعُ الۡبَصِيۡرُ ﴿۲﴾

2. Glory be to Him Who carried His servant by night from the Sacred Mosque to the Distant Mosque, the environs of which We have blessed, that We might show him ***some*** **of Our Signs. Surely, He alone is the Hearing, the Seeing.**

2. Glory be to Him **who took His servant along** by night from the Sacred Mosque to the Distant Mosque, the environs of which We have blessed, that We might show him *some* of Our Signs. Surely, He alone is the Hearing, the Seeing.

6. So when the time for the first of the two warnings came, We sent against you *some* servants of Ours possessed of great might in war, and they penetrated the *innermost parts of your* houses, and it was a warning that was bound to be carried out.

فَاِذَا جَآءَ وَعْدُ اُوْلٰىهُمَا بَعَثْنَا عَلَيْكُمْ عِبَادًا لَّنَآ
اُولِيْ بَاْسٍ شَدِيْدٍ فَجَاسُوْا خِلٰلَ الدِّيَارِ وَكَانَ وَعْدًا
مَّفْعُوْلًا ﴿٦﴾

6. So when the time for the first of the two warnings came **to be fulfilled,** We sent against you *some* servants of Ours possessed of great might in war **who penetrated deep into their houses,** and it was a warning that was bound to be carried out.

8. *Now,* if you do well, you will do well for your own souls; and if you do evil, it will *only go* against them. So when the time for the latter warning came, *We raised a people against you* to cover your faces with grief, and to enter the Mosque as they entered it the first time, and to destroy all that they conquered with utter destruction.

اِنْ اَحْسَنْتُمْ اَحْسَنْتُمْ لِاَنْفُسِكُمْ وَاِنْ اَسَاْتُمْ فَلَهَا
فَاِذَا جَآءَ وَعْدُ الْاٰخِرَةِ لِيَسُوْٓءٗا وُجُوْهَكُمْ وَلِيَدْخُلُوا
الْمَسْجِدَ كَمَا دَخَلُوْهُ اَوَّلَ مَرَّةٍ وَّلِيُتَبِّرُوْا مَا عَلَوْا
تَتْبِيْرًا ﴿٨﴾

8. If you conduct yourselves well you will do the advantage of your own souls, and if you misconduct you will do it to their disadvantage. So when the promised hour of the latter days comes they should bring you to disgrace, and enter the mosque the way they entered therein the first time and destroy utterly everything they conquered.

12. And man asks for evil as he should ask for good; and man is hasty.

وَيَدْعُ الْاِنْسَانُ بِالشَّرِّ دُعَآءَهٗ بِالْخَيْرِ وَكَانَ الْاِنْسَانُ
عَجُوْلًا ﴿١٢﴾

12. **And man begs for evil as though he were begging for good;** and man is hasty.

13. And We have made the night and the day two Signs, and the Sign of night We have made dark, and the Sign of day We have made sight-giving, that you may seek bounty from your Lord, and that you may know the computation of years and *the science of* reckoning. And everything We have explained with a detailed explanation.

وجعلنا الّيل والنهار ايتين فمحونا اية الّيل
وجعلنا اية النهار مبصرة لتبتغوا فضلا من
ربكم ولتعلموا عدد السنين والحساب وكل
شيء فصلنه تفصيلا ⑬

13. And We have made the night and the day two Signs, **and We erased the Sign of night *replacing it with day* and the Sign of day We have made alight,** that you may seek bounty from your Lord, and that you may know the computation of years and *the science of* reckoning. And everything We have explained with a detailed explanation.

14. And every man's works have We fastened to his neck; and on the Day of Resurrection We shall bring out for him a book which he will find wide open.

وكل انسان الزمنه طٰئره في عنقه ونخرج
له يوم القيمة كتبا يلقه منشورا ⑭

14. And every man's **record of deeds have we fastened** to his neck, and on the Day of Resurrection We shall bring out for him a book which he will find wide open.

17. And when We intend to destroy a township, We address Our commandment to its rebellious people, but they transgress therein; so the sentence *of punishment* becomes due against it, and We destroy it with utter destruction.

واذا اردنا ان نهلك قرية امرنا مترفيها
ففسقوا فيها فحق عليها القول فدمرنها تدميرا ⑰

17. And when we intend to destroy a township, we permit the affluent among them *to do as they please.* So they indulge in all manners of sin therein, till the decree is justified to befall it. Then we destroy it utterly.

إِمَّا يَبْلُغَنَّ عِنْدَكَ الْكِبَرَ أَحَدُهُمَا أَوْ كِلٰهُمَا فَلَا تَقُلْ لَهُمَا أُفٍّ وَّلَا تَنْهَرْهُمَا وَقُلْ لَهُمَا قَوْلًا كَرِيمًا ﴿٢٤﴾

24. **If one of them or both of them attain old age with thee, never say unto them any word expressive of disgust nor reproach them, but address them with excellent speech.**

24. If one of them or both of them attain old age with thee, never say unto them any word expressive of disgust nor reproach them, but address them with **kind words.**

وَلَا تَجْعَلْ يَدَكَ مَغْلُوْلَةً إِلٰى عُنُقِكَ وَلَا تَبْسُطْهَا كُلَّ الْبَسْطِ فَتَقْعُدَ مَلُوْمًا مَّحْسُوْرًا ﴿٣٠﴾

30. And keep not thy hand chained to thy neck, nor stretch it out an entire stretching, lest thou sit down blamed *or* exhausted.

30. **And keep not your hand chained to your neck *in utter stinginess* nor extend it in extravagance to the full; or you will end up roundly condemned *and* rendered ineffectual.**

وَّجَعَلْنَا عَلٰى قُلُوْبِهِمْ أَكِنَّةً أَنْ يَّفْقَهُوْهُ وَفِيْٓ اٰذَانِهِمْ وَقْرًا

47. And We put coverings over their hearts lest they should understand it, and in their ears a deafness.

47. **And upon their hearts We have drawn covers so that they do not understand it and inflicted their ears with deafness.**

وَرَبُّكَ أَعْلَمُ بِمَنْ فِي السَّمٰوٰتِ وَالْأَرْضِ ۗ وَلَقَدْ فَضَّلْنَا بَعْضَ النَّبِيّٖنَ عَلٰى بَعْضٍ وَّاٰتَيْنَا دَاوٗدَ زَبُوْرًا ﴿٥٦﴾

56. And thy Lord knows best those that are in the heavens and the earth. And We exalted some of the Prophets over the others, and to David We gave a Book.

56. And thy Lord knows best those that are in the heavens and the earth. And We exalted some of the Prophets over the others and to David **We gave the Zaboor.**

Note: 'Zaboor' means Parchments.

وَّ قُلْنَا مِنْۢ بَعْدِهٖ لِبَنِیْۤ اِسْرَآءِیْلَ اسْكُنُوا الْاَرْضَ
فَاِذَا جَآءَ وَعْدُ الْاٰخِرَةِ جِئْنَا بِكُمْ لَفِیْفًا ﴿۱۰۵﴾

105. And after him We said to the children of Israel, 'Dwell ye in the land; and when *the time of* the promise of the latter days comes, We shall bring you together *out of various peoples.*'

105. And after him We said to the children of Israel, 'Dwell - **you** in the land; and when *the time of* the promise of the latter days comes, We shall bring you together **once again.**

وَ قُرْاٰنًا فَرَقْنٰهُ لِتَقْرَاَهٗ عَلَى النَّاسِ عَلٰی مُكْثٍ
وَّ نَزَّلْنٰهُ تَنْزِیْلًا ﴿۱۰۷﴾

107. And the Qur'ān We have revealed in pieces that thou mayest read it to mankind at intervals, and We have sent it down piecemeal.

107. **And We divided the Qur'an into parts** that you may read it to mankind at intervals, and We have sent it down gradually.

قُلِ ادْعُوا اللّٰهَ اَوِ ادْعُوا الرَّحْمٰنَ ؕ اَیًّا مَّا تَدْعُوْا فَلَهُ الْاَسْمَآءُ
الْحُسْنٰی ۚ وَ لَا تَجْهَرْ بِصَلَاتِكَ وَ لَا تُخَافِتْ بِهَا وَ
ابْتَغِ بَیْنَ ذٰلِكَ سَبِیْلًا ﴿۱۱۱﴾

111. Say, 'Call upon Allah or call upon Raḥmān; *by* whichever name you call on Him, His are the most beautiful names.' And utter not thy prayer aloud, nor utter it *too* low, but seek a way between.

111. **Say, 'Call Allah or call Rahman; by whichever name you pray *to Him,*** His are the most beautiful names.' And utter not thy prayer aloud, nor utter it *too* low, but seek a way between.

AL-KAHF

اَلْحَمْدُ لِلّٰهِ الَّذِیْۤ اَنْزَلَ عَلٰی عَبْدِهِ الْكِتٰبَ وَ لَمْ
یَجْعَلْ لَّهٗ عِوَجًا ﴿۲﴾

2. All praise belongs to Allah Who has sent down the Book to His servant and has not put therein any crookedness.

2. All praise belongs to Allah Who has sent down the book to His servant

and He employed no crookedness in his or in its making.

Note: The pronoun *hoo* (ﻫٗ) in *lahoo* (لَهٗ) equally applies to the servant of Allah — the recipient of the Book — and the Book itself. Hence it cannot be translated into English using a pronoun simultaneously applicable to both. If one translates this as 'God has not placed any crookedness in it', it will exclude the Holy Prophet (peace be upon him) from this promise of purity. If one translates it as, 'He has not placed any crookedness in him', then the Book is left out of this sanctity. To resolve this problem we have translated the verse in a different style keeping absolutely loyal to the spirit rather than overemphasising the letter.

فَضَرَبْنَا عَلَىٰٓ اٰذَانِهِمْ فِي الْكَهْفِ سِنِيْنَ عَدَدًا ﴿۱۲﴾

12. So We sealed up their ears in the Cave for a number of years.

12. So **We prevented them from hearing** ***the news of the outside world*** **for a few years.**

وَتَرَى الشَّمْسَ إِذَا طَلَعَتْ تَّزٰوَرُ عَنْ كَهْفِهِمْ
ذَاتَ الْيَمِيْنِ وَإِذَا غَرَبَتْ تَّقْرِضُهُمْ ذَاتَ
الشِّمَالِ وَهُمْ فِيْ فَجْوَةٍ مِّنْهُ ۚ ذٰلِكَ مِنْ اٰيٰتِ
اللّٰهِ ۚ مَنْ يَّهْدِ اللّٰهُ فَهُوَ الْمُهْتَدِ ۚ وَمَنْ يُّضْلِلْ فَلَنْ
تَجِدَ لَهٗ وَلِيًّا مُّرْشِدًا ﴿۱۸﴾

18. And thou couldst see the sun, as it rose, move away from their Cave on the right, and when it set, turn away from them on the left; and they were in the spacious hollow thereof. This is among the Signs of Allah. He whom Allah guides is rightly guided; but he whom He adjudges astray, for him thou wilt find no helper *or* guide.

18. And **you could** see the sun, as it rose, move away from their Cave on the right, and when it set, **move across them to the left,** and they were in the spacious hollow thereof. This is among the Signs of Allah. He whom Allah guides is rightly guided; but he whom He adjudges astray, for him **you will** find no helper or guide.

إِنَّهُمْ إِنْ يَّظْهَرُوْا عَلَيْكُمْ يَرْجُمُوْكُمْ أَوْ يُعِيْدُوْكُمْ

21. 'For, if they should come to know of you, they would stone you or make you

return to their religion and then will you never prosper.'

فِي مِلَّتِهِمْ وَلَن تُفْلِحُوا إِذًا أَبَدًا ٢١

21. 'For, **if they overcome you,** they would stone you or make you return to their religion and then will you never prosper.'

22. ***And remember the time*** **when people disputed among themselves concerning them, and said, 'Build over them a building.' Their Lord knew them best. Those who won their point said, 'We will, surely, build a place of worship over them.'**

إِذْ يَتَنَازَعُونَ
بَيْنَهُمْ أَمْرَهُمْ فَقَالُوا ابْنُوا عَلَيْهِم بُنْيَانًا ۖ رَّبُّهُمْ
أَعْلَمُ بِهِمْ ۚ قَالَ الَّذِينَ غَلَبُوا عَلَىٰ أَمْرِهِمْ لَنَتَّخِذَنَّ
عَلَيْهِم مَّسْجِدًا ٢٢

22. *And remember the time* when people disputed among themselves concerning them, **and *some* said, 'Erect a building over them.'** Their Lord knew them best. Those who won their point said, 'We will, surely, build a place of worship over them.'

Note: 'Erect a building over them' means to build a memorial at the site of their caves.

23. Say, 'My Lord knows best their number. None knows them except a few.' So argue not concerning them except with arguing ***that is*** **overpowering, nor seek information about them from any one of them.**

قُل رَّبِّي أَعْلَمُ
بِعِدَّتِهِم مَّا يَعْلَمُهُمْ إِلَّا قَلِيلٌ ۗ فَلَا تُمَارِ
فِيهِمْ إِلَّا مِرَاءً ظَاهِرًا وَلَا تَسْتَفْتِ فِيهِم
مِّنْهُمْ أَحَدًا ٢٣

23. Say, 'My Lord knows best **what their real number was. Very few are those who know regarding them. So do not argue concerning them except for a casual discussion,** nor seek information about them from any one of them.

27. Say, 'Allah knows best how long they tarried.' To Him belong the secrets of the heavens and the earth. How Seeing is He! and how Hearing! They have no

قُلِ اللَّهُ أَعْلَمُ بِمَا لَبِثُوا ۖ لَهُ غَيْبُ السَّمَاوَاتِ وَالْأَرْضِ ۖ
أَبْصِرْ بِهِ وَأَسْمِعْ ۚ مَا لَهُم مِّن دُونِهِ مِن وَلِيٍّ

helper beside Him, and He does not let anyone share in His government.

وَّلَا يُشْرِكُ فِيْ حُكْمِهٖٓ اَحَدًا ﴿۲۶﴾

27. Say, 'Allah knows best how long they tarried **therein. To Him belongs the unseen of the heavens and the earth. What a sight He has and what a hearing! There is no friend for them other than He and He does not permit anyone to have a share in His authority.**

38. His companion said to him, while he was arguing with him, "Dost thou disbelieve in Him Who created thee from dust,

قَالَ لَهٗ صَاحِبُهٗ وَهُوَ يُحَاوِرُهٗٓ اَكَفَرْتَ بِالَّذِيْ خَلَقَكَ مِنْ تُرَابٍ ثُمَّ مِنْ نُّطْفَةٍ ثُمَّ سَوّٰىكَ رَجُلًا ﴿۳۸﴾

38. His companion said to him, while he was **conversing with him, 'Do you** disbelieve in Him Who created you from dust,

45. In such **a case** protection *comes only* from Allah, the True. He is the Best in respect of reward, and the Best in respect of consequence.

هُنَالِكَ الْوَلَايَةُ لِلّٰهِ الْحَقِّ هُوَ خَيْرٌ ثَوَابًا وَّخَيْرٌ عُقْبًا ﴿۴۵﴾

45. **At such times the support comes only from Allah,** the True. He is the Best in respect of reward, and the Best in respect of consequence.

47. Wealth and children are an ornament of the life of this world.

اَلْمَالُ وَالْبَنُوْنَ زِيْنَةُ الْحَيٰوةِ الدُّنْيَا

47. Wealth and children **are an adornment of** the life of this world

51. Will you then take him and his offspring for friends instead of Me while they are your enemies? Evil is the exchange for the wrongdoers.

اَفَتَتَّخِذُوْنَهٗ وَذُرِّيَّتَهٗٓ اَوْلِيَآءَ مِنْ دُوْنِيْ وَهُمْ لَكُمْ عَدُوٌّ بِئْسَ لِلظّٰلِمِيْنَ بَدَلًا ﴿۵۱﴾

51. Will you then take him and his **progeny** for friends instead of

Me while they are your enemies? Evil is the exchange for the wrongdoers.

56. And nothing hinders people from believing when the guidance comes to them, and from asking forgiveness of their Lord, except *that they wait* that there should happen to them the precedent of the ancients or that punishment should come upon them face to face.

وَمَا مَنَعَ النَّاسَ اَنۡ يُّؤۡمِنُوۡۤا اِذۡ جَآءَهُمُ الۡهُدٰى
وَيَسۡتَغۡفِرُوۡا رَبَّهُمۡ اِلَّاۤ اَنۡ تَاۡتِيَهُمۡ سُنَّةُ الۡاَوَّلِيۡنَ
اَوۡ يَاۡتِيَهُمُ الۡعَذَابُ قُبُلًا ﴿٥٦﴾

56. And nothing prevented people from believing and seeking forgiveness of their Lord, when guidance came to them, except that they chose to follow the course of the earlier people *with the same consequences* or awaited the punishment *of Allah* to take them head on.

62. But when they reached the place where the two *seas* met, they forgot their fish, and it made its way into the sea *going away* swiftly.

فَلَمَّا بَلَغَا مَجۡمَعَ بَيۡنِهِمَا نَسِيَا حُوۡتَهُمَا فَاتَّخَذَ
سَبِيۡلَهٗ فِى الۡبَحۡرِ سَرَبًا ﴿٦٢﴾

62. But when they reached **the junction of the two *seas*,** they forgot their fish, and it made its way into the sea *going away* swiftly.

64. He replied, 'Didst thou see, when we betook ourselves to the rock for rest, and I forgot the fish—and none but Satan caused me to forget to mention it *to thee*—it took its way into the sea in a marvellous manner?'

قَالَ اَرَءَيۡتَ اِذۡ اَوَيۡنَاۤ اِلَى الصَّخۡرَةِ فَاِنِّىۡ نَسِيۡتُ
الۡحُوۡتَ وَمَاۤ اَنۡسٰنِيۡهُ اِلَّا الشَّيۡطٰنُ اَنۡ اَذۡكُرَهٗ‌ۚ
وَاتَّخَذَ سَبِيۡلَهٗ فِى الۡبَحۡرِ ‌ۖ عَجَبًا ﴿٦٤﴾

64. He replied, 'Did you see, when we betook ourselves to the rock for rest, and I forgot the fish --- and none but Satan caused me to forget to mention it to you **— it took its way to the sea in a strange manner**.

70. He said, 'Thou wilt find me, if Allah please, patient and I shall not disobey any command of thine.'

قَالَ سَتَجِدُنِيٓ إِن شَآءَ ٱللَّهُ صَابِرًا وَلَآ أَعۡصِي لَكَ أَمۡرًا ۝٧٠

70. He said, **'You will** find me, if Allah please, patient and I shall not **disobey you in anything.'**

104. Say, 'Shall We tell you of those who are the greatest losers in respect of their works? —

قُلۡ هَلۡ نُنَبِّئُكُم بِٱلۡأَخۡسَرِينَ أَعۡمَٰلًا ۝١٠٤

104. Say, 'Shall We tell you of those who **are the worst losers with regard to their deeds?**

MARYAM

24. And the pains of childbirth drove her unto the trunk of a palm-tree. She said, 'O! would that I had died before this and had become a thing quite forgotten!'

فَأَجَآءَهَا ٱلۡمَخَاضُ إِلَىٰ جِذۡعِ ٱلنَّخۡلَةِ قَالَتۡ يَٰلَيۡتَنِي مِتُّ قَبۡلَ هَٰذَا وَكُنتُ نَسۡيًا مَّنسِيًّا ۝٢٤

24. And the pains of childbirth drove her to the trunk of a **date- palm.** She said, 'O! would that I had died before this and had become a thing quite forgotten!'

70. Then shall We certainly pick out, from every group, those of them who were most stubborn in rebellion against the Gracious *God.*

ثُمَّ لَنَنزِعَنَّ مِن كُلِّ شِيعَةٍ أَيُّهُمۡ أَشَدُّ عَلَى ٱلرَّحۡمَٰنِ عِتِيًّا ۝٧٠

70. Then shall we certainly **drag out,** from every group, those of them who were most stubborn in rebellion against the Gracious *God.*

87. And We shall drive the guilty to Hell like a herd *of thirsty camels.*

وَنَسُوقُ ٱلۡمُجۡرِمِينَ إِلَىٰ جَهَنَّمَ وِرۡدًا ۝٨٧

87. And We shall drive the guilty to Hell **like a herd to a watering place.**

TA HA

فَلَمَّا أَتَاهَا نُودِيَ يَا مُوسَىٰ ﴿١٢﴾

12. And when he came to it, he was called *by a voice*, 'O Moses,

12. And when he came to it, **it was announced,** 'O, Moses

إِنَّ السَّاعَةَ آتِيَةٌ أَكَادُ أُخْفِيهَا لِتُجْزَىٰ كُلُّ نَفْسٍ
بِمَا تَسْعَىٰ ﴿١٦﴾

16. 'Surely, the Hour is coming; I am going to manifest it, that every soul may be recompensed for its endeavour.

16. Surely, the **Hour will come; I may reveal it,** that every soul may be recompensed for its endeavour.

وَاضْمُمْ يَدَكَ إِلَىٰ جَنَاحِكَ تَخْرُجْ بَيْضَاءَ مِنْ
غَيْرِ سُوءٍ آيَةً أُخْرَىٰ ﴿٢٣﴾

23. 'And draw thy hand close under thy arm-pit. It shall come forth white, without any disease—another Sign,

23. **And press your hand close to your side.** It shall come forth white, without **blemish** — another Sign,

قَالَ رَبِّ اشْرَحْ لِي صَدْرِي ﴿٢٦﴾

26. *Moses* said, 'My Lord, open out for me my breast,

26. **He said, 'My Lord! Open up for me my heart.**

وَاحْلُلْ عُقْدَةً مِنْ لِسَانِي ﴿٢٨﴾

28. 'And loose the knot of my tongue,

28. 'And **unite** the knot of my tongue.'

فَقُولَا لَهُ قَوْلًا لَيِّنًا لَعَلَّهُ يَتَذَكَّرُ أَوْ يَخْشَىٰ ﴿٤٥﴾

45. "But speak to him a gentle speech that he might possibly heed or fear."

45. **'And address him both of you, with gentle words that** he might possibly heed or fear.

61. Then Pharaoh withdrew and concerted his plan and then came *to the place of appointment.*

فَتَوَلّٰى فِرۡعَوۡنُ فَجَمَعَ كَيۡدَهٗ ثُمَّ اَتٰى ۝٦١

61. Then **Pharaoh turned away and mustered all his tricks, then he came *in keeping with the appointment.***

85. He said, 'They are *closely following* in my footsteps and I have hastened to Thee, my Lord, that Thou mightest be pleased.'

قَالَ هُمۡ اُولَآءِ عَلٰٓى اَثَرِىۡ وَعَجِلۡتُ اِلَيۡكَ رَبِّ لِتَرۡضٰى ۝٨٥

85. He said, **'They are close upon my tracks and** I have hastened to **you,** my Lord, that **you may** be pleased.'

89. Then he produced for them a calf—an image producing a lowing sound. And they said, 'This is your God, and the God of Moses.' So he gave up *the religion of Moses.*

فَاَخۡرَجَ لَهُمۡ عِجۡلًا جَسَدًا لَّهٗ خُوَارٌ فَقَالُوۡا هٰذَاۤ اِلٰهُكُمۡ وَاِلٰهُ مُوۡسٰى ۙ فَنَسِىَ ۝٨٩

89. Then he produced for them a calf **— a mere body which emitted** a lowing sound. **Then *he and his companions* said, 'this is your god, and the god of Moses but he forgot *to mention it to you.'***

95. He answered, "O son of my mother, seize me not by my beard, nor by *the hair of* my head. I feared lest thou shouldst say, 'Thou hast caused a division among the children of Israel, and didst not wait for my word.' "

قَالَ يَبۡنَؤُمَّ لَا تَاۡخُذۡ بِلِحۡيَتِىۡ وَلَا بِرَاۡسِىۡ ۚ اِنِّىۡ خَشِيۡتُ اَنۡ تَقُوۡلَ فَرَّقۡتَ بَيۡنَ بَنِىۡۤ اِسۡرَآءِيۡلَ وَلَمۡ تَرۡقُبۡ قَوۡلِىۡ ۝٩٥

Note: The expression 'seize me not by my beard, nor by (the hair of) my head' should not be taken literally. It may simply mean: do not humiliate me.

109. On that day they will follow the Caller *straight,* there being no deviation therefrom; and *all* voices shall be hushed before the Gracious *God* and thou shalt not hear but a subdued sound of footsteps.

يَوۡمَئِذٍ يَّتَّبِعُوۡنَ الدَّاعِىَ لَا عِوَجَ لَهٗ ۚ وَخَشَعَتِ الۡاَصۡوَاتُ لِلرَّحۡمٰنِ فَلَا تَسۡمَعُ اِلَّا هَمۡسًا ۝١٠٩

109. **On that day shall they follow the summoner who is *upright* with no crookedness in him;** and all voices shall be hushed before the Gracious *God* and you will not hear but a subdued sound of footsteps.

114. And thus have We sent it down—the Qur'ān in Arabic—and We have explained therein certain warnings, that they may fear God or that it may give birth to *divine* remembrance in them.

وَكَذَٰلِكَ أَنزَلْنَٰهُ قُرْءَانًا عَرَبِيًّا وَصَرَّفْنَا فِيهِ مِنَ
الْوَعِيدِ لَعَلَّهُمْ يَتَّقُونَ أَوْ يُحْدِثُ لَهُمْ ذِكْرًا ﴿١١٤﴾

114. And thus have We sent it down -- the Qur'an in Arabic — and We have explained therein certain warnings, that they may fear God or **that it may generate in them divine remembrance.**

122. Then they both ate thereof, so that their shame became manifest to them, and they began to stick the leaves of the garden together over themselves. And Adam observed not the commandment of his Lord, so his life became miserable.

فَأَكَلَا مِنْهَا فَبَدَتْ لَهُمَا سَوْءَٰتُهُمَا وَطَفِقَا يَخْصِفَانِ
عَلَيْهِمَا مِن وَرَقِ الْجَنَّةِ ۚ وَعَصَىٰٓ ءَادَمُ رَبَّهُۥ فَغَوَىٰ ﴿١٢٢﴾

122. They both ate thereof; **so their inherent weakness became exposed to them. So they started covering themselves with the leaves from the garden. And Adam disobeyed his Lord and deviated from the path.**

Note: Most translators have taken the scenario too literally while there is enough evidence within the text to rule out a literal application. The sin referred to is obviously related to an internal faltering as indicated by the part of the verse which declares that their *Sau'aatohuma*(سوا تهما)(weakness) became known to them. If it was a bodily nakedness how could they have remained unaware of their nakedness from the time of their birth to the time of the said incident?

It is evident, therefore, that a literal meaning is wrongfully attributed to the Holy Qur'an. The word *sau'aa* (سوا) primarily applies to acts of shame and evil propensities. At the time of faltering the falterer discovers to his horror his own hidden weaknesses. This weakness is psychological and internal, related to mind and heart, and cannot be covered and concealed by sticking leaves over one's body. So in the context of this error, whatever it was, which Adam and Eve committed, coverage can only mean seeking forgiveness from Allah and (seeking protection from Allah). As such leaves of جنّة (garden) must be understood metaphorically to mean seeking shelter under Allah's forgiveness and that is exactly what Adam did according to the Qur'an where it is clearly mentioned that God Himself taught him those words which would rid him of the effects of his error and in response to those words God turned to him with mercy and forgiveness.

وَلَوْلَا كَلِمَةٌ سَبَقَتْ مِن رَّبِّكَ لَكَانَ لِزَامًا وَأَجَلٌ مُّسَمًّى ﴿١٣٠﴾

130. And had it not been for a word already gone forth from thy Lord, and a term *already* fixed, *immediate punishment* would have been inevitable.

130. And had it not been for a word already gone forth from your Lord, and a term *already* fixed, *their punishment* would have been abiding.

وَقَالُوا لَوْلَا يَأْتِينَا بِآيَةٍ مِّن رَّبِّهِ أَوَلَمْ تَأْتِهِم بَيِّنَةُ مَا فِي الصُّحُفِ الْأُولَىٰ ﴿١٣٤﴾

134. And they say, 'Why does he not bring us a Sign from his Lord?' Has there not come to them the clear evidence in what is *contained* in the former Books?

134. And they say, 'Why does he not bring us a Sign from his Lord?' Has there not come to them the clear evidence in what is *contained* in the former **Scriptures?**

AL-ANBIYA

لَاهِيَةً قُلُوبُهُمْ وَأَسَرُّوا النَّجْوَى الَّذِينَ ظَلَمُوا هَلْ هَٰذَا إِلَّا بَشَرٌ مِّثْلُكُمْ أَفَتَأْتُونَ السِّحْرَ وَأَنتُمْ تُبْصِرُونَ ﴿٤﴾

4. *And* their hearts are forgetful. And they keep their counsels secret—those who act wrongfully, *then say,* 'Is this *man* aught but a human being like ourselves? Will you then accede to magic while you see *it?*'

4. *And* their hearts are forgetful. And they keep their counsels secret — those who act wrongfully, *then say,* 'Is this

man **anything** but a human being like **yourselves?** Will you then accede to magic while you see it?'

8. And We sent none *as Messengers* before thee but men to whom We sent revelations. So ask the people of the Reminder, if you know not.

وَمَآ أَرْسَلْنَا قَبْلَكَ إِلَّا رِجَالًا نُّوحِىٓ إِلَيْهِمْ فَسْـَٔلُوٓا
أَهْلَ الذِّكْرِ إِن كُنتُمْ لَا تَعْلَمُونَ ﴿٨﴾

8. And We sent none *as Messengers* before you but men to whom We sent revelations. So ask **those who are well versed in *scriptures*,** if you know not.

11. We have now sent down to **you a** Book wherein lies your *glory and* eminence; will you not then understand?

لَقَدْ أَنزَلْنَآ إِلَيْكُمْ كِتَٰبًا فِيهِ ذِكْرُكُمْ أَفَلَا تَعْقِلُونَ ﴿١١﴾

11. We have now sent down to you a Book wherein lies ***all that you may need for*** **your admonition;** will you not then understand?

14. 'Flee not, but return to the **com**forts in which you exulted, and **to your** dwellings that you might be *approached and* consulted *as before*.'

لَا تَرْكُضُوا وَارْجِعُوٓا إِلَىٰ مَآ أُتْرِفْتُمْ فِيهِ وَمَسَٰكِنِكُمْ
لَعَلَّكُمْ تُسْـَٔلُونَ ﴿١٤﴾

14. 'Flee not, but return to the comforts in which you exulted, and to your dwellings that you might be **brought to account.**

23. If there had been in them (the heavens and the earth) other gods beside Allah, then surely both would have gone to ruin. Glorified then be Allah, the Lord of the Throne, above what they attribute.

لَوْ كَانَ فِيهِمَآ ءَالِهَةٌ إِلَّا اللَّهُ لَفَسَدَتَا فَسُبْحَٰنَ اللَّهِ
رَبِّ الْعَرْشِ عَمَّا يَصِفُونَ ﴿٢٣﴾

23. If there had **been in both *the heaven and the earth* gods other than Allah, then both *the heaven and the earth* would have ended up in chaos.** Glorified then be Allah, the Lord of the Throne, above what they attribute.

64. He replied, 'Aye, somebody has surely done this. Here is their chief. But ask them if they can speak.'

قَالَ بَلْ فَعَلَهُ ۖ كَبِيرُهُمْ هَٰذَا فَاسْأَلُوهُمْ إِن
كَانُوا يَنطِقُونَ ٦٤

64. He replied, 'Aye, somebody has surely done this. Here is the chief ***suspect.*** Ask them if they **are capable of speaking.**

Note: Some translators avoid literal translation of this verse fearing that this would present Abraham as a liar. Obviously it was not the big idols who had smashed the smaller ones but it was Abraham himself who had done it. Therefore attributing the statement to Abraham that 'here is their chief', would be tantamount to attributing an obvious lie to Abraham. It should be noted, however, that it was not a mis-statement but a powerful style of argument. Sometimes a thing is too obvious for anybody to believe and a statement to that effect is never understood as a wilful attempt to mislead others but considered an exposition of the inherent absurdity of a situation. We believe that Abraham did make that statement without the slightest intention of misleading them but only by way of a powerful argument against the falsity of their belief. This is exactly how they took it. Having heard Abraham, none of them retorted by calling him a liar. But according to the Holy Qur'an they were introspectively forced to realise the folly of their belief. This is made clear in the following verses (see verses 65 to 68). Again it should be remembered that before this incident Abraham himself had mentioned in public his resolve to smash their idols (see verse 58).

70. We said, 'O fire, be thou cold and a *means of* safety for Abraham!'

قُلْنَا يَا نَارُ كُونِي بَرْدًا وَسَلَامًا عَلَىٰ إِبْرَاهِيمَ ٧٠

70. We said, **'Turn cold, O Fire, and be a source of peace for Abraham.'**

88. And *remember* Dhu'l-Nūn, when he went away in anger, and he thought that We would never cause him distress and he cried out in *depths of* darkness, *saying*, 'There is no God but Thou, Holy art Thou. I have indeed been of the wrongdoers.'

وَذَا النُّونِ إِذ ذَّهَبَ مُغَاضِبًا فَظَنَّ أَن لَّن نَّقْدِرَ
عَلَيْهِ فَنَادَىٰ فِي الظُّلُمَاتِ أَن لَّا إِلَٰهَ إِلَّا أَنتَ
سُبْحَانَكَ إِنِّي كُنتُ مِنَ الظَّالِمِينَ ٨٨

88. And *remember* Dhu'l-Nun, when he went away in anger. And thought that **We would not bear heavily on him. Then from the depths of darkness he**

cried out: there is no God but **You**, Holy are **You**. I have indeed been of the wrongdoers.'

92. And *remember* her who preserved her chastity; so We breathed into her of Our word and We made her and her son a Sign for peoples.

وَالَّتِيٓ اَحْصَنَتْ فَرْجَهَا فَنَفَخْنَا فِيهَا مِنْ رُّوحِنَا
وَجَعَلْنٰهَا وَابْنَهَآ اٰيَةً لِّلْعٰلَمِينَ ﴿٩٢﴾

92. And *remember* her who **guarded** her chastity; so We breathed into her of Our word and We made her and her son a Sign for peoples.

95. So Whoever does good works and is a believer, his effort will not be disregarded and We shall surely record it.

فَمَنْ يَّعْمَلْ مِنَ الصّٰلِحٰتِ وَهُوَ مُؤْمِنٌ فَلَا
كُفْرَانَ لِسَعْيِهٖ ۚ وَاِنَّا لَهٗ كٰتِبُوْنَ ﴿٩٥﴾

95. So Whoever does good works and is a believer, his effort will **not go unappreciated** and We shall surely record it.

106. And already have We written in the Book *of David*, after the exhortation, that My righteous servants shall inherit the land.

وَلَقَدْ كَتَبْنَا فِي الزَّبُوْرِ مِنْۢ بَعْدِ الذِّكْرِ
اَنَّ الْاَرْضَ يَرِثُهَا عِبَادِيَ الصّٰلِحُوْنَ ﴿١٠٦﴾

106. And already have we written in **the Psalms** of David, after the exhortation, that My righteous servants shall inherit the land.

107. Herein, surely, is a message for people who worship *God*.

اِنَّ فِيْ هٰذَا لَبَلٰغًا لِّقَوْمٍ عٰبِدِيْنَ ﴿١٠٧﴾ ط

107. Herein, surely, is **an important** message for people who worship God.

AL-HAJJ

يَٰٓأَيُّهَا ٱلنَّاسُ ٱتَّقُواْ رَبَّكُمْۚ إِنَّ زَلْزَلَةَ ٱلسَّاعَةِ
شَيْءٌ عَظِيمٌ ٢

2. O people, fear your Lord; verily the earthquake of the Hour is a tremendous thing—

2. O people, fear your Lord; **surely the quaking at the appointed Hour** is a tremendous thing.

يَوْمَ تَرَوْنَهَا تَذْهَلُ كُلُّ مُرْضِعَةٍ عَمَّآ أَرْضَعَتْ
وَتَضَعُ كُلُّ ذَاتِ حَمْلٍ حَمْلَهَا وَتَرَى ٱلنَّاسَ
سُكَٰرَىٰ وَمَا هُم بِسُكَٰرَىٰ وَلَٰكِنَّ عَذَابَ ٱللَّهِ
شَدِيدٌ ٣

3. The day when you see it, every woman giving suck shall forget her suckling and every pregnant woman shall cast her burden; and thou shalt see men as drunken while they will not be drunken, but severe will indeed be the punishment of Allah.

3. The day when you see it, **every nursing mother will** forget her suckling and every pregnant **female will abort** her burden; **and you will** see men as drunken while they will not be drunken, but severe will indeed be the punishment of Allah.

ثُمَّ نُخْرِجُكُمْ طِفْلًا ثُمَّ لِتَبْلُغُوٓاْ أَشُدَّكُمْ وَمِنكُم
مَّن يُتَوَفَّىٰ وَمِنكُم مَّن يُرَدُّ إِلَىٰٓ أَرْذَلِ ٱلْعُمُرِ لِكَيْلَا
يَعْلَمَ مِنۢ بَعْدِ عِلْمٍ شَيْـًٔا

6. We bring you forth as babes; then *We rear you* that you may attain to your *age of* full strength. And there are some of you who are caused to die *prematurely*, and there are others among you who are driven to the worst part of life *with the result* that they know nothing after *having had* knowledge.

6. We **have delivered you as a child so that** ***afterwards*** **you may reach** your age of full **maturity.** And there are **those** among you who **die** and there are others among you who are **made to recede to the age of senility** *with the result* that they know nothing after *having had* knowledge.

Note: The word 'recede' is used to indicate that as in the beginning the child is helpless and incapable of taking care of himself so also a man at an overly advanced age returns to a similar state. This connotation is supported by the verse من نعمره ننكسه فى الخلق. (Yasin Ch: 36 Verse 69)

وَمِنَ النَّاسِ مَنْ يَّعْبُدُ اللّٰهَ عَلٰى حَرْفٍ ۚ فَاِنْ اَصَابَهٗ خَيْرُ ۨ اطْمَاَنَّ بِهٖ ۚ وَاِنْ اَصَابَتْهُ فِتْنَةُ ۨ انْقَلَبَ عَلٰى وَجْهِهٖ ۚ خَسِرَ الدُّنْيَا وَالْاٰخِرَةَ ۭ ذٰلِكَ هُوَ الْخُسْرَانُ الْمُبِيْنُ ﴿۱۲﴾

12. And among men there is he who serves Allah, *standing as it were* on the verge. Then if good befall him, he is content therewith; and if there befall him a trial, he returns to his *former* way. He loses in this world as well as in the Hereafter. That is an evident loss.

12. and among men there is he who **worships Allah on the borderline *of belief,* then if good attends him,** he is content therewith; and if there befall him a trial, **he turns away *from Allah.*** He loses in this world as well as in the Hereafter. That is an evident loss.

وَهُدُوْٓا اِلَى الطَّيِّبِ مِنَ الْقَوْلِ ۚ وَهُدُوْٓا اِلٰى صِرَاطِ الْحَمِيْدِ ﴿۲۵﴾

25. And they will be guided to pure speech, and they will be guided to the path of the Praiseworthy *God.*

25. And they will be guided only to **virtuous** speech, and they will be guided to the path of the Praiseworthy *God.*

ثُمَّ لْيَقْضُوْا تَفَثَهُمْ وَلْيُوْفُوْا نُذُوْرَهُمْ وَلْيَطَّوَّفُوْا بِالْبَيْتِ الْعَتِيْقِ ﴿۳۰﴾

30. 'Then let them accomplish their needful acts of cleansing, and fulfil their vows, and go around the Ancient House.'

30. 'Then let them accomplish **the task of cleansing themselves,** and fulfil their vows, and go around the Ancient House'.

فَاجْتَنِبُوا الرِّجْسَ مِنَ الْاَوْثَانِ وَاجْتَنِبُوْا قَوْلَ الزُّوْرِ ﴿۳۱﴾

31. Shun therefore the abomination of idols, and shun all words of untruth,

31. Shun therefore the abomination of idols, and **shun false speech.**

الَّذِينَ إِذَا ذُكِرَ اللّٰهُ وَجِلَتْ قُلُوبُهُمْ وَالصّٰبِرِينَ
عَلٰى مَآ أَصَابَهُمْ وَالْمُقِيمِي الصَّلٰوةِ وَمِمَّا رَزَقْنٰهُمْ
يُنْفِقُونَ ﴿٣٦﴾

36. Whose hearts are filled with fear when Allah is mentioned, and who patiently endure whatever befalls them, and who observe Prayer, and spend out of what We have provided for them.

36. Whose hearts are filled **with awe** when Allah is mentioned, and who patiently endure whatever befalls them, and who observe Prayer, and spend out of what We have provided for them.

إِنَّ اللّٰهَ لَطِيفٌ خَبِيرٌ ﴿٦٤﴾

64. Allah is indeed the Knower of subtleties, the All-Aware.

64. **Allah is indeed Exquisite, All-Aware.**

وَيُمْسِكُ السَّمَآءَ أَنْ تَقَعَ
عَلَى الْأَرْضِ إِلَّا بِإِذْنِهٖ إِنَّ اللّٰهَ بِالنَّاسِ لَرَءُوفٌ
رَّحِيمٌ ﴿٦٦﴾

66. And He withholds the rain from falling on the earth save by His leave. Surely, Allah is Compassionate *and* Merciful to men.

66. And **He prevents heavenly bodies from falling upon earth except by His leave.** Surely, Allah is Compassionate *and* Merciful to men.

Note: It is likely that the word 'leave' applies to falling of meteors, and other heavenly bodies which constantly bombard the earth.

اَللّٰهُ يَصْطَفِي مِنَ الْمَلٰٓئِكَةِ رُسُلًا وَّمِنَ النَّاسِ

76. Allah chooses *His* Messengers from among angels, and from among men.

76. Allah **chooses Messengers** from among angels, and from among men.

يَعْلَمُ مَا بَيْنَ أَيْدِيهِمْ وَمَا خَلْفَهُمْ وَإِلَى اللّٰهِ تُرْجَعُ
الْأُمُورُ ﴿٧٧﴾

77. He knows what is before them and what is behind them; and to Allah shall *all* affairs be returned *for decision*.

77. He knows what is before them and what is behind them; and to Allah shall ***all* affairs be returned.**

AL-MUMINUN

10. And who are strict in the observance of their Prayers.

وَالَّذِينَ هُمْ عَلَىٰ صَلَوٰتِهِمْ يُحَافِظُونَ ﴿١٠﴾

10. And who **diligently guard** the observance of their prayers.

21. And a tree which springs forth from Mount Sinai; it produces oil and a sauce for those who eat.

وَشَجَرَةً تَخْرُجُ مِن طُورِ سَيْنَآءَ تَنْۢبُتُ بِالدُّهْنِ
وَصِبْغٍ لِّلْآكِلِينَ ﴿٢١﴾

21. And a tree which springs forth from Mount Sinai; **it produces oil and** ***many*** **a condiment** for those who eat.

25. And if Allah had so willed, He could have surely sent down angels *with him*. We have never heard of such *a thing* among our forefathers.

وَلَوْ شَآءَ اللّٰهُ لَأَنْزَلَ
مَلٰٓئِكَةً ۚ مَّا سَمِعْنَا بِهٰذَا فِيٓ اٰبَآئِنَا الْأَوَّلِينَ ﴿٢٥﴾

25. And if Allah had so willed He could have surely sent down angels. We have never heard of such *a thing* among our forefathers.

31. Verily, in this there are Signs. Surely, We did try *the people of Noah*.

إِنَّ فِي ذٰلِكَ لَاٰيٰتٍ وَّإِنْ كُنَّا لَمُبْتَلِينَ ﴿٣١﴾

31. Verily, in this there are Signs. **And verily We have always been bringing** ***people*** **to trial.**

38. 'There is no life other than our present life; we were lifeless and *now* we live, but we shall not be raised up again.

إِنْ هِيَ إِلَّا حَيَاتُنَا الدُّنْيَا نَمُوتُ وَنَحْيَا وَمَا نَحْنُ
بِمَبْعُوثِينَ ﴿٣٨﴾

38. **It is only here that we live our life. Here we die and** ***here*** **we live, and never shall we be raised again.**

51. And We made the son of Mary and his mother a Sign, and gave them refuge on an elevated land of *green* valleys and springs of running water.

وَجَعَلْنَا ابْنَ مَرْيَمَ وَأُمَّهٗٓ اٰيَةً وَّاٰوَيْنٰهُمَآ إِلٰى
رَبْوَةٍ ذَاتِ قَرَارٍ وَّمَعِينٍ ﴿٥١﴾

51. And We made the son of Mary and his mother a Sign, and **We rescued them *and helped them reach* an elevated land, a restful place with springs of running water.**

53. And *know* that this community of your is one community, and I am your Lord. So take Me as *your* Protector.

وَإِنَّ هَٰذِهِۦٓ أُمَّتُكُمْ أُمَّةً وَٰحِدَةً وَأَنَا۠ رَبُّكُمْ
فَٱتَّقُونِ ٥٢

53. And *know* that this community of yours is one community, and I am your Lord. **So fear me *alone.***

54. But they (the people) have cut up their affairs among themselves *forming themselves into* parties, each group rejoicing in what they have.

فَتَقَطَّعُوٓا۟ أَمْرَهُم بَيْنَهُمْ زُبُرًا ۖ كُلُّ حِزْبٍۭ بِمَا لَدَيْهِمْ
فَرِحُونَ ٥٣

54. They split their affairs fragment by fragment among themselves, each party exulting over what they have.

58. Verily, those who fear their Lord, *holding Him* in reverence,

إِنَّ ٱلَّذِينَ هُم مِّنْ خَشْيَةِ رَبِّهِم مُّشْفِقُونَ ٥٧

58. Verily, those who out of fear of their Lord always stand guard *against sins.*

72. And if the Truth had followed their desires, verily, the heavens and the earth and whosoever is therein would have been corrupted. Nay, We have brought them their admonition, but from their own admonition they *now* turn aside.

وَلَوِ ٱتَّبَعَ ٱلْحَقُّ أَهْوَآءَهُمْ لَفَسَدَتِ ٱلسَّمَٰوَٰتُ
وَٱلْأَرْضُ وَمَن فِيهِنَّ ۚ بَلْ أَتَيْنَٰهُم بِذِكْرِهِمْ فَهُمْ
عَن ذِكْرِهِم مُّعْرِضُونَ ٧١

72. **And if the truth were to follow their desires, the heavens and the earth and all that lies therein would have turned into chaos.** Nay, We have brought them their admonition, but from their own admonition they *now* turn aside.

88. They will say, '*They are* Allah's.' Say, 'Will you not then take *Him* as *your* Protector?'

سَيَقُوْلُوْنَ لِلّٰهِ ۚ قُلْ اَفَلَا تَتَّقُوْنَ ﴿٨٨﴾

88. They will say, **'To Allah they belong'. Say, 'Will you not then live in fear?'**

98. And say, 'My Lord, I seek refuge in Thee from the incitements of the evil ones.

وَقُلْ رَّبِّ اَعُوْذُ بِكَ مِنْ هَمَزٰتِ الشَّيٰطِيْنِ ﴿٩٨﴾

98. And say, 'My Lord, I seek refuge in You from the incitements **of the Satans.**

103. Then those whose good works are heavy—these will be prosperous;

فَمَنْ ثَقُلَتْ مَوَازِيْنُهٗ فَاُولٰٓئِكَ هُمُ الْمُفْلِحُوْنَ ﴿١٠٣﴾

103. Then those whose **scales are heavy *in deeds* it is these who will be prosperous.**

105. The Fire will burn their faces and they will grin *with fear* therein.

تَلْفَحُ وُجُوْهَهُمُ النَّارُ وَهُمْ فِيْهَا كٰلِحُوْنَ ﴿١٠٥﴾

105. The Fire will burn their faces and they will grin therein *in agony.*

109. *God* will say, "Away with you, despised therein, and speak not unto Me.

قَالَ اخْسَـُٔوْا فِيْهَا وَلَا تُكَلِّمُوْنِ ﴿١٠٩﴾

109. *God* will say, **'Be lost therein and speak not to Me'.**

117. Exalted then be Allah, the True King. There is no God but He, the Lord of the Glorious Throne.

فَتَعٰلَى اللّٰهُ الْمَلِكُ الْحَقُّ ۚ لَآ اِلٰهَ اِلَّا هُوَ ۚ رَبُّ الْعَرْشِ الْكَرِيْمِ ﴿١١٧﴾

117. Exalted then be Allah, **the Rightful Sovereign,** There is no god but He, the Lord of the Glorious Throne.

AL-NUR

3.
And let not pity for the twain take hold of you in *executing* the judgment of Allah, if you believe in Allah and the Last Day. And let a party of the believers witness their punishment.

وَلَا تَأْخُذْكُم بِهِمَا رَأْفَةٌ فِي دِينِ اللَّهِ إِن
كُنتُمْ تُؤْمِنُونَ بِاللَّهِ وَالْيَوْمِ الْآخِرِ وَلْيَشْهَدْ عَذَابَهُمَا
طَائِفَةٌ مِّنَ الْمُؤْمِنِينَ ③

3. And let not pity for the twain take hold of you **regarding the *execution of the* divine law,** if you believe in Allah and the Last Day. And let a party of the believers witness their punishment.

16. When you received it *and then talked about it* with your tongues, and you uttered with your mouths that of which you had no knowledge, and you thought it to be a light matter, while in the sight of Allah it was *a* grievous *thing*.

إِذْ تَلَقَّوْنَهُ بِأَلْسِنَتِكُمْ وَتَقُولُونَ بِأَفْوَاهِكُم مَّا لَيْسَ
لَكُم بِهِ عِلْمٌ وَتَحْسَبُونَهُ هَيِّنًا وَهُوَ عِندَ اللَّهِ
عَظِيمٌ ⑯

16. **When you pick up the word spread by your tongues and start uttering with your mouths *that* of which you have no real knowledge and consider it to be of no significance, whereas in the sight of Allah it is an enormity.**

23. forgive and pass over *the offence*.

وَلْيَعْفُوا وَلْيَصْفَحُوا

23. Let them forgive and **forbear.**

32. And say to the believing women that they restrain their eyes and guard their private parts, and that they disclose not their *natural and artificial* beauty except that which is apparent thereof, and that they draw their head-coverings over their bosoms, and that they disclose not their beauty save to their husbands, or to their fathers, or the fathers of their husbands or

وَقُل لِّلْمُؤْمِنَاتِ يَغْضُضْنَ مِنْ أَبْصَارِهِنَّ وَيَحْفَظْنَ
فُرُوجَهُنَّ وَلَا يُبْدِينَ زِينَتَهُنَّ إِلَّا مَا ظَهَرَ مِنْهَا
وَلْيَضْرِبْنَ بِخُمُرِهِنَّ عَلَىٰ جُيُوبِهِنَّ وَلَا يُبْدِينَ
زِينَتَهُنَّ إِلَّا لِبُعُولَتِهِنَّ أَوْ آبَائِهِنَّ أَوْ آبَاءِ بُعُولَتِهِنَّ

their sons or the sons of their husbands or their brothers, or the sons of their brothers, or the sons of their sisters, or their women, or what their right hands possess, or such of male attendants as have no sexual appetite, or young children who have no knowledge of the hidden parts of women. And they strike not their feet so that what they hide of their ornaments may become known. And turn ye to Allah all together, O believers, that you may succeed.

اَوْ اَبْنَآئِهِنَّ اَوْ اَبْنَآءِ بُعُوْلَتِهِنَّ اَوْ اِخْوَانِهِنَّ اَوْ
بَنِيْٓ اِخْوَانِهِنَّ اَوْ بَنِيْٓ اَخَوٰتِهِنَّ اَوْ نِسَآئِهِنَّ اَوْ مَا
مَلَكَتْ اَيْمَانُهُنَّ اَوِ التّٰبِعِيْنَ غَيْرِ اُولِي الْاِرْبَةِ
مِنَ الرِّجَالِ اَوِ الطِّفْلِ الَّذِيْنَ لَمْ يَظْهَرُوْا عَلٰى عَوْرٰتِ
النِّسَآءِ ۪ وَلَا يَضْرِبْنَ بِاَرْجُلِهِنَّ لِيُعْلَمَ مَا يُخْفِيْنَ
مِنْ زِيْنَتِهِنَّ ؕ وَتُوْبُوْٓا اِلَى اللّٰهِ جَمِيْعًا اَيُّهَ الْمُؤْمِنُوْنَ
لَعَلَّكُمْ تُفْلِحُوْنَ ﴿٣٢﴾

32. And say to the believing women that they restrain their eyes and guard their private parts, **and they not display their beauty and embellishments except that which is apparent thereof,** and that they draw their headcovers over their bosoms, **and they not display their beauty and embellishments thereof** save to their husbands, or to their fathers, or the fathers of their husbands, or their sons or the sons of their husbands' , or their brothers, or the sons of their brothers, or the sons of their sisters, or their women, or what their right hands possess, or such of male attendants **who have no wickedness in them,** or young children **who have not yet attained any concept of the private parts of women. And they walk not in a style that such of their beauty as they conceal is noticed.** And turn **you** to Allah altogether, O believers, that you may succeed.

34. And those who find no *means of* marriage should keep themselves chaste, until Allah grants them means out of His bounty. And such as desire *a deed of manumission in* writing from among those whom your right hands possess, write it for them if you know any good in them;

وَلْيَسْتَعْفِفِ الَّذِيْنَ لَا يَجِدُوْنَ نِكَاحًا حَتّٰى يُغْنِيَهُمُ
اللّٰهُ مِنْ فَضْلِهٖ ؕ وَالَّذِيْنَ يَبْتَغُوْنَ الْكِتٰبَ مِمَّا مَلَكَتْ
اَيْمَانُكُمْ فَكَاتِبُوْهُمْ اِنْ عَلِمْتُمْ فِيْهِمْ خَيْرًا ۖ وَّاٰتُوْهُمْ

and give them out of the wealth of Allah which He has bestowed upon you.

مِّن مَّالِ اللّٰهِ الَّذِيٓ اٰتٰىكُمْ

34. And those who find no *means of* marriage should keep themselves chaste, until Allah grants them means out of His bounty. **And those of your slaves who desire a deed of liberation to be contracted, write it down for them if you see in them any good *potential* and give them out of that wealth which *truly* belongs to Allah which He has bestowed upon you.**

37. Therein is He glorified in the mornings and the evenings

يُسَبِّحُ لَهٗ فِيْهَا بِالْغُدُوِّ وَالْاٰصَالِ ﴿۳۷﴾

37. Glorify Him therein in the mornings and the evenings;

38. *By* men, whom neither merchandise nor traffic diverts from the remembrance of Allah and the observance of Prayer, and the giving of the Zakāt.

رِجَالٌ ۙ لَّا تُلْهِيْهِمْ تِجَارَةٌ وَّلَا بَيْعٌ عَنْ ذِكْرِ اللّٰهِ وَاِقَامِ الصَّلٰوةِ وَاِيْتَآءِ الزَّكٰوةِ

38. **Men whom neither trade nor commerce makes oblivious of the remembrance of Allah** and the observance of Prayer, and the giving of the Zakat.

40. And *as to* those who disbelieve, their deeds are like a mirage in a desert. The thirsty one thinks it to be water until, when he comes up to it, he finds it to be nothing. And he finds Allah near him, Who then fully pays him his account; and Allah is swift at reckoning.

وَالَّذِيْنَ كَفَرُوْٓا اَعْمَالُهُمْ كَسَرَابٍۭ بِقِيْعَةٍ يَّحْسَبُهُ الظَّمْاٰنُ مَآءً ۗ حَتّٰٓى اِذَا جَآءَهٗ لَمْ يَجِدْهُ شَيْـًٔا وَّوَجَدَ اللّٰهَ عِنْدَهٗ فَوَفّٰىهُ حِسَابَهٗ ۗ وَاللّٰهُ سَرِيْعُ الْحِسَابِ ﴿۴۰﴾

40. And *as to* those who disbelieve, their deeds are like a mirage in a desert. **One who is thirsty considers it to be water** until, when he **comes up to it,** he finds it to be nothing. **And he finds**

Allah to be there Who pays him his account; and Allah is swift at reckoning.

46. And Allah has created every animal from water. Of them are *some* that go upon their bellies, and of them are *some* that go upon two feet, and among them are *some* that go upon four.

وَاللّٰهُ خَلَقَ كُلَّ دَآبَّةٍ مِّنْ مَّآءٍ ۚ فَمِنْهُمْ مَّنْ يَّمْشِيْ
عَلٰى بَطْنِهٖ ۚ وَمِنْهُمْ مَّنْ يَّمْشِيْ عَلٰى رِجْلَيْنِ ۚ وَمِنْهُمْ مَّنْ
يَّمْشِيْ عَلٰٓى اَرْبَعٍ ؕ

46. And Allah has created every animal from water. Of them are some **that crawl upon their bellies,** and of them are *some* that go upon two feet, and among them are *some* that go upon four.

55. Say, 'Obey Allah, and obey the Messenger.' But if you turn away, then upon him is his burden, and upon you is your burden. And if you obey him, you will be rightly guided.

قُلْ اَطِيْعُوا اللّٰهَ وَاَطِيْعُوا الرَّسُوْلَ ۚ فَاِنْ تَوَلَّوْا فَاِنَّمَا
عَلَيْهِ مَا حُمِّلَ وَعَلَيْكُمْ مَّا حُمِّلْتُمْ ؕ وَاِنْ تُطِيْعُوْهُ
تَهْتَدُوْا ؕ

55. Say, 'Obey Allah, and obey the Messenger.' **And if they turn away then *remember, whoever does so* will be held responsible for that reposed in him, as also you will be held responsible for that which is reposed in you.** And if you obey him, you will be rightly guided.

61. *As to* elderly women, who have no desire for marriage—there is no blame on them if they lay aside their *outer* clothing without displaying their beauty. But to abstain *from that even* is better for them. And Allah is All-Hearing, All-Knowing.

وَالْقَوَاعِدُ مِنَ النِّسَآءِ الّٰتِيْ لَا يَرْجُوْنَ نِكَاحًا
فَلَيْسَ عَلَيْهِنَّ جُنَاحٌ اَنْ يَّضَعْنَ ثِيَابَهُنَّ غَيْرَ
مُتَبَرِّجٰتٍۭ بِزِيْنَةٍ ؕ وَاَنْ يَّسْتَعْفِفْنَ خَيْرٌ لَّهُنَّ ؕ
وَاللّٰهُ سَمِيْعٌ عَلِيْمٌ ﴿٦١﴾

61. ***As to* elderly women, who are past marriagable age, there is no blame on them if they lay aside their outer garments but do not deliberately display their charms. And if they prefer to exercise more caution *to guard their purity* it is even better for them.** And Allah is All-Hearing, All-Knowing.

63. Those only are *true* believers who believe in Allah and His Messenger, and who, when they are with him on some matter *of common importance* which has brought *them* together, go not away until they have asked leave of him. Surely those who ask leave of thee, it is they who *really* **believe in Allah and His Messenger. So, when they ask thy leave for some affair of theirs, give leave to those of them whom thou pleasest, and ask forgiveness for them of Allah. Surely, Allah is Most Forgiving, Merciful.**

إِنَّمَا الْمُؤْمِنُونَ الَّذِينَ آمَنُوا بِاللّٰهِ وَرَسُولِهِ وَإِذَا
كَانُوا مَعَهُ عَلَىٰ أَمْرٍ جَامِعٍ لَّمْ يَذْهَبُوا حَتَّىٰ يَسْتَأْذِنُوهُ
إِنَّ الَّذِينَ يَسْتَأْذِنُونَكَ أُولَٰئِكَ الَّذِينَ يُؤْمِنُونَ
بِاللّٰهِ وَرَسُولِهِ ۚ فَإِذَا اسْتَأْذَنُوكَ لِبَعْضِ شَأْنِهِمْ
فَأْذَن لِّمَن شِئْتَ مِنْهُمْ وَاسْتَغْفِرْ لَهُمُ اللّٰهَ ۚ إِنَّ
اللّٰهَ غَفُورٌ رَّحِيمٌ ﴿٦٣﴾

63. **Verily, the true believers are only those who believe in Allah and His Messenger and do not leave without seeking permission from him when they are with him on some matter of collective importance. Surely, those who ask leave of you, it is they who** *really* believe in Allah and His Messenger. So, when they ask your leave for some affair of theirs, give leave to those of them whom you please, and ask forgiveness of Allah for them. Surely Allah is Most Forgiving, Merciful.

65. Hearken ye! To Allah belongs whatsoever is in the heavens and the earth. He does know in what condition you are. And on the day when they will be returned unto Him, He will inform them of what they did. And Allah knows everything full well.

أَلَا إِنَّ لِلّٰهِ مَا فِي السَّمٰوٰتِ وَالْأَرْضِ ۖ قَدْ يَعْلَمُ مَا أَنتُمْ
عَلَيْهِ وَيَوْمَ يُرْجَعُونَ إِلَيْهِ فَيُنَبِّئُهُم بِمَا عَمِلُوا ۗ وَاللّٰهُ
بِكُلِّ شَيْءٍ عَلِيمٌ ﴿٦٥﴾

65. Hearken ye! To Allah belongs whatsoever is in the heavens and the earth. **Verily, He knows what you are.** And on the day when they will be returned to Him, He will inform them of what they did. And Allah knows everything full well.

AL-FURQAN

وَقَدِمْنَآ إِلَىٰ مَا عَمِلُوا۟ مِنْ عَمَلٍ فَجَعَلْنَٰهُ هَبَآءً
مَّنثُورًا ﴿٢٤﴾

24. And We shall turn to the works they did and We shall scatter it into particles of dust.

24. And We will turn to each of their deeds that they performed and render it into scattered particles of dust.

وَيَوْمَ يَعَضُّ ٱلظَّالِمُ عَلَىٰ يَدَيْهِ يَقُولُ يَٰلَيْتَنِى ٱتَّخَذْتُ
مَعَ ٱلرَّسُولِ سَبِيلًا ﴿٢٨﴾

28. *Remember* the day when the wrong-doer will bite his hands; he will say, 'O, would that I had taken *the same* way with the Messenger!

28. *Beware of* the day when the wrongdoer will gnaw at his hands *in utter helplessness;* he will say 'Would, that I had trodden the same path along-with the Messenger'.

وَكُلًّا ضَرَبْنَا لَهُ ٱلْأَمْثَالَ ۖ وَكُلًّا تَبَّرْنَا تَتْبِيرًا ﴿٤٠﴾

40. And to each one We set forth *clear* similitudes; and each one We completely destroyed.

40. And to each of them We related the examples *of earlier people;* and one and all We utterly destroyed.

وَلَقَدْ أَتَوْا۟ عَلَى ٱلْقَرْيَةِ ٱلَّتِىٓ أُمْطِرَتْ مَطَرَ ٱلسَّوْءِ ۚ
أَفَلَمْ يَكُونُوا۟ يَرَوْنَهَا ۚ بَلْ كَانُوا۟ لَا يَرْجُونَ نُشُورًا ﴿٤١﴾

41. And these (Meccans) must have visited the town whereon was rained an evil rain. Have they not then seen it? Nay, they hope not to be raised *after death*.

41. And these must have visited the town **on which** was rained an evil rain. Have they not then seen it? Nay, they hope not to be raised *after death.*

فَلَا تُطِعِ ٱلْكَٰفِرِينَ وَجَٰهِدْهُم بِهِۦ جِهَادًا كَبِيرًا ﴿٥٣﴾

53. So obey not the disbelievers and fight against them by means of it (the Qur'ān) a great fight.

53. So obey not the disbelievers and **strive against them with it** (*the Qur'an*) **a great striving.**

56. And they worship beside Allah that which can do them no good nor harm them. And the disbeliever is a helper of Satan against his Lord.

وَيَعْبُدُوْنَ مِنْ دُوْنِ اللّٰهِ مَا لَا يَنْفَعُهُمْ وَ لَا يَضُرُّهُمْ ۗ وَكَانَ الْكَافِرُ عَلٰى رَبِّهٖ ظَهِيْرًا ﴿٥٦﴾

56. And they worship beside Allah that which can do them no good nor harm them. **And the disbeliever always works** ***in support of those who strive*** **against his Lord.**

60. The Gracious *God!* Ask thou then concerning Him one who knows.

اَلرَّحْمٰنُ فَسْـَٔلْ بِهٖ خَبِيْرًا ﴿٦٠﴾

60. The Most Gracious, **enquire from Him as the one well informed.**

62. Blessed is He Who has made mansions in the heaven and has placed therein a Lamp and a Moon giving light.

تَبٰرَكَ الَّذِيْ جَعَلَ فِي السَّمَآءِ بُرُوْجًا وَّجَعَلَ فِيْهَا سِرٰجًا وَّقَمَرًا مُّنِيْرًا ﴿٦٢﴾

62. Blessed is He **Who made constellations in the heavens and has placed therein the sun and moon** ***both*** **luminous.**

69. nor commit adultery (or fornication), and he who does that shall meet with the punishment of sin.

وَلَا يَزْنُوْنَ ۚ وَمَنْ يَّفْعَلْ ذٰلِكَ يَلْقَ اَثَامًا ﴿٦٩﴾

69. nor commit **fornication** and he who does that shall meet with the punishment of sin.

75. And those who say, 'Our Lord, grant us of our wives and children the delight of *our* eyes, and make us a model for the righteous.'

وَالَّذِيْنَ يَقُوْلُوْنَ رَبَّنَا هَبْ لَنَا مِنْ اَزْوَاجِنَا وَذُرِّيّٰتِنَا قُرَّةَ اَعْيُنٍ وَّاجْعَلْنَا لِلْمُتَّقِيْنَ اِمَامًا ﴿٧٥﴾

75. And those who say, 'Our Lord, grant us of our **spouses and children the delight of our eyes and make *each of* us a leader of the righteous.'**

76. It is such as will be rewarded a high place *in Paradise* because they were steadfast, and they will be received therein with greeting and peace,

أُولَٰٓئِكَ يُجْزَوْنَ ٱلْغُرْفَةَ بِمَا صَبَرُوا۟ وَيُلَقَّوْنَ فِيهَا تَحِيَّةً وَسَلَٰمًا ﴿٧٦﴾

76. It is such as will be rewarded **a lofty station *in Paradise*** because they were steadfast, and they will be received therein with greeting and peace.

AL-SHUARA

15. 'And they have a charge against me, so I fear that they may kill me.'

وَلَهُمْ عَلَىَّ ذَنۢبٌ فَأَخَافُ أَن يَقْتُلُونِ ﴿١٥﴾

15. **'And I am wanted by them for some *alleged* offence,** so I fear that they may kill me.'

22. 'So I fled from you when I feared you; then my Lord granted me *right* judgment and made me *one* of the Messengers.

فَفَرَرْتُ مِنكُمْ لَمَّا خِفْتُكُمْ فَوَهَبَ لِى رَبِّى حُكْمًا وَجَعَلَنِى مِنَ ٱلْمُرْسَلِينَ ﴿٢٢﴾

22. 'So I fled from you when I feared you, then my Lord granted me **authority and wisdom** and made me (one) of the Messengers.

43. He said, 'Yes, and surely then you will be among those who are near *my person*.'

قَالَ نَعَمْ وَإِنَّكُمْ إِذًا لَّمِنَ ٱلْمُقَرَّبِينَ ﴿٤٢﴾

43. He said, 'Yes, and surely then you will be among **the favoured ones'.**

65. And We made others approach that place.

وَأَزْلَفْنَا ثَمَّ ٱلْءَاخَرِينَ ﴿٦٥﴾

65. And We **let** others approach that place.

73. He said, 'Can they listen to you when you call *on them?*

قَالَ هَلْ يَسْمَعُونَكُمْ إِذْ تَدْعُونَ ﴿٧٣﴾

73. He said, 'Can they listen to you **when you call them?'**

80. 'And Who gives me food and gives me drink;

وَالَّذِي هُوَ يُطْعِمُنِي وَيَسْقِينِ ﴿٨٠﴾

80. 'And Who **feeds** me and **provides** **me with** drink;

90. 'But he *alone will be saved* who brings to Allah a sound heart;'

إِلَّا مَنْ أَتَى اللَّهَ بِقَلْبٍ سَلِيمٍ ﴿٩٠﴾

90. 'But he *alone will be saved* who **comes to Allah with a submissive heart.**

92. And Hell shall be opened to those who have gone astray.

وَبُرِّزَتِ الْجَحِيمُ لِلْغَاوِينَ ﴿٩٢﴾

92. And Hell shall be **brought into full view of those gone astray.**

126. 'Surely, I am unto you a Messenger, faithful to *my* trust.

إِنِّي لَكُمْ رَسُولٌ أَمِينٌ ﴿١٢٦﴾

126. 'Surely, I am to you a Messenger, **entirely trustworthy.**

130. 'And do you erect palaces as though you will live for ever?

وَتَتَّخِذُونَ مَصَانِعَ لَعَلَّكُمْ تَخْلُدُونَ ﴿١٣٠﴾

130. 'And you **build fortresses and develop industry so that you may last** forever.'

136. 'Indeed, I fear for you the punishment of an awful day.'

إِنِّي أَخَافُ عَلَيْكُمْ عَذَابَ يَوْمٍ عَظِيمٍ ﴿١٣٦﴾

136. 'Indeed, I fear for you the punishment of an **enormous** day.'

إِنِّي لَكُمْ رَسُولٌ أَمِينٌ ﴿١٤٣﴾

144. 'Surely, I am unto you a Messenger, faithful to *my* trust.

144. 'Surely, I am **to** you a Messenger, **entirely trustworthy.**

وَزُرُوعٍ وَنَخْلٍ طَلْعُهَا هَضِيمٌ ﴿١٤٩﴾

149. 'And cornfields, and date-palms with *heavy* spathes near breaking?

149. 'And **fields of grain** and date-palms **their spathes heavy to the point of breaking?**

وَلَا تَمَسُّوهَا بِسُوٓءٍ فَيَأْخُذَكُمْ عَذَابُ يَوْمٍ عَظِيمٍ ﴿١٥٦﴾

157. 'And touch her not with evil lest there overtake you the punishment of an awful day.'

157. 'And touch her not with evil lest there overtake you the punishment of an **enormous day.'**

إِنِّي لَكُمْ رَسُولٌ أَمِينٌ ﴿١٦٢﴾

163. 'Surely, I am unto you a Messenger, faithful to *my* trust.

163. 'Surely, I am **to** you a Messenger, **entirely trustworthy.**

قَالَ إِنِّي لِعَمَلِكُم مِّنَ الْقَالِينَ ﴿١٦٩﴾

169. He said, 'Certainly I hate your practice.

169. He said, 'I **abhor** your ***evil*** practice.'

وَأَمْطَرْنَا عَلَيْهِم مَّطَرًا فَسَآءَ مَطَرُ الْمُنذَرِينَ ﴿١٧٤﴾

174. And We rained upon them a rain; and evil was the rain for those who were warned.

174. And We rained upon them a rain; and evil **is** the rain **which descends on those who are warned.**

إِنِّي لَكُمْ رَسُولٌ أَمِينٌ ﴿١٧٩﴾

179. 'Surely, I am unto you a Messenger, faithful to *my* trust.'

179. 'Surely, I am **to** you a Messenger, **entirely trustworthy.**

183. 'And weigh with a true balance,

وَزِنُوا بِالْقِسْطَاسِ الْمُسْتَقِيمِ ﴿١٨٣﴾

183. 'And weigh with **an even** balance.

184. 'And diminish not unto people their things, nor act corruptly in the earth, making mischief.

وَلَا تَبْخَسُوا النَّاسَ أَشْيَاءَهُمْ وَلَا تَعْثَوْا فِي الْأَرْضِ مُفْسِدِينَ ﴿١٨٤﴾

184. "And **do not pay people less than the true value of things,** nor act corruptly in the earth, making mischief.

185. 'And fear Him Who created you and the earlier peoples.'

وَاتَّقُوا الَّذِي خَلَقَكُمْ وَالْجِبِلَّةَ الْأَوَّلِينَ ﴿١٨٥﴾

185. 'And fear Him Who created you and the **creatures of earlier make.'**

199. And if We had sent it down to one of the non-Arabs,

وَلَوْ نَزَّلْنَاهُ عَلَىٰ بَعْضِ الْأَعْجَمِينَ ﴿١٩٩﴾

199. And **had We revealed it to a non-Arab.**

200. And he had read it to them, *even then* they would never have believed in it.

فَقَرَأَهُ عَلَيْهِمْ مَا كَانُوا بِهِ مُؤْمِنِينَ ﴿٢٠٠﴾

200. And he had read it **out** to them, they would never have believed in it.

212. They are not fit for it, nor have they the power *to do so.*

وَمَا يَنْبَغِي لَهُمْ وَمَا يَسْتَطِيعُونَ ﴿٢١٢﴾

212. They are **neither worthy of it nor capable of doing so.**

AL-NAML

13. 'And put thy hand into thy bosom; it will come forth white without any disease. *This is* among the nine Signs unto Pharaoh and his people; for they are a rebellious people.'

وَأَدْخِلْ يَدَكَ فِي جَيْبِكَ تَخْرُجْ بَيْضَاءَ مِنْ غَيْرِ سُوءٍ فِي تِسْعِ آيَاتٍ إِلَىٰ فِرْعَوْنَ وَقَوْمِهِ إِنَّهُمْ كَانُوا قَوْمًا فَاسِقِينَ ﴿١٣﴾

13. 'And **insert your** hand **into your bosom under your garment,** it will come forth white, **without blemish.** *This is* among the nine Signs unto Pharaoh and his people; for they are a rebellious people.

19. Until when they came to the Valley of Al-Naml, one woman *of the tribe* of the Naml said, 'O ye Naml, enter your habitations, lest Solomon and his hosts crush you, while they know not.'

حَتّٰۤى اِذَاۤ اَتَوْا عَلٰى وَادِ النَّمْلِ ۙ قَالَتْ نَمْلَةٌ يّٰۤاَيُّهَا
النَّمْلُ ادْخُلُوْا مَسٰكِنَكُمْ ۚ لَا يَحْطِمَنَّكُمْ سُلَيْمٰنُ
وَجُنُوْدُهٗ ۙ وَهُمْ لَا يَشْعُرُوْنَ ﴿١٩﴾

19. Until when they came to the Valley of Al-Naml, a **Namlite woman said,** 'O ye Naml enter your habitations, lest Solomon and his hosts crush you, while they know not.'

20. Thereupon he smiled, laughing at her words, and said, 'My Lord, grant me *the will and power* to be grateful for Thy favour which Thou hast bestowed upon me and upon my parents, and to do *such* good works as would please Thee, and admit me, by Thy mercy, among Thy righteous servants.'

فَتَبَسَّمَ ضَاحِكًا مِّنْ قَوْلِهَا وَقَالَ رَبِّ اَوْزِعْنِيْۤ
اَنْ اَشْكُرَ نِعْمَتَكَ الَّتِيْۤ اَنْعَمْتَ عَلَيَّ وَعَلٰى وَالِدَيَّ
وَاَنْ اَعْمَلَ صَالِحًا تَرْضٰىهُ وَاَدْخِلْنِيْ بِرَحْمَتِكَ
فِيْ عِبَادِكَ الصّٰلِحِيْنَ ﴿٢٠﴾

20. Thereupon he smiled, laughing at her words, and said 'My Lord, **enable me to be grateful** for **Your** favour which **You have** bestowed upon me and upon my parents, and to do *such* good works as would please **You,** and admit me, by **Your** mercy, among **Your** righteous servants.'

21. And he reviewed the birds, and said, 'How is it that I do not see Hudhud? Is he among the absentees?

وَتَفَقَّدَ الطَّيْرَ فَقَالَ مَا لِيَ لَاۤ اَرَى الْهُدْهُدَ ۖ
اَمْ كَانَ مِنَ الْغَآئِبِيْنَ ﴿٢١﴾

21. And he **examined** the birds, and said, 'How is it that I do not see Hudhud? Is he among the absentees?

22. 'I will surely punish him with a severe punishment or I will slay him, unless he bring me a clear reason *for his absence*.'

لَأُعَذِّبَنَّهُ عَذَابًا شَدِيدًا أَوْ لَأَاذْبَحَنَّهُ أَوْ لَيَأْتِيَنِّي بِسُلْطَانٍ مُّبِينٍ ﴿٢٢﴾

22. 'I will **subject him to severe punishment** or I will slay him, unless he brings me a clear reason for *his absence.'*

34. They replied, 'We possess power and we possess great prowess in war, but it is for thee to command; therefore consider thou what thou wilt command.'

قَالُوا نَحْنُ أُولُوا قُوَّةٍ وَّأُولُوا بَأْسٍ شَدِيدٍ ۙ وَّالْأَمْرُ إِلَيْكِ فَانْظُرِي مَاذَا تَأْمُرِينَ ﴿٣٤﴾

34. They replied, 'We possess power and **we are fierce fighters,** but it is for **You** to command; therefore consider **you** what **you will** command'.

39. He said, 'O nobles, which of you will bring me a throne for her before they come to me, submitting?'

قَالَ يَٰٓأَيُّهَا الْمَلَؤُا أَيُّكُمْ يَأْتِينِي بِعَرْشِهَا قَبْلَ أَنْ يَّأْتُونِي مُسْلِمِينَ ﴿٣٩﴾

39. He said, 'O nobles, which of you will bring me **her throne** before they come to me **offering submission?'**

Note: From the following verses, it becomes clear that Solomon does not refer to her throne itself. He either means a throne very similar to her's should be manufactured or that a very faithful replica of her throne should be brought to him. Before her intended visit to the court of Solomon, she is given the surprise of finding a throne very similar to her own but in the possession of Solomon. From the verses which follow, the scenario that emerges clearly indicates that each of the nobles of his court wanted the task to be assigned to him, each boasting to perform the task quicker and better than his rivals. Ultimately, when the replica was first presented to him, he praised God for it and issued instructions to modify it further so that it might resemble the Queen of Saba's throne ever more closely and so deflate her pride in possessing a unique throne. The expression *nakkeroo laha Arshaha* (نكّروا لها عرشها) clearly supports this meaning and implies that if we saw a throne very similar to her own, she would naturally infer that her own throne was not as unique and special as she thought it was. So the meaning of *nakkeroo*(نكّروا) in this context would make her throne seem common looking. When she actually saw the throne built by Solomon's craftsmen, her response was not that of a Queen who only recently had her own throne stolen, nor that of a Queen who could not recognise her own throne because the craftsmen had worked on it to render it unrecognisable. Her response is simply that of a person who finds an article similar to her own. This clearly proves that the scenario we have visualised is more realistic.

41. Said one who had knowledge of the Book, 'I will bring it to thee before thy noble *messengers* return to thee.' And when he saw it set before him, he said, 'This is by the grace of my Lord, that He may try me whether I am grateful or ungrateful.

قَالَ الَّذِي عِنْدَهُ عِلْمٌ مِّنَ الْكِتٰبِ اَنَا اٰتِيْكَ بِهٖ قَبْلَ اَنْ يَّرْتَدَّ اِلَيْكَ طَرْفُكَ فَلَمَّا رَاٰهُ مُسْتَقِرًّا عِنْدَهٗ قَالَ هٰذَا مِنْ فَضْلِ رَبِّيْ لِيَبْلُوَنِيْٓ ءَاَشْكُرُ اَمْ اَكْفُرُ

41. Said one who had knowledge of the Book, 'I will bring it to **you quicker than the blinking of your eye.** And when he saw it set before him, he said, 'This is by the grace of my Lord, that He may try me whether I am grateful or ungrateful.

42. He said, 'Make her throne unrecognizable to her,

قَالَ نَكِّرُوْا لَهَا عَرْشَهَا

42. Make her Throne **appear commonplace to her,**

45. It was said to her, 'Enter the palace.' And when she saw it, she thought it to be a great expanse of water, and she uncovered her shanks. *Solomon* said, 'It is a palace paved smooth with slabs of glass.' She said, 'My Lord, I indeed wronged my soul; and I submit myself with Solomon to Allah, the Lord of the worlds.'

قِيْلَ لَهَا ادْخُلِي الصَّرْحَ فَلَمَّا رَاَتْهُ حَسِبَتْهُ لُجَّةً وَّكَشَفَتْ عَنْ سَاقَيْهَا قَالَ اِنَّهٗ صَرْحٌ مُّمَرَّدٌ مِّنْ قَوَارِيْرَ قَالَتْ رَبِّ اِنِّيْ ظَلَمْتُ نَفْسِيْ وَاَسْلَمْتُ مَعَ سُلَيْمٰنَ لِلّٰهِ رَبِّ الْعٰلَمِيْنَ ﴿٤٥﴾

Note: Clear, high-quality glass, deftly laid, can create the impression of water and that is what actually happened. The message delivered to the Queen, who was exceptionally intelligent, was that sometimes things are very different from the impressions they create, and the qualities they reflect, do not belong to them. Similarly, the impression of glory and power created by the sun, does not belong to it but belongs only to the Creator.

48. They said, 'We auger evil from thee and from those that are with thee.' He said, '*The cause of* your evil fortune is with Allah. Nay, but you are a people who are on trial.'

قَالُوا اطَّيَّرْنَا بِكَ وَبِمَنْ مَّعَكَ ۚ قَالَ طٰٓئِرُكُمْ عِنْدَ
اللّٰهِ بَلْ اَنْتُمْ قَوْمٌ تُفْتَنُوْنَ ﴿۴۸﴾

48. They said, **'We augur ill of you and of those** that are with **you'.** He said, '*the cause of* your evil fortune is with Allah. Nay, but you are a people who are on trial'.

51. And they planned a plan, and We planned a plan, but they perceived *it* not.

وَمَكَرُوْا مَكْرًا وَّمَكَرْنَا مَكْرًا وَّهُمْ لَا يَشْعُرُوْنَ ﴿۵۱﴾

51. And they **wove a plot** and We **wove** a ***counter*** **plot** but they **were unaware of it.**

53. And yonder are their houses empty, because of their wrongdoing. In that, verily, is a Sign for a people who possess knowledge.

فَتِلْكَ بُيُوْتُهُمْ خَاوِيَةًۢ بِمَا ظَلَمُوْا ؕ اِنَّ فِيْ ذٰلِكَ
لَاٰيَةً لِّقَوْمٍ يَّعْلَمُوْنَ ﴿۵۳﴾

53. And yonder **lie** their houses empty, because of their wrongdoing. In that, verily, is a Sign for a people who possess knowledge.

56. 'What! do you approach men lustfully rather than women? Nay, you are indeed an ignorant people.'

اَئِنَّكُمْ لَتَاْتُوْنَ الرِّجَالَ شَهْوَةً مِّنْ دُوْنِ النِّسَآءِ ؕ
بَلْ اَنْتُمْ قَوْمٌ تَجْهَلُوْنَ ﴿۵۶﴾

56. 'What! Do you approach men lustfully rather than women? Nay, you are indeed **a people unmindful of consequences.'**

57. But the answer of his people was naught save that they said, 'Drive out Lot's family from your city. They are a people who would keep clean.'

فَمَا كَانَ جَوَابَ قَوْمِهٖٓ اِلَّآ اَنْ قَالُوْٓا اَخْرِجُوْٓا اٰلَ
لُوْطٍ مِّنْ قَرْيَتِكُمْ ۚ اِنَّهُمْ اُنَاسٌ يَّتَطَهَّرُوْنَ ﴿۵۷﴾

57. But the **response** of his people was **nothing except** that they ***incited the people and*** said, 'Drive out the **followers**

of Lot from your **township.** They are **indeed** a people **who pretend to be pure.'**

60. Say, 'All praise belongs to Allah, and peace be upon those servants of His whom He has chosen. Is Allah better or what they associate *with Him?*'

قُلِ الْحَمْدُ لِلّٰهِ وَسَلٰمٌ عَلٰى عِبَادِهِ الَّذِيْنَ اصْطَفٰى ؕ
آٰللّٰهُ خَيْرٌ اَمَّا يُشْرِكُوْنَ ﴿٦٠﴾

60. Say, 'All praise belongs to Allah, and peace be upon those servants of His whom He has chosen. Is Allah better or **that which** they associate *with Him?*

73. Say, 'It may be that a part of that which you would hasten on may be close behind you.'

قُلْ عَسٰۤى اَنْ يَّكُوْنَ رَدِفَ لَكُمْ بَعْضُ الَّذِيْ
تَسْتَعْجِلُوْنَ ﴿٧٣﴾

73. Say, **'It may be some of that *promised punishment,*** which you ***arrogantly*** **demand to befall you forthwith, is already at your heels.'**

82. And thou canst not guide the blind out of their error. Thou canst make only those to hear who believe in Our Signs, for they submit.

وَمَاۤ اَنْتَ بِهٰدِي الْعُمْيِ عَنْ ضَلٰلَتِهِمْ ؕ اِنْ تُسْمِعُ
اِلَّا مَنْ يُّؤْمِنُ بِاٰيٰتِنَا فَهُمْ مُّسْلِمُوْنَ ﴿٨٢﴾

82. And you cannot guide the blind out of their error. **You can only make** those **listen to you** who believe in Our Signs, so **they become obedient.**

83. And when the sentence is passed against them, We shall bring forth for them a germ out of the earth, which shall wound them because people did not believe in Our Signs.

وَاِذَا وَقَعَ الْقَوْلُ عَلَيْهِمْ اَخْرَجْنَا لَهُمْ دَآبَّةً مِّنَ
الْاَرْضِ تُكَلِّمُهُمْ ۙ اَنَّ النَّاسَ كَانُوْا بِاٰيٰتِنَا
لَا يُوْقِنُوْنَ ﴿٨٣﴾

83. And when the sentence is passed against them, We shall bring forth for them a **creature** out of the earth which shall **injure** them because people did not believe in Our Signs.

85.
'Did you reject My Signs, while you did not embrace them in your knowledge? Or what was it that you were doing?'

أَكَذَّبْتُمْ بِآيَاتِي وَلَمْ تُحِيطُوا بِهَا
عِلْمًا أَمَّاذَا كُنْتُمْ تَعْمَلُونَ ﴿٨٥﴾

85. 'Did you reject My Signs ***hastily*** **while you had not yet gained full knowledge about them?** ***If not this*** **what *else*** was it, that you were doing?'

86. And the sentence shall fall upon them because they did wrong, and they will be speechless.

وَوَقَعَ الْقَوْلُ عَلَيْهِمْ بِمَا ظَلَمُوا فَهُمْ لَا يَنْطِقُونَ ﴿٨٦﴾

86. And the sentence shall fall upon them because they did wrong, and they will **not *be able to*** **speak.**

89. And thou seest the mountains which thou thinkest to be firmly fixed, but they shall pass away like the passing of the clouds—the work of Allah Who has made everything perfect. Verily, He knows full well what you do.

وَتَرَى الْجِبَالَ تَحْسَبُهَا جَامِدَةً وَهِيَ تَمُرُّ مَرَّ
السَّحَابِ صُنْعَ اللَّهِ الَّذِي أَتْقَنَ كُلَّ شَيْءٍ إِنَّهُ خَبِيرٌ
بِمَا تَفْعَلُونَ ﴿٨٩﴾

89. And **you see** the mountains **imagining them to be stationary, while** they **are floating like the floating** of the clouds. **Such is the work of Allah, Who made everything firm and strong.** Verily, He knows full well what you do.

AL-QASAS

4. We rehearse unto thee *a portion* of the story of Moses and Pharaoh with truth, for *the benefit of* a people who would believe.

نَتْلُوا عَلَيْكَ مِنْ نَبَإِ مُوسَىٰ وَفِرْعَوْنَ بِالْحَقِّ
لِقَوْمٍ يُؤْمِنُونَ ﴿٣﴾

4. We rehearse **for you** *a portion* of the story of Moses and Pharaoh with truth, for *the benefit of* a people **who believe.**

9. And the family of Pharaoh picked him up that he might become for them an enemy and a *source of* sorrow. Verily, Pharaoh and Hāmān and their hosts were wrongdoers.

فَالْتَقَطَهُ آلُ فِرْعَوْنَ لِيَكُونَ لَهُمْ عَدُوًّا وَحَزَنًا ۗ
إِنَّ فِرْعَوْنَ وَهَامَانَ وَجُنُودَهُمَا كَانُوا خَاطِئِينَ ⑨

9. And the family of Pharaoh picked him up ***little knowing*** that he **would** become **an enemy and a source of distress for them.** Verily, Pharaoh and Haman and their hosts were wrongdoers.

11. And the heart of the mother of Moses became free *from anxiety*. She had almost disclosed *his identity*, were it not that We had strengthened her heart so that she might be of the *firm* believers.

وَأَصْبَحَ فُؤَادُ أُمِّ مُوسَىٰ فَارِغًا ۖ إِنْ كَادَتْ لَتُبْدِي
بِهِ لَوْلَا أَنْ رَبَطْنَا عَلَىٰ قَلْبِهَا لِتَكُونَ مِنَ الْمُؤْمِنِينَ ⑪

11. And the heart of the mother of Moses became free *from enxiety.* **She might have disclosed** his identity, **had We not** strengthened her heart so that she might be of the *firm* believers.

12. And she said to his sister, 'Follow him up.' So she observed him from afar; and they knew not *of her relationship*.

وَقَالَتْ لِأُخْتِهِ قُصِّيهِ ۖ فَبَصُرَتْ بِهِ عَنْ جُنُبٍ وَهُمْ
لَا يَشْعُرُونَ ⑫

12. And she said to his sister, 'follow him up'**. So she kept an eye on him** from afar **and they knew not.**

13. And We had already ordained that he shall refuse the wet nurses; so she said, 'Shall I tell you of a household who will bring him up for you and will be his sincere well-wishers?'

وَحَرَّمْنَا عَلَيْهِ الْمَرَاضِعَ مِنْ قَبْلُ فَقَالَتْ هَلْ أَدُلُّكُمْ
عَلَىٰ أَهْلِ بَيْتٍ يَكْفُلُونَهُ لَكُمْ وَهُمْ لَهُ نَاصِحُونَ ⑬

13. And We had already **made wet nurses unacceptable to him;** so she said, **'Shall I lead you to** a household who will bring him up for you and will be his sincere well-wishers?'

14. Thus did We restore him to his mother that her eye might be gladdened and that she might not grieve, and that she might know that the promise of Allah is true. But most of them know not.

فَرَدَدْنٰهُ اِلٰۤى اُمِّهٖ كَىْ تَقَرَّ عَيْنُهَا وَلَا تَحْزَنَ وَلِتَعْلَمَ
اَنَّ وَعْدَ اللّٰهِ حَقٌّ وَّلٰكِنَّ اَكْثَرَهُمْ لَا يَعْلَمُوْنَ ﴿١٤﴾

14. Thus did We restore him to his mother that her eye **might rejoice** and **she might not grieve** and that she **might** know that the promise of Allah is true. But most of them know not.

16. And he entered the city at a time when its inhabitants were in a state of heedlessness; and he found therein two men fighting—one of his own party, and the other of his enemies. And he who was of his party sought his help against him who was of his enemies. So Moses smote him with his fist; and *thereby* caused his death. He said, 'This is of Satan's doing; he is indeed an enemy, a manifest misleader.'

وَدَخَلَ الْمَدِيْنَةَ عَلٰى حِيْنِ غَفْلَةٍ مِّنْ اَهْلِهَا
فَوَجَدَ فِيْهَا رَجُلَيْنِ يَقْتَتِلٰنِ هٰذَا مِنْ شِيْعَتِهٖ
وَهٰذَا مِنْ عَدُوِّهٖ فَاسْتَغَاثَهُ الَّذِىْ مِنْ شِيْعَتِهٖ
عَلَى الَّذِىْ مِنْ عَدُوِّهٖ فَوَكَزَهٗ مُوْسٰى فَقَضٰى عَلَيْهِ
قَالَ هٰذَا مِنْ عَمَلِ الشَّيْطٰنِ اِنَّهٗ عَدُوٌّ مُّضِلٌّ مُّبِيْنٌ ﴿١٦﴾

16. And he entered the **town while people were still asleep;** and he found therein two men fighting --- one of his own **people,** and the other of his enemies. And he who was of his **people** sought his help against him who was of his enemies. So Moses **punched** him with his fist, and *thereby* caused his death. He said, 'This is of Satan's doing; he is indeed an enemy, a manifest **deceiver.'**

19. And morning found him in the city, apprehensive, watchful; and lo! he who had sought his help the day before cried out to him *again* for help. Moses said to him: 'Verily, thou art manifestly a misguided fellow.'

فَاَصْبَحَ فِى الْمَدِيْنَةِ خَآئِفًا يَّتَرَقَّبُ فَاِذَا الَّذِى
اسْتَنْصَرَهٗ بِالْاَمْسِ يَسْتَصْرِخُهٗ قَالَ لَهٗ مُوْسٰۤى
اِنَّكَ لَغَوِىٌّ مُّبِيْنٌ ﴿١٩﴾

19. And **he began his day in the town** *walking* **apprehensively,**

watchfully; and lo! He who had sought his help the day before cried out to him *again* for help. Moses said to him, **'Indeed, you are an evident transgressor.'**

25. So he watered *their flocks* for them. Then he turned aside into the shade, and said, 'My Lord, I am in need of whatever good Thou mayest send down to me.'

فَسَقٰى لَهُمَا ثُمَّ تَوَلّٰىٓ اِلَى الظِّلِّ فَقَالَ رَبِّ اِنِّيْ لِمَآ اَنْزَلْتَ اِلَيَّ مِنْ خَيْرٍ فَقِيْرٌ ۝٢٥

25. So he watered *their flocks* for them. Then he turned aside into the shade, and said, **'O my Lord, a beggar I am of whatever good Thou bestows on me.'**

29. Allah watches over what we say.'

وَاللّٰهُ عَلٰى مَا نَقُوْلُ وَكِيْلٌ ۝٢٩

29. Allah **is a Witness** over what we say.'

31.
'O Moses, verily I am, I am Allah, the Lord of the worlds.'

يٰمُوْسٰٓى اِنِّيْٓ اَنَا اللّٰهُ رَبُّ الْعٰلَمِيْنَ ۝٣١

31. 'O Moses, **surely I,** ***none but*** **I, am Allah, the Lord of the worlds.'**

39.
build me a tower, that I may have a look at the God of Moses, though I believe him to be one of the liars.'

فَاجْعَلْ لِّيْ صَرْحًا لَّعَلِّيْٓ اَطَّلِعُ اِلٰٓى اِلٰهِ مُوْسٰى وَاِنِّيْ لَاَظُنُّهٗ مِنَ الْكٰذِبِيْنَ ۝٣٩

39. build me a tower, that I may have a **glimpse** of the God of Moses, though I believe him to be one of the liars'.

48. And had it not been *for the fact* that, if an affliction should befall them because of what their hands have sent before *them*, they would say, 'Our Lord, wherefore didst Thou not send a Messenger to us that we might have followed Thy

وَلَوْلَآ اَنْ تُصِيْبَهُمْ مُّصِيْبَةٌ ۢ بِمَا قَدَّمَتْ اَيْدِيْهِمْ فَيَقُوْلُوْا رَبَّنَا لَوْلَآ اَرْسَلْتَ اِلَيْنَا رَسُوْلًا فَنَتَّبِعَ اٰيٰتِكَ وَنَكُوْنَ مِنَ الْمُؤْمِنِيْنَ ۝٤٨

Signs, and been of the believers?' *We should not have sent thee as a Messenger.*

48. And why do they not, when an affliction befalls them as a result of their own doings, say, 'Our Lord, **why did you not send your Messenger to us so that we could follow Your** Signs, **and be of those who believed?'**

Note: The answer to this question is implied and the reason why they cannot blame Allah, is because God always sends warners to people before punishing them for their misdeeds. See chapter 6 verse 132.

49. But when the truth came to them from Us, they said, 'Why has he not been given the like of what was given to Moses?' Did they not reject that which was given to Moses before? They say, 'Two *works* of sorcery—*the Torah and the Qur'ān*—that back up each other.' And they say, 'We disbelieve in all.'

فَلَمَّا جَآءَهُمُ الْحَقُّ مِنْ عِنْدِنَا قَالُوْا لَوْلَآ اُوْتِيَ
مِثْلَ مَآ اُوْتِيَ مُوْسٰى ؕ اَوَلَمْ يَكْفُرُوْا بِمَآ اُوْتِيَ مُوْسٰى
مِنْ قَبْلُ ۚ قَالُوْا سِحْرٰنِ تَظٰهَرَا ۟ وَ قَالُوْٓا اِنَّا بِكُلٍّ
كٰفِرُوْنَ ﴿۴۹﴾

49. But when the truth came to them from Us, they said, 'Why has he not been given the like of what was given to Moses?' **Had they not rejected what** was given to Moses before **they said,** ***Merely*** **two magicians helping each other'**. And they **said, 'We reject them one and all.'**

Note: Of the three main opponents of Islam --- the Jews, Christians and the idolaters --- the Jews are being addressed in this verse. This statement could only have been made by the Jews. When the Holy Qur'an says that they had rejected what was given to Moses before, it could not have meant that the people of the time of the Holy Prophet of Islam had rejected Moses.

The part of the verse comprising اِنَّا بِكُلٍّ كٰفِرُوْنَ (We reject them one and all) also means that 'we reject all those who come in the name of God with the so-called Signs'. This pinpoints the malady shared by all those who reject the Prophet of their time.

50. Say, 'Then bring a Book from Allah which is a better guide than *these* two, that I may follow it, if you are truthful.'

قُلْ فَاْتُوْا بِكِتٰبٍ مِّنْ عِنْدِ اللّٰهِ هُوَ اَهْدٰى مِنْهُمَآ
اَتَّبِعْهُ اِنْ كُنْتُمْ صٰدِقِيْنَ ﴿۵۰﴾

50. Say, 'then bring a Book from Allah which is a better guide than *these* two - ***the Torah and the Qur'an*** - that I may follow it, if you are truthful.'

67. Then all excuses will become obscure to them on that day, and they shall not *even* ask each other.

فَعَمِيَتْ عَلَيْهِمُ الْأَنْبَآءُ يَوْمَئِذٍ فَهُمْ لَا يَتَسَآءَلُوْنَ ﴿٦٧﴾

67. Then all matters will become obscure to them on that day, and they will not *even* ask each other.

72. Say, 'Tell me, if Allah make the night continue over you till the Day of Resurrection, what God is there besides Allah who could bring you light? Will you not then hearken?'

قُلْ أَرَءَيْتُمْ إِنْ جَعَلَ اللّٰهُ عَلَيْكُمُ الَّيْلَ سَرْمَدًا
إِلٰى يَوْمِ الْقِيٰمَةِ مَنْ إِلٰهٌ غَيْرُ اللّٰهِ يَأْتِيكُمْ بِضِيَآءٍ
أَفَلَا تَسْمَعُوْنَ ﴿٧٢﴾

72. Say, 'tell me, if Allah make the night continue over you till the Day of Resurrection, what **god** is there besides Allah who could bring you light? Will you not then hearken?'

73. Say, 'Tell me, if Allah make the day continue over you till the Day of Resurrection, what God is there besides Allah who could bring you a night wherein you could rest? Will you not then see?'

قُلْ أَرَءَيْتُمْ إِنْ جَعَلَ اللّٰهُ عَلَيْكُمُ النَّهَارَ سَرْمَدًا
إِلٰى يَوْمِ الْقِيٰمَةِ مَنْ إِلٰهٌ غَيْرُ اللّٰهِ يَأْتِيكُمْ بِلَيْلٍ
تَسْكُنُوْنَ فِيْهِ أَفَلَا تُبْصِرُوْنَ ﴿٧٣﴾

73. Say, 'Tell me, if Allah make the day continue over you till the Day of Resurrection, what **god** is there besides Allah who could bring you a night wherein you could rest? Will you not then see?'

77. Verily, Korah was of the people of Moses, but he behaved arrogantly towards them. And We had given him of treasures so much that his hoardings would have weighed down a party of strong men.

إِنَّ قَارُوْنَ كَانَ مِنْ قَوْمِ مُوْسٰى فَبَغٰى عَلَيْهِمْ وَاٰتَيْنٰهُ
مِنَ الْكُنُوْزِ مَآ إِنَّ مَفَاتِحَهٗ لَتَنُوْٓأُ بِالْعُصْبَةِ أُولِي
الْقُوَّةِ

77. Verily, Korah was of the people of Moses, but he behaved **like a tyrant** towards them. And We had given him of treasures so much so that **the keys thereof** would have weighed down a party of strong men.

82. Then We caused the earth to swallow him up and his dwelling; and he had no party to help him against Allah, nor was he of those who can defend themselves.

فَخَسَفْنَا بِهٖ وَبِدَارِهِ الْاَرْضَ فَمَا كَانَ لَهٗ مِنْ فِئَةٍ
يَّنْصُرُوْنَهٗ مِنْ دُوْنِ اللّٰهِ وَمَا كَانَ مِنَ الْمُنْتَصِرِيْنَ ﴿٨٢﴾

82. Then We caused the earth to swallow him up and his dwelling; and he had no party to help him against Allah, nor was he of those who **could overpower** ***Allah's decree.***

AL-ANKABUT

3. Do men think that they will be left alone because they say, 'We believe,' and that they will not be tested?

اَحَسِبَ النَّاسُ اَنْ يُّتْرَكُوْٓا اَنْ يَّقُوْلُوْٓا اٰمَنَّا وَهُمْ
لَا يُفْتَنُوْنَ ﴿٣﴾

3. Do men think that they will be left alone because they say, 'We believe,' and that they will not be **put to trial?**

7. Allah is Independent of all creatures.

اللّٰهَ لَغَنِيٌّ عَنِ الْعٰلَمِيْنَ ﴿٧﴾

7. Allah is Independent of **the entire universe.**

9. And We have enjoined on man kindness to his parents; but if they strive to make thee associate that with Me of which thou hast no knowledge, then obey them not.

وَوَصَّيْنَا الْاِنْسَانَ بِوَالِدَيْهِ حُسْنًا ۗ وَاِنْ جَاهَدٰكَ
لِتُشْرِكَ بِيْ مَا لَيْسَ لَكَ بِهٖ عِلْمٌ فَلَا تُطِعْهُمَا ۗ

9. And We have enjoined on man kindness to his parents; but if they **contend with you so that you** ***too*** **may associate partners with Me; of which**

you have no knowledge whatsoever, then obey them not.

11. Is not Allah best aware of what is in the bosom of *His* creatures?

اَوَلَيۡسَ اللّٰهُ بِاَعۡلَمَ بِمَا فِىۡ صُدُوۡرِ الۡعٰلَمِيۡنَ (١٠)

11. Is not Allah best aware of what is in the **hearts of all the people?**

14. But they shall surely bear their own burdens, and *other* burdens along with their own burdens.

وَلَيَحۡمِلُنَّ اَثۡقَالَهُمۡ وَاَثۡقَالًا مَّعَ اَثۡقَالِهِمۡ

14. But they shall surely bear their own burdens **as well as burdens other than their own.**

15. and he dwelt among them a thousand years save fifty years.

فَلَبِثَ فِيۡهِمۡ اَلۡفَ سَنَةٍ اِلَّا خَمۡسِيۡنَ عَامًا ؕ

15. and he dwelt among them **a thousand years less fifty.**

17. 'Worship Allah and fear Him. That is better for you if you understand.

اعۡبُدُوا اللّٰهَ وَاتَّقُوۡهُ ؕ

ذٰلِكُمۡ خَيۡرٌ لَّكُمۡ اِنۡ كُنۡتُمۡ تَعۡلَمُوۡنَ (١٦)

17. Worship Allah and fear Him. **That would be better for you if only you knew.**

21. He originated the creation. Then will Allah provide the latter creation.' Surely, Allah has power over all things.

بَدَاَ الۡخَلۡقَ

ثُمَّ اللّٰهُ يُنۡشِئُ النَّشۡاَةَ الۡاٰخِرَةَ ؕ اِنَّ اللّٰهَ عَلٰى كُلِّ

شَىۡءٍ قَدِيۡرٌ (٢٠)

21. He originated the creation **then Allah will raise another creation *later.*** Surely Allah has power over all things.

Note: The same scenario has been presented in another similar verse 53:48 (Al-Najm) with a slight change in the choice of a word. Instead of *aakhirah* آخرة there the word *ukhraa* (اُخری) is used. *Aakhirah* (آخرة) Can be simply translated as 'later' *ukhraa* (اُخری) means 'another'. It is obvious therefore the words *ukhraa* (اُخری) and *aakhirah* (آخرة) when combined would mean: another type of creation in a later age.

30.
And you commit abomination in your meetings!'

وَ تَأْتُوْنَ فِيْ نَادِيْكُمُ الْمُنْكَرَ

30. **And you indulge in your meeting in all that is loathsome.**

39. and thus turned them away from the path, sagacious though they were.

فَصَدَّهُمْ عَنِ السَّبِيْلِ وَ كَانُوْا مُسْتَبْصِرِيْنَ ﴿٣٩﴾

39. and thus turned them away from the path **despite their being capable of discerning *the truth.***

45. Allah created the heavens and the earth in accordance with the requirements of wisdom.

خَلَقَ اللّٰهُ السَّمٰوٰتِ وَالْاَرْضَ بِالْحَقِّ

45. Allah created the heavens and the earth **with truth.**

62. How then are they being turned away *from the truth?*

فَاَنّٰى يُؤْفَكُوْنَ ﴿٦٢﴾

62. How then are they **led astray?**

AL-RUM

31. So set thy face to *the service of* religion as one devoted *to God. And follow* the nature made by Allah—the nature in which He has created mankind. There is no altering the creation of Allah. That is the right religion. But most men know not.

فَاَقِمْ وَجْهَكَ لِلدِّيْنِ حَنِيْفًا فِطْرَتَ اللّٰهِ الَّتِيْ فَطَرَ النَّاسَ عَلَيْهَا لَا تَبْدِيْلَ لِخَلْقِ اللّٰهِ ذٰلِكَ الدِّيْنُ الْقَيِّمُ

31. **So set your face towards religion ever inclined *to truth* — *and follow* the nature of Allah after which He fashioned all mankind. There is no altering the creation of Allah. That indeed is the religion which is firmly upright and supports others to be upright.** But most men know not.

Note: Here the nature of Allah refers to His attributes. In this context it means that man has been made capable of imitating the attributes of Allah. That is the only way by which man can spiritually evolve. Evidently other animals cannot share this unique distinction of man. In other words, nearness to Allah can only be acheived if His excellent attributes are acquired. However it should be remembered that Allah is infinite while man is finite. As such man can only imitate Him within the scope of his human limitations.

وَإِذَآ أَذَقْنَا النَّاسَ رَحْمَةً فَرِحُوا بِهَا ۖ وَإِن تُصِبْهُمْ سَيِّئَةٌ بِمَا قَدَّمَتْ أَيْدِيهِمْ إِذَا هُمْ يَقْنَطُونَ ﴿٣٧﴾

37. And when We make mankind taste of mercy, they rejoice therein; but if an evil befall them because of that which their own hands have sent on, behold! they are in despair.

37. And when **We favour mankind with a taste of mercy** they rejoice therein, but if an evil befalls them because of **what their hands have earned** ***themselves*** behold! **They begin to despair.**

فَأَقِمْ وَجْهَكَ لِلدِّينِ الْقَيِّمِ مِن قَبْلِ أَن يَأْتِيَ يَوْمٌ لَّا مَرَدَّ لَهُ مِنَ اللَّهِ ۖ يَوْمَئِذٍ يَصَّدَّعُونَ ﴿٤٣﴾

44. **So set thy face to** ***the service of*** **the right religion before there comes the day from Allah for which there will be no averting. On that day** ***mankind*** **will split up** ***into parts.***

44. So set **your face towards the Religion which is upright and helps others to be upright before there** comes the day from Allah for which there will be no averting. On that day **they will fall into groups distinct from each other.**

وَلَا هُمْ يُسْتَعْتَبُونَ ﴿٥٧﴾

58. nor will they be allowed to make amends.

58. nor will they be allowed **access to** ***His*** **threshold.**

LUQMAN

29. Your creation and your resurrection are only like *the creation and resurrection of* a single soul.

مَا خَلْقُكُمْ وَلَا بَعْثُكُمْ إِلَّا كَنَفْسٍ وَاحِدَةٍ

29. Your creation and your resurrection are only like *the creation and resurrection of* a single **being.**

AL-SAJDAH

10. Then He fashioned him and breathed into him of His spirit. And He has given you ears, and eyes, and hearts. *But* little thanks do you give!

ثُمَّ سَوَّىٰهُ وَنَفَخَ فِيهِ مِن رُّوحِهِ وَجَعَلَ لَكُمُ السَّمْعَ
وَالْأَبْصَارَ وَالْأَفْئِدَةَ قَلِيلًا مَّا تَشْكُرُونَ ﴿١٠﴾

10. Then He **balanced** him and breathed into him of His spirit. And He has given you **hearing and eyes and hearts.** *But* little thanks do you give!

Note: The word *fo'aad* (فؤاد) as used in the Holy Qur'an does not only mean heart, but indicates the ultimate seat of understanding. See 28:11 (Al-Qasas), 53:12 (Al-Najm), 46:27 (Al-Ahqaf) and 14:38 (Ibrahim).

22. And most surely We will make them taste of the nearer punishment before the greater punishment, so that they may return *to Us with repentance.*

وَلَنُذِيقَنَّهُم مِّنَ الْعَذَابِ الْأَدْنَىٰ دُونَ الْعَذَابِ
الْأَكْبَرِ لَعَلَّهُمْ يَرْجِعُونَ ﴿٢٢﴾

22. And most surely We will make them taste of the **lesser** punishment before the greater punishment, so that they may return *to Us with repentance.*

AL-AHZAB

5. Allah has not made for any man two hearts in his breast; nor has He made those of your wives, from whom you keep away by calling them mothers, your *real* mothers, nor has He made your adopted sons your

مَا جَعَلَ اللَّهُ لِرَجُلٍ مِّن قَلْبَيْنِ فِي جَوْفِهِ وَمَا جَعَلَ
أَزْوَاجَكُمُ اللَّائِي تُظَاهِرُونَ مِنْهُنَّ أُمَّهَاتِكُمْ وَمَا جَعَلَ

real sons. That is *merely* a word of your mouths; but Allah speaks the truth, and He guides to the *right* path.

ادعياءكم ابناءكم ذلكم قولكم بافواهكم والله
يقول الحق وهو يهدي السبيل ⑤

5. Allah has not made for any man two hearts in his breast; nor **does He turn your wives into your mothers merely because you address them as your mothers and thereby abstain from maintaining conjugal relations, nor does He turn those whom you adopt into your real sons.** That is *merely* a word of your mouths; but Allah speaks the truth, and He guides to the *right* path.

6. Call them by *the names of* their fathers. That is more equitable in the sight of Allah. But if you know not their fathers, then they are your brothers in faith and your friends. And there is no blame on you in any mistake you may unintentionally make in this *matter*, but *what matters is* that which your hearts intend. And Allah is Most Forgiving, Merciful.

ادعوهم لاباءهم هو اقسط عند الله فان لم
تعلموا اباءهم فاخوانكم في الدين ومواليكم
وليس عليكم جناح فيما اخطاتم به ولكن ما
تعمدت قلوبكم وكان الله غفورا رحيما ⑥

6. Call them by the *names* of their fathers. That is more equitable in the sight of Allah. But if you know not their fathers, then they are your brothers in faith and your friends. And there is no blame on you **for any unintentional mistake which you committed saving that which your hearts wilfully pursued.** And Allah is Most Forgiving, Merciful.

7. The Prophet is nearer to the believers than their own selves, and his wives are *as* mothers to them. And blood-relations are nearer to one another, according to the Book of Allah, than *the rest of* the believers *from among the Helpers* as well as the

النبي اولى بالمؤمنين من انفسهم وازواجه
امهتهم واولوا الارحام بعضهم اولى ببعض
في كتب الله من المؤمنين والمهجرين الا ان

Emigrants, except that you show kindness to your friends. That *also* is written down in the Book.

تَفْعَلُوْٓا اِلٰٓى اَوْلِيٰٓئِكُمْ مَّعْرُوْفًا ۭ كَانَ ذٰلِكَ فِي الْكِتٰبِ
مَسْطُوْرًا ۝٦

7. The Prophet is nearer to the believers than their own selves, and his wives are *as* mothers to them. **And some of the blood relations are nearer to each other than others from among the believers and the Emigrants according to the Book of Allah, except for the voluntary favours you may bestow upon your special friends in a goodly manner. This is what is ingrained in the Book *of Nature*.**

11.
hearts reached to the throats, and you thought *diverse* thoughts about Allah.

بَلَغَتِ الْقُلُوْبُ الْحَنَاجِرَ وَتَظُنُّوْنَ بِاللّٰهِ الظُّنُوْنَا ۝١١

11. and your hearts **leapt to *your* throats and you entertained wayward thoughts about Allah.**

16. And truly they had already covenanted with Allah *that* they would not turn their backs. And a covenant with Allah will have to be answered for.

وَلَقَدْ كَانُوْا عَاهَدُوا اللّٰهَ مِنْ قَبْلُ لَا يُوَلُّوْنَ
الْاَدْبَارَ ۭ وَكَانَ عَهْدُ اللّٰهِ مَسْـُٔوْلًا ۝١٦

16. And truly they had already **made a covenant with Allah** *that* they would not turn their backs. And a covenant with Allah **is certainly accountable for.**

21. They think that the confederates have not gone away; and if the confederates should come *again*, they would wish to be among the nomad Arabs in the desert, asking for news about you. And if they were among you they would not fight save a little.

يَحْسَبُوْنَ الْاَحْزَابَ لَمْ يَذْهَبُوْا ۚ وَاِنْ يَّاْتِ الْاَحْزَابُ
يَوَدُّوْا لَوْ اَنَّهُمْ بَادُوْنَ فِي الْاَعْرَابِ يَسْاَلُوْنَ عَنْ
اَنْۢبَاۗىِٕكُمْ ۭ وَلَوْ كَانُوْا فِيْكُمْ مَّا قٰتَلُوْٓا اِلَّا قَلِيْلًا ۝٢١

21. They think that the ***invading* tribes have not gone away; and in case the tribes invade** *again,* **they would rather** wish to be among the nomad

Arabs in the desert, asking for news about you.

34. And stay in your houses *with dignity*, and do not show off yourselves like the showing off of the former days of ignorance, and observe Prayer, and pay the Zakāt, and obey Allah and His Messenger. Surely Allah desires to remove from you *all* uncleanness, O Members of the Household, and purify you completely.

34. And stay in your houses *with dignity,* **and do not embellish yourselves in the style of embellishment during the days of ignorance** and observe Prayer, and pay the Zakat, and obey Allah and His Messenger. Surely Allah desires to remove from you *all* uncleanness, O Members of the Household, and purify you completely.

وَقَرْنَ فِي بُيُوتِكُنَّ وَلَا تَبَرَّجْنَ تَبَرُّجَ الْجَاهِلِيَّةِ
الْأُولٰى وَأَقِمْنَ الصَّلٰوةَ وَاٰتِيْنَ الزَّكٰوةَ وَأَطِعْنَ
اللّٰهَ وَرَسُوْلَهٗ ۚ إِنَّمَا يُرِيْدُ اللّٰهُ لِيُذْهِبَ عَنْكُمُ
الرِّجْسَ أَهْلَ الْبَيْتِ وَيُطَهِّرَكُمْ تَطْهِيْرًا ﴿٣٤﴾

47. And as a Summoner unto Allah by His command, and as a Lamp that gives

47. And as a Summoner to Allah by His command, **and as a radiant Lamp.**

وَّدَاعِيًا إِلَى اللّٰهِ بِإِذْنِهٖ وَسِرَاجًا مُّنِيْرًا ﴿٤٧﴾

49. And follow not the disbelievers and the hypocrites, and leave alone their annoyance, and put thy trust in Allah; for Allah is sufficient as a Guardian.

49. And follow not the disbelievers and the hypocrites, and **ignore their nuisances,** and put **your** trust in Allah; for Allah is sufficient as a Guardian.

وَلَا تُطِعِ الْكٰفِرِيْنَ وَالْمُنٰفِقِيْنَ وَدَعْ أَذٰىهُمْ وَتَوَكَّلْ
عَلَى اللّٰهِ ۚ وَكَفٰى بِاللّٰهِ وَكِيْلًا ﴿٤٩﴾

50. then you have no right against them with regard to the period of waiting that you reckon.

50. Then you have no right **against them with regard to the *prescribed* period of waiting** that you reckon.

فَمَا لَكُمْ عَلَيْهِنَّ مِنْ عِدَّةٍ تَعْتَدُّوْنَهَا ۚ

52. Thou mayest defer *the marriage of* any of them that thou pleasest, and receive unto thyself whom thou pleasest; and if thou desirest *to take back* any of those whom thou hast put aside, there is no blame on thee. That is more likely that their eyes may be cooled, and that they may not grieve, and that they may all be pleased with that which thou hast given them. And Allah knows what is in your hearts; and Allah is All-Knowing, Forbearing.

52. **You may defer *marrying* anyone among them *if you like* and you may receive unto yourself whom you please. And if you desire *to take back* any of those whom you have put aside, there is no blame on you. This is more likely to result in the cooling of their eyes, and that they may not grieve, and that they may all be pleased with that which you have given them.** And Allah knows what is in your hearts; and Allah is All-knowing, Forbearing.

تُرْجِيْ مَنْ تَشَآءُ مِنْهُنَّ وَتُؤْوِيْٓ اِلَيْكَ مَنْ تَشَآءُ ؕ
وَمَنِ ابْتَغَيْتَ مِمَّنْ عَزَلْتَ فَلَا جُنَاحَ عَلَيْكَ ؕ ذٰلِكَ
اَدْنٰٓى اَنْ تَقَرَّ اَعْيُنُهُنَّ وَلَا يَحْزَنَّ وَيَرْضَيْنَ بِمَآ
اٰتَيْتَهُنَّ كُلُّهُنَّ ؕ وَاللّٰهُ يَعْلَمُ مَا فِيْ قُلُوْبِكُمْ ؕ وَكَانَ
اللّٰهُ عَلِيْمًا حَلِيْمًا ﴿۵۲﴾

54. O ye who believe! enter not the houses of the Prophet unless leave is granted to you for a meal without waiting for its *appointed* time.

54. O ye who believe! Enter not the houses of the Prophet **unless you have been invited to meal and even then not *so early* before the food has been cooked.**

يٰٓاَيُّهَا الَّذِيْنَ اٰمَنُوْا لَا تَدْخُلُوْا بُيُوْتَ النَّبِيِّ اِلَّآ اَنْ
يُّؤْذَنَ لَكُمْ اِلٰى طَعَامٍ غَيْرَ نٰظِرِيْنَ اِنٰىهُ ۙ

58. Verily, those who malign Allah and His Messenger—Allah has cursed them in this world and in the Hereafter, and has prepared for them an abasing punishment.

58. Verily, those who **annoy** Allah and His Messenger --- Allah has cursed them in this world and in the Hereafter, and has prepared for them an abasing punishment.

اِنَّ الَّذِيْنَ يُؤْذُوْنَ اللّٰهَ وَرَسُوْلَهٗ لَعَنَهُمُ اللّٰهُ فِي
الدُّنْيَا وَالْاٰخِرَةِ وَاَعَدَّ لَهُمْ عَذَابًا مُّهِيْنًا ﴿۵۸﴾

يَٰٓأَيُّهَا ٱلنَّبِيُّ قُل لِّأَزْوَٰجِكَ وَبَنَاتِكَ وَنِسَآءِ ٱلْمُؤْمِنِينَ
يُدْنِينَ عَلَيْهِنَّ مِن جَلَٰبِيبِهِنَّ ۚ ذَٰلِكَ أَدْنَىٰٓ أَن
يُعْرَفْنَ فَلَا يُؤْذَيْنَ ۗ وَكَانَ ٱللَّهُ غَفُورًا رَّحِيمًا ﴿٥٩﴾

60. O Prophet! tell thy wives and thy daughters and the women of the believers that they should draw close to them portions of their *loose* outer coverings. That is nearer that they may *thus* be distinguished and not molested. And Allah is Most Forgiving, Merciful.

60. O Prophet! **Tell your wives and your daughters, and the women of the believers, that they should pull down upon them of their outer cloaks *from their heads over their faces.* That is more likely that they may *thus* be recognized** and not molested. And Allah is Most Forgiving, Merciful.

لَّئِن لَّمْ يَنتَهِ ٱلْمُنَٰفِقُونَ وَٱلَّذِينَ فِى قُلُوبِهِم مَّرَضٌ
وَٱلْمُرْجِفُونَ فِى ٱلْمَدِينَةِ لَنُغْرِيَنَّكَ بِهِمْ ثُمَّ لَا
يُجَاوِرُونَكَ فِيهَآ إِلَّا قَلِيلًا ﴿٦٠﴾

61. If the hypocrites, and those in whose heart is a disease, and those who cause agitation in the city, desist not, We shall surely give thee authority over them; then they will not dwell therein as thy neighbours, save for a little while.

61. If the hypocrites , and those in whose hearts **there is disease, and those who spread baseless rumours in the city, do not desist, We shall surely make you stand up against them; then they will no longer tarry around you but a little.**

يَٰٓأَيُّهَا ٱلَّذِينَ ءَامَنُوا۟ لَا تَكُونُوا۟ كَٱلَّذِينَ ءَاذَوْا۟ مُوسَىٰ
فَبَرَّأَهُ ٱللَّهُ مِمَّا قَالُوا۟ ۚ وَكَانَ عِندَ ٱللَّهِ وَجِيهًا ﴿٦٩﴾

70. O ye who believe! be not like those who vexed and slandered Moses; but Allah cleared him of what they spoke *of him.* And he was honourable in the sight of Allah.

70. O ye who believe! Be not like those who vexed *and slandered* Moses; Allah cleared him of what they spoke *of him. And he was honourable in the sight of Allah.*

يُصْلِحْ لَكُمْ أَعْمَٰلَكُمْ وَيَغْفِرْ لَكُمْ ذُنُوبَكُمْ

72. He will bless your works for you and forgive you your sins.

72. *He will* **reform your conduct** for you and forgive you your sins.

73. Indeed, he is *capable of being* unjust *to, and* neglectful *of, himself*.

إِنَّهُۥ كَانَ ظَلُومًا جَهُولًا ﴿٧٣﴾

73. Indeed he was **too cruel to himself, unmindful of the consequences.**

AL-SABA

10. Do they not see what is before them and what is behind them of the heaven and the earth? If We please, We could cause the earth to sink with them, or cause pieces of the sky to fall upon them. In that verily is a Sign for every repentant servant.

أَفَلَمْ يَرَوْا إِلَىٰ مَا بَيْنَ أَيْدِيهِمْ وَمَا خَلْفَهُم مِّنَ السَّمَاءِ وَالْأَرْضِ ۚ إِن نَّشَأْ نَخْسِفْ بِهِمُ الْأَرْضَ أَوْ نُسْقِطْ عَلَيْهِمْ كِسَفًا مِّنَ السَّمَاءِ ۚ إِنَّ فِي ذَٰلِكَ لَآيَةً لِّكُلِّ عَبْدٍ مُّنِيبٍ ﴿١٠﴾

10. Do they not see what is before them and what is behind them of the heaven and the earth? If We please, We could cause the earth to sink with them, **or cause some pieces from the sky to fall upon them.** In that verily is a Sign for every repentant servant.

11. And certainly, We bestowed grace upon David from *Ourselves*: 'O ye mountains, repeat *the praises of Allah* with him,

وَلَقَدْ آتَيْنَا دَاوُودَ مِنَّا فَضْلًا ۖ يَا جِبَالُ أَوِّبِي مَعَهُ

11. And certainly, We bestowed grace upon David from **Ourselves:** 'O ye mountains, **Turn to God with full submission along with him,**

15. And when We decreed his (Solomon's) death, nothing pointed out to them that he was dead save a worm of the earth that ate awayh is staff. So when he fell down, the Jinn plainly realized that if they had known the unseen, they would not have remained in a state of degrading torment.

فَلَمَّا قَضَيْنَا عَلَيْهِ الْمَوْتَ مَا دَلَّهُمْ عَلَىٰ مَوْتِهِ إِلَّا دَابَّةُ الْأَرْضِ تَأْكُلُ مِنسَأَتَهُ ۖ فَلَمَّا خَرَّ تَبَيَّنَتِ الْجِنُّ أَن لَّوْ كَانُوا يَعْلَمُونَ الْغَيْبَ مَا لَبِثُوا فِي الْعَذَابِ الْمُهِينِ ﴿١٥﴾

Note: The word *daa'bah* (دابة) applies to all forms of animal life. So the translation "the worm of the earth" should be taken metaphorically and not literally. This reference is to the son of Solomon who did not inherit any of the spiritual qualities or the art of statecraft which distinguished his illustrious father Solomon. During his rule it became gradually apparent to those powerful chieftains (jinn) who had been subdued and subjugated by Solomon that Solomon was now virtually dead. They successfully rebelled against the state and caused fragmentation of the great empire.

فأعرضوا فأرسلنا عليهم سيل العرم وبدلنهم بجنتيهم جنتين ذواتى أكل خمط وأثل وشىء من سدر قليل ﴿١٧﴾

17. But they turned away; so We sent against them a fierce flood. And We gave them, in lieu of their gardens, two gardens bearing bitter fruit and tamarisk and a few lote-trees.

17. But they turned away; so We sent against them a **fierce flood *from a* burst dam.** And We gave them, in lieu of their gardens, two gardens bearing bitter fruit and tamarisk and a few lote-trees.

وما أرسلنا فى قرية من نذير إلا قال مترفوها إنا بما أرسلتم به كفرون ﴿٣٥﴾

35. And We never sent a Warner to any city but the wealthy ones thereof said, 'Surely, we disbelieve in what you have been sent with.'

35. And We never sent a Warner to any **township** but the wealthy ones thereof said, 'Surely, we disbelieve in what you have been sent with.'

ويوم يحشرهم جميعا ثم يقول للملئكة أهؤلاء إياكم كانوا يعبدون ﴿٤١﴾

41. And *remember* the day, when He will gather them all together; then He will say to the angels: 'Was it you that they worshipped?'

41. And *remember* the day, when He will gather them all together; then He will say to the angels: Was it you ***in particular*** that they worshipped?

Note: The translation of the word *iyyakum* إياكم seems to have been omitted. The insertion of the word 'in particular', therefore, seems to be appropriate.

50. Say, 'The Truth has come, and falsehood could neither originate *any good* nor reproduce *it*.'

قُلْ جَآءَ الْحَقُّ وَمَا يُبْدِئُ الْبَاطِلُ وَمَا يُعِيدُ ﴿٥٠﴾

50. Say, 'the Truth has **arrived'** and falsehood **could neither initiate nor repeat** ***anything*.**

53. And they will say, 'We *now* believe therein.' But how can the attaining *of faith* be possible to them from a position *so* far off,

وَّقَالُوْٓا اٰمَنَّا بِهٖ ۚ وَاَنّٰى لَهُمُ التَّنَاوُشُ مِنْ مَّكَانٍۢ بَعِيْدٍ ۚ ﴿٥٣﴾

Note: It simply means that having distanced themselves earlier from it, they could not attain faith at the time of punishment.

54. While they had disbelieved in it before? And they are uttering conjectures from a far-off place.

وَّقَدْ كَفَرُوْا بِهٖ مِنْ قَبْلُ ۚ وَيَقْذِفُوْنَ بِالْغَيْبِ مِنْ مَّكَانٍۢ بَعِيْدٍ ﴿٥٤﴾

54. **Verily, they had rejected it earlier indulging in wild conjectures from a distant position.**

AL-FATIR

9. Is he, then, to whom the evil of his deed is made *to appear* pleasing, so that he looks upon it as good, *like him who believes and does good deeds?*

اَفَمَنْ زُيِّنَ لَهٗ سُوْٓءُ عَمَلِهٖ فَرَاٰهُ حَسَنًا ۗ فَاِنَّ اللّٰهَ يُضِلُّ مَنْ يَّشَآءُ وَيَهْدِيْ مَنْ يَّشَآءُ ۖ

9. Is he, then, whose deeds are made to appear beautiful to him so he views them as good ***like one who believes and truly does good deeds?***

11. Whoso desires honour, then *let him know that* all honour belongs to Allah. Unto Him ascend good words, and righteous work does He exalt. And those who plot evils—for them is a severe punishment; and the plotting of such will perish.

مَنْ كَانَ يُرِيْدُ الْعِزَّةَ فَلِلّٰهِ الْعِزَّةُ جَمِيْعًا ۗ اِلَيْهِ يَصْعَدُ الْكَلِمُ الطَّيِّبُ وَالْعَمَلُ الصَّالِحُ يَرْفَعُهٗ ۗ وَالَّذِيْنَ يَمْكُرُوْنَ السَّيِّاٰتِ لَهُمْ عَذَابٌ شَدِيْدٌ ۗ وَمَكْرُ اُولٰٓئِكَ هُوَ يَبُوْرُ ﴿١١﴾

11. **Whoever** desires honour, then *let him know that* all honour belongs to

Allah. **To Him ascend good words and righteous work helps them rise.** And those who plot evils, for them is a severe punishment; and the plotting of such will perish.

16. O ye men, it is you that stand in need of Allah, but Allah is He Who is Self-Sufficient, the Praiseworthy.

يَاأَيُّهَا النَّاسُ أَنتُمُ الْفُقَرَاءُ إِلَى اللَّهِ ۖ وَاللَّهُ هُوَ الْغَنِيُّ الْحَمِيدُ ﴿١٦﴾

16. O ye men, **you are mere beggars unto Allah, while Allah is He who stands in need of none, Ever Praiseworthy.**

37. But *as for* those who disbelieve, for them is the fire of Hell. Death will not be decreed for them so that they may die; nor will the punishment thereof be lightened for them. Thus do We requite every ungrateful person.

وَالَّذِينَ كَفَرُوا لَهُمْ نَارُ جَهَنَّمَ لَا يُقْضَىٰ عَلَيْهِمْ فَيَمُوتُوا وَلَا يُخَفَّفُ عَنْهُم مِّنْ عَذَابِهَا ۚ كَذَٰلِكَ نَجْزِي كُلَّ كَفُورٍ ﴿٣٧﴾

37. But *as for* those who disbelieve, for them is the fire of Hell. **It will not be decreed for them that they may die;** nor will the punishment thereof be lightened for them. Thus do We requite every ungrateful person.

46. and when their appointed time comes, then *they will know that* Allah has all His servants under *His* eyes.

مُّسَمًّى ۖ فَإِذَا جَاءَ أَجَلُهُمْ فَإِنَّ اللَّهَ كَانَ بِعِبَادِهِ بَصِيرًا ﴿٤٦﴾

46. and when their appointed time comes, ***beware that* Allah is fully aware of His servants — *the mankind.***

YA SIN

9. We have put, round their necks, chains reaching unto the chins, so that their heads are forced up.

إِنَّا جَعَلْنَا فِي أَعْنَاقِهِمْ أَغْلَالًا فَهِيَ إِلَى الْأَذْقَانِ فَهُم مُّقْمَحُونَ ﴿٩﴾

9. We have put round their necks, **collars** reaching to the chins, so that their heads are forced up.

31. Alas for *My* servants! there comes not a Messenger to them but they mock at him.

يٰحَسْرَةً عَلَى الْعِبَادِ ۚ مَا يَأْتِيهِم مِّن رَّسُولٍ إِلَّا
كَانُوا بِهِ يَسْتَهْزِءُونَ ﴿٣١﴾

31. Alas for **mankind!** There comes not a Messenger to them but they mock at him.

38. And a Sign for them is the night from which We strip off the day, and lo! they are in darkness.

وَآيَةٌ لَّهُمُ اللَّيْلُ ۚ نَسْلَخُ مِنْهُ النَّهَارَ فَإِذَا هُم
مُّظْلِمُونَ ﴿٣٨﴾

38. And a Sign for them is the night from which We **draw forth the day,** and lo! they are in darkness.

39. And the sun is moving on the course *prescribed* for it. That is the decree of the Almighty, the All-Knowing *God*.

وَالشَّمْسُ تَجْرِي لِمُسْتَقَرٍّ لَّهَا ۚ ذَٰلِكَ تَقْدِيرُ
الْعَزِيزِ الْعَلِيمِ ﴿٣٩﴾

39. And the sun is moving on the course **prescribed** for it. That is the decree of the Almighty, the All-Knowing *God.*

43. And We have created for them the like thereof whereon they ride.

وَخَلَقْنَا لَهُم مِّن مِّثْلِهِ مَا يَرْكَبُونَ ﴿٤٣﴾

43. And We **will create** for them the like thereof **on which they will ride.**

56. Verily the inmates of Heaven will, on that day, be happy in *their* occupation.

إِنَّ أَصْحَابَ الْجَنَّةِ الْيَوْمَ فِي شُغُلٍ فَاكِهُونَ ﴿٥٦﴾

56. Verily, the inhabitants of Heaven, on that day, will be happily employed in several occupations.

69. And him whom We grant long life—We revert him to a weak *condition of* creation. Will they not then understand?

وَمَن نُّعَمِّرْهُ نُنَكِّسْهُ فِي الْخَلْقِ ۖ أَفَلَا يَعْقِلُونَ ﴿٦٩﴾

69. And him whom We grant long life, **We cause him to revert to a state of senility.** Will they not then understand?

70. And We have not taught him poetry, nor does that suit it (the Qur'ān). It is but a Reminder and a Qur'ān that makes *things* plain,

وَمَا عَلَّمْنٰهُ الشِّعْرَ وَمَا يَنْۢبَغِيْ لَهٗ ۭ اِنْ هُوَ اِلَّا
ذِكْرٌ وَّقُرْاٰنٌ مُّبِيْنٌ ﴿٧٠﴾

70. And We have not taught him poetry, **nor does it befit him.** It is but a Reminder and a Qur'an that makes *things* plain,

71. So that it may warn all who live, and that the word *of punishment* be justified against the disbelievers.

لِّيُنْذِرَ مَنْ كَانَ حَيًّا وَّيَحِقَّ الْقَوْلُ عَلَى الْكٰفِرِيْنَ ﴿٧١﴾

71. So that it may warn all who live, and that **the decree against the disbelievers may come to pass.**

76. They are not able to help them, but they will be brought *before God* as their *allied* host.

لَا يَسْتَطِيْعُوْنَ نَصْرَهُمْ ۙ وَهُمْ لَهُمْ جُنْدٌ مُّحْضَرُوْنَ ﴿٧٦﴾

76. They will not be able to help them; *on the contrary,* they themselves will be made to appear along with them as hosts.

83. Verily His command, when He intends a thing, is *only* that He says to it, 'Be!', and it is.

اِنَّمَآ اَمْرُهٗٓ اِذَآ اَرَادَ شَيْـًٔا اَنْ يَّقُوْلَ لَهٗ كُنْ فَيَكُوْنُ ﴿٨٣﴾

83. Verily His command, when He intends a thing, is *only* that He says to it, 'Be!', **and it begins to be.**

AL-SAFFAT

7. We have adorned the lowest heaven with an adornment—the planets;

إِنَّا زَيَّنَّا السَّمَاءَ الدُّنْيَا بِزِينَةٍ الْكَوَاكِبِ ⑥

7. We have adorned the lowest heaven with **an adornment of stars;**

9. They cannot hear *anything* from the exalted assembly *of angels*—and they are pelted from every side,

لَا يَسَّمَّعُونَ إِلَى الْمَلَإِ الْأَعْلَىٰ وَيُقْذَفُونَ مِن كُلِّ جَانِبٍ ⑧

9. **They shall not be able to listen to** the Exalted Assembly **despite straining hard — being** pelted from **all** sides.

12. So ask them whether it is they who are harder to create, or *others* whom We have created? Them We have created of cohesive clay.

فَاسْتَفْتِهِمْ أَهُمْ أَشَدُّ خَلْقًا أَم مَّنْ خَلَقْنَا ۚ إِنَّا خَلَقْنَاهُم مِّن طِينٍ لَّازِبٍ ⑪

12. So ask them **if what they can create is more enduring than what We have created?** Them We have created of cohesive clay.

20. Then it will be but one shout of reproach, and behold, they will begin to see.

فَإِنَّمَا هِيَ زَجْرَةٌ وَاحِدَةٌ فَإِذَا هُمْ يَنظُرُونَ ⑲

20. Then it will **be a single stern call,** and behold, they will begin to see.

29. They will say, 'Verily, you used to come to us, swearing *that you were truthful.*'

قَالُوا إِنَّكُمْ كُنتُمْ تَأْتُونَنَا عَنِ الْيَمِينِ ㉘

29. They will say, 'Verily, you used to come **at us from the right.'**

50. As though they were sheltered eggs.

كَأَنَّهُنَّ بَيْضٌ مَّكْنُونٌ ㊾

Note: *baizun* بيض as *baizatun* بيضة An egg of an ostrich or of any bird. When said in praise, *huwa baizatul balad* (هو بيضة البلد) means : He is like an ostrich egg in which is the young bird, because the male ostrich in that case protects it; or he is unequalled in nobility, like the egg that is left alone; or he is a lord, or chief; or he is the unequalled of the *balad* بلد (or country or the like) to whom others resort, and whose words they accept or he is celebrated, or well-known, person. Thus *baizun maknoon* (بیض مکنون) would mean the pride of paradise well guarded and well protected.

سَلٰمٌ عَلٰى نُوْحٍ فِي الْعٰلَمِيْنَ ﴿٨٠﴾

80. 'Peace be upon Noah among the peoples!'

80. Peace be upon Noah **among *people of* the worlds.**

اِذْ جَآءَ رَبَّهٗ بِقَلْبٍ سَلِيْمٍ ﴿٨٥﴾

85. When he came to his Lord with a sound heart;

85. When he came to his Lord with a **submissive heart.**

اَئِفْكًا اٰلِهَةً دُوْنَ اللّٰهِ تُرِيْدُوْنَ ﴿٨٦﴾

87. 'Do you falsely seek gods beside Allah?

87. **Do you seek lies as** gods **instead** of Allah?

فَلَمَّآ اَسْلَمَا وَتَلَّهٗ لِلْجَبِيْنِ ﴿١٠٣﴾

104. And when they both submitted *to the will of God*, and he had thrown him down on his forehead,

104. And when they both submitted *to the Will of God* and **he laid him *on the ground* face down,**

وَبٰرَكْنَا عَلَيْهِ وَعَلٰٓى اِسْحٰقَ وَمِنْ ذُرِّيَّتِهِمَا مُحْسِنٌ وَّظَالِمٌ لِّنَفْسِهٖ مُبِيْنٌ ﴿١١٣﴾

114. And We bestowed blessings on him and Isaac. And among their progeny are *some* who do good and others who clearly wrong themselves.

114. And We bestowed blessings on him and Isaac. **And from among the progeny of both there is many a doer of good and many a one who is manifestly cruel to himself.**

Note: The word *zalim* ظالم (cruel) or *zulm* ظلم (cruelty) is not always used as condemnation without exception in the Holy Qur'an. When used in this sense it covers all categories of deviation from the right path. Yet, there are some exceptions where it is used to signify praiseworthiness.

In 35:33 (Al-Fatir), it is evident that God has included amongst His chosen servants, such people as are *zalimun li nafsihi*(ظالم لنفسه) who treat themselves cruelly as they strive in the path of Allah. In the same category those belonging to the comparatively higher order are mentioned as *muqtasid* مقتصد and *sabiq bil khairat*(سابق بالخيرات). (Al-Fatir Ch:35 Verse 33)

Similarly, to bring oneself to do good deeds requires a measure of harshness and cruelty to oneself during early stages of spiritual struggle. Those who do it for the sake of God are evidently praisworthy yet they are spoken of as *zalimun linafsihi* (ظالم لنفسه) (cruel to himself).

118. And We gave them the Book that made *things* clear;

وَاٰتَيْنٰهُمَا الْكِتٰبَ الْمُسْتَبِيْنَ ﴿١١٨﴾

118. And We gave them the manifestly clear Book.

142. And he cast lots *with the crew of the ship* and was of the losers.

فَسَاهَمَ فَكَانَ مِنَ الْمُدْحَضِيْنَ ﴿١٤٢﴾

142. And he drew lots ***at the bidding of his shipmates*** **and was of the losers.**

152. Now, surely it is one of their fabrications that they say,

اَلَاۤ اِنَّهُمْ مِّنْ اِفْكِهِمْ لَيَقُوْلُوْنَ ﴿١٥٢﴾

152. **Beware, verily it is of their fabrication when they say,**

159. And they assert a blood relationship between Him and the Jinn, while the Jinn *themselves* know that they will be brought *before God for judgment.*

وَجَعَلُوْا بَيْنَهٗ وَبَيْنَ الْجِنَّةِ نَسَبًا ؕ وَلَقَدْ عَلِمَتِ الْجِنَّةُ اِنَّهُمْ لَمُحْضَرُوْنَ ﴿١٥٩﴾

159. And they assert a blood relationship between Him and the Jinn, while the Jinn **know full well that they** ***too*** **will be summoned** ***to His presence.***

SAD

6. 'Does he make the gods to be one God? This is indeed a strange thing.'

اَجَعَلَ الْاٰلِهَةَ اِلٰهًا وَّاحِدًا ۖۚ اِنَّ هٰذَا لَشَیْءٌ عُجَابٌ ﴿٦﴾

6. **'Has he forged the gods into One God?** This, **verily,** is the strangest thing ***we have heard'***

وَانْطَلَقَ الْمَلَأُ مِنْهُمْ أَنِ امْشُوا وَاصْبِرُوا عَلَىٰ
آلِهَتِكُمْ ۖ إِنَّ هَٰذَا لَشَيْءٌ يُرَادُ ⑦

7. And the leaders among them spoke out, 'Go and stick to your gods. This is a thing designed.

7. **At that, their** leaders **disputed** ***admonishing them,*** 'Go **hold fast** to your gods. This is a thing **much desired.**

مَا سَمِعْنَا بِهَٰذَا فِي الْمِلَّةِ الْآخِرَةِ إِنْ هَٰذَا إِلَّا
اخْتِلَاقٌ ⑧

8. 'We have not heard of this *even* in the latest religion. This is nothing but a fabrication.

8. **'We never heard of such a thing in any other religion.** This is nothing but a fabrication.

أَأُنْزِلَ عَلَيْهِ الذِّكْرُ مِنْ بَيْنِنَا ۚ بَلْ هُمْ فِي شَكٍّ
مِنْ ذِكْرِي ۖ بَلْ لَمَّا يَذُوقُوا عَذَابِ ⑨

9. 'Has the exhortation been sent down to him *in preference to all* of us?' Nay, they are in doubt concerning My exhortation. Nay, but they have not yet tasted My punishment.

9. **'What, is he out of all of us the one to whom exhortation is sent down?'** Nay they are in doubt concerning My exhortation. Nay, but they have not yet tasted My punishment.

كَذَّبَتْ قَبْلَهُمْ قَوْمُ نُوحٍ وَعَادٌ وَفِرْعَوْنُ
ذُو الْأَوْتَادِ ⑬

13. Before them *too* the people of Noah, and *the tribe of* 'Ād and Pharaoh, the lord of stakes, treated *the Messengers* as liars;

13. **Much as before them the people of Noah and the *tribe of* □d and Pharaoh, the lord of encampments, had rejected.**

وَثَمُودُ وَقَوْمُ لُوطٍ وَأَصْحَابُ لْئَيْكَةِ ۚ أُولَٰئِكَ
الْأَحْزَابُ ⑭

14. And *the tribe of* Thamūd, and the people of Lot, and the dwellers of the Wood—these were the confederates.

14. **So** *the tribe of* Thamud, and the people of Lot, and the dwellers of the Wood --- **these were the hordes *routed one and all.***

15. There was not one *of them* but treated *their* Messengers as liars, so My punishment rightly overtook *them*.

إِن كُلٌّ إِلَّا كَذَّبَ الرُّسُلَ فَحَقَّ عِقَابِ ﴿١٥﴾

15. **All without exception rejected the Messengers, thus My punishment became inevitable.**

16. And these only wait for a single blast, and there shall be no delaying it.

وَمَا يَنظُرُ هَٰٓؤُلَآءِ إِلَّا صَيْحَةً وَاحِدَةً مَّا لَهَا مِن فَوَاقٍ ﴿١٦﴾

16. **They wait not but for a long drawn out scream from which there is no respite.**

18. Bear patiently what they say, and remember Our servant David, *man* of *strong* hands; surely he was always turning *to God*.

اِصْبِرْ عَلَىٰ مَا يَقُولُونَ وَاذْكُرْ عَبْدَنَا دَاوُدَ ذَا الْأَيْدِ

إِنَّهُ أَوَّابٌ ﴿١٨﴾

18. Bear patiently **with** what they say, and remember our servant David, **a man of many powers;** surely he was always turning *to God.*

19. We subjected *to him* the mountains. They celebrated God's praises with him at nightfall and sunrise.

إِنَّا سَخَّرْنَا الْجِبَالَ مَعَهُ يُسَبِّحْنَ بِالْعَشِيِّ وَ

الْإِشْرَاقِ ﴿١٩﴾

Note: The word *jibal* (جبال) (mountains) may apply to the powerful mountainous tribes which were subjugated by David or it may also refer to the mineral wealth of mountains which was well exploited in his time.

20. And *We subjected to him* the birds gathered together: all turned to him.

وَالطَّيْرَ مَحْشُورَةً ۖ كُلٌّ لَّهُ أَوَّابٌ ﴿٢٠﴾

Note: The word *attair* (الطير) (birds) means men of exceptional talents who soar high on the wings of their achievements.

21. And We strengthened his kingdom, and gave him wisdom and decisive judgment.

وَشَدَدْنَا مُلْكَهُ وَآتَيْنَاهُ الْحِكْمَةَ وَفَصْلَ

الْخِطَابِ ﴿٢١﴾

21. And We strengthened his kingdom, and gave him wisdom and ***talent for* decisive speech.**

33. He said, 'I love the love of horses because of the remembrance of my Lord.' *So great was his love of them that* when they were hidden behind the veil, ***he said,***

فَقَالَ إِنِّيٓ أَحۡبَبۡتُ حُبَّ ٱلۡخَيۡرِ عَن ذِكۡرِ رَبِّي
حَتَّىٰ تَوَارَتۡ بِٱلۡحِجَابِ وقفة ٣٣

33. He said, 'The love of horses is dear to me because they remind me of my Lord. *So he sat* until they disappeared behind the veil.

34. 'Bring them back to me.' Then he began to pass his hand over *their* legs and *their* necks.

رُدُّوهَا عَلَيَّۖ فَطَفِقَ مَسۡحَۢا بِٱلسُّوقِ وَٱلۡأَعۡنَاقِ ٣٤

34. ***He said,*** 'Bring them back to me'. Then he **started stroking *their* legs and *their* necks.**

36. He said, 'O my Lord, grant me forgiveness and bestow on me a kingdom that will not suit anyone after me; surely Thou art the Great Bestower.'

قَالَ رَبِّ ٱغۡفِرۡ لِي وَهَبۡ لِي مُلۡكٗا لَّا يَنۢبَغِي لِأَحَدٖ
مِّنۢ بَعۡدِيٓۖ إِنَّكَ أَنتَ ٱلۡوَهَّابُ ٣٦

36. He said, 'O my Lord, grant me forgiveness and bestow on me a kingdom **which non unworthy of it may possess after me. Surely Thou art so Generous.'**

43. 'Strike *and urge thy riding beast* with thy foot. Here is cool water to wash with and a drink.'

ٱرۡكُضۡ بِرِجۡلِكَۖ هَٰذَا مُغۡتَسَلُۢ بَارِدٞ وَشَرَابٞ ٤٣

43. **'Spur on *your mount.*** Here is cool water to wash with and a drink.'

44. And We bestowed on him his family and as many more with them, *by way of* mercy from Us, and as a reminder to men of understanding.

وَوَهَبۡنَا لَهُۥٓ أَهۡلَهُۥ وَمِثۡلَهُم مَّعَهُمۡ رَحۡمَةٗ مِّنَّا
وَذِكۡرَىٰ لِأُوْلِي ٱلۡأَلۡبَٰبِ ٤٤

44. And We bestowed on him his family **and many like them along with them,** by way of mercy from Us, and as a reminder to men of understanding.

46. And remember Our servants Abraham, and Isaac, and Jacob, *men* of strong hands and *powerful* vision.

وَاذْكُرْ عِبٰدَنَآ اِبْرٰهِيْمَ وَاِسْحٰقَ وَيَعْقُوْبَ اُولِي
الْاَيْدِيْ وَالْاَبْصَارِ ﴿۴۶﴾

46. And remember Our servants Abraham, and Isaac, and Jacob, men of **might and vision.**

47. We chose them for a special *purpose* — reminding *people* of the abode *of the Hereafter.*

اِنَّآ اَخْلَصْنٰهُمْ بِخَالِصَةٍ ذِكْرَى الدَّارِ ﴿۴۷﴾

47. We chose **them especially to remind *people* of the abode of the Here-after.**

65. Surely, this is a fact—the disputing together of the people of the Fire.

اِنَّ ذٰلِكَ لَحَقٌّ تَخَاصُمُ اَهْلِ النَّارِ ﴿۶۵﴾

65. **Verily, it is true** --- the disputing together of the people of the Fire.

76. *God* said, 'O Iblīs, what hindered thee from submitting to what I had created with My two hands? Is it that thou art *too* proud or art thou *really* of the exalted ones?'

قَالَ يٰٓاِبْلِيْسُ مَا مَنَعَكَ اَنْ تَسْجُدَ لِمَا خَلَقْتُ
بِيَدَيَّ ؕ اَسْتَكْبَرْتَ اَمْ كُنْتَ مِنَ الْعَالِيْنَ ﴿۷۶﴾

76. *God* said, 'O Iblis, what hindered **you** from submitting to what I had created with My two hands? **Have you acted out of pride or you really belong to the exalted ones?**

89. 'And you shall surely know the truth of it after a while.'

وَلَتَعْلَمُنَّ نَبَاَهٗ بَعْدَ حِيْنٍ ﴿۸۹﴾

89. 'And you **will surely learn its implication** after a while.'

AL-ZUMAR

3. Surely it is We Who have revealed the Book to thee with truth; so worship Allah, being sincere to Him in obedience.

اِنَّآ اَنْزَلْنَآ اِلَيْكَ الْكِتٰبَ بِالْحَقِّ فَاعْبُدِ اللّٰهَ مُخْلِصًا
لَّهُ الدِّيْنَ ﴿۳﴾

3. Surely it is We Who have revealed the Book to you with truth; so **worship Allah, dedicating your faith to Him in all sincerity.**

5. He is Allah, the One, the Most Supreme.

هُوَ اللّٰهُ الْوَاحِدُ الْقَهَّارُ ⑤

5. He is Allah, **the only One, the Dominant.**

7. He creates you in the wombs of your mothers, creation after creation, in threefold darkness. This is Allah, your Lord.

يَخْلُقُكُمْ فِيْ بُطُوْنِ اُمَّهٰتِكُمْ خَلْقًا مِّنْۢ بَعْدِ خَلْقٍ فِيْ ظُلُمٰتٍ ثَلٰثٍ ذٰلِكُمُ اللّٰهُ رَبُّكُمْ

7. He creates you in the wombs of your mothers, creation after creation, **in three tiers of darkness.** This is Allah, your Lord . . .

10. Say, 'Are those who know equal to those who know not?' Verily, only those endowed with understanding will take heed.

قُلْ هَلْ يَسْتَوِي الَّذِيْنَ يَعْلَمُوْنَ وَالَّذِيْنَ لَا يَعْلَمُوْنَ اِنَّمَا يَتَذَكَّرُ اُولُوا الْاَلْبَابِ ⑩

10. who does not do so? **Say, 'Can those who know and those who do not know be equal?'** Verily, only those endowed with understanding will take heed.

17. 'O My servants, take Me, then, for your Protector.'

يٰعِبَادِ فَاتَّقُوْنِ ⑰

17. **Hence 'O My servants! Fear Me alone.'**

29. ***We have revealed*** **the Qur'ān in Arabic wherein there is no deviation from rectitude, that they may become righteous.**

قُرْاٰنًا عَرَبِيًّا غَيْرَ ذِيْ عِوَجٍ لَّعَلَّهُمْ يَتَّقُوْنَ ㉙

29. We *have revealed* the Qur'an **manifestly clear, with no crookedness** ***about it,*** that they may become righteous.

30. Allah sets forth a parable: a man belonging to several partners, disagreeing with one another, and a man belonging wholly to one man. Are they both equal in condition?

ضَرَبَ اللّٰهُ مَثَلًا رَّجُلًا فِيهِ شُرَكَآءُ مُتَشٰكِسُونَ
وَرَجُلًا سَلَمًا لِّرَجُلٍ هَلْ يَسْتَوِيٰنِ مَثَلًا

30. Allah sets forth a parable; a man belonging to several partners, disagreeing with one another, **and a man belonging exclusively to one man.** Are they both equal **in example?**

43. Allah takes away the souls of human beings at the time of their death;

اَللّٰهُ يَتَوَفَّى الْاَنْفُسَ حِيْنَ مَوْتِهَا

43. Allah takes away the souls of **the living** at the time of their death;

46. And when Allah alone is mentioned the hearts of those who believe not in the Hereafter shrink with aversion; but when those beside Him are mentioned, behold, they begin to rejoice.

وَاِذَا ذُكِرَ اللّٰهُ وَحْدَهُ اشْمَاَزَّتْ قُلُوْبُ الَّذِيْنَ
لَا يُؤْمِنُوْنَ بِالْاٰخِرَةِ ۚ وَاِذَا ذُكِرَ الَّذِيْنَ مِنْ دُوْنِهٖٓ
اِذَا هُمْ يَسْتَبْشِرُوْنَ ﴿٤٥﴾

46. **And when Allah alone is mentioned the hearts of those who believe not in the Hereafter wince in aversion;** but when those beside Him are mentioned, behold, they begin to rejoice.

57. "Lest a soul should say, 'O my grief for my remissness *in my duty* in respect of Allah! and surely I was among those who scoffed;'

اَنْ تَقُوْلَ نَفْسٌ يّٰحَسْرَتٰى عَلٰى مَا فَرَّطْتُّ فِيْ جَنْۢبِ
اللّٰهِ وَاِنْ كُنْتُ لَمِنَ السّٰخِرِيْنَ ﴿٥٦﴾

57. Lest a soul should say, 'O, my grief! **I fell short *in my conduct* despite being in the presence of Allah and surely I was of those who scoffed.'**

62. And Allah will deliver the righteous *and lead them* to a place of security and success;

وَيُنَجِّى اللّٰهُ الَّذِيْنَ اتَّقَوْا بِمَفَازَتِهِمْ

62. Allah delivers those who fear *Him* to their rightful place of security *and success;*

وَمَا قَدَرُوا اللّٰهَ حَقَّ قَدْرِهٖ وَالْاَرْضُ جَمِيْعًا
قَبْضَتُهٗ يَوْمَ الْقِيٰمَةِ وَالسَّمٰوٰتُ مَطْوِيّٰتٌۢ بِيَمِيْنِهٖ
سُبْحٰنَهٗ وَتَعٰلٰى عَمَّا يُشْرِكُوْنَ ﴿٦٨﴾

68. And they do not esteem Allah, with the esteem that is due to Him. And the whole earth will be *but* His handful on the Day of Resurrection, and the heavens will be rolled up in His right hand. Glory to Him and exalted is He above that which they associate *with Him.*

68. They did not pay proper respect to the Majesty of Allah as was due to it. And the earth will be entirely in His grasp on Doomsday; so will the heavens be rolled up by His right hand. Glory to Him and Exalted is He above that which they associate with Him.

AL-MUMIN

اِنَّ الَّذِيْنَ كَفَرُوْا يُنَادَوْنَ لَمَقْتُ اللّٰهِ اَكْبَرُ
مِنْ مَّقْتِكُمْ اَنْفُسَكُمْ اِذْ تُدْعَوْنَ اِلَى الْاِيْمَانِ
فَتَكْفُرُوْنَ ﴿١١﴾

11. An announcement will be made to those who disbelieve *in the words:* 'Greater was the abhorrence of Allah when you were called to the faith and you disbelieved than your *own* abhorrence of yourselves *today.*'

11. Certainly to those who disbelieved a call will be made to them, 'The detestation of Allah is greater than your detestation of yourselves, when you were called to have faith and you rejected it.'

ذٰلِكُمْ بِاَنَّهٗٓ اِذَا دُعِيَ اللّٰهُ وَحْدَهٗ كَفَرْتُمْ
وَاِنْ يُّشْرَكْ بِهٖ تُؤْمِنُوْا فَالْحُكْمُ لِلّٰهِ الْعَلِيِّ
الْكَبِيْرِ ﴿١٣﴾

13. *It will be said to them,* 'This is because, when Allah was proclaimed as One, you disbelieved, but when partners were associated with Him, you believed. The decision *now* belongs only to Allah, the High, the Incomparably Great.'

13. That is because when Allah alone was proclaimed you rejected *the call* but when partners were associated with Him, you believed. But the *last*

word belongs to Allah, the Lofty, the Great.

15. Call ye then on **Allah**, being sincere to Him in religion,

15. Call you then Allah, being sincere to Him in **faith.**

فَادْعُوا اللّٰهَ مُخْلِصِيْنَ لَهُ الدِّيْنَ

16. *He is* of most exalted attributes, Lord of the Throne. He sends the Word by His command to whomsoever of His servants He pleases, that He may give warning of the Day of Meeting,

16. **The Exalter of ranks, the Lord of the Throne. He causes the spirit to descend with His Command** to whomsoever of His servants He pleases, that He may give warning of the Day of Meeting ***Him***.

رَفِيْعُ الدَّرَجٰتِ ذُو الْعَرْشِ ۚ يُلْقِي الرُّوْحَ مِنْ
اَمْرِهٖ عَلٰى مَنْ يَّشَآءُ مِنْ عِبَادِهٖ لِيُنْذِرَ يَوْمَ
التَّلَاقِ ﴿١٦﴾

17. The day when they will *all* come forth; nothing concerning them will be hidden from Allah. 'Whose is the kingdom this day?' '*It is* Allah's, the One, the Most Supreme.

17. The day when they will *all* come forth; nothing concerning them will be hidden from Allah. **'To whom belongs the kingdom this day?' To Allah, the One, the Most Supreme.**

يَوْمَ هُمْ بٰرِزُوْنَ ۚ لَا يَخْفٰى عَلَى اللّٰهِ مِنْهُمْ
شَيْءٌ ۭ لِمَنِ الْمُلْكُ الْيَوْمَ ۭ لِلّٰهِ الْوَاحِدِ الْقَهَّارِ ﴿١٧﴾

21. And Allah judges with truth, but those on whom they call beside Him cannot judge at all. Surely, Allah is the All-Hearing, the All-Seeing.

21. And Allah judges with truth **while those on whom they call beside Him judge nothing.** Surely, Allah is the All-Hearing, the All-Seeing.

وَاللّٰهُ يَقْضِيْ بِالْحَقِّ ۭ وَالَّذِيْنَ يَدْعُوْنَ مِنْ
دُوْنِهٖ لَا يَقْضُوْنَ بِشَيْءٍ ۭ اِنَّ اللّٰهَ هُوَ السَّمِيْعُ
الْبَصِيْرُ ﴿٢١﴾

22. Have they not travelled in the earth and seen what was the end of those before them? They were mightier than these in power and *in* the marks *they left* in the earth. But Allah seized them for their sins, and they had no protector against Allah.

أَوَلَمْ يَسِيرُوا فِي الْأَرْضِ فَيَنْظُرُوا كَيْفَ
كَانَ عَاقِبَةُ الَّذِينَ كَانُوا مِنْ قَبْلِهِمْ ۚ كَانُوا هُمْ أَشَدَّ
مِنْهُمْ قُوَّةً وَآثَارًا فِي الْأَرْضِ فَأَخَذَهُمُ اللَّهُ بِذُنُوبِهِمْ ۗ
وَمَا كَانَ لَهُمْ مِنَ اللَّهِ مِنْ وَاقٍ ﴿٢٢﴾

22. Have they not travelled in the earth and seen what was the end of those before them? **They were far more powerful than these and stronger in the marks they left in the earth.** But Allah seized them for their sins, and they had no protector against Allah.

26. But the design of the disbelievers is but a thing wasted.

وَمَا كَيْدُ الْكَافِرِينَ إِلَّا فِي ضَلَالٍ ﴿٢٦﴾

26. But the design **of the disbelievers is nothing but wasteful.**

27. **I fear** lest he should change your religion or cause disorder to show itself in the land.'

إِنِّي أَخَافُ أَنْ يُبَدِّلَ دِينَكُمْ أَوْ أَنْ يُظْهِرَ
فِي الْأَرْضِ الْفَسَادَ ﴿٢٧﴾

27. I fear lest he should change your religion or **inundate the land with disorder *and curruption.***

31. And he who believed said: "O my people, I fear for you *something* like the day of the parties,

وَقَالَ الَّذِي آمَنَ يَا قَوْمِ إِنِّي أَخَافُ عَلَيْكُمْ مِثْلَ
يَوْمِ الْأَحْزَابِ ﴿٣١﴾

31. And he who believed said: 'O my people, I fear for **you like the *fateful* time of the confederates.**

33. "And O my people, I fear for you the day of mutual calling *and wailing*,

وَيَا قَوْمِ إِنِّي أَخَافُ عَلَيْكُمْ يَوْمَ التَّنَادِ ﴿٣٣﴾

33. 'And O my people, I fear for you the day of **calling each other *for help.***

37. And Pharaoh said: 'O Hāmān, build thou for me a lofty building that I may attain to the means of approach,

وَقَالَ فِرْعَوْنُ يَا هَامَانُ ابْنِ لِي صَرْحًا لَعَلِّي
أَبْلُغُ الْأَسْبَابَ ﴿٣٧﴾

37. And Pharaoh said: 'O Haman, **build for me a lofty mansion that I may gain access,**

38. 'The means of approach to the heavens, so that I may have a look at the God of Moses, and I surely think him to be a liar.' And thus the evil of his doing was made

أَسْبَابَ السَّمٰوٰتِ فَأَطَّلِعَ إِلَىٰ إِلٰهِ مُوسَىٰ وَإِنِّي لَأَظُنُّهُ كَاذِبًا ۚ وَكَذٰلِكَ زُيِّنَ لِفِرْعَوْنَ سُوءُ عَمَلِهِ

38. 'The means of **approach to the heavens, so that** I may have a look at the God of Moses, and I surely think him to be a liar.' And thus the evil of his doing was made . .. . .

57. –there is nothing in their breasts but *a feeling of* greatness which they will never attain. So seek refuge in Allah. Surely He is the All-Hearing, the All-Seeing.

إِن فِي صُدُورِهِمْ إِلَّا كِبْرٌ مَّا هُم بِبَالِغِيهِ ۚ فَاسْتَعِذْ بِاللَّهِ ۖ إِنَّهُ هُوَ السَّمِيعُ الْبَصِيرُ ﴿٥٧﴾

57. There is nothing in their breasts **but a conceit of greatness which they will never achieve.** So seek refuge in Allah. Surely He is the All-Hearing, the All-Seeing.

65. Allah it is Who has made for you the earth a resting-place, and the heaven a canopy, and has given you shape and made your shapes perfect, and has provided you with good things. Such is Allah, your Lord. So blessed is Allah, the Lord of the worlds.

اللَّهُ الَّذِي جَعَلَ لَكُمُ الْأَرْضَ قَرَارًا وَالسَّمَاءَ بِنَاءً وَصَوَّرَكُمْ فَأَحْسَنَ صُوَرَكُمْ وَرَزَقَكُم مِّنَ الطَّيِّبَاتِ ۚ ذٰلِكُمُ اللَّهُ رَبُّكُمْ ۖ فَتَبَارَكَ اللَّهُ رَبُّ الْعَالَمِينَ ﴿٦٥﴾

65. Allah it is Who has made for you the earth a resting- place, **and the heaven a means of dependence and into figures He fashioned you and made your shapes excellent and provided you with wholesome provisions.** Such is Allah, your Lord. So blessed is Allah, the Lord of the worlds.

HA MIM SAJDAH

4. A Book, the verses of which have been expounded in detail—the Qur'ān in clear, eloquent language—for a people who have knowledge,

كِتٰبٌ فُصِّلَتْ اٰيٰتُهٗ قُرْاٰنًا عَرَبِيًّا لِّقَوْمٍ يَّعْلَمُوْنَ ﴿٤﴾

4. A book, the verses of which have been expounded in detail — **oft recited made manifestly clear** — for a people who have knowledge.

6. and between us and thee there is a screen. So carry on thy work; we *too* are working.'

وَّمِنْۢ بَيْنِنَا وَبَيْنِكَ حِجَابٌ فَاعْمَلْ اِنَّنَا عٰمِلُوْنَ ﴿٦﴾

6. and between us and **you there is a veil,** so carry on **your** work; we *too* are working.'

10. Say: 'Do you really disbelieve in Him Who created the earth in two days?

قُلْ اَئِنَّكُمْ لَتَكْفُرُوْنَ بِالَّذِيْ خَلَقَ الْاَرْضَ فِيْ يَوْمَيْنِ

10. Say: 'Do you really disbelieve in Him Who created the earth in two **periods?**

11. He placed therein firm mountains rising above its *surface*, and blessed it *with abundance*, and provided therein its foods in proper measure in four days—alike for *all* seekers.

وَجَعَلَ فِيْهَا رَوَاسِيَ مِنْ فَوْقِهَا وَبٰرَكَ فِيْهَا وَقَدَّرَ فِيْهَاۤ اَقْوَاتَهَا فِيْۤ اَرْبَعَةِ اَيَّامٍ سَوَآءً لِّلسَّآئِلِيْنَ ﴿١١﴾

11. He **set** therein firm mountains rising above its *surface,* and **placed blessings therein and finely balanced its means of sustenance in four periods — alike for all who seek.**

20. And on the day when the enemies of Allah will be gathered together and driven to the Fire, they will be goaded on.

وَيَوْمَ يُحْشَرُ اَعْدَآءُ اللّٰهِ اِلَى النَّارِ فَهُمْ يُوْزَعُوْنَ ﴿٢٠﴾

20. And on the day when the enemies of Allah **will be flocked together and**

led to the fire, they will be marched in order.

25. Now if they can endure, the Fire is their abode; and if they ask for forgiveness, they are not of those whom forgiveness can be shown.

فَإِن يَصْبِرُوا فَالنَّارُ مَثْوًى لَّهُمْ وَإِن يَسْتَعْتِبُوا
فَمَا هُم مِّنَ الْمُعْتَبِينَ ٢٥

25. Now if they can endure, the Fire is their abode; and if they **seek a hearing** they will not be **of those who are heard.**

26. And We had assigned for them companions who made *to appear* attractive to them what was before them and what was behind them; and the sentence became due against them along with the communities of Jinn and mankind that had gone before them. Surely, they were *the* losers.

وَقَيَّضْنَا لَهُمْ قُرَنَاءَ فَزَيَّنُوا لَهُم مَّا بَيْنَ
أَيْدِيهِمْ وَمَا خَلْفَهُمْ وَحَقَّ عَلَيْهِمُ الْقَوْلُ
فِي أُمَمٍ قَدْ خَلَتْ مِن قَبْلِهِم مِّنَ الْجِنِّ وَالْإِنسِ
إِنَّهُمْ كَانُوا خَاسِرِينَ ٢٦

26. And We had assigned for them companions who made *to appear* attractive to them **that which had gone before and that which lay ahead of them; and the judgement was passed against them as it was passed regarding the peoples before them belonging to the Jinn - *great people* or common men.** Surely, they were *the* losers.

36. But none is granted it save those who are steadfast; and none is granted it save those who possess a large share of good.

وَمَا يُلَقَّاهَا إِلَّا الَّذِينَ صَبَرُوا وَمَا يُلَقَّاهَا
إِلَّا ذُو حَظٍّ عَظِيمٍ ٣٦

36. But none is granted **that** save those who are steadfast; and none is granted **that except the one who possesses a large share *of excellence*.**

40. And among His Signs is *this:* that thou seest the earth *lying* withered, but when We send down water on it, it stirs and swells *with verdure*. Surely, He Who

وَمِنْ آيَاتِهِ أَنَّكَ تَرَى الْأَرْضَ خَاشِعَةً فَإِذَا أَنزَلْنَا
عَلَيْهَا الْمَاءَ اهْتَزَّتْ وَرَبَتْ إِنَّ الَّذِي أَحْيَاهَا

quickened it can quicken the dead. Verily He has power over all things.

لَمُحۡیِ الۡمَوۡتٰی ؕ اِنَّهٗ عَلٰی كُلِّ شَیۡءٍ قَدِیۡرٌ ﴿۴۰﴾

40. And among His Signs is this: that you see the earth **dried up,** but when We send down water on it, it stirs and swells *with verdure.* Surely, He Who quickened it can quicken the dead. Verily He has power over all things.

41. Surely, those who deviate *from the right path* with respect to Our Signs are not hidden from Us.

اِنَّ الَّذِیۡنَ یُلۡحِدُوۡنَ فِیۡۤ اٰیٰتِنَا لَا یَخۡفَوۡنَ عَلَیۡنَا ؕ

41. Surely, **Those who quarrel regarding Our Signs** are not hidden from Us.

48. And on the day when He will call unto them, *saying,* "Where are My 'partners'?" they will say, 'We declare unto Thee, not one of us is a witness *thereto.*'

وَ یَوۡمَ یُنَادِیۡهِمۡ اَیۡنَ شُرَكَآءِیۡ ۙ قَالُوۡۤا اٰذَنّٰكَ ۙ مَا مِنَّا مِنۡ شَهِیۡدٍ ﴿۴۸﴾

48. And ***think of* the day when He will call them, *saying,* 'Where are the partners attributed to Me?' They will say, 'We declare to You, there is none among us as witness *to that.*'**

49. And all that they used to call upon before will be lost to them, and they will know for certain that they have no place of escape.

وَ ضَلَّ عَنۡهُمۡ مَّا كَانُوۡا یَدۡعُوۡنَ مِنۡ قَبۡلُ وَ ظَنُّوۡا مَا لَهُمۡ مِّنۡ مَّحِیۡصٍ ﴿۴۹﴾

49. And all that they used to call upon before will be lost to them, **then will they realise that there is no escape for them.**

52. And when We bestow a favour on man, he goes away, turning aside; but when evil touches him, lo! he *starts* offering long prayers.

وَ اِذَاۤ اَنۡعَمۡنَا عَلَی الۡاِنۡسَانِ اَعۡرَضَ وَ نَاٰ بِجَانِبِهٖ ۚ وَ اِذَا مَسَّهُ الشَّرُّ فَذُوۡ دُعَآءٍ عَرِیۡضٍ ﴿۵۲﴾

52. And when We bestow a favour on man, **he ignores *it* and turns aside; but when evil touches him, lo! there he is a supplicant of long prayers.**

54. Soon We will show them Our Signs in all parts *of the earth*, and among their own people until it becomes manifest to them that it is the truth. Is it not enough that thy Lord is Witness over all things?

سَنُرِيهِمْ آيٰتِنَا فِي الْآفَاقِ وَفِيٓ أَنْفُسِهِمْ حَتّٰى
يَتَبَيَّنَ لَهُمْ أَنَّهُ الْحَقُّ ۗ أَوَلَمْ يَكْفِ بِرَبِّكَ أَنَّهُ
عَلٰى كُلِّ شَيْءٍ شَهِيدٌ ﴿٥٤﴾

54. Soon We will show them Our Signs ***appearing* on the horizon** and **within themselves** until it becomes manifest to them that it is the truth.

AL-SHURA

4. Thus has Allah, the Mighty, the Wise, been revealing to thee and to those that preceded thee.

كَذٰلِكَ يُوحِيٓ إِلَيْكَ وَإِلَى الَّذِينَ مِنْ قَبْلِكَ ۙ
اللّٰهُ الْعَزِيزُ الْحَكِيمُ ﴿٤﴾

4. Thus Allah, the Mighty, the Wise, reveals to you and has revealed to those that preceded you.

6. The heavens may well-nigh rend asunder from above them; and the angels glorify their Lord with His praise and ask forgiveness for those on the earth. Behold! it is surely Allah Who is the Most Forgiving, the Merciful.

تَكَادُ السَّمٰوٰتُ يَتَفَطَّرْنَ مِنْ فَوْقِهِنَّ وَالْمَلٰٓئِكَةُ
يُسَبِّحُونَ بِحَمْدِ رَبِّهِمْ وَيَسْتَغْفِرُونَ لِمَنْ فِي
الْأَرْضِ ۗ أَلَآ إِنَّ اللّٰهَ هُوَ الْغَفُورُ الرَّحِيمُ ﴿٦﴾

6. **The heavens may rend asunder in their celestial heights;** and the angels glorify their Lord with His praise and ask forgiveness for those on the earth. Behold! It is surely Allah Who is the Most Forgiving, the Merciful.

8. Thus have We revealed to thee the Qur'ān in Arabic, that thou mayest warn the Mother of towns, and all around it; and *that* thou mayest warn *them* of the

وَكَذٰلِكَ أَوْحَيْنَآ إِلَيْكَ قُرْاٰنًا عَرَبِيًّا لِّتُنْذِرَ أُمَّ
الْقُرٰى وَمَنْ حَوْلَهَا وَتُنْذِرَ يَوْمَ الْجَمْعِ لَا رَيْبَ

Day of Gathering whereof there is no doubt: A party *will be* in the Garden, and a party in the blazing Fire.

فِيهِ فَرِيقٌ فِي الْجَنَّةِ وَفَرِيقٌ فِي السَّعِيرِ ۝

8. Thus have We revealed to **you** the Qur'an in Arabic that **you may** warn the Mother of **townships,** and all around it; and *that* **you may** warn *them* of the Day of Gathering whereof there is no doubt: **A section will abide in the gardens *of paradise* and a section will be in a blazing Fire.**

Note: The first house ever built for the purpose of worship of Allah was *al-kaaba* الكعبة situated in a township named Mecca. It is this township which is referred to as *umm-ul-Qura'* اُمّ القرىٰ (the mother of all townships).

This expression may signify its importance with relation to all other cities or it may also literally mean to be the first township ever built. In that case it would imply that in the ancient times, in the same place where Mecca is situated, a township gradually grew around the house of God when it was initially built by some unknown people. Mankind learned to build townships in immitation of this. As such it can be referred to as the mother of all townships.

12. *He is* the Maker of the heavens and the earth. He has made for you pairs of your own selves, andof the cattle *also He has made* pairs. He multiplies you therein.

فَاطِرُ السَّمٰوٰتِ وَالْاَرْضِ جَعَلَ لَكُمْ مِّنْ اَنْفُسِكُمْ اَزْوَاجًا وَّمِنَ الْاَنْعَامِ اَزْوَاجًا يَذْرَؤُكُمْ فِيْهِ

12. *He is* the **Prime Creator** of the heavens and the earth. **He made pairs from among you and also pairs from among the cattle for your benefit.** He multiplies you therein.

15. And they did not become divided but after knowledge had come to them, through jealousy among themselves.

وَمَا تَفَرَّقُوْٓا اِلَّا مِنْۢ بَعْدِ مَا جَآءَهُمُ الْعِلْمُ بَغْيًا بَيْنَهُمْ

15. **They did not differ and split, but after knowledge had come to them, *they did so* out of envy against each other.**

20. Allah is Benignant to His servants. He provides for whom He pleases. And He is the Powerful, the Mighty.

اَللّٰهُ لَطِيۡفٌۢ بِعِبَادِهٖ يَرۡزُقُ مَنۡ يَّشَآءُ ۚ وَهُوَ
الۡقَوِيُّ الۡعَزِيۡزُ ﴿۲۰﴾

20. Allah is **exquisitely kind** to His servants. He provides for whom He pleases. And He is the Powerful, the Mighty.

24. Say: 'I ask of you no reward for it, except *that I am inviting you to God because of* love of kinship.' And whoso earns a good deed, We give him increase of good therein. Surely, Allah is Most Forgiving, Most Appreciating.

قُلۡ لَّاۤ اَسۡـَٔلُكُمۡ عَلَيۡهِ اَجۡرًا اِلَّا الۡمَوَدَّةَ
فِي الۡقُرۡبٰى ؕ وَمَنۡ يَّقۡتَرِفۡ حَسَنَةً نَّزِدۡ لَهٗ فِيۡهَا
حُسۡنًا ؕ اِنَّ اللّٰهَ غَفُوۡرٌ شَكُوۡرٌ ﴿۲۴﴾

24. Say: 'I ask of you no reward for it, except **a love displayed among kith and kin. And whoever does an act of goodness, We further enhance for him the beauty of his goodness.**

25. Do they say, 'He has forged a lie against Allah?' If Allah had *so* willed, He could seal thy heart *as He has sealed the hearts of thy enemies*. But Allah is blotting out falsehood *through thee* and is establishing the truth by His words. Surely, He knows full well what is in the breasts.

اَمۡ يَقُوۡلُوۡنَ افۡتَرٰى عَلَى اللّٰهِ كَذِبًا ۚ فَاِنۡ يَّشَاِ اللّٰهُ
يَخۡتِمۡ عَلٰى قَلۡبِكَ ؕ وَيَمۡحُ اللّٰهُ الۡبَاطِلَ وَيُحِقُّ الۡحَقَّ
بِكَلِمٰتِهٖ ؕ اِنَّهٗ عَلِيۡمٌۢ بِذَاتِ الصُّدُوۡرِ ﴿۲۵﴾

25. Do they say, 'He has forged a lie against Allah? **If Allah so willed He could have sealed your heart. But Allah blots out falsehood and establishes truth by His Commands.** Surely, He knows full well what is in the breasts.

AL-ZUKHRUF

5. And surely, it is *safe* with Us in the Mother of the Book, exalted *and* full of wisdom.

وَاِنَّهٗ فِيۡۤ اُمِّ الۡكِتٰبِ لَدَيۡنَا لَعَلِيٌّ حَكِيۡمٌ ﴿۵﴾

Note: The phrase *umm-ul-Kitab* ام الكتاب (Mother of the Book) is commonly applied to the opening chapter of the Qur'an *al-fatiha* الفاتحة which like a seed has all the basic teachings and characteristics of the Qur'an. But here it seems to apply to the blueprint of the Divine Book which in some form is preserved with God, in dimensions not fully fathomable by man.

9. And We destroyed *those* who were stronger in power than these, and the example of the earlier peoples has gone before.

فَأَهْلَكْنَآ أَشَدَّ مِنْهُم بَطْشًا وَمَضَىٰ مَثَلُ ٱلْأَوَّلِينَ ﴿٩﴾

9. And We destroyed those who **were stronger in grip than these,** and the example of the earlier peoples has gone before.

14. 'Holy is He Who has subjected this to us, and we had not the strength to subdue it *ourselves*.

سُبْحَٰنَ ٱلَّذِى سَخَّرَ لَنَا هَٰذَا وَمَا كُنَّا لَهُۥ مُقْرِنِينَ ﴿١٤﴾

14. 'Holy is He Who has subjected this to us, and we, **by ourselves, were unable to harness it.**

16. And a portion of His servants they assert to be His *children*. Indeed man is clearly ungrateful.

وَجَعَلُوا۟ لَهُۥ مِنْ عِبَادِهِۦ جُزْءًا ۚ إِنَّ ٱلْإِنسَٰنَ لَكَفُورٌ مُّبِينٌ ﴿١٦﴾

16. **And they assert some of His servants to be a part of Him.** Indeed man is **manifestly** ungrateful.

24. And thus *has it always been* that We never sent any Warner before thee to any township but the evil leaders thereof said: 'We found our fathers following a *certain* course, and we are following in their footsteps.'

وَكَذَٰلِكَ مَآ أَرْسَلْنَا مِن قَبْلِكَ فِى قَرْيَةٍ مِّن نَّذِيرٍ إِلَّا قَالَ مُتْرَفُوهَآ إِنَّا وَجَدْنَآ ءَابَآءَنَا عَلَىٰٓ أُمَّةٍ وَإِنَّا عَلَىٰٓ ءَاثَٰرِهِم مُّقْتَدُونَ ﴿٢٤﴾

24. And thus *has it always been* that We never sent any Warner before **you** to any township but **the prosperous thereof said: 'We found our ancestors set on a** *certain* course; and we are following in their footsteps.'

26. So We punished them. Behold then what was the end of those who rejected *the Prophets!*

فَانْتَقَمْنَا مِنْهُمْ فَانْظُرْ كَيْفَ كَانَ عَاقِبَةُ
الْمُكَذِّبِينَ ﴿٢٦﴾

26. So **We exacted retribution from them.** Behold then what was the end of those who rejected *the Prophets!*

33. and We exalt some of them above others in degrees *of rank*, so that some of them may make others subservient *to themselves*. And the mercy of thy Lord is better than that which they amass.

وَرَفَعْنَا بَعْضَهُمْ
فَوْقَ بَعْضٍ دَرَجٰتٍ لِيَتَّخِذَ بَعْضُهُمْ بَعْضًا سُخْرِيًّا
وَرَحْمَتُ رَبِّكَ خَيْرٌ مِمَّا يَجْمَعُونَ ﴿٣٣﴾

33. and We exalt some of them above others in degrees of rank, **but alas merely to result in the subjugation of some by others.** And the mercy of **your** Lord is better than that which they amass.

40. 'And *the fact* that you are partners in punishment will not profit you this day for you have acted wrongfully.'

وَلَنْ يَنْفَعَكُمُ الْيَوْمَ إِذْ ظَلَمْتُمْ أَنَّكُمْ فِي الْعَذَابِ
مُشْتَرِكُونَ ﴿٤٠﴾

40. **'Having transgressed as you did, your being partners in punishment will be of no avail to you this day.'**

45. And, truly, it is *a source of* eminence for thee and for thy people; and you will be inquired about.

وَإِنَّهُ لَذِكْرٌ لَكَ وَلِقَوْمِكَ وَسَوْفَ تُسْأَلُونَ ﴿٤٥﴾

45. And, truly, it is **a reminder for you and for your people, and you shall be called to account.**

58. And when the son of Mary is mentioned as an instance, lo! thy people raise a clamour thereat;

وَلَمَّا ضُرِبَ ابْنُ مَرْيَمَ مَثَلًا إِذَا قَوْمُكَ مِنْهُ
يَصِدُّونَ ﴿٥٨﴾

58. And when the son of Mary is mentioned as a **parable,** lo! **your** People raise a clamour thereat;

وَإِنَّهُ لَعِلْمٌ لِّلسَّاعَةِ فَلَا تَمْتَرُنَّ بِهَا وَاتَّبِعُونِ ۚ هَٰذَا صِرَاطٌ مُّسْتَقِيمٌ ﴿٦٢﴾

62. But verily, he was a sign of the Hour. So have no doubt about it, but follow me. This is the right path.

62. But verily, he **is** a sign of the Hour. So have no doubt about it, but follow me. This is the right path.

Note: The word الساعة literally translated as 'the Hour' should be understood in the light of the same expression used in (Ch: 54:2) Sura Al-Qamar. There the revolutionary changes which were destined to be brought about by the advent of the Holy Prophet Muhammad (peace be upon him) are referred to as الساعة. And the splitting of the moon is presented as evidence in favour of the spiritual revolution which was about to take place. The connotation of this term as applied to Jesus in the verse under study should be understood on the same lines. Hence 'the Hour' refers to the advent of Jesus in the latter days and the spiritual revolution attendant upon it.

الَّذِينَ آمَنُوا بِآيَاتِنَا وَكَانُوا مُسْلِمِينَ ﴿٧٠﴾

70. '*You* who believed in Our Signs and submitted,

70. '**Those** who believed in Our Signs and submitted,

ادْخُلُوا الْجَنَّةَ أَنتُمْ وَأَزْوَاجُكُمْ تُحْبَرُونَ ﴿٧١﴾

71. 'Enter ye the Garden, you and your wives, honoured and happy.'

71. 'Enter ye the Garden, you and your **spouses will be honoured and made happy.'**

وَنَادَوْا يَا مَالِكُ لِيَقْضِ عَلَيْنَا رَبُّكَ ۖ قَالَ إِنَّكُم مَّاكِثُونَ ﴿٧٨﴾

78. And they will cry: 'O master! let thy Lord finish with us.' He will say, 'You must remain.'

78. **And they will cry out, 'O custodian *of Hell*, let your Lord cause us to perish. He will reply,** 'You must remain'.

AL-JATHIYAH

15. Tell those who believe to forgive those who *persecute them and* fear not the Days of Allah, that He may requite a people for what they earn.

قُلْ لِّلَّذِيْنَ اٰمَنُوْا يَغْفِرُوْا لِلَّذِيْنَ لَا يَرْجُوْنَ اَيَّامَ اللّٰهِ
لِيَجْزِيَ قَوْمًا بِمَا كَانُوْا يَكْسِبُوْنَ ﴿۱۵﴾

15. **Say to those who believe, that they exercise forgiveness towards those who do not expect the promised days of Allah** ***to come to pass,*** that He may requite a people for what they earn.

18. And We gave them clear Signs regarding this affair.

وَاٰتَيْنٰهُمْ بَيِّنٰتٍ مِّنَ الْاَمْرِ

18. And We gave them clear **instructions** regarding **the Law.**

19. Then We set thee on a clear path in the matter *of religion;* so follow it, and follow not the evil inclinations of those who know not.

ثُمَّ جَعَلْنٰكَ عَلٰى شَرِيْعَةٍ مِّنَ الْاَمْرِ فَاتَّبِعْهَا وَ
لَا تَتَّبِعْ اَهْوَآءَ الَّذِيْنَ لَا يَعْلَمُوْنَ ﴿۱۹﴾

19. Then We set **you upon a clear path of the Law;** so follow it, and follow not the evil inclinations of those who know not.

24. Hast thou seen him who conceives of his god according to his own fancy, and whom Allah has adjudged astray on the basis of *His* knowledge, and whose ears and whose heart He has sealed up, and on whose eyes He has put a covering? Who, then, will guide him after Allah *has condemned him?* Will you not then heed?

اَفَرَءَيْتَ مَنِ اتَّخَذَ اِلٰهَهٗ هَوٰىهُ وَاَضَلَّهُ اللّٰهُ
عَلٰى عِلْمٍ وَّخَتَمَ عَلٰى سَمْعِهٖ وَقَلْبِهٖ وَجَعَلَ عَلٰى
بَصَرِهٖ غِشٰوَةً ؕ فَمَنْ يَّهْدِيْهِ مِنْۢ بَعْدِ اللّٰهِ ؕ
اَفَلَا تَذَكَّرُوْنَ ﴿۲۴﴾

24. **Have you seen him who makes his own desire his lord,** and whom Allah has adjudged astray **knowingly,** and whose ears and whose heart He has sealed up, and on whose eyes He has put a covering? Who, then, will guide him

after Allah *has condemned him?* Will you not then heed?

28. on that day those who follow falsehood will be the losers.

يَوْمَئِذٍ يَّخْسَرُ الْمُبْطِلُوْنَ ﴿٢٨﴾

28. on that day those who **reject the truth will suffer.**

36. 'This *is so*, because you made a jest of the Signs of Allah, and the life of the world deceived you.' Therefore, that day they will not be taken out from thence, nor will they be taken back into favour.

ذٰلِكُمْ بِاَنَّكُمُ اتَّخَذْتُمْ اٰيٰتِ اللّٰهِ هُزُوًا وَّ غَرَّتْكُمُ الْحَيٰوةُ الدُّنْيَا ۚ فَالْيَوْمَ لَا يُخْرَجُوْنَ مِنْهَا وَ لَا هُمْ يُسْتَعْتَبُوْنَ ﴿٣٦﴾

36. 'This *is so*, because you made a jest of the Signs of Allah, and the life of the world deceived you.' Therefore, that day they will not be taken out from thence, nor will they be **granted access to the threshold.**

AL-AHQAF

28. And We did destroy townships round about you; and We have varied the Signs, that they might turn *to Us*.

وَ لَقَدْ اَهْلَكْنَا مَا حَوْلَكُمْ مِّنَ الْقُرٰى وَ صَرَّفْنَا الْاٰيٰتِ لَعَلَّهُمْ يَرْجِعُوْنَ ﴿٢٨﴾

28. and We did destroy townships **all around you** and We have varied the Signs, that they might turn *to Us*.

MUHAMMAD

3. —He removes from them their sins and improves their condition.

كَفَّرَ عَنْهُمْ سَيِّاٰتِهِمْ وَ اَصْلَحَ بَالَهُمْ ﴿٣﴾

3. **He will remove from them their evils and will reform their conduct.**

5. And if Allah had *so* pleased, He could have punished them *Himself*, but *He has willed* that He may try some of you by others.

وَلَوْ يَشَآءُ
اللّٰهُ لَانْتَصَرَ مِنْهُمْ وَلٰكِنْ لِّيَبْلُوَا۟ بَعْضَكُمْ بِبَعْضٍ ؕ

5. And if Allah had so **decided, He could have Himself exacted retribution from them, but He puts some of you to trial at the hands of some others.**

6. He will guide them and improve their condition,

سَيَهْدِيْهِمْ وَيُصْلِحُ بَالَهُمْ ۚ ﴿۶﴾

6. He will guide them and **reform their conduct.**

7. And admit them into the Garden which He has made known to them.

وَيُدْخِلُهُمُ الْجَنَّةَ عَرَّفَهَا لَهُمْ ﴿۷﴾

7. And admit them into the garden which **He beautified and made distinguished for them.**

21. thou seest those in whose hearts is a disease looking towards thee with the look of one who is fainting on account of *approaching* death. So ruin seize them!

رَاَيْتَ
الَّذِيْنَ فِيْ قُلُوْبِهِمْ مَّرَضٌ يَّنْظُرُوْنَ اِلَيْكَ نَظَرَ
الْمَغْشِيِّ عَلَيْهِ مِنَ الْمَوْتِ ؕ فَاَوْلٰى لَهُمْ ۚ ﴿۲۱﴾

21. **You will see those whose hearts are diseased looking at you with a look of one dazed by the shadow cast upon him by death.** So ruin seize them!

25. Will they not, then, ponder over the Qur'ān, or is it that on the hearts are their locks?

اَفَلَا يَتَدَبَّرُوْنَ الْقُرْاٰنَ اَمْ عَلٰى قُلُوْبٍ اَقْفَالُهَا ﴿۲۵﴾

25. Will they not, then, ponder over the Qur'an, or is it that **upon their hearts are locks of their own *making?***

32. And We will surely try you until We distinguish those among you who strive *for the cause of God* and those who are

وَلَنَبْلُوَنَّكُمْ حَتّٰى نَعْلَمَ الْمُجٰهِدِيْنَ مِنْكُمْ وَ

الصّٰبِرِيْنَ وَنَبْلُوَاْ اَخْبَارَكُمْ ﴿٣٢﴾

steadfast. And We will make known the facts about you.

32. And We will surely try you **until We know the true strivers among you and the steadfast, and *by trial* We will bring out your real worth.**

فَلَا تَهِنُوْا وَتَدْعُوْٓا اِلَى السَّلْمِ ۖ وَاَنْتُمُ الْاَعْلَوْنَ ۖ وَاللّٰهُ مَعَكُمْ وَلَنْ يَّتِرَكُمْ اَعْمَالَكُمْ ﴿٣٦﴾

36. So be not slack and sue not for peace; for you will *certainly* have the upper hand. And Allah is with you, and He will not deprive you of *the reward of* your actions.

36. Do not slacken lest you should sue for peace while you are bound to emerge victorious. And Allah is with you, and He will not deprive you of *the reward of* your actions.

AL-FATH

عَلَيْهِمْ دَآئِرَةُ السَّوْءِ ۚ

7. On them *shall fall* an evil calamity;

7. Against them will turn the wheel of misfortune.

وَظَنَنْتُمْ ظَنَّ السَّوْءِ ۖ وَكُنْتُمْ قَوْمًاۢ بُوْرًا ﴿١٣﴾

13. and you thought an evil thought, and you were a ruined people.'

13. **and you entertained an evil thought,** and you were a ruined people.'

سُنَّةَ اللّٰهِ الَّتِيْ قَدْ خَلَتْ مِنْ قَبْلُ ۖ وَلَنْ تَجِدَ لِسُنَّةِ اللّٰهِ تَبْدِيْلًا ﴿٢٤﴾

24. Such is the law of Allah that has been *in operation* before; and thou shalt not find any change in the law of Allah.

24. Such **has been the established practice of Allah that has been *in operation* before and you shall not find any change in the established practice of Allah.**

27. and made them cleave to the principle of righteousness, and they were better entitled to it and more worthy of it. And Allah knows everything full well.

وَأَلْزَمَهُمْ كَلِمَةَ التَّقْوٰى وَكَانُوْٓا أَحَقَّ بِهَا وَأَهْلَهَا ۚ وَكَانَ اللّٰهُ بِكُلِّ شَيْءٍ عَلِيْمًا ﴿٢٧﴾

27. and made them **cleave to the word of righteousness** and they were better entitled to it and more worthy of it. And Allah knows everything full well.

30. Muḥammad is the Messenger of Allah. And those who are with him are hard against the disbelievers, tender among themselves.

مُحَمَّدٌ رَّسُوْلُ اللّٰهِ ۚ وَالَّذِيْنَ مَعَهٗٓ أَشِدَّآءُ عَلَى الْكُفَّارِ رُحَمَآءُ بَيْنَهُمْ

30. Muhammad is the Messenger of Allah. And those who are with him are **firm against the non-believers,** tender among themselves.

AL-HUJURAT

2. O ye who believe! be not forward in the presence of Allah and His Messenger, but fear Allah. Verily, Allah is All-Hearing, All-Knowing.

يٰٓأَيُّهَا الَّذِيْنَ اٰمَنُوْا لَا تُقَدِّمُوْا بَيْنَ يَدَيِ اللّٰهِ وَرَسُوْلِهٖ وَاتَّقُوا اللّٰهَ ۚ إِنَّ اللّٰهَ سَمِيْعٌ عَلِيْمٌ ﴿٢﴾

2. O, Ye who believe! **be not forward with respect to Allah and His Messenger,** but fear Allah. Verily, Allah is All-Hearing, All-Knowing.

4. Verily those who lower their voices in the presence of the Messenger of Allah are the ones whose hearts Allah has purified for righteousness. For them is forgiveness and a great reward.

إِنَّ الَّذِيْنَ يَغُضُّوْنَ أَصْوَاتَهُمْ عِنْدَ رَسُوْلِ اللّٰهِ أُولٰٓئِكَ الَّذِيْنَ امْتَحَنَ اللّٰهُ قُلُوْبَهُمْ لِلتَّقْوٰى ۚ لَهُمْ مَّغْفِرَةٌ وَّأَجْرٌ عَظِيْمٌ ﴿۴﴾

4. Verily those who lower their voices in the presence of the Messenger of Allah are the ones whose hearts Allah has **made righteous through trials.** For them is forgiveness and a great reward.

5. Those who shout out to thee from without *thy private* apartments—most of them lack understanding.

5. Surely those who start addressing you loudly while as yet at a distance from *your* houses — most of them lack understanding.

إِنَّ الَّذِينَ يُنَادُونَكَ مِن وَرَاءِ الْحُجُرَاتِ
أَكْثَرُهُمْ لَا يَعْقِلُونَ ﴿٥﴾

12.
And defame not your own people, nor call *one another* by nick-names. Bad *indeed* is evil reputation after *the profession of* belief; and those who repent not are the wrong-doers.

12. **Do not slander your own people, nor taunt each other with nicknames. It is bad indeed to earn foul reputation after *professing* the faith;** and those who repent not are the wrongdoers.

وَلَا تَلْمِزُوا أَنفُسَكُمْ وَلَا
تَنَابَزُوا بِالْأَلْقَابِ بِئْسَ الِاسْمُ الْفُسُوقُ بَعْدَ
الْإِيمَانِ وَمَن لَّمْ يَتُبْ فَأُولَٰئِكَ هُمُ الظَّالِمُونَ ﴿١٢﴾

13. O ye who believe! avoid most of suspicions; for suspicion in some cases is a sin. And spy not, nor back-bite one another. Would any of you like to eat the flesh of his brother who is dead? Certainly you would loathe it. And fear Allah, surely, Allah is Oft-Returning *with compassion and is* Merciful.

13. O ye who believe! Avoid **too frequent indulgence in suspicion; for some suspicions are certainly sin.** And spy not, nor backbite one another. Would any of you like to eat the flesh of his brother who is dead? Certainly you would loath it. And fear Allah, surely, Allah is Oft-Returning *with compassion and is* Merciful.

يَا أَيُّهَا الَّذِينَ آمَنُوا اجْتَنِبُوا كَثِيرًا مِّنَ الظَّنِّ إِنَّ
بَعْضَ الظَّنِّ إِثْمٌ وَلَا تَجَسَّسُوا وَلَا يَغْتَب
بَّعْضُكُم بَعْضًا أَيُحِبُّ أَحَدُكُمْ أَن يَأْكُلَ لَحْمَ
أَخِيهِ مَيْتًا فَكَرِهْتُمُوهُ وَاتَّقُوا اللَّهَ إِنَّ اللَّهَ
تَوَّابٌ رَّحِيمٌ ﴿١٣﴾

14. O mankind, We have created you from a male and a female; and We have made you into tribes and sub-tribes that you may recognize one another.

يَا أَيُّهَا النَّاسُ إِنَّا خَلَقْنَاكُم مِّن ذَكَرٍ وَأُنثَىٰ
وَجَعَلْنَاكُمْ شُعُوبًا وَقَبَائِلَ لِتَعَارَفُوا

14. O mankind, We have created you from **male and female;** and We have made you into **clans and tribes** that you may recognize one another.

18. Say, 'Deem not your embracing Islam a favour unto me. On the contrary, Allah has bestowed a favour upon you in that He has guided you to the *true* Faith, if you are truthful.'

قُلْ لَّا تَمُنُّوْا عَلَيَّ إِسْلَامَكُمْ ۚ بَلِ اللّٰهُ يَمُنُّ عَلَيْكُمْ أَنْ هَدٰىكُمْ لِلْإِيْمَانِ إِنْ كُنْتُمْ صٰدِقِيْنَ ﴿۱۸﴾

18. Say, 'Do not show off your acceptance of Islam as a favour to me. It is you on the contrary, whom Allah has favoured by guiding you to the true faith, if you are true *in your claim to be believers.'*

QAF

2. Qāf*. By the glorious Qur'ān, *thou art a Messenger of God.*

قٓ ۚ وَالْقُرْاٰنِ الْمَجِيْدِ ﴿۲﴾

2. Qaf. ***We present*** **the Glorious Qur'an** ***as a witness to your truth.***

17. And assuredly, We have created man and We know what his *physical* self whispers *to him*, and We are nearer to him than *even his* jugular vein.

وَلَقَدْ خَلَقْنَا الْإِنْسَانَ وَنَعْلَمُ مَا تُوَسْوِسُ بِهٖ نَفْسُهٗ ۚ وَنَحْنُ أَقْرَبُ إِلَيْهِ مِنْ حَبْلِ الْوَرِيْدِ ﴿۱۷﴾

17. And assuredly, We have created man and **We are aware of what his ego whispers to him,** and We are nearer to him than *even his* jugular vein.

43. The day when they will hear the blast in truth;

يَّوْمَ يَسْمَعُوْنَ الصَّيْحَةَ بِالْحَقِّ ۚ

43. **The Day when they will certainly hear the blast.**

AL-DHARIYAT

وَالذّٰرِيٰتِ ذَرْوًا ﴿٢﴾

2. By *the winds* that scatter *seeds with a true* scattering,

2. By the scatterers who scatter — a thorough scattering.

فَالْحٰمِلٰتِ وِقْرًا ﴿٣﴾

3. Then by *the clouds* that carry the load *of moisture,*

3. Then by those who carry heavy loads.

فَالْجٰرِيٰتِ يُسْرًا ﴿٤﴾

4. Then by *the rivers* that flow gently,

4. Then by those who move along effortlessly.

فَالْمُقَسِّمٰتِ اَمْرًا ﴿٥﴾

5. *And* then by *the angels* that finally administer and execute affairs,

5. Then by those who distribute authority,

اِنَّكُمْ لَفِيْ قَوْلٍ مُّخْتَلِفٍ ﴿٩﴾

9. Truly you are discordant in *your* utterances.

9. Verily you hold different views.

يُّؤْفَكُ عَنْهُ مَنْ اُفِكَ ﴿١٠﴾

10. He *alone* is turned away from *the truth* who is *destined to be thus* turned away.

10. Only he will be led away from *the promised truth* who is *fit* to be led away.

قُتِلَ الْخَرّٰصُوْنَ ﴿١١﴾

11. Cursed be the liars,

11. Cursed be the conjecturers,

الَّذِيْنَ هُمْ فِيْ غَمْرَةٍ سَاهُوْنَ ﴿١٢﴾

12. Who are heedless in the depth *of ignorance.*

12. Who are drowned deep in negligence.

15. **'Taste ye your torment. This is what you would hasten.'**

ذُوقُوا فِتْنَتَكُمْ هَٰذَا الَّذِي كُنتُم بِهِ تَسْتَعْجِلُونَ ﴿١٥﴾

15. 'Taste ye ***the consequence of*** **your mischief. This is what you were hastening towards.**

20. And in their **wealth was a share** for one who asked for help **and** *for* one who could not.

وَفِي أَمْوَالِهِمْ حَقٌّ لِّلسَّائِلِ وَالْمَحْرُومِ ﴿٢٠﴾

20. **And in their wealth is a share belonging to the beggar and the destitute.**

29. And he felt a fear on account of **them. They said, 'Fear not.' And they gave** him glad tidings of ***the birth of*** **a** son **possessing** knowledge.

فَأَوْجَسَ مِنْهُمْ خِيفَةً ۖ قَالُوا لَا تَخَفْ ۖ وَبَشَّرُوهُ بِغُلَامٍ عَلِيمٍ ﴿٢٩﴾

29. **He grew apprehensive of them.** They said, 'Fear not.' And they gave him glad tidings of *the birth of* a **knowledgeable** son.

40. But he turned away *from Moses* in his *pride of* power, and said, 'A sorcerer, or a madman.'

فَتَوَلَّىٰ بِرُكْنِهِ وَقَالَ سَاحِرٌ أَوْ مَجْنُونٌ ﴿٤٠﴾

40. **He turned away along with his chieftains** and said, 'A sorcerer, or a madman.'

48. And We have built the heaven with *Our own* hands, and verily We have vast powers.

وَالسَّمَاءَ بَنَيْنَاهَا بِأَيْدٍ وَإِنَّا لَمُوسِعُونَ ﴿٤٨﴾

48. And We have built the heaven **with might and We continue to expand it indeed.**

56. And keep on exhorting; for verily, exhortation benefits those who would believe.

وَذَكِّرْ فَإِنَّ الذِّكْرَىٰ تَنفَعُ الْمُؤْمِنِينَ ﴿٥٦﴾

56. And keep on exhorting; **certainly** exhortation benefits **the believers.**

فإن للذين ظلموا ذنوبا مثل ذنوب أصحابهم فلا يستعجلون ﴿٦٠﴾

60. And for those who do wrong there is a share *of comfort* like the share *enjoyed by* their fellows *of the earlier times;* so let them not ask Me to hasten on *the punishment.*

60. Surely, the fate of those who did wrong shall be like that of the people of their ilk; so let them not ask Me to hasten on *the punishment.*

AL-TUR

يوم تمور السماء مورا ﴿١٠﴾

10. On the day when the heaven will heave *with awful* heaving,

10. On the day when the heaven will heave **with great commotion.**

وتسير الجبال سيرا ﴿١١﴾

11. And the mountains will move, *with terrible* moving,

11. And the mountains will move **a great moving,**

كلوا واشربوا هنيئا بما كنتم تعملون ﴿٢٠﴾

20. 'Eat and drink in happiness because of what you used to do,

20. 'Eat and drink **joyfully, as a reward for** what you used to do.

فليأتوا بحديث مثله إن كانوا صادقين ﴿٣٥﴾

35. Let them, then, bring forth an announcement like this, if they speak the truth!

35. Let them, then, bring forth **a narration like this,** if they speak the truth.

أم خلقوا من غير شيء أم هم الخالقون ﴿٣٦﴾

36. Have they been created for nothing, or are they themselves the creators?

36. Have they been created **out of nothing,** or are they themselves the creators?

45. And if they should see a piece of the cloud falling down, they would say, 'Clouds piled up.'

45. And if they see a piece of cloud descending, they say; *soon will follow* clouds layer upon layer.'

وَإِنْ يَرَوْا كِسْفًا مِّنَ السَّمَآءِ سَاقِطًا يَقُولُوا سَحَابٌ مَّرْكُومٌ ﴿٤٥﴾

46. So leave them until they meet that day of theirs, on which they will be overtaken by a thunderbolt,

46. So leave them **alone** until they **confront their *promised* day** on which they will be **thunderstruck.**

فَذَرْهُمْ حَتّٰى يُلٰقُوا يَوْمَهُمُ الَّذِي فِيهِ يُصْعَقُونَ ﴿٤٦﴾

AL-NAJM

2. By the stemless plant when it falls,

2. By the star when it falls,

وَالنَّجْمِ إِذَا هَوٰى ﴿٢﴾

7. *The One* Possessor of strength. So He manifested His ascendance *over everything*,

7. Of Great Might. Who then settled *upon His Throne*,

ذُو مِرَّةٍ فَاسْتَوٰى ﴿٧﴾

8. And *He revealed His Word* when he was on the uppermost horizon,

8. When He was at the loftiest Horizon,

وَهُوَ بِالْأُفُقِ الْأَعْلٰى ﴿٨﴾

12. The heart *of the Prophet* was not untrue to that which he saw.

12. **The heart of the Prophet lied not regarding what he saw.**

مَا كَذَبَ الْفُؤَادُ مَا رَأٰى ﴿١٢﴾

25. Can man have whatever he desires?

25. **Is there for man all that he desires?**

أَمْ لِلْإِنْسَانِ مَا تَمَنّٰى ﴿٢٥﴾

26. Nay, to Allah belong the Hereafter and this *world*.

فَلِلّٰهِ الْاٰخِرَةُ وَالْاُوْلٰى ٢٦

26. *Nay* to Allah belongs the end *of everything* and all that precedes.

31. That is the utmost limit of their knowledge.

ذٰلِكَ مَبْلَغُهُمْ مِّنَ الْعِلْمِ

31. That is the utmost **they have of knowledge.**

33. Those who shun the grave sins and immoral actions except minor faults—verily, thy Lord is very liberal in forgiving.

اَلَّذِيْنَ يَجْتَنِبُوْنَ كَبٰٓئِرَ الْاِثْمِ وَالْفَوَاحِشَ اِلَّا
اللَّمَمَ ۭ اِنَّ رَبَّكَ وَاسِعُ الْمَغْفِرَةِ

33. **Those who shun major sins and indecencies except for minor slips — verily, your Lord is expansive in forgiveness.**

40. And that man will have nothing but what he strives for;

وَاَنْ لَّيْسَ لِلْاِنْسَانِ اِلَّا مَا سَعٰى ٤٠

40. **And there is nothing for man but *the fruits of* his endeavours;**

41. And that his striving shall soon be seen;

وَاَنَّ سَعْيَهٗ سَوْفَ يُرٰى ٤١

41. **And that his endeavour will soon be acknowledged;**

54. And He overthrew the subverted cities *of the people of Lot*,

وَالْمُؤْتَفِكَةَ اَهْوٰى ٥٤

54. And He overthrew the subverted **townships** *of the people of Lot.*

55. So that there covered them that which was to cover.

فَغَشّٰىهَا مَا غَشّٰى ٥٥

55. **So covered them that which did cover them.**

AL-QAMAR

25. Then indeed we would be in manifest error, and *would be* mad.

إِنَّآ إِذًا لَّفِى ضَلَٰلٍ وَسُعُرٍ ﴿٢٥﴾

25. Indeed then we shall be in grave error and ***afflicted with* madness.**

29. 'And tell them that the water is shared *only* between them, *but as for the she-camel* every drinking time may be attended *by her*.'

وَنَبِّئْهُمْ أَنَّ الْمَآءَ قِسْمَةٌۢ بَيْنَهُمْ كُلُّ شِرْبٍ مُّحْتَضَرٌ ﴿٢٩﴾

29. 'And tell them that the water is shared between them, **every drinking time shall be observed.'**

30. But they called their comrade, and he seized *a sword* and hamstrung *her*.

فَنَادَوْا صَاحِبَهُمْ فَتَعَاطَىٰ فَعَقَرَ ﴿٣٠﴾

30. But they called their comarade, **and he poised himself to strike and hamstrung her.**

AL-RAHMAN

5. He has taught him plain speech.

عَلَّمَهُ الْبَيَانَ ﴿٥﴾

5. He taught him **the skill of expression.**

20. He has made the two bodies of water flow. They will *one day* meet.

مَرَجَ الْبَحْرَيْنِ يَلْتَقِيَانِ ﴿٢٠﴾

20. **Verily He will merge the two oceans, joining them together.**

32. Soon shall We attend to you, O ye two big groups!

سَنَفْرُغُ لَكُمْ أَيُّهَ الثَّقَلَانِ ﴿٣٢﴾

32. Soon shall We attend to you, O ye two **mighty powers!**

يُرۡسَلُ عَلَيۡكُمَا شُوَاظٞ مِّن نَّارٖ وَنُحَاسٞ فَلَا تَنتَصِرَانِ ٣٥

36. There shall be sent against you a flame of fire, and smoke; and you shall not be able to help yourselves.

36. There shall be sent against you a **smokeless tongue of fire and a fireless** ***column of*** **smoke and you shall not be able to help one another.**

وَلِمَنۡ خَافَ مَقَامَ رَبِّهِۦ جَنَّتَانِ ٤٦

47. But for him who fears to stand before his Lord there are two Gardens—

47. But for him **who is awed by the lofty station of his Lord, there are two gardens.**

ذَوَاتَآ أَفۡنَانٖ ٤٨

49. Having many varieties *of trees*.

49. Both having many branches.

AL-WAQIAH

لَيۡسَ لِوَقۡعَتِهَا كَاذِبَةٌ ٢

3. None can say that its coming to pass is a lie—

3. **There is no denying its occurrence —**

خَافِضَةٞ رَّافِعَةٌ ٣

4. *Some* it will bring low, *others* it will exalt.

4. **Lowering some and exalting others.**

فَأَصۡحَٰبُ ٱلۡمَيۡمَنَةِ مَآ أَصۡحَٰبُ ٱلۡمَيۡمَنَةِ ٨

9. *First,* those on the right hand—how *lucky* are those on the right hand!—

9. **And the people of the right and what of the people of the right!**

وَأَصۡحَٰبُ ٱلۡمَشۡـَٔمَةِ مَآ أَصۡحَٰبُ ٱلۡمَشۡـَٔمَةِ ٩

10. *Second,* those on the left hand—how *unlucky* are those on the left hand!—

10. **And the people of the left and what of those who are of the left!**

ثُلَّةٞ مِّنَ ٱلۡأَوَّلِينَ ١٣

14. A large party from among the early ***Muslims***,

14. A large party from among the earlier people,

وَ قَلِيلٌ مِّنَ الْاٰخِرِيْنَ ﴿۱۵﴾

15. And a few from the later ones,

15. And a smaller group from among the people of the latter days,

كَاَمْثَالِ اللُّؤْلُؤِ الْمَكْنُوْنِ ﴿۲۴﴾

24. Like pearls, well preserved,

24. Like pearls, **well concealed *and protected.***

وَاَصْحٰبُ الْيَمِيْنِ ۙ مَآ اَصْحٰبُ الْيَمِيْنِ ﴿۲۸﴾

28. And *as for* those on the right hand—how *lucky* are those on the right hand!—

28. The people of the right and what of the people of the right!

لِّاَصْحٰبِ الْيَمِيْنِ ﴿۳۹﴾

39. With those on the right hand:

39. **For people of the right.**

وَ اَصْحٰبُ الشِّمَالِ ۙ مَآ اَصْحٰبُ الشِّمَالِ ﴿۴۲﴾

42. But *as for* those on the left hand—how *unlucky* are those on the left hand!—

42. And the people belonging to the left and what of those who belong to the left!

فَشٰرِبُوْنَ شُرْبَ الْهِيْمِ ﴿۵۶﴾

56. 'Drinking like the drinking of the camels that suffer from an insatiable thirst.'

56. 'Drinking like an ever thirsty camel.'

نَحْنُ خَلَقْنٰكُمْ فَلَوْلَا تُصَدِّقُوْنَ ﴿۵۸﴾

58. We have created you. Why, then, do you not accept *the truth?*

58. We have created you. Why, then, do you not **acknowledge *it?***

عَلٰٓى اَنْ نُّبَدِّلَ اَمْثَالَكُمْ وَ نُنْشِئَكُمْ فِيْ مَا لَا تَعْلَمُوْنَ ﴿۶۲﴾

62. From bringing in your place others like you, and *from* developing you into a form which *at present* you know not.

62. From changing your *present* forms and raising you into something of which you have no idea.

لَوْ نَشَآءُ لَجَعَلْنٰهُ حُطَامًا فَظَلْتُمْ تَفَكَّهُوْنَ ٦٦

66. If We *so* pleased, We could reduce it all to broken pieces, then you would keep lamenting:

66. Had We so wanted We could have turned it into chaff, then you would be left lamenting.

فَلَآ اُقْسِمُ بِمَوٰقِعِ النُّجُوْمِ ٧٦

76. Nay, I swear by the shooting of the stars—

76. Nay, I swear by the moorings of the stars —

اَفَبِهٰذَا الْحَدِيْثِ اَنْتُمْ مُّدْهِنُوْنَ ٨٢

82. Is it this *Divine* discourse that you would reject?

82. Will you then treat this *divine* discourse with hypocracy?

AL-HADID

اِعْلَمُوْٓا اَنَّ اللّٰهَ يُحْيِ الْاَرْضَ بَعْدَ مَوْتِهَا ۭ قَدْ
بَيَّنَّا لَكُمُ الْاٰيٰتِ لَعَلَّكُمْ تَعْقِلُوْنَ ١٨

18. Know that Allah is *now* quickening the earth after its death. We have made the Signs manifest to you, that you may understand.

18. Know **that Allah quickens the earth after its death.** We have made the Signs manifest to you, that you may understand.

سَابِقُوْٓا اِلٰى مَغْفِرَةٍ مِّنْ رَّبِّكُمْ وَجَنَّةٍ عَرْضُهَا
كَعَرْضِ السَّمَآءِ وَالْاَرْضِ ۙ اُعِدَّتْ لِلَّذِيْنَ اٰمَنُوْا
بِاللّٰهِ وَرُسُلِهٖ

22. Vie with one another in seeking forgiveness from your Lord and for a Garden the value whereof is equal to the value of the heaven and the earth; it has been prepared for those who believe in Allah and His Messenger.

22. Vie with one another in seeking forgiveness from your Lord and for a **paradise, whose span is like the span of**

the heaven and the earth; it has been prepared for those who believe in Allah and His Messenger.

26. and that Allah may distinguish those who help Him and His Messengers without having seen *Him*. Surely, Allah is Powerful, Mighty.

وَلِيَعْلَمَ اللّٰهُ مَنْ يَّنْصُرُهٗ وَرُسُلَهٗ بِالْغَيْبِ ؕ اِنَّ اللّٰهَ قَوِيٌّ عَزِيْزٌ ﴿٢٦﴾

26. and that Allah may distinguish those who help Him and His Messengers **albeit He remains unseen.** Surely, Allah is Powerful, Mighty.

28. **But monasticism which they invented for themselves—We did not prescribe it for them—for the seeking of Allah's pleasure; but they did not observe it with due observance.**

وَرَهْبَانِيَّةَ ابْتَدَعُوْهَا مَا كَتَبْنٰهَا عَلَيْهِمْ اِلَّا ابْتِغَآءَ رِضْوَانِ اللّٰهِ فَمَا رَعَوْهَا حَقَّ رِعَايَتِهَا ۚ

28. The monasticism **which they innovated We did not prescribe it for them but for the sake of gaining Allah's favour; but they did not practise it in accordance with its true spirit.**

AL-MUJADILAH

13. O ye who believe! when you consult the Messenger in private, give alms before your consultation.

يٰۤاَيُّهَا الَّذِيْنَ اٰمَنُوْۤا اِذَا نَاجَيْتُمُ الرَّسُوْلَ فَقَدِّمُوْا بَيْنَ يَدَيْ نَجْوٰىكُمْ صَدَقَةً ؕ

13. O ye who believe! When you consult the Messenger in private, **present an offering before your consultation.**

14. Are you afraid of giving alms before your consultation? So, when you do not do so and Allah has been merciful to you, then observe Prayer and pay the Zakāt and obey Allah and His Messenger. And Allah is Well-Aware of what you do.

ءَاَشْفَقْتُمْ اَنْ تُقَدِّمُوْا بَيْنَ يَدَيْ نَجْوٰىكُمْ صَدَقٰتٍ ؕ فَاِذْ لَمْ تَفْعَلُوْا وَتَابَ اللّٰهُ عَلَيْكُمْ فَاَقِيْمُوا الصَّلٰوةَ وَاٰتُوا الزَّكٰوةَ وَاَطِيْعُوا اللّٰهَ وَرَسُوْلَهٗ ؕ وَاللّٰهُ خَبِيْرٌ بِمَا تَعْمَلُوْنَ ﴿١٤﴾

14. Are you afraid of giving **offerings before your consultation? But if you do not and may Allah forgive you, then *it should be enough that*** you observe Prayer and pay the Zakat and obey Allah and His Messenger. And Allah is Well-Aware of what you do.

AL-HASHR

7. but Allah grants power to His Messenger over whomsoever He pleases;

وَلٰكِنَّ اللّٰهَ يُسَلِّطُ رُسُلَهٗ عَلٰى مَنْ يَّشَآءُ

7. But Allah grants power to His **Messengers** over **whomever** He pleases.

10. but prefer *the Refugees* to themselves, even though poverty be their *own lot*.

وَيُؤْثِرُوْنَ عَلٰٓى اَنْفُسِهِمْ وَلَوْ كَانَ بِهِمْ خَصَاصَةٌ

10. but prefer **others to themselves** even though poverty be their own lot.

20. And be not like those who forgot Allah, and whom He has *consequently* caused to forget their own souls.

وَلَا تَكُوْنُوْا كَالَّذِيْنَ نَسُوا اللّٰهَ فَاَنْسٰهُمْ اَنْفُسَهُمْ

20. And be not like those who forgot Allah, **So He made them forget themselves.**

23. He is Allah, and there is no God beside Him,

هُوَ اللّٰهُ الَّذِىْ لَآ اِلٰهَ اِلَّا هُوَ

23. **There is none worthy of worship except Him,**

24. He is Allah, and there is no God beside Him,

هُوَ اللّٰهُ الَّذِىْ لَآ اِلٰهَ اِلَّا هُوَ

24. **There is none worthy of worship except Him,**

AL-MUMTAHANAH

3. If they get the upper hand of you, they show themselves to be your *active* enemies,

إِن يَثْقَفُوكُمْ يَكُونُوا لَكُمْ أَعْدَآءً

3. Only if they gain ascendency over you will they emerge as *open* enemies to you.

AL-SAFF

6. And *remember* when Moses said to his people, 'O my people, why do you vex and slander me and you know that I am Allah's Messenger unto you?'

وَإِذْ قَالَ مُوسَىٰ لِقَوْمِهِۦ يَٰقَوْمِ لِمَ تُؤْذُونَنِى وَقَد تَّعْلَمُونَ أَنِّى رَسُولُ ٱللَّهِ إِلَيْكُمْ

6. And *remember* when Moses said to his people, 'O my people, why do you **hurt me** and you know that I am Allah's Messenger to you?'

15.
Then We gave power to those who believed against their enemy, and they became victorious.

فَأَيَّدْنَا ٱلَّذِينَ ءَامَنُوا عَلَىٰ عَدُوِّهِمْ فَأَصْبَحُوا ظَٰهِرِينَ ﴿١٥﴾

15. Then We **helped** those who believed against their enemy, and they became victorious.

AL-MUNAFIQUN

5. And when thou seest them, their figures please thee; and if they speak, thou listenest to their speech. *They are* as though they were *blocks of* wood propped up. They think that every cry is against them. They are the enemy, so beware of them. Allah's curse be upon them! How are they being turned away!

وَإِذَا رَأَيْتَهُمْ تُعْجِبُكَ أَجْسَامُهُمْ وَإِن يَقُولُوا تَسْمَعْ لِقَوْلِهِمْ كَأَنَّهُمْ خُشُبٌ مُّسَنَّدَةٌ يَحْسَبُونَ كُلَّ صَيْحَةٍ عَلَيْهِمْ هُمُ ٱلْعَدُوُّ فَٱحْذَرْهُمْ قَٰتَلَهُمُ ٱللَّهُ أَنَّىٰ يُؤْفَكُونَ ﴿٥﴾

5. And when **you see** them, their figures please **you;** and if they speak,

you listen to their speech. ***Whereas* they are like dry twigs propped up. They fear every calamity to befall them.** They are the enemy, so beware of them. Allah's curse be upon them. How are they being turned away!

8. They it is who say, 'Spend not on those who are with the Messenger of Allah that they may disperse *and leave him;*' while to Allah belong the treasures of the heavens and the earth; but the hypocrites understand not.

هُمُ الَّذِينَ يَقُولُونَ لَا تُنْفِقُوا عَلَىٰ مَنْ عِنْدَ رَسُولِ
اللَّهِ حَتَّىٰ يَنْفَضُّوا ۗ وَلِلَّهِ خَزَائِنُ السَّمَاوَاتِ وَالْأَرْضِ
وَلَٰكِنَّ الْمُنَافِقِينَ لَا يَفْقَهُونَ ۝٨

8. They it is who say, 'Spend not on those who are with the Messenger of Allah **until they disperse** ***deserting him;'*** while to Allah belong the treasures of the heavens and the earth; but the hypocrites understand not.

AL-TAGHABUN

3. It is He Who has created you, but *some* of you are disbelievers and *some* of you are believers; and Allah sees what you do.

هُوَ الَّذِي خَلَقَكُمْ فَمِنْكُمْ كَافِرٌ وَمِنْكُمْ مُؤْمِنٌ ۚ
وَاللَّهُ بِمَا تَعْمَلُونَ بَصِيرٌ ۝٣

3. It is He who has created you, **then some of you become disbelievers and some of you become believers.** And Allah sees what you do.

4. He created the heavens and the earth with truth, and He shaped you and made your shapes beautiful, and to Him is the *ultimate* return.

خَلَقَ السَّمَاوَاتِ وَالْأَرْضَ بِالْحَقِّ وَصَوَّرَكُمْ فَأَحْسَنَ
صُوَرَكُمْ ۖ وَإِلَيْهِ الْمَصِيرُ ۝٤

4. He created the heavens and the earth with truth, and **He fashioned you and made your shapes excellent,** and to Him is the *ultimate* return.

7. That was because their Messengers came to them with manifest Signs, but they said, 'Shall mortals guide us?'

ذٰلِكَ بِأَنَّهٗ كَانَتْ تَّأْتِيْهِمْ رُسُلُهُمْ بِالْبَيِّنٰتِ فَقَالُوْٓا اَبَشَرٌ يَّهْدُوْنَنَا

7. That was because their Messengers came to them with manifest Signs, but they said, 'Shall **humans** guide us?'

17. And whoso is rid of the covetousness of his own soul—it is such who shall be successful.

وَمَنْ يُّوْقَ شُحَّ نَفْسِهٖ فَاُولٰٓئِكَ هُمُ الْمُفْلِحُوْنَ ۝١٧

17. And whoso is **saved from his own covetousness — it is these** who shall be successful.

AL-TALAQ

2. O Prophet! when you divorce women, divorce them for the *prescribed* period, and reckon the period; and fear Allah.

يٰٓاَيُّهَا النَّبِيُّ اِذَا طَلَّقْتُمُ النِّسَآءَ فَطَلِّقُوْهُنَّ لِعِدَّتِهِنَّ وَاَحْصُوا الْعِدَّةَ ۚ وَاتَّقُوا اللّٰهَ رَبَّكُمْ ۚ

2. O Prophet! When you divorce women, divorce them for the *prescribed* period, and reckon the period; and fear Allah, **your Lord.**

5. And whoso fears Allah, He will provide facilities for him in his affair.

وَمَنْ يَّتَّقِ اللّٰهَ يَجْعَلْ لَّهٗ مِنْ اَمْرِهٖ يُسْرًا ۝٥

5. And whoso fears Allah, **He will facilitate his affairs for him.**

7. and consult with one another in kindness; but if you meet with difficulty from each other, then another *woman shall* suckle *the child* for him (the father).

وَاْتَمِرُوْا بَيْنَكُمْ بِمَعْرُوْفٍ ۚ وَاِنْ تَعَاسَرْتُمْ فَسَتُرْضِعُ لَهٗٓ اُخْرٰى ۝٧

7. and **decide your affairs by mutual consultation with fairness;** but if you meet with difficulty from each other, then another *woman shall* suckle *the child* for him (the father).

AL-TAHRIM

قَدْ فَرَضَ اللّٰهُ لَكُمْ تَحِلَّةَ أَيْمَانِكُمْ وَاللّٰهُ مَوْلٰكُمْ وَهُوَ الْعَلِيمُ الْحَكِيمُ (٣)

3. Allah has indeed allowed to you the dissolution of your oaths, and Allah is your Friend; and He is All-Knowing, Wise.

3. Allah has indeed **made incumbent upon you** the dissolution of **your vows,** ***concerning the aforementioned,*** and Allah is your **Guardian;** and He is All-Knowing, Wise.

وَمَأْوٰهُمْ جَهَنَّمُ وَبِئْسَ الْمَصِيرُ (١٠)

10. Their home is Hell, and an evil destination it is!

10. Their **resort** is Hell, and an evil destination it is!

AL-MULK

ثُمَّ ارْجِعِ الْبَصَرَ كَرَّتَيْنِ يَنْقَلِبْ إِلَيْكَ الْبَصَرُ خَاسِئًا وَهُوَ حَسِيرٌ (٥)

5. Aye, look again, and yet again, thy sight will *only* return unto thee confused and fatigued.

5. Aye, look again, and yet again, **your** sight will *only* return **to you frustrated** and fatigued.

فَاعْتَرَفُوا بِذَنْبِهِمْ فَسُحْقًا لِأَصْحٰبِ السَّعِيرِ (١١)

12. Then will they confess their sins; but far away are the inmates of the blazing Fire *from God's mercy.*

12. Then will they confess their sins; **but damnation be for the inmates of the Fire.**

إِنَّ الَّذِينَ يَخْشَوْنَ رَبَّهُمْ بِالْغَيْبِ لَهُمْ مَغْفِرَةٌ وَأَجْرٌ كَبِيرٌ (١٢)

13. Verily, those who fear their Lord in secret—for them is forgiveness and a great reward.

13. Verily, those who fear their Lord **while He is hidden *from them*** — for them is forgiveness and a great reward.

قُلْ أَرَءَيْتُمْ إِنْ أَصْبَحَ مَآؤُكُمْ غَوْرًا فَمَن يَأْتِيكُم بِمَآءٍ مَّعِينٍ ﴿٣١﴾

31. Say, 'Tell me, if *all* your water were to disappear *in the earth*, who then will bring you *clear* flowing water?'

31. Say, 'Tell me, if *all* your water **sinks into a deep recess,** who then will bring you *clear* flowing water?'

AL-QALAM

أَنِ اغْدُوا عَلَىٰ حَرْثِكُمْ إِن كُنتُمْ صَارِمِينَ ﴿٢٣﴾

23. Saying, 'Go forth early in the morning to your field, if you would gather the fruit.'

23. Saying, 'Go forth early in the morning to your field, **if you are to reap the harvest.'**

أَن لَّا يَدْخُلَنَّهَا الْيَوْمَ عَلَيْكُم مِّسْكِينٌ ﴿٢٥﴾

25. Saying, 'Let no poor man today enter it against you.'

25. Saying, **'Let no poor man enter therein today against your interest.'**

وَغَدَوْا عَلَىٰ حَرْدٍ قَادِرِينَ ﴿٢٦﴾

26. And they went forth early in the morning, determined to *achieve their* purpose.

26. **And they set out early in the morning with full might.**

قَالُوا يَا وَيْلَنَا إِنَّا كُنَّا طَاغِينَ ﴿٣٢﴾

32. They said, 'Woe to us! We were indeed rebellious *against God*.

32. They said, 'Woe to us! **Verily, we were transgressors indeed.**

وَمَا هُوَ إِلَّا ذِكْرٌ لِّلْعَالَمِينَ ﴿٥٣﴾

53. Nay, it is naught but *a source of* honour for all the worlds.

53. Nay, it is naught **but a reminder** for all the worlds.

AL-HAQQAH

كَذَّبَتْ ثَمُودُ وَعَادٌۢ بِالْقَارِعَةِ ۝٥

5. *The tribe of* Thamūd and *the tribe of* 'Ād treated as a lie the *sudden* calamity.

5. The *tribe of* Thamud and *the tribe of 'Ad* ***refused to believe in the shattering calamity.***

Note: This in fact is taken from the Qur'anic expression itself wherein *al qariah* (القارعة) has been expressed as يوم يكون الناس كالفراش المبثوث وتكون الجبال كالعهن المنفوش (101:5-6 (Al-Qari'ah)). The day when mankind will be like scattered moths, and the mountains will be like carded wool.

So it is not an ordinary shatter but refers to a gigantic clamity such as produced by H-bombs and neutron bombs etc. The magnitude of the explosion mentioned is such as could pulverise mountains.

فَعَصَوْا رَسُولَ رَبِّهِمْ فَأَخَذَهُمْ أَخْذَةً رَّابِيَةً ۝١١

11. And they disobeyed the Messenger of their Lord, therefore He seized them—a severe seizing.

11. And they disobeyed the Messenger of their Lord, therefore He seized **them with an ever-tightening grip.**

وَالْمَلَكُ عَلَىٰ أَرْجَائِهَا ۚ وَيَحْمِلُ عَرْشَ رَبِّكَ فَوْقَهُمْ
يَوْمَئِذٍ ثَمَانِيَةٌ ۝١٨

18. And the angels will be *standing* on the sides thereof, and above them on that day eight *angels* will bear the throne of thy Lord.

18. And the Angels will be *standing* on the sides thereof, and above them on that day **the** eight *angels* will bear the throne of **your** Lord.

يَا لَيْتَهَا كَانَتِ الْقَاضِيَةَ ۝٢٨

28. 'O would that *death* had made an end *of me* !

28. 'How I wish that that *judgement* were a decree for me to perish!

37. 'Nor any food save blood mixed with water,

وَّلَا طَعَامٌ اِلَّا مِنْ غِسْلِيْنٍ ﴿٣٧﴾

37. 'Nor any food **save the washing of wounds,**

45. And if he had forged *and attributed* any sayings to Us,

وَلَوْ تَقَوَّلَ عَلَيْنَا بَعْضَ الْاَقَاوِيْلِ ﴿٤٥﴾

45. And if he had falsely attributed even a trivial statement to Us,

47. And then surely We would have severed his life-artery,

ثُمَّ لَقَطَعْنَا مِنْهُ الْوَتِيْنَ ﴿٤٧﴾

47. And then surely We would have severed his **jugular vein.**

48. And not one of you could have held *Us* off from him.

فَمَا مِنْكُمْ مِّنْ اَحَدٍ عَنْهُ حٰجِزِيْنَ ﴿٤٨﴾

48. And none of you could shield him *from Us.*

AL-MA'ARIJ

26. For one who asks *for help* and *for one* who does not.

لِّلسَّآئِلِ وَالْمَحْرُوْمِ ﴿٢٦﴾

26. For the beggar and the destitute who begs not.

29. Verily the punishment of their Lord is not *a thing* to feel secure from—

اِنَّ عَذَابَ رَبِّهِمْ غَيْرُ مَاْمُوْنٍ ﴿٢٩﴾

29. Verily the punishment of their **Lord is unsparing.**

35. And those who are strict in the observance of their Prayer.

وَالَّذِيْنَ هُمْ عَلٰى صَلَاتِهِمْ يُحَافِظُوْنَ ﴿٣٥﴾

35. And those **who stand guard over their prayers.**

44. The day when they will come forth from their graves hastening, as though they were racing to a target,

يَوْمَ يَخْرُجُوْنَ مِنَ الْاَجْدَاثِ سِرَاعًا كَاَنَّهُمْ اِلٰى نُصُبٍ يُّوْفِضُوْنَ ﴿٤٤﴾

44. The day when they would emerge from their graves rushing forth as if they were hastening towards their targets,

NUH

8. and covered up their hearts, and persisted *in their iniquity*, and were disdainfully proud.

وَاسْتَغْشَوْا ثِيَابَهُمْ وَأَصَرُّوا وَاسْتَكْبَرُوا اسْتِكْبَارًا ۝

8. **and wrapped their garments around them** and persisted *in their iniquity,* and **behaved with exceeding arrogance.**

9. "Then, I called them *to righteousness* openly.

ثُمَّ إِنِّي دَعَوْتُهُمْ جِهَارًا ۝

9. 'Then I **invited them *to your path*** openly.

11. "And I said, 'Seek forgiveness of your Lord; for He is the Great Forgiver.

فَقُلْتُ اسْتَغْفِرُوا رَبَّكُمْ إِنَّهُ كَانَ غَفَّارًا ۝

11. 'And I said, 'Seek forgiveness of your Lord; for He is **Exceedingly Forgiving.**

14. 'What is the matter with you that you expect not wisdom and staidness from Allah?

مَا لَكُمْ لَا تَرْجُونَ لِلَّهِ وَقَارًا ۝

14. 'What is the matter with you **that you do not ascribe dignity to Allah.**

15. 'And He has created you in *different* forms and *different* conditions.

وَقَدْ خَلَقَكُمْ أَطْوَارًا ۝

15. **'And certainly He has created you in stages.**

16. 'Have you not seen how Allah has created seven heavens in *perfect* harmony,

أَلَمْ تَرَوْا كَيْفَ خَلَقَ اللَّهُ سَبْعَ سَمَاوَاتٍ طِبَاقًا ۝

16. 'Have you not observed how Allah has created seven heavens tier upon tier?

18. 'And Allah has caused you to grow as a *good* growth from the earth,

وَاللّٰهُ اَنْۢبَتَكُمْ مِّنَ الْاَرْضِ نَبَاتًا ﴿۱۸﴾

18. 'And Allah has raised you from the earth like the raising of vegetation.

19. 'Then will He cause you to return thereto, and He will bring you forth *a new* bringing forth.

ثُمَّ يُعِيْدُكُمْ فِيْهَا وَيُخْرِجُكُمْ اِخْرَاجًا ﴿۱۹﴾

19. 'Then will He return you therein and bring you forth in a special way.

27. And Noah said, 'My Lord, leave not in the land a single one of the disbelievers;

وَقَالَ نُوْحٌ رَّبِّ لَا تَذَرْ عَلَى الْاَرْضِ مِنَ الْكٰفِرِيْنَ
دَيَّارًا ﴿۲۷﴾

27. And Noah said, 'My Lord leave not in the land a single one of the disbelievers **as dwellers therein;**

AL-JINN

27. *He is the* Knower of the unseen; and He reveals not His secrets to any one,

عٰلِمُ الْغَيْبِ فَلَا يُظْهِرُ عَلٰى غَيْبِهٖۤ اَحَدًا ﴿۲۷﴾

27. *He is the* Knower of the unseen, **and He does not grant anyone ascendency over His domain of the unseen.**

28. Except to him whom He chooses, namely a Messenger *of His*. And then He causes an escort *of guarding angels* to go before him and behind him,

اِلَّا مَنِ ارْتَضٰى مِنْ رَّسُوْلٍ فَاِنَّهٗ يَسْلُكُ مِنْۢ بَيْنِ
يَدَيْهِ وَمِنْ خَلْفِهٖ رَصَدًا ﴿۲۸﴾

28. Except him whom He chooses as *His* Messenger. And in front of him and at the back of him march *angels* as sentinels.

AL-MUZZAMMIL

يٰۤاَيُّهَا الْمُزَّمِّلُ ۝٢

2. O thou who art bearing *a heavy responsibility*,

2. **O' you who has wrapped *himself* in a robe.**

فَكَيْفَ تَتَّقُوْنَ اِنْ كَفَرْتُمْ يَوْمًا يَّجْعَلُ الْوِلْدَانَ شِيْبَا ۝١٨

18. How will you then, if you disbelieve, guard yourselves against a day which will turn children grey-headed?

18. How will you then, if you disbelieve, guard yourselves against a day which will **turn the children's hair grey.**

AL-MUDDATHTHIR

وَرَبَّكَ فَكَبِّرْ ۝٤

4. And thy Lord do thou magnify.

4. And **your** Lord do **extol.**

وَثِيَابَكَ فَطَهِّرْ ۝٥

5. And thy heart do thou purify,

5. **And your garment do purify,**

Note: The word *thiyabaka* (ثيابك) may mean heart but only if it were taken as a figure of speech. But the problem is that the word *thiyab* ثياب literally means clothes or garments. So if one treats it as a figure of speech then the heart is not the only possible interpretation. More likely perhaps *thiyabaka* ثيابك in this context could refer to the companions of the Holy Prophet, peace be upon him, and the others close to him. Hence the suggested alternative translation is literal providing the reader a wider choice of interpretation.

سَاُصْلِيْهِ سَقَرَ ۝٢٧

27. Soon shall I cast him into the fire of Hell.

27. Soon shall I cast **him into 'Saqar'.**

وَمَآ اَدْرٰىكَ مَا سَقَرُ ۝٢٨

28. And what makes thee know what Hell-fire is?

28. And what can make you know what 'Saqar' is?

لَا تُبۡقِي وَلَا تَذَرُ ﴿٢٩﴾

29. It spares not and it leaves naught.

29. It spares not and leaves nothing.

لَوَّاحَةٌ لِّلۡبَشَرِ ﴿٣٠﴾

30. It scorches the face.

30. It scorches the skin.

مَا سَلَكَكُمۡ فِي سَقَرَ ﴿٤٢﴾

43. 'What has brought you into the Fire of Hell?'

43. 'What has brought **you into 'Saqar'?**

AL-QIYAMAH

وَلَآ أُقۡسِمُ بِٱلنَّفۡسِ ٱللَّوَّامَةِ ﴿٢﴾

3. And I do call to witness the self-accusing soul, *that the Day of Judgment is a certainty*.

3. And I call to witness **the oft - blaming concience.**

بَلۡ يُرِيدُ ٱلۡإِنسَٰنُ لِيَفۡجُرَ أَمَامَهُۥ ﴿٥﴾

6. But man desires to continue to send forth evil deeds in front of him.

6. But man desires to continue to sin as he proceeds.

بَلِ ٱلۡإِنسَٰنُ عَلَىٰ نَفۡسِهِۦ بَصِيرَةٌ ﴿١٤﴾

15. Nay, man is a witness against himself;

15. Nay, man is fully aware of his own self.

كَلَّا بَلۡ تُحِبُّونَ ٱلۡعَاجِلَةَ ﴿٢٠﴾

21. Nay, but you love the present life;

21. Nay, but you love that which is near at hand.

وَتَذَرُونَ ٱلۡأٓخِرَةَ ﴿٢١﴾

22. And you neglect the Hereafter.

22. And disregard the Hereafter.

37. Does man think that he is to be left *to himself* uncontrolled?

أَيَحْسَبُ الْإِنْسَانُ أَنْ يُتْرَكَ سُدًى ۝٣٧

37. Does man think that he will be left free to wander.

AL-DAHR

3. We have created man from a mingled sperm-drop that We might try him; so We made him hearing, seeing.

إِنَّا خَلَقْنَا الْإِنْسَانَ مِنْ نُّطْفَةٍ أَمْشَاجٍ نَّبْتَلِيهِ
فَجَعَلْنٰهُ سَمِيعًا بَصِيرًا ۝٣

3. We created man from a mingled sperm-drop which We cause to pass through trials; then We turned him into a hearing, seeing being.

17. *Bright as* glass *but made* of silver, which they will measure according to *their own* measure.

قَوَارِيرَا مِنْ فِضَّةٍ قَدَّرُوهَا تَقْدِيرًا ۝١٧

17. **Glass of silver which they fashioned with outstanding skill.**

22. On them will be garments of fine green silk and thick brocade. And they will be made to wear bracelets of silver. And their Lord will give them to drink a pure beverage.

عٰلِيَهُمْ ثِيَابُ سُنْدُسٍ خُضْرٌ وَّإِسْتَبْرَقٌ وَّحُلُّوا
أَسَاوِرَ مِنْ فِضَّةٍ وَسَقٰهُمْ رَبُّهُمْ شَرَابًا طَهُورًا ۝٢٢

22. On them will be garments of fine green silk and brocade. And they will be **decked with** bracelets of silver. And their Lord will give them to drink a pure beverage.

31. And you exercise your will because Allah has *so* willed. Verily, Allah is All-Knowing, Wise.

وَمَا تَشَآءُونَ إِلَّآ أَنْ يَّشَآءَ اللّٰهُ إِنَّ اللّٰهَ كَانَ
عَلِيمًا حَكِيمًا ۝٣١

31. **And you cannot exercise your desires except when Allah so wills.** Verily, Allah is All-Knowing, Wise.

AL-MURSALAT

وَالْمُرْسَلٰتِ عُرْفًا ۝٢

2. By *the angels* who are sent forth with goodness,

2. By those which are sent off gently,

فَالْعٰصِفٰتِ عَصْفًا ۝٣

3. *And* then they push on with a forceful pushing,

3. Then gather speed and blow swiftly,

وَّالنّٰشِرٰتِ نَشْرًا ۝٤

4. And by *the forces* that spread *the truth*, a good spreading,

4. And by those who spread a thorough spreading,

فَالْفٰرِقٰتِ فَرْقًا ۝٥

5. *And* then they distinguish fully *between good and evil.*

5. And then they make clear distinctions,

فَالْمُلْقِيٰتِ ذِكْرًا ۝٦

6. Then they carry the exhortation *far and wide*

6. And by those who deliver the Reminder,

عُذْرًا اَوْ نُذْرًا ۝٧

7. To excuse *some* and warn *others.*

7. Absolving themselves of responsibility or by way of warning,

اِنَّهَا تَرْمِيْ بِشَرَرٍ كَالْقَصْرِ ۝٣٢

33. It throws up sparks like *huge* castles,

33. It throws up flames like castles,

كَاَنَّهٗ جِمٰلَتٌ صُفْرٌ ۝٣٣

34. As if they were camels of dim colour.

34. As if it were made up of many copper-coloured camels.

AL-NABA

3. About the great Event, عَنِ النَّبَاِ الْعَظِيْمِ ۝٣

3. About the news of great import,

12. And We have made the day for the activities of life. وَّجَعَلْنَا النَّهَارَ مَعَاشًا ۝١١

12. And We have made **the day for the sake of sustenance.**

19. The day when the trumpet will be blown; and you will come in large groups; يَّوْمَ يُنْفَخُ فِي الصُّوْرِ فَتَاْتُوْنَ اَفْوَاجًا ۝١٩

19. The day **when the trumpet will be blown; and you will come horde after horde.**

25. They will taste therein neither sleep nor drink, لَا يَذُوْقُوْنَ فِيْهَا بَرْدًا وَّلَا شَرَابًا ۝٢٥

25. **They will taste therein neither cool nor a drink of any kind,**

26. Save boiling water and a stinking fluid — اِلَّا حَمِيْمًا وَّغَسَّاقًا ۝٢٦

26. **Except water boiling hot or freezing cold.**

27. A meet requital. جَزَآءً وِّفَاقًا ۝٢٧

27. **A befitting requital.**

38. They shall not have the power to address Him. لَا يَمْلِكُوْنَ مِنْهُ خِطَابًا ۝٣٨

38. **They will possess no right to address Him.**

AL-NAZI'AT

2. By those beings who draw *people to true faith* vigorously, وَالنّٰزِعٰتِ غَرْقًا ۝٢

2. By those who move submerged and drag and pull with the purpose of sinking,

وَّالنّٰشِطٰتِ نَشْطًا ۙ﴿٣﴾

3. And *by* those who tie *their* knots firmly,

3. And by those who move swiftly across countries,

وَّالسّٰبِحٰتِ سَبْحًا ۙ﴿٤﴾

4. And *by* those who glide along swiftly,

4. And by those who swiftly travel long distances over the surface of oceans,

فَالسّٰبِقٰتِ سَبْقًا ۙ﴿٥﴾

5. Then they *advance* and greatly excel *others*,

5. And by those who vie with each other for supremacy,

فَالْمُدَبِّرٰتِ اَمْرًا ۘ﴿٦﴾

6. Then they manage the affair *entrusted to them*.

6. And by those who plan and execute their task well,

AL-BURUJ

وَشَاهِدٍ وَّمَشْهُوْدٍ ؕ﴿٤﴾

4. And *by* the Witness and that about whom witness has been borne,

4. By the testifier and the one who is testified.

قُتِلَ اَصْحٰبُ الْاُخْدُوْدِ ۙ﴿٥﴾

5. Cursed be the Fellows of the Trench—

5. Cursed be the people of the trenches ---

اِنَّهٗ هُوَ يُبْدِئُ وَيُعِيْدُ ۚ﴿١٤﴾

14. He it is Who originates and reproduces;

14. He it is who initiates and repeats.

فَعَّالٌ لِّمَا يُرِيدُ ﴿١٦﴾

17. Doer of whatever He wills.

17. A thorough Executer of what He wills.

وَّاللّٰهُ مِنْ وَّرَآئِهِمْ مُّحِيْطٌ ﴿٢١﴾

21. And Allah encompasses *them* from before them and from behind them.

21. And Allah encompasses them **in a manner they perceive not.**

AL-TARIQ

وَالسَّمَآءِ ذَاتِ الرَّجْعِ ﴿١٢﴾

12. By the cloud which gives rain after rain,

12. By the heavens oft-returning (with rain),

اِنَّهُمْ يَكِيْدُوْنَ كَيْدًا ﴿١٦﴾

16. Surely they plan a plan,

16. Verily they are hatching a plot.

وَّاَكِيْدُ كَيْدًا ﴿١٧﴾

17. And I *also* plan a plan.

17. I, too, am devising a counter plot.

AL-GHASHIYAH

وَاِلَى الْجِبَالِ كَيْفَ نُصِبَتْ ﴿٢٠﴾

20. And at the mountains, how they are set up?

20. And at the mountains, **how they are firmly rooted?**

لَسْتَ عَلَيْهِمْ بِمُصَيْطِرٍ ﴿٢٢﴾

23. Thou hast no authority to *compel* them.

23. **You are not a warden over them.**

AL-FAJR

9. The like of whom have not been created in *these* parts— الَّتِي لَمْ يُخْلَقْ مِثْلُهَا فِي الْبِلَادِ ⁹

9. Buildings like theirs were never built before in the lands.

12. Who transgressed in the cities, الَّذِينَ طَغَوْا فِي الْبِلَادِ ¹²

12. Who transgressed in the **lands.**

22. Nay, when the earth is completely broken into pieces and made level; كَلَّا إِذَا دُكَّتِ الْأَرْضُ دَكًّا دَكًّا ²²

22. Nay, when the earth **is pounded a thorough pounding;**

AL-BALAD

11. And We have pointed out to him the two highways *of good and evil.* وَهَدَيْنَاهُ النَّجْدَيْنِ ¹¹

11. And **We showed him two ascending paths of nobility.**

12. But he attempted not the ascent *courageously.* فَلَا اقْتَحَمَ الْعَقَبَةَ ¹²

12. But he did not follow the path of 'Aqabah.'

13. And what should make thee know what the ascent is? وَمَا أَدْرَاكَ مَا الْعَقَبَةُ ¹³

13. **And what should make you know what the 'Aqabah' is?**

21. Around them will be a fire closed over. عَلَيْهِمْ نَارٌ مُؤْصَدَةٌ ²¹

21. **Upon them is** *to leap* **a fire kept enclosed.**

AL-SHAMS

وَالشَّمْسِ وَضُحٰهَا ﴿٢﴾

2. By the sun and its growing brightness,

2. By the sun and the time when it begins to radiate,

قَدْ اَفْلَحَ مَنْ زَكّٰهَا ﴿١٠﴾

10. He indeed *truly* prospers who purifies it,

10. Surely, he prospers who augments it,

فَكَذَّبُوْهُ فَعَقَرُوْهَا فَدَمْدَمَ عَلَيْهِمْ رَبُّهُمْ بِذَنْۢبِهِمْ فَسَوّٰىهَا ﴿١٥﴾

15. But they rejected him and hamstrung her, so their Lord destroyed them completely because of their sin, and made it (destruction) *overtake all of them* alike.

15. But they rejected him and hamstrung her, so their Lord destroyed them completely because of their sin, and **levelled them *to the ground.***

AL-LAIL

وَصَدَّقَ بِالْحُسْنٰى ﴿٧﴾

7. And testifies to *the truth of* what is right,

7. And he testifies to all that is good,

AL-DUHA

وَاَمَّا السَّآئِلَ فَلَا تَنْهَرْ ﴿١١﴾

11. And him who seeks *thy help,* chide not,

11. And as for the beggar, chide him not,

وَاَمَّا بِنِعْمَةِ رَبِّكَ فَحَدِّثْ ﴿١٢﴾

12. And the bounty of thy Lord, proclaim.

12. And as for the bounty of your Lord do relate *it to others.*

AL-INSHIRAH

9. And to thy Lord do thou attend *whole-heartedly*. وَإِلَىٰ رَبِّكَ فَارْغَبْ ۝٩

9. And to thy Lord do you turn seeking Him eagerly.

AL-TIN

4. And *by* this Town of Security, وَهَٰذَا الْبَلَدِ الْأَمِينِ ۝٤

4. And by this Town, the abode of peace.

5. Surely, We have created man in the best make; لَقَدْ خَلَقْنَا الْإِنْسَانَ فِي أَحْسَنِ تَقْوِيمٍ ۝٥

5. Surely, We have created man in the best of creative plans.

6. Then, *if he works iniquity*, We reject him as the lowest of the low, ثُمَّ رَدَدْنَاهُ أَسْفَلَ سَافِلِينَ ۝٦

6. Then We reverted him to *the state of* the lowest of the low.

AL-ALAQ

2. Convey thou in the name of thy Lord Who created, اقْرَأْ بِاسْمِ رَبِّكَ الَّذِي خَلَقَ ۝٢

2. Recite in the name of your Lord Who created,

3. Created man from a clot of blood. خَلَقَ الْإِنْسَانَ مِنْ عَلَقٍ ۝٣

3. Created man from **an adhesive clot.**

4. Convey! And thy Lord is Most Generous, اقْرَأْ وَرَبُّكَ الْأَكْرَمُ ۝٤

4. Recite! And your Lord is the Noblest.

الَّذِىْ عَلَّمَ بِالْقَلَمِ ٥

5. Who taught *man* by the pen,

5. Who taught by the pen.

أَرَءَيْتَ إِن كَانَ عَلَى الْهُدَىٰٓ ١٢

12. Tell me if he (Our servant) follows the guidance

12. ***Beware*** **what if he were to be on the right,**

أَوْ أَمَرَ بِالتَّقْوَىٰ ١٣

13. Or enjoins righteousness, *what will be the end of the forbidder?*

13. **Or had admonished righteousness?**

أَرَءَيْتَ إِن كَذَّبَ وَتَوَلَّىٰٓ ١٤

14. Tell me if he (the forbidder) rejects and turns his back,

14. **Again have you considered if he falsified the truth** ***instead*** **and turned away,**

أَلَمْ يَعْلَم بِأَنَّ اللَّهَ يَرَىٰ ١٥

15. Does he not know that Allah sees *him?*

15. **Does he not realise that Allah sees?**

كَلَّا لَئِن لَّمْ يَنتَهِ لَنَسْفَعًا بِالنَّاصِيَةِ ١٦

16. Nay, if he desist not, We will assuredly *seize and* drag him by the forelock,

16. Nay if he desist not, **We will certainly drag him by the forelock,**

نَاصِيَةٍ كَاذِبَةٍ خَاطِئَةٍ ١٧

17. A forelock lying, sinful.

17. A forelock **false,** sinful.

فَلْيَدْعُ نَادِيَهُ ١٨

18. Then let him call his associates,

18. Then let him call his **companions,**

AL-QADR

تَنَزَّلُ الْمَلٰٓئِكَةُ وَالرُّوْحُ فِيْهَا بِإِذْنِ رَبِّهِمْ مِنْ كُلِّ أَمْرٍ ﴿٥﴾

5. Therein descend angels and the Spirit by the command of their Lord—with every matter.

5. Therein descend angels and the spirit with their Lord's decree concerning everything.

سَلٰمٌ هِيَ حَتّٰى مَطْلَعِ الْفَجْرِ ﴿٦﴾

6. *It is all* peace till the rising of the dawn.

6. Peace - so will it be even at the rising of the dawn.

AL-BAYYINAH

رَسُوْلٌ مِّنَ اللّٰهِ يَتْلُوْا صُحُفًا مُّطَهَّرَةً ﴿٣﴾

3. A Messenger from Allah, reciting *unto them the* pure Scriptures.

3. A Messenger from Allah recites Scriptures purified.

فِيْهَا كُتُبٌ قَيِّمَةٌ ﴿٤﴾

4. Therein are lasting commandments.

4. Therein are the everlasting teachings.

AL-ZILZAL

بِأَنَّ رَبَّكَ أَوْحٰى لَهَا ﴿٦﴾

6. For thy Lord will have revealed about her.

6. It will be because your Lord would have so revealed to her.

AL-ADIYAT

فَوَسَطْنَ بِهٖ جَمْعًا ﴿٦﴾

6. And penetrating thereby into the centre of *the enemy* forces,

6. And penetrating thereby the heart of the *enemy* ranks.

AL-QARI'AH

10. Hell will be his *nursing* mother.

فَأُمُّهُۥ هَاوِيَةٌ ۝١٠

10. His mother will be 'Haviyah.'

AL-TAKATHUR

2. Mutual rivalry in *seeking worldly* increase diverts you *from God*

أَلْهَىٰكُمُ ٱلتَّكَاثُرُ ۝٢

2. Vying with each other for amassing wealth had made you oblivious,

3. Till you reach the graves.

حَتَّىٰ زُرْتُمُ ٱلْمَقَابِرَ ۝٣

3. Even you reached the graveyards.

6. Nay! if you only knew with certain knowledge,

كَلَّا لَوْ تَعْلَمُونَ عِلْمَ ٱلْيَقِينِ ۝٥

6. Nay, were you to know the certain knowledge,

AL-ASR

2. By the *fleeting* Time,

وَٱلْعَصْرِ ۝١

2. By the testimony of time,

AL-HUMAZAH

5. Nay! he shall surely be cast into the crushing punishment.

كَلَّا لَيُنۢبَذَنَّ فِى ٱلْحُطَمَةِ ۝٤

5. Nay, he shall surely be cast into 'Al-Hutamah'?

6. And what should make thee know what the crushing punishment is?

وَمَآ أَدْرَىٰكَ مَا ٱلْحُطَمَةُ ۝٥

6. And what should make you know what the 'Hutamah' is?

الَّتِىۡ تَطَّلِعُ عَلَى الۡاَفۡـِٕدَةِؕ‏ ﴿۸﴾

8. Which rises over the hearts.

8. Which will leap at hearts.

اِنَّهَا عَلَيۡهِمۡ مُّؤۡصَدَةٌ ۙ‏ ﴿۹﴾

9. It will be closed in on them

9. It will be enclosed against them.

فِىۡ عَمَدٍ مُّمَدَّدَةٍ ‏﴿۱۰﴾

10. In *the form of* extended columns.

10. In extended columns.

AL-QURAISH

لِاِيۡلٰفِ قُرَيۡشٍۙ‏ ﴿۲﴾

2. Because of the attachment of the Quraish—

2. To bind the Quraish together,

اِلٰفِهِمۡ رِحۡلَةَ الشِّتَآءِ وَالصَّيۡفِۚ‏ ﴿۳﴾

3. *His* making them attached to *their* journey in winter and summer—

3. *and* to promote their alliance *We have devised trade* journeys of the winter and the summer ---

فَلۡيَـعۡبُدُوۡا رَبَّ هٰذَا الۡبَيۡتِۙ‏ ﴿۴﴾

4. They should worship the Lord of this House,

4. Hence they should worship the Lord of this House,

AL-MA'UN

الَّذِيۡنَ هُمۡ يُرَآءُوۡنَۙ‏ ﴿۷﴾

7. They like to be seen *of men*,

7. Those who show off.

وَيَمۡنَعُوۡنَ الۡمَاعُوۡنَ ‏﴿۸﴾

8. And withhold *legal* alms.

8. and they deprive people of even small benefits.

AL-LAHAB

تَبَّتْ يَدَآ اَبِيْ لَهَبٍ وَّتَبَّ ۝٢

2. Perished be the two hands of Abū Lahab, and he will perish.

2. **Perished be the two hands of** Abu Lahab, **and so perish he.**

Note: Abu Lahab, *father of the flames,* is applicable to a person of fiery and rebellious nature and to one who inflames others.

وَّامْرَاَتُهٗ ۭ حَمَّالَةَ الْحَطَبِ ۝٥

5. And his wife *too*, who goes about slandering.

5. **And his woman *too*, who goes about carrying the firewood.**

AL-FALAQ

قُلْ اَعُوْذُ بِرَبِّ الْفَلَقِ ۝٢

2. Say, 'I seek refuge in the Lord of the dawn,

2. Say, 'I seek refuge with the Lord of **cleaving,**